**Norman Foster** Works 1

Die Deutsche Bibliothek –
CIP-Cataloguing-in-
Publication-Data.
A catalogue record for this
publication is available from
Die Deutsche Bibliothek

Library of Congress
Cataloguing-in-Publication
is available

©2002, Foster and Partners,
London, and Prestel Verlag,
Munich · Berlin · London ·
New York

Prestel Verlag
Königinstrasse 9
80539 Munich
Germany
Tel +49 (089) 381709-0
Fax +49 (089) 381709-35
www.prestel.de

175 Fifth Ave.
Suite 402
New York NY 10010
USA
Tel +1 (212) 995-2720
Fax +1 (212) 995-2733

4 Bloomsbury Place
London WC1A 2QA
United Kingdom
Tel +44 (020) 7323-5004
Fax +44 (020) 7636-8004
www.prestel.com

Printed in Germany
on acid-free paper
ISBN 3-7913-2534-5

# Norman Foster Works 1

Contributors

Chris Abel
Reyner Banham
Alastair Best
Peter Buchanan
Francis Duffy
Norman Foster
Brian Hatton
Louis Hellman
Ian Lambot
Tim Ostler
Martin Pawley
Kenneth Powell
Robert A M Stern
Graham Vickers
John Walker

Editor

David Jenkins

Prestel  Munich · London · New York

Editor's Note

This volume is the first of a new series devoted to the Complete Works of Norman Foster. It spans the period 1963 to 1983 – from student days to the completion of the Renault Centre. As with succeeding volumes, it is organised broadly chronologically. However, within that chronology some projects have been grouped into 'themes' or 'families' in order to facilitate a better understanding of their underlying ideas, to represent a body of work with a particular client or collaborator, or – as in the case of the Sainsbury Centre – to enable the extended building to be studied alongside the original.

Many of the essays and project descriptions published here were first included in two earlier books: *Norman Foster, Buildings and Projects*, Volumes 1 and 2, published in 1990 and 1989 respectively. These texts have been republished with the benefit of ten years' perspective. Some have been edited or abridged and others updated; and much new material has been introduced. A similar approach has been adopted with the projects. Where the opportunity exists, many of the buildings have been re-photographed, allowing comparisons with their original condition or highlighting changing patterns of usage. In some cases – such as Willis Faber & Dumas – this has been particularly telling.

Running along the top of each page is a strip – which has come to be known as 'the film'. This provides an additional commentary on the relevant project or essay, and takes the form of 'visual footnotes', ephemera, critical commentaries and 'voices off'. It is hoped that this material will add to the reader's enjoyment and aid those who wish to research the work of the Foster studio further.

In editing this volume I am particularly fortunate to have enjoyed the encouragement of Norman Foster, whose great skill is always to be able to push things that bit further to get the very best from everyone. I am grateful also to Per Arnoldi, who helped to shape the concept of this new series; to Thomas Manss and Lisa Sjukur, who have brought it graphically to life; to Sophie Carter, assistant editor for the series, who has provided invaluable editorial and research support; to Kate Stirling, chief research assistant, who with the support of Katy Harris and Stephan Potchatek has mined the office archive; to Julia Dawson for proof-reading the text; to Sophie Hartley for picture research; and to the many contributors who have made this such a rich and varied work.

David Jenkins
London, August 2002

# Contents

| | | | |
|---|---|---|---|
| 10 | Preface – Norman Foster | 280 | The Years of Innovation – Martin Pawley |
| 12 | Measured Drawings | 292 | Connections – Willis Faber & Dumas |
| | | 294 | Willis Faber & Dumas |
| 18 | The Impact of Yale – Robert A M Stern | 338 | Social Ends, Technical Means – Norman Foster |
| 34 | Early Projects | 346 | Sapa Factory |
| 38 | Connections – The Cockpit | 350 | Modern Art Glass |
| 40 | The Cockpit | 356 | Shopping and Leisure Centres |
| 46 | Creak Vean House | 360 | Orange Hand Shops |
| 66 | Waterfront Housing | 362 | German Car Centre |
| 70 | Murray Mews | | |
| 76 | Wates Housing | 366 | Meeting the Sainsburys – Norman Foster |
| 82 | Skybreak House | 368 | Connections – Sainsbury Centre for Visual Arts |
| 88 | High Density Housing | 370 | Sainsbury Centre for Visual Arts |
| 90 | Forest Road Annexe | 422 | With Wendy – Norman Foster |
| | | 430 | The Crescent Wing |
| 92 | The Early Years – John Walker | | |
| 96 | Connections – Reliance Controls Electronics Factory | 450 | Beyond the Yellow Bicycle – Reyner Banham |
| 98 | Reliance Controls Electronics Factory | 464 | Masterplan for St Helier Harbour |
| | | 466 | Hammersmith Centre |
| 116 | In the Beginning – Alastair Best | 480 | Joseph Shop |
| 128 | Connections – Newport School | 482 | Foster Residence |
| 130 | Newport School | 486 | London Gliding Club |
| 138 | Factory Systems | 488 | Open House |
| | | 490 | Granada Entertainment Centre |
| 144 | Design for Living – Norman Foster | 492 | Renault Distribution Centre |
| 148 | Projects and Masterplanning for Fred Olsen | | |
| 150 | Fred Olsen Amenity Centre | 532 | Richard Buckminster Fuller – Martin Pawley |
| 166 | Fred Olsen Passenger Terminal | 536 | Projects with Buckminster Fuller |
| 172 | Country Offices | 538 | Samuel Beckett Theatre |
| 176 | Son Recreation Centre and Oslo Offices | 540 | Climatroffice |
| 178 | Fred Olsen Travel Agency | 542 | International Energy Expo '82 |
| 180 | Gomera Regional Planning Study | 544 | Autonomous House |
| 192 | Systems Thinking Revisited – Francis Duffy | 548 | Bucky and Beyond – Norman Foster |
| 202 | Projects for Computer Technology | 556 | The Team |
| 204 | Air-Supported Office | 560 | Project Credits |
| 208 | Computer Technology | 567 | Project Bibliography |
| 214 | IBM Pilot Head Office | 570 | Contributors |
| | | 572 | Index |
| 234 | LL/LF/LE v Foster – Reyner Banham | 578 | Credits |
| 238 | Fitzroy Street Studio | | |
| 242 | IBM Technical Park | | |
| 266 | Special Care Unit | | |
| 270 | Palmerston Special School | | |
| 274 | Bean Hill Housing | | |

11. Air-Supported Office
    Hemel Hempstead,
    England
    1969-1970
12. Fred Olsen Passenger
    Terminal
    London, England
    1969-1970
13. Samuel Beckett
    Theatre
    Oxford, England
    1971
14. IBM Pilot Head Office
    Cosham, England
    1970-1971
15. Computer Technology
    Hemel Hempstead,
    England
    1969-1970
16. Special Care Unit
    London, England
    1970-1972
17. German Car Centre
    Milton Keynes, England
    1972
18. Climatroffice
    1971

9. Newport School
   Gwent, Wales
   1967
10. Fred Olsen Amenity
    Centre
    London, England
    1968-1970

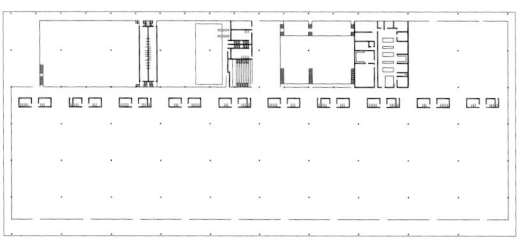
9

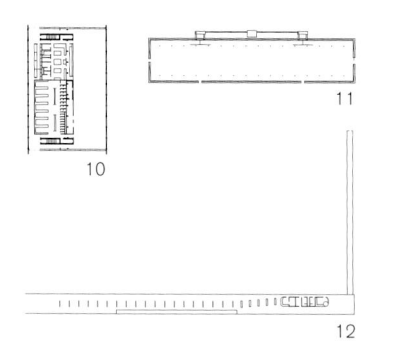
10
11
12

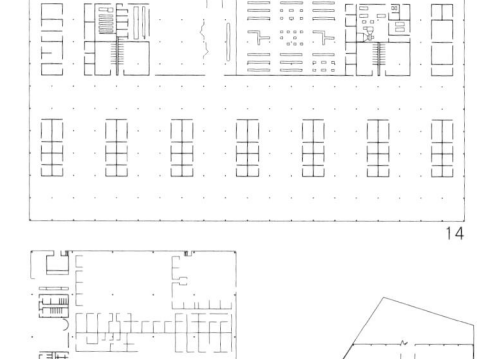
14

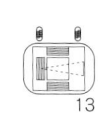
13

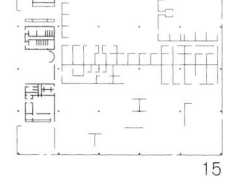
15

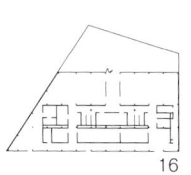
16

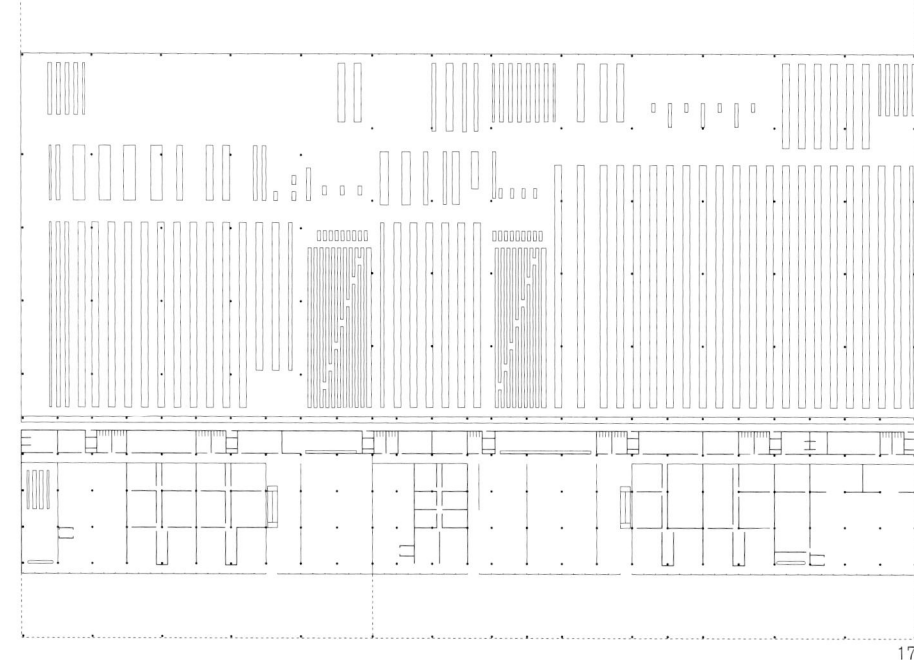
17

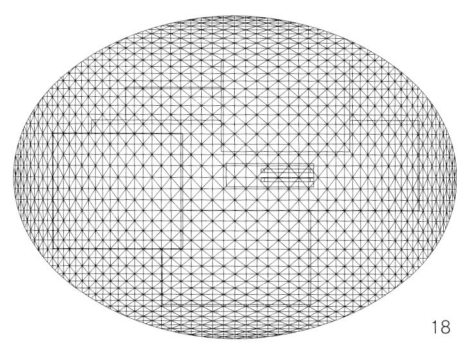
18

**1967**  **1969**  **1971**

Key

1. Office Building project
   Yale University, USA
   1962
2. The Cockpit
   Pill Creek, Cornwall,
   England
   1964
3. Murray Mews Houses
   London, England
   1965
4. Wates Housing
   Coulsdon, England
   1965
5. Creek Vean House
   Pill Creek, Cornwall,
   England
   1964-1966
6. Reliance Controls
   Swindon, England
   1965-1966
7. Skybreak House
   Radlett, England
   1965-1966
8. Forest Road Annexe
   East Horsley, England
   1966

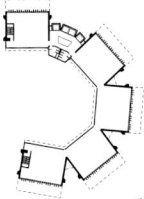
1

2

3

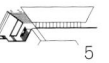
4

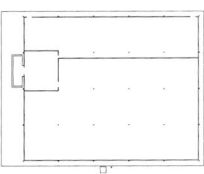
5

6

7

8

**1961**      **1963**      **1965**

**Timeline of Plans**

32. Hammersmith Centre
London, England
1977-1979

33. Granada Entertainment Centre
Milton Keynes, England
1979

34. Foster Residence
London, England
1978-1979

35. IBM Technical Park
Greenford, England
1975-1980

36. Renault Centre
Swindon, England
1979-1982

37. Autonomous House
Los Angeles, USA
1982-1983

32

36

37

33

34

35

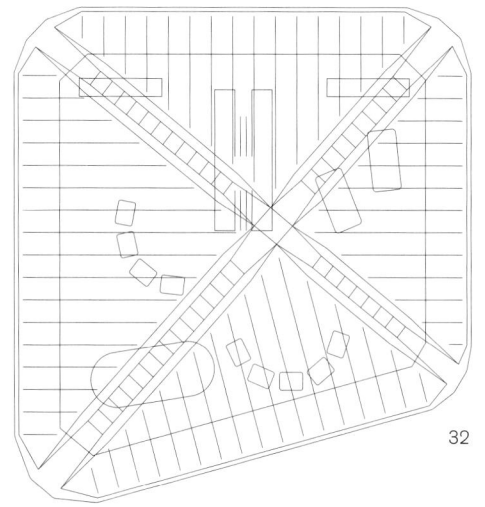

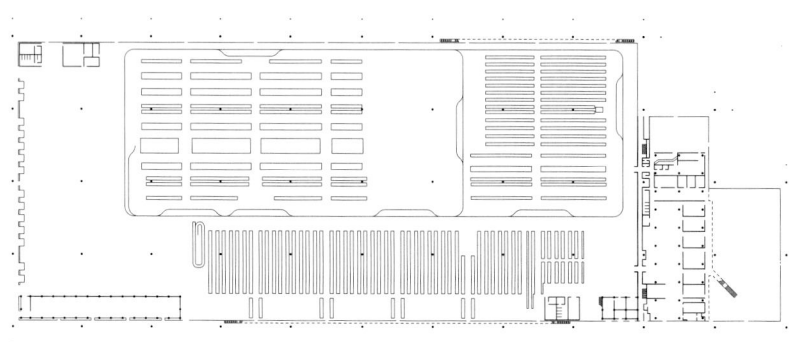

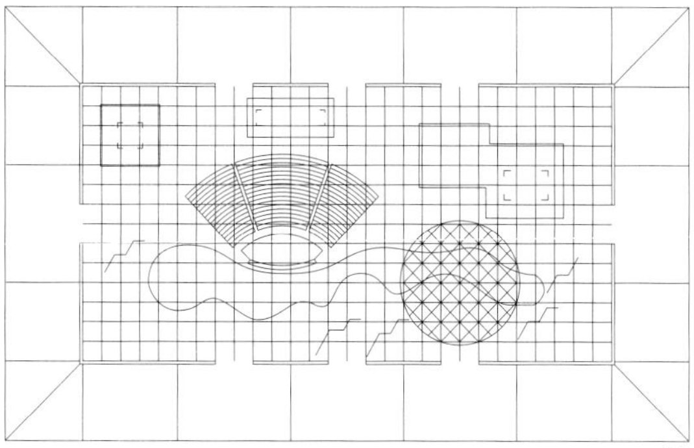

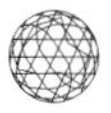

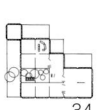

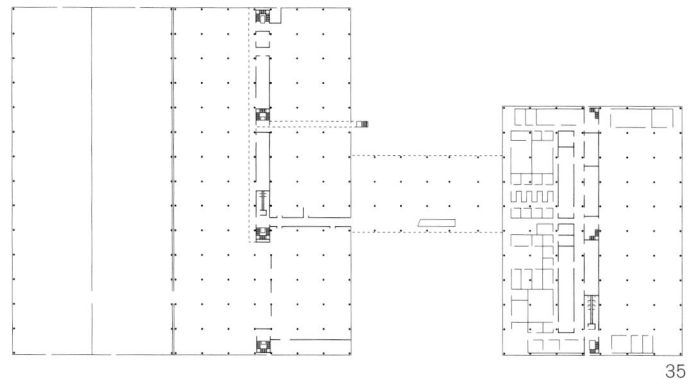

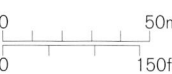

**1979**

**1981**

**1983**

19. Sapa Factory
    Tibshelf, England
    1972-1973
20. Bean Hill Housing
    Milton Keynes, England
    1971-1973
21. Modern Art Glass
    Thamesmead, England
    1972-1973
22. Willis Faber & Dumas
    Ipswich, England
    1971-1975
23. Pavilion Leisure Centre
    Knowsley, England
    1972-1973
24. Country Offices
    Vestby, Norway
    1973
25. Fred Olsen Travel Agency
    London, England
    1975
26. Sainsbury Centre for Visual Arts and Crescent Wing
    Norwich, England
    1974-1978, 1986-1991
27. Palmerston Special School
    Liverpool, England
    1973-1976
28. London Gliding Club
    Dunstable Downs, England
    1978
29. Open House
    Cwmbran, South Wales
    1978
30. Joseph Shop
    London, England
    1978
31. International Energy Expo
    Knoxville, USA
    1978

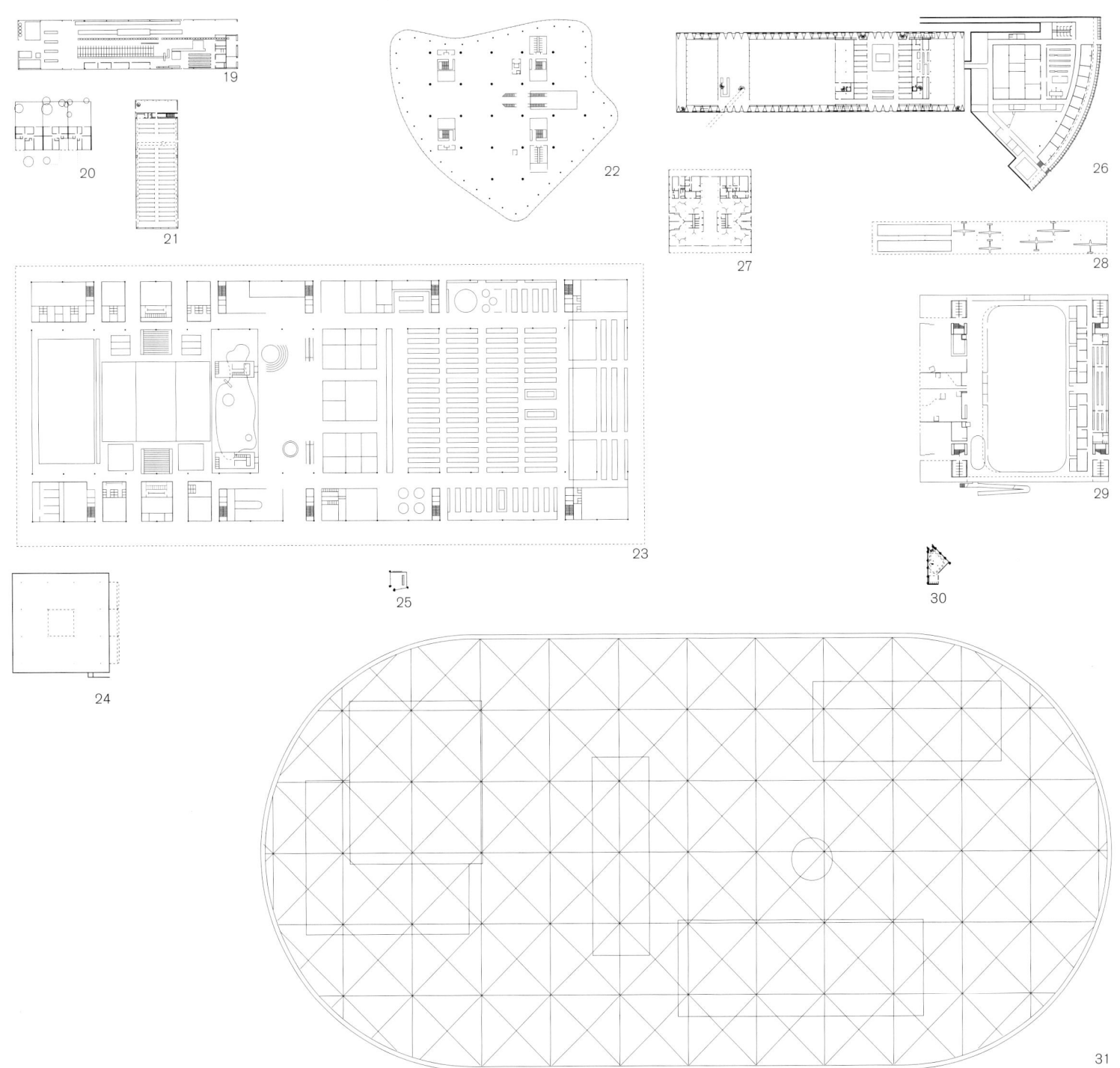

1973     1975     1977

# Preface
Norman Foster

Previous page: 'Seated at a table and engaged in almost conspiratorial discussion': Tim Street-Porter's famous photograph of Buckminster Fuller with Norman Foster and members of the project team for the Samuel Beckett Theatre was taken in Foster Associates' Bedford Street studio in 1971. From left are: Buckminster Fuller, Michael Hopkins, Tony Hunt, John Walker, Norman Foster and James Meller.

This new volume is the first of a series of books about our work. I say 'our' with some emphasis because architecture and building are team activities: many people are involved, both in the foreground and behind the scenes. And many of them have contributed to this book, whether that be in the form of sketches and drawings done at the time, or by recording their recollections of the projects, which you will find as you explore further.

The work illustrated here, almost all of it by Foster Associates, spans nearly two decades. This volume also includes transitional work from the brief period of Team 4. I met Richard Rogers at Yale and we collaborated on two student projects. Returning to England, in 1963, this was to be the foundation of Team 4 with two architect sisters, Georgie and Wendy Cheesman. When the practice dissolved, less than four years later, Wendy – by then my wife – and I established Foster Associates.

Looking back on this early period, it was a time in which the seeds of our current practice took root. Themes explored then would come to inform our later work. For example, the little 'dug-in' Cockpit – our first project to be built – established a site-sensitive strategy that would be re-explored many times at a far greater scale, most recently in the Great Glasshouse at the National Botanic Gardens of Wales.

With another early project, Reliance Controls, we made the case for 'democracy in the workplace'. In the 1960s, the 'them and us' mentality in factories in Britain found built form in the workers' 'shed' fronted by the management 'box' and extended into the provision of segregated canteens and the like. Reliance Controls rejected those conventions and provided a high standard of amenities shared by all employees. We went on to work with other enlightened clients – Fred Olsen among them – who echoed a belief that the workplace could provide a pleasant, stimulating environment.

Reliance Controls also introduced the concept of the 'integrated enclosure' in which a variety of functions usually housed separately would be brought together under one roof. This idea was developed through later projects such as the Newport School and the Sainsbury Centre, and on an unprecedented scale in the terminal building at Hong Kong's International Airport at Chek Lap Kok.

This formative period also saw us develop, refine and ultimately reject one particular approach – the top-serviced shed. It is a journey that can be traced from Reliance Controls, via buildings for IBM and the Sainsbury and Renault Centres to Stansted Airport. In the process we would exchange solid roofs and overhead services for transparent enclosures and natural light.

Along the way, in the Vestby offices, our ecological agenda led us to develop sunlight reflectors that would ultimately appear in the Hongkong Bank and again in the Reichstag. The environmental theme continues in the development study for the Canary Island of Gomera, which formulated clear ideas about sustainability long before the green agenda was seriously being discussed. Likewise, with Willis Faber & Dumas we began to investigate ideas for greening the workplace that would lead us to the Commerzbank and a new generation of environmentally responsible office buildings in Duisburg.

Willis Faber is also significant in other ways. Designed for long-term flexibility – another recurring theme – we specified raised floors in the office spaces at a time when such floors were used exclusively in computer rooms. A decade later – almost alone among its competitors – the company was able to confront the revolution in information technology without disruption. Considered radical at the time, the building's low-rise, deep-plan form, with its central atrium would also prove influential: today it is regarded by developers as the norm.

Similarly, with the Hammersmith Centre we first explored ideas about the nature of public space in the city that were to be crucial to the development of the Great Court at the British Museum.

In the early 1970s we also took our first steps towards becoming an international practice, opening a studio in Oslo. At the end of that decade we would open another office in Hong Kong. During that time in London we moved three times. Perhaps the biggest step was from a domestic flat in Hampstead Hill Gardens to our first 'real' studio in Bedford Street, Covent Garden – which we shared with Tony Hunt, the structural engineer for all of Foster Associates' early projects. From there we practised what we preached by moving to custom-designed studios, first in Fitzroy Street and then in Great Portland Street.

It was Wendy who instigated the move to our present studio at Riverside, in 1990. For me, Riverside is a rare combination of a wonderful team and a great place to work. It is a cosmopolitan powerhouse of youthful energy. Open twenty-four hours a day, seven days a week, you will find people working there at all hours.

As individuals we are all shaped by our background, our influences, education and experience and these are reflected in the work of the practice. Going back to very early days, it has been suggested that the antecedents for some of our later work can be glimpsed in student schemes. The editor, David Jenkins, has accordingly devoted space to projects that I undertook at university, first at Manchester, and later as a graduate student at Yale.

I have special debts to America and Europe and two teachers at Yale – Paul Rudolph and Serge Chermayeff – personify for me the cultures of America and Europe at their best. The studio under Rudolph was a 'can-do' world in which almost anything was possible if you only worked hard enough: concepts could be rejected one day and reformulated overnight. Rudolph was only interested in the hard evidence of drawings and models. For Chermayeff, in contrast, debate and theory took precedence over imagery: analysis dominated action. Rudolph was a blast of fresh air, but Chermayeff's more reflective approach was an important counterpoint.

Looking back I can see that our practice is similar in many ways to that Yale studio, inspired by the same polarities of analysis and action. That means trying to ask the right questions, allied with a curiosity about how things work – whether they are organisations or mechanical systems. It also means believing in the social context, that architecture is about people and their needs, both material and spiritual.

My current partners – Spencer de Grey, David Nelson, Graham Phillips and Ken Shuttleworth – have helped to develop this approach. All of them joined the practice during the early days, more than twenty-five years ago. For a brief time Michael Hopkins was a partner and he is still a kindred spirit. Both personally and professionally I am fortunate to have had so many generous collaborators over the years – the architects who have contributed to the life of the studio and the exceptional consultants, particularly engineers and quantity surveyors.

Less obvious perhaps is the creative role of those that commission a building: so often the final result is as good as the dialogue with the client. I am indebted to those special clients, some of whom – like Fred Olsen – helped to establish the practice in that lean time when I had begun to believe that emigration was the only answer. And I am especially grateful to the late Sir Robert Sainsbury and his wife Lisa – patrons to many emerging artists over the years – who became like second parents to me.

Other mentors include Buckminster Fuller, whom I was privileged to work with. He was a true master of technology, but he also offered a moral conscience, reminding us of the fragility of our planet, and with an ecological awareness that grows ever more relevant today. Bucky remains a guiding spirit; so too does Otl Aicher. (It is interesting how the theme of America, with Bucky, and Europe, with Otl, continues.) Otl was renowned as a graphic designer, but in reality he was far more. He had a way of working and living in which the creation of a new typeface, the design of a book, attitudes to war, politics, writing or communication, or how you peeled an onion, were related parts of a personal philosophy.

It was with Otl, that we first set out to record the work of the practice in book form. Otl devised a concept that would allow the books to communicate at many levels. He was concerned to reveal the processes behind the work, to show the relationship of drawings, models and prototypes to the final product. He aimed to provide an overall order within which there could be an almost infinite scope for choice and variation.

We published two volumes of that series before Otl's untimely death – and then two more. But without him it was not the same. It proved impossible to recreate his highly personal working method. And so we decided to start again, from the beginning, remaining faithful to Otl's guiding principles, but with a new graphic language. Starting again also allowed us to make connections between the early projects and those we are working on today – to trace the development of ideas over time.

This book, like the buildings it portrays, is a team effort. I am especially grateful to David Jenkins who has conceived and edited this and forthcoming volumes, drawing together an extraordinarily varied range of threads; to Per Arnoldi and Thomas Manss, who together have formulated a new graphic discipline; to the writers – far too many to mention individually – who have offered new insights into our work; and to all the other people who have worked together, behind the scenes, to make this book a reality. It has been a fascinating process for me and I hope that some of that sense of discovery is communicated in the following pages.

# Measured Drawings
## 1956–1961

Each year at Manchester University the best student measured drawings were put forward for awards, so from an early stage Norman Foster became aware of the power of clear, concise presentation techniques.

1-5. In the summer of 1959 Foster spent several days at Rufford Old Hall in Lancashire, an elaborate fifteenth-century timber-framed manor house. Elevations and sections were drawn, but it was the construction of the pegged oak roof structure that captured his imagination. He made a series of some thirty detailed sketches, some concentrating on the major joints and assemblies, others exploring the simplest elements and the most ingenious traditional timber connection methods.

In my early days as a student at Manchester University I was fascinated by structure and by buildings that were hardly architecture in the accepted sense – the vernacular.

There was a discipline at Manchester of measured drawing. Every summer you had to go out and measure a building and make notes, and then you would come back and draw it up. In a school that was still locked into the Beaux-Arts tradition you were expected to draw Classical buildings with columns and mouldings. It was not that I rejected that tradition – I enjoyed it immensely – but the obsession with drawing up decorative details, year after year, almost by rote, seemed questionable at best.

I was pulled instead to what J M Richards characterised in The Architectural Review as the 'functional tradition' in architecture: early industrial buildings, such as windmills, or medieval structures such as barns. I would travel widely to find them – a Welsh barn, which had once been the great hall of a fortified house, or a post mill in Cambridgeshire.

I would lovingly detail how they worked; I would draw the cross sections of their structural members. But this was considered revolutionary; it was a heresy to draw something that might not even be regarded as a proper building. It caused a lot of controversy at the University, but nobody could really challenge what I was doing because I was winning prizes for these drawings. For example, in my third year I won the RIBA Silver Medal, which was worth a hundred pounds. In 1959 that was a lot of money, probably the equivalent of several thousand pounds today and I used it to fund my summer travels.

That enthusiasm for discovering how things work, how they fit together, how the design of one component impacts on another has been a constant over the years and remains with me now.

Norman Foster

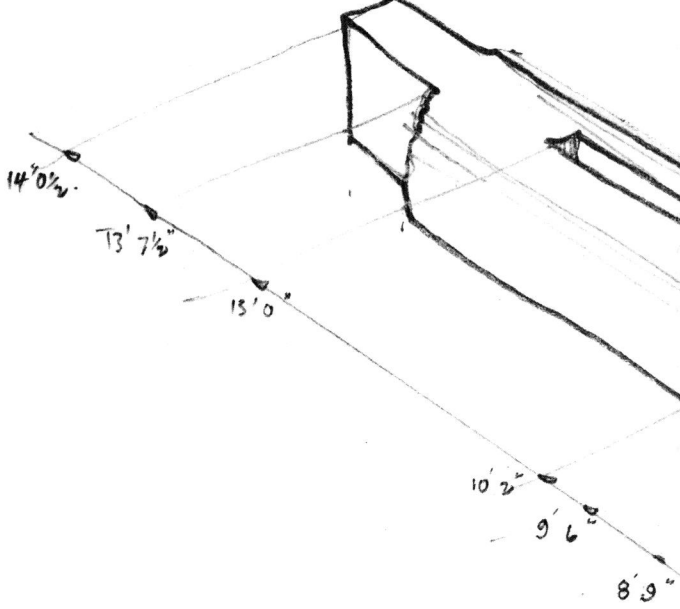

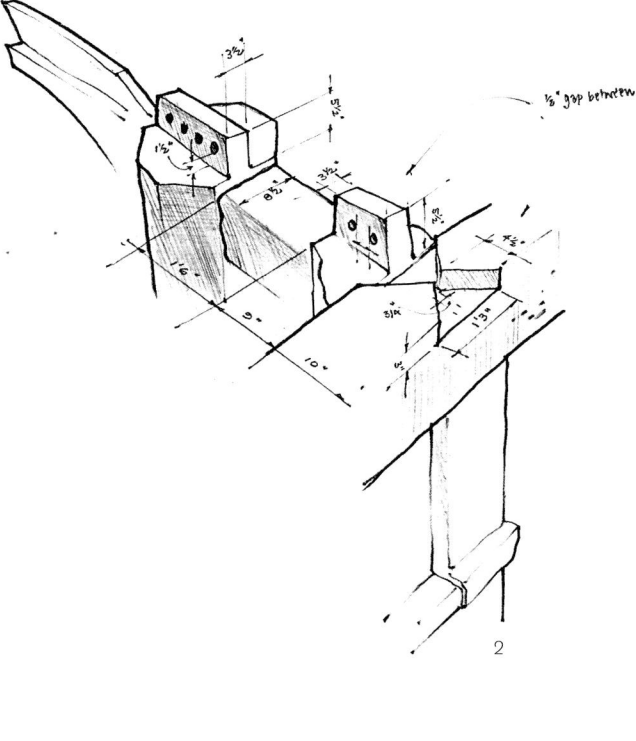

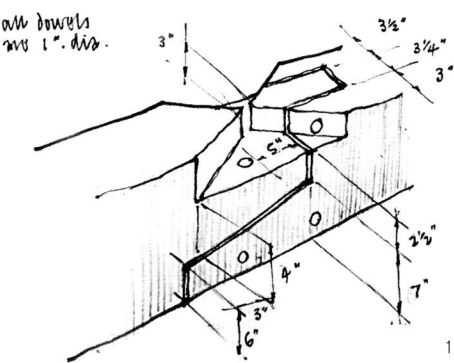

Manchester University was very traditional. It was nothing like, say, the Architectural Association, or what was then the Regent Street Polytechnic here in London. I remember visiting studios there and finding an unbelievably creative environment. Manchester, on the other hand, was very conventional, very disciplined. It was frustrating because you never had the opportunity to debate. You would know what was expected, you would produce the work, it would be assessed, and maybe a week later you would get it back with a mark. You would never present your work, and there was no dialogue. Norman Foster, in conversation with Yoshio Futagawa, 1999

Left: Rufford Old Hall, in Lancashire, is one of the finest examples of late medieval architecture in the UK. Built by Sir Thomas Hesketh in the early fifteenth century, only the Great Hall with its timber studding and mullioned windows survives, forming one wing of an otherwise late seventeenth-century building. The hall is 14 metres (46 feet) long and 6.7 metres (22 feet) wide, crowned by a magnificently ornate hammer beam roof with quatrefoil motifs, while an elaborately carved wooden screen separates the hall from what was once the kitchen at its eastern end.

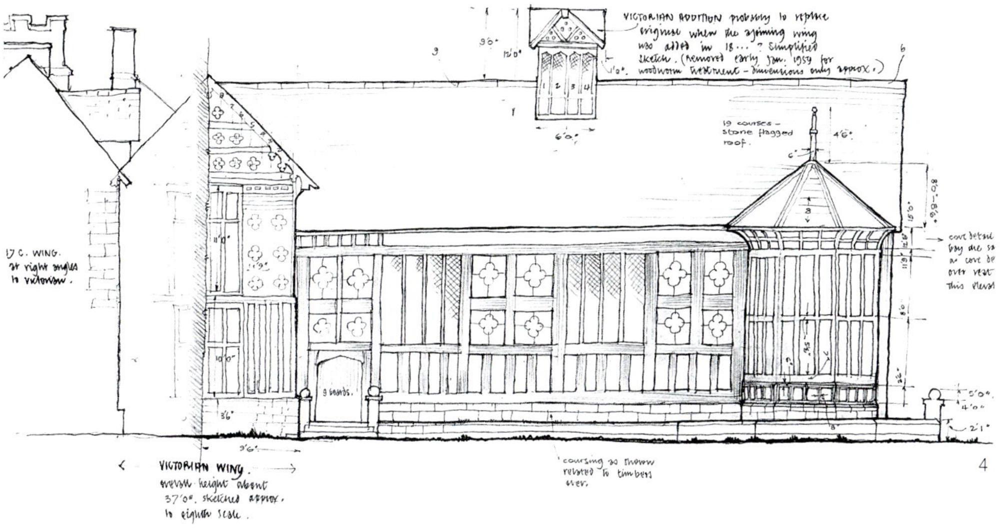

Measured Drawings 13

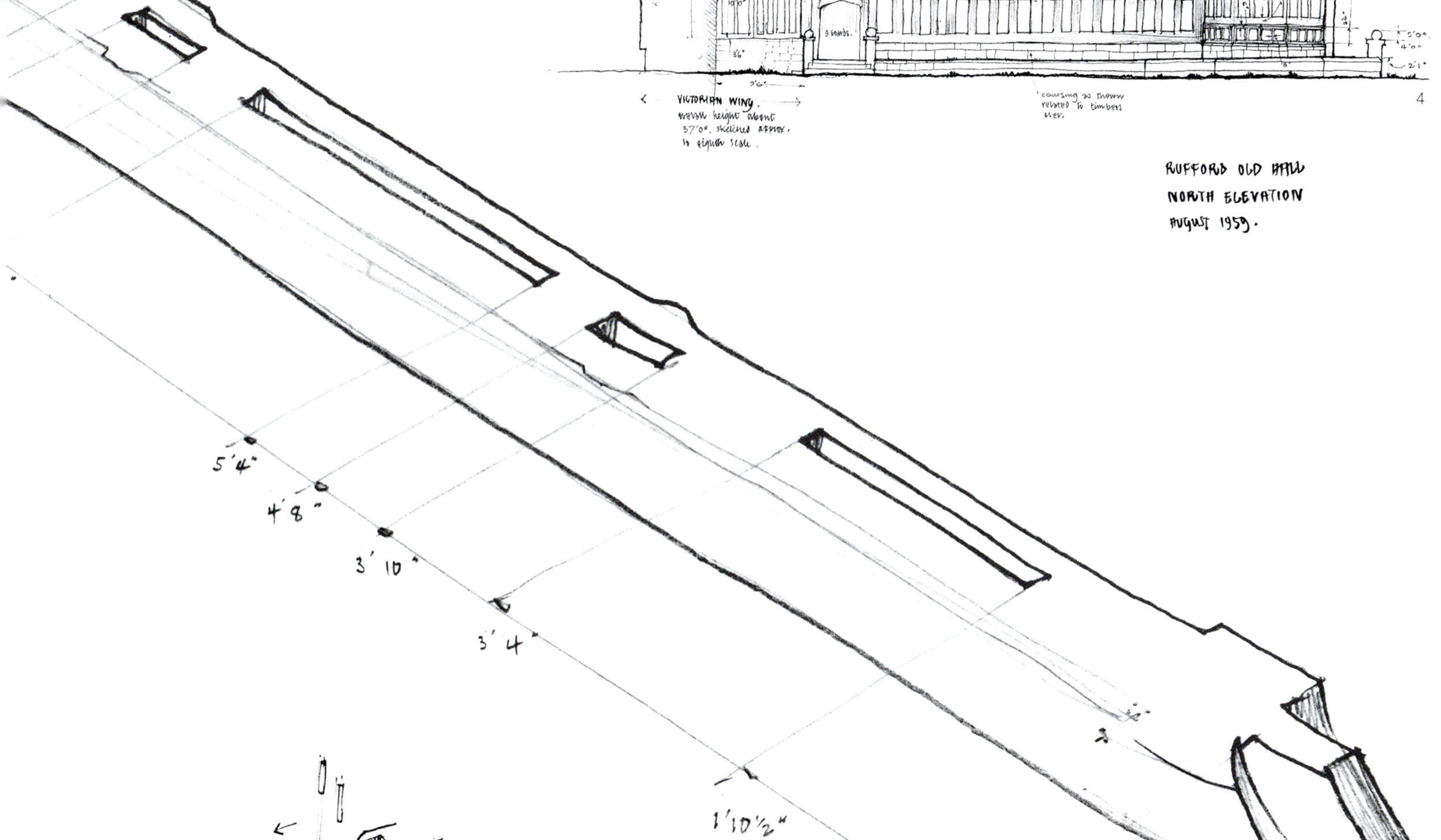

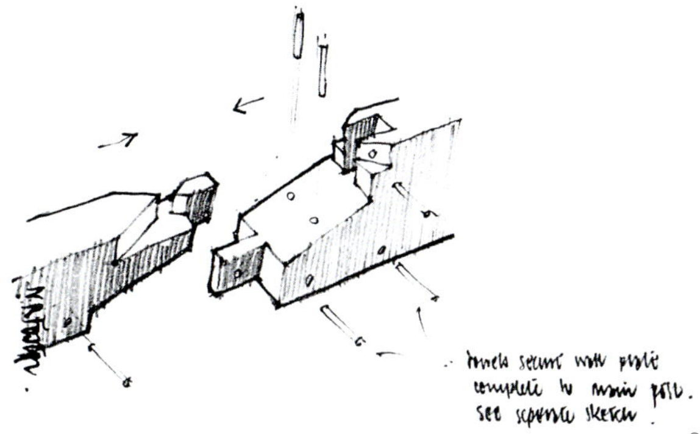

**Ever since his student years at Manchester University in the 1950s (a working class boy, he paid his way through school with a variety of jobs, including a stint as a nightclub bouncer) Foster loved utilitarian buildings: barns, factories, windmills. He did measured drawings of them when other students were drawing buildings they had never seen: Greek temples, Palladian villas. Foster would learn from those too, but his immersion in common language and uses translates into a feeling of rightness, which works as completely in small structures as in large.** Robert Hughes, *Time* magazine, 19 April 1999

**There is a negative side to the current explosion of computer-generated imagery. I worry about students who might feel that the power of such sophisticated equipment has somehow rendered the humble pencil if not obsolete, then certainly second rate … The pencil and computer are, if left to their own devices, equally dumb and only as good as the person driving them.** Norman Foster, *Norman Foster: Sketches*, 1992

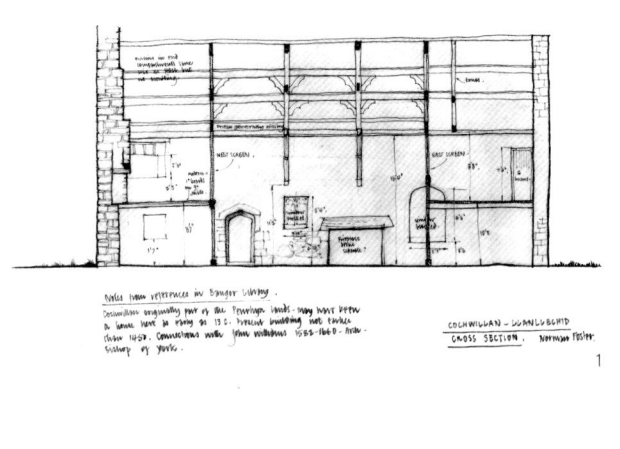

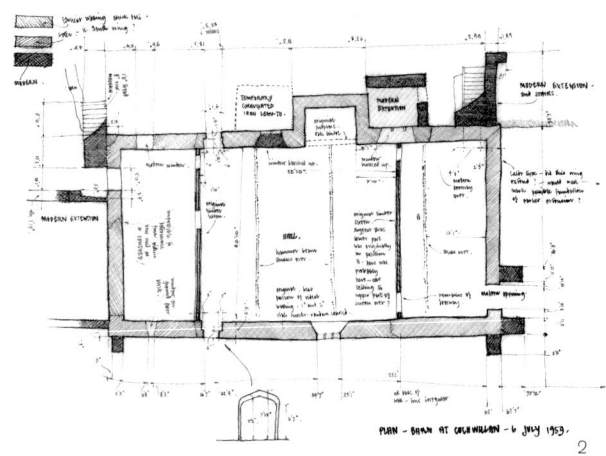

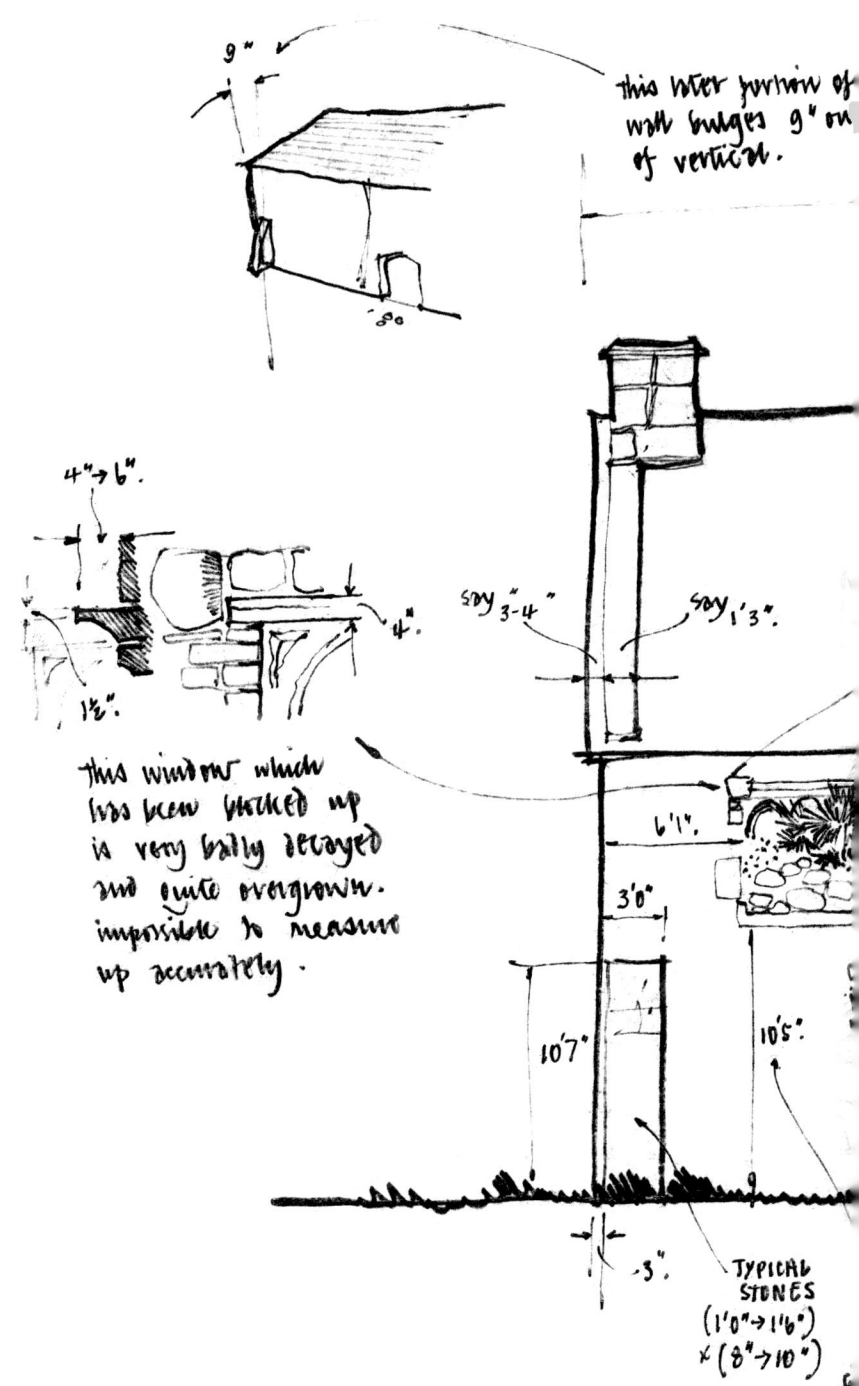

1-3. Extracts from a series of Norman Foster's survey drawings of a Welsh barn at Cochwillan, Llanllechid, drawn in July 1959. The Cochwillan barn can be dated back, with some certainty, to the mid-1400s when it was the great hall of a fortified house. The plan indicates the positions of wooden screens, obviously remnants from the building's earlier history. Following the guidelines that all survey notes should be clear enough for someone else to be able to draw up, all of Foster's sketches are richly annotated.

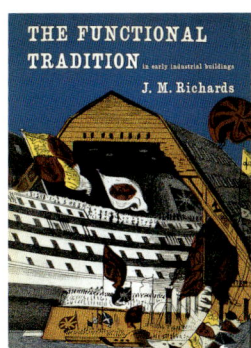

**Buildings belonging to the functional tradition derive their artistic character directly from the way the challenge of function is met, and all the qualities they have in common – forthrightness and simplicity, the use of building materials in a way that brings out most strongly their intrinsic qualities – are equally a product of the hard-headed relationship of ends and means that functionalism in this sense implies.** J M Richards, *The Functional Tradition*, 1958

Far left, left: Cover and pages from J M Richards' book, illustrated by legendary *Architectural Review* photographer Eric de Maré. This work inspired Foster as a student and holds a particular fascination to this day: in fact, he suggests the book be re-issued as *The Right Stuff*.

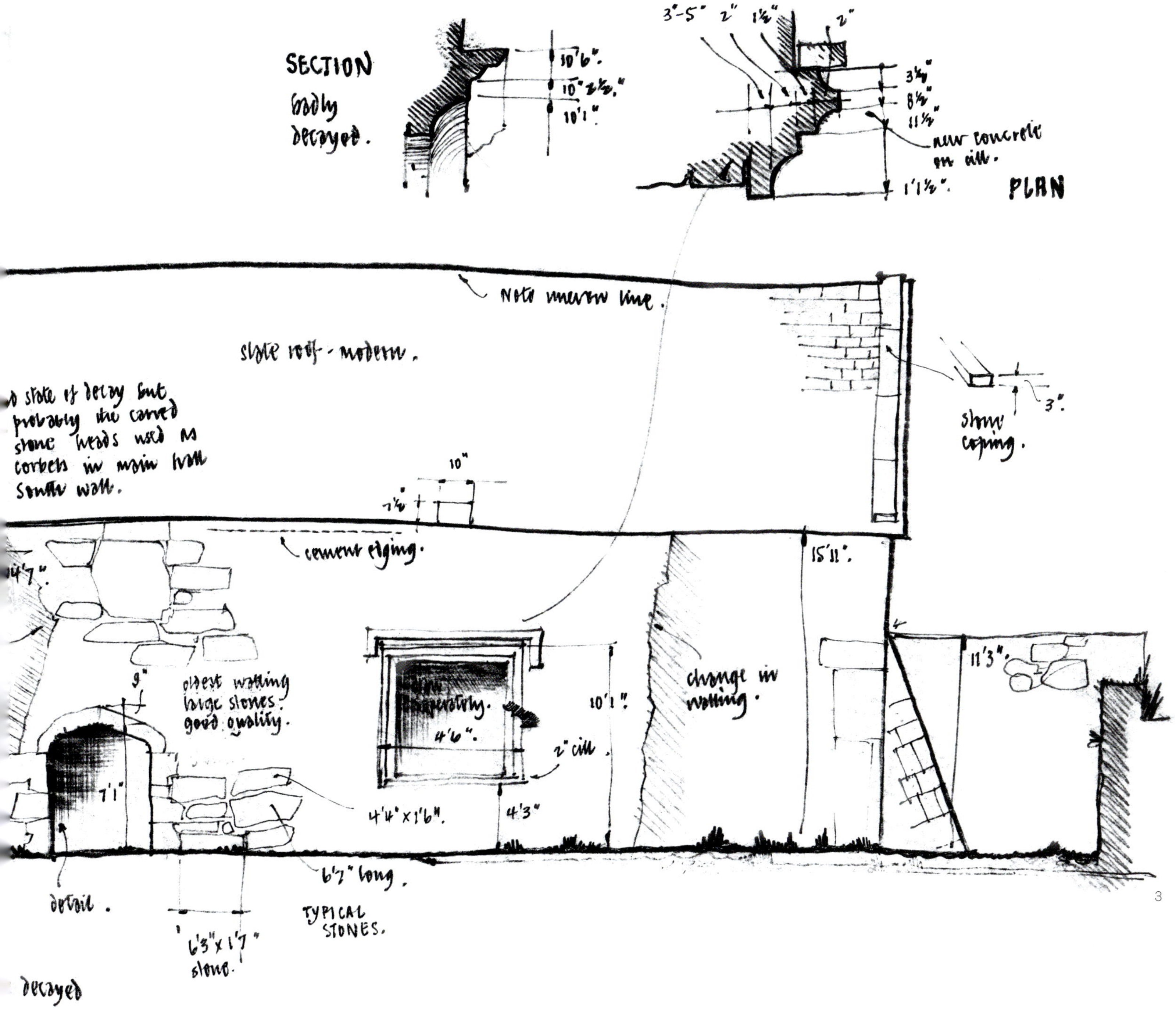

Measured Drawings 15

**This is real high-performance design, entirely functional and yet, for me, it has its own kind of beauty and elegance. It almost grows out of the landscape. Bourn Mill will certainly have a place in my personal history of architecture.** Norman Foster, quoted in the *Sunday Telegraph*, 18 November 2001

Right: Norman Foster's photograph of the post mill at Bourn, an early example of the pre-industrial vernacular. Far Right: Some forty years after Foster executed the drawings of the Bourn mill, the practice was to develop the E66 wind turbine with Enercon, the German power company. The result is the most advanced turbine of its kind. The two structures are seen here modelled to the same scale.

**A particularly interesting stream of work in our studio has been the design and development of wind turbines ... Working with industry, we have been attempting to learn from a kind of lateral transfer of technology and knowledge from aerodynamics and from NASA programmes.** Norman Foster, lecture at the Fourth European Conference on Solar Energy in Architecture and Urban Planning, Berlin, 29 March 1996

1-5. Norman Foster's drawings of the post mill at Bourn, in Cambridgeshire, which he surveyed in August 1958, are among his most successful and complete measured drawings, winning him an RIBA award. This little structure has become an enduring reference point for Foster – an example of the unselfconscious early industrial vernacular that he has called 'the right stuff'. His detailed notes record the building in the most meticulous detail, from the intricacy of its workings to the jointing methods of its timber frame.

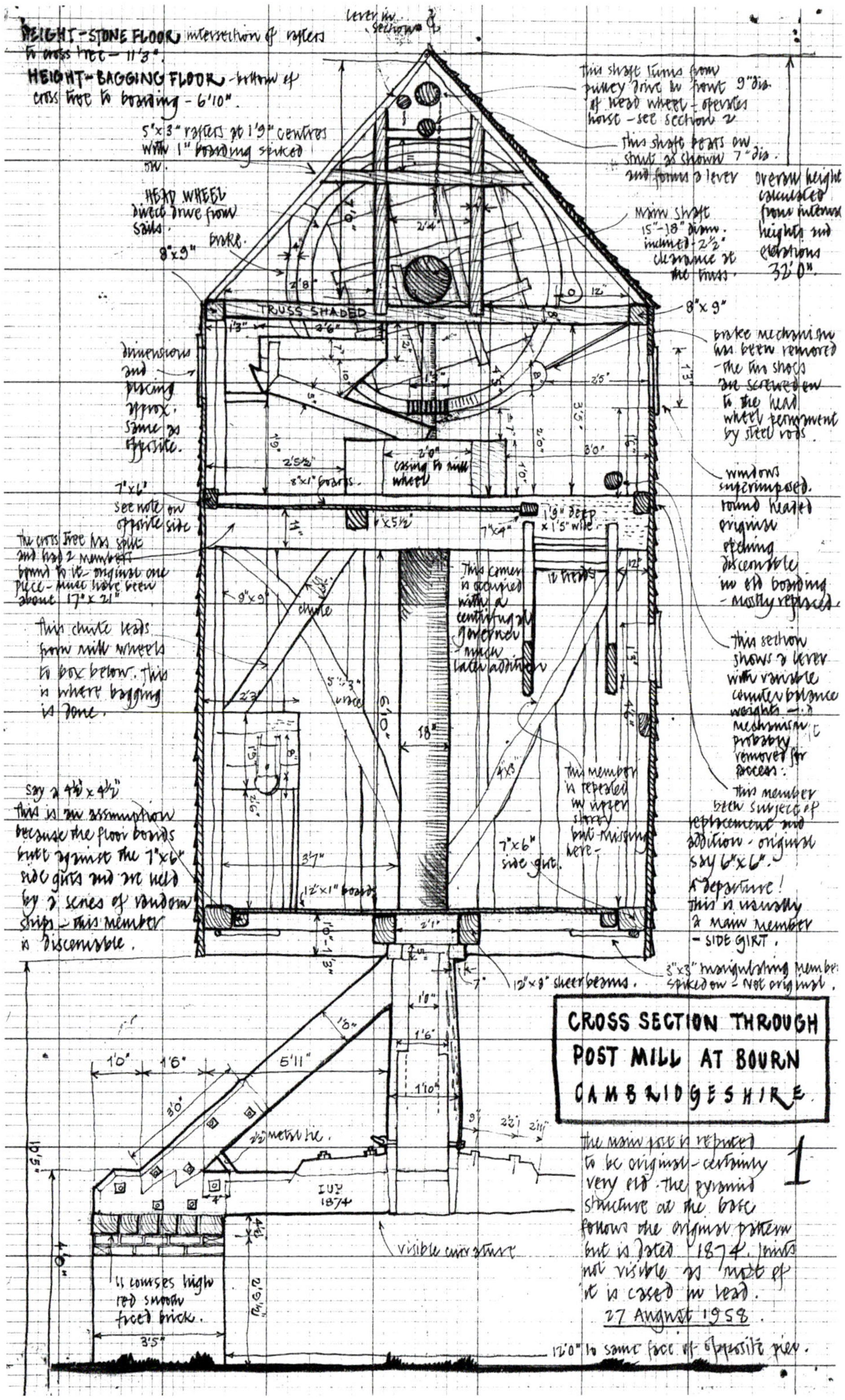

16 Norman Foster Works 1

**I am fascinated by going back to basics. I was amazed by windmills when I was a student, and made numerous drawings of these marvellous structures. Interestingly, we have recently been commissioned to work with a manufacturer to develop a large wind turbine.** Norman Foster, lecture at the Solar Energy Conference, Florence, 17 May 1993
Right to far right: The E66 wind turbine (1993) has an individual power rating of 1.8 megawatts. One hundred metres high, with a wing span of 66 metres, each turbine can generate enough clean, renewable energy to supply up to 1,500 homes (far right). The first completed UK example was installed at Swaffam in Norfolk, seen here.

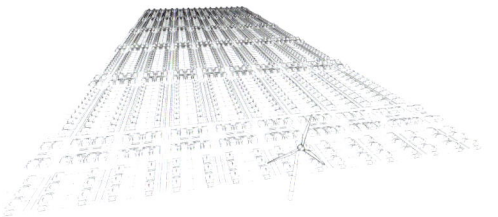

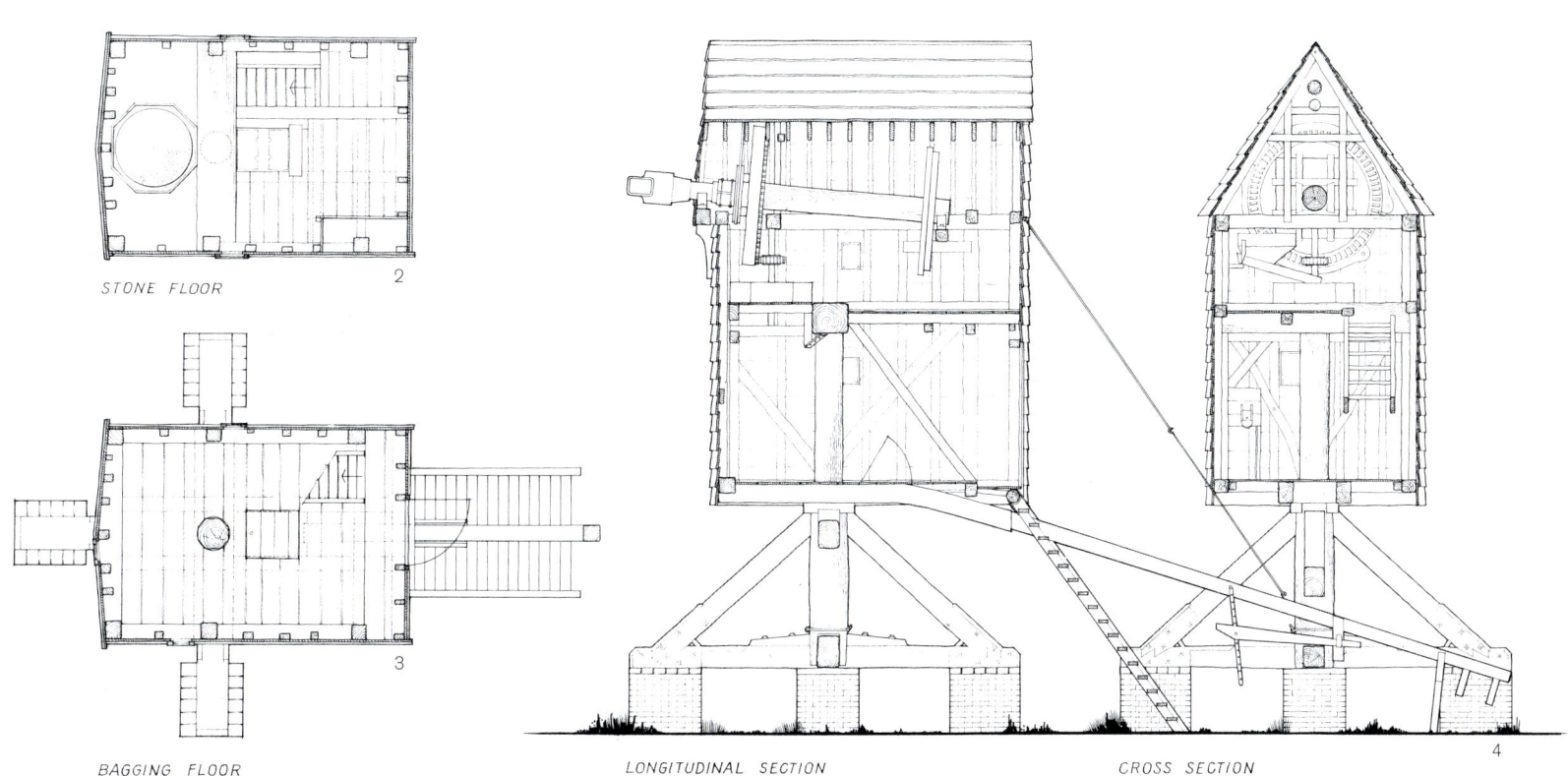

STONE FLOOR  2

BAGGING FLOOR  3

LONGITUDINAL SECTION    CROSS SECTION   4

SIDE ELEVATION    FRONT ELEVATION    REAR ELEVATION   5

Measured Drawings  17

# The Impact of Yale
Robert A M Stern 1999

Norman Foster is without question one of the most accomplished and most influential architects of our time. What interests me in particular about Foster's career is the continuing exchange of English, European, and American ideas and techniques. The Anglo-American part of this exchange has its practical, experience-based beginning in 1961 at Yale University, where both Foster and I were architecture students. Our time at Yale had a profound and different effect on each of us, leading me to question the then 'constituent facts' of modernism and modernity, and Foster to open his work up to the various 'constituent facts' of the American experience, including its vast landscape and its unabashed commercialism.

In 1951, ten years before going to Yale, Norman Foster, then aged sixteen, had already begun to develop a healthy interest in architecture, in part stimulated by trips to the local public library in Levenshulme, the Manchester suburb where he grew up. It was there, as he recalled recently, that he '… discovered the different worlds of Frank Lloyd Wright and Le Corbusier. Imagine the contrast of a home on the Prairie with a villa on a Paris boulevard. Yet I remember being equally fascinated by both at the time.'

**What interests me about Foster's career is the continuing exchange of English, European and American ideas and techniques. The Anglo-American part of this exchange has its beginning in 1961 at Yale University.**

At just the moment that Foster was educating himself in the history of architecture, however, he was called up for two years' mandatory National Service, which he elected to serve in the Royal Air Force. Following his return to civilian life and his subsequent graduation from Manchester University School of Architecture, Foster arrived in New Haven in the autumn of 1961 aided by a Henry Fellowship which each year enables selected British students to study either at Yale or Harvard universities while their opposite numbers study at Oxford or Cambridge. Foster was a Guest Fellow in Jonathan Edwards College, one of Yale's residential colleges modelled on those found in Oxbridge. Interestingly, Foster had been offered a Fulbright Travel Scholarship, but declined the award because it would have inhibited his freedom to work in the United States.

Foster's decision to go to Yale was not easily arrived at, nor did the value of the place immediately manifest itself to him. For a time he wondered if he might not have done better to have gone to the University of Pennsylvania and studied under Louis Kahn. Soon enough, however, Foster found Yale to be a liberating place, alive to the possibilities of architecture as an art and to the cross-currents of prevailing styles, ideologies, and passions.

**I first came to America as a student over 30 years ago. America was the land of my heroes – a very long list – and it still is. I had great expectations and they were fulfilled beyond the dreams that I dared not dream ... When I came to the United States I felt that I had come home. There was a pride in working and serving. I felt liberated. It is no exaggeration to say that I discovered myself through America.** Norman Foster, AIA Gold Medal address, Washington, 1 February 1994

Right: Although the University boasts major works by twentieth-century Modernists such as Louis Kahn, Eero Saarinen and Paul Rudolph, the Yale campus is characterised predominantly by nineteenth-century pastiche collegiate architecture, complete with Oxbridge-inspired spires and quadrangles.

A small school, at the time – really a department in the School of Art and Architecture – Yale was dominated by two great teachers: the architect Paul Rudolph and the architectural historian Vincent Scully. There were, of course, other permanent faculty members but the great strength of the school lay in the interplay between Scully and Rudolph and, in turn, in their interplay with a host of visiting critics, including American architects such as Philip Johnson, Henry Cobb, Craig Ellwood, and Ulrich Franzen, to name a few. They were joined by Europeans such as Frei Otto, Henning Larsen, and Shadrach Woods and especially the British architects James Stirling and Colin St. John Wilson.

In Foster's year at Yale, the Masters class benefited not only from his presence but from that of two other brilliant English students: Eldred Evans and Richard Rogers. The confluence at Yale of the three – who had not known each other in England – proved to be remarkably important for the future of architecture, as was their interaction with American students in the class, such as Carl Abbott, as well as others in the four-year-long Baccalaureate programme, including Charles Gwathmey, Jonathan Barnett, M J Long, David Sellers, Peter Gluck, and David Childs.

Paul Rudolph's Yale was a phenomenon, a surprise newcomer on an American architectural scene that had been dominated by Harvard since the late 1930s when Walter Gropius took over as Chairman of its architecture programme. When Rudolph became head of the Yale programme, in 1958, it was in a state of disarray, despite a burst of energy in the early 1950s when George Howe – assisted by Louis Kahn and Philip Johnson – had revived it.

Following Howe's retirement, in 1954, the school became rank with contentiousness under his short-term successor, Paul Schweikher; but Rudolph's regime changed all that. By the time Foster arrived, Yale occupied a position of international prominence in architectural education. It was arguably the most talked about architecture programme in the world.

Rudolph's appointment had required a great leap of faith. He was no 'educator' in the generally accepted sense of the term, but he was a brilliantly talented architect, whose reputation rested on the bedrock of a dazzling series of small houses, mostly in Sarasota, Florida. In the late 1950s Rudolph's practice was blossoming. His first major work, the Jewett Arts Center at Wellesley College, was nearing completion and was already regarded as a serious challenge to the uniformity and placelessness of the American version of the International Style which Gropius and Breuer had advocated at Harvard in the 1940s.

## Foster's decision to go to Yale was not easily arrived at. But he found Yale to be a liberating place, alive to the possibilities of architecture as an art and to the cross-currents of prevailing styles, ideologies, and passions.

Rudolph was not only not an educator, he was not very well educated himself. He was in no way like his courtly and well-connected predecessor, George Howe, who had come from wealth, attended Groton and Harvard with Franklin Roosevelt, and spent four years in Paris at the Ecole des Beaux-Arts. Rudolph, a Methodist minister's son raised in a variety of Southern towns, lacked cultivation and was brusque in a way many found refreshing – and many did not. He had studied at Alabama Polytechnical Institute (now Auburn University) and although he had gone on to complete two years in the Masters class at Harvard, at the time of his appointment to Yale, his professional academic experience was confined to a succession of posts as visiting critic at a dozen or more provincial universities.

1. For his final year thesis at Manchester University Norman Foster designed a new museum for the Faculty of Anthropology at Cambridge University. The proposed building's centre piece was a three-storey glass walled gallery to house the largest items in the collection.

2. A cross-section through the scheme reveals an early concern with bringing natural light into an interior – a theme that has been developed across a range of projects in the course of Foster's career.

3. Norman Foster, photographed with fellow Yale students Richard Rogers and Carl Abbott, on their pilgrimage to see the architecture of Chicago, well wrapped up against the extreme chill of the Midwest winter.

3

**Perhaps the strongest common thread that linked Rudolph the architect and Rudolph the teacher was a sense of absolute commitment, a moral imperative in which no effort was spared, however late in the process, to improve the quality of architecture, whether in his own buildings or, by inspiration, in the work of his students. It is an example that will live on in all of those who shared his influence.** Norman Foster, *Paul Rudolph*, 1999

**By the time he designed the Art and Architecture Building at Yale, [Rudolph's] personal style was assured: violent contrasts of scale and colossal piers in rough corduroy concrete gave the whole building a vaguely primitive air. Silhouettes and sequences were expressed in an exaggeratedly irregular external volume.** William J R Curtis, *Modern Architecture since 1900,* 1996
Left: Rudolph's Yale School of Art and Architecture, completed in 1963, the year that Foster finished his studies at Yale. Prior to the completion of this building, the architecture school occupied a studio on the top floor of Louis Kahn's Yale University Art Gallery.

1. Paul Rudolph's zeal and enthusiasm are captured in this photograph taken during a typical crit at Yale. Head of Yale's architecture programme from 1958 to 1965 – while running his own practice with studios in Connecticut, Florida, Massachusetts and New York – Rudolph was, Foster says, the main reason he chose to study at Yale for his Masters.

2. Rudolph working vertically on a large-scale presentation drawing of the kind that made so definitive an impact on Norman Foster.

Rudolph, forty years old when he took over Yale, was not that much older than some of his students, whose education had been interrupted by the Korean War. He lacked a theory of education, and did not seem particularly interested in developing one. But he was intensely interested in the 'learning process'. He viewed the art of building in strictly heroic terms and passionately believed in the capacity of the architectural idea – and the architect – to prevail over day-to-day circumstances. For him theory was synonymous with the big idea that carried the day:

'Theory', he argued, 'must again overtake action … Architectural education's first concern is to perpetuate a climate where the student is acutely and perceptively aware of the creative process. He must understand that after all the building committees, the conflicting interests, the budget considerations and the limitations of his fellow man have been taken into consideration, that his responsibility has just begun. He must understand that in the exhilarating, awesome moment when he takes pencil in hand, and holds it poised above a white sheet of paper, that he has suspended there all that will ever be. The creative act is all that matters.'

The zenith of Rudolph's effectiveness as a teacher can be said to be the years 1960 through 1963, when his career as a practising architect was in full flood and he worked intensely on the design of the watershed building that would become the new home of Yale's School of Art and Architecture.

Vincent Scully was the other important guiding force at Yale at the time. Scully played a key role not only as a brilliant Professor of Art History, but as an active participant in the crits and juries in the design studio. Cut from the same cloth as Malraux or Camus, Scully was an engaged intellectual. Typical of his often controversial stands on contemporary architecture was his endorsement of the then vigorously debated late work of Le Corbusier.

**A small school at the time – really a department in the School of Art and Architecture – Yale was dominated by two great teachers. The great strength of the school lay in the interplay between Scully and Rudolph and, in turn, in their interplay with a host of visiting critics.**

Scully, a local boy from New Haven, was a graduate of Yale College and its graduate school. He had seen active service in the Second World War and had been teaching at Yale since the late 1940s. By the 1960s, Scully's lectures were the stuff of legend; indeed, he was among the first of the academic media stars, working with film-makers and frequently quoted in the press.

20  Norman Foster Works 1

> Vincent Scully's insights opened my eyes to the interaction between the Old World and the New. He made more meaningful those European cities whose urban spaces and modern works I had studied on my travels as a student at Manchester.
> Norman Foster, Pritzker Prize acceptance speech, Berlin, 7 June 1999

Right, far right: Vincent Scully's *American Architecture and Urbanism*, published in 1969, and *The Earth, the Temple and the Gods*, published in 1962, illustrate the breadth and scope of Scully's work.

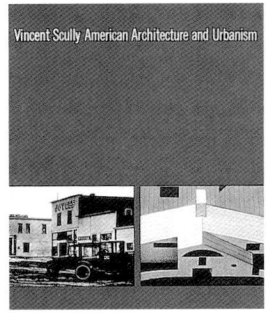
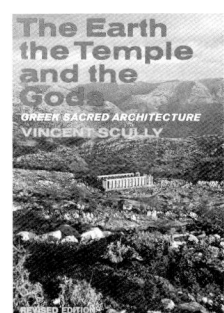

David McCullough, in a profile in 1959, in *Architectural Forum*, dubbed Scully an 'Architectural Spellbinder'. Scully's theatrical lectures electrified his audiences, challenging architects and would-be architects while fostering a profound interest in the built world among Yale's other undergraduates who would carry this new-found awareness to their work in different fields.

Scully taught a generation to view buildings as the embodiment of ideas and ideals. He also taught them how to see, bringing inert matter to life as – with a scholar's knowledge and an actor's passion – he brought out the empathetic relationship between mankind and masterworks of the built environment, be they Greek temples sited in the landscape, or the taut abstractions of post-war industrialization. To a remarkable extent, Scully's perceptions helped to shape those of his most talented students – including Foster – and his powerful convictions became central to his students' own concerns about architecture. At the deepest level, Scully's influence was based on his feeling for the interrelation of man, building and place. And his reach extended far beyond the lectern; he published prolifically in the early 1960s, completing monographs on Frank Lloyd Wright and Louis Kahn, as well as *Modern Architecture: The Architecture of Democracy* and *The Earth, the Temple, and the Gods: Greek Sacred Architecture*, both published in 1962.

In specific historical terms, Scully stressed the great differences between European and American architecture, elevating the latter from its then lowly status as a mere footnote to the former. He dramatically and memorably presented the work of Henry Hobson Richardson, Louis Sullivan, and particularly that of Frank Lloyd Wright, as part of a continuum across national borders yet uniquely expressive of American issues of landscape and culture. In 1999, when accepting one of the architectural profession's highest honours, the Pritzker Prize, Foster pinpointed a key aspect of his teacher's impact, asserting that 'the insights of Vincent Scully … opened my eyes to the interaction between the Old World and the New'.

Louis Kahn was another highly consequential force at Yale when Foster arrived, although he was no longer teaching there. Kahn and Rudolph did not get on and the University of Pennsylvania, Kahn's alma mater, offered a more convenient and to his mind, congenial, setting. Kahn nonetheless seemed ubiquitous. Scully had got to know Kahn during the architect's Yale years in the 1940s and 1950s and Scully's lectures often promoted, and interpreted new projects by him long before they were published in the journals. As a result, Kahn's work was vigorously debated in the Yale studios.

3. Vincent Scully, world renowned architectural historian and mainstay of the Yale Art History Department since 1947. Scully's panoramic and insightful approach to architectural history ranged from explorations of the 'Shingle Style' of the New England beach house to the development of urbanism in America, taking in Classical architecture, and the work of Modernists such as Frank Lloyd Wright and Louis Kahn along the way. His work is unified by its consistent exploration of the relationship between man, building and place.

4. The 'Architectural Spellbinder' at work. Scully delivers a lecture to a packed auditorium in the Yale School of Art and Architecture. A typically encyclopaedic lecture might range from discussions of the film currently showing at the local cinema or the work being undertaken at Eero Saarinen's New Haven office to why the Greeks built temples.

**Jim really brings together three forces: teacher, draughtsman and designer – all inextricably linked as James Stirling, the architect. Regardless of workload, he has been a visiting Professor at Yale for over twenty years now; and it was as a graduate student at Yale that I first came into contact with him. He was the kind of tutor who refused to say how he would do it, but would rather force you back on your own resources by posing the awkward questions, and quite right too.** Norman Foster, introducing James Stirling as Royal Gold Medallist, RIBA, London, 21 June 1980
Right: A cutaway drawing of Stirling and Gowan's Ham Common Flats, 1955-1958, a project that Norman Foster visited and admired.

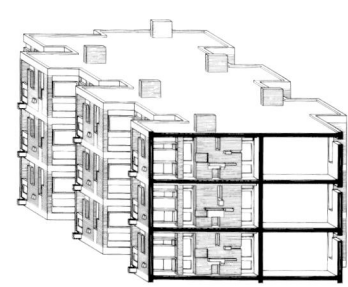

1. James Stirling's connection with Yale spanned twenty-four years. He was visiting critic in 1959 and 1961, and from 1966 to 1983 he was Davenport Professor for one semester each year.

Kahn also came to New Haven for juries and public lectures, a typical one of which was published in 1965 in Volume 9-10 of *Perspecta*, the student-run Yale journal which had begun publishing in 1952. Perhaps Kahn's biggest impact on Yale architecture students in the early 1960s was through his Art Gallery, completed in 1953, an epochal building which married the influences of Mies van der Rohe, Le Corbusier, and Richard Buckminster Fuller. The building exerted a powerful, positive influence on virtually all those students who spent seemingly endless days and nights in its extensively glazed, concrete-trussed, fourth-floor drafting room.

During the early 1960s the presence of brilliant visiting English architects immeasurably enriched the New Haven scene and brought to it a much-needed cosmopolitan approach that Rudolph's inherent provincialism lacked. The English offered an alternative way of looking at things. Their admiration of the uninhibited formal exuberance of American architecture, especially roadside and other commercial vernacular work, came as a surprise to the locals who were still embarrassed by the absence of high cultural aspirations in so much native building.

Moreover, the English not only seemed to admire the everyday buildings which embarrassed the Americans, they also found most American high-art efforts pretentious. According to M J Long – a Canadian educated at an American college, and a student at Yale between 1960 and 1964 – the English afforded a nexus of countervailing criticism against '… the forced and rather blousy monumentality prevalent at the school'. In the mid-1970s, Long recalled the English influence at Yale: 'The English used *humble* materials (brick rather than concrete) and displayed a natural reticence which sometimes emerged as anti-monumentality. They talked about Aalto as much as about Corbu. They showed that it was not necessary to resort to anaemic form as an antidote to overblown form – their buildings at best had a kind of animal toughness and boniness. It was a set of images which we could use and it took hold, just before Moore and Venturi pointed to the possibilities in traditional American wood buildings and gave to others of us a similarly usable alternative set of images … They were also interested in issues of planning and saw them in design terms … And, they were never anti-intellectual; on the contrary, they were highly articulate and historically conscious.'

**During the early 1960s the presence of brilliant visiting English architects immeasurably enriched the New Haven scene and brought to it a much-needed cosmopolitan approach. The English offered an alternative way of looking at things.**

Among the visiting British critics at Yale, James Stirling exerted the most profound and lasting influence. In a break with the historical 'know-nothingism' of the 1940s and 1950s, Stirling made it respectable for Yale students to consider the past. In this he was complemented by Philip Johnson who in 1959 began a lecture at Yale by writing on the chalkboard: 'You cannot not know history.'

1

**The list of influences and inspirations from my days in America is a long one – Frank Lloyd Wright, Mies, Eames, airstream caravans, Cape Canaveral, trucks, indigenous Indian dwellings, colonial houses, bridges and endless highways that disappeared with infinite perspective to the horizon.** Norman Foster, *Norman Foster: Sketches*, 1992
Right: Norman Foster's photograph of the gleaming rig of a North American truck.

To students who were still in the thrall of anti-traditionalist Modernism, Stirling offered a strong dose of its opposite – a Modernism that drew from both the Modernist and the pre-Modernist past. Like Rudolph, Stirling tended to see history as a justification for romantic formalism, but Stirling's grasp of the past was deeper and broader. Stirling was keenly aware of – and troubled by – the limited definition of modern architecture that had come to be accepted. In his essay, 'The Functional Tradition and Expression', published in 1960 in Volume 6 of *Perspecta*, Stirling not only made a plea for an expanded vocabulary of form but also exposed his own work to direct comparison with the best of the past.

He showed Blenheim Palace alongside unidentified medieval fortifications and walled cities, as well as passed-over nineteenth-century English brick vernacular architecture, and the late work of Le Corbusier which he suggested did not subscribe to the extreme reductionism of the Cubist work of the 1920s, or similarly minimalist work by Gropius and Mies van der Rohe. This was remarkable and largely new to American architects, and perhaps also to Foster, who first got to know Stirling at Yale.

Though in one sense Stirling's argument suggested that enriched form should arise from a more careful and imaginative representation of a building's functional programme, on the other hand, he chose to illustrate his text with images from the past coupled with those of his own recent work. To be 'modern' was no longer enough. Stirling presented Trinity College in contrast to his and his partner James Gowan's Churchill College scheme of 1958, as well as a traditional English farmhouse paired with his own Woolton House of 1954, and nineteenth-century English commercial and industrial buildings seen in counterpoint with his and Gowan's Ham Common flats of 1955-1958.

As a result of their publication in *Perspecta*, Stirling and Gowan's housing projects at Ham Common and Stirling and Alan Cordingley's work for Sheffield University became stylistic touchstones for Yale students, and for Rudolph as well. At a time when heroic, self-invented and self-inventing architecture was very much the model, Stirling's bold move to show how his and Gowan's work derived from the forms of high and low buildings from the past was almost unique.

## By the time Foster arrived, Yale occupied a position of international prominence in architectural education. It was, arguably, the most talked about architecture programme in the world.

Three other Britons – Colin St. John Wilson and Alison and Peter Smithson – significantly contributed to Yale's intellectual climate, although all of them preceded Foster by a year and did not have direct contact with him at Yale. Nonetheless, their impact on the school was still apparent in 1961-1962. Colin St. John Wilson – 'Sandy' to students and faculty alike – offered a yet more complicated reading of the recent past than did Stirling. Wilson loved things American in a way the British frequently then did: he loved jazz, especially Miles Davis, even though most young Americans were not that interested in it, preferring folk music or rock and roll. Yet despite his love of jazz – and the English version of pop art – he was appalled by pop culture as it really was in America, sharing with many American intellectuals a highbrow dislike of commercial design that Peter Blake would elaborate upon in his book, *God's Own Junkyard,* of 1964.

Alison and Peter Smithson were better known for their writings and exhibitions than for their buildings, although Scully admired extravagantly their school at Hunstanton and showed it in his classes. Of the Smithsons' ideas, that of 'ordinariness' proved the most compelling. The idea rooted itself more deeply and lastingly into the Yale psyche than any other, resonating for years to come, perhaps as an antidote to Rudolph's heroic bluster.

**The Yale University Art Gallery ... responded to the many levels and textures of an elective urban environment with a subtle, inward-looking design. The interior spaces seemed to evoke an entirely different world from the brash, mass-produced environment of standardised panels and suspended ceilings then prevalent in the United States, by subtle effects of light falling over the triangulated web of the concrete ceiling and by the direct use of materials, evident in the bare yet elegant concrete piers.** William J R Curtis, *Modern Architecture since 1900*, 1996
Right: Louis Kahn's Yale University Art Gallery, completed in 1953. During Foster's time at Yale the architecture studio was located on the top floor of this building.

**The school, housed in a Louis Kahn building, was next to where I lived and was open 24 hours a day from the first day of term to the last. This was an incredible luxury, as I was used to a university where everything closed at 5.00pm, and you had to pack your work up, take it home, carry on, and then come back the next day and set it up again. Being able to integrate work and life was an extraordinary experience. That school of architecture at Yale became, consciously, the model for our office today, as it too is a 24-hour, seven-days-a-week environment, providing the flexibility to accommodate individual needs and the demands of circumstances.** Norman Foster, lecture at Stuttgart University, 14 May 1997

1. During Norman Foster's time at Yale the drafting studio was located on the top floor of Louis Kahn's Yale University Art Gallery. Foster's own rooms in Jonathan Edwards College were mere minutes away.

2. Norman Foster with Masters class colleagues John Chisholm, Richard Rogers and Roy Mason.

Another British influence on the early 1960s Yale scene – disproportionately strong perhaps given the brevity of the contact – was that of Peter Reyner Banham, an engineer turned architectural critic and historian, who was at Yale in 1960-1961 and returned in the spring of 1962 to visit the recently completed Morse and Stiles Colleges, a posthumous work of Eero Saarinen. Perhaps the most emblematic American architect of his generation, Saarinen was a graduate of the Yale architecture school and a close advisor to Whitney Griswold, the Yale president whose passionate support of modern architecture fuelled the university's extensive post-war building programme.

Saarinen's proto-Postmodernist Morse and Stiles residential colleges 'disgusted' Banham 'at sight' and still appalled him four weeks later when he slammed them in a review in the *New Statesman*, stating that there were 'no extenuating circumstances' to justify the design for which 'the client gave the architect plenty of rope'. Although Banham disliked Saarinen's special kind of concrete, he really saved his venom for what he lambasted as 'Gordon Craig-type scenic effects' which he felt were achieved at the price of the 'medieval standards' of student accommodation. Banham had already denounced Saarinen, architect of the US Embassy in Grosvenor Square, London, as one of America's 'most trivial performers'.

For many in New Haven, Banham's hatchet-job on the Yale residential colleges went too far in a too public way. Not content to take a swipe at the recently deceased Saarinen's design, he also went after the architect's wife, the art critic Aline B Louchheim, dismissing her as the 'formidable Saarinen widow', and then lamented that the dormitories employed 'that creeping malady that causes an increasing number of returning Europeans to say "Yale is a very sick place", the malady of gratuitous affluences irresponsibly exploited ...'

## Architectural education's first concern is to perpetuate a climate where the student is acutely and perceptively aware of the creative process.

Such was the backdrop of stimulating, if sometimes overheated design and intellectual debate that greeted Foster in 1961. In Manchester, lacking a grant and forced to fund his own way through his studies, he had been compelled to live at home and to work at an array of part-time jobs, from manning the night-shift in a bakery to being a bouncer in a rough cinema. New Haven, in contrast, offered the luxury of time to study and think and debate.

While the students in the architecture department were intensely focused on their work as designers – the drafting room was open to students twenty-four hours a day – the programme of studies also encouraged students to pursue interests in architectural history and planning and, in fact, whatever else attracted them from among the university's broad course offerings. Moreover, in a time when there was still comparatively little cross-fertilisation among cultures, Foster and the other Britons then studying in the architecture department – together with Rogers' wife Su, who was studying for a Masters degree in City Planning – found themselves challenged, even confounded, by the American way of doing things.

**At the end of a programme we often worked through the last couple of nights, thanks to Paul Rudolph's habit of appearing just in time to savage every scheme in sight so that it all had to be done again.** Norman Foster, introduction to *Pierre Koenig*, 1998

**There were some thirteen students working on the top floor in Louis Kahn's beautiful Yale Art Museum. Rudolph expected full commitment, 24 hours a day, with surprise tutorials at 2am. Those who collapsed at their drawing boards didn't make it. Fortunately, there was a couch on which we took turns to sleep. We certainly learned to work extremely hard and to use our eyes – not an English tradition.** Richard Rogers, 'Team 4', 1991

This situation was exacerbated by the fact that the English visitors were a little older than most of their American counterparts. They considered themselves to be not quite students – or at least in a different league from their Yankee student cousins. The English would-be architects did not want to be instructed, per se, preferring to discuss, debate and deliberate at length; they put off committing their ideas to paper for as long as possible.

One day Foster and his compatriots found posted above their desks a sign that read: 'Start drawing'. The English response was to post another sign that read: 'Start thinking'. While these strikingly different approaches produced a certain degree of tension, their juxtaposition ultimately proved fertile ground for Foster's imagination. Foster has said of his time at Yale, '… looking back with the perspective of nearly forty years I can see that our practice has been inspired by [those] polarities of analysis and action.'

Though the American and English students differed in many ways, Foster got on quite well with his American classmates. In particular, he formed a close friendship with Carl Abbott, who was from the west coast of Florida. Abbott would return there after his time at Yale – and a stint in London when he worked with Foster and Rogers – to establish his own practice in Sarasota that to this day extends the spirit of Rudolph's early architectural achievements in that city.

While at Yale Foster also began a life-long friendship with Richard Rogers. How amazing that friendship was between two gifted students who would later practise together. How ironic, as well, that the two architects who, working separately, would subsequently dominate British architecture for decades, first met as they prepared to leave their home country – at a reception for English students who had been offered Fulbright Travel Scholarships.

Both Foster and Rogers were bowled over by Yale – each in his own way. Rudolph's driven and hard-driving working and teaching styles were a complete surprise. He constantly pressured students to work fast and around the clock and would stage surprise late night crits. Foster found his pressure-cooker methods exhilarating. A superb draughtsman and model-maker, Foster was used to racing the clock; having worked his way through school in Manchester he understood that time was precious.

2

**Rudolph had created a studio atmosphere of fevered activity, highly competitive and fuelled by a succession of visiting luminaries. Crits were open and accessible – often combative. It was a 'can-do' approach in which concepts could be shredded one day and reborn overnight.**
Norman Foster

The Impact of Yale 25

**At Yale Foster sharpened up his drawing technique under Paul Rudolph – the exploded section and heavily shaded elevations with which all Foster buildings from Reliance Controls on are presented owe something to Rudolph.**
Alastair Best, *The Architectural Review*, April 1986
Left: Rudolph's perspective section of the Yale School of Art and Architecture is typical of the presentational style which so impressed Foster as a student. The cutaway section was Rudolph's preferred method of explaining his own projects, and Foster was later to make this drawing style very much his own.

1. Norman Foster's first project at Yale was for an American high school. Paul Rudolph, renowned at Yale for his 'no-holds-barred' approach to crits, was impressed with the scheme and praised Foster for 'thinking like an architect', even if his trees 'looked like cauliflowers'.

Foster recalls: 'Rudolph had created a studio atmosphere of fevered activity, highly competitive and fuelled by a succession of visiting luminaries. Crits were open and accessible – often combative. It was a "can-do" approach in which concepts could be shredded one day and reborn overnight. But the only criterion was the quality of the work presented – the architecture of the drawings and models. There was no room for excuses, no substitutes of rhetoric.'

At Yale Foster learned to look hard at what was around him and what was on the drawing board before him. As Rogers, who later described his time in New Haven as 'wonderful heady days', would note, the Britons at Yale learned 'to use our eyes, not an English tradition'. In the studio the importance of 'using one's eyes' was stressed most of all by Rudolph who was brilliantly and instinctively visual. In the lecture hall, this same approach was emphasised by Scully. So compelling did Foster find Scully's presentation and interpretation of Wright's uniquely American architecture that on one short, between-terms break, he, together with Carl Abbott and Richard and Su Rogers, squeezed into Abbott's Volkswagen Beetle and visited nearly every Wright building in the Midwest.

Foster's first studio project at Yale not surprisingly reflected Rudolph's influence. Rudolph had assigned the design of a public high school, a relatively workaday building type which – three years earlier – he had raised to the level of architectural art in Sarasota, Florida, by imaginatively translating Le Corbusier's High Court Building at Chandigarh through the medium of American technology and the realities of American programmes and budgets. At the final project crit, Rudolph praised Foster for 'thinking like an architect', even if the trees in his Rudolph-inspired renderings 'looked like cauliflowers'.

Foster considers his project for an office building to be the best of his Yale work. The design problem Rudolph assigned was once again a reconsideration of one of his actual commissions – in this case his massive concrete, Blue Cross-Blue Shield building, completed in Boston in 1957. Foster's project consisted of a cluster of towers which marched round the corner, 'where office space was supported by a structural service core with great splayed feet', as Rogers later put it. The project incorporated a structurally expressive building profile, exposed service elements, and a strong programmatic mix that represented a distinct break with the Rudolph model and strongly suggested spatial and structural lessons learned from Louis Kahn.

**One day Foster and his compatriots found posted above their desks a sign that read: 'Start drawing'. The English response was to post another sign that read: 'Start thinking'.**

Foster's design also stood in sharp contrast to the prevailing open-field neutrality pioneered by Mies van der Rohe. In Foster's design the areas of office space were broken up into column-free sections spanning concrete towers that housed vertical services, surely an anticipation of his Hongkong and Shanghai Banking Corporation headquarters building in Hong Kong, an architectural and engineering *tour de force* completed in 1985.

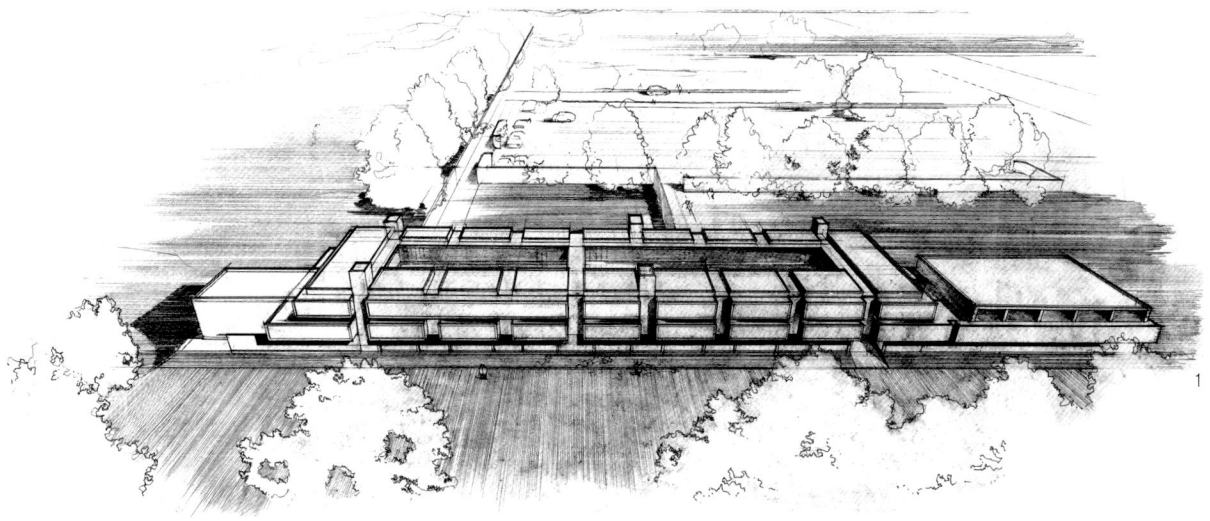

> There was a kind of missionary zeal about Rudolph. He could be daunting in the manner and content of his criticism – but you also knew that he was equally tough on himself. I found that out first-hand by working in his office as a lowly draughtsman. Those immaculate illustrations that I had long admired turned out to be giant-sized ink drawings on white boards – the grain of lines would be designed for later reduction in scale. Details of the perspectives would be changed by pasting over pieces of white card like a patchwork quilt and I would redraw the areas under scrutiny – matching up the thousands of hand-crafted lines.
> Norman Foster, *Paul Rudolph*, 1999

> During a presentation of our project for a science laboratory complex, Paul Rudolph was joined by Philip Johnson. They surveyed our presentation material and Philip immediately questioned some stepped buildings branching off a central spine – 'I've already told them what I think about that' said Paul. Whereupon Philip set about the model, ripping off all the offending pieces – and finally pronouncing that we now had a very good scheme indeed! In retrospect they were both right – the model looked much better.
> Norman Foster, *Norman Foster: Sketches*, 1992

While at Yale, Foster and Rogers collaborated on a studio design problem, the Pierson Sage Science Laboratories in the Hillhouse section of the university's campus – a complex actually entrusted to Philip Johnson, whose resulting Kline Science Center deferred to the site's older medieval-inspired buildings by Delano & Aldrich and others, while incorporating the misconceived Modernist Gibbs Physics Laboratory designed by Howe's successor as architecture department head, Paul Schweikher.

In this project, Rudolph challenged the students to take into consideration not merely programmatic requirements but also what he believed to be the deplorable state of contemporary architecture as a whole. The brief he presented to the students stated: 'This is an urban problem. It is also the problem of the architect, as planners and developers have failed to rebuild our cities. They are obsessed with numbers (people, money, acreage, units, cars, roads, etc.) and forget life itself and the spirit of man.'

According to Rogers, he and Foster worked on the project together, 'to the horror of Rudolph'. Nonetheless, their scheme was a marvel, introducing to the local scene, and perhaps to American practice as a whole, a mega-structural approach that was a radical departure from the typical, isolated, building-by-building campus model. Foster and Rogers proposed a central spine of car parking, from which lecture halls and other facilities projected at right angles forming wings that stepped downhill to confront existing buildings at an appropriate scale.

Though the scheme's mega-structural scale and diagrammatic approach were distinctly English, or at least not American, there were aspects to the proposals that were quite familiar – especially the Kahn-inspired service towers. Philip Johnson, one of the guest jurors at the final review, adopted a typically robust approach to architectural criticism. He took a strong dislike to the buildings placed on top of the spine. After staring at the balsa wood model of the project, he proceeded to crush these blocks in his fist, saying: 'Have to do something about these'. Whatever the project's weaknesses, however, Foster and Rogers' explosion of scale and their ability to command the entirety of the large and complex site were nothing short of astonishing.

Foster's last Yale project was for a new city. The project was realised in collaboration with four other students but verbally presented for jury review by Foster, who had been elected by his co-designers to act as spokesman. It was clear even then that besides talent and drive Foster possessed an attribute deemed by many to be quintessentially that of American business practice: the ability not only to work in a team but also to become its leader. The design of the new city incorporated aspects of Foster's earlier office tower project, constituting a form of self-quotation that had characterised the urban proposals of Le Corbusier and Frank Lloyd Wright.

Foster's scheme was developed under the guidance of the European-born Serge Chermayeff, whom Rudolph had brought to Yale from Harvard in a deliberate if possibly misguided attempt to lodge an anti-heroic, anti-aesthetic point of view in the curriculum. Whatever the complex intentions behind Chermayeff's appointment as Professor of Architecture, his influence, particularly on Foster, was lasting and profound. Chermayeff added a distinctively European seasoning to the already rich Anglo-American soup.

Foster has argued that, 'My timing at Yale in 1961 was more fortunate than I could ever have foreseen because it marked the change of leadership to Serge Chermayeff. He was as European as Rudolph was American. It was not just in dress or manner, but deeply rooted differences in philosophy. For Chermayeff debate and theory took precedence over imagery – questioning was to the fore – analysis dominated action'.

2. The cutaway section was a favourite drawing of Rudolph's which he often used to explain his own projects. Norman Foster explored the technique in this project for a private house. For Foster the scheme was not a success but, as a means to understanding the integration and assembly of components, he was later to make this type of drawing very much his own.

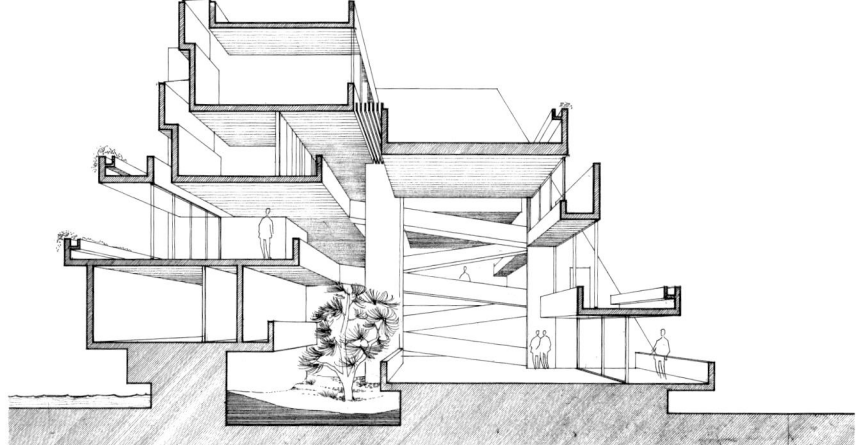

**When Rudolph issued a new design assignment, we always assumed it was the latest commission that had just come into his practice. He delighted in using the Masters class that way – and it was certainly good for us!** Norman Foster in conversation with Malcolm Quantrill, 1999
Right: Paul Rudolph's Blue Cross-Blue Shield building in Boston, completed in 1967. Rudolph set this commission as a design project for his students, in response to which Foster produced his design for an office tower, below.
Far right: The free-spanning office floors sandwiched between edge service zones explored in Foster's student project were ultimately to be realised in the Hongkong and Shanghai Bank (1979-1986).

**In the design project for a high-rise building I completed as a student, bays of flexible space were suspended between towers of structure, services and vertical circulation, with a cross-section that was staggered to express the different kind of spaces and to create a more distinctive profile on the skyline. It is interesting to note that this could be a word picture for the Hongkong Bank project which we completed some twenty years later.** Norman Foster, RIBA Royal Gold Medal address, London, 21 June 1983

1. Norman Foster's scheme for an office building was an early lesson in integrating a large building into a tight urban context. The plan responded to the curve of the site while also creating a series of protected plazas that linked the new offices to an existing shopping mall.

2. There was a tradition at Yale for first year students of the architecture school to help Masters students on selected projects. A young Japanese student worked with Foster to produce this immaculate white card model of the office towers.

3. Considered by Foster to be the best of his Yale projects, the office tower was influenced by Louis Kahn's concept of served and servant spaces, incorporating open-planned office floors spanning between edge service zones, a model that would later inform the development of the headquarters for the Hongkong and Shanghai Bank (1979-1986). A mixture of smaller professional suites, at the lower levels, with larger corporate offices above, invited a broad spectrum of potential users.

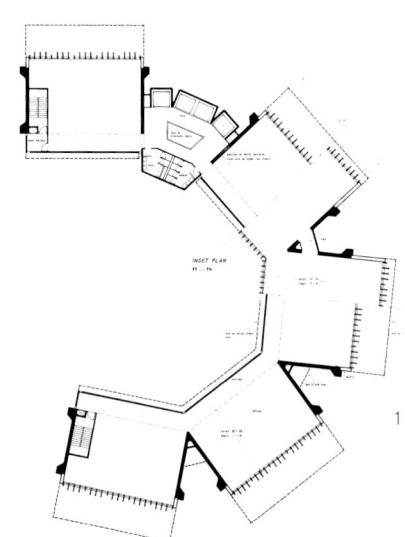

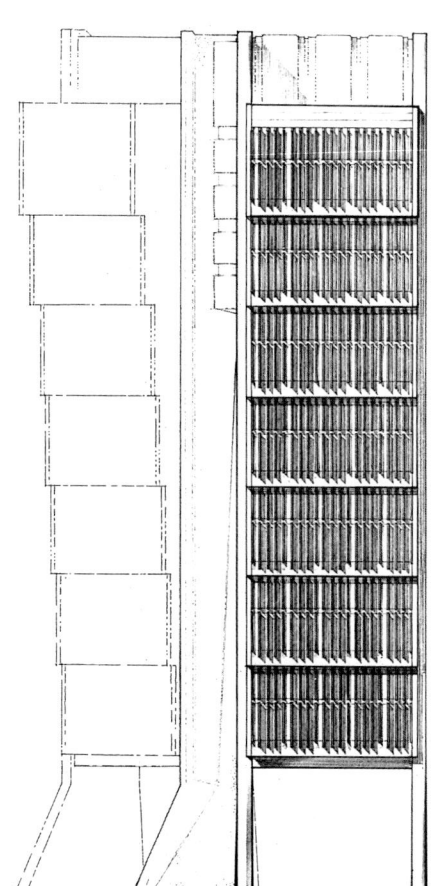
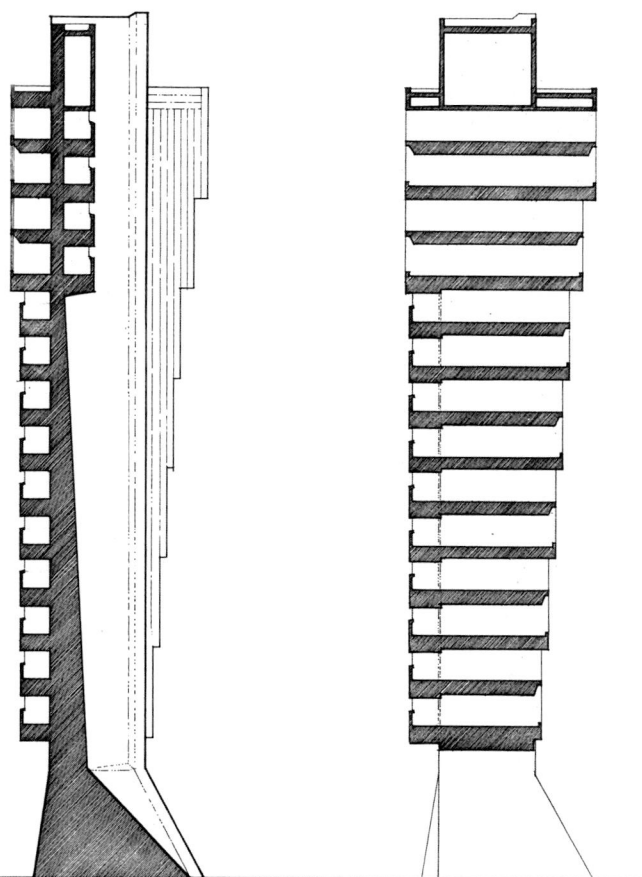

**In this architecture, form comes from the characteristics of the spaces and how they are served ... a plan should be recognisable as belonging to an era. This handling of our complicated servant spaces belongs to the twentieth century just as a Pompeian plan belongs to its era.** Louis Kahn, quoted in *Louis I Kahn: Complete Work 1935-1974*, 1987
Left: Louis Kahn's Richards Medical Research Laboratories at the University of Pennsylvania, of 1957-1965: towers housing service functions were a dominant feature of Foster's student scheme for a new city, below.

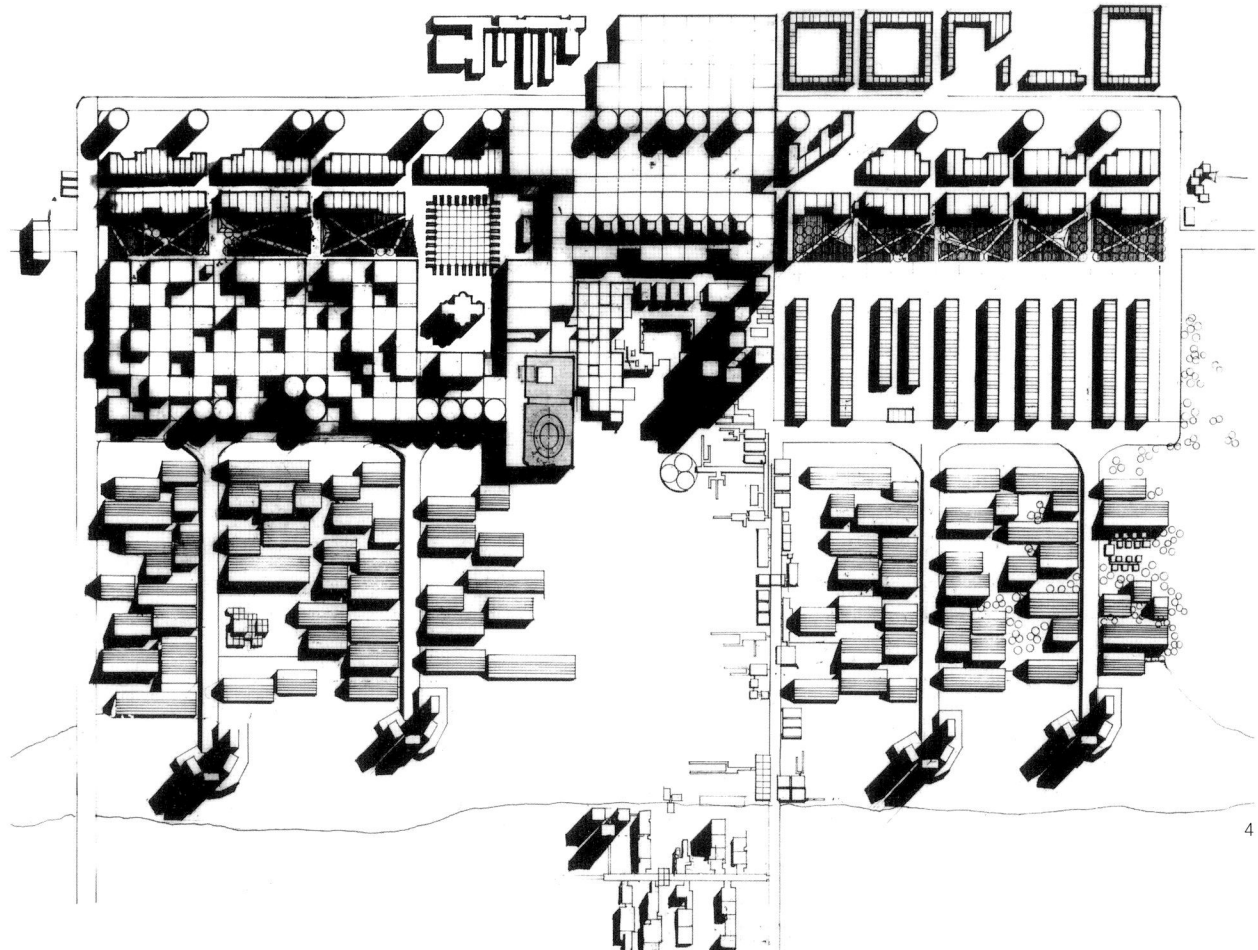

4. The final 'group project' at Yale was a scheme for a new city, directly inspired by Chermayeff's theories on community and privacy. A rich variety of drawings and models was prepared which even incorporated Foster's earlier office tower project.

5. Foster had been making models of his designs ever since his early years at Manchester, but few matched the precision of the model for the new city project. Another such model, constructed for a different assignment, was to suffer a particularly energetic crit at the hands of visiting assessor Philip Johnson.

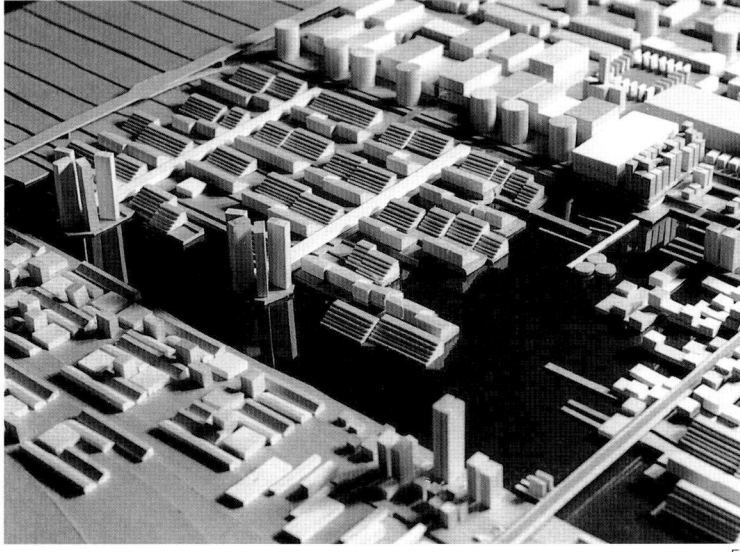

**Rudolph was a legend. He would summon the Masters class a few days before the hand-in of a major design assignment for a snap 'crit'. This might mean that the entire project would be discarded but there would be renewed pressure on everyone to produce a new, even better design in the remaining few days.**
Norman Foster

The Impact of Yale 29

**It would be hard to imagine two characters more different than Rudolph and Chermayeff. Rudolph had a haircut which must have been done with a spirit level, and tended to wear trousers that were slightly too high, and white socks. If there was a drawing there then there was something to talk about. Chermayeff was exactly the opposite, with hair slicked back like a tango dancer and a sort of aristocratic air, immaculately dressed. He didn't really want to look at drawings – if you were doing a project you should be thinking about where it was sited, and whether it should be built. And we were very fortunate to get the best of both these approaches.** Norman Foster, lecture at the Mellon Centre, London, 29 October 1998

Right: Thirty years after Norman Foster studied under Chermayeff at Yale, Foster and Partners undertook the extension and renovation of the Chelsea house built by Chermayeff and Erich Mendelsohn (1887-1953) in 1935 for the playwright Denis Cohen.

1. A characteristically urbane Serge Chermayeff, Professor of Architecture at Yale between 1962 and 1970. Chermayeff's distinctively European philosophy was to provide an important counterpoint to the American influences Foster absorbed at Yale.

2. Elevations and section of a scheme for the Pierson Sage Science Laboratories on the Yale campus, a joint effort by Norman Foster and Richard Rogers. A central spine of car parking bisects the development whose profile is stepped to confront surrounding buildings at an appropriate scale.

Overleaf: Norman Foster presents his final project at Yale – a group scheme undertaken by five students for which Foster was elected spokesman.

Ironically, the European influence at Yale emanated not only from the Russian-born Chermayeff, but also from the quintessentially American Rudolph; as Foster has noted, '… in some ways I went to Yale to discover a European heritage because America had embraced those émigrés such as Gropius who taught Rudolph at Harvard and was, I quote, *his point of reference*.'

Foster's project for a new city, executed while he was studying with Chermayeff, was decidedly European, with rationally sited Siedlung-like rows of houses punctuated by towers. In a way, the project directly illustrated the theoretical studies which would lead to Chermayeff's book, *Community and Privacy*, co-written with Christopher Alexander and published in 1963.

After completing his studies at Yale in 1962, Foster was invited by Chermayeff to stay in New Haven and join him as a research fellow. Tempted as he was, Foster chose instead to work as a city planner in Massachusetts before moving on to San Francisco to work with John Carl Warnecke and Anshen & Allen who were engaged in planning a new University of California campus at Santa Cruz. Rogers was also working in California at the time and the two young architects were excited by Ezra Ehrenkrantz's School Construction Systems Development Program.

Through journals and Scully's lectures they had already been introduced to the California Case Study houses designed by Raphael Soriano, Pierre Koenig, Craig Ellwood, Richard Neutra, and Charles and Ray Eames, which they admired. Of these, the house that Eames built for himself, in 1949, in Pacific Palisades, with its creative assemblage of off-the-shelf industrial components, exerted a lasting influence on Foster's work. So too did the compelling imagery of Koenig's hillside Case Study House #22 with its impossibly slender cantilevers. Foster was also captivated by the forms of American technology: highways, Airstream trailers, and the rockets and launching pad structures of Cape Canaveral.

However, it was not just specific American buildings, nor even American approaches to architecture, construction and large-scale planning, that captured the young Britons' imaginations as they criss-crossed the country together. It was the entire sweep of the continental landscape and the national character that fired them up. As Rogers has said: 'America enthralled us [with] its scale, energy, optimism and openness. We travelled by thumb, by car and by Greyhound bus, voraciously absorbing the culture, both of the massive open spaces and the tall, taut, energetic cities.'

For Foster, Yale had in some ways been emblematic of America: 'The emphasis on tangible results in the studio summed up an American world in which everything was possible if you were willing to try hard enough. For me that was a breath of fresh air … America gave me a sense of confidence, freedom and self-discovery.'

**Serge Chermayeff was as European as Rudolph was American. For Chermayeff debate and theory took precedence over imagery – questioning was to the fore – analysis dominated action.** Norman Foster

**America presented a rich imagery of artefacts, which still continue to fascinate me. Not only the hardware of space exploration, but also the built spaces that it generates, such as the vertical Assembly Building at Cape Canaveral.**
Norman Foster, RIBA Royal Gold Medal address, London, 21 June 1983
Far left, left: Foster's own photographs of the space age structures that so impressed him on his travels around America, and which continue to provide inspiration.

In 1963, Foster returned to England where he joined Richard Rogers to found the trend-setting firm Team 4. The remaining two of the 'four' were the architect sisters, Wendy and Georgie Cheesman, although the latter was a member in name only; as the only qualified architect of the group, it was she that initially allowed Team 4 to meet the legal requirements of architectural practice. Soon enough, however, Foster would be on his own. After only four years together, in 1967, Team 4 split up. Foster and Wendy (by then his wife) established themselves as Foster Associates and pursued an independent direction, quite different from Rogers', although the three of them remained close.

Foster's is an architecture which, in its functional rigour, compositional clarity, and high finish, as well as its concern with means of production and far-reaching issues of urban planning and the social context of buildings, continues to reflect his experience at Yale and in America. It inspires architects everywhere to realise the expressive possibilities of advanced technology and the sheer optimism of the act and art of building. Most of all, in the generosity of his open-mindedness, Foster has demonstrated, as too few architects do, that 'Architects learn from architects – past and present.'

**Yale opened my eyes and my mind. In the process I discovered myself. Anything positive that I have achieved as an architect is linked in some way to my Yale experience.**
Norman Foster

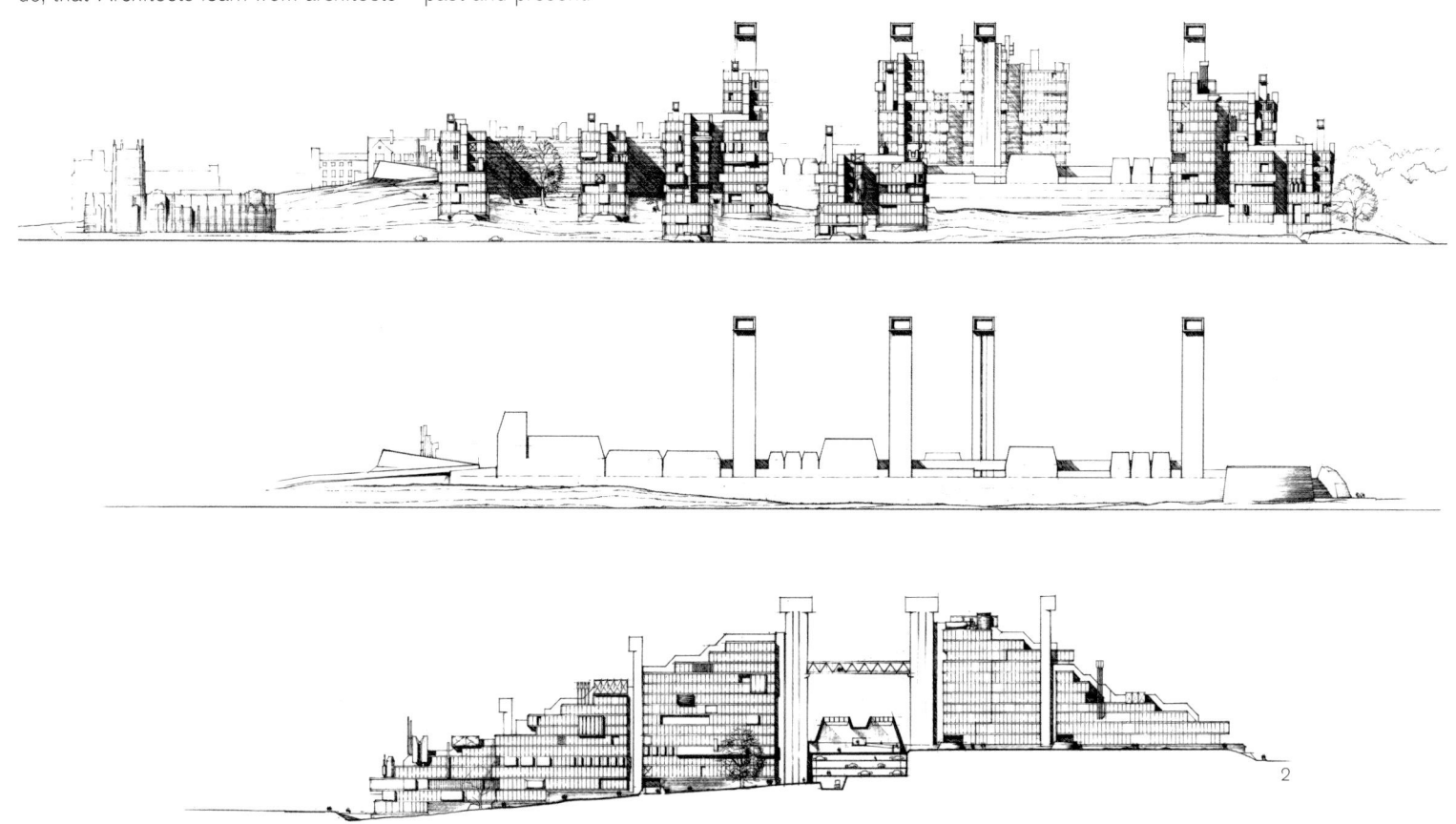

The Impact of Yale   31

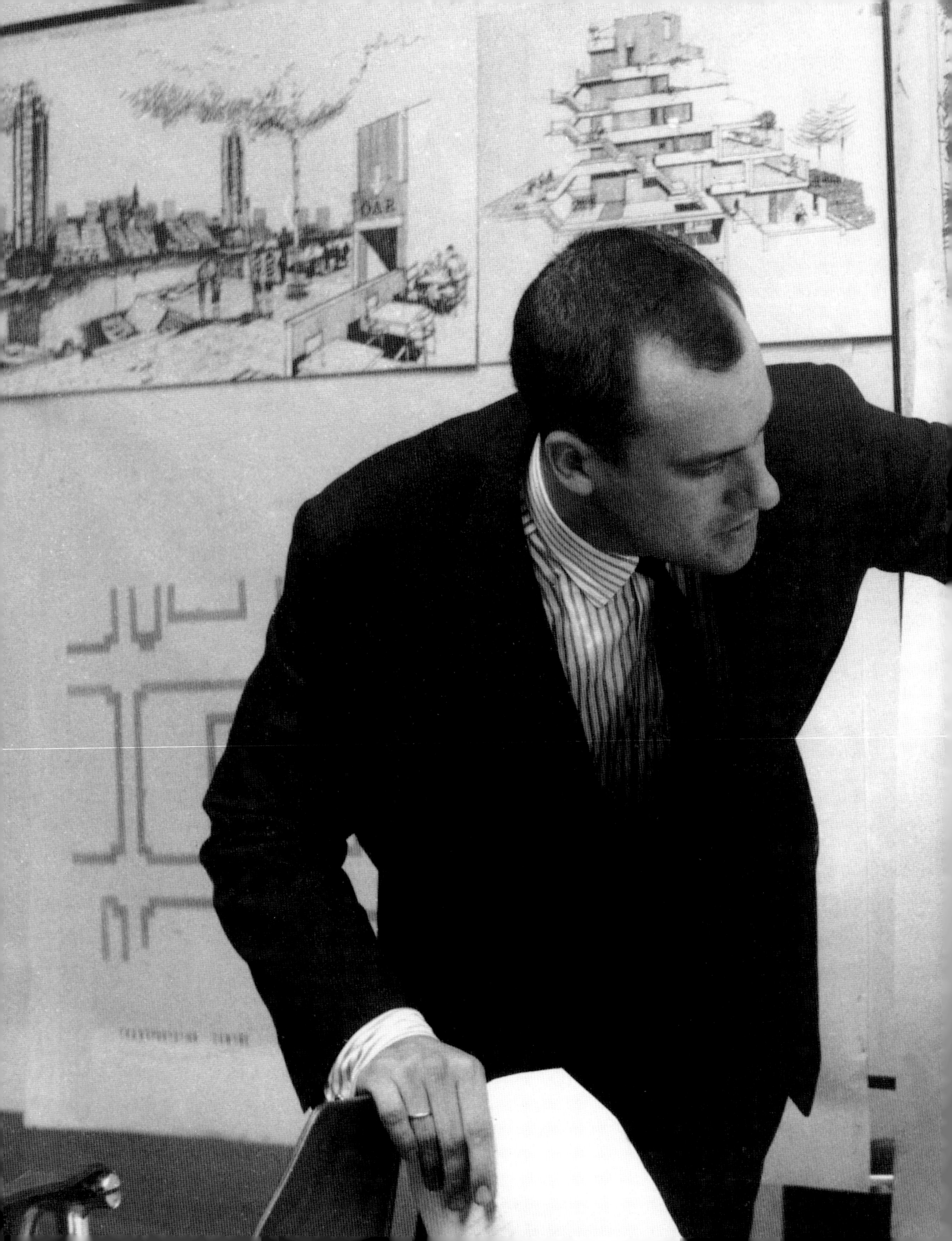

TRANSPORTATION CENTRE

BUS LEVEL

**Early Projects**
1963–1964

**The Henrion project experimented with a number of themes that would run through many of the projects undertaken by Team 4 over the next few years.**
Brian Hatton

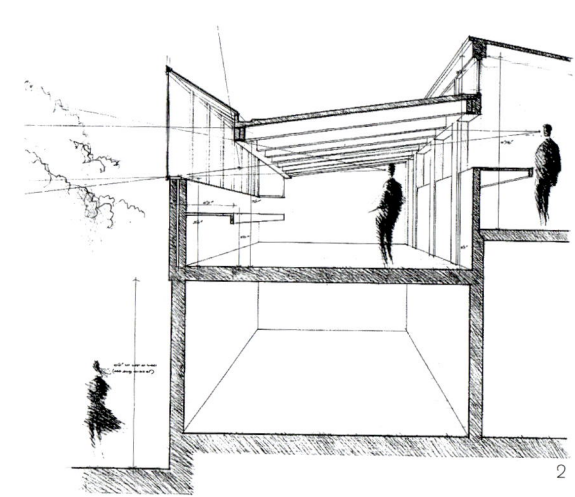

**When the practice began, Team 4's first clients were a series of 'trusting friends and relations'. The work pattern involved 'long and hard hours, although seldom through the night'.** Malcolm Quantrill, *The Norman Foster Studio*, 1999
Left: Team 4 photographed in 1966. Standing, left to right: Tony Hunt and Frank Peacock. Seated, left to right: Sally Appleby, Wendy Foster, Richard Rogers, Su Rogers, Norman Foster and Maurice Phillips.

One of Team 4's earliest commissions came from the graphic designer F H K Henrion: a design studio built as an annexe behind his Georgian terraced house needed to be enlarged. The studio looked northwards over a garden from an upper floor. Instead of continuing the existing floor level, Team 4 proposed that the new extension be lowered to create a stepped section that included a built-in desk and window for each floor.

At the upper level, the window was split into a clerestory, which admitted north light into the depth of the older studio, and a lower opening looking out from the new extension across the built-in desk. An unbroken view to the garden was thus possible at both levels, despite the deep section of the rear studio, and openness to the sky was amplified by glazing the adjoining roof along its re-entrant pitch.

The Henrion studio, modest though it was, experimented with a number of themes that would run through many of the projects undertaken by Team 4 over the next few years. Chief among these were: the distinction in the disposition of windows between daylighting (using skylights to bring light into deep sections, for example) and outlook (orienting windows towards the best views); and the ranging of section by terrace and mezzanine-like elements, as if in a domestic theatre with the window as proscenium giving an outlook on the world.

Internally this overview-format was often repeated so that, for instance, a kitchen work-range would look out over a social or play area. There was also a commitment to varying and variable degrees of open plan, sometimes involving moveable partitions to enable a flexible facility for various occasions.

The influence of Serge Chermayeff, who had tutored Norman Foster and Richard Rogers at Yale, is clearly apparent in the planning of these early houses. Entrance from the public domain was most often made through what might be termed the back elevation, presented as a closed defensive aspect in contrast to a very open outlook on the private side of the house.

Lateral aspects were left blank, implying party-walls and a possible repetition of the unit as a typological element in a terrace, sometimes in contour-following echelon rather than strict alignment. Such typological extrapolations were proposed, with some modifications, from the individual houses, such as Creek Vean, while the houses in Murray Mews were expressly repetitive in implication.

One unbuilt model for this form of domestic planning was a project proposed for Camden Mews in London. Here, a row of studio houses – consciously influenced by the work of Louis Kahn and Paul Rudolph – was to be sited in the back gardens of some Victorian villas, with a small, high-walled courtyard between each new house and the mews. The side of the houses facing the villas was to be a blank wall, so, in principle, they could have been built back-to-back on the old north of England pattern. Compensation for this confinement was provided by the great openness of each house to its courtyard and of its rooms to each other. This was effected not by means of a sliding door, as would be used at the later Skybreak house, but by wide, centre-pivoted panels, which could turn like revolving doors to forge the living room, the playroom and the courtyard into a continuum.

1. The Henrion studio seen from the garden. Built as an extension to a Georgian house in Hampstead, the studio faced north, the generous glazing rising from desk height to maximise views out. The prismatic glazing was a recurring theme, which would be restated in early versions of the Skybreak house.

2. Norman Foster's cross-section through the Henrion studio. Modest though it was, the studio explored a number of themes that would come to characterise Team 4's subsequent work: using skylights to bring daylight into deep sections; orienting the plan and section to take advantage of, or frame the best views; and manipulating the section to forge a number of discrete spaces into a continuum.

3. An early Norman Foster sketch of a courtyard house with a raised kitchen and dining area; the sectional arrangement prefigures the Murray Mews houses.

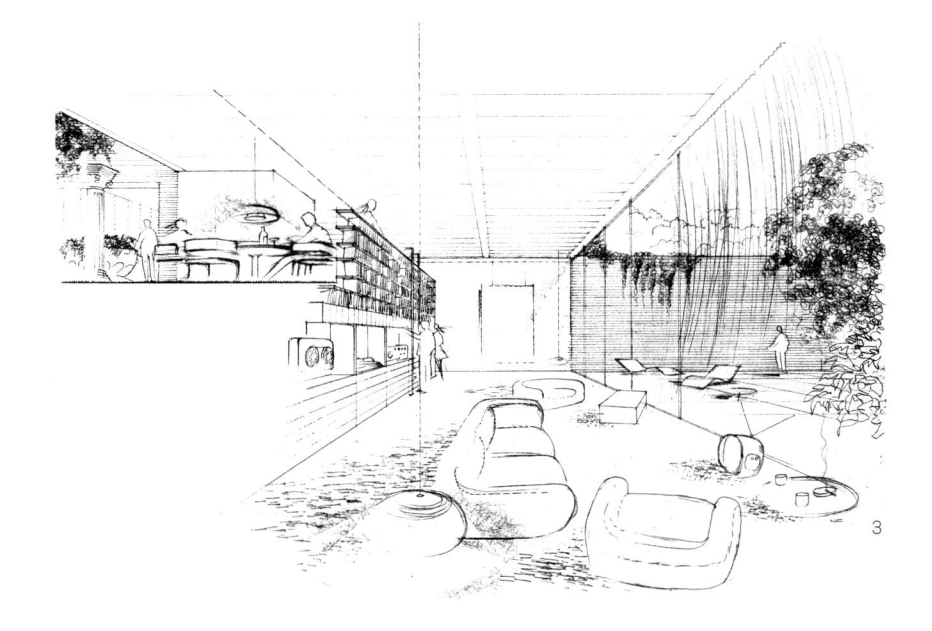

Early Projects  35

**An early job by Foster and Rogers to extend the back of the house helped define the aura that surrounded Henrion: looking to the Continent; in touch with books and ideas; just slightly bohemian; bow-tied and jacketed even in the age of smart suits.** Robin Kinross, *Blueprint*, September 1990

Far left: F H K Henrion photographed in 1966. A significant force in twentieth-century graphic design, Henrion's career spanned government work during the war, advertising, publishing, commercial and corporate design.

Left: A poster designed by Henrion for CND in 1963.

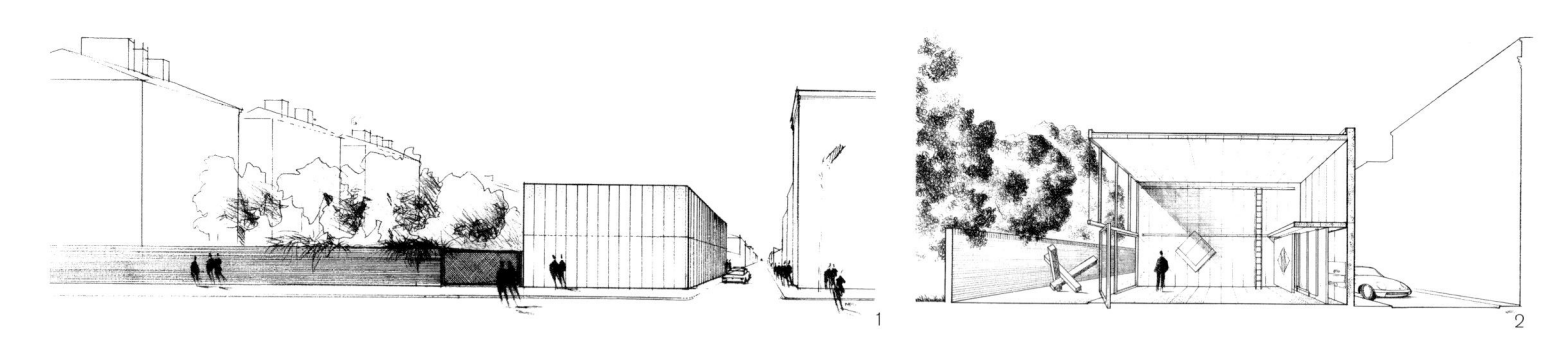

1, 2. Norman Foster's perspective view and section of an early London mews house proposal – one of the first projects in which he suggests the use of steel-frame construction, industrial glazing and prefabricated cladding.

3. In this perspective study of the living area of the Camden Mews houses, Norman Foster investigates the spatial possibilities that could be created by using centre-pivoting screens.

The kitchen was raised a few steps in order to survey this space across its worktop. The living room itself was to be double-height with open stairs leading up to a mezzanine – a studio with top-light and steps up to a roof terrace. On the ground floor, a bathroom and lavatory were enclosed in an island block that stood between the playroom and children's bedroom – a space that was open to allow variable partition. Above, a door from the stairs led to an upper bathroom and a main bedroom could open, by another revolving wall, to the void above the living room. This ingenious Raumplan was compact, yet still provided 1,350 square feet of enclosed space.

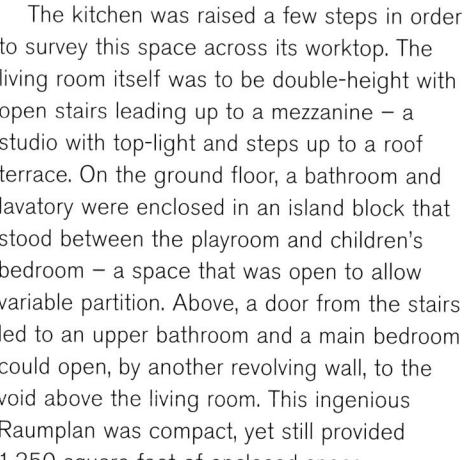

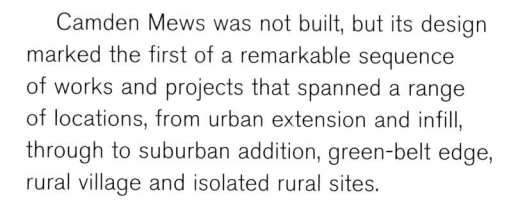

Camden Mews was not built, but its design marked the first of a remarkable sequence of works and projects that spanned a range of locations, from urban extension and infill, through to suburban addition, green-belt edge, rural village and isolated rural sites.

## Each building adapted clients' idiosyncrasies and transformed local idioms to generate specific solutions of great individual character.

The material and constructional means, however, were to remain broadly the same throughout: industrial stock brick, concrete blocks, steel joists and plate glass, all brought together by a traditional builder. These materials were deployed with and in their own character. Similarly, a common set of spatial and formal prototypes informed the whole sequence. Local idioms and clients' idiosyncrasies were transformed into prototypical formats. Each building, however, adapted these common conditions to create intensely specific solutions of great individual character.

Brian Hatton

Left: The Henrion studio's 'light-cage' would provide a model for many of Foster and Team 4's subsequent London mews house schemes.
Right: The 'light-cage' as reinvestigated in the Murray Mews houses, completed in 1965.

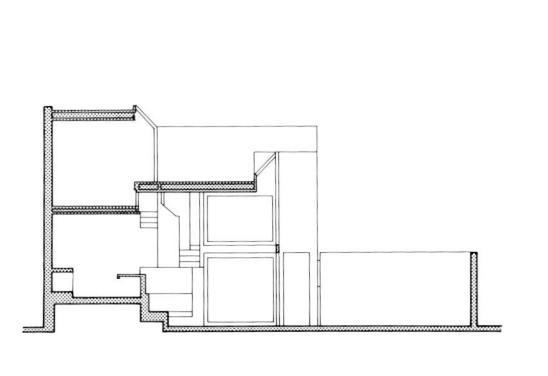

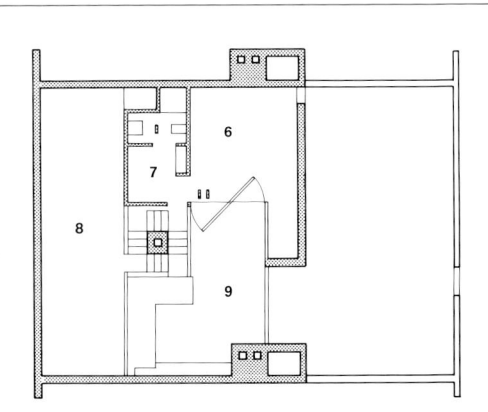

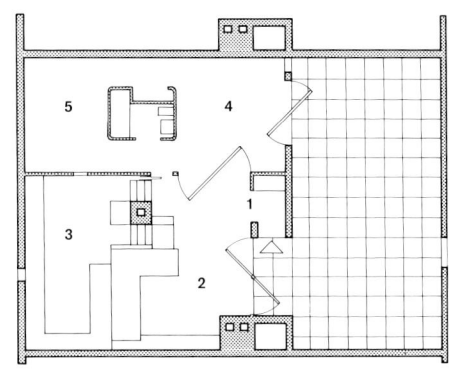

4. Section and plans of the Camden Mews houses. The planning of these small, single-aspect houses made ingenious use of spiralling floor levels around a central staircase to maximise the sense of spatial freedom within a small volume.

1 entrance
2 living room
3 kitchen
4 playroom
5 child's bedroom
6 master bedroom
7 bathroom
8 studio gallery
9 void

5. Norman Foster's sketch of the four Camden Mews houses, characterised by their rhythmically repeated roofline and 6-metre set-back from the high site boundary wall.

6. A perspective study by Norman Foster of a notional courtyard family house, which makes strong use of natural top-lighting, via prismatic roof-lights, and sliding doors – consistent motifs of the early houses. The tiled floors and built-in furniture are suggestive of the Murray Mews houses.

Early Projects

# Connections The Cockpit

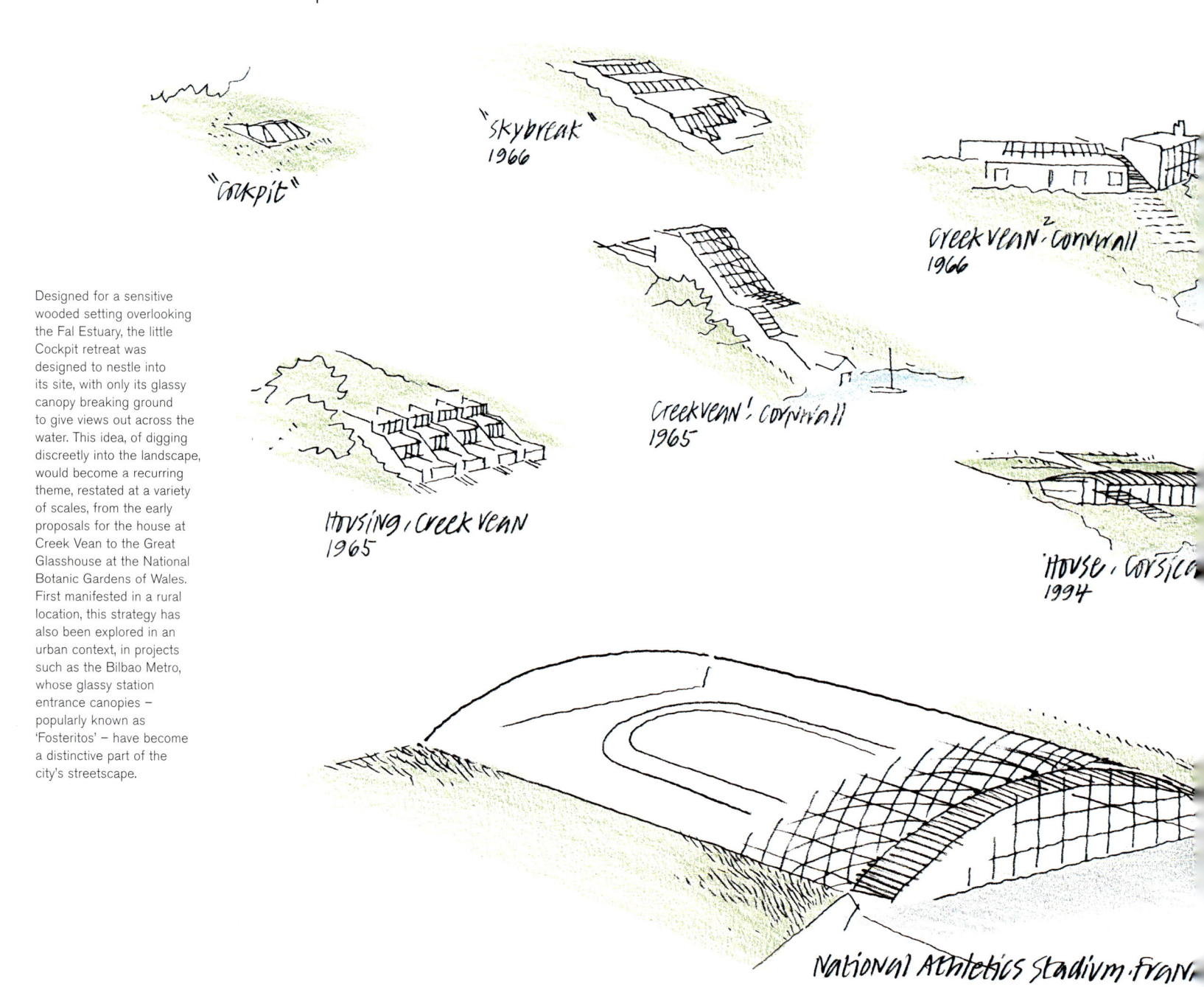

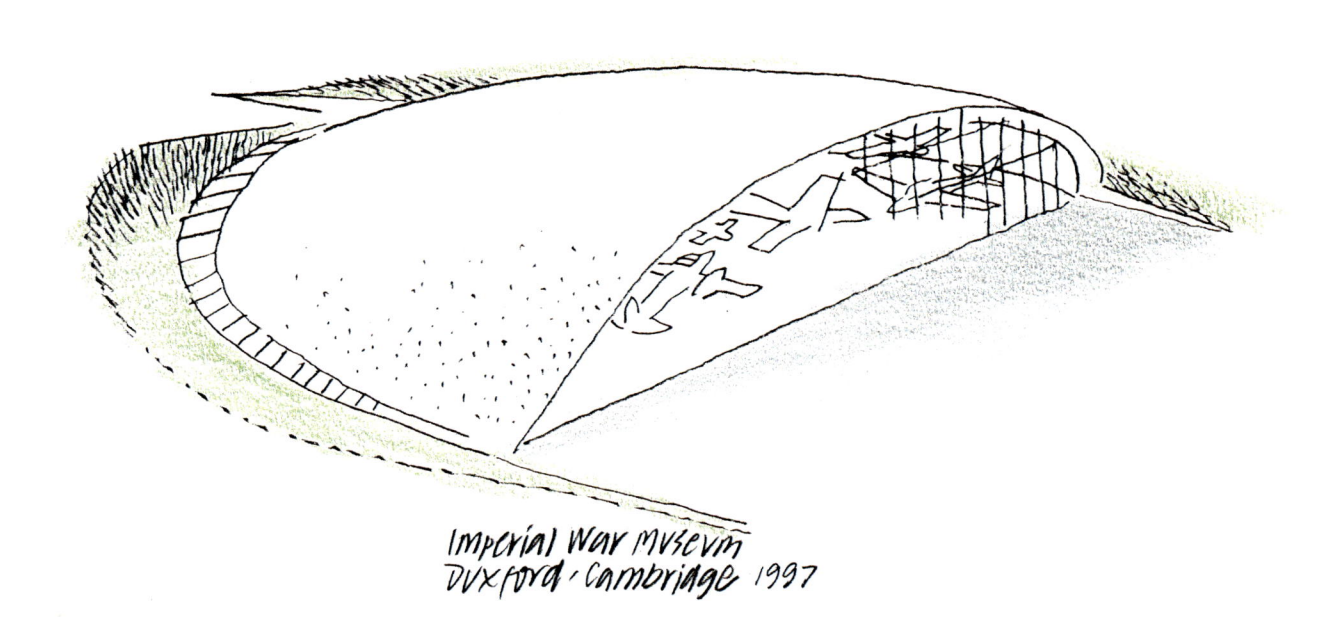

Designed for a sensitive wooded setting overlooking the Fal Estuary, the little Cockpit retreat was designed to nestle into its site, with only its glassy canopy breaking ground to give views out across the water. This idea, of digging discreetly into the landscape, would become a recurring theme, restated at a variety of scales, from the early proposals for the house at Creek Vean to the Great Glasshouse at the National Botanic Gardens of Wales. First manifested in a rural location, this strategy has also been explored in an urban context, in projects such as the Bilbao Metro, whose glassy station entrance canopies – popularly known as 'Fosteritos' – have become a distinctive part of the city's streetscape.

"Cockpit"

"Skybreak" 1966

Creek Vean, Cornwall 1966

Creek Vean, Cornwall 1965

Housing, Creek Vean 1965

House, Corsica 1994

National Athletics Stadium, France

Imperial War Museum Duxford, Cambridge 1997

Son Club
Norway 1973

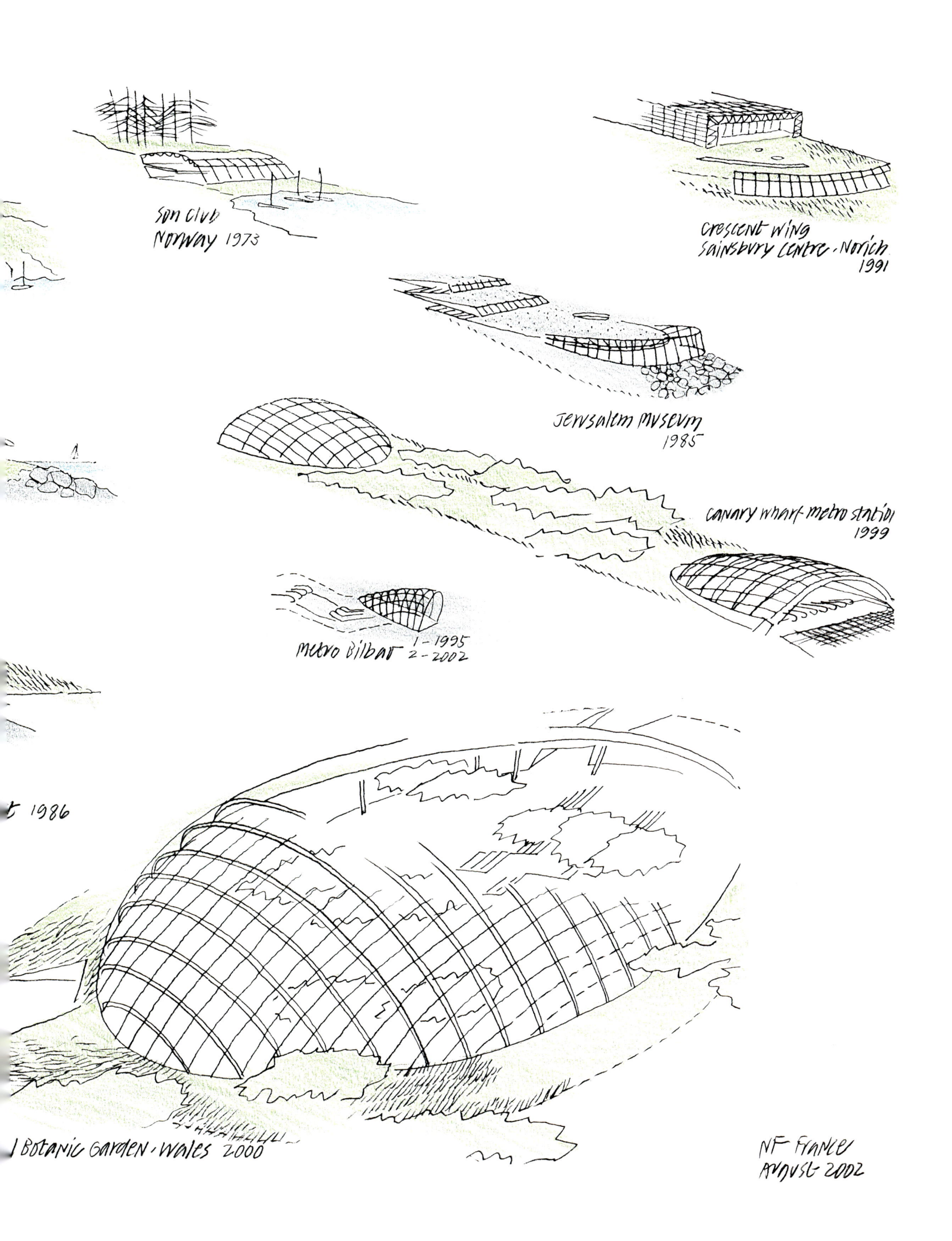

Crescent Wing
Sainsbury Centre - Norich
1991

Jerusalem Museum
1985

Canary Wharf - metro station
1999

Metro Bilbao 1 - 1995
2 - 2002

t 1986

Botanic Garden - Wales 2000

NF France
August 2002

# The Cockpit
Pill Creek, Cornwall, England 1964

Left: In this early sketch Norman Foster explores an alternative strategy for the Cockpit retreat, casting the building as a cool Miesian pavilion in the woods.

The 'Cockpit' or 'Retreat' at Feock was not the first major work designed by Team 4, but it merits priority by virtue of its radical singularity of purpose and clarity of solution. In certain respects it has proved the most advanced of the early projects; notably in respect of technical devices such as the gaskets that sealed its windows, and in the sense that it prefigured the severe distinction in later works – the Sainsbury Centre and Frankfurt National Athletics Stadium, for example – between heavily-embedded groundworks and diaphanous, lightweight superstructures.

**In certain respects the Retreat was the most advanced of the early projects, prefiguring a distinction in later works between light-weight superstructures and heavily-embedded groundworks.**

Like the house at Creek Vean, the Cockpit was commissioned by Marcus Brumwell and his wife Rene. Sailing was for them an intrinsic part of life in Cornwall: at the waterfront at Creek Vean was a boathouse from which they could sail down Pill Creek into the Fal estuary. A mile or so down the creek, on the opposite bank, lies the wooded promontory of Feock. From here a wide prospect of the branching estuary opens, while a gentle water margin enables boats to be brought up to the shore.

The Brumwells and their family were fond of taking picnics at this place, and kept a hut for that purpose there, but following the design of Creek Vean they asked Norman Foster and Richard Rogers to create a special building for the site. It was to be an all-weather gazebo, with electricity for a small stove and piped water to a sink; otherwise it was to be as simple as possible.

The architects adapted the splayed, trapezoid shape that had planned Creek Vean, but now let it generate both plan and section to make a complex crystalline polyhedron with triangular, rectangular and trapezoid facets. Fanning outward from a notional source within the earth, the gazebo breaks surface from the slope of the bank, and faces towards the sea like the cockpit of a plane or boat.

The main structure is a concrete shell, set into the earth. Into this shell are set the bases of the seats, sink and cooker. The stainless-steel sink is covered by a teak lid with brass hinges; the drawers beneath the stove are also of stainless steel. Entrance is through a sliding panel in the windows, whose wooden frames required some careful geometry in their joinery.

For a budget of about £500, the architects provided 100 square feet of well-serviced shelter, establishing a bridgehead to life on the water, and leaving the sward of a pine wood intact in the process. This definitely non-primitive hut may be said to fulfil within Norman Foster's oeuvre the same archetypal role as Abbé Laugier's mythological edifice: an idyllic cell, come down from Eden to make a prototype for paradise.

Brian Hatton

1. The view down the Fal estuary, as seen from inside the Cockpit. An all-weather gazebo with modest facilities for tea and warmth, this diminutive structure was used for family picnics, a quiet place to read or to watch regattas on the river. Although tiny, the Cockpit explored design ideas that would be pursued at a far greater scale in much of Norman Foster's later work.

2. Norman Foster's early sketch section through the Cockpit. The simple, dug-in structure, discreet in its woodland setting, opens out in a crystalline bubble of glazing to maximise views of the waterfront.

3. The balsa-wood used to construct this study model suggests analogies with model aircraft and hints at connections with the cockpit of the wooden framed Hurricane (see overleaf). Part of the timber glazing frame slid sideways for access.

Left: Norman Foster has cited the distinctive sliding canopy of the Hawker Hurricane as a reference point in the design of the Cockpit. Designed by Sidney Camm in 1934, this wooden-framed fighter plane was incredibly agile and versatile in flight and played a key role in the Battle of Britain.

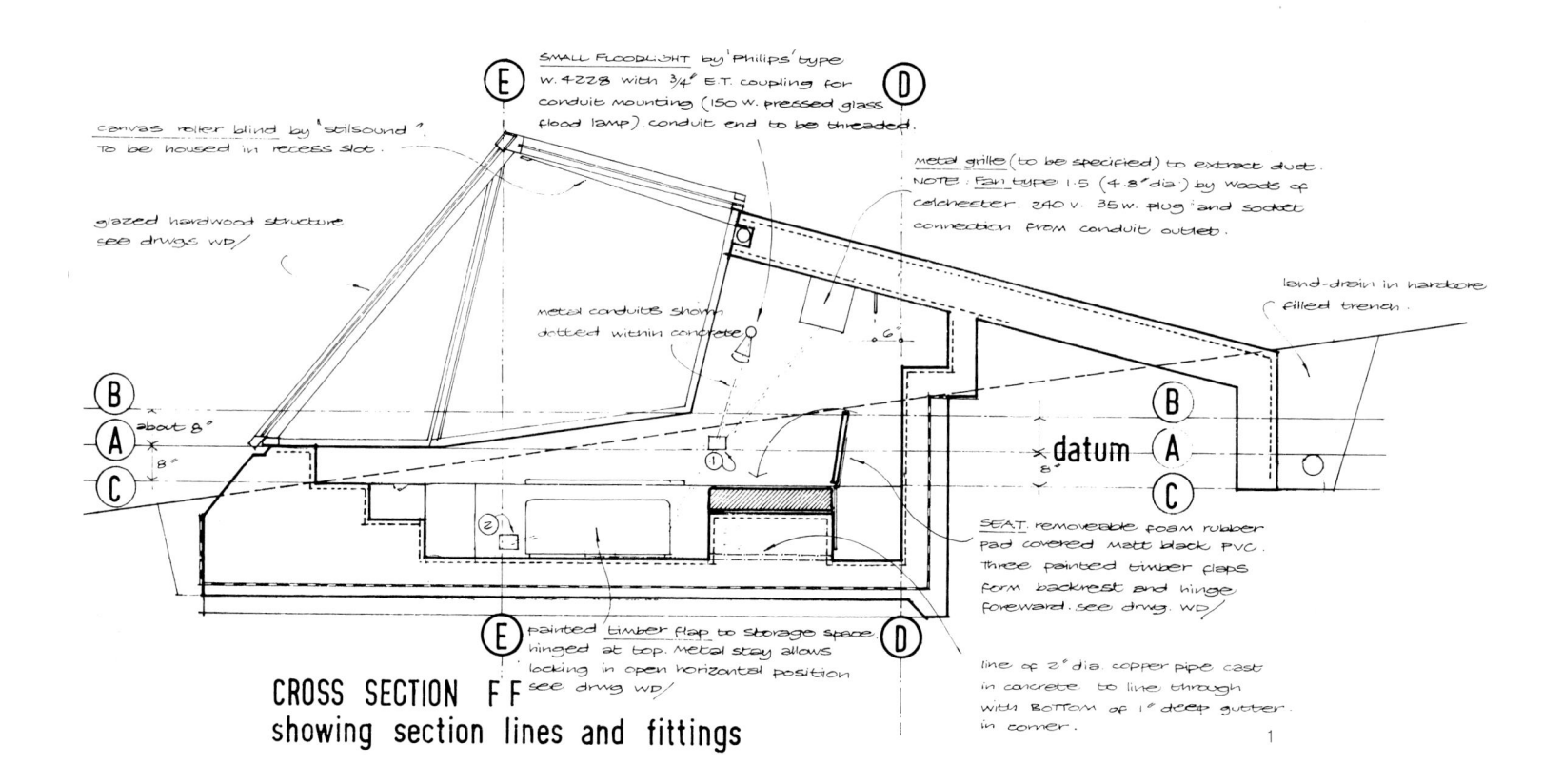

**CROSS SECTION FF**
showing section lines and fittings

1. A detailed cross-section through the Cockpit – one sheet from a set of contract drawings drawn by Norman Foster himself. The materials and finishes specified are simple and direct: exposed concrete, timber framing and glass. This was Team 4's first completed building and the first of a long series of collaborations with Anthony Hunt, who was to be the structural engineer for all Team 4's projects.

2. Plan and cross-section to the same scale; the overall plan dimension, from front to back, is approximately 5 metres.

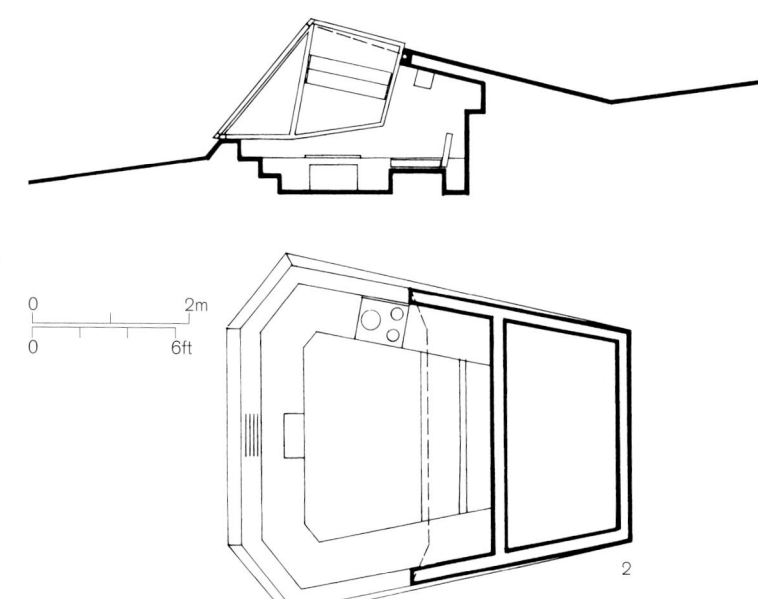

> **We were seeking to create a minimalist glass bubble – a 'cockpit' looking out to views of the Fal estuary – an 'away place' in which to read, contemplate or hold picnics.**
>
> Norman Foster

**The delicate tracery of metal and glass envisaged in the sketches was frankly beyond our technical capability at the time and was translated into timber, which worked well but never achieved the sparse elegance that one associates with traditional structures such as early timber greenhouses. However, it was still a magical place to escape to.** Norman Foster, *Norman Foster: Sketches*, 1992

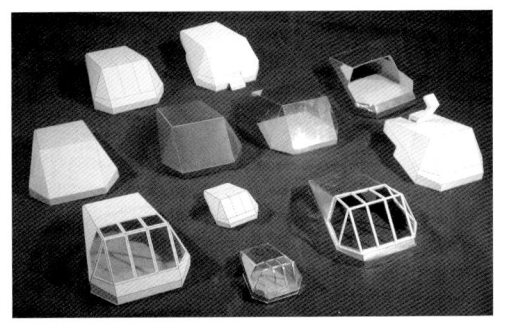

Left: From 25 October to 30 December 2001, the Museum fur Angewandte Kunst in Cologne mounted a retrospective exhibition of Norman Foster's work entitled 'Norman Foster: architecture is about people'. In association with this exhibition, architecture students from the Cologne University of Applied Sciences conducted research on the Pill Creek Cockpit and produced a series of models offering contemporary interpretations of the structure. The research project culminated in the construction of a full-scale model of the Cockpit in the museum forecourt.

3. Looking in through the sliding entrance door. The floor, worktop and seats were cast in-situ; storage units, a vestigial kitchen and a simple glazing frame were fixed directly to the concrete structure.

4. The wooden glazing frame required complex joinery to ensure the polyhedron form was entirely sealed. Foster had wanted to build it in metal, but cost and the skills of the local builder prevailed to realise the form in timber.

5. Norman Foster's sketch stresses the Cockpit's minimal structure and maximum transparency.

Overleaf: Marcus Brumwell photographed in the Cockpit.

The Cockpit

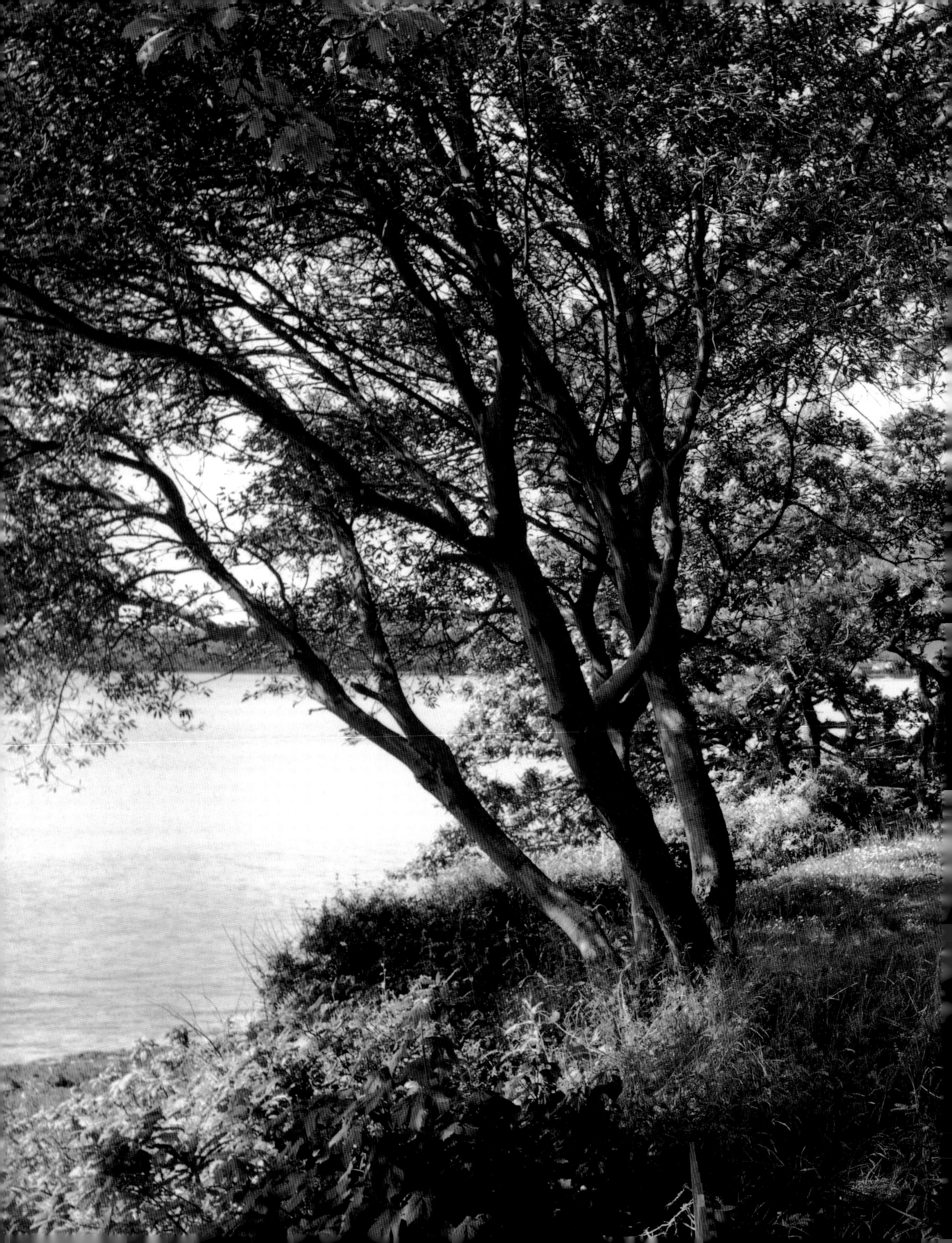

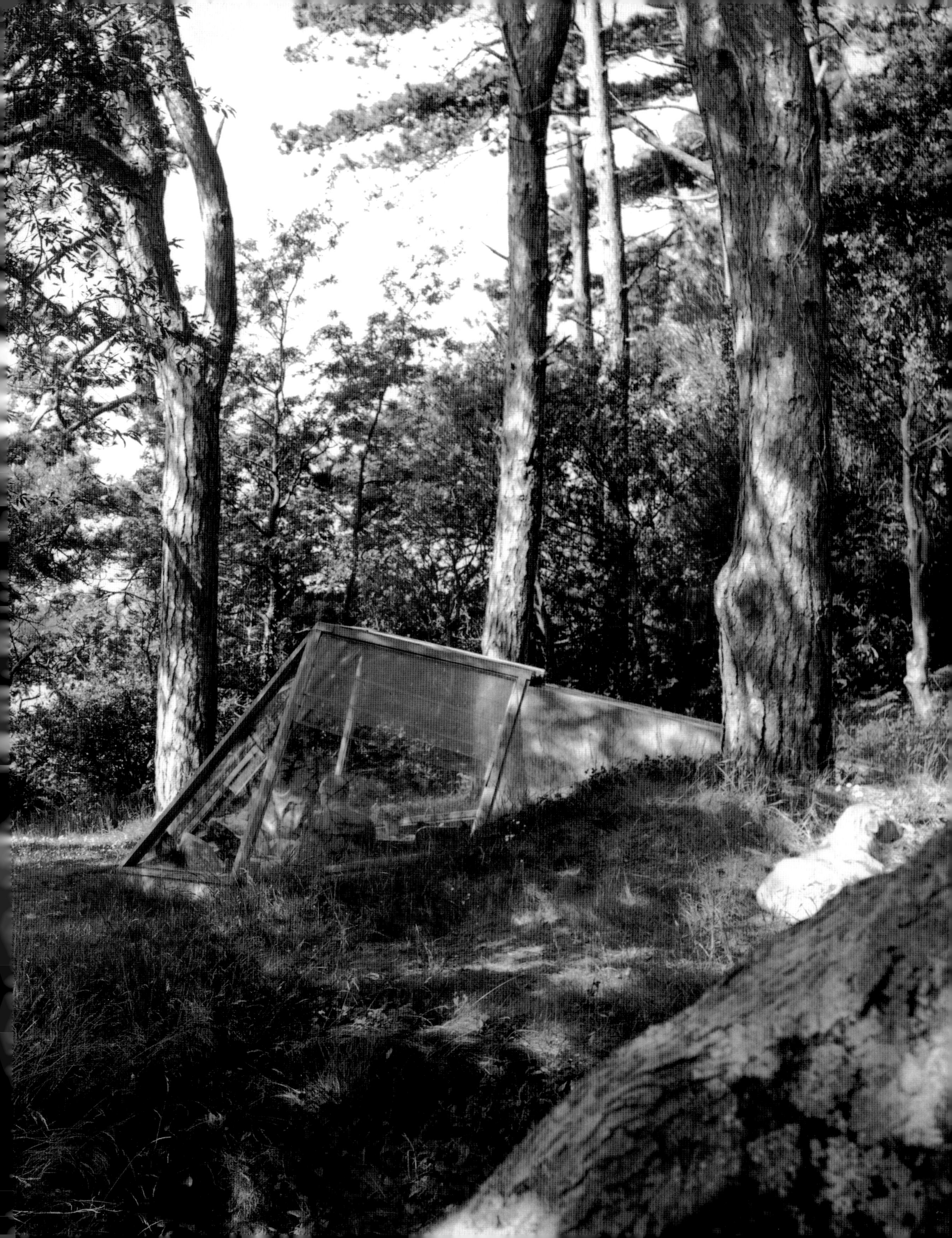

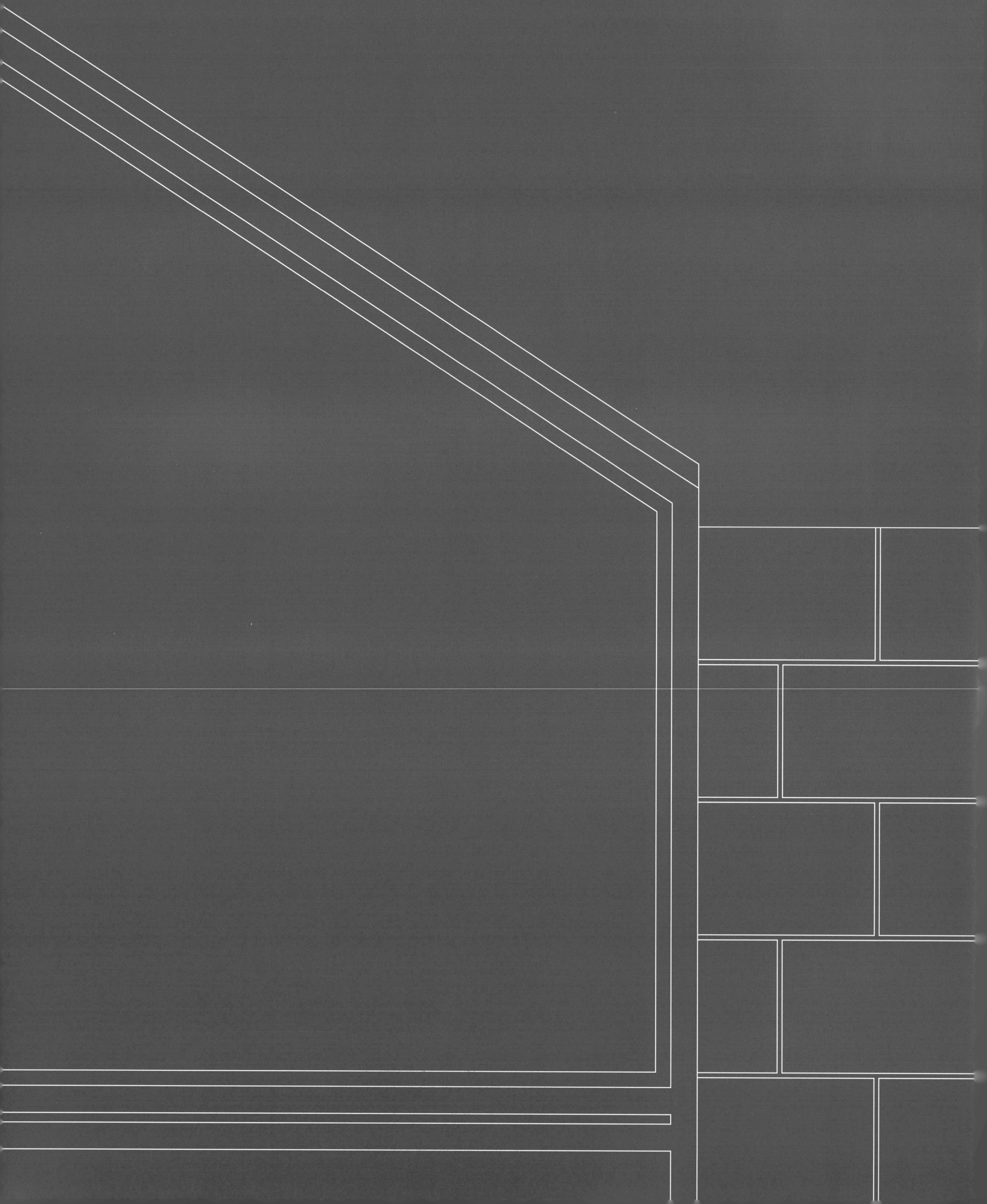

**Creek Vean House**
Pill Creek, Cornwall, England 1964–1966

This private house, built on a steeply sloping site, was designed to exploit classic Cornish views, its rooms fanning out to face the broad sweep of the Fal estuary. It is organised around two routes. One is external and visually divides the house in two, leading from the road across a bridge to the front door and down a flight of grassy steps to the waterfront. The other is internal, in the form of a top-lit picture gallery. The section follows the contour line, forging all the living spaces into a continuum. Creek Vean mixes traditional materials with industrial components; the structure is open-ended and manifested both internally and externally. Except for the landscaped roof – shades of a later Willis Faber – such a description would fit exactly the Sainsbury Centre of some ten years later, although the departure points in materials, techniques and flexibility are of an opposite extreme.

Norman Foster

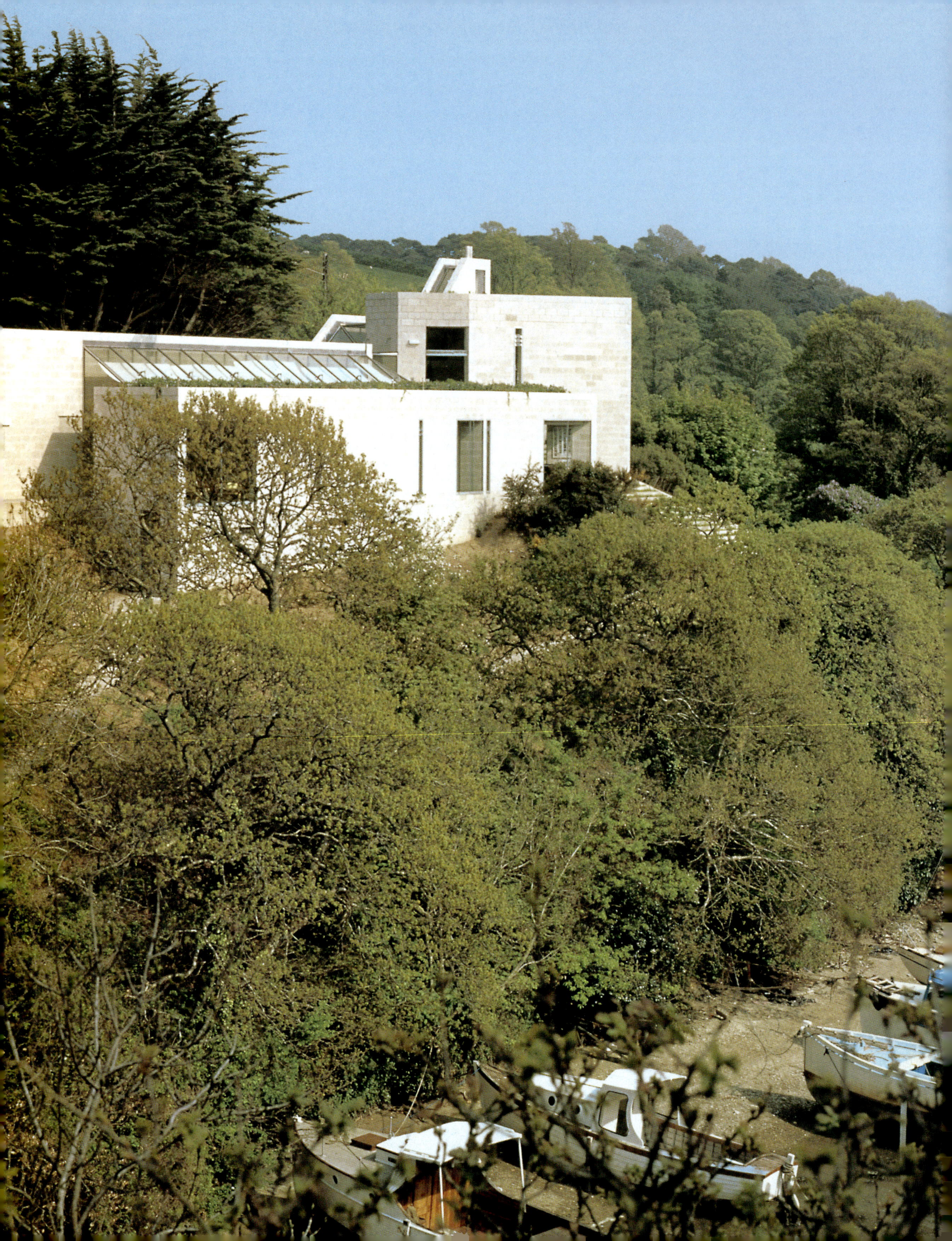

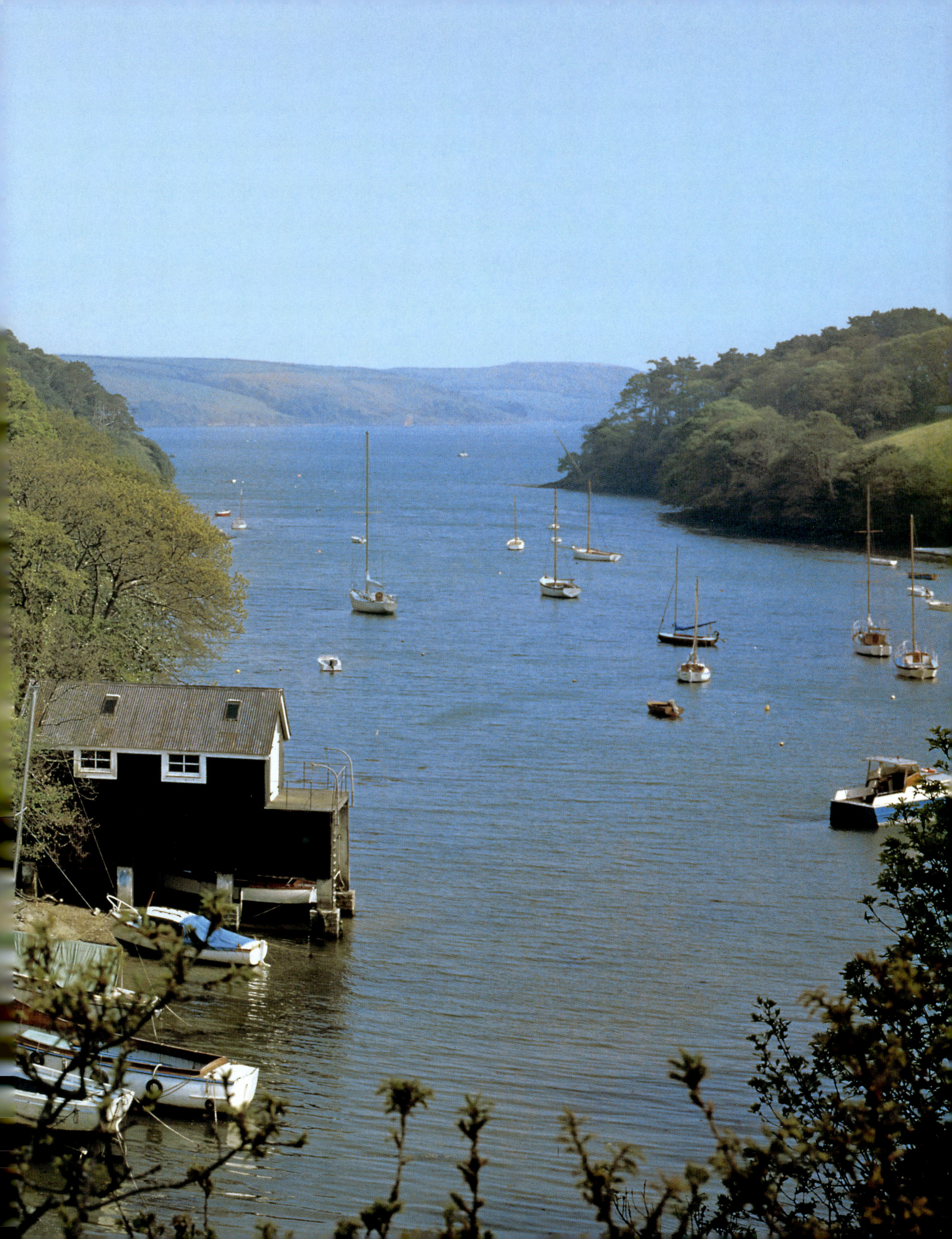

Marcus Brumwell was a man of great business, scientific and artistic talent whose interests came together in his running of the Design Research Unit, which had been set up in 1943 with idealistic and visionary aims as an integrated design service, equipped to tackle the demands of post-war reconstruction. Its first head had been the great critic and historian Herbert Read ... When the war ended, Marcus Brumwell became proprietor and the DRU took off. Kenneth Powell, *Richard Rogers*, 1999
Right: Marcus Brumwell photographed in his boat in Pill Creek; Creek Vean house and its boathouse are visible on the opposite bank.

The scheme started life as the conversion of an existing house but eventually the new work became so dominant that it threatened to bury almost every trace of the original building. I remember ... concluding that the only way forward was to demolish and start from scratch. We then agonised about how to break the news to the clients. Norman Foster, *Norman Foster: Sketches*, 1992
Right: Seated in the dining room of the Creek Vean house, Marcus and Rene Brumwell and guest enjoy the view out to the wooded bank and the creek below.

Previous page: The Creek Vean house, photographed shortly after completion. It is seen here from across Pill Creek, which leads into the Fal estuary. The boathouse below it was built for an earlier bungalow that was demolished to make way for the house.

1. Norman Foster's sketch of the Creek Vean house in its first incarnation as an extension to the existing bungalow on the site, which he purposefully omitted from this drawing. The house's periodic emergence and disappearance from behind the surrounding vegetation was already hinted at here.

The house at Creek Vean is far more complex than the Retreat, but it is as connected to the road and village as the Retreat is to sea and sky, and is as embedded in artistic culture as the cell is in its wooded bank. The project began as a proposed extension to a house already on the site and, at first, stacked up three floors behind a raking window wall not unlike the profile of the Feock Cockpit or the later terraces at Skybreak. It was Foster's initiative to break free of the existing house to create a liberated new structure as opposed to the limitations of a conversion. As a result, a linear plan emerged, stretching 50 metres along its steep bank site, which falls to meet the boathouse and creek at its foot.

The linear plan implied extensibility, in accordance with the Brumwells' brief, but it also accommodated another singular requirement, namely a gallery for the display of a collection of modern art: the Brumwells' great passion, along with sailing. Other requirements were for a degree of flexibility and openness for entertainment, provision of a study and self-contained guest flat and, of course, orientation to the light and views, west across the creek and southwards down the Fal estuary.

The way that this was done was to articulate the house by a dramatic coup that transformed it from a solitaire to a small yet vivid rehearsal in urbanism. The new plan arranged the house on a natural terrace immediately beneath the man-made terrace of the lane. Along this lower terrace a 5.5-metre-high blank wall was run, shielding the house from the lane and creating a kind of dry moat. Main entry to the house was via a bridge across this gap to a door at first floor level. A path to the water continued down a flight of steps, broadening as it descended between the two wings of the house to form virtually a miniature open-air theatre.

**The project began as a proposed extension to the house already on the site, and, at first, stacked up three floors behind a raking window wall not unlike the profile of the Feock Cockpit or the later terraces at Skybreak.**

This grassy stair, like that at Alvar Aalto's Säynätsalo town hall, in fact forms part of the roof, for the two wings are connected beneath its upper flight. Several commentators have described the house as organised by this crossing of two 'axes' – one over and down the bank, the other under and along the contour. Yet 'axial' is hardly an accurate description of the actual experience there, because whereas one axis designates an exterior wedge of space, the other refers to an interior route which is repeatedly impinged by encounters with oblique openings and planes at the insistence of the light and view to one side.

1

The Retreat naturally led on to the Creek Vean house itself. At this stage, it was still seen as an extension to an existing Victorian building on the site. It was clear Norman and Richard would have preferred to remove the old building but did not know how to suggest the idea to Marcus Brumwell, the client … Eventually, it was decided I should do a survey of it and I was able to report, quite honestly, that retaining the building would present major problems: it was in poor condition and differential settlement would have been difficult to control. Tony Hunt, 'In at the Beginning', 1991

We worked fifteen hours a day, seven days a week. No one invited us to dinner as we would invariably fall asleep during the first course. It took the team three years to build the Brumwells' Creek Vean house, the first house to win an RIBA Award. This slowness of production, when related to the national housing shortage, stimulated us to reconsider our architectural direction.
Richard Rogers, 'Team 4', 1991

2, 3. Cross-sections through the house in its earliest form, drawn by Norman Foster. The huge cascading glass roof facing the water was later much reduced to survive only in the narrow roof-light over the interior gallery. The plunging buttress walls to the creek disappeared altogether.

4. An early Norman Foster sketch, looking across the living/dining area and out to sea.

**We wanted to ensure that all the interior spaces maintained a connection with the landscape and, in particular, with the river running beneath the site.**
Norman Foster

Creek Vean House

**Richard Rogers ... felt that his parents-in-law, who through friendships with Cornwall-based artists such as Ben Nicholson, Henry Moore and Barbara Hepworth had assembled an important personal art collection ... should select an architect 'of the calibre, or at least of the potential calibre, of the artists whose art work you buy. I feel that your beautiful works should have a setting which shows them off to their best advantage, at the same time harmonising with them.'** Kenneth Powell, *Richard Rogers,* 1999

The Brumwells' art collection featured several important works by painter Ben Nicholson. Nicholson first met the Brumwells in London, but was a regular visitor to their Feock home. It is not entirely fanciful to suggest that the elegant clarity of Nicholson's abstract works must have appealed to the Brumwells in much the same way as the light-bathed spaces of the Creek Vean house.
Left: Nicholson's *Pill Creek by Moonlight,* 1928
Right: Ben Nicholson photographed in 1954 in his St Ives studio.

1. The success of the earlier annexe scheme convinced the Brumwells that the existing bungalow should be demolished and an entirely new house designed. In this view into the living room Norman Foster indicates planting on the roof for the first time.

2. Norman Foster's elevation of the evolving house design shows a sloping, low-lying glass wall stretching along the contours of the site.

The true organiser is not a dogmatic imposition of axes, but a formalised staging of prospects and sightlines. The 'open-air theatre' of the stairway is one such, but the whole of the south wing sets up a proscenium to nature by its broad-span canopy and giant glazed wall, which can slide back to open up the kitchen-dining room to the garden. Above the kitchen, slung on a single concrete tray like the balcony or circle in a theatre, is a bridging mezzanine that functions as a sitting room and library. This has even better views down the creek than the dining room or 'stalls' below.

Yet it is from the kitchen bench – a long, cantilevered concrete and stainless-steel worktop – that a sovereign view of the interior as a whole is gained. For at that point a sightline follows along the top-lit gallery to a glass door and little terrace at the end of the north wing of the house. It is a view that Vermeer or Velázquez would have relished – a succession of light and dark openings in perspective, corresponding to the discrete yet continuous phasing of access, reserve, and privacy in the house.

On the long 'back' wall of the gallery are hung paintings and drawings by Ben Nicholson, Barbara Hepworth, Patrick Heron and others from the English Modern Movement. Along the other wall are ranged the study, bedroom and guest flat. These are shaped, like the south wing, as trapezoids, fanning outwards to the creek, over which their windows look. Yet they do not form, as does the south wing, a 'proscenium to nature'. Rather the opposite: for the screen that divides them from the long corridor slides back, so that the theatre is reversed: the proscenium opens to the picture gallery from the three separate rooms, rather in the way that in Melnikov's Rusakov Club a single stage plays to three fanning, cantilevered auditoria. This indoor proscenium looks to art, not nature, as the setting for conviviality, relaxation and culture.

The three 'theatres' – one outdoor, one indoor, and one on the threshold, form the salient social spaces at Creek Vean, but they by no means exhaust its intricacies. There are, for instance, three entrances. The house is approached from a sunken garage along a path to the terrace at the end of the gallery, while, at the southern end, steps lead down from the lane to a service door which connects to the kitchen through a small laundry.

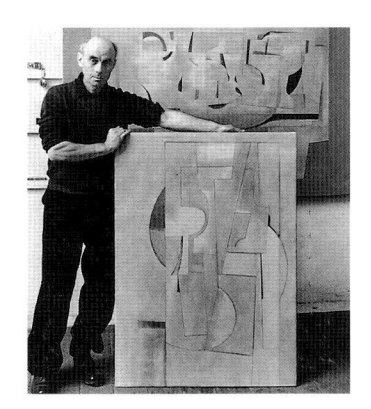

**Modernist design could produce posters welcomed by adventurous people in commerce and also abreast of the most avant-garde international art. A commission came to Nicholson in 1938 from Marcus Brumwell and the Stuart Advertising Agency. What was required was a poster for Imperial Airways, featuring the words faster air services. Nicholson produced a powerful image ... Everything in it was asymmetrical and dynamic; the means were strikingly minimal for the date.** Norbert Lynton, *Ben Nicholson,* 1993
Right: A poster for Imperial Airways designed by Ben Nicholson in 1938. This powerful and dynamic image was commissioned by Marcus Brumwell, then head of the Stuart Advertising Agency.

There are very few right-angles anywhere in the plan, but at the point where the two wings join, the geometries (which offered some challenges to the builders) become particularly involved. Such torsions may bring to mind some of Frank Lloyd Wright's elaborate compositions; indeed there are many 'organic' dispositions at Creek Vean. Yet, as with talk of axes, it may be misleading to 'over-Wright' the plan, which eludes a rigorously geometric definition. In Wright's 1950 Usonian Palmer house, for example, a flowing plan conforms to a controlling grid of equilateral triangular modules. For all its intimate relation to site, its genetic principle stems from commitment to an idea of 'composition' which is hard to discern in the essentially more picturesque, even theatrical, Creek Vean.

**The house at Creek Vean is far more complex than the Retreat, but it is as connected to the road and village as the Retreat is to sea and sky, and is as embedded in artistic culture as the cell is in its wooded bank.**

These abstract considerations barely intrude upon one's experience of the house, however, which is encountered as a sequence of scenes and vantage-points rather than a manifest rationale. For instance, on entering, a double vantage is immediately presented to the visitor, who can, as he hangs up his coat, view both the kitchen-dining room below and the lounge-mezzanine a few steps above. Will he be received below or above? The answer is there, for he can see and hear his hosts at either level as clearly as if they were on stage and he in the stalls (if he glances across the gap to the mezzanine) or the circle (if he glances down through the gap to the kitchen).

In fact, this little 'theatre' replicates the proscenium structure of the mezzanine and kitchen themselves, but with those spaces playing the stage, not the auditorium.

A third, still higher, view is to be had by ascending a steep cathedral-stair from the mezzanine to the roof. These steps, like the flooring throughout the house, are of blue Welsh slate, and contrast with the honey-coloured concrete blocks of the walls. They make a precipitous cascade, but like a rock formation in a Mackintosh watercolour, their almost mannerist elegance fashions a functional structure. In fact, this corner of the house seems to be its most restless, least resolved aspect, and the top-lit staircase culminates in a door that breaks the roofline in a late-Corbusian gesture, like the belltower at La Tourette.

3. An early upper level plan of the house corresponding with the elevation opposite. An irregular plan with stair access at each end was proposed, the entrance bridge on the left being diverted to a lower terrace and steps down to the old boathouse.

4. The lower floor plan bears similarities to the final, built scheme in its distribution of rooms, though the irregularly shaped storage and games room was to be put to much better use in the completed building.

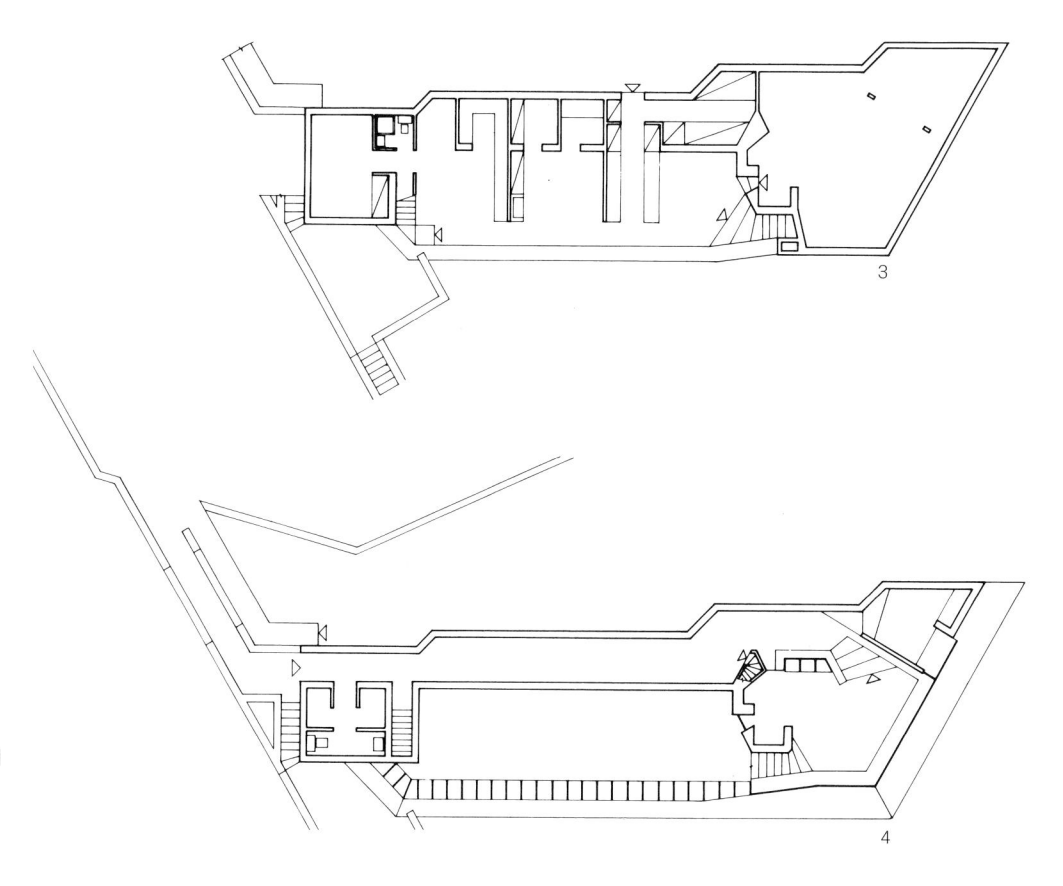

**We would take that despised outcast of the building industry – the concrete block – out from underfoot or from the gutter – find a hitherto unsuspected soul in it – make it live as a thing of beauty – textured like the trees. All we would have to do would be to educate the concrete block, refine it and knit it together.** Frank Lloyd Wright, *An Autobiography*, 1932
Right: Frank Lloyd Wright's Millard House, of 1923. Like Creek Vean, this house manages to achieve an organic unity with its surroundings while remaining formally and structurally distinct, and, like Creek Vean, it is constructed from concrete blocks.

**A vital part of my experience at Yale University was the total immersion in the work of great and talented designers across the breadth of America: architects learn from architects past and present. I would set off in a car and sometimes travel huge distances to visit buildings. And I saw a great deal, including all the Frank Lloyd Wright buildings in the Midwest.** Norman Foster, in conversation with Yoshio Futagawa, 1998

1. Site plan. The house sits along a natural terrace in an otherwise steeply sloping site, the walls of its two wings sharply angled to make the most of the views. The entrance bridge spans across from the access road, the path created continuing over the house as a flight of steps spilling down to the waterfront and boathouse.

From the roof terrace, another inspiration becomes apparent in the planted canopy that covers the north wing: Siedlung Halen, the terraced estate near Berne by Atelier 5. Here, three ranks of adjoining houses overlap down a south-facing slope in a compact range of terraces on a grid of stepped alleys and interstitial driveways.

## The true organiser is not a dogmatic imposition of axes, but a formalised staging of sightlines.

Creek Vean, in contrast, is but a villa, yet the logic of its stairway-and-gallery plan, and its balcony staging of horizontal planes condenses the collective idiom of Siedlung Halen to a highly-tuned individual variant. A year or two later, Team 4 was to propose its own bolder version of the Atelier 5 scheme in a project for waterfront housing across the estuary from Creek Vean.

The waterfront housing project never proceeded, and today another house, by John Miller and Su Rogers, stands on that site. It is occupied by the family and friends during holidays and often at weekends, so that life at Creek Vean is often carried on by boat between the two homes. As Deyan Sudjic remarked in the television programme *Building Sights*, 'breakfast might be taken in one house and tea in another'.

For Rene Brumwell the house is inseparable from the sea: '… one would sit upstairs; the windows above open by means of a winch on the wall there. Upstairs you get more view, you see the boats going past on the Fal, racing. That's when you are indoors, but quite often you are outdoors – in the boats!' In the winter, however, the mezzanine lounge is also the warmest place in the south wing, for the house is heated by warm air, which is ducted through the ceiling.

Rene Brumwell recalls the change when she moved in from the Victorian house across the creek: 'It was so easy to run, so well thought out. We took to it very well. This room (the kitchen-dining room) is beautiful to sit in and have your meals. Even as I cook I can enjoy the view. One important thing is you don't feel shut in, and getting older, you don't feel, "Oh, I must get out", because you can actually get exercise in the house, too. Children enjoy running up and down the gallery. Delivery boys who come to the front door, look at it and say "This is a marvellous place!" They really like it, and I don't think it's put on. And what have we spent on decoration? Local people are always doing up their places. We haven't spent a penny on decoration.' For the bare block walls are still as crisp as on their day of completion.

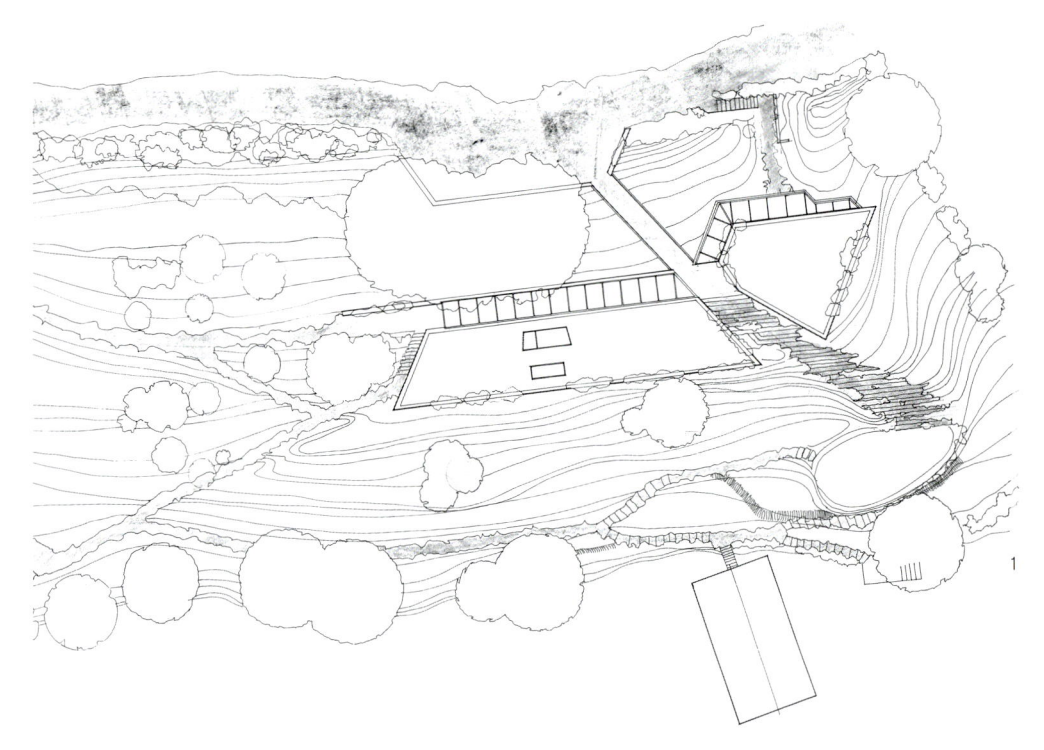

**An adherence to Fuller's Dymaxion principle, or 'maximum advantage gain for minimum energy input', was to characterise Foster's work from the outset, although his first efforts in this direction were hardly of the High-tech, lightweight structural range that one normally associates with Fuller. On the contrary, the initial Team 4 partnership ... first took a decidedly low-tech approach to the issues of building economy and energy conservation. This much is evident from their early joint work in Cornwall – the Creek Vean house of 1964-1966, designed for a steeply sloping site in the Fal estuary.** Kenneth Frampton, *On Foster ... Foster On*, 2000

**The building attempts to fit more snugly into its waterfront surroundings by generating a garden on the roof. As this starts to become overgrown, the house will recede into its creek-side Cornish setting.** Norman Foster, Arthur Batchelor lecture at UEA, 7 February 1978

Auguste Perret, who declared that his Naval Ministry contained 'not an ounce of plaster', would undoubtedly have concurred. Le Corbusier also; in *The Decorative Art of Today* he declared: 'If decorative art has no reason to exist, tools, on the other hand, do exist, and there exists also architecture and the work of art'. The house is indeed decorated by the vitality it facilitates; its ornaments are indices of an integral lifestyle.

Oven, fridge and cupboards are built into the backdrop of the kitchen workbench, with books on sailing ranged across the facing wall. Upstairs, a collection of classic art books of the 1940s and '50s line the mezzanine shelves; many of their subjects are represented among the paintings and sculptures throughout the house, and many of their authors lived in Cornwall, among the Brumwells' circle.

**At the point where the two wings of the house join, the geometries become particularly involved. Such torsions may bring to mind Frank Lloyd Wright's elaborate compositions; yet it may be misleading to 'over-Wright' the plan, which eludes a rigorously geometric definition.**

In the history of English Modernism, Cornwall occupies a special place and, in Cornwall, Creek Vean sums up the feeling of a generation for that same place. Like Jim Ede's house at Kettle's Yard in Cambridge, Creek Vean convenes a vivid museum of the modern in the setting of a private home. Better than Kettle's Yard, though, is that the house is itself the main thing, and, of course, is still lived in.

Adrian Stokes, I believe, never visited Creek Vean, but the house can be seen to share much of his sensibility. It can be sensed in a passage from 'Inside Out'; an essay in the *Psychology and Aesthetic Appeal of Space* in which he describes his encounter at Rapallo with the Mediterranean: 'I had the sensation that the air was touching things; that the space between things touched them, belonged in common, that space itself was utterly revealed. There was heatness in the light. Nothing hid or was hidden. We are looking on Nature, but at the same time we look on a clearer distribution of forces within ourselves, a clearer interaction, one more Homeric, more in style and therefore more disinterested than is the case. Would that inner conflict were thus wind-swept, that visitation of the deeper caverns of the mind were subject to such causes as those that govern tides.'

Brian Hatton

2, 3. Upper and lower-level plans of the house as built. It is organised around two routes: one is external and visually divides the house in two; the other is internal, in the form of the long picture gallery, which connects all the major living spaces.

1 main entrance
2 entrance gallery
3 studio living room
4 kitchen/dining room
5 laundry
6 store
7 study
8 bedroom
9 dressing room
10 guest suite
11 gallery
12 garden terrace

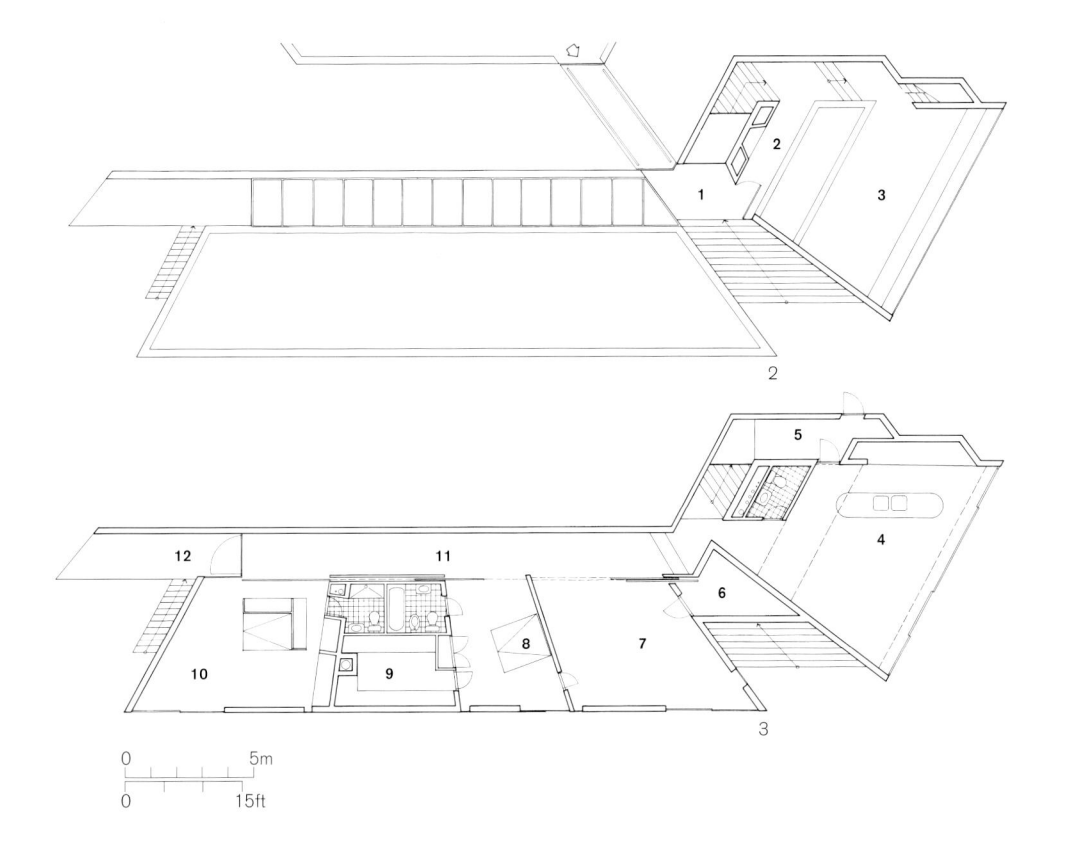

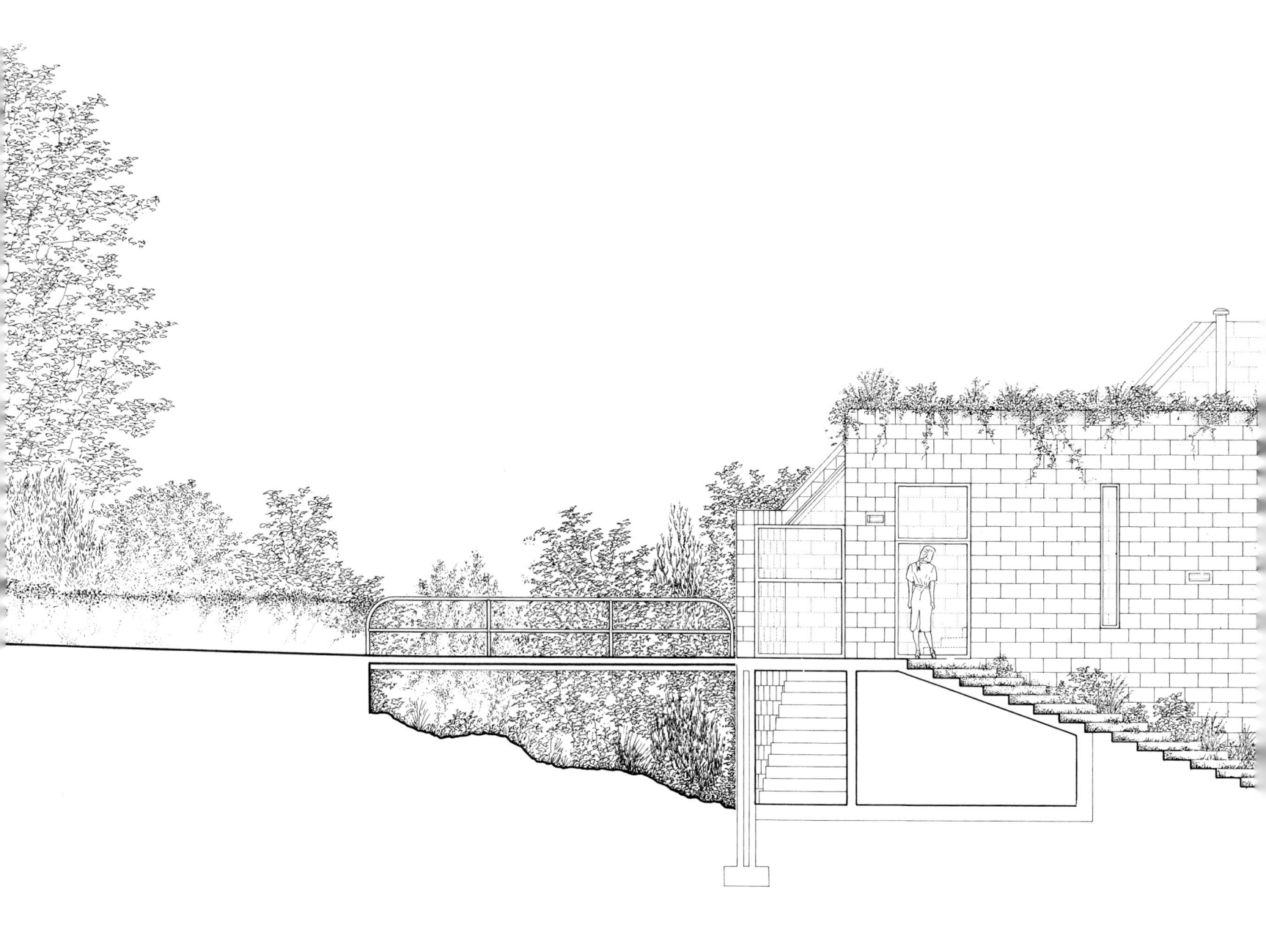

**One important thing is that you don't feel shut in, and getting older I don't feel, 'Oh, I must get out', because you can actually get exercise in the house too ... Delivery boys who come to the front door, look at it and say 'This is a marvellous place!' they really like it and I don't think it's put on.**

Rene Brumwell

A cross-section through the planted flight of steps that articulate the house, looking towards the two-storey living wing and the glass entrance door. Standing at the top of these steps the visitor has the choice of entering the house or proceeding down towards the river, through the garden.

**There is a distinctly mysterious aspect to the house as it emerges from the cliff in sections defined solely by the particular condition of the vegetation at the time. There is thus an indeterminacy about the appearance which contrasts with the finality of the blank wall on the road side. For the planting is not disciplined but rough, forcing its way through the steps and right up against the house.** Bryan Appleyard, *Richard Rogers*, 1986

**Visiting Aalto's Town Hall at Säynätsalo I was especially struck both by how small the complex was physically and yet how generous it was in spirit. Entering the central courtyard, which is sheltered by red brick walls and low-pitched roofs, and reached by a flight of shallow grassy steps, one perceives it immediately as more 'village' than single building. Looking back on the design of Creek Vean, it is easy to trace the impression that Säynätsalo made on its fledgling designers.** Norman Foster, *Alvar Aalto: Process and Culture*, 1999
Left: The planted steps at Alvar Aalto's Säynätsalo Town Hall, of 1952, which inspired those at Creek Vean.

1. Perhaps the single most memorable external feature of Creek Vean, is the planting on the roof of the bedrooms in the gallery wing. The roof-lights shown here light and ventilate the internal bathrooms, while the slanting glazing to the right top-lights the back wall of the gallery.

2. The planted steps that lead down from the entrance towards the creek and the boathouse. The irregular geometry of the plan means that the apparent curvature of the steps and the right-angle formed by the corner of the gallery wing are both optical illusions.

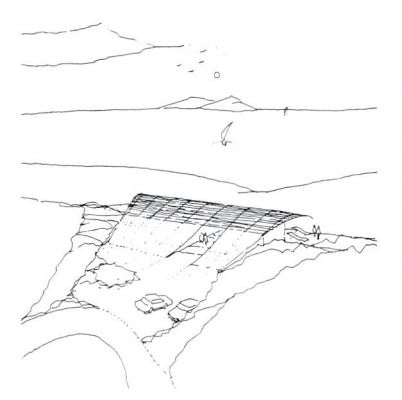

**Martin Pawley has drawn analogies between the early Creek Vean house in Cornwall – which was built in blockwork with a turf roof – and the more recent house in Corsica, in the sense that both have a rather dramatic relationship with the principal views of the site.** Norman Foster, in conversation with Malcolm Quantrill, 1999
Left: The house in Corsica (1992-1993). A single sweeping roof covers the house in a bold, simple gesture, ending in a curved canopy of louvres to provide shade for the south-facing terrace.

**In the history of English Modernism, Cornwall occupies a special place, and, in Cornwall, the Creek Vean house sums up the feeling of a generation for that same place.**
Brian Hatton

3. The complex arrangement of glazing provides top-light to the stairs beneath, which lead from the entrance gallery down to the kitchen, or up to the roof. In the foreground is the entrance footbridge.

4. The small sun terrace outside the dining room and kitchen of the two-storey living wing. The mezzanine floor of the living room studio above is set back from the flush glass walls, which have storey-height sliding glass panels at both levels.

5. The gallery wall projects out beyond the house, sheltering the line of the long top-lit gallery until it becomes a path that divides and leads off in two different directions, one passing along the side of the house down towards the creek, the other leading to a garage.

Creek Vean House  59

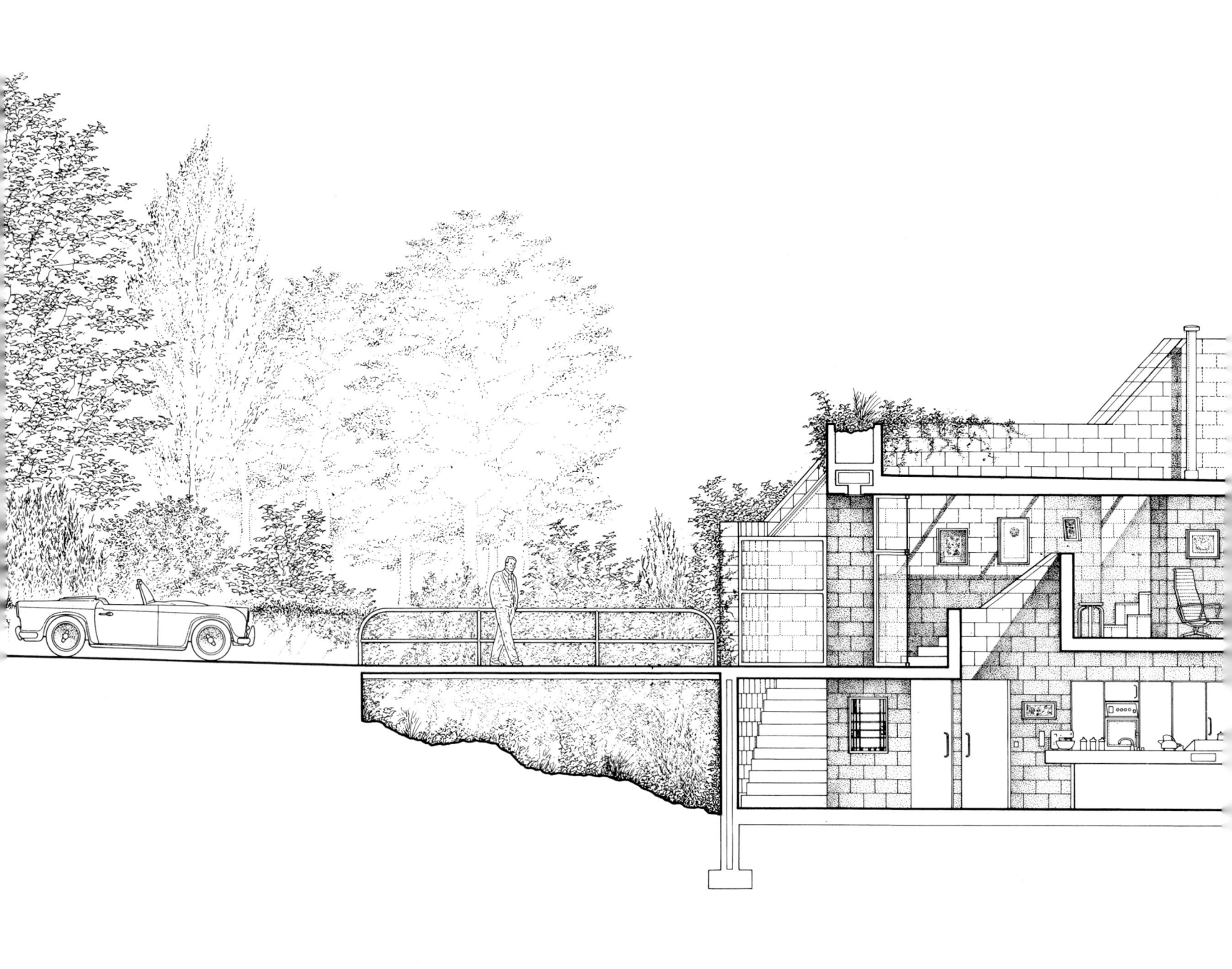

**What I love about this house is that it is really inseparable from the sea. You sit upstairs and you see the boats going past on the Fal, racing. That's when you are indoors, but quite often you are outdoors – in the boats!**
Rene Brumwell

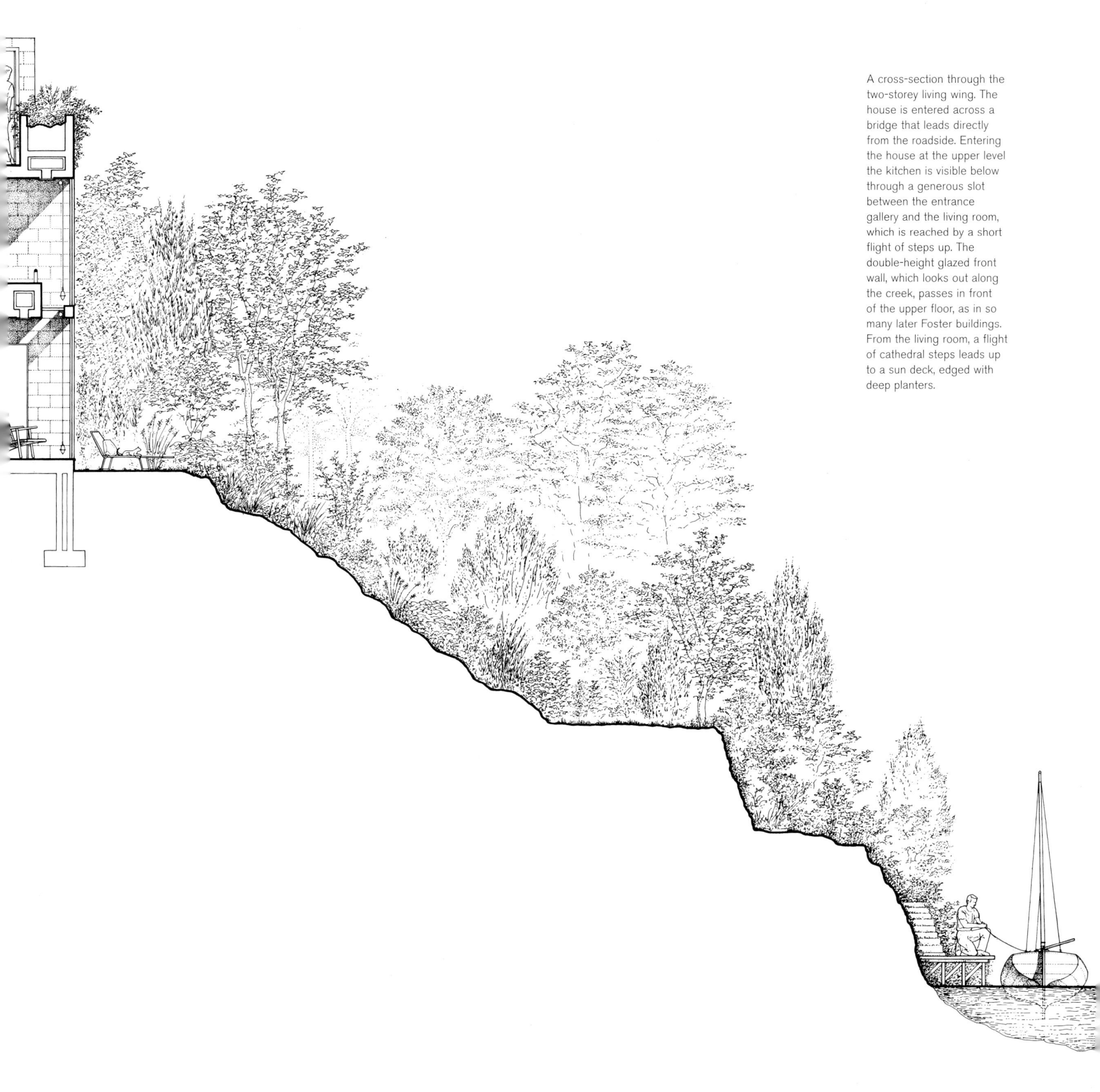

A cross-section through the two-storey living wing. The house is entered across a bridge that leads directly from the roadside. Entering the house at the upper level the kitchen is visible below through a generous slot between the entrance gallery and the living room, which is reached by a short flight of steps up. The double-height glazed front wall, which looks out along the creek, passes in front of the upper floor, as in so many later Foster buildings. From the living room, a flight of cathedral steps leads up to a sun deck, edged with deep planters.

Left: Norman Foster's photograph of Kettle's Yard, taken as part of his research for the design of the Sainsbury Centre, emphasises the sympathetic integration of art works in a top-lit domestic space – also a key element of the house at Creek Vean. Kettle's Yard was created by Jim Ede (1895-1971). Whilst working as a curator at the Tate Gallery he formed close friendships with British and European artists such as Ben Nicholson and Henri Gaudier-Brzeska, and built a substantial collection of art works. In 1956, with the help of architect Roland Aldridge, he remodelled four cottages in Cambridge to create an informal domestic setting for the collection.

1. The studio living room spans the main wing of the house and has wide slots on either side of the floor, allowing it to form a single space with the kitchen and dining areas below.

2. Looking down from the living room towards the glass entrance door and, beyond, the external steps that divide the two parts of the house.

3. As befits a home for a couple who loved sailing, the kitchen looks out over Pill Creek, while the studio living room above looks down the estuary and out to sea.

4. A view into the master bedroom, accessed from the top-lit picture gallery by means of sliding doors.

5. The dining area with its sliding glass doors giving on to the terrace.

6. Looking along the picture gallery towards the garden door and terrace.

**Like Jim Ede's house at Kettle's Yard in Cambridge, Creek Vean convenes a vivid museum of the modern in the setting of a private home. Better than Kettle's Yard, though, is that the house is itself the main thing, and, of course, is still lived in.**
Brian Hatton

In our opinion this small building is a work of outstanding quality. The architects have achieved an imaginative and highly original building without resorting to clichés or gimmickry. The design is carried through with commendable consistency using a self-imposed discipline in the choice of colours and materials. The general impression is that every arrangement in this design is an essential and significant part of the concept as a whole. Extract from the jurors' report for the RIBA Award, 1969

Creek Vean is, in our view, one of the most significant houses of its era. It is notable as a work of the Team 4 practice in which Foster and Rogers, two of the most influential British architects of the late twentieth century, were partners, and reflects the influence of American architecture on the youthful architects who both pursued Masters courses at Yale … It is our view that no other house of the 1960s is the equal of Creek Vean in terms of the integrity of the house and contents and its general historical significance. Extract from a submission made by Kenneth Powell, Consultant Director of the Twentieth Century Society, to the National Trust, August 1999. Creek Vean House received Grade II listing in 1998

The problems of quality control on straightforward exposed blockwork seemed almost insuperable; I suppose it was a house that was built several times before it was left alone. Norman Foster, lecture at Hong Kong University, 2 February 1980

Creek Vean House 63

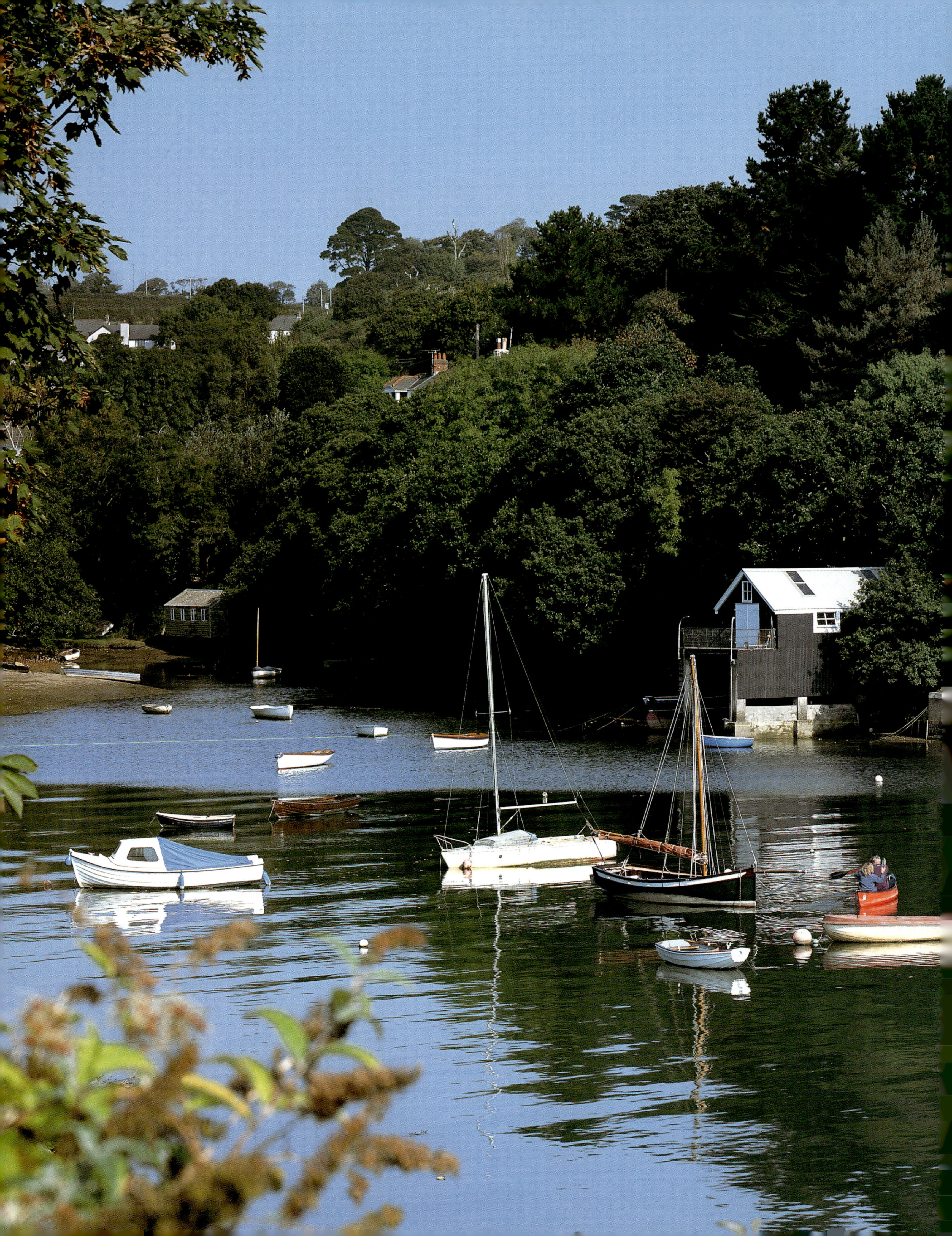

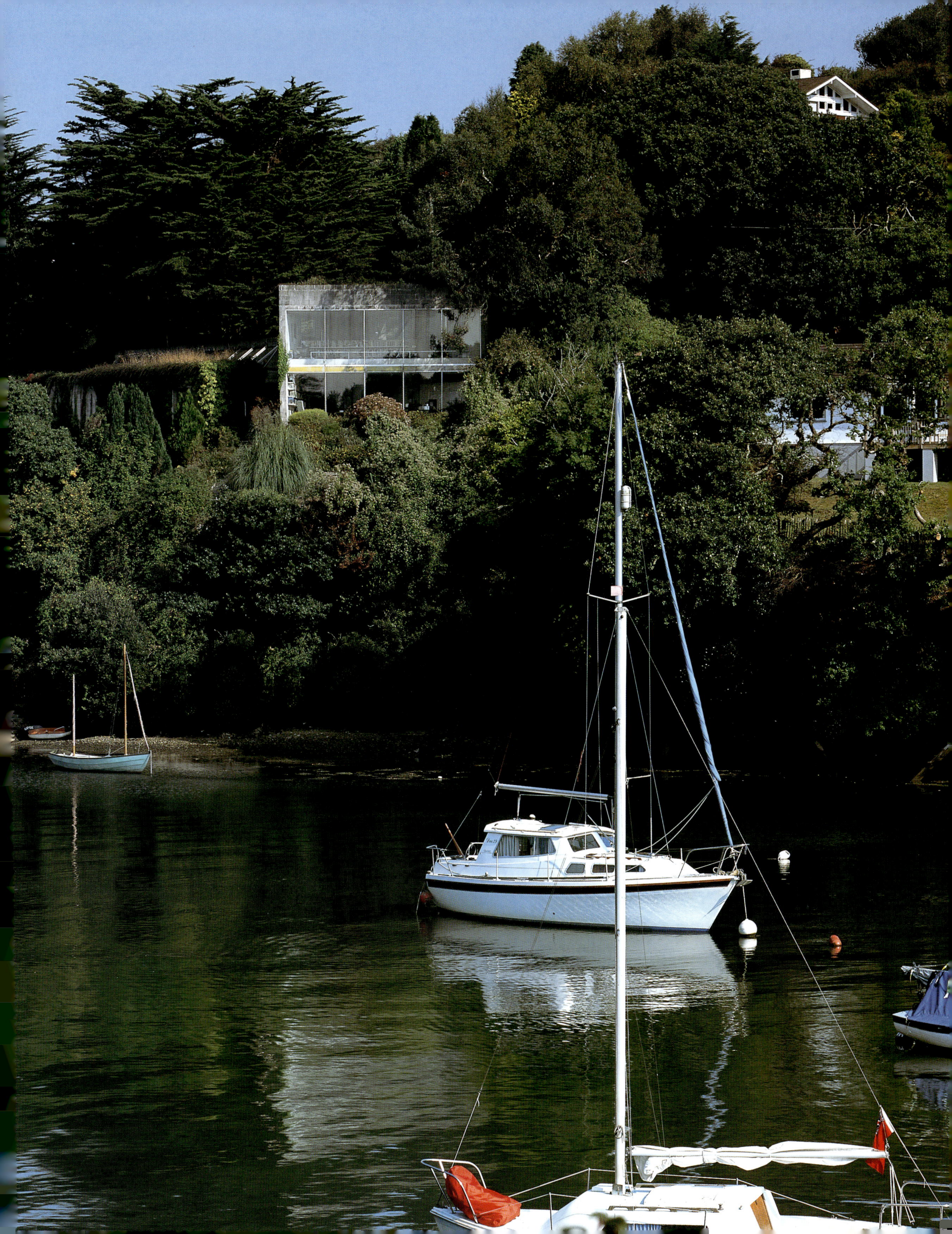

# Waterfront Housing
Feock, Cornwall, England 1964–1965

**Waterfront Housing was a protest against the suburbanisation of a precious coastline with low density developments.**
Norman Foster

**Feock is a small village. The core comprises a church, graveyard, vicarage, school and shop. The character of this area is changing rapidly for the worse as unsympathetic, sporadic development increases. The village has little contact with the water although from surrounding areas there are fine views out to the Fal estuary. But despite this heritage more and more individual houses, each with their own acreage, accumulate.** Part of the architects' written evidence to the local authority planning committee, 1965

**Feock, on the Fal estuary, is typical of the environmental disintegration which threatens coastal areas where there is increasing demand for homes by retired people. About fifty applications are approved each year in the parish for individual houses, mainly bungalows. Marcus Brumwell, who has had a home in Feock all his life, wanted to demonstrate an alternative: that, by grouping new houses in fairly dense clusters, the rest of the coast could be preserved unspoilt.**
Nicholas Taylor, *The Sunday Times*, 14 April 1968
Right: The proposed site for the Waterfront Housing scheme is visible on the opposite bank of the estuary from the dining room of the Creek Vean house.

A consequence of the Brumwells' move into the Creek Vean house was that the site of their earlier home could be reconsidered for new use. Marcus Brumwell was quick to agree with the architects' view that the piecemeal development of isolated bungalows was spoiling the Cornish coastline, whereas a traditional pattern of compact settlement fitted its intricate creeks far better. Terraced cottages, on the other hand, presented car-parking problems and tended to occlude views to the sea. However, the steep slope to the water at Feock offered a natural theatre for a tiered arrangement of overlapping terraces of a kind implicit in the section of the Creek Vean house.

Brumwell commissioned from Team 4 a plan for nineteen houses on the 1.21 hectare site, grouped in the earliest scheme as a staggered echelon facing the creek. This echelon appeared as a natural consequence of turning each house obliquely to the line of contours in order to face down the creek to the Fal estuary. But, interspersed with clumped trees so as not to obstruct any view, it also set out a broken and picturesque rhythm. Garages were clustered at each end and there was a plan for a community hall at the village end of the site. A stone footpath was to run along the frontage, stepping down to the water at certain points; while the road, as at Creek Vean, ran along the crest of the bank behind a long shielding wall.

The terrace was cut at intervals by steps between houses, which comprised two to four bedrooms in several variants within a standard type. Party walls of concrete blocks framed three-level dwellings, consisting of reinforced-concrete shelves that descended in terraced courtyards facing out to the sea. The uppermost rooms were for kitchen, dining and living.

In the final scheme, as at Creek Vean, a pitched skylight and planted roof were anticipated (the early version showed a range of sloping glass walls, later made vertical) while an interstitial alley ran between parallel ranks along the site, and car ports were located at the top of each terrace, rather than in clustered garages at the ends.

The aim was to recreate, at a collective scale, the individual experience of Creek Vean. Numerous drawings by Norman Foster attest to a recurrent idyllic theme in these projects. A table is sketched in the foreground, set with fruit bowl, glasses and wine, forming the first in a layered series of planes looking out through a transparent glass wall to the stage of a patio and beyond to the sea. Le Corbusier, in his drawings for houses at Rio de Janeiro, depicted a similar scene, commenting, 'the house is installed before its site'. Sadly, after lengthy discussions, the scheme was rejected by the local planning authority.

Brian Hatton

1. Norman Foster's sketch of the first version of the Waterfront scheme explores the idea of prominent sloped glazing facing the water, which was a feature of the early designs for the house at Creek Vean. In the first site layout, small groups of terraced houses step down the hillside, connected by a central path that runs between garage courts at each end of the site.

2. The stepped, single-outlook houses had no windows in the party walls but opened to the south-west to spectacular views of the creek and estuary. As Norman Foster's sketch illustrates, by responding to the contours of the site, the houses could be arranged to avoid overlooking neighbouring terraces.

3. Taken from the planning report prepared by Norman Foster, this annotated plan shows the village of Feock surrounded by sporadic development. The Waterfront Housing site is directly south of the village on the north bank of the Creek, giving oblique views of the Fal estuary to the west.

1. Norman Foster's sketch shows how a single footpath ran along the site giving access to the individual houses above, stepping up the hill.

2. This sectional perspective of the final scheme, drawn by Norman Foster, clearly shows the influence of the Atelier 5 housing at Siedlung Halen, though the large under-footpath service and drainage duct was an innovative feature ahead of its time.

3. The plans of the two-storey houses were oriented to maximise views and daylighting to both floors. Several variations in plan and section were designed – one with a double-height living room – the different configurations responding to the changing slope.

**The scheme applied the lessons to be learnt from the traditional clustering of buildings, accepting inevitable growth, but protecting as much of the countryside as possible.**
Norman Foster

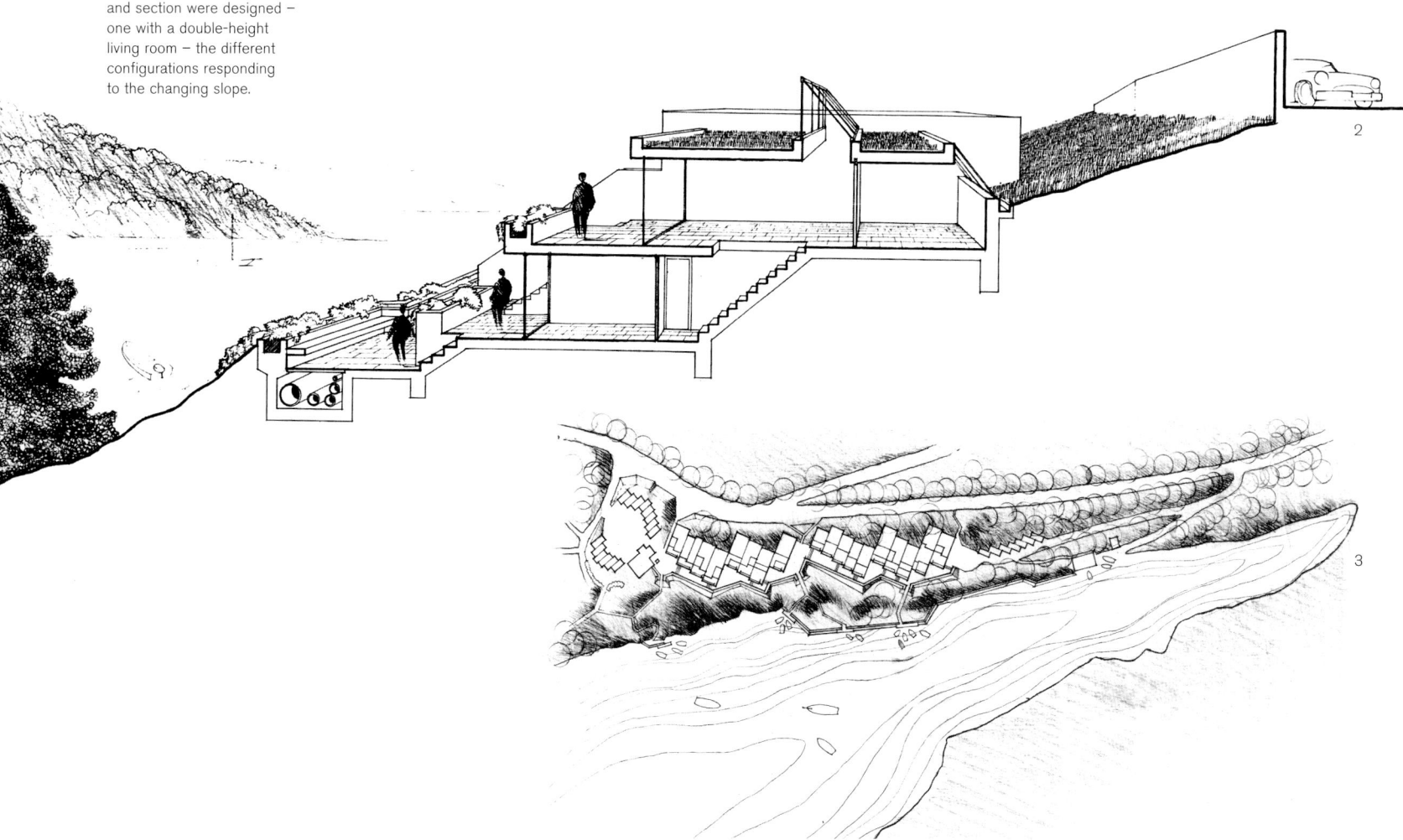

**The older, more traditional buildings on the site are absolutely right in their setting; they cluster economically, complementing the landscape and leaving large stretches undisturbed and rural.**
Norman Foster, notes on sketches of the Waterfront Housing site, 1964

Left and right: As part of his early research for the Waterfront Housing project, Norman Foster spent a week at Feock sketching the village and surrounding area, and making notes. The view on the extreme left looks across Pill Creek to the site of the Creek Vean house, showing the original bungalow and waterside boathouse.

4. A view of the model of the final scheme, in which all the housing units enjoy a uniform aspect towards the creek and the Fal estuary.

5. A partial section and elevation drawn by Norman Foster to illustrate how the terraced houses adapted a modern idiom to traditional Cornish village densities.

Waterfront Housing 69

**Murray Mews Houses**
Camden, London, England 1965

**This was a tiny pocket-handkerchief site, so to optimise the very tight area available the building came right up to the public pavement with a minimal courtyard tucked behind.** Norman Foster, 'Delight in Design' lecture at UEA, Norwich, 27 November 1978

**None of us appreciated the difficulties of running a practice without experience. I remember episodes such as crying under a tree on Hampstead Heath and thinking, I will never be an architect; a client asking me what I thought his damp-proof membrane was made of and finding it was the *Daily Mail* painted black; unplanned-for springs of water bursting into beautifully conceived living rooms; and our precious unopened drawings being used by contractors to wrap their fish and chips.** Richard Rogers, 'Team 4', 1991
Left: A view of the Murray Mews site during construction.

Team 4's earliest scheme for a terraced house, in Camden Mews, did not transpire, but in nearby Murray Mews a row of three houses was built. Here, however, the site was confined, and local circumstances determined that only two of the three houses conformed to the architects' original ideas.

The Murray Mews houses face directly onto the street along the building line of adjacent converted stables, while courtyards at the rear of the site adjoin the back gardens of the former villas. Although the street wall is pierced by both house and garage doors, it is predominantly blank. From the upper bedrooms, slit windows look out at right-angles to the mews facade, while the ground floor is illuminated by a sloping top-light invisible from the pavement. The aspect is severe and private, not to say, solipsistic: minimal solids and voids in ABABA rank.

The street door opens straight into the kitchen which is raised a few steps, as in the Skybreak house, to look over a worktop and built-in concrete table to the living room and a glazed wall with the courtyard beyond. The glass wall of the living room, like that of the kitchen-dining room at Creek Vean, is placed a metre or so forward of where the ceiling ends, so that more day-lit space is created. Standing in the kitchen, one is aware of bright top-lighting, then of a band of dimmer, intimate space in the living room, and then again of a band of brighter space along the window wall.

At an angle parallel to the sloping, glazed roof in the double-height kitchen, an open staircase runs up to the bathroom and bedrooms, with a few more steps leading up to a long top-lit picture gallery. From the balcony wall of this space one can look down into the kitchen as if from a minstrel gallery.

Courtyard, living room, kitchen and glazed 'attic' are thus related in a continuous spatial liaison; only the bedrooms and bathroom in the U-shaped middle level of the house are enclosed and separate. It is as if the medieval English 'Great Hall' has been miniaturised and centred around the kitchen.

Brian Hatton

Opposite: The three mews houses photographed shortly after completion. From the street they are inscrutable, the result of placing the courtyards at the rear, away from the front, instead of the front, as was proposed for the earlier houses in Camden Mews. The dramatic nature of the interiors can hardly be imagined from what is visible from outside.

1. Norman Foster's sectional study of one of the houses shows it very much in the form it was eventually built.

2. This early sketch of the mews by Norman Foster explores the idea of glazing in the flank walls of the two-storey blocks, an option that was not pursued.

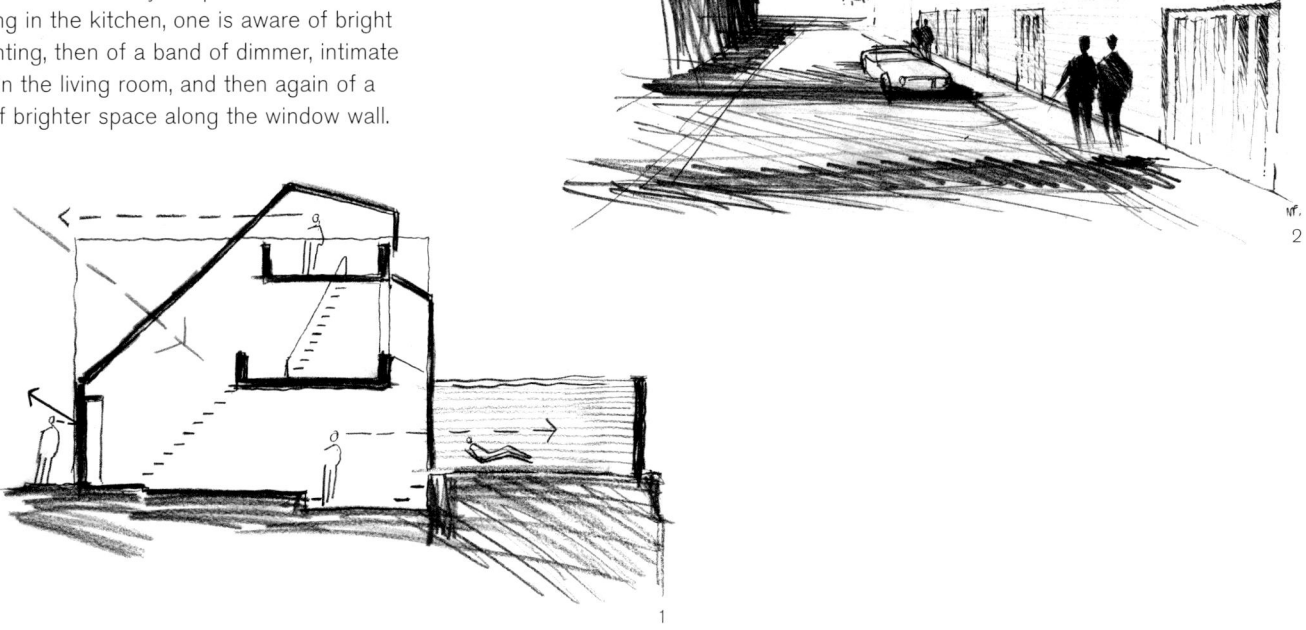

**Aalto's ability to signal the presence of a building in its setting with simple rugged forms is matched by an ability to break down its detailing wth seemingly infinite loving care.** Norman Foster, *RIBA Journal*, July 1976

Right: Alvar Aalto's 'experimental house' at Muuratsalo, of 1935, was a source of inspiration for the Murray Mews houses, particularly in the way that it presents an inscrutable aspect to the arriving visitor.

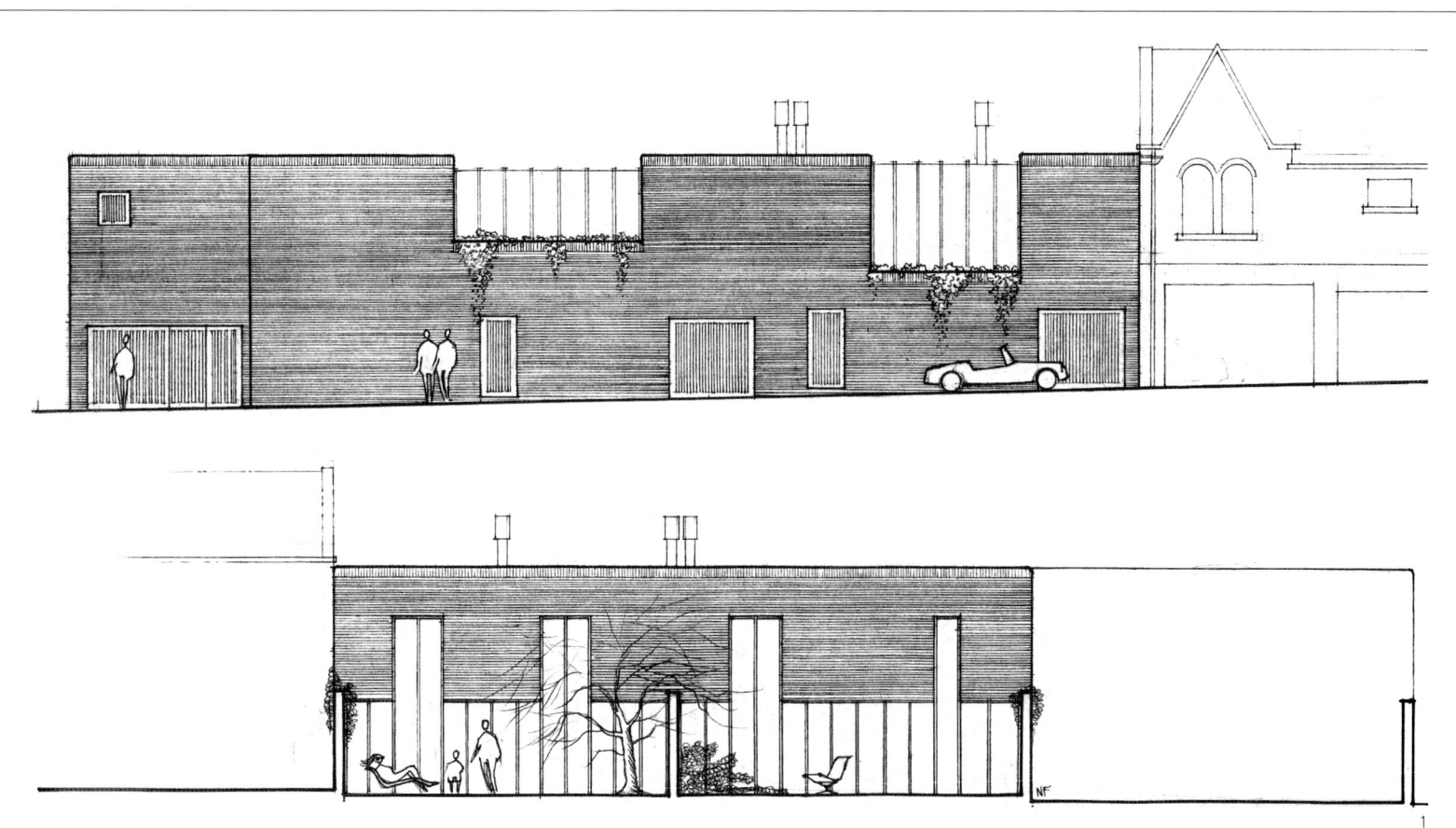

**Courtyard, living room, kitchen and glazed 'attic' are related in a continuous spatial liaison; only the bedrooms and bathroom in the U-shaped middle level of the house are enclosed. It is as though the medieval English 'Great Hall' has been miniaturised and centred around the kitchen.**

Brian Hatton

Overall, Murray Mews amounted to a competent synthesis of a large number of ideas about housing which were in the air at the time, and this quality means that the homes are still visited today by students of the use of small urban sites. The occupants have grown so accustomed to this that they start unrolling the original plans the moment the doorbell rings unexpectedly.
Bryan Appleyard, *Richard Rogers*, 1986

The early Team 4 mews houses, although exhibiting determinedly non-transparent brick walls to the street, have full-width glass walls to the garden courts. In a similar way, another Team 4 design, Reliance Controls at Swindon, of 1967, had three of the main walls *closed* by metal cladding, while the other is entirely *opened* by full-height glazing. This pattern established a dominant glass element within the architecture of Team 4.
Malcolm Quantrill, *The Norman Foster Studio*, 1999
Left: The glazed end wall at Reliance Controls.

1. In these early elevational studies by Norman Foster only the two houses on the right conform to the final design. The front doors open directly into the kitchen and dining areas, the large doors into the garages. The glass walls to the courtyards with first floor 'bays', are drawn much as built.

2. Norman Foster's sectional perspective of the Murray Mews 'system'. Each house, though adjusted to suit the requirements of its owner, has common characteristics: through visibility at ground level from front to back; a double-height living room; and a second-floor gallery beneath the peak of the patent glazing roof.

3. In their final form the sloping glass roofs resemble those proposed but never employed for the early Creek Vean and Waterfront Housing projects. Team 4's early success with advanced materials would encourage Foster in later years.

4. This section shows the high glazing ridge as built, together with the stair arrangement to the first floor and gallery above. In an echo of the Henrion studio, the sunken living room allowed the kitchen to enjoy courtyard views.

5. Ground-floor plan:

   1 entrance lobby
   2 kitchen/dining room
   3 living room
   4 study
   5 garage

Right: Taking up an idea introduced at Camden Mews, Foster proposed in one sketch the use of pivoting wall panels between the kitchen and living room.

1. The kitchen/dining room with its built-in concrete table and steps down to the living room. The main stairs lead up to three bedrooms at first-floor; the cathedral steps access the gallery at the top of the house.

2. Looking across the full width of the sunken living room into the study. The raised kitchen/dining area is on the right behind the permanent seating built into the balustrade wall.

3. A view along the dining table towards the living room. The quarry tile finish was carried across all the concrete surfaces in the kitchen, including the balustrade/planter, the worktops and the table.

4. The rear of the house at night. The ability to open up the full width of the ground floor to the courtyard gave a sense of spaciousness to an otherwise compact house. Bay windows on the first floor define the two rear bedrooms, the third being at the front of the house above the garage.

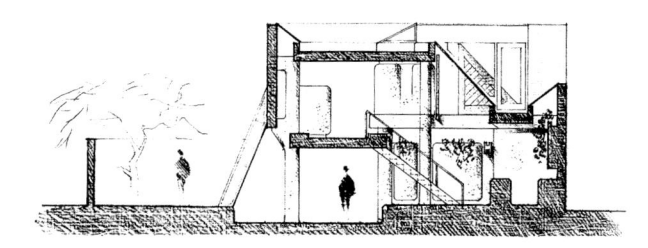

**The internal planning of each house responded to the particular needs of the occupants, a doctor with a strong interest in art, a husband and wife who were both barristers, and a skilled trade craftsman. The introduction of top-light and a concern for individual privacy were the major elements of the design.** Norman Foster, *Foster Associates*, 1979

Left: Norman Foster's sketch of an early design for Dr Owen Franklin's house in Murray Mews.

**Wates Housing**
Coulsdon, England 1965

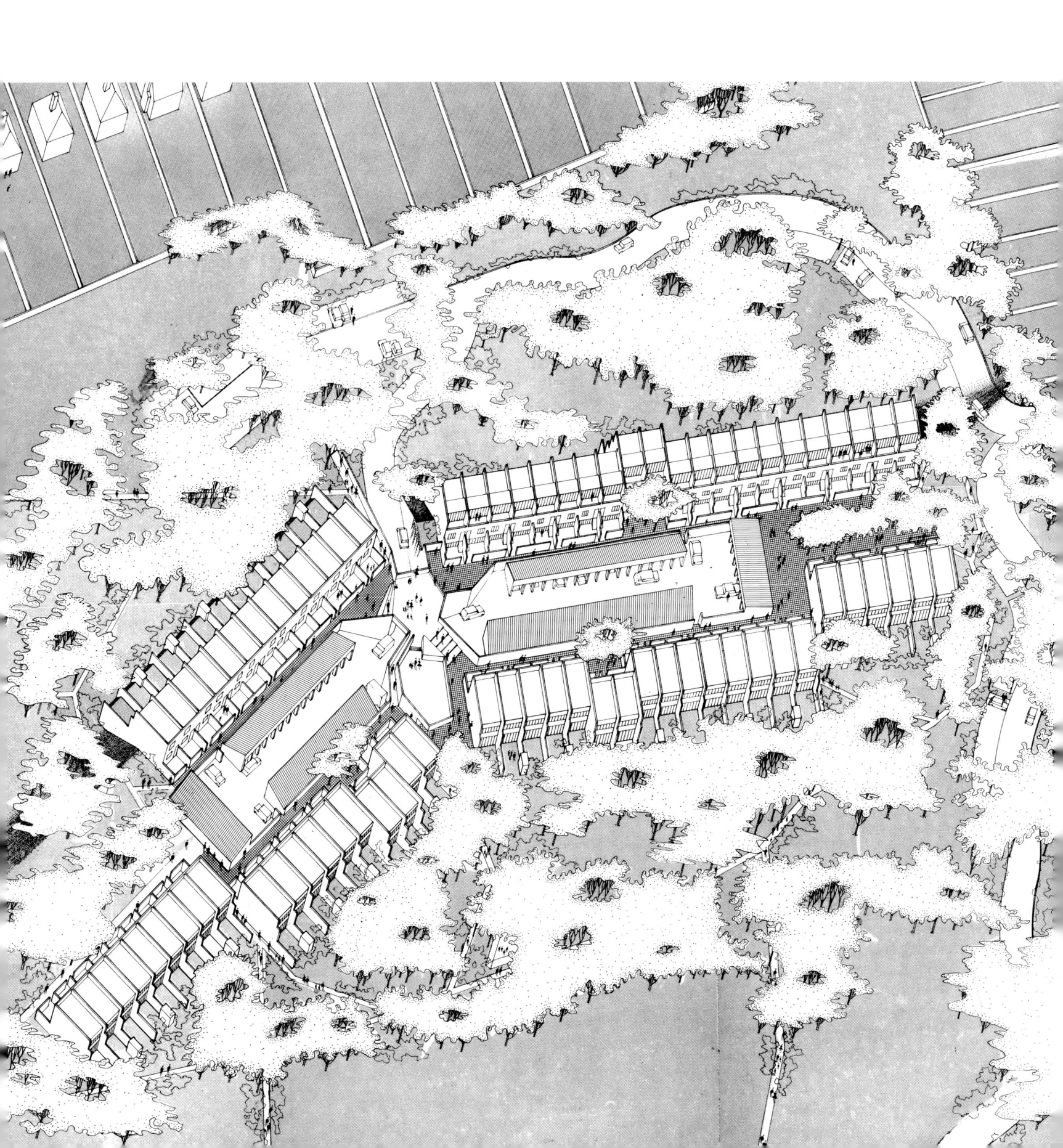

**Wendy and I had visited Siedlung Halen, the pioneering scheme by Atelier 5 near Berne, and had seen at first hand how exceptional privacy was achieved in a high-density layout with separation of cars and pedestrians.** Norman Foster, *Norman Foster: Sketches*, 1992

**The prototype of a kasbah may have influenced the planning of Siedlung Halen outside Berne (1961), by the Atelier 5 group, a 'squashed Unité' packed down to conform to the patterns of the landscape. The social relations of Siedlung Halen were directly expressed in the gradual transition in scales, from the main piazza and street in the middle to the secondary routes, to the gardens, and then to the individual quarters.** William J R Curtis, *Modern Architecture since 1900*, 1996

Left: An aerial view of Atelier 5's Siedlung Halen scheme – a reference point in the design of Wates Housing.

Wates Built Homes, a housing development and contracting company, had secured an option on 69 acres of suburban backland for housing development at Coulsdon in Surrey, 35 miles from the centre of London. The site was well covered with trees, bounded by existing paths and divided by a steep bank, with a maximum drop of nearly 4 metres running north-south across its centre. These were topographical challenges that ruled out conventional off-the-peg developer's housing.

Wates had its own architects department but decided that in this instance it needed innovative architectural advice. Ken Bland, the company's chief architect, visited a number of firms of which Team 4 was by far the youngest and least experienced. However, as a result of that process, Norman and Wendy Foster and Richard Rogers were interviewed by Neil Wates and Ken Bland, who asked their advice on how best to tackle the Coulsdon site.

Norman Foster recalls: 'We suggested that they should seek out Atelier 5 in Switzerland and see their Siedlung Halen housing near Berne. This caused an exchange of surprised looks – they had planned to do that anyway'. The outcome was that Team 4 was engaged to produce a feasibility study for the whole site, suitable for an outline planning submission, together with detailed proposals for a small pilot scheme. A landscape architect and, interestingly, a sociologist were also appointed.

Like the Siedlung Halen scheme, which was completed in 1961, Team 4's pilot studies proposed a high-density solution with the houses arranged in terraces on either side of a central hard-landscaped parking court. And like their earlier waterfront housing in Cornwall, the houses were 'dug-in' to the sloping site, with cars and pedestrians segregated so that the paths on the estate could be kept free of vehicular traffic.

The pilot scheme for Wates was to have been built on a 9-acre plot consisting of two large clearings. The use of these clearings, together with the retention of as many trees as possible, led to the arrangement of four east or west facing terraces.

Opposite: In this early presentation drawing the main features of the pilot scheme are established but the terraces are arranged at a more pronounced angle than in the final scheme.

1. The site model of the final scheme looking south along the line of terraces.

2. In its final form, the pilot scheme accommodated 130 houses. Access roads ran through the site north-south creating private, self-contained areas.

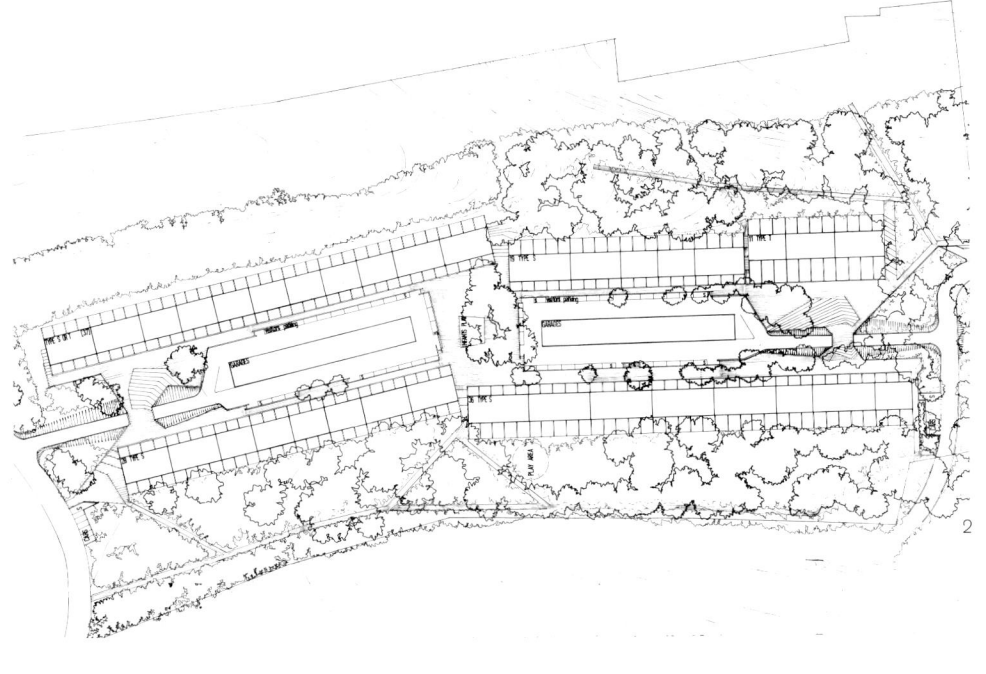

**The design is based on a clear progression from public and communal 'hard' areas, through private access courts to the houses, and on to gardens facing the woodlands. The house types respond to this concept in having small windows to the urban elevations and full glazing to the gardens. The scheme takes advantage of a sense of community whilst giving at the same time good privacy and pleasant outlooks for the individual houses.**
Extract from the assessors' report, *Architectural Design* Project Award, 1965

Norman Foster's sketches illustrate the textural qualities of the scheme.

1, 2. Terraces step down the site, separated by a central covered parking area. At the meeting point, a ramp leads up, separating pedestrians from the vehicle access. This segregation was maintained along the walkways that give access to each house's courtyard entrance, where children might play.

3. The wooded strip in the middle of the site was to have been developed as a pedestrian spine crossed with footpaths.

4. Where the fall on the site was sufficient, vehicular access was directed through cuttings at the lower level.

Within the masterplan the existing landscape features were, as far as possible, preserved or manipulated to achieve a strikingly well-ordered site layout. A densely wooded strip running along the centre of the site was retained and developed as a pedestrian spine with a network of paths running through it; shorter spurs lead off to each of the housing areas. Interconnecting open spaces accommodated children's play areas and allowed a richer variety of walks through the trees together with more direct routes to the local railway station, bus-stops, schools and shops.

Vehicles were confined to a road running around the edge of the site with smaller feeder roads giving off at strategic points into the centre of the housing clusters. The four major entry points into the site were conceived as 'locks' where cars would be slowed down by cattle grids and then allowed to pick up speed on the peripheral road. In conceptual terms, this organisation can be seen as analogous to Louis Kahn's 1956-1962 plan for the centre of Philadelphia, where streets were thought of as 'rivers' or 'canals' and parking areas became 'harbours' or 'docks'. Other routes were freed of cars and given over to pedestrians, the two types of movement being separated from one another not for speed of travel but for order and convenience.

Forming the vehicular route from the peripheral road to the parking area for the first two housing clusters involved excavating a cutting into the land bank; above that was a pedestrian viewing platform reached by a ramp. After this initial level separation, the segregation of cars and pedestrian routes was maintained horizontally by screened alleyways. This arrangement allowed cars to feed into the heart of the scheme and be parked close to each front door, while making convenient use of the 21-metre statutory open space required between facing terraces. The terrace layout was deliberately open-ended so that it could be easily extended or built incrementally.

## Like Team 4's Waterfront Housing project in Cornwall, the Wates houses were 'dug-in' to the site, with cars and pedestrians segregated.

Wates' original intention was to begin development by building the pilot scheme on an approximately 9-acre plot that incorporated two clearings in the south-east corner of the site. Altogether, ten such clearings existed, each defined by surrounding woodland. The initial phase was to have comprised 131 houses with one garage or parking space per house, together with additional visitors' parking and a communal clubhouse, which was to be run by a residents' association.

Right: Serge Chermayeff and Christopher Alexander's *Community and Privacy*, first published in 1963, was a key influence on the development of the Wates scheme. Norman Foster had been given a draft copy of the book by Chermayeff while still a student at Yale University and was offered a research fellowship to continue those studies with Chermayeff at Yale.
Far right: Chermayeff and Alexander's diagrammatic analysis of contrasting models of urban development from around the world.

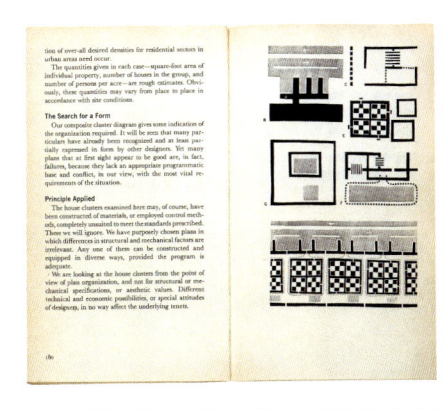

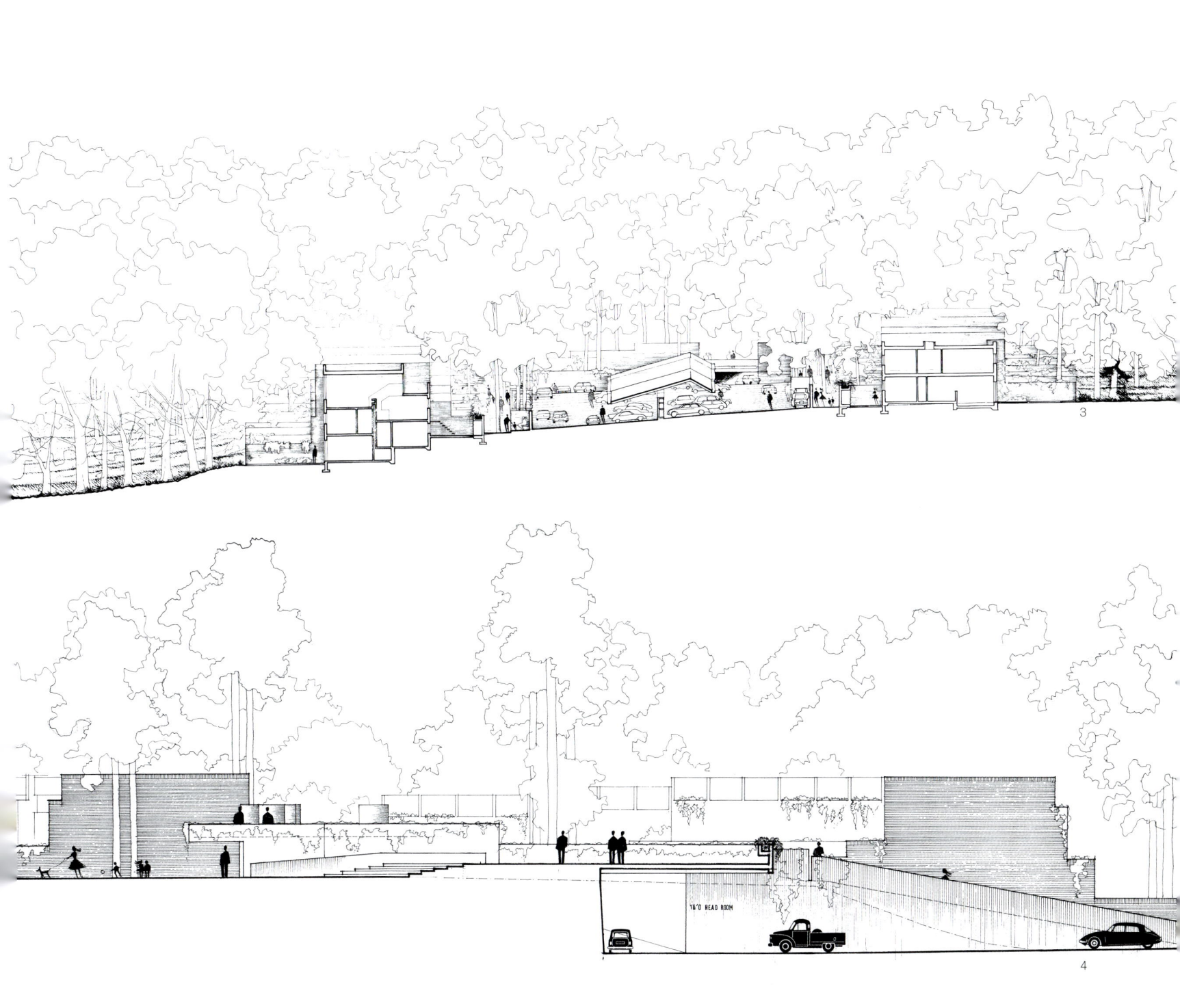

Wates Housing

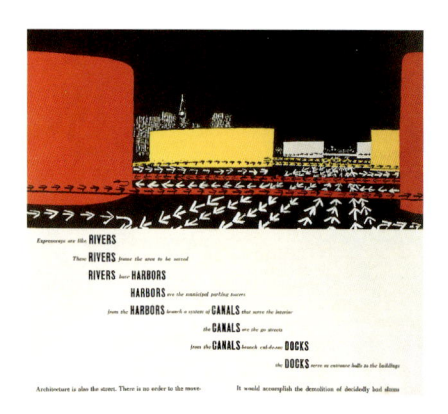

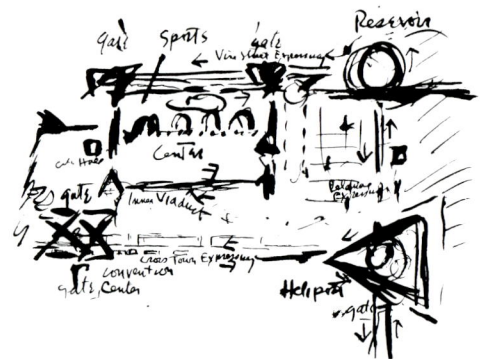

> Express ways are rivers that need harbours ...
> Streets are canals that need docks ... The motor
> car has completely upset the form of the city.
> I feel that the time has come to make the distinction
> between the viaduct architecture of the car and
> the architecture of man's activities. Louis Kahn,
> quoted in *Louis Kahn: Complete Work 1935-1974*, 1987
> Left: Louis Kahn's diagram and plan sketch
> for the Philadelphia Midtown Development of 1956-
> 1962. Kahn's zoning of pedestrians and cars can
> be seen to be reprised in the development of the
> Wates scheme.

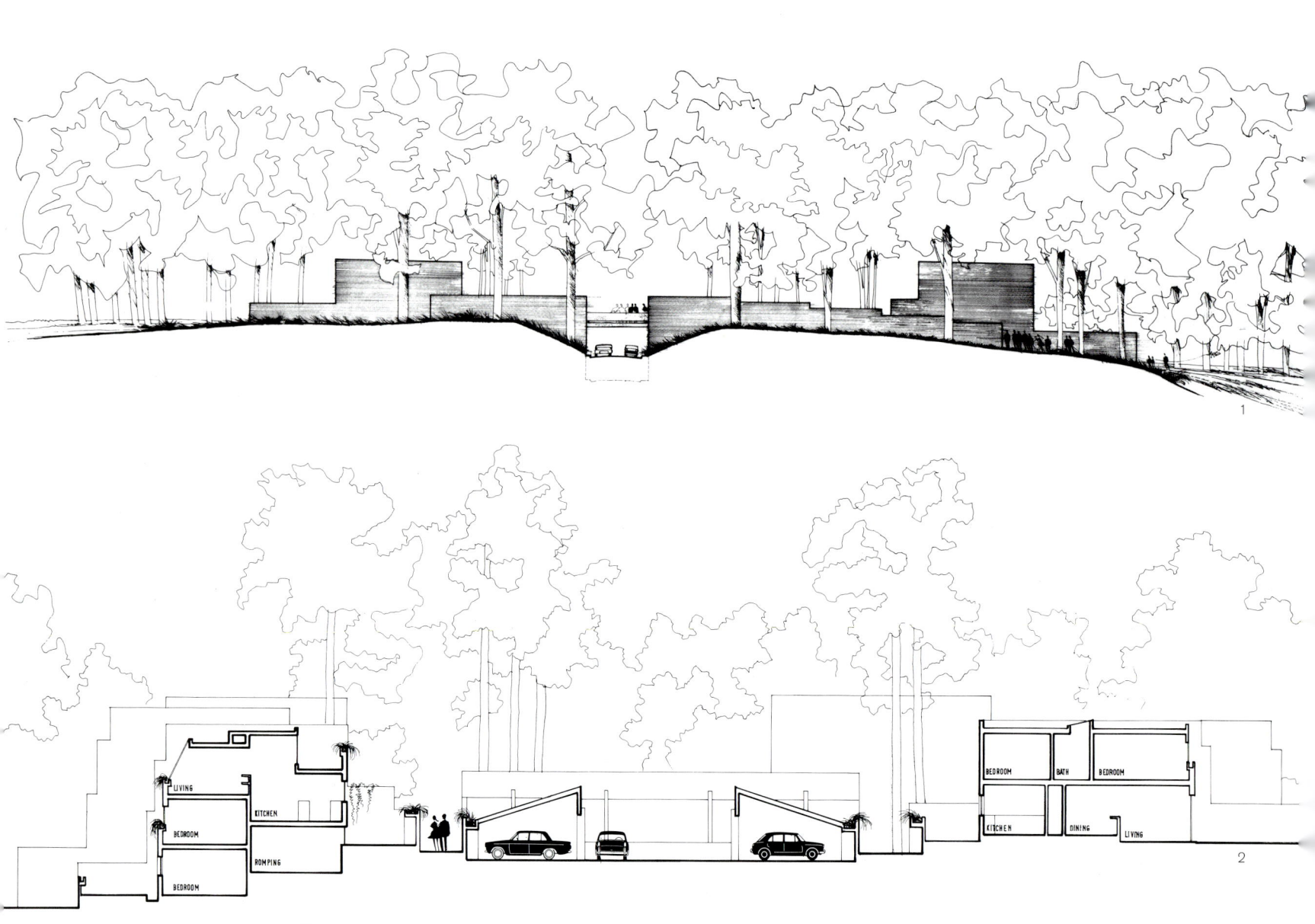

**Team 4's pilot studies proposed a high-density solution with the houses arranged in terraces on either side of a central hard-landscaped court.**

David Jenkins

80  Norman Foster Works 1

**With open spaces and landscaping, Lafayette Park provides the best of suburban living ... It is a new structure predicated on human values, disciplined but not dominated by the automobile.**
David Spaeth, *Mies van der Rohe*, 1985
Right: Mies' Lafayette Park, in Detroit, Michigan, of 1955-1963, was a source of inspiration for the Wates scheme, particularly in the way that it segregated cars, from landscaped areas, using subtle changes of level to maintain clear views through the gardens.

**The Team 4 scheme pays unusually close attention to the disposition of families and their vehicles on a residential site with the result that their design suggests what is really a new architectural form for a housing estate.** Extract from assessors' report, *Architectural Design* Project Award, 1965

There were two main house types, the first of two storeys and three bedrooms, the second of three storeys and three to four bedrooms. Both were traditionally constructed with flat roofs and aimed at middle-income families. The two-storey house was conventionally planned with living accommodation on the ground floor and bedrooms above. The living rooms opened on to a private garden with the woodland beyond. The kitchens overlooked a paved entrance court and the parking area.

The three-storey house stepped in section following the natural bank, with a split-level living space at the top. This gave on to a private terrace, allowing residents to feel close to the trees on the wooded side. As in the smaller house, the kitchen looked down into the entrance courtyard. The dining area was located in the double-height zone generated between the kitchen and the sitting room, which was situated in the half level above it.

Spatially the upper floors of these houses had much of the free-flowing quality of the Skybreak house, an impression that comes across clearly in Norman Foster's perspective sketches. And, again as with the Skybreak house, the influence of Serge Chermayeff's planning theories is apparent, with a clear hierarchy of spaces leading from the public to private realms.

Below the living space the bedroom floors again worked on the half level, with children's bedrooms occupying the lowest level, giving them direct access into the back garden on one side and the entrance courtyard on the other.

Organising the house into parent and child domains allowed for mutual privacy and a high degree of independence, including the potential of converting the lower floor into a separate flat for teenagers or an elderly relative.

The elevational treatment of the terraces reinforced the conceptual progression from communal 'hard' areas, via private entrance courts to the houses and out on to the 'soft' gardens facing the woodland. On the hard side the windows were treated as holes punched in the red brick walls, reflecting a defensible, mews-like urban character; while on the garden side the glazing stretched in horizontal bands from party-wall to party-wall, opening up the living spaces to sunlight and views.

Wates was granted outline planning permission in April 1965 but decided not to proceed with the Team 4 scheme. Looking back, Norman Foster feels that Wates was not really the right client, noting that 'traditional housing developer values prevailed, with the respectable minimum of safe experiment'.

David Jenkins

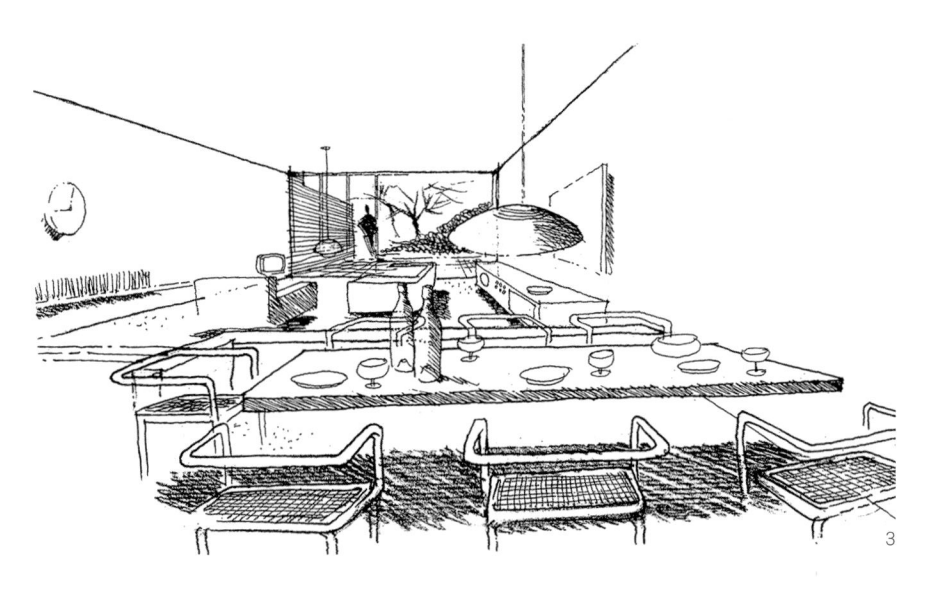

1. Vehicular circulation was confined to the perimeter of the site, while access to the covered parking courts at the centre of each pair of terraces was to be by feeder roads; vehicle speeds were controlled by the use of cattle grids.

2. Different solutions had to be found to accommodate the compound fall across the site; from north to south this reached a maximum of 3.5 metres. Certain house designs incorporated stepped sections that responded to the slope.

3, 4. Norman Foster's sketch studies of the interiors of a typical upper-level terrace house, with its private walled garden. As later in the high-density housing at Radlett, narrow frontages with cross-wall construction would have permitted large glazed areas.

# Skybreak House
Radlett, England 1965–1966

**It is an aesthetic experience to progress down through the main space of this house from platform to platform, through alternating areas of brightness, from the top glazing, and shade, always with the view to the green countryside opening up as one approaches the lowest level.** Richard Einzig, *Classic Modern Houses in Europe*, 1981

**The Skybreak house was really an attempt to squeeze the maximum house from the minimum resources, and it is characterised by an interest and a belief in the potential and joy of natural light – particularly natural top light.** Norman Foster, Arthur Batchelor lecture at UEA, Norwich, 7 February 1978

The type of stepped house envisaged for the Cornish Waterfront Housing project was to be developed individually in the Skybreak house at Radlett, although on a gentler slope that allowed all of its rooms to be disposed as open-plan stages on terraces within a single continuous space. That each level in the house could thus be top-lit by skylights doubtless gave rise to its name.

Skybreak was simpler in format than Creek Vean, for its site offered none of the vantages and views that so invited articulation and drama from its designers. Instead, the location was a gentle, north-facing slope on a dry, shallow dell at the edge of an incipient suburb. A straggle of detached houses had begun along the road, to which Team 4 reacted much as they did at Feock, with a study for an extension of the Skybreak unit into a continuous range of terraced houses, an idea later developed more fully by Norman and Wendy Foster in the high-density housing project.

Skybreak gave rise to radical experiments and initiated thoughts on interior space that would be explored with increasing vigour in Foster's later work. It exploits the elementary ranging of the house between two parallel walls which could easily become party-walls between adjoining neighbours. But while the low, single-storey profile and sloping, glazed end-walls might be considered unusual in its suburban setting, the real innovations at Skybreak are found on the inside. Here is a conception of living based not only on an open plan but also on a level of flexibility that facilitates change.

The Jaffés, who commissioned the house, had asked for a place that could be adapted to a variety of uses, for both family and social occasions, and which could be extended easily as required. Additionally, an arrangement was envisaged whereby the kitchen could overlook a play area. With regard to the best use of site and sunlight, a solution consistent with Team 4's work elsewhere clearly suggested itself: the distinction, in the disposition of windows,

1. A view from the highest level of the house down through the open-plan living area. Sliding doors allow the space to be used in a variety of configurations, while sunlight and views provide a pervasive theme.

2. Norman Foster's sketch analysis of the house and site. Sunlight from the south is 'captured' by rooflights in an echelon roof. The house is otherwise closed to the south, but opens up to the north to maximise views across open countryside. Even in diagrammatic form the possibilities for terraced housing (later taken up in the high-density housing project) can be clearly seen.

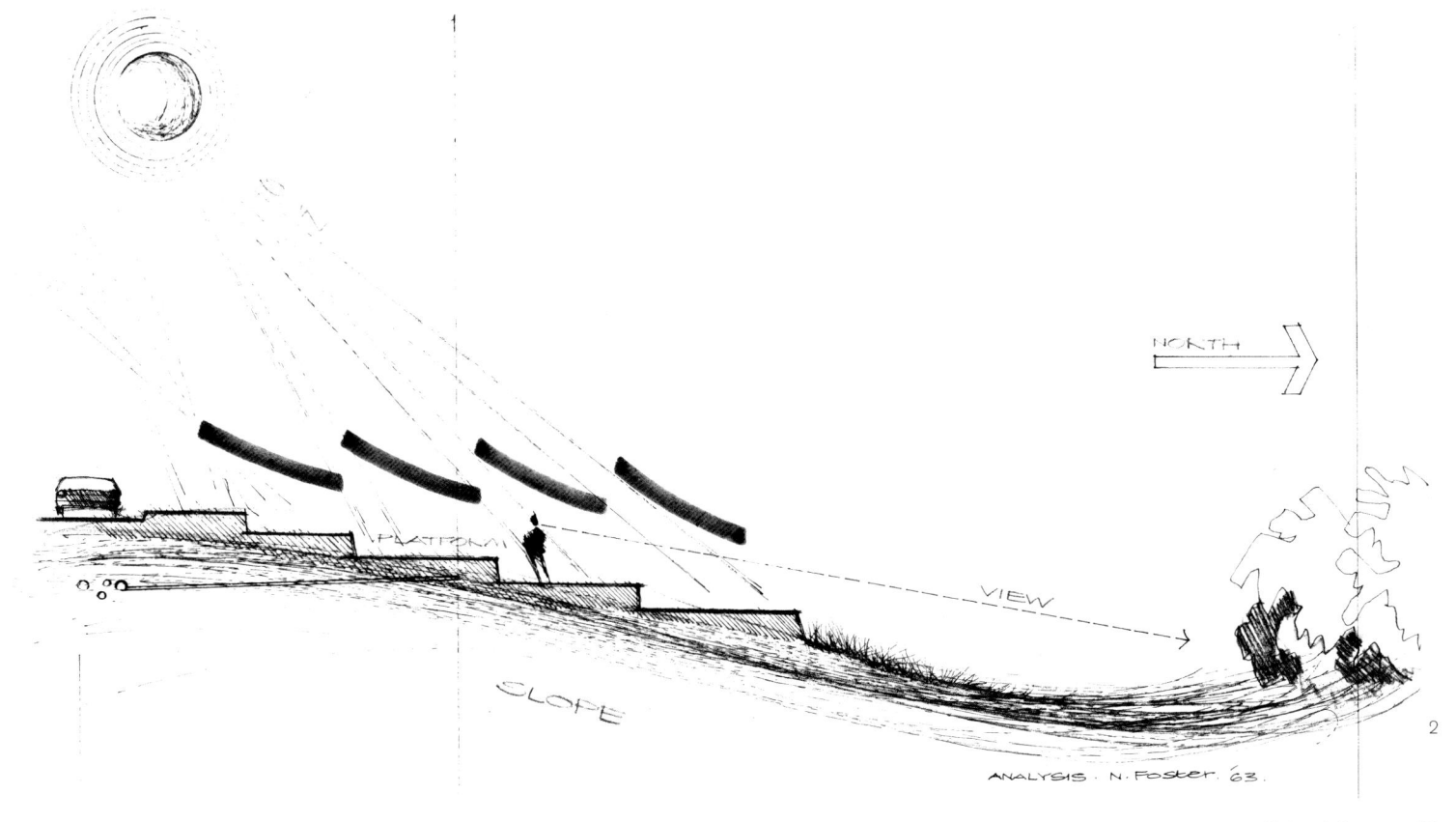

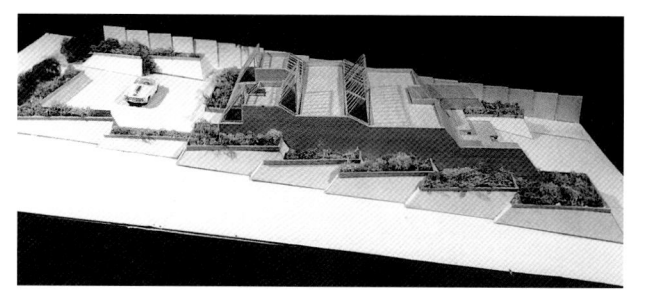

Left: A model of the prismatic roof-light system originally proposed for Skybreak house, applied differently across the three planning zones. The vertical glass elements were intended to reflect light through the angled panes into the interior – a detail that would ultimately be 'designed out'.

1. Norman Foster's elevation of the house. With its single level stepping down the slope, the house is quite at variance with its suburban surroundings.

2. The three linear zones of the house move from the 'public' living area, through a 'semi-private' family zone, to the privacy of the bedrooms.

3. This axonometric drawing by Norman Foster reveals how the stepped levels are divided into parallel planning zones, each defined by cross walls with different degrees of openness.

4, 5. The three internal planning zones are defined externally by the staggered planes of the glazing and the echelon of the brick cross walls. Sliding doors open out onto a terrace that enjoys views across the surrounding countryside.

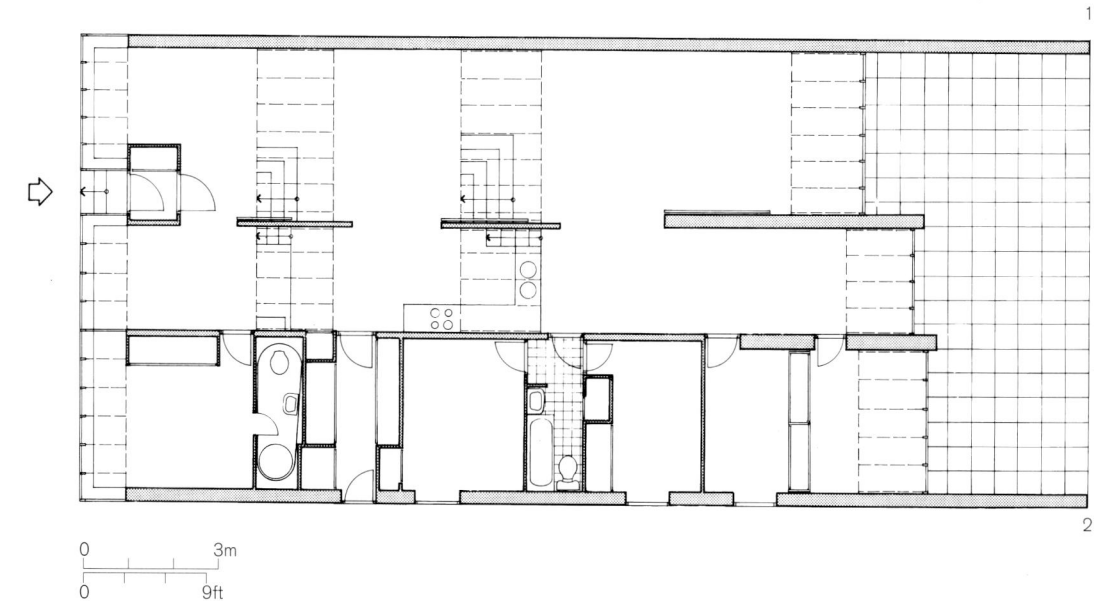

**One of the themes that weaves itself between our projects over the years is the handling of natural light: how it might inform, diffuse and add another dimension to an interior, whether it's a domestic interior, an airport, a building you work in, or a gallery where you look at works of art.**
Norman Foster, inaugural Academy Architecture lecture, Royal Academy, London, 15 June 1991

Left: Norman Foster's sketch for the Fred Olsen country offices in Vestby, Norway (1973) presented a logical extension of the top-lighting at Skybreak. The Olsen scheme proposed the use of solar reflectors – or 'sunscoops' – which would track the sun, drawing the maximum amount of natural light into the buildings.

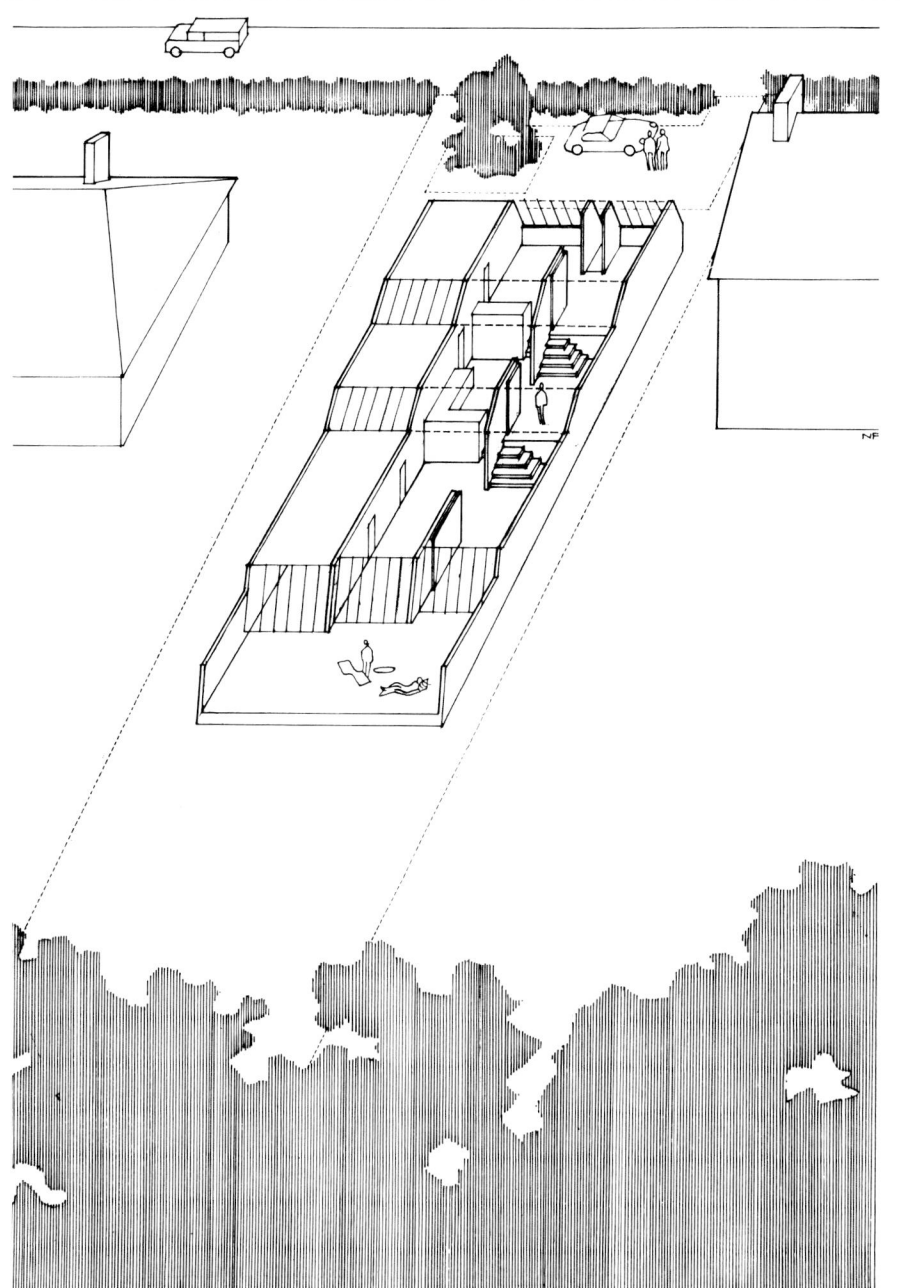

# Skybreak gave rise to radical experiments and initiated thoughts on interior space that would be explored with increasing vigour in Foster's later work.

Brian Hatton

**Skybreak house is one of my favourites and when the original owners decided to move on, Wendy and I very seriously considered buying it. It was only the problem of our children commuting to their London schools that stopped us.**
Norman Foster, *Norman Foster: Sketches*, 1992
Right: Norman Foster photographed on a site visit to Skybreak house during its construction.

**While the low, single-storey profile and sloping, glazed end-walls might be considered unusual in its suburban setting, the real innovations at Skybreak are found on the inside. Here is a conception of living based not only on an open plan but also on a level of flexibility that facilitates change.**
Brian Hatton

**Skybreak achieved a rather non-architectural fame in that its interior was used for some of the scenes of ultra-violence in the film *A Clockwork Orange*. But Stanley Kubrick, the director, was not interested in the outside so he cheated by implying that the house had a different, traditional exterior.** Bryan Appleyard, *Richard Rogers*, 1986
Right: Skybreak provided the setting for *A Clockwork Orange*'s infamous rape scene. Released in 1971, Stanley Kubrick's film (based on Anthony Burgess' 1961 novella) engendered intense critical controversy and was eventually withdrawn from circulation by Warner Bros on Kubrick's instruction.
Far right: The film's poster, famous in its own right.

An early sketch by Norman Foster shows how the stepped section was conceived with a view north to open countryside, while sunlight fell from above and behind through breaks in an echelon roof. Such a drawing makes no definite indications as to planning, but it does imply certain possibilities. One is of great length and extendability – indeed, the echelon skylight roof is an industrial form developed for assembly shops and production lines. Another possibility would be of rooms without lateral windows, a form characteristic of museums and art galleries. Skybreak transferred the form, however, to a residential scale.

An initial division by two parallel walls running the length of the space was made the tool for this transference, creating two distinct zones on plan, one open, the other enclosed. The eastern zone contains closed rooms for sleeping, washing and utility. The western zone is a fluid open space, a domestic concourse in three terraced stages. Two flights of spreading steps each connect the stages. The upper two stages are square and the lowest, leading through sliding windows to the patio and garden, a double square. These stages were designated respectively for study, dining and living. At the far end of the lowest level, a piano was placed before the window, so that the upper two terraces, with their balcony rails, assume the role of tiers in a theatre. In a house designed expressly with the aim of entertaining guests, this is a role they must often have assumed, at least informally.

A low wall separates the kitchen from the conservatory behind, which is reached by three narrow steps. With access in four directions to playroom, dining room, conservatory and the outside, through a utility room, and with oblique views to study and living rooms, the kitchen is not just the physical centre of the house but, again as at Creek Vean, its principal vantage-point.

At Skybreak the bedroom walls are non-structural to allow for change. Indeed the whole house presents implications of thorough flexibility that were subsequently explored by both Foster and Rogers; implications that would lead rapidly away from wet-build methods and heavy structures towards prefabrication, light materials and new technologies. Interesting and noteworthy here is that such innovations were prompted less in the pursuit of maximised production of unit modules, than by a desire to refine and tune the quality and controllability of individual environments.

That controllability is indeed remarkable in a building which, contrary to appearances, is really quite small. As the Jaffé family grew, however, the possibility for extension was not taken up. Instead they decided to move and, for a while, Foster seriously contemplated moving there with his own young family.

Brian Hatton

1. Though the roof-lights are relatively narrow, the house is suffused with daylight.

2. The placement of the piano encourages a reading of the three stepped floors of the living area as tiers in a domestic theatre. Tubular-steel balustrades enhance the resemblance to an auditorium, and lead the eye to the highest level.

3. Looking up into the kitchen from the playroom. The steps on the left are repeated in a short flight that leads up from the kitchen to a conservatory at the top of the house.

4. The living room at the lowest level of the 'domestic' zone. The sliding door to the right is open to reveal the children's playroom.

5. A view from the highest level of the house looking down through the dining area; the sliding door on the right leads to the kitchen.

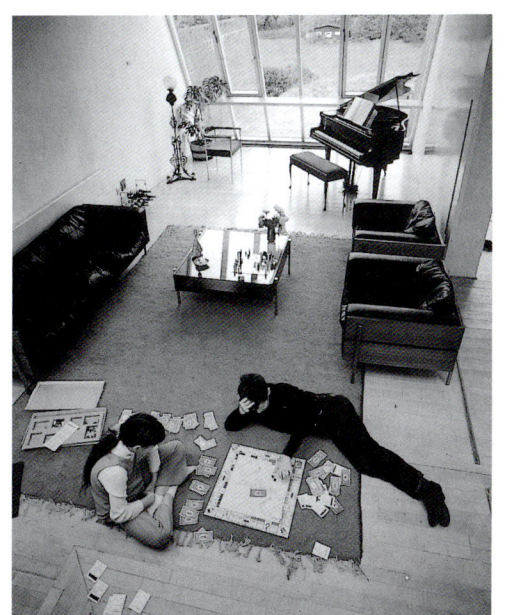

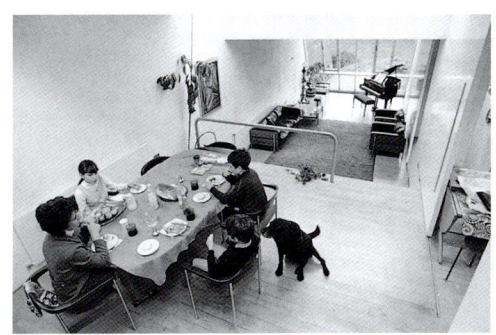

# High-Density Housing
Radlett, England 1967

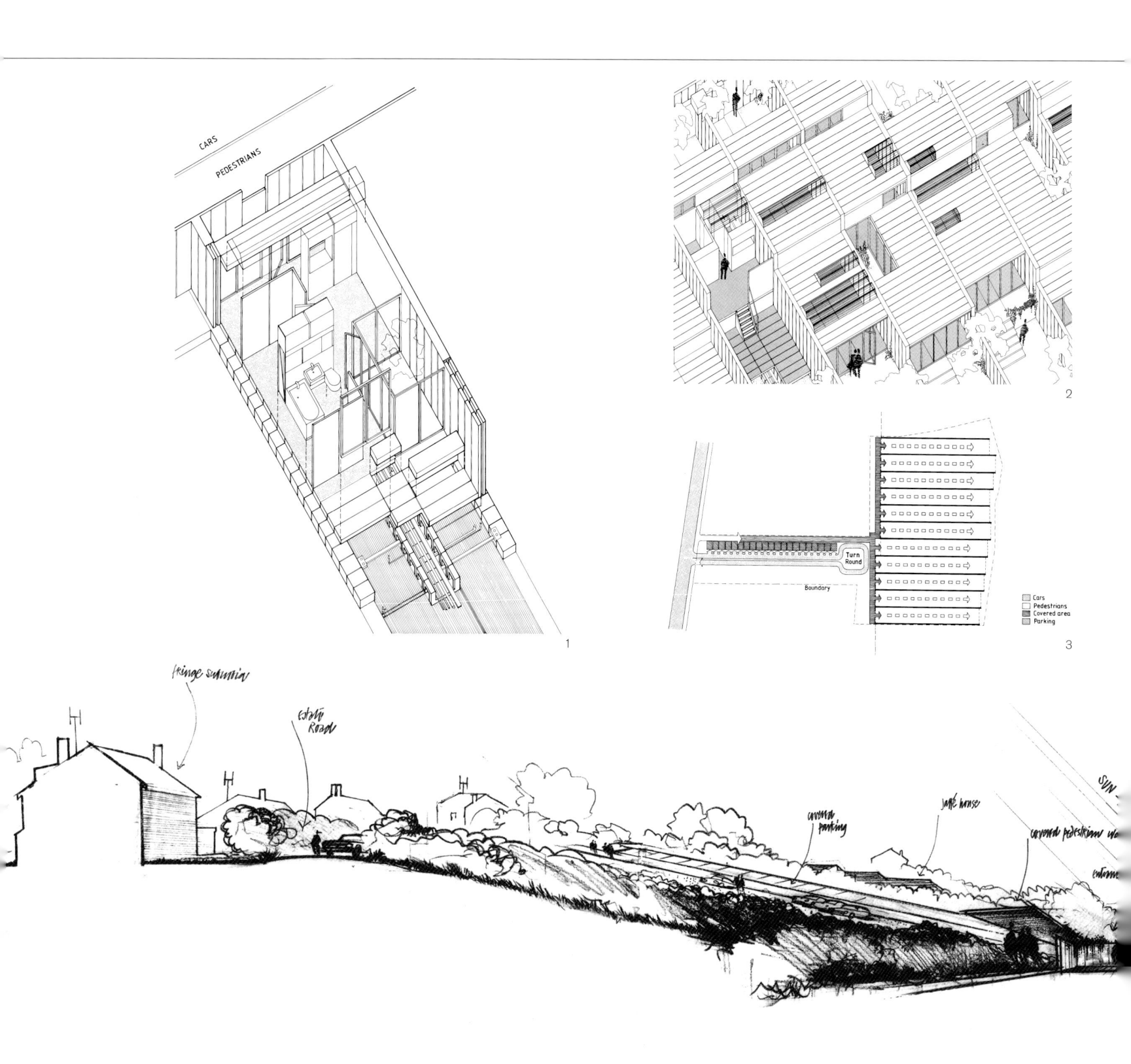

**Our buildings will have to be planned for flexibility so that they can change, grow and adapt. As land becomes more precious we must reconcile these needs with buildings which are sensitive to areas of scenic beauty.** Norman Foster, *BP Shield*, March 1969

**We are approaching a state of technical proficiency when it will become possible to rationalise buildings and mass-produce them in factories by resolving their structure into a number of component parts. Like boxes of toy bricks they will be assembled into various formal compositions.** Walter Gropius, quoted in Sutherland Lyall, *The State of British Architecture*, 1980
Left: Prefabricated housing techniques being realised on the Farm Lane Estate in Fulham, 1976.

This experimental project for a high-density development of eleven single-storey houses drew together concurrent ideas that were explored separately in the housing for Wates at Coulsdon and in the Jaffé Skybreak house, both designed while Norman and Wendy Foster were members of Team 4. It was Mr Jaffé's delight in the earlier house that led him to appoint Foster Associates to design this scheme, initially proposed for a site adjoining the Skybreak house but later explored in detail as a model for application elsewhere.

As with the Coulsdon project, cars are parked away from the houses and vehicular and pedestrian routes are segregated. Here too, the progression from public to private follows the route into the scheme, from access road to car-port, via a covered walkway to a protected entrance courtyard that gives on to individual front doors. Again, the influence of Serge Chermayeff is clear. Chermayeff had been one of Foster's tutors at Yale and had involved the dedicated student in the final draft of his polemical book *Community and Privacy*. Foster readily cites the importance of this work, and the early houses – most notably Skybreak – explore the ideas contained in that book in their most direct form.

Other recognisable themes from Skybreak are also present: the accommodation steps down in a series of platforms that follow the sloping site, opening out to views to the north, while at roof-level, aluminium patent glazing is employed to allow sunlight into the long, thin plan. Here, this latter device is elaborated upon with the introduction of glazed courtyards.

The constructional system relies entirely on factory-made structural components and lightweight partitioning materials. Precast concrete units form the party walls and floors, allowing services to be ducted under-floor beneath a central circulation zone. These were intended to be the only fixed elements of the design; a shell within which each house could be customised using varying layouts, materials and finishes to suit the purchaser's individual requirements.

In exploring the design of high-density housing on the edge of the green belt the development can be seen to be far ahead of its time, addressing themes that are of increasingly pressing concern today.

David Jenkins

1. A cutaway drawing of a typically 'customised' interior space, formed using non-load-bearing partitions, which could be erected in a number of different ways. The large central service duct was an advanced feature for the time.

2. A high degree of planning variation was possible within the standard pattern of narrow frontage houses. As each unit stepped down the site, different patterns of roof-lights and courtyards could be explored.

3. The plan in diagrammatic form. Eleven units, each with excellent green-belt views and privacy, were arranged on the irregularly shaped backlands site.

4. Norman Foster's sketch section shows the essential topography of the scheme. Like the Skybreak house, the project hugs the slope of the site, screening the units from the noise of the road behind and maximising views out towards the open countryside.

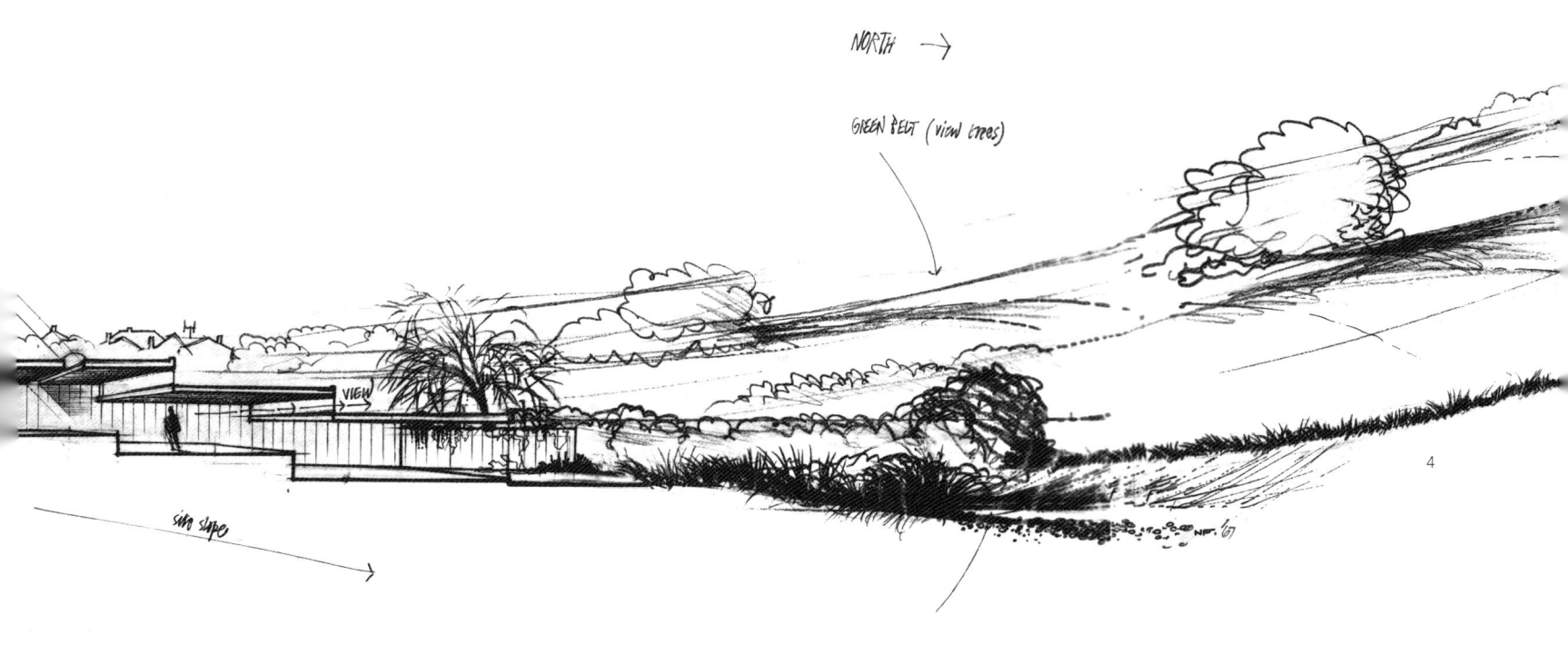

# Forest Road Annexe
East Horsley, England 1966

One of the more unusual projects Team 4 designed and built was an annexe to Wendy Foster's mother's house in Forest Road, East Horsley, Surrey. The plan is formed of five interlocking rectangles in echelon, containing a single apartment and, separated at the far end, a garage.

Here the aspect of a serial minimalism, at least in the most publicised view of the scheme, is striking enough to prompt the question of influence. In the same year, 1966, Don Judd and Robert Smithson were exhibiting staggered arrays of prismatic blank volumes. Smithson would go on, in his essay 'Entropy and the New Monuments' to describe such echelons of low-order structures – 'the much-derided glass boxes of Park Avenue' – in terms of timelessness and infinitude, as specimens of a pervasive industrial sublime. Certainly, that one published image of the project, devoid as it is of window or door, defeats any sense of measure. Only the texture of the bricks evident in the walls indicates the scale.

In fact, the annexe is a modest suburban extension. The main house was altered to open up its plan and perimeter by glazed walls, but rather than extending its older fabric, with attendant problems of compatibility, a radical alternative was proposed in the form of a new free-standing building. The walls facing the house are blank, but the walls facing outwards are pierced at the corners of each step in the echelon by windows which look out upon trees while respecting neighbouring privacy sightlines.

**At Forest Road the aspect of a serial minimalism is striking enough to prompt the question of influence. In the same year Don Judd was exhibiting staggered arrays of blank volumes.**
Brian Hatton

**Pure, closed, impenetrable, rectangular blocks – by Le Corbusier at one extreme, and Minimalist sculptors like Donald Judd, at the other – are supposed to bring us close to the permanent truths of geometry, form without compromise and therefore impervious to decay.** Reyner Banham, *Foster Associates*, 1979

Right: Donald Judd's *Untitled* of 1966 has been cited as an influence in the development of the Forest Road scheme. Quite apart from certain formal resonances, the radical simplicity, clarity and precision of Judd's work chimes with Foster's design philosophy, then as now.

Contrary to the impression given by the 'minimalist' photographs, the roof is not flat but a continuous monopitch, echoing, in a certain view, the roof-pitch of the main house. In this way the annexe both continues and rejects the 'context' of the older house, and the gap between the old and new buildings is sensitised by virtue of asserting a clean break, in much the way that Modernist painting and sculpture since Cézanne has dealt in reversing the notion of *Gestalt*, affording voids as much stress as solids and replacing composition by a configuration of tensions.

For those familiar only with the stereotype of a 'High-tech' Norman Foster, the variety of qualities and concerns in these early works may come as a surprise. A range of lyric figures can be found at work here which, if at times appears repressed in favour of that rigorous concentration required to reach precision and refinement, in fact continues to inform and organise a concept of design far broader than the purely 'technical'. Moreover, we may find in these early works a genetic resource to be returned to, as well as the promise of reanimations yet to come.

Brian Hatton

1. This cross-section through the main house highlights the relationship between the existing house and the separate annexe, revealing the surprising size of the latter in relation to the more compact main dwelling.

2. A view into the small annexe apartment, looking from the kitchen/dining area towards the living room; the glazed doors lead to the terrace and garden beyond.

3. The project also involved remodelling the existing house. Much of the ground floor was opened up by means of a conservatory, which wrapped around three sides of the house.

4. This photograph by Norman Foster, the best-known view of the annexe, was taken from the lawn at the back of the main house. The forced perspective of the diminishing wall planes results from the line of the sloping roof behind their parapets.

5. The plan illustrates the close relationship between the annexe garage, which serves the house, and the rest of the building which is effectively a self-contained flat with its own small terrace garden.

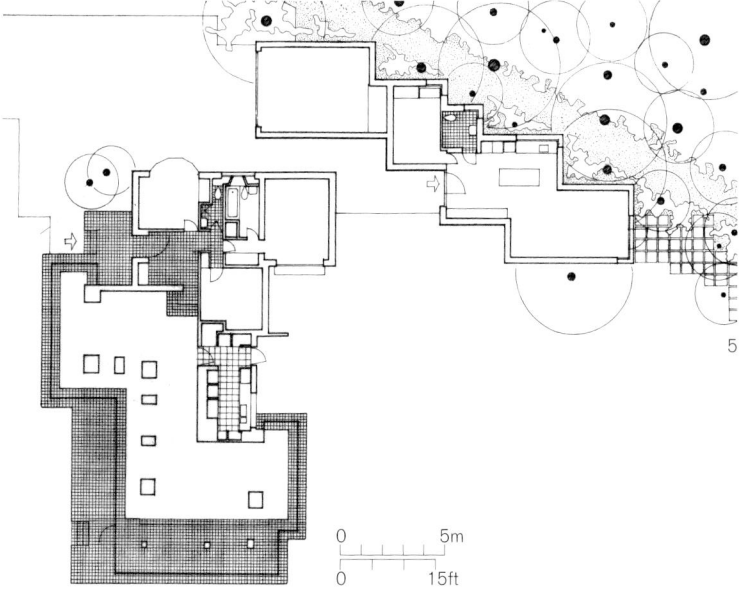

Forest Road Annexe

**The Early Years**
John Walker 1991

**The close working relationship that evolved between Norman, Tony Hunt, Loren Butt and myself was an example of teamwork at its best. Respect for one another's abilities was earned by a willingness to accept that any opinion would be challenged and must be successfully defended.**
John Walker

Norman and Wendy were actually living in the Hampstead flat-cum-office, and its combination of functions constantly presented problems of privacy … When a genuine client – that is, one beyond the clan of family and friends came in prospect … the space lived in by Norman and Wendy was turned into an extension of the work area … Hilary Walker, the wife of Team 4's quantity surveyor, brought in a typewriter, and the living room was disguised as a conference space. Then Hilary set up her typewriter in the kitchen next door so that she could make secretarial noises off. Malcolm Quantrill, *The Norman Foster Studio*, 1999
Left: The first floor flat at 16 Hampstead Hill Gardens, which provided Team 4 with their first 'office'.

To most people the living area of our flat with its Eames furniture already looked like an office, but that image was not helped by the presence of a very large bed. The problem was promptly solved by constructing an equally large box, in two pieces, the joints carefully masked by a display of glossy magazines. Norman Foster, *Norman Foster: Sketches*, 1992

Writing about someone you know well and have worked with at length, who has since achieved fame, is an interesting task; particularly if, as I did, you moved half-a-world away just at the onset of his success. I have watched with interest as the ever-widening circles of reputation have finally reached my new home. Now, on the west coast of Canada, I bask in reflected glory because I once worked closely with Norman Foster, who today is a household name. At least, that is, among the architects, bankers and Hong Kong émigrés with which Vancouver abounds.

Many of the projects in this book were engineered by Anthony Hunt and had the Hanscomb Partnership (or, more specifically, myself) as quantity surveyor. Many of them also had mechanical installations designed by Loren Butt. This group came together in the Team 4 and early Foster Associates days by a process of trial and error. None of us was the first member of our particular speciality to work with Norman, but each of us happened into the group in his turn and, for a decade or so, we stuck together. That we did so resulted from a number of factors. We were similar in age; we were at a similar stage in our careers; and each of us had a greater than average interest in disciplines other than his own.

Architects who believe that buildings can be economical, as well as elegant, are not unique but, at that time, they were unusual. So too, were engineers who believed that stable, but inelegant structures represented a different, but no less important, kind of structural failure. For my part, a real interest in both architecture and engineering meant suggestions for savings were much more likely to be accepted by other members of the team. All of which, taken together, made it exciting, challenging and fun to be part of the group. Few things stimulate humans more strongly than pride in being a member of a winning team and there was, in this group, a strong sense from the beginning of being involved in something new and vital in the world of the built environment. As a result, work no longer seemed entirely like work and sessions which continued late into the night competed readily with rival attractions such as the pub, the cinema or even, sometimes, the family.

Strong reinforcement of this *esprit de corps* came in the form of architectural rewards. It was not unique to produce buildings that were completed on time and within budget, although a depressingly large number of projects by other architects failed in this respect. But it was, if not unique, then very nearly so, to achieve these ends while winning praise from the buildings' occupants and awards for the excellence of their architecture.

**Architects who believe that buildings can be economical, as well as elegant, are not unique but, at that time, they were unusual. So too, were engineers who believed that stable, but inelegant structures represented a different, but no less important, kind of structural failure.**

Perhaps not surprisingly, it is for me the combination of excellence and economy which gives the great sense of pride in looking back at these projects. Even with unlimited resources it is easy to produce garbage. To produce cheap garbage is even easier. But to have been part of the team which achieved this level of excellence at these all-time low prices is something really worth remembering.

The close working relationship that evolved between Norman, Tony Hunt, Loren Butt and myself was an example of teamwork at its best. As a group we had a strongly questioning attitude. Respect for one another's abilities grew as time went by, but it was respect that was earned by a willingness to accept that any opinion would probably be challenged and must be successfully defended.

1. From right, Norman Foster, John Walker and engineer Anthony Hunt, captured in 1971 during a typical 'brainstorming' session on the Samuel Beckett Theatre (1971), a project developed with Buckminster Fuller.

**The team of Norman, Richard, John Walker and myself was now so well established that, if we didn't quite read each other's minds, we certainly worked together using the simplest of 'shorthands'. It's very difficult, now, to remember who made which decision or how. We met once a week and were joined, at quite an early stage, by Loren Butt, a services engineer then working for Haden's, but he, too, quickly became an ally and launched himself into our collaborative ways.** Tony Hunt, 'In at the Beginning', 1988

**Foster chaired every site meeting from the beginning of the Reliance Controls contract to its completion. [Although] he had no experience whatsoever of actual site procedures, Norman describes [these meetings] as 'lessons in psychology and life'. He was quite spellbound by John Walker's worldliness in the cut and thrust of life on the site, as well as being impressed by the quantity surveyor's thorough grasp of building knowledge and cost accountancy.** Malcolm Quantrill, *The Norman Foster Studio*, 1999

**Traditionally ... the architect is expected to design a building, which the engineer then makes stand up. For me the first project which challenged this approach was Reliance Controls. There was the structural engineer Tony Hunt, the talented mechanical engineer Loren Butt and a brilliant quantity surveyor called John Walker. It was the nucleus of a highly creative design team – the exact opposite of the traditional sequential approach.** Norman Foster, in conversation with Malcolm Quantrill, 1999

1. In this site photograph by Norman Foster, the structural frame of the Reliance Controls factory is seen under construction. John Walker describes this as perhaps the 'most memorable' project he was to undertake with Norman Foster.

While each was a specialist, he had also a reasonable working knowledge of all the other disciplines. No one felt inhibited about challenging an expert's preconception and often those challenges caused the expert to re-examine his own point of view. The result was seldom that he agreed completely with the challenger but often that an entirely novel concept emerged. Most of the innovative thinking evident in the designs of that period emerged as a result of this 'brainstorming' approach.

But in the early 1960s success was far from assured. Norman, then a part of Team 4, was faced with the new architect's old problem – until you have done it, no one will trust you to do it. Catch 22, so you have to cheat a little. On a certain day a potential client arrived at Team 4's office and was sufficiently impressed to award a commission. He did not know that the 'draughtsmen' he saw included a number of friends (myself among them) and that the sound of typing from the adjoining room was Hilary, my wife, pretending to be a specifications department. He certainly didn't know that under the conference table was a bed, hastily boxed in and covered with white plastic the previous weekend. Note the vague date. He probably still doesn't know.

Even then, however, the key to success was there. First and foremost, was determination: Norman refused to be satisfied with anything less than the best. Not necessarily the most expensive, for those early buildings were built within rigorous cost limits. But the best solution that could possibly be found given the resources available.

Best because nothing was accepted without being challenged and challenged and challenged again. Talented designers, yes, but that alone would not have been enough. It was the determination to keep trying long after others would have said 'good enough' that proved decisive.

Of course, this had its negative side. A certain bricklayer's labourer, who had distributed about a thousand bricks in neat, orderly piles ready to be laid, was not pleased when a better, cheaper brick was found. He wheeled them back up the hill to the road. He replaced them with neat, orderly piles of the new bricks. Alas, it was not the end. An even better, cheaper brick appeared. The labourer paused to speak with me as he struggled up the hill. 'If that ... architect changes his ... mind one more ... time, I'm going to stick these ... bricks up his ... sideways.'

Perhaps the most memorable building from the early years was Reliance Controls. Winner of the first ever Financial Times Award for Industrial Architecture, it was a first in many other ways as well. The structure was clean, simple and elegant. It was also repetitive, lean and very carefully engineered to cover the space at the most economical possible cost. The cladding spanned clear from the structure above to the slab beneath, an unusually economical arrangement. Drains were carefully grouped in certain predetermined areas so that, everywhere else, the simple floor slabs could be laid quickly and on undisturbed ground. The entire rear elevation was clad in a low-cost glazing system, the metal support bars carefully positioned so that the balance between their cost and that of the sheets of glass was optimised to an overall minimum. There is no doubt that Norman's later buildings are far more spectacular but the spare economy of Reliance still compares favourably with the best of them.

In 1967 I spent a year in Canada. I returned to discover that, alas, Norman and Richard had agreed to part company and Team 4 was no more. Foster Associates, consisting then of only Norman and Wendy was one of the two spin-offs. It had but one commission: the conversion of an old house into three or four apartments.

**Dear Mr Cox,**
**You may remember that we met when our factory for Reliance Controls was awarded the Financial Times Industrial Architecture Award. You asked me to let you know if this resulted in any jobs. Sadly, the answer is no – absolutely nothing! Apart, that is, from: endless requests from students to visit the factory; continual requests for work opportunities in this office; and continual requests for photos and data from architectural magazines and schools. If you have any ideas on how we might make use of the award to get work, these would be much appreciated. The present job situation is somewhat desperate.**
**Yours sincerely, Norman Foster**

Left: A letter written on 24 October 1968 by Norman Foster to Anthony Cox of the Architect's Co-Partnership – one year after the formation of Foster Associates – indicates the precarious situation of the practice. A few weeks later, Foster would meet Fred Olsen.

Not an exciting architectural opportunity but, when it was complete, a project marked with special attention to detail and determination to 'do it better', which was to continue to distinguish Norman's later work.

Norman's response to difficulties stands him apart from the common herd. For example, when it proved impossible to find the kind of curtain wall he wanted for the Olsen building at Millwall Dock in England, he jumped on a plane to America. While most of us would have been bogged down with doubt about whether the client would pay for such a trip, Norman simply went. To him, it did not matter whether he was reimbursed. He went and got what he needed, then argued later. To this day, I do not know whether the expenses were recovered. I do know, however, that photographs of that wall, or the reflections on it, were priceless to the practice. The same wall was used on IBM Cosham, with similar results. The commissions that resulted from the success of those buildings alone paid for innumerable trips.

He also has excellent instincts for discovering what will be acceptable to a particular client, and the necessary powers of persuasion to make his intuitive judgments come true. The idea of housing Computer Technology in an air-supported bubble while building a new facility for them was not, as I recall, Norman's. But, without his instinct that the client would accept such a concept or his persuasiveness in selling the idea, I doubt that it would ever have happened. The ability to recognise that an idea's time has come is perhaps more important in the innovative process than the spark which produces the concept in the first place.

IBM Cosham is an object lesson in the art of 'more for less'. The basic building is very cheap. A simple short-span shed with a flat, low-cost roof and packaged, roof-mounted air-conditioning units was the cheapest possible way of protecting its occupants from the elements. Adding high-quality carpet and lighting made it feel luxurious. The deep-plan concept made the unusually beautiful curtain wall affordable. The money saved on pad foundations by floating a lightly loaded raft slab over the former rubbish dump site was spent on these 'where it shows' items and the result was a resounding success in commercial as well as architectural terms.

No cranes were used. The structure was light enough to erect using rubber-tyred fork-lift trucks. And there was no digging. The flat ground slab had some extra mesh reinforcement under the columns and the short-span structure imposed such light loads that even the poor bearing capacity of the old rubbish dump proved adequate to its task. Grouping the lavatories and other services requiring below-slab drainage and collecting rainwater by horizontal pipework in the roof space with strictly limited drops to floor level, made it possible to lay thousands of square feet of floor slab quickly, economically and without interruption.

Many of these design concepts came about as a direct result of the desire to achieve more for less cost and some were my ideas. But whatever contribution I made to the success of Foster Associates was amply repaid. Partly directly by fees, of course, and partly by pride in the results. But also in less direct ways.

**Norman absolutely refused to be satisfied with anything less than the best. Not necessarily the most expensive, for those early buildings were all built within rigorous cost limits. Best because nothing was accepted without being challenged and challenged again.**

Norman and Wendy were exceptionally generous by nature. For several months, when penniless and first married, Hilary and I sat in style on two of their Eames chairs. When, slightly less penniless but still decidedly hard up, we arrived back in England after our first stay in Canada, we bombed around London, free of charge, for several months in the Fosters' Land Rover.

Alas, Wendy is gone and her infectious laugh is heard no more. Without her, Norman has said, he would have been nothing. Personally, I doubt that. Without in any way under-valuing her contribution, I believe that Norman would have succeeded. But it matters not. What is important is that he continues as she would have wished. And succeeds.

# Connections  Reliance Controls Electronics Factory

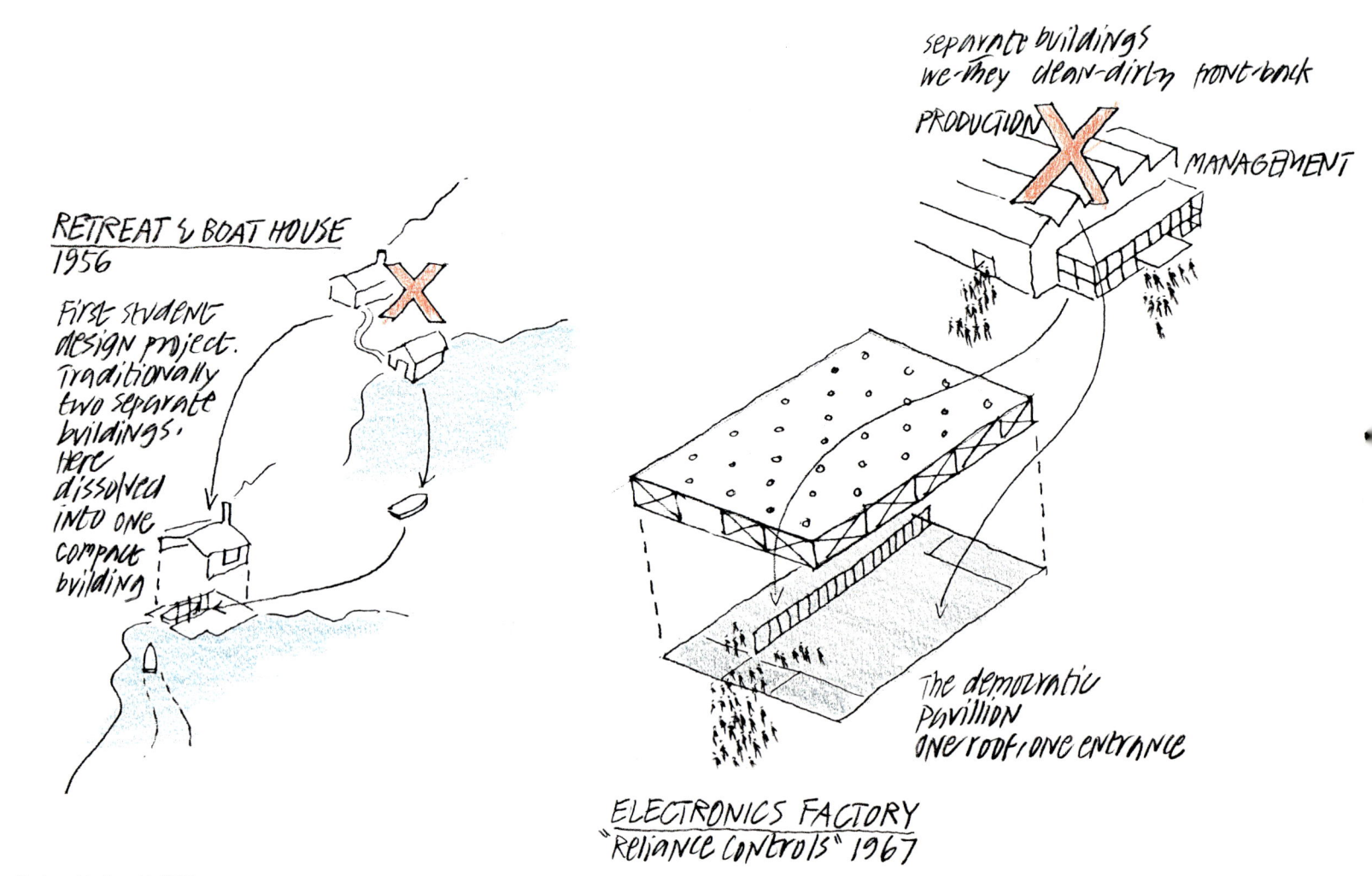

**RETREAT & BOAT HOUSE 1956**
First student design project. Traditionally two separate buildings. Here dissolved into one compact building

*separate buildings we-they clean-dirty front-back*
PRODUCTION  MANAGEMENT

*the democratic pavillion one roof, one entrance*

**ELECTRONICS FACTORY "Reliance Controls" 1967**

Designed in the mid-1960s, when British industry still observed the social codes of the Victorian era, the factory for Reliance Controls took the unprecedented step of bringing management and workforce together under one roof, with equal amenities for all. This concept of 'integration' – both spatial and social – is an idea that runs throughout the Foster oeuvre and can be traced to Norman Foster's first student project for a Retreat and Boathouse, which integrated two separate entities into one compact enclosure. This theme would find new emphasis in projects such as Newport School, which aimed to create a sense of community by bringing the diverse amenities of a comprehensive school together under one roof and the IBM Pilot Head Office, which pioneered the integration of the mainframe computer – typically housed in a separate 'shrine' – into the office building.

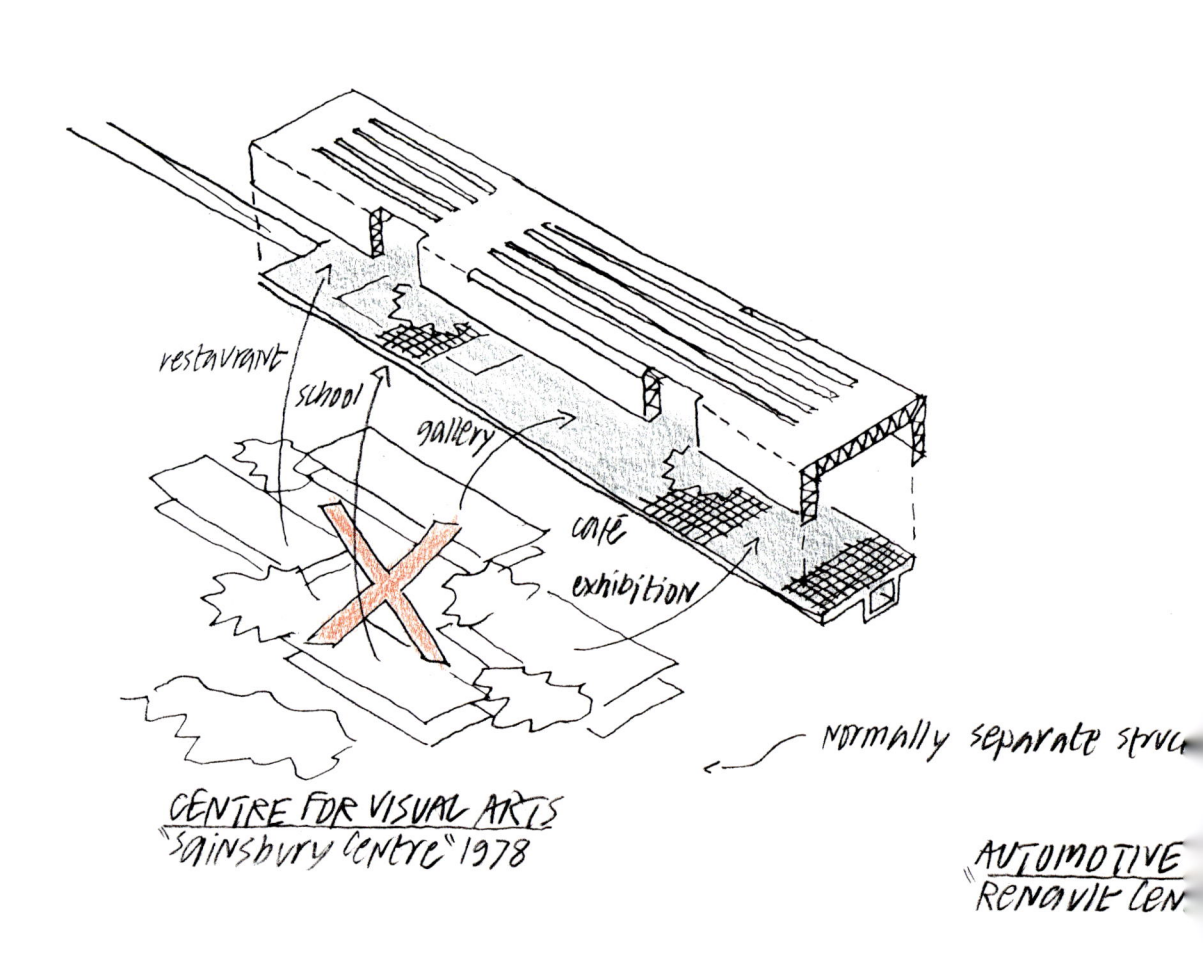

restaurant  school  gallery  café  exhibition

*normally separate structures*

**CENTRE FOR VISUAL ARTS "Sainsbury Centre" 1978**

"AUTOMOTIVE RENAULT CEN

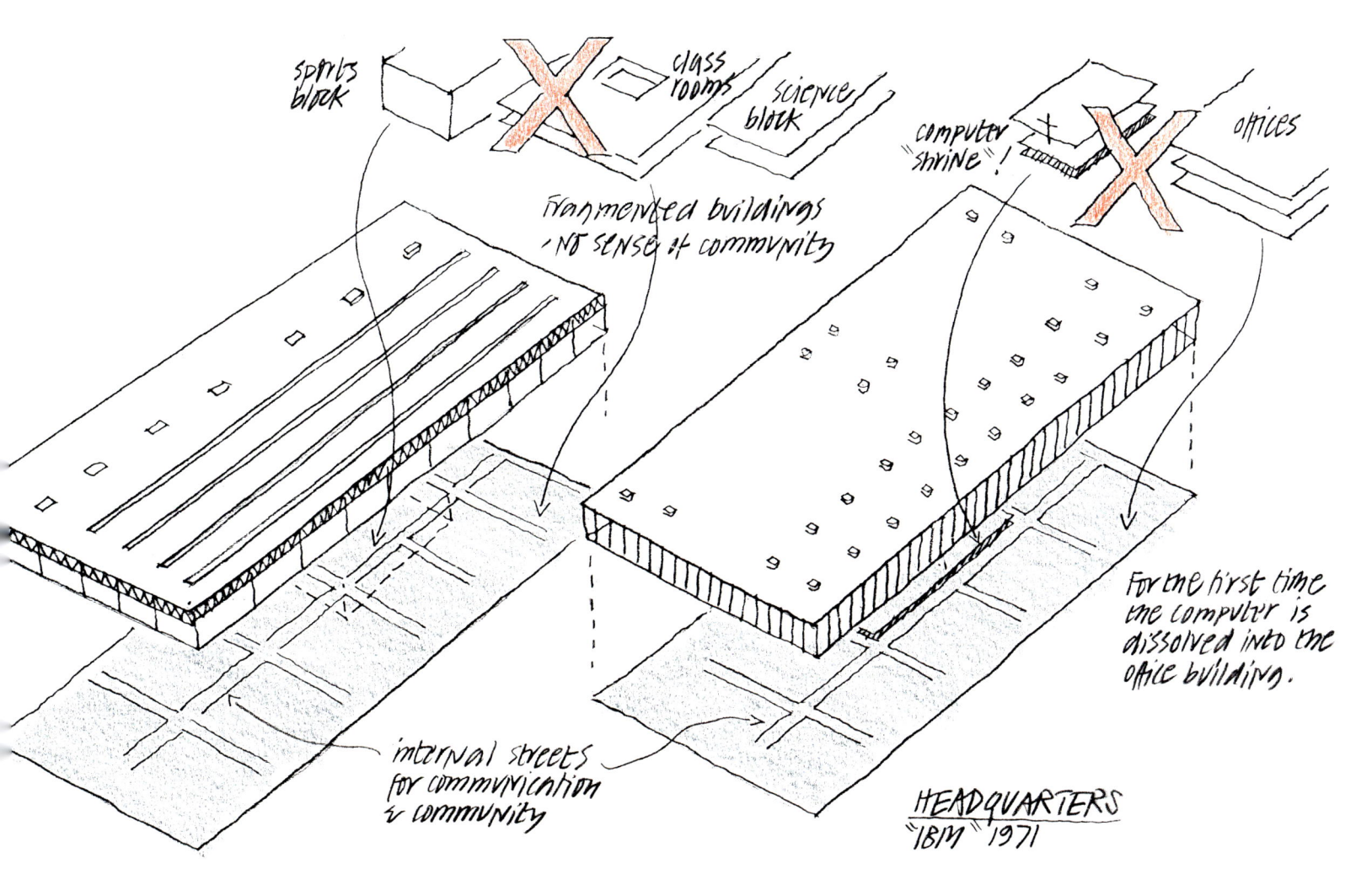

**spirits block** — **class rooms** — **science block** — **offices** — **computer "shrine"!**

fragmented buildings - no sense of community

internal streets for communication & community

For the first time the computer is dissolved into the office building.

**COMPREHENSIVE SCHOOL** Newport 1967

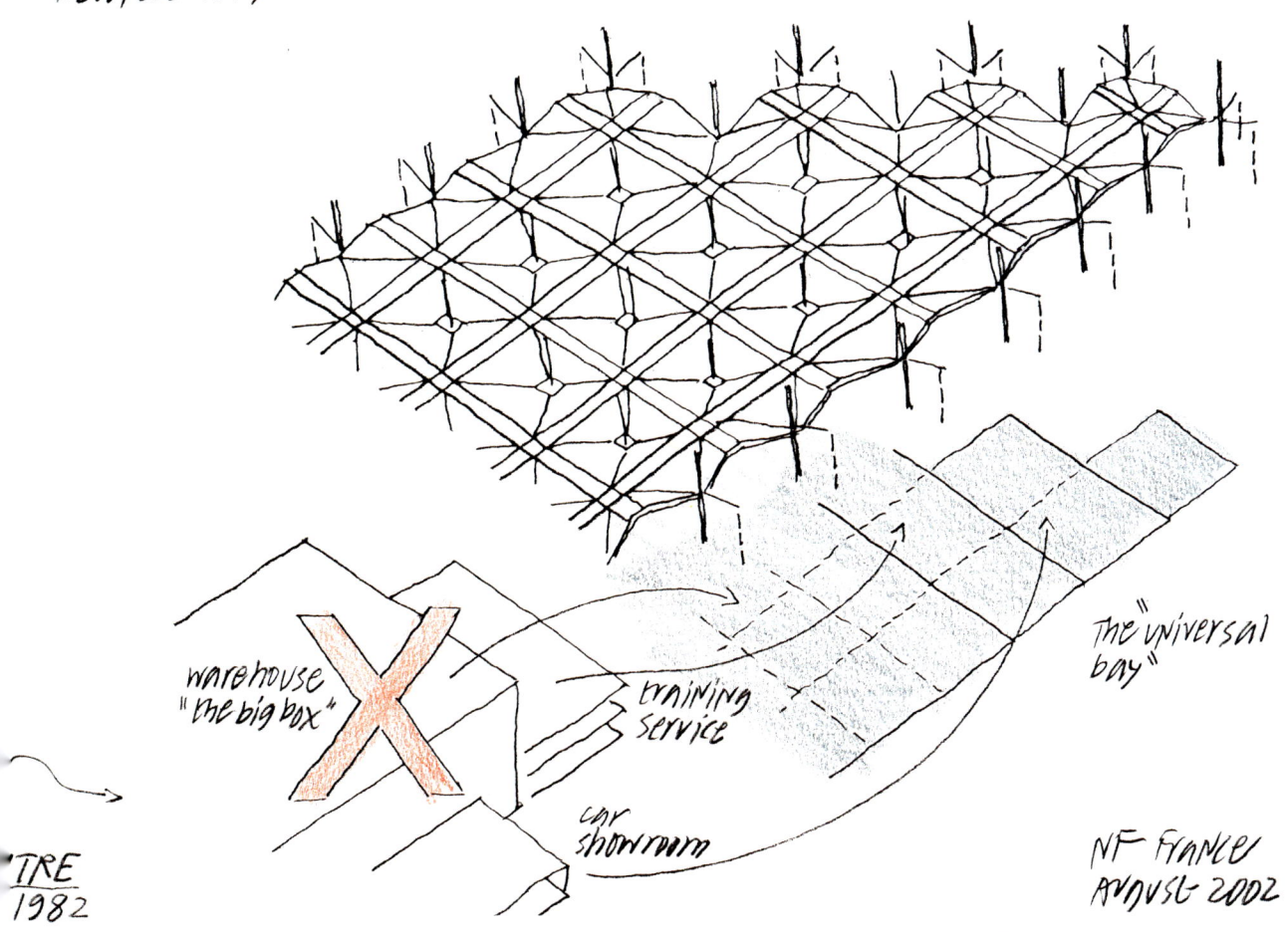

**HEADQUARTERS** "IBM" 1971

warehouse "the big box" — training service — car showroom — the "universal bay"

TRE 1982

NF France August 2002

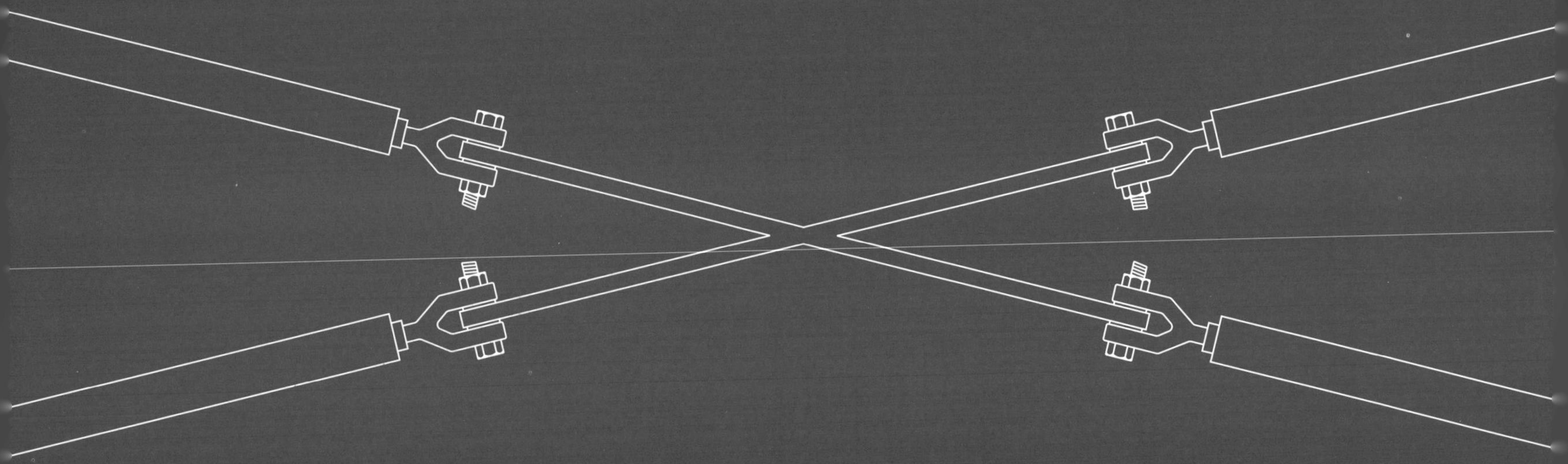

**Reliance Controls Electronics Factory**
Swindon, England 1965–1966

**Designed for an electronics industry then in its infancy, this democratic pavilion broke new ground, both socially and technologically. It was the opposite of the traditional management box and workers' shed with its overtones of 'us and them', 'clean and dirty', 'front and back'. Management and employees shared a single entrance and a single restaurant, a practice unheard of at the time. Its emphasis on prefabricated components allowed the structure to be built in under a year, at very low cost. The structural steel frame enclosed a single volume within which only the toilets, kitchen and plant rooms were permanent structures, which meant that the plan could be reconfigured simply by moving the partitioning. This flexibility paid off when the client, in a sudden production surge, was able to increase his production area by a third.**
Norman Foster

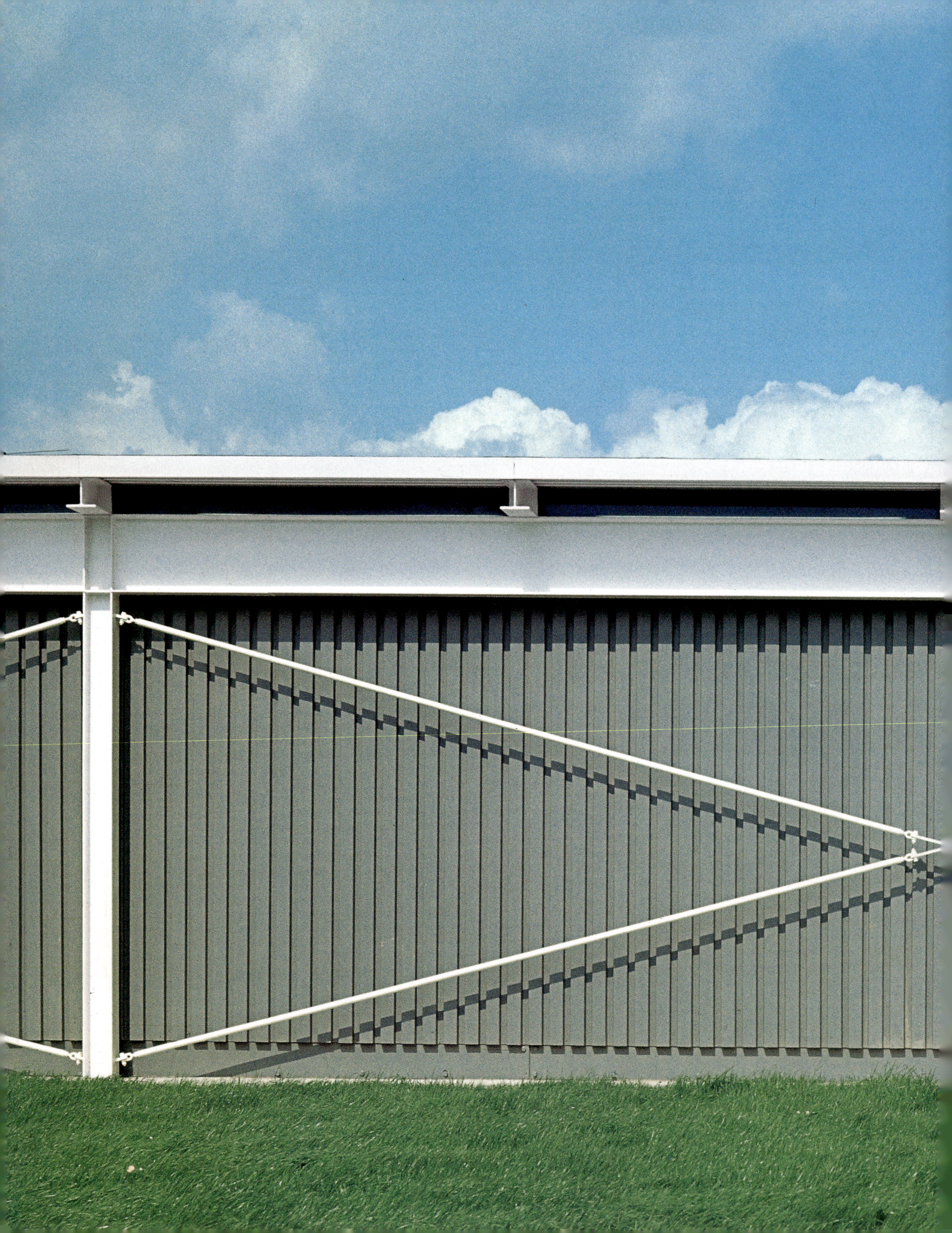

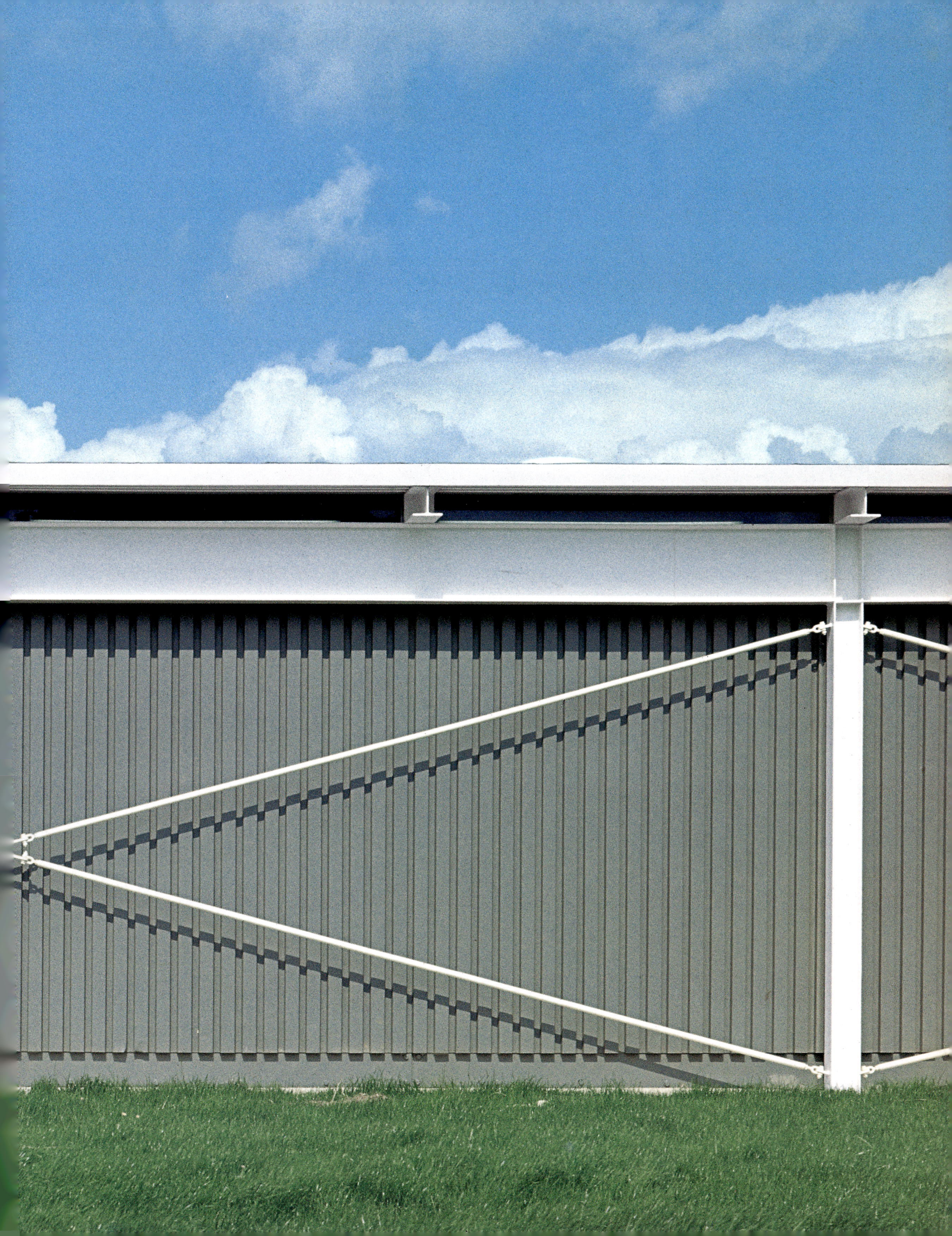

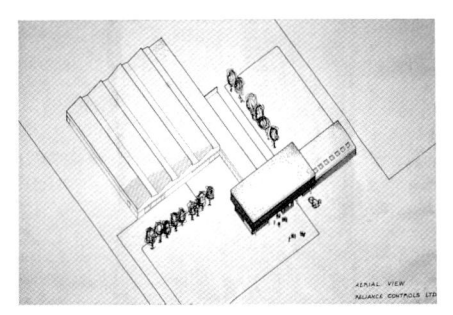

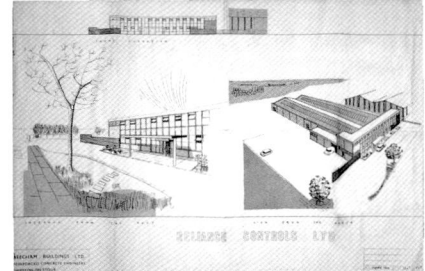

**A pavilion form was considered more socially appropriate for a clean and rapid growth electronics industry than the usual workers' shed and management box with its implication of 'we and they', 'clean and dirty', 'posh and scruffy', 'back and front'. Technically such a form also offered a degree of rationalisation, which was more responsive to optimising limited resources of time and money, as well as providing the potential for quick and easy change.** Norman Foster, Foster Associates, 1979

Left: These two early developers' proposals for Reliance Controls' new building perpetuated the traditional, segregated model of the workplace that Foster describes, and which he and the client so clearly rejected.

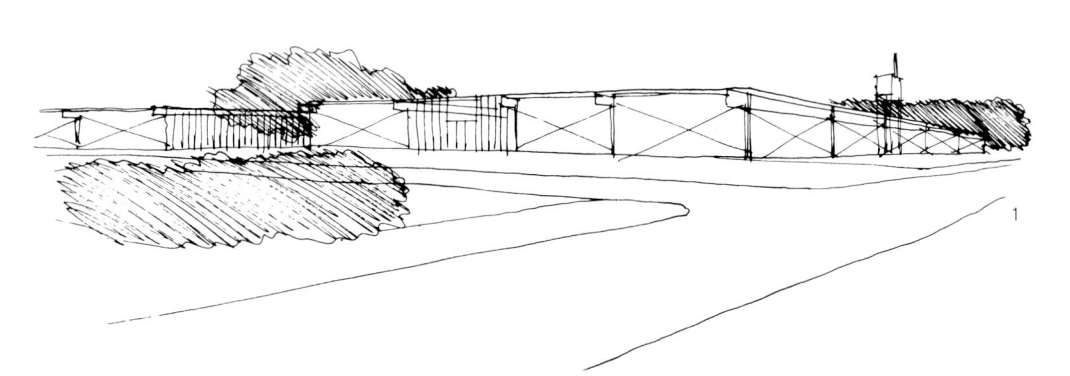

More than just a turning point in Norman Foster's early career, the electronics factory for Reliance Controls is a seminal building in the post-war history of the Modern Movement, reaffirming basic Modernist principles whilst at the same time injecting new – sorely needed – social and professional values.

The circumstances and timing of the project could not have been less propitious, however. Designed and built at breakneck speed – ten and a half months from the first client meeting to operation – it was completed in the same year that Robert Venturi published his influential critique of Modernism, *Complexity and Contradiction in Architecture*. Venturi gave voice to a rising tide of doubts about Modern architecture, and its common lack of humanising qualities. Crucially, however, his arguments were all about aesthetics, and how to recreate the visual pleasures and subtleties achieved in earlier historical movements. Other concerns, whether functional, social or technological, were swept under the carpet – weaknesses that would later fatally undermine Postmodern architecture.

**Reliance Controls took a very simple stance about the kind of building that might be appropriate to the electronics industry. An open-ended pavilion, flexible, with moveable walls under an umbrella roof, it had the ability to adapt and change as circumstances required.**
Norman Foster

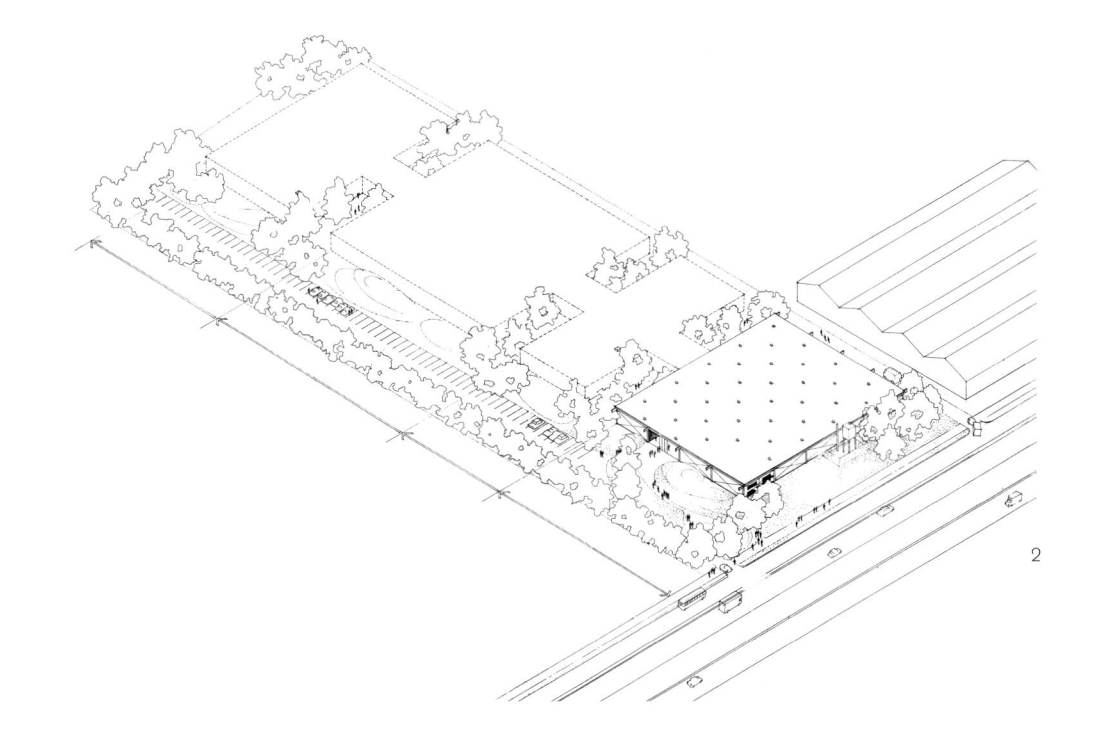

Left: Norman Foster's sketches illustrate the thinking behind the Reliance Controls building: an approach that broke with every industrial convention in the 1960s to reinvent the workplace for the electronic age.

In the same period, Archigram was enjoying huge success in the UK with its futuristic visions, enhanced by comic book imagery. Though apparently at odds with Venturi's thesis, Archigram's uncritical love affair with mass-production technology, short-life product design and pop art techniques, was as much an endorsement of consumerist extravagance and conspicuous waste as Venturi's later celebration of Las Vegas.

It seemed that hardly anyone was interested anymore in how buildings were really made, how they worked and how people used them – least of all what they cost. Except Team 4. Reliance Controls was the last design to be produced before Team 4 broke up, and the first industrial project of any kind the practice had undertaken. Yet, the project embodies a sizeable number of the features and techniques that were to become the hallmark of Foster's independent practice and design approach for the next few decades.

Primary themes are memorably encapsulated in one simple, iconic drawing – a diagrammatic cross-section through the structure. Drawn by Foster himself in the manner of a medical dissection of the human body, the anatomical section presents an architecture that is simultaneously both reductionist and holistic. Looking at one level like an assemblage of ready made parts, each layer of material and structure is peeled back to reveal the one beneath. The drawing also unveils Foster's first convincing demonstration of his now familiar integrated design philosophy, in which social function, structure, services and production methods are all tightly integrated into one, indivisible and meticulously executed whole.

The holistic qualities of the building are a direct result of the 'systems design' approach, borrowed from the aerospace industry, which had been successfully applied in getting man into orbit. Also evident is the impact of Foster's studies of American architecture, especially Ezra Ehrenkrantz's Southern California Schools Development (SCSD) project. Like Ehrenkrantz, Foster and his colleagues understood the systems approach to be more about process and getting everything to work together, from concept to production line, construction and use, than the reviled 'building systems' that had come to be associated with it.

The fruits of that thinking can be seen, not only in the extraordinary clarity and coherence of the design, but in the economy of use to which almost every part of the building was put. Repetitive elements throughout ensured that most could be factory made, speeding construction, buying valuable design time and raising quality control. Anticipating Foster's later, more complex exercises in integrated design and tailor-made components, many elements served more than one function, exceeding both the purpose and performance for which they were originally designed by their manufacturers. Thus standard, corrugated-metal roof decking also provided a stiffening diaphragm for the structural frame and was used as both wall cladding and ceiling finish, doubling up yet again as a built-in reflector for the bare lighting tubes, which were placed in between the corrugations. Spanning clear from floor to roof, the plastic-coated, rigid decking also conveniently did away with the need for intermediate wall supports or external finishes.

Previous page: A single structural bay from Reliance Controls. The simplicity of the design and the elegance of its detailing belie the fact that this was Team 4's (and engineer Tony Hunt's) first steel-structured building.

1, 2. As Norman Foster's drawings indicate, the initial design envisaged a series of pavilions, linked by plant rooms positioned above an under-floor service duct. Only the 3,200-square-metre first phase of this scheme was built, although it was later extended by one bay to the north.

3. Of extreme simplicity, the front elevation consisted of five 12-metre bays with distinctive, diagonal cross bracing. With its plastic-coated corrugated steel cladding and white-painted steel stanchions and beams, the building was otherwise astonishingly discreet, even anonymous. Initially, there was not even a company sign. The sculptural steel water tower and flue offered a subtle homage to Alison and Peter Smithson's Hunstanton School.

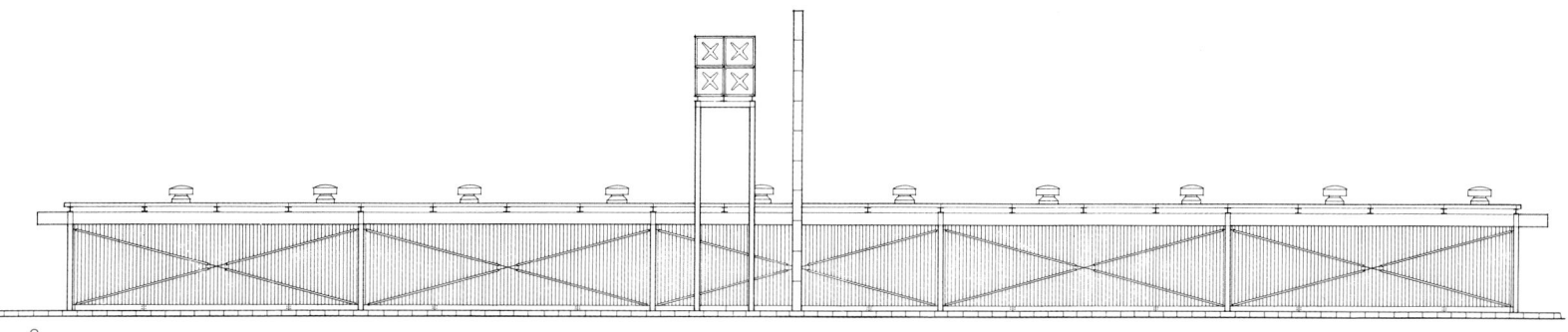

Reliance Controls would make a better village building than most new housing estates. The site, long and narrow, is just the kind of left-over land – an orchard or paddock, maybe – which turns up so often in villages. The factory makes tiny electronic components, which are used in objects as different as heart-pacing machines and servo mechanisms for aircraft controls. So the operation is completely clean inside and out. In a sense, Reliance's elegance is wasted on the Greenbridge estate in Swindon. Ian Nairn, *The Observer*, 10 December 1967

Reliance Controls incorporated or hinted at many of the innovations Norman Foster was to bring to industrial and commercial architecture over the following three decades: a rational deep-plan design for minimal superstructure surface area; large module, clear-span steel construction with light metal cladding; the minimisation of wet trades; the extensive use of metal components for quick construction; a multi-functional internal space that could be reconfigured rapidly; a rational distribution of services from above and below; and, last but not least, workplace democracy achieved through design. Martin Pawley, *Norman Foster: A Global Architecture*, 1999

There is a genuine structural logic to the building, a real, not spurious, functionalism. Editorial, *BP Shield*, March 1969

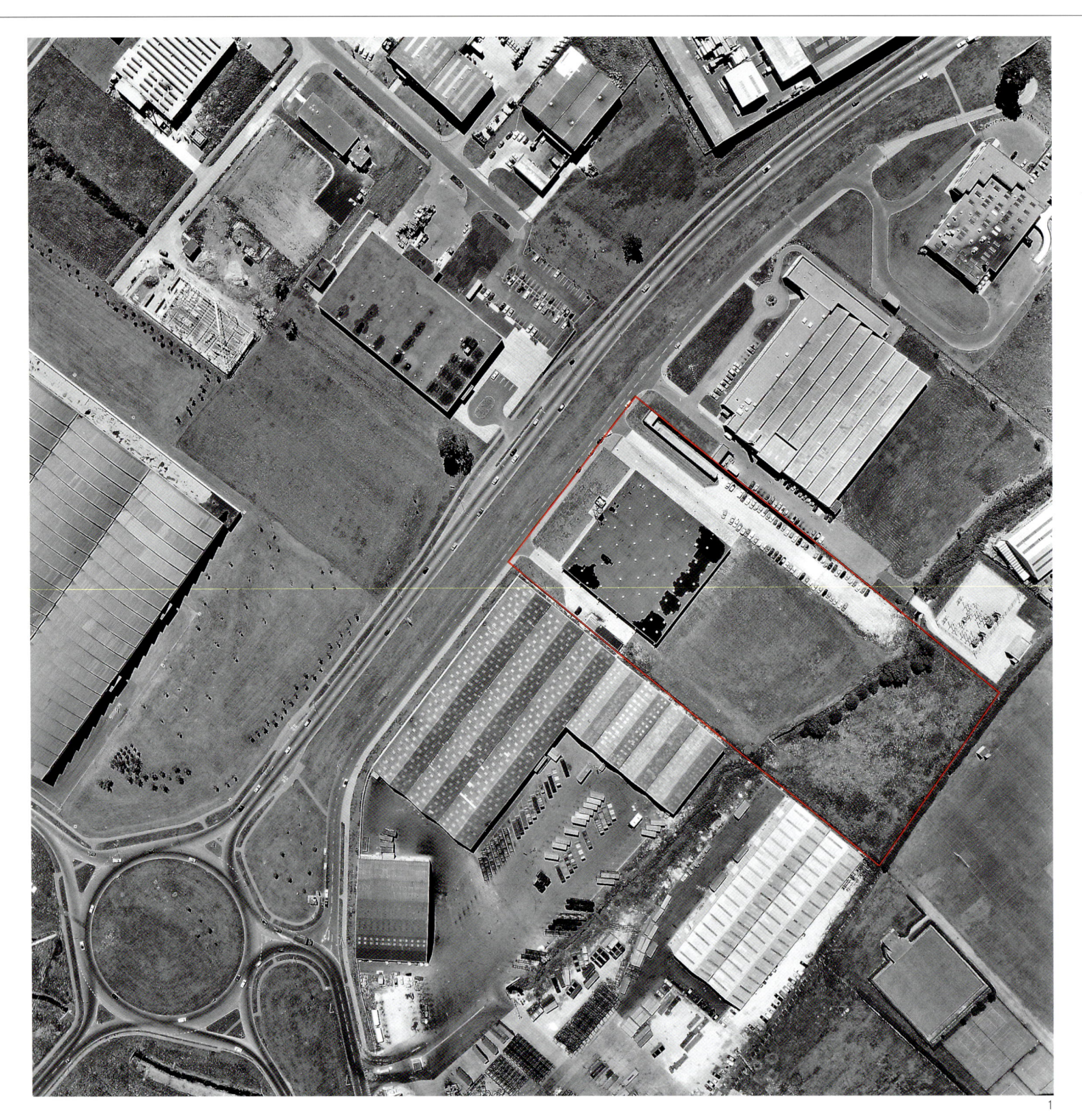

Left: Many of the themes first investigated in the Reliance Controls building are re-explored in the Microelectronic Centre in Duisburg, Germany, 1988-1996. However, whereas in the 1960s the nascent electronics industry was confined to industrial estates, on the outskirts of town, the Microelectronic Centre and its associated buildings are integrated within a predominantly residential district, focused on a new public park. The Duisburg project demonstrates how, with the trend towards clean and quiet manufacturing industries, the potential exists to create new kinds of urban neighbourhoods that integrate places to live, work and play.

Such agility indicates an exceptional level of investigative rigour and intimate knowledge of the capabilities of the components and materials available. This is evinced by Foster's own free-hand drawings of the construction system, which were so accurately detailed and annotated that they made more extensive working drawings unnecessary. Here, at long last, with Foster and Team 4, was a group of architects who were prepared to go beyond the mere imagery of industrialised production, which had plagued Modern architecture from Le Corbusier to Archigram, and to take the business of building into their own hands. Moreover, they did it all with the kind of panache only seen before on the other side of the Atlantic.

The famed minimalist aesthetic of Reliance Controls was also, as John Walker (Team 4's regular quantity surveyor during this period) has explained, as much driven by cost and reality as by anything to do with ideology, though there was that too. The repetitive steel structure itself – one of many collaborations with engineer Tony Hunt – defines the maximum possible space with the fewest and thinnest members. Partly welded in the factory and partly on site, it was designed in response to the lack of any suitable ready-made systems on the market. The central channel for under-floor services, which features so prominently in Foster's cross-sectional drawing, also permitted the simplest and most economical floor slab.

The aesthetic, like the systems approach, was also strongly influenced by American architecture on the West Coast – notably the steel-framed 'Case Study' houses and by the work of Craig Ellwood in particular. Mies van der Rohe may have invented Minimalism by saying 'less is more' and Charles and Ray Eames may have rationalised it with their use of off-the-shelf components for their own Case Study house, but Ellwood gave it sex appeal. While Reliance Controls is often described, by Foster himself, as well as by others, as a 'pavilion building', it is worlds apart from the austere Neoclassicism of Mies' work.

Whereas a Miesian pavilion presents a finite composition and is all repose and constraint, Reliance Controls fairly bursts with energy, bristling with extended I-beams projecting from the sides and the ends of the structure.

Such details were consciously designed with an expressive purpose. For Team 4, the idea of growth and change – not only within the building, as Mies' universal space concept suggested, but also of the enclosure itself – was a still essential and increasingly relevant feature of Modern architecture, not least in the industrial sector. The simple rectangular enclosure was later envisaged by Foster as the first element of a building that would extend along the line of the central services channel, punctuated by landscaped courtyards. However, only the first stage was ever built, the extended I-beams being the sole, eloquent indication of a building whose boundaries were intended to grow along with the company that occupied it.

## Whereas a Miesian pavilion presents a finite composition and is all repose and constraint, Reliance Controls fairly bursts with energy.

Similarly, whereas Mies, with rare exception, would design both cladding and structure in the same plane like a tight corset restricting a potential bulge, the cladding at Reliance Controls is set just behind the steel columns, exposing the taut cross-braces. The separation of cladding and structure was a common feature of the Case Study houses, and from Reliance Controls onwards it became an accepted sign of technological savvy for a generation of European architects. Such a move leaves open the possibility, with a bit of juggling, of one stepping beyond the other, or being otherwise changed at will. (Later, Foster would sometimes move the cladding in front of the structure, as with the Pilot Head Office for IBM and Willis Faber & Dumas, but he would seldom place them in the same plane.)

1. An aerial view of the Reliance Controls site, built on a newly developed industrial estate on the outskirts of Swindon. In this photograph the building is seen as extended in the 1970s. Originally four by five structural bays, it was enlarged by one 12-metre bay to the north to form a square plan. In the process the glazed north facade was lost, to be replaced by solid cladding with punctured proprietary windows.

Eames had reversed the normal design process of creating a house design and then choosing the materials by starting off with American builders' suppliers catalogues and assembling his design, rather like a kit of parts, from readily available components. From [this] approach … there developed a hard-edged architectural type which Reyner Banham aptly described as the 'serviced shed' … The Reliance Controls factory was reckoned at the time to be a turning point in built factory design and represents the modest beginning of the serviced shed aesthetic.
Sutherland Lyall, *The State of British Architecture*, 1980
Right: Sutherland Lyall suggests a formal connection between the Eames House and Reliance Controls.

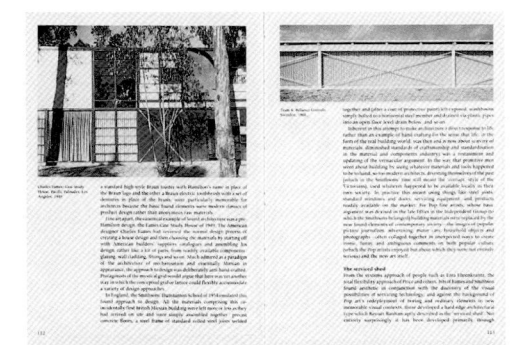

The Reliance Controls factory plays with light and shadow on its subtly contoured steel structure, which offers homage to the California houses of two decades before, and particularly to the house built by Eames. Much taken with Eames' idea of building with parts that could be ordered from catalogues, Foster took the concept further. 'Once, using technology meant repetitive, standard, boring serialisations. Now there's an incentive to use the customising ability of twentieth-century production methods so that you can get the qualities of an individual building at the same price as serial production', he says.
Hugh Aldersey-Williams, *Metropolis*, December 1997

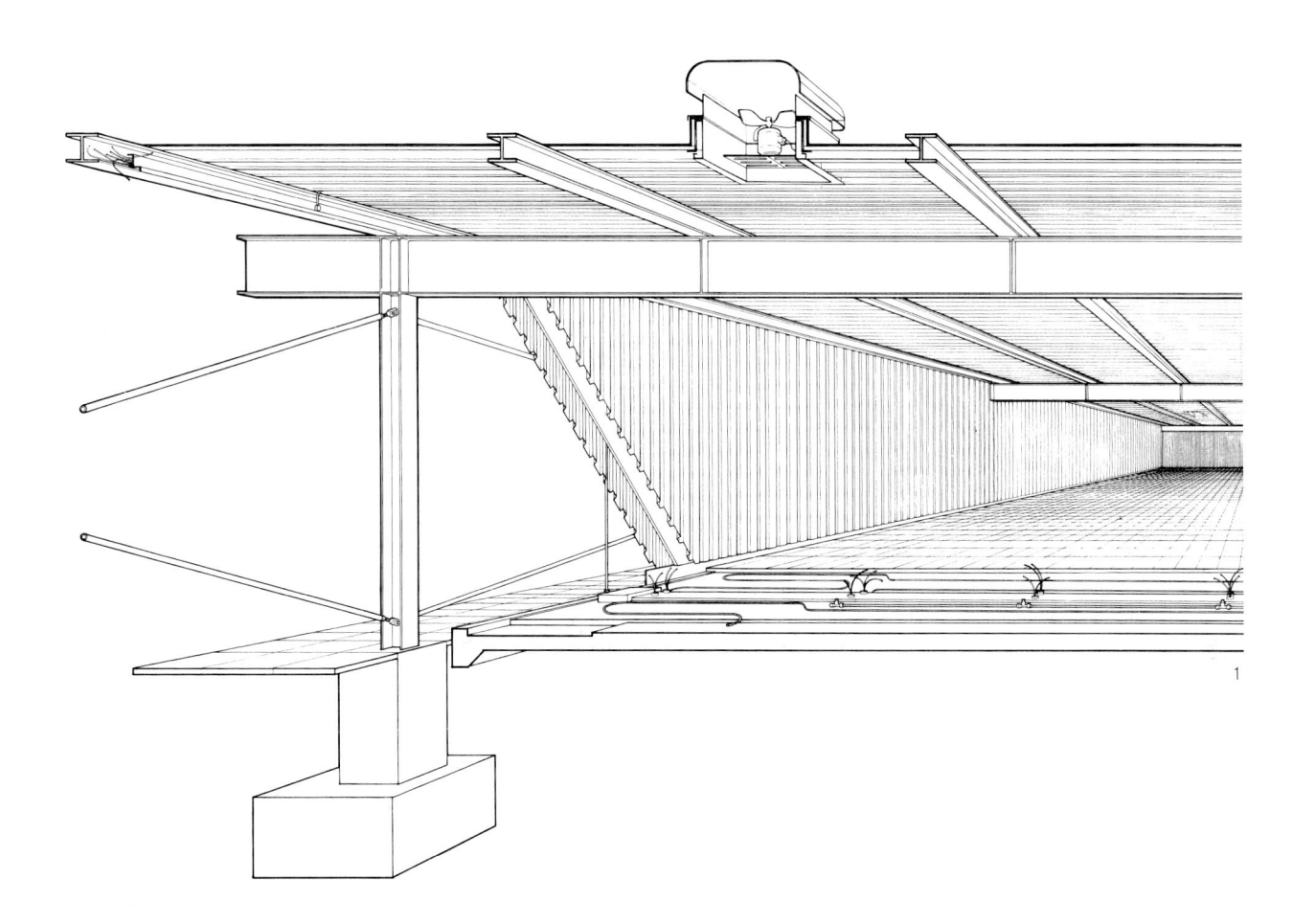

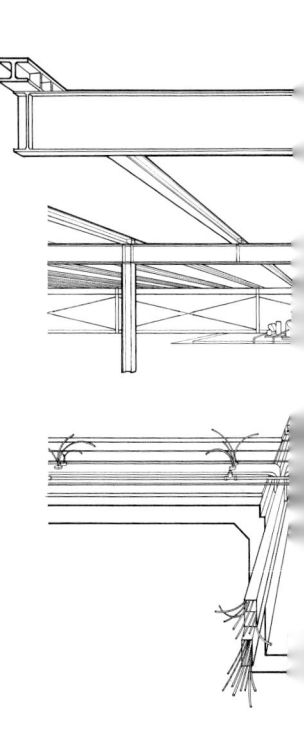

1. This sectional perspective, looking north along the building's central axis, shows all the principal features of its construction. Set up by Norman Foster, the drawing was completed by Mark Sutcliffe. The main columns stand on short-piled foundations. The power-floated site slab is indented along the axis line to provide an under-floor service duct. The sandwich construction, corrugated steel cladding panels spanned 4 metres from wall plate to eaves without intermediate support.

'Reliance Controls [is] one of those very rare European buildings that can be compared with the work of Craig Ellwood in California, and loses nothing in the comparison ... Like Ellwood, Team 4 managed to eliminate the lurking monumentality of the Miesian tradition in metal framing ... Team 4 had escaped from it, not into the slightly vapid neutralism of Saarinen's work for General Motors, but into something like the tough self-sufficient indifference of the true 'architecture of the bottom line'.' Reyner Banham, *Foster Associates*, 1979
Left: Craig Ellwood's Scientific Data Systems of 1966.

'Norman was my tutor during my second year at the Regent Street Polytechnic and later, in 1963, he took me on as Team 4's first 'year-out' student. Norman had already drawn all the working details and had set up most of the presentation drawings for Reliance Controls. I remember very clearly working on the cutaway perspective drawing, which was supposed to illustrate everything about the building's structure in a single clear diagram. I inked in the drawing, working over Norman's pencil original. It was quite a labour of love. I also remember that this was my introduction to the concept of the working weekend!' Mark Sutcliffe, now a director of the practice, in conversation with the editor, February 2002

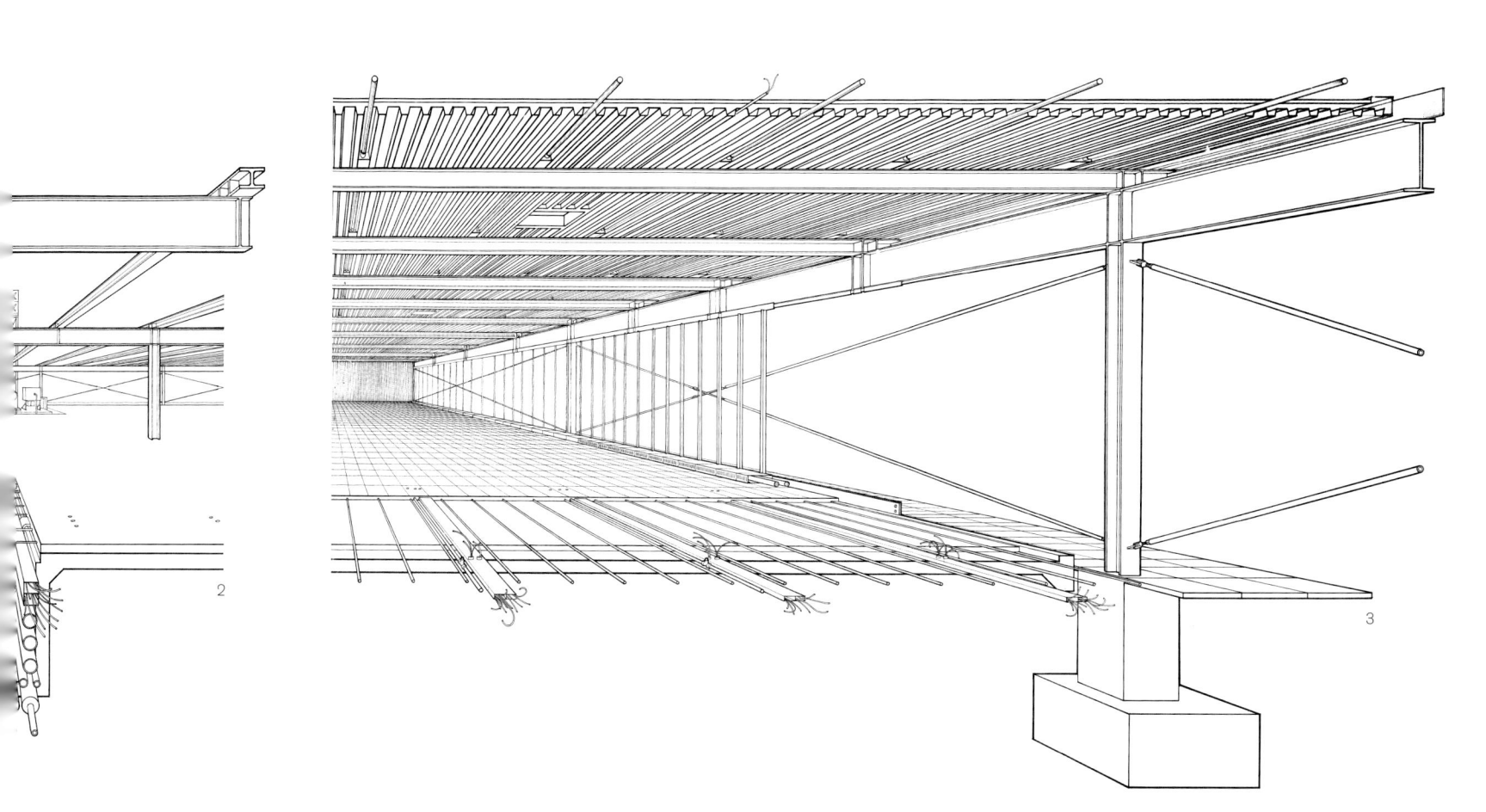

# Reliance Controls marked a turning point, in moving from 'traditional' heavy materials to factory-made, lightweight components.

Norman Foster

2. The underfloor service duct carried electrical and telephone wiring, water, gas and heating pipes, and compressed air runs. Nearly 2 metres deep, it permitted routine maintenance to be effected without disturbing the factory floor. Pipes from the oil-fired heating system were buried in the floor slab.

3. The glazed north wall spanned unsupported from ground slab to eaves beam. Like the wall panels, the profiled roof decking proved strong enough to act as a stiff diaphragm, spanning 3 metres without rafters.

Reliance Controls Electronics Factory

Left: In an early sketch, Norman Foster explored the possibility of floor-to-ceiling perimeter glazing for all four sides of the building, a concept that was to be realised in the Pilot Head Office for IBM at Cosham, some four years later.
Right: A detail of IBM Cosham's all-glass curtain wall.

1. Hidden from the main road, the building's entire north elevation was glazed, full-height glass panels being supported in a minimal frame. This view, at night, looks into the staff canteen.

2. Norman Foster's drawing of the courtyard system proposed for the northward extension of the building. Drawn after the break-up of Team 4, it shows a more organic response to expansion and humanising the deep-planned space.

3. The interior of the factory, seen soon after completion, before it was occupied.

4. The elegance of the elevational treatment is evident in this extended drawing. To the left, what appears to be the projecting end of the steel eaves beam is in fact half of one of the prefabricated cross-head pieces; together with their stanchions, these were erected at the first stage of construction. The beams linking these cross-heads were subsequently site-welded into position.

Internally, the reduction of elements and components to a small number of repetitive systems, each designed and finished to an unusually high standard for a building of this type, was designed to facilitate changes of use between office and production areas, or research and development, which are frequently needed in such a fast-moving industry. Demountable, fully glazed internal partitions matched the glazed north wall, which would have looked out onto one of the landscaped courtyards, had the building been extended as Foster anticipated.

Additionally, the building's built-in flexibility and uniform level of finishes was driven by an explicit and radical social agenda every bit as important, if not more so to Foster, as the functional programme, with which it was closely interrelated. The coming of the Electronic Age had thrown up a host of new 'clean industries', where the assembly of electronic components and products required environmental conditions just as spotless in many cases as those of a hospital. Despite this, architects and clients stubbornly clung to a model of factory planning dating back to the Industrial Revolution, with factory and office workers getting separate buildings, entrances and canteens, not to mention pay packets and perks.

Such deeply entrenched social prejudice was anathema to Foster, whose working-class childhood is now part of architectural folklore. The all-in-one functional space planning of Reliance Controls is a direct outcome of these social considerations, as well as others already discussed. Flexibility required it; economy required it and, as Foster puts it, social justice required it: 'Reliance Controls challenged the idea of the management box and the worker's shed, the distinctions between "we and they", "posh and scruffy", "clean and dirty", "back and front", and suggested a more egalitarian, more flexible, more appropriate response'.

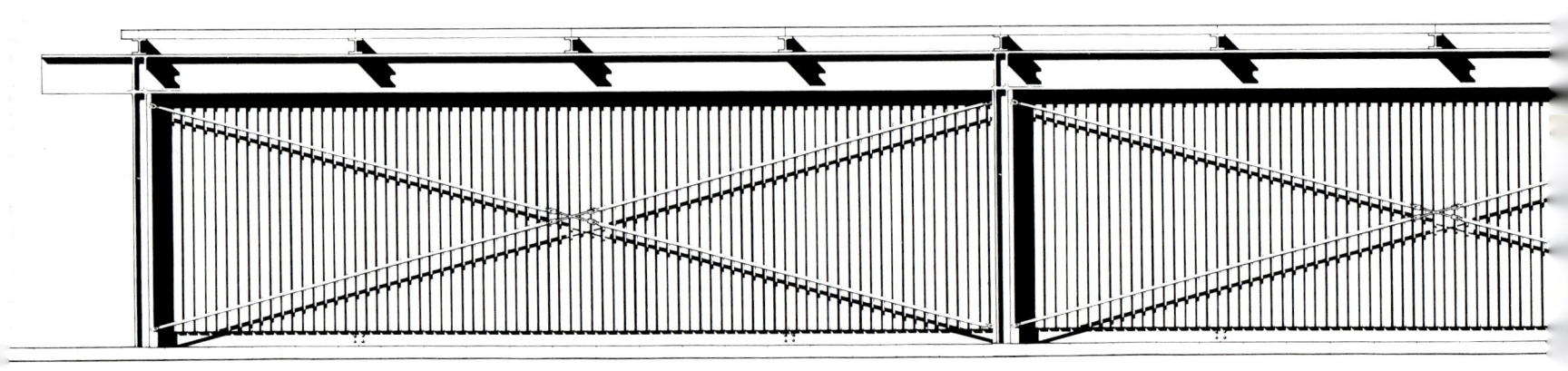

**Whenever possible, elements were designed to do double or even triple duty – for example, the metal roof profile also acted as a lighting reflector for recessed fluorescent tubes as well as performing structurally as a stiff diaphragm.**
Norman Foster, *Foster Associates*, 1979

**Of course, the point that I always have to answer for now is the multiple cross-bracing, not only along the sides that would have required some diagonal support anyway, but also along the two elevations that did not require it at all. I am still a little embarrassed: it is not a 'pure' structure, so the engineer in me can never be entirely satisfied. The designer in me, however, tends to agree it makes the building look better. The real irony was that Norman, who had used all his charm to persuade me to accept multiple cross-bracing for the building, then decided the water tower would be better without it. As a very tall, very slender portal frame, this really did present some problems!** Tony Hunt, 'In at the Beginning', 1991

**The thin steel cross-brace is the Doric column of High-tech – its visual sign and ordering device – and has been so ever since Foster and Rogers completed the Reliance Controls building in 1967. A cluster of cross-braces in the air can look like a cats' cradle of spindly lines, making them often the most expressive device in a shed-like structure.**
Charles Jencks, *The New Moderns*, 1990

Amongst all the other challenges thrown down by the project at the time, knowingly tinkering with the established social structure was perhaps the riskiest of them all. Social engineering, or architectural determinism as it is sometimes called, has in the wrong hands given Modernism as much of a bad name as leaking roofs and dull, ugly buildings. Yet this radical move was accepted not only by the client at Reliance Controls (as it has been by numerous Foster clients ever since) but also by increasing numbers of architects, clients and managers around the world. Such developments suggest that wider and more positive processes were at work here, beyond Foster's or any other architect's direct control, but not beyond their influence or ability to express.

The fact that Foster and his colleagues succeeded in this most difficult of areas, as in others, where so many well-meaning Modernists failed before them, speaks for itself. Incongruously, a cheap but sleek, well-made, worker-friendly factory on the edge of Swindon, marked the beginning of the rehabilitation of Modern architecture, precisely at the point of its deepest decline. A new kid was on the block.

Chris Abel

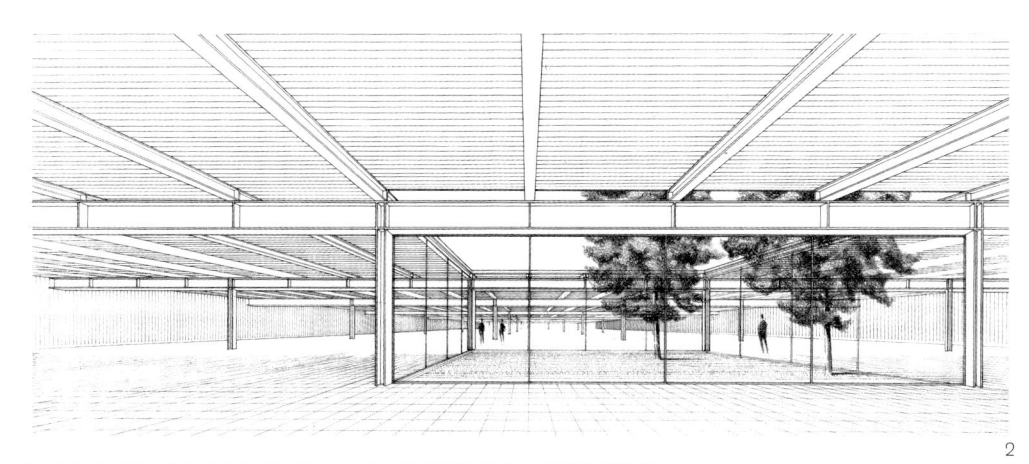

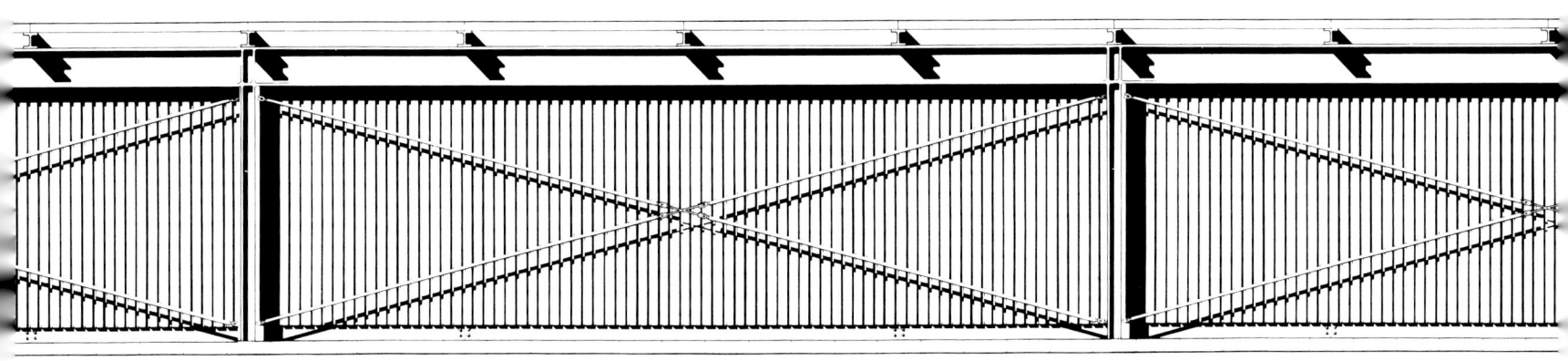

2

3

4

**I can still remember all the Reliance Controls critical dimensions by heart, because it was the first building that I was totally immersed in, from the concept down to the smallest detail.** Norman Foster, in conversation with Malcolm Quantrill, 1999

**Both internally and externally the total anatomy of the factory is revealed – incredibly revealed – incredibly simple and therefore, by necessity, extraordinarily well detailed.** John Chisholm, *Daily Telegraph*, 30 December 1968

The elegance of the structural framing – or 'anatomy' – of Reliance Controls evidently owed much to Norman Foster's understanding of a range of architectural and engineering traditions, not least the vernacular. Right: Foster's measured drawings of an eighteenth-century timber-framed clunch barn, which he made during his studies at Manchester University: the kit-of-parts aesthetic in the pre-industrial age.

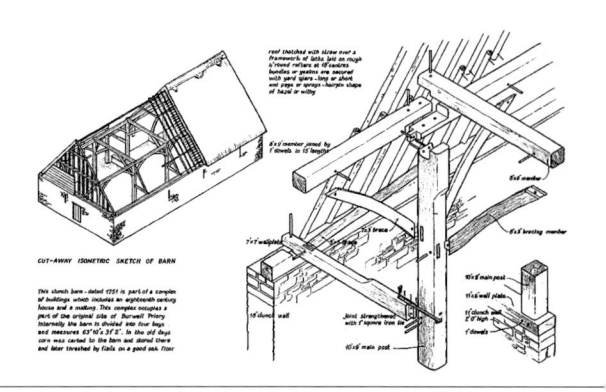

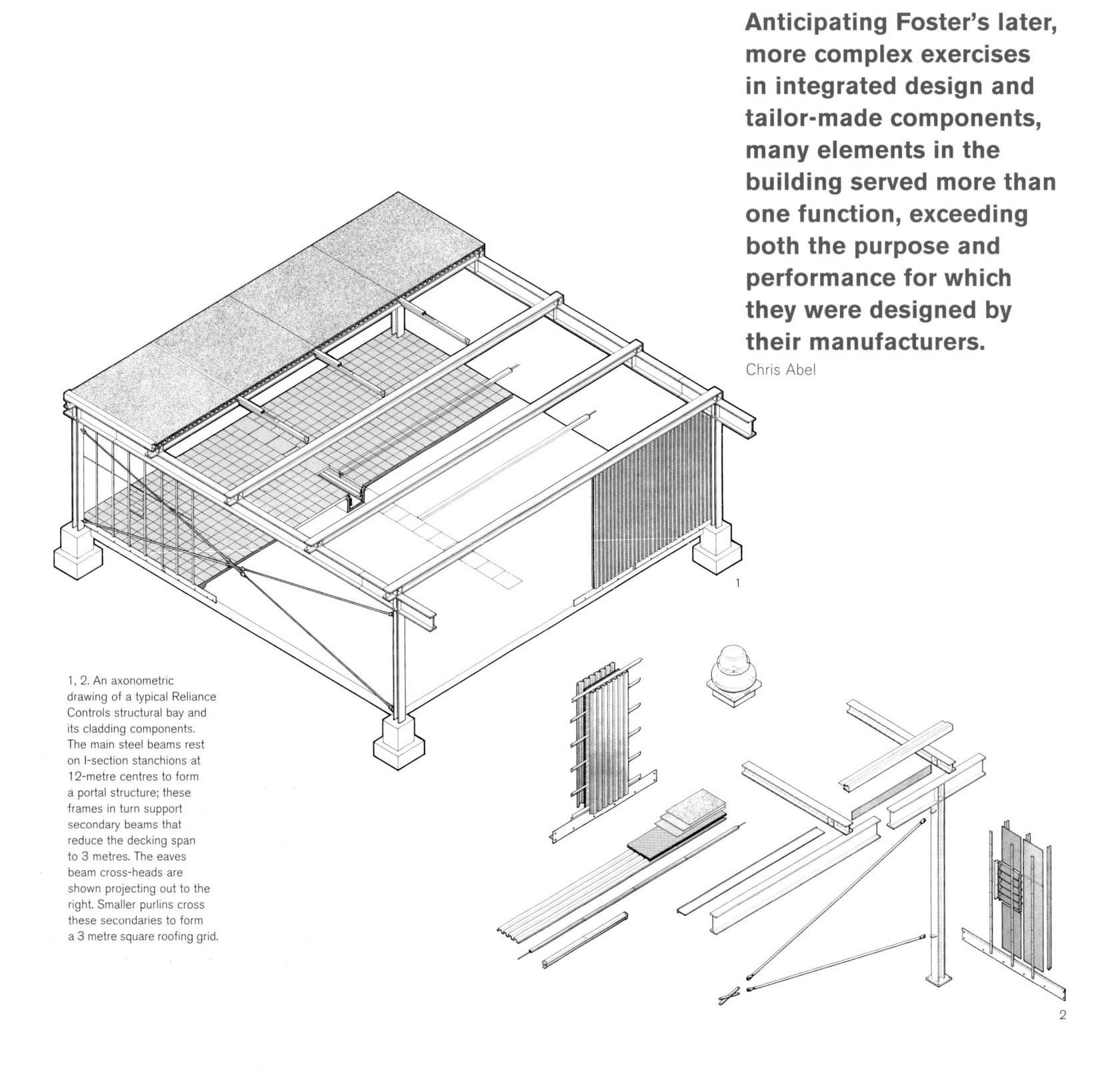

**Anticipating Foster's later, more complex exercises in integrated design and tailor-made components, many elements in the building served more than one function, exceeding both the purpose and performance for which they were designed by their manufacturers.** Chris Abel

1, 2. An axonometric drawing of a typical Reliance Controls structural bay and its cladding components. The main steel beams rest on I-section stanchions at 12-metre centres to form a portal structure; these frames in turn support secondary beams that reduce the decking span to 3 metres. The eaves beam cross-heads are shown projecting out to the right. Smaller purlins cross these secondaries to form a 3 metre square roofing grid.

**Steel is not something you can take up and put down. It is a way of life.** Pierre Koenig, quoted in *Domus*, December 1989
Left: Norman Foster's photograph of a prefabricated corner cross-head during construction illustrates Reliance Controls' economical use of materials, and its empathy with the approach espoused by Koenig.
Right: Pierre Koenig's Case Study House #22 of 1960.

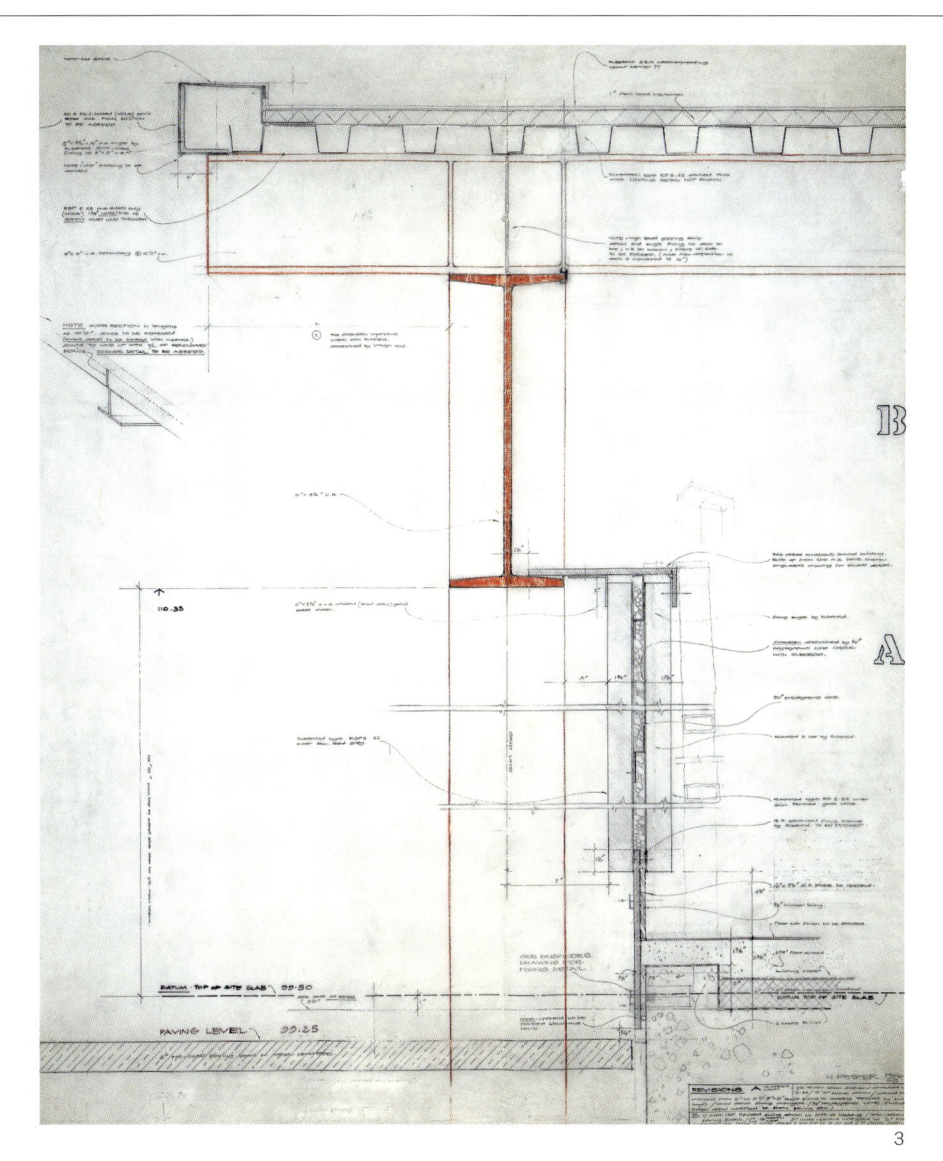

3. Norman Foster prepared all the working drawings for Reliance Controls himself. He set out to describe all the major conditions at the edge of the building, thereby collating information from consultants, suppliers and subcontractors. This drawing worked so well that a more extensive set of working details proved unnecessary; together with the structural and mechanical engineers' drawings, a series of these 'sketches' formed the basic shop drawings from which Reliance Controls was built.

4. The roof edge condition as built; the clarity of the structure meant that many of engineer Anthony Hunt's construction drawings could be issued to the contractor as hand-drawn sketches.

5. Examples of Anthony Hunt's comparative structural systems for Reliance Controls, prepared for cost analysis at an early stage in the project.

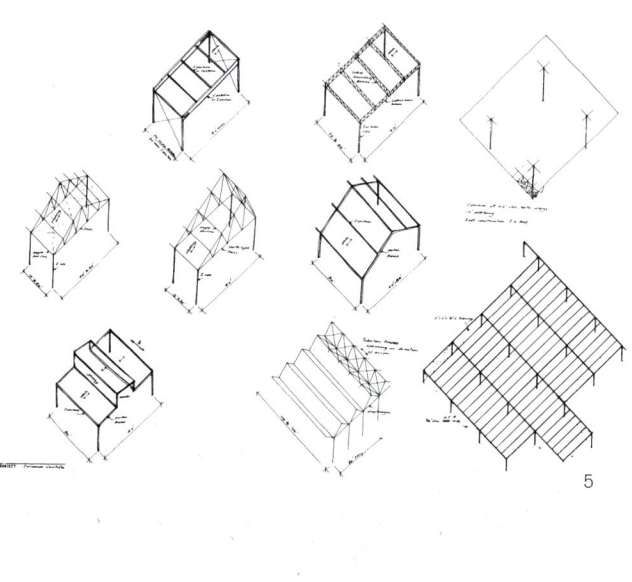

Reliance Controls Electronics Factory

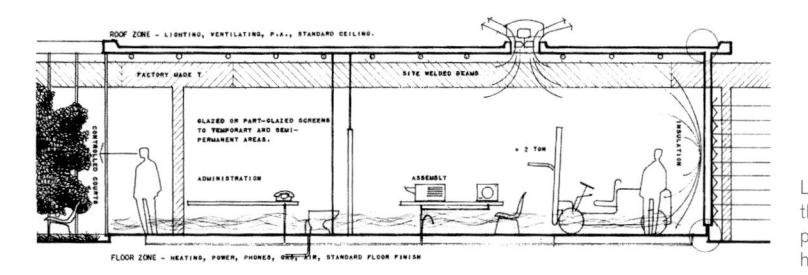

Left: In this early drawing Norman Foster explored the containment of fumes, noise and vibration in the production area by means of insulated wall panels, head-height screens, and powerful roof extract fans.

**On entering the visitor is immediately aware, even if he has not noticed from the outside (for it is consistent both externally and internally) that he is in a distinguished building. Its uncompromising simplicity and unity of general conception and detailed design create an atmosphere that is not only pervasive but notably comfortable to be in. It is refreshing to find something so beautifully direct that it looks like a lost vernacular.** Extract from jury report, Financial Times Industrial Architecture Award, 1967

The building included several items of purpose-designed fixed furniture, which extended the vocabulary of welded steel construction down to the smallest detail.
Right: The steel-framed undercarriages of the desking system produced specially for the building.

1. The main production area spanned the centre of the building. Any sense of closure was mitigated by the extensive use of full-height glass partitions. Finishes were reduced to the fewest number of coordinated elements, as demonstrated by the fluorescent lighting which used the recesses of the roof decking as a reflector; the secondary beams being spaced to allow standard tubes to fit exactly.

2. A view of the entrance hall area, with its purpose-designed reception desk.

3. A view of the canteen, which was shared by all the company's staff. Against Norman Foster's wishes, when the building was extended northwards the wall of glazing seen here was not reinstated. Instead it was replaced with solid corrugated panels, much to the detriment of the central working areas (see overleaf).

**Reliance Controls confronted the politics of integrating the workplace. Instead of accepting the status quo, it suggested a far more egalitarian, flexible and appropriate response.**
Norman Foster

Reliance Controls Electronics Factory

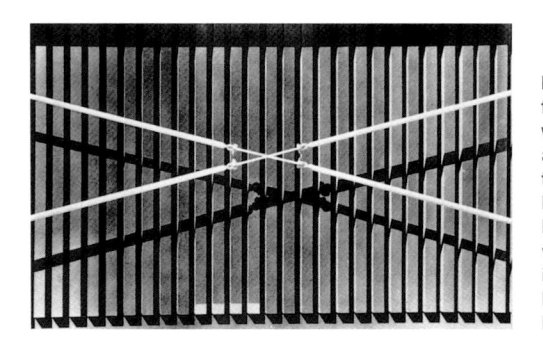

**In the end you cannot separate Norman Foster from his work process. Once you have seen the way the office attacks a project you realise that an enormous expenditure of energy is directed towards a social as well as a technical goal.** Ben Johnson, in conversation with Ian Lambot, 1990
Left: Painted in 1973 (acrylic on canvas), 'Cross-Bracing' was Ben Johnson's first work to use a Foster project as its subject. Based on a press photograph, it was only later than Johnson found out that it was Norman Foster himself who had been the photographer.

**This single-storey, windowless, trabeated, cross-braced structure has become a milestone in the development of twentieth-century architecture. It seems however, that the building will soon be nothing more than history. In a recent conversation with the director of the company occupying the building – one Fred Welfare – Martin Pawley discovered that the building – always referred to as 'the biscuit tin' – is to be demolished in June to make way for a DIY store. Was Welfare sorry, wondered Pawley. Far from it: Welfare hoped to push the button himself.** 'Astragal' commenting on the imminent demolition of Reliance Controls, *The Architects' Journal*, 28 February 1990

**More than just a turning point in Norman Foster's early career, the factory for Reliance Controls is a seminal building in the post-war history of the Modern Movement, reaffirming basic Modernist principles whilst at the same time injecting new – sorely needed – social and professional values.**
Chris Abel

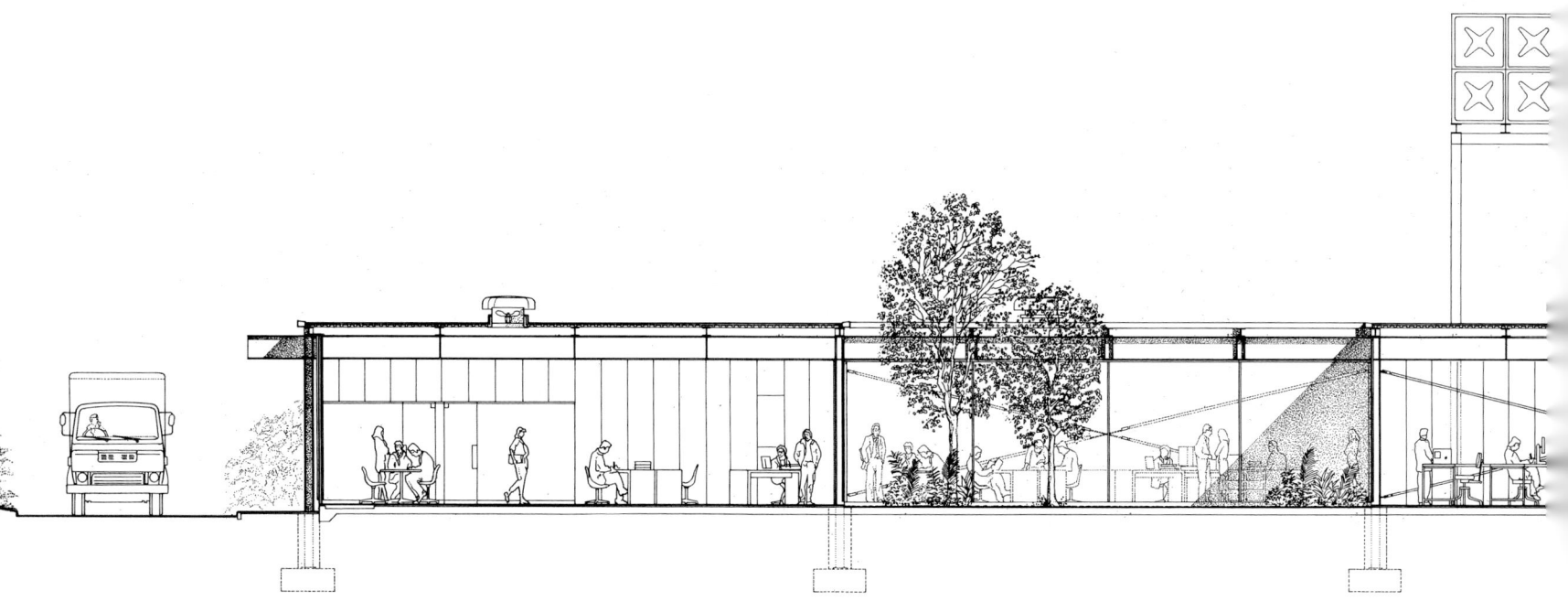

114  Norman Foster  Works 1

Over the years the management of the Reliance Controls factory changed several times. A newly appointed American director decided to extend the building and turn it into a windowless box just like 'back home'. I implored him to reconsider, pointing out that the window wall served everyone who worked there, but to no avail. Their minds were made up and it went ahead ... It was only a short time after the extension was finished that the director summoned me to say that he now had to have a window for his office. The irony of his demand was lost on him, but then he did not have too much of a sense of humour either. I pointed out that the logical solution would be to infill with full-height glazing. Quite apart from the visual implications, to do otherwise would result in complex and expensive intermediate structures ... No – he was adamant. Perversity prevailed and the director's little status symbol of a window was popped in – it looked like the aftermath of a collision with a council house!
Norman Foster, *Norman Foster: Sketches*, 1992
Left: The Reliance Controls building as altered by its owner, despite Norman Foster's protestations.

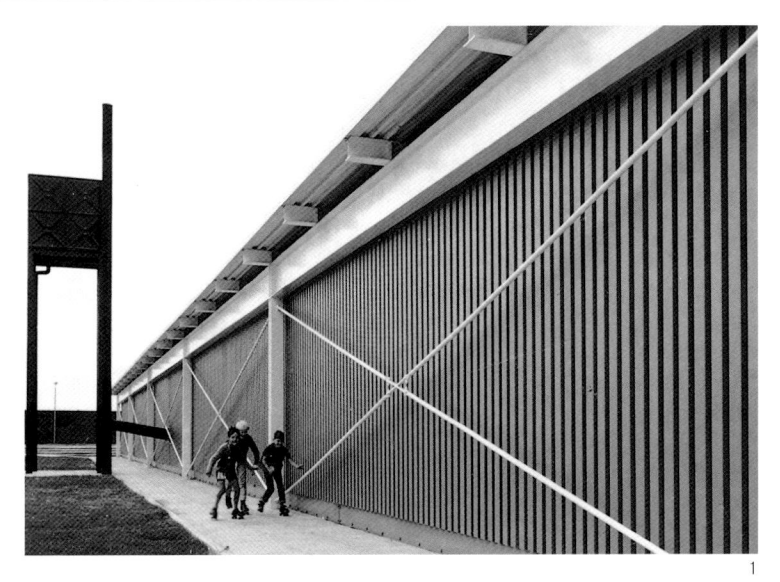

1. The road elevation of Reliance Controls looking west. The linked, welded frames in the east-west direction act as contiguous portal frames in which the cross-bracing is, in fact, redundant. Norman Foster, however, insisted the cross-bracing be applied to every bay, in both this and the north-south directions, creating a distinct device which laced the building together and established much of its individual character. Only at the entrance and where escape doors were located in the glazed north facade was the cross-bracing omitted, its absence signalling the significance of these bays.

2. A long section through the building's original five bays showing the varying internal conditions, including the planted courtyards, which would have been realised had the building been extended as originally planned (see page 102).

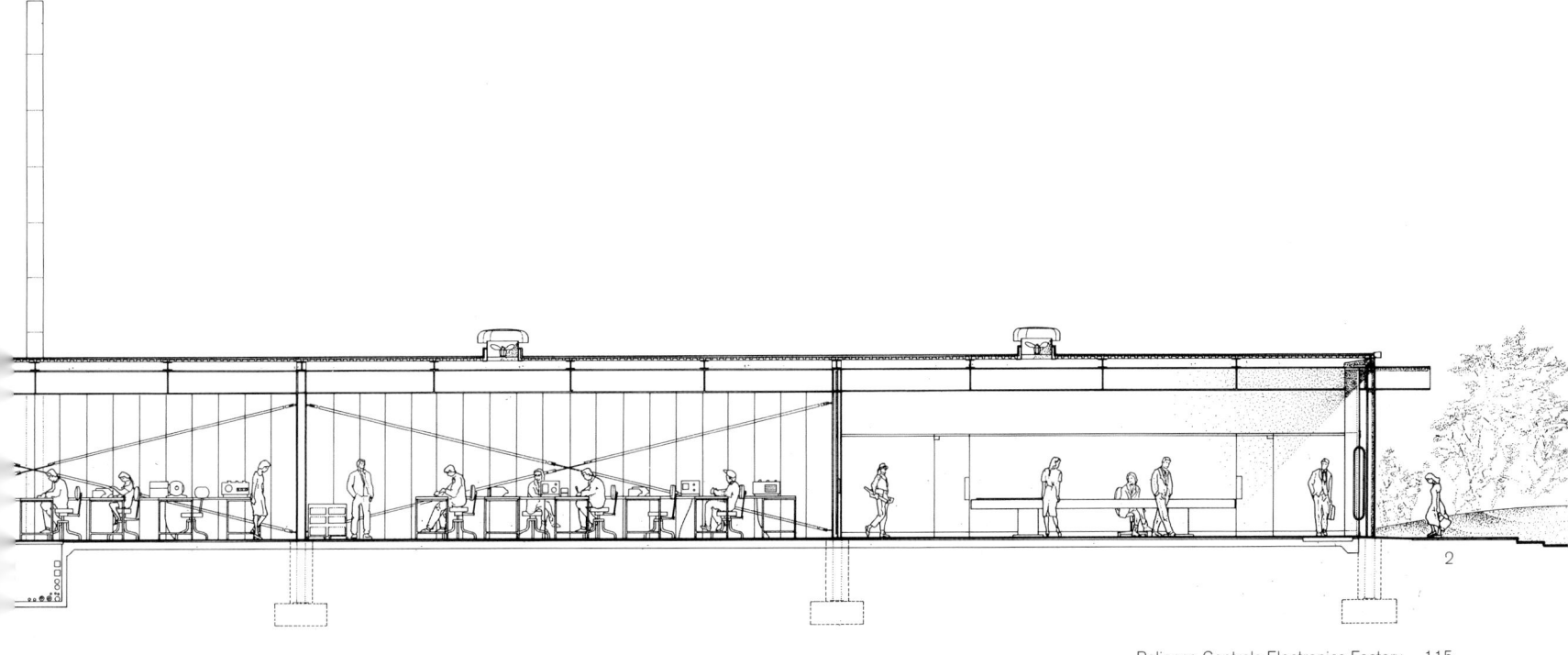

Reliance Controls Electronics Factory

## In the Beginning
Alastair Best 2000

When I look to the early years of Foster Associates, the recurring image is of a group, seated at a table and engaged in intense, almost conspiratorial discussion. I am thinking of the celebrated Tim Street-Porter photograph, taken during the course of a session with the late Buckminster Fuller. Among those clustered round the table are Norman himself, Michael Hopkins, Anthony Hunt, James Meller, John Walker and one or two others I cannot now identify. All are leaning forward intently to hear what the sage is saying. Again, I remember entering a Pizza Express in the Fulham Road and coming across almost the whole office seated at a large circular table. They were conducting an earnest post-mortem on a pitch they had just made to Chelsea Football Club – in those days top of the First Division and planning to build a new stand.

It was, of course, fashionable in the 1960s to talk about the design 'team'; but I find it difficult in those early years to detach Foster from his associates or, for that matter, from the professional consultants – like the engineer, Anthony Hunt, or the quantity surveyor, John Walker – with whom he surrounded himself. Partly, perhaps, this was window-dressing: clients like to see a multidisciplinary array of skills. Partly, of course, it was the result of Foster's extremely thorough, even cautious, approach to architecture. The process that he calls 'exploring the client's range of options' is an exact description of the painstaking, sometimes almost diffident, way in which he feels towards a solution.

Nobody who has seen the design exercises that went into the proposed Radio Centre for the BBC could ever believe that Foster produces buildings like rabbits out of hats, and the brilliance of the Fred Olsen schemes in this volume is rooted in some very unflashy strategic research. Foster proceeds by marshalling all the arguments and taking the best available advice. Only when he is convinced that his own position is unassailable will he make a move; and when he does he is unstoppable. It was the same with his own entry into the architectural profession: oblique and diffident at first; but once the fuse had been lit – explosive.

**It was fashionable in the 1960s to talk about the design 'team'; but I find it difficult in those early years to detach Foster from his associates or, for that matter, from the professional consultants with whom he surrounded himself.**

Norman Foster grew up in Levenshulme, a working class suburb of Manchester, and was raised in an atmosphere of thrift and self-help. He attended the local high school and did well, but given his social milieu, and the fact that he left school early, a career in one of the professions seemed out of the question. Yet even as a schoolboy he was exceptionally well-informed about architecture. One of his earliest possessions was a history of architecture written by Frederick Gibberd, and while still a teenager he had immersed himself in two key influences: Frank Lloyd Wright and Le Corbusier. Wright he imbibed via Henry-Russell Hitchcock's *In the Nature of Materials* – especially the science fiction images of shimmering glass in the Johnson Wax building. Whereas what impressed him most about *Vers une architecture* was the startling juxtaposition of past and present images it contained – a cornice detail from the Parthenon paired with the cockpit of a Caproni flying boat.

1

**Through my local library I discovered the different worlds of Frank Lloyd Wright and Le Corbusier. Imagine the contrast of a house on a prairie with a villa on a Paris boulevard. Yet I remember being equally fascinated by both at the time.** Norman Foster, Pritzker Prize address, Berlin, 7 June 1999
Left: A spread from Henry-Russell Hitchcock's *In The Nature of Materials*, 1942, illustrating Frank Lloyd Wright's Johnson Wax buildings.
Right: Pages from Le Corbusier's *Vers une architecture*, translated as *Towards a New Architecture* in 1927.

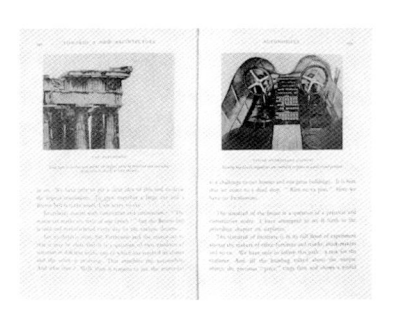

He had also begun to respond to architecture at first hand. His first job in the Treasurer's department of Manchester Town Hall exposed him to Waterhouse's remarkable building from the inside. And what impressed him, he told the RIBA in his Gold Medal address of 1983, was 'not only the internal spaces and the presence on Albert Square, but also the details: the handrails and the light fittings, even the glass-sided cisterns in the toilets'. Other buildings in Manchester also left their mark: the delicate tracery of the Barton and Lancaster arcades, and, perhaps most of all, the Daily Express building, by Owen Williams, in Great Ancoats Street, with its sleek curves and dark reflective bands of glass – an obvious blood ancestor of Willis Faber & Dumas in Ipswich.

It's difficult to say exactly when Foster came to terms with the fact that a career in architecture was inevitable, but by the time he joined the Royal Air Force for his National Service the idea of studying architecture had begun to take hold. At least he knew that he had to escape from the Town Hall; and the RAF, where he was trained to work on airborne Radar systems, gave him the opportunity to acquire another skill. He worked in a turf-covered hangar (another portent?) which was high on camouflage and low on natural light; but, as he told the RIBA: 'there was a certain futility to our struggles: the Radar systems we repaired were designed for propeller driven bombers; their response was too slow for the new generation of jets and by the time the navigator had established a fix, the aircraft had already travelled a long way to somewhere else'.

His National Service over, Foster took on a variety of short-term jobs, doing almost anything to postpone his return to the Town Hall. Paradoxically, it was his book-keeping skills, acquired while working at the Town Hall, that finally gave him an oblique entry into architecture. He got a job as an assistant in the contracts department of John Beardshaw & Partners, a large Manchester commercial practice installed in a Georgian house near the University. Here, for the first time, he started mixing with architects, or embryonic architects, and he discovered to his surprise that he was rather better informed than some of them.

A chance conversation with an apprentice student, on a year out from Manchester School of Art, ran as follows: Foster: 'What do you think of Frank Lloyd Wright's work?' Student: 'Frank Lloyd Wright? I don't think there's anyone of that name on the course'.

Foster decided that he would apply to Manchester University. The problem was that he had no portfolio to show – he had never done an architectural drawing. Then he had a bright idea. He began to take drawings from the office at the end of each day and produce his own versions of them after hours. Each morning – always the first one in – he would put the drawings back, so nobody knew that they had disappeared overnight.

Before he applied to the University, however, he thought he ought to tell his boss. Foster recalls: 'One day I knocked on his door and said, 'I just wanted to tell you that I am trying to get into the University.' He said, 'But you have to have work to show.' I told him that it was not a problem: I had lots of drawings. He asked how that was possible. So I explained and he was amused and asked to see what I had done. When I showed him he said: 'You're a square peg in a round hole. Come with me'. There and then he produced a drawing board, a T-square, a book of graphic standards and a project. That afternoon I became part of the office. And then he tried very hard to persuade me to stay with him and not to study.'

Meanwhile he had discovered that he could obtain a grant to study architecture at the School of Art but not at the University – and the University ran a better course. And so, American style, he worked his way through college, performing a bizarre range of jobs: from a bouncer in a rough cinema to selling ice cream from a van.

1. 'Seated at a table and engaged in almost conspiratorial discussion': Tim Street-Porter's celebrated photograph of Norman Foster, James Meller, John Walker, Anthony Hunt and Michael Hopkins in a design meeting with Buckminster Fuller in the Bedford Street studio in Covent Garden.

2. Norman Foster as a teenager, photographed with his parents.

# The best favour that Manchester did for me was to refuse me a grant for study at the University. What better challenge could there be to try to prove them wrong?

Norman Foster

**Manchester, like the Britain of which it is a part, probably brings out the best and the worst in me. It has taken me most of my lifetime to realise how fortunate I have been. For a long time I believed that I came from a poor background because I had to work to pay my way through university at the same time as studying; but all the things that I thought were barriers have turned out to be incentives.** Norman Foster, Honorary Degree address at Manchester University, 12 May 1993
Left: The Manchester of Foster's early years, with its rich mix of Victorian industrial and civic architecture, is perhaps most evocatively portrayed in the paintings of L S Lowry; here the city is depicted in *VE Day Celebrations*, of 1945.

1,2. Norman Foster's very first design project as a student at Manchester University was for a holiday cottage with its own boathouse in the Lake District. However, rather than design separate pavilions, as was expected of him, Foster combined the two functions within a single enclosure. From the outset the idea of 'integration' has been fundamental to Foster's design philosophy.

He was also amassing prizes and scholarships at the University. Many of the prizes were for foreign travel, and he managed to see a great deal of Europe in five years. He did the usual tour (town-planning studies of the Campo at Siena) and went to Denmark to look at the housing of Utzon and Jacobsen. The Manchester school placed a strong emphasis on history and drawing, both traditions stemming from Professor R A Cordingly, editor of the seventeenth edition of *Banister Fletcher*, but there was very little in the way of verbal communication or debate. In many ways Foster was out on a limb and it was only when he won a Henry Fellowship to study for a Masters degree at Yale that his period of isolation came to an end.

For someone with his background and temperament Yale was the perfect finishing school. The course was run on rigid lines by Paul Rudolph. There were marks every week and a strict regime of projects. All assignments were run against the clock – a vital early lesson in the importance of time as an ingredient of design. Foster thrived in this atmosphere of regulated hard work – more so than his classmate Richard Rogers, with whom, back in Britain, he would enter partnership under the umbrella of Team 4.

But more than Yale, more than his mentors – Rudolph, Serge Chermayeff and Vincent Scully – it was America itself that made the most powerful impression. The Britain that Foster had left behind was still drab and impoverished; the architectural profession still dominated by such essentially herbivorous characters as Sir Basil Spence or Sir Hugh Casson – for whom Foster had worked during his year out in 1959. The imagery of man-made America – its freeway architecture, its Airstream caravans and all the hardware of space travel – exerted a seductive influence.

Then there was the architecture. It is tempting, with hindsight, to suppose that the Case Study houses and Californian steel systems buildings he saw then made the greatest impact, since their influence was to resurface so decisively in Reliance Controls and the Newport School competition. But it would probably be more accurate to say that they were just some of the many powerful impressions that he docketed and filed away for retrieval later on.

In fact one needs to look back further, to Foster's Manchester days, to trace the roots of a generative theme that runs through the work of Foster Associates, and continues to characterise the work of the practice today – the idea of 'integration'. The very first Manchester design project was a boathouse and retreat in the Lake District. Foster recalls:

'The expectation was that you would design a shed for the boat and a little cottage alongside to stay in at the weekend. But I took a very different approach. I integrated the boathouse and retreat to form a single building on the waterfront. The boat went directly inside the building and the living accommodation was located behind a glass screen facing out onto the river. I had this incredible image in my mind of a Riva motorboat – a kind of Ferrari of the water – and I could imagine sitting in this cottage, perhaps with a glass of wine, looking out through a glass wall onto that beautiful boat. It made perfect sense to bring those two experiences together under one roof.

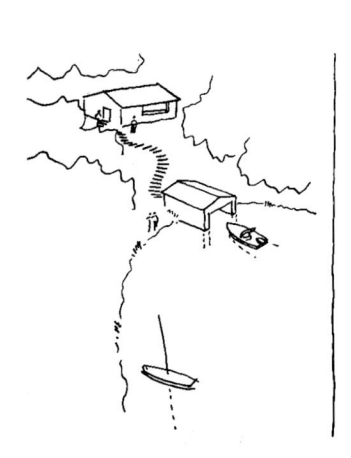

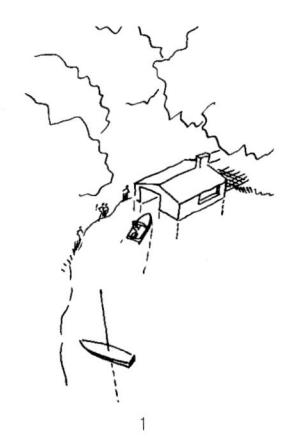

118  Norman Foster Works 1

**After school I marked time working in the city accountant's office, in the splendid Town Hall building by Alfred Waterhouse. I have strong recollections not only of its internal spaces and its presence on Albert Square, but also of its details, the handrails and light fittings, down to the glass-sided water cisterns in the lavatories. If the Town Hall was like a Victorian Cave then I remember being excited by its counterpoint, the tent-like tracery of Barton Arcade.** Norman Foster, RIBA Royal Gold Medal address, London, 21 June 1983
Far left: Lancaster Avenue Arcade, Manchester, 1873; demolished 1980.
Centre: Barton Arcade, Manchester, 1871.
Left: Manchester Town Hall, 1868-1877.

'If you look at the projects in the office today and study their history – whether you take an early project such as Reliance Controls, or a mid-career one such as the Sainsbury Centre, or a very recent one such as Hong Kong Airport at Chek Lap Kok, you will find that they are all about integration.

**One needs to look back further, to Foster's Manchester days, to trace the roots of a generative theme that runs through the work of Foster Associates, and continues to characterise the work of the practice today – the idea of 'integration'.**

'Reliance Controls innovated on several levels. It was a rejection of the prevailing us and them, posh and scruffy, front and back idea of the traditional factory, which typically had a management box at the front and a workers' shed at the back, the former clean the latter most probably dirty. Instead, Reliance Controls brought everybody together in one democratic pavilion, with only a non-structural glass wall between the administrative and factory spaces. You could not expand the old kind of factory because it was fragmented, but Reliance Controls had a very simple structure that allowed the building to grow.

'Similarly, when we came to design the Sainsbury Centre for Visual Arts, we sought to unify a number of disparate functions – an art gallery, a faculty of art history, a senior common room, a public restaurant – within a single, open top-lit space. Essentially we thought that these buildings would be richer if they were flexible and if the edges between functions were broken down. Coming right up to date, Hong Kong Airport – which is arguably the largest construction project in the world – has many different activities all under one roof, but a roof of monumental size: something like 18 hectares (45 acres) of roof over a single space with a perimeter 5.6 kilometres long.'

From the first, Foster seems to have known instinctively how to be both challenging and appealing. In founding Team 4, for example, the very name struck precisely the right note, midway between the world of pop and serious architecture. There were echoes of groups such as the Beatles – the 'Fab Four', who cut their first LP in 1963 – and in architecture of Atelier 5, whose Siedlung Halen housing scheme, on a forested hillside outside Berne, was the sought-for antidote to the English picturesque versions of Le Corbusier on the LCC's Roehampton Estate, or Sir Basil Spence's University of Sussex campus.

Those who worked for Team 4 in the early 1960s – usually the most talented students plucked from the Architectural Association or the Regent Street Polytechnic – remember a stylish atmosphere of creative tension, underpinned by good living. Furniture, walls and floor in Wendy's flat – by now the office – were white, as in a Dick Lester film. Sir Herbert Read's daughter Sophie, complete with Afghan hound, manned the reception. Su Rogers did the accounts and Norman and Richard, seated on either side of a large table, scribbled, or squabbled, over endless rolls of buff paper. The coffee, then as now, was exceptional. They were both fortunate and unfortunate in their early clients.

3. Norman Foster's concept sketch for Hong Kong International Airport at Chek Lap Kok (1992-1998) illustrates how the building integrates and rationalises the different functions of the modern airport terminal beneath a single, all-embracing enclosure, in order to maximise clarity and efficiency in use.

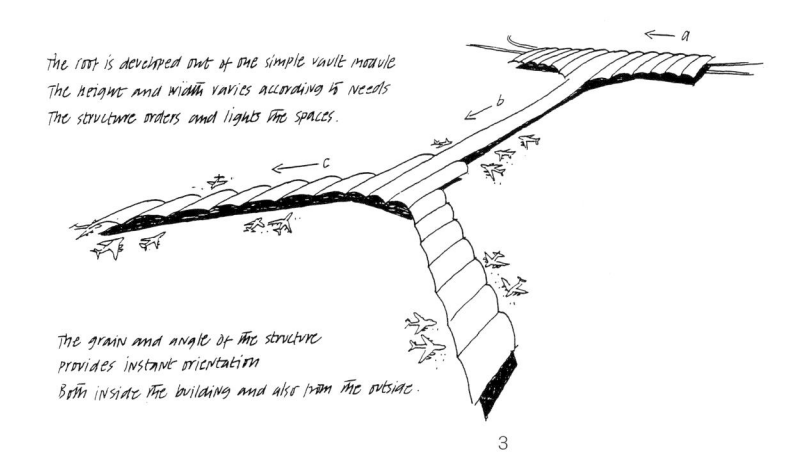

**This giant glistening dewdrop that appears to have been distilled on the Carmarthenshire countryside was intended to echo the gentle contours of the surrounding hills. Never have steel and glass – those ubiquitous components of modern architecture – been employed more effectively.** *The Independent on Sunday*, 8 October 2000
Right: The Great Glasshouse at the National Botanic Gardens of Wales (1995-1999), continues the theme of dug-in, or groung-hugging buildings in Foster's work that was pioneered by the Cockpit at Creek Vean.

In Marcus Brumwell, Su Rogers' father, they found a cultivated and indulgent patron who presented them with two commissions, one on either side of the small wooded creek that flows into the Fal estuary in Cornwall. First and chief of these was for a house on a steeply sloping site at Pill Creek; the second, facing it across the water, was for a small 'retreat' situated on a favourite picnic spot.

The resulting 'Cockpit', which has a commanding view over the Fal estuary, takes the form of a sunken gazebo, buried between the pine trees. It is a light, elegant industrial object – Brumwell had suggested something resembling the draught shield on the side of a car – and it sits uncompromisingly in its natural setting. As such it recalls later Foster works in established landscapes, notably the proposed office complex for Fred Olsen in the ecologically sensitive pine forests at Vestby, outside Oslo, in 1973, or much more recently, the glasshouse for the National Botanic Gardens of Wales, at Middleton. As with Le Corbusier's Villa Savoye, the aesthetic pleasure of these buildings is generated by the tension between the untouched natural setting and the pristine, man-made object in its midst.

The house was quite different. Creek Vean took three years to complete and won an RIBA Award in 1969. When I visited it, the house was still lived in quite happily by Brumwell's widow Rene, and I was touched to note that the storage jars and coffee percolator were still arranged on the free-standing stainless-steel worktop in exactly the configuration in which they appear in the early Richard Einzig photographs. The established planting has helped to soften the rather stark concrete block elevations, but it is still possible to detect the influence of two Modern masters.

**From the first, Foster seems to have known instinctively how to be both challenging and appealing. In founding Team 4, for example, the very name struck precisely the right note, midway between the world of pop and serious architecture.**
Alastair Best

**All Aalto's buildings have this strong sense of orientation, possibly because you can always relate back to a key space, which defines the heart of the scheme. At Aalborg this would surely be the main gallery and its immediately related areas, all beautifully top-lit.** Norman Foster, *RIBA Journal*, July 1976

Left: Alvar Aalto's Aalborg Museum, completed in 1972; its distinctive reflectors draw daylight into the building. Right: An array of solar reflectors at the Hongkong Bank building (1979-1986) ingeniously ensure that the vast atrium is flooded with natural light.

Both in its internal planning – with a sequence of bedrooms arranged off a gallery – and in the way it snuggles into the protective hillside, it is reminiscent of Wright; while the planted roof, and the steep flight of grassy steps that fan out between the sleeping and living quarters are suggestive of Aalto's Säynätsalo Town Hall.

But perhaps the major indication of future developments in Foster's independent work is the ingenious use of top light – another Aalto connection. He recalls visiting Aalto's Aalborg Art Museum, in Denmark, where the galleries are cleverly top-lit, with a variety of reflectors that direct and control the light, 'without blanking off the sky, or excluding a glimpse of the sun'. This was a concept that Foster had similarly explored in the Vestby project, using roof-top mirrors to project sunlight into office interiors. He was later to realise this idea in the 'sunscoop' of the Hongkong and Shanghai Bank, although perhaps its ultimate incarnation can be seen in the cupola of the rebuilt Reichstag, where a mirrored cone functions as a Fresnel lens reflecting daylight (and some sunlight) from a 360-degree horizon down into the parliamentary chamber.

Before the completion of Creek Vean, Team 4 had wrestled with other less rewarding schemes and less accommodating clients. Murray Mews, for example, a development of three brick terraced houses for three different but highly demanding clients, was continually plagued by water penetration, shoddy finishes, incomplete junctions – in fact all the vices of traditional, on-site building methods.

Galvanised in this crucible, Foster and Rogers knew that, in future, they had to pursue alternative methods that would avoid outmoded building techniques. This led them to investigate flexible plan forms, which could also accommodate the clients' evolving needs, and to lightweight structures composed as far as possible from standardised components. By removing fabrication from the site to the factory it was possible to control standards of workmanship in a way that was unheard of in conventional building with its procession of semi-skilled labourers and wet trades. All this led back to the Californian buildings of Eames, Ellwood and Ehrenkrantz's SCSD.

The Reliance Controls factory, which spanned the break-up of Team 4 and the formation of Foster Associates, marks a significant turning point in the careers of both Foster and Rogers. Reliance may owe something to the Smithsons' influential Hunstanton School of 1954 (the water tower at Swindon is a direct quote) but in most crucial respects it is closer to its Californian counterparts. The low, slim profile recalls the work of Ellwood and Koenig and the cross-bracing – carried round all sides outside the ribbed metal cladding – recalls the cross-bracing on the Eames house at Pacific Palisades. In strict structural terms, the cross-bracing was only required on the two long elevations, but then it was entirely superfluous on the Eames house.

> **Perhaps the major indication of future developments in Foster's independent work is the ingenious use of top light. He recalls visiting Aalto's Aalborg Art Museum, in Denmark, where the galleries are cleverly top-lit, with a variety of reflectors that direct and control the light, 'without blanking off the sky, or excluding a glimpse of the sun'.**

Foster ran all the project meetings and produced most of the drawings (with assistance from Mark Sutcliffe) and in many ways Reliance Controls seems to have far more Foster in it than Rogers. The suppression of services, the expressed – but not over-expressed – structure, all recur in Foster Associates' subsequent work.

It was for Reliance Controls, too, that he perfected a presentational style that was to become standard at Foster Associates. The elevation is drawn with structural members in deep shadow; the structural options are drawn out; the kit-of-parts drawing shows the respective components coming together; and most characteristically, the exploded section reveals flexible service runs buried in the floor slab (in the case of Reliance Controls) or wriggling out of the ceiling void. The theory and practice may have been California inspired, but Foster refined them into a taut, razor-sharp architecture quite distinct from the West Coast originals.

1. The Cockpit at Creek Vean established Norman Foster's approach to the integration of a building into its natural context and explored what was to become a distinctive theme of subsequent Foster projects – that of digging a building into its site.

2. The planted roof at Creek Vean ensures that the house blends discreetly into its wooded sloping site. The grassy flight of steps leading down to the water's edge also points to Foster's enduring fascination with the work of Alvar Aalto – and specifically with his Säynätsalo Town Hall of 1949-1952.

**Although our domestic work for friends and relations had been well-received and our factory for Reliance Controls was singled out for the first Financial Times Industrial Architecture Award, in the late 1960s we were virtually out of work and talking of emigrating to the United States.** Norman Foster, *Norman Foster: Sketches*, 1992

**There were hardly any architectural competitions thirty years ago, and I remember that it was in some desperation that we submitted our entry to the Newport School competition – it was the great exception: it was the only competition, although there were no jury reports and there was no exhibition. If you compare that with the situation now, it's fantastic – new practices starting out can go through journals and tick which projects they would like to compete for, and there is a lot of discussion.** Norman Foster, lecture at Glasgow Royal Concert Hall, 8 May 1987

1. The Olsen Amenity Centre seen from the deck of one of Fred Olsen's ships in Millwall Dock. The relaxed sociability engendered by the range of facilities the building offered to dock workers – to a standard unheard of at the time – epitomises the key social dimension of Foster's approach.

And although Reliance Controls was designed to accommodate growth and change – the projecting I-beams emphasised that fact – it still gives the strong impression of a building complete in itself, with a lingering monumentality that betrays European roots along with its American ancestry.

Reliance Controls won the first Financial Times Award for Industrial Architecture in 1967, but, like many highly regarded buildings, it did not lead to further commissions for its architects. When Team 4 was disbanded, Norman and Wendy established Foster Associates in the same Hampstead Hill Gardens flat that had been home to Team 4. At this stage, in 1967, the practice included Mickey Kuch and Alan Stanton, as well as Martin Francis, an ex-furniture student from the Central School. But work soon began to dry up and Foster remembers it as a frustrating period. A building boom was under way – housing schemes, new university campuses, shopping centres, motorway service stations were all being designed and built – but Foster waited on the sidelines. In fact they had so little work that Norman and Wendy came close to leaving Britain in search of 'a more open society'; the only question was whether they would emigrate to the United States or Canada.

The one significant project on the drawing boards was an entry for the Newport School competition. It was a period when the term 'architecture' was seldom used in connection with education. There was an influential school of thought (led colourfully by Cedric Price) which held that the educational process could – and perhaps should – be conducted outside of conventional settings, in mobile enclosures or in multi-purpose centres.

Foster's Newport School entry posited an optimistic view of British comprehensive education as a forum for pedagogic experimentation, backed up by a wide array of advanced technical aids. It narrowly missed winning the competition, but it gave him the opportunity to work up a British version of the SCSD system. He proposed a constant-height roof 'umbrella' combining structure and environmental control, floating above a variety of teaching and administrative spaces. Though unbuilt, Newport sowed the seeds for a succession of buildings – mostly for industrial or commercial clients – that would become the mainstay of the practice.

As Foster recalls: 'Wendy and I survived by appealing to a niche where architects had not traditionally been involved, which was industry'. The exemplar in this regard is the Amenity Centre for Fred Olsen at Millwall Dock, perhaps the key building of Foster's early career. It consolidated a democratic agenda for the architecture of the workplace. Taking its cue from Reliance Controls, the Amenity Centre provided integrated facilities for workers and management, but to unprecedented standards.

The Olsen project was a classic Foster *tour de force*. Proceeding from a simple but restricted brief to design a small amenities building on a remote part of the site, Foster began to question the fundamentals of the company's entire mode of operations. This resulted in a masterplan for the site, which demonstrated conclusively that instead of being banished to the hinterland, the amenities and management should be combined in a single building at dockside, right at the centre of operations. It is probable that Foster had already decided that the logical site for the building was the firebreak slot between the two transit sheds. But it is characteristic of him that he should have cleared all other options out of the way before forging ahead with complete conviction.

**We would ask questions, listen to what the client said, then ask more questions. We made sure that we understood the client's objectives in terms of the functional and the social organisation of the company.**
Norman Foster

I had just moved into new offices in Bedford Street, Covent Garden. A four-storey building, it was far too large for me then but offices were difficult to come by and I intended to sublet. I was still unpacking when Norman phoned in some agitation to say that IBM had rung and would like to visit his office. At this time Norman and Wendy – and half a dozen others – were still working out of their flat in Hampstead Hill Gardens, which was effective but rather chaotic. We agreed he should borrow one of my floors and, virtually overnight, a nameplate appeared on the door, screens were found, Zeev Aram lent us some furniture and Foster Associates' Bedford Street office was in operation. Tony Hunt, 'In at the Beginning', 1991

I remember the [Covent Garden] office quite well. Its atmosphere was curiously hard to describe. The general impression was of galvanic creative forces barely under control. Somewhere at the heart of it all … lurked the contradictory figure of Foster himself: edgy, gum-chewing, exuding chutzpah. In some ways this was the most exhilarating Foster phase. It was characterised by a fevered, *Boy's Own Paper*-ish admiration for technology in all its forms, and an endearing reverence for transatlantic business practices, imbibed during Foster's graduate spell at Yale.
Alastair Best, *Design*, June 1983
Left: The entrance to Foster Associates' first studio in Bedford Street, Covent Garden, 1968-1971.

Fred Olsen was an enlightened employer and was keen to provide his workforce with good amenities. Prompted, as he has since explained, by Foster's ability to 'ask the right questions', Olsen expanded the brief to include office space for clerical staff and commissioned a passenger handling facility. Foster remembers the early presentations to Olsen:

'The first challenge was to win the client over from the competition, which was not easy. I was not up against other architects but contractors. Typically the competition would come in and make a presentation and they would talk about how the building would look. My approach was very different. I would ask questions, listen to what the client said and go away. Then I would come back and ask more questions. I made sure that I understood the client's needs both in terms of the functional and the social organisation of the company.'

**A building boom was under way but Foster waited on the sidelines. In fact they had so little work that Norman and Wendy came close to leaving Britain in search of 'a more open society'; it was only a question of whether they would emigrate to the United States or Canada.**

'Then I demonstrated that we could offer three things. Firstly, I showed that by playing the open market – buying a structure here, a cladding there – I could produce a good building for less than a builder could produce a bad one. Secondly, I proved that we could do all of that very quickly. And thirdly, I was able to bring a dimension to the project that a builder never could: to speak to industrialists in their own language. A client's needs will change. I used that fact to our advantage by stressing the importance of flexibility. I said: "You cannot know what you will need tomorrow. Your requirements could be very different in a year from now, or over the life of the building." Typically I tried to develop a project without permanently locking in how much space was designated for administration, or production and so on.

'The development period was incredibly short and so we had to challenge conventions in all kinds of ways. For example, we could not possibly have designed and prototyped the glazed curtain-wall that we wanted in the time available. And so I went on a research trip to the United States and brought back a sophisticated system that used brand new products such as heat- and light-reflective glass. Nobody had ever taken that initiative before.'

The Olsen project was a prime example of Foster's wit, his daring, his originality and his unmatchable eye for the main chance. It was this building which so impressed a string of major commercial clients, including Willis Faber & Dumas, IBM and Sir Robert Sainsbury. Foster again: 'When new clients visited the building and talked to the managers and workers, they realised just how penetrating our understanding of the needs of those users had been, and the positive effect it had on the design of the building.'

It was this freshness of approach that, in 1974, persuaded Sir Robert and Lady Sainsbury to commission Foster to design the Sainsbury Centre for Visual Arts. And the same inquisitive process was the secret of his success in winning the Hongkong and Shanghai Bank project in 1979. Long after the other competitors had left, Foster and his team stayed on in Hong Kong to discover how banking worked there and to establish what you could put in a banking hall. It was that research which led to the idea of raising the banking hall in the air, giving it a glass underbelly, and creating a public space at ground level.

2. Norman and Wendy Foster photographed by Tim Street-Porter, shortly after moving from Bedford Street into a new studio in Fitzroy Street, in 1972.

**Inflatables have been around for some time. Balloons date from the eighteenth century, airships from the nineteenth, covered life rafts from the Second World War and buildings from the AEC portable theatre of 1959. However, what went up on a frosty Sunday morning in January outside Hemel Hempstead was something rather different ... For on that day – with a great deal of snap, crackle and pop – the world's first inflatable office lifted off the snow covered ground to full inflation in 55 minutes.** Martin Pawley, *Design*, March 1970

Right: Foster's air-supported office – in the process of being inflated – on the cover of *Design*, March 1970.

1. Given a tight budget and time-frame that assumed an 'off-the-shelf' solution, Foster Associates instead designed for IBM at Cosham a 'temporary' building that has remained in constant use for more than 30 years. During that period it has been adapted several times in response to changing needs and has witnessed a revolution in communications technology.

More immediately, at the time of its completion, the Olsen project established Foster Associates – then newly settled in a studio in Bedford Street, in a still vegetable-strewn Covent Garden – as a leading practice in the new architecture of the early 1970s. But what exactly did this new architecture consist of? In many ways it was rooted in old values. One of the most attractive tenets of the Modern Movement – largely ignored by its detractors – was a genuine democracy of design.

It has been suggested that some of the social dimension in Foster's work comes from his own subconscious, from the experience of growing up in working-class Manchester and seeing the possibility of improving the quality of life for everybody. But as he says, 'irrespective of personal circumstances or environment, if you are passionate about an idea, something can come of it.'

Reliance Controls and the Olsen Amenity Centre were both, in that sense, built manifestos. Whatever his other virtues or defects, it seems to me that in his understanding of the corporate animal, and his unswerving commitment to the architecture of the bottom line, Foster in the 1970s was operating in a different league from the majority of his British contemporaries.

## In his understanding of the corporate animal and his unswerving commitment to the architecture of the bottom line, Foster in the 1970s was operating in a different league from his British contemporaries.

Noting the shift in attitudes presaged by the Olsen project, Foster talks with conviction about 'reinventing the workplace' just as in the context of the Hongkong Bank or Stansted Airport, he talks about 'reinventing the tall building' or 'reinventing the airport'. Olsen created a working environment rooted in the social realities of the present rather than the preconceptions or prejudices of the past. Foster recalls:

'One of the most satisfying aspects of the project was to see the transformation of lifestyle that followed from it. We pioneered the notion that the workplace could be a pleasant environment. We did not just provide the basics, such as showers, but also facilities for table tennis, billiards and television; and we put art on the walls. That might not seem radical now, but in the context of the period these were startling new ideas. In the docks at that time the toilet facilities were disgusting; most workers in industry were treated little better than animals. But at Olsen we found that a workforce, once notorious for its vandalism, was transformed to the point of being so possessive about its new building that they would not allow visiting truck drivers to use it because of their bad habits.'

This is not a plea for architectural determinism. 'I am not suggesting', Foster continues, 'that this apparent miracle in industrial relations – characterised by a virtual absence of unofficial strikes during the working life of the building – was due to the architecture in isolation. Rather it was the integration of a progressive management philosophy and a belief in the value of good communications between people.'

While the Olsen project was making headlines, Foster was tackling another industrial brief, for Computer Technology, an equally forward-looking client led by the charismatic Iann Barron. Computer Technology – the first company in Britain to make microchips – was expanding so quickly that it was rapidly running out of space in its existing facility, an old canning factory already transformed by Foster Associates.

**The inflatable scene is getting pretty densely populated and spreads wide: from a window full of blow-up furniture at Habitat, to a contract between Cedric Price, Frank Newby and the M of PBW for advanced research in inflatable structures: from the aluminized Warhol *Clouds* floating round Robert Fraser's gallery, to ... an exhibition of 'Structures Gonflables' last month in Paris. You name it, someone is blowing it up right now.** Reyner Banham, *New Society*, 18 April 1968

Right: Second World War barrage balloons – antecedents of the inflatable technology described by Banham.

Plans to construct a new building alongside were crucially delayed by planning red tape. The brief – precisely the kind that inspired Foster to his most brilliantly inventive solutions – was to provide 8,000 square feet of temporary office accommodation in only twelve weeks, including ordering and fitting out. All 'off-the-peg' forms of temporary building were investigated and, as later at IBM, found wanting. The quickest, cheapest and by far the most elegant option was an air-supported bubble.

There was great interest in air structures among the architectural avant-garde in the early 1970s. They had been used for a wide range of purposes, from military stores to golf driving ranges, but never before for offices. There were some doubts about their thermal and acoustic performance. And there was the small matter of convincing the local authority that it was safe to put office workers into a structure that could swiftly deflate and engulf them all. The last of these problems was resolved with characteristic panache: a row of angled booms, running along each of the long sides of the tent which carried the fluorescent lighting fixtures – designed to reflect light off the white PVC skin – would also have held the deflating fabric clear of the escape routes in the event of a collapse.

The elegance of this solution is a form of thrift: typical of the manner in which Foster was able to extract 'more with less'. It was a similarly 'against the clock' brief that inspired perhaps the most admired building of Foster's early period, the pilot head office building – or 'instant office' – designed for IBM at Cosham on the outskirts of Portsmouth. To understand the scope of Foster's achievement at Cosham, it is important to grasp that IBM had intended to install its 750 staff members on the site in temporary wooden structures until the permanent head office it planned to build nearby was ready. The challenge was to demonstrate that it was possible to provide an equally economical, but far more elegant purpose-designed pavilion within the allotted budget and time scale. As usual, all the options were explored, and set out in an immaculate, yellow-covered design report. This demonstrated how a single-storey envelope could preserve views, retain trees, provide ample space for car parking and still allow for expansion if required: all at less cost per square foot than the equivalent 'off-the-shelf' structures.

Notwithstanding its temporary status, the deep-plan building was designed for maximum long-term flexibility, and 'integration' was a dominating theme, as Foster recalls: 'We challenged the conventional wisdom that the (then mainframe) computer should have its own separate *shrine* and integrated it within our office building. We anticipated the fact that computer usage would ephemeralise and change, that it was not a sacred object.'

## There was great interest in air structures among the architectural avant-garde in the early 1970s. They had been used for a wide range of purposes, from military stores to golf driving ranges, but never for offices.

The key to the building's long life and evolving usage is Foster's prescient attitude to services provision. Except for the computer room, which had a raised floor, all the service runs were contained in the depth of the roof space (SCSD again) and carried down the structural columns to rectangular 'dice boxes' for local distribution. IBM has several times availed itself of the flexibility thus offered: the staff restaurant has been moved and the computer room expanded twice. In 1985, the building, which by then had far exceeded its design life, was repainted and recarpeted and a massive amount of extra cabling inserted in the ceiling void to extend its lease of life still further.

2. The air-supported structure for Computer Technology – 800 square metres of temporary office space provided in just eight weeks, including ordering and fitting out – is the most ephemeral of Foster's buildings and perhaps illustrates most convincingly his ability to do 'more with less'.

> I have always believed that architecture is about people. At one extreme is the private inner sanctum that it can create, at the other are those outdoor public spaces which are, in turn, 'enclosed' by it. In between such public and private domains the edges can be consciously or unconsciously blurred, to create or modify communities by sustaining, erecting or breaking down social barriers. Such an approach involves value judgements by attempting to ask the right questions. It suggests an interactive process between those who initiate buildings, those who use them, and those who design them. Another way of saying teamwork. Norman Foster, RIBA Royal Gold Medal address, London, 21 June 1983

1. The Hackney special care unit's 'kit-of-parts' approach and flexible plan set the standard for the design of schools for handicapped children. This was to be the first of a series of Foster projects to meet the challenge of designing buildings for people with special needs.

Until the advent of Willis Faber & Dumas, the deep-plan serviced shed, with fixed services but undifferentiated floor space, was the building type for which Foster Associates was known. But the practice's appeal extended well beyond the kind of client who might normally be interested in commissioning industrial buildings. In fact the 'industrialised' nature of those early buildings resulted more from a quest for economy of means – doing 'more with less' – than from any aesthetic preoccupation. For Foster, 'prefabrication has never been a goal in itself. It is simply a way of achieving higher standards for the building and its users in an economical way.'

It is indicative of the universality of this approach that it could be applied, with equal success, to a domestic scale when the Spastics Society commissioned a special care unit, for handicapped children suffering from a broad range of mental and physical disabilities. Until a change in legislation brought them under the umbrella of the Department of Education and Science, such children were looked after either at home, or in a hospital or, if they were lucky, in junior training centres run by the local authority. The special care unit that Foster designed in the London borough of Hackney was therefore intended as a prototype school. A cheap, portable kit-of-parts, it was designed to be bolted on to existing property, set up alongside special schools or form a building in its own right.

Ever since Lubetkin and Tecton's Finsbury Health Centre, in the 1930s, there has been an honourable link in Britain between modern architecture and care. The special care unit at Hackney, like Finsbury, was an attempt to bring rational principles and modern construction techniques to bear on the problem. Essentially it was the shed solution in microcosm: a large core contained lavatories and bathing facilities for often severely incontinent children, with lots of flexible space divided by full-height sliding screens leading out on to a hard play area.

I greatly admired this modest little building, especially the courage with which it tackled head-on one of the main problems of spasticity – incontinence – and made it the focus of the scheme. The Palmerston Special School, located in a tough, vandal-prone area of Liverpool, extended these ideas into a larger building, with top-lighting and a less severe roof line based on lightweight steel portals linked into five bays.

Not many architectural practices can claim to have covered such a wide span of work in their first few years as Foster Associates. But then few architects have ever exhibited quite the same insatiable desire to design and build. Looking through this book one is immediately struck by the range of projects that Foster was prepared to take on.

## Looking back on this early period it is obvious that this is a young man's work, full of freshness, vitality and optimism.

While the core of the practice was centred on industrial or commercial buildings, there are also forays into town planning, private and public housing, shops and showrooms, and special schools. Most surprising of all perhaps, was the planning study carried out for Fred Olsen on the island of Gomera, then the only island in the Canaries group still unravaged by tourism. This extremely sensitive little document questioned such *idées fixes* as the construction of an airport and ring roads, and proposed a revival of vernacular building techniques and alternative energy sources. If only it had been put into effect.

Looking back on this early period it is obvious that this is a young man's work, full of freshness, vitality and optimism. Norman once said of Buckminster Fuller: 'The thing about Bucky is that he makes you believe anything is possible'. The same could be said, in those exhilarating first years, of Foster himself.

**Foster Associates' work is not stylistically unified; rather, a series of master-concepts – the glass box, the metal shed, the downtown polygon – have leapfrogged cyclically through their work, appearing in modified form at each reincarnation. What continues consistently throughout is a fastidious, elegant but conspicuous minimalism in detailing, usually involving the edge-to-edge conditions of lightweight materials.** Reyner Banham, *Foster Associates*, 1979
Right: The cover of the catalogue accompanying the 1979 RIBA Heinz Gallery exhibition of the work of Foster Associates.

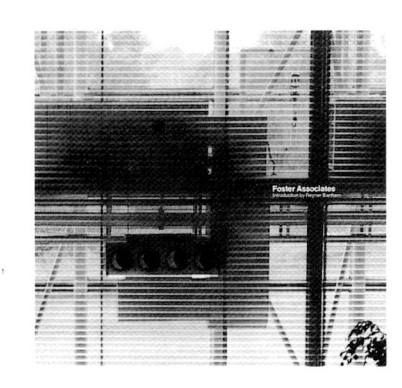

2. Norman Foster photographed with John Harris, curator of the RIBA Drawings Collection, outside the 'Foster Associates' exhibition at the Heinz Gallery in London, 1979. A full-size mock-up of the structural system for the Foster residence – one of the projects featured in the exhibition – was erected outside the gallery.

In The Beginning

# Connections  Newport School

Newport School introduced a concept that was explored widely in the Foster oeuvre throughout the 1970s and '80s – the serviced umbrella roof. Designed to create almost infinitely flexible, 'universal' enclosures, which could be easily reconfigured to meet changing uses and evolving needs, the umbrella concept informed projects as diverse as Norman Foster's factory systems studies of 1969, through shopping and leisure building projects to facilities for IBM at Cosham and Greenford. Indeed IBM Greenford represents both the zenith and the end of the umbrella concept. In later projects, such as the Renault Centre and Stansted Airport, a radically different approach to flexible space was developed, in which heavy structure and overhead servicing gave way to diaphanous enclosures with an emphasis on natural toplight. Clues to this new direction can be detected in the early 'umbrella' projects. For example, the structure of the Leisure Centres heralds the Stansted 'trees', while the internal street of the German Car Centre anticipates Stansted's internal servicing road.

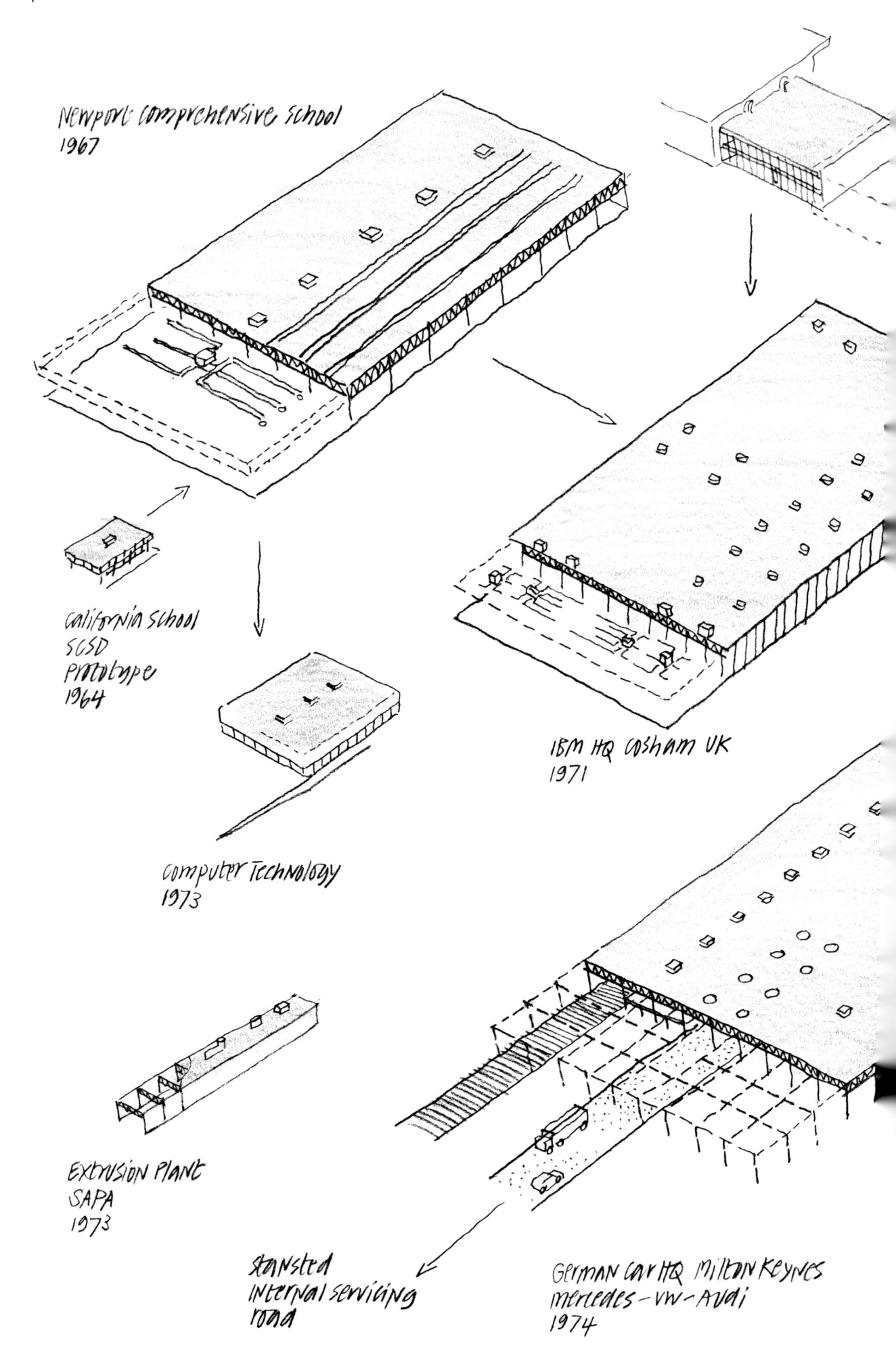

Newport Comprehensive School 1967

California School SCSD Prototype 1964

IBM HQ Cosham UK 1971

Computer Technology 1973

Extrusion Plant SAPA 1973

Stansted internal servicing road

German Car HQ Milton Keynes Mercedes – VW – Audi 1974

Olsen Centre Millwall Dock
London 1970

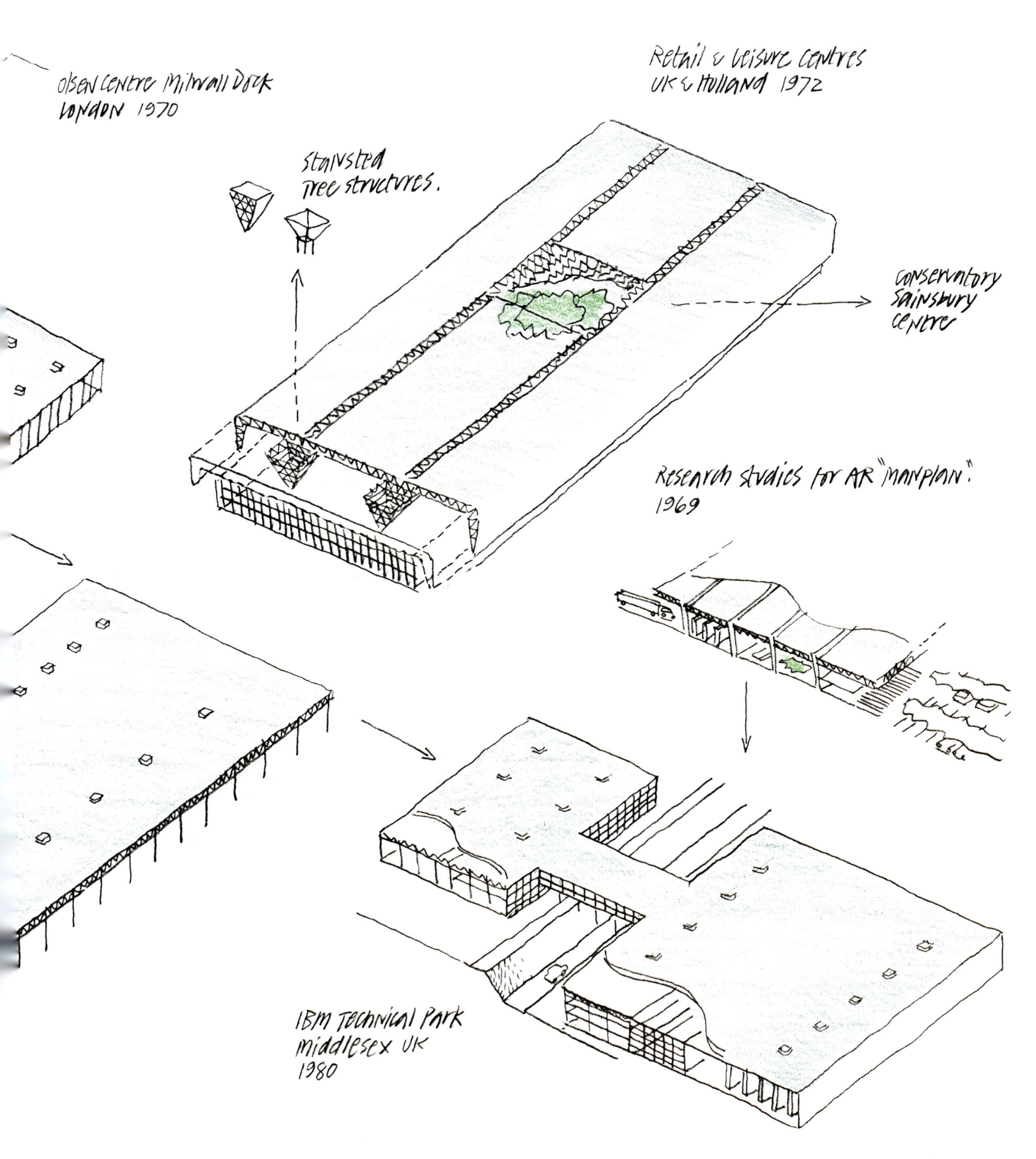

Retail & Leisure Centres
UK & Holland 1972

Stansted
tree structures.

Conservatory
Sainsbury
Centre

Research studies for AR "manplan"
1969

IBM Technical Park
Middlesex UK
1980

NF France
August 2002

# Newport School
Gwent, Wales 1967

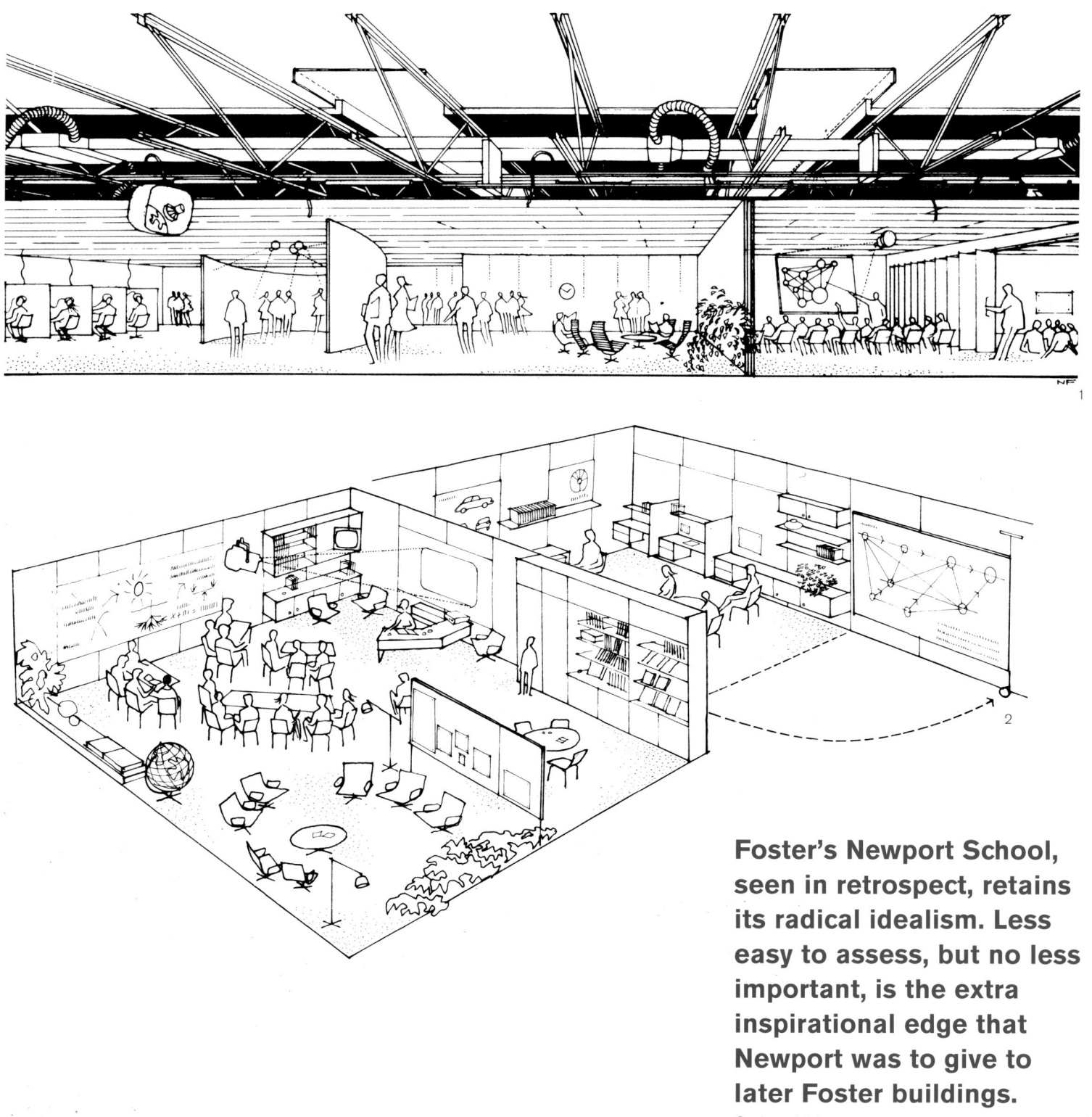

**Foster's Newport School, seen in retrospect, retains its radical idealism. Less easy to assess, but no less important, is the extra inspirational edge that Newport was to give to later Foster buildings.**
Graham Vickers

**The Newport School had a very special place in our memories because, although unbuilt, it did strongly influence our later work. It was very disappointing not to win, but we continued to draw and develop the project long after the competition itself. In many ways it proved to be a model for the IBM Pilot Head Office at Cosham which could not otherwise have been realised in that form so quickly.** Norman Foster, *Norman Foster: Sketches*, 1992

**The intention at Newport was to show that a generous roof umbrella could accommodate not only the requirements of the brief – which were absolutely traditional – but other approaches to education as well. If there had been a will to explore these other approaches – which were to do with newer technologies and the breaking down of the more rigid educational patterns associated with repetitive classroom units – then this scheme would have been very sensitive to such uses. It was more an educational tool than a fixed building.** Norman Foster in conversation with Graham Vickers, 1989

Foster Associates' 1967 Newport School competition entry can be seen as one of the most important buildings the practice never built. Today, Norman Foster will go so far as to say that: 'Without the knowledge we gained from Newport, it would not have been possible to do IBM Cosham. Arguably, Newport also made the Olsen Amenity Centre the very swift reality it turned out to be, and IBM Greenford, too, is more easily explained in terms of what we learnt there'. Certainly some links – notably those to do with the relationship of structure, services, skin and overall flexibility – are clearly traceable in these buildings.

However, Newport also symbolises another of Foster's long-term preoccupations. It answers the brief on its own terms while at the same time seeking to introduce an extra social dimension. That dimension often surfaces as a possibility, as some encouragement to change the accepted order of things or at least to look anew at how people are accommodated by buildings, which can too easily perpetuate outmoded attitudes.

On the surface the Newport competition brief did not encourage innovation. Traditional requirements, based upon conventional classrooms, had to be realised within (then) Department of Education and Science cost limits. Foster's response was particularly imaginative. It used the school as a vehicle for exploring a systems approach to a multi-use building. Various alternative uses for the building as a whole were proposed and encouraged. Module-free flexible spaces were posited. New educational possibilities were enabled.

The building envelope conceived to contain this was a compact single-storey structure with a constant-height roof umbrella incorporating all the mechanical and electrical services. A proportion of deep-planned teaching spaces was assumed, although other possibilities were implied: for example, internal lightwells and outdoor courts could be introduced where appropriate. The whole building system was designed to stimulate an immediate sense of orientation and community. The main circulation hall was a social focus and, with its views into teaching spaces, promoted spectator involvement in a wide range of activities. Direct access to outdoors and a variety of internal spaces were intended to make for a pleasing mix of aspects in use. Whether consciously or otherwise, this planning arrangement was to serve as a model for the IBM pilot head office, which followed a few years later.

1. Norman Foster discovered at Yale the importance of communicating radical ideas in a simple and 'friendly' way, as in this drawing. The sectional perspective, which mixed the technical and social aspects of a design, was to become one of the key drawings in Foster Associates' repertoire.

2. Norman Foster prepared several drawings to convey the social possibilities of the scheme. With top-down servicing (note the projector) and moveable partitions, independent of a structural grid, these demonstrated how larger or smaller teaching spaces could be created at will.

3. In response to a request by Cedric Price, who wanted a drawing of the Newport project for a special edition of *AD* he was preparing, Norman Foster drew this sketch in an attempt to capture the essence of the scheme in a single image.

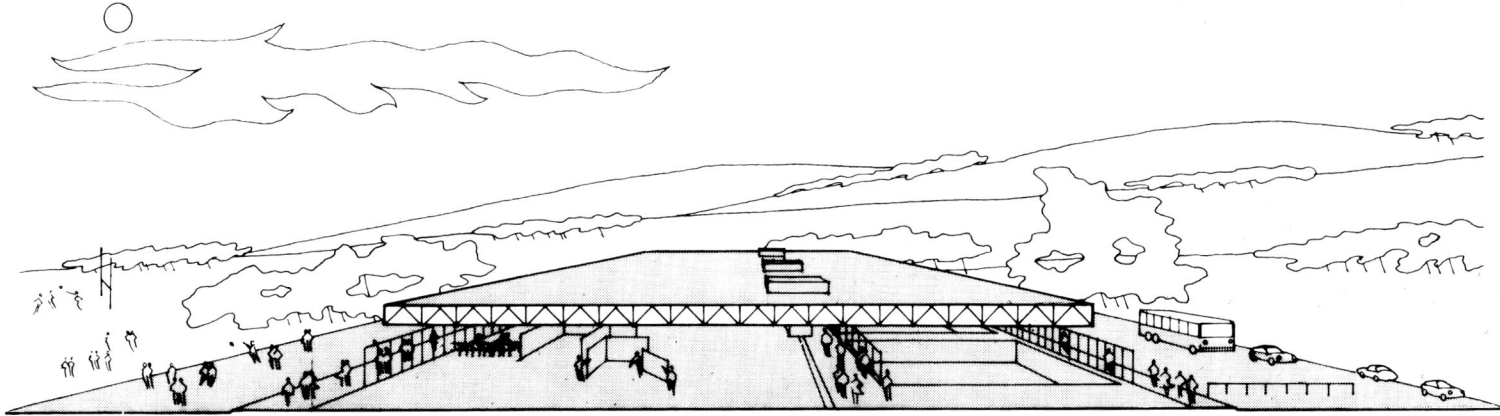

**Much of Foster's early work was influenced by the SCSD model. As well as offering economic advantages and ease of prefabrication, this highly-flexible structural and planning concept suited Foster's functional and social aims of providing for changes of use and improving the workplace by pooling resources and encouraging conventionally separate classes of workers to share the same spaces and amenities.** Chris Abel, 'From Hard to Soft Machines', 1991
Left: Ezra Ehrenkrantz's prototype SCSD (School Construction Systems Development) building of 1964.

**Newport Comprehensive School was used as a vehicle for exploring a systems approach to multi-use buildings. The deep-plan form was a response to social aims and to the economics of flexibility. By rationalising the components down to relatively few, highly repetitive elements, and balancing an expensive infill against a more straightforward low-cost enclosure, the scheme was priced within the then current cost limits.** Norman Foster, *RIBA Journal*, June 1970

1, 2. The 137 metre by 80 metre rectangle of the school was covered by a 1.2-metre deep space-frame roof of welded steel lattice trusses, whose edges would have been exposed on all sides. The only elements to project through the roof were plant rooms and air-conditioning units. The building's structural grid was rectangular; this is reflected in the perimeter column spacing of 17 metres on the long elevations and 12 metres at each end.

3. The shading effect of the deep overhang was explored in detailed elevation studies – something that would become a characteristic Foster Associates' technique.

**On the surface the Newport brief did not encourage innovation. Traditional requirements had to be realised within DES cost limits, but Foster's response was particularly imaginative. It used the school as the vehicle for exploring a systems approach to what was a multi-use building.**
Graham Vickers

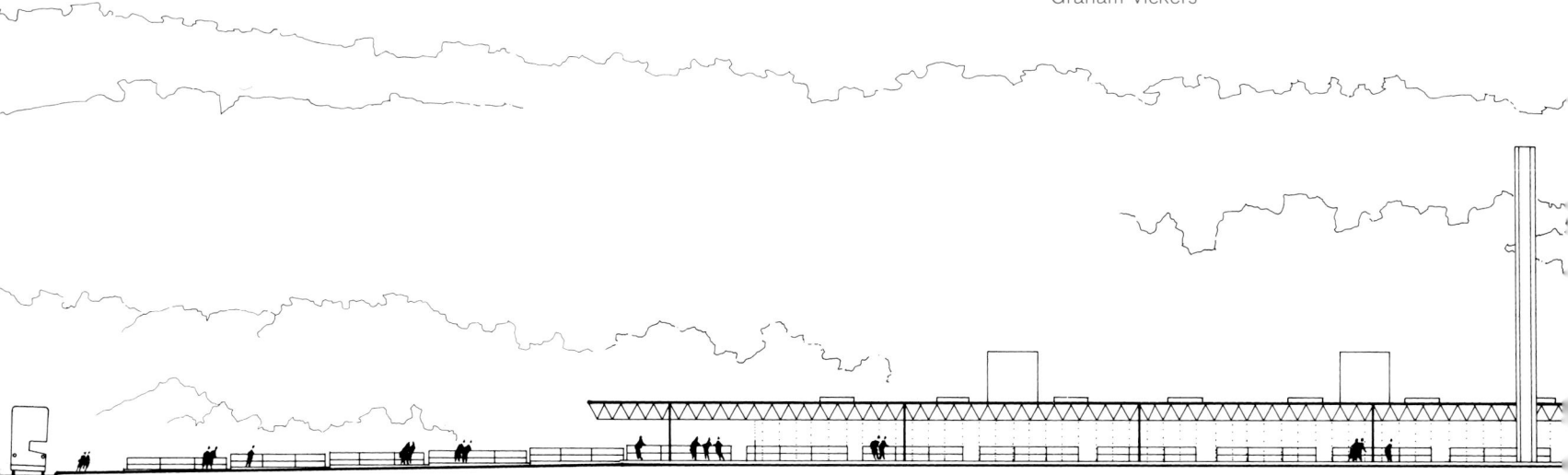

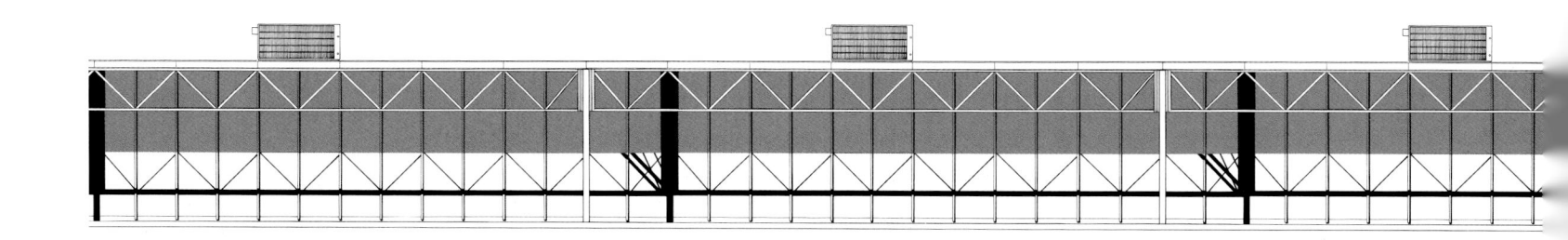

**If the major concern is to increase the capacity of the individual to learn throughout life, then an entirely different attitude to the conditions under which such learning can take place is necessary. … The classroom is probably the strongest of all educational totems – its very name presupposing a rigidness irrelevant to present day educational patterning.** Cedric Price, *Architectural Design*, May 1968.
Right: Cedric Price edited this special edition of *AD* on the subject of building for education, in which Foster's Newport School scheme was cited as a model for a new 'flexible and realistic' approach towards facility design.
Far right: Pages from the issue illustrate variations in classroom design and their corresponding impact on modes of teaching and learning.

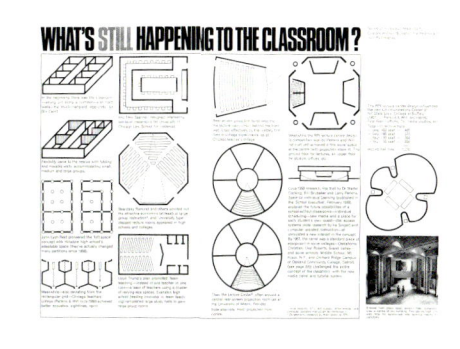

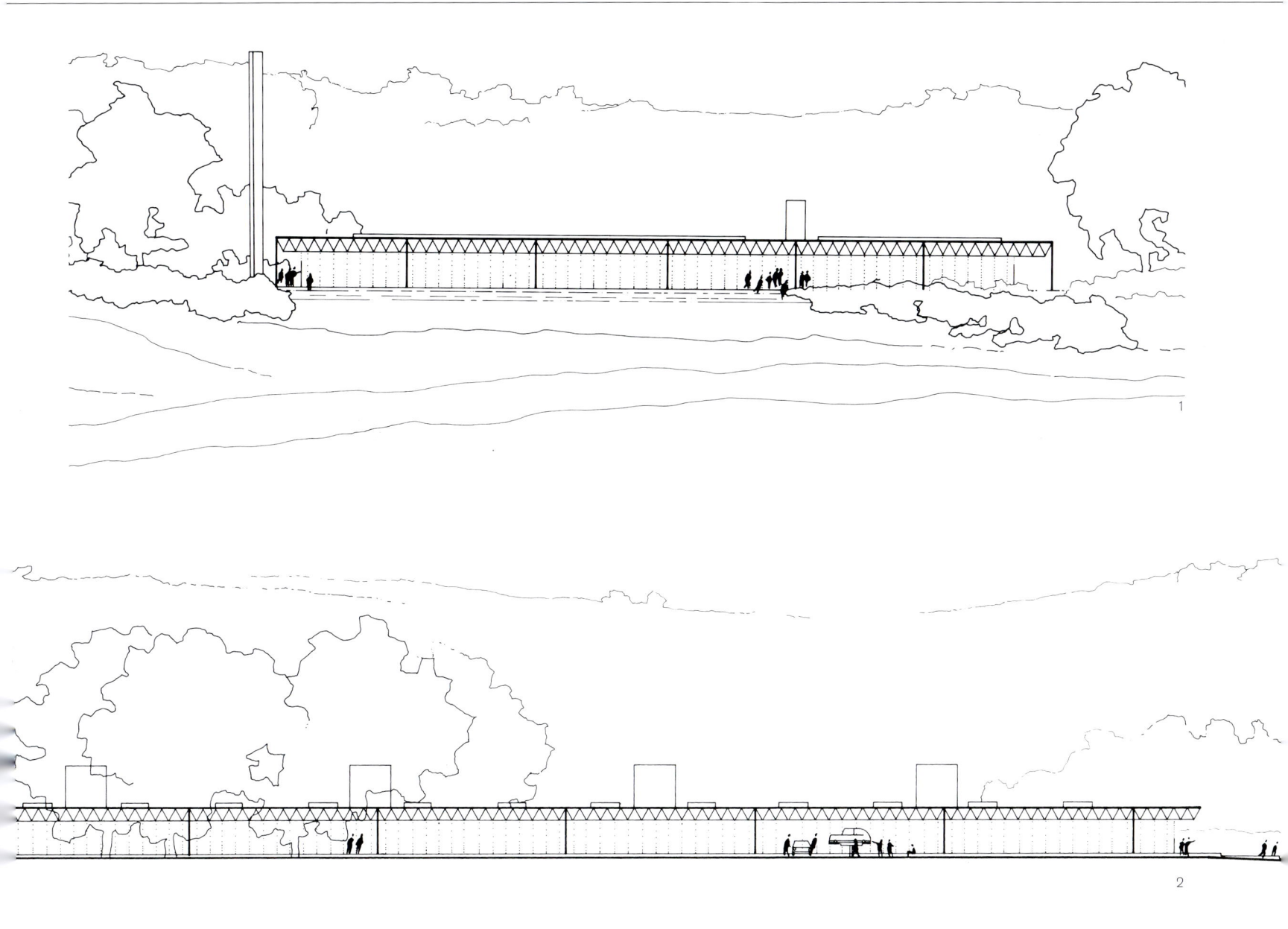

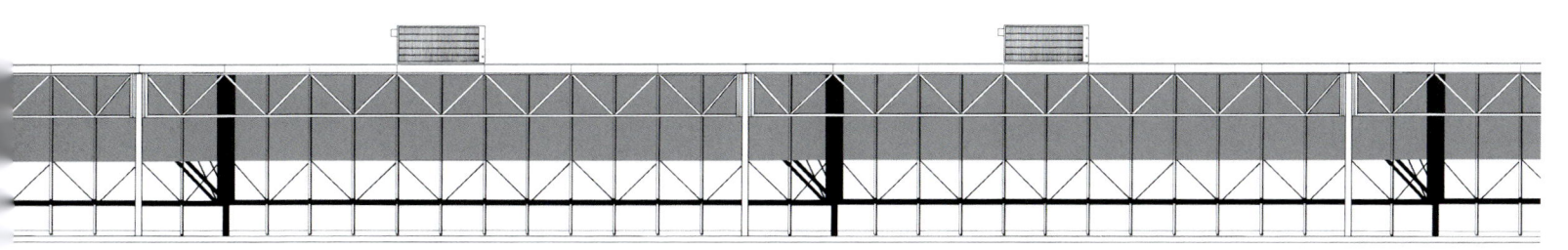

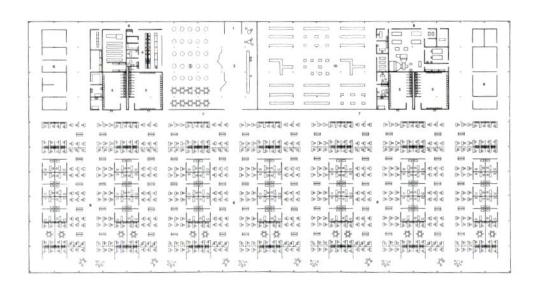

**The Newport School systems study showed the perimeter of the building as a lattice structure, giving an overhang for circulation with the glass wall set back. On the IBM project we introduced the glass skin outside and took advantage of the same perimeter walkway, but now inside the building itself.** Norman Foster, lecture at Hong Kong University, 2 February 1980

Left: An early plan of the space utilisation at IBM Cosham illustrates the family resemblance.
Right: The perimeter walkway at IBM Cosham which developed an idea first explored in the Newport School.

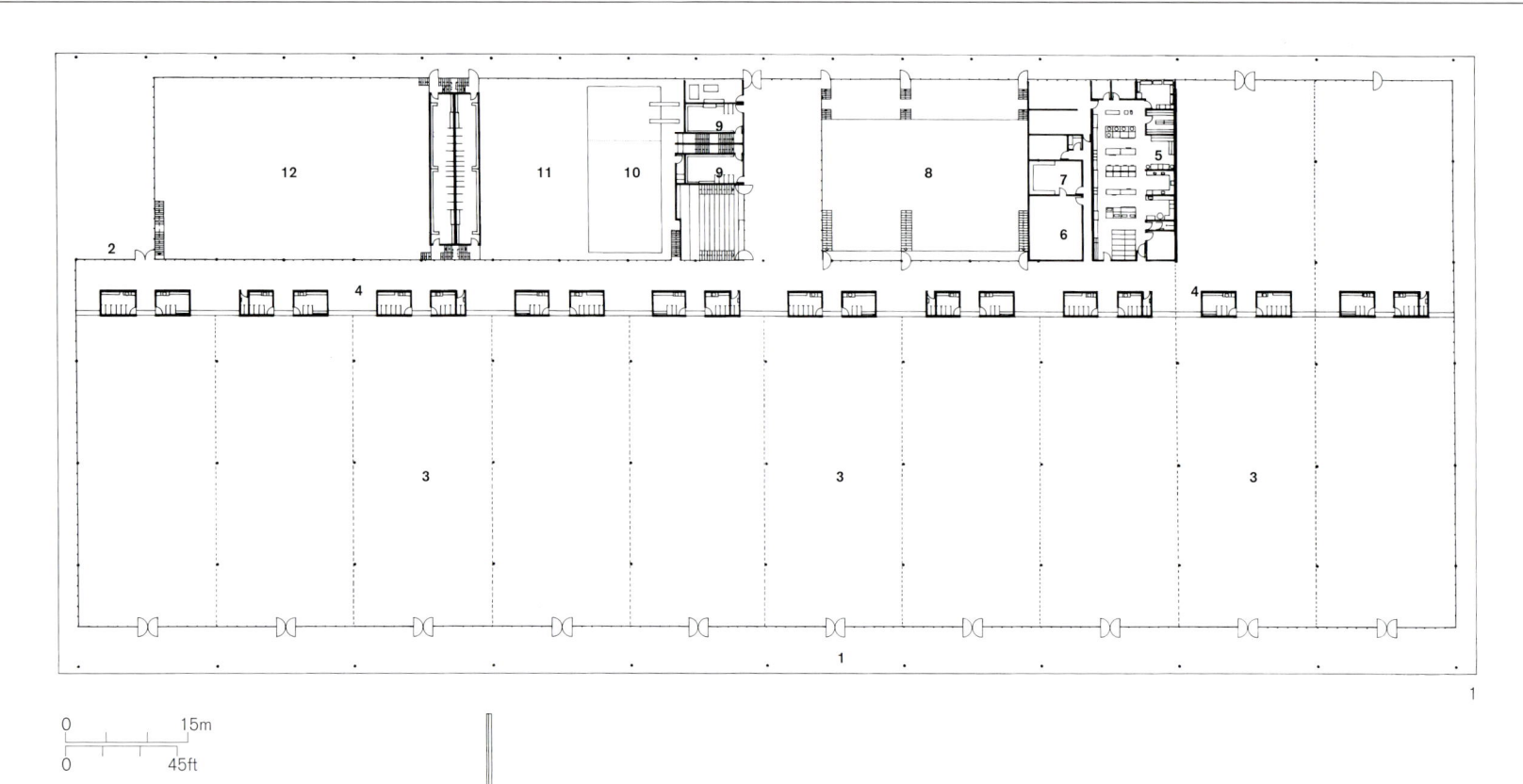

1, 2. Two-thirds of the plan consisted of flexible, top-lit teaching space that could be subdivided in an almost limitless number of ways. The remaining third, which contained a wide variety of fixed functions, was articulated by a spine of cloakrooms and lavatories above a long service duct.

1 covered circulation area
2 entrance
3 teaching areas
4 lavatories
5 kitchen
6 plant room
7 store
8 assembly hall
9 changing rooms
10 swimming pool
11 gymnasium
12 sports hall

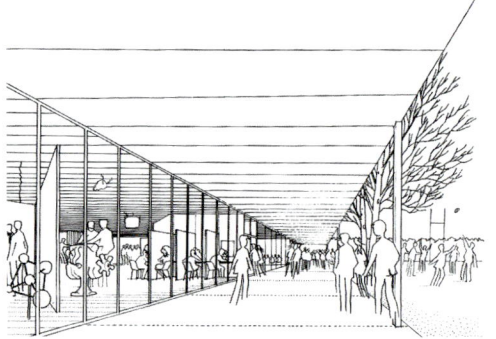

134  Norman Foster  Works 1

Right: The concept of flexibility in use, which the Newport School pioneered, is again being investigated by the Foster studio in the design of the City Academies (2001-2004), a new type of school which will provide a sports-oriented education for eleven to eighteen-year-olds. The school has no corridors; instead, running the full length of the building, is a full-height galleria or internal 'street'. The street is wide enough to create a sense of space – even during busy change-over periods. Again, as in Newport, classrooms are arranged in two bands on either side of the street, one deeper than the other to facilitate variations in internal planning.

**The scheme meant that you could have a school that would have corridors and classrooms and so on, but you could also have independent planning geometries. I don't believe that we've done anything else, before or since, with quite that extraordinary degree of flexibility.**

Norman Foster

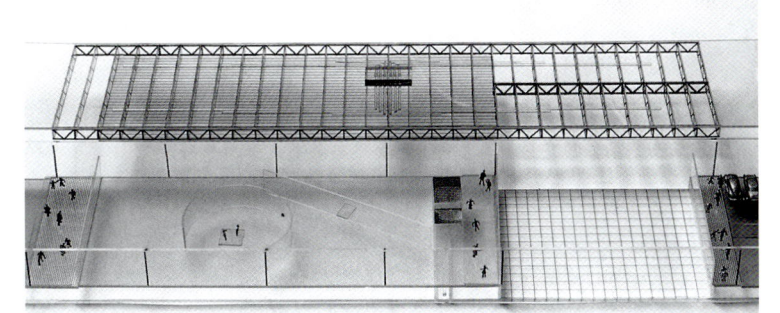

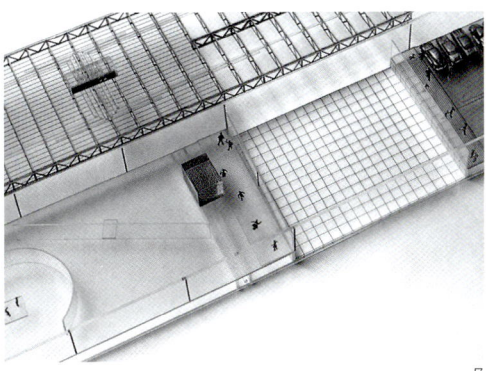

3. Norman Foster's sketch shows how apparently incompatible activities might be accommodated beneath the school's generous roof umbrella, with acoustic isolation facilitated by glazed, high-performance moveable partitions.

4. In an age before solar-reflective glass, full-height glazing required effective shading. Following the SCSD model, Foster put this practical constraint to good use, creating a protected circulation zone right round the building.

5. The roof service zone seen in plan, with the air conditioning and other service runs standardised within the space-frame.

6, 7. Photographs of the competition model showing the basic structural frame, the roof service zone and some of the free-form planning possibilities that could be explored.

Newport School 135

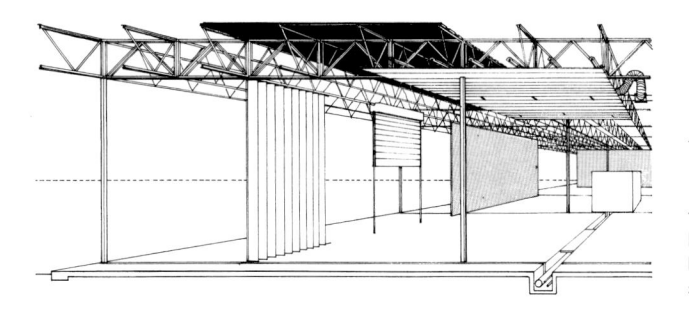

Left: A cutaway drawing of the Newport School illustrates the family resemblance between this project and Reliance Controls (right). However, the small service duct recessed into the ground slab is the only relic of the floor distribution system used at Swindon. As shown here, the perimeter of the building could include horizontal and vertical sliding doors, and sandwich panel solid wall sections, as well as full-height standard glazing.

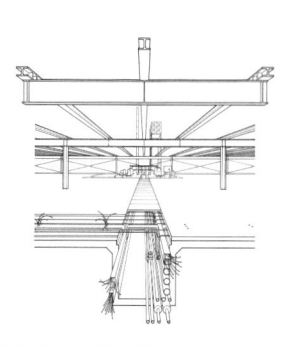

1. A perspective section showing the air-conditioning ducting inside the roof service zone above one of the fixed-plan areas of the school. The large cowlings to the right are part of the ventilation and extraction system for the school's kitchens.

Norman Foster suggests that an important aspect of the Newport scheme, which has occasionally been overlooked, was the practical aspect of creating adaptable spaces – areas that could be flexible because of their design:

'The scheme meant that you could have an orthogonal structural geometry', says Foster, 'In other words you could have a school that would have corridors and classrooms and so on. But you could also have independent planning geometries. I don't believe that we've done anything else, before or since, with quite that extraordinary degree of flexibility. There was no module, and the idea of a very simple bungee rubber gasket at the junction of wall and ceiling meant that we were freed from the grid. Architects – and we are no exception – can tend to get wedded to a grid.'

Working closely with a number of potential manufacturers and consultants, the practice was able to reduce the building's elements to relatively few. Furthermore, a reliance upon lightweight steel construction, widely available components and a high degree of off-site prefabrication, conferred significant cost and programme advantages. This systems approach, combined with the decision to balance a sophisticated, flexible interior against a simple low-cost enclosure, enabled Foster to price the scheme within the stipulated cost limits.

Since those limits traditionally implied solutions that were cheap in the pejorative as well as the financial sense of the word, a scheme as rich as this represented an unexpected level of quality.

**Long-term flexibility was enabled by a variety of means, capable of altering what might normally be treated as immovable features: external doors could be repositioned, or lavatories relocated at any point along the spine duct, and even the building itself could be extended.**

This approach clearly reflected the work of the SCSD (School Construction Systems Development) programme initiated by Ezra Ehrenkrantz in California in 1964, which had already embodied the notion of active participation by industry in this field.

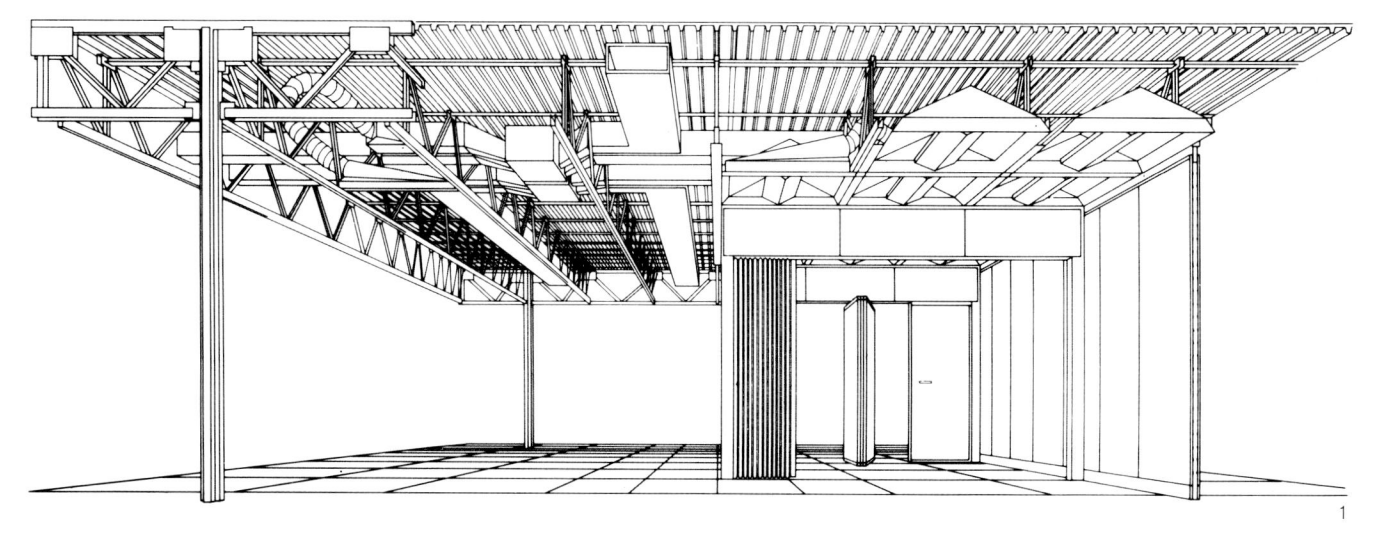

The Newport School scheme allowed Foster to explore and resolve the operational flexibility which would be crucial to later projects such as the offices for Willis Faber & Dumas (1971-1975). As proposed in the Newport School scheme, Willis Faber's services are contained in the floor and ceiling zones, affording maximum versatility in the use of floor space and ensuring that any desired changes can be effected both swiftly and economically.
Left and right: Willis Faber's purpose-designed ceiling system integrates lighting and air distribution.

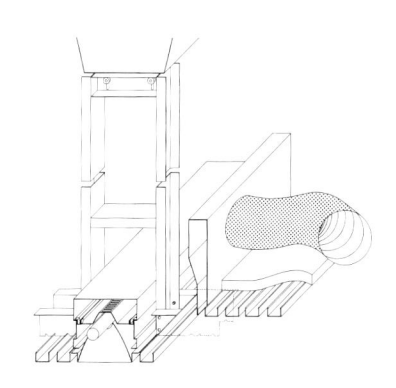

Along with the free interior plan, a flexible heating and cooling system was proposed in order to respond to layout changes by means of precise zoning control. With all roof-lights sealed, this was intended to achieve a highly controllable internal environment within a deep-plan building. In teaching and administrative areas, the cooling target was to reduce internal heat gains on hot days to match external shade temperatures. While comfort conditions would not have been those of a fully air-conditioned school, they would certainly have been superior to those provided in an ordinary perimeter-glazed school with opening windows.

Three levels of operational flexibility were envisaged for the building. An immediate degree of flexibility would come from the rearrangement of proprietary pvc-faced steel partitions, bleacher seating, loose furniture and external barrier rails. Short-term flexibility, such as alternative weekend or vacation usage, for example, could be achieved by rearranging the demountable partitions. Long-term flexibility was enabled by a variety of means, capable of altering what might normally be treated as immovable features: external doors could be repositioned, lavatories relocated at any point along the spine duct, and even the building itself could be extended.

**Without the knowledge we gained from Newport, it would not have been possible to do IBM Cosham. Arguably, Newport also made the Olsen Amenity Centre the very swift reality it turned out to be, and IBM Greenford, too, is more easily explained in terms of what we learnt there.**
Norman Foster

Such provisions revealed the depth of the practice's early commitment to the notion of flexibility. Clearly that commitment went beyond using ingenious 'quick-release' design solutions, and extended to the concept of a more elastic, creative and cost-effective use of the building all year round.

Like many unrealised projects, Foster's Newport School, seen in retrospect, retains its radical idealism. Less easy to assess, but no less important, is the extra inspirational edge that Newport was to give to later Foster buildings. The practice was primed to tackle future problems not only with a far greater knowledge of integrated systems, but also with a degree of what might be called creative impatience, an eagerness to show just how well such systems could work. That eagerness was soon to be rewarded.

Graham Vickers

2. An assembly detail of the roof service zone, which was contained by a flush ceiling of Georgian wired glass. The ceiling allowed daylight transmission through the service zone, from rooflights above, without disrupting the service runs. It also allowed leaks or malfunctions within the service zone to be found and remedied immediately, protected the light-fittings, and provided a secure surface to receive the foam rubber acoustic seals of the moveable partitions.

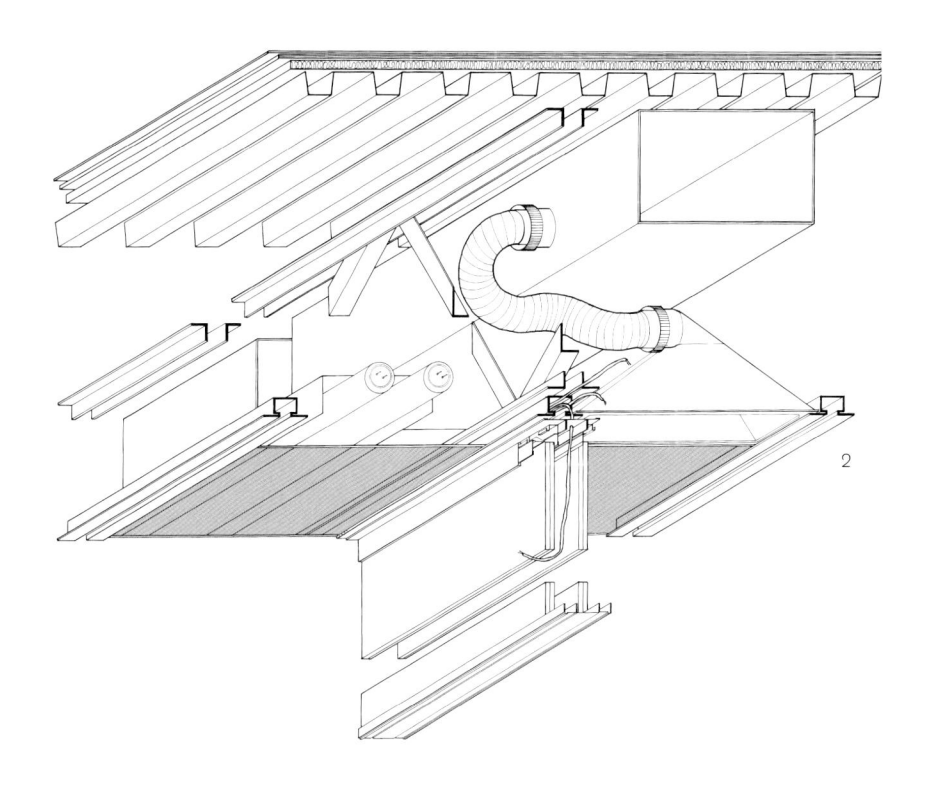

# Factory Systems

1969–1972

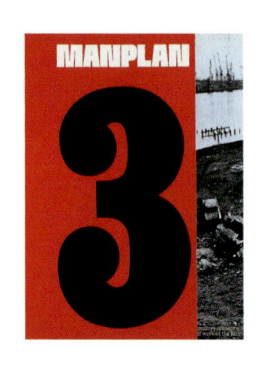

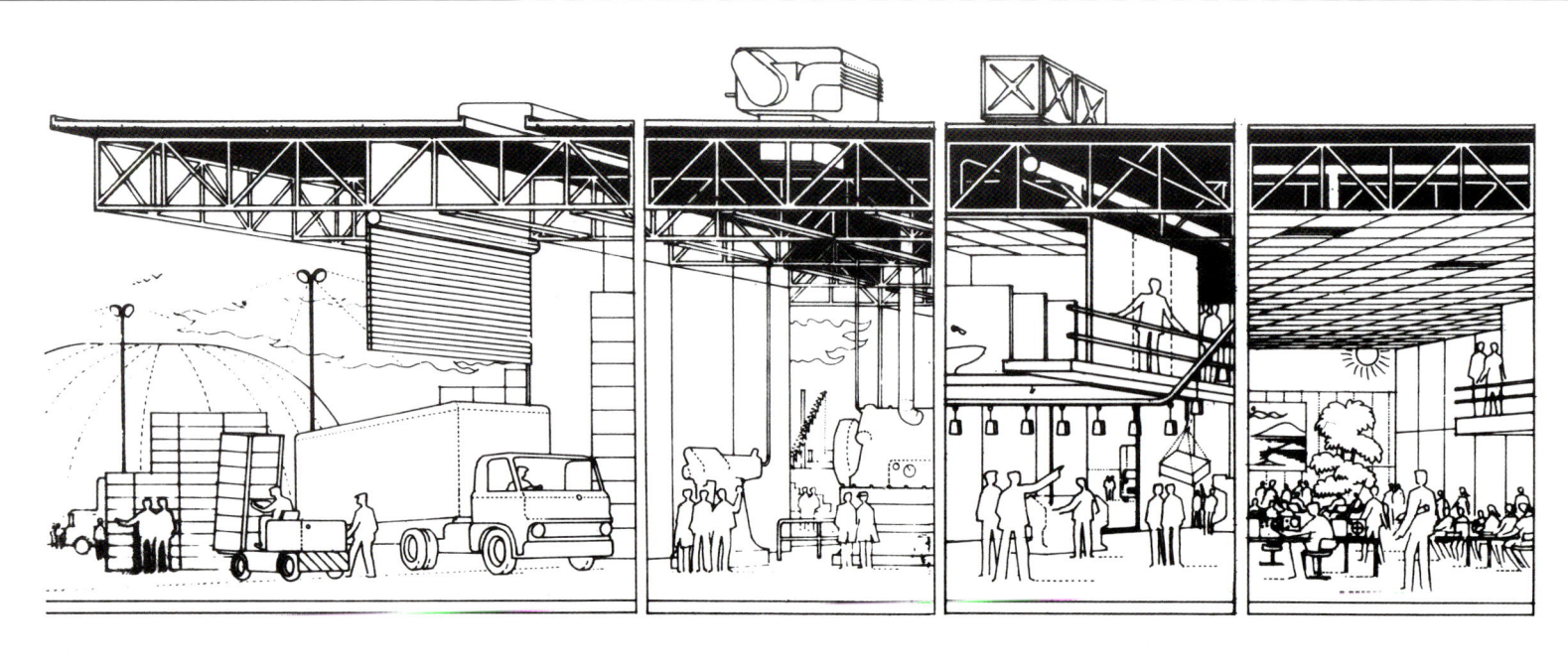

> **The advance factory system should never be taken by surprise, whatever activity the incoming firms want to pursue inside it.**
> Norman Foster

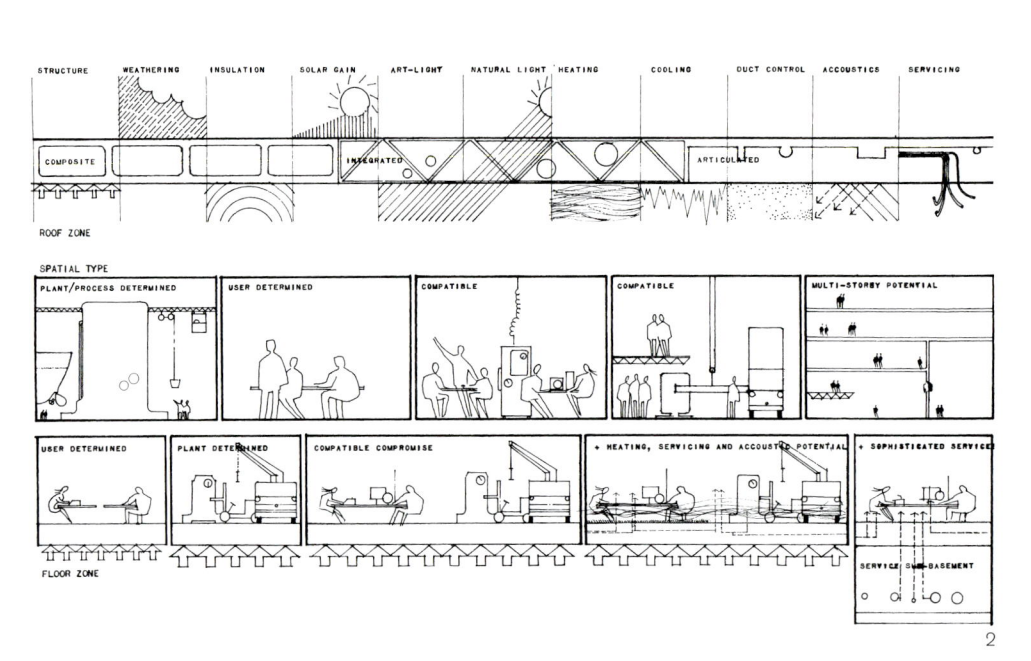

**Traditional barriers in industry are falling. The management box-production shack ... is fast being replaced in some of the newer industries by buildings in which the physical boundaries between production and administration are disappearing ... Whatever the scale, the architectural emphasis is on flexibility and the capacity to expand. Modern industry is no longer able to think in terms of finite monuments. No more should architects.** Editorial from 'Manplan 3', *The Architectural Review*, November 1969
Left: The title page of 'Manplan 3', which was guest-edited by Norman Foster.
Right: Examples of the decay and social dislocation of the British industrial landscape in the late 1960s.

1. Norman Foster seized the opportunity of 'Manplan' to develop ideas raised by the Newport School competition. Drawn by Foster himself, this sectional perspective became a key image of the period, demonstrating in one immediately understandable drawing the practice's total commitment and philosophy. It embodies all the issues and concerns that would command the practice's full attention over the next few years. Under a space-frame umbrella roof – housing services, with roof-top tanks and air-conditioning units – a double-height space can be adapted to a multiplicity of functions: less a town workshop, more a workshop embracing a town.

2. The different demands placed on a fully flexible factory system were itemised by Norman Foster in one simple diagram. It includes alternative roof structures of varying benefits and potential, as well as enclosed spaces with different industrial functions made flexible and compatible by design.

During 1969 when politicians and pundits were eagerly preparing for the 1970s, Norman Foster was invited by editor Tim Rock to guest-edit 'Manplan 3', one of a series of eight special issues published by *The Architectural Review* during late 1969 and early 1970.

With little work in the office, Norman and Wendy Foster were contemplating a move to the richer pastures of North America. There is a certain irony, therefore, that it was Manplan's aim to review the 'state of the nation', covering everything from education to religion and from housing to industry. Subtitled 'Town Workshop', 'Manplan 3' came out in November 1969 and was devoted to industrial buildings. It asked, 'Is technology for or against us?', expressed alarm at the general acceptance of industrial squalor and proposed positive alternatives. Part of Foster's contribution to the issue was a proposal for a multi-purpose industrial building system. In 1969 statistics showed that almost one in ten people employed in manufacturing worked for companies that had either moved or opened branch factories since the War. It was primarily for these industrialists' needs that Foster's 'advance factory' was designed.

Much of the industrial expansion of the period was taking place in new towns and development areas within industrial estates, which might contain a variety of activities from light engineering to electronics or even office use. The prerequisite of the advance factory was that it 'should never be taken by surprise, whatever activity the incoming firms want to pursue inside it'. With this in mind, Foster produced a composite perspective drawing demonstrating the logic of a multi-purpose system. Within a uniform structural envelope he housed a factory with its production areas, offices and storage, a teaching space, even a supermarket and a visitors' centre.

Foster noted that for every industrialist prepared to consult an architect in planning his company's short- and long-term needs, there were hundreds who were not. Most could be expected to haggle over the price and specification of a complex piece of plant to the last ball-bearing or nut and bolt, but would buy an off-the-peg shed costing ten times as much with no clearer brief than 'a great big space at a rock-bottom price'. Questions about maintenance, heating and lighting costs were often never asked.

**If his early architecture is influenced by the SCSD building type, Foster never accepted the implied defeatism in Ehrenkrantz's approach ... which left architects bereft of any design role. The Foster team's highly professional skills as both industrial designers and architects separates their factory-made architecture from that of the industrialised building movement as a whole.** Chris Abel, 'From Hard to Soft Machines', 1991
Left: A view into the roof servicing zone of Ezra Ehrenkrantz's iconic SCSD prototype building of 1964.
Right: A worm's-eye view of the SCSD model reveals the steel construction, corrugated decking and integration of heating and ventilation trunking, all of which were to feature in Foster's early factory and office buildings.

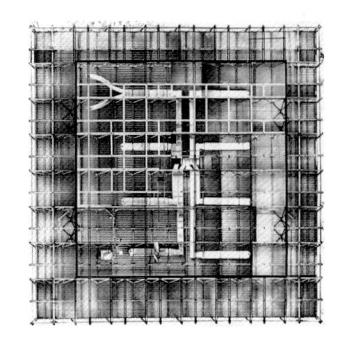

1. An early application of the 'Manplan' factory systems studies, which also demonstrated the influence of the SCSD programme, was the Cincinnati Milacron factory project of 1970.

2. Cincinnati Milacron was a deep-plan project with cellular and open-plan elements deployed beneath a roof of long-span steel lattice beams supported by widely spaced columns. While this arrangement is similiar to that achieved the following year at IBM Cosham, there was no attempt to develop a glass curtain-walling system.

3, 4. The family connection between the buildings for Cincinnati Milacron and IBM is apparent in these part section and part elevation drawings. Roof-zone servicing, typical of the factory systems studies, is coupled with a covered perimeter walkway inherited from the Newport School project. The roof-top air-conditioning units are located directly above the columns to minimise loadings on the beams.

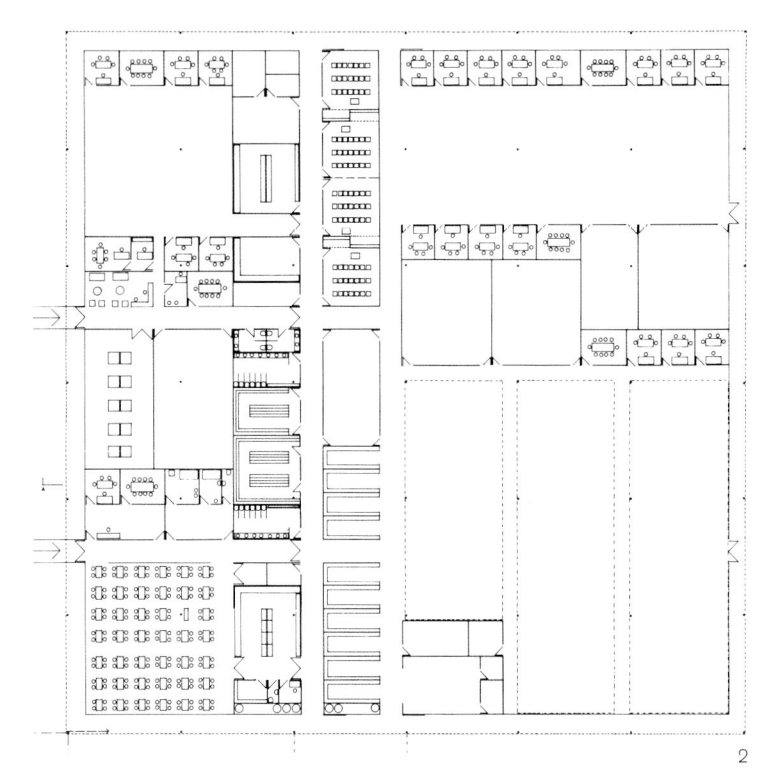

The advance factory unit was intended to compete economically with the package dealer's shed and accommodate these 'impulse buyers' as a government report had called them. In fact, independent studies in the USA had shown that a multi-purpose, flexible pre-fabricated system could meet the requirements of 75 per cent of industry and obsolescence could be more or less eliminated. In the UK, an unpublished government-sponsored report had recommended investing in a prototype commissioned system akin to the California School Construction Systems Development (SCSD), but it had been shelved and forgotten.

In essence, the system Foster proposed was the bigger and smarter brother of SCSD. Ehrenkrantz's schools prototype had been a formative influence in the design of Foster's Newport School compctition cntry. And the concept of a lightweight, modular steel structure supported off a reinforced-concrete floor slab, with services distributed horizontally in the deep roof zone, using roof-top air-conditioning units and flexible trunking, is one that appears in many of the practice's later buildings, most notably in the German Car Centre project of 1972 and two projects for IBM at Cosham and Greenford, in 1971 and 1980 respectively.

The key requirement was flexibility, so that the buildings could be expanded or modified over time to suit an owner's changing needs. This was to lead Foster to the identification of four basic design criteria: long-span structures, movable partitions, full thermal environmental control and an adaptable lighting provision.

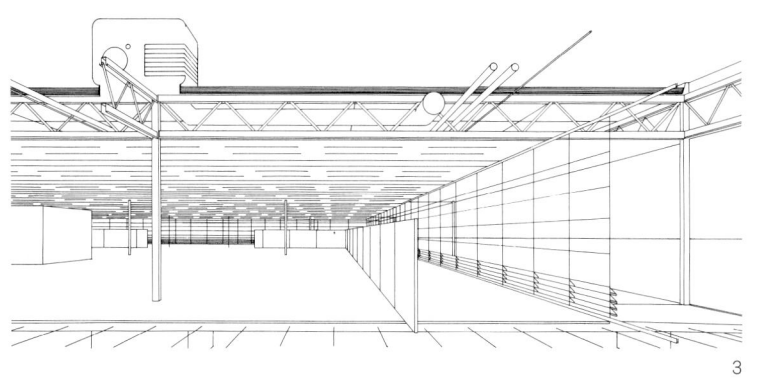

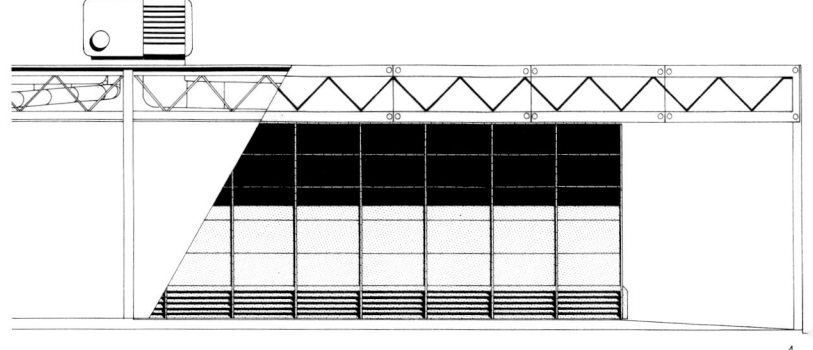

The response to sociologists' questionnaires about work satisfaction has – for mass-production workers on assembly lines – overwhelmingly shown that much industrial work is fragmentary and monotonous, almost beyond bearing point. The car workers of Detroit, who two years ago stuck 'Humanise Working Conditions' on their bumpers and persuaded the United Automobile workers throughout America to follow suit, were not asking for more wages and shorter hours, but for a radical change in industrial life. 'Manplan 3', *The Architectural Review*, November 1964

As a practice we began in a difficult period when the building boom had ebbed and the development boom had not yet started. In order to build, we poached on the traditional activities of the package dealers and contractors. We played them at their own game, but built better, more flexible buildings with an element of joy. We took a progression of these techniques and applied them to a wider range of building types than anybody else. Norman Foster, *Design*, October 1971

---

The system also had to be used for a wide variety of applications by different architects and unknown contractors. The framework was consequently described as a set of basic 'rules' contained within a comprehensive performance specification. This allowed design details to be varied, while ensuring competitive tendering.

**The key requirement was flexibility, so that the buildings could easily be expanded or modified over time to suit an owner's changing needs.**

Structural, cladding and services sub-contract packages were all covered by an integrated specification, which ensured that each bidder was fully aware of the design implications of not just his own package, but of the context in which he would be working.

By embodying these basic principles the advance factory system greatly increased the scope and scale of possible modifications. Beneath the serviced roof 'umbrella', the space could be used as a single clear volume high enough to allow overhead walkways and conveyors above machines, or stacking with fork-lift trucks.

Ancillary accommodation such as offices and canteens could make use of mezzanine floors above service cores, substations or enclosed environmentally-regulated areas. In response to each industrialist's particular brief, the basic shell could be fitted out or 'customised' by adding to, or subtracting from, a kit that included partitions, suspended ceilings, light fittings and heating units. The floor slab was structured to support a range of potential activities from heavily-loaded trucks to major pieces of machinery. And ancillary components or cores could be located anywhere within the modular framework and plugged into the services network like moveable plant.

In 1970, the newly-established Milton Keynes Development Corporation (MKDC) had a mandate to respond to a probable demand of some 50,000 square metres of industrial floorspace per year and required just such a system. Foster was commissioned as systems consultant, with Anthony Hunt as structural engineer, to work with MKDC's own architects department on the development of the Systems Building for Industry (SBI). Foster was also responsible for the servicing concept, its detail design and installation.

5, 6. Norman Foster's cross-section and perspective of a heavy industrial exhibition unit proposed for Scottish Foundries. The elegant but massive steel beam structure supports a 25-ton travelling crane. The display area is at ground level, 13 metres beneath the heavy steel roof beams. Ingenious features include external lighting and adjustable perimeter sun screens.

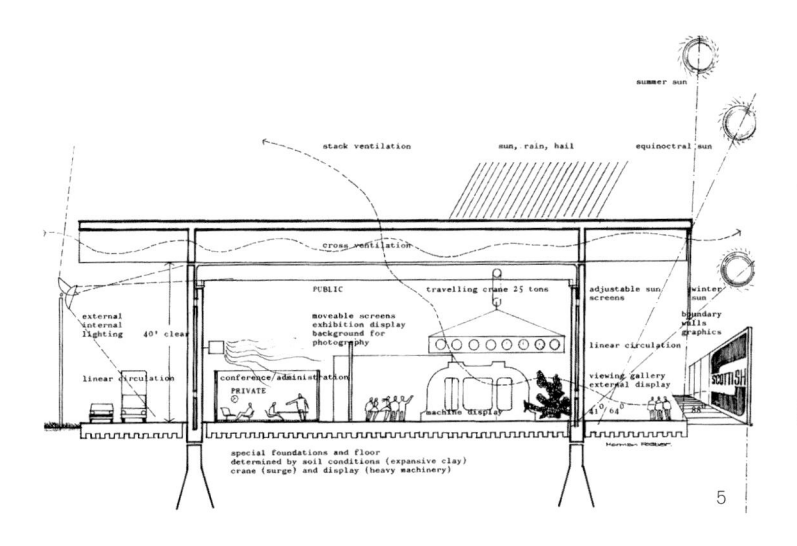

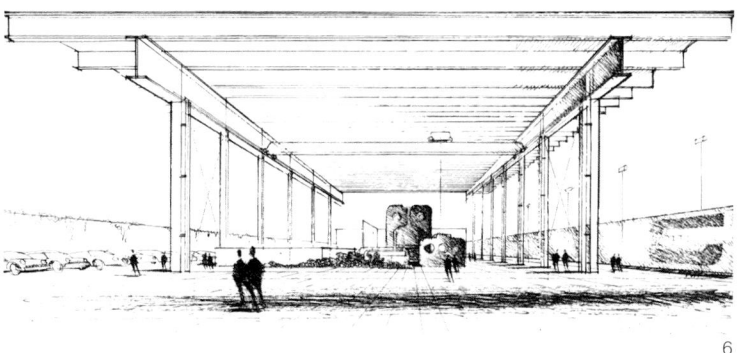

**The British New Town experience has slowly led planners to the conclusion that concentrating industry in designated areas is an unnecessarily expensive and wrongly conceived policy.**
'Manplan 3', *The Architectural Review*, November 1969
Left and right: Diagrams produced for Manplan illustrated how the planners of Milton Keynes sought to generate a functional bond between industry and its labour pool by avoiding the conventional zoning of residential and industrial areas.

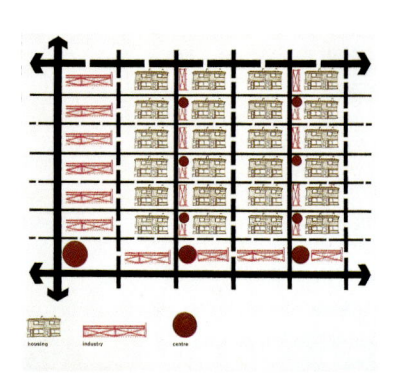

1-3. One of the earliest applications of Foster's factory systems studies was at Milton Keynes where a prototype 1,200 square-metre multi-functional SBI (Systems Building for Industry) unit was erected for the Development Corporation in 1972 to house its own architects' department. The design of Unit P70 shared the deep roof zone, low-level perimeter windows and high-level servicing of the Computer Technology building, completed a year earlier, but with a more open lattice roof structure instead of castellated beams. The extraordinary choice of colour was made by MKDC.

MKDC's research showed that, with few exceptions, the preferred factory was single storey and small in size. SBI offered a variety of solutions using a lightweight steel frame with 12 x 12-metre multi-directional spans, clear height options of 3.5, 5.5 and 7.5 metres, a roof service zone, increased roof and floor loadings, different cladding arrangements, a two-storey potential, and a range of environmental control, natural and artificial lighting possibilities. However, unlike the earlier advance factory system, SBI was never intended to operate entirely from a performance specification; rather, it offered a 'constrained' performance specification, giving a degree of final planning control over materials and finishes to ensure continuity in large-scale developments.

To prove its economy, MKDC built a low-budget SBI prototype, the small P70 unit at Wavendon, which was three bays or 36 metres square with a clear height of 5.5 metres. The latter dimension was calculated to allow a central service core with a mezzanine above.

The cladding was a mix of glazed and flat, white, stove-enamelled insulated panels in a gasketed sub-frame assembly. The building was completed in 1972 and used as a drawing office for the architects' department before becoming a publicity centre, thus proving its flexibility. At Kiln Farm in 1973, the system was used in a courtyard arrangement that allowed the industrial flotsam that litters most estates to be contained within the confines of the building blocks.

The full potential of SBI was never realised, however, partly because design tendering and production procedures could not be fully rationalised. And serial contracting in a fast-moving but sometimes erratic industrial development programme was made more difficult by the galloping UK inflation and rising building costs that characterised the period. Derek Walker, who as Chief Architect and Planner was responsible for initiating SBI, regrets the loss. These obstacles, he believes, 'baulked a very earnestly researched system that offered such a sensible and simplified service to the incoming industrialist'.

David Jenkins

The trading estate is not the weapon Manplan suggests for refashioning the industrial environment ... Because stinking industry so long dominated the lives of thousands of men and women, the planner's prescription has been a violent, puritanical and dogmatic policy of apartheid putting asunder industry and housing for ever ... But why? Industry in Britain is in the midst of a gigantic capital spending spree. The architecture ... is ready. Where are the clients?
'Manplan 3', *The Architectural Review*, November 1969
In spite of its evident benefits, various factors conspired to prevent the wide-ranging adoption of the SBI system. Right: The Kiln Farm development, of 1973, represented the largest application of the SBI factory system.

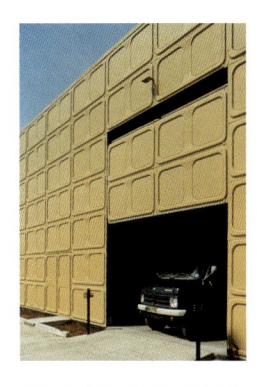

The interior of the prototype SBI building was particularly striking – a bright red structure with yellow partitions, desks and drawing boards – and was occupied by the architects' department of the Milton Keynes Development Corporation. I tried to persuade all the architects to wear red shoes to match the colour scheme ... I thought the connection to Judy Garland in *The Wizard of Oz* might be amusing. They were understandably reluctant – even though this was the 1970s! Derek Walker, in conversation with the editor, November 2001

**Building for industry really is a no-frills situation; there is a crispness, a need to build quickly, and a need to create generous uncluttered areas; to do it with a minimum of fuss; and to do it within tight cost limits and extremely demanding timescales.**
Norman Foster

Factory Systems 143

# Design for Living
Norman Foster 1969

**The architect is traditionally responsible for design. But design is not a fashionable 'ism': it is born out of the needs of people.** Norman Foster, AIA Gold Medal address, Washington, 1 February 1994

There is a tendency for a certain mystique to develop around such words as 'design', especially 'good design'. This is unfortunate because it tends to cloud the importance that design decisions have in our lives. Virtually everything man-made has been subject to a design process involving deliberate choices and decisions; in our Western civilisation that means nearly everything that we see, hear, touch and smell. As in all things, this is something that we can do well, badly or indifferently with corresponding end results. To this extent the very quality of our day-to-day living is profoundly influenced by the quality of our design.

Our environment is a compound of many objects and enclosures whose designers may be anonymous, often hidden in bureaucratic and business organisations, or sometimes independent consultants. Their main role, in essence, is problem-solving. It is this fundamental aspect of their work that is so often overlooked.

The 'style' in which the problem is solved is far less important and it is unfortunate that this aspect is often over-emphasised. This dilemma can be seen in two current attitudes. Firstly, there is a public apathy and indifference to the most fundamental aspects of design as they affect our very existence. Secondly, there is a tendency among designers to over-indulge in the more superficial aspects of their trade to the exclusion of the fundamental problems. The ensuing dialogue with its overtones of 'good taste' and mystique is largely irrelevant to a world going about its business.

**Virtually everything man-made has been subject to a design process involving deliberate choices and decisions; in our Western civilisation that means nearly everything that we see, hear, touch and smell. As in all things, this is something that we can do well, badly or indifferently with corresponding end results.**

As a random example of the above dilemma it is worth considering the 'tower block' of flats in the form which is currently designed and built in Britain. As a design for a family with young children it is chronically unsuitable. Despite all popular conceptions it is not the only way to achieve high densities; students of architecture were devising low-rise, high-density schemes many years ago.

**Good design emerges, perhaps above all, from listening. If you listen, you ask the right questions and understand the needs that generate the building. Good design also involves motivating not just yourself and those immediately around you, but the larger team, which can run into thousands. It is about stimulating, anticipating and auditing, and about adapting to change.** Norman Foster, lecture at Stuttgart University, 14 May 1997

**We have artists with no scientific knowledge and scientists with no artistic knowledge and both with no spiritual sense of gravity at all, and the result is not just bad, it is ghastly. The time for real reunification of art and technology is really long overdue.** From *Zen and the Art of Motorcycle Maintenance* by Robert M Pirsig, first published in 1974, an extract often quoted by Norman Foster

Nevertheless, it is commonplace for architects and critics endlessly to debate at the level of imagery and detail those 'tower blocks' that are 'good' and those that are 'bad'. Obviously some are better than others at a superficial level; but fundamentally a tower block is a tower block, regardless of whether it is neo-Georgian, mock-Tudor or plastic-faced.

It is amazing how long outdated design concepts can survive. At least our housing has attempted many new forms and experiments since the Industrial Revolution. By comparison, our design for industry has been virtually at a standstill since the 1800s. We still persist in building management 'boxes' and workers' 'sheds' even though this may in fact conflict with the needs of processes, expansion, flexibility and management policies. Obviously, some types of industries and processes are still rooted in a 'clean and dirty', 'we and they' social structure, but they are a growing exception. The traditional factory building and so-called industrial estate is currently one of our most unpleasant, uncomfortable, inefficient and expensive hangovers from the past.

These examples are only part of a totality. The family living in the tower block may be twenty miles from a major airport but deafened by one of its flight paths; traffic jams may separate the worker's factory from home; other facilities such as shopping, schools and recreation may be similarly unrelated. It is an indictment of our educational system that we accept such patterns almost without question as the mythical price of progress and frequently continue to regard good design as 'arting-up' or cosmetic treatment that can be applied 'after the act'.

At the risk of over-simplification, the designer's task could be summed up as analysing set problems in the widest sense and organising the best available resources to achieve the highest-performance solution in the most economical manner. It follows that the end result will have accommodated and integrated often conflicting and competing requirements. The core of the problems and the way they are resolved will largely generate the style.

It should not be thought that so fundamental an approach is insensitive to the full range of our spiritual and material needs. Most of the historical places that today continue to delight us were originally a calculated response to well-defined requirements.

## The traditional factory building and so-called industrial estate is currently one of our most unpleasant, uncomfortable, inefficient and expensive hangovers from the past.

For example, Bath was a speculative developers' 'New Town', based on a simple structural system of cross walls and repeated narrow window openings; an eloquent design totally embracing the social, topographical, technical and financial aspects of its site. It is interesting to compare Bath with the scale of our present opportunities and the quality of our own resulting New Towns and other speculative developments.

In an age of social and technological change, the designer's tasks become increasingly complex. The overlaps and interactions between the hardware and software of our time (cars, planes, television, communications, computers) and our building fabric make it increasingly difficult to conceive of architecture in terms of the traditional past.

The age-old definition of architecture as 'commodity, firmness and delight' is, however, still valid even if the 'firmness' is realised by plastic or alloy instead of masonry, and the 'delight' is extended by current developments in electronic communications and climatic control.

1. The Ronan Point tower blocks in the London borough of Newham (1966-1968) typified the high-rise accommodation – now recognised as 'chronically unsuitable' – built from the 1960s onwards to replace run-down nineteenth-century city housing with smart new 'homes in the sky'. In May 1968 an explosion in an eighteenth-floor flat caused the collapse of the south-east corner of the tower. The accident killed four people and signalled the gradual decline of urban planners' love affair with this particular form of city dwelling.

2. The distinctive sweep of Bath's Royal Crescent, designed by John Wood the Younger and built between 1767 and 1774.

3. A typical post-war industrial development consisting of management 'boxes' and worker 'sheds'. These industrial ghettos were drab, inhospitable, inflexible and ultimately entirely unsuited to both use and users.

> 'The lesson of building history is not that one particular type of construction is superior or less wasteful or more natural than others, but that many modes of construction have long been understood to be subtly appropriate to different sorts or conditions of buildings – the proof is in the performance ... Undisturbed by the Gadarene rush of theorists and moralists down from 'high' technology to 'low', Foster has gone the less facile route of 'appropriate technology'.' Reyner Banham, *Foster Associates*, 1979

1. An example of the sprawling trailer parks which are proliferating across America.

2, 3. The MUST (Medical Unit, Self-contained Transportable) inflatable hospital, developed by the US military during the Vietnam War to provide portable, durable and quick-assembly shelter for field medical treatment. A prototype MUST unit was erected at Tay Ninh, Vietnam, in October 1966 (shown here during and after erection) to house the 45th Surgical Hospital. Its successful performance prompted the installation of five further inflatable hospitals in Vietnam.

The scope for new design solutions to meet both established and emerging needs is tremendous. It does not follow that we have to use untried techniques or ideas to innovate. Initiatives taken on a prototype can determine vast potential on the open market. At one end of the scale new planning ideas allied with traditional techniques can often prove as significant as the utilisation of new materials and techniques in isolation. The real scope lies in the fusion of both, whatever the scale of assignment, from product design to city and regional planning, whether one-off projects or vast collective enterprises.

Design innovations, which could change the appearance of buildings and make them more sensitive to our real needs, can spring from a number of sources. These could be broadly classed under new techniques of planning, engineering and management. They can be separated out for examination in more detail, but in reality the design process itself would integrate these and other key factors.

Firstly, new planning techniques. These are needed to satisfy today's rapidly changing social and technological patterns. Our spaces are becoming smaller but very highly mechanised. Like industrial plant it becomes uneconomic not to utilise them to the maximum effect. In planning terms this might mean spaces that have multi-purpose use. We also demand mobility and rapid change. More than five million people in the USA are living in trailer homes, which are increasing at the rate of 300,000 a year.

Obsolescence, whether based on fashion or real change, will have radical implications. Our buildings will have to be planned for flexibility so that they can change, grow and adapt. As land becomes more precious we must reconcile these needs with buildings that are sensitive to areas of scenic beauty. There is no reason why our present pattern of squandering natural resources, both visual and material, should continue. Intensive coastal development for housing and industry, for example, could be achieved without extending our present 'suburbia-on-sea'.

**The scope for new design solutions to meet established or emerging needs is tremendous. New planning ideas allied with traditional techniques can often prove as significant as the utilisation of new materials and techniques in isolation. The real scope lies in the fusion of both.**

Similarly, by abandoning out-of-date planning forms, which are currently based on hangovers from the past, we could preserve the genuinely historic parts of our cities and revitalise them with a modern, twentieth-century equivalent.

Secondly, new engineering techniques. Examples of these are new materials, structures, total energy concepts and the feedback of ideas from other sources such as the electronics and aerospace industries. At one extreme we have the large-scale potential. Vast areas can be enclosed within lightweight space-frame structures or inflatable membranes. Full climatic control is feasible; the polar regions could be 'tropicalised' and desert areas cooled.

It is a sad reflection on our society that it takes the stimulus of warfare to promote instant hospitals. A full surgical hospital unit, just about our most complex building type, was dropped by helicopter on barren ground at Tay Ninh, in Vietnam. Complete with self-contained power-packs, its rubber-coated Dacron walls were inflated and the unit fully operational within a few hours.

1

Left: Norman Foster's interest in inflatable structures found practical application in the air-supported office for Computer Technology (1969-1970), which offered virtually instantaneous temporary office accommodation for a rapidly expanding new-technology company.

Traditional site-based techniques are being replaced by factory-controlled components using new materials to achieve higher standards, speed and value-for-money. Some traditional materials, such as carpets, are being completely reinterpreted by current technology. Mechanical equipment has become a major and fast-increasing proportion of the total building cost. Nevertheless, it is still in a very crude form (it is difficult to imagine anything more crude than our lavatories and waste disposal systems) and we generally insert this equipment into an obsolescent shell, complete with traditional plumbing. At present we are still in limbo; half embracing a craft-based past and half aware of a new engineering potential.

Thirdly, new techniques of management. Increasingly complex organisations involved with problem-posing (clients, communities) and problem-solving (designers, contractors, manufacturers) can no longer rely on intuitive judgements. Skilled programming and briefing techniques are becoming increasingly important. Cost and time factors should be welcomed as further performance disciplines. Cost-in-use will become an increasingly critical factor. Our cost planning, often based on first cost in isolation, is quite misleading.

Although the framework for teamwork exists, all too often designers act in isolation, leaving other specialists to 'make it work' in a passive role. The scope for really integrated teams with wide-ranging skills is considerable. Current divisions between design and production will be reduced, involving the designer in new and exciting roles closely allied to industry. It is paradoxical that as the organisations involved get larger, the scope for smaller groups to innovate will increase, either from within or from outside.

Although greater rationalisation will produce ever more sophisticated components and kits-of-parts, there is every reason to suppose that, as in the field of business and politics, key individuals will still play a decisive role in the field of design. In many ways, the design process is probably one of our cheapest commodities. It allows us the scope to explore many alternatives and possibilities before making any commitment in reality. All too often, however, it is the subject of short-cuts; an unnecessary fringe benefit to which lip service is occasionally paid, or a luxury for those prestige occasions. The results we suffer surround us, and the loss at all levels is entirely our own.

## It is a sad reflection on our society that it takes the stimulus of warfare to promote instant hospitals.

Norman Foster

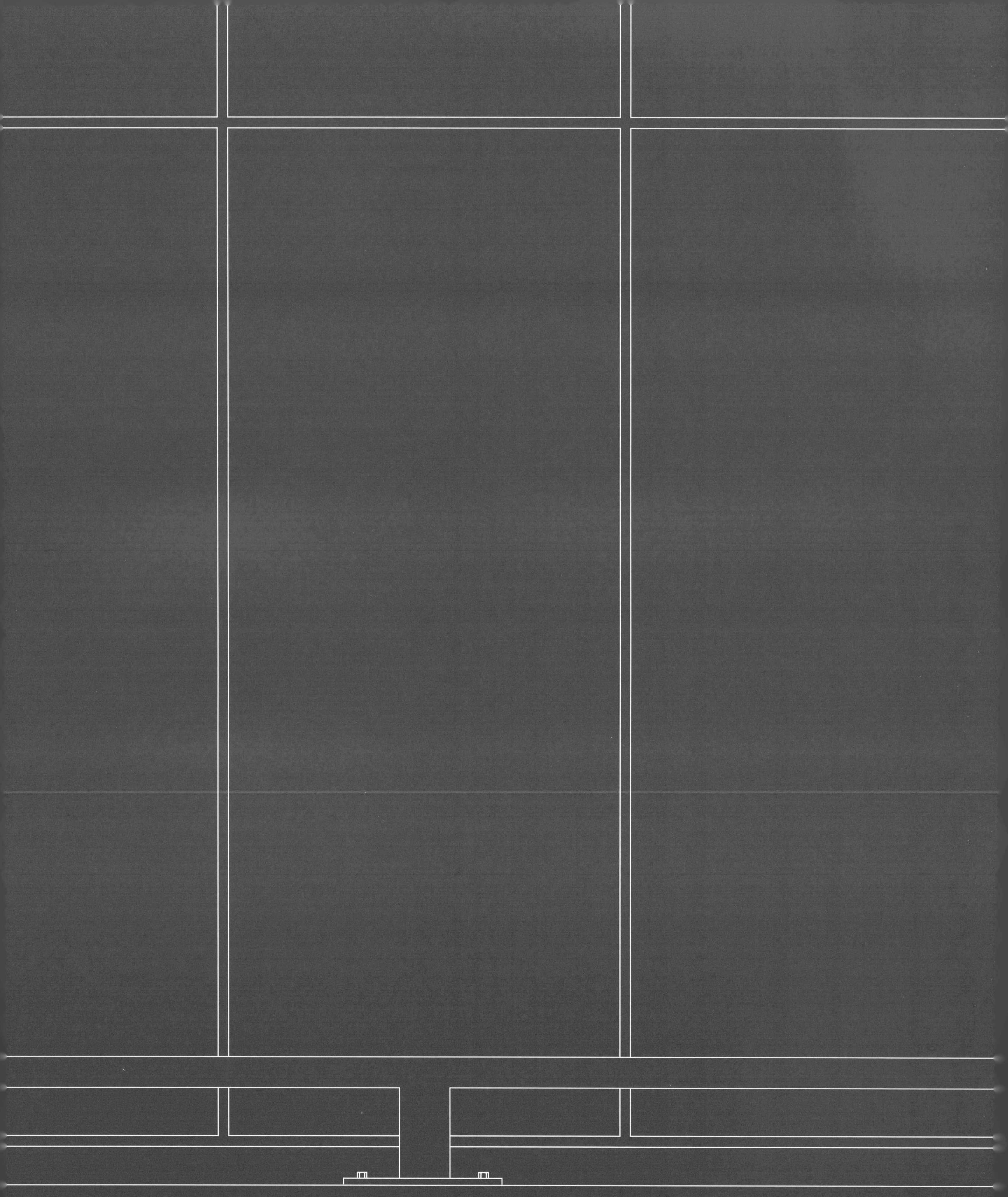

**Projects and Masterplanning for Fred Olsen**
1968–1975

The many projects undertaken with Fred Olsen ranged from a modest travel agency to a comprehensive exercise in sustainable masterplanning for Gomera, in the Canary Islands. In the process, the practice established its first overseas office, in Oslo, and introduced European ideas about workplace design into the benighted London Docks. The largest completed buildings to arise from this collaboration, the Amenity Centre – and the Passenger Terminal that followed alongside – originated from a brief to design a canteen and amenity building for dock workers at the Olsen berth in Millwall. However, our alternative studies generated a radical proposal to unite white and blue-collar workers in a single combined operations and amenity building, which offered the same high standards to everyone in the company, regardless of class or collar.
Norman Foster

**Fred Olsen Amenity Centre**
Millwall Dock, London, England 1968–1970

**Thinking back, the consultative process we established worked well. It combined the skills of Fred Olsen, with his Nordic distance from our weary pattern of labour relations, together with Mike Thompson, the then dock manager, and Tom Jones, the union leader. There was also my own naive belief that nobody had to be a victim of the past.** Norman Foster, *Norman Foster: Sketches*, 1992

Left: Millwall Dock before the construction of the Amenity Centre. In this view, the Fred Olsen wharf is to the right of the dock.

The formation of Foster Associates in 1967 marked a sea change for Norman and Wendy Foster. However, despite the confident ring of the practice's new name, not only were there no associates, there were very few clients either. Norman Foster recalls, 'We had so little work that we came very close to leaving Britain. The question was whether or not we would emigrate to North America or Canada. We survived by appealing to a niche where architects had not traditionally been involved, which was industry'.

In doing so, Foster's first challenge was to win the client over from the competition, which was not other architects, but contractors. To do so, he had to demonstrate that he could not only beat the opposition by producing a good building for less than a contractor would supply a poor one, but that he could do so to tight deadlines. He succeeded by using professional skills to research the best solutions: 'We could buy a structure here, a cladding there and since we didn't have a commercial axe to grind, we could justify a fair fee to do it', he recalls. More importantly, by entering into a dialogue and analysing a client's needs objectively, Foster was able to bring an extra dimension to the project that a contractor never could.

Foster's first foray into industry, with Reliance Controls – completed under the umbrella of Team 4 – was the antithesis of the prevailing factory building, characterised by Foster as a 'workers' shed and management box', which was finite, inflexible and reinforced social barriers. With its flexible enclosure, open planning and democratic provision of amenities Reliance Controls revolutionised the design of the workplace in Britain. And these themes were to be explored further in Foster's next industrial building, the Amenity Centre for Fred Olsen in Millwall Dock, commissioned in 1968.

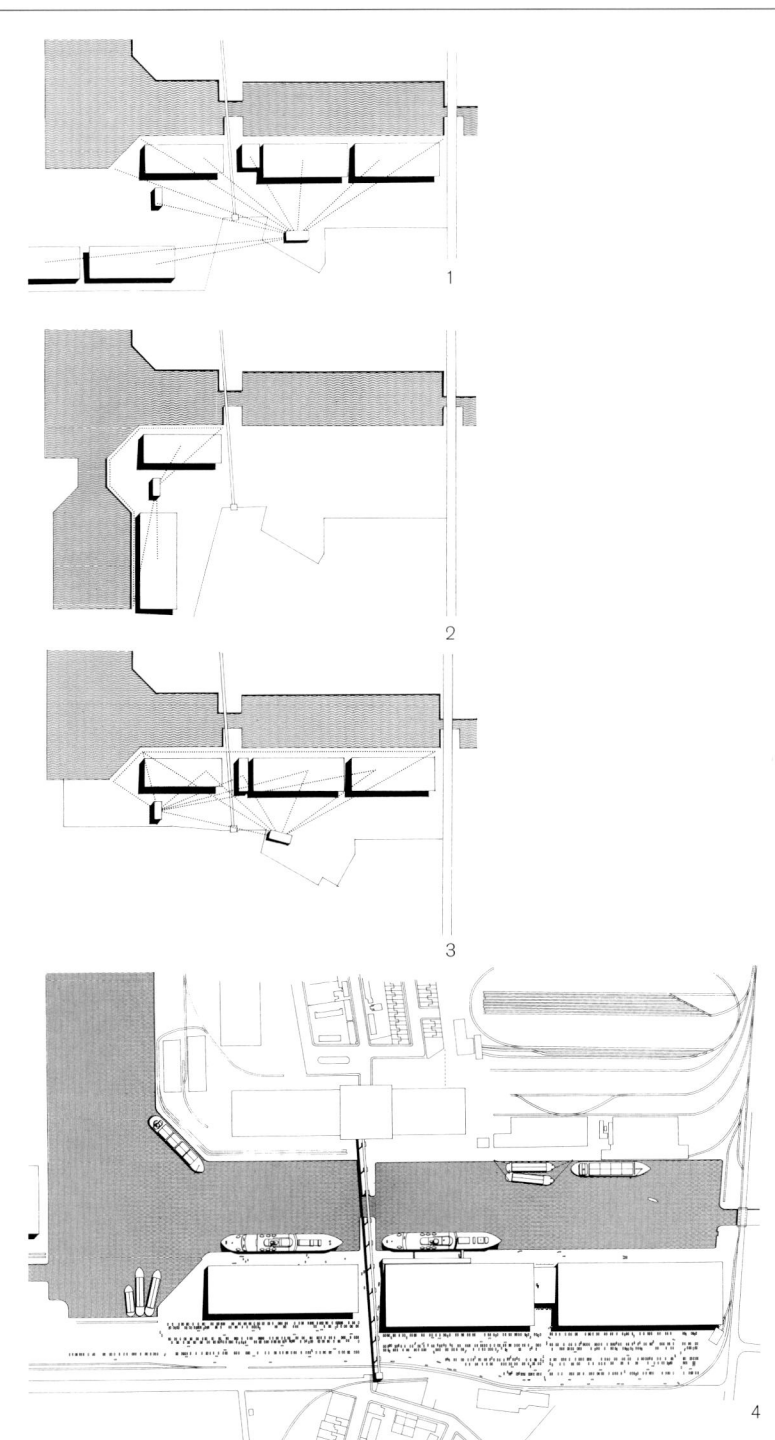

Opposite: A view of Millwall Dock and the Fred Olsen terminal, photographed in the early 1970s.

1-3. Foster Associates' initial brief was for the construction of a small canteen and amenity centre for dock workers, but Norman Foster's analysis of where this would be best located, and how it would relate to Olsen's other activities on the site, convinced Fred Olsen to expand the scope of the project.

4. The final scheme combined the operations and amenity functions in a single building, which bridged the firebreak gap between two transit sheds then being constructed in Millwall Dock by the Port of London Authority.

Overleaf: Ships reflected in the two-storey glass dockside facade. The steel kerb structure prevented damage to the glass by fork-lift trucks working on the quay.

Fred Olsen Amenity Centre

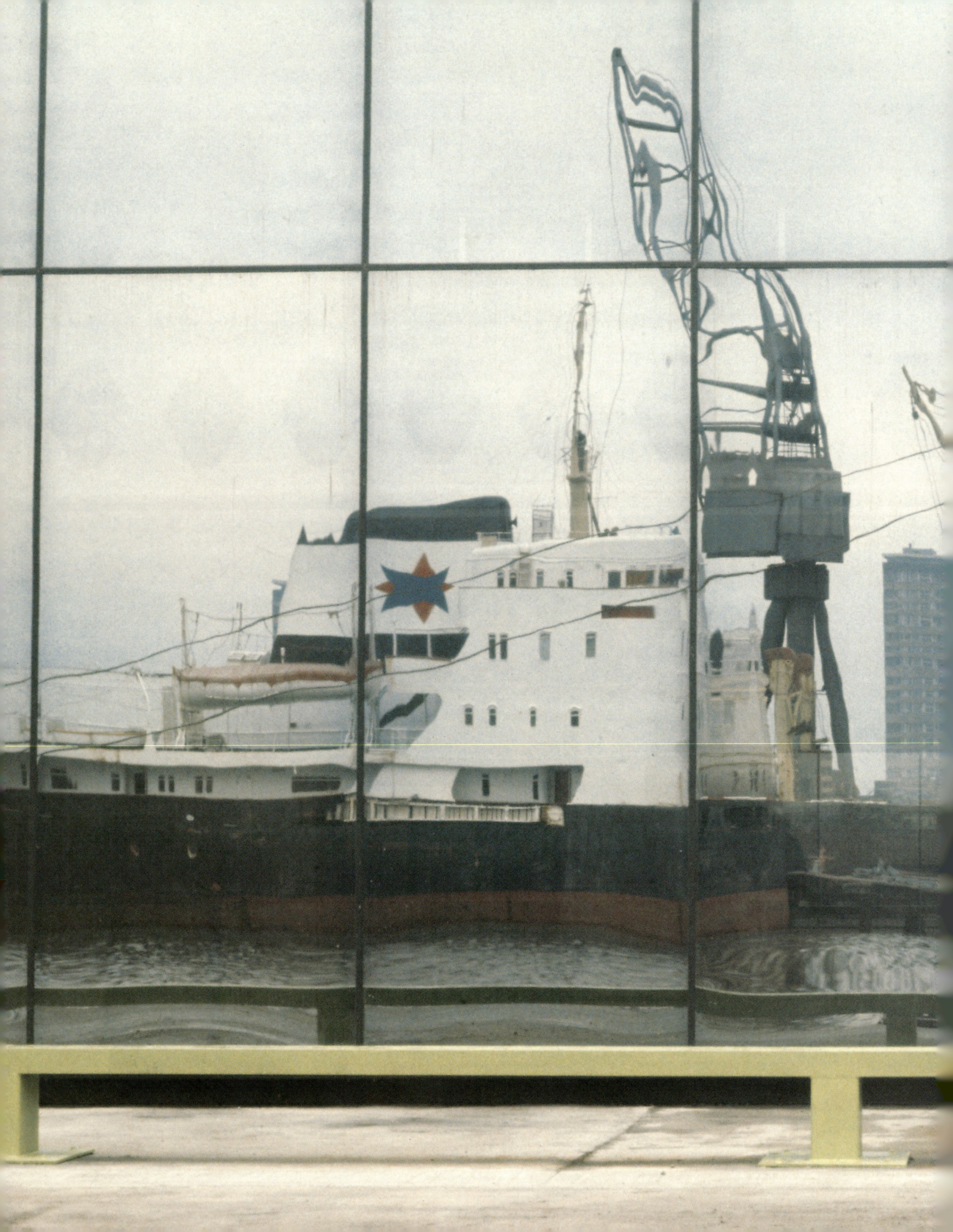

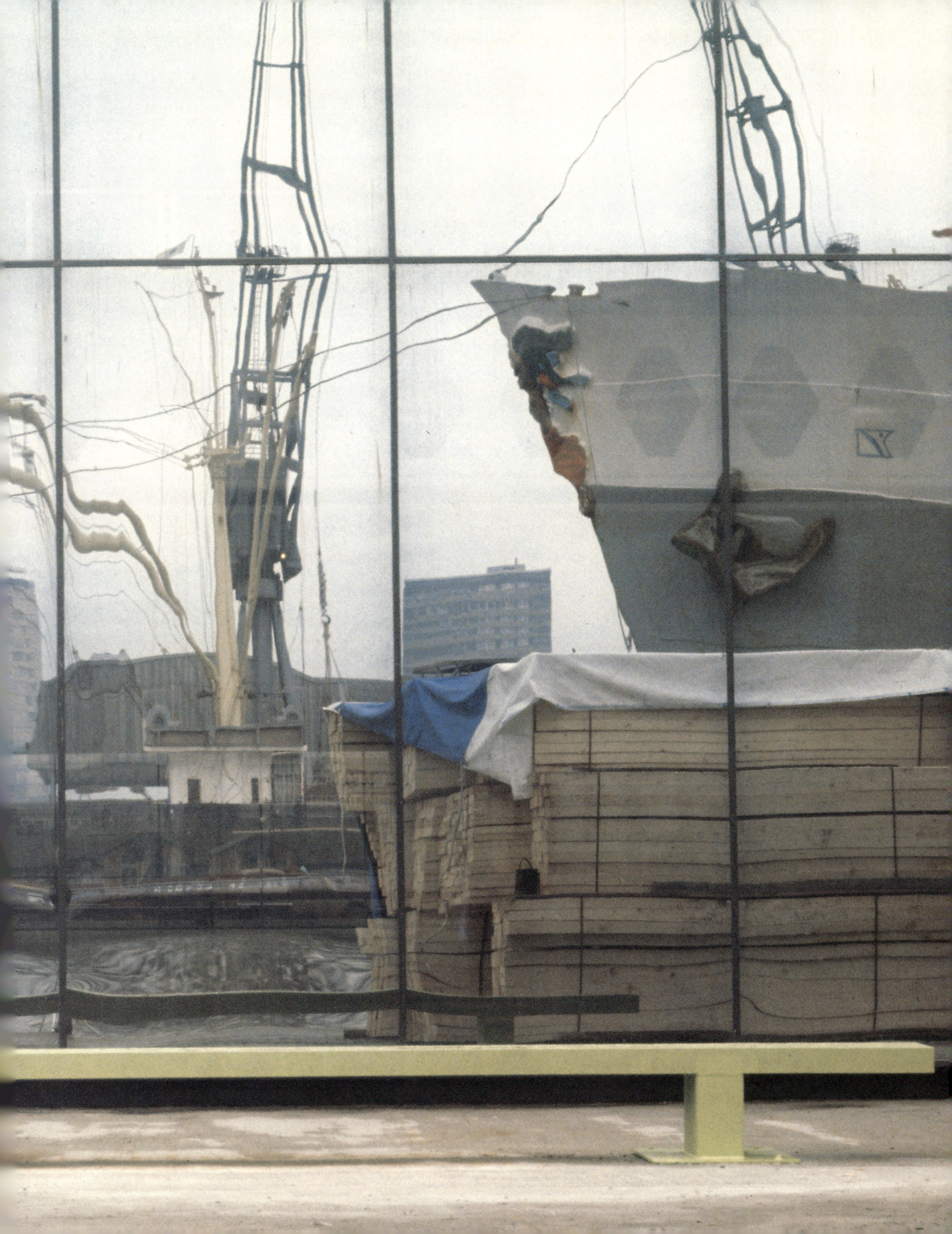

> We had heard that Olsen was seeking contractors for a small shower block and canteen at Millwall. We joined the interview queue and met the Dock Manager, Mike Thompson. Unlike the contractors, whose questions were about the proposed building itself, I was much more concerned with the 'hows and whys' behind the decision to have such a building in the first place. I heard enough to question intuitively the wisdom of providing amenity facilities remote from the working centre of gravity of such a large dock site. Norman Foster, *Norman Foster: Sketches*, 1992

> **The main aims were to improve significantly communications and efficiency, to integrate related activities and to achieve maximum site utilisation.**
> Norman Foster

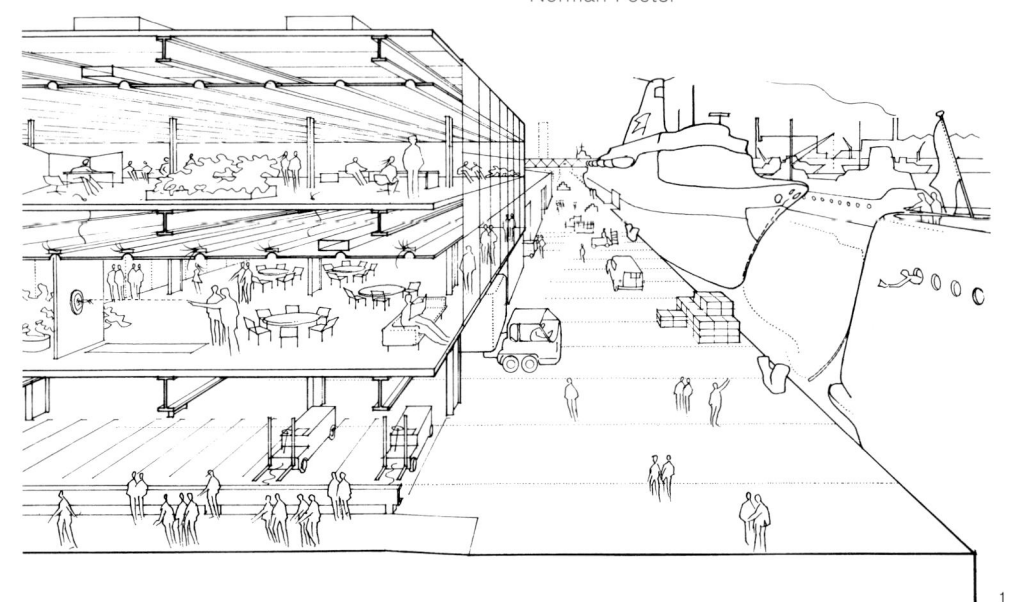

In the late 1960s, working conditions in the Port of London were among the worst in Britain and labour relations were little better. Foster describes the workers' accommodation he found on his first visit to Millwall Dock, as 'barbaric'. The lavatories were filthy and racially segregated, there were no proper canteen facilities and only rudimentary shelter was provided from the elements during breaks.

Fred Olsen, Foster's client, was a relative newcomer to the British scene who brought with him an enlightened, Scandinavian attitude towards the workplace that echoed Foster's own. Olsen sought to reverse ingrained social prejudices and he placed a high priority on the provision of amenities. The personal chemistry between these two like-minded men was very positive; in fact, Foster believes that it was one of the keys to the success of the project.

1. The first scheme rose to three storeys, with clear access to the quayside for trucks at ground level. The top floor was given over to operations, with the Amenity Centre taking over the entire middle level. However, the realisation that vehicular access could be carried out through the adjacent transit sheds removed the need for this level and established the final two-storey scheme.

2. The three-storey scheme would have risen above the transit sheds on either side. Glass cladding was intended from the beginning but the framing suggested here is more conventional than that finally employed.

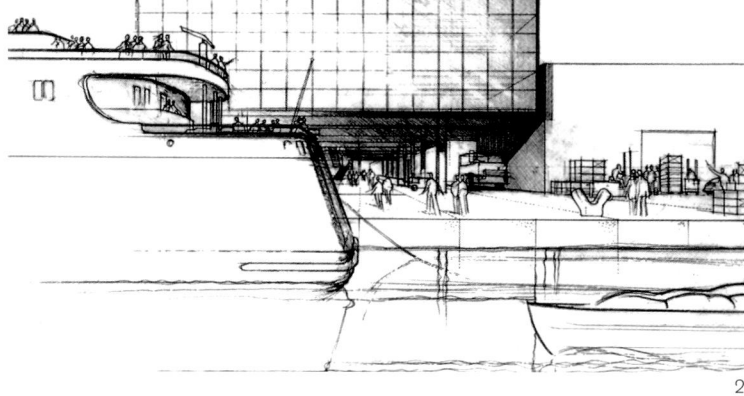

154  Norman Foster  Works 1

**An earlier design was elevated to allow trucks to pass under for access to the quayside. This version gave way to a simpler two-storey scheme which was strategically placed on the quayside between two massive transit sheds. It produced the desired immediacy – those who operated and those who managed were part of the same team, on the spot and in the same premises. But this arrangement could also be justified in other ways. The fire risks of such vast adjoining enclosures would normally require open wasted space between them. By designing the building as an eight-hour fire break the site was more efficiently developed.** Norman Foster, *Norman Foster: Sketches*, 1992

**Norman Foster changed the way we at Fred Olsen think about buildings. The principles established in dealing with the movement of people and their working environment are still ingrained in the company.** John Wallace, Chairman of Fred Olsen, in conversation with Martin Pawley, 1991

---

Fred Olsen had taken the initiative and decided to decasualise his workforce, ahead of recommendations contained within the Devlin Report, and he was determined to provide his staff with working conditions of a standard far higher than generally provided in the Port of London. Olsen had bravely promised the dock workers that they would have their new amenity building in twelve months. In order to meet this deadline, as Foster recalls, 'The building employed one or two fairly simple devices, like prefabrication, modular construction, dry trades, and designing the structure way ahead in such a way that it was really designed around the services'.

The introduction to Olsen came originally via Barry Copeland, a young architect working for Foster Associates in his year out, whose father worked for Olsen at Millwall. Copeland learned that the company was interviewing bidders for the amenity building, and so Norman Foster went to see Mike Thompson, the dock manager. Foster's approach was very different from that of his competitors. Foster remembers: 'Typically they would come in and make a presentation, and talk about how their building would look. Instead, I asked questions, listened to what the client wanted and came away. Then I went back and asked more questions – I made sure I understood the client's objectives both in terms of the functional and the social organisation of the company'.

At that time the redevelopment of Millwall Dock included the imminent construction of two large warehouses on the quayside. Olsen's new amenity building and a separate administration block were to be located behind these sheds, at the back of the site. However, it quickly became clear to Foster that locating this accommodation away from the activity of the quayside was far from ideal. It would have resulted in long walking times, reduced levels of communication and lost productivity. Convinced of the need for an alternative strategy, on his own initiative Foster undertook a planning study that looked at all the company's activities – administration, servicing, cargo, passenger and vehicular access – in a systematic way.

Olsen's principal trade from London was with the Canary Islands. On the outward journey its ships would carry a mixed cargo, and they would return with bananas. However, in order to maximise the use of his ships, Olsen cleverly combined this trade with holiday cruises, carrying passengers and freight in the same vessel. Foster saw that a similar organisational strategy could be deployed to bring together dock workers and administrative staff. He recognised that these two apparently contradictory functions could be integrated in a complementary way, much as they were on the ships, which is perhaps why Fred Olsen was so receptive to the idea and was persuaded to expand the brief.

3. These two comparative drawings show how the operations and amenity facilities, rather than being isolated behind the transit sheds on the dockside, could be related directly to operations on the quayside.

4. As Norman Foster's sketch demonstrates, the Amenity Centre reflects the organisational logic of the ships themselves. Facilities for dockers are at ground level, giving direct access to the quayside and cargo holds. Administration is above, relating to the ships' staff accommodation and passenger levels.

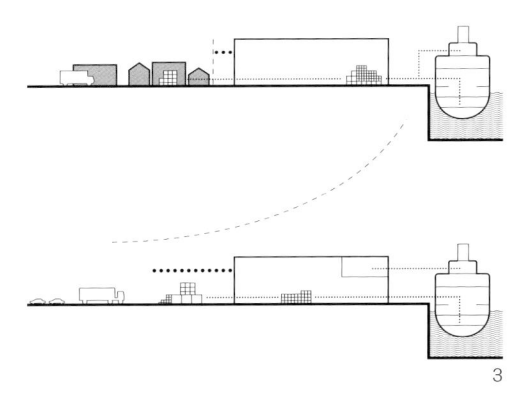

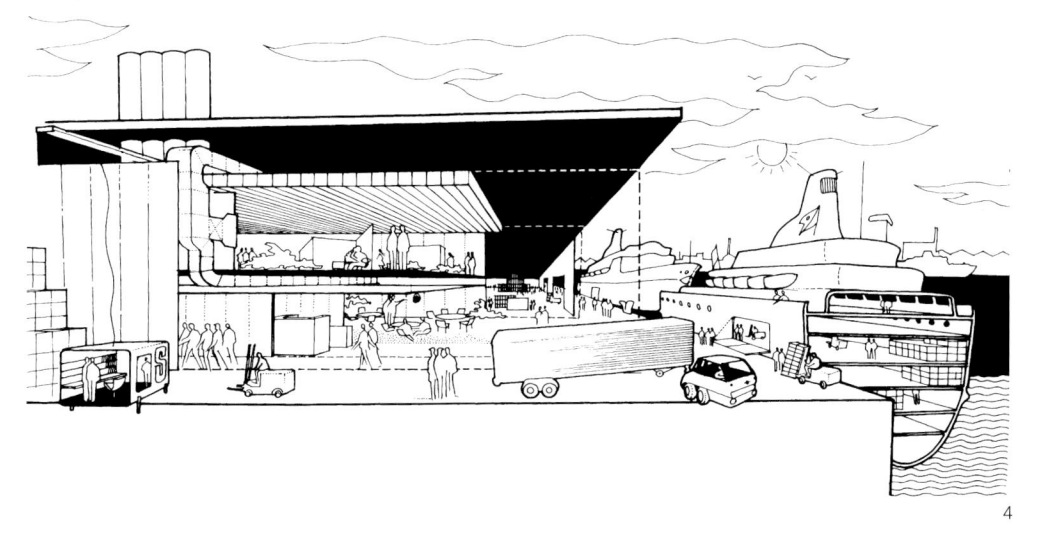

Right: A map of Canary Wharf and Millwall Dock as redeveloped in the 1990s. The Harbour Exchange development now occupies the northern half of the Fred Olsen site. The southern part is occupied by the London Arena, adjacent to the new Docklands Light Railway station at Crossharbour.

Far right: The former West India Docks, which run east-west in the aerial view below, have been reincarnated as Canary Wharf, a major new business and financial quarter. Seen here are three Foster and Partners projects: in the foreground are offices for Citibank (1996-2000) and the glazed canopies of Canary Wharf Underground station; behind is the emerging form of the 42-storey HSBC Headquarters (1997-2002).

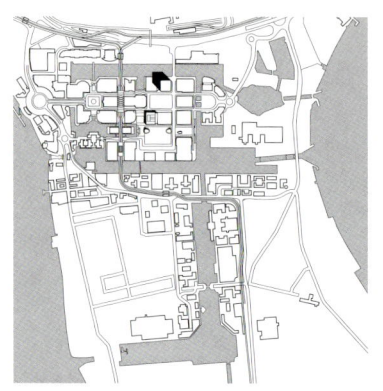

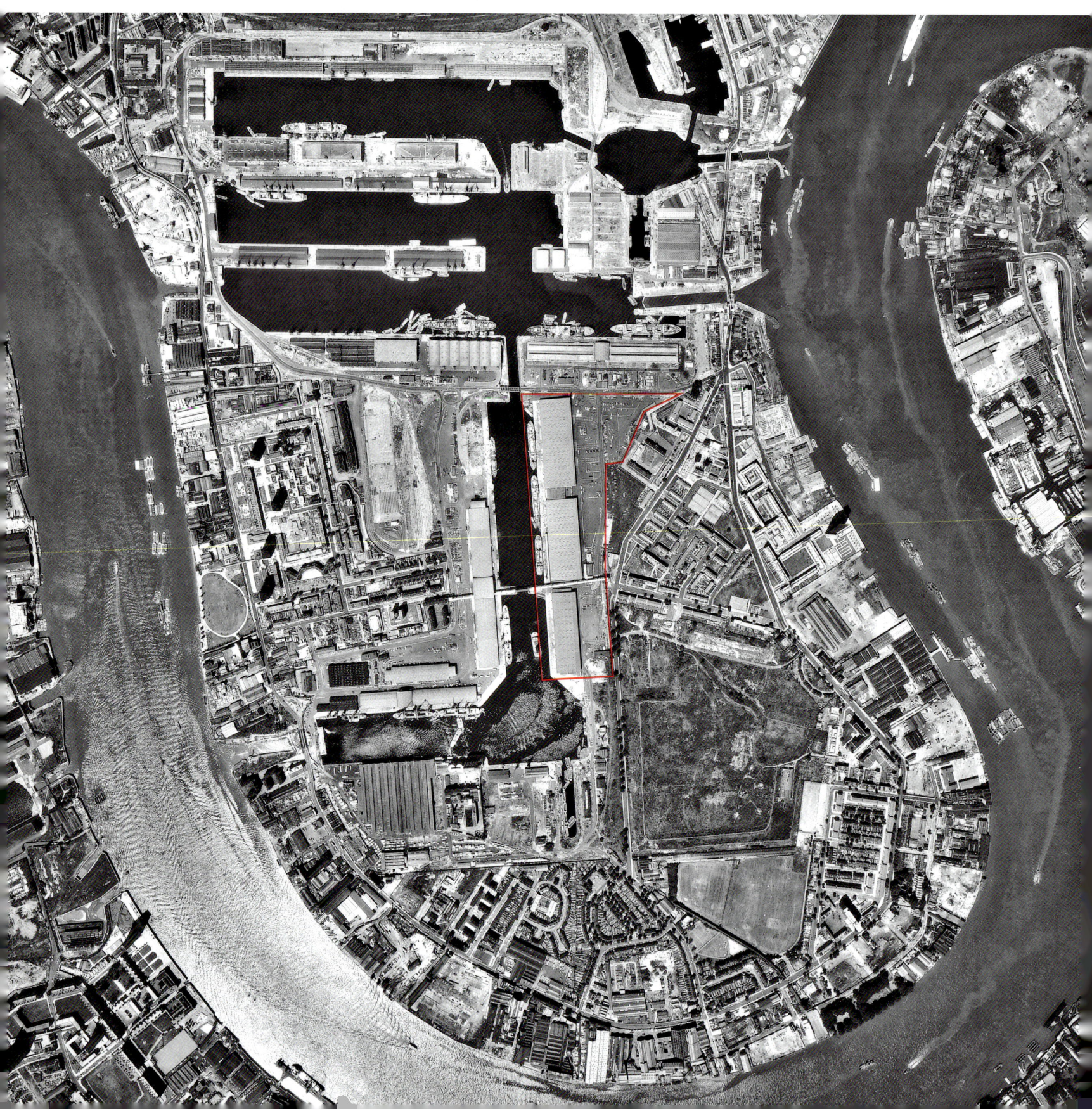

Right: The London Underground Jubilee Line extension is one of the greatest acts of architectural patronage of recent times, comprising eleven new stations by as many architects. Canary Wharf station (1991-1999) is the largest of these – when the development of the area is complete it will be used by more people at peak times than Oxford Circus. The station is built within the hollow of the former West India Dock using cut-and-cover construction techniques. At 300 metres in length, it is as long as the Canary Wharf Tower is tall. The roof of the station is laid out as a green park, creating Canary Wharf's principal public recreation space. Its only visible elements above ground are the swelling glass canopies, which cover the three entrances and bring natural light deep into the station platforms.

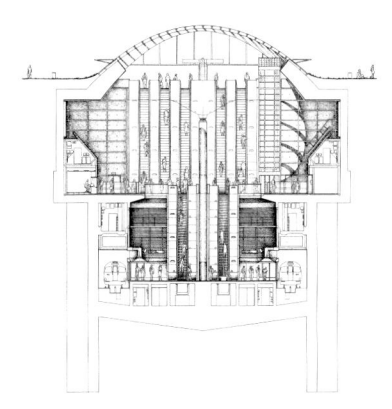

Foster's chosen site was the 27-metre-wide fire-break between the two warehouses on the dockside. Locating the administrative and amenity functions at the very hub of activity in this way achieved a far more efficient site utilisation than Olsen had anticipated. More significantly, it brought together clerical staff and dock workers in a building that offered the same high standards for everyone, regardless of class or collar – nothing short of a revolutionary idea at the time.

Although Fred Olsen himself was strongly supportive, the English management was far more sceptical. Foster recalls comments such as 'How can we possibly have the dockers in the same building? They're dirty, they swear, the secretaries will walk out'. Ultimately, of course, the building was very quickly accepted and Olsen's employees were demonstrably proud of it. So much so, that returning to Millwall a year after the Amenity Centre opened, Foster was surprised to discover a thriving industry of portable cafés on the site catering for truck drivers: 'I didn't understand it', he says, 'I asked, why there were separate facilities for the truck drivers and why they weren't using the staff restaurant. And the dockers said, "But the drivers are dirty people, they can't come in here …"'

Over time the Amenity Centre transformed patterns of behaviour on the Olsen wharf, not just socially, but also in terms of industrial relations. The fact that Foster was able to achieve such a constructive break with the past reflects the nature of the dialogue between the different parties involved. From the outset, Foster became part of the working group for the project that included both management and union representatives – 'a middle man that both sides could trust' – and the floor plans were drawn up after exhaustive consultations with all the different user groups: 'We all worked together and there was a lot at stake', he says.

In total, the Amenity Centre provided 2,500 square metres of air-conditioned accommodation on two floors. On the ground level, entered directly from the quayside, there were lavatories and showers for up to 240 dock workers, together with a restaurant and a games and relaxation area, while the first floor provided open-plan offices for sixty managerial and administrative staff. The interiors were bright, colourful and welcoming: grass-green floors complemented warm brown facings to the service core, a peppermint-green carpet and purple stair rails. And there were unheard of luxuries: table tennis and billiard tables in the relaxation area, and modern paintings on the walls, from Fred Olsen's personal art collection.

**Fred Olsen, Foster's client, was a relative newcomer to the British scene who brought with him an enlightened, Scandinavian attitude towards the workplace that echoed Foster's own.**

Along with its social innovations, the most revolutionary aspect of the project at the time – and the source of its most memorable image – was its glass curtain walling, which clad both open ends of the building. It was the beginning of Foster's romance with the reflective glass skin, which would continue with the Pilot Head Office at Cosham, for IBM, and culminate with Willis Faber & Dumas in Ipswich.

An aerial view of the Isle of Dogs and the Millwall and West India Docks in the late 1970s. Within ten years the advent of containerisation of cargo would lead to the removal of the entire Port of London to Tilbury. Olsen's operations were relocated to Southampton. The dock running east-west at the top of the photograph is Canary Wharf (see above). In this view, the Fred Olsen wharf is to the right of Millwall Dock. The Olsen terminal was demolished in 1988 prior to the comprehensive redevelopment of the entire London Docks.

We pioneered the notion that the workplace could be a pleasant environment ... At Olsen we did not just provide the basics, such as showers, but also facilities for table tennis, billiards and television; and we put art on the walls. That might not seem radical now, but in the context of the 1960s these were startling new ideas. In the docks at that time, the toilet facilities were disgusting. Workers in industry were treated little better than animals.
Norman Foster, *GA Extra*, February 1999

This building brought various groups together in a mix that was supposed to be explosive. It was explosive, but in quite unpredictable terms. Traditionally, all facilities were open to truck drivers, but the dockers wouldn't let them in if they didn't work for Olsen. They became so possessive about the building that a minor industry sprang up outside with small canteens and hot dog bars. It became such a threat to the established order in the docks that people were taking pot-shots at the windows with air-rifles.
Norman Foster, lecture at Hille Seminar, London, 8 July 1980

**The idea of integrating in a single building those concerned with operating the docks and those who managed the docks, was considered outrageous at the time. We proceeded with the concept very much against the wishes of the junior management who said 'How can we possibly have the dockers in the same building?'**
Norman Foster

**Over the duration of the building's life, Olsen did not suffer from unofficial strikes, or indeed any kind of industrial action for which the docks are notorious. I don't know how you quantify that in terms of cost plans.** Norman Foster, lecture to the Construction Industry Conference, London, 15 May 1980

**Asked years later why he had chosen Foster Associates for the Millwall project, Fred Olsen gave a reply that Norman Foster still quotes with pride: 'He asked the right questions.'** Martin Pawley, Foundation, Spring 1991

1-4. At the beginning of the project Norman Foster commissioned Tim Street-Porter to take a series of photographs of dockers at work on the Olsen quays. Their work, while much mechanised, still remained arduous because of unsocial hours and lack of protection from the weather.

5-8. The sociological significance of the building's location at the heart of the Olsen complex is not easy to understand in retrospect, but at the time it marked a revolution in labour relations. Its amenities – including table tennis – were entirely without parallel, not just in the docks but in British industry at large.

**Promises made to the dockers were honoured and often exceeded. The gentle hints of a better life-style extended to billiards and television as well as darts. Office walls were graced with paintings which Fred Olsen sent over from Norway, in addition to the promised carpet and landscaping.** Norman Foster, *Norman Foster: Sketches*, 1992
Left: A selection of abstract works from Fred Olsen's contemporary art collection graced the office spaces.

**Inside, colour has been used with an exquisite sensibility ... Grass-green floor surfaces, warm brown facings to the service core and peppermint-green linings in Swedish melamine are the ground elements. Other details, such as purple stair rails ... and bold semi-abstract paintings provided by Fred Olsen himself add up to an environment more in tune with limp-wristed aesthetes than with the brawny, matter-of-fact habitués of the London docks.** Alastair Best, *Design*, May 1970

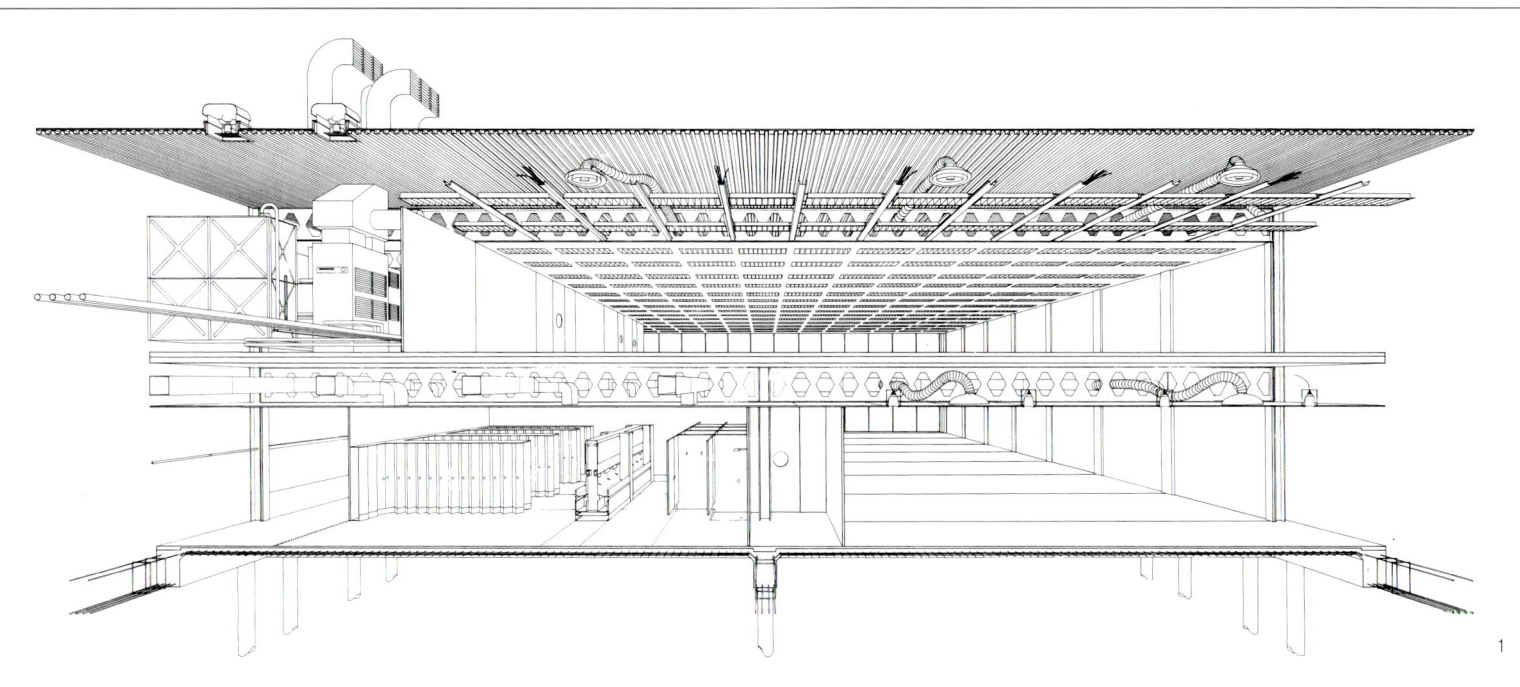

1. The structure comprised 1-metre deep castellated beams spanning the full 27 metres between the two transit sheds, supported on columns at either end. All services – including air-conditioning ductwork – were distributed through the ceiling zones, supplied via a plant room at first floor level.

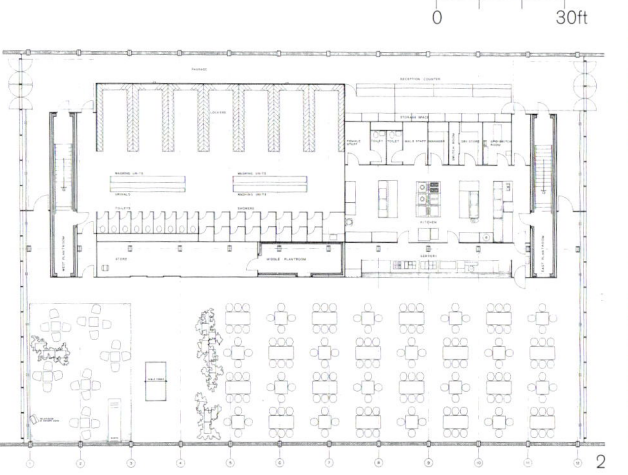

**The relationship between social and technical aspects of design is best illustrated by an incident at the official opening ceremony. A journalist trying to score points suggested to the union representative Tom Jones that the glazing was a sort of one-way mirror – a management device to spy on workers on the quayside. His reply was brief and to the point: he explained that everyone knew about the glass before it arrived on site because they were fully involved in what was happening. The level of social integration achieved on this project was evidently the exception rather than the rule.** Norman Foster, 'Flexibility in Design' lecture, Brighton, 7 April 1981

Left: The press conference to mark the official opening of the Olsen Amenity Centre. Seated left to right are Tom Jones, union representative, Fred Olsen, H M Lloyd, M A Thompson, Fred Olsen Centre manager, and J H Gabony, Millwall Dock manager.

The glazing system used here was not unique to the project: the short development period meant that Foster could not possibly have designed and prototyped a curtain wall in the time available. However, research revealed that an American company, Pittsburgh Plate Glass, had recently introduced a new, rubber-gasketed glazing system, which was the first to make use of solar-reflective glass. It had been designed for single-storey applications (the system would subsequently be used in its original form for the IBM Pilot Head Office) but Foster was quick to recognise its potential for two-storeys. His reaction was to jump on a plane to the United States to discuss with the company's technical team how the details might be resolved. He returned with a full set of working drawings, and the glazing was duly shipped and installed by Modern Art Glass, for whom Foster would, in turn, design a building two years later.

On completion the building garnered so much press coverage that it brought Foster to the attention of a string of new clients, Sir Robert Sainsbury among them. He visited the building, talked to the managers and workers, and came away impressed both by its design and the extent of its social innovation. It was the Olsen building that convinced him that he had found his architect for what was to become the Sainsbury Centre for Visual Arts.

Technically the Olsen building was a significant advance on Reliance Controls. With its sophisticated componentry and tight engineering tolerances it represented the state of the art. Foster notes that it also marked a move towards closer links with industry, which has come to characterise the practice's working method ever since. This was manifested not only in terms of the glazing system and product development, but also in the use of 'fast-track' management contracting, which Foster pioneered in the UK at Olsen.

2. The ground floor provided amenities for dock workers. The core contained locker, lavatory, washing and storage areas, to the left, and kitchen, servery and plant rooms to the right. The rest of the space was taken up with a restaurant and recreation facilities.

3. Like the rest of the building, the restaurant was air-conditioned and finished to a very high standard. To cater for shift workers, the servery remained open twenty-four hours a day.

4. The first floor spanned the full 27 metres from party-wall to party-wall without internal columns. A small service core, with plant rooms and lavatories, ran along one party wall.

5. The first floor was mainly given over to administrative offices, open-planned to accommodate up to sixty people. Managers and clerical staff shared the same space. Planting and cabinets were carefully arranged to mask meeting areas and managers' offices where a greater degree of privacy was required.

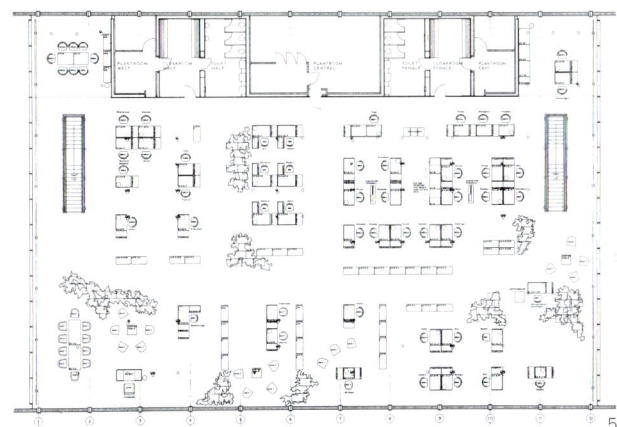

**The development period for the first Olsen project was incredibly short, and so we had to challenge conventions; for example, we could not possibly have designed and prototyped the glazed curtain-wall that we wanted in the time available. And so I went on a research trip to the States and brought back a sophisticated system that used brand new products such as heat and light reflective glasses. Nobody had ever taken that initiative before.** Norman Foster, *GA Extra*, February 1999

Left: One of the sheets of glass being lifted into place. Despite the large sheet size of 4.25 x 1.5 metres, remarkably fine tolerances of plus or minus 1.5mm over 10 metres were achieved on the glazing frame.

1. The implications of air conditioning on the design of the two glass walls were very carefully studied, and various combinations of internal shading, venetian blinds and curtains, external louvres and heat-absorbing glass were evaluated. In the end a 6mm-thick low heat and light transmission American glass called Solargray was chosen. The glass was supported by a full-height, silver-anodised aluminium box-section frame with a neoprene gasket fixing system developed by Pittsburgh Plate Glass. The sealing sequence for the gasket is shown here.

2. As at IBM Cosham, the ceiling service zone was expressed behind the glass facade and was clearly visible in the evening.

3. Within a tolerance of a few millimetres, the first floor cantilevers out to touch – but not support – the curtain-wall's aluminium framing. A free-standing handrail offers security.

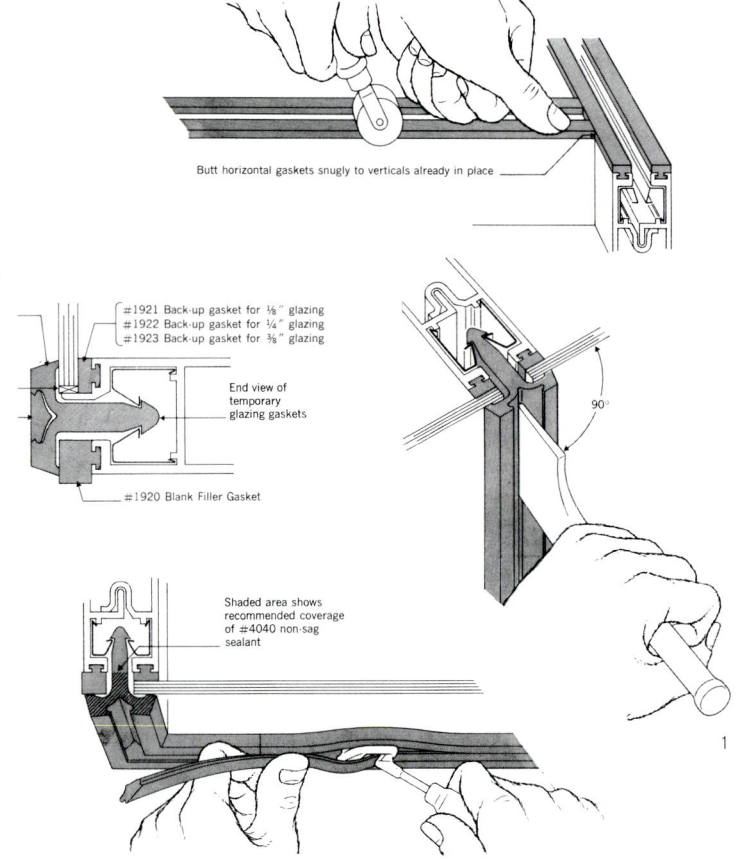

Yet, while Reliance Controls was built for the rapidly expanding electronics industry, then in its infancy, the Amenity Centre was designed for a sector already in steep decline. Within fifteen years of the building's completion, the docks would move downstream to Tilbury and the area now known as 'Docklands' would become the largest new development area in the capital. When Fred Olsen left Millwall for Southampton the building briefly enjoyed a new lease of life as the headquarters of the London Docklands Development Corporation – proof indeed of Foster's argument for flexibility – until it too was demolished in 1988 to make way for the Harbour Exchange development.

Foster himself would return to Docklands to design on a scale he could not possibly have imagined when he won the Olsen commission. In 1991 the practice was commissioned to design a new Underground station on the Jubilee Line extension, and within the next ten years would complete major headquarters buildings for Citibank and HSBC in the new business and financial quarter of Canary Wharf – all within sight of the old Millwall Dock.

David Jenkins

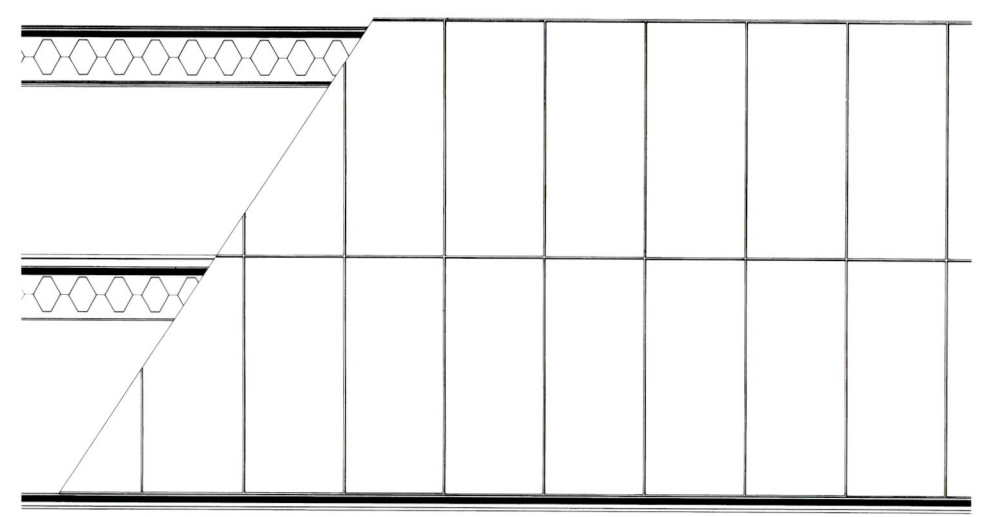

**Norman Foster makes an expressive virtue of the wobbly flat, an effect which has been focused on by the painter Ben Johnson. In his *Dock Reflections*, we find the reflected world broken up into rectangular patches by a very thin mullion line while the reflections themselves wobble as they cross the panels and bend. The painting brings out another rhetorical property of the mirror-wall: as a *trompe l'oeil* it distorts reality slightly and enhances its cleanliness and precision.** Charles Jencks, *Current Architecture*, 1982
Right: Ben Johnson's painting *Dock Reflections*, of 1971. This work was purchased by Norman Foster in 1974.

4. The tinted glass cladding of the Amenity Centre seen from the deck of an Olsen ship berthed at the quay. At the time of its completion, the building's pristine quality stood it apart from any other building in the docks.

Overleaf: At night the reflectiveness of the tinted glass gave way to a dramatic transparency, exposing the inner workings of the building in all their detail.

**The two award-winning buildings were so far above the others that there was no doubt among us that they were the best.** Arthur G Aldersley-Williams, Juror, *AD* Project Awards, January 1969
The Olsen Amenity Centre was the recipient of an *AD* Project Award in 1969; the first year in which awards were restricted to the category of service buildings.

**The Olsen Amenity Centre was an attempt by a well-intentioned employer to address the positively medieval working practices of the dock industry … and indeed it was a remarkable achievement. Britain suddenly seemed to escape from the black and white cloth cap caricature of labour relations, to emerge blinking into a new world of vivid colour. Foster showed that it was possible to create a working environment for dockers that could get into the glossy magazines … Two radically different worlds, usually in collision, were for the first time brought together.**
Deyan Sudjic, *On Foster … Foster On*, 2000

**It is the reflective glazing of the amenity building – more usually connected with the rich executive pastures of Manhattan and Chicago – that is its most unexpected feature. By day the glass, which was made in Pittsburgh to the architects' specification, throws back a rippling image of the dockside scene; by night the picture is reversed and the eye has an uninterrupted view of the ground-floor canteen and landscaped first floor offices, separated by castellated steel beams.**
Alastair Best, *Design*, May 1970

**The idea of the workplace as a democratic environment has been a key issue for Foster ever since Reliance Controls, and the Olsen Lines building in the London Docks. It is a poignant witness to the pace of change that both these once revolutionary buildings have been demolished, superseded by the shifts in the world of work.** Deyan Sudjic, *On Foster … Foster On*, 2000

Right: After serving for several years as the headquarters of the London Docklands Development Corporation the Amenity Centre was demolished in 1988 to make way for the wholesale redevelopment of Millwall Dock.

# Fred Olsen Passenger Terminal
Millwall Dock, London, England 1969–1970

**Designed to accommodate departing or arriving cruise passengers, the building sat lightly on the dockside, an appropriately machine-like presence in a wholly industrialised landscape.**
David Jenkins

**The passenger terminal has a simplicity of approach and clarity of structure which belies the level of thought and research behind its design.**
Jose Manser, *Design*, January 1971
Left: An aerial view of the Olsen Amenity Centre taken following the completion of the Passenger Terminal.

**The elevated passenger terminal is never in continuous use. Even during the winter months – the peak cruise season – the building is in action at most three times weekly. It was therefore difficult to justify a structure which was more than a weatherproof link from ship to shore (and vice versa).** *Industrial Buildings: A Client's Guide*, pamphlet produced by Foster Associates, 1977

Norman Foster has said that for him the projects for Fred Olsen in Millwall Dock, were more interesting socially than technically; certainly the Amenity Centre pioneered the integration of white and blue-collar staff and brought unprecedented standards of accommodation to the otherwise benighted docks. But, together, the Olsen Amenity Centre and Passenger Terminal are also remarkable in terms of their design and construction. The Amenity Centre was notable for its glass curtain wall – which introduced new materials and assembly methods to the UK – but each of them also offered a compelling demonstration of how to achieve 'more with less', and did so within the confines of an exceptionally tight programme.

Foster's strategic analysis of Fred Olsen's operations at Millwall Dock, the catalyst for the design of the Amenity Centre, was concerned in part with the efficient movement of goods and people on the site, and the segregation of freight and passenger activities. The Passenger Terminal, commissioned the following year, sprang directly from this logic and might be read in Foster's phrase as 'built circulation'.

Designed to accommodate departing or arriving cruise passengers, the building sat lightly on the dockside, an appropriately machine-like presence in a wholly industrialised landscape. Its section echoed that of Olsen's ships, separating passengers above from cargo below and delivered them and their baggage to the ship at the appropriate deck level.

The enclosure was formed simply and economically from two slender tubes that fitted tightly around the corner of one of the transit sheds. The larger tube, 6.5 metres wide, ran horizontally for 70 metres along the dockside and formed a passenger concourse. The smaller tube provided a covered access ramp. The raised tube structure was supported on I-beam stanchions pin-jointed to concrete pads – engineered to resist impact from forklift trucks – and was stayed laterally against the transit shed behind.

Early studies envisaged a rigid monocoque tube formed from two skins of cold-rolled plastic-coated profiled steel decking, similar to that used at Reliance Controls. However, this option was rejected for cost reasons and a far lighter structural system adopted in which the steel-framed tubes were clad in a single skin of ribbed aluminium.

1. Seen from the deck of one of Fred Olsen's moored ships, the barrel-vaulted passenger terminal blended imperceptibly with the sloping aluminium roof of the transit shed beyond.

2. An end view and cut-away elevation of the terminal in close to its final form. Structurally it is little more than a 6.5 metre wide, 70 metre long steel beam platform, supported on steel stanchions pin-jointed to the quayside and stayed against the existing transit shed. The cladding is a single skin of profiled aluminium sheet.

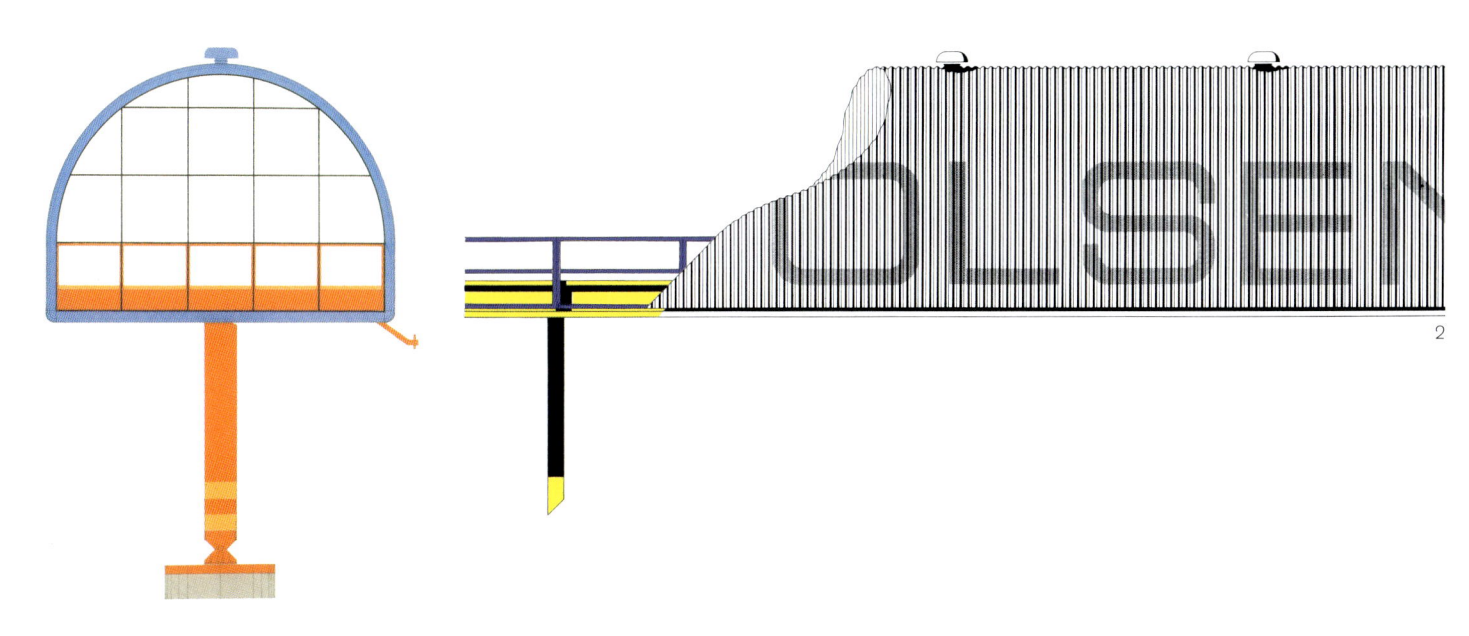

**The more one simplifies a construction the more it acquires character.** Jean Prouvé, lecture at the Arts et Métiers, Paris, 1961
From the 1950s onwards, Prouvé explored the potential of pressed or folded metal structures in a series of curved building shapes. His pioneering work to extend the principles of high quality manufacturing into the world of architecture clearly influenced the design of the Olsen Passenger Terminal.
Left: Detail of an organically elegant aluminium shutter designed by Prouvé for the Manufacture des Tabacs in Marseilles (1954).

**The elegant economy of the Passenger Terminal's pressed-metal skin and the dexterity with which its constituent parts were assembled evoke the intellectual clarity of Jean Prouvé, the master of prefabricated construction and one of Foster's acknowledged heroes.**
David Jenkins

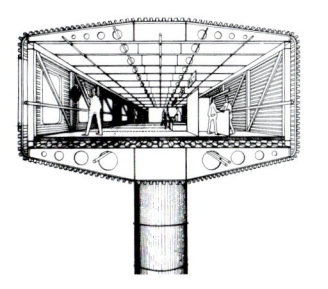

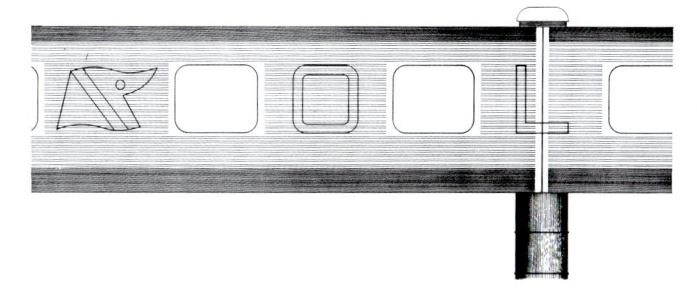

**The passenger terminal pursued a particular direction that appeared in other projects of the period – the concept of the wrap-around skin, which reduced the number of components and traded on the common denominators between roof and wall cladding.** Norman Foster, 'Delight in Design' lecture at UEA, Norwich, 27 November 1978

Left: The first version of the terminal was a relatively heavy affair relying on a cantilevered structure of tapered steel frames, the weight-reducing holes in their webs doubling as service runs. Horizontally profiled aluminium sheeting was to have been wrapped around the 'tube', with purpose-made windows inserted into the sides.

1, 2. The relationship between the terminal and the ships it served could not be simpler. Raised up to permit uninterrupted cargo operations at quay level, the tube of the Passenger Terminal links horizontally with the passenger decks of the berthed liners.

3, 4. To compensate for an otherwise windowless tube, the two ends of the terminal were fully glazed, offering spectacular views of the working dock below.

5. Close to the threshold that separates architecture from mere industrial enclosure, and erected in only three weeks, the Olsen terminal was an exercise in structural minimalism.

6. Together with the Fred Olsen name, the shipping line's flag – the company's logo – was painted on to the aluminium cladding.

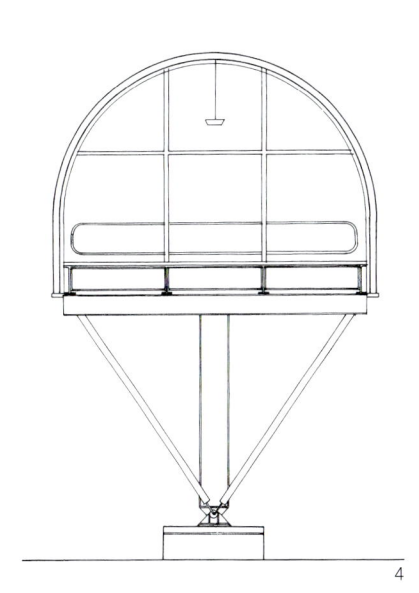

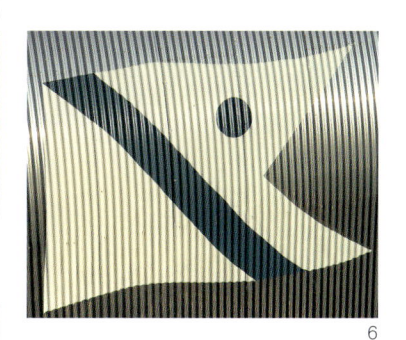

Fred Olsen Passenger Terminal

**The Doug was designed with innate style by people who cared about designing airliners and built a good one ... they are the aircraft which set the standard by which all other jets fail. Built like tanks with professionalism in every detail – you should see those patterns of rivet heads on the wing!** Reyner Banham, *The Architects' Journal*, 1 August 1962

Left: The semi-monocoque fuselage of the DC-3 aircraft is echoed in the structure of the Olsen Passenger Terminal. Launched by Douglas in 1936, the DC-3's elegant airframe design incorporated the first effective production-line application of stressed-skin structures and represented a milestone in the development of commercial air travel.

1-5. The terminal in use. Its aluminium cladding was supported on a minimal steel frame. Simple square-cut 'portholes' provided access to the ships; roller-shutter doors sealed the openings when not in use. Lighting was a combination of daylight – via the translucent corrugated pvc sheets that replaced the aluminium at regular intervals – and fluorescent tubes positioned in a suspended metal trough running the length of the terminal. Mainly used as a staff link, the spiral staircase – encircled in perforated steel sheet – gave access to the quay below. A free-standing cabin contained lavatories and washrooms.

**As with Reliance Controls, the elements forming the structure and enclosure were used to their fullest effect and maximum use was made of 'found' materials and products. The customs and ticket office, for example, was formed from truck sections and the baggage-handling conveyor was made from customised agricultural machinery.**
David Jenkins

170  Norman Foster  Works 1

**There is a rising breed, amongst whom Foster Associates are a notable example, who are on easy terms with contemporary conditions, have a decent working relationship with industry and commerce, and who are in their seemingly relaxed way producing some of the most interesting and appropriate modern architecture. Foster Associates, particularly, are doing it with a steely dedication and disregard for prescriptive methods that makes all those prima donnas look like flabby leftovers from another age.** Jose Manser, *Design*, January 1971

**Certainly, Foster Associates have not gone out of the way to evolve an architectural style or an iconography of details that says unequivocally 'Look at me, I'm appropriate!' And they are probably right: the simple-mindedly low-tech have their windmills and pisé walls, the woolly-minded high-tech have their highly coloured exposed ductwork; the 'appropriate-tech' must have whatever is usefully at hand, whatever it may be.** Reyner Banham, *Foster Associates*, 1979

---

Natural light was introduced through the transparent panels that articulated the aluminium cladding and through the glazed walls at either end, which also revealed the thinness of the structure. Simple, square-cut 'portholes' with roller shutters allowed access to the ships at the required points.

As with Reliance Controls, the elements forming the structure and enclosure were used to their fullest effect and maximum use was made of 'found' materials and products. The customs and ticket office, for example, was formed from truck sections and the baggage-handling conveyor was made from customised agricultural machinery. Similarly, a mobile maintenance platform, originally designed for servicing jet aircraft, was adapted to form a gangway between the terminal and the ship.

The cladding was of natural-finished ribbed aluminium, emblazoned with the Olsen logo, while the remaining structural elements were articulated in primary colours – the steelwork and window frames in blue, the escape stairs and 'pods' containing offices in yellow. Like the interior of the Amenity Centre, bright colour was used with great effect to create a break with the grime of the dockside and, in Foster's words, 'to introduce a little joy'.

The elegant economy of the Passenger Terminal's pressed-metal skin and the dexterity with which its constituent parts were assembled evoke the intellectual clarity of Jean Prouvé, the master of prefabricated construction and one of Foster's acknowledged heroes.

There are suggestions too of technological influences from outside the building industry. In the view down the concourse there is more than a hint of the pioneering stressed-skin airframe of the Dakota DC-3, a milestone in aircraft design. And from outside, at certain angles, there are echoes of the silvery skin of the Airstream caravan, which so captivated Foster as a student in the United States. In retrospect, although the aims of this little building were modest, it was a bravura performance.

David Jenkins

6. An axonometric drawing of the terminal in its early colour plastic-coated skin. Designed to fit tightly round the corner of the existing warehouse, the terminal was approached via a long covered ramp which kept cars and buses well away from the activity of the quayside. Luggage-handling and customs facilities were contained in the main tube.

7. A mobile maintenance platform, originally designed for servicing jet aircraft, was adapted to support a simple adjustable gangway linking terminal to ship.

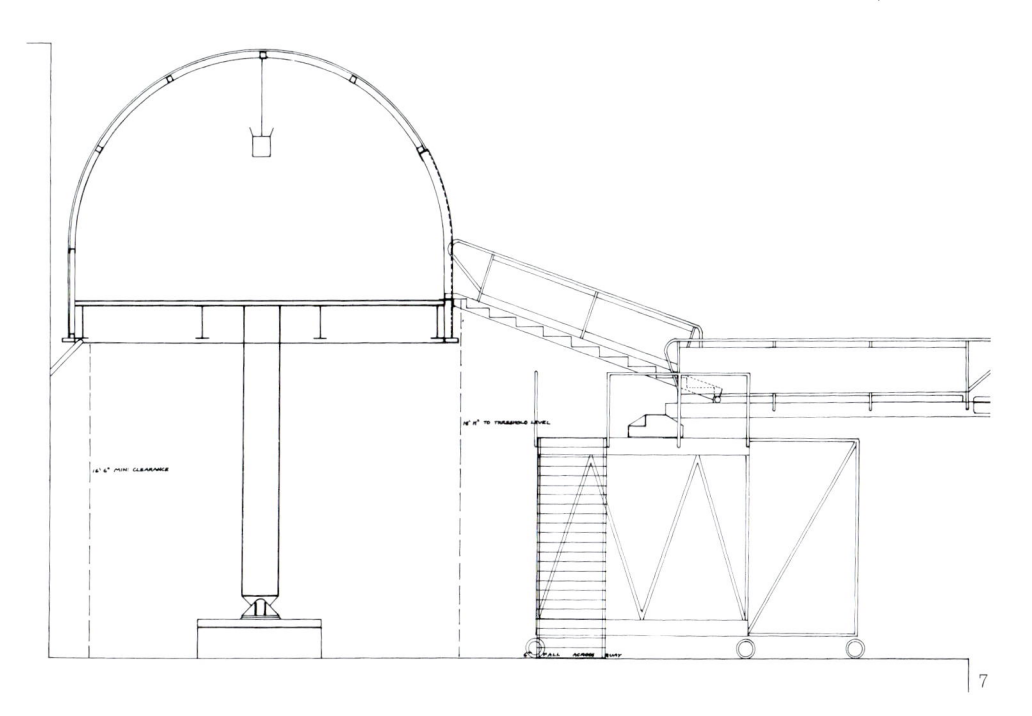

# Country Offices
Vestby, Norway 1973

Located deep in a woodland setting, south of Oslo, the Vestby pavilions 'touched the ground lightly', structurally and environmentally.

1. In this Helmut Jacoby perspective drawing, the glassy pavilions seem to hover weightlessly above the forest floor. High-performance glazing was specified, similar to that used at the Olsen Amenity Centre and IBM Cosham.

2, 3. Circulation within the Vestby complex was to have been entirely on foot, with all vehicles confined to the perimeter. Norman Foster's sketch of the proposed forest paths shows how they were to follow the routes of existing ski trails. These walkways were to be raised above the ground level to permit water, power and communications services to run beneath them, where they would be concealed but easily accessible.

**Vestby was to clarify many of the environmental ideas that would form the basis of our later work – the sunlight reflector, for example, is just one element that has since become a recurring theme.**
Norman Foster

**When the Vestby project ... was presented, laden with signs of energy conservation, many assumed an about-face had occurred in Foster Associates' attitudes to technology. For on close inspection the raised pavilions, that silently infiltrated the forest and so deceptively looked like High-tech boxes, proved to be Pandora's boxes packed with appropriate technology surprises.** *Architectural Design*, March 1976
Left: The Vestby project sought inspiration from many surprisingly low-tech sources, such as these vernacular dwellings and platform structures, illustrated by Bernard Rudofsky in his seminal *Architecture Without Architects*. Like the Vestby buildings, they 'touch the ground lightly'.

Left: The roof-top reflectors proposed at Vestby would inform the design of the 'sunscoop' incorporated within the Hongkong and Shanghai Bank Headquarters (1979-1986). The sunscoop, fitted with a battery of angled mirrors, reflects sunlight down through the central atrium to the floor of the open public plaza below.

The rapport that Norman Foster established with Fred Olsen in London led to commissions for a series of projects in Olsen's native Norway. These were to take the practice in new architectural directions and would provide the impetus for opening its first overseas office. The Vestby project resulted from a proposal by Olsen and two associated companies to relocate their headquarters from Oslo to a wooded, rural site overlooking Oslo Fjord, 50 kilometres south of the city.

The site was a mature pine forest, hitherto untouched by development, which was cut through with ski trails and sloped down towards the water. Foster sensed immediately the need to establish a strategy for building there that would 'touch the ground lightly' and preserve the delicate forest ecology. That concern was allied with a desire to make the buildings as energy efficient as possible by exploiting natural methods of lighting and ventilation. The convergence of these imperatives would lead the design team to explore a wide range of ecologically informed solutions to constructing and servicing the new buildings.

4. This early sketch by Wendy Foster demonstrates how the pavilions were to have been raised on pilotis, allowing them to span the irregular forest floor, which was left untouched below. The roof-top reflectors, designed to direct sunlight through roof-lights into the deep plan, are suggestive of the sunscoop that Foster would design for the Hongkong and Shanghai Bank nearly a decade later.

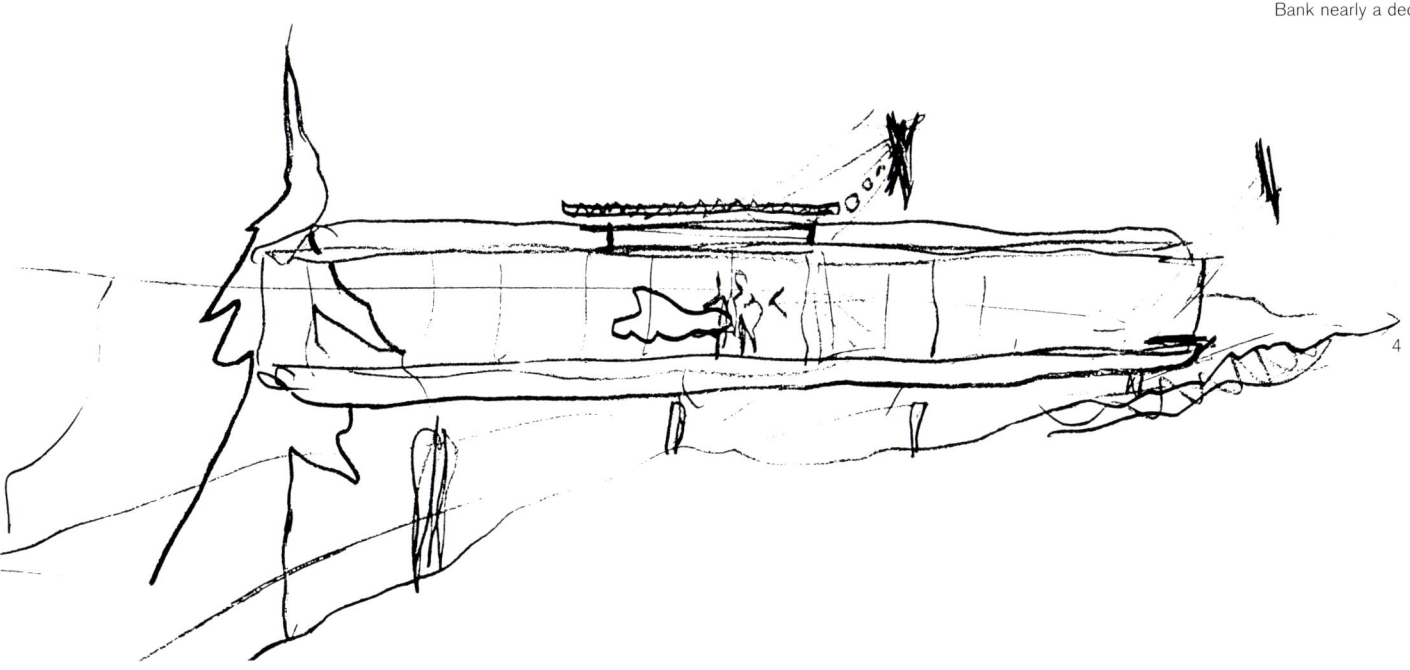

Country Offices 173

Right: The Chesa Futura in St Moritz (2000-2002) returns to the themes of minimising environmental impact and situating a building sensitively in its surroundings explored in the Vestby project. The apartment building utilises local sustainable timber construction techniques and its bubble-like form is a response to the planning envelope, views and the sun, as well as the microclimate. Like the Vestby offices, the building stands on pilotis, referencing indigenous architectural traditions while maximising the spectacular vista offered out on to the Engadin valley below.

**The Vestby scheme sits on undercarriages to conserve the forest and protect it from the ravages of builders' and contractors' plant. Lightweight components, easily transportable by helicopter to more remote locations, can be bolted together quickly by small teams ... This approach also embraces the energy concepts to drive the building – its waste systems would recycle to avoid polluting the fjord with human waste.** Norman Foster, *Foster Associates*, 1979.
Right: A series of sketches by Birkin Haward was used to communicate to the client the benefits of appropriate technology in supplying energy, and managing environmental systems.

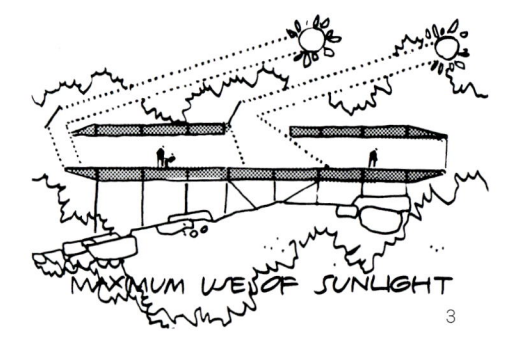

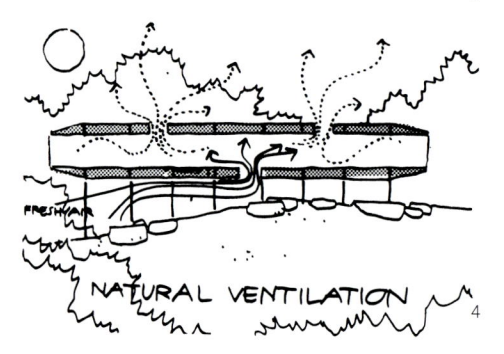

The resulting building form was a single-storey, free standing pavilion, raised clear of the forest floor on pilotis and oriented to exploit views of the fjord. These pavilions would be located discretely within the forest. Vehicular traffic stopped at the edge of the forest and circulation within the site was to be entirely on foot, using raised pathways that followed the existing ski trails.

The buildings were to be prefabricated, thus ensuring a minimum of site work, and the lightweight components could have been manoeuvred easily along forest paths, or brought in by helicopter. Ducts for water, power and cabling were incorporated within the pathways thereby avoiding the need for excavations.

The pavilion's external envelope was well insulated and reflective, incorporating louvres to reduce solar gain. Norman Foster hints at the 'chameleon-like' characteristics of the buildings in their setting: 'Depending on how the external blinds were activated, the pavilions could have appeared as solid forms – coloured, metallic or ribbed', he recalls: 'Or with the throw of a switch they could become reflective mirrors'. The design team also explored ways in which the sides of the buildings might be opened up completely in warm weather, allowing those inside to almost reach out and touch the trees.

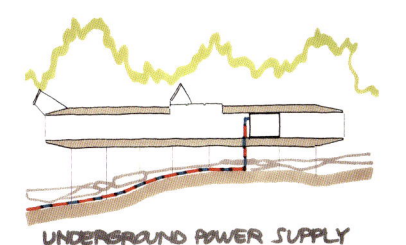

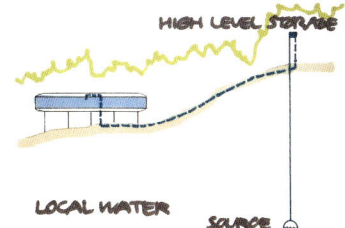

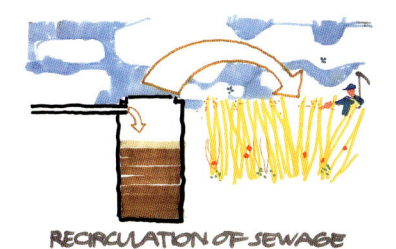

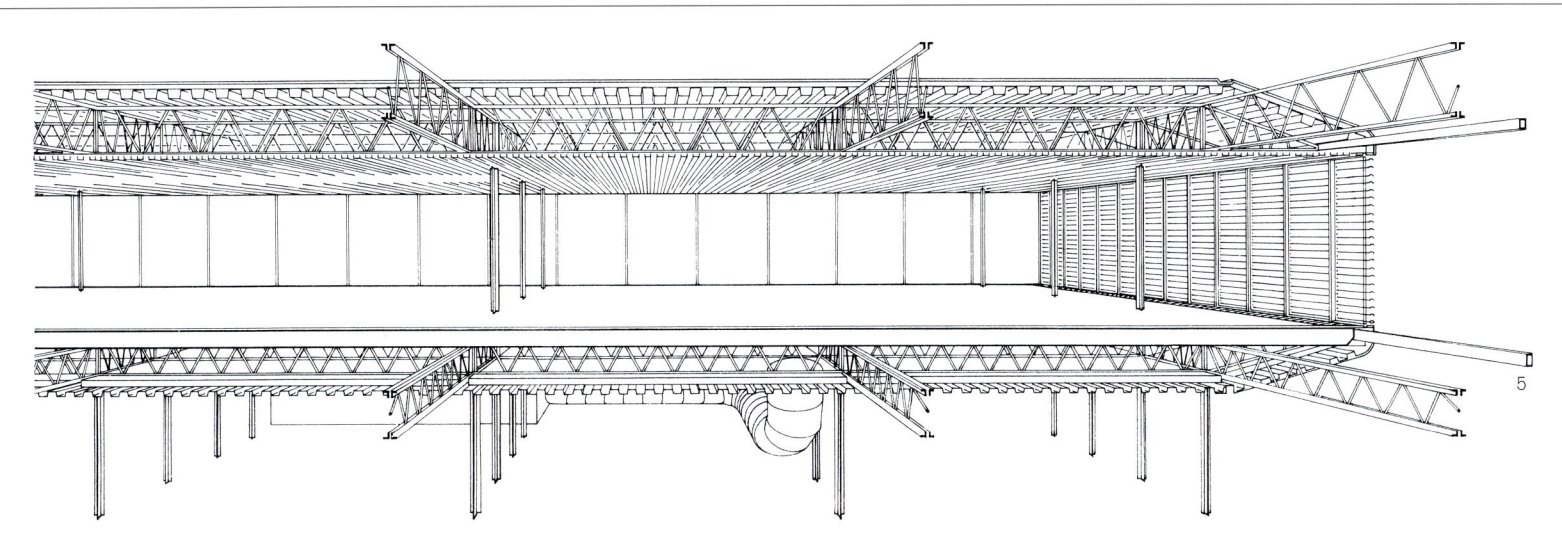

Lifting the pavilions free of the ground allowed air to circulate around the external envelope; enabling it to be drawn in at floor level to supply a natural ventilation system that relied on large air volume and the stack effect, thus avoiding the need for high energy consuming air conditioning. On the roof, banks of motorised reflectors were designed to track the low northern sun, to reflect warming sunlight into the centre of the plan. They could also direct the sun's heat to melt winter snow along the northern elevations; rainwater and melt water would be channelled and used to flush lavatories. Drainage and sanitary systems were in turn designed to recycle waste matter organically to avoid polluting the fjord, which supplied Vestby with its fresh water.

Although the Vestby project was not realised, its ecological agenda would have a significant influence on the future direction of the practice's work, not least the regional planning study for Gomera, which followed shortly afterwards. And the sunlight reflector – perhaps Vestby's most significant invention – would transmute through many subsequent incarnations, from the 'sunscoop' in the Hongkong Bank to the mirrored cone in the cupola of the Reichstag.

David Jenkins

**Many of the technical features we pioneered at Vestby were subsequently monitored by the Norwegian government for potential application in new and remote settlements.**

Norman Foster

1. This elevational study shows the external louvres, which would have responded automatically to prevailing weather conditions.

2, 6. The Vestby model reveals the sunlight reflectors on the roof and the ventilation equipment slung below each pavilion.

3, 4. Birkin Haward's sketches explain the building's lighting and ventilating systems.

5. The structure was a long-span steel lattice system, designed to rely on minimal ground support to reduce environmental impact. Components were small and lightweight to take account of limited site access.

Country Offices 175

# Son Recreation Centre and Oslo Offices
Norway 1973

1. The Son country club and marina, situated on a peninsula projecting into Oslo Fjord, 50 kilometres south of the capital, included the adaptive use of existing barns as well as new buildings, boatyard facilities and a heliport. Birkin Haward's sketch interior of the recreation building proposed column-supported balconies projecting into an open-plan space on which facilities for different activities could be easily combined.

> **As with Vestby, Foster's approach was one of minimal intervention in the landscape, although here this intention was articulated quite differently.**
> David Jenkins

The preliminary studies that Foster Associates made for the waterside Recreation Centre in Son, in Norway, 50 kilometres south of the capital, were prompted by the nearby Vestby development. The building was to provide recreational facilities for Olsen's employees at Vestby and form a social focus for the entire local community. Additionally, there was a possibility that it could include a small conference hotel and provide a yacht marina, while an existing barn on the site could be converted to provide a base for picnics.

The site lay on a peninsula projecting into Oslo Fjord and the building was envisaged as a lightweight, glazed dome structure, located close to the water's edge. As with the Vestby pavilions, Foster's approach was one of minimal intervention in the landscape, although here this intention was articulated quite differently. Rather than sitting on pilotis the building nestles into its site and the section is organised as a series of stepped terraces, which follow the contours of the embankment. In 'digging into' the site in this way – and presenting a glassy cowling above ground – the building follows the precedent set by the little Cockpit at Creek Vean. It is a theme that recurs at varying scales throughout Foster's later oeuvre, culminating perhaps in the Great Glasshouse for the National Botanic Garden of Wales, completed in 2000.

176  Norman Foster  Works 1

Left: The ground-hugging or dug-in building has been a consistent theme in Foster's work, from the little Cockpit retreat at Feock, to the Great Glasshouse at the National Botanic Garden of Wales (1995-2000) described here in Norman Foster's sketch section. The latter reinvents the glasshouse for the twenty-first century, offering a model for sustainability; elliptical in plan, its toroidal roof swells from the ground like a glassy hillock, echoing the undulations of the surrounding landscape.

**When Norman set up the practice in 1967 he was seen as a radical new force in contemporary architecture. At that time, the idea that the practice might develop to encompass creative rehabilitation – the art of bringing life back to historical buildings – was unthinkable.** Spencer de Grey, in conversation with Malcolm Quantrill, 1999
Left: The Sackler Galleries at the Royal Academy of Arts, completed in 1991, is typical of Foster's innovative response to the 'creative rehabilitation' of historical buildings. The Olsen offices in Oslo can be seen as the first of a long series of projects in the Foster oeuvre that have approached this challenge with sensitivity.

Fred Olsen's proposal to move his headquarters from the centre of Oslo to Vestby generated a further planning study, which focused on the city block in which the existing headquarters was situated. It was a project that gave Foster his first opportunity to work within the context of a major historical building – a nineteenth-century timber-framed structure that had housed Olsen's offices – and to rehearse themes that would become highly significant in his later work.

The 'hands-off' approach that Foster had explored in the Vestby schemes – where the natural landscape is respected and left untouched as far as possible – was translated into an urban context. The existing building is retained intact and a new building placed alongside it, the street between them being roofed over to form a glazed atrium. The atrium mediates between the private realm of the offices and the city beyond and continues an Oslo tradition, echoing the glazed courtyards to be found in many historical buildings, including the Olsen offices, which provide shelter from the extremes of the Norwegian climate.

The strategy that Foster adopted in Oslo stemmed from his belief that 'every era produces its own vocabulary, has its own integrity and makes its own mark'. He attributes the architectural richness and variety that we take for granted in so many cities to each age having had the confidence to express itself in its own distinctive way, looking forward optimistically while respecting the past. That approach, at the scale of the city, anticipates his subsequent interventions within individual buildings that have grown or been extended over time: first with the Royal Academy of Arts, and later in the Reichstag and the British Museum. In each case Foster creates a conscious dialogue between the new work and the old, enriching both in the process.

David Jenkins

2. Norman Foster's sketch section through the principal Son building, a discreet large-scale glazed dome at the water's edge. Terraced internally and dug into the contours of the land so as to be inconspicuous despite its size, the structure would have provided unrivalled views of the Fjord.

3. This drawing, by Helmut Jacoby, was prepared as part of a proposal for the Fred Olsen offices in Oslo. One of Foster Associates' first opportunities to work within the context of a historical building, the scheme left the existing building intact and turned the adjacent street into an atrium. The Oslo project was linked to the move to Vestby and was unfortunately lost with that scheme.

**I believe that every era produces its own vocabulary, has its own integrity and makes its own mark – and if they are expressed honestly, the old and the new can complement each other in an enriching way.**
Norman Foster

# Fred Olsen Travel Agency
London, England 1975

**One of the most innovative aspects of the Olsen Travel Agency was the use of banks of videos to sell holidays to its customers – and it worked!**
Norman Foster, in conversation with the editor, 2001
Right: A typical example of the staid printed promotional material used hitherto by Olsen to promote its cruises.

Fred Olsen Lines had operated a sales agency in Regent Street, London for many years. When the time came for refurbishment, the company was stimulated by new concepts in marketing to commission Foster Associates to redesign the showroom.

Norman Foster's approach was to break with the usual sales reliance on printed materials and to incorporate banks of video screens that could offer a far more vivid impression of life on an Olsen cruise. The showroom made the most of its corner location on one of London's busiest shopping routes, opening up both street elevations with full-height glass walls. The street was thus drawn into the shop and vice versa, creating a feeling of generous and accessible space.

This sense of openness was reinforced by the simplest of interiors based on the company colours. A blue carpet was set against walls and a ceiling lined with polished aluminium slats. Furniture was finished in the same blue as the carpet and the whole area was suffused with the cool light of two neon signs set high on the interior walls. These signs were clearly visible from the street, especially at night when the whole shop shone like a lantern.

Ian Lambot

1. The Olsen agency, located at the corner of Hanover Street and Regent Street, in the West End of London, was completely glazed on its two street frontages. The passer-by was drawn into the space by the apparent short cut, a feeling further emphasised by the diagonal direction of the ceiling slats.

2. A bank of video screens showed film footage of life on board the cruise ships and their destinations.

3. Seen at night, the shop's brightly lit interior became part of the life of the street.

4. The space contained an information and booking desk, with a table and chairs in front of a bank of video screens. Video equipment, storage and staff facilities were located separately and accessed via a slatted door that blended into the walls.

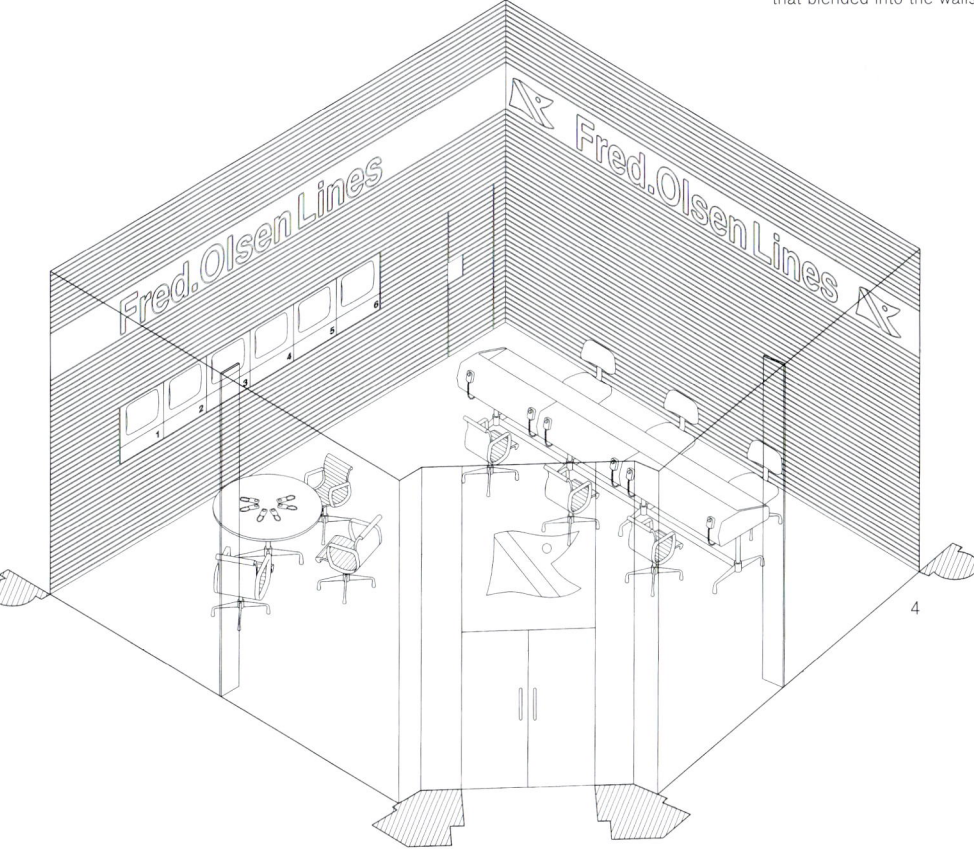

Fred Olsen Travel Agency

# Gomera Regional Planning Study
Island of Gomera, Canary Islands 1975

> The brief was to draw up a plan that showed how the island could embrace tourism without wrecking its coastline, and how the island could harness its natural resources.
>
> Norman Foster

Right: By 1975, the main Canary Island of Tenerife was already developing rapidly as a tourist resort, placing pressure on the nearby islands to follow suit. Though it is the closest island to Tenerife, at the time of this study Gomera had been unaffected by the tourist boom. However, a newly opened Fred Olsen Lines ferry link between the two islands was seen as the first step in Gomera's possible development as a tourist destination.

**Gomera at present exhibits all the characteristics of an island in decline. Its population is dwindling; the road network is inadequate; public transport negligible. The island's economy depends heavily on Tenerife, to which it has been linked since 1973 by a daily ferry. Both Gomera's mainstays – agriculture and fishing – are heavily depleted. And, with the exception of one 40 bedroom hotel, there are no organised facilities on the island for tourists.** Excerpt from Foster Associates' Gomera project report, 1975

When looked back on from today, two Foster Associates projects from the early and mid-1970s stand out for the teasingly provocative questions they raise. They are the Vestby Country Offices (and the associated Son Recreation Centre) and the Gomera Regional Planning Study. Both were commissioned by the Norwegian shipping magnate Fred Olsen, following the completion of the amenity centre and passenger terminal in London's Millwall Dock, and they reflect the inspiration both of his ideals and the ideas of Buckminster Fuller. What if they had been realised, instead of marking (for a prolonged period at least) a cul-de-sac in Foster Associates' exploration of a particular approach to environmental design? Might Norman Foster have adopted much earlier the genuinely twenty-first-century approaches to design to which the practice's architecture is now progressing, instead of pursuing what, at the time, might have seemed to be a more futuristically oriented approach?

The Vestby and Gomera schemes both speak eloquently to our ecologically minded times. Both would have nestled gently into their natural settings and harvested ambient energies (sunlight in the former, solar heat and wind in the latter) to reduce a dependence on fossil-fuel derived energy. However, the projects were very different architecturally. Vestby's glass-walled office buildings were rather like spaceships that hovered above and barely touched the land. Yet these blocks would also have settled within a Nordic pine forest and opened up to natural ventilation, while what resembled the tailplanes of the spaceships were projecting banks of mirrors to reflect low northern sun into the deep-plan offices. By contrast, elements of the tourist housing proposed for the arid island slopes of Gomera were derived from the local vernacular. The buildings were earthbound with heavy tile roofs backed against the walls of what had been agricultural terracing so that they too would have been barely visible from any distance.

There is another key difference between the schemes. For the Vestby offices and Son Recreation Centre, there is clear precedent in the work of Foster and Fuller, as well as later offspring; but for Gomera there is no real precedent in Foster's work nor, as yet, progeny. The recessive yet extroverted office blocks at Vestby might evoke something of the diminutive early Cockpit at Pill Creek. But instead of hovering above the earth, the Cockpit barely protrudes from it – and is thus much closer in spirit to the Recreation Centre that was to have served the Vestby complex. The Recreation Centre was clearly inspired by Fuller's domes and reworks the themes of the Climatroffice explored in collaboration by Foster and Fuller. (The concept of a dome snuggling into sloping ground was at last realised in the glasshouse of the National Botanic Gardens in Wales – though, instead of Fuller's spherical geometry there it is toroidal.)

However, the real precedent for the Vestby offices is surely to be found in Buckminster Fuller's projects, in particular those for mast-suspended houses and housing which, no matter how different they look, were also to be lightly poised above and minimally disruptive of the earth. (Vestby's projecting solar reflectors could be seen as the equivalent of the rotating rudder-vent of the Wichita House or the teardrop-shaped and tail-finned wind fairing of the 4D Dymaxion House, both of which would have brought advantages in energy efficiency.)

These photographs, taken by the Foster Associates project team, record Gomera as it existed at the time of their visit in February 1975.

1-4. The island was dying of desiccation. Devoid of trees to aid transpiration and thus cloud formation on its southern side, the prevailing trade winds tended to gather clouds against only the northern side of the island's central peak. Some green valleys with small banana plantations persisted on the island's northern slopes, while abandoned agricultural terracing bore testimony to wetter, more fertile times.

5. The island's rugged coastline is characterised by remote beaches of black volcanic rock and sand.

**The biggest difficulty of all was convincing the locals that they didn't need that prestige symbol, the airport. It was the only place that didn't have one and that was why it was so civilised.**
Norman Foster, lecture at the AIA Conference, London, October 1977

Right: A map of the main shipping and ferry routes to and from the Canary Islands, located close to the Tropic of Cancer off the north-west coast of Africa. Although it had a small airstrip, at the time of the study Gomera was fully accessible only by sea.

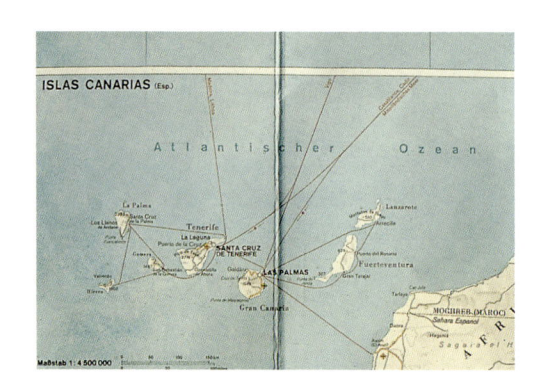

**Much of our work is dedicated to avoiding the built cliché. Gomera was the only island in the Canaries group which had not suffered the consequences of package tourism, and our study sought to develop a sympathetic alternative: to revive labour intensive local industries and traditional housing forms, and to show how the island might develop gradually without succumbing to a rash of international airports, ring-roads and high-rise hotels.** Norman Foster, lecture at the AIA Conference, London, October 1977
Left: An example of the effect that the Gomera study sought to avoid: the jostling high-rise hotels of Tenerife.

As for progeny, a contemporary project that has returned to some of the same themes as the Vestby offices (and Fuller's housing blocks) is the Chesa Futura apartment block for St Moritz. Here, however, instead of hiding amongst trees, the building's pumpkin form (which recalls the Wichita House) is framed in timber and clad in wood shingles, a sustainable material that is also visually sympathetic to the trees that the building hovers above.

Compared with Vestby or any other Foster project before or since, the Gomera study was much wider ranging and more radical. Its proposals would have settled seamlessly into and brought about the rejuvenation of all aspects of its setting: socio-cultural as well as environmental-architectural. Like Vestby, Gomera reveals the influence (probably indirect as much as direct) of Fuller, especially in its advocacy of what was then known as 'intermediate technology', which Fuller had largely inspired. Some might also detect echoes of the Waterside Housing project for Feock in Gomera's proposed tourist housing. But whereas the Feock housing was sculpturally assertive, in the British manner of the times, and flat roofed, the Gomera housing was gently recessive, with elements derived from the local vernacular, in particular the pitched clay-tile roofs (like those on Jørn Utzon's Kingo Housing). Others keen to trace the legacy of Gomera in Foster's more recent work might find affinities in the way that the Malaysian Petronas University fits itself into the topography and is adapted to its tropical climate.

However, more telling and fruitful parallels for Gomera are to be found, both for some of its particular sources (such as the tiled roofs) as well as for more general strategies, in the times in which the study was conducted. Paradoxically, it is precisely because it now seems to be so much a period piece that the Gomera study was also a herald of the future. Just as the intensifying environmental crisis has provoked a reappraisal of Fuller's ideas and legacy, so the Gomera study was, and still is today, an immensely evocative and exciting model of how to approach the quest for what we now call 'sustainability'.

Prepared for an as yet undeveloped island in the wake of the first oil crisis provoked by an Arab-Israeli war, it was perhaps predictable that the Gomera study would propose the liberal use of the sort of intermediate technology that filled the voluminous *Whole Earth Catalogue*, which was again explicitly inspired by and dedicated to Fuller. The sympathy for the local vernacular buildings also echoes Bernard Rudofsky's then cult *Architecture without Architects*; and the many ways in which the scheme sought to achieve mutually beneficial reciprocities with nature recalls the spirit of books such as Ian McHarg's immensely influential late-1960s classic, *Design with Nature*.

Today such concerns are even more urgently germane, not only because of global warming and the ecological holocaust, but also due to the widespread destruction, by rampantly intrusive tourism, of the local eco-systems and cultures that originally attracted that tourism. Indeed, the twenty-first century promises to differ from the twentieth in precisely the ways the Gomera study exemplified so evocatively.

1. An aerial view of Gomera and its neighbour Tenerife, the largest of the Canary Islands, which lies to the east. The Canaries form an autonomous region of Spain; the name is said to derive from the Latin *canis*, meaning 'dog', one of the islands having been noted in Roman times for large dogs.

2, 3. The Tenerife effect: in these two contrasting drawings the Foster team recorded some of the problems associated with tourism and the accelerating commercialisation of the Canary Islands. In the newly developed areas of Tenerife, focused on the capital Las Palmas, perimeter roads and obtrusive high-rise hotels scarred the coastline, while elsewhere traditional patterns of settlement remained unspoiled.

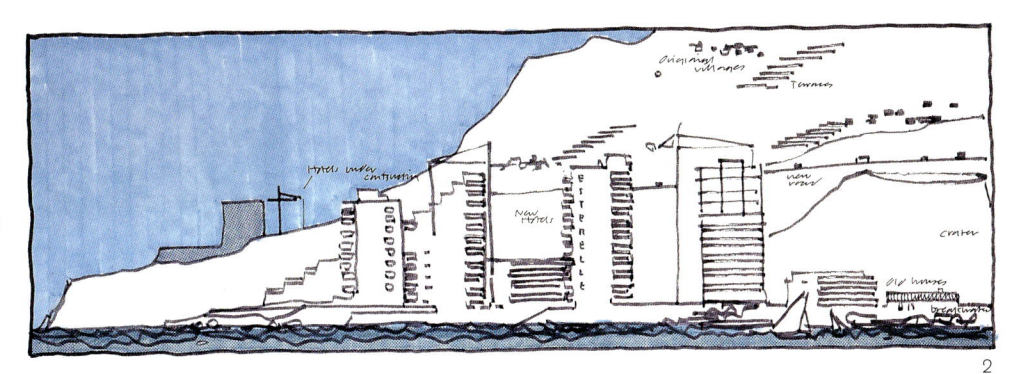

Right: Norman Foster with members of the Gomera team on their first study trip to the island, in February 1975. Far right: Because of the undeveloped nature of the island, and the poor quality of the existing roads, journeys to the more remote areas were made by helicopter.

1. This survey map of a section of the southern side of the island, west of the main port of San Sebastian, was annotated to indicate new roads and identify areas suitable for tourist housing development. A rudimentary existing airstrip is indicated, as is the potential site of a golf course nearby.

More measured and discerning in its use of technology, particularly in relation to its ecological impact, there is also evidence of a renewed appreciation of and desire to engage with the local, its traditional cultures and customs as well as its characteristic topography, climate and vegetation. And there is increasing demand for an ecologically and culturally sensitive tourism.

**Lacking an airport or tourist facilities and with only few small beaches of black volcanic sand, the island was still unspoilt at the time of the study.**

Gomera is the once-verdant Canary Island immediately to the west of Tenerife. Columbus had stopped there to take on fresh food and water before sailing on to the Americas. Later ships crossing the Atlantic followed this precedent. As a result, the island's population and agricultural production had grown. Over time this led to deforestation, and so also to soil erosion and decreased rainfall.

Without the transpiration to aid cloud formation elsewhere, the prevailing north-east trade winds tend to gather rain-bearing clouds and damp mists against only the northern side of the island's high central peak. Beneath these vapours, some lush valleys with banana plantations, palms and papaya trees persist on the island's northern slopes. But on the island's now arid southern half, only the ubiquitous agricultural terracing bears testimony to wetter, more fertile times. It is witness to a pattern of ecological destruction that has been a recurrent cost of civilisation to date, and which our populous planet can no longer afford.

Lacking an airport or tourist facilities, and with only few small beaches of black volcanic sand, the island was still unspoilt in 1975, the time of the study. It was referred to as one of the 'forgotten islands of the Canaries', despite its proximity to the main island of Tenerife. The latter was already a rapidly developing tourist resort, due in part to the ferry services between Europe and the Canaries that Fred Olsen's shipping line had been running for several years. His companies also had other interests in the islands. On Gomera, where Olsen owned a large villa, they were involved in agricultural development, including banana and avocado plantations. At the end of 1974, Olsen initiated a regular ferry service between Tenerife and Gomera's main port of San Sebastian to export fruit from the island and bring visitors to it. Anticipating the inevitable tourist influx, he commissioned Norman Foster to undertake a strategic planning study of potential tourist developments which, rather than being deleterious to the character of the island, might aid its future regeneration.

The Foster team approached the study through its usual process of conducting thorough research and then generating several alternative solutions to critique and from which to choose a preferred option for development. But however typical the process, the outcome was rather atypical of Foster Associates (or at least of how the practice would later be perceived) if less so of the times.

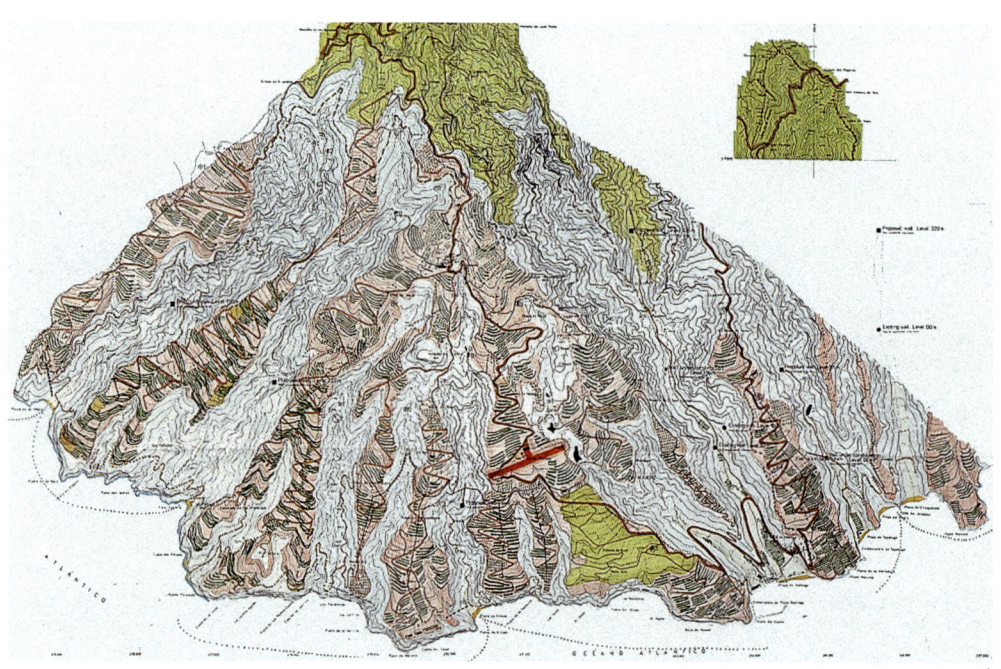

If Fred Olsen's brief had been addressed towards the opportunities for local tourist development, Foster's own studies concentrated on more fundamental environmental issues. If development was to take place, Foster argued, there had to be a basic framework that could support that development and benefit Gomera as a whole.
Ian Lambot, 'Gomera Regional Planning Study', 1989

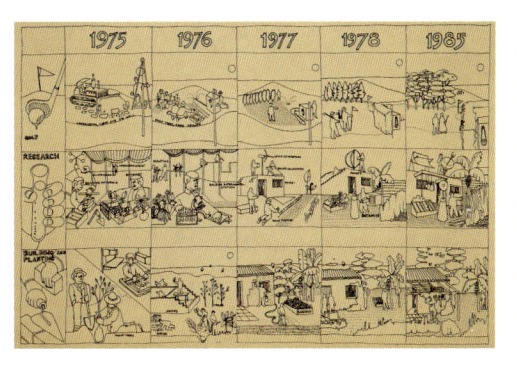

The core of the strategy is the need to protect the island's coastline and waterfront, and integrate tourist development with the local community. But the future growth of the island will hinge on its ability to tap and deploy latent resources. These could be immense: a subterranean water supply – the extent of which is unknown; wind on the higher levels; and almost unlimited solar energy. We therefore recommend, as a matter of urgency, the setting up of a UN backed research and development laboratory on Gomera, to study low energy techniques.
Excerpt from Foster Associates' Gomera report, 1975
Left: The cover of the Gomera report.

Low key, low or intermediate tech, and even unabashedly neo-vernacular (or at least proposing to reconstitute the vernacular in places and revive elements of its vocabulary elsewhere) the scheme would have quietly deferred to and settled into its natural and cultural context. Some might deem it feminine in its spirit of accommodation and the richness of its proposals – which constituted a set of holistic, healing strategies to tackle all aspects of the island's life and development – just as a typical Foster Associates' project of the period might be regarded as masculine in its elegantly reductive single-mindedness.

The striking and exotic setting, with its climatically apt and charming vernacular buildings, which make the most of the island's limited natural and technological resources, no doubt provoked much of the (what some might see as surprising) character of the proposals. But this character also reflects the composition of the team that prepared the study. Besides Norman Foster and Birkin Haward, and a local collaborating architect, Pepe Martell, there were three other key members of the team. These were the ecological consultant, Professor Kenneth Mellanby, and two architects then with Foster Associates who had been born and raised outside Europe: the Argentinian, Orlando Modesti, and the Mozambican-Portuguese, Pedro Guedes. The Iberian lineage of the latter pair, along with their familiarity with less developed countries, probably contributed to the team's sensitive appreciation of the local culture and vernacular buildings, and to the low-key pragmatism of the proposals.

Yet another major influence on the spirit of the scheme was Fred Olsen himself. He knew and loved the island, felt a great responsibility towards social issues and reverence for nature typical of Scandinavians, and headed an organisation that was far ahead of its time in reflecting these concerns (as had already been demonstrated in the Vestby proposals).

Birkin Haward's sketches from an early study trip reveal an island of diversity and contrasts. He records fertile valleys and arid ridges, volcanic peaks whose slopes are stepped with terraces, and roads winding up these slopes, their precipitous edges offering panoramic views. But however impressive these natural and historic features, it was also apparent that the islanders and their agriculture already faced serious challenges that would be compounded by the added pressures of tourist hordes. It was obvious to Norman Foster and his team that if their study was to offer truly workable conclusions and proposals it could not restrict its focus to tourist developments. Instead it had to deal with all aspects of the island's environment and the problems these posed. Any plan that did not benefit Gomera as a whole would also fail to achieve a form of tourist development that would be viable in the long term, that is to say sustainable.

2. A small airstrip existed on the south of the island, but the study argued against constructing an airport, preferring ferry services for normal demands and helicopters for emergencies.

3. Modern agricultural and irrigation techniques had proved successful in helping to reinstate some of the old terraced fields as plantations for bananas and avocados. However, water supplies from underground reservoirs had yet to be exploited. The layout of established plantations was recorded in sketches as an indication for the design team in planning future development.

4. The stark beauty of the island impressed the whole design team. The dramatic contrast between areas of barren mountainside and the small areas of agriculture, as at Barranco de Santiago, were vividly depicted in Birkin Haward's sketches, which formed part of the Gomera report.

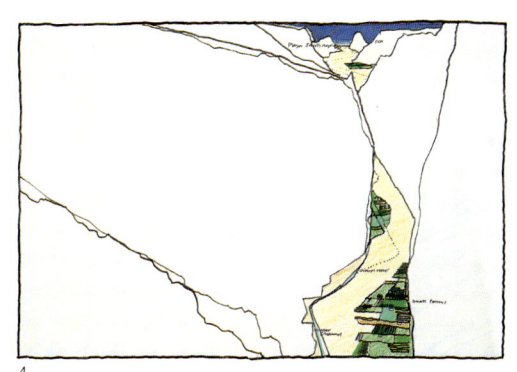

Gomera Regional Planning Study

**At the time of Columbus' visit, in the fifteenth century, Gomera had enjoyed a rich layer of vegetation and forest. With the opening up of the Americas, the island had developed a measure of importance as the last staging post before the great trip across the Atlantic. Consequent population growth, however, took its toll, with steady clearance of the forest bringing soil erosion and, more seriously, reduced rainfall.**
Ian Lambot, 'Gomera Regional Planning Study', 1989

Right: Birkin Haward's drawings suggest how new tourist activities might be developed on the island to take full advantage of its spectacular coastline and open natural landscape; from left to right these included sailing, hang-gliding, horse riding and walking.

---

1. Two earlier reports had recommended that a new coastal ring-road should be constructed. However, the Foster team foresaw the danger of strip development following this route and proposed instead to upgrade and complete the existing inland system. The high central part of the island was to be reforested as a 'national park', while the lower slopes were to be returned to agricultural use, integrated with new tourist housing.

2. As this sequence of drawings illustrates, the island's originally dense forestation had been stripped away over the centuries, resulting in soil erosion and reduced rainfall. It was estimated that there had been a progressive drying of the island over the preceding 100 years: below a level of 400 metres there was hardly a green plant except in the irrigated areas. Renewal of the protective tree cover was regarded as an integral part of any new development and as an essential prerequisite to securing a sustainable future for the island.

Two early exercises that informed the study were an ecological survey of the island by Mellanby and a critical analysis of two previous planning studies that had been prepared by other consultants. Because the island's steady decline had been mostly brought about by a lack of water, much of Mellanby's report was an assessment of the availability of this crucial resource, without which tourist development and the restoration of agriculture and indigenous vegetation would have been impossible. Though rainfall was sparse on the southern side of the island, rainwater falling on the north percolated through to underground reservoirs from which wells could supply water to most of the island. Contemporary analysis by other specialist consultants suggested that this water was sufficient to support tourist development (even a golf course) and some agricultural irrigation, as well as the replanting of indigenous vegetation. Nevertheless, Mellanby also recommended investigating intermediate technologies, both to derive fresh water from the sea and to decrease the island's dependence on imported fossil fuels.

In particular, two forms of energy that were consistently available on the island – sun and wind – could have been harnessed. Solar stills could be used to desalinate salt water for domestic use, while solar panels could provide energy to heat that water. And windmills could be deployed throughout the island to pump water and generate electricity.

**The Gomera study was – and still is – an immensely evocative and exciting model of how to approach the quest for what we now call 'sustainability'.**

Following further expert advice, the Foster team was reluctant to depend only on the underground water lest its over-extraction encouraged inward seepage and contamination by seawater. So it was suggested that surface water might also be captured by completing an earlier project of constructing a catchment system around the upper levels of the island.

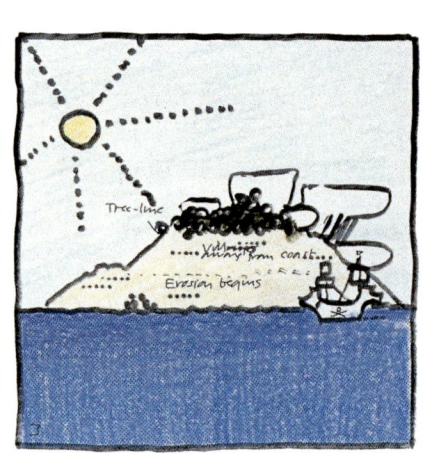

1400     1550     1750

Rainwater was to be conducted to reservoirs around the island via old and new channels, which were to be lined and roofed with polythene sheeting to prevent leakage and evaporation. This water was to be used for agricultural irrigation. (More polythene sheets were to be spread over the earth to trap the water that would otherwise evaporate under the fierce heat of the sun.)

As well as advocating such low-tech devices, the team explored other intermediate technologies suggested by Mellanby, as recorded in the distinctive sketches of both Haward and Guedes. Ways were investigated to make the dwellings independent of piped water and the electricity grid, allowing them — in the jargon of the period — to be as 'autonomous' as possible. Various methods of using, and combining the use of, fresh and salt water were examined. The latter was to be used for flushing toilets as well as in the solar stills. In the fully autonomous scenario, salt water was to be delivered by a tanker truck to each house to be distilled and heated there by solar energy. Waste water was to be used in the gardens; the composting toilets were to be connected to an anaerobic digester, the methane from which was to be used for cooking; and wind generators would be deployed to charge batteries to power lights and other appliances.

The Foster team's assessment of the two earlier planning studies concluded that, for broadly similar reasons, the proposals of neither were satisfactory. Each had proposed that tourist developments, oriented to the short-stay, package-holiday trade, were to be restricted to a rim along the shore. Isolated there they would have contributed nothing, beyond bringing in money, to the overall development of the island. An airport was also proposed close to the shore, connected to the tourist developments and San Sebastian by a coastal road. The Foster proposals were quite different. Tourist development (for those on long and medium stay, as well as those on package holidays) was to spread up the slopes from the coast and deeper inland. The airport (which was deemed to be, at best, of questionable desirability) was moved as high up and far away from the beach as possible. And, rather than constructing a coastal road, the network of existing roads that criss-crossed the island was to be upgraded and extended.

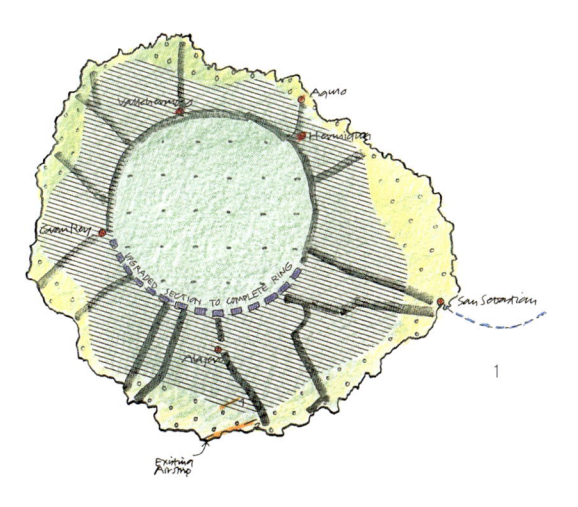

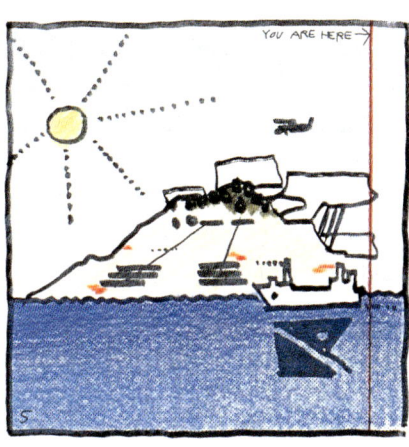

1950  1975  2000

Right: One of the existing irrigation channels on the dry southern side of the island, which had fallen into disrepair. This system was to be brought back into use and supplemented with soil moisture retention measures to encourage agriculture and reforestation on the island.

**Analysis of indigenous buildings, local labour and available materials led to proposals for traditionally constructed shells which respected the island's surplus labour problems and the high cost of shipping in materials. At the same time we suggested that new light industries could be established to prefabricate more specialised infill concerned with energy systems, kitchens, bathrooms and the like.** Norman Foster, *Building Design*, 26 October 1979

1. This sequence of sketches by Birkin Haward surveys the existing freshwater sources on the island, including a defunct dam and channel system. The report suggested that these facilities could be reused and a rainwater catchment created around the upper contours of the island. This would combine with a new system of boreholes to provide the island's freshwater supplies.

2. Existing irrigation channels were to be brought back into use, lined with polythene and covered to prevent water loss through leakage or evaporation.

**Ways were investigated to make the dwellings independent of piped water and the electricity grid, allowing them – in the jargon of the times – to be as autonomous as possible.**

Peter Buchanan

These broad proposals were consistent with two key intentions that informed all aspects of the Foster plan: that it would bring about the regeneration of the entire island; and that it would do so, as much as possible, by reusing or reinterpreting (by upgrading or updating) what already existed there. These imperatives would complement a third major goal: that while both the density of habitation and intensity of agriculture were to increase considerably, they would do so in a manner that would be benevolent in its impact. Any new development was to be as seamlessly integrated into its setting as possible. The design team took the view that catering for longer stay tourists would help to further these goals, as such visitors would be more likely to familiarise themselves with and integrate into island life than those on short package tours. Today, development and design ideals such as these seem both laudably correct and inescapably obvious; yet they were rare at the time, as most contemporaneous tourist developments testify.

The existing man-made elements to be reused and upgraded were to include not only the water channels and roads, but also the settlements and agricultural terraces where tourists would be housed in a way that regenerated both villages and vegetation. Upgrading the existing road pattern rather than building a coastal road would have better served both islander and tourist, improving connections for the former and spreading the latter deeper into the island to integrate with, and so help with the regeneration of, life on the island. More than that, it would have helped maintain the perceived diversity and experiential richness of the island. The coastal road would have blurred the boundaries between, and identities of, individual settlements, which would have been reduced to mere incidents along it. By contrast, the retention of the existing road pattern would have kept each settlement as a distinct terminal destination, thus enhancing its unique identity and special characteristics. Additionally, every beach – rather than being adjacent to a coastal road – would have remained a special destination.

**In our studies, we put a tremendous amount of energy into encouraging local, labour-intensive industries on the island for the development of roads, airfields and housing. In our proposals, windmills and mud bricks figure much more prominently than bathroom capsules.** Norman Foster, Whitworth Exhibition catalogue, May 1984

Right: Pedro Guedes' drawings from the Gomera report illustrate how traditional brick-making skills might be revived on the island. Simple mud bricks, with an admixture of cement to make them waterproof, were to be formed in a portable, high-pressure filter press and then sun dried in the open air.

3, 4. The study proposed energy self-sufficient houses, as described here in Pedro Guedes' drawings. The house on the left is reliant on conventional services. The drawing on the right shows how the house could be supported by natural resources; wind power generates electricity for lighting; sea-water deliveries allow drinking water to be distilled in solar stills; and anaerobic generators digest household waste to create methane gas for cooking.

5, 6. The combination of almost constant sunshine and reliable winds made the island a perfect test-bed for alternative energy sources. Several such systems were proposed – including this wind-powered water pump and electricity generator – and it was proposed that a United Nations funded research centre should be established to further their development.

7, 8. Solar collectors fitted to the roofs of the houses, or arranged in banks along the coast, would generate sufficient heat energy to provide domestic hot water and to power solar stills for sea-water desalination.

Gomera Regional Planning Study   189

**We took helicopters to the more remote villages where you could look at the original settlements, and we found that there was an indigenous plan – a single aspect strip development which looks out to the sun, and has as much related covered area outside as it has enclosed habitable area inside. From these ingredients we produced a possible building type – a high-density, low-rise solution – that responded well to the climate.** Norman Foster, lecture at the AIA Conference, London, October 1977
Left: The different forms of vernacular construction were carefully recorded. One interesting adaptation was the change from flat to pitched roofs corresponding to the uneven pattern of rainfall on the island.

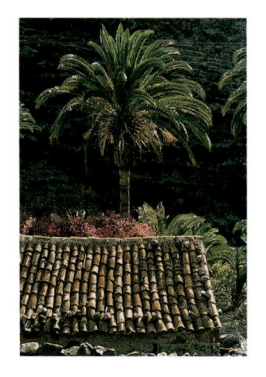

1. Simple village-like housing developments were proposed, laid out among banana plantations, using the stepped contours of the surviving agricultural terraces.

2. A plan and section of a linear house of the type envisaged in the terraced arrangement above. The ratio of enclosed to semi-enclosed or 'modified external' space was roughly equal. Built into the retaining walls of the terraces, each single-aspect unit was oriented to ensure privacy while enjoying views out to sea over the roof-tops of its neighbour below.

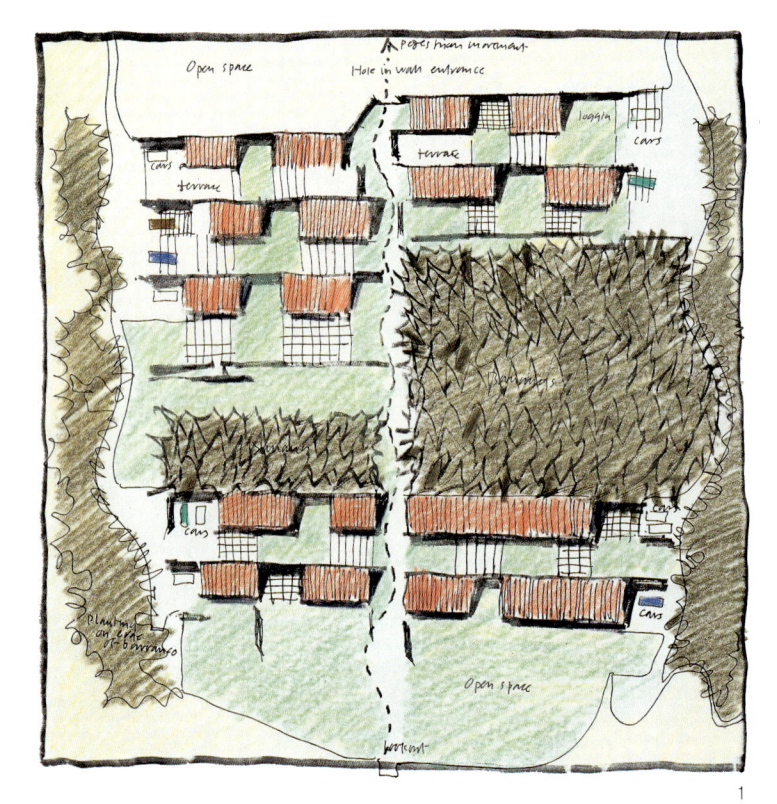

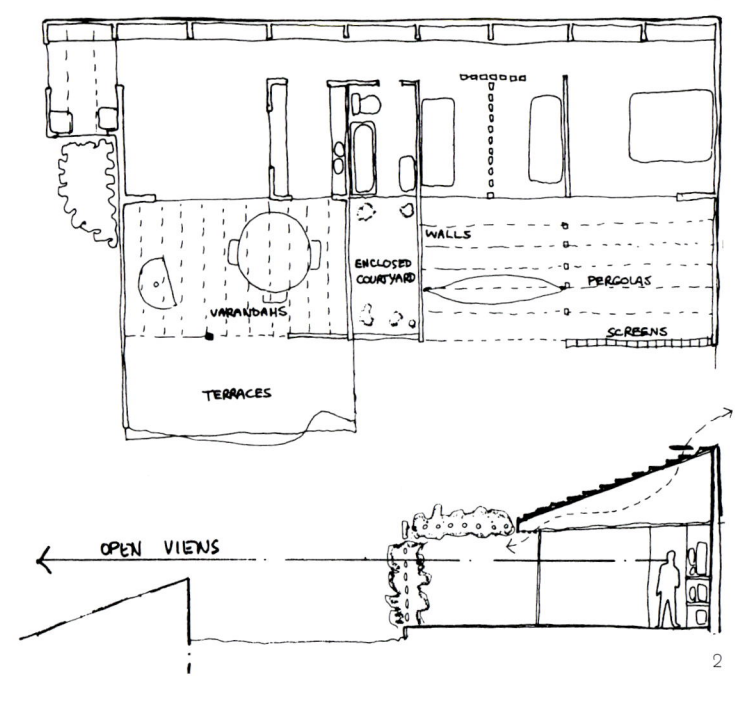

In the Foster proposal the beaches were to reached from above by path or from the sea by boat. The modesty of the paths and landing jetties would have ensured that they remained as natural and unspoilt as possible.

The design of the tourist accommodation also derived from the study of the vernacular. The new buildings would thus have been well suited to the climate and could be made from local rather than imported materials. Many might be surprised today to find that Foster once proposed using (or at least investigated the use of) traditional clay tile roofs and walls of bricks pressed using 'intermediate technology' equipment, as well as verandas and pergolas shaded by awnings and blinds of slatted reeds. The vernacular was to be emulated most exactly when building in or extending the old villages. Here, the new buildings would have been identifiable only by the solar panels and windmills they sported; that is until the islanders adopted similar devices over time.

**The most radical aspect of the Gomera study was that it promised to create what was almost a new ecology.**

In one of the few predictable Foster touches – inspired once again by a Fuller invention – the bathroom and service cores were to have been factory made and shipped pre-assembled to site. Just as Olsen's ships maximised their potential by combining passengers and cargo (hence Foster's passenger terminal at Millwall Dock) so the bathroom units would have been shipped in the holds of the incoming boats, which would then carry bananas on their outward journey.

Most of the tourists were to have stayed in houses, which were to be backed against the walls of the agricultural terraces, so hugging the contours of the land. The houses would thus have been arranged independently of the roads that zigzagged across the terraces as they climbed up and down the slopes.

Various vernacular forms of construction were recorded on the island and valuable lessons learned from them.
Far left: Locally made clay tile roofs as used on a traditional farmhouse.
Left: Passive environmental control was proposed using the most elementary of methods – split-cane blinds and rolled canvas awnings, both of which were in use on the island.
Right: Fine examples of traditional architecture were recorded in the larger communities. The projecting balcony shown here, enclosed in its simple yet decorative wooden slats, brings shade while encouraging natural through ventilation.

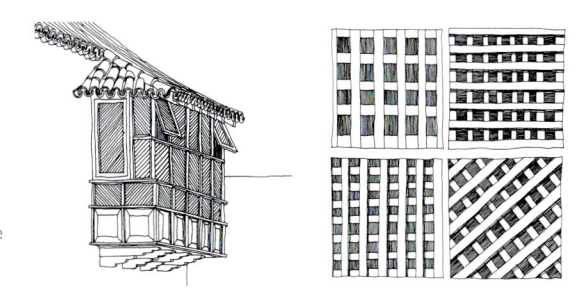

Seen from a distance, only the clay tile roofs would have been visible; and even these earth-coloured elements would have been nearly as recessive and inconspicuous as the glass walls hiding in the shade of the overhanging roofs. From parking courts along the roads, paths would have connected the linear or clustered groups of houses. If some external elements were vernacular, the simple plans – which allowed all the rooms to look out to sea and sun – in part drew from contemporary Scandinavian holiday houses, which were also designed to blend with their forested and waterside settings. Once the planting was established, this architecture-as-landform would have almost disappeared as it came to be an integral part of the island.

Ultimately, the most radical aspect of the Gomera study was that it promised to create what was almost a new ecology. It combined the man-made and the natural in a loose-knit symbiosis of buildings (new and old), infrastructure (roads, channels and terracing) and vegetation (indigenous, agricultural and gardens). If its proposals had been realised, the scheme could have been a shortcut to the future towards which Foster is still travelling: a future that must heal our planet, its local cultures and the relationships between them. The gauntlet laid down by the Gomera study then, and still today, is for architects to have the courage to forgo restrictive obsessions with such things as the technological imperative and the cautious conventions of taste (particularly that of their professional peers). Instead they must become true problem solvers: broad ranging and open-minded in the service of people and planet.

In retrospect perhaps it was to be no bad thing that the Gomera scheme was abandoned. Unrealised, and so not compromised by the dilution of its ideals, nor by the only partial realisation of its proposals, the Gomera study remains a beautifully compelling dream. So much so that it might yet inspire the sort of design approach to the larger environment that becomes more urgent with every passing day.

Peter Buchanan

3. Responding to climate and local precedent, new buildings would incorporate nearly as much external space as conventional enclosed rooms. In the cloistered housing units, which formed an alternative typology to the terraced arrangement opposite, communal social spaces were oriented to look out to sea. Simple walls, pergolas and planting provided shade.

4, 5. In response to the demands of modern tourism, larger self-contained hotels and spas were proposed. Here communal activities and sports could be catered for alongside tennis courts and swimming pools, even discotheques.

# Systems Thinking Revisited
Francis Duffy 2000

1. In section, Stansted Airport (1981-1991) reveals its systemic relationship to both the Sainsbury Centre and the Renault Centre. In a development of the service basement at the Sainsbury Centre, an undercroft runs beneath the entire Stansted concourse, accommodating environmental services, baggage handling equipment and even a mainline railway station. Vertical services distribution is contained within the trunks of the structural 'trees' which echo those at the Renault Centre. At Stansted, they support a lightweight roof which is freed of services to admit the maximum amount of daylight to the concourse.

Norman Foster's greatest achievement in his early works of the 1970s – which are illustrated in this volume – was to reify certain powerful ideas that had been articulated by such thinkers as Charles and Ray Eames, Buckminster Fuller and Cedric Price but which had remained embryonic – at least in architectural terms. Subsequently Foster has continued to embody these ideas with a precise and highly buildable logic, a craftsman-like perfection of finish, a compelling beauty that no other architect can rival.

Throughout the 1980s and 1990s Foster has been able to apply the same integrated vision of what architecture ought to be but at a far larger scale. Offices, airports, university faculties, a telecommunications tower, a national stadium, the Berlin parliament, demonstrate his application of systemic ideas – which have meanwhile largely been dropped from the conventional discourse of increasingly fashion-dominated architecture – to the emerging technological, commercial and political circumstances of our times.

What makes Foster so different and distinguishes him so sharply from many of his rivals? Because systemic thinking is so important to him, Foster has been able to transcend the self-imposed limitations of those of his contemporaries who have chosen to define architecture within the terms of fine art. It is Foster's recurrent habit of radical systems thinking that sets him apart. Taking a longer view of those early works and of his subsequent development, it is now possible to discern much more clearly than before the artistic consequences of Foster's characteristic modes of thinking and designing.

Two recurrent themes provide particularly strong evidence to support this proposition. The first is a long sequence of innovative projects in which developments in the design of structure and environmental services are linked by the architect's determination to construct the most perfectly integrated and highly 'serviced shed'. The second is a subsequent and even more radical series of projects in which the potential for the dematerialisation of environmental services is carefully explored. These preoccupations, neither of which can be properly understood without the underpinning of systems thinking, are the connecting ideas that explain the development of some of Foster's most innovative projects.

**Foster has been able to transcend the self-imposed limitations of those of his contemporaries who have chosen to define architecture within the terms of fine art. It is Foster's recurrent habit of radical systems thinking that sets him apart.**

The integrating idea that led to the 'serviced shed' sequence of projects was already implicit in the striking simplicity of the single-storey IBM Pilot Head Office project at Cosham, of 1970. It recurs in Willis Faber & Dumas, also conceived in the same year. However, the idea emerges with even greater clarity in the Sainsbury Centre, of 1974-1977, in which the primary steel structure and the double skins of the big shed are clearly articulated in order to allow environmental and maintenance services to be neatly and programmatically accommodated within the two layers. Overhead servicing is pushed to the limit. The reference to integrated aerodynamic design, in which the design of the skin has always been so critical, is obvious.

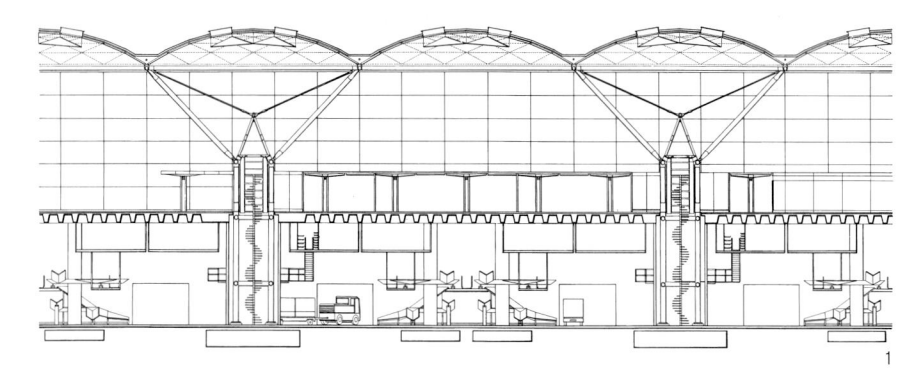

I often wonder how Paxton would react to systems building now, and to the opportunities and achievements of a new age? He had the confidence and optimism to produce a systems building for an industrial exhibition – the Crystal Palace – which was later re-assembled on another site for a different use. If only we had the same confidence to continue in his tradition with today's systems.
Norman Foster, lecture at RIBA Annual Conference, University of Hull, 14 July 1976
Left: The transept of Joseph Paxton's remarkable Crystal Palace, completed for the Great Exhibition in 1851

The BBC Radio proposal of 1982, one of London's great unbuilt projects, is the result of a similarly systemic design approach. In the Renault Distribution Centre, 1980, the yellow structural steel frame is pushed through the skin. This move anticipates the next big step at Stansted, 1981-1991, in which the servicing idea that shaped the Sainsbury Centre is inverted – environmental services come from below the concourse rather than from above. Structural 'trees' support but do not penetrate the overarching roof. This allows light to flood in from above and from the sides of the shed and makes possible a lightness and grace that have a lot to do with understanding gravity and even more with the systemic imagination. They are the result of Foster's insistence that the design of structure, environmental services, natural and artificial lighting and space planning should all work together to achieve the client's goals in the most efficient and elegant way.

That is how aircraft are designed. That is what systems design is all about. You can feel in this sequence of projects how, in the course of design, each building's emerging formal, servicing and structural systems have been mentally pulled, pushed, turned over and round about in order to squeeze more and more performance out of highly integrated design.

The second series of projects addresses a related but rather different problem: how to dematerialise architecture; that is, how to use the least physical resources to maximum effect – to do 'more with less'. The objective is to get rid of the environmental waste, the opaque circulation patterns and the hermetic separation of inside and outside that are the three chief – and most deadening – characteristics of cheap and, paradoxically, highly wasteful, conventional office building design.

Willis Faber, with the help of escalators, has an unmistakable pattern of circulation. The turfed roof garden, the swimming pool and the solar glass are early responses to bringing the park into the office, to what has become the critically important problem of designing the working environment in a sustainable way. By 1979, in his first tall office building – the Hongkong and Shanghai Banking Corporation Headquarters – Foster made his first attempt to reinvent the gas-guzzling limitations of the North American model of the skyscraper. The use of a ten-storey atrium (with an ambitious, reflective sunscoop) as a place-making device is the most obvious manifestation of this impatience.

The proposed use of solar panels and the innovative application of chilled ceilings in the Duisburg Business Promotion Centre, 1988, demonstrate a heightened interest in the dematerialisation of environmental services. From a systems point of view, the strategic significance of the Duisburg project is that the design of building elements and the design of environmental services have become interdependent. The ceilings, the services, the multi-layered outer skin and the structure itself have been designed in such an integrated way that the lumbering apparatus network of ducts and the volume-devouring plant of conventional office buildings are no longer needed. Environmental control is achieved lightly and delicately without the inefficient and energy consuming pumping of vast amounts of treated air.

The Commerzbank Headquarters, 1991-1997, with its ingenious environmental engineering, its big central ventilating atrium and its unfolding and continuous spiral of four-storey-high 'sky gardens' addresses simultaneously and head-on the triple challenge of providing transparency, greenness and orientation in a 53-storey office building.

2. The Business Promotion Centre (1990-1993) forms the landmark building within the Duisburg Microelectronic Park, located in the former 'rust belt' of the Ruhr region. Part of a masterplan designed to integrate new, clean industries within a mostly residential area, the building incorporates highly advanced technological systems to ensure energy efficiency.

3. The multi-layered outer envelope of the Business Promotion Centre is so thermally efficient that no heating is required during the winter months. The triple-layered cladding system consists of an external single-glazed glass wall, a continuous insulating cavity, housing computer controlled blinds, and a glazed inner layer.

4. Rather than occupying a conventional floor or ceiling void, the Business Promotion Centre's environmental control systems have been miniaturised and integrated within the fabric of the building. Chilled ceilings provide cooling, while fresh air is introduced through grilles at floor level.

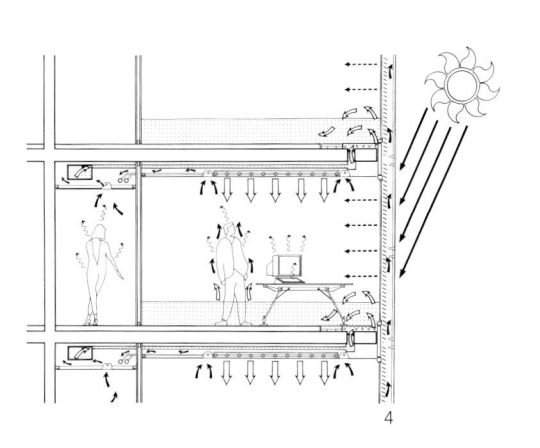

**On a freezing winter morning in February 1996, a huge 1:20 model of the dome and chamber, minutely detailed and large enough for us to stand inside, was hoisted on to the Reichstag roof. This would provide us with conclusive evidence as to whether the mirrored cone at the centre of the cupola would be able to reflect sufficient light into the chamber below. Using a light meter, Claude measured the light being reflected into the chamber. The cone worked beautifully – our instincts had proved to be correct.** Norman Foster, *Rebuilding the Reichstag*, 2000
Far left: The model of the cupola against the Berlin sky.
Left: Inside the model, from right, Norman Foster, Claude Engle and David Nelson.

Similarly the roof of the new Reichstag, 1992-1999, has been designed to harvest energy, to deflect light into the interior, to make natural ventilation possible and to be the iconic heart of the democratic process. The same systemic design principles are currently being applied, with even more ambition and rigour, in the extraordinary design of the skyscraper for Swiss Re in the City of London.

At the beginning of the age of e-commerce, Foster is not aiming simply to apply gadgetry or even to lay down the infrastructure to accommodate new generations of information technology. More and more frequently he is attempting to integrate structure with the design of circulation, and with data and environmental systems to anticipate high-tech organisations' demand for rapid change. He is using systems thinking to design not conventional offices but buildings that are 'intelligent'.

There is another level of Foster's success, which is just as striking and potentially even more durable. The output from Foster's studio in London and from outposts in Hong Kong, the US, France, Germany and Spain is impressive. Foster is one of the very few architects to have used his growing base of international fame to create a reliable machine capable of delivering the highest quality of architecture anywhere in the world. He has created a practice that is quite as powerful and technically at least as competent and sophisticated as the best of the great American architectural practices of the 1950s and early 1960s.

The rapid globalisation of world trade and the growth of mergers and acquisitions throughout the corporate world are encouraging clients to search for the best architectural talents wherever they can find them, regardless of national barriers, historic patterns of procurement or inherited cultural influences. It is this open, international economic context that makes Foster's current body of work so impressive.

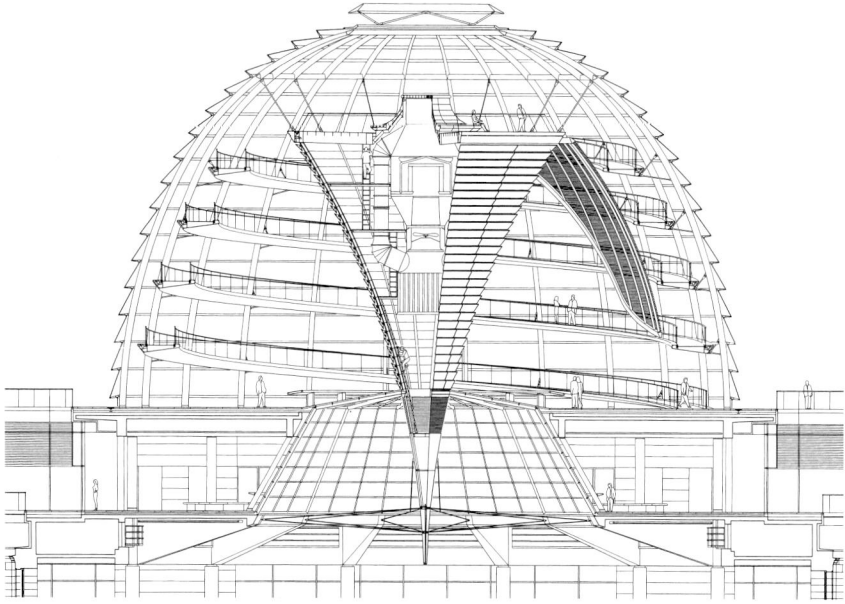

**Foster is not aiming simply to apply gadgetry or even to lay down the infrastructure to accommodate new generations of information technology. He is using systems thinking to design not conventional offices but buildings that are 'intelligent'.**
Francis Duffy

**It is salutary to consider how frequently in our society it seems to take the stimulus of warfare to promote design or systems innovation.** Norman Foster, lecture at Stuttgart University, 14 May 1997
Right: The Combined Operations command centre for the Western Approaches, photographed during the Second World War. Systems analysis appeared in a rudimentary form to tackle the industrial problems of mass production during the 1920s and '30s, but it was the pressures of war that saw its first major advances and a growing acceptance of its methods.

Foster's architecture is always best when he is tackling an emerging idea, and when he can bring his own formidable powers of concentration – reinforced by the resources of his increasingly powerful studio – to bear upon a newly identified, practical problem. That he has been able to do this so successfully so often is because he understands that buildings are systems.

From this perspective, performance is what matters. Projects with the toughest programmes and the tightest budgets – for example, the Cambridge Law Faculty and Imperial College – are perhaps more challenging to Foster than prestige office projects, designed to a speculative brief, such as the Canary Wharf tower for Citibank, or the London Bridge City office complex. Projects with real user content, for example, the substantial challenge of relating old to new – such as the Nîmes Carré d'Art, 1984, the Reichstag and the British Museum, 1994-2000 – produce much more interesting results than more generic proposals. Whenever a real environmental conundrum is addressed – as in the Commerzbank – the results have the most lasting impact. When social and operational issues are added to the problematic mix, the results are even better. This is because Foster is today, and always has been, a systems designer as well as an architect.

An early Foster project, mentioned above and discussed below, remains the best example of what Foster's systems approach really means in practice to clients. This is the 'temporary' office for IBM at Cosham, of 1970, in which he broke the rules of early 1970s office design in order to meet a stringent brief within severe constraints of time and cost. The alternative would have been a genuinely short term – and far less cost effective – array of prefabricated cabins. The rationale was brilliant, the business case excellent, the results measurable and the finished building is still the epitome of elegance. The project is one of the earliest examples of Foster's characteristic ability to combine lateral solutions to intractable client problems with the highest and most fastidious standard of design and construction. That remains the hallmark – and the test – of the master. No other architect anywhere has ever raised systems thinking to such an elevated level of artistic achievement.

Looking at the period into which the development of IBM Cosham falls, if one word can encapsulate a quarter of a century, then 'systems' sums up the years from 1950 to 1975. Disciplines ran riot, renounced conventional boundaries, sought interconnections between phenomena, thought big, started again from scratch. They began, in short, to connect the kneebone to the thighbone. Architects, never backward in such pursuits, sought throughout this whole period a fresh vision. Many expected this to emerge from a radical analysis of their clients' needs. For most the vision never quite materialised. For some, as the skylines of innumerable cities testify, an all too concrete imagery emerged in the form of a thousand tower blocks. Foster, in contrast, wholeheartedly embraced the idea of systems architecture and came away in 1975 with a clutch of buildings that were not only different but obviously superior.

## Foster is today, and always has been, a systems designer as well as an architect.

Why was this idea of systems so attractive to architects in this period? Perhaps more important, what is it about Norman Foster which enabled him to turn the systems thinking which turned out to be so empty an inspiration for so many architects, into an utterly convincing architecture? These questions need to be answered if the foundations of Foster's particular architectural contribution are to be properly surveyed and understood. With the right answers Foster's early career can also be used to illuminate what is likely to become an increasingly evanescent and hard-to-understand episode in cultural and technological history.

Related to the interdisciplinary thinking, which in the early 1940s was the basis of the invention of operational research, systems thinking carried the aura of big public sector programmes such as the Tennessee Valley Authority scheme of the Roosevelt era, wartime Combined Operations and the Manhattan Project implicit within it. The very word was worth a lot: it had the effect of a simultaneous claim to intellectual respectability and practicality.

1. In addition to creating a new public vantage point from which to view both the city and the workings of parliament, the cupola of the Reichstag (1992-1999) is crucial to the building's lighting and ventilation strategies. At its core a 'light sculptor' reflects horizon light into the chamber below while a sun-shade controlled by electronic sensors and powered by photovoltaic cells prevents solar gain and glare. Within the cone an air-extraction system draws stale air out from the chamber.

2. Dynamically contrasted with the Reichstag's nineteenth-century facades, the cupola combines the energy efficiency of the truly 'intelligent building' with the dignity and symbolism of a civic and national landmark.

**Foster is an architect of flexibility, and his instinct to design for the inevitability of change is rooted in the unselfconscious factory sheds of England's Industrial Revolution and the modest Case Study Houses of Los Angeles by Charles and Ray Eames ... Foster found the direction he would pursue for most of his career in an industrialised, off-the-peg approach conceived to raise standards and minimise costs ... Like the Californians and the anonymous designers of England's industrial sheds, Foster was not shaping one-off forms but inventing and deploying systems.** Joseph Giovannini, *The Pritzker Architecture Prize*, 1999
Left: The spare anatomy of the Eames' Case Study House #8, 1949, as seen during construction.

1. Ezra Ehrenkrantz's School Construction Systems Development (SCSD) prototype (1964), constructed on the campus of Stanford University, in Southern California, has been cited regularly by Norman Foster in lectures and presentations as a key inspiration. Under the direction of Ehrenkrantz, the SCSD programme of the early 1960s was the first major application of systems thinking related to the building industry; among its many innovations it is notable for having introduced the performance specification approach to design and procurement.

Eric Trist of the Tavistock Institute was a typical systems intellectual of the period. In the late 1940s, when British social science still meant something, he demonstrated that systems thinking could profitably be applied to designing the interface between men and machines in the newly nationalised collieries. Trist showed that it was essential not just to import wholesale the latest American coal-cutting technology, but to introduce it in such a way that it did not destroy the mutual support in risk-taking between miners which had grown up over centuries in the Durham coal fields. Men and machines were, in effect, an 'open socio-technical system'. Social systems, reward systems, technological systems, all had to be interwoven to make it possible for the newly founded National Coal Board to achieve its organisational objectives. Four key examples are enough to show how similar systems ideas were introduced into architecture.

The earliest and best innovators in this field were American: Charles Eames, who created a brilliant metaphor of systems thinking in his own house – all standard components from builders' catalogues and *objéts trouvés* – not to mention his highly innovative product design and exhibitions; and Buckminster Fuller whose whole career is in itself a core study of the abolition of intellectual boundaries and the search for systems solutions.

In Britain the obvious contemporary parallel was the post-war work of the development groups in the old Ministry of Education, so well described by Andrew Saint in his book *Towards a Social Architecture*. At that time resources were scarce and demand for school places heavy: how could a miracle in the procurement of school buildings be achieved?

By systems thinking, of course: bringing architects and educationalists, physicists and builders, scientists and quantity surveyors together to rethink not just how to build the old kind of school faster, but how to build new schools, with new curricula, new plan forms and new ways of teaching. The logic was simple: relax the old constraints, bring intellect to bear, rethink the problem, and out comes new teaching, new architecture and a bright new world.

Not only in Britain and not only in education did such miracles of the Modern Movement happen. In Germany in the mid-1950s the Schnelle brothers began to think about office buildings from first principles. The same conditions applied: great economic stringency, a heavy demand for office space because of the rapid rebuilding of the German economy, a crossing and intermingling of disciplines, the urgent need for cheap physical solutions to pressing organisational problems. The result was the dazzling new concept of Bürolandschaft, the famous open-plan office layouts that were designed to maximise organisational communications and which, from the inside out, determined the shape of a totally new generation of office buildings. Bürolandschaft instantly encapsulated generations of management thinking from Taylorism, to human relations, to cybernetics – all by way of systems.

Equally important to the success of these precursors was memorable imagery and a fully articulated intellectual programme. Foster's work is best understood in the context of this dualist tradition. He can be compared, for example, to contemporaries who seemed in earlier phases of their careers to be equally promising for the same reasons. Cedric Price is the best British example, with his eloquence, radicalism and rage for a more soundly based, more rational architecture. Ezra Ehrenkrantz, who had absorbed the radical British tradition in his years at the Building Research Station, appeared as a star in the Californian skies in the early 1960s with his innovative 'performance specification' approach to procuring school buildings called the School Construction Systems Development (SCSD). In fact certain images from the SCSD programme were present as icons in Foster's earliest office in Covent Garden. However, neither Price's nor Ehrenkrantz's built work ever succeeded in capturing the systems idea strongly enough in architectural terms; ideology always seemed stronger than imagery (and, in the case of Ehrenkrantz, the ideology too seems to have faded with time).

**The School Construction Systems Development (SCSD) project is a lineal descendant of the English post-war industrialised component building systems. However, whereas the Hertfordshire systems ... came to life amid post-war material and labour shortages, and a desperate backlog of building, SCSD inserted itself into the already highly active and competitive American building industry.** Editorial, *Architectural Design*, July 1956
Left: *Building Bulletin*, published from October 1949 onwards by the then Ministry of Education, promoted the wider application of systems building for schools.

**Hertfordshire's 'rolling programme' [was] revolutionary in British Architecture. A continuous, organised process of design, production, feedback and development was to be linked to a means of construction which would be simple, fast, economic and unifying, yet flexible enough to permit regular revision.** Andrew Saint, *Towards a Social Architecture*, 1967
Right: The 1949 Aboyne Lodge Primary School was typical of the buildings produced under the auspices of the Hertfordshire schools building programme. This exemplary systems approach was subsequently reflected in Foster Associates' Newport School scheme of 1967.

Foster had all the advantages of single-mindedness and a late start. The position from which he began, in the late 1960s, allowed him to establish quickly his own vision of what systems buildings ought to be like. The models were available, an architectural language existed and an appropriate ideology had already been worked out. The extent of Foster's acceptance of this inheritance is abundantly clear in the Newport School competition of 1967.

Billed as sophisticated package within Department of Education and Science cost limits, the proposal manages to combine the lively and imaginative interest in users so characteristic of the best DES work of the time – compare Foster's sketches with those in contemporary Building Bulletins – with an enthusiastic acceptance of the deep, open-plan (owing a lot to North American influence, for example, from schools being publicised at the time by the Educational Facilities Laboratories) and with an energetic and practical sense of the way buildings should be put together (that owed as much to the engineer Anthony Hunt as to the example of SCSD).

However, there is a toughness and rigour about the Newport plan, which is new. Care is taken to demonstrate that the rigid rectangular building envelope can accommodate both the 'traditional' classroom layout and a 'plan arrangement based on new educational techniques'. While the sketches hint that the latter style is preferred, the basic systems network will accommodate both. Something of what Newport promised for school buildings was achieved in the Palmerston School for Handicapped Children.

This is a school building conceived as a shed – five linked portal frames, with four service cores 'to define the various zones of activity'. The project combines typical features of the period on a glum unpromising site: the severe, deep plan; the taut, nervous, almost aerodynamic building skin; the construction-kit grid; the visible integration of services and structure; and relatively loose, almost rhapsodic interior planning. Somehow the children and all their paraphernalia are independent of and yet counterpoint the architecture.

Similar features can be found in the Hertfordshire and local authority consortium schools of the 1940s, '50s and early '60s illustrated by Andrew Saint. But in none of these buildings do the various elements fuse in the almost obsessive, holistic way that had already become the touchstone of Foster's genius.

The first commercial building Foster built (with Team 4) carried this holistic passion into a different world, one that had previously tolerated very low standards of building and design. This was the steel-framed electronics factory for Reliance Controls at Swindon built in 1967 – for which Peter Paul-Huhne was the enlightened (and fortunate) client.

Foster and his colleagues rose to the challenge of a dynamic client in an emerging industry with a combination of fast track design, speedy erection, low cost, flexibility to accommodate growth and change, and a progressive image. In plan, the distinctions between office and factory were swept away. Throughout the design, provision for adaptability and for service was the priority.

Three factors indicative of the future direction of Foster's work are present in this building: first, stretching the use of familiar components far beyond the conventional view of their capacity (for example, the use of corrugated deck units with no intermediate supporting rails); second, the integration of all components into a comprehensive system (for example, the reflective nature of the underside of the roof decking doubling as a ceiling); and third, the extreme, practical, minimalist elegance of the construction. Nothing superfluous, everything deft, all components working together. This is why Foster's perspective section through the building is an important drawing: it is a heuristic device to eliminate redundancy but explaining, after the fact, what was done.

2. Norman Foster's 1967 drawing of the Newport School competition scheme demonstrates his complete understanding of the SCSD model – and the fact that he was already developing it further to achieve new levels of planning flexibility.

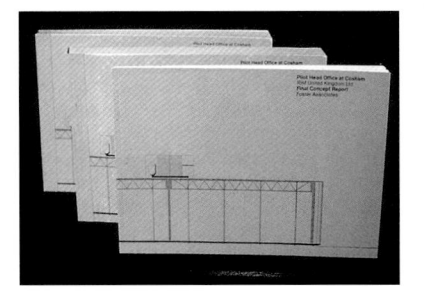

**Communication is really vital in any attempt to break the deadlock around what is traditionally taken for granted in the construction industry. To this end, the documentation we sent out to the IBM contractors included a report which instanced how the building would be built, showing a cost plan and detailed timetables. And the advantage of this was that this glossy document did not end up going to some director while the main documentation went to the estimator – it all went to the same man. This sort of communication is critically important.** Norman Foster, lecture at the Construction Industry Conference, London, 15 May 1980
Left: The reports that convinced IBM of the practical advantages of Foster's flexible deep-plan building.

1. A perspective section of the Olsen Amenity Centre (1968-1970) shows the two-storey structure with services integrated into the roof zone.

2. 'One of the great architectural images of the period', the perspective section of Pilot Head Office for IBM, Cosham (1970-1971) relates in one simple drawing virtually all there is to know about the building's construction and assembly. As at the Olsen Amenity Centre, the services are integrated in the roof zone to create clear, uninterrupted spaces with maximum flexibility of use.

The projects for Fred Olsen at Millwall Dock follow directly in this line. Now the architect has the bit between his teeth – the pencil flying over the pages of the notebook, diagramming, reducing, explaining all at once. The challenge (in what was then a real Docklands) was operational – how to move large numbers of people from taxis and coaches, through ticketing and customs on to ships; and how to provide amenities for Fred Olsen's staff. In the design of the passenger terminal, 1970, the shell design is simplified into a search for the least number of the simplest possible components. The planning equally becomes a process of remorseless simplification. Nothing is left unresolved, everything is made into an intellectual challenge – an opportunity to think laterally, to cut the Gordian knot, to reduce, to solve the problem with the least expenditure of energy in the most elegant way.

'Less is more' was already a famous axiom by the 1970s, but nothing in the work of Mies van der Rohe prepared one for the nervy, obsessive, impatient quality that was already characteristic of Foster's work by the time the Fred Olsen buildings were completed. In Chicago, Mies van der Rohe was attractive to developers because his view of architecture did not particularly contradict theirs. Foster, in a much more positive way, had become by this stage highly attractive to certain sophisticated industrial 'user' clients, because it had become obvious that he was capable of exploiting scarce resources to achieve organisational objectives through the design of buildings in very much the same way as they did in their various businesses. The Fred Olsen Amenity Centre and the later passenger terminal, showed how Foster was able not just to build economically but also to plan intelligently with management to achieve operational goals – which, in this case, meant working collaboratively with the dockers as well as anticipating passenger requirements.

IBM was the epitome of the enlightened client. For an architect to work with IBM in the 1960s and 1970s was to experience excellent project management – just as capable in procuring buildings as in developing new computer systems, of using the corporation's immense experience, as well as seeking innovative ways of solving new problems. So it is not surprising that in 1970 IBM picked Norman Foster, given his recent experience in the electronics industry, to design what originally was to have been temporary offices at Cosham. These 'temporary' offices are still there today as crisp and sharp as ever.

## Clarity is everything. The brochure produced by Foster to describe the IBM scheme is itself a didactic masterpiece.

The plan form at Cosham is almost exactly that of the Newport School – if you are Norman Foster you never waste a good idea – a huge single-storey rectangle (146 x 73 metres) with absolutely clear access and circulation, served by asymmetrically placed cores and highly serviced areas.

Here again is the ghost of Hertfordshire schools, but with their wayward planning exorcised and their clumsy detailing transmuted into the most exquisite delicacy and lightness of construction. Birkin Haward's drawing of the section is itself a masterpiece rivalling Ehrenkrantz's, and one of the great architectural images of the period. The slowly accumulated experience of two decades of public sector work has been captured and raised to another level for the service of the most sophisticated computer company in the world. And this was achieved not by elaboration but by reduction, by the simplest, most intensely focused means.

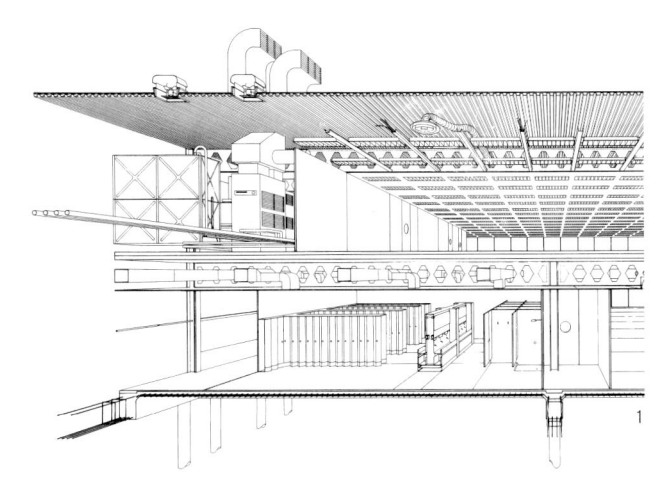

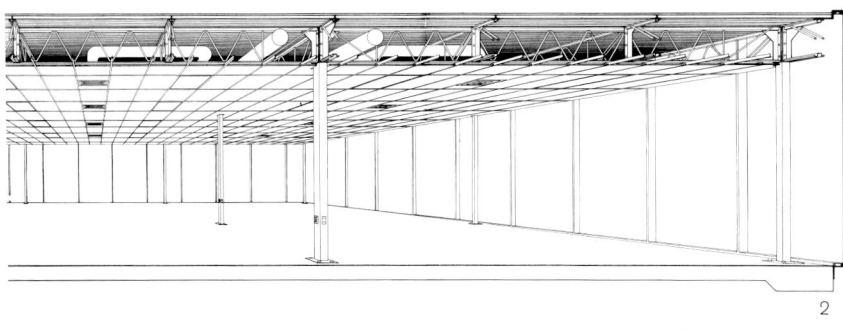

**At Modern Art Glass … the particular combination of architect and client has naturally led to a glass wall which is a bit of a showpiece, which pushes glazing technology forward, and which the architects accept is experimental … However, the architects are being unduly modest, for this glass wall is far too technically assured to be described as experimental.** John Winter, *The Architectural Review*, July 1974

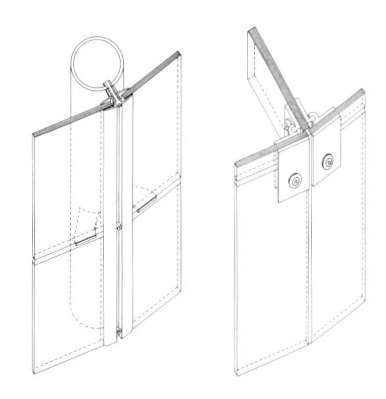

Far left: Detail of the glazing system at Modern Art Glass, in which panels of glass rest upon flanges projecting from stainless-steel mullions. The practical application of this system at Modern Art Glass allowed Foster to explore an alternative to the curtain walling then in development for Willis Faber & Dumas.
Left: Detail of the suspended glazing system developed in association with Pilkington Glass which facilitated the construction of Willis Faber's spectacular glass cladding.

Clarity is everything. The brochure produced by Foster to describe the scheme is itself a didactic masterpiece. Data and electrical services are integrated into the column grid, which in turn neatly complements the layout of desks and internal rooms. The distribution of air-conditioning units on the roof follows a precise and confident modular plan – so unlike the clutter that still disfigures buildings today in dozens of so-called business parks. Site planning, services, structure, construction, layout, have all been comprehended and ordered. It is so simple, so direct that it is still possible to ask: why isn't all building like this?

Two other commercial projects of this period should be mentioned: the 1973 building for Modern Art Glass at Thamesmead and the earlier building (or rather degree-zero building) for Computer Technology of 1970.

What the Modern Art Glass building – a warehouse and office/showroom – demonstrated again was Foster's capacity to seize any opportunity to develop component design as far as he could take it. The client had been a subcontractor on earlier Foster Associates' projects and wanted to use his own building as a showcase for glazing technology. Foster rose to the challenge – '12mm bronze-tinted toughened glass positioned on lugs welded to tubular steel supports, with vertical mullions of bolted neoprene and horizontal joints filled with silicone – all pretty impressive'. Modern Art Glass may be a showpiece but it is also unabashedly still an industrial shed. In the end it is the extraordinary way in which ordinary components have been put together which impressed. Unlike, for example, Richard Rogers' much later Lloyd's building, where innovation proceeded grandly on a hundred fronts simultaneously, Foster was content, in 1973, to focus on the smallest number of most feasible means to improve one assembly – the glazing system.

That such synergetic improvements quickly raised building components to a totally different level of quality has direct parallels with Japanese industry today. Corporations such as Sony, Toshiba and Nissan concentrate on the continuing improvement of the quality of ordinary things to produce some of the most refined products in the world.

Foster's most radical exercise in minimalist design during this period was the temporary air-supported structure for Computer Technology at Hemel Hempstead: 800 square metres of space was commenced, erected and occupied in eight weeks, providing basic office accommodation while the more permanent (and, one has to admit, rather less memorable) structure was built.

Summing up this extraordinary period from 1968 to 1974, we can see a process of progressive refinement during which Foster turned the industrial shed into an art form. This is conveyed perfectly in the diagram produced for *Architectural Design* which tacitly claims, project by project, a Darwinian line of refinement very much in the Buckminster Fuller tradition, from Reliance Controls to the 'ephemeralised' air structure for Computer Technology. Christopher Alexander, author of *Notes on the Synthesis of Form* and *The Pattern Language*, might even have been tempted to cite this sequential pattern of development as an example of progressive adaptation and improvement in one of the most basic components of architectural enclosure.

**You can feel how, in the course of design, each building's emerging formal, servicing and structural systems have been mentally pulled, pushed, turned over and round about in order to squeeze more and more performance out of highly integrated design.**

Note, however, the extent of understatement in the Foster style – by a sleight of hand, technological progress is made to look impersonal and inevitable. In fact, such continuing refinement can only be the consequence of an individual vision, of one man's overriding drive.

3. The glazed wall of the Modern Art Glass building (1972-1973) – essentially a dry run for the glazing system initially proposed for Willis Faber & Dumas (1971-1975) – illustrates Norman Foster's capacity to seize any opportunity to further develop the design of component systems.

**Whereas Willis Faber celebrated the continuous, open workspace, [Herman Hertzberger's] Centraal Beheer Office Building at Apeldoorn concentrated on the private domain of the individual worker ... assembled inside to out on the basis of small standardised units related to activity and human scale ... The rough concrete blocks, precast beams and irregular trays of the 'workers' village' embodied the ideal of participation and implied that the structure would be incomplete until dressed in ... knick-knacks, plants and place-making symbols.** William J R Curtis, *Modern Architecture Since 1900*, 1996
Right: The interior of Hertzberger's Centraal Beheer office building (1968-1972).

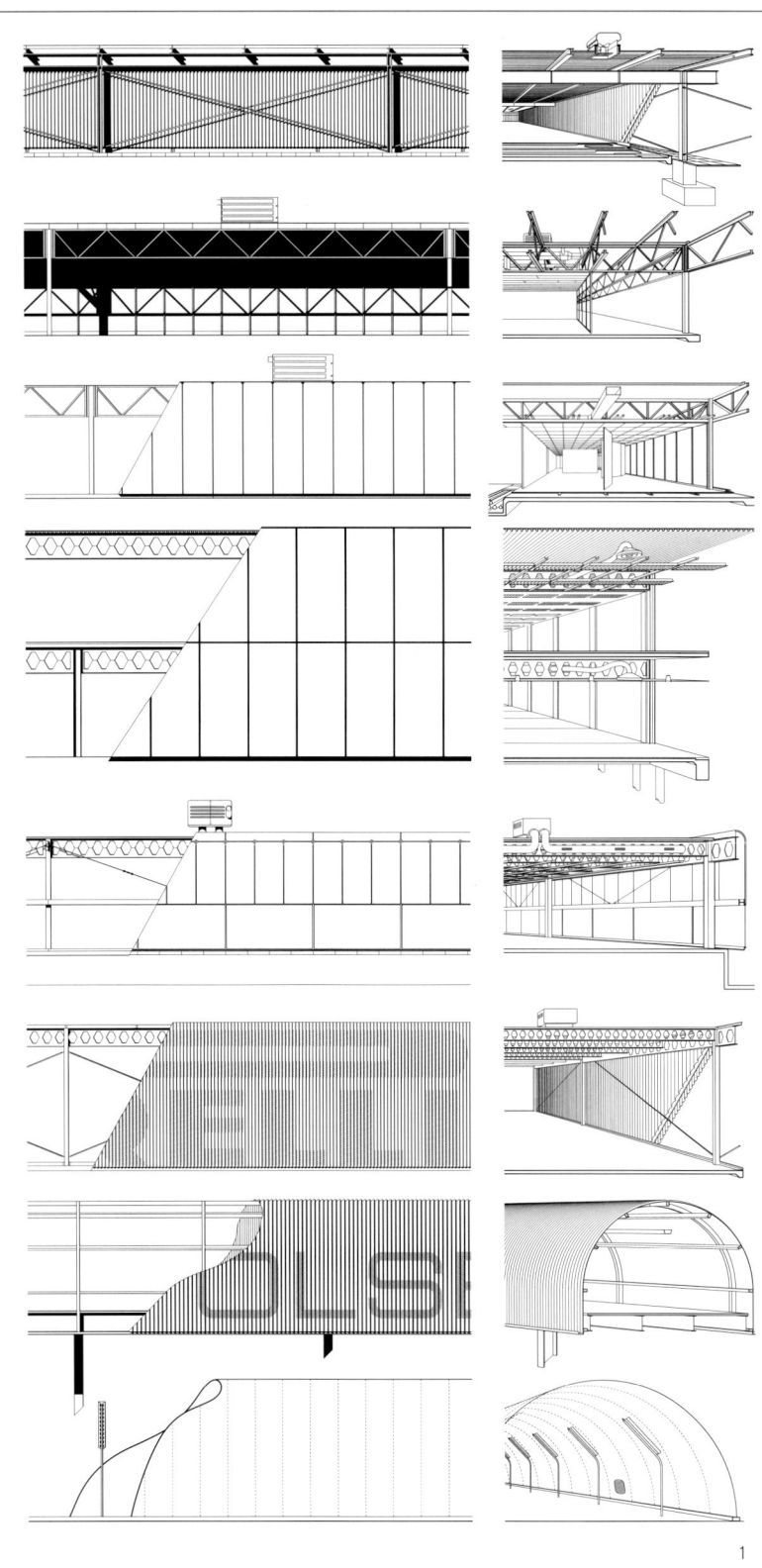

By 1975 Foster had demonstrated in the unglamorous and highly competitive and commercial arena of the design of deep-plan industrial sheds that: firstly, he had not only learned everything that there was to know from two decades of patient development work in the public sector schools programme, but was capable of transferring it to another sphere; secondly, his particular architectural skills were relevant to achieving clients' operational goals in the fastest growing sector of the economy at that time; thirdly, he could use individual projects as a means to achieve the equivalent of a continuing programme of development; and finally, that building components could be as easily and effectively developed as building types themselves.

**In the Foster buildings of this period there is no attempt to emulate the growing German interest in complex building forms intended to articulate and reinforce group spaces – it always seems more important to stress the rationalist, corporate orthogonal than to explore the potential of unusual grids.**

That all this was possible in a series of low budget projects on dismal industrial estates – unfashionable locations at best – simply adds to the magnitude of the achievement. The groundwork had been done and the objectives established for subsequent far more conspicuous and complex projects such as the IBM Technical Park at Greenford and Willis Faber in Ipswich. If one analyses Foster Associates' major achievements of the 1980s, such as the Hongkong Bank and Stansted Airport terminal, the genesis of the approach can be traced back to the same integrating and reductionist discipline that led to the success of Reliance Controls.

Foster found very early in his career a system-based ideology that combined satisfying client requirements with innovative thinking about how to put buildings together. It was a severe, puritanical, purging kind of ideology with little scope for sentimentality or second thoughts. Under its scorching, excoriating glare, there was little room for the wilful self-indulgence of Bürolandschaft layouts – a tougher, service-based discipline had to be found.

**The concept of the Hongkong Bank modules was a logical extension of Foster's attempt to re-analyse high-rise construction. If you could eliminate the central service core ... you could also eliminate floors packed with mechanical and electrical plant ... If plant could be dispersed throughout the building it would not only save valuable floorspace but also energy.**
Stephanie Williams, *Hongkong Bank: The Building of Norman Foster's Masterpiece*, 1989
Right: The Hongkong Bank service modules contain lavatories and air-handling plant and were shipped to site ready to be plugged into the service risers.
Far right: Modules were delivered to site and hoisted into place during the early hours of the morning.

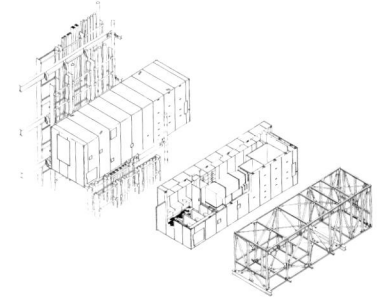

Nor could there be any sympathy for the romantic elaboration of heavy concrete construction that lies at the heart of Herman Hertzberger's contemporary attempts to reconcile long-term corporate culture with short-term individual worker discretions. The objective is always to do the most with the least. There is, in fact, scant evidence of tolerance, or of whimsy or choice on the part of the end users – corporate clarity always tends to dominate.

In the Foster buildings of this period there is no attempt to emulate the growing German interest in complex building forms intended to articulate and reinforce group spaces – it always seems more important to stress the rationalist, corporate orthogonal than to explore the potential of unusual grids. Steel is the ideal material given its lightness and precision. In this way, Foster avoided at a stroke the over complexity and rigidity of attempts to integrate services with concrete structures. Meeting short-term objectives is always more challenging than catering for vague notions of long-term capacity. There is no attempt to follow Louis Kahn's love of the articulation of building form to express served and servant spaces except in the most abstract terms. Understatement is more attractive to Foster than an architecture that needs mass to expound its meaning. There is no playfulness, no waste, no redundancy, no attempt to speak in any regional dialect. Simplicity is the thing.

All the relevant commercial and educational buildings from this period have deep open plans. The significance of the deep plan is not just that such plan configurations are sensible for the purposes these particular buildings serve (as they certainly are) but for three underlying and much more important reasons. The first is that the deep open plan represented at this time an ideology, a particular, no-nonsense, approach to building design.

Breaking down barriers between offices and workshops, between front and back, between high and low status was very much an open systems attitude of the time: 'Long Life, Loose Fit, Low Energy'. Second, and more important, the radical simplification that open planning entailed allowed Norman Foster to concentrate on the development and refinement of certain recurrent constructional details – in the sense that he removed planning from the problem: all the plans of his early commercial buildings are the same. Third, and most importantly, deepness and openness allowed Foster to make 'visible' his intention to integrate systems.

There is a strong, partly unconscious, didactic programme running throughout all these buildings – 'systems integration is good; therefore it should be seen'. For this mission, smaller, more fragmentary building types would not have suited Foster's purposes at all. In a sense, the accident (or the singlemindedness) of being commissioned to design a series of similar buildings made Foster the architect he is. These buildings, in a very real sense, both chose and made him.

Did Foster really need the intellectual baggage of systems thinking? The answer is undoubtedly yes. Without this open-ended, conceptual framework his energies would have been both dissipated and too narrowly channelled. Would systems thinking in itself have been enough to create what Foster has subsequently achieved? The answer is certainly no – the legacy of the schools' programme is sufficient testament to the weakness of good intentions without great talent. Foster's reductionist genius required a starting point. In the end, this series of projects leaves one breathless at the intensity of imagination, at the alchemy that could reduce such ordinary material, such temporary and mundane projects, into purest gold.

1. In this drawing specially prepared for a profile of the practice in *Architectural Design*, in May 1970, Norman Foster tacitly acknowledges an almost Darwinian line of refinement through the early projects, from Reliance Controls to Computer Technology. With the air structure – also for Computer Technology – the process of ephemeralisation was brought to an absolute peak. That Foster was able to establish so much in this, a series of essentially low-budget projects, only adds to the magnitude of the achievement.

2. With the Hongkong Bank, Foster went back to first principles, questioning every aspect of how an office building is used. Hidden by the more eye-catching advances in construction technology, it is as much the development of social systems in his early projects that made this building possible.

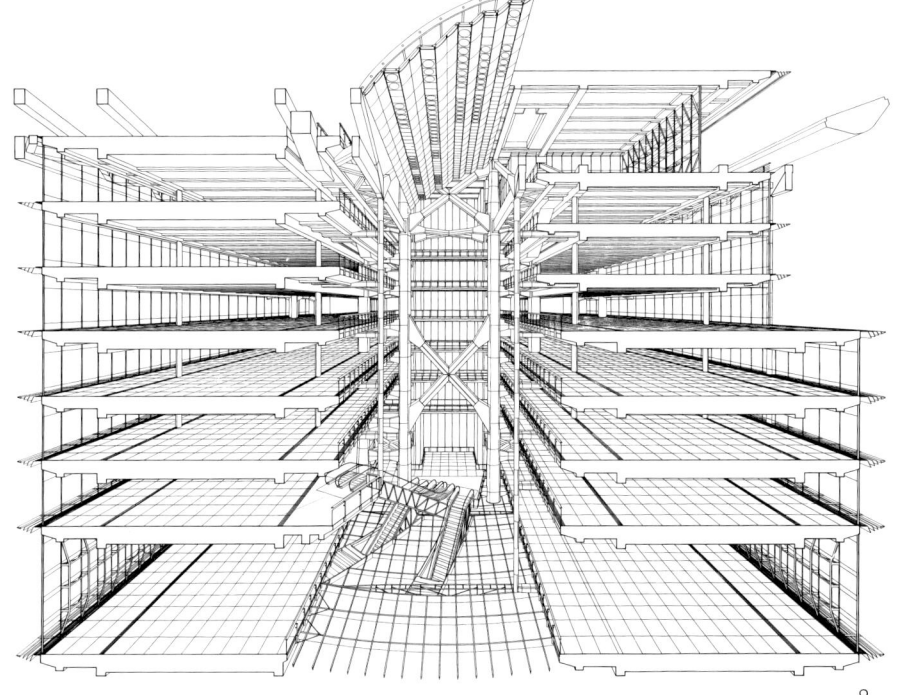

Systems Thinking Revisited 201

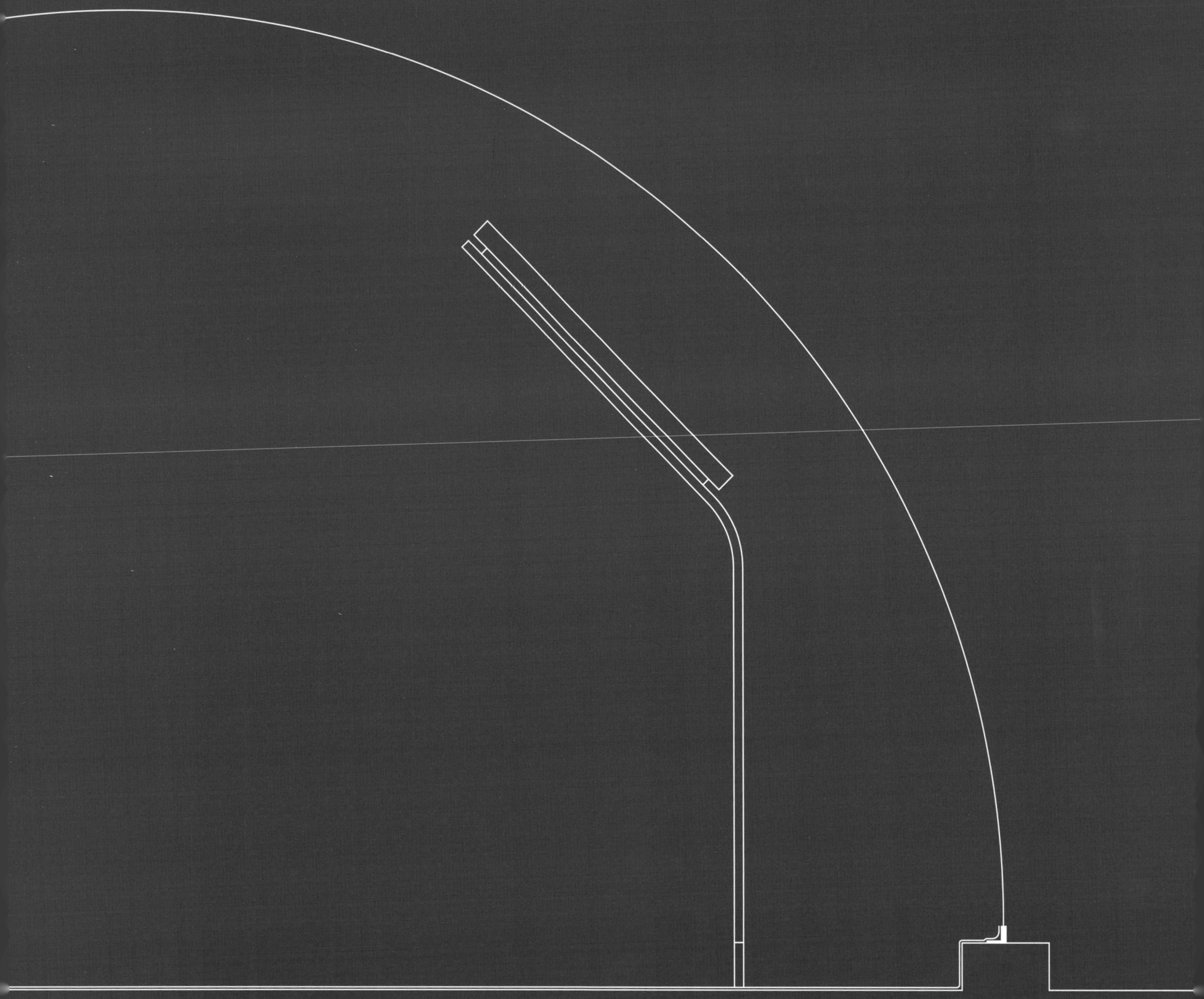

**Projects for Computer Technology**
1969–1971

In the late 1960s Computer Technology was a rapidly expanding young company – the first in Britain to make microchips. Our first project was the conversion of an old canning factory on an incredibly tight budget. We built furniture from white melamine panels bolted together; we cut the legs off standard plastic seats and bent them to create easy chairs; we carpeted the whole building; and in the process we transformed social habits. Previously people flicked solder on to the floor, because it was dirty; but no longer – we had created a space in which they took pride. We were in the process of designing a new building for them when unexpected planning difficulties made temporary accommodation a priority – office space for seventy employees was required within twelve weeks. The solution was an 'instant' structure – a purpose-designed inflatable – which was erected in less than an hour and lasted for more than a year.

Norman Foster

# Air-Supported Office
Hemel Hempstead, England 1969–1970

**In that 'can-do' spirit that had so enthralled me in America, we convinced ourselves, and the company, that we could create the first air-supported office structure.**
Norman Foster

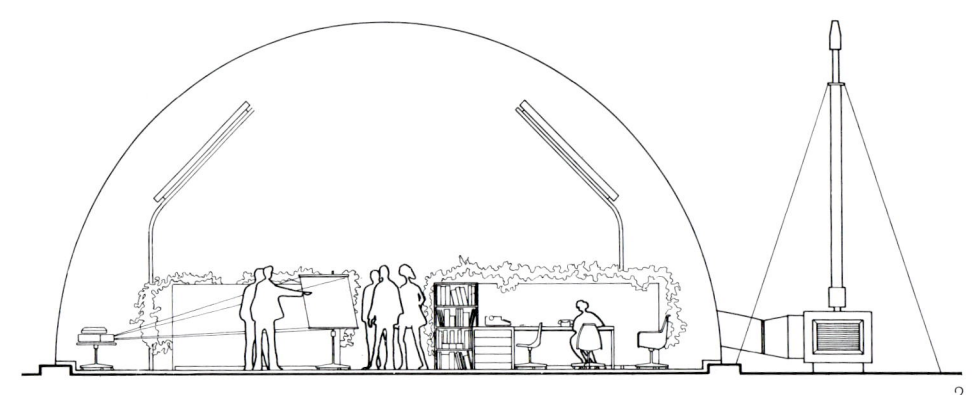

**Perhaps our most minimal exercise in serviced space was the air-supported office for Computer Technology. The structure was environmentally engineered to enable 70 people to work throughout a year in conditions more comfortable than the standard factory shed to which it was attached. This was the first application of an ultra-thin membrane enclosure for sedentary activities.** Norman Foster, *Foster Associates*, 1979

**The taste that has been turned off by the regular format of modern architecture ... is turned right on by the apparent do-it-yourself potentialities of low-pressure inflatable technology.** Reyner Banham, *New Society*, 18 April 1968

Inflatables enjoyed a distinct vogue among architects in the late 1960s, culminating in the Osaka World's Fair, of 1970, for which a range of pneumatic structures were designed.
Left: Yakuta Murata's Fuji Group pavilion at the 1970 World's Fair. Shown here in the process of being erected, the pavilion consisted of sixteen immense 'air beams', inflated and then belted together to form an enclosure capable of withstanding typhoons.

The notion of an 800 square-metre office building being delivered to site in a single compact bundle is something of a novelty. Seeing that structure take shape in less than an hour may even hint at a slightly capricious architectural response to a client's office overspill crisis. In fact, nothing could be further from the truth. The air-supported office for Computer Technology, designed in 1970, not only demonstrated Foster Associates' commitment to appropriate technology and the solution of problems by a return to first principles, it was also a highly rational and cost-effective response.

In the late 1960s, Computer Technology was a dynamic young company driven by the sudden and rapid success of its 'Modular One' computer series. But the speed of that success had brought with it accommodation problems.

Foster had already converted for office use an old canning factory on the company's Hemel Hempstead site and was about to build an adjacent permanent headquarters when unexpected planning permission difficulties made the provision of temporary office space an urgent priority. Work space for 70 employees was required within twelve weeks, to last over a period of twelve months.

Foster was asked to carry out comparative studies of a number of different options. Contractors' huts, portable cabins, dome structures and other conventional and unconventional solutions all proved far more expensive than the one that Foster preferred: a purpose-designed inflatable tent. No one was in any doubt that this was the cheapest solution, but questions of stability, security, temperature control and lighting were still unanswered. Inflatable structures in themselves were hardly new, but their previous industrial use had been limited to warehousing; it was the office-space application that raised the key questions – and simultaneously offered the opportunity to re-examine a number of more familiar problems in this new and unfamiliar context.

The site for the inflatable structure was the area destined to become the car park for the final building. On this rectangle of tarmac the structure was anchored by means of a concrete perimeter ground beam.

1. The world's first inflatable office building, seen in the snow of winter, 1970.

2. Throughout its short life the crucial issue was thermal performance. Twin external air-inlet fans pressurised the envelope and supplied warm air for space heating. Cold radiation through the fabric was controlled by the heaters and the creation of a no-go 'reservation' around the perimeter of the open-plan space. Summer overheating was prevented yet more simply by water evaporation from the surface of the skin, sprayed on by nothing more complicated than a standard garden sprinkler. The lighting stanchions supported standard fluorescent tubes which reflected their light off the inner surface of the nylon/pvc envelope. They also provided practical emergency support in the event of a sudden deflation.

3. The plan presented a spacious office arrangement, organised around a central aisle. A main 'air-lock' entrance at one end was supplemented by three escape doors, for use in emergencies only.

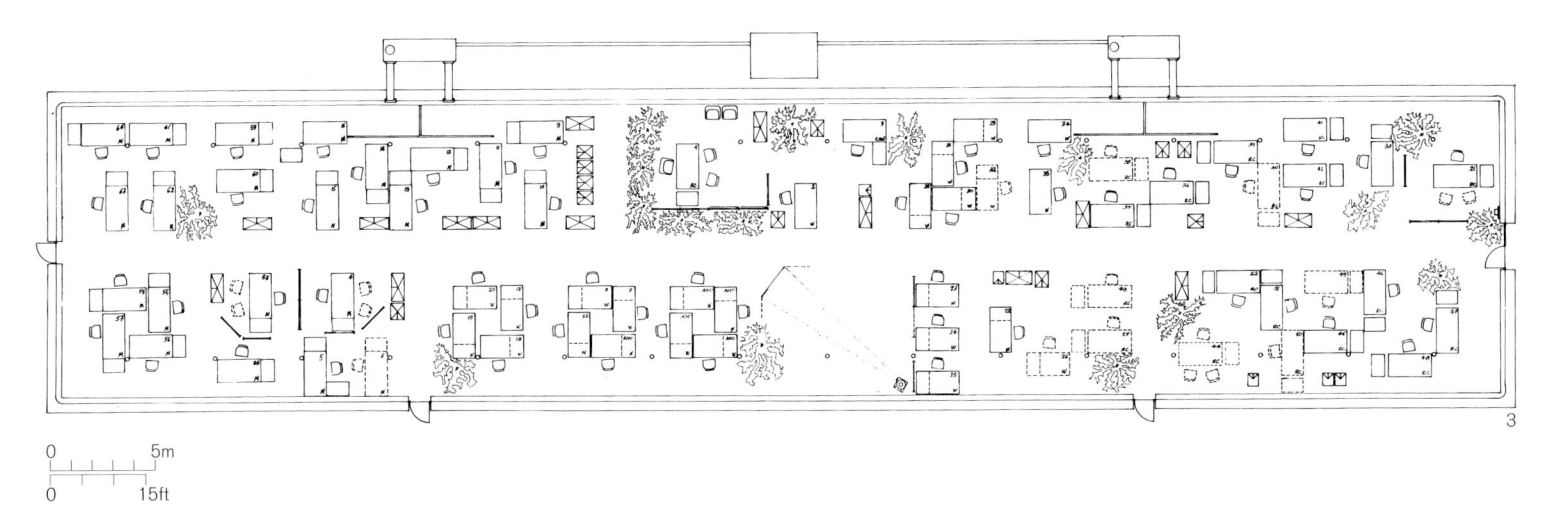

1-3. A central aisle proved the most efficient form of circulation for the space, while providing the most direct means of escape in the event of fire or rapid deflation. The perimeter 'reservation' was used as an additional circulation route, with workstation screens positioned to act as baffles in front of the air inlets. The fluorescent tubes supplied such a good standard of ambient light – supplemented during the day by a 10 per cent transmission of daylight through the translucent envelope – that the task lights were rarely used.

4. Delivered to site as a 2-metre diameter bundle, the 70 x 13 metre envelope was craned into position on the car park, unrolled and secured to its perimeter beam prior to inflation. The envelope was inflated in just 55 minutes, and Computer Technology's staff moved in 14 days later.

Electrical and telephone cabling ran around the top of the beam, encircling the 70 x 13-metre enclosure and supplying all the internal equipment, none of which, incidentally, required a current exceeding 2 amps. The subsequent economies made in wiring and insulation exemplified an approach that at no point sacrificed cost to innovation.

The translucent envelope itself, made from a nylon and pvc fabric purchased from the company Swedish Polydrom, remained something of an unknown quantity in certain respects, despite its obvious structural suitability. Twin inlet fans inflated the structure via baffles that were designed to minimise noise and distribute the air evenly. By heating the incoming air to 90°F, an internal temperature of 70°F could be maintained in winter – the structure was erected in January – although an unpredictable variation in the insulation value of the envelope's skin took some time to identify. The presence or absence of daylight, it was eventually found, caused a perceptible change in the material's U-value: loss of heat by radiation being significantly greater at night. Further fine-tuning was also required when it was discovered that a slight slope in the car park was causing noticeable heat stratification.

Lighting and safety considerations were happily united in a single elegant solution: a double row of canted steel tubes, cantilevered out of the floor slab and supporting standard fluorescent fittings, would act as supporting ribs should the structure for any reason fail.

The lights themselves, directed on to the inner surface of the envelope, provided ample background lighting. Tungsten desk lighting combined with the specially chosen, bright red broadloom carpet to bring a sense of warmth to a translucent structure which, perhaps inevitably, carried psychological overtones of coolness.

Psychological reactions were also a concern with regard to the structure's lack of windows. In reality, the very openness and height of the space seemed to allay any sense of being closed in for most people. Curiously, the space was more responsive to the outside world than most traditional structures, changing perceptibly when sunny or overcast and responding directly to the sound of falling rain.

When summer came, the need to reduce the inside temperature resulted in the installation of 'an evaporative cooling system' or – more prosaically – ten lawn sprinklers which were draped over the structure. The simplicity of this solution perhaps detracts from its remarkable effectiveness and its almost absurd cheapness. The same might be said of the whole tent itself. Before the structure was finally dismantled and sold, to be replaced by the permanent building, Computer Technology had enjoyed a pioneering piece of 'instant' architecture at a fraction of conventional costs. As for Foster, the experiment had provided a focal point for a long-standing area of fascination, while making its own unique contribution to the cumulative knowledge of the practice.

Graham Vickers

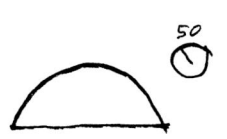

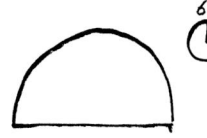

**The 800-square-metre bundle, fabricated to our specifications in Sweden, was off-loaded and inflated one cold Sunday morning in some 55 minutes, and we cut ourselves in with a Stanley knife!** Norman Foster, *RIBA Journal*, June 1970
Left: As this sequence of photographs records, the fabric structure was delivered to site in a 2-metre bundle and took little under an hour to inflate; it was fitted out and occupied within 14 days.

**Its semi-transparency to light gave it a delicate air of transience, yet its form (like that of many other inflated structures) was not so different from that of, say, a long heap of clay piled up at its natural angle of permanent repose. That particular form makes functional and economic sense (something more bubble-like would have enclosed wasteful amounts of volume) but it still left a powerful sense of visual ambiguity, which is perhaps proper to an 'impermanent' structure.** Reyner Banham, *Foster Associates*, 1979

**At minimal cost a cheerful space unfolded. We installed red carpets that gave the space a warm glow, and erected light fittings that supported the structure, so that if there was a sudden deflation the structure would not fall on top of you.** Norman Foster

REMOVED DAY 365

Air-Supported Office  207

# Computer Technology
Hemel Hempstead, England 1969–1971

It was a difficult period because we had so little work. However, we were finally asked to design a building for Computer Technology – the first company in Britain to make microchips. We gave as much to that project as any before or since. It was the most important thing in our lives, and I recall real passion in the way that we went to work on it ... Out of an old canning factory we produced something quite luxurious – a space in which people could take pride. Norman Foster, lecture at Stuttgart University, 14 May 1997
Right: The canning factory in its original state.

Computer Technology is run by young whizz-kids in a hurry ... They needed premises fast so they leased a prime example of the traditional inflexible box and shack variety standing in three acres in a New Town. They then commissioned Foster Associates to transform it into the kind of environment which the go-ahead electronics industry demands as a matter of course. Within an impressively low budget of 35 shillings [£1.75] per square foot the proverbial pig's ear was turned into a silk purse. Terry Wright, *The Architectural Review*, November 1969

If IBM Cosham achieved a minimalist elegance in the face of a tight budget, Foster Associates' next permanent building in Hemel Hempstead was to be visually much bolder. Even so, the Computer Technology permanent building, which was to work in conjunction with the company's earlier canning factory refit and succeed the temporary air-supported structure, was also realised on a limited budget. Here again Foster was to provide a flexible internal space, serviced entirely overhead, leaving the maximum floor area clear of structure.

For the final stage of his involvement with the young computer company, Foster proposed a single-storey, deep-plan building enclosing a generous air-conditioned and landscaped space. From the beginning, Computer Technology's managing director, Iann Barron, had enthusiastically agreed with Foster's proposal that there should be a single enclosure for varied activities, with a common entrance. Internal divisions would be totally flexible and their location determined only by operational demands. Apart from a few enclosed spaces, which had to take account of acoustic or other special requirements, there was to be a single dynamic space in which a wide range of activities, from research to product assembly, could be undertaken.

Barron had enthusiastically endorsed Foster's earlier proposals for the air-supported office and had worked in it for twelve months. Norman Foster's own preoccupation with the social benefits of breaking down traditional barriers within the workplace here found overt support from the client.

The new building, linked to the converted canning factory by a glazed corridor, was to be both a continuation and a more satisfactory realisation of intentions first executed there. In the old building some features already enshrined the spirit of the new building to come: its wall-to-wall carpeting symbolised a flexible, socially integrated and humane working space: extending through the assembly areas, the carpet had dramatically improved work practices, which became far cleaner.

The earlier building had even prompted Norman Foster's first venture into furniture systems. Working with associate Martin Francis he later repeated the exercise for the new building. Assembly benches, internal walls, desks, tables and kitchen worktops were all made from a simple system of knock-down components and partitions.

1. Computer Technology was among the pioneers of a new breed of 'clean' industries whose precision work and skilled staff required a fresh approach to factory building.

2. The ground floor of Computer Technology's first building – a converted canning factory. An omni-directional service zone was created beneath a suspended ceiling; all services dropped vertically to the workstations.

3. A view into the reception area of the converted canning factory.

**Computer Technology provided a single dynamic space in which all kinds of activity from research analysis to computer assembly could take place.**
Norman Foster

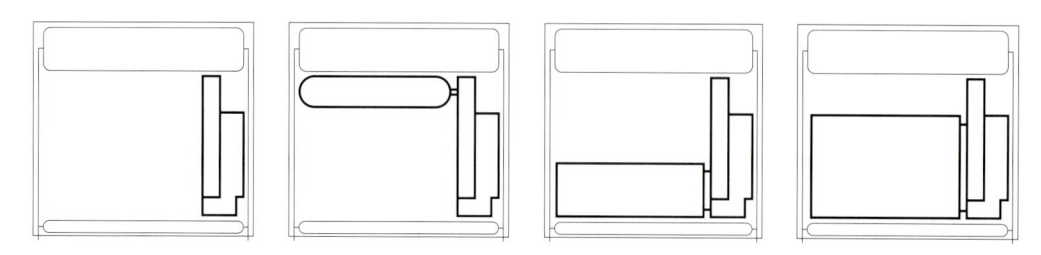

**Taking the expansion programme for Computer Technology as a whole, the factory will have grown from 6,000 square feet to 48,000 square feet in five easy stages in the space of four years … Computer Technology will have nearly doubled in size every year. That's what phrases like 'the fast-growing computer industry' really mean.**
Terry Wright, *The Architectural Review*, November 1969

Left: A series of plans shows the sequential development of the Computer Technology site. The first phase involved altering and refurbishing the former canning factory. The second phase was the creation of the temporary air-supported office. The final phase was the design of a permanent research and development building, itself capable of expansion.

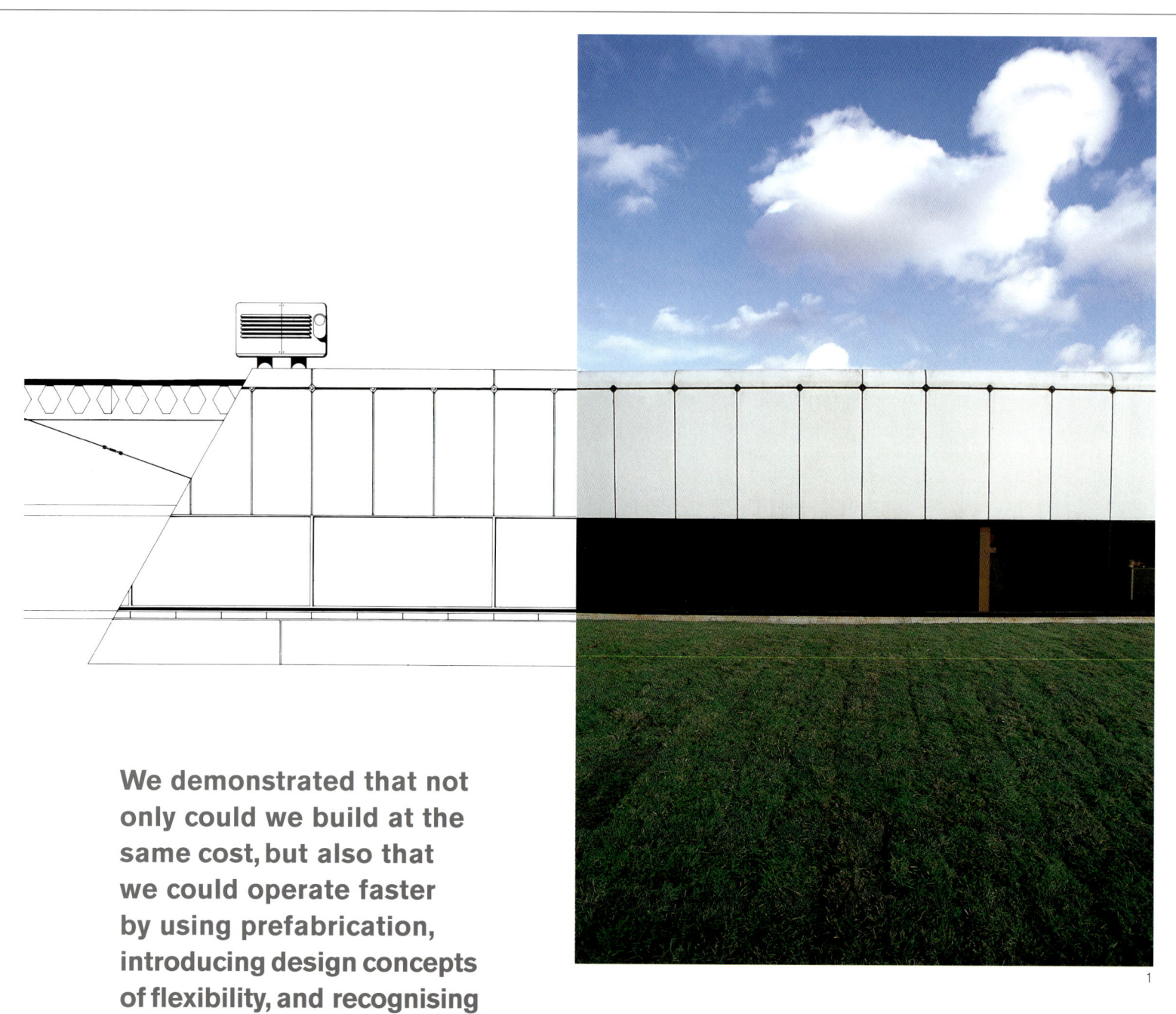

**We demonstrated that not only could we build at the same cost, but also that we could operate faster by using prefabrication, introducing design concepts of flexibility, and recognising that the only constant for most of our commercial clients was change itself.**
Norman Foster

**With the Fred Olsen company we established a vital link to the user in the form of regular sessions with the works committee. This was extended to include office committees and has proved as valuable in realising the project as the more traditional exchanges with the company's directors. A similar pattern was established with the Computer Technology programme and on one occasion involved a presentation to the whole company as an open forum.** Norman Foster, *RIBA Journal*, June 1970

**The exterior of this single-storey building is simple, direct, yet distinctive in expression. A large trade symbol fulfils its purpose while at the same time forming an interesting part of the appearance of the building seen as a whole.** Extract from the jurors' report for the Financial Times Industrial Architecture Award, 1971

The building itself demands to be assessed not only in its physical context – a visually uninspiring industrial estate – but also in terms of its cost and timeframe. The heady days of the (then) burgeoning computer industry demanded a flexibility of approach, which made Foster the ideal choice of architect, but which also brought unusual conditions, not least from the company's financiers.

## Computer Technology was early in addressing questions about the organisation and operation of deep-plan, barrier-free office spaces.

Engineer Loren Butt explains: 'The spacing of the structure was interesting because the financing of the building came from ICFC (Industrial Construction Finance Corporation) which was very concerned about its future usage, beyond the time when Computer Technology might occupy it. So the structural bay, the heights and structural spans were all influenced by financing. We looked at all that with glee, because future flexibility was what we were always talking about. It is true to say that Computer Technology was a firm changing rapidly at the time. The degree of change in this building was far in excess of anything that happened in an IBM building. The mix of office and design space, and assembly areas was very flexible. One weekend, I recall, they took all of one department out and simply extended the assembly area – all in the same building. Computer Technology was using the flexibility that had, at least in part, been designed for future users at the behest of the financiers who paid for the building.'

Despite this happy meeting of aims, cost limitations meant that the facility's practicality and visual expression of intention often needed to be extremely simply stated. Loren Butt suggests that in terms of temperature control, although the Computer Technology building represented an advance on the system installed at IBM Cosham, it was still not ideal. 'Here we had the roof-mounted package solution that I would have preferred at Cosham', he says. 'Even so, initially it had to go in with only heating and ventilating capability. The facility to add a cooling unit came later on, when more money became available.'

The idea that there would never be any need for full-height partitions inside the building also meant that there would be no need for a ceiling to provide an acoustic function. This led to the notion of exposing all the services throughout the building and expressing them in a way that would be both practical and visually exciting. As a result, the interior was to achieve a visual boldness that might not have been appropriate for a more traditional client.

1. This cutaway elevation exposes the castellated beam roof structure and diagonal bracing wires behind the building's white-painted cladding panels. Derived from freezer-truck technology these insulated panels – jointed with neoprene strips – provide what appears to be a sealed 'umbrella' above the glazed section of the walls. In fact the curved cornice section conceals a flat roof.

2. The grassed area outside the glazing aligns with the floor level inside. Only the vehicle access ramp and car park are set at a lower level.

With his Beatles haircut and office gear of pink towelling sweater, black cord jeans and open toe sandals, Iann Barron doesn't look much like a conventional managing director. To many in the computer industry he is the enfant terrible of the business; many of them still talk of the advertisement, two years ago, in which he appeared nude in the bath to give his newly-launched computer a mass-market image.
*The Observer*, 25 October 1970

Left: Iann Barron, Computer Technology's managing director, at work in the new building soon after its completion. It was Barron's enthusiasm for Foster Associates' innovations that made the sequence of projects for Computer Technology possible.

**The concept of dropping services from the factory ceiling is a long-standing industrial tradition. But to extend it, to help blur the edges between office space and production space, was, I think, an interesting idea.**

Norman Foster

**There is nothing soft about Computer Technology, except its software and the fact that its Hemel Hempstead plant is the first factory in Britain where the production area is fully carpeted. The computer men were keen to break down the traditional white collar/blue collar division of British industry. Architecturally they agreed wholeheartedly with their architects that there should be only one shed with one entrance for everyone, and that divisions within the shed should be completely flexible without distinction of class or collar.** Nicholas Taylor, *The Sunday Times*, 5 May 1968

**We were particularly impressed with the handling of the interiors where, for instance, brightly coloured exposed pipework and air ducts, suspended from above, add interest to the whole. Carpeting of a neutral colour, extending over the whole of the floor area, including the entrance stairs and stairwells, gives a handsome uniform impression. The careful detailing and competent treatment of every part of the building is very impressive.** Extract from the jurors' report for the Financial Times Industrial Architecture Award, 1971

---

Concern for insulation resulted in a much better standard than full-height glazing could have provided: only the lower section of the walls was glazed to retain an outside view. This lower band of Pilkington's umber-tinted Spectrafloat glass, which sat above a plinth of bolted concrete panels, contrasted dramatically with the highly insulated, snow-white panels above. It was a solution that, in a way, prefigured the Sainsbury Centre.

The cladding panels used were made of aluminium-faced polyurethane, with finished interior and exterior faces and a vapour barrier laminated into a single prefabricated unit. Being light and demountable, they were ideally suited to phased building operations. The junctions between panels, derived from container construction techniques, used neoprene and aluminium extrusions to make airtight joints.

Interestingly – and atypically for Foster – the building employed a minor trick of visual deception, again necessitated by the low budget. Seen from ground level, it looks as though its sides continue up and over the building in an unbroken line, as was the case in the later Sainsbury Centre. Here, however, there is a disguised flat roof. The illusion of continuity is created by curved panels at the eaves and the corners of the walls.

Computer Technology was early in addressing questions about the organisation and operation of deep-plan, barrier-free office spaces. The inclination of its users to clutter a generous space is one which the architect can discourage, but never prevent. However, in this case, Foster's decision to use an overhead electrical power distribution to drop power cables directly from the roof zone suggested an interesting self-regulating solution.

As Norman Foster says, 'The idea of dropping services from the ceiling in a factory is a long-standing industrial tradition. To extend it, to help blur the edges between office space and production space, was, I think, an interesting idea. Of course, there is a very real risk of visual pollution in use, especially when there are high concentrations of connections and wiring. In defence – or, perhaps, if I wanted to play devil's advocate – I could argue that such a system might be more self-policing. What tends to happen now is that the average highly-serviced building has probably got more redundant wiring hidden out of sight than it has current wiring. "Out of sight, out of mind" gets you into bad housekeeping habits that might not happen with a more visible system.'

Graham Vickers

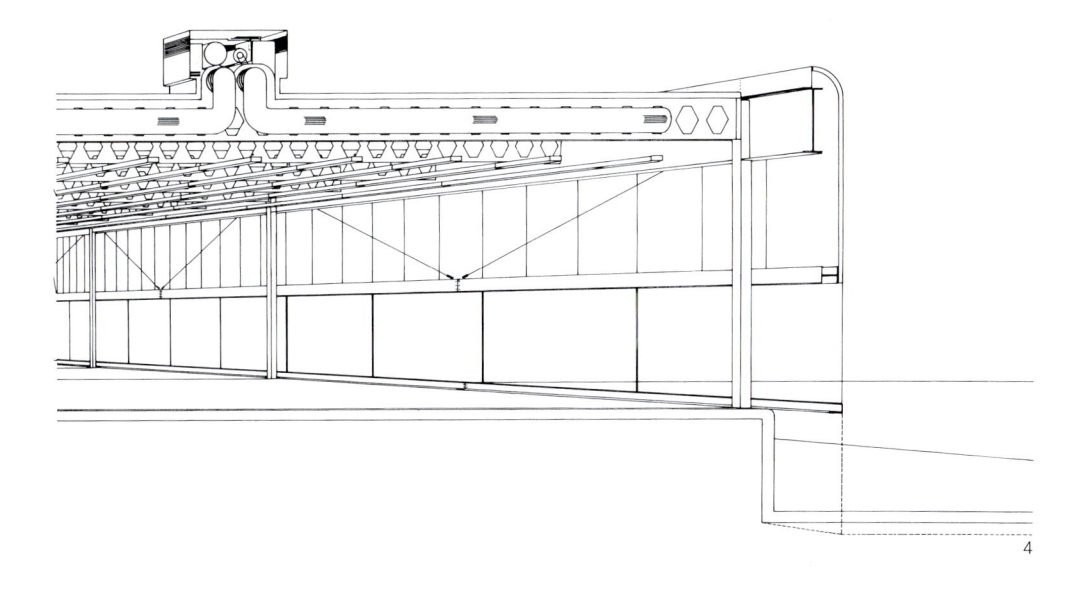

1-3. The interior of the Computer Technology building, photographed at the time of the Financial Times Award in 1971. The exposed castellated beams support and permit the passage of colour-coded electricity and telephone cables, air-conditioning ducts and air pressure lines, while the fluorescent lighting is suspended on continuous tracks below. As Norman Foster observed, the one great advantage of high-level servicing was its visibility: redundant sections could not be ignored as they might have been in under-floor ducts.

4. A part section through the building. Air-conditioning units were roof-mounted, which allowed the free passage of all services and ducting. Unlike IBM Cosham, which this arrangement prefigures, the service zone was concealed externally by solid cladding panels fixed above the glazing.

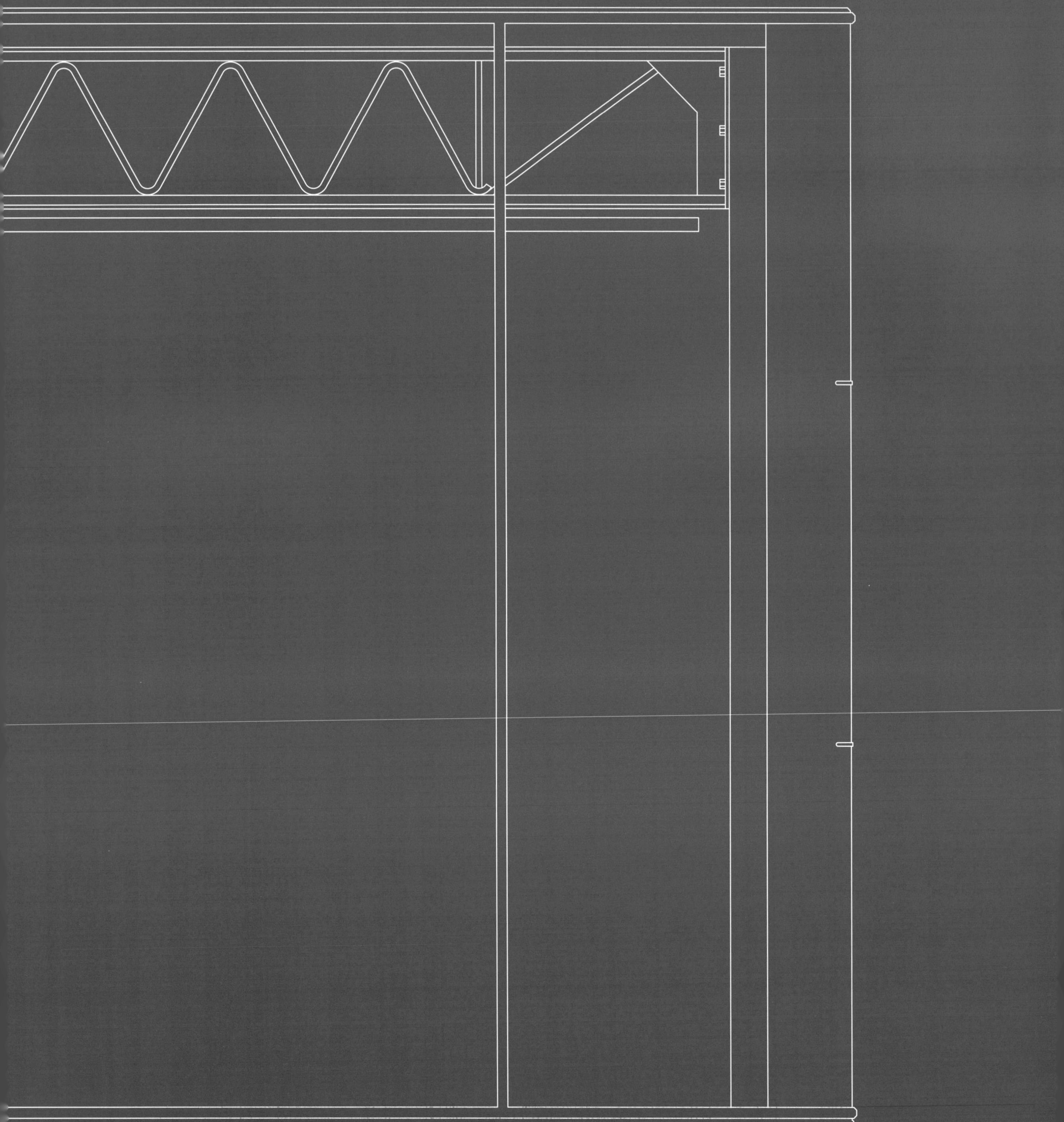

**IBM Pilot Head Office**
Cosham, England 1970–1971

Like many rapidly expanding companies at the time, IBM relied on an ad hoc mixture of permanent and temporary accommodation. The brief initially was to research the available 'off-the-peg' systems and propose a site layout. But we were able to demonstrate that for the same cost and within the same tight time-scale, IBM could have a purpose-designed building that embraced high architectural and environmental standards. In its inherent flexibility and anticipation of computer technology, the building was many years ahead of its time. In the early 1970s the computer was still regarded almost as a sacred object, and the convention was to house it in a separate 'shrine'. Yet all it needed was a raised floor. To demystify the computer and integrate it into the main office space was a radical departure. And although the building was expected only to be a stop-gap, its ability to respond to changing needs has ensured its long-term survival.

Norman Foster

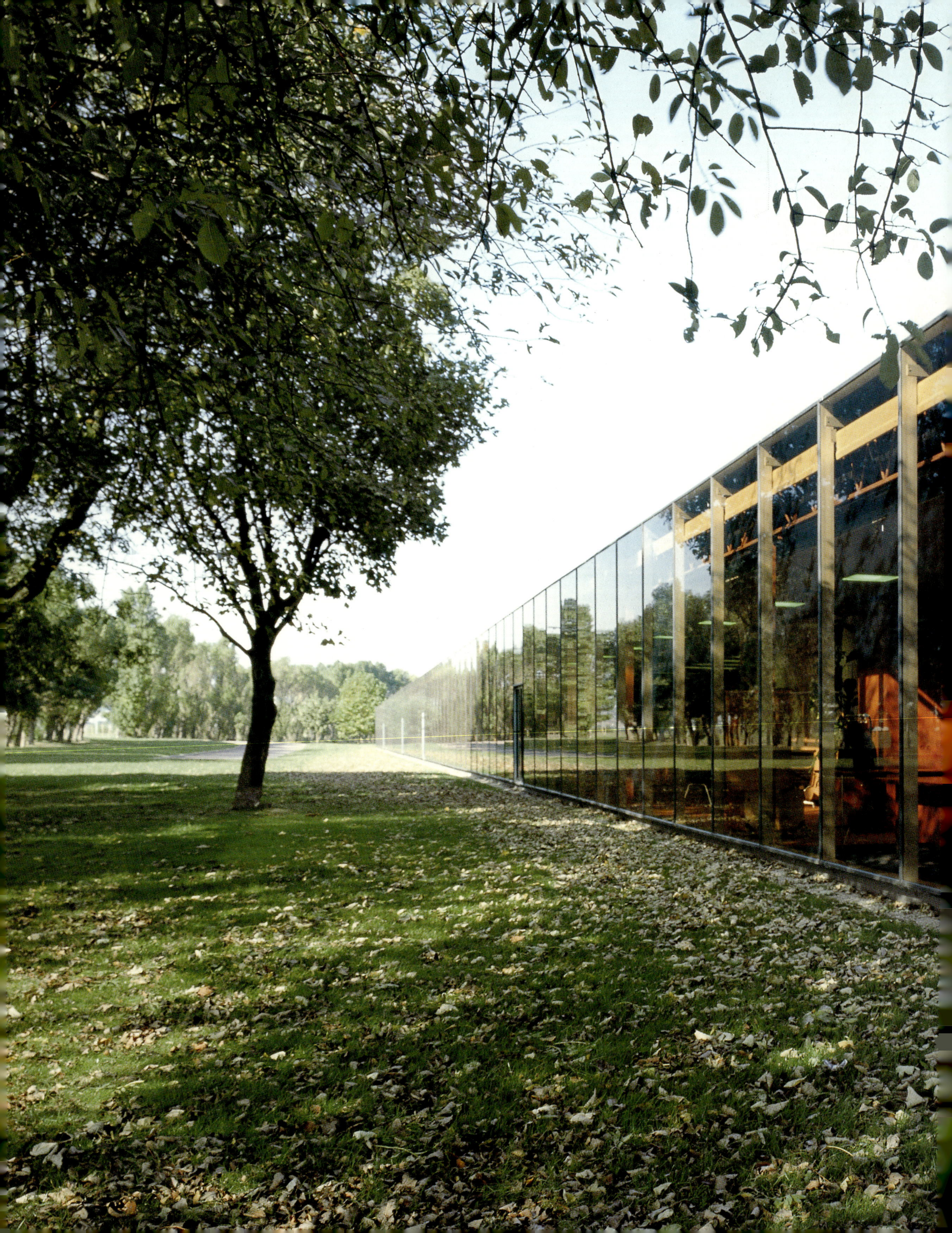

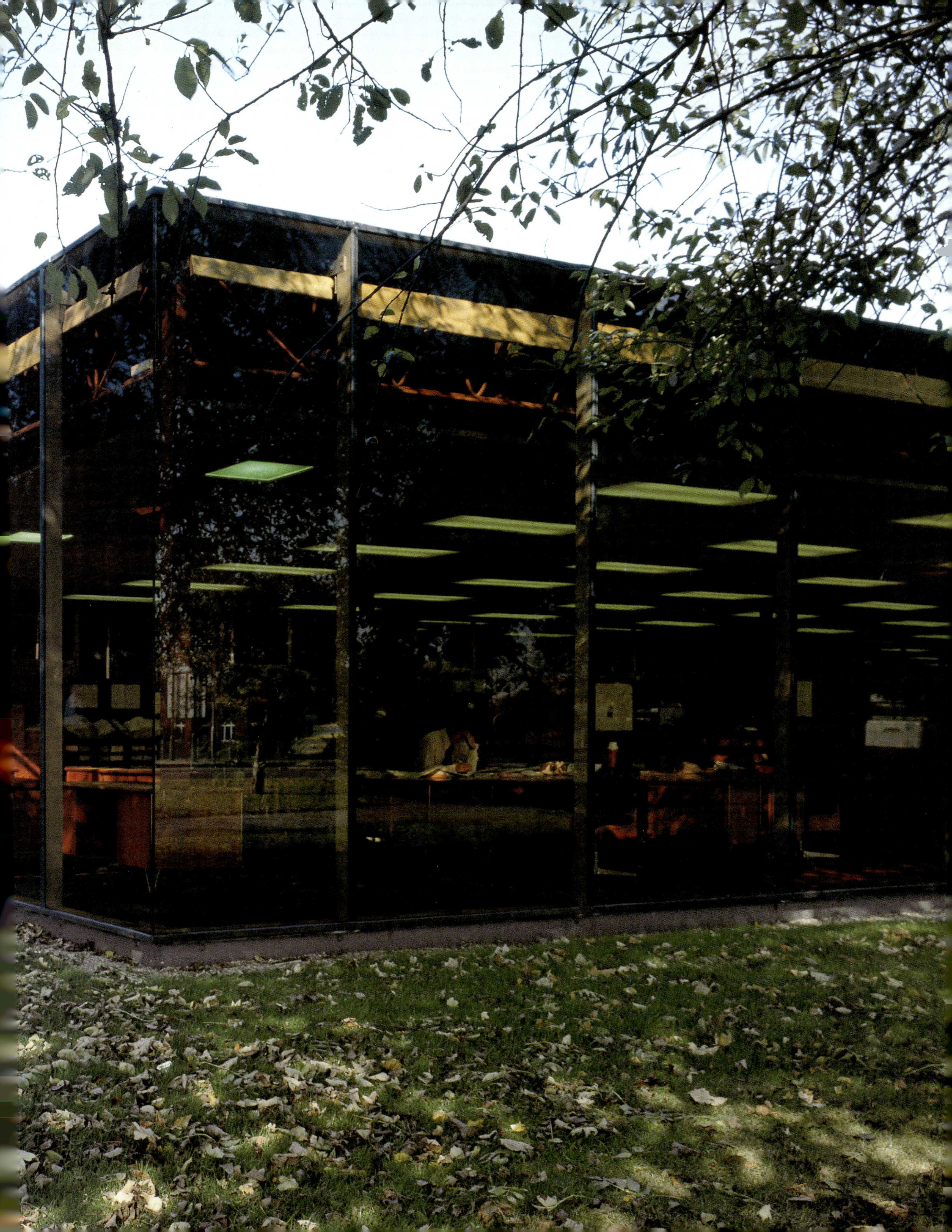

**IBM asked us to design a temporary building. I took the brief as a challenge. Having looked at the cost and the time needed to build such a structure we instead designed what was in effect a permanent building for the same very low budget, which could be completed to the same very fast time-scale.** Norman Foster, lecture in Santiago, Chile, 15 October 1997

Left: Typical proprietary temporary buildings that had already been used by IBM at its Havant site in 1970.

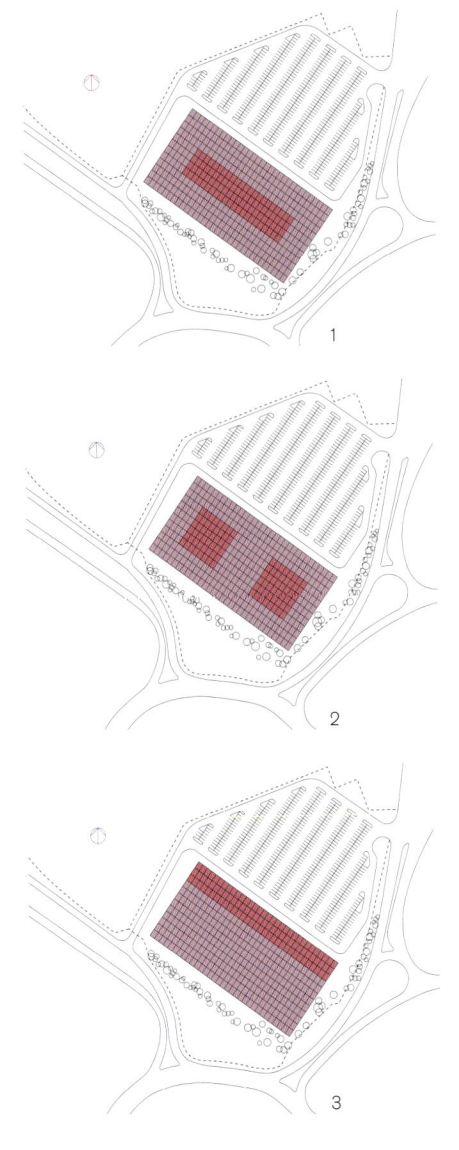

In March 1970, Foster Associates was invited to consider the feasibility of providing a pilot – or perhaps more appropriately – an 'instant' head office for IBM at Cosham in Hampshire. The proposed site adjoined land designated for the company's main UK offices. The need for what was planned as a temporary headquarters building was generated by the scheduling of a land reclamation programme.

The site lay just north of Portsmouth. Formed by refuse-tip reclamation in the 1930s, it was bounded by playing fields and Cosham Park to the north-west and east, and lay adjacent to the (then) proposed M27 motorway linking Havant, Portsmouth and Southampton.

## Initially, the brief was to research the best available systems and propose a site layout – exactly the situation Foster had argued against in his factory systems studies.

As was common for many rapidly expanding companies at that time, IBM was happy to rely on a mixture of permanent and temporary accommodation. At some locations as much as half its office space was provided in proprietary prefabricated buildings. It was no surprise, therefore, that Foster's first brief was simply to research the best available systems and propose a site layout. It was exactly the situation Foster had argued against in his factory systems studies and 'Manplan' articles of the year before. He raised objections again, arguing that any new building, as well as being fast and cheap, should also embrace high architectural and environmental standards.

IBM, for its part, required accommodation for 750 employees, with expansion potential for up to 1,000. This suggested a gross floor area of 15,000 square metres, with possible future expansion up to 20,000 square metres.

Furthermore, there was some uncertainty about the detailed use of the building over its expected life-span, and so maximum flexibility was required. Two months of discussion elapsed before the commission was finally awarded, leaving Foster, in effect, only four months in which to develop a design solution. IBM had made important concessions during this time, however. Most significantly, following a visit to Fred Olsen's Amenity Centre at Millwall Dock, Gerry Deighton, head of IBM's estates and construction division, had agreed to Foster drawing up a new systems building.

However, Foster was also asked to evaluate a complete range of possible solutions with regard to phasing, expansion and site utilisation. The cheapest option, an air-supported structure as used at Computer Technology, was rejected as being unsuitable on security grounds, because of the valuable equipment it would house. The remaining options were quickly narrowed down to two 'off-the-peg' solutions and a new building.

The first proposal investigated a system then being employed by IBM at nearby Havant: a single-storey Youngman patent prefabricated timber frame, shallow-planned on a 12 x 12-metre office bay with courtyards giving natural through ventilation. This scheme was rejected on several counts: it did not allow sufficient space for car parking and possible expansion; it required opening windows which would result in traffic noise, disturbance and pollution from the adjoining highway; and electricity and telephone cable distribution were restricted to the perimeter of the bays. Furthermore, vital services and facilities could not be incorporated without expensive and complex conversion of the standard units.

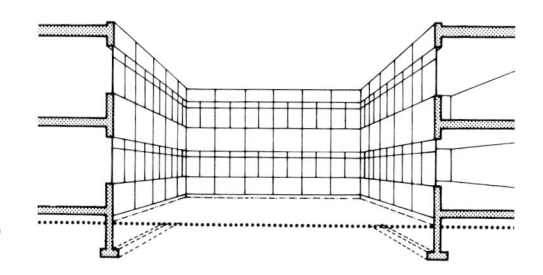

Right: A two storey proprietary office system was initially considered for the IBM site. Although covering much reduced site area, this solution would have required deep foundations in reclaimed land of poor bearing capacity.

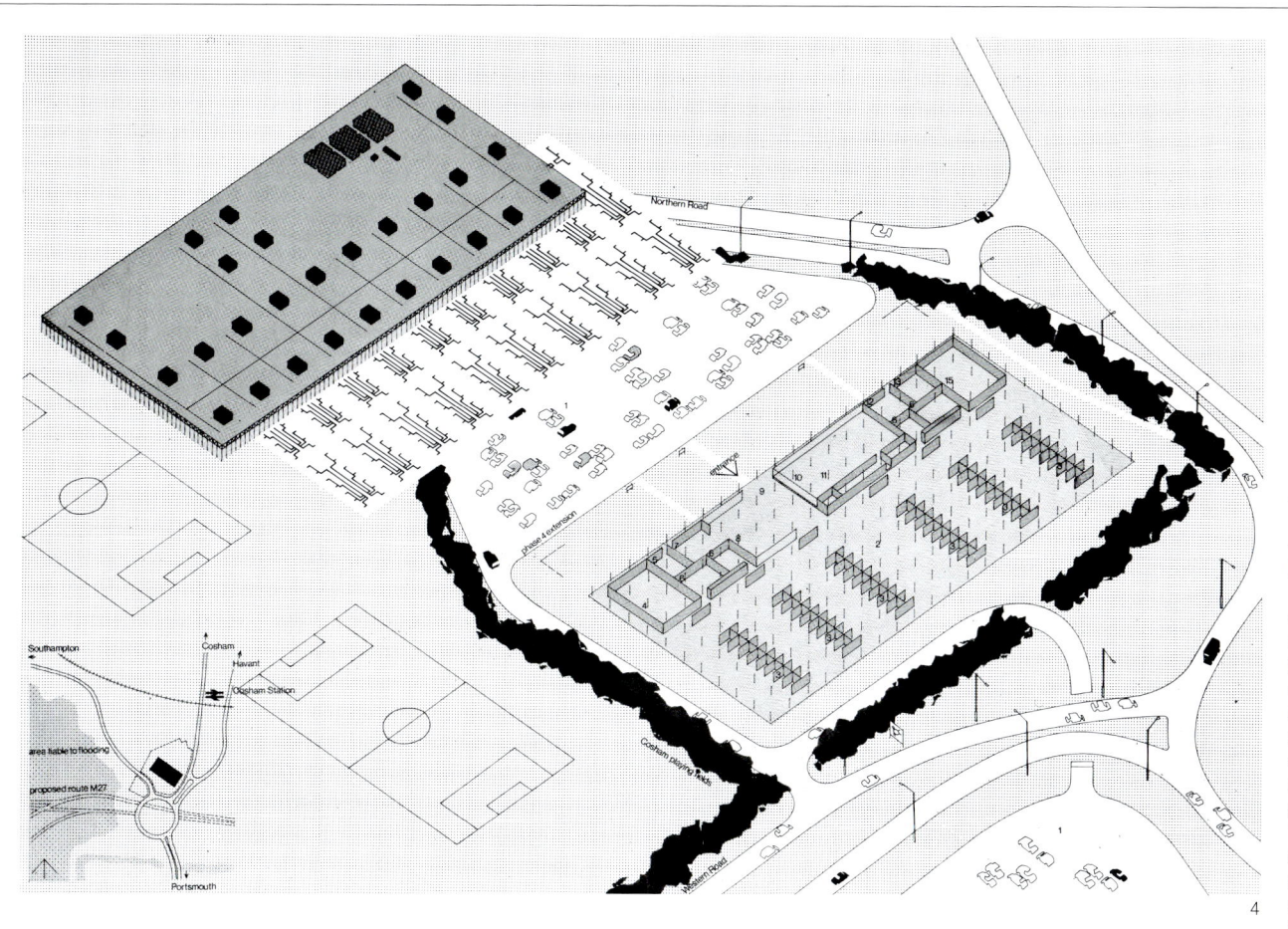

Although IBM's brief had called for no more than the use of the 'best temporary buildings available', Foster Associates' research proved that a deep-plan permanent structure would offer better value for money and could be completed within the same time-frame.

1-3. In Foster's initial report to IBM, service zones of identical size were overlaid on plans for comparative purposes. IBM agreed that central service cores reduced flexibility and accepted the recommended option (bottom) to run all highly serviced areas along the north side of the building.

4. In this exploded isometric the roof, complete with its air-handling units and chillers, is removed to expose the network of air distribution ducts and the internal planning arrangement of the building as it was on completion in 1971. Over the years this arrangement has been extensively altered, but the possible extension indicated has never materialised.

5. This sketch from the report bears a strong resemblance to the final building. The tinted glass was retained but the large logo was dropped.

6. The site layout proposed in the report is remarkably close to its final form.

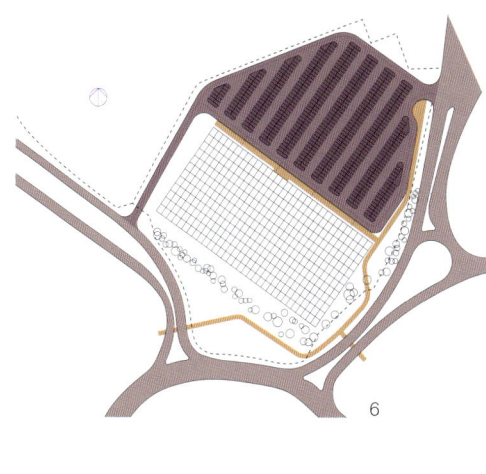

IBM Pilot Head Office

**We have never really had the luxury of that utopian vision where a client isolates a brief and hands it over to a design team who, in glorious isolation, design a fixed building and then hand it over to a contractor who produces a fixed building. In our experience life is not like that. The only constant is change.** Norman Foster, lecture at the Construction Industry Conference, London, 15 May 1980

**The brief was to provide space for computers, offices, restaurants and a communications centre. Now, normally this would sprout a multitude of separate buildings, each, say, with connecting corridors. In this instance, the solution was to put them all under one umbrella. In this way the activities could flux and change over a period of time, and that is what has actually happened. Over a period of ten years the building has been subject to constant change.** Norman Foster, lecture at the RIBA Annual Conference, University of Hull, 14 July 1976

**IBM seem to have toyed originally with the idea that if you want speed and cheapness you should go 'straight to industry': that you should go straight to a building system knocked up by some hard-headed businessman-cum-engineer, whose mind is unclouded by idle aesthetic preferences, who knows his market like the back of his hand, etc etc. What is principally gratifying about this job, therefore, is that Foster was able not merely to provide something much better than anything which could be bought off the peg, but to do it more quickly and at less cost.** Lance Wright, *The Architectural Review*, January 1972

---

The second proposal – essentially a two-storey version of the first – was rejected for much the same reasons and because the extra parking space advantage gained was offset by expensive pile foundations, necessary because of the low bearing capacity of the reclaimed land. Foster's preferred – and intended option – offered a custom-designed, deep-plan building with full environmental control. Its advantages were clear. The lightweight structure would need no deep foundations as it could sit on a shallow concrete raft.

The elimination of internal courtyards for ventilation meant that a compact building form was possible, and the large, uninterrupted internal space allowed the gross building area to be reduced. Air conditioning allowed sealed glazing to eliminate traffic noise and, finally, the use of an open industrialised component system allowed selection to suit specific standards within the costs and time available. Foster's proposal was adopted and within days work began on site.

**There was some uncertainty about the exact use of the building over its expected life-span, and so maximum flexibility was required.**

What is missing from this analysis is a theme that Norman Foster still considers to be a central and radical aspect of IBM Cosham. Again, as at Reliance Controls or the Fred Olsen Amenity Centre, there is evidence of the practice looking below the pragmatic surface to produce a psychological reading of the brief.

'We were very much entrepreneurs of the concept', Foster explains. 'You must remember that for this client at that time it would have been far more usual to have made three separate buildings – an office building, an amenity building and a computer building. Of these the computer building would have been the "shrine", and the ground slab would have been customised for it. The idea that you could put all those buildings under one roof umbrella and then have this capability for moving them around beneath it has its roots in the Newport School competition and before. It is a recurring theme. The Sainsbury Centre did exactly the same thing for a very different kind of institution. The same thinking can be seen in the Renault Distribution Centre and in Reliance Controls too.'

More demanding at the time must have been the extreme speed and the degree of flexibility required by IBM. The ramifications of this are apparent in the practice's report at the time: 'The building is considered as a synthesis of systems – the integration of structure, environmental control, movement and location. These systems are organised specifically as a direct response to a brief, which is typical of a company with a high growth rate.

'It is in the nature of such a brief that requirements can only be defined broadly at the time when design is initiated and will develop during the design and construction period. The internal accommodation should be capable of adaptation, change and growth during occupation.'

Engineer Loren Butt joined the practice while IBM Cosham was under way. He recalls the speed with which the pilot building was erected. 'The way the activities overlapped on site was very interesting', he notes. 'At one end the structure was being erected whilst at the other end internal finishes were already starting – it was almost as if the building were coming from an extrusion machine.'

1. An aerial view of the IBM site. Primary road access and parking is to the north of the rectangular building. The Portsbridge intersection, to the south, is linked to the M27 motorway.

The programme was so tight (less than a year for design and build) that IBM had assumed that an 'off-the-peg' timber building would be the only answer. The budget had been set accordingly at around half the price of a traditional permanent building. Interestingly IBM had around half of its total UK accommodation in such temporary structures and the remainder in permanent buildings which tells a great deal about the constant of change. Within such constraints the only solution was an integration of essential dry systems which could be likened to a Meccano set. Ironically this has produced a 'permanent' building. Norman Foster, *Foster Associates*, 1979

The most heartening and invigorating thing about Foster's design sense is its clarity, the insistence that the poetics of a building must grow out of its legible and fully expressed structure. Foster has never been even faintly tempted by the clutter of second-hand allusion and quotation that infested so much Postmodernist building in America and elsewhere. Robert Hughes, *Time* magazine, 19 April 1999

Steel means speed. Ever since the Crystal Palace – designed and built in less than a year – steel has been synonymous with rapid construction. Time can be saved at all stages of the process. Lightweight, prefabricated sections can be transported swiftly and cheaply on site in all weathers. If the rest of the programme is planned to allow other contractors to keep pace, no other form of construction can improve on the completion dates possible with steel. *Industrial Buildings: A Client's Guide*, pamphlet produced by Foster Associates, 1977

1. Engineer Anthony Hunt presented a series of alternative structural systems ranging from heavy 'I' sections, as used at Reliance Controls, to an omnidirectional space-frame. In the event Foster chose 7.5-metre Metsec lattice beams at 2.4-metre centres (centre bottom).

2. This standard intersection of 600mm welded-steel lattice girder beams bolted to square steel columns is the key to the construction of the building. The large openings between top and bottom chords created a service area deep enough to permit the suspension of cables and ducts, while allowing the whole roof zone to serve as a return air plenum. Even the square tube stanchions serve a secondary function as cable drops for power and telephones, and as supports for outlet boxes above floor level.

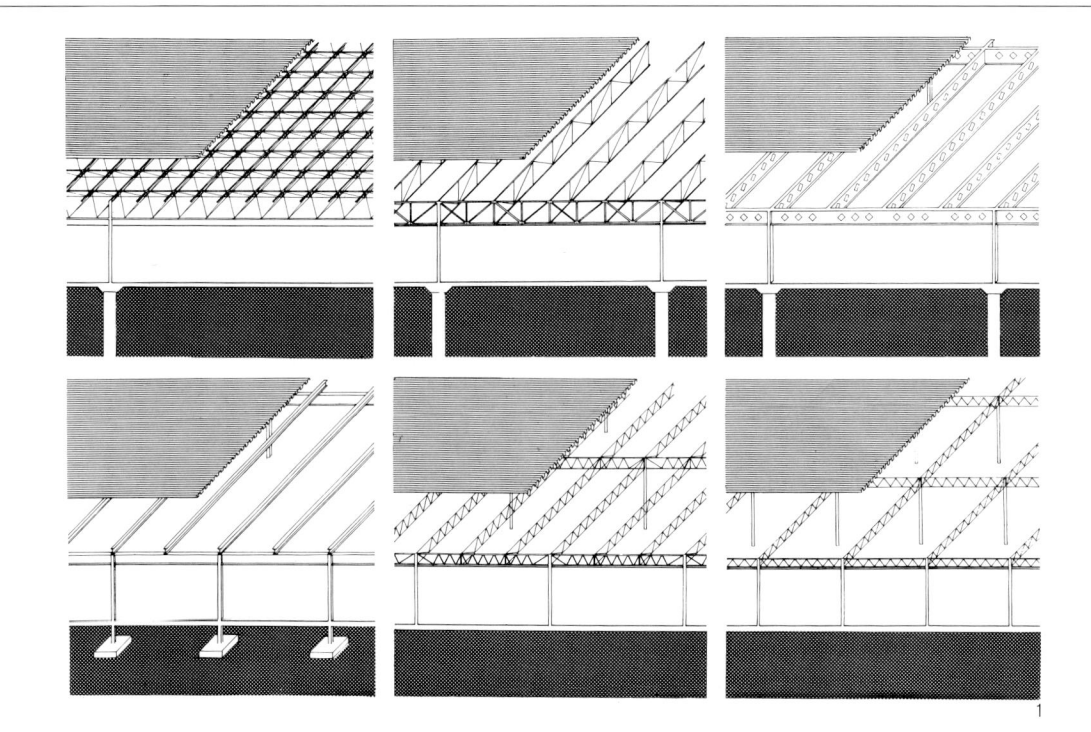

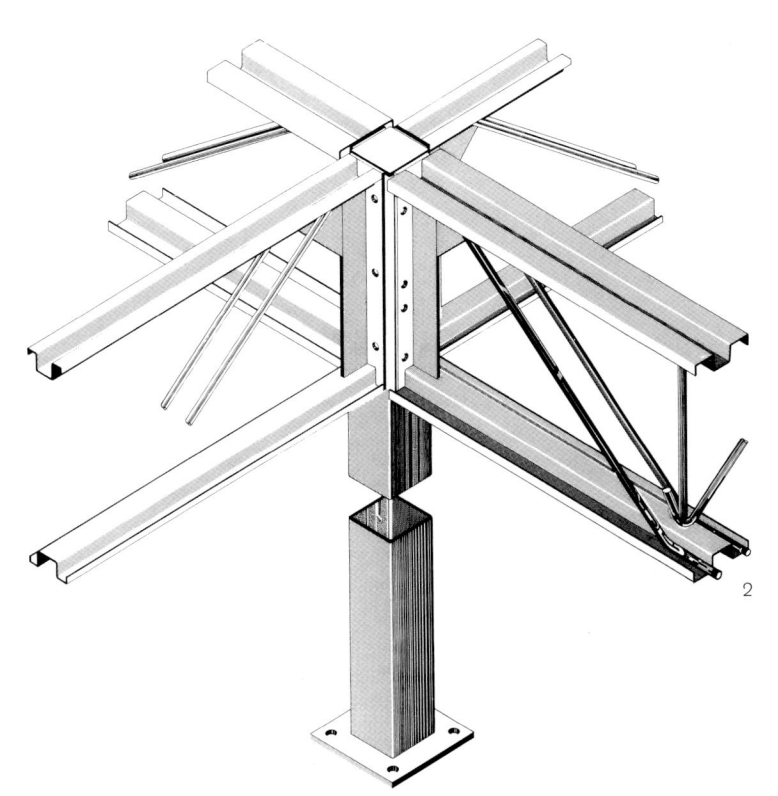

**At that time, it would have been usual for the client to have made separate buildings for offices, amenities and computers. The idea that you could put all these under one roof umbrella and have the capacity for moving them around beneath has its roots in the Newport School competition, and is a recurring theme.**
Norman Foster

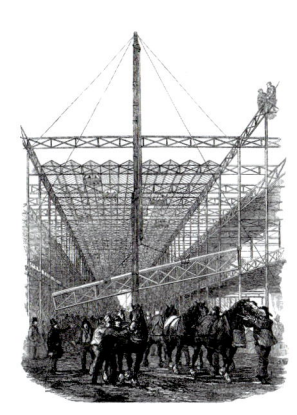

Left, far left: In an unlikely coincidence, it was discovered that IBM Cosham and Crystal Palace shared both an identical structural grid and construction period. A period drawing was found which showed that even construction techniques were similar, though, at Cosham a fork-lift truck superseded the horse.

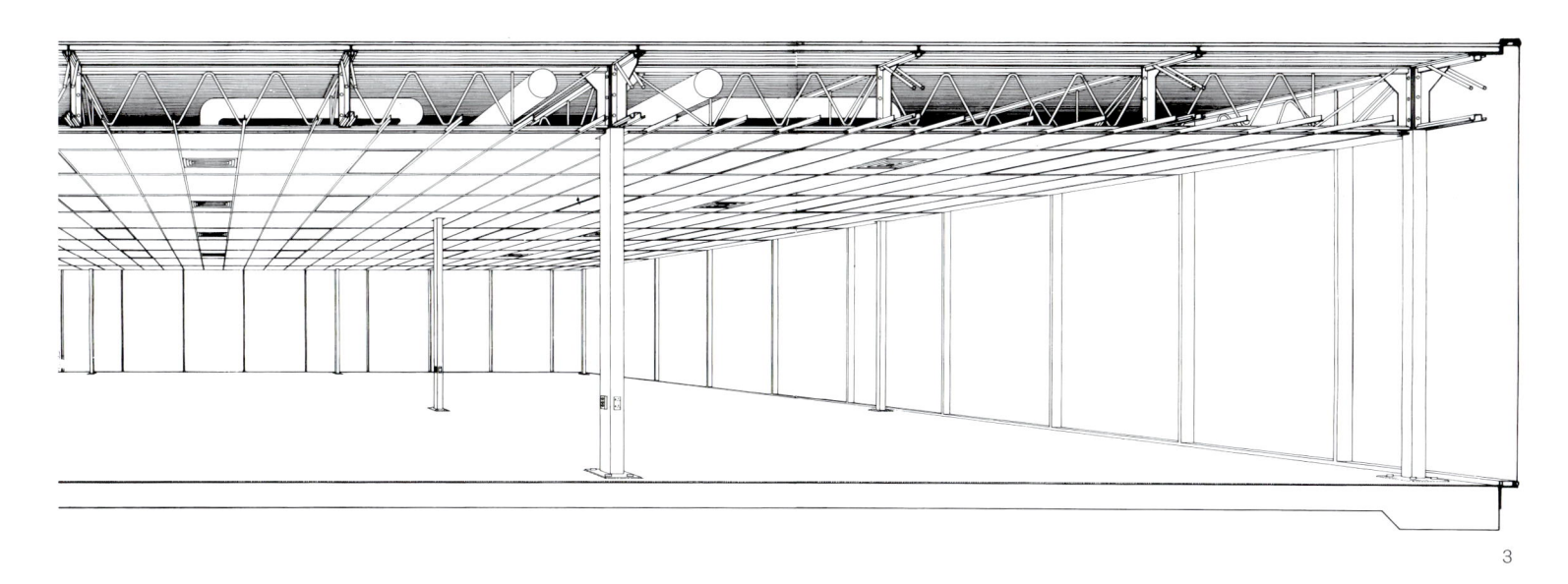

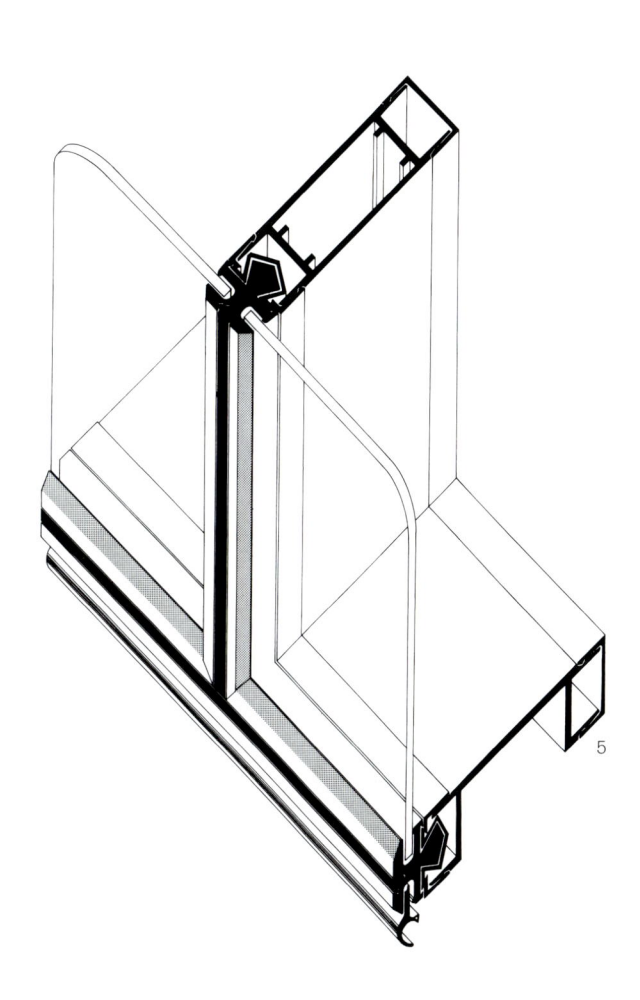

3

3. The building's structure and servicing explained in a single drawing. The corrugated steel roof decking is supported by lattice beams bolted to square stanchions, which are bolted directly to the reinforced-concrete ground slab. The roof zone and the hollow columns carry ducted services and wiring.

4. The glass envelope is formed using aluminium box section glazing frames. The vertical mullions span from slab level to the top chord of the perimeter lattice roof beams and support 4 x 2-metre bronze-tinted solar glass panels.

5. Engineered so as to be entirely behind the glazing line, each box section of the glazing frame is slotted on its outside edge to receive a thin neoprene extrusion, which is designed to hold two sheets of glass.

IBM Pilot Head Office 223

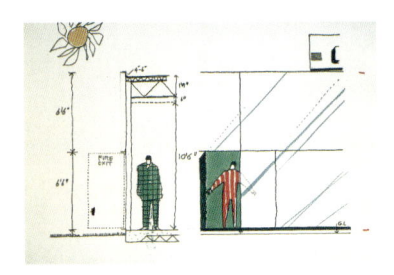

Left: An early sketch for a possible escape route proposed an outward opening fire door inserted into the cladding system as a half-height door hung between the mullions. Within a more formal frame, this system is used on the completed building.

The phrase which repeatedly comes to mind on a Norman Foster job is 'engaging simplicity'. So many of the complications and structural props that we have learnt to live with are shorn away. What could be simpler than a single power-floated slab 480 by 240 feet (bang goes piles, footings, underfloor ducts, screeds)? Or than glass panels running from floor to eaves capping, held in neoprene gaskets (bang goes transoms, fascias, coverstrips, frames, opening lights)? Or than bringing all heat, light and power down from above (bang goes perimeter ducts, wall fittings, radiators, cable runs through partitions and under carpets)? And so it goes on. Lance Wright, *The Architectural Review*, January 1972

1. An early plan of the space utilisation, much as completed but omitting the low-level partitions used throughout the open-plan office areas. Soon after the building opened, the main entrance was moved to the east, at the end of the 'street', and the computer suite extended through to the restaurant area.

1 main entrance
2 reception
3 restaurant
4 kitchen
5 lavatories
6 cellular offices
7 central 'street'
8 open-plan offices
9 computer suite

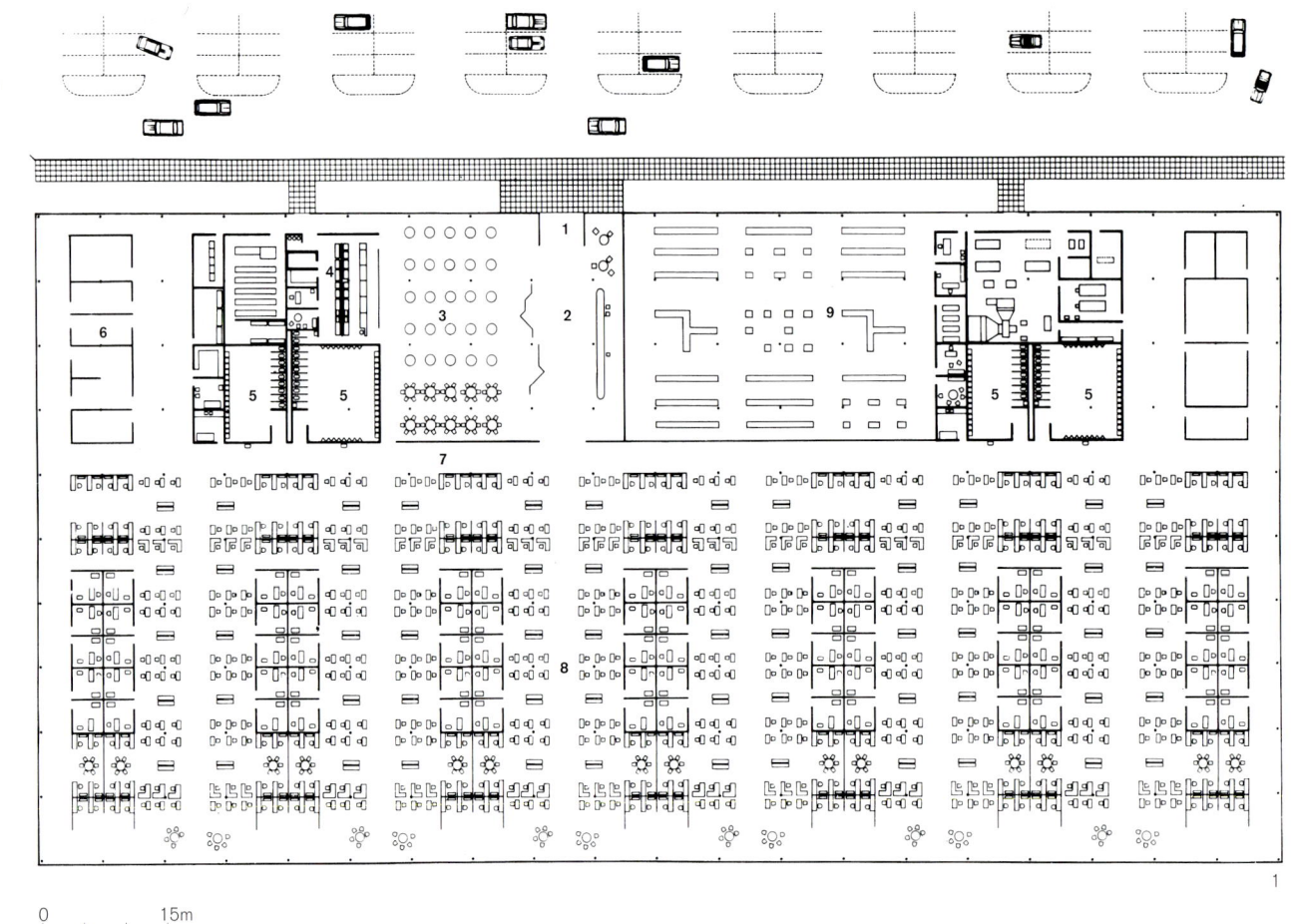

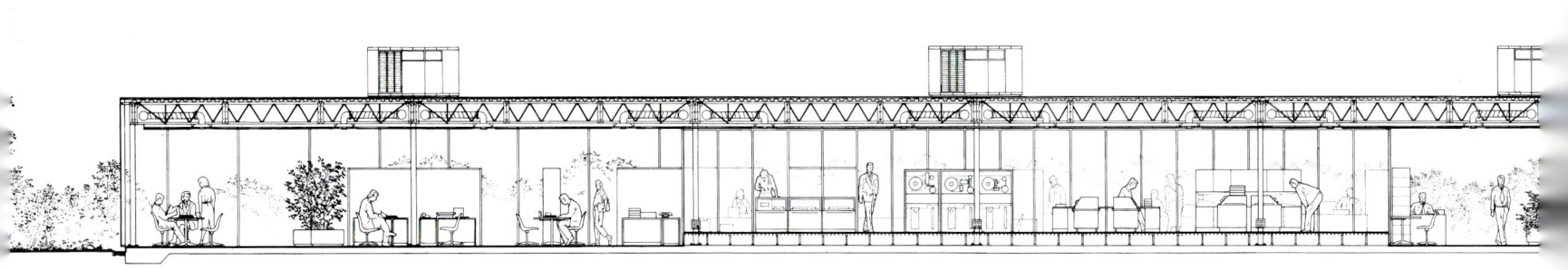

Right: A diagrammatic representation of some of the service systems of the building. Roof-mounted air-conditioning units – positioned over the columns – connect directly to high-level flow and return ducting. All services are supplied from the roof zone, telephone and electrical cabling being run down the columns to worktop height. Eye-level height partitions allow privacy for individual workstations.

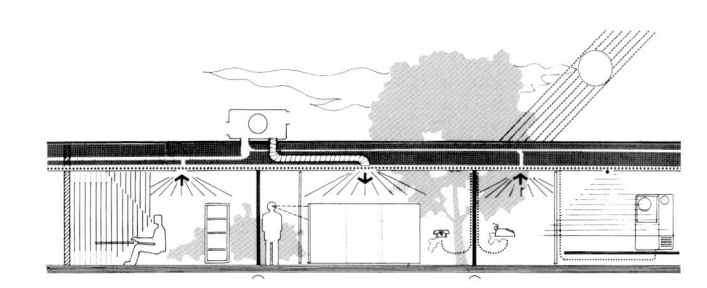

Loren Butt also points out an unlikely set of coincidences between IBM Cosham and the Crystal Palace. 'I worked out that the two construction periods were the same, the same structural bay module was used (24 feet), and that the start and finish dates were exactly 120 years apart, almost to the day!' To complete the parallel, remarkably similar images exist of the two buildings under construction. IBM Cosham introduced the notion of using the peripheral areas of the building for secondary circulation and meeting places, later to be used at Willis Faber & Dumas. No desks are located against the windows, where local solar gain might prove too uncomfortable.

Instead, the circulation zone allows the external views to be enjoyed by the office workers as well as their managers. Again one suspects that Foster rather enjoyed the social inversion here: the enclosed managerial offices, traditionally the 'prime' spaces closest to the windows, are in this instance located towards the middle of the building, away from the views.

Such manipulation indicates a desire for social integration that has proved as durable a theme as many of Foster's structural or practical philosophies. At Reliance Controls and the Olsen Amenity Centre, workers and managers were brought together under the same roof, but in carefully delineated areas.

At IBM, for the first time, Foster introduced a much closer integration, reversing social convention in the process. It was later to provide an exact model for the planning of the Hongkong Bank's new headquarters – an institution that might be considered a bastion of such convention – and was even further exploited at Willis Faber where partitioned managerial offices were eliminated.

## This was an award-winning building achieved for the sort of money normally associated with mediocrity.

Another product of Foster's integrated approach was the location of the 'machine' or computer room. Conventionally, the solution would have been to provide special facilities – a separate building, or 'shrine' to the computer. At Cosham, however, the machine room is dissolved into the rest of the building. A raised floor – with a shallow ramp access – and standard internal partitions satisfy the services and humidity control such spaces need.

Ingenious, cost-effective solutions within such an elegant office building are easy to miss, despite its size. When Cosham was completed and in use, it was acclaimed for its efficiency. At a senior management seminar, an IBM executive once introduced Foster as the architect of the only IBM building which, 'if it burned down today, would be instantly rebuilt tomorrow', such was its flexibility.

2. A composite cross-section through the building running from the car park, through the reception area and circulation mall that runs east-west across the building, to the computer room and the open-plan office areas. Semi-private workstation areas deploy low-level partitions to provide privacy for seated deskwork while allowing extended views across the building from a standing position.

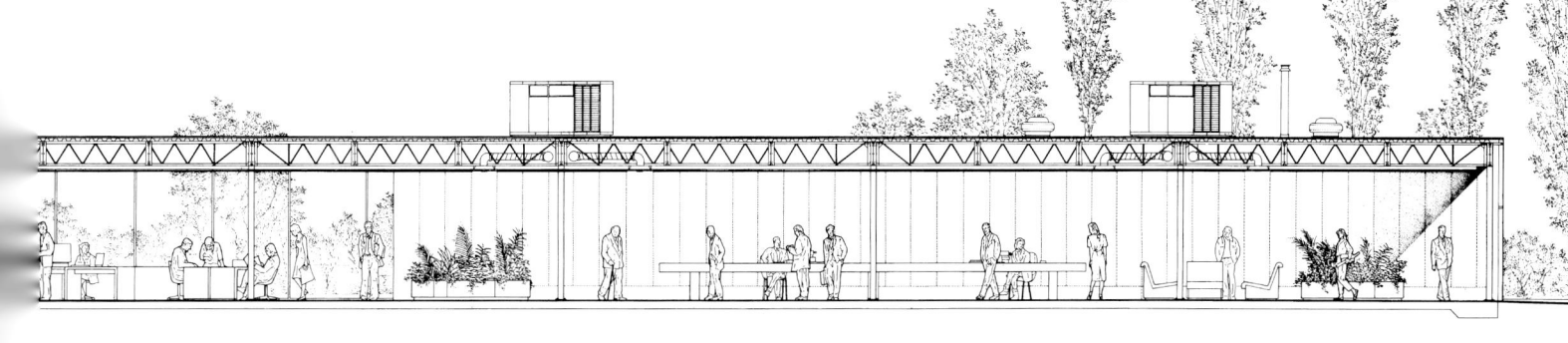

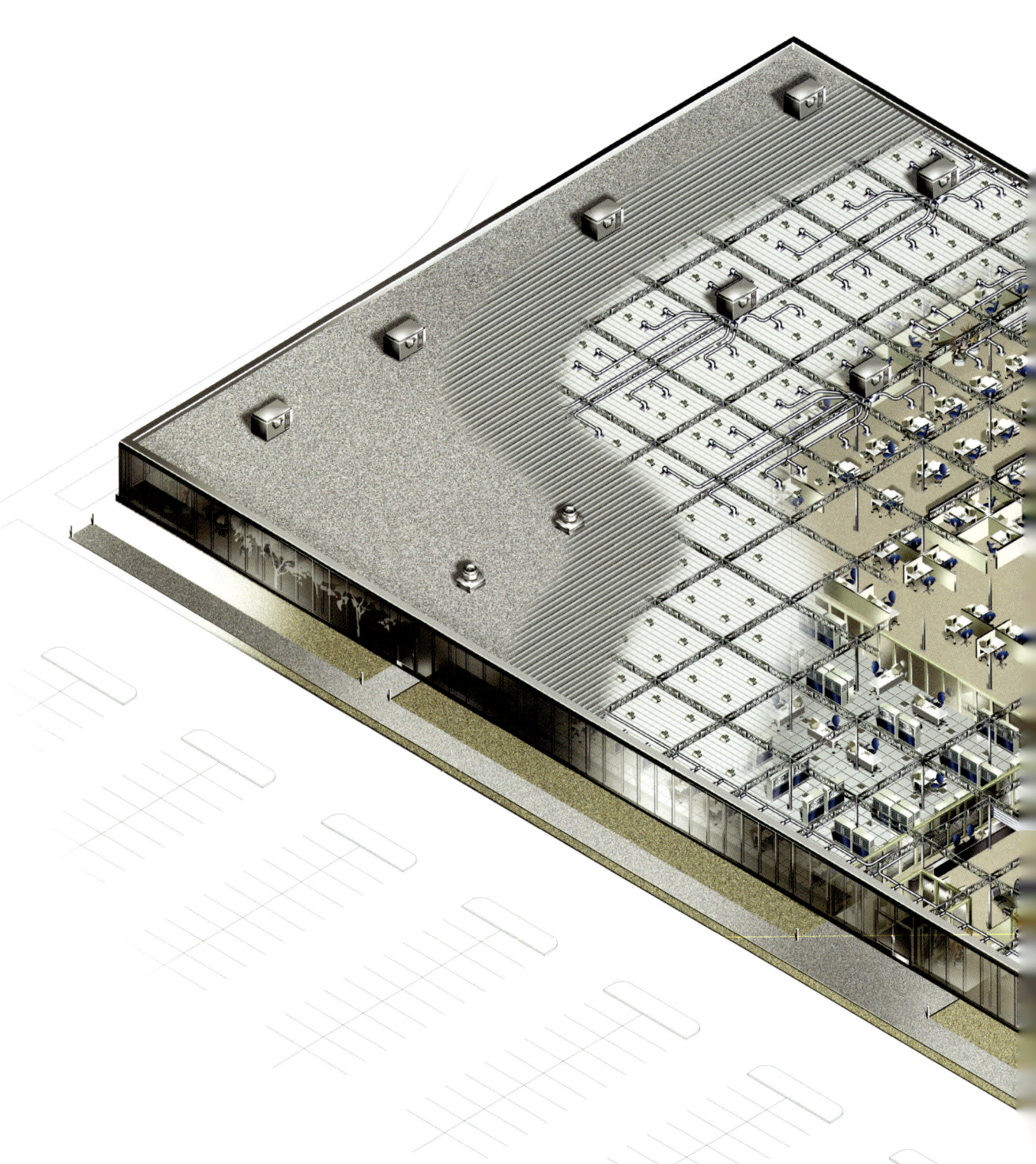

A cutaway drawing of the building as completed. Early plans offered a rich variety of space-utilisation arrangements for the offices, including open and partitioned workstations, cellular management offices, and conference facilities. The perimeter circulation zone is punctuated by conference areas, which are shielded by indoor planting. Roof-mounted air-conditioning units – positioned directly above the columns – connect to high-level flow and return ducting. All services are supplied from the roof zone, telephone and electrical cabling running down the columns to worktop height. Eye-level height partitions allow privacy for individual workstations.

IBM Pilot Head Office   227

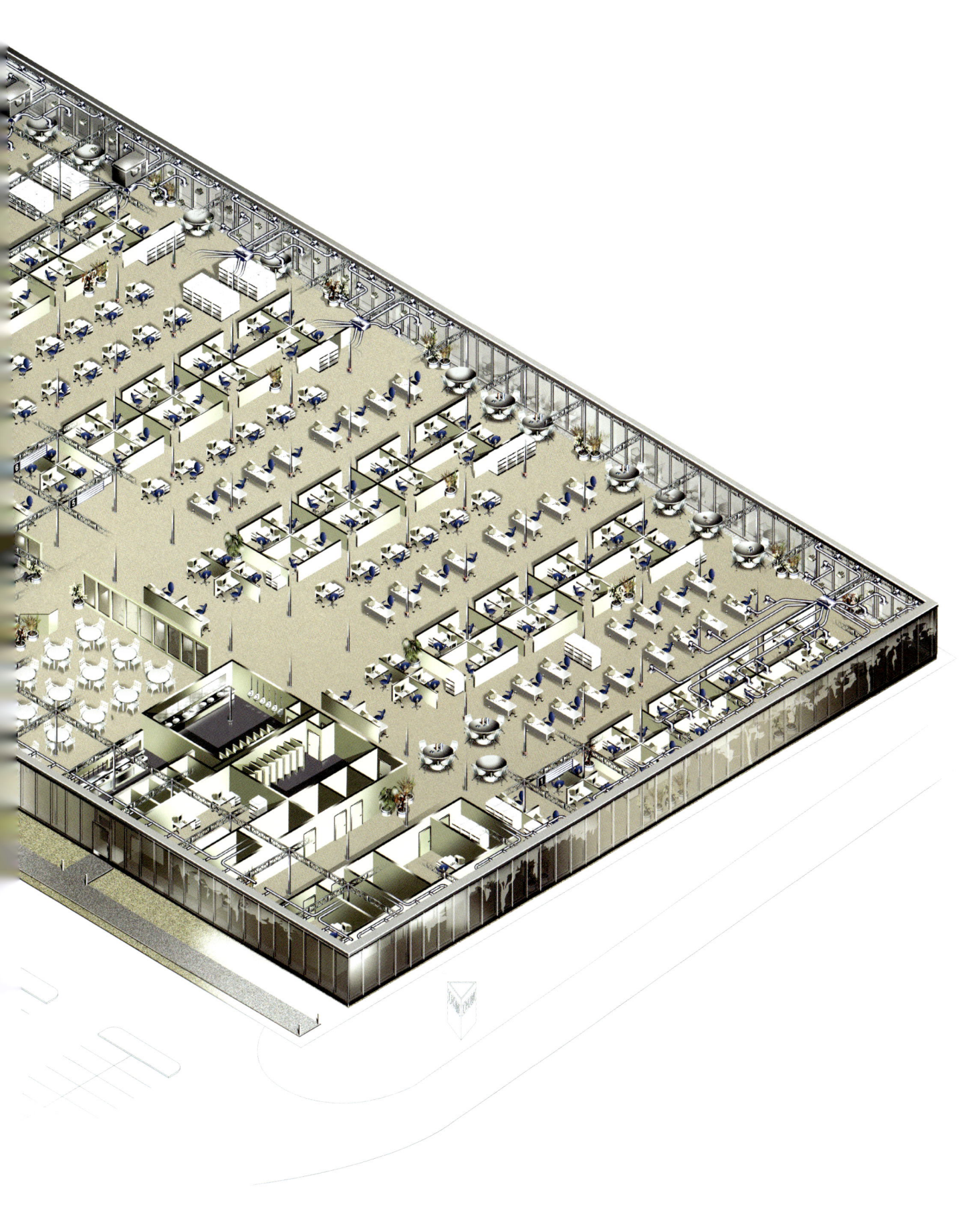

**The building initially housed computers, offices, amenities and a centre for communications, but has been in a constant state of flux. Major internal changes over the years have been aided by the ability to pop in external doors in place of the gasketed panels.** Norman Foster, in conversation with the editor, 2001

**From the economics derived from the simple envelope, the architect has found money to pay for complete air conditioning, carpet throughout, and a high standard of equipment. He has clearly fulfilled his task of giving good value for money, and the building demonstrates that architecture can be produced from a tough commercial situation by the exercise of ingenuity and imagination.** Extract from the assessors' report for the RIBA Award, 1972

**You cannot innovate on every project. That would be impossible. But I think we have a very strong interest in innovation. Take the work we did for IBM in the 1970s. The computer had never been placed inside the office; it had always been in a hallowed shrine of its own. To demystify that and bring it onto the office floor was a radical departure … Access floors, large spans, central spaces, atria – all of those were absolutely radical and revolutionary in the mid-1970s. Now they are absolutely standard practice for development.** Norman Foster in conversation with Robert Ivy, *Architectural Record*, July 1999

---

1. A variety of office layouts were created in the building. Low-level partitions throughout the general area maintained a sense of openness, while desks closer to the perimeter seemed to become part of the outside landscape. Only the computer room needed a contained environment. Using the perimeter zone for circulation proved so successful that the same solution was integrated into the planning of subsequent buildings, most notably Willis Faber & Dumas.

2. Four-way power and telephone service outlets were fixed to (and supplied via) each column. Alternative distribution systems from these were drawn for comparison, the fixed desk-height trunking (top) quickly giving way to a more flexible floor-level arrangement.

Such assessments are justifiable, and yet it is important to remember that IBM Cosham was also built very quickly and at very little cost. This was an award-winning building achieved for the sort of money normally associated with mediocrity. However, if cost limitations failed to compromise the structure's overall quality, they did at times pare some features to the bone.

'To do what we did was possible only by being quite ruthless', Foster recalls. 'You laid the ground slab as if it were a road and put a carpet straight on to it knowing that this would have repercussions on flexibility of services.' But overhead servicing proved to be the answer, with cables routed down through the columns. Access to telephone and power lines, it was originally assumed, would then be via flush-mounted points at the mid-point or base of each column. As the design progressed, however, increased demand necessitated the addition of what came to be known as 'dice-boxes'. Mounted on the columns, these could be directly accessed or, more usually, could feed cables to free-standing boxes.

The internal layout was a model of clarity. A main circulation corridor, known as the 'street', connected all the facilities: restaurant, computer room, lavatories and word-processing areas. From the 'street', smaller subsidiary 'lanes' led down between the work spaces. The extensive use of low-level partitions and occasional full-height glazing, where acoustic privacy was required, meant that it was more or less impossible to become disorientated. Interestingly, the design could eschew the notion of a grand entrance and a fixed circulation pattern aligned to it: 'For a long time the entrance was at one end of the building', says Foster. 'Then one day we popped it out and moved it down to the other end. It seemed to work better that way.'

IBM Cosham must be considered one of the most influential buildings in the Foster oeuvre, an extraordinary position given its tight budget and short time-frame. Its standing was apparent on completion. IBM's UK management was put in the embarrassing position of explaining to the American head office just why so much supposedly cheap, temporary accommodation had been commissioned in the years before Cosham, when it had clearly been proved that far better results could be obtained just as quickly and at lower cost.

More impressively, the building has stood the test of time. It was expected to last only three or four years until a permanent headquarters building by Arup Associates was completed on a site nearby. When the time came, however, the building had proved so popular that IBM decided to retain it as a research office – expanding the computer room in the process.

In 1988, seventeen years after completion, the building interior was completely refurbished by Foster, following almost exactly the design intentions laid out all those years before. Major planning changes were implemented without difficulty, and of the major elements only the flat roof has been upgraded and the air-handling units replaced. The structure and glazing have survived as good as new.

Graham Vickers

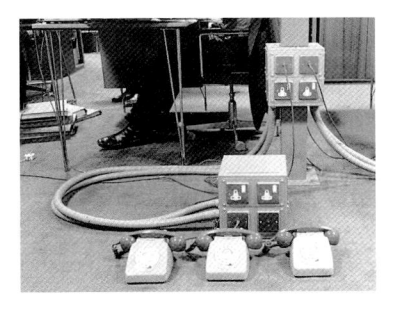

Far left: In the final design the four-way service outlets mounted near the foot of each column were augmented by free-standing satellite outlets know as 'dice boxes'. These were fixed to the floor where required and fed by tough, flexible metal conduits.

Left: Low-level partitions provide privacy for deskwork while allowing extended views across the building from a standing position.

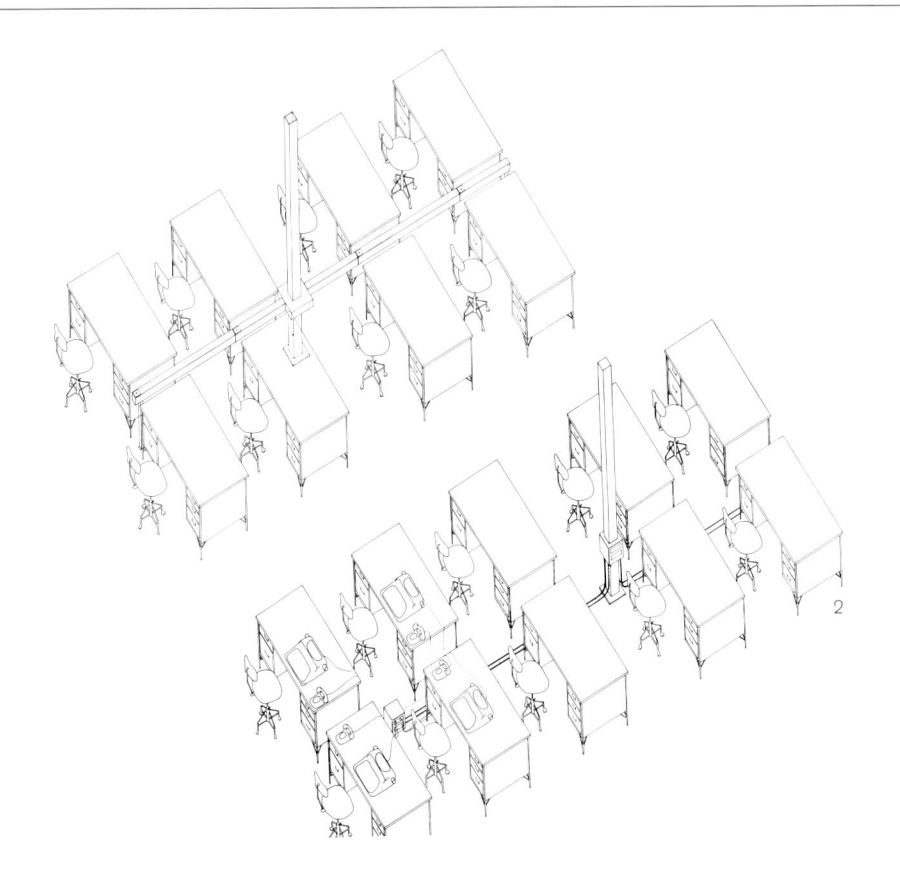

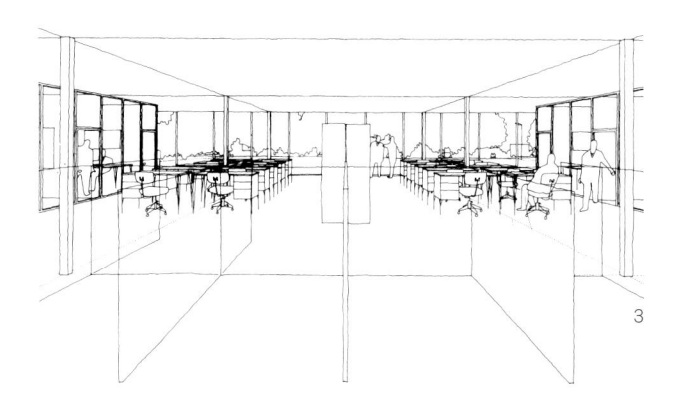

3. A conceptual view between cellular offices of one of the large open-plan office areas. Over the years of IBM's occupation, the proportion of open office space has been greatly reduced as specialists have replaced clerical workers.

4. The cafeteria was initially placed next to the reception area, but when the computer room needed to expand, it was relocated to the north-west corner of the building.

5. The interior of the computer room – originally the 'machine' room. Apart from its air conditioning requirements, it was treated much as any other part of the building, the standard ceiling treatment being made possible by the installation of a 300mm raised floor system to accept the required cabling.

IBM Pilot Head Office 229

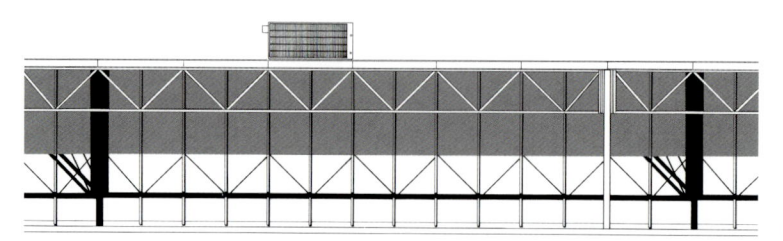

**Much of our thinking on flexible, lightweight construction systems was triggered by the Newport School competition that expanded a kit-of-parts approach to produce interior layouts that would be responsive to dynamic change within an infinite variety of plan forms. Essentially these were highly integrated and lightweight service umbrellas developed with a strong awareness of the SCSD California Schools.**
Norman Foster, *Foster Associates*, 1979.
Left: The exposed truss and deep overhanging eaves of the Newport School scheme created a circulation area around the perimeter of the building. It can be seen as a precursor of the IBM project, although at IBM this perimeter zone was enclosed behind the glass wall.

1. At the edge of the building the suspended ceiling is stopped deliberately short, exposing the steel structure above. Yellow roller-blinds were installed along those elevations where the deep penetration of sunlight might prove distracting or uncomfortable, but they are rarely used, the office staff preferring the views out through the full-height glazing.

2. An informal sitting area located in the perimeter zone and given privacy by indoor plants.

3. In certain light conditions the ephemeralisation of the building envelope can be remarkable. Under strong sunlight the rich bronze tinting of the solar-reflective glass becomes very apparent and, with their minimal neoprene fixing beads for head, foot and mullion, the individual panes seem almost to float in the landscape. There is no corner mullion, the two abutting sheets of glass being joined instead with an early form of silicone sealant. Two stainless-steel clips provide extra support.

Overleaf: Richard Einzig's celebrated photograph of IBM's long south-west facing elevation, reflecting the setting sun.

**Our earlier school system studies showed the perimeter of the building as a lattice structure, with the glass wall set back. On the IBM project we introduced the glass skin on the outside with a perimeter walkway inside the building itself.**
Norman Foster

**IBM takes [the Paxton] tradition to its logical conclusion and makes the whole building a window. Of course the roof and floor aren't glass, but one assumes Foster Associates will solve this rather minor inconsistency in time.** Charles Jencks, *A+U*, September 1975

The building is not disguised in any way. It is an honest, straightforward glass box. But when you look at it you don't see a glass box, you see the surrounding trees and things like that. This is probably carrying self-effacement to the point of lunacy, except, of course, it has given the building a very powerful image quality – of a curiously negative or back-to-front kind – which Foster was to exploit brilliantly, I think, in his Willis Faber building. Reyner Banham, 'Beyond the Yellow Bicycle', lecture at UEA, Norwich, 27 June 1985

**I remember once thinking that light in buildings must have had an importance for Norman that stretched right back to his childhood. He grew up in Manchester in the post-war years, surrounded by a crumbling heritage of neglected, dark Victorian buildings. I think that part of the reason he seized on glass as a material and pioneered such spectacular innovations in glass cladding was because of the memory of this older dark architecture and the grimness of the environment it created.** Ben Johnson, 'Art and Architecture', 1991
Right: Johnson's painting *Neoprene Gasket Supporting Curtain Wall Reflection*, a work commissioned by Foster in 1974 and based on a photograph by Richard Einzig.

**When you drive up to the IBM building it isn't there. All you find is a duplication of reality: two parking lots, two sets of trees, a symmetrical sky and yourself doubled – most of it disappearing to infinity.** Charles Jencks, *A+U*, September 1975

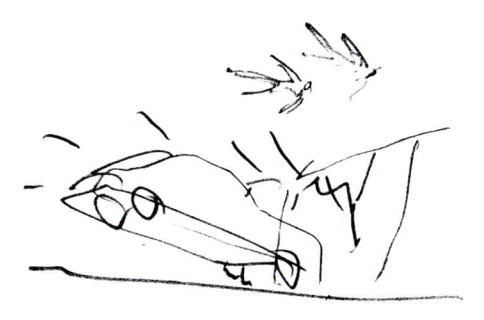

**Oh my God! ... I have to say that when we designed the building to be fully flexible this wasn't quite what I had in mind!** Norman Foster, in conversation with the editor, 2001

Right: A rather incongruous Postmodern entrance portico was added to the building after it was vacated by IBM in 1995. Now occupied by the Inland Revenue, it has been renamed Lynx House.

Left: Norman Foster's interpretation of this collision between two conflicting architectural styles.

# LL/LF/LE v Foster
Reyner Banham 1972

Foster Associates have been getting their work on the fronts of architectural magazines again – not surprisingly. Glassy, simple, it's a colour photographer's dream. In real life, much of it is in places and circumstances where the general public won't get much chance to see it. So students of the contemporary scene should be pleased that they now work in London's first store-front design studio, handily located in Fitzroy Street. Even so, it's easy to miss what's going on inside – the wall-to-wall, floor-to-ceiling glazing is flush, grey-tinted and highly reflective. With the sun at the wrong angle, the interior can only be seen if you get up on the rubber-paved podium and peer rudely through the glass at close range.

Inside you'll see a fully carpeted open-plan office à la mode, divided into work spaces by Herman Miller AO-2 'advertised in *Scientific American*' system furniture, in a colour gamut that tends to yellows and acky greens. A ditto-green wall down one side is punctuated by snub-cornered spaceship doors, giving access to kitchen, lavatories and the usual etceteras. On the other wall leans the boss's racing bike (yellow, naturally), and the staff tend to affect basic Brook-Street-temp gear, tan jeans, moustaches-of-the-month, and accents that span the globe.

It's a success scene; it's an architectural office doing its thing for fun and profit. The work style suits them, the product visibly suits the sort of client who wants to project a keen liberal image without ceasing to turn a fast buck. Typically it was said of one client: 'Every time he opens his mouth, a quarter of a million comes off the budget.' But the building made all the magazines, and still attracts architectural pilgrims.

Foster Associates' kind of architecture – lean, elegant, shiny, mechanistic – is the kind of thing that, for half a century, the Modern Movement believed itself to be about. Lightweight, standardised, advanced-technology stuff that the masters of modern design kept trying to build all through the 1920s, '30s and '40s and finally got around to in the 1950s (except Le Corbusier, who'd given up trying). It seems that the professional establishment in architecture recognises that Foster Associates have achieved at least one of the ideals of the Movement, because one of their jobs – for IBM (of course) at Portsmouth – received the 1972 RIBA Award for the southern area of England, and duly appeared on the cover of the *RIBA Journal* last July. Its appearance, in so prominent a place in that particular *RIBAJ*, involved an irony so cutting as to be satirical, and has had architects tittering everywhere.

To explain why requires a short excursion along the frontier between technology and envy. The converse of that RIBA Award is architects wondering out loud how Foster 'gets away with it?' Nothing to do with financial skulduggery, but about sheer nerve in making buildings. The walls of that IBM building consist of sheets of glass over 12 feet high, held in place by almost nothing; just aluminium glazing bars about an inch wide.

On 12 July, the good old *Architects' Journal* published Working Detail No 408 (in a series that seems to have been running since Christopher Wren was a lad) which revealed that Foster had achieved this skinny detail at the top of the wall by securing the aluminium bar to a flat capping-strip of steel along the concealed edge of the roof behind. On 19 July a baffled reader writes to *AJ*, expressing admiration for the way Foster Associates are developing 'invisible structures', but adding that, 'There seems to be a perfect vehicle for condensation … in the uninsulated mild steel roof capping. Perhaps Mr Foster would care to comment before we all start doing it.'

1

**Reyner Banham brought together a critical eye with scholarly research and a piercing wit.**
Norman Foster, introduction to the film 'Reyner Banham Loves Los Angeles', 1 May 1988
Right: Banham photographed on his Moulton bicycle in Queen Anne's Gate, home of *The Architectural Review*.

Certainly the absence of the usual clutter of gaskets, sealing strips, foamed polyurethane and general gunge at this point was impressive. Foster Associates clearly didn't see this as an inviolable trade secret. On 26 July, Loren Butt, their mechanical engineer, wrote, in a short, businesslike letter to the *AJ*, that the movement of conditioned air under this detail removed any risk of condensation; but that if they had applied anything to the under side of the steel, there might have been condensation between it and the metal, and 'the insulation has been specifically omitted in order to prevent a condensation problem occurring'.

**Foster Associates' kind of architecture – lean, elegant, shiny, mechanistic – is the kind of thing that the masters of modern design kept trying to build all through the 1920s, '30s and '40s and finally got around to in the 1950s (except Le Corbusier, who'd given up trying).**

One week later, the full import of Butt's explanation dawned on Astragal, the *AJ*'s Pendennis: 'IBM's air-conditioning plant has to be on all the time at night, and during the weekends, to prevent condensation … heat has to be thrown at the glass wall – to be radiated outwards in vast quantities – to keep the building habitable. The process can only be extremely wasteful. Foster might now turn his back on lightweights and try to design heavy buildings which have many advantages – including an inbuilt resistance to condensation.' Anybody who has tried to cook in the kitchen of a Glasgow tenement with condensation streaming down its (heavy) stone-built walls, anyone who has battled with black mould growing in the standing water on the walls of a tower block built in the once-vaunted 'heavy prefabricated concrete panel' systems, is bound to wonder how Astragal can be so morally positive about so unreliable an 'inbuilt' quality – except that you can never be morally positive in the real world without ignoring contingent factors. Who or what is Astragal that he can presume to ignore factors quite as consequential as these?

A crypto-LL/LF/LE is what he is! He, or one of his demi-independent writing limbs, must be an unavowed member of this new and officially sponsored amalgam of (mostly tame) young ecological radicals and good greying architectural liberals in waistcoats. The official backing comes from the RIBA (it's all a bit like the Festival of Light, somehow) and the unusually modish set of initials stand for Long Life/Loose Fit/Low Energy. This means that buildings ought to last rather longer than the current expectation of about 60 years; that they should not be too tightly tailored to their present functions, so that they can be adapted to other uses over time, not scrapped; and that they shouldn't consume heat, light and other kinds of energy at the wasteful rates now tolerated (not to say encouraged by present tax structures and the like).

All this high-sounding stuff was launched with due presidential pomp and circumstance in a lead editorial in the *RIBAJ*. That's right, irony-spotters, the self-same issue that belaurelled Foster's IBM building.

The PRIBA commended Long Life/Loose Fit/Low Energy to the membership as a 'study … an attempt to work towards a set of professional ideas to meet the environmental crisis'. That may be how the President sees it. Some hairier adherents to the idea seem to see it as something of a crusade, not a study, and the initials as a kind of magic formula for 'solving' the environmental crisis.

1. The entrance to Foster Associate's Fitzroy Street studio, London's 'first storefront design studio' where the practice was based from 1971 to 1981.

2, 3. Compare and contrast: the London premises of the Architectural Association – based in a Georgian terrace – at 34-36 Bedford Square (left), and the Pilot Head Office for IBM Cosham. One is traditionally constructed and conventionally heated and has been in use for more than 200 years; the other is lightweight, fully glazed and air conditioned. But, as Banham enquired, which has the better claim to the Long Life/Loose Fit/Low Energy agenda?

**Foster Associates' original brief for this building in 1970 was to provide low-budget offices of 'high architectural and environmental standards' with a life-span of up to ten years ... in spite of its deceptively simple appearance this is not a 'loose-fit' building. Its success – and it has now been refurbished to ensure a life-span of at least twenty-five years – is due to it being carefully tailored to meet very particular requirements.**
'Working Details Revisited', *The Architects' Journal*, 28 June 1989
Right: When the *AJ*'s Working Details team revisited IBM Cosham, seventeen years after the publication of Working Detail No. 408, they found a building in the very best of health and still going strong.

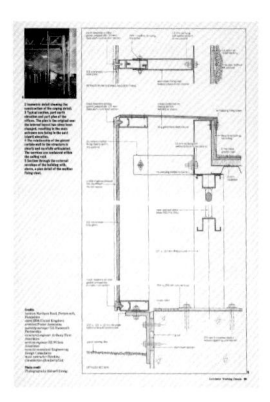

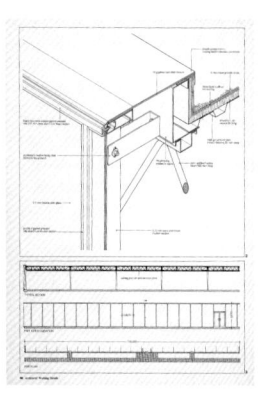

1, 2. Working Detail No. 408 from *The Architects' Journal*, 12 July 1972. This study of the Pilot Head Office for IBM Cosham – illustrated with Richard Einzig's iconic image of the reflective glass curtain wall – provided a detailed analysis of the relationship between glazing and structure and prompted critical correspondence in the magazine's letters page.

Others, understandably, see it more cynically. Disgruntled RIBA members tend to regard it as an attempt to distract attention from the internal political mess at the institute's headquarters. Trend-watchers saw it as a last desperate scramble on to Raine Dartmouth's environmental bandwagon before it rolled off to the Stockholm Conference with a nude at the prow and not a solitary architect on board.

All are agreed (me, too) that in plugging Long Life/Loose Fit/Low Energy as a quasi-political nostrum, the RIBA is attacking exactly the kind of architecture which it rewarded at IBM. That was specifically a temporary facility, tightly fitted round the client's functional needs, and consuming quite a lot of energy (chiefly because it is virtually impossible to run computers except in air-conditioned environments, and Foster Associates were capitalising on this fact to economise on structure). So either the RIBA is speaking with a forked tongue or a split personality.

Not that there's anything wrong with the RIBA doing some serious work on environment problems. If the present alleged study has diverted talent into designing a Long Life-etc campaign emblem (bearing an unintendedly ironical resemblance to the trademark of Kimberly-Clark paper, who have done so much to contribute to the world's waste-disposal crisis) it has also provided an establishment platform for serious eco-radicals like Andrew McKillop.

But in going bull-headed for the slogan concept of LL/LF/LE, the RIBA must appear to be (as the President himself was admitting, almost as soon as that issue of *RIBAJ* came out) 'wanting to pre-empt the result of our study', and making serious research almost impossible. How could a well-intended operation (as I know it to be) have managed to get up the proverbial gum tree so fast?

One reason is the well-known polarisation effect, which eliminates third (fourth ... nth) alternatives in all quasi-political debate, and is very marked in architectural polemic. We go straight from high-rise to low-rise, from permissiveness to determinism, from scientism to intuitionism, Classical to Romantic, monumental to ephemeral; you have to be for or against Le Corbusier, the New Towns, pneumatic structures, Utopia is always the opposite direction to the way we are headed. If people like Foster are building lightweight, short-life, energy-consuming, highly precise structures, and we are heading for an energy crisis, then the only salvation lies in the exact opposite of everything Foster Associates are doing.

I exaggerate, but not that much. There is another factor at work. In architecture, as in other arts of the possible, a problem is rarely perceived until the answer to it already exists. Architects, understandably, tend to work from example. When they see others doing it, they call it cribbing. When they do it themselves, it's called a fact-finding tour, or the 'study of typologies'. If the RIBA is plugging LL/LF/LE as the 'solution', the institute must have actual buildings in mind that exist.

They do. The original submission to Lady D made it easier to guess what they were, because it also mentioned heavy construction and less complicated exterior forms. And if ever there was a type of building that had tidy outlines, heavy construction, has lasted a long time, was designed to consume very little energy and is a loose fit on what goes on inside it now, it's the kind of building most of Britain's most influential architects were trained in – the Georgian terrace house! At Liverpool, Cambridge, Edinburgh, Bristol (I can't remember the full list), and above all at the Architectural Association, generations of students have been conditioned by up to seven years of daily exposure to accept Georgian as a kind of universal environmental fail-safe. The Loose Fit myth, in particular, has been bred in the bone at the AA, which is located in Bedford Square, where other similar houses contain, without strain, functions as seemingly diverse as publishing, moral welfare and various other administrative all-sorts.

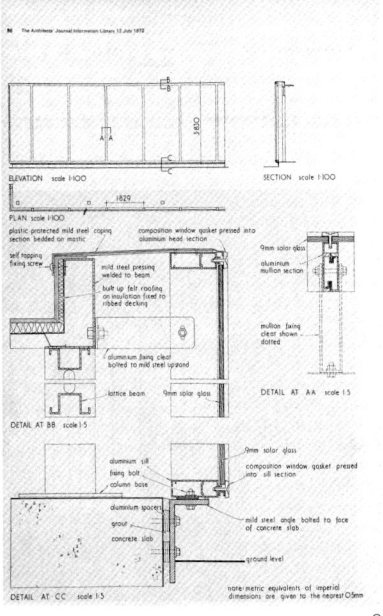

1  2

236  Norman Foster Works 1

**Foster Associates' attitude to energy from the 1960s through the 'oil crisis' and to the present time has remained consistent. Energy is a servant not a master; it is there to be used ... intelligently. That obviously implies a concern for conservation, but in the context of striving first for the highest possible standards of design and in doing so making buildings as effective as possible for the activities they house ... Energy conservation is just one of the main constraints of architectural design and can be acknowledged in positive ways; it should never be an excuse for poor design.**
Loren Butt, *Foster Associates*, 1979

**Foster Associates ... is of interest as an example of a highly tuned operation producing efficient and sometimes innovative buildings in the real world.** Editorial, *Architectural Design*, November 1972
Right: Trevor Sutton's interpretation of Foster Associates and their work on the cover of *AD*, November 1972. Shown from front to back, as if at the prow of the Olsen Amenity Centre, are: Norman Foster, Wendy Foster, Loren Butt, Mark Sutcliffe, Michael Hopkins, Birkin Haward, Frank Peacock and Michael Kuch.

---

So, radical eco-chic and greyheaded eco-told-you-so can unite on almost the only premise that all the generations of English architects hold in common. United, they have been saying some pretty alarming things already: one of the greyheads, who is now delighted to find himself 'leading the profession from the rear', told this year's RIBA conference that for years 'we've been saying you could build buildings simpler, cheaper, better … with fewer drains (spend the money on important things like decent brickwork)'. Did he really mean that architectural values are more important than health and life-support? He's a nice guy, a humane guy. It just shows how silly the debate can get.

**The fact remains that there is no habitable building at all that doesn't use energy of some sort, and quite a lot of it. In Georgian terrace houses the energy source was called Serving Wench, and the fact that she doesn't appear on the architect's plan doesn't mean she wasn't there.**

Each term of the LL/LF/LE slogan contains a potential silliness of this sort. If we are really going to be as short of land as is currently being doomsaid, then we shall need shorter-life buildings that can all be cleared away when they're not needed, to free the land. Loose fit may be fine for fundamentally similar functions like sitting at office desks in Bedford Square. But how many swimming pools, blast furnaces, cold stores, lifeboat houses and Anglican cathedrals are there in those admired purlieus? And how many cold stores, for instance, could be a loose enough fit to serve as Anglican cathedrals – though plenty of the latter might work wastefully as the former!

The biggest potential silliness concerns the relationship existing between loose fit and low energy. Holding forth about this kind of thing lately to a student at the Architectural Association, I was suddenly struck by the visible fact that adapting two Georgian front parlours into the lecture hall where we had found ourselves – a simple enough piece of loose fitting, you'd think – involved quite a startling amount of electric lights and similar gadgetry, whereupon a well-informed non-student voice from the floor volunteered the most up-to-date figures available: that the AA pays £900 a year rent and £2000 a year for electricity. Even allowing that the AA currently pays a less than economic rent, the disparity should give the LL/LF/LE campaigners a pause.

Quite a long pause, we architecture-consumers must hope. Long enough for serious reflection, and genuine study. Such research may well show that the kind of adaptability looked for in the Loose Fit concept can only be bought at an expenditure of energy that is too high to be acceptable when our energy sources are under strain; and that it would make better sense to design Tight Fit buildings that can take better advantage of the energy that's got to be used anyhow, Foster-style.

For the fact remains that there is no habitable building at all that doesn't use energy of some sort, and quite a lot of it. In Georgian terrace houses the energy source was called Serving Wench, and the fact that she doesn't appear on the architect's plan doesn't mean she wasn't there.

To go back to where we came in. You can only prevent humidity-saturated atmospheres from depositing moisture on walls by having warm enough walls, by throwing heat at them sometime, in the manner Astragal found so shocking. That is why you have put an infra-red heater or a hot towel-rail in your tiled bathroom: right? And if your bathroom has thick brick walls, you may dissipate less heat to the outside world than IBM's glass ones do. Except that you've also opened the window to let the bloody steam out, taking heat with it; and IBM has a closed and controlled air-conditioning system that knows, pretty accurately, where all its heat is going.

If the LL/LF/LE concept is ever properly studied, and the balance of trade-offs between its elements fully understood, it could be that someone is going to have to apologise to Norman Foster. They may have to, since he'll probably be PRIBA by then. If there's any RIBA left to be P of.

# Fitzroy Street Studio
London, England 1971–1981

In 1971, after two years in Bedford Street, in Covent Garden, Foster Associates moved to a new studio in Fitzroy Street, just as design work was beginning on Willis Faber & Dumas, the project that would come to cement the practice's international reputation. Foster Associates remained in this studio for ten years, until 1981, when the move was made to a much larger studio in Great Portland Street. Some of the leading members of the Foster team are captured here in Tim Street-Porter's photographs, together with consultants of the period and other regular faces in the studio. Many of those pictured have gone on to establish independent practices of their own.

Right: The Fitzroy Street studio on the cover of the September 1972 issue of *The Architectural Review*. The full-height glazing at Fitzroy Street had to be built twice. The first installation, which employed aluminium mullions, was destroyed by an IRA bomb planted in the nearby Post Office Tower. Norman Foster seized the opportunity to improve on this with a second version using Pilkington's newly developed all-glass system.

**I well remember receiving an invitation to attend an interview on that wonderful, original headed notepaper with 'Foster Associates' printed in neon green. The plastic shell chair in which I sat in the reception area of Fosters' black-windowed studio in Fitzroy Street was also green. It wasn't any normal office; it was more like a starship, with its rubber gaskets, bulkhead doors and a crew wearing carefully coordinated day-glo tank-tops.**
Graham Phillips, in conversation with Malcolm Quantrill, 1999

**Inside you'll see a fully carpeted open-plan office à la mode, divided into work spaces by Herman Miller system furniture, in a colour gamut that tends to yellows and greens. A green wall down one side is punctuated by snub-cornered spaceship doors, giving access to kitchen, lavatories and the usual etceteras. On the other wall leans the boss's racing bike (yellow, naturally).**
Reyner Banham

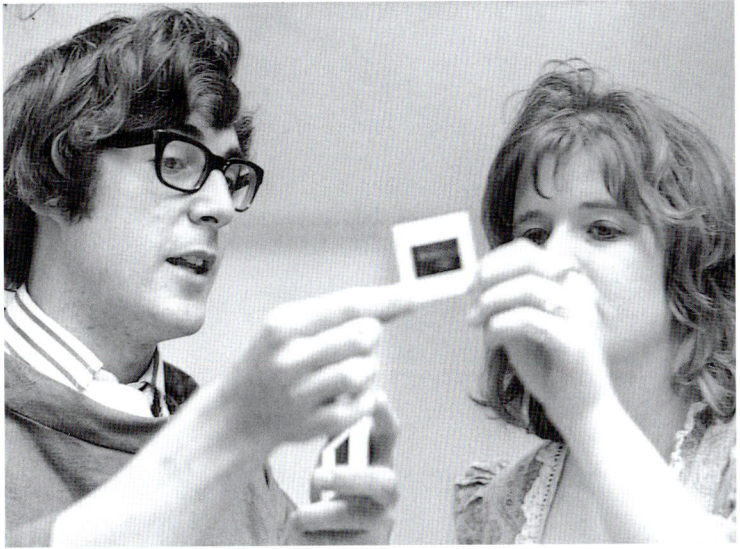

1. Consultants and members of the Foster Associates design team meet to discuss the Willis Faber & Dumas project; seated clockwise from left are David Clapp, Laurie Fogg, John Wharton, Clyde Malby, Loren Butt and Mark Sutcliffe. A Bucky Fuller dome occupies the foreground.

2-6. Clockwise from top left: Norman and Wendy Foster, Mark Sutcliffe, Jamie Troughton and David Bailey, Max Aiken and Diana Goddard, and Joanna van Heyningen.

Fitzroy Street Studio 239

With its acidulous lime-green paintwork and jet-black service core reached by submarine doors, rimmed, inevitably, in neoprene, Fitzroy Street resembled the offices of an advertising agency or even an airline, rather than an architectural practice. Alastair Best, *Design*, June 1983

1-6. Clockwise from top left: Loren Butt and Chubby Chhabra, Louis Piller, Archie Phillips, Jenny Wharton, Reg Bradley, and Max Aiken.

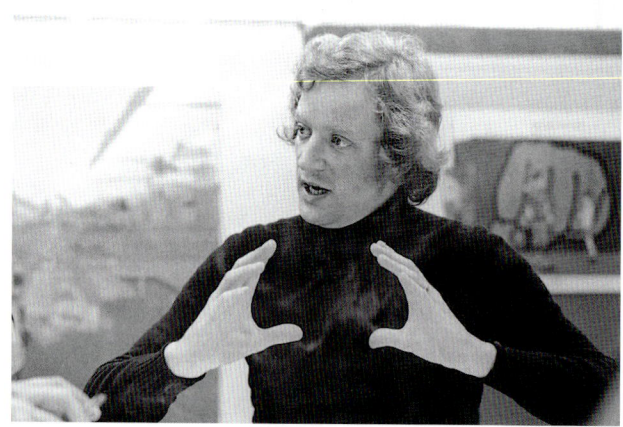

**The staff tend to affect jeans, moustaches-of-the-month, and accents that span the globe. It's an architectural office doing its thing for fun and profit. The product visibly suits the sort of client who wants to project a keen liberal image without ceasing to turn a fast buck.**
Reyner Banham

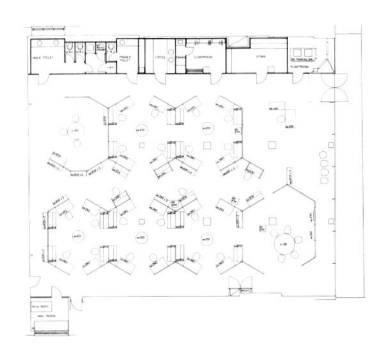

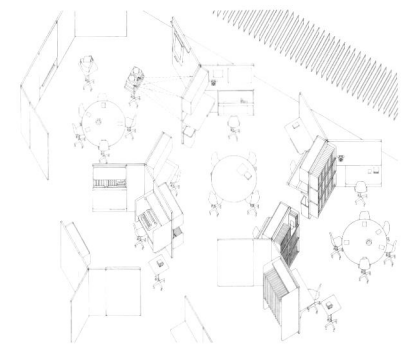

Right, far right: By enclosing all service requirements along one side wall, the plan of the Fitzroy Street studio became a rectangle inside a rectangle. This was then occupied with a molecular structure of Herman Miller furniture and fittings, augmented and arranged in ways its inventor had never imagined.

7-12. Clockwise from top left: Norman Foster, Ian Ritchie, Birkin Haward, Michael Hopkins, Giles Downes, and Frank Peacock

Fitzroy Street Studio 241

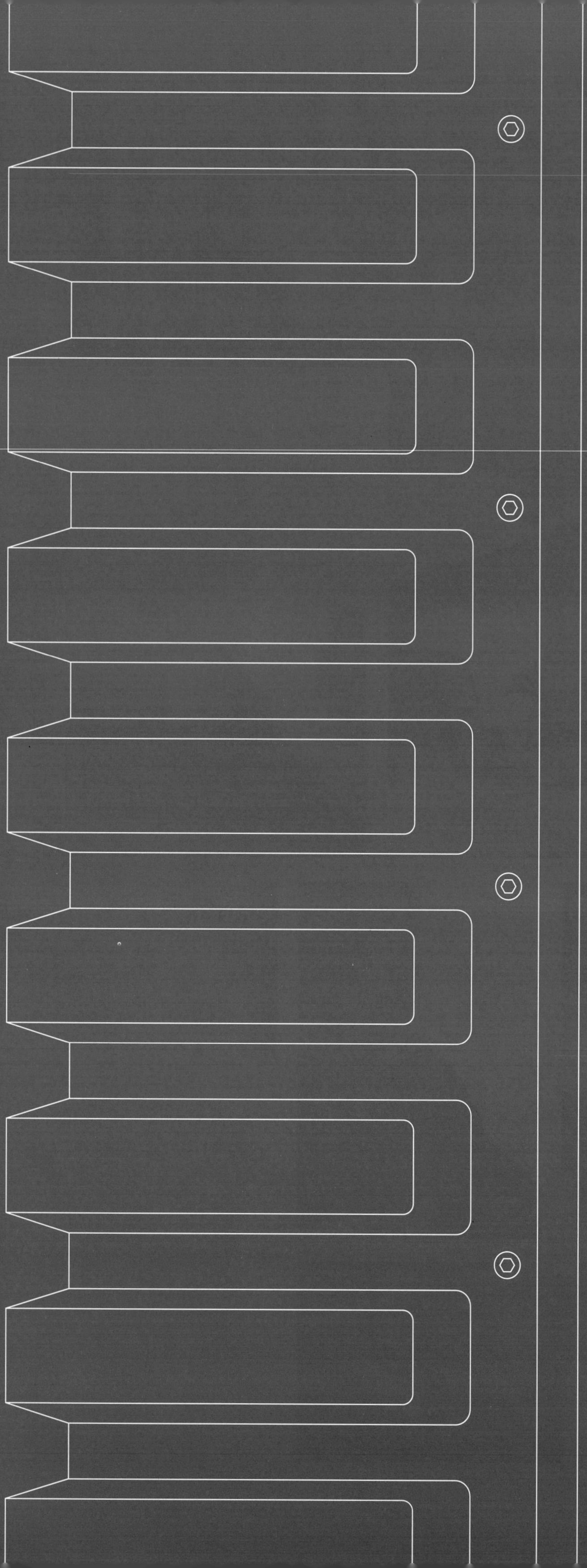

**IBM Technical Park**
Greenford, England 1975–1980

The technical park for IBM sought to give form to new patterns of social and technological change by pursuing democracy in the workplace and high environmental standards – both internally and externally. The scheme has two distinct elements, delineated at ground level by a service road but linked at high-level by a suspended pedestrian walkway and an inhabited bridge of offices, which serve both buildings. Activities with widely different spatial and environmental requirements are grouped within enclosures designed around unified component systems, which are flexible for change and growth. Double-height warehousing and loading docks, maintenance and repair centres, small parts storage, offices, staff facilities and an air-conditioned machine hall are all accommodated beneath a common 12-metre roofline, an arrangement that has its roots in our factory systems studies of five years earlier.
Norman Foster

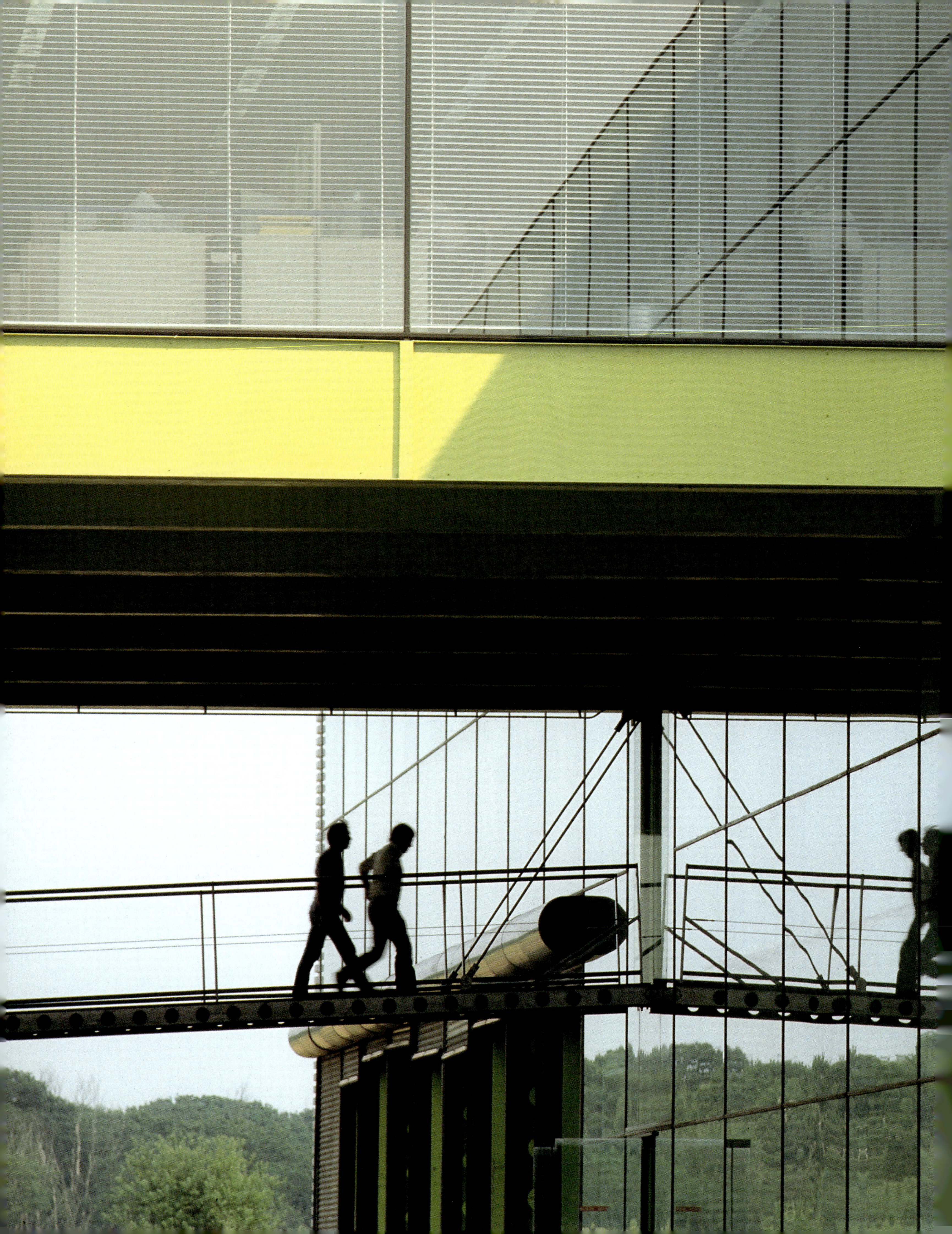

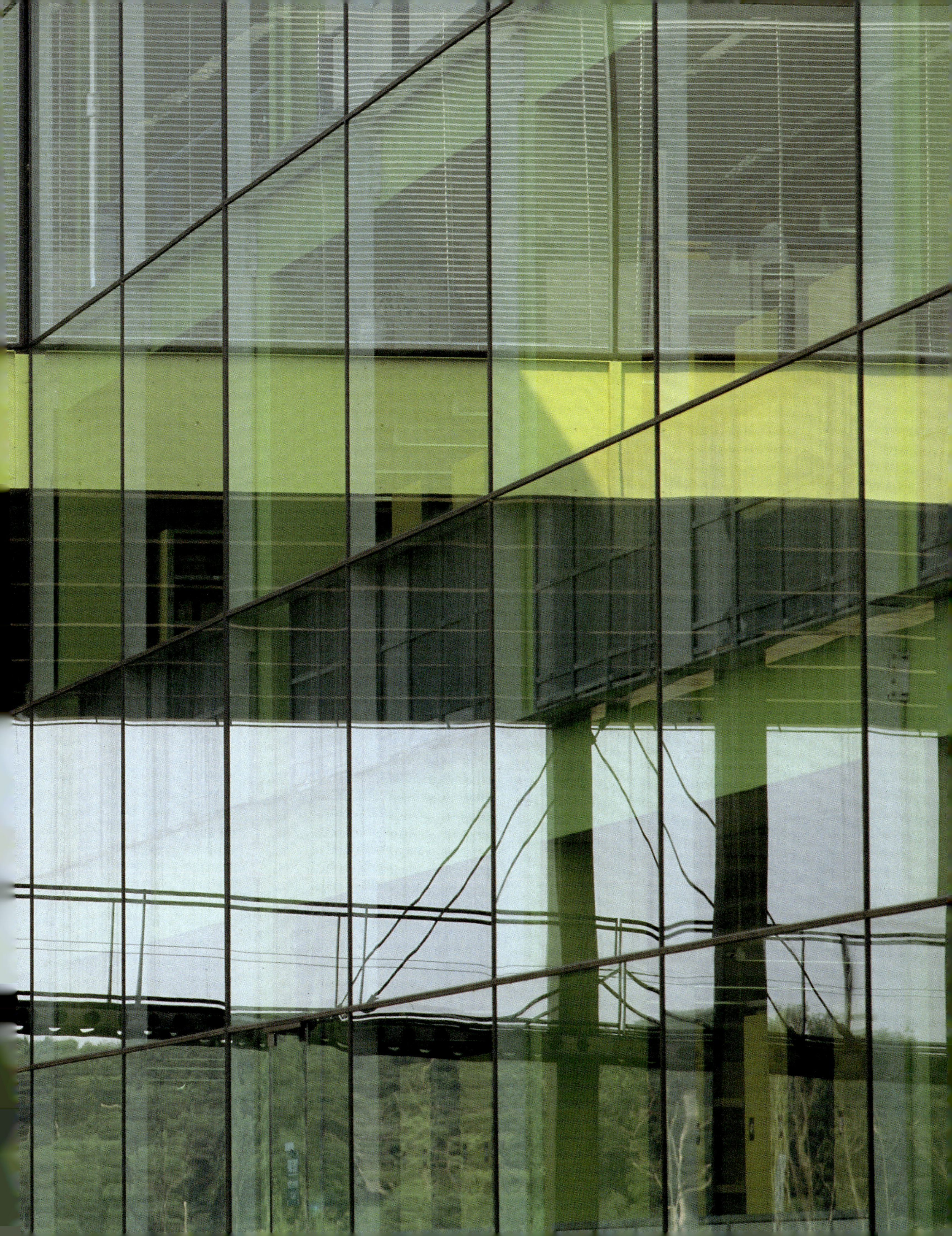

The location, 15 miles from London's West End and only four miles from Heathrow Airport, was typical of the blighted and outmoded industry of the United Kingdom. In contrast to this, the brief from IBM has been translated into a technical park which seeks to give form to new patterns of social and technological change reflected in high environmental standards, generous landscaping and the recognition of democratic influences at work. *A+U*, February 1981

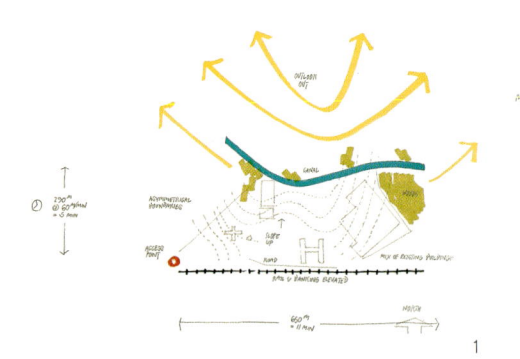

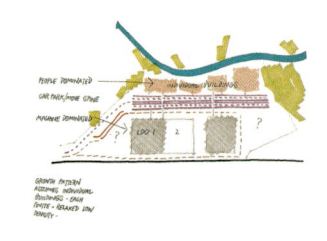

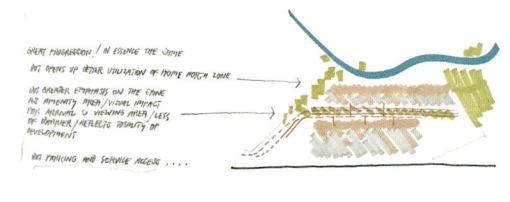

1-5. Norman Foster's site analysis was presented in a series of sketches. For reasons of access and outlook Foster favoured the north-west corner of the site for the 'people dominated' accommodation, and the lower south-western area for the 'machine dominated' distribution centre. Future expansion would be to the east. Foster had already begun to explore ways of linking the various functions beneath a constant roofline.

6, 7. The site, formerly occupied by the Rockware Glass factory, was bounded to the north by a canal, and to the south by a road and railway. Demolition made possible a new south-west access road.

In the west London Technical Park for IBM, we see a satisfying conclusion to the sequence of architectural ideas and preoccupations that inform earlier Foster buildings such as IBM Cosham, Computer Technology and other descendants of the pioneering Newport School competition. This is in no way to suggest that all these buildings were taken as opportunities to apply the practice's theories, rather it is to identify Norman Foster's developing awareness of the architectural possibilities presented by a section of British industry which was prepared to look beyond traditional architectural attitudes, and had declared itself ready to commission buildings that reflected this spirit.

The 40-acre site, 15 miles from central London, had previously been occupied by a tenant using buildings very much in the haphazard tradition so typical of British industrial estates; management boxes and worker sheds had been dotted around a site disfigured by outdoor storage dumps and other detritus. The Greenford site had hitherto enshrined the industrial attitudes that Norman Foster abhorred and which, in various ways, in previous projects, he had tried to overcome.

In 1975 Foster was asked to prepare a feasibility study for the site, which IBM had acquired in order to build a distribution centre for its range of business machines. IBM's own ambitions for the site were to create a technical park – not in the now familiar sense of the phrase, but rather in the sense of siting a well-designed industrial building in park-like surroundings. Clearly, this was an idea very much in tune with Foster's commitment to create high-quality working environments, both inside and out.

## The Greenford site had hitherto enshrined the industrial attitudes that Foster abhorred.

Early discussions focused on the provision of a single enclosure incorporating double-height and mezzanine spaces within the same building. This would have formed phase one of the site development, allowing subsequent smaller buildings to be placed to the north of it. Intended to contain a warehouse, repair shop and small parts storage, this original building was approved, and design work began.

However, 18 months down that road, a new element was abruptly added to the brief, superseding the original building in urgency. Incremental site acquisition and changing business patterns had resulted in new instructions from IBM's parent company in the United States. This, in turn, meant that there was a sudden opportunity for IBM to build an additional building on another part of the site.

**Foster Associates was asked to make a feasibility study in 1974 when IBM had already carried out its own study for a package-deal warehouse. In a re-run of IBM Cosham, they were asked to design the building for the same budget.** Christopher Woodward, *The Architectural Review*, August 1980

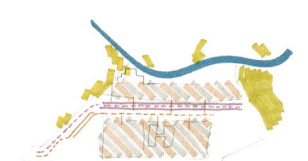

The Installation Support Centre (ISC), as it was to be known, would house the company's very large computers for demonstration purposes. Crucially, the chance to build the ISC at Greenford only existed if it could be realised within a year – otherwise IBM had decided it would be built elsewhere in Europe.

Initially, few people thought this was feasible, least of all the client, and indeed in a sense it was not possible to build such a structure from scratch in such a short time. But Foster's design work on the original United Kingdom Distribution Centre (UKDC) building had been characterised by great flexibility of planning, occupancy and provision for future changes of use. This meant, invaluably, that the design work already undertaken on the distribution centre could be usefully applied to the task of designing and constructing the ISC, even though its function was to be quite different.

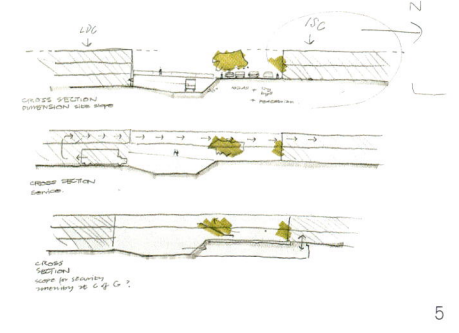

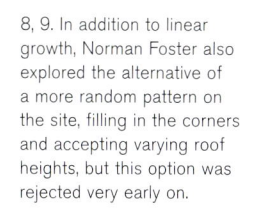

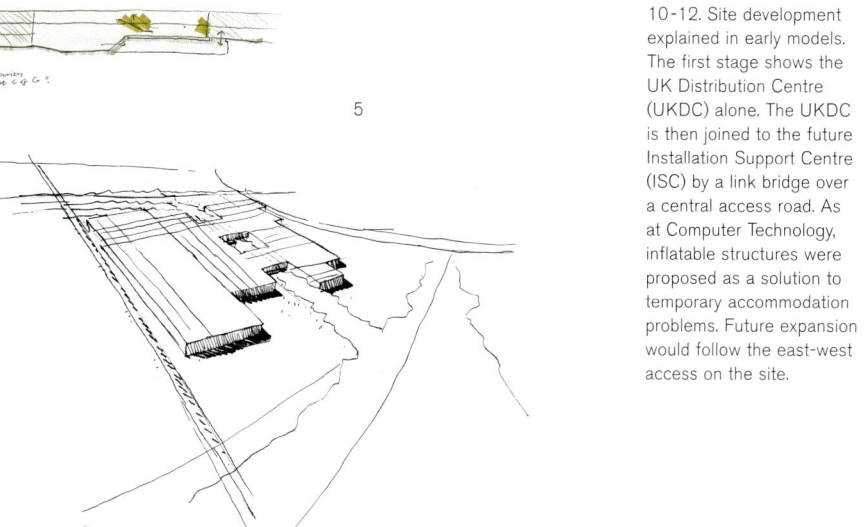

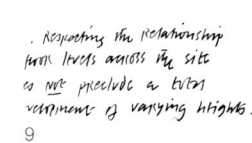

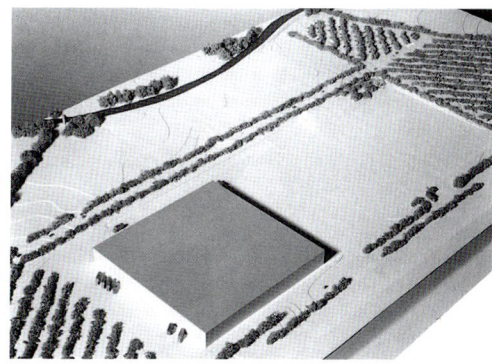

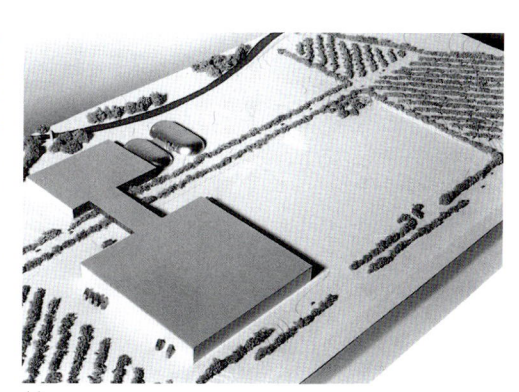

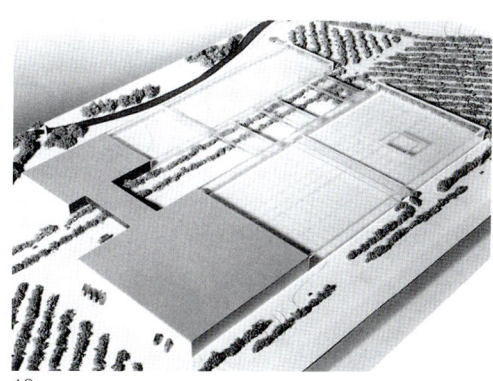

8, 9. In addition to linear growth, Norman Foster also explored the alternative of a more random pattern on the site, filling in the corners and accepting varying roof heights, but this option was rejected very early on.

10-12. Site development explained in early models. The first stage shows the UK Distribution Centre (UKDC) alone. The UKDC is then joined to the future Installation Support Centre (ISC) by a link bridge over a central access road. As at Computer Technology, inflatable structures were proposed as a solution to temporary accommodation problems. Future expansion would follow the east-west access on the site.

**The image of the industrial estate of the 1980s is no longer grim acres of corrugated iron set in wastes of tarmac. Some of Britain's best architects are now being employed to produce industrial buildings, and they are proving that decent surroundings can have a measurable effect on productivity and labour relations.** Deyan Sudjic, *Design*, August 1980

**On my first day at Foster Associates I was given the 'external works' package on the IBM Greenford project. I immediately got down to producing detailed drawings indicating all the necessary layers of tarmac, British Standard kerb dimensions, drainage falls and invert levels! At the next design review you can imagine my surprise when I was told to just forget everything I had learned at other practices. The result was that the entire three weeks of work was torn up ... and in that first encounter with Norman I began to understand why his work was so exceptional.** Graham Phillips, in conversation with Malcolm Quantrill, 1999

Left: Norman Foster's sketch exploring the experience of arrival at the building from the viewpoint of the car driver.

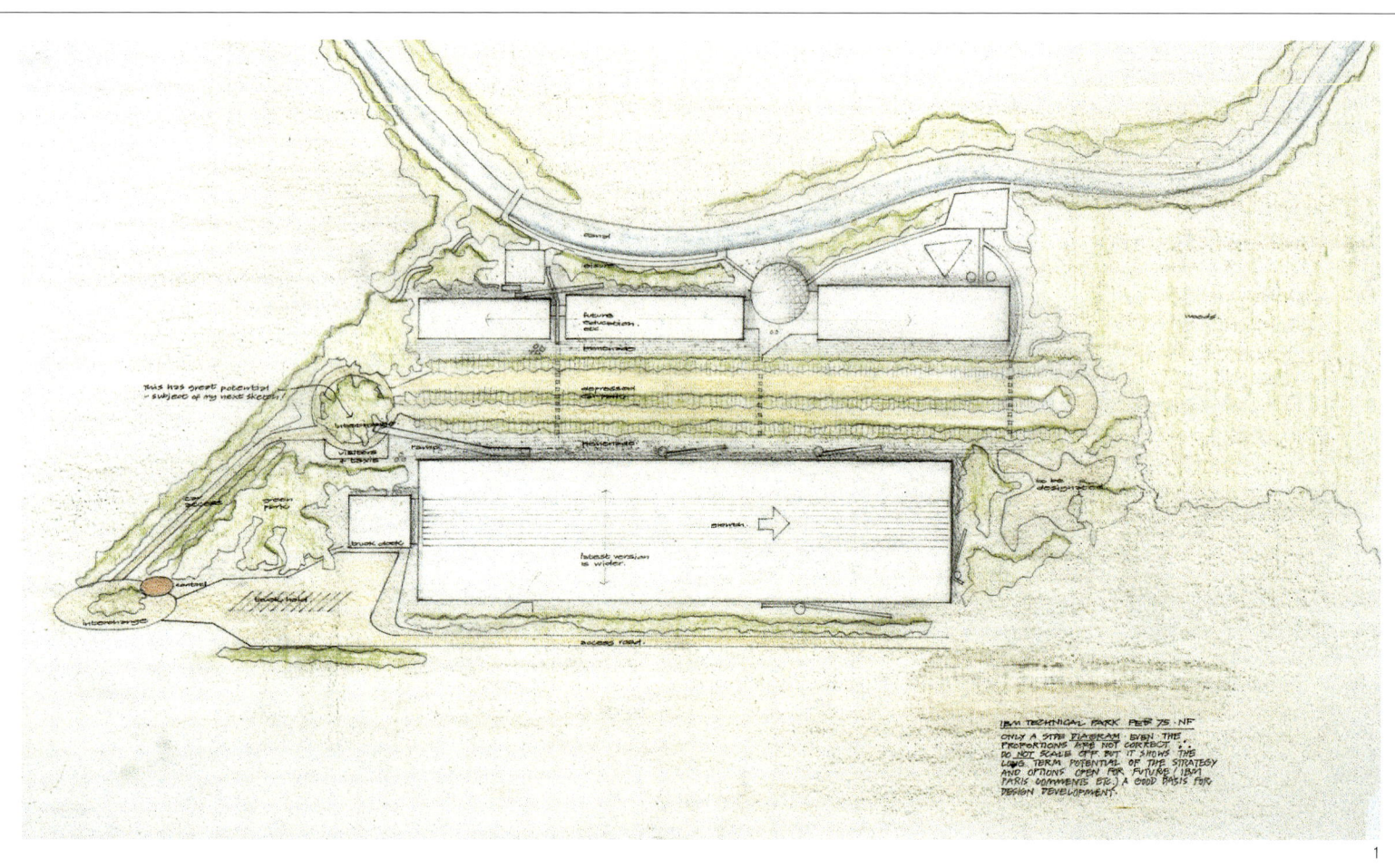

1. This early presentation sketch by Norman Foster shows the first scheme. As he points out, it is still a diagram, but all the main elements are in place. Only the broad central mall, including the car park, would be lost in the final scheme.

2. Another early sketch by Foster explores the possibility of introducing daylighting into the deep-plan UKDC by means of glazed roof-lights.

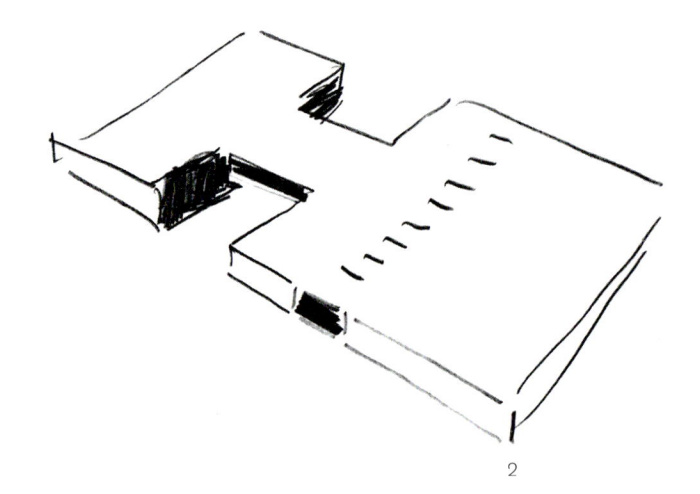

**I wanted to show that the masterplan was about zoning and movement. Because our earlier buildings had certain edge lines and certain rooflines, I thought it might have been felt that this was a dictate in our work, but I wanted to show that things could be much freer.** Norman Foster

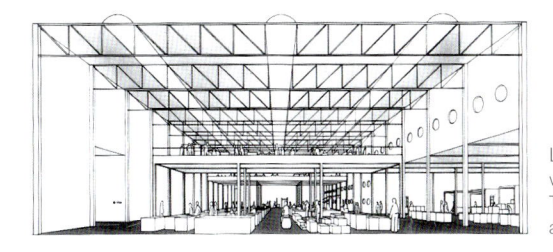

Left: A sectional perspective of the 27-metre wide workshop bay of the UKDC from the first scheme. The same space is incorporated in the final scheme with additional full-height glazing inserted into side elevations.

This crucial fact enabled the realisation of the ISC to a remarkable timetable: Foster was instructed to proceed in February 1977. The following month, the contractor was on site and preliminary works commenced. Planning permission was granted at the end of the same month. The contract period was 32 weeks and the building was handed over at the end of October in the same year. The time span for the ISC part of the complex, from inception to occupation, was less than nine months.

Early sketches and plans prefigure this flexible and dynamic process. Foster was anxious to explore a number of possibilities for the original building which, he believed, could be treated in a variety of ways. It did not need to be rectilinear; it did not need to adhere to the single roofline, which was, in fact, to become a reality. This preoccupation with fluidity of concept seems to have been prompted by worries that the practice's philosophical approach might be regarded as having only one form of expression. 'I wanted to show that the masterplan was about zoning and movement', Foster explains. 'Because our earlier buildings had certain edge lines, certain rooflines, I thought it might have been felt that this was a dictate in our work, but I wanted to show that things could be much freer.'

In fact, that freedom was eventually to be realised not in the asymmetrical perimeter shown in some of Foster's early sketches, nor was it to be expressed in differing roof levels or the introduction of atria. It was to be shown in the skilful promotion of mixed uses within the building. The resulting structure has a constant roofline with integrated services, and is designed to expand in its eastern and western zones. This parti responds well to the Greenford site, drawing in service vehicles and visitors rather than segregating them, and encourages new patterns of social and industrial change. The site, irregularly shaped and incrementally acquired, also slopes upwards towards a canal. This means that, in order to maintain an unbroken roofline, internal spaces necessarily vary in height. The treatment of that variation became one of the strong points of the design.

With the ISC and the UKDC now forming the brief, a plan was evolved to connect the two buildings by means of an upper-storey link spanning a central mall. The form they were eventually to take was recorded by the practice in its final report to IBM in these terms:

'The ISC is realised as a large-span steel structure clad with ribbed-aluminium sheeting combined with fully glazed facades. The frameless, glazed entrance and exit doors are suspended from the structure without support from the external walls. Inside, the highly serviced computer room, in the form of a machine hall, is a double-height space fully glazed to the north and designed so that an intermediate floor can be added if required.

'Both the machine hall and the office spaces use a 900mm modular partitioning system. That system is pressed into unusual service in the machine halls when used in the horizontal plane to provide a roof for single-storey cabins within the double-height space.

'The UKDC is both larger and more complex in construction than the linked ISC building. The cross-section varies structurally, reflecting the variety of activities being carried out under one roof. The 12-metre high "very narrow aisle" warehouse spaces are steel-framed with lattice beams on an 8.1 x 27-metre grid. The office area, small parts storage and workshops are a two-storey reinforced-concrete frame topped by a single-storey steel roof structure running contiguously with the ISC building.

'The servicing of the complex is integrated with the structural systems throughout. Necessarily, it too varies in response to the activity zones. At the northern end, the highly-serviced zone of the machine hall changes to the simpler comfort-cooled office area which employs a basic system of fresh air exhaust and replacement. Unit heaters provide an appropriate degree of environmental control to the large warehouse spaces.'

3. An early site model explores the possibility of random rather than linear growth on the site, and includes 'finger' units extending north to follow more closely the curve of the canal. However, the rudimentary nature of the model indicates that it is more a means of proving the concept wrong than a serious alternative to the linear scheme.

4. Birkin Haward's cutaway aerial perspective shows the final site arrangement, with the ISC and UKDC buildings linked by a bridge spanning the central access road.

**The part of Greenford immediately to the north of London Transport's Central Line is in the state that Alison Smithson once aptly described as 'English mess', and IBM's choice of the old Rockware Glass manufacturing site must have been made more for its nearness to Heathrow than for its intrinsic qualities.** Christopher Woodward, *The Architectural Review*, August 1980

**For many years IBM has represented one of architecture's most prestigious patrons. Lasdun, Foster, Arups, Hopkins ... Architects deeply appreciated the fact that here was one organisation that still believed good design was good business. Not only was it an enlightened client, but it was also perceived to be a 'sunrise' industry, with great potential for the future ... For architects the rooms full of corporate execs and machine rooms of silent boxes and whirring tapes were ideal citizens of a minimalist Miesian Utopia.** Tim Ostler, *World Architecture*, May 1993

'Throughout the complex, servicing is both centralised within the "core" areas as well as decentralised with externally-mounted locally positioned plant on the roof. The track-supported roof plant permits flexibility of movement in tandem with changes in building use and fabric.'

Useful as such summaries may be in grasping the overall nature of the building, they belie a design process that needed to be highly responsive to change. Foster's wish to introduce natural light to the middle of the building was initially frustrated by IBM, only to be reinstated when some employees expressed concern about the lack of external awareness. A roof-light and end glazing were eventually introduced to the relevant zone to ameliorate this condition.

## IBM's ambitions of siting a good industrial building in park-like surroundings was very much in tune with Foster's commitment to create high-quality working environments.

Financial restraint precluded the practice's favoured solution for cladding the building: a panel system. In this case the solution was to use what must be considered an unexceptional profile cladding. However, in an exceptionally well-judged piece of detailing, special corner pieces were devised to create the impression that the profile ran unbroken around the corners. This simple idea — which had to be expressed in two different forms, one corner piece to join profile to profile, another to butt profile to the glazing — greatly enhances the building's appearance.

Both Norman Foster and the architect in charge of the project, Graham Phillips, stress the unpredictability of the scheme. Foster points out that, 'the clarity of the diagram was always difficult to achieve. IBM bought the site in increments and they were forced to act expediently, so it was never the ideal linear sequence where you would have a known site, do a masterplan and then implement it'. This created severe practical problems as Phillips explains: 'We had to order all the steelwork and put in the foundations before we even knew what was going in the building'.

Even the low cost of the building — although naturally a source of satisfaction — had its down side. The final result was so successful and so prestigious in appearance that the parent company, distanced from the realities of the situation, used it as an example to express dissatisfaction with other IBM buildings which had taken longer to achieve, looked inferior and, more often than not, had cost more.

Despite these constraints, there is little evidence of compromise in the completed building. If the raised floor is revealed for what it is by the glazing, which extends below it, then no attempt has been made to disguise the exposed supports — instead they are painted bright yellow and celebrated for what they are.

IBM Greenford remains a remarkable achievement. The complexity of the internal activities it successfully accommodates, together with the satisfying realisation of the continuing services/structure integration theme and the quality of its detailing, belie the uncertainty of its genesis.

1. An aerial view of the IBM Greenford site, which lies alongside the Grand Union Canal in west London. Built on the site of a former glass factory, the UK Distribution Centre (UKDC) is aligned with the main road to the south and connected to the Installation Support Centre (ISC) by an inhabited bridge of offices, which spans a central vehicle access road. Separate truck and car circulation was made possible by moving the car parking to the western side of the UKDC. The undeveloped site to the east was earmarked by IBM for future linear expansion, which has not been realised.

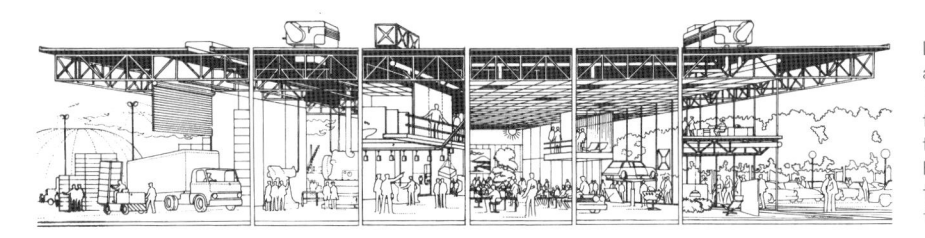

Left: Norman Foster's cutaway sectional perspective of a fully flexible factory enclosure produced in November 1969 for *The Architectural Review* shows how a space-frame roof could accommodate services, with roof-top tanks and air-conditioning units, while creating a double-height space which could be adapted to a variety of functions. These principles were to be fully explored for the first time at IBM Greenford.

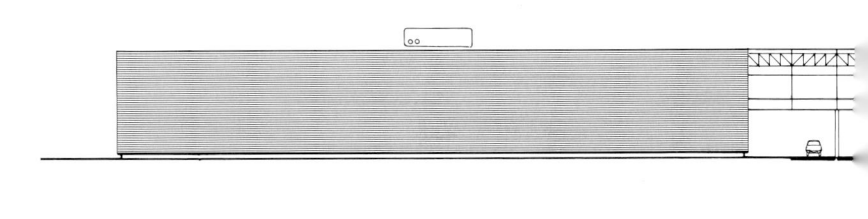

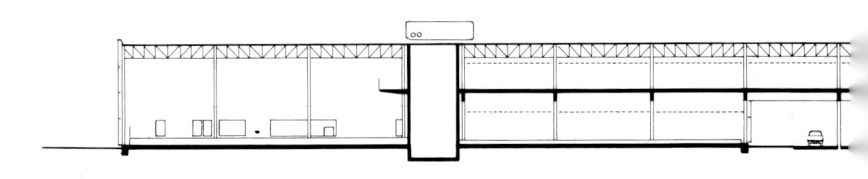

1,2. The west elevation and corresponding section show the integrity achieved by maintaining the same roofline and virtually unbroken cladding in two such clearly articulated buildings. The circulation mall between the buildings resolves the problem of changing levels on the site by separating car and truck routes, while the complex of bridges and steps ties the two parts of this large structure together.

3. A composite section through the building's different areas shows how a wide variety of facilities are accommodated beneath its constant roofline. From left: the machine hall – a showroom for IBM's mainframe computers – is double-height, with a raised floor and fully glazed north facade; the ISC houses administration areas and staff facilities; the three-level sections of the UKDC are linked by a glass-enclosed hydraulic lift around which spirals the main access stair. Beyond the main service spine are a double-height packaging and dispatch area with top-lit workshops above. A fire wall separates the warehouse areas from the rest of the building.

**Servicing is centralised within the 'core' areas as well as decentralised with externally mounted plant on the roof, which permits flexibility of movement in tandem with changes in building use and fabric.**

Norman Foster

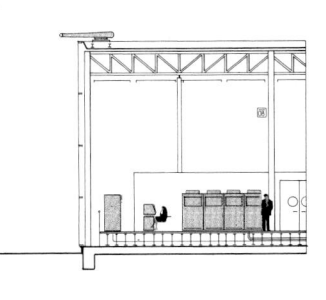

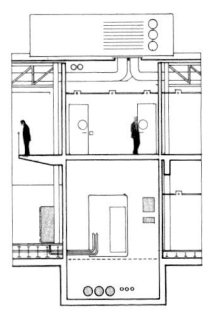

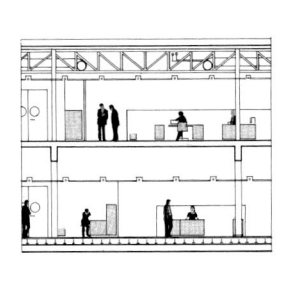

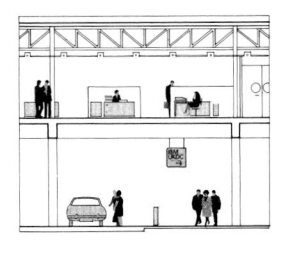

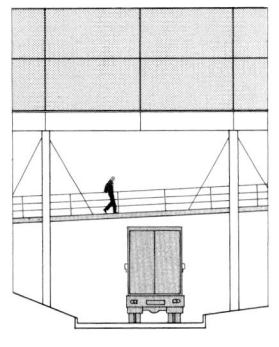

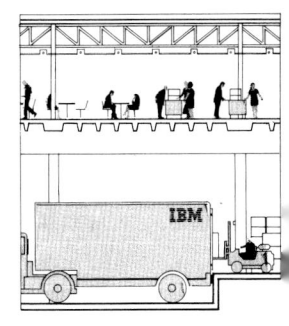

**The new building was placed to the north of the warehouse and joined to it by a bridge across the now central service road. The resulting 'elementarist' composition is, coincidentally, the same as that of the Dessau Bauhaus.**
Christopher Woodward, *The Architectural Review*, August 1980

Right: A drawing from Norman Foster's sketchbook explores how the new ISC could be integrated into the original scheme, a physical link being proposed by means of a high-level office bridge. The distance between the two service spines and the mall was determined by fire regulations.

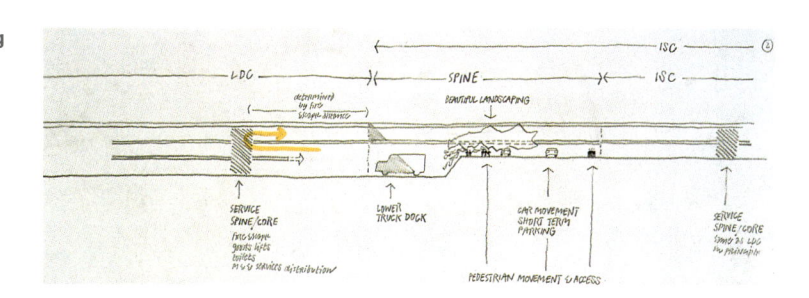

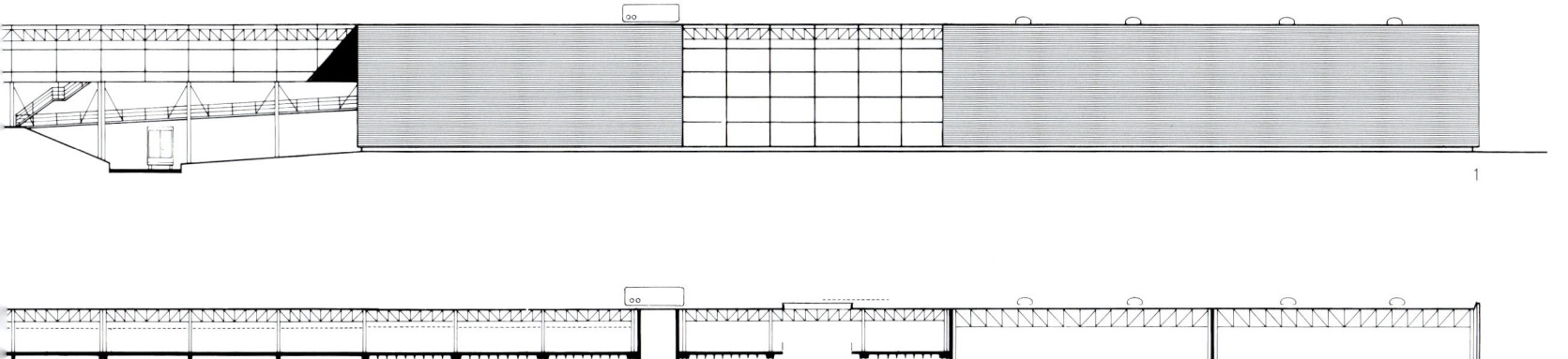

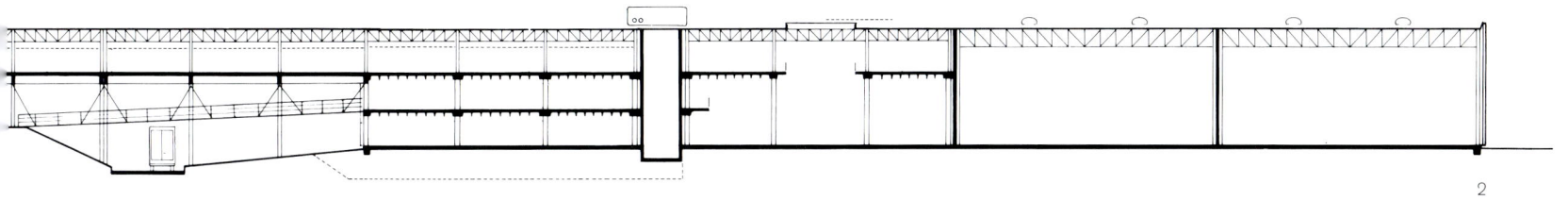

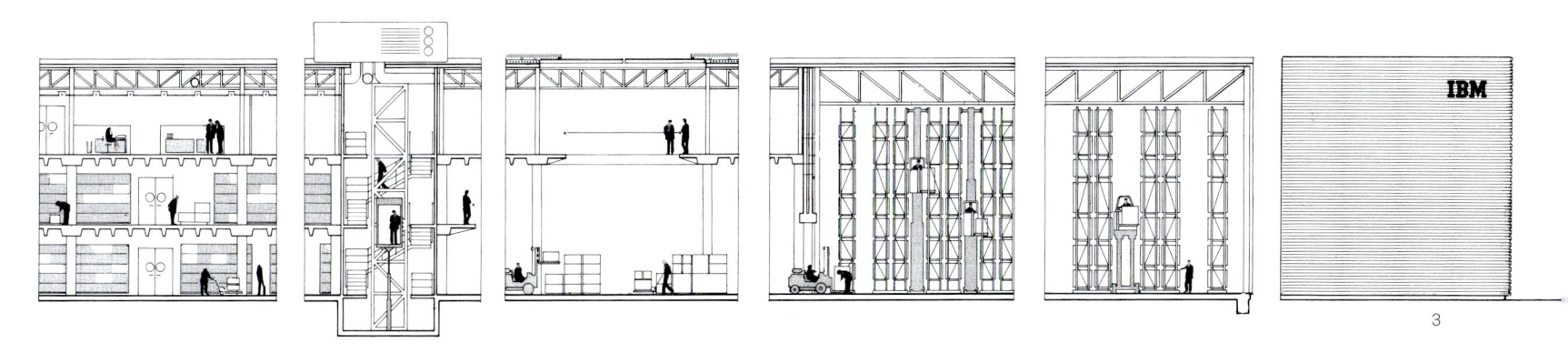

A cutaway drawing of the UK Distribution Centre (UKDC) – seen in the foreground – and the Installation Support Centre (ISC). The ISC is dominated by the double-height machine hall, designed as a showroom for IBM's mainframe computers. The ISC is linked to the three-storey UKDC by a high-level bridge, with a footbridge below. The UKDC consists of four 27-metre bays. The bay to the north of the main services spine is split east-west – one half contains a truck delivery bay, with a staff restaurant above, the other has offices above two floors of small parts storage. The bay to the south of the services spine houses a double-height packing and dispatch area with top-lit workshops above. A fire wall forms a barrier between the automated warehouse areas and the remainder of the accommodation, access ways being protected by automatic fire shutters.

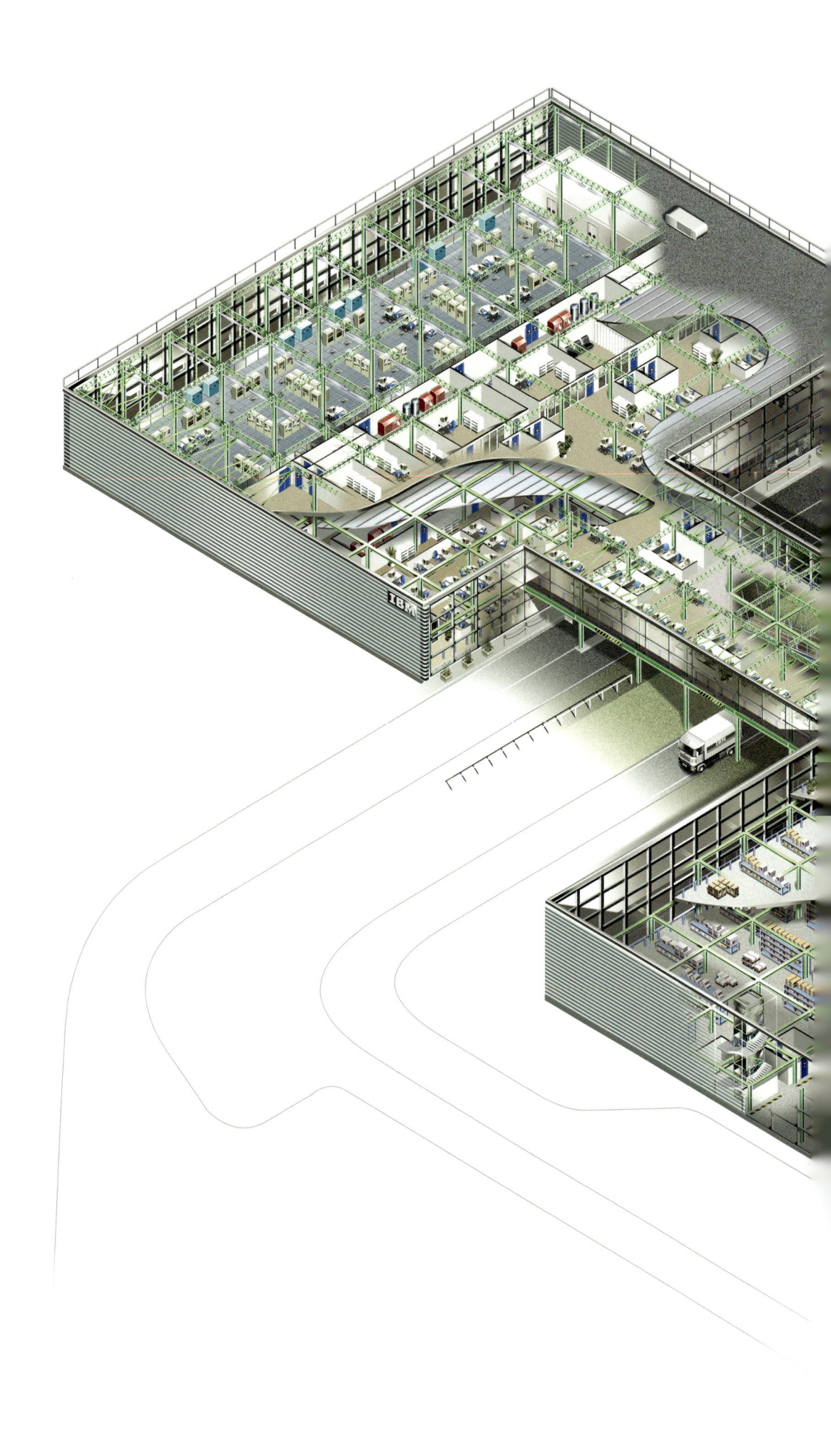

IBM Technical Park 255

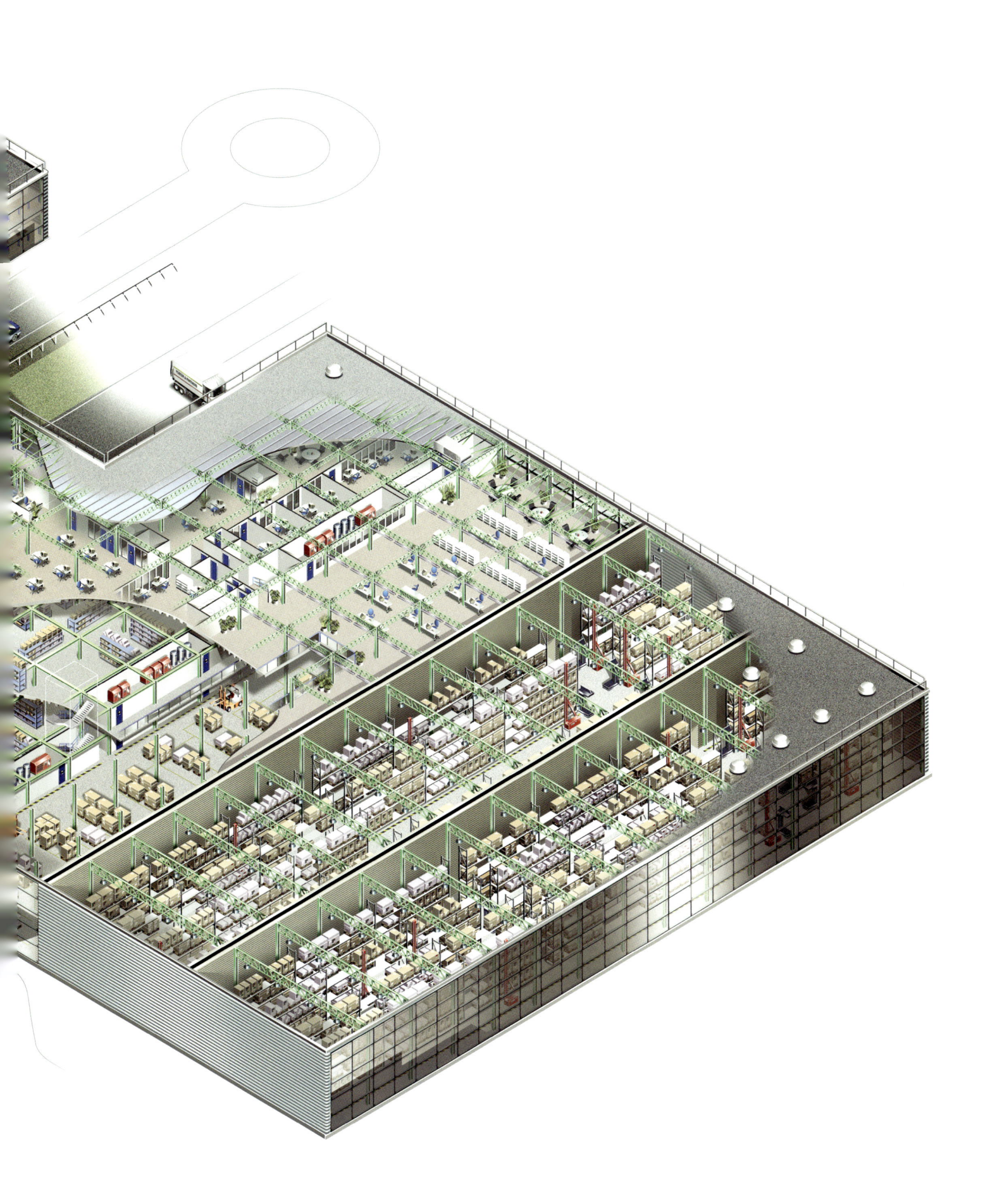

**In keeping with IBM's longstanding concern with good design, high environmental standards were envisaged, both inside the building and around it. Foster Associates' masterplan for the area set out to provide a development strategy that was both flexible and capable of coping with unforeseen growth. At the same time it represented a shift away from hierarchical working patterns toward a more democratic model.** Deyan Sudjic, *Design*, August 1980

**The interesting thing, stylistically speaking, about the buildings of the Foster office is that they have taken the aesthetic of the SOM Chicago office, but removed the magic of structure while retaining its order. The result is a lightness of appearance. This lightness, and the lack of structural ordering, take us some way outside the traditions of architecture that have been handed down to us from the past, and into the realm of industrial design where colours, lettering and finish set the mood.** John Winter, *A+U*, September 1985

**IBM came to the office and said: 'Forget the London Distribution Centre, we need to get the Installation Support Centre going. If it can be built in nine months we can build it here in London. If we can't it will have to go to the Continent. We don't think we can get it built for two years. What do you think?' We said we could build it in nine months, knowing we could put the same components together in a different way.'** Loren Butt, in conversation with Graham Vickers, 1989

1. Offices on the second floor of the UKDC, looking out over the mall with the bridge building and ISC beyond. Colours are muted, dominated by the beige of the carpet, desks and cabinets. Highlights of blue are provided by chairs, doors and handrails.

2. Staff make use of IBM's branch of the National Westminster Bank, located in the office bridge.

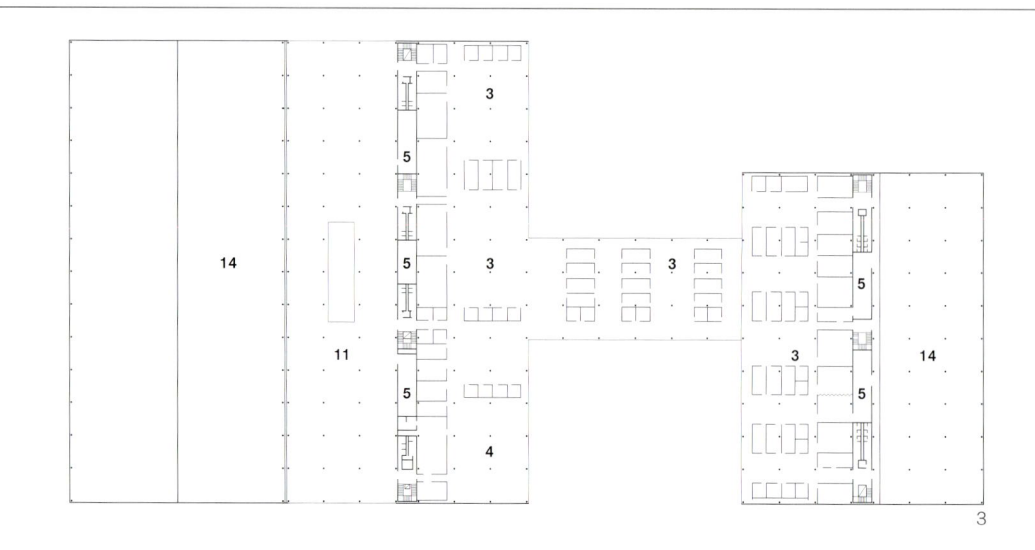

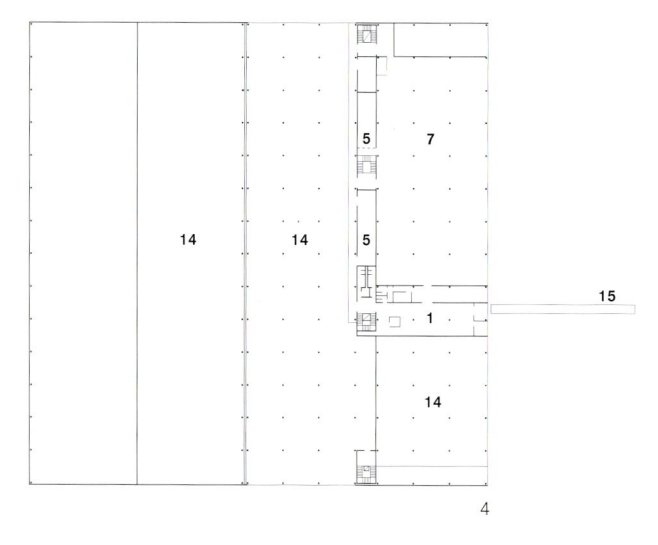

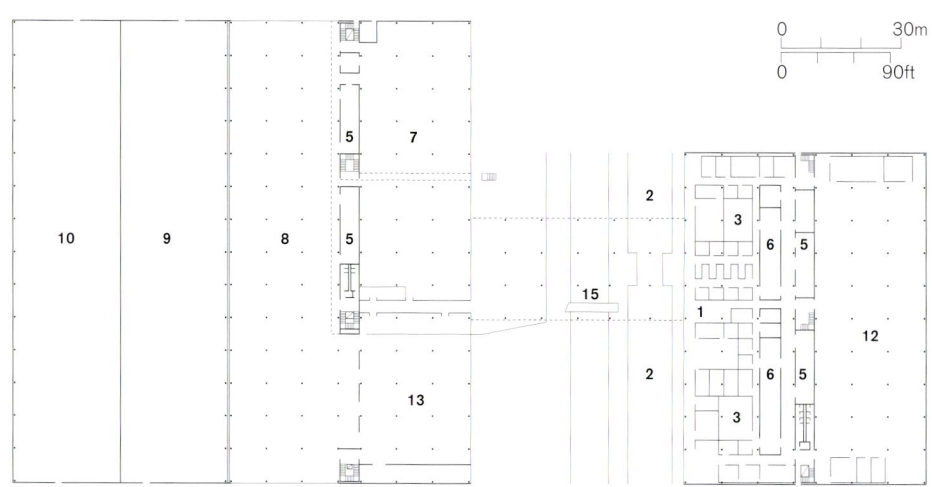

256 Norman Foster Works 1

Far left: A view of the IBM computer hall, looking down from the mezzanine-level gallery. With its full-height glazing, looking north towards the Grand Union Canal, the space follows in the Victorian industrial tradition, updated here to suit late-twentieth-century technology.
Left: The equivalent view across the Foster and Partners studio beside the Thames at Riverside Three (1986-1990). It echoes almost exactly the sense of space and openness created at IBM Greenford.

3. Second floor plan of the ISC and UKDC, which are linked at this level.

4. First floor plan of the UKDC. Access from ground level is via a footbridge across the mall from the vehicle drop-off point.

5. Ground floor plan. Both parts of the building are arranged around a constant 9 x 8.1 metre grid, the only exception being the two UKDC warehouse bays, which are 9 x 27 metres.

1 reception
2 visitors' parking
3 offices
4 restaurant
5 plant rooms
6 secondary plant
7 small parts store
8 dispatch
9 warehouse one
10 warehouse two
11 workshop
12 computer hall
13 loading dock
14 void
15 footbridge

6. The vast machine hall where IBM's computers were demonstrated.

7. The glass enclosed lift-shaft and surrounding access stair in the UKDC.

8. A detail of the roof-lights and ducting above the UKDC's workshop bay.

> **At IBM Greenford we continued the application of our democratic approach to office design; we wanted to get away from the divisions between 'posh and scruffy', 'front and back' which were being perpetuated in so many workplaces of the time.**
> Norman Foster

IBM Technical Park 257

**In a capitalist economy the conventions of industrial design consider aesthetic surface as no less important than functional and economic efficiency. By treating architecture as industrial design Norman Foster legitimises his search for aesthetic excellence along with technical competence. Architecture is reduced to a client-directed package, but the package includes architecture.** Robert Maxwell, *A+U*, September 1975

**The corners at IBM Greenford illustrate Foster's ability to identify critical points of detail, place them within a programmatic hierarchy, and budget resources accordingly.** Darl Rastorfer, *Architectural Record*, August 1985

Using a standard panelling system, IBM Greenford brought a new level of refinement to metal cladding by carefully controlling the positioning of joints and fixing bolts.

1. The special corner cladding pieces were moulded in glass-fibre – metal tooling being too expensive – and secured with hexagonal bolts. At the glazed facade the connection is made directly to the curtain-wall framing; a neoprene strip seals the gap between panel and glass.

2, 3. Norman Foster's sketches explore the design of the corner cladding elements.

4. The glass-fibre corner panels are of a slightly darker colour than their metal counterparts, but the tonal change serves to articulate the ends of the walls.

5. A detailed section through the machine hall. The principle of exposing the mechanics of the building's structure and servicing, introduced at IBM Cosham, is taken a stage further at Greenford where the edge of the computer floor is also exposed, set back from the facade and sealed with a glass balustrade. Housing secondary air-conditioning ducts and computer wiring, the floor void also acts as a return air plenum.

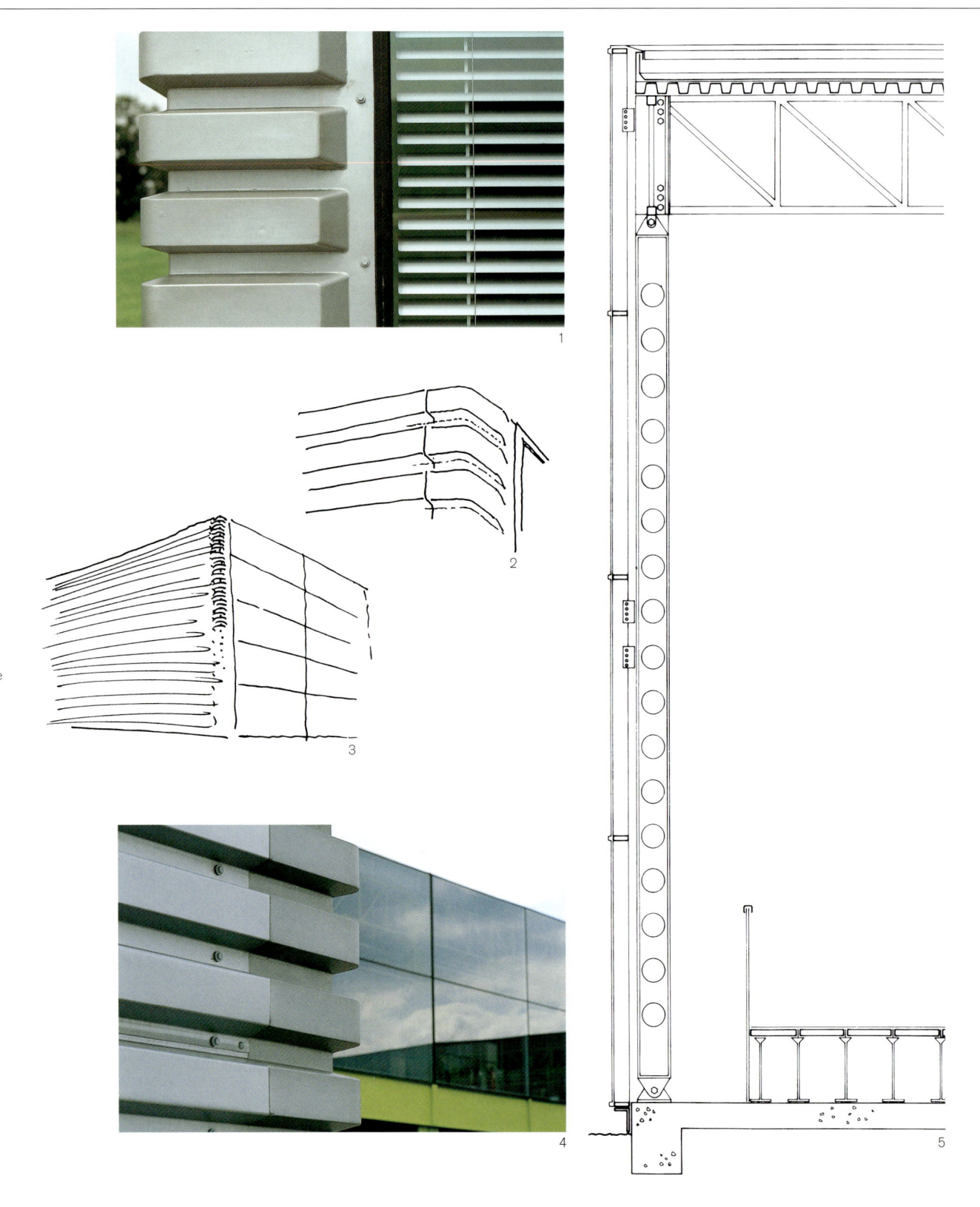

258  Norman Foster Works 1

Left: The roof zone accommodates air-movement ducting and other services, which can be reconfigured to suit changing needs, encouraging a reading of the building as a work in transition. It is interesting to compare this detail with the reflected view of the SCSD roof services zone on page 140.

**This is Foster's first 'joined-up' building. It can most plausibly be viewed as the first part of a continuum, 'always complete, never finished', although the absence of any of the rhetoric of incompleteness – blockwork temporary end walls, beam stumps left sticking out – makes this difficult.** Christopher Woodward, *The Architectural Review*, August 1980

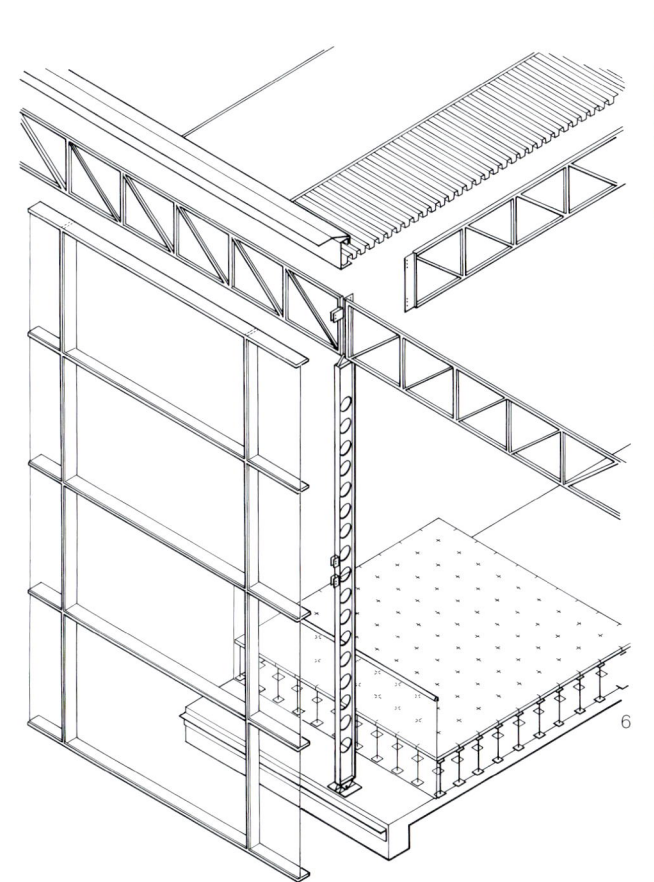

6. The framing for the machine hall glazing is wholly supported at ground level; connections to the stanchions and intermediate mullions, at mid-height and roof level, provide lateral wind-bracing only.

7. The workshop roof zone in the UKDC; the perforations of the glazing mullions are echoed in the supporting structure for the roof-lights.

8. A detail of the glazed curtain-wall of the UKDC. A development of the Pitco T-wall system used at the Olsen Amenity Centre, the aluminium framing was stretched to its limits to accept panes of glass measuring 2.4 x 4 metres.

**Financial restraint precluded the use of a panel cladding system. However, in a well-judged bit of detailing, special corner pieces were devised to create the impression that the profile cladding ran unbroken around the building's corners.**
Graham Vickers

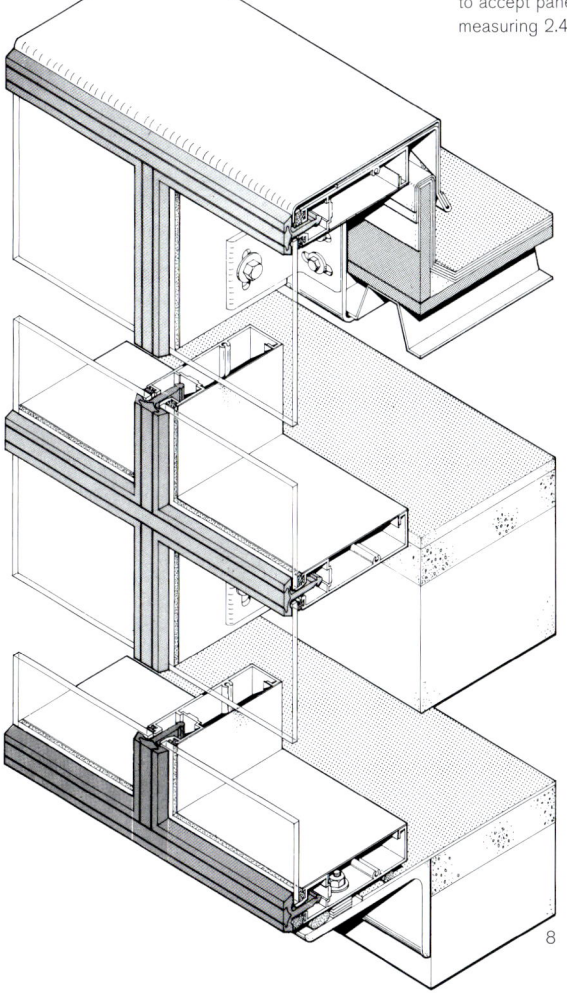

IBM Technical Park 259

IBM Greenford achieves something close to the perfect transparency – philosophical as well as literal – that lies at the heart of all great modern architecture. Even the edges of its computer floors are clear glass ... in many ways the Greenford complex represents the culmination of Norman Foster's 'universal building' period, which began with the large multi-functional space and overhead servicing at Reliance Controls. Computer Technology, the Fred Olsen buildings, IBM Cosham and IBM Greenford all stem from this vision of steel-framed multifunctional space, which in the decade stretching from 1967 to 1978 was used for numerous warehouse, office, retail and entertainment clients. All of this work comes together at IBM Greenford in a demonstration of what lucid thinking about structure, servicing and quality of life can contribute to a democratic architecture of the workplace. Martin Pawley, *Norman Foster: A Global Architecture*, 1999

It is now ten years since IBM started to think about their pilot head office at Cosham, time in which Foster Associates have been able to try out and develop their ideas ... These are, broadly, that few functions are inimical to each other, and that on the contrary much is usually to be gained from bringing them closer together; that democracy, however circumscribed, is best served by side-stepping or inverting the conventional hierarchies both of institutions and of architecture; and that buildings now must exploit those technologies which underpin our culture, with the aim of providing more for less. Christopher Woodward, *The Architectural Review*, August 1980

European Factories are designed as civilised working environments, but in Britain they all too often serve as bricks-and-mortar monuments to class divisions and poor labour relations. British industrialists have seen little point in spending more than an absolute minimum on buildings and their architects have often treated the work with equally little enthusiasm. But ... a few enlightened firms have set an example which is beginning to be taken more widely. Deyan Sudjic, *Design*, August 1980

Norman's initial mention of a country park 'style' developed into his vision of an entirely flush, hard and soft landscaping scheme, which at one point included green tarmacadam! And whenever anyone challenged this vision with such practical problems as those of cars driving on the pavement, or lack of definition under snow cover, he simply generated such amazing suggestions as rows of bollards, or reflecting fluorescent pink cat's eyes to delineate hard surface areas. Graham Phillips, in conversation with Malcolm Quantrill, 1999

1. The office bridge seen from the east; suspended beneath it is the blue-painted ramp that slopes up to the UKDC. The glass cladding floats in front of the roof structure to provide the thinnest possible eaves detail. As in IBM Cosham, the line of the false ceiling within is barely perceptible.

2. The pedestrian ramp leading from the visitor drop-off point in the mall to the mezzanine level of the distribution centre. The steel staircase leads directly up into the offices inside the bridge building. The blue-painted handrails continue inside both main buildings as safety barriers in front of the full-height glazing.

3. The vivid green-painted structure of the bridge building dominates an otherwise subdued facade. The landscaping of the mall and the central pedestrian route accentuates the change in level from the lower truck route to the upper access road.

**The final result was so successful that IBM used it as an example to express dissatisfaction with other buildings which had taken longer to achieve, looked inferior, and had cost more.** Graham Vickers

In 1985 IBM commissioned a revised masterplan and a new administrative building on the site. The project resulted from a major restructuring of IBM's European operations. However, even as design work proceeded, these internal changes continued, leading eventually to the project being abandoned.

1. The new buildings stretch eastwards from the UKDC and ISC on either side of an extended central mall. Small extensions also appear to the west maximising use of an expanded site.

2, 3. The south elevation as drawn and modelled. North-south service spines articulate the facade. Vertical service risers with roof-top plant alternate with glass-fronted stair and lift cores.

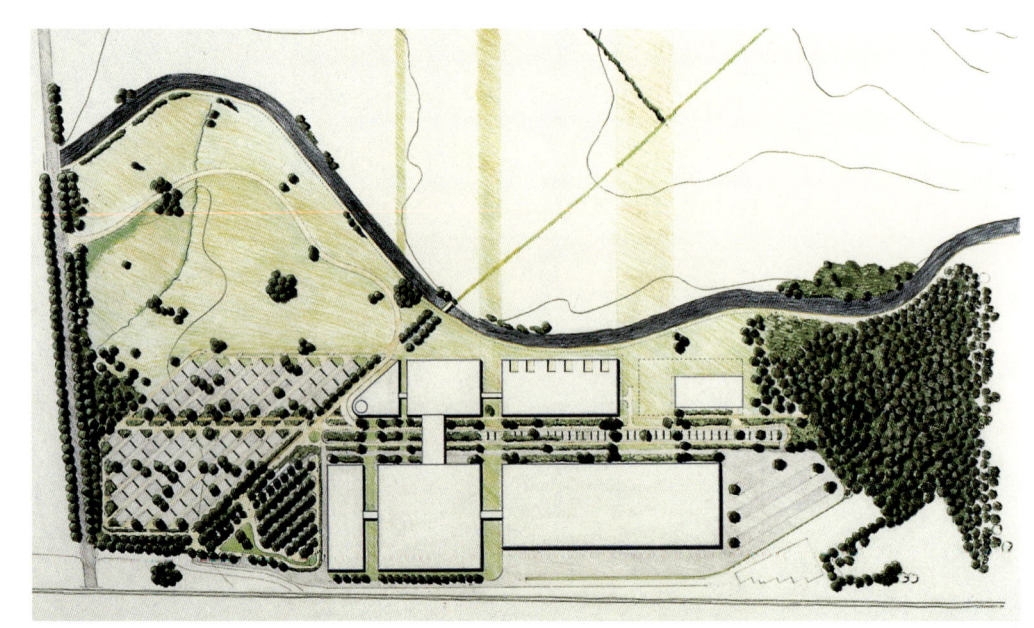

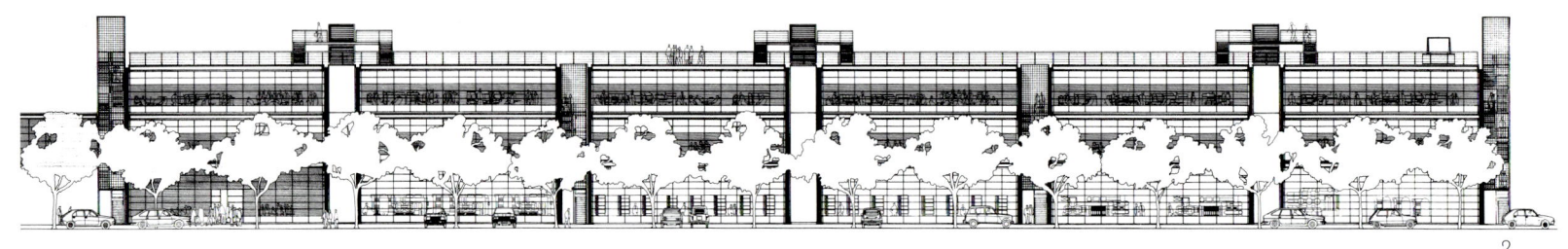

Left, far left: Project architect Ken Shuttleworth's early sketch elevations for the new administrative building. Continuing the eastward thrust determined by the first masterplan, this is the south elevation seen across the tree-lined central mall. A small bridge link to the original ISC is seen on the left. With service cores and atria running east-west parallel to this elevation, the different elevational treatments emphasise the continuous horizontal sweep of office space behind the facade.

**As one surrenders the visitor's plastic security tag on leaving Greenford, it is tempting to dismiss the building as no more than one of the pleasant homes of a wealthy multi-national ... West London, though, quickly reminds one of the rotten conditions in which most of us are still condemned to work, and that what serves IBM so handsomely and economically would do very well for a northern workers' co-operative.** Christopher Woodward, *The Architectural Review*, August 1980

The story does not stop there, however. With flexibility and future growth always assumed, in 1985 Norman Foster was again invited to look at the site. By this time IBM's requirements had changed significantly. It no longer required the originally assumed style of extension to an open-plan 'shed'. Instead a cellular solution was proposed in which an additional building would be sited to the east of the ISC and nominally linked to it. Various explorations of this theme were undertaken. A rectangular building with atria was proposed and so was a building with finger-like wings.

Although this extension was eventually abandoned for reasons related to IBM's internal organisation and fast-changing requirements, the exercise remains of interest for two primary reasons. Firstly, it is a reminder that the sort of dynamic industry, which first enabled the practice to express its ideas about industrial buildings, continued to be dynamic throughout the 1980s: the extension reflects requirements, which the old brief could not have anticipated.

Secondly, it shows how the practice – post Willis Faber & Dumas and more importantly, the Hongkong Bank – was much more committed to the notion of atria and the admission of natural light. Foster's preoccupation with integrating services and structure within deep-plan buildings had not so much subsided in this case – it remains central to his philosophy – as served its purpose. IBM Greenford can be seen to summarise a line of architectural thought that began with Reliance Controls and the Newport School competition. Future work by Foster would build on that achievement, and it would begin by letting in the daylight.

Graham Vickers

4. Zoned as a deep-plan structure to be built to the east of the ISC, in this sketch Norman Foster returned to an earlier idea for top-lit courtyards and atria conceived for the original UKDC but never implemented.

5. A model of the new administration building in its final form, with service cores now running north-south across a major 'front' building and finger extensions stretching northwards behind.

Overleaf: The restaurant on the second floor of the distribution centre illuminated at night. Directly beneath is the loading dock, its overhead service zone visible above its doors with their red warning lights.

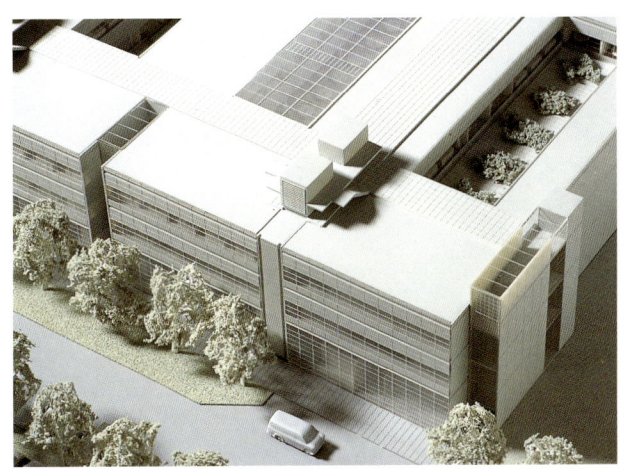

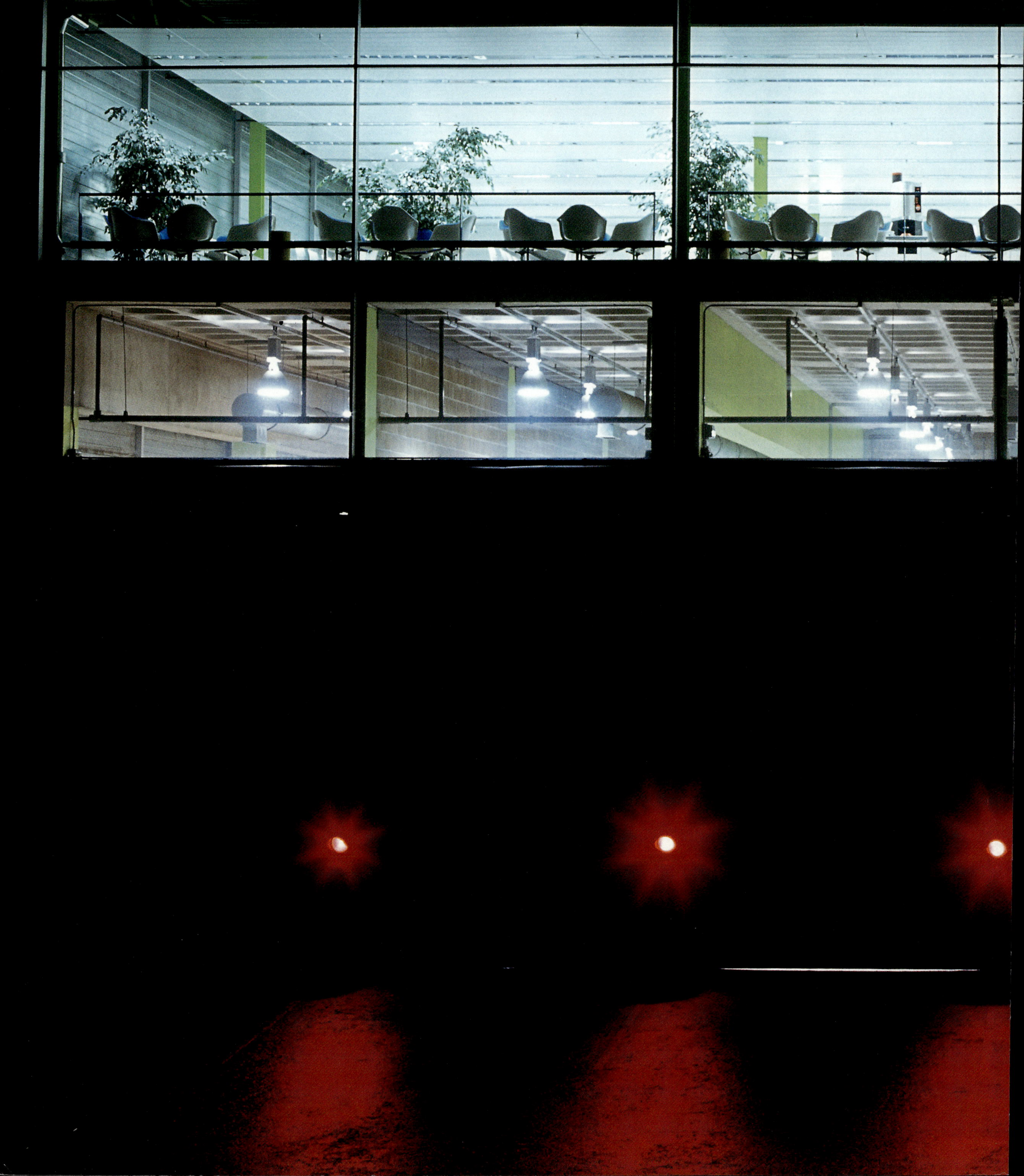

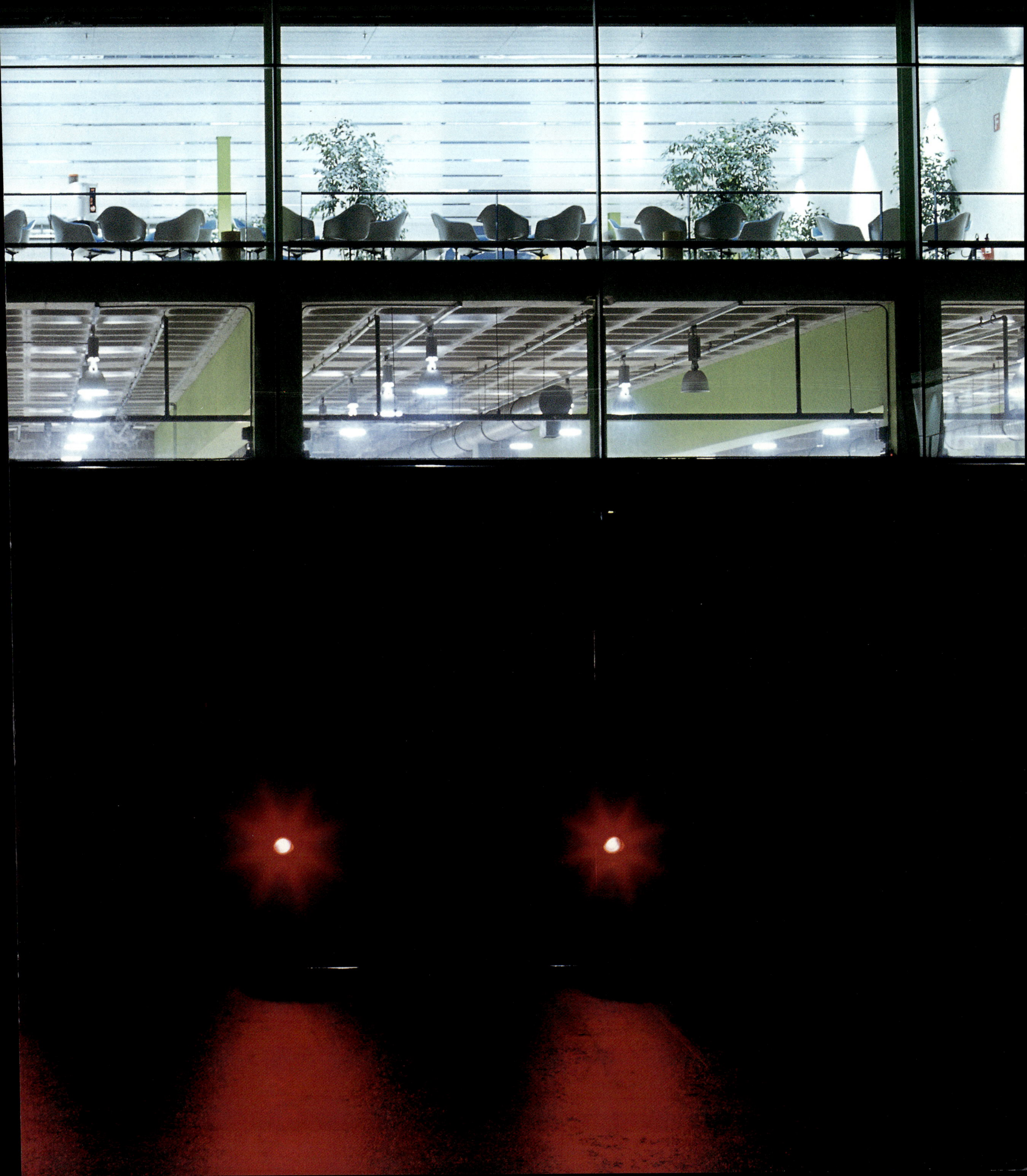

# Special Care Unit
Hackney, London, England 1970–1972

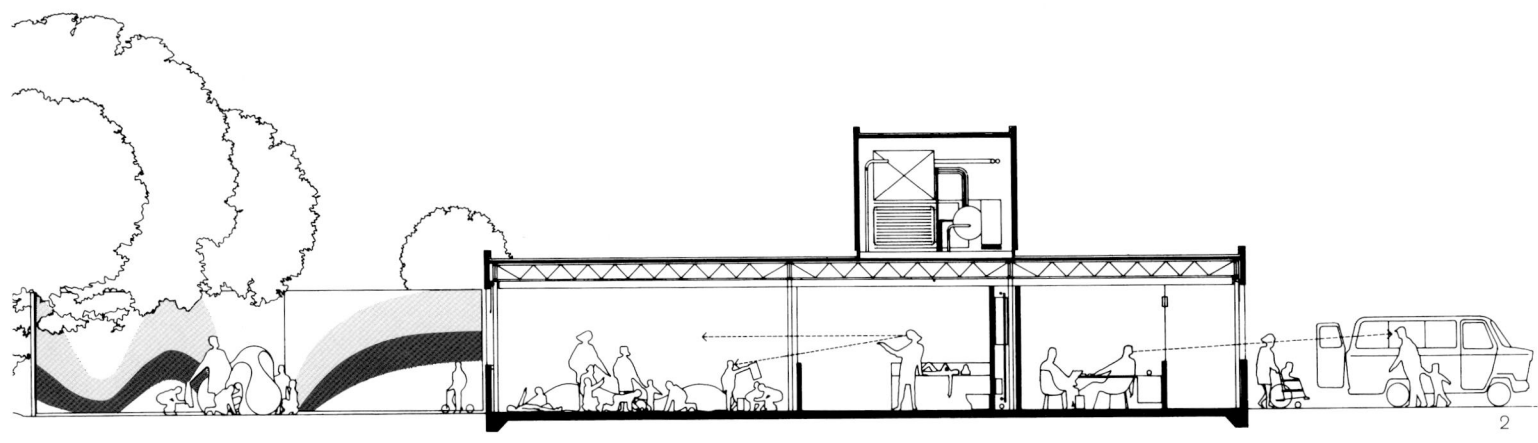

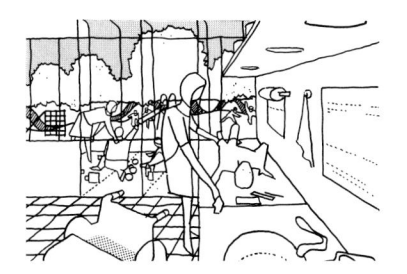

**In the Special Care Unit we aimed to develop an experimental prototype; one which could be monitored in use, and used to establish a standardised set of parameters to be applied to future projects.** Norman Foster, *Foster Associates*, 1979

Left: Re-thinking the role of the care and sanitary facilities required by children with special needs was the key to the design of the unit, as explored here in Birkin Haward's concept drawing.

There is a fine tradition in modern British school building to do with the interrelationship between technically advanced architecture and progressive educational philosophies. In the 1930s, the combination of Walter Gropius and his aims for an architecture that was simple, practical, universal and imaginative, and the egalitarian educationalist Henry Morris, found expression in Impington Village College. From this collaboration developed the notion of a non-assertive architecture of steel-framed buildings and light-filled, colourful interiors complementing and reinforcing brave new pedagogical ideas. The Hertfordshire schools of the 1950s and the acclaimed Consortium of Local Authorities Special Programme (CLASP) system in the 1960s followed in this tradition and, in turn, influenced the California School Construction Systems Development (SCSD) building programme.

In the early 1970s Foster Associates designed two schools for children with special needs in which the practice's by now well-established architectural philosophy was applied to low-cost public/voluntary sector educational buildings. The brief for each building evolved under the sponsorship of the Spastics Society and both were, to a large extent, experimental in concept and design.

The late 1960s had witnessed a radical reappraisal of primary level schooling, which culminated in the Plowden Report with its emphasis on informal, child-centred teaching derived from the ideas of educationalist pioneers such as Froebel and Peztalozzi. Mentally or physically 'handicapped' children were, however, considered 'uneducable' and were still dealt with under the jurisdiction of Medical Officers of Health whether in psychiatric hospitals, residential homes, junior training colleges, special units, or under the care of their parents. In 1971 the Education (Handicapped Children) Act brought the then categorised 'educationally subnormal' under the Department of Education and Science and the concept of special schools was introduced.

The first school that Foster designed was essentially an experimental prototype, which would supply a range of parameters applicable to future projects, whether they be conversions, extensions or new buildings. To this end the architects were interested in developing a standardised 'kit of parts' capable of widespread application.

1. The courtyard, with its distinctive mural, provides a protected outdoor play area.

2. The open cross-section facilitates observation: from the lavatories through to the outdoor play area, and from the offices to the car park and entrance lobby.

3. The building occupies the width of the site. Two activity areas, with a 'wet play' area in between, overlook the courtyard. An office/service core contains the lavatories and sluice room together with store rooms, a laundry, offices, therapy rooms, and a small doctor's surgery.

4. As all the children are doubly or singly incontinent, providing clear lines of sight into and out of the lavatories was a key consideration.

5. Indoor activities take place on a big carpeted area equipped with a 'landscape' of inflatables designed and made by the Psychiatric Rehabilitation Association.

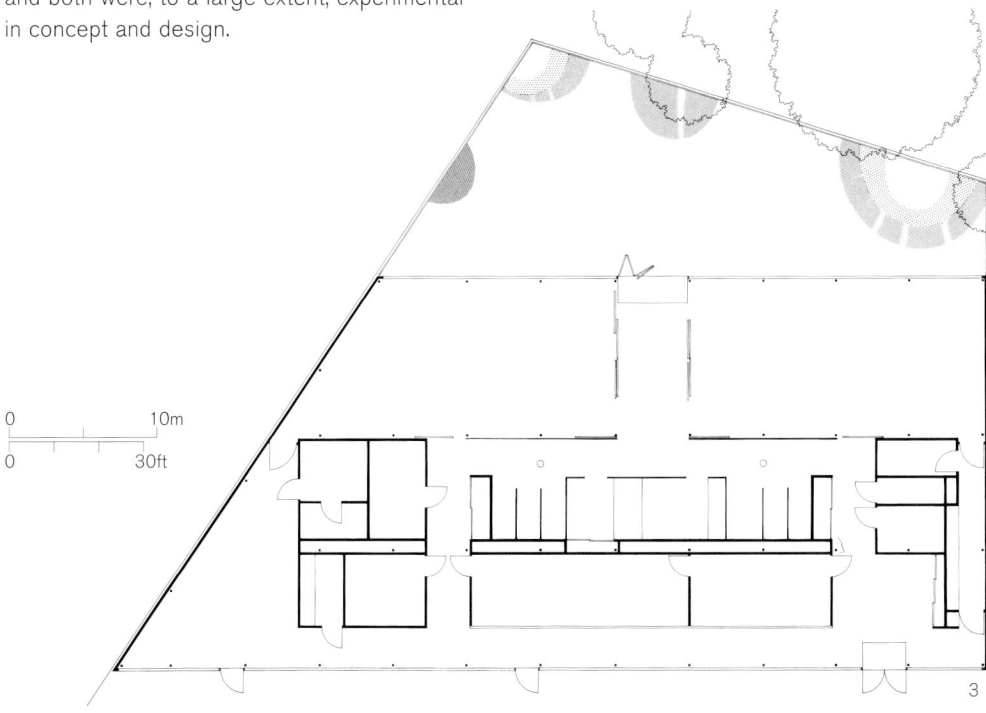

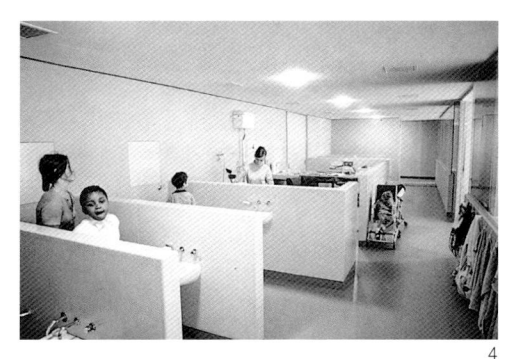

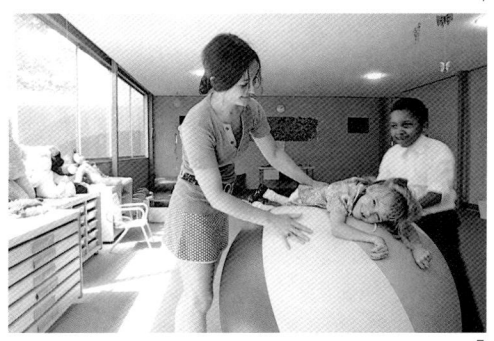

Special Care Unit 267

**The architects may be right: one can't in this case ask the customers. They may get more than one suspects from the warmly coloured scene. The bright yellow walls, the orange stanchions and the vivid pink sliding doors are certainly visually compelling.** Selwyn Goldsmith, *Design*, July 1973

**At a detailed level the problems of heating and lighting such buildings were quite challenging when it was realised that some children could burn themselves on radiators or suffer eye damage by staring up at bright light sources … The successful resolution of these and other problems enabled better utilisation of the teachers' time, allowing them to devote their attention to the real priority – the children's therapy.** Norman Foster, *Foster Associates*, 1979

Right: Norman Foster and members of Foster Associates staff contributed to the completion of the special care unit by painting the walls and ground of the outdoor play area in a bright yellow and blue design.

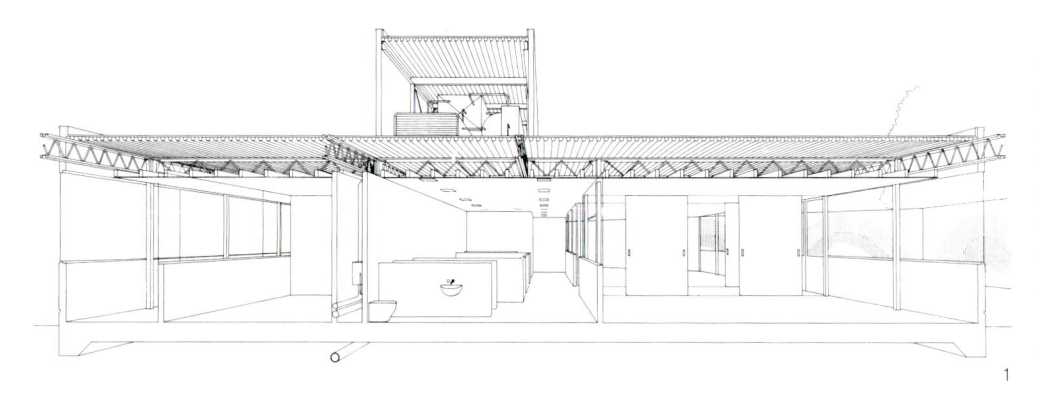

In 1970, the London Borough of Hackney was approached and agreed to provide land on the site of an existing junior training college. A special care unit was proposed for fourteen to twenty-four severely mentally and physically disabled children who were either unable to talk or walk, were incontinent, or were generally thought to be unresponsive to stimulation. Their educational needs would involve an attempt to provide increased stimulation through play and dedicated care.

In addition to consultation with the Spastics Society, the Foster team was able to draw on experience in the field from Hackney and the Inner London Education Authority who would take over the running of the school. The architects' investigation of existing provision showed it to be woefully lacking, unnecessarily rigid or simply inappropriate. In the face of an innovative and changing educational climate, the approach that Foster developed – in terms of flexibility and user choice, the application of appropriate technology as a means to a social end, and the disengagement of structure and services from space – seemed apt.

The single-storey unit was conceived as three linear zones extending right across the width of the site to leave an enclosed play court in the south-facing corner. The first (public) zone contained the main entrance, reception, medical and therapy rooms; the second (service core) provided lavatories, laundry and storage; and the third (private) zone comprised the activity/teaching areas leading on to the court. The lavatories were conceived as open, light areas with internal windows, which functioned both in terms of views out and for ease of supervision from the teaching areas. Certainly, when the building opened, it was immediately liked by both teachers and children, and it remains in use today.

Louis Hellman

**We wanted to design a building that met the specific needs of both teachers and pupils; but more than that, we wanted to create a space which the children would enjoy and which would enhance the learning process.**
Norman Foster

The Hackney Special Care Unit pioneered a design philosophy that continues in the studio's more recent projects for people with special needs.
Left: The Forth Valley Community Care Village (1993-1995) houses long-term mental health patients in a domestically scaled environment.
Right: The ASPIRE National Training Centre (1995-1998) provides training and rehabilitation facilities which are fully accessible to users with a wide range of mobility, hearing and visual impairments as well as those with learning difficulties.

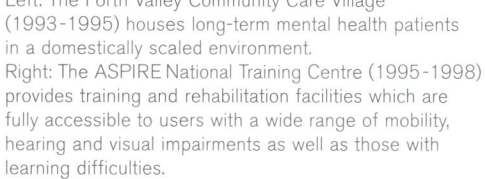

1. All servicing systems are housed in a plant room above the roof deck. The ceiling carries radiant heating panels, a safe heat source for handicapped children.

2. Sliding doors separate the larger activity areas from a central 'wet play' area, which has additional sliding-folding doors on to the outdoor play area.

3. The bright orange and yellow colour scheme is maintained throughout the building, with an easily cleaned nylon carpet, yellow painted walls, and yellow roller blinds.

4. The lavatory stalls are painted yellow to avoid an institutional appearance. Extract fans in the ceiling draw smells into the plant room overhead where they can be dissipated easily.

5. Looking through to the sheltered outdoor play area.

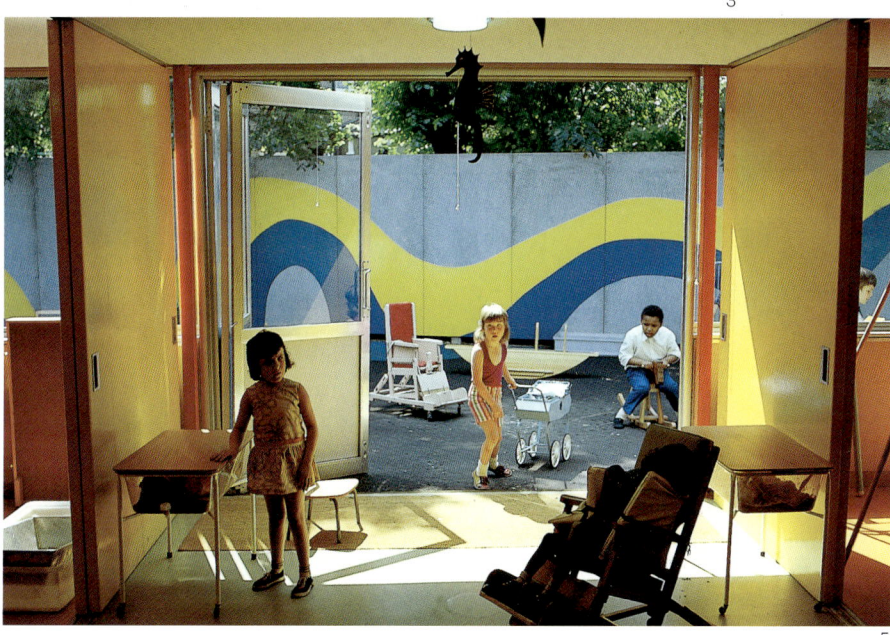

Special Care Unit   269

# Palmerston Special School
Liverpool, England 1973–1976

At the heart of the school we created a generous light-filled space designed to aid child supervision. We avoided architectural gymnastics and instead invested in the cheapest possible structure so that we could improve services and make this the freshest place in the building.

Norman Foster

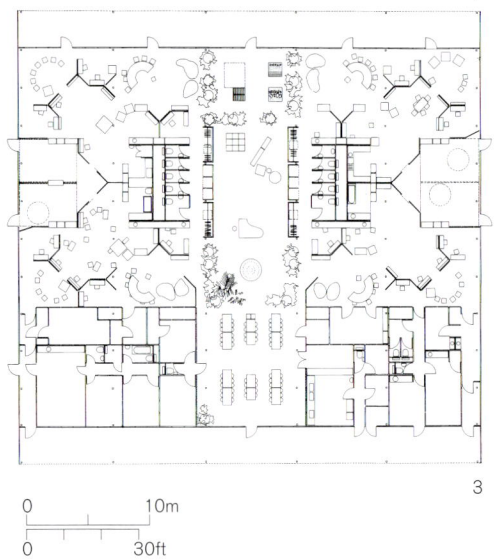

**This school for handicapped children reveals an objectivity in solving the requirements of the brief that is often lacking in more complex buildings. This approach to the design is equally apparent in the selection of the structure, materials and service systems which, although utilitarian in appearance and unconcealed within the building, are combined with the furnishings and colour there to create an environment of sparkling warmth and interest.** Extract from the assessors' report for the RIBA Award, 1977

**Before I joined Foster Associates I had been working for the London Borough of Merton, where I was responsible for the design of a new middle school in South London. The design was influenced by the SCSD system, and also by Norman's submission for the Newport School competition. As Foster Associates was just starting work on a school for handicapped children in Liverpool – Palmerston School – it seemed perfectly natural for me to join the practice when the middle school was complete.** Spencer de Grey, in conversation with Malcolm Quantrill, 1999

**The chief interest of the interior is the contrast between the relatively massive, rounded forms of the high-level ductwork (fed by air-handling units in one of the northern cores) and the spindly, square-section outline of the structural steel frame. The steelwork, in fact, is something of a minor *tour de force*; the hollow section portals are cantilevered off continuous strip footings, obviating the need for additional bracing: a really elegant use of steel.** *Design*, December 1976

---

The innovative approach to the design of schools for mentally and physically disabled children initiated by Foster Associates at Hackney was further developed at the much larger Palmerston Special School. The project was commissioned jointly by Liverpool's education department and the Spastics Society to provide facilities for sixty disabled children between the ages of fourteen and sixteen, with a special care unit for an additional severely and doubly disabled group.

While Palmerston was on the drawing board, the Department of Education and Science (DES) published its *Design Note 10: Designing for the Severely Handicapped*. This report recommended that 'handicapped' and 'severely handicapped' children be educated in special schools, which could provide flexibility in teaching spaces, simple spatial relationships, a friendly and reassuring atmosphere, freedom of movement, covered play areas and the integration of special care units, all within the same building.

The DES guide also drew on a report by Kenneth Bayes, an architect with the Design Research Unit, published in 1964, entitled 'The Therapeutic Effect of Environment on Mentally Handicapped and Emotionally Disturbed Children'. This theory of the therapeutic environment holds that space, light, colour, pattern and texture can be manipulated to elicit a positive response in otherwise passive children and to calm those who are hyperactive. These various findings were entirely consistent with Foster's conclusions following the design team's investigations prior to planning the Hackney special care unit.

The planning at Palmerston represented a more subtle variation of the 'zoning' approach at Hackney. The structural system linked hollow section portal frames in five bays. This simple arrangement allowed a flexible, open-ended plan form with freedom to dispose the internal elements in any desired pattern. Wrap-around, yellow-painted corrugated asbestos cladding to the roof and walls confined windows to the two ends, which were fully glazed and set back.

One glazed end adjoined the approach road to the north and formed the main entrance, the second provided sheltered, south-facing play areas. The relatively rigid service core zone at Hackney was here broken down into four nodes – two flanking the entrance contained staff and service areas, and two provided lavatories and cloakrooms easily accessed from the teaching areas. A 'public' zone extended through the centre of the building under a translucent roof to accommodate entrance, dining and shared resource areas.

Four open-plan teaching spaces allowed flexibility for teachers experimenting with different teaching methods. Each area was distinguished by screens of a different colour – green, yellow, orange or blue – which could be arranged to meet varying spatial requirements and create specific areas: quiet, practical, play, wet or general. Integrated both by colour and size with the screens was a furniture system providing storage boxes, work surfaces, cupboards, trolleys and play equipment. The contents of the teaching areas thus aimed to provide both mobility and stimulus for children and teachers alike.

Louis Hellman

1. Close-carpeted, open-planned from front to back and easily reached from any part of the school, the central common play area was daylit through its two glazed gable ends and by means of skylights.

2. As a simple solution to the problem of producing a small covered area for outdoor activities, the one-bay recessed glazing line on the north and south elevations gives elegance to what would otherwise be a very direct industrial configuration. The simple plan, with multiple exits on all sides, obviated the need for fire protection to the steel and resulted in a remarkable lightness of structure.

3. Ground floor plan: the only fixed elements were the four service cores.

4, 5. The school in use. Moveable, low-level screens were colour-coded to define the four main teaching areas. High-level ducting, running below the ridge in each of the five bays, provided ventilation, fed by air-handling equipment in the main plant room.

**Palmerston was an exemplary lesson for me in how the design of services must be carefully considered and coordinated into the building as a whole – an early training for what was to be one of the most important aspects of the subsequent projects we undertook accommodating people with special needs.** Spencer de Grey, in conversation with Malcolm Quantrill, 1999

Left: Birkin Haward's early concept sketch envisages a large, 'single-pitch' building, but the planning principles remain the same. Flexible screens and moveable furniture would allow the staff to experiment with a variety of arrangements within the single space, restricted in the completed building only by the four fixed service cores.

**Spaces around the cores flow pleasantly into one another, but have been roughly demarcated into four zones by means of simple coloured screens, each zone, in turn, being furnished with play equipment and boxes.** Alastair Best, *The Architectural Review*, November 1976

Roughly 3000 handicapped children are born in the UK each year. Of these, some 15 per cent will be in need of special care. All these children will be severely mentally handicapped; and some may also suffer from one or more physical disabilities.

Before April 1971 all such children were beyond the educational pale. Some were cared for in hospitals or residential homes; others were looked after by their parents under the eye of the Medical Officer of Health.

In April 1971, the Education (Handicapped Children) Act brought all educationally subnormal children under the care of the Department of Education and Science.

Against this background of changing attitudes, the Spastic Society and Foster Associates started to plan for a special care unit for Hackney. We read the (all too little) available literature, spoke to the (all too few) specialists and visited the (all to rare) built examples. With a tight budget, we determined on a systems approach using readily available off-the-peg components.

With no fixed rules for special care, we concluded than any new building would have to be able to adapt readily to new roles. We developed an arrangement for Hackney that placed the maximum of flexible space around a fixed service core.

Now, with Palmerston Special School on the drawing board, the DES has published *Design Note 10* on special schools. With its emphasis on flexibility and simple plan forms, it seems to confirm many of the design principles developed for Hackney.

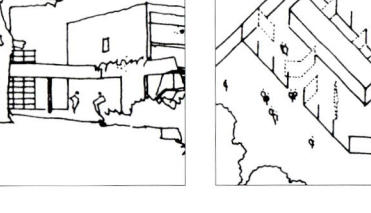

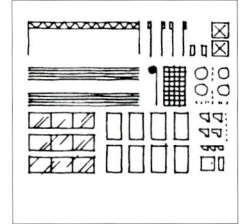

**The single gable at Thamesmead here becomes a series of five portals; and the glazing, which for Modern Art Glass formed a very appropriate shop window outside the steel frame and flush with the cladding, is now recessed to the depth of one bay, allowing the skinny steelwork to form a kind of covered arcade at either end. The effect of all this – a typical Foster Associates' device – is to convey the impression of a section cut through a seemingly endless building envelope; steel portal frames, cladding rails, cladding, all sharp and distinct.** Alastair Best, *The Architectural Review*, November 1976
Right: Comparative curved corner cladding details of Modern Art Glass and Palmerston respectively.

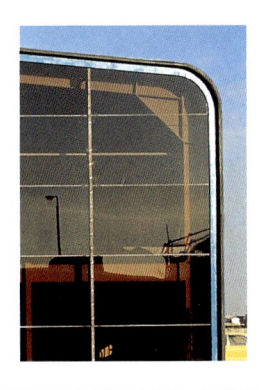

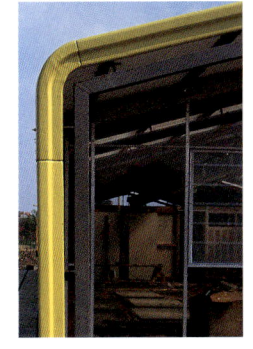

**A row exploded in Liverpool yesterday over a 'Marie Celeste' school which boasts valuable fixtures and fittings – but no pupils. Stunned city education chiefs heard that a wide range of equipment had been left behind when the special school was abandoned more than a year ago. Liverpool City Council closed Palmerston Special School at Belle Vale because it was riddled with dangerous asbestos.** *Liverpool Echo*, 2 November 1988
This was one of many local newspaper stories provoked by the premature closure of Palmerston, in 1987.

Unlike Hackney, however, the DES publication makes a strong case for integrating the special care aspects of education into the general running of a more broad-based special school. So at Palmerston, handicapped and severely handicapped children will be cared for side by side.

Our first designs assumed one large open-plan space flowing around four fixed service cores, all under one simple 'single-pitch' roof.

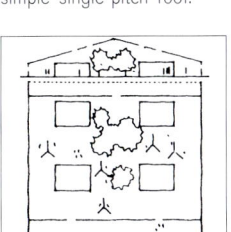

The structural form of the single-pitch design has not proved to be the most cost effective. We now propose a multi-pitch building based on a series of linked portal frames. The low-profile structure will be lighter and easier to build. A variety of cladding systems are being considered.

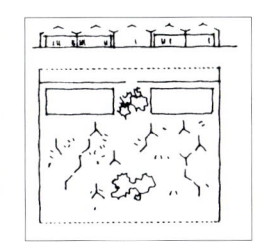

Internally the open-plan arrangement of the first scheme will be retained, though with possible variations in the location of service cores.

Most importantly, the building is being designed around the simplest (and cheapest) available systems for structure and enclosure, so as to release as large a part of the budget as possible for fitting out the internal environment.

Our research is continuing, notably on how best to service the building; not only with regard to comfort, but also to future maintenance.

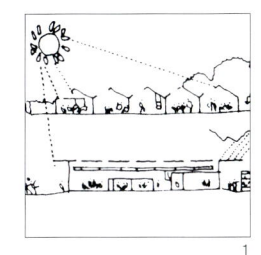

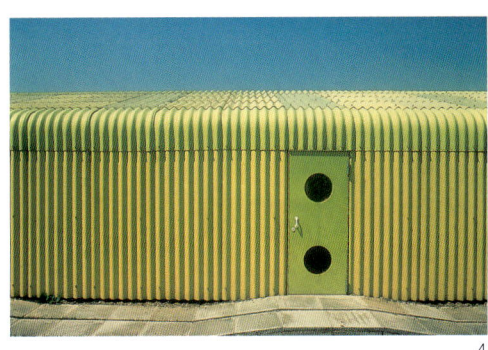

1. Annotated extracts from Foster Associates' illustrated report to the client.

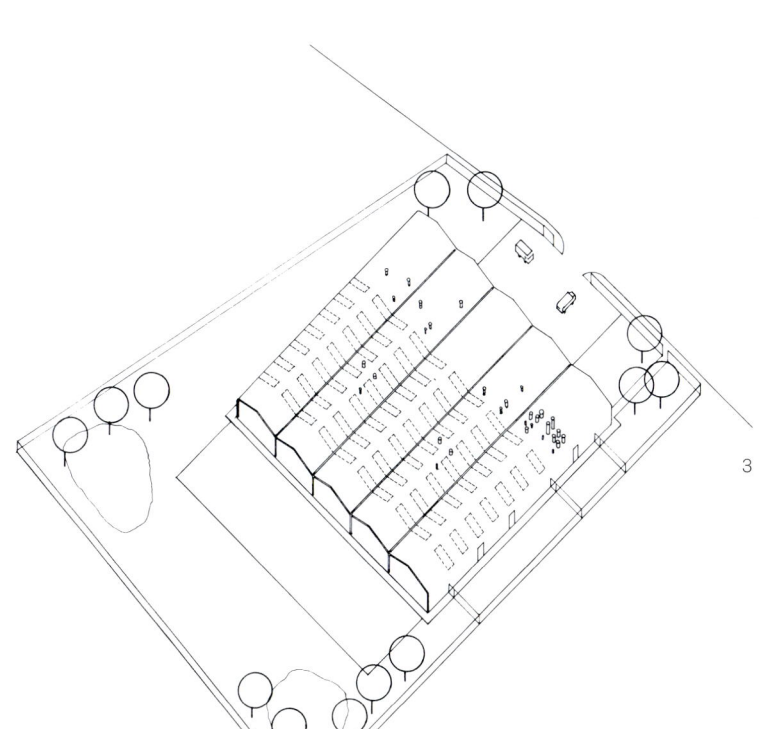

2. The pitched roofs gave the building a domestic scale, while its openness to daylight was matched by the night-time transparency of its gable elevations.

3. An early axonometric drawing. To maintain a bright atmosphere in the deep-plan interior a high degree of top-lighting was envisaged.

4. Many small details, such as the ramped paths for wheelchair access, demonstrate the degree of thoughtfulness applied throughout the school.

**Bean Hill Housing**
Milton Keynes, England 1971–1973

**We face a crisis in housing which most of us working on the subject on a day-to-day basis view with increasing pessimism. It is not just that we cannot build enough – it is also about the quality of what we can build.** Derek Walker, *The Architecture and Planning of Milton Keynes*, 1981

The Milton Keynes Masterplan, drawn up in 1970, established a framework for the development of a 9,000 hectare New Town. Although open to adaptation as the town developed, the masterplan established a template that balanced housing and employment so that the town could be self-contained without large numbers of people having to commute to work.
Right: An aerial view of central Milton Keynes illustrates its distinctive gridded layout.

The most urgent problem facing the Milton Keynes Development Corporation in the early 1970s was the need to build sufficient housing to draw settlers to the embryonic city. Derek Walker, as founding Chief Architect and Planner, set out to establish a positive identity for Milton Keynes by promoting new ideas in housing design. He pursued an energetic commissioning policy, allocating 40 per cent of the design work to outside architects and selecting innovative firms to meet this challenge. Foster Associates was among the very first to be appointed, with a commission for Bean Hill, a 100-acre site at Woughton, south of the city centre.

## In Walker's words, the developing city was a 'frontier town' with almost no indigenous industry or labour force.

Bean Hill reinvestigated many of the concepts explored by Norman and Wendy Foster in early Team 4 houses and housing schemes which were variously concerned with the notions of privacy, flexibility and adaptability. Skybreak house, for example, uses sliding partitions to open up a range of spatial options, and splits the living accommodation into living and sleeping areas while a central zone acts as a 'noise buffer'. This idea was taken further in the high-density housing project at Radlett, where clear main services and circulation zoning allowed the freedom to fit out each house to suit individual needs. In the Wates project, the houses were organised into parent and children realms, allowing each a degree of independence.

Significantly, all these schemes employed 'heavy' in-situ masonry or precast construction techniques. The shift away from this at Bean Hill was an integral part of the Milton Keynes brief. In Walker's words, the developing city was a 'frontier town' with almost no indigenous industry or labour force. Construction projects were reliant on building workers bussed in from nearby towns such as Stevenage or Northampton; and operating Britain's largest house-building programme, with a goal of 3,000 houses per year, suddenly turned traditional building materials into a very rare commodity. Systems building seemed to offer the only short-term answer.

Opposite: A Helmut Jacoby rendering of one of the single-storey areas of Bean Hill. Short rows of houses were grouped orthogonally around cul-de-sac roads, penetrated by the 'reinforced hedgerow' lines of the pedestrian and cycle routes. Old people's houses were placed at the ends of each terrace overlooking green spaces, and all the houses were planned so that the living rooms looked out onto private gardens.

1. The plan of phase one at Bean Hill – laid out at only 11 dwellings to the acre – is in marked contrast to the earlier high-density Team 4 housing schemes.

In the late 1970s prefabrication has been taken up more successfully by timber manufacturers. Formerly an expensive material, timber has, after the wild fluctuations in the price of building materials around 1973, become economic. Although prefabricated wall and floor panels are still relatively unusual, prefabricated timber roof trusses are the rule rather than the exception on late '70s housing sites. Sutherland Lyall, *The State of British Architecture*, 1980

**By using a high degree of prefabrication we were able to raise standards and lower costs. But prefabrication was not – and never has been – a goal in itself. It was a means to achieving higher standards for the building and its users in an economical way.** Norman Foster, in conversation with Malcolm Quantrill, 1999
Left: Pre-assembled timber frame components from the Walter Llewellyn Quick-Build system being lowered by crane during the construction of the Bean Hill housing. This system allowed individual shells to be erected and roofed in a single day.

1. An exploded axonometric showing the prefabricated timber elements used at Bean Hill. The Quick-Build system comprised load-bearing, stud-frame gables, party and partition walls supporting a composite stressed roof deck of plywood, all resting on a concrete ground slab.

2. A cutaway drawing of the front wall of a typical house showing stud framing and windows and the dark grey corrugated aluminium sheet cladding.

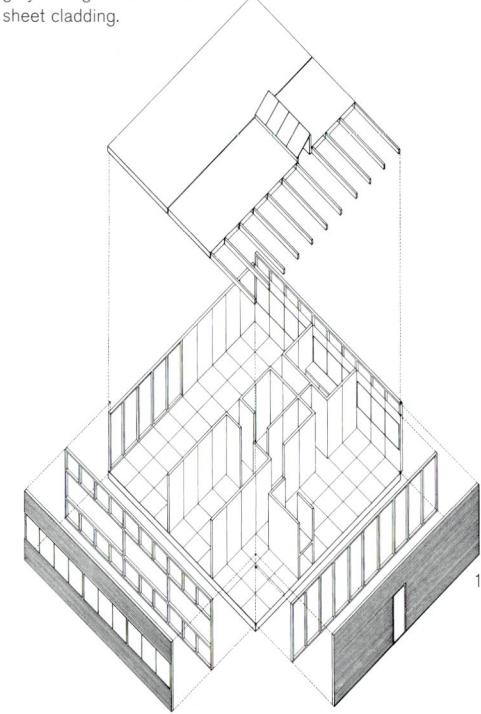

The Corporation was also committed to providing low-rise housing, and had determined that a two-storey development was most likely to meet stringent government cost yardsticks. However, poor load-bearing site conditions and a low development density of only eleven dwellings per acre raised the possibility of achieving a single-storey scheme within similar cost limits. Engineer Tony Hunt's structural studies confirmed that only part of the site could accommodate two storeys without the use of deep foundations, while detailed costing demonstrated that a single-storey solution could be more viable provided that a lightweight construction system was adopted.

A variety of off-the-peg steel-framing options were considered, from agricultural sheds to industrial structures, but none was available within the budget. Foster's instinct for going direct to industry led to further research with manufacturers in the UK and Scandinavia, and to the conclusion that a timber frame offered the best value. The outcome was the adoption of the Walter Llewellyn 'Quick-Build' prefabricated system which allowed relocatable internal walls and could satisfy a range of plan types, from two to six-person units.

The timber frame comprises load-bearing party walls and partitions supporting a stressed plywood roof deck, all sitting on a reinforced-concrete slab. The external walls also have a plywood skin, lined with bitumen-impregnated insulation and clad with stove-enamelled profiled aluminium sheet.

Foster now believes that a timber panel cladding might have been more appropriate; his elaboration that this might have been a self-weathering wood, turning silver-grey with time, emphasises this shift of attitude.

In Foster's first proposals, the single-storey solution was explored to open up related plan areas, making the most of the Parker Morris yardstick space standards. Clear openings were introduced between dining, kitchen and living rooms to reveal the full width of the house. In the family houses, sliding partitions meant that the dining space could be enlarged into a daytime play area by connecting it to the children's bedroom, while the living room could be linked to the parents' bedroom.

**Foster's instinct for going 'direct to industry' led the design team to adopt the Walter Llewellyn 'Quick-Build' prefabricated system which allowed relocatable internal walls and could satisfy a wide range of plan types.**

Houses were effectively zoned into 'quiet' and 'noisy' areas on either side of a combined kitchen and bathroom service core, which provided acoustic privacy. It also offered the traditional advantages of the bungalow – adaptability with minimal physical alteration and ease of management for a young family or the elderly.

Walker remembers this scheme as 'a remarkably ingenious solution which maximised every square inch of space, keeping circulation to the absolute minimum'. However, in the face of pressure to cut costs, the layout gradually stiffened from its early spatial freedom to a much more conventionally organised *Raumplan* with car ports notched into a continuous terrace, rather than between paired units as originally envisaged.

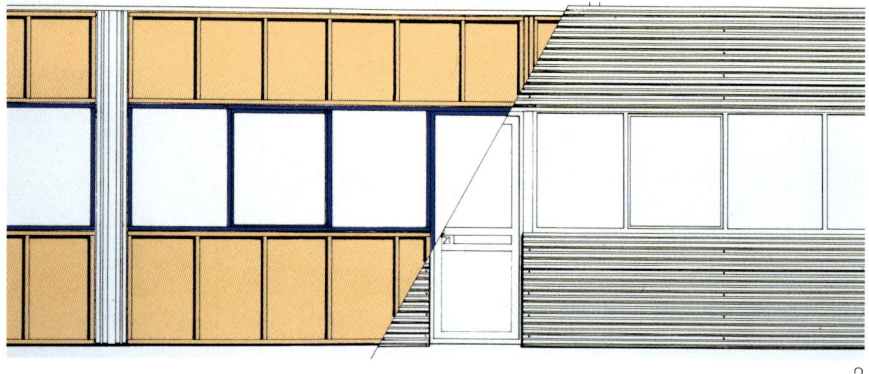

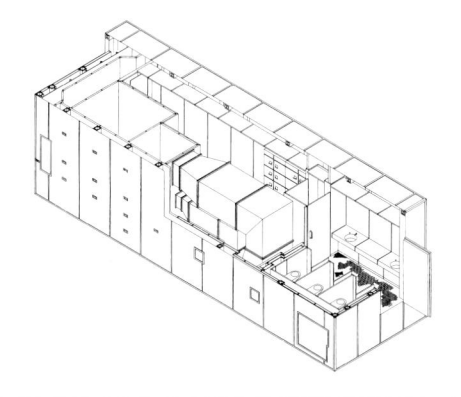

Left: Six years after the completion of the Bean Hill estate, prefabricated technology was employed in the construction of the Hongkong Bank, albeit on a larger scale. A typical prefabricated service module, contains lavatories and air-handling plant. Each one was fully finished in the factory, ready to be shipped to the site.

As completed in 1973, phase one of Bean Hill (phase two was built later under the Corporation's supervision) consists of 492 single-storey and 77 two-storey family houses, grouped in terraces around short culs-de-sac giving on to open spaces. Groups of houses for the elderly are distributed throughout the site, overlooking more generous green spaces.

The houses relate comfortably to the gardens. All rooms have direct views of a private plot, and the existing trees and hedgerows, which weave through the site, have a greater visual impact in the context of a single-storey layout. Where necessary the hedgerows were to be reinforced to delineate cycle paths and pedestrian ways. Where these routes cross, a variety of outdoor spaces were intended to form sitting and play areas related to corner shops, clubrooms and the like, which the Corporation planned to build over time.

One of Foster's great regrets is that the lush landscaping proposals were never carried out. Helmut Jacoby's aerial perspective offers the clearest picture of how Bean Hill might have looked, the low terraces nestling among dense planting. Foster also believes that the earlier, open-plan scheme came closer in spirit to the aims of the motor-generated garden city, in the way it reconciled house, garden, green space and car.

Another frustration was the imposition of flat roofs. Preliminary schemes had explored the use of a continuous monopitched roof for the terraces, but this solution – heavily debated within the team – was ruled out by the Development Corporation on cost grounds: an ironic decision in the light of the later re-roofing with similar pitches by the Corporation's own architects. Foster's preference for a flat built-up felt roof was also rejected in spite of the practice's successful use of the method elsewhere. The Corporation insisted on the proprietary low-pitch aluminium system specified at Netherfield with, as it transpired, similarly problematic results.

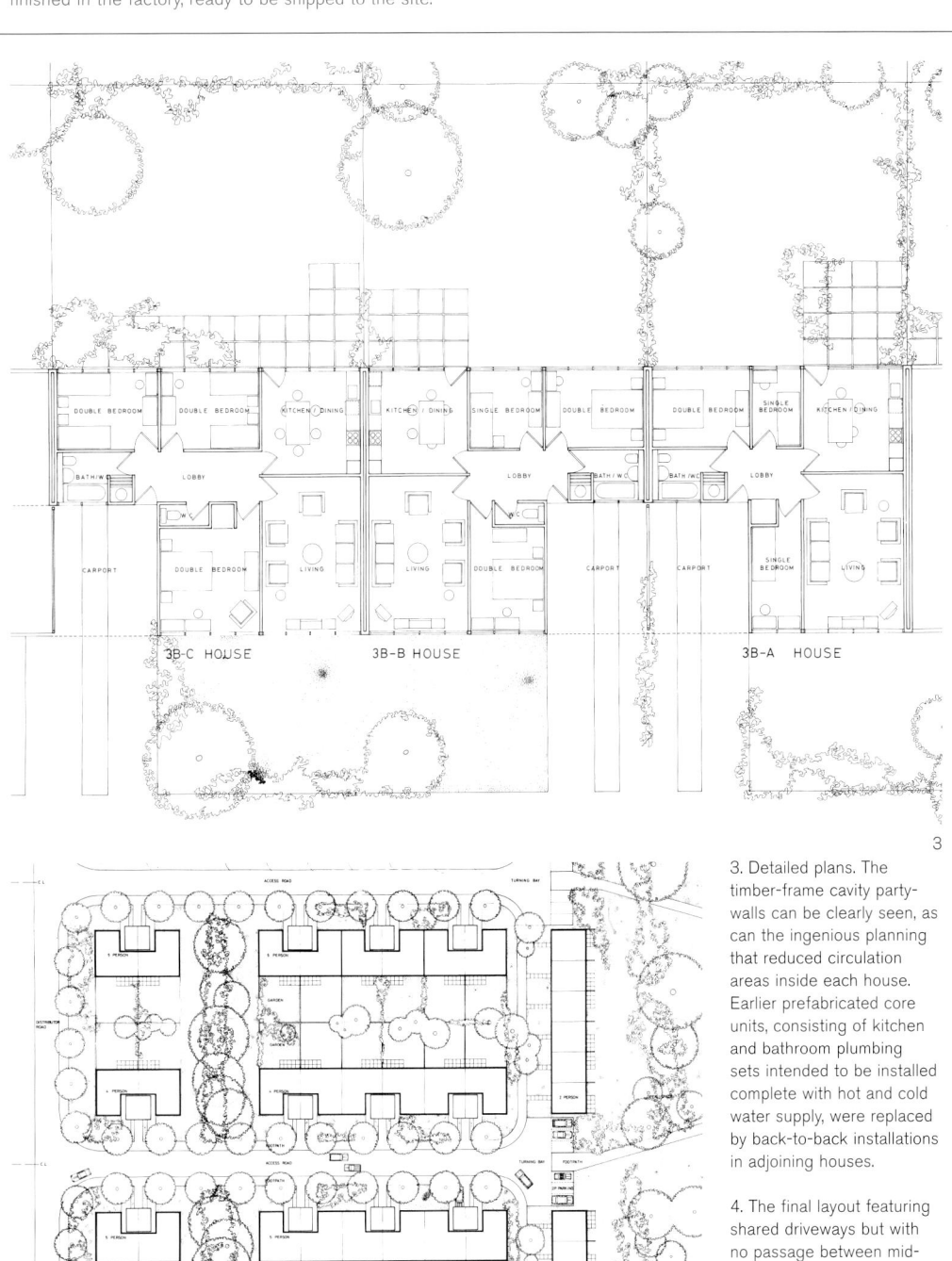

3. Detailed plans. The timber-frame cavity party-walls can be clearly seen, as can the ingenious planning that reduced circulation areas inside each house. Earlier prefabricated core units, consisting of kitchen and bathroom plumbing sets intended to be installed complete with hot and cold water supply, were replaced by back-to-back installations in adjoining houses.

4. The final layout featuring shared driveways but with no passage between mid-terrace houses to link front and back gardens.

**For all its regularity, Bean Hill makes a notable contrast with its bloody-minded neighbour, Netherfield ... But as John Betjeman has shown, the essence of suburbia is that, however banal, its physical components allow an infinite variety of individual expression. Even if the 'mature hedgerow structure' guides late party-goers back to their own particular cul-de-sac, will Foster Associates' eminently rational design provide for this irrational human need?** *The Architects' Journal*, 9 May 1973
Left: A child's climbing frame, one of the few communal facilities provided by the Development Corporation in the final scheme.

**Bean Hill accepts the implications of a low-density city that has been specifically designed for car ownership. To my knowledge it is the only scheme in Milton Keynes where you can drive your car to your front door, live on one level, and have a private garden.** Norman Foster, *A + U*, September 1975

1. A view across the rooftops of the single-storey housing at Bean Hill. Single-storey housing predominated in the development and this rather leafy view gives some idea of how the scheme would have appeared overall if the desired landscaping had been implemented.

2. One of the pedestrian and cycle paths between the two-storey terraced houses. Included in phase one of Bean Hill – as completed in 1973 – were a small number of two-storey family houses. Because of their narrow frontages these were allocated separate garaging instead of integral car ports.

3. Three of the single-storey houses built at Bean Hill, in their original form showing the shared driveway with its lower roofed car ports.

With hindsight, it is clear that relentless cost cutting to meet an over-tight budget lies at the root of many of Bean Hill's subsequent shortcomings. Other problems resulted from unnecessary expenditure. The Corporation would not accept Tony Hunt's raft foundations and insisted on deep footings at the slab edge. And access roads were heavily over-structured due to the marshy ground, which added to escalating infrastructure costs and reduced the money available for the houses themselves.

**In the four decades since Bean Hill was commissioned, the pioneering ideas that drove Milton Keynes have been trampled underfoot by private sector house builders and a fashion for the neo-vernacular.**

In a final irony, the scheme was eventually found to be ten per cent under budget – a discovery that caused justifiable anger in the Foster office. The Corporation and its quantity surveyors had been dramatically over-prudent. Even this had ramifications. It was a set policy to fix new rents as a proportion of build-costs. Because Bean Hill was so far under budget it naturally became one of the cheapest estates and attracted a high proportion of 'disadvantaged' families; a situation compounded by a decision to reduce the mix of houses for rent and for sale from an initial ratio of 60:40 to a final 75:25.

The Corporation had, largely through its own efforts, turned what was once a housing problem into a stock of problem housing, eventually having to spend more money on its refurbishment than it had cost to build.

Walker acknowledges that in the first few years of Milton Keynes' life, the learning curve was too steep. The scale and speed of the housing programme demanded financial management expertise that the Corporation simply did not possess. He now accepts that the optimum number of units that can be successfully built simultaneously is probably 100. At Bean Hill there were nearly 600 in the first phase and quality control became impossible. 'If it had been built five years later, when these problems were more familiar', he suggests, 'we might have pulled it off.'

Foster offers his favourite analogy of the architect as aircraft pilot to illuminate the relationship between architect and client. 'We were under ground control for most of the flight. But whatever the conflicts, the pilot is charged with the responsibility for the safety of his aircraft, whatever instructions he might have been given.' After the unqualified successes of Foster's earlier work, Bean Hill might be seen as a somewhat bumpy landing.

In the four decades since Bean Hill was commissioned, the pioneering ideas that drove Milton Keynes have been trampled underfoot by private sector house builders and a fashion for the neo-vernacular. Bean Hill is not alone in being abused as much for its looks as its leaks. Reporting in March 1989 on an RIBA seminar on the repair of post-war buildings, 'Astragal', in *The Architects' Journal*, noticed how the speaker responsible for the wholesale imposition of pitched roofs at Bean Hill had described in detail how the new roofs were deliberately varied, with a choice of slates or tiles and a hipped or gabled form. 'Altering the image', observed Astragal, 'seems almost to have been the primary objective.'

David Jenkins

Right: Photographed seventeen years after completion, the scheme is now virtually unrecognisable after re-roofing in variegated slates and tiles. Carried out for the Development Corporation prior to its sale to owner-occupiers, Bean Hill has been renamed 'The Gables'.

**Bean Hill accepts the implications of a low-density city designed for car ownership. To my knowledge it's the only scheme at Milton Keynes where you can drive your car to your front door, live on one level, and have a private garden.**
Norman Foster

# The Years of Innovation
Martin Pawley 1989

A building, a plan or a project by Norman Foster is always interesting – all the more interesting for being at once as useful as a pair of jeans or a bicycle, and as beautiful as a violin or a racing yacht. A shop for Joseph Ettedgui; a plan for the harbour at Saint Helier in Jersey or the island of Gomera in the Canaries; an office building for a multi-national corporation or a sports hall for a German city; a project for a flying club or a private house – the scale is unimportant, for every one displays the same qualities of lucidity, conviction, completeness and, ultimately, perfection. Each comes from the application of an intelligence and creative ability that is unique. If it is a building it will not be built to a style – Modern, Postmodern, Revivalist or Futuristic. Instead it will be a complete answer to a series of problems that locks into its site with the same conviction that it locks into its economic purpose and the lives of those who will use it.

At the beginning of the 1970s, Norman Foster was a promising young architect with a small office in the West End of London and a short string of unusual commissions behind him. The buildings he had designed included an 800-square-metre inflatable office for a computer company, which was erected in 55 minutes. It depreciated in one year at a cost of £10 per square metre including furniture. Another project was the 15,000-square-metre air-conditioned headquarters for IBM, a structure that (to its corporate surprise) the company discovered would cost less than the equivalent accommodation in temporary wooden huts. Another client had, no doubt to its equal amazement, been convinced by the architect that better space planning would obviate the need for a new building at all. That was the Foster of 1971, an architect known, where he was known at all, for his unorthodox approach and his capacity to produce highly advanced buildings at a remarkably low cost.

It is one measure of the following twelve years of achievement that on the evening of 21 June 1983, when he rose to accept the award of the Royal Gold Medal for Architecture from the hands of the President of the Royal Institute of British Architects, his reputation was no longer that of a promising designer, but of a world-famous architect.

He was in 1983 already a man in the throes of one of the most prestigious commissions of modern times: the 47-storey, £600 million, 100,000-square-metre new headquarters for the Hongkong and Shanghai Banking Corporation – a structure that, when it was completed, was destined to be recognised not only as a work of sublime architectural genius but also as the most expensive building in the world.

Though few could have foreseen it in 1967, the break-up of Foster's Team 4 partnership with Richard Rogers, shortly after the completion of the award-winning Reliance Controls building in Swindon, marked the debut of a powerful and wayward force in world architecture. Foster's period of apprenticeship, remembered as a time of 'guinea-pig clients who were really relatives', had ended long before. Now four years of close association with another gifted architect were over too, and he had crossed an important threshold. Largely unknown outside the profession, Foster was destined within a decade to execute triumphantly commissions of such seminal importance that they elevated him above the battleground of modern versus traditional values that raged throughout the rest of the profession, giving him the almost magical immunity from stylistic controversy that he retains to this day.

**The moment I entered his airy white office on Great Portland Street the spacious interior, peppered with scarlet Anglepoise lamps over distant drawing boards, instantly communicated a message about Foster's attitudes to architecture and life – space, time and relaxation.** Stephen Gardiner, *The Listener*, 17 February 1983
Left: A Foster Associates team photograph in the Great Portland Street studio, May 1982.

In the short space of time covered by the design and completion of three major British buildings – the offices for insurance brokers Willis Faber & Dumas in Ipswich, the Sainsbury Centre for Visual Arts at the University of East Anglia, and the Renault Distribution Centre in Swindon – Foster was to pass through a period of unprecedented creativity, the results of which were not so much national as international in their impact. Taken together, the built and unbuilt projects of this period revealed a rare capacity for innovation coupled with an intuitive grasp of the synoptic needs of broad outline and structural detail. At a more fundamental, but frequently overlooked, level they gave evidence of an organisational and logistical capability that few British architects have ever been called upon to deploy.

As his practice steadily grew, Foster moved his office twice: from Covent Garden to Fitzroy Street, and from Fitzroy Street to Great Portland Street. Varied industrial, commercial and planning projects for such clients as the Department of Education and Science, London Transport Executive, the Fred Olsen shipping line, IBM and Computer Technology tested his abilities and prepared the ground for buildings that were to follow.

As Foster himself is the first to agree, each of these projects contributed to its successor in the most direct and fundamental way. Without the 1967 Newport School study, with its deep plan and roof services distribution system, there would have been no 1968-1970 Operations and Amenity Centre in London's Docklands for Fred Olsen and, in due course, no headquarters for the London Docklands Development Corporation, the then unborn organisation that was destined to take over the building in 1981. Without the floor-to-ceiling glazing at Fred Olsen, there would have been no pure glass box at IBM Cosham. Without IBM Cosham, no suspended glass facade at Willis Faber & Dumas. Without the huge floor plates and escalator circulation at Willis Faber & Dumas, no confident mastery of vertical movement and no Hongkong Bank in its present form.

A similar progression can be shown to run from one of the alternative roof structures considered for Willis Faber & Dumas, through the massive 1977-1979 Hammersmith redevelopment project for London Transport, to the 1981-1986 Frankfurt Athletics Stadium – and even to the 1987 King's Cross transport interchange scheme.

**The immense variety in the nature and scale of Foster's work during these early years is not, however, its most remarkable feature. Of far greater historical significance is its supremely innovative nature.**

Yet another line can be shown to connect the structural concept of the 1974-1978 Sainsbury Centre for Visual Arts with the unbuilt 1978-1979 project for the architect's own house. A fourth can be discerned in the progression from the 'umbrella' structural system of the 1980-1982 Renault Distribution Centre to the omnidirectional, space-enclosing structure for London's third airport at Stansted in Essex. The immense variety in the nature and scale of Foster's work during these years is not, however, its most remarkable feature. Of far greater historical significance is its supremely innovative nature. None of the buildings completed in this period is conventional or traditional, and the departure from standard practice begins early, with the writing of the brief, and ends late, with the pattern of project management during construction itself.

1. Extracts from Foster Associates' 1975 regional planning study for the Canary Island of Gomera. These sketches by Birkin Haward record first impressions and the different environmental conditions found on the verdant northern (top row), and arid southern halves of the island. The study was ahead of its time in stressing that a sensitive consideration of local needs and traditional building practices should form the basis for sustainable future development.

2, 3. The 1970 Fred Olsen Amenity Centre (left) and the 1967 Newport School competition entry (right) marked further steps in the development of a highly pragmatic Foster typology: the glass-walled, horizontally serviced, deep-plan, single-storey, multi-purpose space.

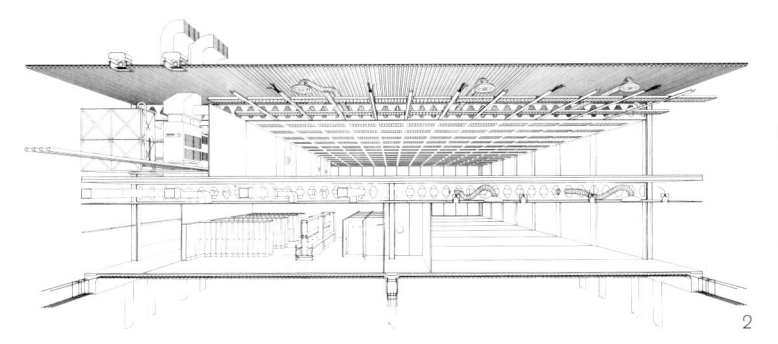

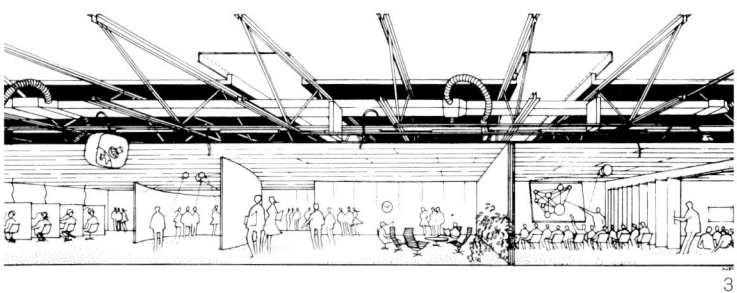

**The design process begins with a fairly active probing of the programme. We might completely redefine it, or at worst confirm and audit it, an exercise which could probably be summarised as trying to ask the right questions.** Norman Foster, in conversation with Malcolm Quantrill, 1999.
Right: Norman Foster's series of sketches, produced during the development of the BBC Radio Centre scheme (1982-1985), illustrates this complex process of communication and client consultation.

1. Escalators rising through the atrium at the heart of the Willis Faber & Dumas building (1971-1975) provide the primary means of circulation for occupants. A radical innovation at the time, this avoidance of the traditional office bank of lifts enhanced the sense of openness and social contact throughout the building.

2. At the Hongkong Bank (1979-1986), escalators lead up from the public plaza beneath the building to the main banking hall in the atrium, a 'confident mastery of vertical movement' first explored in the Willis Faber & Dumas building.

In a way that was perhaps foreshadowed by a sequence of drawings produced in 1970 to show how the structural system evolved for Reliance Controls developed first into the monocoque structure of a proposed passenger terminal at Millwall Dock, and then into the evanescent nylon-reinforced PVC envelope of the Computer Technology Air-Supported Office, each project represented a step towards a new approach to architectural design and practice.

Today this approach can be seen to have drawn closer and closer to the omnivorous methodology of industrial product development, and farther away from the traditional architect's manipulation of visual images. In this sense Foster's buildings and projects of the decade to 1983 are not only numerous, diverse and complex, but conceptually uncharted as well. Though to a lesser extent than the global component sourcing brought to such a triumphant pitch of organisational perfection in the specification of the Hongkong Bank, Willis Faber & Dumas and the Sainsbury Centre and Renault Centre were all buildings whose key architectural elements were developed with the aid of the research and development engineers of major international component manufacturers.

As such, they had to be conceived in an entirely novel way. The structural and cladding elements that gave each of these buildings a unique identity were not taken from standard ranges or chosen from catalogues, but envisioned in the architect's office and developed by the manufacturer according to the architect's specification.

Foster not only designed and built landmark buildings in the years before 1983; he designed and built them in a way that had never been successfully achieved before – even by the pioneers of prefabrication who, fifty years earlier, had called for the creation of a whole new building components industry. Although confined to individual buildings, Foster's architecture succeeded precisely where theirs had failed. Instead of demanding the replacement of an old industry, he achieved the same goal by stretching its capacity and forcing the pace of development amongst the established manufacturers of steel, glass, plastics and alloys.

**By learning more about his client's needs than the client himself knows, Foster the architect has frequently been able to 'move from a situation of inferiority to one of superiority' – and redraft the user's definition of what he needs from his building.**

In comparison with the design leadership that was necessary to produce the suspended Pilkington glazing system at Willis Faber & Dumas, the superplastic aluminium cladding at the Sainsbury Centre or the vast, undulating, seamless PVC welded roof at Renault, Foster's capacity to master the administrative complexities generated by major commissions, rapid growth, repeated office relocation and fluctuating workload during the years to 1983 falls into its correct perspective. For his real achievement was the sustained innovation that was the end-product of this management triumph.

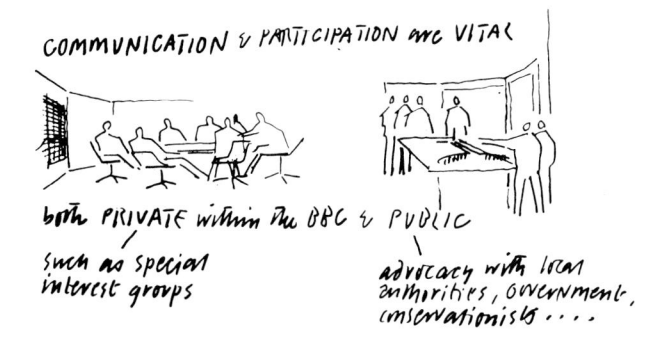

It is a measure of his diverse abilities that he was able, during this short period, to deploy not only the traditional architectural skills of clear thinking, programming and delegation, but also serendipitously to attract and maintain the allegiance of a growing number of gifted staff, manage the massive expansion of his studio, and lose neither his overall direction nor control of the fine-tuning of projects that were so complex and diverse that they would have driven lesser men into a hopeless morass of indecision and compromise.

So universally accepted now is Foster's reputation for combined attention to strategic thrust and crucial detail, that it is not widely appreciated that the skills that enabled him to gain it were self-taught, and learned in a remarkably short space of time. It is a testimony to the rapidity of Foster's own learning curve that many people still do not know that, prior to the Hongkong Bank, the practice had never built a building more than three storeys high.

It is perhaps inevitable that the magnificent achievement of the Hongkong Bank should become the lens through which the entire Foster *oeuvre* to that point has come to be viewed. This is understandable, but it presents a problem to the historian, for it becomes as difficult to concentrate on the work of the architect before that epic voyage of discovery as it is to study the career of Winston Churchill before the Second World War, or to consider the work of Ferdinand Porsche before the design of the Volkswagen. In all such cases, the only way to approach the earlier period without hindsight is to seek out threads of meaning that are not only perceptible before the great event, but still exist after it.

In the case of Churchill one such thread is to be found in his historical writing. With the immortal engineer Porsche it might be considered to be his transcending interest in power transmission. With Foster the key is, perhaps surprisingly, the indissoluble link between the redefinition of the brief and the achievement of a new architecture.

**Without the neoprene and aluminium floor-to-ceiling glazing at Fred Olsen, there would have been no pure glass box at IBM Cosham. Without IBM Cosham, no suspended glass facade at Willis Faber & Dumas.**

The Austrian psychologist Alfred Adler (1870-1937) is best known for the importance in the structure of human personality that he ascribed to the will to dominate. In this connection Adler invented the term 'lifestyle' – since debased and misused until it has come to mean little more than a collection of consumer choices. What Adler meant by it originally was the unique process by which every individual in a competitive situation endeavours to move from a subservient to a commanding role. In Adler's original formulation, an individual's lifestyle was the behavioural technique he or she evolved in early childhood for dealing with feelings of inferiority. Properly understood this lifestyle can not only be recognised in individual responses to personal experience, but can also be seen as an integral part of the creative personality.

3-5. Details from a succession of projects featuring glazed walls illustrate the technological progress, project on project, that has become a hallmark of the Foster approach. Left to right are the Olsen Amenity Centre (1968-1970), IBM Cosham (1970-1971) and Willis Faber & Dumas (1971-1975), each can be seen to pave the way for the project following it.

The Years of Innovation

Left: A checklist of priorities for the Hongkong Bank building and its occupants produced by Norman Foster during a design team brainstorming session in the early phase of development.

Architects, designers, artists and creative individuals of all kinds continually confront challenges in their professional lives, all of which can be analysed in Adlerian terms. Successful creative individuals surmount or rationalise these challenges; if they did not they could not survive in an environment dogged by frustration and disappointment. When a designer surmounts a challenge to the authority of his or her conception of a project, he or she does it – according to Adler's analysis – by converting the threat of inferiority, or defeat, into superiority, or victory. In this sense, lifestyle becomes more than a part of their personality, it becomes a professional tool that makes them successful where others fail, and drives them on when others fall back.

In the Adlerian sense there is a way in which Foster's characteristic initial approach to any architectural commission – which takes the form of an energetic research phase designed to enable him, if necessary, to seize the initiative from his client by challenging the precepts of the brief – can be seen as a classic manifestation of the successful professional lifestyle. By learning more about his client's needs than the client himself knows, Foster the architect has frequently been able to 'move from a situation of inferiority to one of superiority' – and redraft the user's definition of what he needs from his building.

There is evidence of the remarkable success of this technique from Foster's very earliest commissions to his most recent. It is a thread that runs right through his work in the decade leading up to 1983 and beyond. In psychological terms, an important part of Foster's astonishing success as an 'advanced technology' architect, in an era that professes to distrust advanced technology, is to be found in the very early moves prompted by his lifestyle. Of course, this technique alone can never guarantee success, but lifestyle coupled with a carefully developed reinforcing expertise is a powerful combination.

As a practice today, Foster Associates deploys powerful design skills and more research and development expertise than ten conventional firms of architects. But Foster's ultimate skill is his first line of attack – the practice knows how to seize the initiative by questioning and rewriting the brief by analysis – and this is a skill that has grown from the personality of Norman Foster himself.

As an architect Foster has never hesitated to question any prospective client's conception of the kind of building, plan or organisation that he needs, even when such questioning might appear to endanger his own position at the very beginning of delicate negotiations. It is a bold course, and it is not always successful, but time after time it has laid the foundations of great architecture.

Foster has always been dedicated to the business of solving organisational, environmental and people problems rather than inventing architectural imagery. As Foster himself characterised it in 1970: 'Clients tend to put problems to us in building terms but, with analysis, the solutions to those problems often emerge as not architectural at all. In this sense we are a new kind of architectural office, a bridge between the potential of new ideas and their realisation in practical terms. Each project, for us, is a kind of challenge to do more with less.'

**Foster not only designed and built landmark buildings in the years before 1983; he designed and built them in a way that had never been successfully achieved before – even by the pioneers of prefabrication who, fifty years earlier, had called for the creation of a whole new building components industry.**

In one case – that is dramatic in its illustration of the difference between this approach and the understandable desire of most young and ambitious architects for work at any price – a client approached Foster for a new building but was convinced by dispassionate analysis that the real answer lay in a more efficient pattern of space utilisation within his existing buildings. Berco Corporation actually bought space planning, not architecture, from Foster. Instead of a building, the company was rewarded with a pioneering example of a technique that was soon to become a recognised discipline in itself.

**Prefabrication no longer means repetition and standardisation; it can mean total customisation, economic customisation which opens up a whole new world of possibilities.** Norman Foster, Eric Lyons Memorial Lecture, London, 25 November 1986
Far left: An early model of prefabrication, the 1946 AIROH house was a sectionalised dwelling intended to be built at the rate of one every twelve minutes in the factories of the Bristol Aeroplane Company. However, rising costs led to its discontinuation in 1948.
Left: Forty years after the AIROH house, one of 139 prefabricated service modules is hoisted into place in the Hongkong Bank.

Needless to say, doing more with less did not always mean convincing a potential client that a new building was not needed. On a subsequent occasion it meant pioneering something that ten years later was to become famous in city office development as the American technique of 'fast-track construction' – the deliberate overlapping of briefing, design and construction stages and the elimination of a single main contractor through the exercise of expert project management and the use of multiple prime contracts with different suppliers.

Where Berco had retired satisfied without a new building, Foster's next client found himself enthusiastically commissioning a 10,000-square-metre head office building when his initial approach had been about the organisation of some temporary hutted accommodation. This client was IBM, the UK subsidiary of the American computer giant, which in 1970 submitted part of its decentralisation plan from Central London to Foster for analysis.

After considering the economics of moving the corporation's head office to temporary buildings on a pilot site for five years, Foster concluded that rapid construction of a single-storey, air-conditioned glass box with a vast 10,000-square-metre floor area would actually be cheaper – as well as reducing the site coverage to create more car parking. As a computer company, IBM was in the business of logic and it knew how to be convinced.

**It is a testimony to the rapidity of Foster's learning curve that many people still do not know that, prior to the Hongkong Bank, the practice had never built a building more than three storeys high.**

The decision that no new building was necessary for Berco, and the decision that a new building would be better than a temporary collection of huts for IBM, are examples of Foster's Adlerian lifestyle in professional action. At Willis Faber & Dumas, it expressed itself again, but this time in the leap of imagination that led from the conventional notion of a multi-storey office building on an irregular site, to a three-storey, deep-plan structure with 100 per cent site coverage. Once again an essentially conservative corporate client – one of the longest-established insurance brokers in the world – allowed itself to be convinced by logic. 'Willis Faber & Dumas never in their wildest dreams expected the sort of building they ended up with,' recalls Foster. 'What we achieved was an architectural coup. We captured the spirit of the company.'

1. 'The lens through which the Foster oeuvre has come to be viewed' – the north elevation of the Hongkong Bank (1979-1986), which faces onto open public space at the water's edge.

What strikes the visitor so often about the interior of Foster's buildings – the Sainsbury Centre, for example – is the sense of detail: the beautifully judged gradation of large to small components.
Alastair Best, *Norman Foster*, 1986

It is interesting to note how frequently good architectural solutions bring secondary benefits. It is the process of 'achieving more with less'. There are numerous cases within the Sainsbury Centre where economy is achieved through making components do more than one job. I will instance a small one: the neoprene gaskets which form the seal between the structure and cladding panel system form 'gutters' to carry rainwater off the roof down to drainage channels running along the sides of the building. There is no internal rainwater piping – no costs, therefore, and no blockages, leakage or maintenance problems.
Loren Butt, lecture at the Construction Industry Conference, London, 15 May 1980

1. A building 'about light and space never achieved before': the Sainsbury Centre for the Visual Arts (1974-1978). Its smooth-skinned structure brought a new degree of refinement to the lightweight, steel-framed enclosures designed for industrial clients in the early years of the practice.

2. Viewed from the roof the dynamic outrigged structure of the Renault Centre (1980-1982) contrasts strikingly with the smooth exterior of the Sainsbury Centre. At Renault, 30,000 square metres of multi-functional space are enclosed beneath a single roof membrane.

3. An elevation of the Renault Centre shows how the primary structure runs outside the perimeter walls, allowing all elements of the architectural skeleton to be expressed. The nautical joints, guy rods and drilled-out webs animate the facade with constantly changing shadow patterns.

Foster's design sketches for Willis Faber & Dumas perfectly reflect the process of questioning and probing for the initiative that enabled such a coup to take place. They start with an awkwardly-angled geometrical building that leaves slivers of its amoebic medieval site on all sides; from there they develop into various ziggurat forms which are dismissed as structurally unsatisfactory; and finally they venture into a fully glazed envelope with an inverted ziggurat within. 'Great possibilities! But we lack time and technical expertise,' noted Foster at the time – and indeed this idea was not to be developed until later, for the Hammersmith redevelopment project and, more recently, at King's Cross.

The final solution to the problem at Willis Faber & Dumas only emerged after all these possibilities had been pursued to the limit. Eventually the sketches begin to define with increasing confidence the wide structural grid, stepped escalator circulation, faceted, transomless, mullionless glass walls, and the helipad-equipped roof garden of the final version. Today Foster's sole regret is that the proposed *porte-cochère* entrance to the reception was not retained.

At the Sainsbury Centre for Visual Arts, 1974-1978, the Foster process of analytical redefinition was more complicated. The Sainsbury collection and the accommodation for the Arts Department of the University of East Anglia were not only originally conceived as occupying separate buildings, but the architectural commission itself was at first to have been shared between Foster and the Dutch-Indonesian architect Kho Lang Ie. The tragic death of Kho Lang Ie early on in the project inevitably led to a reassessment of the whole commission and it was only then, after considerable discussion between Norman Foster, Sir Robert and Lady Sainsbury and the University authorities, that the single-building solution emerged.

**At the Sainsbury Centre everything that is not space is hidden within structure, and where there is no structure – as at each end of the great inverted 'U' – there is glass. As Foster's former associate Richard Horden has said, the building is 'about light and space never achieved before'.**

When it did the project was one of breathtaking simplicity. The Sainsbury Centre is a 120-metre long inverted 'U' with its two 7.5-metre legs joined by a 35-metre wide roof. The structural 'U' shape is built up from welded-steel tubes so as to create a 'thick wall' effect. Within the 2.4-metre zone between the inner and outer skins are located lobbies, lavatories, stores, darkrooms and plant. Far from being two buildings, the Sainsbury Centre brings the collection and the department together in a single, astounding interior space with its own advanced artificial and daylight control system. The 'thick wall' concept creates a simplicity and purity of outline, inside and out, that is as different from the 'bolt-on' appearance of his former partner's Centre Pompidou, in Paris, as it is possible to imagine. At the Sainsbury Centre everything that is not space is hidden within structure, and where there is no structure – as at each end of the great inverted 'U' – there is glass. As Foster's former associate Richard Horden has said, the building is 'about light and space never achieved before'.

**Discussing his office's most recently completed and most articulated project, the Renault Centre, Foster says: 'There is no need to expose everything or conceal everything. One has to integrate. Renault is surprisingly Classical in what it expresses' – rather like the Comet jet airliner of 1949 or NASA's space shuttle – all reference points.** Jonathan Glancey, *The Architectural Review*, July 1983

Left: The streamlined fuselage and gracefully swept wings of the de Havilland Comet, the first generation of commercial passenger jet aircraft, which opened a new era of commercial air travel in 1952.
Right: The space shuttle, the first and only reusable space vehicle, which made its maiden flight in April 1981.

In one way the building for Renault at Swindon, 1980-1982, is unique in that there was no apparent redefinition of the brief in the early stages. Sébastien de la Selle, Renault's Coordinateur d'Expression Visuelle at the time, commissioned Foster after visiting Willis Faber & Dumas and the Sainsbury Centre and, apart from the exigent functional requirements of the building, the French car company had no preconceptions about the design.

Foster was asked to provide a vast 30,000-square-metre enclosure for parts storage, training, showroom and office purposes, with the prospect of a later enlargement to 40,000 square metres. With the brief established, the expression of lifestyle here took the form of an abandonment of the previous Foster trademark of enveloping form, and the adoption instead of a structure-driven umbrella roofing system. This consists of a forest of steel masts supporting projecting beams stayed by steel tension rods. At Renault the conventional wisdom that roof penetrations should be avoided is stood on its head: there are no fewer than 456 separate penetrations of the huge, continuous, solvent-welded PVC roof membrane in the form of structural members, roof-lights and smoke vents. The result is a radical silhouette in which structure, for the first time in Foster's work, completely dominates the building's appearance.

We should also note two further examples of analytical brief redefinition in Foster's career. The first, and perhaps most dramatic, occurred at the competition stage of the commission for a new headquarters for the Hongkong and Shanghai Banking Corporation, which started out with two options already prepared by the client. It was only at the end of a research phase, equalled by none of the other invited entrants, that Foster was able to win the commission by proposing a third solution that transcended both original strategies.

More recently, the King's Cross redevelopment project – which began with Foster being asked by London Regeneration Consortium to contribute a single building to a masterplan prepared by another firm of architects – quickly evolved into a commission to prepare an alternative masterplan. This masterplan featured the creation of a large park and a complex transport interchange, clear-spanned by an advanced-technology envelope, neither of which had existed in the earlier version.

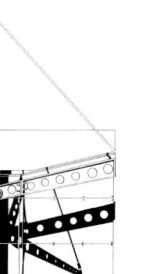

The Years of Innovation 287

**When Charles Jencks announced in 1977 that the demolition of Pruitt Igoe represented the death of modern architecture, he invoked an interpretation of the project that has today gained widespread acceptance. Anyone remotely familiar with the recent history of American architecture automatically associates Pruitt Igoe with the failure of High Modernism.** Katherine G Bristol, *Journal of Architectural Education,* May 1991
Right: Initially lauded for its cost-effectiveness, Helmuth, Yamasaki and Leinweber's Pruitt Igoe public housing project (1955) was demolished in 1972, following decades of neglect and criticism of its design flaws.

**Every time I see a television documentary or a critical article on the state of modern architecture I've got rather accustomed to being told that this movement 'happily died' – to quote Charles Jencks – at the precise time of three o'clock in the afternoon on 15 July 1972, with the demolition of the Pruitt Igoe block of flats.** Norman Foster, lecture at the UIA Conference, Brighton, 13 July 1987

These examples of the application of Foster's design lifestyle to the practice of architecture clearly show the pattern and force of a technique that can be detected throughout his career. In each case the same analytical skills are deployed from the very first moment of client approach, and it is in the exercise of them that the seeds are planted for his unique buildings. As the artist Ben Johnson – who has executed remarkable paintings of many of Foster's buildings, including several bold interiors of Willis Faber – once said: 'I know it is the "concept" of that building that created the masterpiece, because I watched what happened to the people who came from the old office in Southend and went to work there. It transformed them; it turned them into better, healthier and happier human beings.'

## Foster's buildings were not rearguard actions fought by the old Modernism. Instead they were the pioneering structures of another, newer rationality.

While it is partly due to their unique process of inception that Willis Faber & Dumas, the Sainsbury Centre and the Renault Distribution Centre attract the admiring and the curious from all over the world, there is another powerful reason for the unique status they hold in the architectural firmament. Not only are they buildings that emerged from a new process of design, but they are also the sole masterpieces of a discredited era.

In conception they are all buildings of the 1970s (although Renault came at the very end of the decade) and the 1970s were the years of the death of Modern architecture: a time that by common agreement produced few architectural landmarks.

The decade of the 1970s was a period of ideological bankruptcy in politics, economics and architecture. It marked the end of many of the unquestioned certainties of the post-war years; the end of unquestioned deficit spending by the governments of the Western nations; the end of unquestioned public-sector investment in housing and social welfare building; the end of unquestioned cheap energy and guiltless environmental damage; and the end of an unquestioned public consensus in favour of Modern architecture. If a single date must be assigned to the commencement of this era of disillusionment, it is not the parochial but much-quoted 15 July 1972 when the low cost public housing project of Pruitt Igoe was filmed being dynamited to the ground in St Louis, but 6 October 1973 when engineers of the Egyptian Army bridged the Suez Canal under fire and began the Yom Kippur War.

From that war flowed the Arab oil embargo, and from the oil embargo the massive inflationary shock to the economies of the West that resulted from an overnight 500 per cent increase in the price of Middle Eastern oil. Adjustment to this shock, and the state of economic and political uncertainty that accompanied it, was the story of the rest of the decade. It was a time of fear, a time of disaster, and a time of opportunity. From the wreckage of the old socialised states of Europe emerged new political and economic attitudes, and nowhere more drastically than in Britain.

From the 1973 oil embargo onwards, successive governments struggled to maintain the status quo and failed. Modern architecture, its limitless state funding removed, drifted from the penumbra of mild disappointment into a black pit of public loathing. Slashed budgets and abandoned plans downgraded the built environment and as the environment deteriorated so the architects who had built it were blamed for its failure. It was not a good time to be a Modern architect.

1

But notwithstanding the well-documented manifestations of this era of uncertainty – the property boom, the energy crisis, the three-day week and the winter of discontent – Foster's architecture not only survived but prospered. It prospered because by its very nature it contrived to connect itself to the public consciousness, not with the past – the post-war architecture of social welfare that had failed – but with the future. The future of an advanced-technology, 'more-for-less', design science that would manifest itself in a new kind of architecture. In addition to their technological ingenuity, their speed of erection and their economy, their appearance as something utterly different to the heavy *béton brut* of the final years of public-sector Modern architecture, Foster's buildings of the 1970s possessed another quality that was unique: they radiated competence, control, performance and beauty in an environment of fear, incompetence, failure and ugliness. The magnetism of those buildings, perhaps their true significance, derives from this.

Willis Faber, the Sainsbury Centre and Renault were each in their way buildings of crisis. They were designed and constructed at a time of inflation, strikes and recession, but there was nothing about them that spoke of failure or even half-failure. They were something in the field of architecture that had not been seen for fifty years: they were triumphs of anticipatory design that radiated new possibilities. Like the early villas of Le Corbusier, the prefabricated housing of Ernst May, and the whole creative ethos of the Bauhaus, they were socially and environmentally predictive. Foster's buildings showed how people might live and work in another way in the future – once the bad times were over.

Just as the early skyscraper projects of Mies van der Rohe radiated an order and optimism belied by the inflationary chaos of Weimar Germany, so Willis Faber & Dumas, the Sainsbury Centre and Renault promised a better ordering of the elements of life and a new harmony after the passing of the 'winter of discontent'.

Unlike many of the buildings of the 1970s – London's Alexandra Road housing scheme is a classic example – Foster's buildings were not rearguard actions fought by the old Modernism. Instead they were the pioneering structures of another, newer rationality. Light, where Alexandra Road was heavy; private, where Alexandra Road was public; fast, where Alexandra Road was slow; innovative, where Alexandra Road harked back to a concrete technology that was new in the 1920s; each of Foster's buildings in its way was a promise for the future.

## Foster's buildings of the 1970s radiated competence, control, performance and beauty in an environment of ugliness.

Fifteen years before 'Big Bang', Willis Faber & Dumas had open-planned, 4,000-square-metre office floors, complete with under-floor servicing, still – at the time of writing – larger than any dealing room in the City of London. Designed before the Yom Kippur War, Willis Faber & Dumas anticipated the energy crisis in an uncanny way with its heavily insulated grass roof; deep plan, giving minimal surface area for internal volume; and power by natural gas. Although it was constructed during the February 1974 crisis of the three-day week when the normal forty-hour working week was cut to twenty-four hours, it was completed ahead of schedule by a characteristically masterful reprogramming of construction to anticipate material shortages.

1. Foster Associates' 1987 King's Cross masterplan had as its centrepiece a new international terminal situated between King's Cross and St Pancras stations. A vast glass envelope was to enclose the triangular geometry of the site to create a daylit concourse.

2. The light and elegant Frankfurt Leichtathletikhalle project (1981-1986). With its massive clear span and low silhouette surrounded by trees it is clearly a progenitor of the King's Cross Terminal structure.

**Domed-over cities have extraordinary economic advantage. A two-mile diameter dome ... calculated to cover Mid-Manhattan Island ... has a surface area which is only 1/85 the total area of the buildings which it would cover. It would reduce the energy losses either in winter heating or summer cooling to 1/85 the present energy cost obviating snow removals. The cost saving in ten years would pay for the dome.** Richard Buckminster Fuller, *Utopia or Oblivion*, 1969

Right: Buckminster Fuller's 1950 Dome over Manhattan project. Two decades later, Foster and Fuller were to collaborate on a further exploration of the practical applications of an environmental envelope structure, albeit on a smaller scale, in the Climatroffice project.

---

1. 'Great possibilities!' An early Norman Foster sketch for Willis Faber & Dumas (1971-1975) proposes a fully glazed envelope and internal cantilevered floors. This proposal was not pursued, but the practice was to further explore the concept in the form of the Climatroffice project (1971) undertaken with Richard Buckminster Fuller.

2. 'A modern classic', the Willis Faber & Dumas building's innovative democratisation of the workplace and pioneering energy-conscious design have come to be regarded as commonplace features of the contemporary office.

Like the 1971 IBM building, which absorbed an 800 per cent increase in computing power over fifteen years without structural alteration, or the Hongkong Bank which is poised to permit the same revolution in the future with its aircraft-style raised floor system, Willis Faber was a perfect example of anticipatory design – a building that combined all its elements into a whole that was greater, and more valuable, than the sum of its parts.

Unlike the pyramids of Egypt, St Paul's Cathedral or Alexandra Road; Willis Faber, the Sainsbury Centre and the Renault building are all synergetic buildings. In one sense they are simply objects of usefulness, but in another they have already transcended usefulness to attain another scale of value altogether. They are in a literal sense anachronisms – timeless achievements in an age of continuous technical development that gives a shelf-life to its artistic creations as much as its manufactures. There are cars, aeroplanes, yachts and computers that hold the status of Foster buildings, but all of them are rare and all of them achieved their status in defiance of the general law of late twentieth-century industrial production which says, because technical development is continuous, that no single product must dawdle in the limelight but must either vacate it swiftly in favour of something cheaper and better, or else become part of some other composite product in a synergetic fusion.

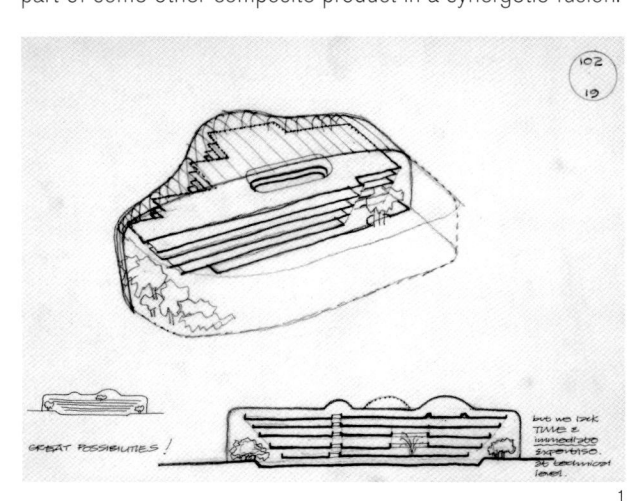

Richard Buckminster Fuller (1895-1983), who originated the concept of cumulative technical advantage that is called synergy, called this evolutionary process the 'Law of Ephemeralisation'. For him it explained the transformation of the eighteenth-century craftsman's timepiece into the twentieth-century's mass-produced quartz watch – a device that is not only infinitely smaller, lighter and more accurate than its handmade predecessor, but is priceless in another way: it has become so universally available as to be almost without value.

For Fuller the watch, the pen, the telephone, the calculator, the camera, the bicycle, electric power, water supply, artificial heating and cooling, the car and the building were all goods or services destined for ephemeralisation – objects fated to evolve into something as effortlessly available as the seeds of plants, or merge as easily with other goods and services as the unseen parasites that live upon the human body.

Before he died in 1983, Fuller saw the entire process coming true. Today there is no car without a clock; soon there will be no car without a telephone. Today there is no building – at least in the developed world – without water and electric power. Soon there will be no building without climate control. One day there will be a climate-controlled environment – and the component parts of it will not even be called buildings.

One of the most important things that Foster's career shows us is what it means to be a successful architect in this age of ephemeralisation. In his work we can see how, amid a cascade of innovations that diffuse and coalesce with bewildering speed, there can be individual artistic creations called buildings that still become objects of pilgrimage. As Willis Faber & Dumas, the Sainsbury Centre and the Renault Centre demonstrate, it is only by truly extraordinary feats of synergetic design that the evolving complexes of environmental technology, which we call buildings, can survive. These masterpieces will retain their identity because they have become benchmarks of technological and artistic advance; objects whose recognition is semantically necessary for the understanding of the age of ephemeralisation itself. Without such designed objects there would be no landmarks on the map of synergy; no signposts to direct product evolution; no true history of design at all.

Change is inevitable and irreversible – indeed it is probably the only constant as people come and go. And yet there are a very few important and fascinating examples of design whose balance of flexibility and integrity ensures their status as 'design classics'. Norman Foster, 'Flexibility in Design' lecture, Brighton, 7 April 1981
Right: The Volkswagen Beetle, designed by Ferdinand Porsche. Prototyped in 1936, it was officially launched in 1947 and continued in production in Germany until 1975. In 1972 it surpassed the 15,007,033 car production record set by the Model T Ford.

Since the end of the Second World War, the design of motor cars has been in constant revolution, but the standard against which most cars have been judged and found wanting … has been the Volkswagen … It had, until recently and with very few exceptions, a more advanced technical specification than any other vehicle produced in quantity … In a world of automotive flux its appearance remained constant and … when cars grew larger year by year, it remained the same size.
Reyner Banham, *The Architectural Review*, July 1961

Seen in this way a modern classic like the Willis Faber & Dumas building is an evolutionary archetype. It cannot be timeless in the sense claimed for the great historical achievements of architecture – which are regarded by art historians as objects of value irrespective of their usefulness (or lack of it) or their relevance (or lack of it) to present needs and skills. Instead it possesses evolutionary significance: and evolutionary significance means value as a sign, not as a symbol.

**There are cars, aeroplanes, yachts and computers that hold the status of Foster buildings, but all of them are rare and all of them achieved their status in defiance of the general law of late twentieth-century industrial production which says that no single product must dawdle in the limelight.**

It is in this archetypal sense that a sixty-year-old aircraft design like Donald Douglas' DC-3, or a car like Ferdinand Porsche's 1936 Volkswagen Beetle, or a building like Willis Faber & Dumas is a 'modern classic'. Such objects display in elegant form the resolution of so many functional demands and creative insights that they will remain alive in the minds of designers long after they cease to be new. They will remain alive as long as the concept 'aeroplane' or the concept 'automobile' or the concept 'building' has meaning in the world around us.

Machine-made objects that become part of the alphabet of technological ephemeralisation in this way are rare – as rare as individuals whose creative energies do not wane with age, the corruption of failure, or the distractions of success. In architecture their very existence transcends the art historical value system that recognises 'timeless' values instead of those timed by the clock of technological evolution. Foster's key buildings of the 1970s belong to a select company. Like the steel frame buildings of Mies van der Rohe, the Usonian houses of Frank Lloyd Wright and the concrete villas of Le Corbusier, they possess that unique combination of rich invention and technical completeness that is forever immune to the vagaries of fashion.

No student of the evolution of the modern house can ignore Farnsworth, Fallingwater or the Villa Savoye, for all these buildings embody formal and structural relationships that are not the creations of fashion or financial speculation, but stem from the exercise of a creative genius that works at a higher level. All of them are objective achievements which, as Mies van der Rohe said, 'express the inner structure of our time'. Thus it is with the form of the deep-plan commercial building after Willis Faber & Dumas or the art gallery after the Sainsbury Centre. No student of commerce or art can ignore these buildings, for they are modern classics of synergy and ephemeralisation; archetypes whose design is part of the basic vocabulary of art and science in the service of man. They are, in a literal sense, part of the language of twentieth-century architecture, for it is a language that cannot be spoken without them.

# Connections  Willis Faber & Dumas

Willis Faber & Dumas pioneered the concept of 'lifestyle' in the workplace, introducing 'flexi-time' and providing a range of amenities, including a swimming pool, roof garden, restaurant, café and bar. This 'lifestyle' approach has since been developed further for other owner-occupier clients, such as Electronic Arts. In the early 1970s, with its low-rise form, deep-plan, large-span office floors, access flooring and atria, Willis Faber was considered radical. This approach is echoed in the design of the unbuilt BBC Radio Centre, and Willis Faber has since become the model for a new generation of developer-led 'groundscrapers', which are replacing high-rise 1960s office buildings in the City of London. The Willis Faber concept of 'gardens in the sky' was also inspirational in the development of a sequence of high-rise office buildings, such as the Commerzbank, and informed the 'social garden' for the twenty-four-hour workforce of HACTL, the world's most advanced automated container warehouse.

Willis Faber Ipswich 1975

BBC Centre

Electronic Arts - European HQ 2000
UK

Paragon - McLaren Centre 2002
UK

Tower Place
London 2002

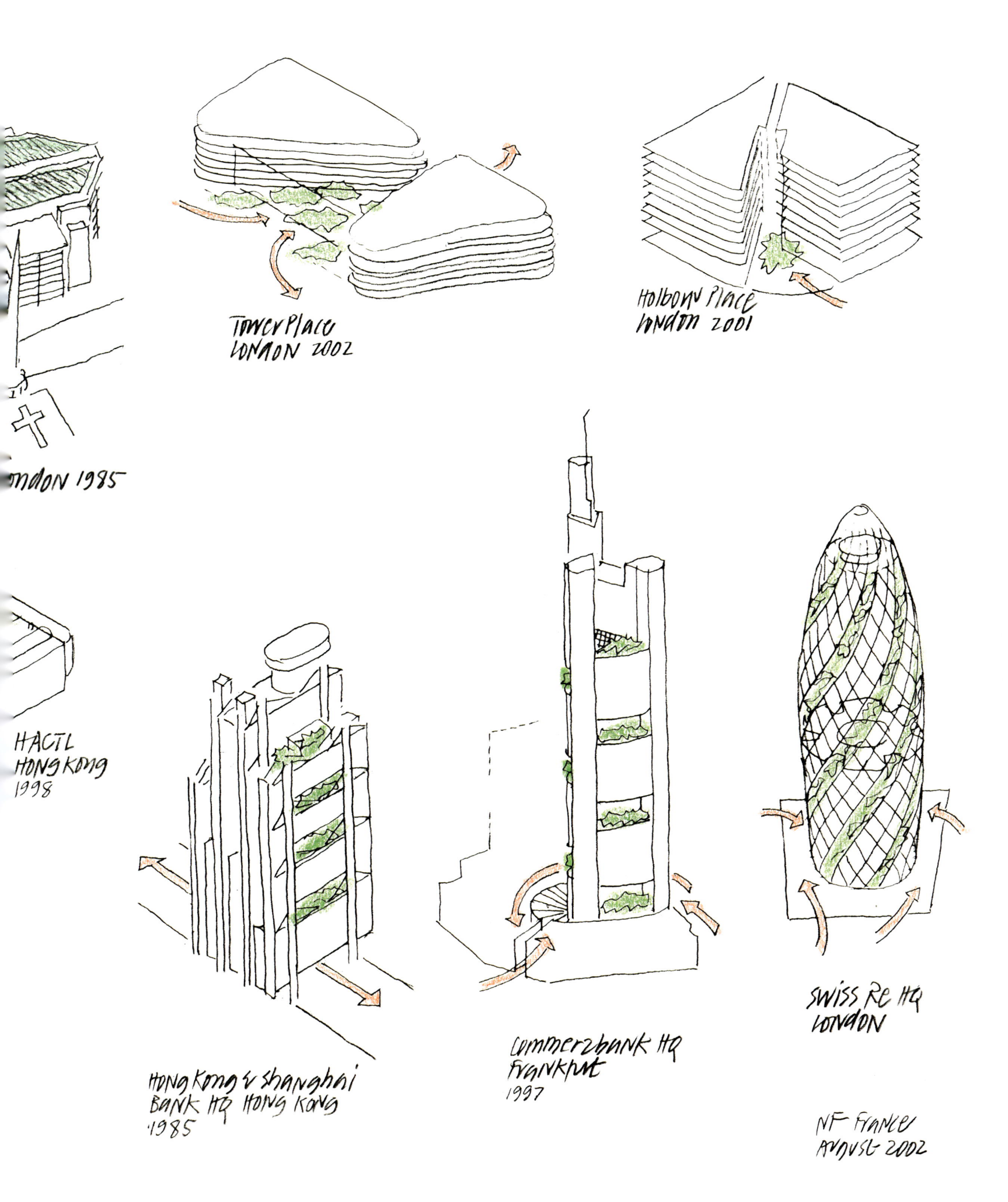

Holborn Place
London 2001

London 1985

HACTL
Hong Kong
1998

Hong Kong & Shanghai
Bank HQ Hong Kong
1985

Commerzbank HQ
Frankfurt
1997

Swiss Re HQ
London

NF Frances
August 2002

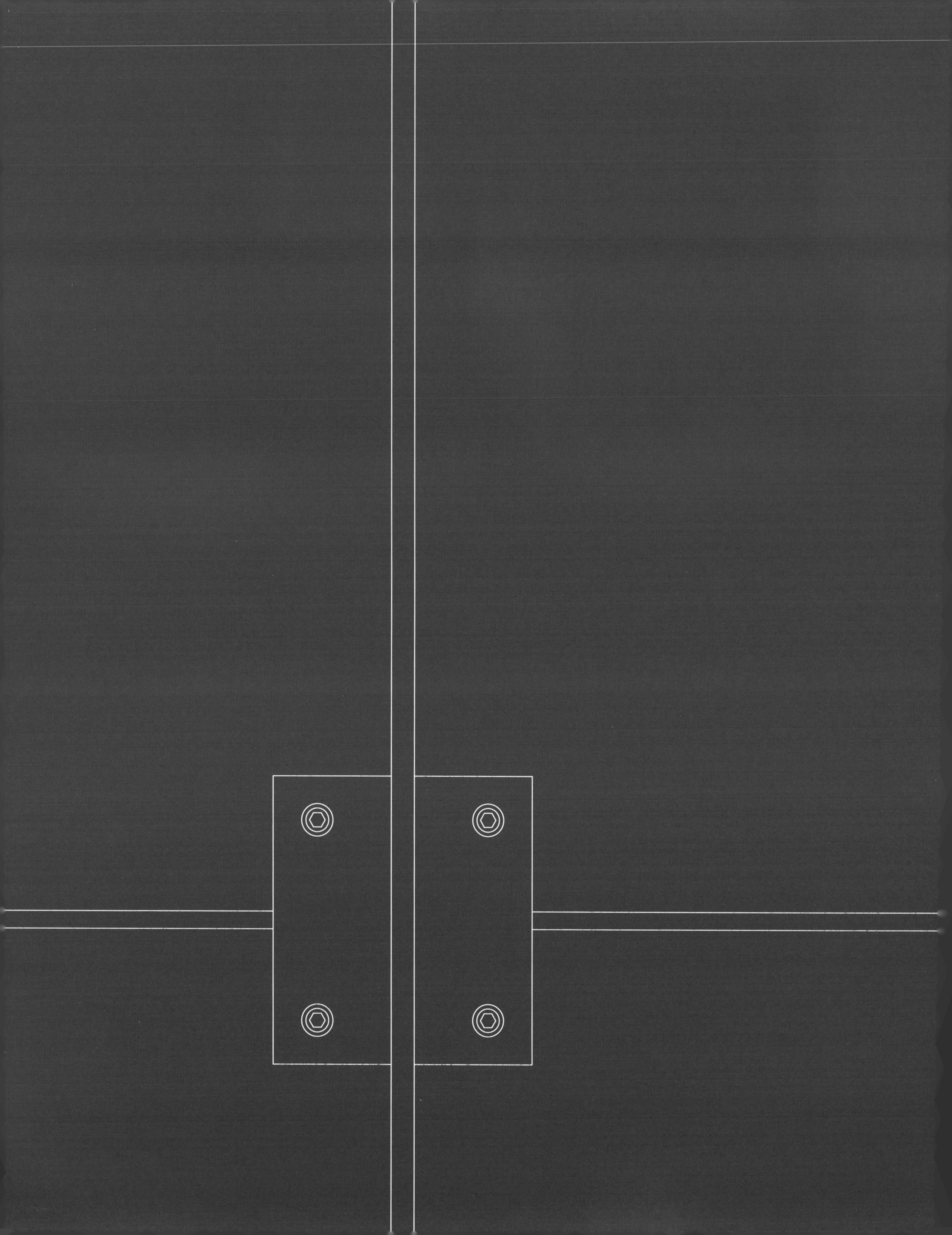

**Willis Faber & Dumas**
Ipswich, England 1971–1975

Willis Faber & Dumas challenged almost every preconception about office buildings. The atrium with its escalators, the social dimension of its roof garden and restaurant all help to engender a sense of community. Above all it is concerned with quality of life, and light – with introducing a little joy into the workplace. Conceived before the oil crises of the mid-1970s, and designed to burn natural gas, it was a pioneer of energy conscious design. It was also technologically advanced: the glass curtain wall pushed technology to its limits; and it was far sighted in anticipating the revolution in information technology by incorporating raised office floors – so much so that Willis Faber was virtually alone amongst insurance companies in being able to introduce computerisation without disruption. Uniquely for a post-war office building, it now enjoys Grade 1 listed status, which means that it cannot be changed – surely a contradiction in a building designed for flexibility!
Norman Foster

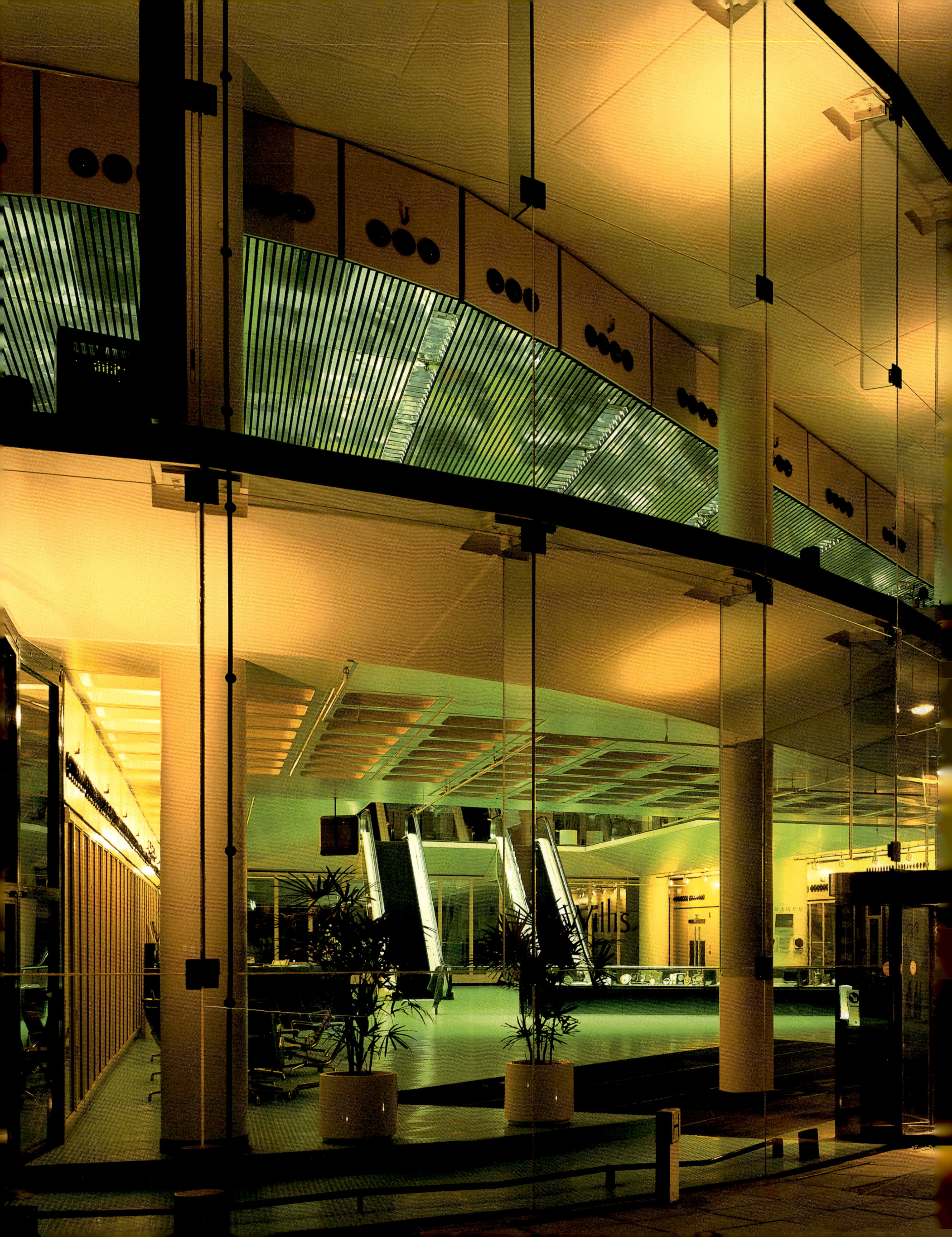

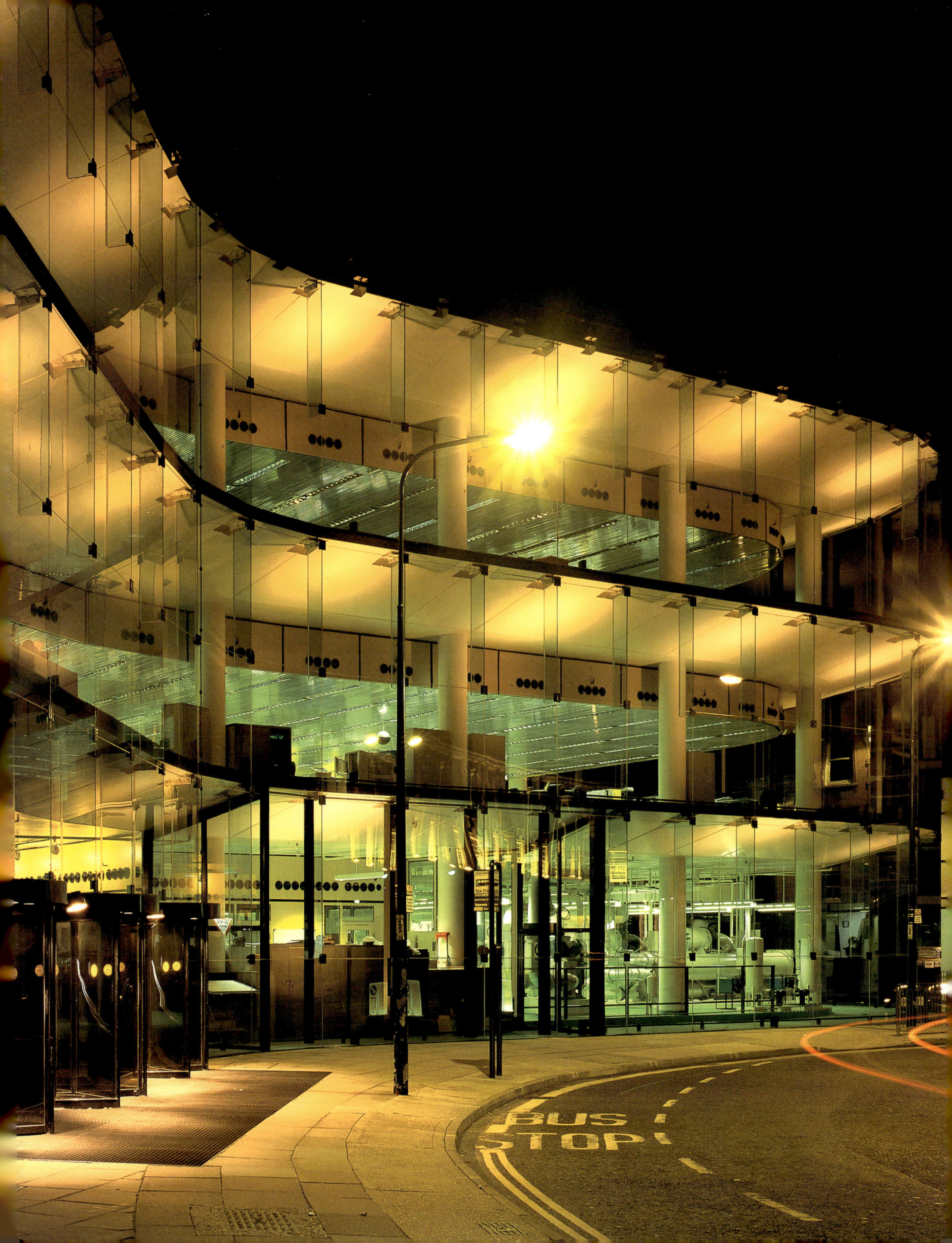
BUS
STOP

In a fundamental sense, the Willis Faber building is really about people and their place of work. Herman Kahn, American futurologist of the Hudson Institute, once made the point that those office buildings that failed to anticipate what he saw as inevitable social changes would simply become obsolete if they did not respond by raising standards and providing a high proportion of amenities. In his view these were not philanthropic gestures, just the hard cutting edges of changing real estate values. Our own experience bears this out. Norman Foster, *Architectural Design* 9-10, September-October 1977

Foster has always maintained that a better working environment improves morale and labour relations and he has used these arguments persuasively in countless commissions. At Willis Faber, for example, he was able to make the swimming pool the centrepiece of the main entrance by arguing that recreation should be an integral part of the working environment. This preoccupation with the social aspects of the architect's role, like his undiminished enthusiasm for state-of-the-art technology, marks Foster out as a late Modern who has survived the crisis of Postmodernism with his social rhetoric intact. Alastair Best, *Norman Foster*, 1986

**Ipswich is characterised by low-rise, articulated buildings bound together with winding streets of random geometry. Any new building had to respond to the scale of these surroundings and the pattern of streets.**

Norman Foster

Left: During the earliest phases of analysing the brief, members of the design team spent time at Willis Faber's Southend office recording staff working methods and practices. The offices there – accumulated in an ad hoc manner during the company's rapid expansion of the 1960s, and which the new building was to replace – demonstrated all the disagreeable symptoms associated with a typical insurance company's 'paper factory'. Photographs of the old offices were used in early presentations to convince the client that creating a better working environment should be a key concern in the new building.

9The country head office building for Willis Faber & Dumas in Ipswich represents an important turning point in the development of the Foster office. Not only was it Foster's largest building at that time, but it was by far the practice's greatest challenge. It developed and consolidated themes already explored in earlier projects – including the rapid relocation of office staff and the development of glass cladding systems – while with its raised floors, central atrium and banks of escalators, it is an important precursor of the Hongkong Bank. Significantly, it also anticipated the advent of flexible, deep-plan City office buildings by more than a decade.

Foster Associates' two most significant buildings prior to the Willis Faber commission – the single-storey pavilion for IBM in Cosham and the Fred Olsen Amenity Centre at Millwall Docks – had been smaller, simpler undertakings. Although they would inform the spirit of the project, they had offered only limited scope to explore the themes of social integration and democratic, flexible workplace design, which Willis Faber allowed Foster to develop to an unprecedented degree.

Willis Faber's business is insurance. The bulk of an insurance company's work, even in an electronic age, comprises 'paperwork' management on a heroic scale. While Willis Faber retained a head office in London, in the late 1960s its offices in Southend had – literally – housed this activity. However, due to the rising costs of being in the capital, the company wanted to concentrate a wider range of its activities in a country head office, capable of accommodating everything from computer data-processing to large-scale manual operations involving approximately 1,300 members of staff.

In August 1970, when Willis Faber made the decision to move out of London in force, it had a total of 2,100 employees, split between London and Southend. It was still almost a family firm. The directors knew many of the staff by their Christian names, having worked with them over many years; and the company had a relaxed management structure, with an 'open door' policy, which encouraged easy lines of communication at all levels.

Before deciding to move, the Willis Faber board had identified certain relocation criteria. These included: availability of a suitable freehold site near to a town centre; a sympathetic local authority; good road and rail communications with London; availability of staff and housing; good education facilities; and a pleasant working environment. Ipswich came out on top on a simple points basis.

**Willis Faber was by far the practice's greatest challenge. It developed and consolidated themes already explored in earlier projects and anticipated the advent of flexible, deep-plan office buildings by more than a decade.**

With guidance from the RIBA, Willis Faber prepared a shortlist of 'distinguished' architects. Kenneth Knight, then company secretary – and later coordinator of the project team that monitored the relocation exercise – summarised the chief selection criteria:

The brief: could the architects make a proper assessment of not only what the client wanted, but of what he ought to want? New technologies: did they take into account future environmental and other systems and have the ability to handle these possibilities? Detailed design: would it conform to the brief; were they looking at functional efficiency as well as aesthetic qualities?

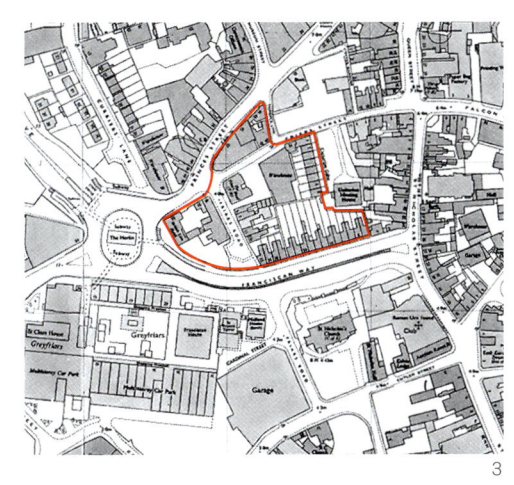

1. An aerial view of the Ipswich site before redevelopment. In the foreground can be seen a section of traffic roundabout and Franciscan Way – part of an aborted ring-road system that marked the edge of the old town.

2. The character and topography of Ipswich, with its ancient and twisting street pattern, was to be profoundly influential in the design of the building, and would lead the design team to a radical reappraisal of conventional attitudes to the design of large office blocks in urban centres.

3. The potential site area – indicated by the heavier outline – was split by two existing roads into three independent parcels of land. It was only several months into the project that Willis Faber secured the entire area for redevelopment.

Willis Faber & Dumas    299

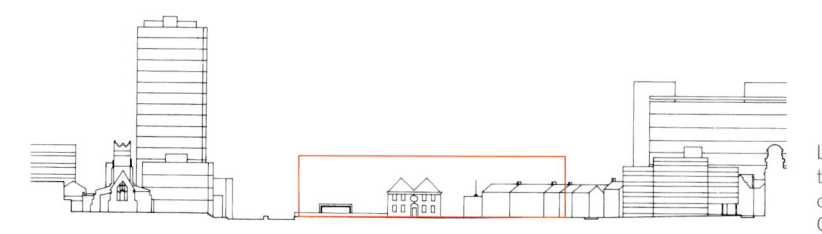

Left: A diagrammatic site section contrasts the profile of the final Willis Faber & Dumas scheme – shown in heavy outline – with the insensitive towers of the neighbouring Greyfriars development.

This sequence of sixteen annotated sketches by Norman Foster – from a total of 21 – clarifies his early ideas for the form of the building.

1. Simple geometry not acceptable for environmental reasons.

2. Valuable site area unused – awkward corners negate simple runs, pin-wheel solutions and centre well.

3. Overall podium block does not have enough capacity. Consider set-backs.

4. Suggests this – accommodates changes of height and light angles but structurally awkward with plan/section/space conflict.

5. OK but problems of separate access escape structure and why two not one building?

6. Difficult to divert services along preferred route – difficult to build over part of site – suggests one form.

7. Combination of pool / movement /café terraces in heart of building. Makes for social and technical conflicts – a building type not related to overlaps. Socially suggests usable space reduced significantly.

8. Ideal pool construction but unless larger 60-foot span feasible then problems.

9. Preferred location for pool and other larger span elements – socially (day and weekend) more interesting – compatible with strata studies.

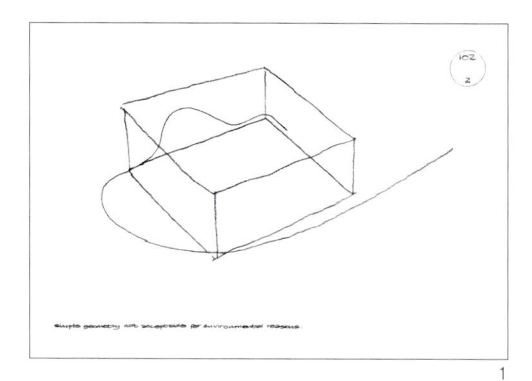

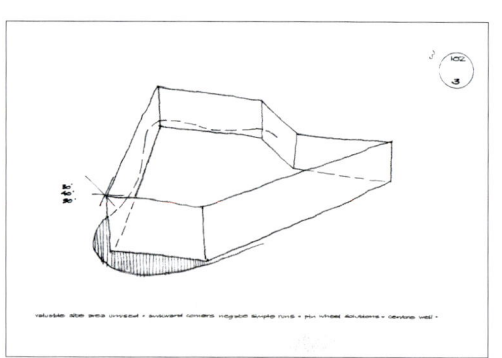

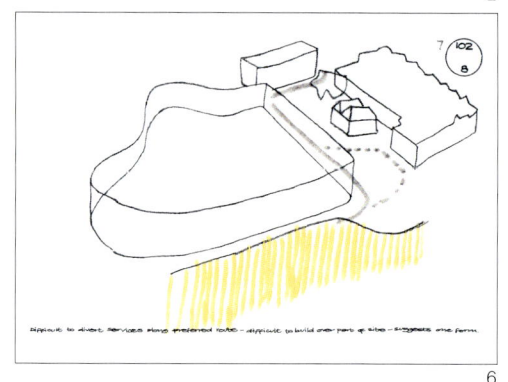

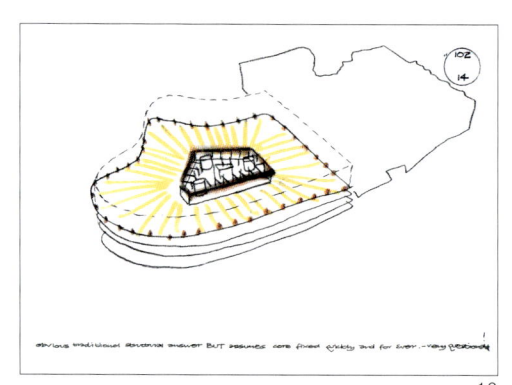

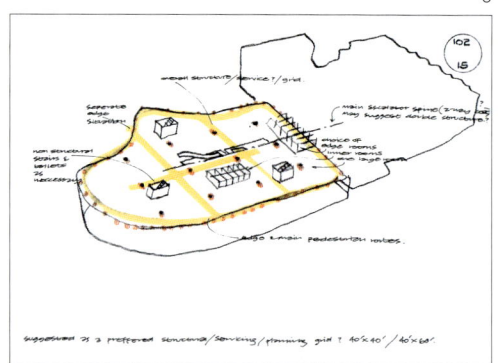

> **The most sympathetic and efficient building form was a low-profile, deep-plan building that could swell to the edges of the containing street pattern like a pancake in a pan.**
> Norman Foster

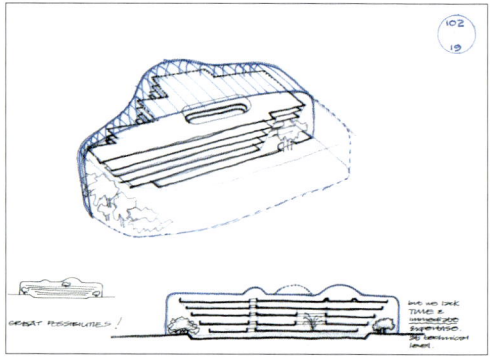

300  Norman Foster Works 1

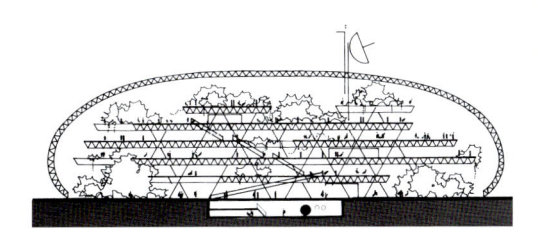

'One of our early ideas for the Willis Faber & Dumas building – the 'Climatroffice' – was inspired by Bucky and his vision of a bubble over New York. Beneath an artificial sky of filigree, so thin that there was almost nothing between you and the real heavens, would be a temperate microclimate filled with greenery and comfortable, low-energy spaces.'
Norman Foster, lecture at Stuttgart University,
14 May 1997
Left: A section throught the Climatroffice (1971).

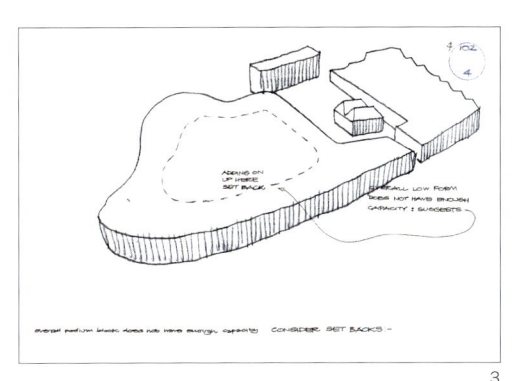

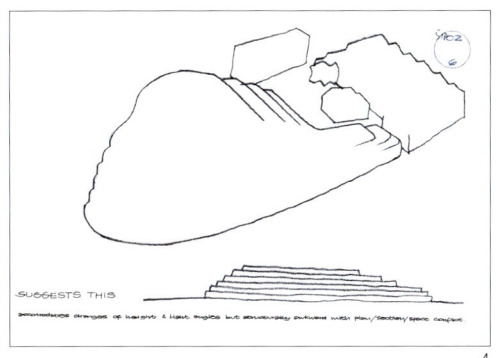

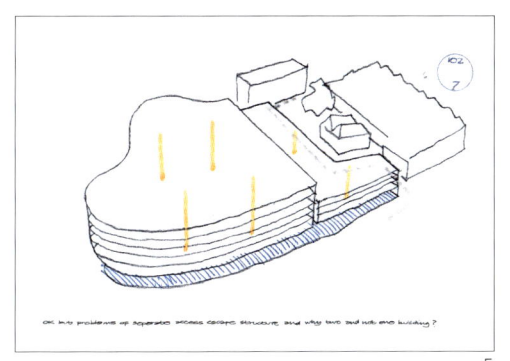

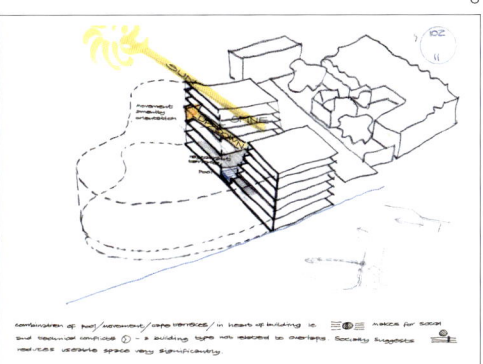

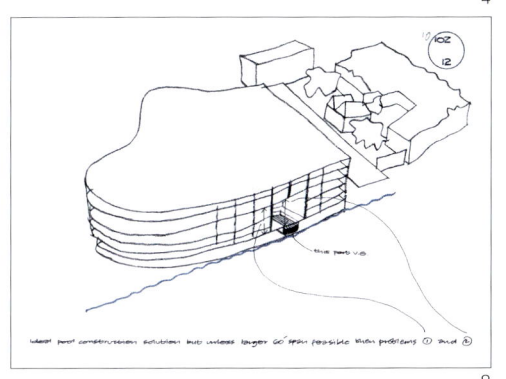

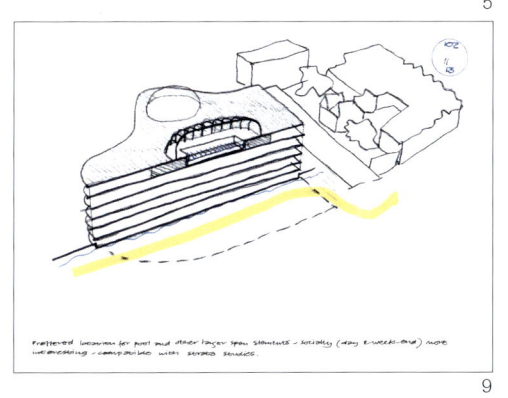

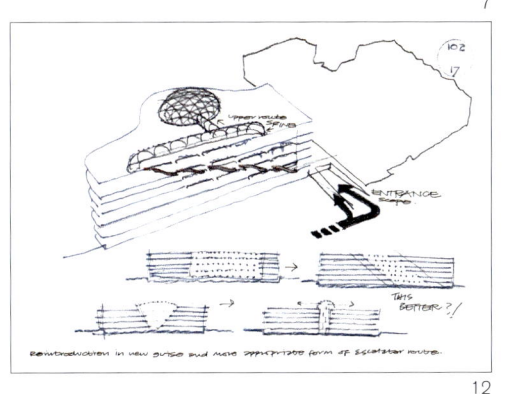

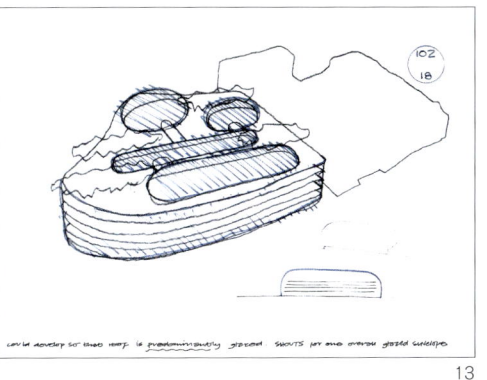

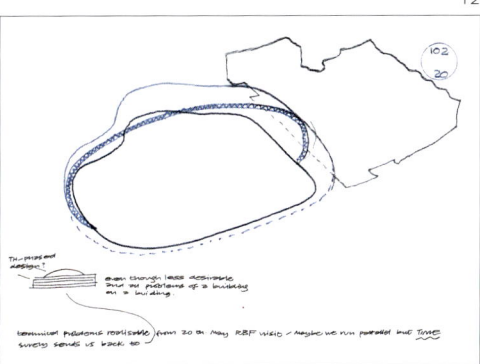

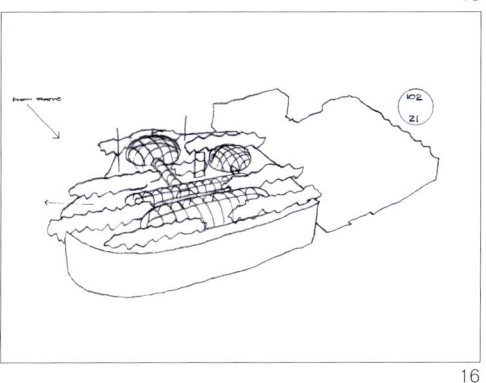

10. Obvious traditional structural answer but assumes core fixed quickly and for ever – questionable.

11. Suggested as a preferred structural/servicing/planning grid. 40 x 40, or 40 x 60 foot?

12. Reintroduction in new guise and more appropriate form of escalator route.

13. Could develop so that roof predominantly glazed. Shouts for overall glazed envelope.

14. Great possibilities! But we lack time and immediate expertise at technical level.

15. Technical problems realisable from 20 May RBF visit – maybe we run parallel but time surely sends us back to:

16. Could generate a unique roofscape/trees/gardens/sun/views out.

Willis Faber & Dumas  301

**With Willis Faber & Dumas, Foster Associates reaped the harvest of the social equalising management theory they had sown at Millwall Dock in collaboration with Fred Olsen Ltd ...**
**In this way, architecture becomes less of a grand cultural statement and more of a facilitator of socially balanced environments and a democratic rendezvous.** Malcolm Quantrill, *The Norman Foster Studio*, 1999

Right: Observations of routine collaborations between staff were recorded in colour-coded sketches and led to early proposals that a 'planned open office' would form the best organisational solution for the new building. Further probing of the client's brief included the compilation of a lengthy staff questionnaire.

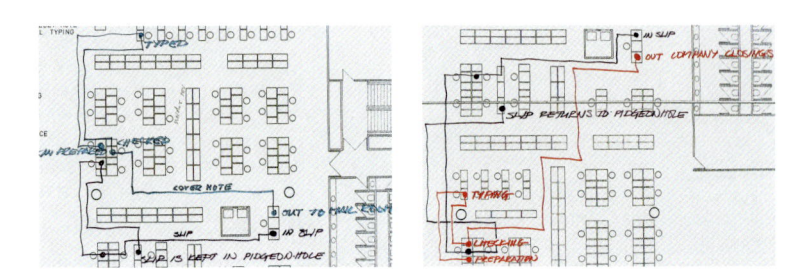

---

1. Norman Foster's sketch highlights the case against building a typical office tower on the site and calls for a more contextually sensitive solution.

2. The Willis Faber site lay next to a historic meeting house; the surrounding traditional buildings were low and extended to the edges of their sites to form narrow winding streets.

3. Time was short, which meant that the design and site acquisition had to proceed together. There were many unknowns – was the site a, b, c, and d or a combination of two or three of these? Could streets be closed or would they have to remain open, possibly with buildings spanning over them?

The construction process: how would they handle the choice of contractor and his detailed supervision to ensure completion within programme and to a controlled budget? Project supervision: a relatively minor point; was the practice of such a size that a partner would be involved at all stages?

The emphasis shifted focus, from the pragmatic to the sympathetic, as the interviews continued. Kenneth Knight identified another criterion: 'We sought to create at Ipswich a working environment at least as good as anything that had been achieved so far.' But in a telling caveat he added: 'We also required an architect who was cost-conscious and would not add to cost to achieve a good environment.'

## The Ipswich site was a hotchpotch of unrelated buildings beached on an island between the historic northern part of the town and a run-down southern zone.

Kenneth Knight recalls: 'Foster had developed a reputation for building quickly, keeping to timescale and achieving success within controlled budgets. In an inflationary climate, adherence to timescale has a great deal to do with maintaining budgets. Bearing in mind the three-day week and its consequences, Foster's timescale for the building was very fast – his appointment was in January 1971 and the formal opening on 2 June 1975.'

Norman Foster himself suggests that it was the charismatic figure of Johnny Roscoe – ex-chairman of Willis Faber and an influential member of the selection committee – who was largely responsible for his appointment. 'Every client needs one man in the organisation who will take the bold decision', says Foster. 'He is the first "architect" of the building and his presence helps to get proposals accepted which more conservative members of the board might otherwise reject.'

Roscoe and the Willis Faber board might be congratulated for their boldness in rewarding a then young, relatively unproven architect, with such a major building. That boldness is only slightly diminished by the fact that – IBM Cosham and Fred Olsen notwithstanding – they perhaps did not fully grasp how radical Foster's approach might be.

Prior to Foster's appointment, Willis Faber had prepared what Knight described a 'vast tome' on the company, its staff structure and procedures. That was swiftly balanced with a briefing document, prepared by the Foster team, which the client completed in the form of a questionnaire. It covered all aspects of the company's operations, down to the details of work flow and staff employment. Armed with this information, and backed up by staff interviews at all levels, the Foster team started to plan.

The site initially identified in Ipswich was a hotchpotch of unrelated buildings beached on an island between the historic northern part of the town and a run-down southern zone. Among its many challenges it was found to have a high water table; it was crossed by rights of way, which belonged to the Crown because no one else could prove ownership; it was cut in two by a road; and beneath that road was a series of telephone cables and a three-foot diameter sewer. To complicate matters further, it was uncertain how much land was actually available at the outset of the commission as the acquisition process was still ongoing.

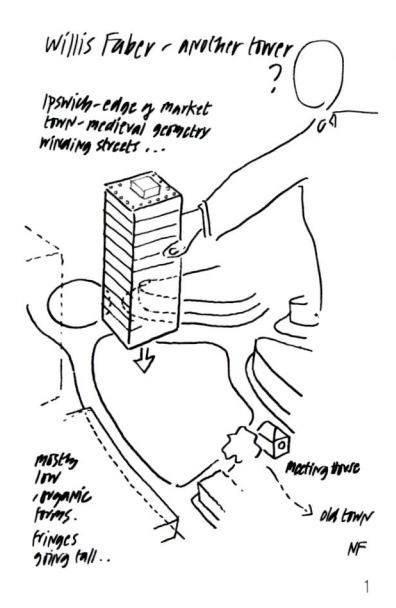

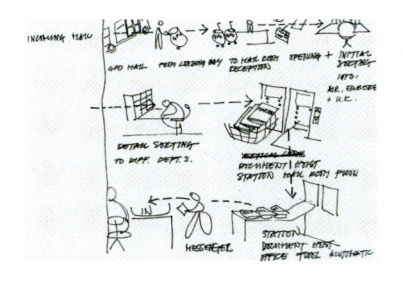

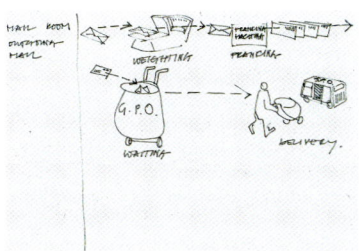

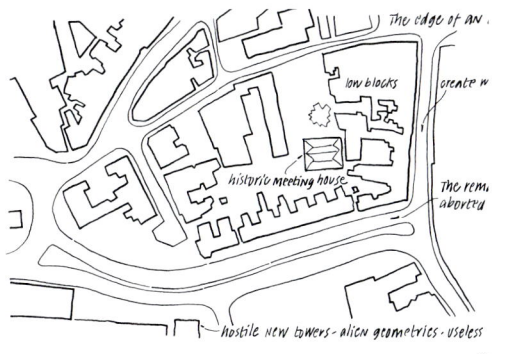

4. The proposal was deliberately open-ended and had two components – an inboard structure on a 14-metre square grid and an edge 'necklace' of columns. The inner structure was ideal for flexible offices and was capable of bridging over roads and a swimming pool.

5. In the final scheme the roads were closed allowing the building a clear and cohesive form. The edge necklace of columns followed the site boundary, while the main structure was aligned to accommodate an atrium and swimming pool in the best position in overall planning terms.

6. Four discrete minor cores were used – an arrangement that responded to servicing and escape requirements as well as the subdivision of the floors requested in the brief to allow possible sub-tenancies at a future date.

7. Two sketches lucidly demonstrate the urban spatial value of the low-rise deep-plan form adopted for the final scheme, as opposed to a conventional tower block solution.

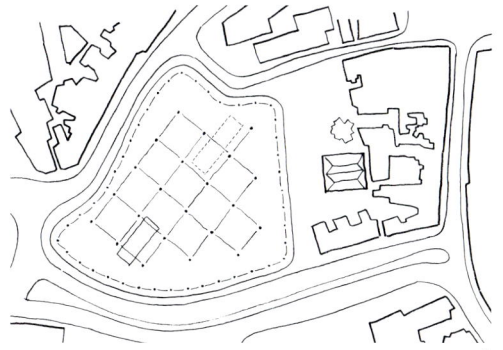

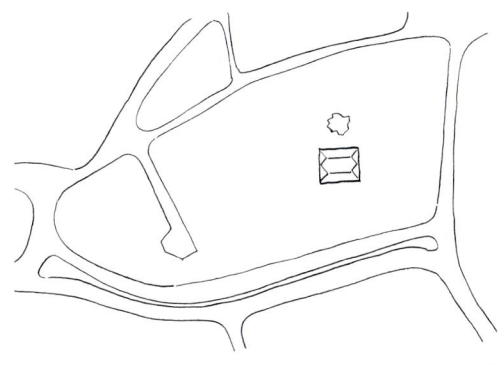

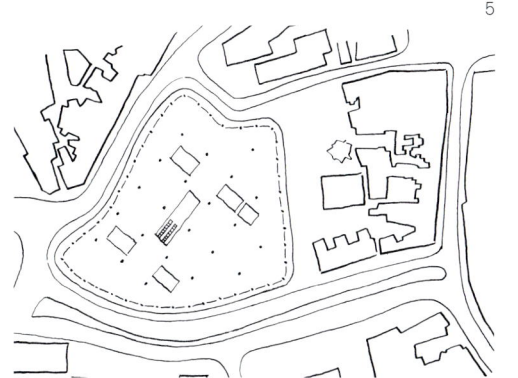

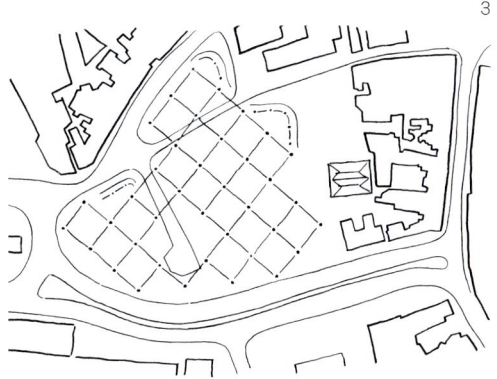

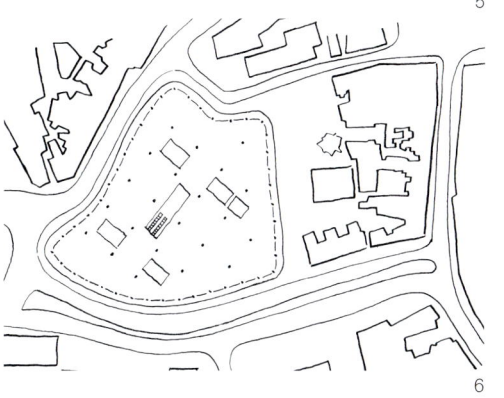

**The profile of the Willis Faber & Dumas building is a more civilised and humane response to a medieval market town than pushing towers up into the sky.**

Norman Foster

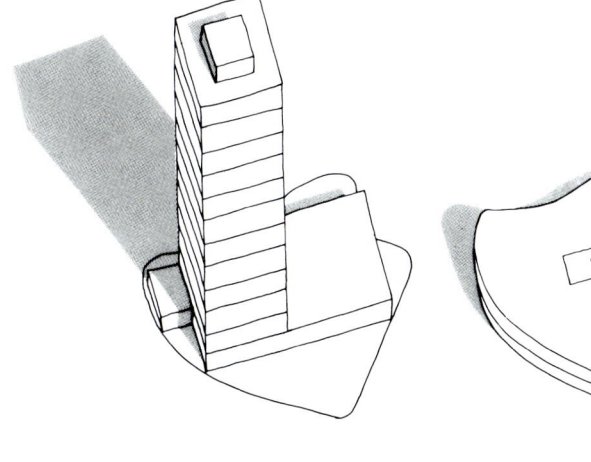

Willis Faber & Dumas  303

**Foster's buildings are technical contraptions; they come from another planet; they are unconcerned, tolerant, amnesiac Martians who land on earth with remarkable ease. One only has to see the serenity with which the most urban to date of Foster's buildings, the Ipswich offices for Willis Faber & Dumas, have taken their place on a humdrum site, the series of concavities and convexities coolly reflecting the surrounding townscape, integrating, defining and domesticating the chaotic environment.** François Chaslin, *Norman Foster*, 1986

**The ruthless and apparently automatic way in which the shape of a plan has been determined more by the accidents of the site rather than by the building's internal organisation, has … called for an architectural language which can do again what the corners of most Victorian blocks, especially pubs, could do so well in towns not having the convenient assistance of an orthogonal street grid … The line of the street, its origin now as obscure as that of a country lane, can be reaffirmed, and the street itself transformed, but with materials and techniques only available within the last decade.** Christopher Woodward, *The Architectural Review*, September 1975

**Clients are brave to take on Foster, for he may reorganise their idea of their own organisation through meticulous and inventive searching for a brief. Brave, also, to accept his architecture, for his process ensures that the buildings will never appear expected, however quickly they become accepted after the first shock.** John McKean, *The Architects' Journal*, 30 March 1983

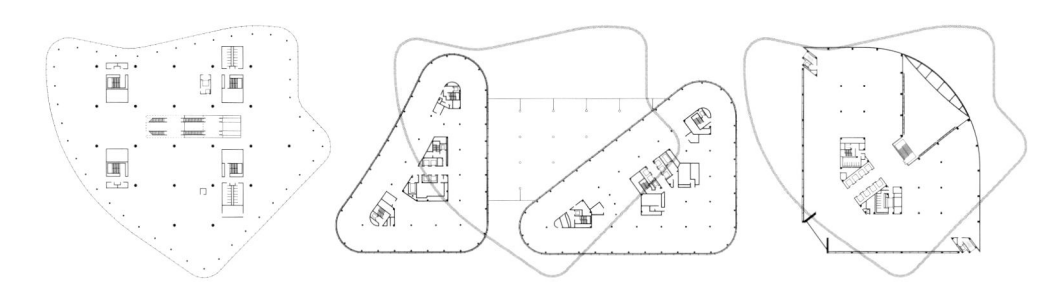

**My experience is that genuine innovation in office design is pioneered by owner-occupiers. Changes that stand the test of time then filter down to be adopted by the market. For example, in the 1970s Willis Faber pioneered the use of low-rise, deep-plan office floors. Today, with projects such as Tower Place and Holborn Place, we are replacing obsolete 1960s office towers with lower-rise structures. Although each is special to its site the design specifications are remarkably similar to those of Willis Faber. What was once avant-garde has become mainstream for developers.** Norman Foster, in conversation with the editor, 2002
Left: Comparative plans of Willis Faber & Dumas, Tower Place and Holborn Place respectively.

Norman Foster recalls: 'We were on board as architects from day one, working with the planners while the client was still purchasing the site, segment by segment. So we were responding on several fronts: to the needs of the client organisation, to the scope of a constantly evolving site and to the urban context of this small market town. Ipswich is characterised by low-rise buildings all bound together with winding streets of random geometry from a medieval past. Any new building had to respond to the scale of these surroundings – the streets being the most important spaces in the town.'

These factors prompted a series of early responses. Many alternative building forms were considered. Towers were examined, but rejected because they were inefficient or out of character with the neighbouring buildings, particularly the adjoining Unitarian Meeting House, a listed building of 1700.

Norman Foster again: 'Our response to the unknowable site was to develop a system that, if necessary, could cover the whole of Ipswich. It is based on a 14-metre-square structural grid with a fluid edge necklace of columns that follow the street contours. The main structural bay is wide enough to leap across a swimming pool, or span a road. So when the client acquired what he called the Legal & General site, we just said "yes" and extended the system. The existing building was pulled down, the road was closed, another road was diverted and the site became a different shape. The response was really to create a building that could preserve and reinforce the street pattern, rather than impose an alien geometry on the site and then have to cope with the problems of left-over space.'

This evolutionary process can be charted through Foster's sketches of the period; all the key concerns and elements were explored, though not at this stage fully resolved. An atrium was introduced to bring sun into the heart of the building; various locations for a swimming pool were suggested – possibly as part of the atrium, possibly in its own enclosure on the roof – and other secondary structures were suggested for the roof-top, together with a rich covering of planting.

The problems of servicing from a central core were also contrasted with a clearly preferred solution for a grid of 'mini-cores' to allow the possibility of subletting one or more floors, while escalators are introduced into the atrium, which develops through several configurations.

'Shouts for one overall glazed envelope', read Foster's notes at one point. Significantly, it was in response to the highly fluid early stages of Willis Faber that Foster developed the concept of the 'Climatroffice' – a transparent, glazed lightweight dome with its own interior micro-climate – doubtless inspired by his active collaboration with Buckminster Fuller at that time. Foster remembers Fuller observing one day how much easier the whole Willis Faber exercise would have been, 'if you just put a big space enclosure over the whole thing – existing and new'. Foster bounced this idea around and Climatroffice was the result. It raised the possibility of limitless flexibility because the division between the inside and outside worlds could be completely dissolved.

Climatroffice remained an abstract concept, but it informed the design team's thinking. Flexibility in the form of multi-functional spaces, energy conservation, enclosing the maximum space within the minimum envelope, and maximising natural light are recurrent themes in Foster's work, then and now. Early visualisations bear witness to Foster's rapid working methods and to the crucial importance of developing an understanding of not only how the building would work, but also how it might look and feel.

1. An aerial view of the completed building in its context. The medieval pattern of winding streets at the edge of the old city reads very clearly, the building flowing to the edges of its irregular site 'like a pancake in a pan'. Though not unprecedented, the decision to 'recreate the site' at roof level by covering it with grass was unusual: it was certainly unique for an office building. The first aim of the initial proposal had been to provide the users of the building with a positive amenity for their enjoyment and relaxation. But it also had significant practical advantages: the roof offered such good insulation value that it was possible to eliminate, at a stroke, the need for any expansion joints within the structure.

The Willis Faber building could perhaps be related to something that I am personally very familiar with. There are not many left. It is a building type from the north of England, the traditional Corn Exchange. The Corn Exchange is a nineteenth-century building and has some interesting ingredients: you always knew where you were in it; it had a public space which was at the heart of it; you changed level in that public space; it had working areas either side; and it had a generosity of top light. Norman Foster, lecture at the Metropolitan Museum of Art, New York, 24 November 1982
Right: Leeds Corn Exchange, completed by Cuthbert Broderick in 1863: one of the finest of its type.

1. The earliest drawings of the scheme show two floors of offices sandwiched between ground level amenities and a landscaped roof with independent pavilions. The roof-lit 'escalator hall' lies at the heart of the building. Only the roof-top plant rooms are obviously at variance with the completed scheme.

2, 3. These sketches by Norman Foster capture the diagrammatic simplicity of the final planning concept: escalators move up through the building to arrive at sunlight and greenery.

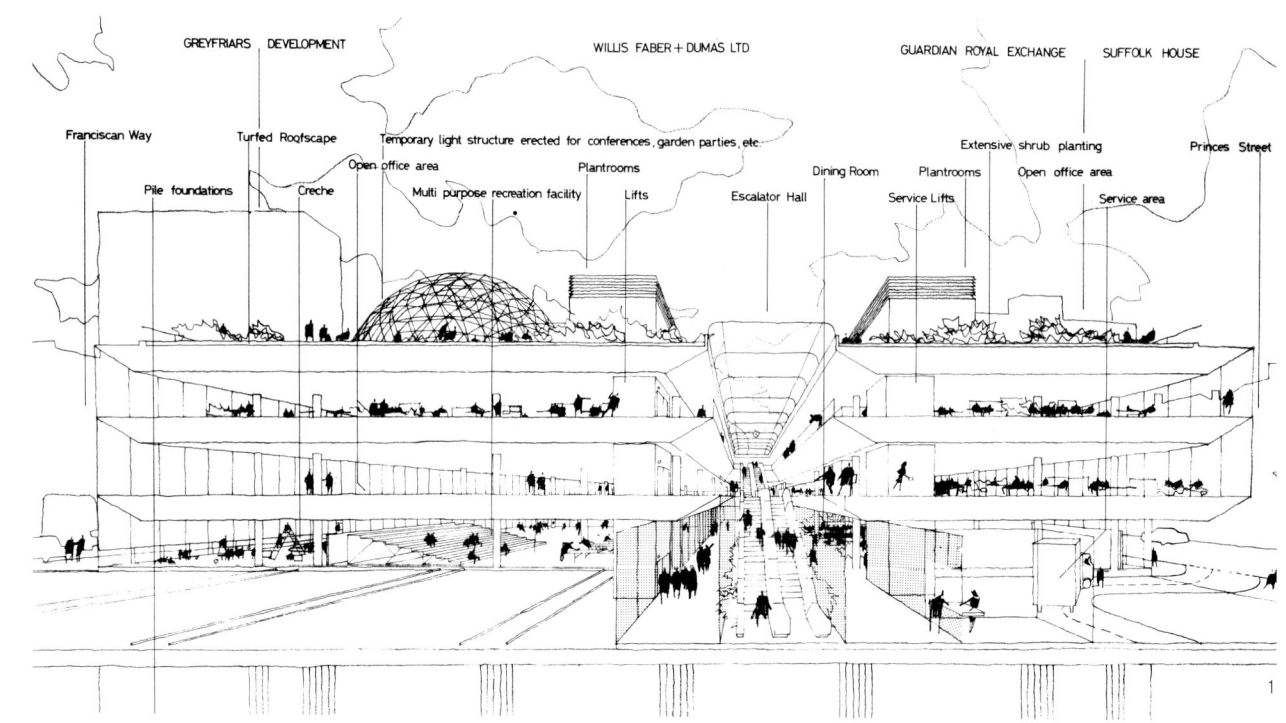

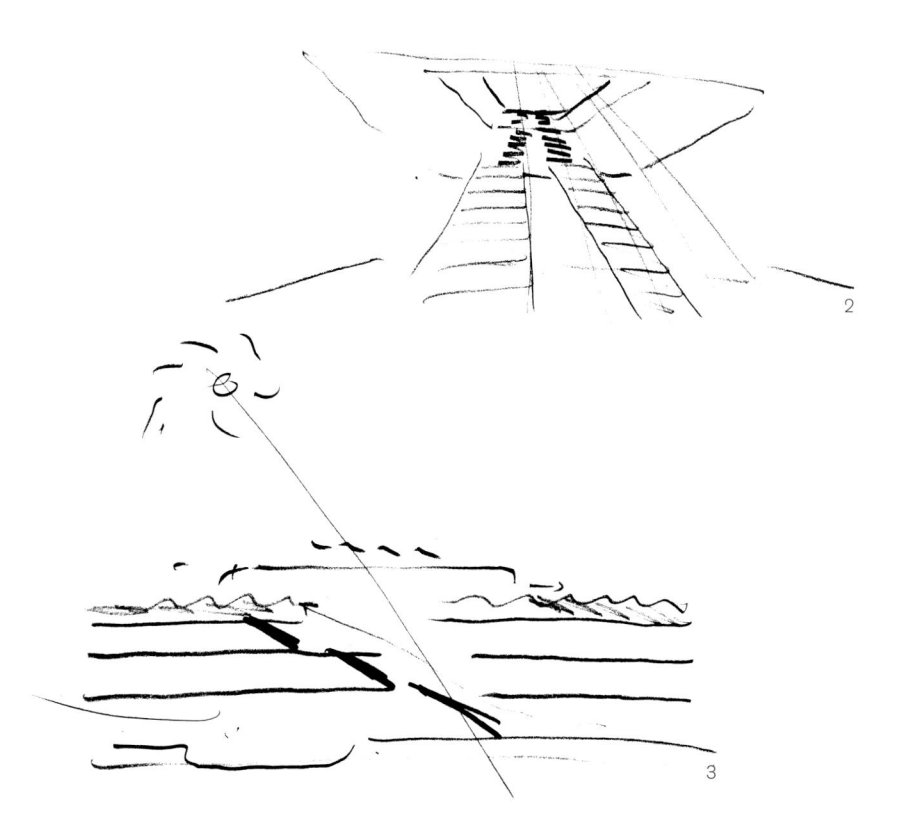

**In a deep-plan building the need for a central focus is crucial. In a solution that made a glorious virtue out of practical necessity, the escalator atrium brought space, light, movement and social intercourse to the heart of the building.**
Graham Vickers

306  Norman Foster  Works 1

It has been helpful to refer back to historical examples when questioning the nature of vertical movement in modern high-rise buildings; the trip in a typical lift-car is, at best, a third-rate experience. Compare this with the drama of movement through ... the Bradbury Building in Los Angeles. Here, transparent lifts move through a glass-roofed courtyard to serve the tiers of office floors which ring the site. Norman Foster, RIBA Royal Gold Medal address, London, 21 June 1983
Right: The glass-topped atrium of the Bradbury Building, the oldest commercial building in downtown Los Angeles, designed by George Wyman in 1893.

Increasingly, Foster has been drawn into a concern for urbanism. This, however, is not new. From his student days Foster has never been without sketchbooks on trips and he still fills dozens of them with details or street scenes that catch his imagination. Nevertheless, few of Foster's buildings have needed to fit into a specific context. The Willis Faber building in Ipswich, perhaps the first to do so, was a truly urban building that not only recreated the contours of an old street pattern but extended the street inside and through the building itself. So the experience of movement through the building was like walking through covered streets. Jonathan Glancey, *World Architecture*, April 1989

The central features of atrium, escalators and roof garden, established in the early sketches, were developed through early schematic sections. The principle of generous natural light entering through the roof and atrium space provided the key to how the entire building would function. In such a deep-plan building, the need for a central focus is crucial. In a solution that was to make a glorious virtue out of practical necessity, Foster created the escalator atrium – thereby introducing space, natural light, movement and social intercourse at the heart of the plan. Escalators form the primary method of moving people throughout the building; only one secondary lift is provided for the necessary goods and service delivery. This solution was to confer social benefits as well as a major psychological one, and would be deployed again as the basis of the primary public and private circulation in the Hongkong Bank.

Around its central open core, the Willis Faber building is layered in a very clear way. Norman Foster explains: 'We located the office spaces and the majority of the workforce in the middle two floors – like the filling in a hamburger. The ground floor is given over to support systems such as a swimming pool, plant rooms, computers, reception and loading docks (it does not have a conventional front or a back, so the loading dock comes inside the building). And then we put a landscaped roof and a restaurant on top. The atrium is the unifying element.'

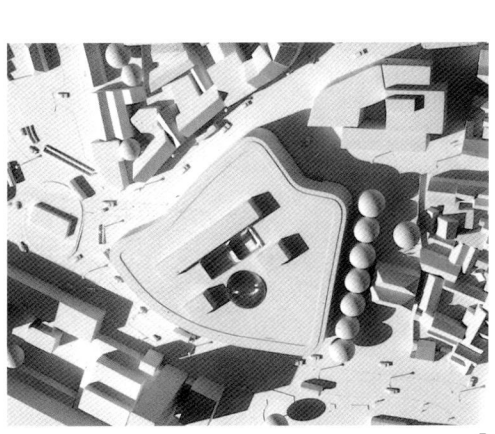

4. Only along the eastern side of the site does the glass wall break away from its exact tracing of the site boundary, forming instead the one straight elevation in the building and thereby creating a less assertive backdrop for the nearby Unitarian Meeting House.

5. The first study model shows the form of the final scheme and its location in the surrounding streetscape. Only the detail of the rooftop pavilions is unresolved.

6. Early drawings explored the mirror effect of the faceted glass facade.

**The purity of the glass wall system is an extreme development of Mies' 'less is more' philosophy. But once away from the glass, that attitude is superseded by a kind of laissez-faire, whereby separate systems – for sound control, circulation, mechanical services, lighting – are allowed highly visible presences but are seldom allowed to touch. It is this additive character that makes the building a three-dimensional catalogue of ingenious solutions to problems of which, otherwise, one might not have been aware. Problem solving replaces 'expression'.** Arthur Drexler, *Transformations in Modern Architecture*, 1979

**With its glass wall and complete air conditioning it is perhaps hard to see how [the Willis Faber building] can be considered to be an energy-conserving design … But it serves beautifully to illustrate a fundamental relationship between form, construction and energy use. This is that in compact forms, the area of wall represents only a small proportion of the total external envelope and, relatively speaking, has an insignificant effect on the total energy consumption. In a building of this type, economies of energy can best be made by paying attention to the design of plant and controls and through improvements in the technology of artificial lighting.** Dean Hawkes, *RIBA Journal*, February 1981

1. The earliest structural solution for the roof-top pavilion took the form of 'folded' triangular lattice trusses. However, this was to prove impossible due to the restrictions of the three-day working week (imposed by the UK government in response to industrial disputes in 1974). A simpler solution was subsequently erected in its place.

2. The width of the glass panels had to balance their ability to match the perimeter curves with an economical number of joints. Early sketch models explored the options.

3. A detailed model of the glass wall begins to create a very realistic impression of its final effect.

The concept of a single volume is central to the building's philosophy. There are no partitions or barriers to break the flow between the escalators and office areas or between office areas and the roof-top restaurant. Apart from the computer rooms, only the swimming pool was isolated, by means of a glass wall, while retaining a visual link to the lobby and atrium areas. Foster discovered much later that, although they had been outwardly supportive, the board had privately entertained doubts about the practical implications of the single volume. They were worried that noise and food smells might permeate the building; and in fact they had set aside a secret fund to install partitions around the restaurant should they be required. Ultimately, of course, their fears were groundless.

As Kenneth Knight recalls, 'Foster was always keen that we should have an open-plan office, or to be precise a "planned open office". We as clients were happy to go along with him, for with our ever-changing structure, changes in accommodation layout had cost us a fortune over the years.'

The 'planned open office' was well-suited to Willis Faber's operations in Ipswich and met many of the remits of the brief: it offered ease of communication; it maximised space utilisation and reduced status factors; it allowed the efficient use of air conditioning, thus reducing energy usage; and with its raised floors it allowed versatility in the use of floor space and economies in making changes, thereby ensuring future flexibility.

Indeed, flexibility – a key characteristic of Foster's early buildings – was to prove crucial at Ipswich, and not only as a response to a complex pattern of site acquisition. Detailed analysis of the work patterns at Willis Faber's base in Southend revealed that there were very considerable commercial advantages to be gained from the sort of flexibility that would allow individual departments to regroup or expand at short notice. In practice, only companies that have had to contend with the disruption of major departmental changes will fully appreciate the advantages of a genuinely flexible building. To be able to unplug a workstation, reconnect it elsewhere and make a simple change at the control centre means that major physical reorganisations can be effected quickly, simply and cheaply.

Foster addressed this issue with a far-reaching vision that has since paid dividends. Even the dramatic growth of information technology – a development that could hardly have been anticipated in the 1970s – has been effortlessly accommodated by the building. Although raised floors were then commonly being used to contain the heavy cabling required by early mainframe computer rooms – a 'computer floor' had been installed at IBM Cosham – Foster pioneered the use of this method at Willis Faber to accommodate all cable management.

Left: A full-size mock-up of a typical Willis Faber office floor was assembled employing, where possible, real elements and materials to allow both the design team and the client the opportunity to resolve final details.

Ultimately, the structure was the only site-based wet trade. Everything else was shop fabricated to maximise quality control and speed of erection. These were not the only reasons ... a belief and joy in using the materials of the age, allied with an economy of means, were important additional factors. This approach involved a shift in roles because if the product we wanted was not available 'off the peg' (and hardly anything was) we designed a new one and collaborated with the manufacturers to produce it. This meant **secondment to industry where appropriate and the frequent use of full-scale mock-ups.**
Norman Foster, *Architectural Design* 9-10, September-October 1977

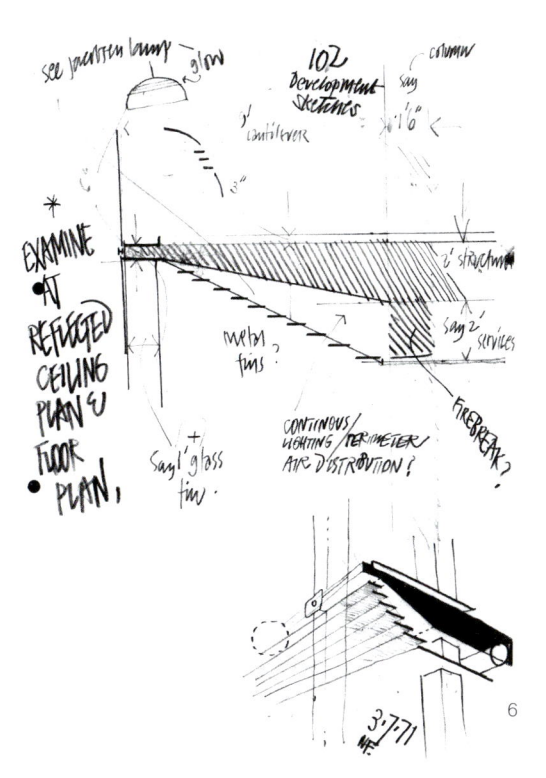

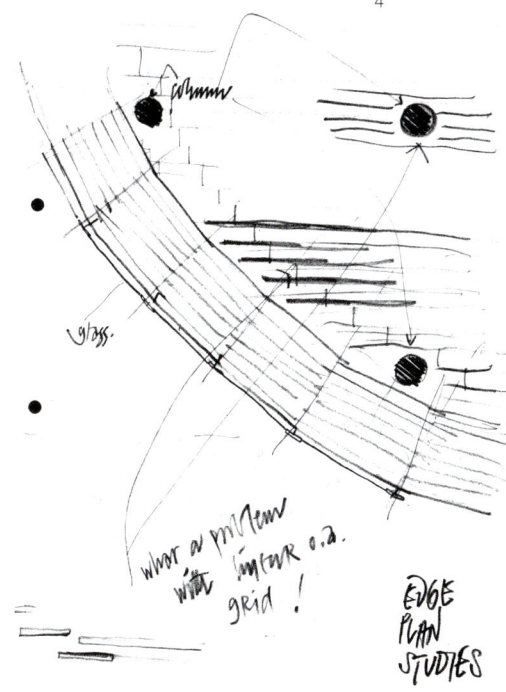

4. In the final scheme, the suspended ceiling stops inside the outer ring of 'necklace columns' and only the structural concrete slab continues out to the glass wall, tapering to present the thinnest possible section where the two elements meet. Earlier models and sketches assumed that some form of ceiling system would also be necessary and attempted to overcome the practical difficulties of such a solution.

5. A purpose-designed ceiling was developed as the only solution that would satisfactorily resolve the junction with the curved edge of the building.

6, 7. Norman Foster's sketches define the problem of how to treat the floor slab and soffit where it meets the glass wall.

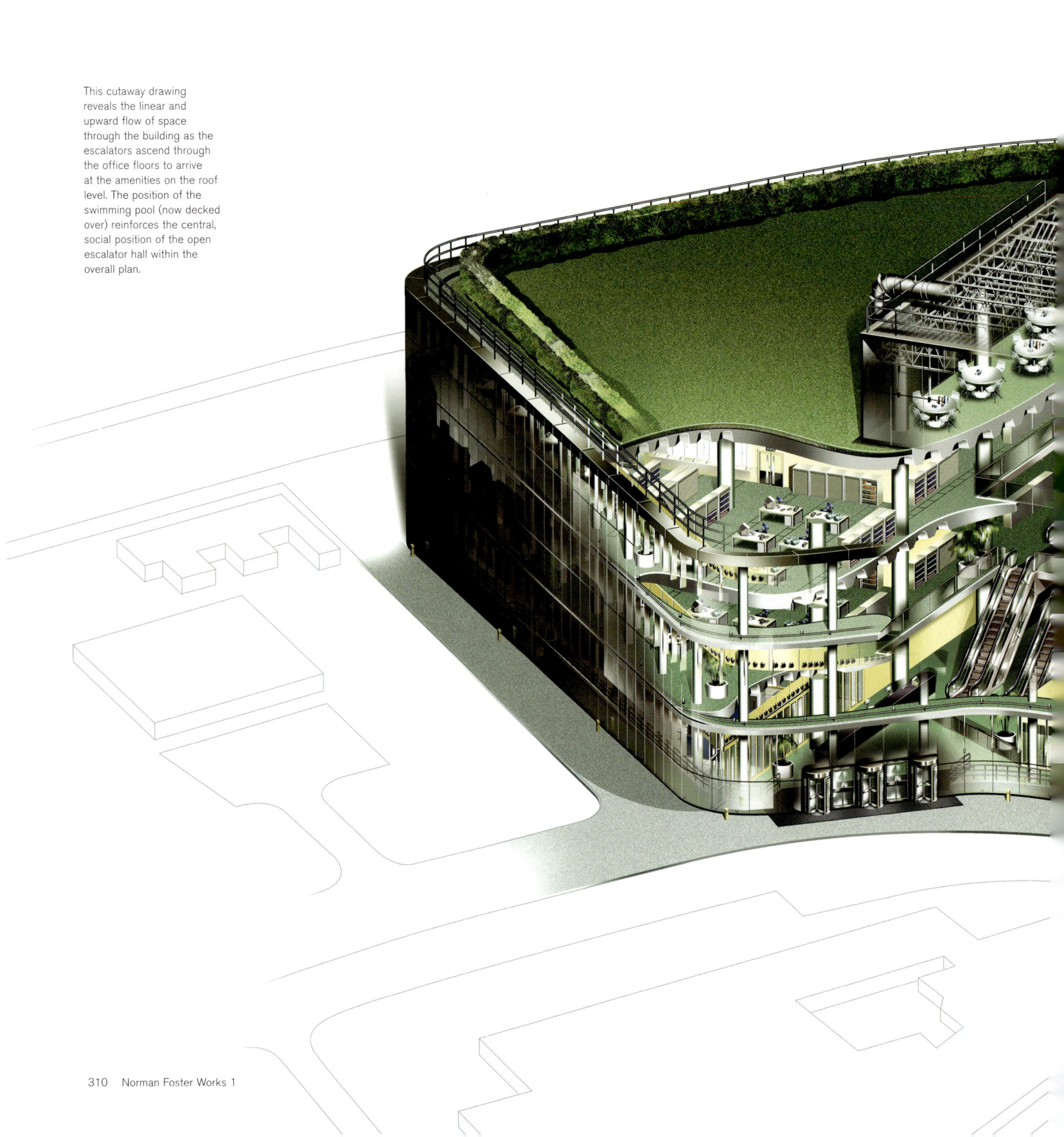

This cutaway drawing reveals the linear and upward flow of space through the building as the escalators ascend through the office floors to arrive at the amenities on the roof level. The position of the swimming pool (now decked over) reinforces the central, social position of the open escalator hall within the overall plan.

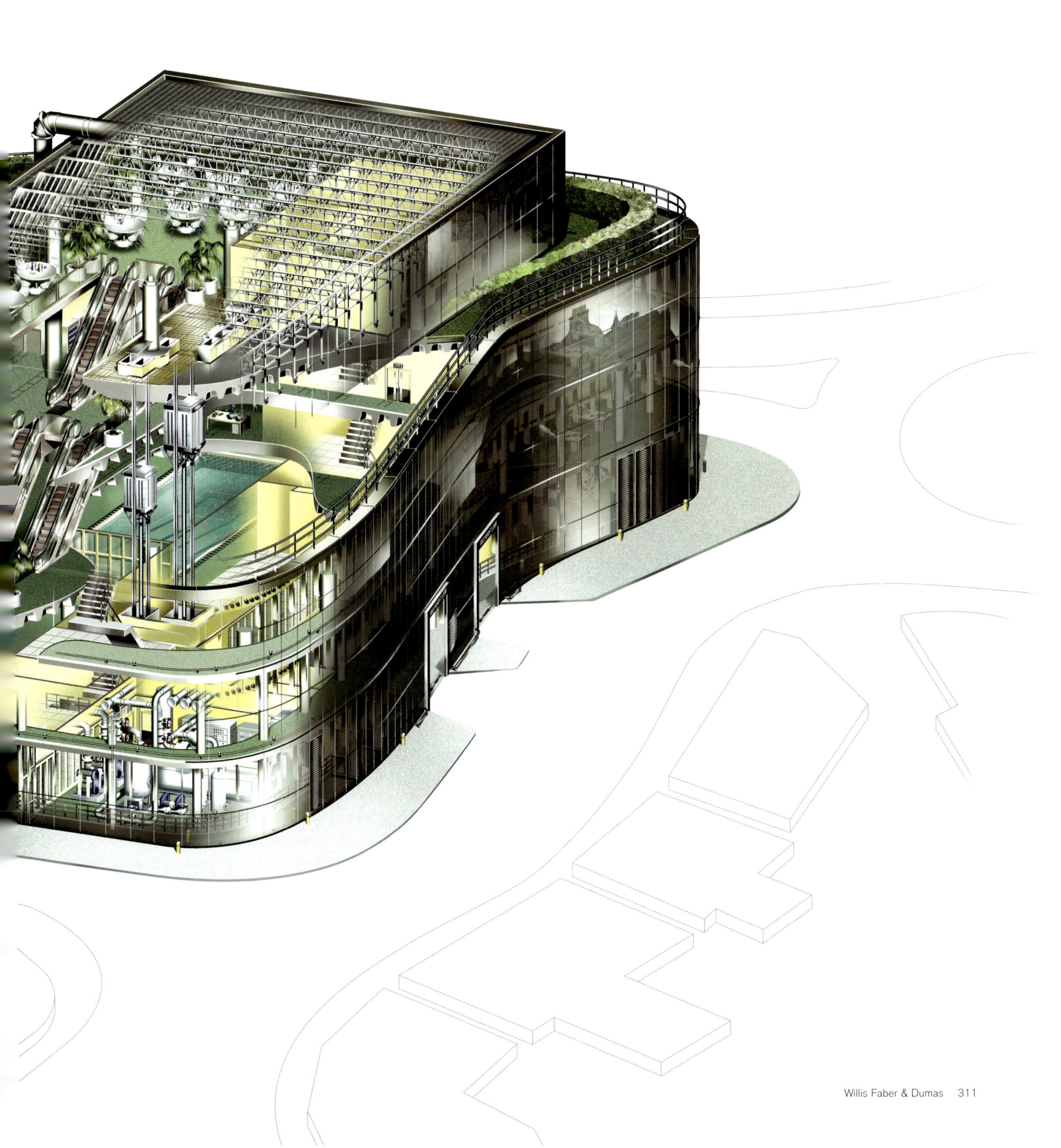

Willis Faber & Dumas

**One of the few buildings mentioned as an influence in Foster's RIBA Royal Gold Medal address, in 1983, was the Daily Express building in Great Ancoats Street, Manchester. And it is not difficult to see in the smooth lines and polished curves of Sir Owen Williams' building, of 1939, a forerunner of the Willis Faber building in Ipswich, completed 45 years later.** Alastair Best, *Norman Foster*, 1986
Left: Owen Williams' Daily Express building in Manchester, 1939.

The building grew from its foundations to completion of the glass curtain over a sixteen month period, from March 1973 to July 1974. The formal opening followed a year later on 2 June 1975.

1. May 1973: with the foundations completed construction of the ground floor slab begins; the excavation for the swimming pool is visible in the centre foreground.

2. September 1973: a 'stepped' construction procedure was adopted so that sections of the ground, first and second floor slabs were under construction at the same time.

If anything about this building is ahead of the state of the art it is the glass curtain wall around the perimeter. In it, the state of the art finally catches up with an old Modern Movement dream, a dream as old as Mies van der Rohe's first skyscraper projects in Berlin – the dream of pure glass wall uninterrupted by gratuitous and light-wasting glazing bars. It is a dream that can only be approximated by the state of the art, of course, because something has to support the glass and stop it falling out into the street.' Reyner Banham, *Foster Associates*, 1979
Right: Mies van der Rohe's Berlin glass skyscraper project of 1922.

We live for the most part in closed rooms. If we want our culture to rise to a higher level, we must change our architecture. We can only do that by introducing glass architecture which lets in the sun, the stars and the moon, not merely through a few windows, but through every possible wall, which will be made entirely of glass. The new environment we thus create will bring us a new culture.' Paul Scheerbart, *Glasarchitektur*, 1914
Left: Bruno Taut's 1914 Glass Pavilion, Cologne.

3. January 1974: although this was the 'winter of discontent' and the three-day week, construction proceeded smoothly due to management contractor Bovis' flexible working procedures.

4. March 1974: as the main concrete structure neared completion, preparation for erection of the glass wall began.

5. May 1974: the suspended glass wall already at the half-way point. On the roof, the lattice-truss structure of the restaurant pavilion was nearing completion.

6. September 1974: the glass wall is complete; internal fit-out is proceeding.

7, 8. The suspended glass wall is erected.

9. Joints between the solar-tinted glass panels are sealed with silicone.

10, 11. The glass panels were lifted into position individually using a pneumatic hoist, which also held the panel in position until the patch fittings were bolted into place.

Willis Faber & Dumas

TURNED ON ITS SIDE, THE WILLIS FABER + DUMAS GLASS WALL IS CAPABLE OF WITHSTANDING LIGHT OFFICE LOADS

**The edge of the building is on a route to Ipswich football ground and there were a good many reservations about the ability of the glass wall to withstand the onslaught of the Ipswich football supporters en route. The question was posed, 'What would happen if somebody threw a brick at it?' We tested this on a mock-up and what happened was that it bounced back.** Norman Foster, lecture at Aspen Design Conference, 16 June 1980
Left: Birkin Haward's sketch plays tricks with gravity to offer a quirky illustration of the resilience of the building's glass facade.

1. Discussions were held with several manufacturers during the early development stages of the glass wall. One of the key documents to emerge from this process was the 'parameters' drawing that Martin Francis prepared to outline all the key constraints that the system would have to tolerate. These ranged from dimensional limitations set by the geometry of having the wall follow the site boundary and considerations of constructional tolerances and building movement to less easily quantifiable concerns such as thermal shock, wind loading, impact or even a sonic boom.

2, 3. Very precise setting out allowed all the glass panels to be factory-cut, even the lowest ones which, due to changes in level around the site, had to change height to suit specific locations. A grating at pavement level conceals the bottom edge of the glazing and doubles as a continuous drainage gulley encircling the building. On the office floors the perimeter zone is left free for circulation or occasional meetings.

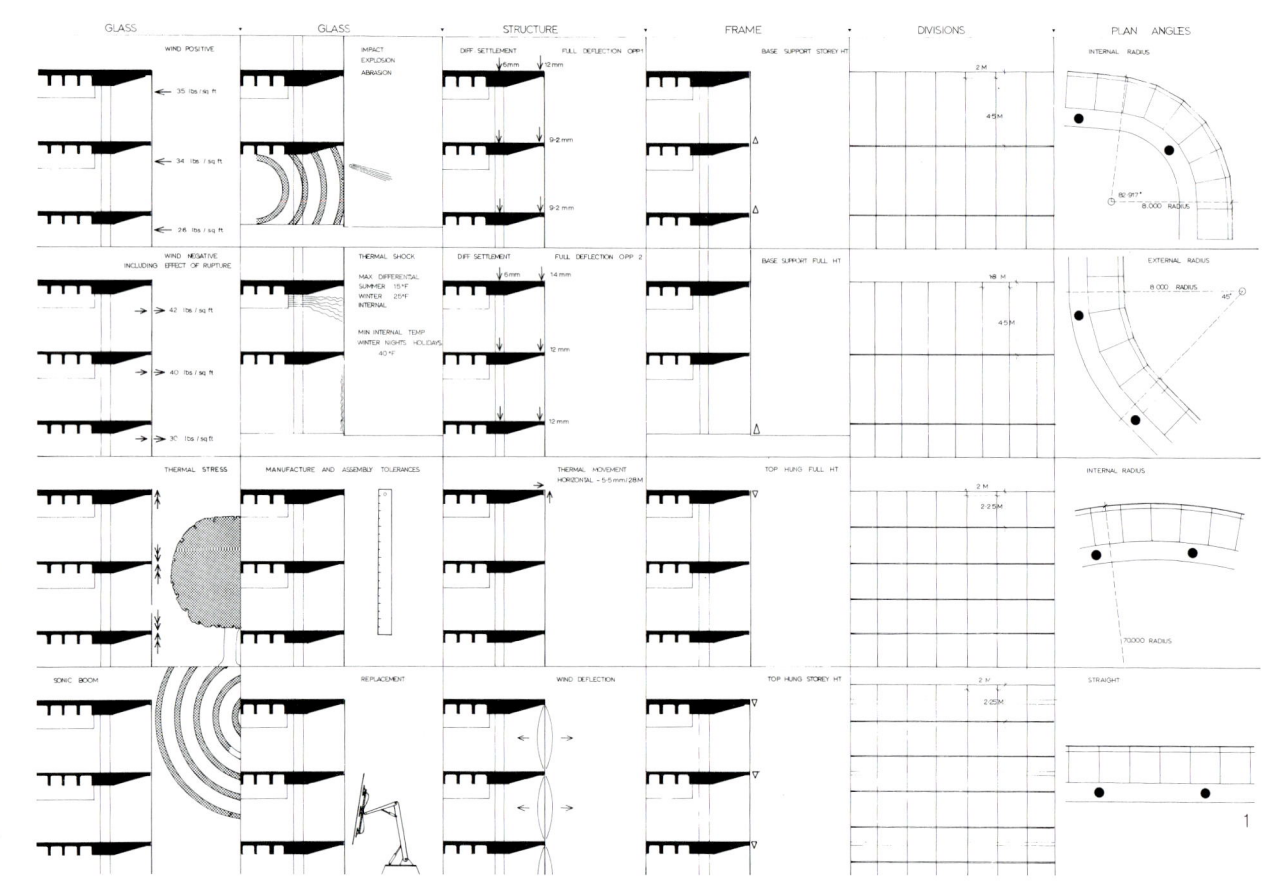

**It was only by doing our own independent technical research and detailed drawings that we were able to convince a manufacturer that glazing without mullions really was achievable.**
Norman Foster

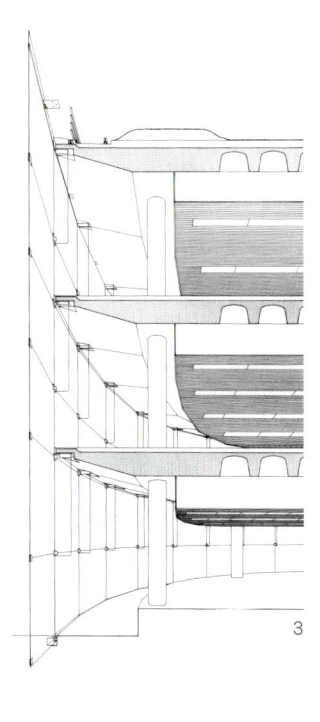

**An awareness that glass is at its strongest in tension prompted the concept of a glazed curtain suspended from the top edge of the building ... Eventually, enough calculations and technical details emerged to convince specialist sub-contractors that the idea was not only viable but also looked very attractive in cost terms (hardly surprising since it reduced the major elements down to just glass and glue).** Norman Foster, *Architectural Design* 9-10, September-October 1977

Left: In June 1975, only a week after the building's official opening, a single pane of glass shattered, puncturing the building's reflective facade to surreal effect. Although six panes of glass are suspended in series from each clamping strip at the top of the building, the panes beneath will not break if there is a breakage higher up, as the silicone joints allow structural loads to be transferred sideways.

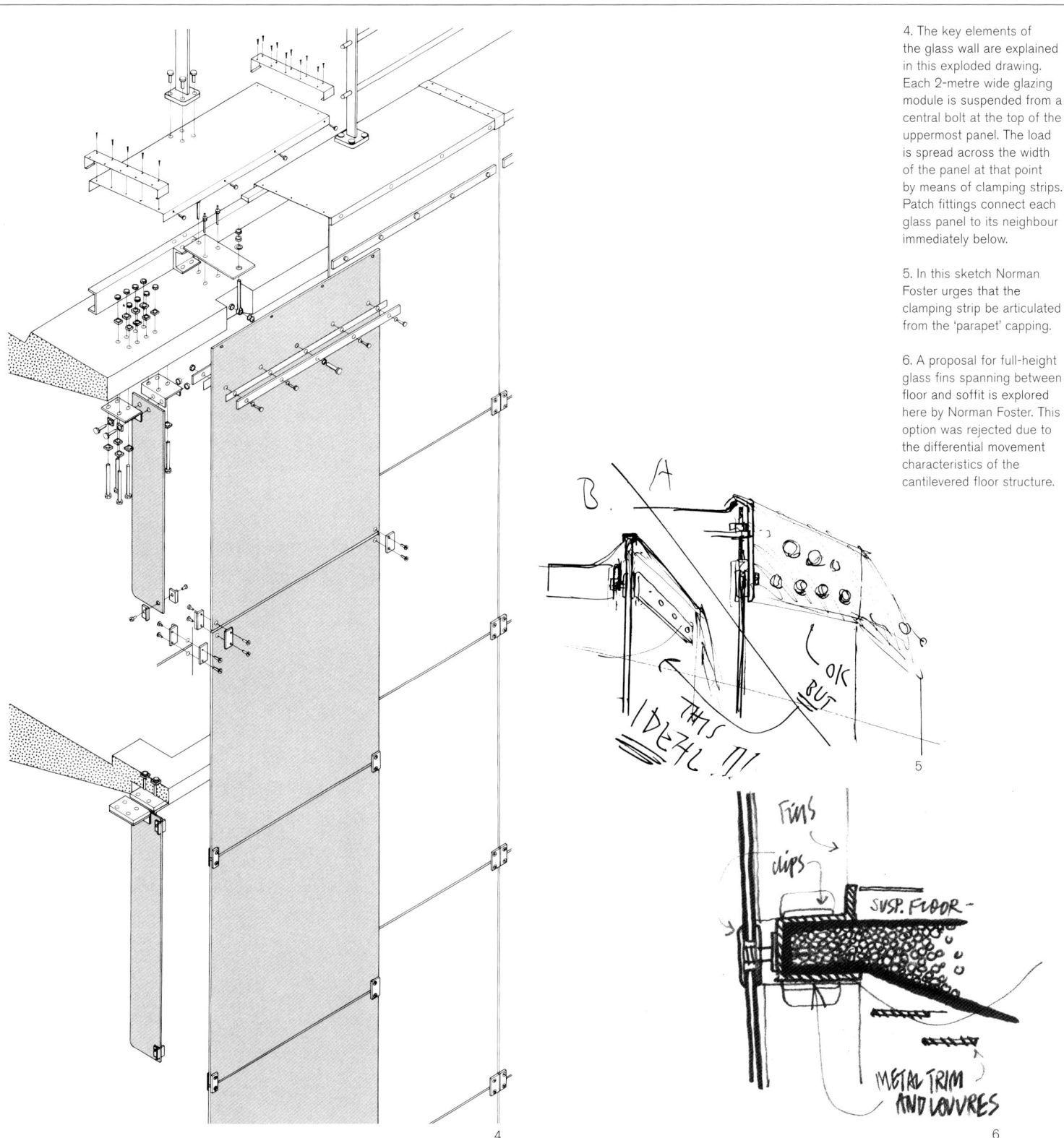

4. The key elements of the glass wall are explained in this exploded drawing. Each 2-metre wide glazing module is suspended from a central bolt at the top of the uppermost panel. The load is spread across the width of the panel at that point by means of clamping strips. Patch fittings connect each glass panel to its neighbour immediately below.

5. In this sketch Norman Foster urges that the clamping strip be articulated from the 'parapet' capping.

6. A proposal for full-height glass fins spanning between floor and soffit is explored here by Norman Foster. This option was rejected due to the differential movement characteristics of the cantilevered floor structure.

**If anything about this building is ahead of the state of the art it is the glass curtain wall around the perimeter ... Support has been refined away almost, but not quite, to nothing, a clamp bar to hang the glass from the top, and a patch plate at each corner where four sheets meet. Otherwise there is nothing except a translucent line of sealant between each sheet and the next, optically lost in the inevitable refractions and reflections that occur at any cut edge in glass.**
Reyner Banham, *Foster Associates*, 1979

1. Lateral restraint against wind loads is provided by half-storey-height glass fins at each floor. These are independently attached to the concrete structure and are linked to the main facade by means of a sliding patch fitting which restrains horizontal movement but permits vertical movement caused by thermal effects and building movement. Joints between the individual panels of glass are sealed with translucent silicone.

**An alternative steel mullion system was designed for the Wilis Faber project and test-bedded in a smaller installation in Thamesmead.** Norman Foster, *Architectural Design* 9-10, September-October 1977

Left: Diagram of the glazing system employed at the Modern Art Glass building (1972), in which suspended steel mullions support glass panels vertically with the aid of an external clamping strip.

Right: The Modern Art Glass wall offers a hint of how Willis Faber might have looked, had the alternative glazing system not been adopted.

2, 5. Details of a typical patch-plate fitting, seen from inside and outside the building respectively.

3. A detail of a standard interlocking patch fitting from the Pilkington system. The patch fittings allow vertical movement between the glass panels of the facade and the half-storey-height glass fins. The fittings secure one sheet of glass to the sheets immediately above or below, never to those sheets on either side.

4. The standard interlocking patch fitting only needed one subtle modification to cope with the angled junctions created by the building's curves. The usual rectangular slot of the flat-wall system was changed to an open-hinge arrangement, the geometry of which was carefully calculated to suit all requirements.

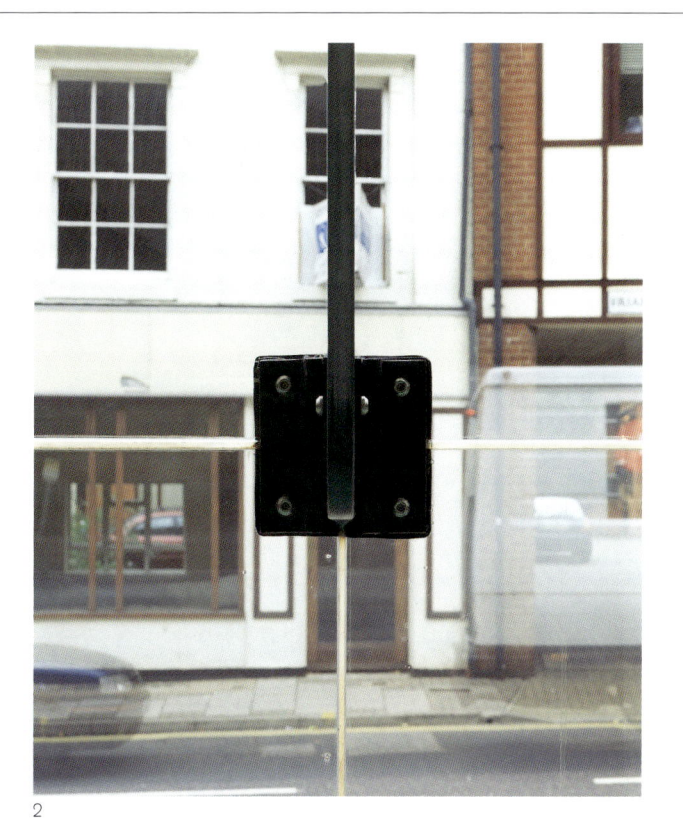

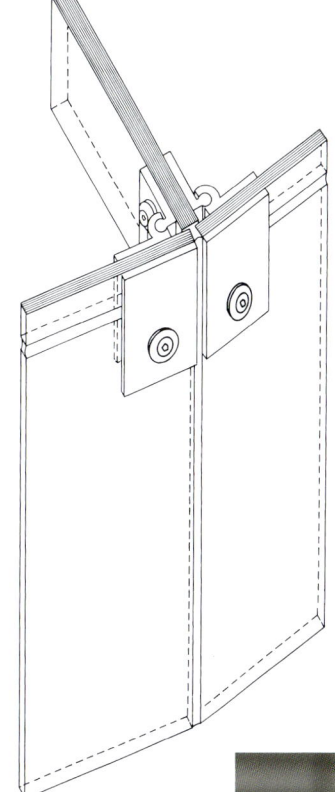

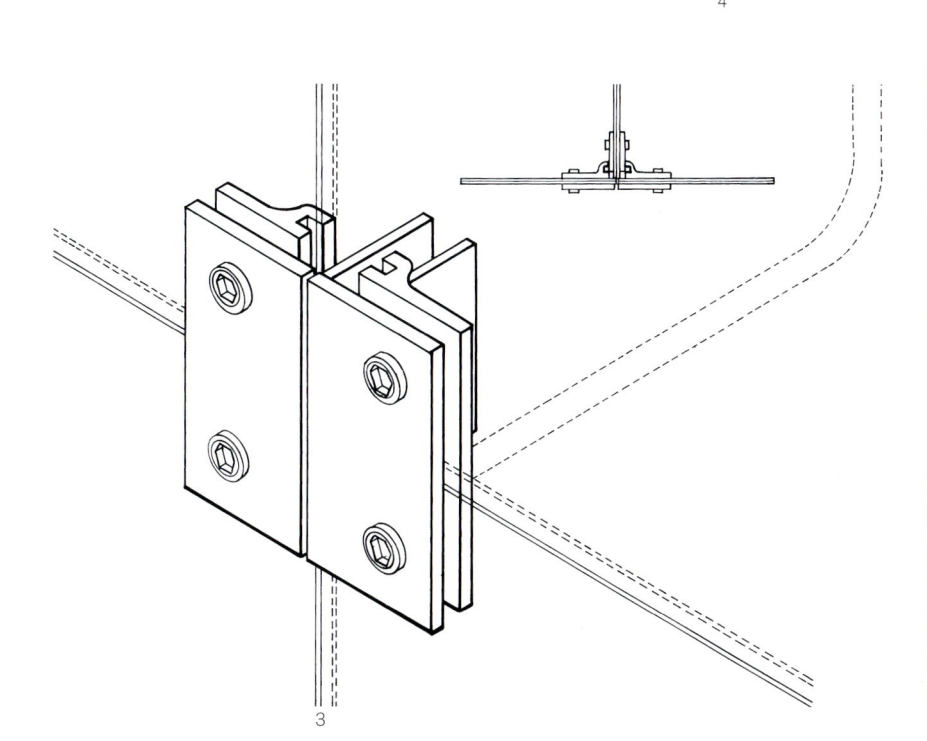

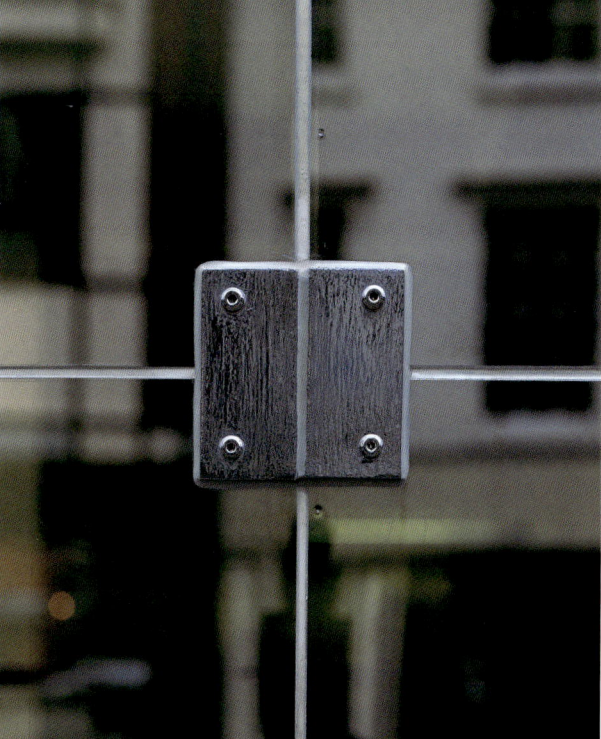

Willis Faber & Dumas 317

**Questions of scale are neatly avoided. What is the size of the building's subdivisions? Is it the interval of the scarcely visible floor slabs, or the individually faceted and dynamic reflections of the sky, the buildings opposite or, occasionally, of the building reflecting itself?** Christopher Woodward, *The Architectural Review*, September 1975
Left: The cover of *The Architectural Review* in which Chirstopher Woodward's critical evaluation of Willis Faber & Dumas was published.

**Now 'everybody knows' that glass is an energy-wasteful material. Yet Foster Associates have the gall and the figures to show that this is a reasonably energy-efficient structure – partly because its very deep-plan four-storey format gives a low ratio of glass to internal volume, and the glass is deeply bronzed as well; and partly because much of its roof is clad in one of the oldest and most reliable insulating materials known to vernacular wisdom – growing turf!** Reyner Banham, *New Society*, 6 October 1977

1. In creating the all-glass sheath that wraps around the building, the design team was presented with the problem of what could be placed behind the glass at the ground floor, where it would be clearly visible to passers-by. The decision to locate the main plant at this level solved the dilemma. The concept of showing how a building works and using the consequent detail to provide visual interest had been explored in earlier projects, but here the process was taken further with all-glass partitions used inside the building as well, so that all sides of the plant rooms are clearly visible.

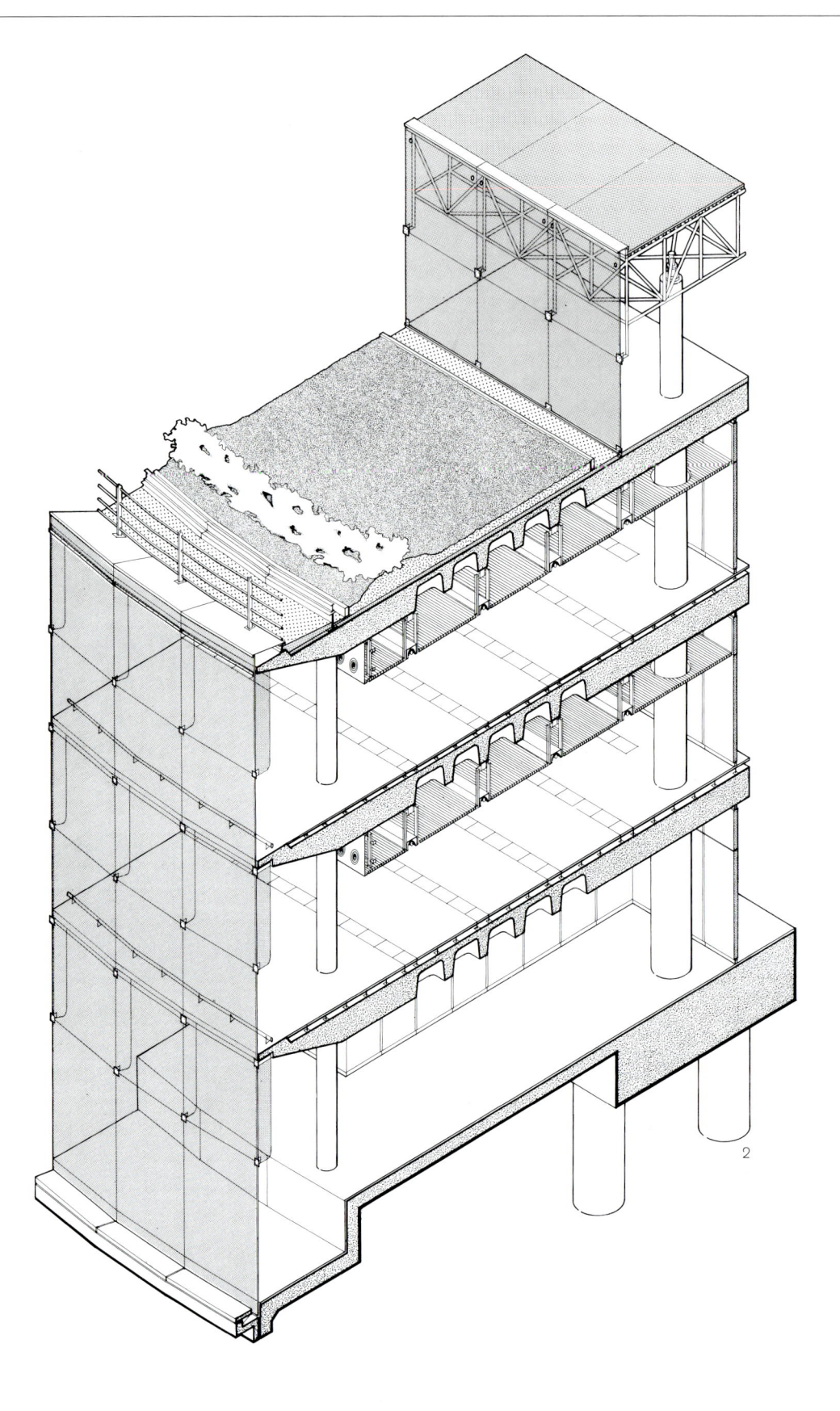

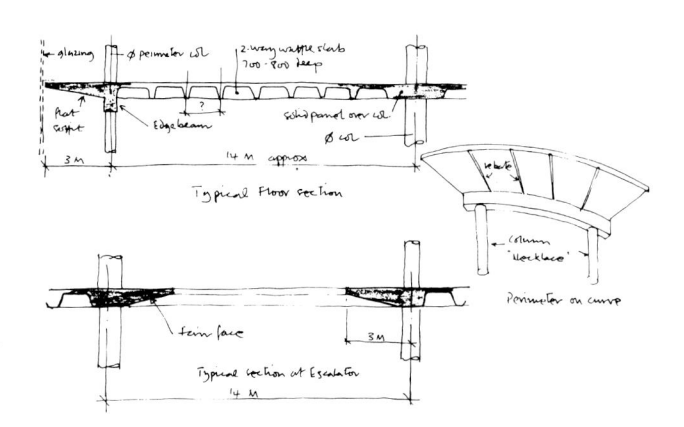

Right: Structural engineer Tony Hunt's design sketches were a response to Foster's desire to cantilever and taper the edge of the floor slab so that it would not impact visually behind the glass skin.

The accepted method at the time was to bury trunking in the floor finish, a system that inevitably resulted in outlets being located in the 'wrong place' whenever a move was contemplated. So while the idea of a continuous raised floor was introduced at Willis Faber to deal with general office equipment – telephone and typewriter cables and the like – the real benefits of this approach only became significant later with the ephemeralisation of computers. Today the building handles two and a half times the business it did originally, with comparable numbers of staff, and office layouts have been reconfigured many times.

## The finished building represents a satisfyingly holistic conclusion to an extraordinarily complex design process.

The single open volume and open escalator well is unusual at another level in that it does not offer conventional fire compartmentation. However, the case for this arrangement was supported by the provision of a fully automatic sprinkler system, which protects the entire building. The use of four subsidiary circulation cores was also beneficial in this respect, allowing a higher provision of protected stairs than required by the regulations. The cost of the fire detection and sprinkler systems was more than offset by savings made from omitting internal partitions.

The finished building represents a satisfyingly holistic conclusion to an extraordinarily complex design process. The building is suffused with natural light, and the sense of spaciousness and accessibility has to be experienced to be fully understood. Behind the solution, and indeed behind the numerous individual design problems, lies Foster's philosophy that only a fully integrated design approach can result in a harmonious building which is as efficient to service as it is coherent to look at.

Informing Willis Faber's remarkably clear parti is a highly complex balancing act, as Norman Foster explains: 'Our design philosophy is perhaps best expressed as a process of resolving and integrating views and polarities which might otherwise be in conflict. For example, the company versus the community; public versus private; new versus old; time and cost versus quality and innovation; socially acceptable versus commercially viable. Another part of the approach is a conscious attempt to put all those dry objective pieces of the jigsaw – whether research, statistics, cost plan, site analysis, structural options: the checklist is endless – together with some subjective joy.'

The 'joy' in this case manifested itself in the Corbusian virtues of 'space, light and greenery' and an unprecedented level of staff amenities. Kenneth Knight's observation that the client should be given, 'not only what he wants, but what he ought to want', reflects a corporate instinct that was highly sympathetic to Foster's proposals.

2. The main components of the building's construction are readily identifiable in this isometric drawing of a 'typical' slice through the edge of the building. The glazing of the roof-top pavilion is similar in most respects to the main facade, the glass being supported by special rocking-arms from the top edge of the steel roof trusses. A proposal to provide not only turf to the roof but a hedge on a built-up bank around the edge of the building – to complete the illusion that this might indeed be a park raised from the ground level – was also carried through on the completed building.

3. The floors are constructed from a 70mm deep waffle-slab, supported on cast in-situ reinforced-concrete columns. The depth of the slab was calculated to avoid the need for downstand beams. Solid concrete panels, 6-metres square, form the junction between the columns and the integrated flat beams.

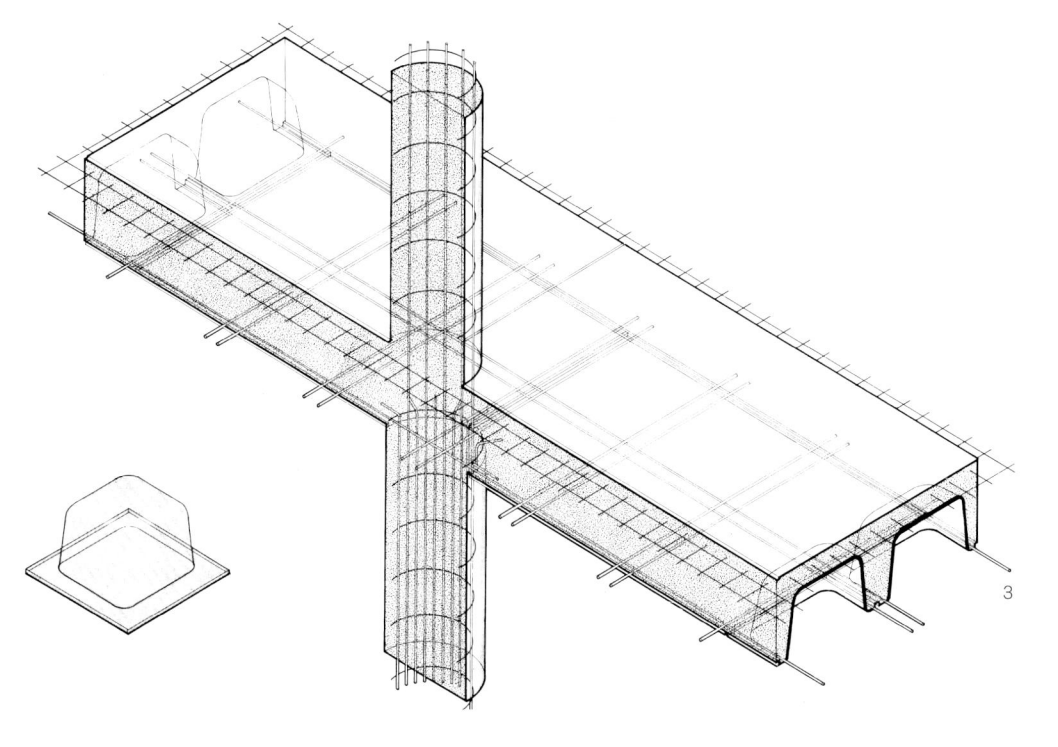

**The parabolic light fittings, which are integrated within the ceiling, are designed to accommodate the air distribution and extract grilles for office areas and house sprinkler runs, as well as providing a separate emergency lighting system. Additionally, the power and cable runs on the office floors telegraph through the lighting grid above and below. Compare this with the more usual proliferation (and redundancy) of separate suspended elements, which are typically brought together in the equivalent of a last-minute shotgun marriage.** Norman Foster, *Architectural Design* 9-10, September-October 1977

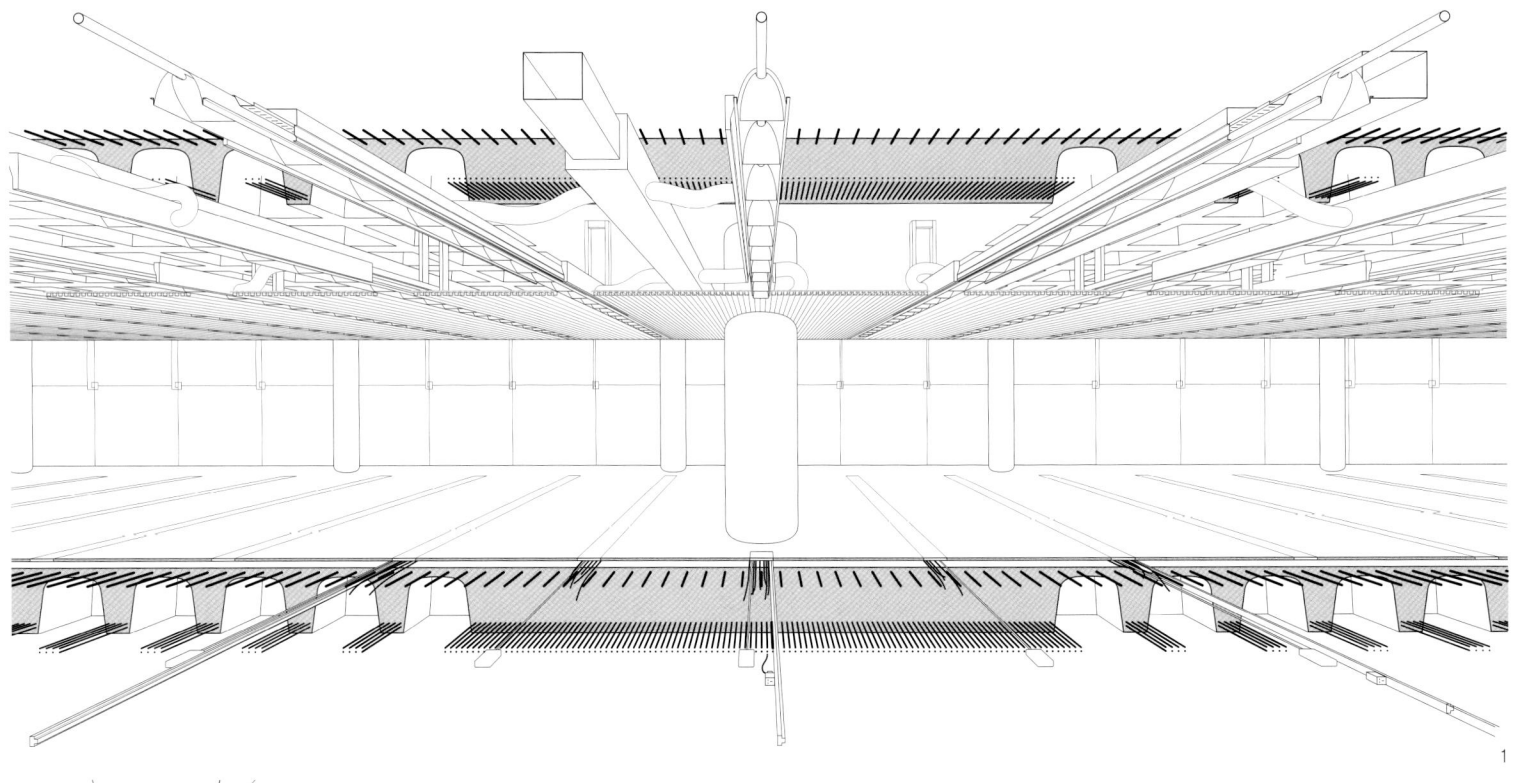

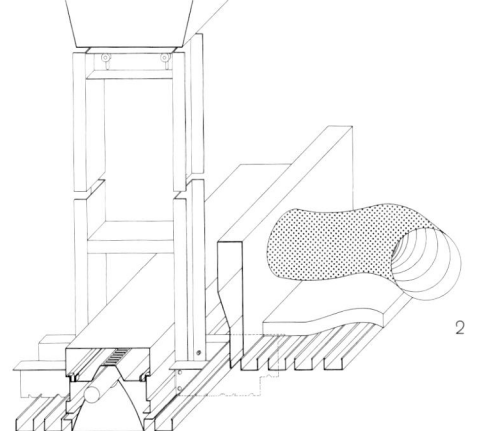

A swimming pool, coffee bar, roof garden and restaurant – with the added capability for a gymnasium, and possibly a helipad – were strongly advocated in the early stages of brief definition. They marked a bid to break away from the concept of the traditional company sports ground and the thinking that accompanied it. Not all of these survived, but the swimming pool, built to Olympic standard, represents a remarkable commitment to the provision of leisure amenities. The fact that the pool has since been decked over to accommodate expanding staff numbers, which at one level is a 'loss', is also an example of the building's inherent flexibility – a balancing 'gain'.

Early impressions of how the finished building would look were produced to stimulate discussion both within the architectural team and with the client. One of these drawings shows an early proposal, later abandoned, for a new plaza adjacent to the historical Unitarian Meeting House, part of a plan to create more open space in front of this distinguished neighbouring building.

The renderings of this period are as interesting for their discrepancies as for their similarities to the final building. For example, one drawing shows a far more transparent entrance section, with a distinct canopy formed by sweeping the glazing inside the footprint at ground-floor level. By now, the radical concept of the all-glass wall suggested in Foster's notes had been embraced. Another rendering shows an early proposal for the glass wall, in which suspended, tubular-steel mullions were still being explored as a fall-back option.

Loren Butt, a former Foster associate, and a member of the design team recalls: 'This project was always throwing up extraordinary challenges. The glass wall was of course a key issue. The traditional engineering view is "you can't do that", which is odd because the most ambitious of our nineteenth-century engineers were very adventurous. Yet in this century engineering has become a matter of "good practice", of always looking over your shoulder to see what other engineers might think.'

**A feeling of freedom and openness is conveyed, particularly in the photograph that shows the space uncluttered by furniture or people. This might be a parterre at Louis XIV's Versailles, or a green carpet (with concealed electrical outlets) and a repetition of columns, mechanical ducts, and long, very long, lines of acoustic baffles … And the transformation of these pragmatic considerations into signs of the sublime is achieved by Foster, as it was by Le Nôtre in the gardens of Versailles, by taking repetitive devices of order beyond their usual extent and rendering them with a pristine absoluteness.** Charles Jencks, *Current Architecture*, 1982

**There is a subtle economy in the integration of functional design between the ceiling surface, the colour of the carpet and the office lighting. The planning grid of the building is 2 x 2 metres, which leads to a wider spacing of lighting; however, the use of green carpet to reflect the predominant colour component of the lights, together with secondary reflection from the polished aluminium ceiling, eliminates the potential problem of patchy lighting levels on the desks. Creative interaction … resulted in a better and more economical solution than a conventional 'keep the cost down' approach would have achieved.** Loren Butt, lecture at the Construction Industry Conference, London, 15 May 1980

1. The quality of servicing to the office floors was designed for long-term flexibility and considerably exceeded standards of installation accepted at that time. Accessible cable ducts run throughout the offices at 2-metre centres under a totally raised floor. This farsightedness was to ensure that subsequent developments in computer technology could be accepted with ease.

2. The light-fittings were specially designed to give very efficient illumination without glare at spacings wider than the norm. Interconnecting wiring channels within the chassis of each fitting eliminate much of the usual conduit and trunking. The fittings themselves are fixed to the structural slab by a special frame which also provides support for the sprinkler system, suspended ceiling and air ducts. Return air is drawn up through the light fittings to absorb heat at source.

3. The offices are fully air-conditioned, with supply and return air being distributed through the suspended ceiling. Directional nozzles feed a constant supply of air on to the glass wall to avoid possible condensation. Air is drawn back through the light fittings to absorb their heat at source. The cost effectiveness of the specially designed systems was assisted by the size of the building: components and materials were relatively inexpensive because of the large orders. For example, 60 kilometres of aluminium channel was required for the ceiling of just one floor.

**This was one of the few occasions when a building exceeded my expectations. I think it is a superb job – beautiful and of extraordinary technical interest. It also states some of the philosophical questions of modern architecture as forcefully as possible. It's a really marvellous building and I'm delighted that we are going to have the model.** Excerpt from a letter to Norman Foster from Arthur Drexler, Director of the Museum of Modern Art, New York, December 1981
Left: A detail of the Willis Faber & Dumas model, which is now included in MOMA's permanent collection.

**Willis Faber seems like some Spielbergian spaceship that has settled into the weave of the town. Opaque and visually silent by day, transparent and winking with light after sunset.**
Jonathan Glancey, *The Architectural Review*, July 1983

1. Ground floor plan. Only at this level are partitions required for acoustic control and occasional special servicing requirements. Where possible, all-glass screens are used to maintain the sense of openness.

 1 entrance
 2 reception
 3 escalators
 4 coffee bar
 5 swimming pool
 6 changing rooms
 7 gymnasium
 8 crèche
 9 data processing
10 computers
11 telex room
12 chillers
13 generator
14 loading bay
15 plant

2, 3. First and second floor plans. Up to 600 people work on each office floor. All staff and management – including the company chairman – work in open-plan offices. Four minor cores provide service and escape facilities.

 1 escalator atrium
 2 service lift
 3 document lift
 4 plant
 5 storerooms

4. The roof level provides a staff restaurant and access to the garden, with its perimeter running track.

 1 roof garden
 2 cooling tower
 3 perimeter walk
 4 plant
 5 kitchen
 6 servery
 7 cafeteria
 8 restaurant

5, 6. The main structure, with columns set out on a 14-metre square grid, is combined with an edge band of columns at 7-metre centres, which respond to the edge of the site.

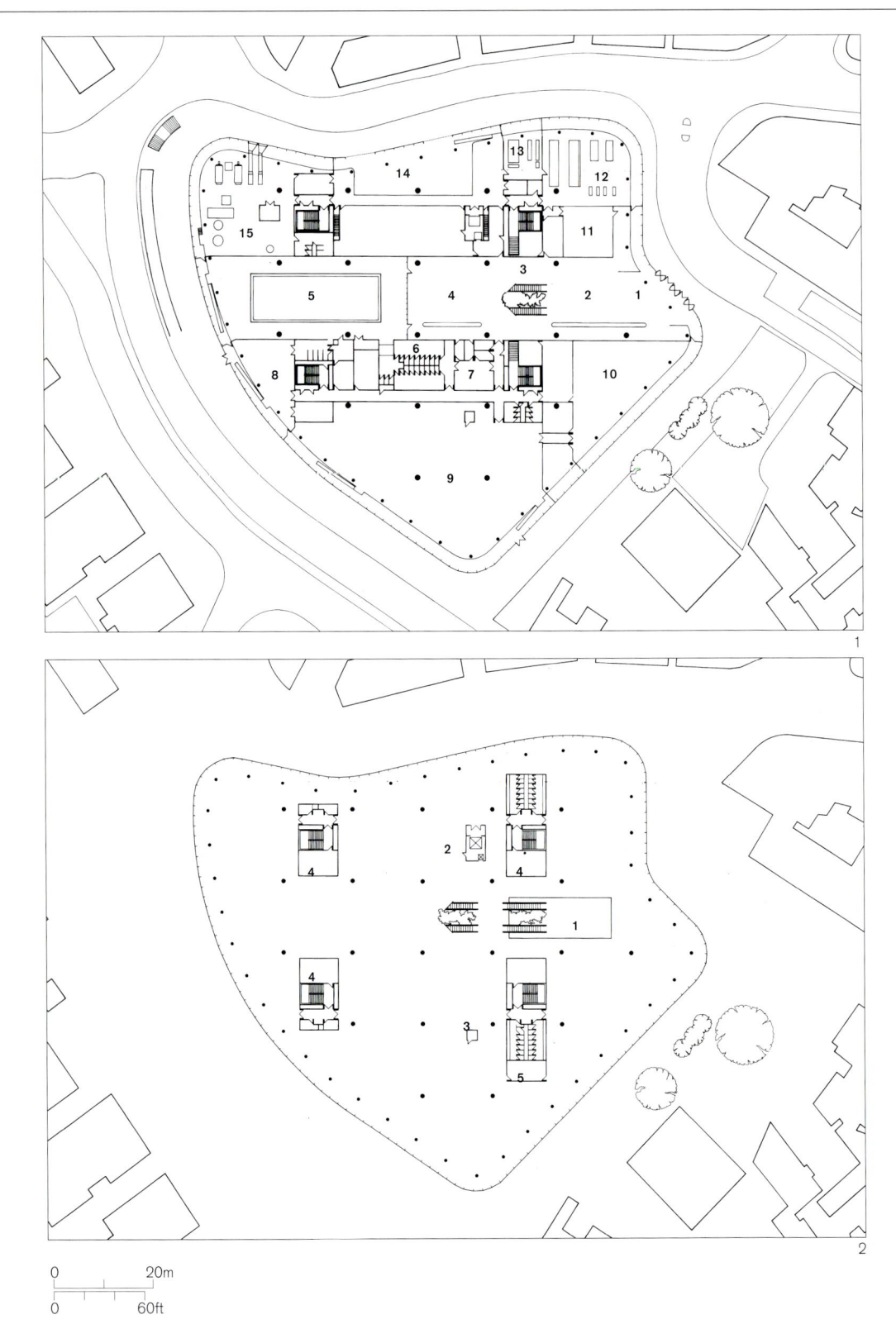

**The issue of a building's relationship with its site boundaries reached its extreme limit with Norman Foster's Willis Faber & Dumas offices, Ipswich (1975), a three-storey building whose sheer glass walls, reflective in daylight and translucent by night, follow the irregular site boundary exactly.** Banister Fletcher, *A History of Architecture*, 1996

Right: As a result of its iconic status, the Willis Faber building has appeared in a range of contexts and occasionally surprising guises. The building's distinctive outline lent itself naturally to a cake prepared to commemorate the publication of the centenary edition of Banister Fletcher's *A History of Architecture* in 1996.

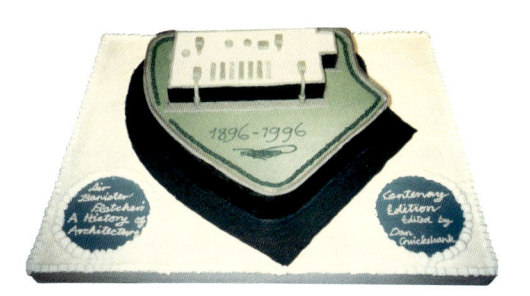

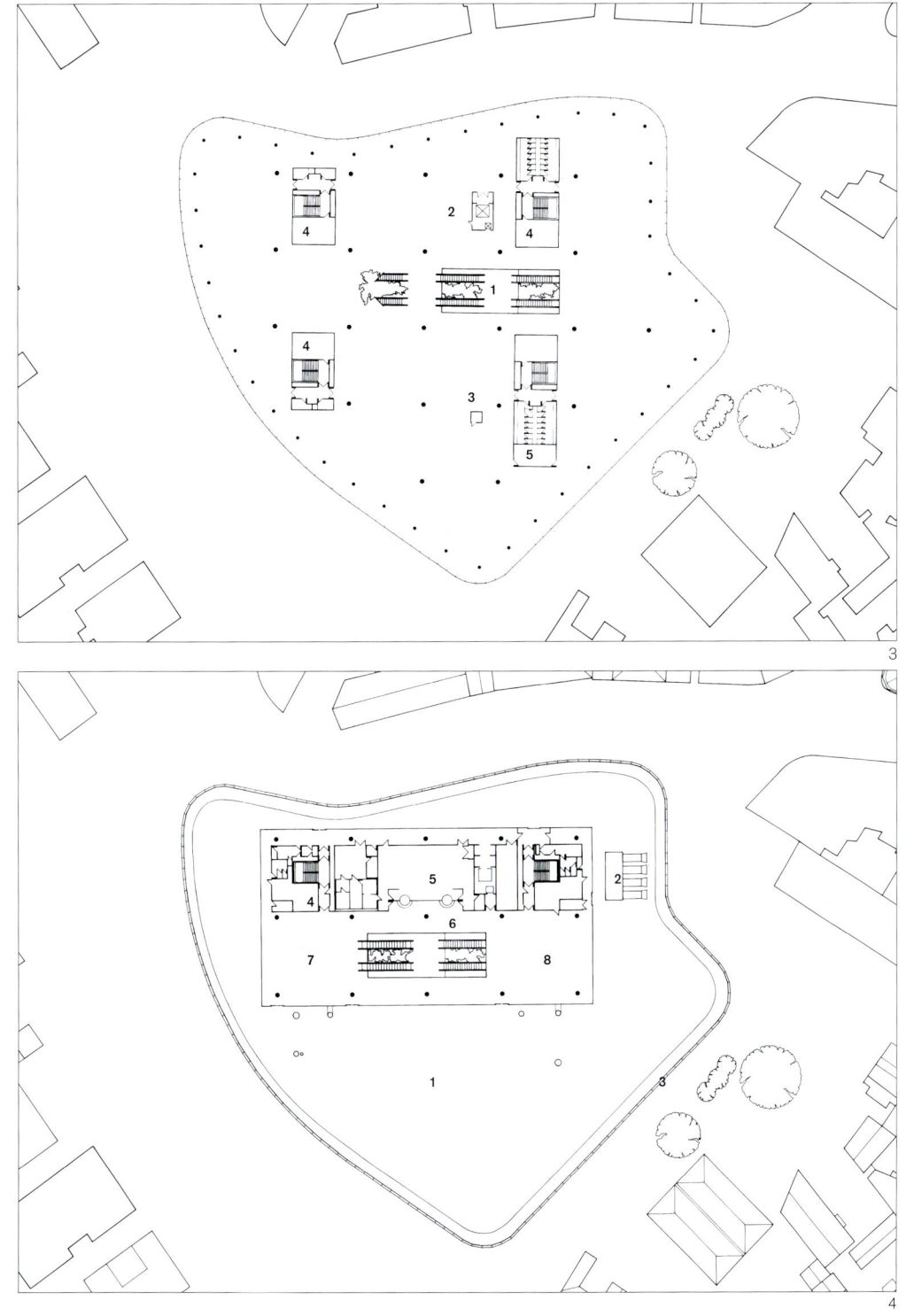

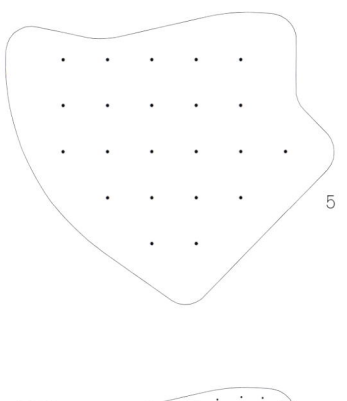

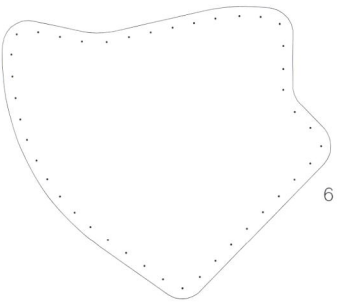

> **We located the office spaces in the middle two floors. The ground floor is given over to support systems such as a swimming pool, plant room, computers, reception and loading docks. And then we put a landscaped roof and a restaurant on top, with the open atrium as a unifying element.**
> Norman Foster

**Look upon its featureless facades, and you shall see every period of East Anglian suburban architecture from Low Gothic to High Brutalist, and almost every catalogued historical detail from abacus to zygus. Spire and dome are there, chimney and gable, column and pilaster, arches round, ogival and pointed. Better still, by choosing your viewpoints with creative care, you can manoeuvre an artisan-mannerist gable (reflected) on top of a modern matt-black ventilating grille (real) and make them fit together exactly.** Reyner Banham, *New Society*, 6 October 1977

**The Willis Faber building in Ipswich even dematerialises architecture: the reflections in the glass skin are as important as the breathtaking finesse with which that skin is put together. This is the ultimate celebration of technology as art.** Ada Louise Huxtable, *The Troubled State of Modern Architecture*, January 1987

**At a glance, this singular presence might be an enormous blob of black ink – because the vast sheets of glass are butted end-to-end and frameless; we are simply presented with a startling enclosure for space inside, which, when discovered, is all the more astonishing for the inscrutable appearance of the thing outside – suddenly, we find light, distance, clear colours, escalators, height.** Stephen Gardiner, *The Listener*, 13 February 1983

So while the team advanced the solution that everyone preferred, a more conservative option was developed as a fall-back. Norman Foster: 'We actually built the glass wall that we felt we would be forced to build at Willis Faber on another building, for Modern Art Glass (who would later install the Willis Faber glass wall). It was only by doing our own independent technical research and detailed drawings that we were able to convince a manufacturer that glazing without mullions really was achievable.'

Foster's method of anticipating the final appearance and feel of the building extended to the glass wall's less obvious ramifications. If the technical feat of actually suspending it impresses, no less important is the integrated design of the interior detail juxtapositions and related environmental services.

It is no exaggeration to say that Foster could not have conceived the all-glass solution successfully without an equally thorough commitment to the detailed design of the whole building. For example, the glass wall would have been inconceivable without a complementary method of preventing the formation of condensation on its inner surface.

The solution was to route the air supply ducts around the perimeter, directing a constant flow of air onto the glass. This also offered a solution to the ceiling edge problem: the suspended ceiling system ends some 2 metres from the glass, inside the line of the perimeter columns, and the panel that houses the air ducts returns vertically to meet the concrete soffit. This allows the soffit alone to taper out to meet the glass wall, presenting the thinnest possible visible edge at the junction.

Other technical problems posed by the all-glass perimeter included the installation of smoke barriers in the tolerance gap between the horizontal slab and the vertical wall. A flexible neoprene fin with the necessary fire resistance was found, and it very satisfyingly provides both effective sound insulation and the required smoke seal between floors.

This and other detailed design issues were explored in a full-scale mock-up, constructed in a warehouse, which brought together elements of the ceiling, the raised floor panels and the partitioning system. It provided both architect and client with a reassuringly 'real' expression of the solution that would eventually be built, offering opportunities for both to assess and fine-tune the design at an early stage.

The mock-up played a particularly important role in the development of the ceiling system. The problems generated by the building's distinctive curved perimeter militated against a conventional grid-based system; no existing product could be found that did not require major modification. Foster characteristically took advantage of this fact to develop a purpose-designed system, which proved cost-effective by virtue of the large amount required.

**Approached through Ipswich's narrow streets, the building is seen in fragmentary glimpses. Only close-to is its transparency appreciated.**
Norman Foster

**In daylight, the one acre of mirror glass exterior wall uniformly reflects and augments the historic neighbouring structures. At night, with its customised, mirror-finished aluminium ceiling reflecting an evenly illuminated interior, the building becomes an enclosed urban plaza. The darkened and quiet neighbourhood which inscribes it after nightfall is then provided with an exciting vista into the active world within.**
R S Reynolds Memorial Award Citation, April 1976

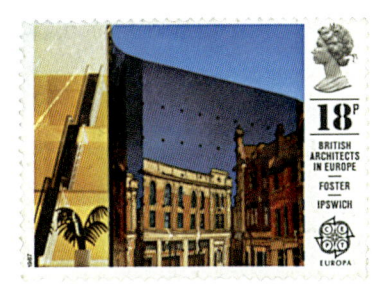

Left: Willis Faber was one of four outstanding buildings selected to feature on a series of stamps celebrating the work of British architects in Europe issued by the Post Office in May 1987.

1, 2. Situated on the edge of the old town, the building is approached for the most part via small-scale twisting medieval streets that reveal only fragmentary views of its reflective glass facade.

3. Only at close quarters is a broader view of the building possible.

4. The only straight elevation creates an unassertive backdrop for the historical Unitarian Meeting House.

5. As night falls the otherwise reticent facade dissolves dramatically to reveal the inner workings and organisation of the building. The uplighters that were designed to illuminate the soffits of the floor slabs are no longer used.

In this long section through the building the transparency of its internal spaces can be appreciated. The buildings compact overall form offered good energy-conserving characteristics despite the large areas of glass. Due to a high water table and poor ground conditions, basements were avoided and the natural fall of the site was used to minimise excavation for the swimming pool.

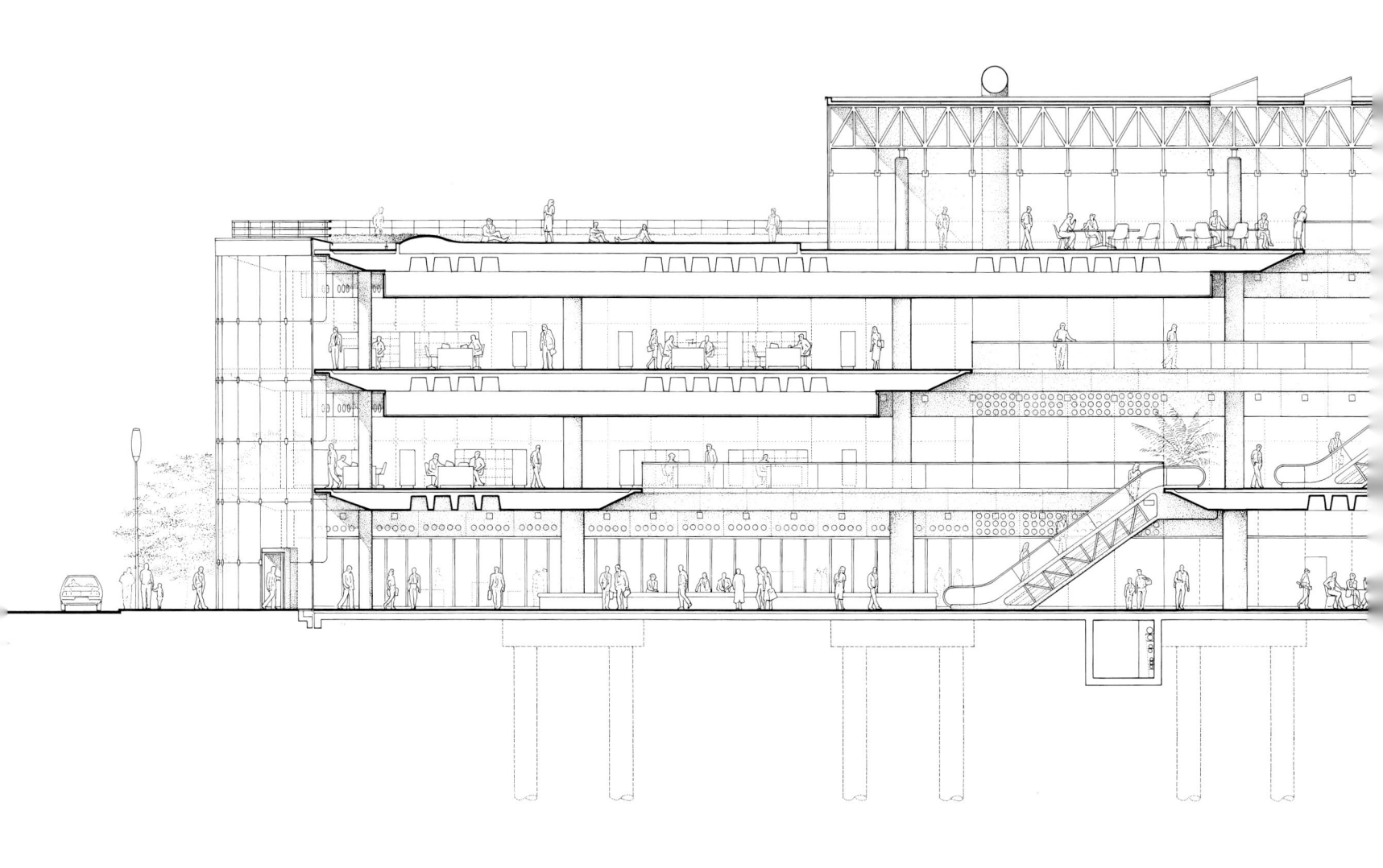

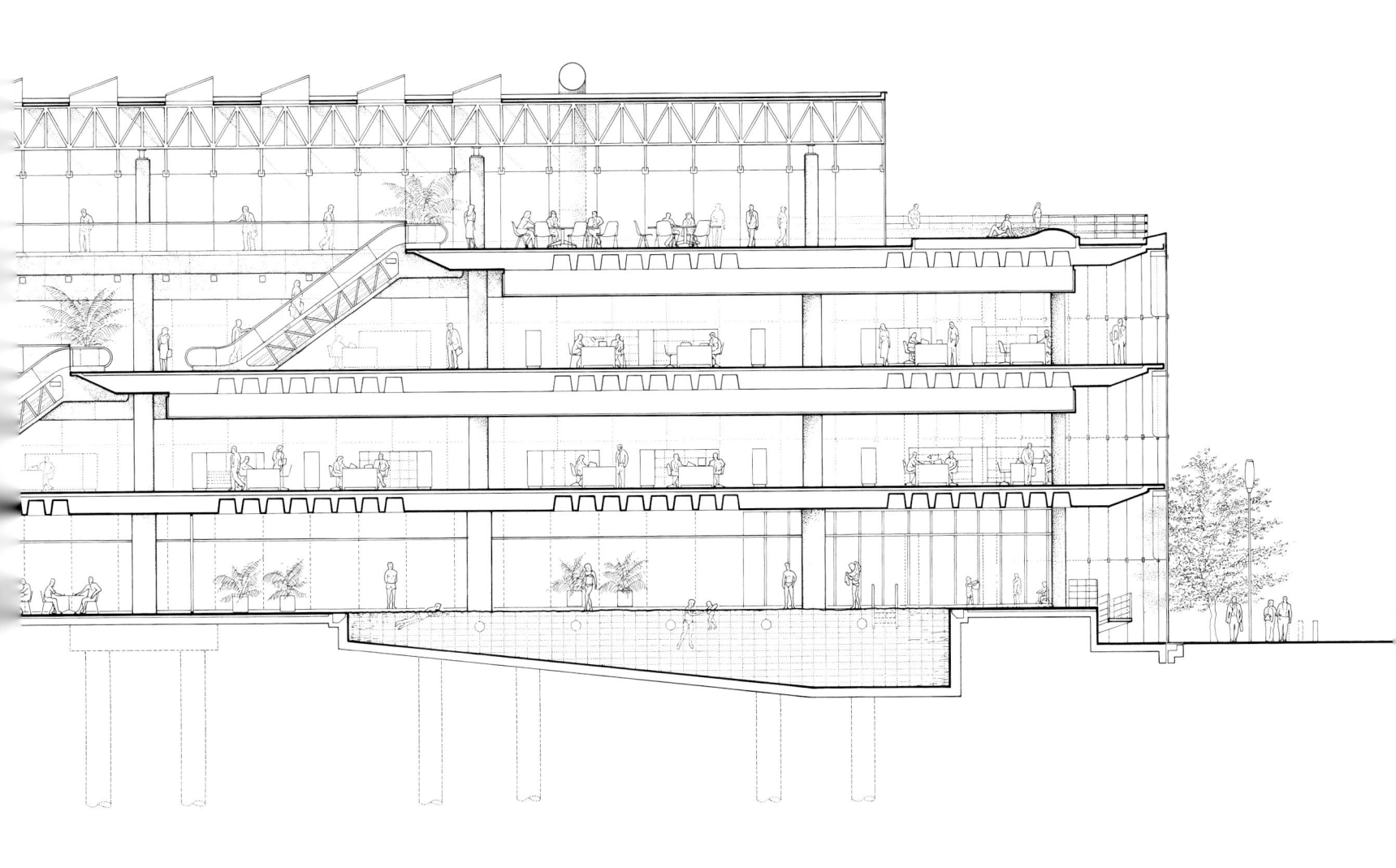

Willis Faber & Dumas

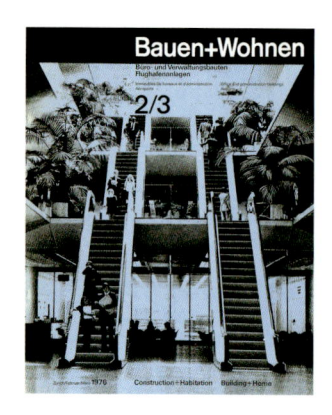

Left: Willis Faber featured on the covers of many architectural magazines of the period. It is seen here on the cover of *Bauen+Wohnen*, February 1976. The atrium with its bank of escalators offers a striking illustration of the philosophy at the heart of the building.

The rock-bottom, bottom-line fact about the work of Foster Associates is that you can't tell just by looking: you have to go inside ... The wavy form of Willis Faber & Dumas contains more space than we can guess from without, but it is not immediately apparent on entry because the rising plane of the escalator through the generous central lightwell makes one look at, and think about, other matters. It is a building to be explored before it is understood, and for this reason its levels of technology, servicing and energy consumption are not to be read by snap-judgement or any single viewpoint. Reyner Banham, *Foster Associates*, 1979

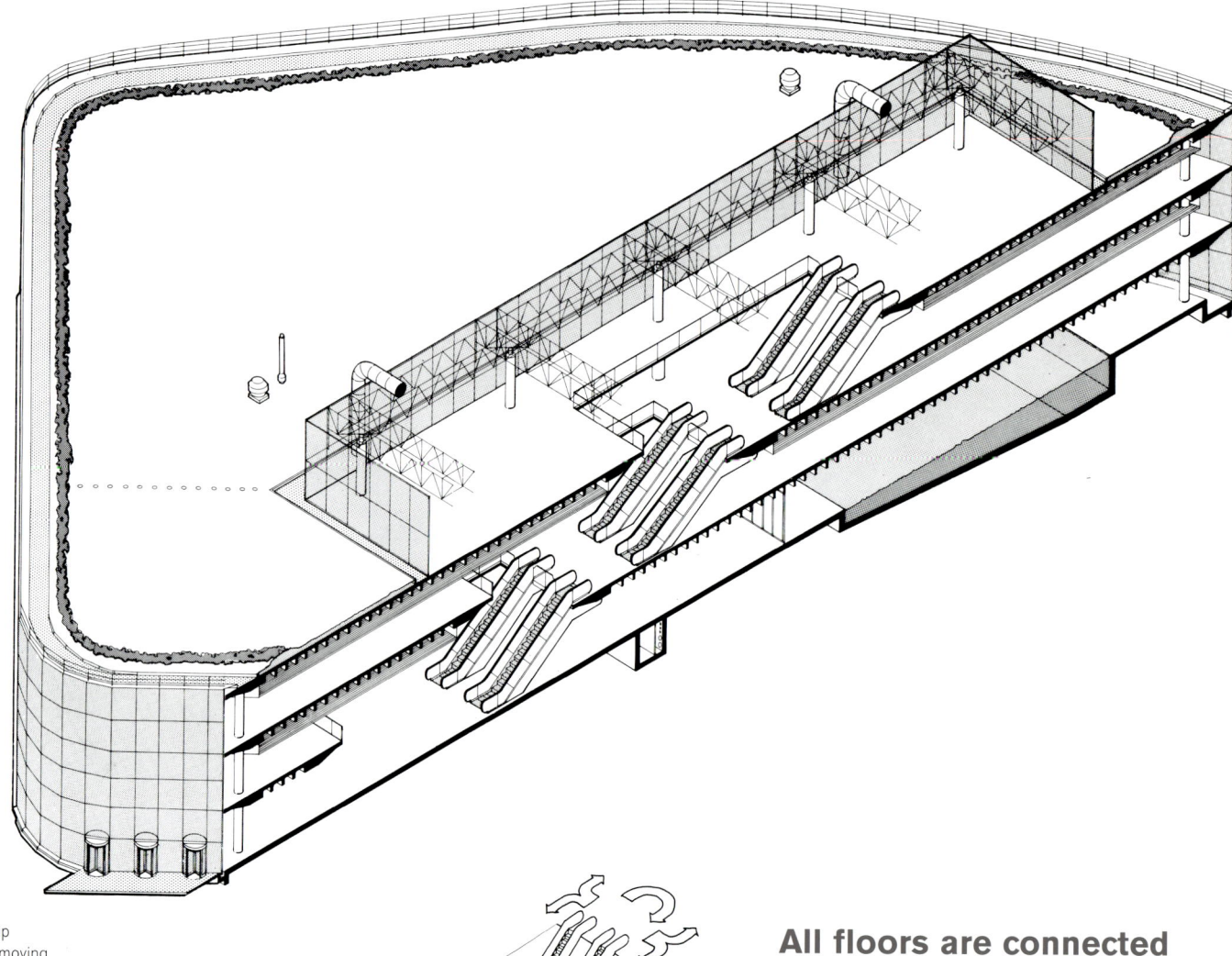

1-3. Escalators rise up through the building, moving from the entrance foyer towards the light and the amenities of roof level. To allow the roof to be left as free as possible, all the building's central services were located on the ground floor. This level also housed loading docks, computer rooms, data processing and a swimming pool (now decked over). A 'coffee shop', placed between the escalators and the swimming pool, formed an extension to the foyer and acted as a social hub during lunch-times and evenings.

**All floors are connected and penetrated by a vertical movement space containing banks of escalators. This space is the building's centre of gravity – it is important functionally, socially and symbolically.**

Norman Foster

328 Norman Foster Works 1

Looking at the wonderful amenities here, I am reminded of a story many years ago, when ICI built what was thought to be one of the most modern offices in London. The founder of the enterprise, Sir Alfred Mond, was taking a visitor around the building when his guest asked 'How many people work here?' 'Oh,' said Sir Alfred, 'ten per cent, not more.' I hope that in spite of all these amenities, or perhaps because of them, you will be able to advance to a higher figure.
The Rt Hon Harold Macmillan, speech at the official opening of Willis Faber & Dumas, Monday 2 June 1975
Right: The foundation stone, which Harold Macmillan had laid two years prior to opening the building.

**There were some things we did just because they seemed wild and wonderful ... As a reaction to an innate dislike of swimming in a washbasin with a rim, we designed a swimming pool where the water level is flush with the surrounding floor.**
Norman Foster, *Architectural Design* 9-10, September-October 1977

The imagery of Norman Foster's architecture has proved particularly compelling for artist Ben Johnson, and Willis Faber is no exception. Johnson executed two paintings of aspects of the Willis Faber building at the time of its completion and returned in 1984 to fulfil a commission from Michael Manser, then President of the RIBA, to be sponsored by British Gas.
Left: The resulting painting focused on the remarkable juxtaposition of the plant room, with its gas boilers and piping, and the limpid surface of the swimming pool.

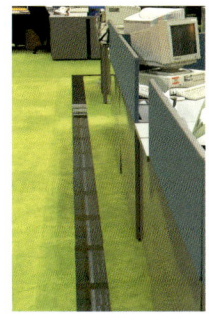

**Owning Britain's youngest Grade 1 listed building should have been a cause for celebration, but the accolade for the Willis Faber building in Ipswich has left insurance brokers Willis Corroon frustrated and disappointed for it has effectively thwarted a plan to cover its ground-floor swimming pool to create new offices.** *The Mail on Sunday*, 5 May 1991

In April 1991, Willis Faber proposed to cover up the swimming pool to create 2,136 square metres of office space. However, the Department of the Environment intervened and listed the building.
Left: The pool was subsequently decked over with a temporary structure that can be removed in the future if required. Glass panels reveal the line of the pool edge.

This system was able to combine a number of functions and so provide an integrated solution, which would not have been possible using individual 'off-the-shelf' elements. In this case the light-fittings, sprinkler outlets and parts of the air-conditioning return-air ducts are commonly supported within a ceiling formed from unidirectional polished aluminium slats.

## Willis Faber embodies Foster's commitment to an efficient and benign working environment.

With the freedom of purpose-built systems comes the responsibility of creating an efficient building. A popular misconception about Willis Faber is that its large area of glass must make the building inefficient in energy terms. But in fact the reverse is true. The solar-control glass successfully blocks solar gain and the deep plan means that the ratio of glass to floor area is approximately half that of most conventional office buildings. Additionally, the landscaped roof – while significant enough for its amenity value alone – provides the building with a highly insulating quilt, which further improves its overall thermal performance.

More impressively, the degree of insulation was so good that it eliminated the need for an expansion joint across the building, removing at a stroke an entire line of columns and associated foundations. Remember also that the designers presciently anticipated the oil crisis by specifying a natural gas-fired heating plant. It comes as no surprise, therefore, to discover that over the years the building has won as many awards for energy efficiency as it has for architectural merit.

Acknowledging, however, that the glazed edge condition involves the risk of greater extremes of temperature, the perimeter zone is identified as a 'thermal cushion' and used for circulation and informal meeting areas rather than seated office space.

This last aspect was one of Willis Faber's chief criteria in choosing a relocation site. Equally important was communicating the qualities and benefits of their new environment to the incoming staff. Part of the project team's remit was to introduce Willis Faber's staff to the town and, later, to the building itself. Foster did this with characteristic élan.

Most of the staff were readers of the London *Evening Standard* newspaper which featured the 'Bristow' cartoon strip. Bristow's life is dominated by 'the office', which made him the ideal medium for contrasting the effects of good and bad office environments. Foster commissioned Frank Dickens, Bristow's creator, to communicate the benefits of the new building in an amusing, accessible way.

Opposite: Perhaps the most radical element of the brief was the inclusion of a competition-standard swimming pool, an amenity hitherto unheard of in an office building. It was to prove immediately and enduringly popular both with members of staff and their families, who were invited to use it in the evenings and at weekends. At its peak it was used by an average of more than 70 people a day.

1. The quality of the installation was very high, with the green studded-rubber flooring running flush to the water level. The pool plant room was visible through all-glass partitions.

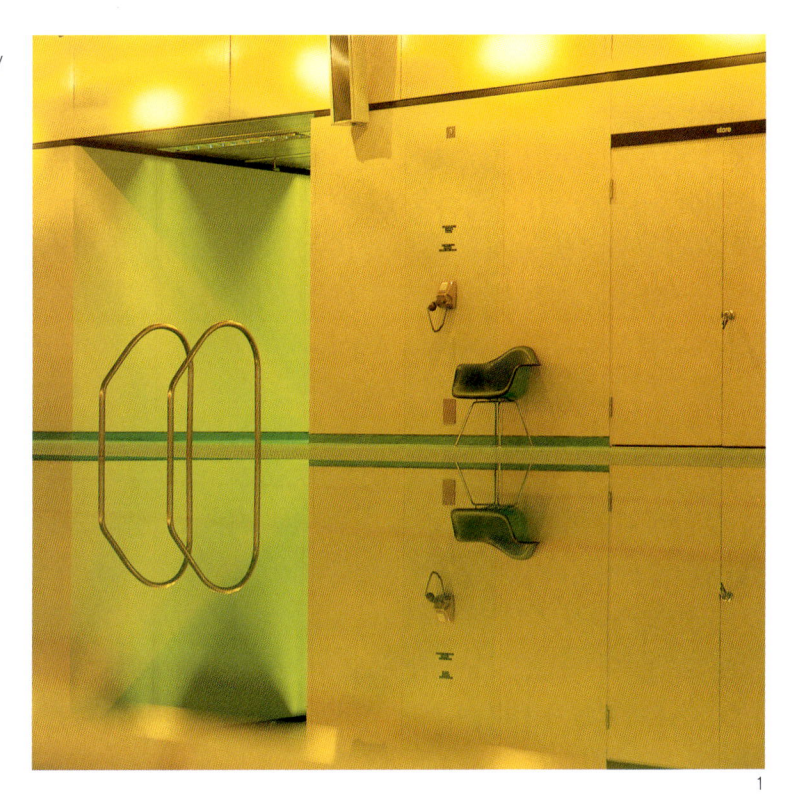

**I have always been interested in how buildings respond to change ... Our approach in the case of Willis Faber anticipated the information revolution and was a commercial lifeline to the company. Because we had provided suspended access floors throughout all their office areas, Willis Faber, unlike their competitors, did not have to embark on a new building programme in the 1980s. When the building was designed it was unheard of to provide this degree of flexibility outside computer rooms.** Norman Foster, in conversation with Malcolm Quantrill, 1999

**The degree to which the building works can be judged by the enthusiasm expressed for it by the person most likely to loathe it: the facilities manager. Peter Smith is the natural enemy of the badly designed building – but he is almost disconcertingly positive about Willis Faber: 'There has been an explosion in technology since 1975, but everything still works ... the air conditioning, the floor-loading of the building, the lighting, the floor ducts for cabling. Much of this technology was new at the time and using it may have seemed risky. But ... the architect's foresight has saved us a fortune.'** Dan Cruickshank, *RIBA Journal*, June 1997

1, 2. Following the principle that all main service installations would be open to view, even the escalators were redesigned to better integrate structure and cladding, and to incorporate glass-sided panels that would reveal their inner workings.

3. The use of escalators as the main form of circulation brought unexpected benefits. Several directors commented that the company had developed a true family spirit in the new building because people now stopped and talked on the escalators, creating a social focus at the heart of the building.

**The open office floors, centrally located escalators, and floor to ceiling glass walls offer a foretaste of the spaces Foster was to design ten years later for the Hongkong Bank.** Graham Vickers

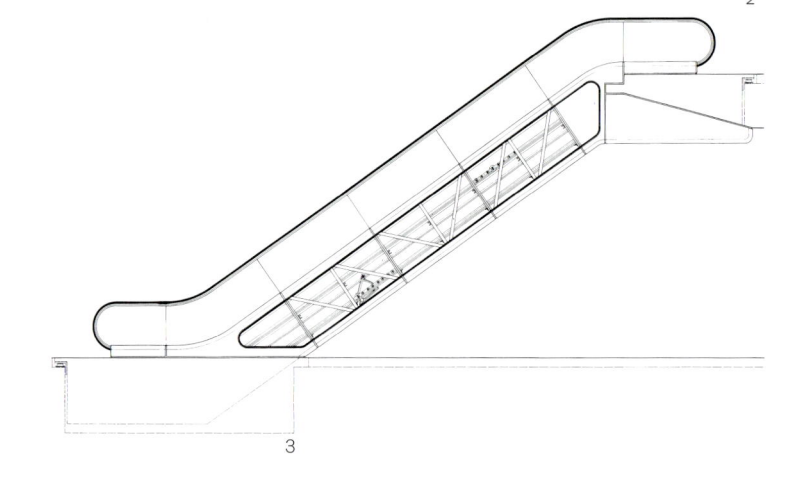

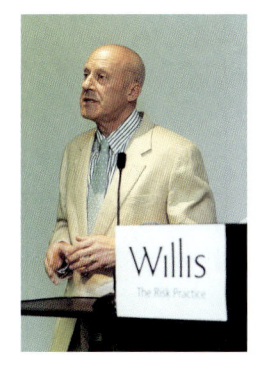

**This building has stood the test of time. It has seen the introduction of new technology without any problem and it's still as good as new. Only the original carpets are up for renewal, but 25 years is a good life for any carpet!** Norman Foster, speech at the reception to mark the 25th anniversary of the Willis Faber building, June 2000.
Right: Willis Faber staff past and present celebrated the occasion with a garden party on the roof of the building.

In its realisation, the Willis Faber building embodies Foster's early commitment to an efficient and benign working environment as illustrated in the Bristow cartoons. Fundamental to that commitment were the assumptions that people generally prefer green open spaces to rectilinear concrete blocks and natural light over artificial. More specifically, it was thought that within a large organisation, lifts would tend to inhibit communication while escalators might encourage social contact. The resulting loss of floor space may be cited in opposition to this view, but the social advantages are obvious and not as difficult to evaluate in financial terms as is sometimes assumed.
Similarly, to give restaurants and snack bars mean little spaces on the grounds that they are 'non-productive' areas is surely to misread the value of a happy workforce. Cellular offices, with the associated problems of isolation and temperature control, were taken to be inferior to a sympathetic interpretation of Bürolandschaft – at the time an unusual solution in the UK. With Willis Faber Foster created a building in which staff well-being is not simply a slogan but – as the roof garden demonstrates – an integral part of the structure. As his sketches show, Foster recognised the amenity value of the roof very early on. What better, in a tightly-knit urban setting, than to recreate the site at roof level in the form of an open park?

Foster uses the Corbusian term, the 'fifth elevation', aware that in an age of high-rise buildings roofs are no longer invisible. It is an acknowledgement also that the Willis Faber garden has its roots in the roof deck of Le Corbusier's Marseilles Unité d'Habitation, with its marvellous views and liner-like sun deck. To convince the client of the merits of this idea, Foster took the client to see London's (then) closest equivalent, the roof-top tea garden of the Derry & Toms building in Kensington. They were immediately won over.

Offering as it does a typically Fosterian combination of amenity with economy, the Willis Faber roof garden has more than justified its existence. Filled with sunbathers in the summer, and host to the occasional morning jogger on its running track, it has been a source of delight for staff and visitors alike over the years.

The artist Ben Johnson, for whom the Willis Faber building has been a continuing source of inspiration and subject matter, watched the building progress towards completion and saw the first employees move in: 'Norman has always been deeply concerned about the working conditions of the occupants of his buildings. I saw how this worked at first hand. The employees would arrive from the old building in Southend and after only a few days in the new building you could see the physical change in them. Their quality of life had been transformed.'

4, 5. These two photographs, taken 20 years apart, in 1975 and 1995 respectively, show how the building has adapted to changing information technology. Designed for flexibility, the building incorporated raised floors throughout all the office spaces. This has enabled Willis Faber to accommodate greatly increased amounts of computer cabling with ease, avoiding the costly alternative of moving to new premises, a choice that faced many of its competitors.

4

5

**I always think it is somewhat tragic that when you contemplate the view of any city from a high-rise building that the possibility of recreating the ground level site at the top of a building is generally squandered.** Norman Foster, lecture at Aspen Design Conference, 16 June 1980
Left: The sixth-storey roof garden of the former Derry & Toms building in Kensington, London – built in the 1920s – was a favourite source of reference when discussing with the client the benefits of a landscaped roof.

**In Foster's buildings it is the quantitative aspect of ephemeralisation that has attracted most attention: the light lattice structures, the neoprene gasketry, the frameless glazing. But it is the less conspicuous work done on the space itself which is most significant: the improvement, by an appropriate disposition of the structure, of the quality of space contained within; enriching and diversifying the range of options either presently offered by the space, or easily attainable by virtue of its inherent flexibility.** Richard Padovan, *International Architect*, No. 1, 1979

**Foster recognised the amenity value of the roof very early on in the design process. What better, in a tightly-knit urban setting, than to recreate the site at roof level in the form of an open park?**
Graham Vickers

You look up through the floors to the white painted, tubular-steel space-frame supporting the glazed roof, and to the sunlight. Escalators carry you there – you glide soundlessly upwards, floor by floor of apple-green carpet, in your commercial dream. At the top you surface, and the green carpet leads out to the turf of the restaurant's green roof garden which overlooks the real world. Stephen Gardiner, *Observer Review*, 22 June 1975

**One unusual aspect of the Willis Faber building is that it now has Grade 1 listed building status – which puts it on a par with an historical monument such as Ely Cathedral! interestingly, both buildings can be seen as appropriate technological responses to the architectural challenges of their age – right at the cutting edge of what was possible at the time, and far removed from the romantic associations that might follow in a later age.** Norman Foster, in conversation with the editor, June 2001

Left: The austere form of Ely Cathedral rises from the flat East Anglian landscape.

Since its completion, Willis Faber's glass wall has proved the most controversial aspect of the design, receiving praise and criticism in almost equal measure. The design team was aware from the start that the glass, which is deeply tinted to reduce solar gain, might generate a visually heavy, solid dark form. However, experience from earlier projects also revealed the architectural potential of reflected images; Ipswich, with its rich tapestry of tightly circumscribing buildings, provided ample scope for such visual delights.

Kenneth Knight offers his own perspective: 'Having seen it all by day, the building takes on a new look by night. No longer is it the black building at the bottom of Prince's Street, but rather the "goldfish bowl". At night it discloses its inner self, and all is revealed for the world to see.' Aware that the new building was attracting visitors – their noses pressed against the glass – Willis Faber set up numerous visits for local societies and organisations, which lasted over a period of two years.

Kenneth Knight again: 'It was our view that the local public should be invited to understand the purpose of this building and the manner in which it works. Having been given a tour, their hearts have been won in admiration. They appreciate the building as a splendid place in which to work. Often at the end of a tour, people would say how much they wished that they, or maybe their children, could work within those black glass walls.'

Willis Faber's all-glass wall is a technological achievement of the highest order – a brilliant distillation of experience gained from the earlier buildings for IBM and Olsen. And although much copied, it has never been improved on.

But to focus on Willis Faber's external form is to miss a crucial aspect of the design: the indivisible relationship between inside and outside and the qualities of its interiors. The open office floors, centrally located escalators, and floor to ceiling glass walls offer a foretaste of the spaces Foster was to design some ten years later for the Hongkong Bank. Even the technical details of Willis Faber's raised floors and the use of distributed service cores would be developed further in that project.

It is perhaps fitting that Willis Faber should be one of the very few post-war buildings to enjoy Grade 1 listed status – the highest level of legal protection – putting it on a par with historical landmarks such as Ely Cathedral. Interestingly, as Norman Foster has observed, both buildings are appropriate technological responses to the architectural challenges of their age, both operating at the cutting edge of what was achievable at the time.

Graham Vickers

1-3. The use of escalators as the only means of vertical circulation for the office staff was a direct response to the kind of work carried out by the client company, with its strong emphasis on regular but rather ad hoc inter-departmental meetings. Their success was to have far-reaching effects: ten years later the directors of the Hongkong Bank were so impressed that they accepted the use of escalators in their new headquarters.

4-6. The English weather may mean that the roof garden is not used as often as liked – although it is very popular in the summer – but the pleasant aspect it affords the restaurant makes it more than worthwhile.

Overleaf: Brian Clarke's distinctive Willis Faber tapestry now hangs at the head of the escalators.

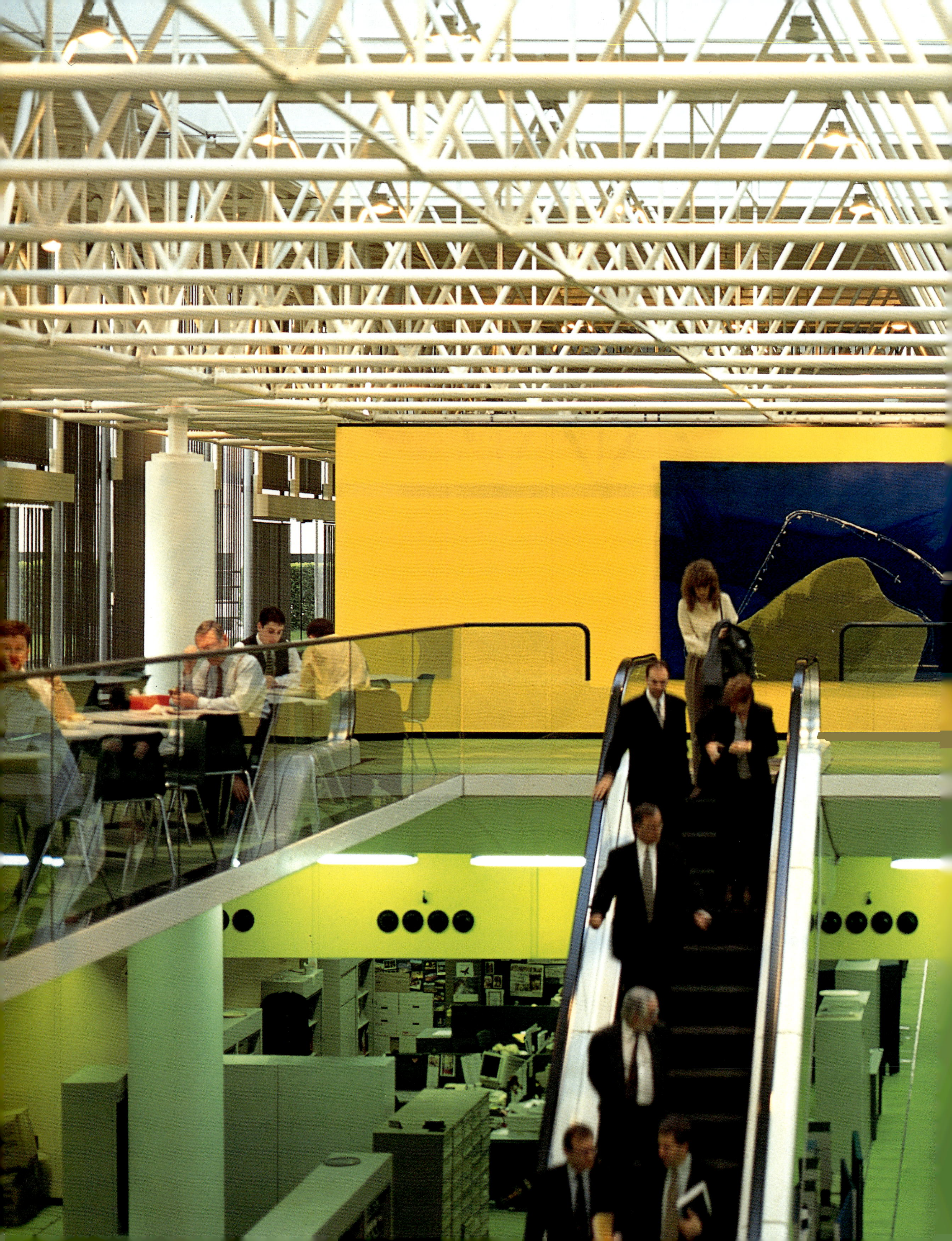

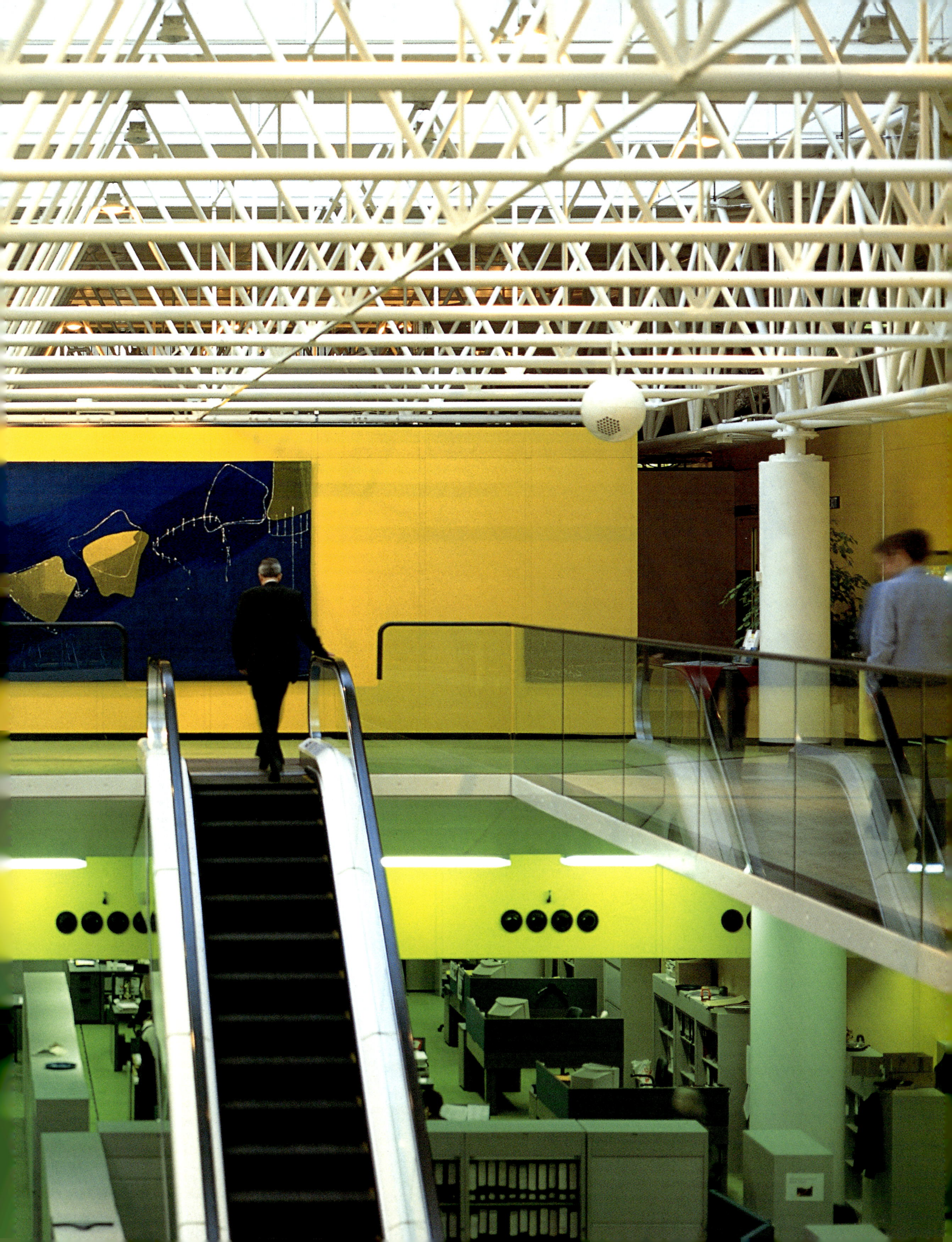

# Social Ends, Technical Means
Norman Foster 1977

When the Willis Faber and Dumas building was first published, most magazines at the time began and ended their coverage of the building with pictures of curved glass walls and high technology. Whilst one should not underestimate the importance of such technical means, for me they have never been ends in themselves. The ends are always social – generated by people rather than the hardware of buildings. However, the relationship between ends and means is a vital part of our approach. Together with my known association with Buckminster Fuller, any study of the practice's earlier work, from 1963 onwards (without which it would have been impossible to contemplate this design) should make clear our position on adopting what we believe to be appropriate technologies in achieving social goals.

In a fundamental sense the building is really about people and their place of work. Socially, of course, this is a moving target. Herman Kahn, American futurologist of the Hudson Institute, once made the point that those office buildings that failed to anticipate what he saw as inevitable social changes would simply become obsolete if they did not respond by raising standards and providing a high proportion of amenities. In his view, these were not just philanthropic gestures, simply the hard cutting edges of changing real estate values. My own experience bears this out.

It is perhaps worth giving a reminder of the concept – the parti – of the Willis Faber building. Essentially, two office floors – for around 1,300 people – are elevated and sandwiched between amenity and support areas above and below them. The ground level comprises a concourse, swimming pool, coffee bar, gymnasium, crèche (since changed), mechanical and electrical plant, computer suite and internal truck-loading docks. The roof level comprises a glass restaurant pavilion set in a landscaped garden.

All floors are connected and penetrated by a vertical movement space containing banks of escalators. This space is filled with palm trees and flooded with daylight from generously glazed rooflights; it forms the centre of gravity of the building and is important functionally, socially and symbolically. Giving it a precise name or label is difficult; the various titles of 'winter garden', 'internal court' or 'atrium' provide clues to its character but do not adequately convey the spirit of the place.

The proportion of amenity area to work area is high, especially if the near acre of roof garden is included in the equation. This is due in large part to design ingenuity as well as resource allocation. This emphasis on amenity in the workplace and raising standards represented a virtual about-face from the office buildings of the time, whether prestige one-offs or reach-me-down spec developments. Most office buildings raise standards for the visitor 'front of house' – gobbling up disproportionate slices of funds in the process – and gradually dilute them as you move further 'backstage' towards the users.

**To help explain our proposals for Willis Faber & Dumas to the client, we contacted Frank Dickens who did the Bristow cartoons to broach the idea that he might use his skills to communicate the spirit of the building and why it might be different from the traditional office. He got completely carried away with the idea and produced a sequence of about 40 of these messages.** Norman Foster, lecture at Hong Kong University, 2 February 1980
Right to far right and overleaf: Frank Dickens' vignettes contrast the inefficient and unsympathetic working environment of the traditional office – as endured by Bristow, the archetypal white-collar employee – with the radically improved conditions to be found in the new Willis Faber building.

The reverse is true at Willis Faber. The entrance has exposed concrete structure (enlivened with emulsion paint), studded rubber flooring (the same as the boiler room and the lavatories) and demountable metal partitions (just like everywhere else). This compares in the two office floors with carpet (the same carpet, incidentally, that was laid in the 1970s) and custom-designed ceilings with glare-free light fittings. This is not a reaction against fine finishes; it is more a question of how you define priorities and reflect them in the allocation of fixed financial resources.

**Whilst one should not underestimate the importance of technical means, for me they have never been ends in themselves. The ends are always social – generated by people rather than by the hardware of buildings.**

If the workplace is so vital that it determines the priority of finishes, then the spaces themselves are conceived in the same spirit. In a typical office building the working areas are 'out of sight and out of mind'; the only aids to orientation are the lift floor button you push, the number on the door. The better-designed versions might have sleeker skins but they are fundamentally the same animal underneath. The reverse is everywhere apparent at Willis Faber. Movement is open, literally in the sun, and social contact is natural and relaxed across the entire spectrum of the company. Orientation is immediate; you always know where you are. The barriers are few and seldom visual.

A management approach characterised by an open-door policy in Willis Faber's original building is here reflected by a virtual absence of doors. The only planned cellular office – for the Deputy Chairman – was lost en route in the design process; and by the same token the 'directors' dining room' became an exercise in furniture design to define a part of the main restaurant. Even that space has now become a 'visitors' dining room'. The kinds of spaces described here are in no manner fixed for the future. Indeed the technology that enables them to work at present also provides the flexibility for them to reflex at some future point into quite different patterns.

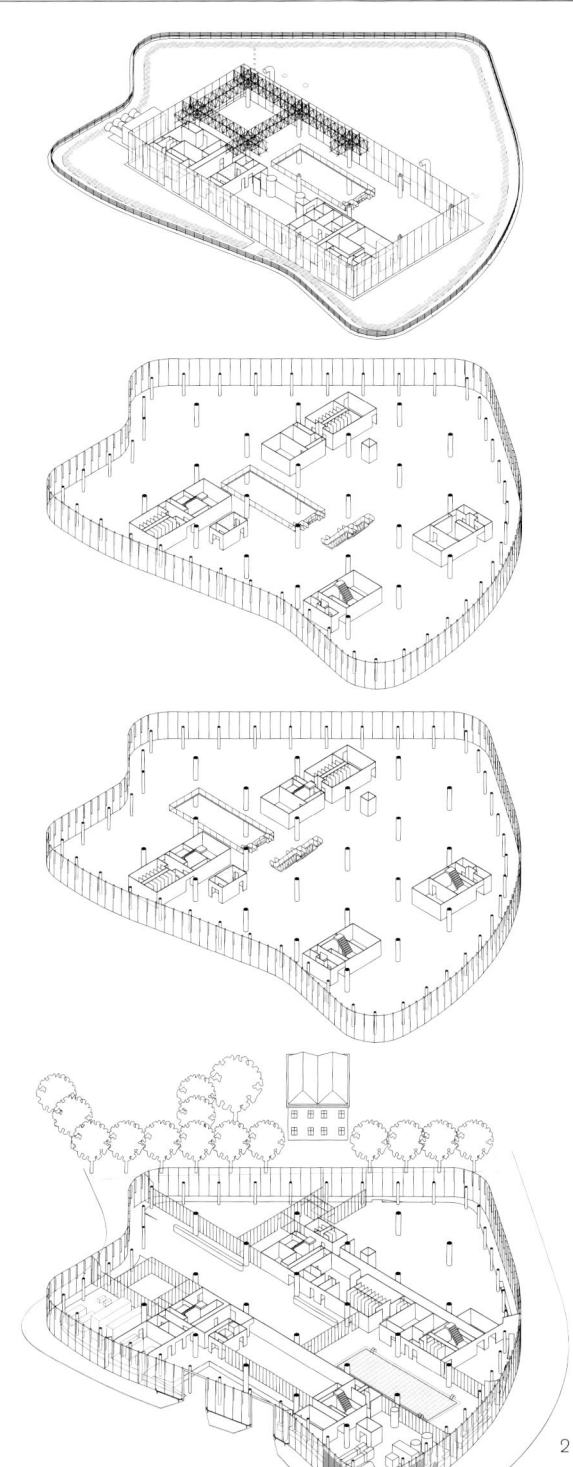

1. At night the building becomes transparent, revealing its inner workings to view. Although critical attention has tended to focus on the technological advances of the glass wall, it is the building's radical social programme that really marks it as unique.

2. By stretching the building out to the site boundaries, and covering the entire site area, the required 21,000 square metres of space specified in the brief could be provided on three floors. The whole administrative function of the building was grouped on just two of these floors, both almost entirely open plan and housing up to 600 people. Support facilities and communal staff amenities, including a swimming pool, restaurant and roof garden, occupy the ground and uppermost floors. Escalators connect the different levels and provide the building with a social focus – the animated equivalent of the village pump.

1. The use of open-plan offices for all members of staff was initially regarded with scepticism by some. But in practice the layout has proved very successful over the years. The glare-free light fittings have been particularly effective, and no additional task lighting has ever been required.

2. Rather than present the best finishes to the visitor and then gradually dilute them towards the user, the reverse approach was adopted at Willis Faber. The entrance hall has an exposed concrete structure, enlivened only with emulsion paint, and studded rubber flooring: the same finishes as found in the plant rooms, the swimming pool and the lavatories. This compares with carpet and custom-designed ceilings with glare-free lighting throughout the two office floors.

The plan form and cross section are a response to balancing and reconciling a range of priorities that are frequently in conflict: namely how to achieve the sympathetic integration of the company and the community. Or, to put it another way, how to relate a large new building on the edge of a historical town. The key factor was to adopt a very low deep building which enables a commercially viable content to equate with a low profile. There are other significant benefits; for example: fewer larger floors allow more efficient space utilisation, greater flexibility and far lower energy consumption.

At this point it is worth considering the kinds of outdoor space that typify a town like Ipswich. They must surely be its streets? It seemed to me that so many modern buildings have largely ignored random street patterns by imposing hard rectilinear geometries. That might be appropriate on a green-field site or in low-density suburbia, but it is alien to dense, complex urban areas (excepting, of course, those cities that come with 90-degree gridiron plans). Apart from destroying the coherence of the street pattern, the leftover spaces produced by such developments tend to be hostile and unusable. In Ipswich, by pushing the building to the limit of the site boundaries the original street pattern was reinforced. This is the complete opposite of arbitrary shape making, whether rectilinear or free form.

The remainder of our townscape proposals are as yet unrealised. Our early drawings show a gravelled urban space with trees, forming a forecourt to the Unitarian Meeting House. In the tradition of pedestrian thoroughfares elsewhere in the town, it was intended to link this forecourt through the existing passageway to St Nicholas Street to encourage small-scale additions to the adjacent shops, restaurants and cafés.

**At Willis Faber movement is open and social contact is natural and relaxed across the spectrum of the company. Orientation is immediate; you always know where you are. The barriers are few and seldom visual.**

The building was the outcome of leading a team approach, in which the key was to shift the traditional roles of those concerned with designing and fabrication. For example, many activities were streamed in parallel in the early stages of the project. This was essential on a crash programme: two years of feverish design and building activity with a minimum run-up period. The client's lawyers described the site as having 'every problem in the book', but we found new ones to swell its pages. During the complexities of demolitions and services diversions, as architects we were more involved in what might be better described as management consultancy than the exercise of any normal design-based skill. In any discussion of 'means' one should not forget the operational and management techniques that we virtually take for granted; management can never be divorced from the design process.

A briefing guide was specifically developed for the project to provide insight into the client's organisation and its working methods. In collaboration with Willis Faber a joint management committee was established to oversee the project; it was chaired by the Company Secretary and involved the past company Chairman. This working group, with permanent architect representation, was able to co-opt other consultants as necessary. It could monitor progress and review options and had direct communication with the main Board at regular intervals.

This collaboration began so early in the life of the project that it actually preceded the final definition and purchase of the site itself. We developed many preliminary design strategies in response to varying early site options – some involved closing roads, others spanning over them. It soon became apparent, however, that the real estate process was so volatile that it was impossible to reflex quickly enough with traditional on-off design responses. Allied with a detailed understanding of the brief and its major fixes, a careful analysis of ground conditions beneath the building, and an insight into the process of site acquisition, provided the main clues.

We found that an overall column grid of 14 x14 metres – which kept within an acceptable cost threshold – related well to office planning constraints and allowed us to straddle such fixes as a swimming pool and, if necessary, to span roads and truck docks. In a building that has no 'back' or 'front', the latter have to be located inside the building, at least if good street manners are to be respected. Furthermore, providing an edge 'necklace' of columns allowed us to tune the perimeter to follow closely the lines of existing street boundaries.

The detailed development of the structure was also influenced by the constraints of mechanical and electrical engineering systems. The integrated nature of the practice was a key factor at all times. Working with Tony Hunt we devised an ingenious modular system based on a specially designed plastic mould. This eliminated downstand beams throughout – which kept the overall height of the building down while providing the maximum flexibility for duct runs – and provided a structure that is handsome enough to stand in its own right. This was good for the budget (no need to paste over it) and good for the programme (fewer on-site trades). In its final form the structure was boiled down to remarkably few elements: columns and floor slabs internally; and a necklace of columns with a cantilevered slab at the perimeter. In designing the structure we also had to anticipate the mechanics of building swiftly and economically on a tight urban site.

**The building attempted to challenge preconceptions about office buildings, to introduce more joy, sunlight, a swimming pool, roof gardens. The achievement of such luxuries within the realities of a tight commercial budget represented a special kind of design challenge.**
Norman Foster

1. At the top of the building, staff in the restaurant look out onto the roof garden, the first of a series of 'gardens in the sky' that reappear in the Foster oeuvre. Willis Faber's 'elevated park' would prompt the design of the unrealised sky gardens of the Hongkong Bank and, in turn, the spiralling gardens in the Commerzbank, in Frankfurt.

Ultimately, the structure was the only site-based wet trade. Everything else was shop fabricated to maximise quality control and speed of erection. These were not the only reasons, although they are fairly persuasive, especially when programme, cost and attention to detail are taken into account. A belief and joy in using the materials of the age, allied with an economy of means, were important additional factors. This approach also involved a shift in roles because if the product we wanted was not available 'off the peg' (and hardly anything was in the integrated sense of the word) then we designed a new one and collaborated with the manufacturers to produce it. This meant secondment to industry where appropriate and the frequent use of full-scale tests and mock-ups. A brief summary of how some key purpose-designed elements were developed might give an insight into the relationship between design and the management techniques that made our creative goals technically feasible.

The suspended glass wall was a response to the notion that most people are happier inside a building when they are able to see outside, provided that they do not suffer some discomfort as a consequence. That concept could no doubt be phrased in a more scientific manner but it would come down to the same sentiments. Unlike shallow-plan buildings – where a fully glazed perimeter can have a drastic effect on energy loads – in a deep-plan building such as this the effect is relatively insignificant. Furthermore, unlike shallow plans where a hole in the wall will suffice, to ensure that everybody in a deep building (not just those closest to the perimeter) enjoys visual contact with the outside world, the proportion of glass has to be generous. This led us to consider several alternative glazing systems that would combine such qualities of transparency with acoustic and solar control.

**This emphasis on amenity in the workplace and raising standards represented a virtual about-face in the office buildings of the time.**

An awareness that glass is at its strongest in tension prompted the concept of a glazed curtain suspended from the top edge of the building. Unfortunately we were unable to convince anyone outside the office that it was technically feasible. For that reason all the interior perspectives of that period show a steel mullion system designed for the project and test-bedded in a smaller installation for Modern Art Glass, in Thamesmead. Eventually, however, enough calculations and technical details emerged to convince specialist suppliers and subcontractors that the idea was not only viable but also looked very attractive in cost terms (hardly surprising since it reduced the major elements down to just glass and glue). At this point we found that industry was so keen to get in on the act that Pilkington (the glazing subcontractor) happily traded design warranties in exchange for rights to our details.

The office floor and ceiling systems followed similar development paths; in both cases the design process was driven by a desire to integrate what had hitherto been separate products in single-system solutions. The parabolic light fittings, for example, which are integrated within the ceiling, are designed to accommodate the air-distribution and extract grilles for office areas and house sprinkler runs, as well as providing a separate emergency lighting system. Additionally, the power and cable runs on the office floors telegraph through the lighting grid above and below. Compare this with the more usual proliferation (and redundancy) of separate suspended elements, which are typically brought together on-site in the equivalent of a last-minute shotgun marriage.

Conscious that future flexibility would be thwarted by fixed cable trunking runs (then the norm) and aware that wet screeds take for ever to install and cure, we searched for more viable alternatives. The result is a suspended floor system, with continuous lines of easily removable access panels, which we developed specifically for this project by working with a manufacturer. Our goals were high speed, low cost, optimum appearance and maximum flexibility, although not necessarily in that order (then, as now, it was extremely difficult to consider these factors in a precise hierarchy since they are so closely related).

Similarly, the design development and final definition of facilities and standards was inextricably linked with continuous financial appraisals: quite the opposite of a static brief and cost response. A wide variety of options were examined, always related back to a base yardstick of minimum shell cost. One analogy was the Ford Mustang which, given a basic chassis, could produce infinite variations of models. Alternatives were evaluated with particular sensitivity to cost-in-use. The exterior of the building, for example, is virtually maintenance-free; the glass wall almost wipes its own face and apart from an occasional haircut, the turf roof looks after itself. Considerable ingenuity was deployed to minimise the on-cost of potential fringe benefits and thereby encourage their introduction. For example, in capital terms, a landscaped roof is certainly more expensive than asphalt. However, by beefing it up a little it provided such a good insulating quilt that we were able to eliminate expansion joints across the entire building, with their attendant (and costly) double rows of columns and piles. Allied to that are considerable long-term energy savings.

For financial justification the building had to be potentially sublettable. Three factors make such an option quite straightforward. Firstly, the internal court with its escalators is capable of functioning as a semi-public space used by all office tenants. Secondly, each floor has four cores enclosing escape stairs and utilities to allow up to four major sub-divisions of space from a common access gallery formed by the escalator well. Smaller suites would be possible with shared rather than private toilets. Thirdly, the internal servicing systems allow total subdivision into cellular offices if required.

This design approach is perhaps best characterised as a process of integration, reconciling views and polarities which might otherwise be in conflict; for example: the company versus the community; public versus private; new versus old; time and cost versus quality and innovation; socially acceptable versus commercially viable. Another vital part of the approach is a conscious attempt to put all those dry objective pieces of the jigsaw (research, statistics, cost plan, site analysis, structural options – the check list is endless) together with some very subjective joy.

2. The swimming pool was to prove immensely popular with Willis Faber's staff. Records for 1981, for example, show that 23,000 people used the pool during that year – an average of more than 70 a day. Out of hours, the pool was open to both staff and their families.

Overleaf: Taken shortly after the building's completion, this memorable photograph by John Donat, of a mother teaching her child to swim, must surely rank as one of the most touching images from British Modernism.

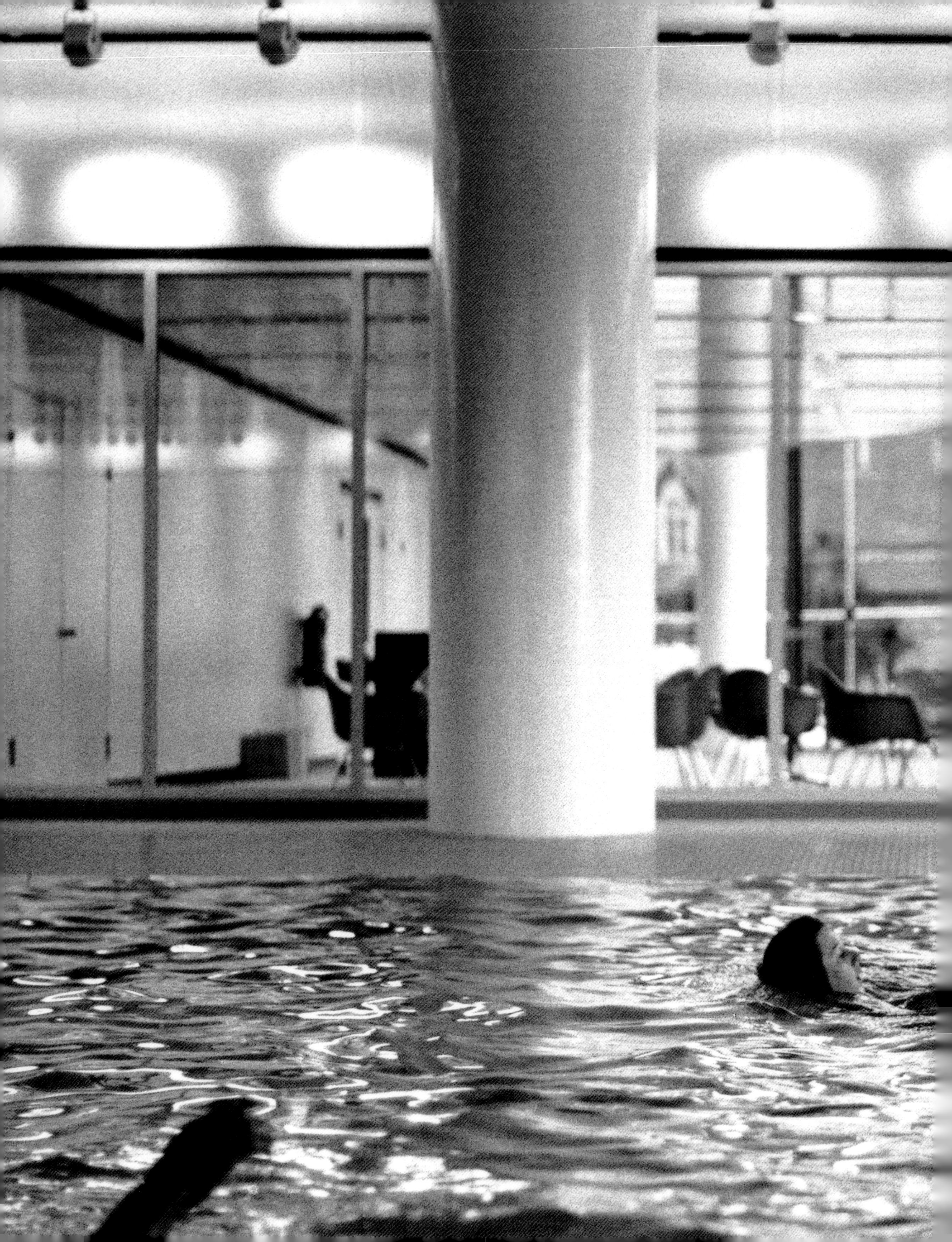

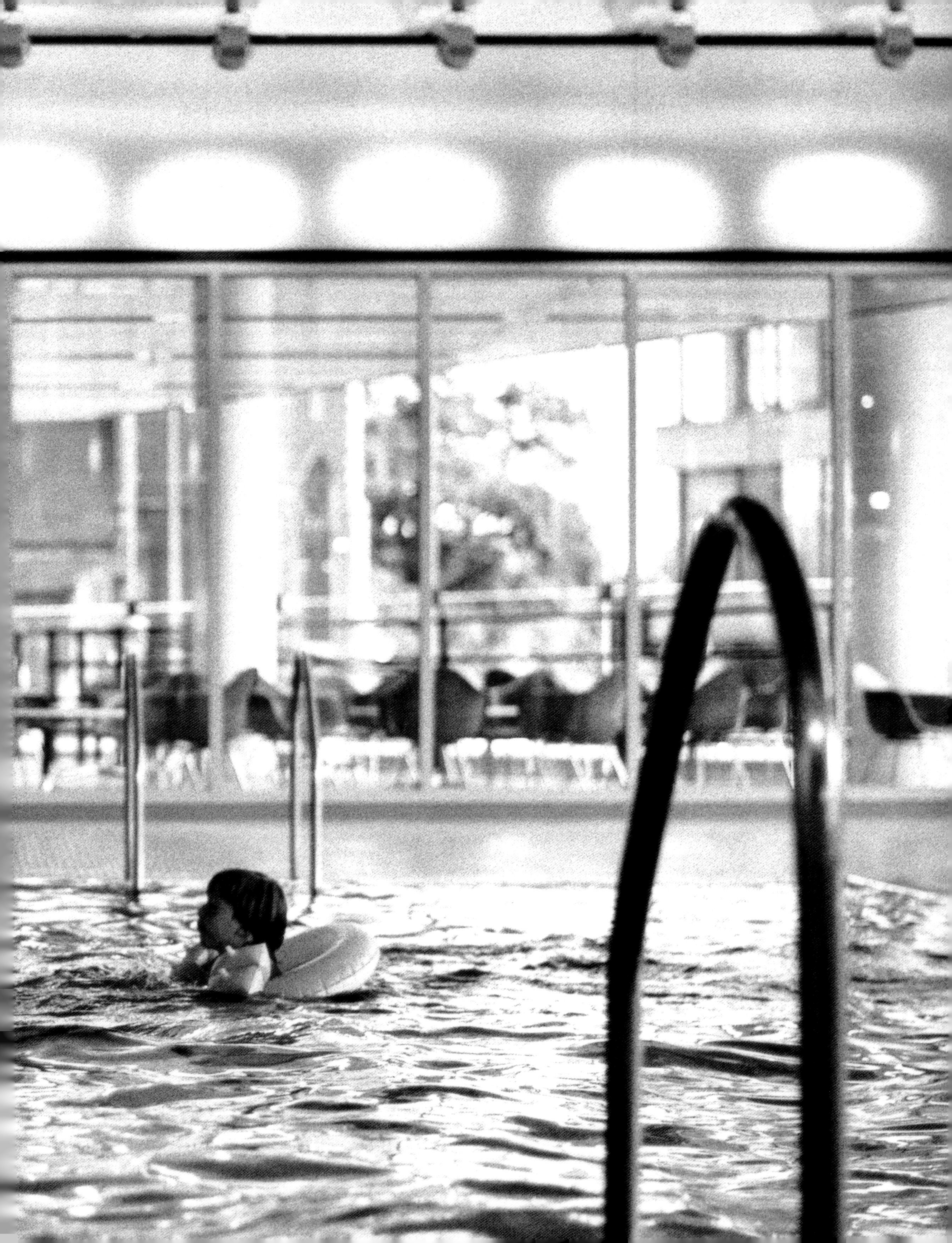

# Sapa Factory
Tibshelf, England 1972–1973

**Sapa Factory**

**Yes, we are still here. The building was a little bit ahead of its time when it was built, but it's very nice to work in.** Sapa receptionist, in telephone conversation with the editor, 2001

**Gaunt shed and crude office, the Sapa building certainly stands out. Amid general numbing environmental pain just a sore thumb would be unnoticed. But the view from dismal surrounding suburbia may anyway be concealed in two decades, for the site edges are banked and unusually generously planted. Perhaps the bland factory exterior is a fair reaction to the brief and to the site, while it hides the surprise of the brightly (and entirely artificially) lit interior. Under the pallid skin are green and red, blue and orange arteries and muscles, sinews and heart.**
*The Architects' Journal*, November 1973

In the spring of 1972, having committed to building a British manufacturing plant, the Swedish metal extrusion company Sapa commissioned Foster Associates to undertake joint site searches and production engineering studies. Investigations into plant and layouts were carried out in Sweden and Holland, then related to equipment available on short delivery times. Eventually a 4.26-acre site was found in a newly designated industrial estate just off the M1 motorway. Within a year the factory had been completed, ready to start full production.

## The smooth-running 'industrial machine' ticks over regularly under a plain bonnet, relieved only by the bright blue Sapa logo emblazoned on the facade.

Items normally outside the building brief were drawn into the ten-month period allowed for design and construction. The Foster team met a full production-engineering brief and the contract included ordering and installing all manufacturing equipment. The first phase factory building housed an extrusion press and associated machinery; by March 1977 it had expanded to comprise two presses, an anodising plant, a fabrication shop and additional staff facilities. Ultimately the site could accommodate expansion of up to four times the original building volume.

The internal plan organisation follows the manufacturing process in its essentially linear progression, beginning with vehicle entry and ingot storage, followed by the extrusion press, water and air quenchers, and the run-out table, with production offices located alongside. Packing, weighing and dispatch are located at the far end of the factory.

The phase-two expansion tripled the factory floor area. With a lead-time of only four months, the new plant was fully operational within a total of nine months. Machinery was installed while the building was being completed and full production was maintained throughout.

Sapa had a progressive attitude to industrial democracy. Its declared objective was to 'make profits and have fun doing it'. Creating a high-quality working environment was central to that approach. With the company's encouragement, Foster consulted employees prior to the phase-two expansion. Some workers, for example those in the die shop, were allowed to define their own requirements.

In contrast to this self-expression, the building takes the 'undecorated shed' to the nth degree. The smooth-running industrial machine ticks over regularly beneath a plain bonnet, relieved only by the bright blue Sapa logo emblazoned on the facade. Like the factory process, which is self-contained, the working environment respects the client's directive to be closed and secure and entirely artificially lit. From outside, the structural frame is concealed – a move away from the articulation of, for example, Reliance Controls, where the notion of extension is explicit, the projecting beams declaring the possibility of growth. With Sapa, the potential for expansion remains discreet, subsumed within the concept of a 'smooth skin', which would eventually result in the gleaming silver extrusion of the Sainsbury Centre.

David Jenkins

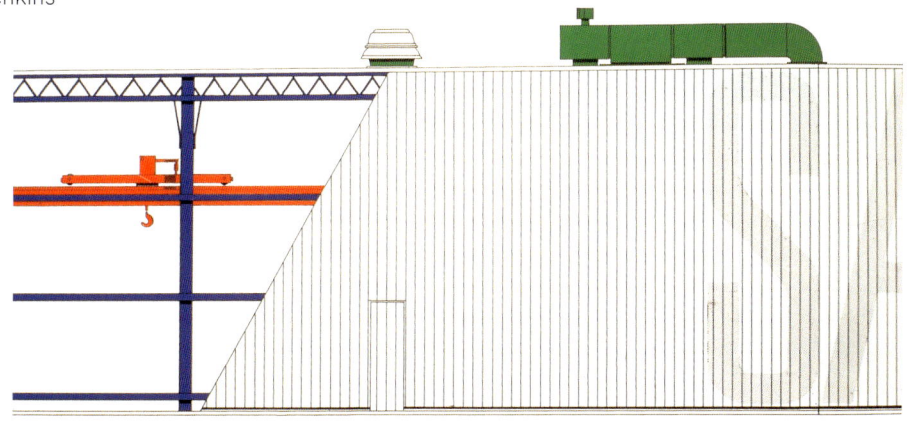

1. The full scale of the 100-metre long phase-one Sapa 'supershed' could only be grasped from a distance. With no views in or out, its white rectangular shape is seen here beyond a green field and a water course on the edge of the Derbyshire industrial estate. Apart from the doors and the servicing elements on the roof, all colour was confined to the inside of the building. To relieve this starkness when phase two was completed, the company logo was of the building at one end of the long elevation.

2. The essential elements of the building in the final colours used. White profiled-steel-sandwich cladding panels rise full height to a flat roof on which sits green servicing equipment. Internally, dark blue steel framing supports the cladding and an orange overhead travelling crane.

**Ellwood's Scientific Data Systems was a carnival of colours – shocking pinks and lime greens juxtaposed with the primaries – each colour applied to codify a particular element of the building.** Norman Foster, *Craig Ellwood*, 2G, 1999
Right: The colour-coded interior of Craig Ellwood's SDS building illustrated in *Domus* magazine, February 1967. Foster applied a similar coding system to the interior of the Sapa factory, so that the high capacity ventilators, crane, machinery, walls and even the concrete floor slab were rendered distinct.

**The interior of the building is articifially lit – the colours of the production plant, handling equipment, piping, structure and services were all chosen for their response to the visible spectrum of the light output.** Norman Foster, in conversation with the editor, 2001

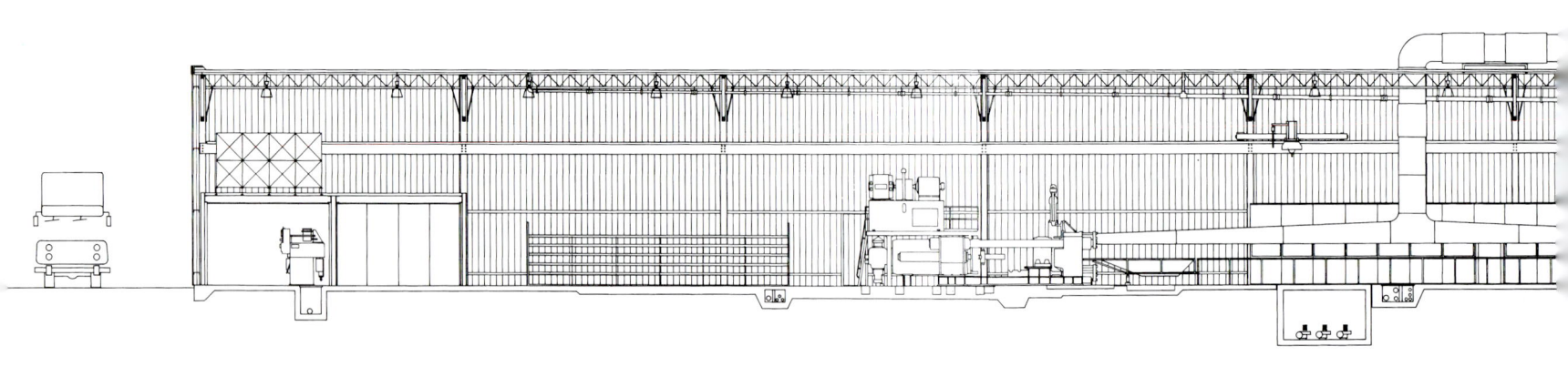

1. Long section through the phase-one building. A clear head-height of 6 metres was required beneath the travelling crane to carry it over all machinery and racked storage.

2-5. The Sapa factory in use. Internal partitions, services and machines are picked out in primary colours. The structure is painted mid-blue, meshed overhead with orange gantries and the silver octopus arms of the air-quenchers.

6. A glazed canteen area was provided at mezzanine level in the phase-two expansion.

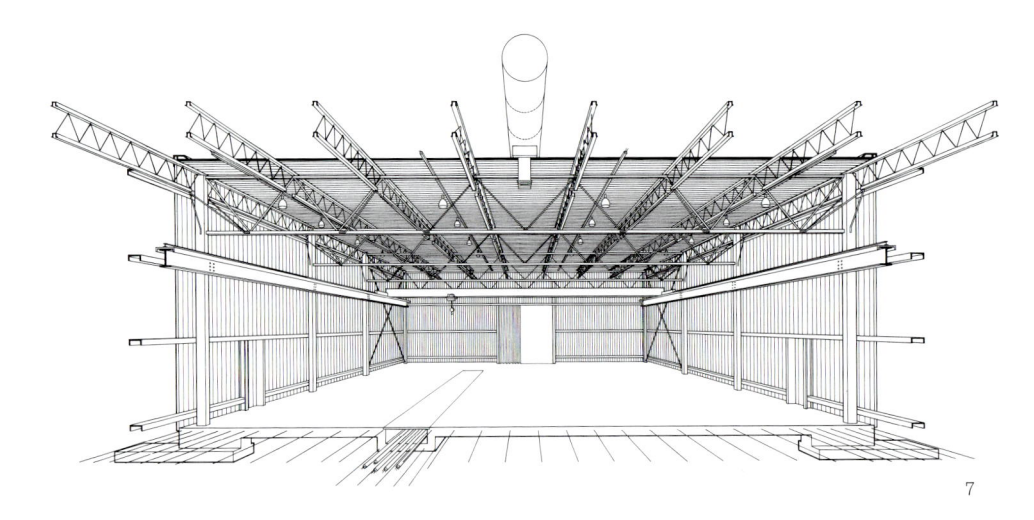

348 Norman Foster Works 1

**It is seldom that the flexibility of modular buildings – so frequently a central concern of designers – is made use of in reality. When it is used it is even less often that it works. Yet the expansion of Sapa's factory shows that it is possible.** *The Architects' Journal,* September 1977
Left: A view of the enlarged factory.
Right: A grand dinner for 200 guests and employees was given in the Sapa building in September 1977 to celebrate the opening of the second phase of the plant by Eric Varley, then Secretary of State for Industry. An indication of the size of the building can be gained from the diminutive heavy trucks in the background and the fact that the area shown is only the south-west corner of the enclosure.

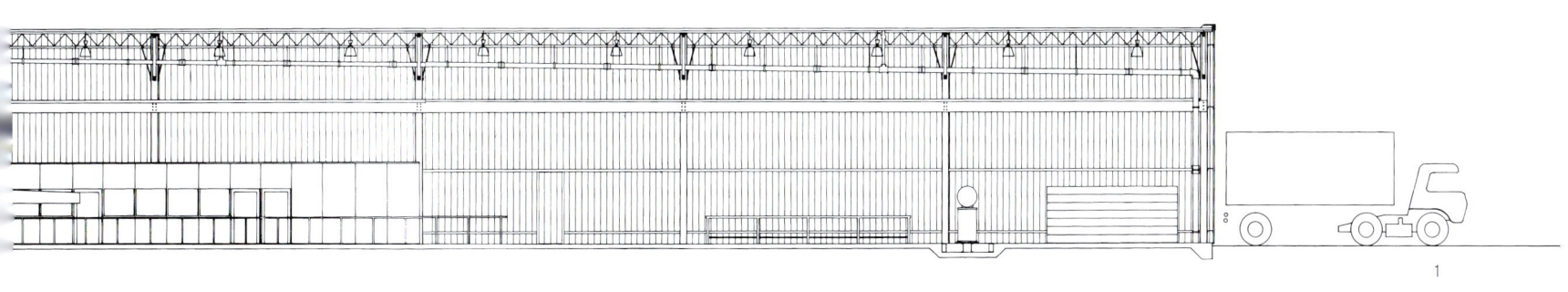

7. Perspective section. The structural frame was sized so as to permit modular expansion in any direction and the building was eventually extended to three times its original size.

8. The phase one plan was determined by the needs of the extrusion process. Vehicle entry was at the eastern end, next to storage and service cores. The extrusion press and a long run-out table filled the main space, with storage racks located next to the exit.

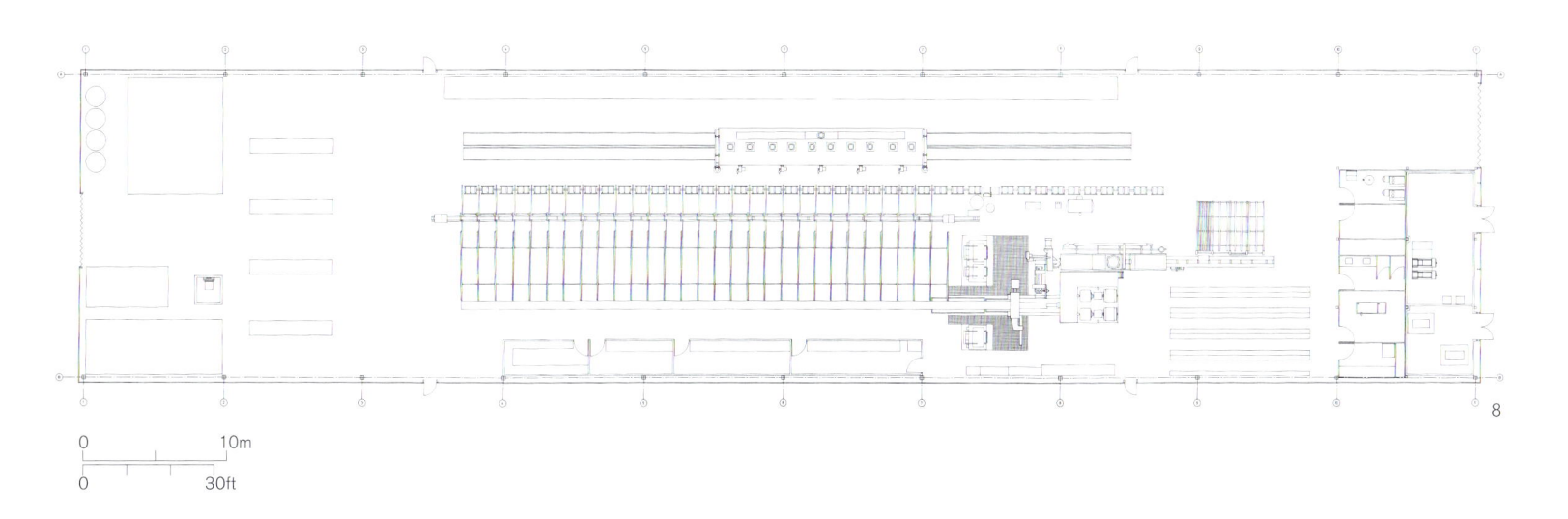

**Modern Art Glass**
Thamesmead, England 1972–1973

**All the Foster Associates big shed buildings of the 1970s were prophetic in their emphasis upon ground-hugging horizontality and existing transport infrastructure. Seen in retrospect, their work of nearly 20 years confirms that the idea of huge, flat rectangles of serviced floorspace, cruising half-buried through the landscape like submarines running on the surface, yet connected by the umbilical cords of access to road and rail networks, must have taken root in Norman Foster's mind at the end of the 1960s and worked through one commission after another to achieve its most developed realisation.** Martin Pawley, *Monografias de Arquitectura y Vivienda*, 1992

Foster Associates' relationship with Modern Art Glass began in 1970 when the company installed the glazed curtain wall at the Fred Olsen Amenity Centre in Millwall Dock – Foster's first glass-walled building. That was followed by IBM Cosham in 1971. Both of these early projects adopted the Pitco 'T'-wall mirror-glass and neoprene curtain-wall system. In the summer of the following year, Modern Art Glass commissioned Foster to design its own building at Thamesmead. Foster recalls that he had given them such a hard time on those projects that they decided he would be equally tough on their behalf.

The brief was for a low-cost warehouse, with offices and showroom, to replace the company's existing premises, which it had outgrown. Modern Art Glass was at the time one of the largest glazing contractors and importers of glass wall assembly systems in the UK. It wanted a building that would perform efficiently, provide a high standard of working conditions and act as a showcase where clients – architects, designers and builders – could view its products.

## The building stands out from its surroundings, confident and colourful.

The site was a windswept area of reclaimed land on the Thamesmead Industrial Estate. As landlord, the Greater London Council laid down strict planning guidelines for the estate including the use of materials, colour and building height, with the aim of harmonising new development. In some respects this was a pioneering move. Aesthetic controls rarely figure in the detailed design of industrial estates. But at Thamesmead the controls themselves had an adverse effect, inducing a banal monotony. To conform, the GLC wanted the new building to be no more than 5.5 metres high and faced with Staffordshire blue/grey bricks like its (then very few) neighbours.

This presented immediate problems. Norman Foster summarises his objections: 'We were in the middle of a brick shortage and, in any case, we should have needed extra piling and monumental piers to hold up the walls. Added to which quality control over bricklaying is practically nil'.

Fortunately, it proved possible to negotiate a path through the rules. Foster made a case for cladding the structure in profiled aluminium and for going higher than the recommended limit to accommodate an overhead travelling crane in the warehouse, thus allowing room for a mezzanine-level office above the showroom at one fully-glazed end of the building. The GLC agreed, with the proviso that the cladding be painted blue/grey in lieu of the brick.

The building stands out from its bland surroundings, confident and colourful. Once completed, however, it became apparent that shades of colour are, of course, open to degrees of interpretation. Foster maintained that the deep-blue factory-coated cladding represented 'a more appropriate interpretation of the spirit of the controls'. But Bexley, the local planning authority concerned, disagreed and served an enforcement notice, ordering that the building be repainted dark grey. In a cartoon in *The Architects' Journal* Louis Hellman wryly observed that to harmonise with the existing environment, the Modern Art Glass building would have to be 'grey and drab'.

1. The Modern Art Glass warehouse and showroom in its factory finished blue aluminium cladding. Objections from local planners raised the possibility that the newly completed building would have to be repainted grey, but on appeal Foster Associates won the right to retain the bright blue. The double-height roller door was a proprietary component, selected from a catalogue, but painted blue to match the cladding. At its base, a blue and yellow strip matches crash barriers that protect the building from vehicle impact.

2. An early axonometric showing the building in close to its final form.

3. An aerial view from the south. Wrap-over cladding envelops a simple portal structure, with only the south-facing end elevation glazed. Behind this are located the showroom and mezzanine-level offices.

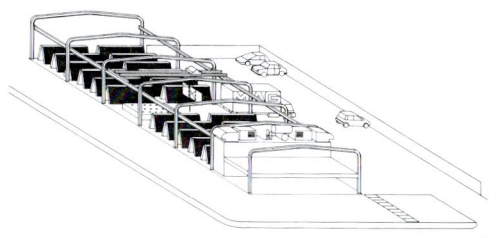

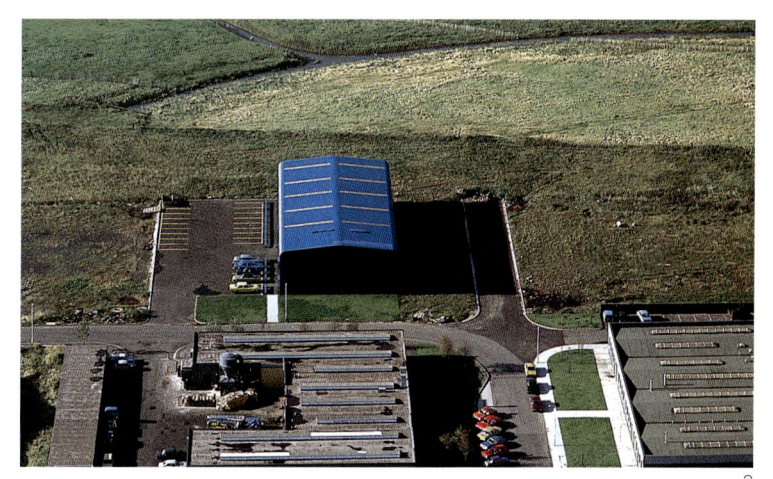

**The building retains its impact through superb detailing and a fierce insistence on graphic colour. That a sense of architecture should emerge from such modest means is an indication of the intensity of control employed.** Robert Maxwell, *A+U*, September 1975

**The Modern Art Glass building is still there, it's still blue, and I think everyone is very happy with it.** Norman Foster, in conversation with the editor, 2001

**There is something surreal about the industrial estate at Thamesmead. Some dull factories, some pylons, a lot of flat space waiting for something to happen, and the massive Ford complex across the river giving a different industrial scale. There are also fields of horses and a battered sign saying Manor Farm. It is a confused no-man's-land, the sort of area that Gertrude Stein had in mind when she said 'There is no there there'. Now it has acquired a 'there', a landmark, Foster Associates' big blue box for Modern Art Glass.** John Winter, *The Architectural Review*, July 1974
Right: Louis Hellman's cartoon in *The Architects' Journal*, March 1974, offered a wry commentary on the building's contested colour scheme.

1. The completed 605-square-metre warehouse seen from the south-east. External landscaping was minimal, with only a small car park and a wide grass verge beside the main access road.

2. The building's essential elements: blue profiled-aluminium cladding wraps yellow steel framing with purlins and diagonal bracing; the orange rails are for the overhead travelling crane.

**With Modern Art Glass, Foster pursued a direction that can be observed in other projects of the period – the concept of the wrap-around skin.** David Jenkins

Modern Art Glass' modest new building quickly became a reluctant cause célèbre. An appeal was lodged but Foster reassured the client: 'I said if it has to go grey then we'll repaint it. And he asked if I would give him that assurance in writing. I said there was no question of that – he either took my word for it or not, and he did. If it had gone grey then it would have done so at our expense'.

Had the appeal been lost, Foster was prepared to arm the whole office with spray guns and take them to Thamesmead, television cameras in tow, and personally help with the repainting. The huge press coverage the case had by then received would have guaranteed a slot on the evening news. However, the problem quickly evaporated once the Government-appointed planning inspector visited the site. He liked the building and judged it 'the best kept blue/grey building on the estate'.

With Modern Art Glass, Foster pursued a direction that can be observed in other projects of the period – the concept of the wrap-around skin. Here the corrugated aluminium cladding envelops the flank walls and roof – the wrapping and the configuration of the structure prefiguring the form of the Sainsbury Centre in its early stages. Structurally, the building is conceived as a series of rigid steel portal frames forming eight 7-metre bays, standing on a piled, reinforced-concrete raft foundation. Diagonal tubular strutting in the second and seventh bays provides wind-bracing and regularly spaced purlins span between the frames to form a substructure for the cladding.

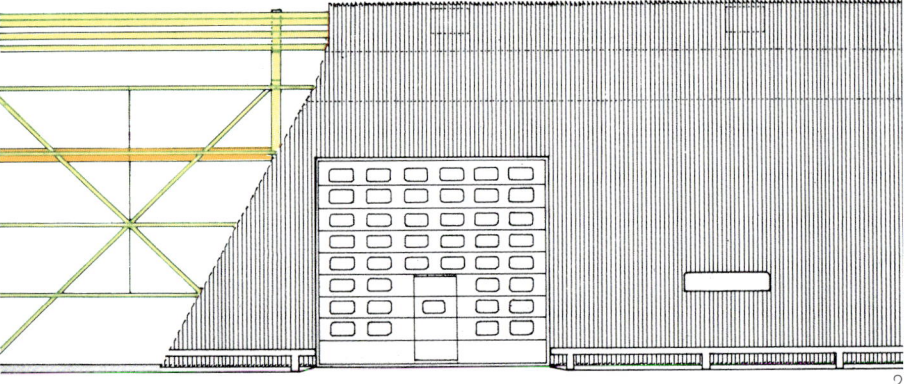

The cladding is a double-skin sandwich system with a glass-fibre core, colour-coated externally and natural-finished aluminium internally. The cladding kit consists of four basic panel types, two for the pitched roof and two for the walls, with capping pieces running along the ridge, with panels curved to the smallest practicable radius forming the eaves.

**In a cartoon in *The Architects' Journal*, Louis Hellman wryly observed that to harmonise with the existing environment, the Modern Art Glass building would have to be 'grey and drab'.**

Rainwater is allowed to run off the roof and down the walls to collection in a gutter at ground level, thus doing away with the paraphernalia of high-level gutters and downpipes (another idea developed further at the Sainsbury Centre). Tough steel barriers at ground level, dazzle-painted yellow and blue, protect the cladding from impact damage by cars and trucks.

Inside the warehouse the bright yellow steel frame is revealed. Overhead, the crane gear, which has a special glass-handling attachment, is picked out in a vivid orange. The warehouse once had facilities for glass storage, cutting and racking but is no longer used as originally intended, Modern Art Glass having moved on.

Between the warehouse and the 190 square metres of office and showroom, the required two-hour, fire-resisting wall was 'fattened' into a circulation and service core which houses lavatories, utility and store rooms. This creates a densely planned filter between the two major accommodation elements and forms an effective fire lock. The same planning device was used at the Renault Centre ten years later. An escape staircase from the upper-level office leads directly to the open air, while a free-standing spiral stair provides the main internal link between the ground-floor showroom and offices above.

These special areas occupy a shallow, single-bay zone behind the glazed southern wall, but neither has opening windows nor air conditioning. Problems of overheating or discomfort, are avoided by the careful combination of passive and active measures: the glass has a reflective bronze tint to reduce solar gain and the first-floor slab stops 120mm short of the glazing, allowing air movement between the two levels. Mechanical ventilation assists the natural stack effect; warm air is drawn out at high level while fans push in fresh air at a comparatively low level.

3. The structural frame is built off a short-piled ground slab because of the poor ground conditions. It consists of eight structural bays, each of which is defined by portal frames. These are connected by purlins, which also provide support for the cladding. Two bays are cross-braced for lateral support.

4. Internally, the cladding is left in its natural aluminium finish, as is the loading door. The structural frame was painted yellow, with the different services colour-coded for easy identification.

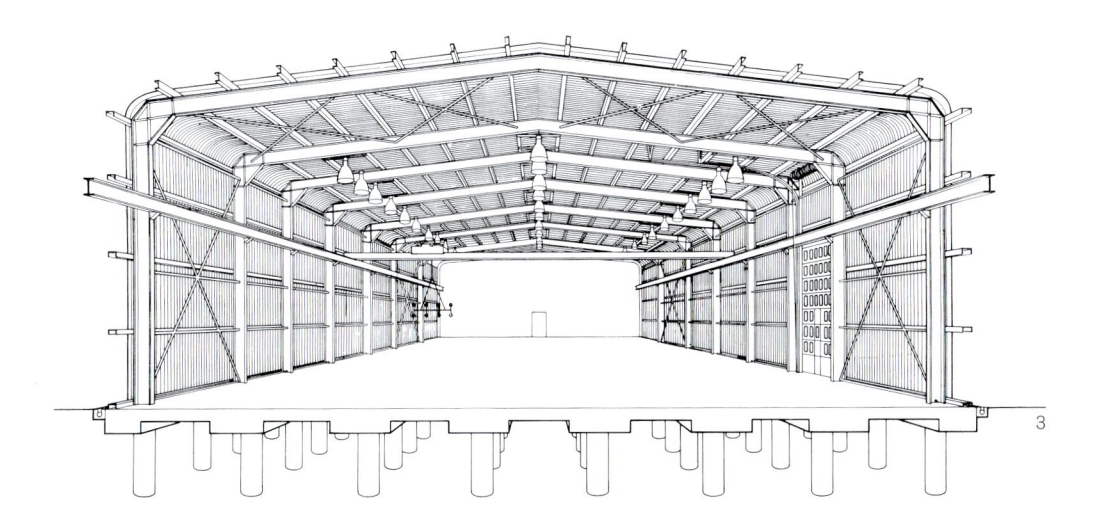

**This is an excellent example of a low-cost industrial building, of ordinary materials, handled in all its detailing as if it were the most significant construction possible, a most distinguished achievement assembled from a basic vocabulary of corrugated sheeting, steel and glass. The care in detailing throughout demonstrates the possibility of transforming ordinary development, even within strict cost limits, into an exciting environment for its obviously contented users.**
Extract from the jurors' report for the Financial Times Industrial Architecture Award, 1974

Right: Helmut Jacoby's early interior perspective of the Willis Faber & Dumas building shows the glass wall supported by the steel mullion system developed at Modern Art Glass.

1. The entire south elevation is a wall of bronze-tinted glazing carried on tubular mullions. The design of this wall represents an important evolutionary step in the journey from the proprietary system used at the Olsen Amenity Centre and IBM Cosham to the 'Planar' system developed for Willis Faber & Dumas.

2. Suspended tubular-steel mullions restrain the glass panels vertically with the aid of an external clamping strip held in place with stainless-steel fixing nuts: an assembly that was daringly minimal at the time but now looks surprisingly heavy-handed. Built while the Willis Faber project was on the drawing board, it was initially assumed that this system would be used there too.

**The glass wall was a dry-run for the system that Foster thought he might be forced into using at Willis Faber & Dumas.**
David Jenkins

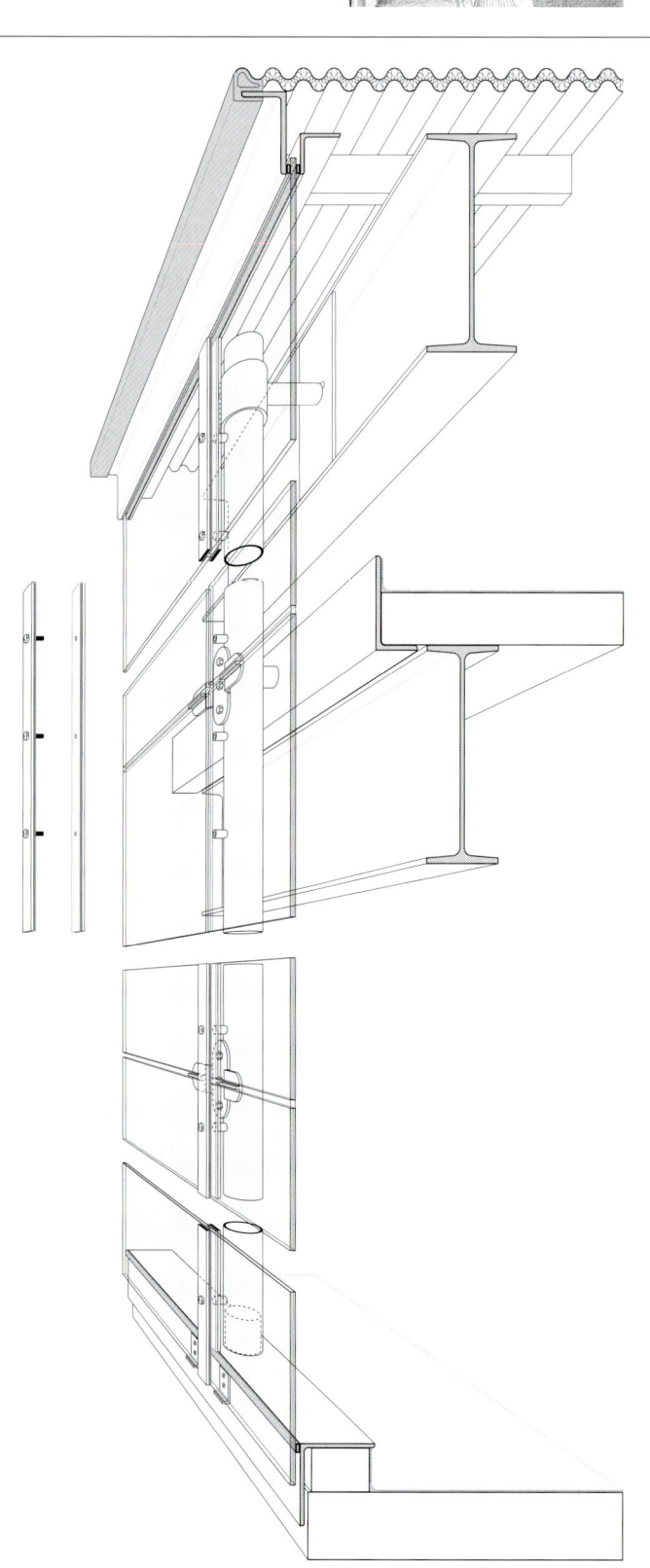

Left, far left: The glazing at Modern Art Glass contrasted with that at Willis Faber & Dumas. Although entirely suitable for the Modern Art Glass building, this glazing system would not have afforded the seamless appearance that the Willis Faber glass wall achieved.

At the time, Foster insisted that the design was not expensive when seen against the typical package-deal shed that proliferates on most industrial estates. The 'square-foot' prices that might initially be quoted by a package dealer do not include under the line expenses, as an industrialist would discover sooner or later to his cost. For example, the extensive piling and raft foundation, and the office fit-out would all have been extras. So too would the glass wall, which Modern Art Glass itself erected as a test-bed installation.

This wall was, in fact, a dry-run for the system that Foster thought he might be forced to use at Willis Faber & Dumas where a solution for the glass curtain wall did not emerge until late in the day. To force the pace on both projects, Foster worked closely on the glass wall with Martin Francis, whom he had last worked with on the Computer Technology building in 1970.

The aim at Willis Faber & Dumas was to achieve a mullion-free glass wall. Pilkington Glass was approached because the company already had an all-glass system; but this was ground-supported and not suitable for Willis Faber's three floors. Pilkington was also experimenting with a suspended system using toughened glass with patch plates at the corner of each sheet and silicone-sealed joints, but that too had only been used for straight runs over a single storey. Adapting it for three storeys required the development of special intermediate supports. A further complication was the requirement for tinted toughened glass: toughening large panels of tinted glass still presented technical problems.

Pilkington was reluctant to commit itself. And so a fall-back system was detailed that relied on suspended stainless-steel mullions to give the glass structural support. It was this system that was manufactured by Modern Art Glass and installed on its own building. The mullions have projecting flanges with lugs on which each 12mm-thick panel of glass can rest. Simple, vertical steel and neoprene sandwich strips provide weather seals and hold the glass securely in position.

**Foster insisted that the design was not expensive when seen against the typical industrial estate package-deal shed. The 'square foot' prices quoted by package dealers do not include under-the-line expenses, as an industrialist would soon discover to his cost.**

Helmut Jacoby's early perspectives of Willis Faber & Dumas show how the serpentine glass wall might have looked had the Modern Art Glass solution been applied. Foster admits that the building would have lost something – the vertical joints tending to bunch on the curves spoiling its smooth, clean lines.

Eventually, at the eleventh hour, Pilkington agreed to be included on the tender list for Willis Faber, returned the lowest tender and finally provided full warranties in return for rights to many of the details developed by Foster and Francis. Modern Art Glass brought the story full circle by then being appointed erector for the Willis Faber glass wall.

David Jenkins

3. The edge of the office mezzanine floor level is set 120mm inside the glass cladding line, thus permitting the tubular glazing mullions to pass uninterrupted from the concrete ground slab to special top connections, which are cantilevered off the portal frame.

4. Staff access between the ground-floor showroom and offices above is provided by a simple spiral staircase. The showroom and offices were fully carpeted, the carpet colour matching that of the structure exactly.

# Shopping and Leisure Centres
1972–1973

**The Pavilion concept used the hypermarket – a typeform then unknown in Britain – as a catalyst for creating a wide range of social and recreational facilities, some of which would be subsidised by commercial operations.**
David Jenkins

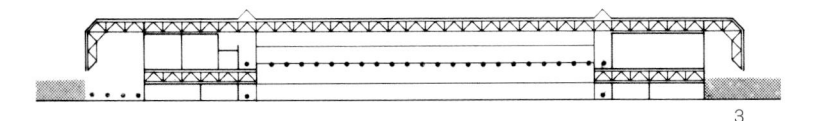

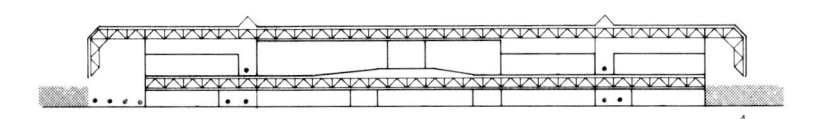

**The building has been designed as an 'umbrella', under which all activities can be accommodated, rather than a collection of smaller buildings each housing different activities – a building for a swimming pool, a building for the retail element, another building for the sports hall, and so on. The umbrella has a low profile, is two storeys internally and is deep plan.** Excerpt from Foster Associates' Pavilion Leisure Centres project report, 1973
Left: As part of the research for the Pavilion project, Norman Foster and the client visited a number of hypermarkets in Europe, including Carrefour, in France.

**These buildings would bring together under one roof activities which were in many senses related but which conventionally found themselves in separate buildings ... The design demonstrated that ease of internal movement and visual excitement, which the combination of retail shopping, sport, leisure and recreation would bring, had the strong commercial potential of providing a venue for the whole family rather than just shopping in isolation.** Norman Foster, *Foster Associates*, 1979

When Foster Associates first investigated the concept of integrated shopping and leisure centres there were few out-of-town developments of any kind in the UK and nothing as novel elsewhere in Europe. The 'integrated' concept had been developed together with MPC & Associates, a firm of marketing and planning consultants, following research into retail and leisure trends in Western Europe and the United States.

Catering for personal recreation was identified as a growth area. The Pavilion concept responded by using the hypermarket – a typeform then unknown in Britain – as a catalyst for creating a wide range of social and recreational facilities, some of which would be subsidised by the commercial operation. This made the proposition attractive to the planning authorities and more importantly provided a valuable local amenity.

MPC's subsidiary, Pavilion Recreation, commissioned Foster to design two prototype centres, one each in England and Holland, on a site adjacent to the M57 at Knowsley, near Liverpool, and at Badhoevedorp, close to the Amsterdam-Haarlem motorway, respectively. Both projects employed all-embracing, wide-span 'umbrella' structures. Large facilities – the superstore, sports hall, pool and plaza – were located in a central full-height zone with smaller spaces arranged in two floors along each side.

At Knowsley, of the total floor area of 47,000 square metres, just under half was taken up by recreational facilities, including a swimming pool and sports hall, bars and restaurants. The Badhoevedorp Pavilion contained a similarly rich mix of commercial and recreational elements. Finding the right ingredients for this mix was fundamental to what Foster described as, 'translating the hypermarket into a centre for all the family'. The strength of the attractions on offer, from shopping to sporting activities and places to eat, meant that there was something to encourage everyone, young and old, to make the journey out of town.

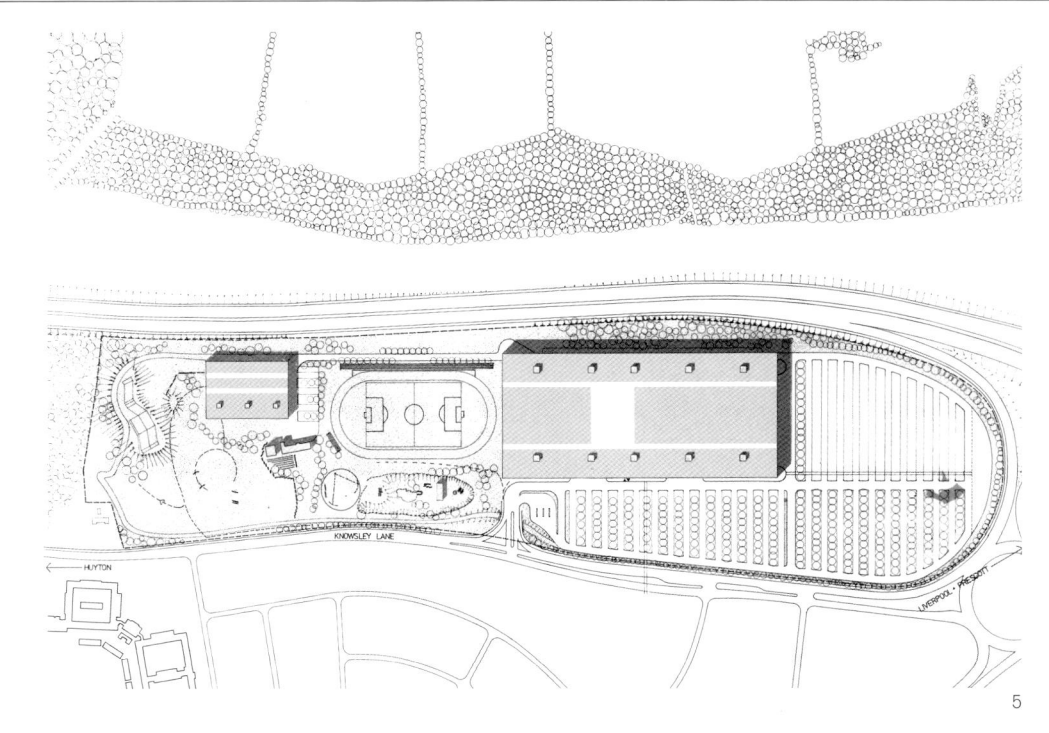

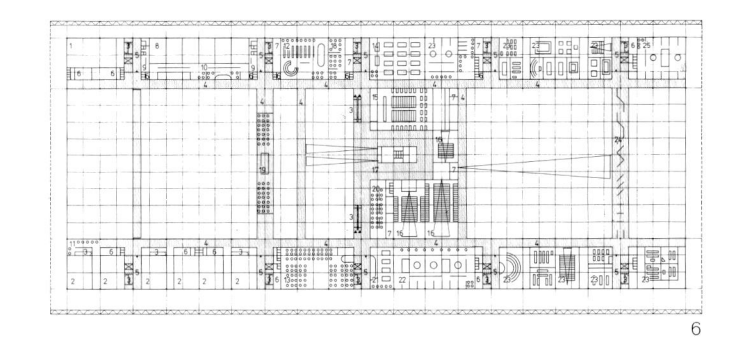

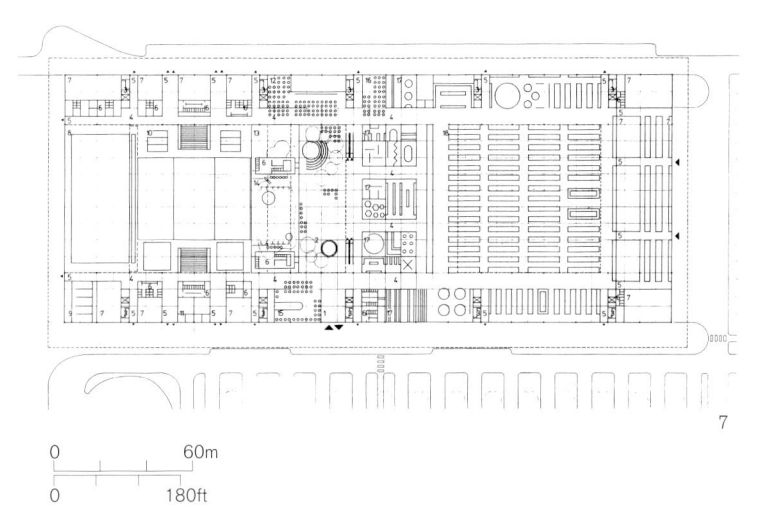

1. The Knowsley Pavilion, 1972-1973, viewed from the outdoor activities area.

2-4. Cross-sections through the Knowsley Pavilion.

5. Located near a major motorway interchange, the Knowsley site could draw on a potential catchment area of 1.5 million people. Anticipating developments such as the Gateshead Metro Centre by many years, the scheme incorporated soccer pitches, athletics and cycle tracks and a riding school in addition to the superstore and parking for 2,500 cars.

6, 7. Upper level and ground floor plans of the Knowsley Pavilion. The superstore and smaller retail outlets were entered via a plaza from which escalators led to the upper-level galleries, which were dominated by a three-screen cinema.

Shopping and Leisure Centres 357

**The plaza is the hub of the Knowsley Pavilion and can be described as a contemporary agora. People entering the pavilion will arrive in the plaza where they can obtain information, deposit luggage, drink, eat, sit, watch, listen, meet and move off to participate in the activities within the pavilion. It will be landscaped with trees and plants to allow part of the plaza to become a small community theatre or provide space for small shows and exhibitions.** Excerpt from Foster Associates' Pavilion Leisure Centres project report, 1973

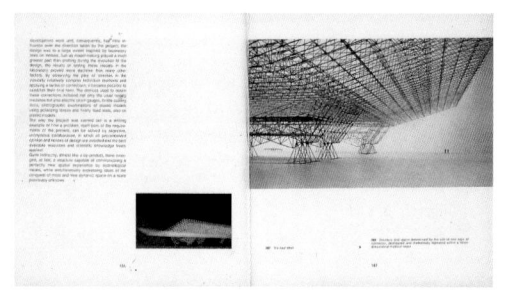

**Structure and space determined by the use of one type of connector, distributed and rhythmically repeated within a three-dimensional modular order.**
Konrad Wachsmann, excerpt from *The Turning Point of Building*, 1961.
Left: In 1951 Wachsmann was commissioned by the United States Air Force to develop a structural system for very large hangars. The super-lightweight space-frame structure pictured here, which spanned 36 metres between supports, would inform the design of Foster's Pavilion and Lord's Hill centres.

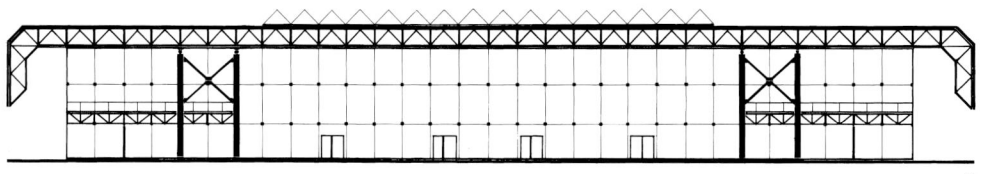

1. A photomontage of the proposed Badhoevedorp Pavilion in the Netherlands, 1972-1973. Though smaller overall than the Knowsley centre, it enjoyed excellent motorway access and incorporated extensive leisure and sports facilities alongside shopping.

2. The Badhoevedorp Pavilion's structure was to have been a large-span, space-frame 'umbrella' with a cantilevered eaves overhang providing an extensive covered set-down and pick-up area.

With the shops open until late in the evening, and restaurants and clubs open even beyond that, the centres would have been lively and welcoming places to visit at any time of the day. It was envisaged that the sports facilities would be used by local schools on weekday mornings when the centre might expect few visitors. All amenities were to be available to the public without a membership fee, and some facilities, such as the crèche and swimming pool, would have been free, thus preventing the centre from becoming an exclusive 'club' for middle- and high-income families.

Furthermore, the Knowsley Pavilion would have provided 400 full-time jobs and employed 450 people part-time: in all a very impressive set of credentials to present to the planning committee. In fact, presenting the schemes became a regular event. Ian Ritchie, who worked most closely with Norman Foster on the project, remembers travelling with the 'Pavilion Roadshow' – a multi-visual production that relied on banks of slide projectors and other hired bits of kit.

Foster and MPC consulted a host of interest groups including local chambers of commerce, the Sports Council, youth club leaders and a cross-section of inhabitants within each catchment area. This area was potentially very great. At Knowsley, for example, a survey showed a population of up to 1.5 million living within a half-hour drive of the centre.

It seemed that economically and socially the Pavilion centres had everything to offer. Yet MPC was not able to make the commercial leap from concept to reality and the project was never pursued. Perhaps in retrospect they were simply too far ahead of their time. However, the ideas explored in the Pavilion centres would inform the design of Foster's competition entry for the Lord's Hill Centre, in Derby, of 1973. And the structural and spatial principles established in all three schemes would be echoed in the design of the universalising enclosure of Stansted Airport Terminal, begun less than a decade later.

David Jenkins

**In a way, Stansted can be seen as the culmination of many of the earlier ideas and philosophies of the practice. It provides a single, elegant enclosure, housing many diverse activities under one roof to give the client great flexibility but above all, through economy of form, to create a memorable space clearly ordered by its striking structure.** Spencer de Grey in conversation with Malcolm Quantrill, 1999
Left: The spatial and structural clarity of Stansted Airport (1981-1991), which developed and refined the concept of the umbrella enclosure proposed for the Pavilion and Lord's Hill centres.

**The first integrated shopping and leisure centres designed by the practice in the early 1970s explored the idea of the centre as a destination in its own right. Functioning almost around the clock, they were envisaged as powerful magnets in their respective communities.**
Norman Foster

3. The Lord's Hill Centre, in Derby, 1973, was an unrealised competition entry based on Foster Associates' pioneering work at Knowsley and Badhoevedorp. With its branching structural 'trees' supporting the roof, the project can be seen as a direct progenitor of the Stansted Airport terminal.

4. An interior view of the Badhoevedorp Pavilion. Here, a swimming pool and large landscaped atrium were to be included beneath the 15-metre clear height of the space-frame roof.

Shopping and Leisure Centres  359

**Orange Hand Shops**
England 1972

1. A view of the completed Nottingham Orange Hand store in 1972. The full width of the shop opened on to the street – security being offered by fold-away glazing and a roller shutter.

2. An early cutaway perspective illustrates the kit-of-parts approach, which proposed high-level servicing and removable display units instead of fixtures. Storage areas were separate, possibly in a basement, while air-handling equipment was suspended undisguised from the ceiling.

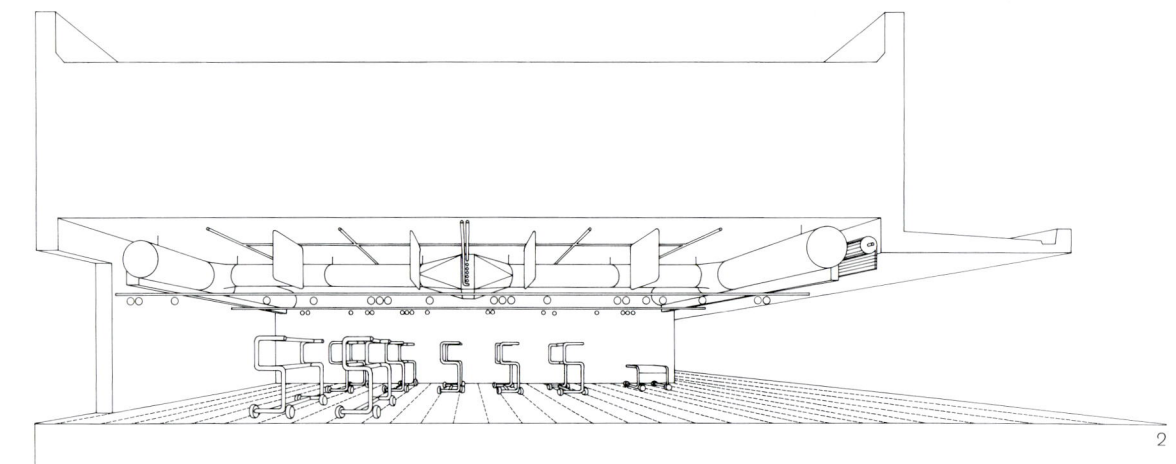

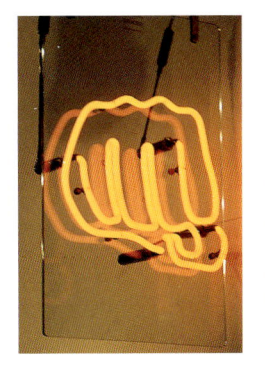

Left: The Orange Hand symbol, devised for Burtons by Wolff Olins. Intended for application to all shop fronts, this neon version was used on only the Reading store. Other local planning authorities considered its 'clenched fist' symbolism offensive and it was not used again.
Right: One of a series of Burton clothing group advertisements for Orange Hand. The target customer profile was active boys aged between five and fifteen.

**The Foster Associates system is cheap. It also provides visual unity and allows staff to move units to suit daily needs, even moving them on to the pavement. Also, because the units can be used vertically or horizontally, only one type of unit has to be considered, ordered and deployed according to the merchandise available. But this very flexibility is a drawback: a visually unaware salesman can move units to such a degree that the clean line of the design becomes muddled. The architect is considering a systems manual; a humorous solution which might just work.**
Isle Gray, *Design*, May 1973

Orange Hand was a retail concept created by the Burton group, in the early 1970s, aimed at boys between the ages of five and fifteen. The idea had been tested in three prototype shops, with varying degrees of success, but these had little unifying style or identity. Foster Associates was asked to 'develop the concept further by design innovation'. The brief included project management; defining cost targets; and 'breaking through the opening late syndrome'.

The first five sites were standard shop units, each of approximately 100 square metres in prominent locations; one in London on Sloane Square and others in Brighton, Nottingham, Reading and Uxbridge.

Most shops are custom-fitted which means that fittings are lost at the end of the lease. In a volatile retail market, Foster concluded that this made no sense. It only discouraged mobility, which might otherwise be commercially desirable. Instead, he proposed a standardised kit-of-parts that could be assembled quickly. The kit included shop-front and fascia, heating and ventilating equipment and display systems, which, if necessary, 'you could take with you'.

The shop front was designed for maximum transparency allowing the clothes to make an immediate visual impact. Consisting of sliding glass panels, with a neon Orange Hand logo suspended above, it eliminated any physical barrier between shop and customer. Work to the shell was reduced to a minimum: floors were tiled, and walls and ceilings painted white to form a neutral backdrop against which the bright-yellow-framed shop fittings and service ducts were superimposed.

In retrospect it is difficult to separate the Orange Hand project from the ethos of its time. Foster's solution is best understood as a radical response to the 'throw-away' mentality of the period and the – then – equally radical concept of a chain specialising in clothes for boys.

David Jenkins

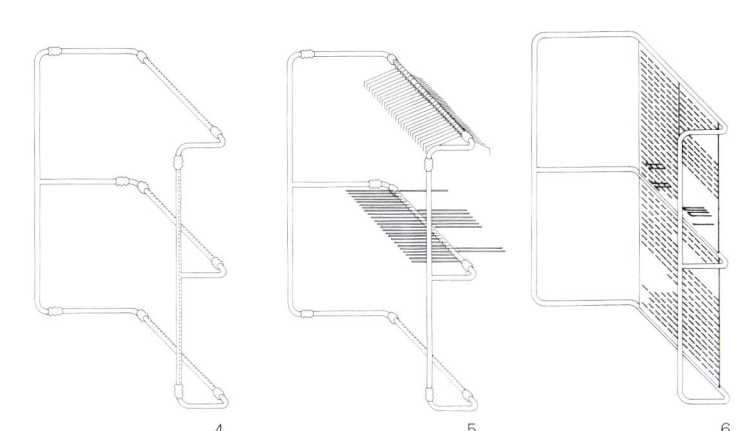

3. Brightly coloured standard industrial warehouse storage components were adapted for use as a low-cost shop display system that could contain anything from shoes to shirts.

4–6. Elements from the mobile demountable retailing system. High and low-level hanging racks and shelving units were assembled from chrome or painted steel tubing and pressed metal sheets. Dressing cubicles could be formed with additional acrylic panels.

7. Every element in the fit-out kit was exposed, including the ductwork for a specially developed reversible heating and ventilating system supplying warm or ambient air to the back or front of the shop. Lighting was a high/low voltage spot system selected for its flexibility and accurate colour rendering.

**We have always viewed the design of shop interiors as a spatial rather than a stylistic exercise.**
Norman Foster

Orange Hand Shops 361

# German Car Centre

Milton Keynes, England 1972–1974

> Two of the major foreign car importers in Britain, Volkswagen and Audi NSU, have been merged by their holding company, Thomas Tilling. The new company will be substantially the single largest importer of foreign vehicles and is expected to break the 100,000-vehicle figure this year for the first time. *The Guardian*, 23 March 1973

**A modular, dimensionally rational structure would accommodate future needs without costly or inefficient compromises. In addition, its compact footprint enabled the site's wooded areas to be preserved.**

Norman Foster

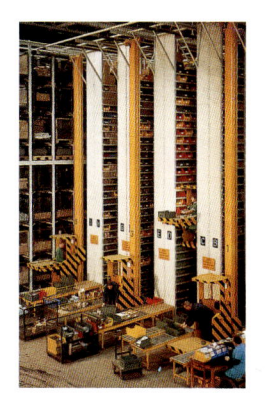

**Movement through a warehouse should represent a smooth flow between the three basic elements, namely: reception, storage and dispatch.** Excerpt from Foster Associates' German Car Centre project report, 1974
Left: An illustration from the section of the report that investigated warehouse systems. Even though the project did not proceed, this research was to prove invaluable in the context of later work for IBM, at Greenford, and for Renault in Swindon.

'New city building', observes Derek Walker, 'is remarkably like a fishing trip: the most significant fish are inevitably those that got away'. In the first half of the 1970s when he was Chief Architect and Planner, and Milton Keynes was enjoying its peak building period, the city lost a number of projects that would undoubtedly have become landmarks, among them a sculpture park, James Stirling's Olivetti headquarters and Foster Associates' German Car Centre.

Foster was commissioned by Thomas Tilling, the UK franchise holder for Volkswagen, Audi and Mercedes-Benz, who planned to build a headquarters on a site at Linford Wood. The scheme included offices, workshops, training facilities, warehousing, staff amenities, and accommodation for trainees. The commission came via Walker, who had convinced the company to reject the design/build package-deal it had been offered.

**The design concept drew on Foster's early factory systems studies, where a modular frame allowed a range of infill solutions with services distributed horizontally in the deep roof structure zone.**

Working with Tilling's management consultants and distribution systems experts, Foster evaluated alternative building forms and site arrangements. The conventional approach, which VW had followed in its North American headquarters, would have resulted in a 'campus' with each company occupying separate parts of the site, fragmenting accommodation and duplicating many functions. However, studies of the three companies' operations in Germany and the United States showed that strong inter-connections between their prime activities were possible. Indeed, many of Foster's observations were taken up by VW/Audi – then in the process of merging.

Foster's goal was to develop a single architectural form that would optimise these relationships while reinforcing significant design, financial and operational advantages – a concept that drew on his early factory systems studies, where a modular frame allowed a range of infill solutions with all services distributed horizontally in the deep roof structure zone.

Studies of German warehousing systems showed that the optimum clear height in these areas was 8 metres, with a 24 x 24-metre bay size giving maximum flexibility for various aisle options, permitting a mix of bin, pallet and rack storage. This, in turn, generated the overall structural umbrella enclosing a rectangular volume within which easy interrelationships between various activities were possible. Mercedes-Benz was located at one end of the building with VW and Audi placed together at the other, allowing either section to grow independently as required.

However, in January 1973 Tilling's Mercedes Benz franchise expired, and Daimler-Benz announced that it would establish its own British dealership network within a year. This immediately put the brakes on the project.

1. Helmut Jacoby's drawing of the Volkswagen element of the proposed centre. Open-framed around the perimeter of the building, the immense structural bays projected to form large covered parking areas.

2, 3. Early sectional studies explored a variety of options. Mezzanine floors carry offices and training centres, with vehicle maintenance and lecture rooms below. Roof-lights bring daylight to double-height atria and internal streets serving the extensive warehouse areas.

4. The Linford Wood site. The main building, to be shared by the three companies, was designed to expand to a maximum 800-metres in length, its compact footprint making it possible to preserve as much of the natural woodland as possible. A separate amenity centre (top) was to be connected to the main building by existing footpaths running across the site.

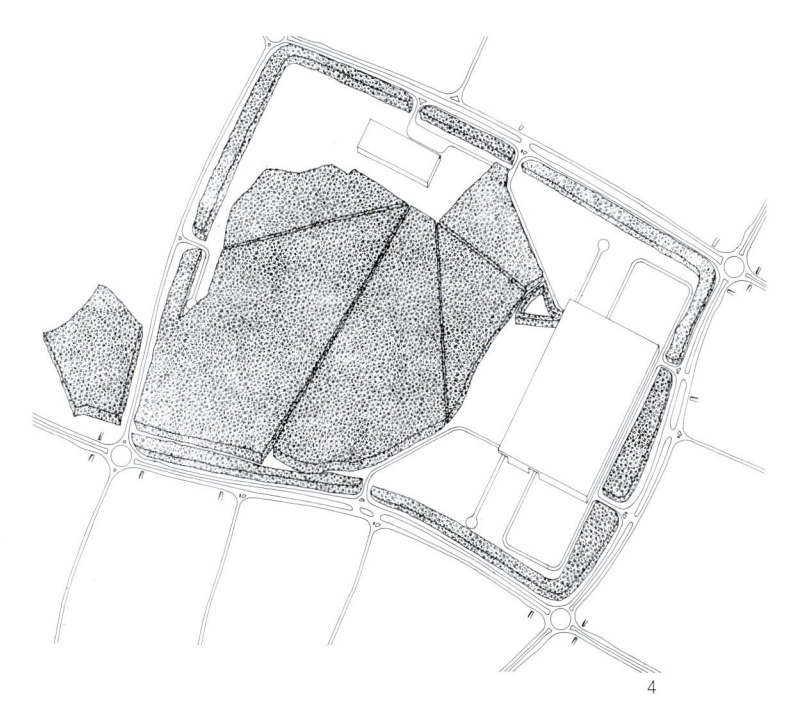

**It became demonstrable that if the common denominators between the companies could be integrated there would be considerable advantages in organisational efficiency, staffing levels, operating costs and capital building costs. In that sense the study anticipated the later full component interchangeability programme which formed a central part of the VW/Audi strategy for the 1980s.** Norman Foster, *Foster Associates*, 1979

**Milton Keynes has lost through ill-luck, over-optimism, international recession and timidity, a number of projects that would help make the city beautiful: Stirling's Olivetti headquarters and Foster's German Car Centre among them.** Derek Walker, *Unbuilt Milton Keynes*, 1981

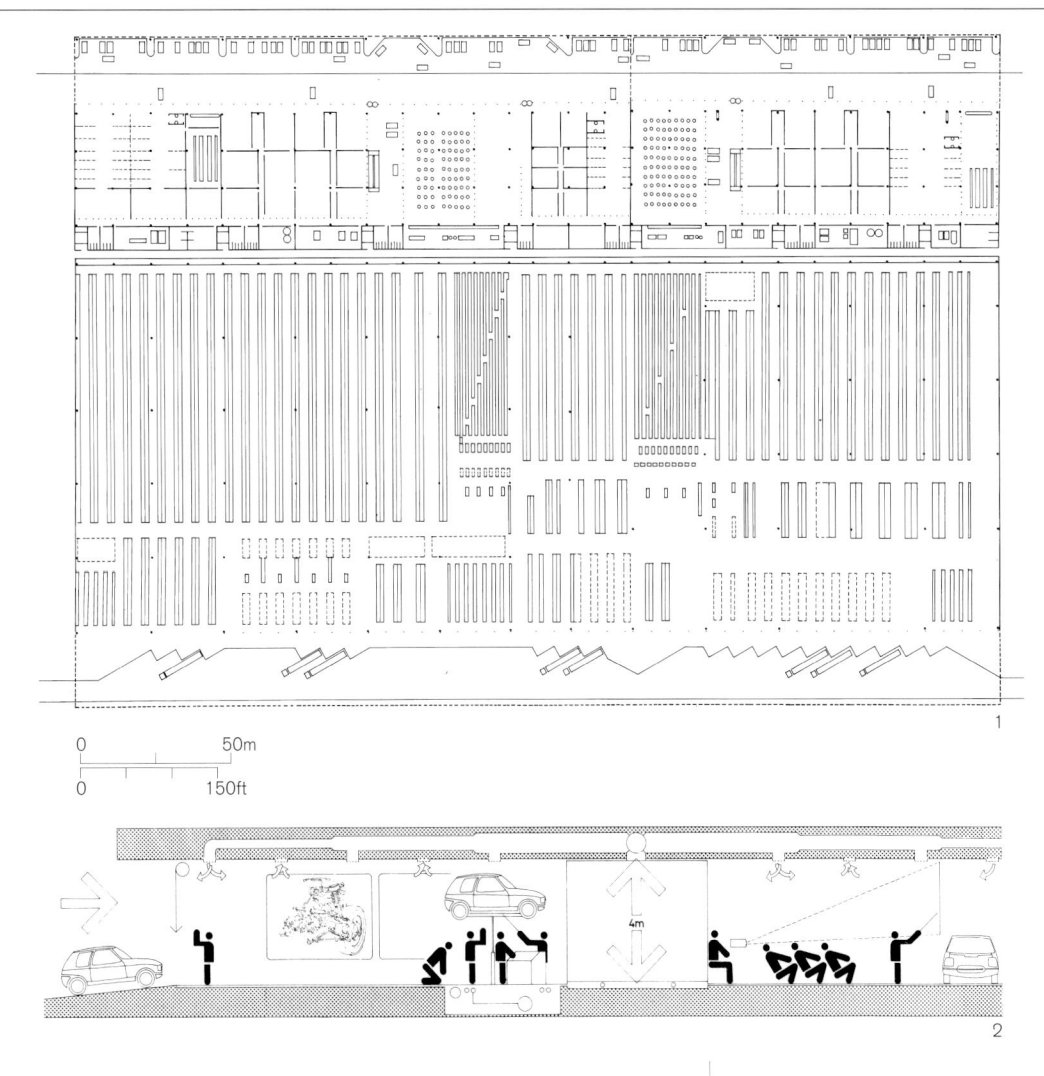

1. The ground floor plan was developed into a highly rational diagram. A strip of training rooms and motor workshops (beneath an administration mezzanine) was separated from the larger warehouse racking area and loading docks by a solid services core.

2, 3. In response to extensive handling and storage studies Foster proposed a 4-metre high motor workshop area, a 6-metre high commercial vehicle workshop and a 9-metre high area for heavy goods vehicles. Workshops could be serviced from the constant-height roof zone.

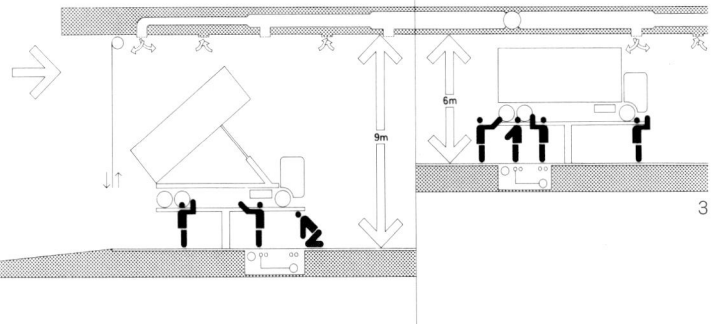

By March, Tilling had merged its VW and Audi holdings, in line with moves completed in Germany, making it Britain's largest car importer. In October, Tilling commissioned Foster to work with Demag, VW's warehousing systems supplier, on a modified facility on the same site. It was to accommodate a centralised administration and an intake of 5,000 trainees a year, from workshop mechanics to salesmen. But the brief was dominated by an automated warehouse, which required a 20-metre high-bay area to accommodate Demag's preferred overhead crane retrieval system.

A variety of structural and cladding solutions was considered before the adoption of a low-cost panel system with a curved eaves detail similar to that used on the Sainsbury Centre. The cladding was stretched taut over roof and walls – unlike the first project where the roof structure was clearly expressed – the roof projecting out along one elevation to create a public arrival space.

The final scheme made fundamental concessions to cost and the limitations of its more restricted site. To reduce ground works, part of the services core was dug into the sloping ground, allowing the building to step from a 4-metre high single storey, accommodating offices and the training school at one end, to an 8-metre high warehouse at the other, keeping a constant eaves line above which only the high-bay area projected.

It was an elegant and economical solution, but by September 1974 Tilling's business was failing. Like other car importers, it had been hit badly by the falling value of Sterling against the Deutschmark and sales were dropping. Tilling was forced to sell VW (GB) Ltd to Lonrho, who would eventually proceed with the Milton Keynes Centre, but on a less sensitive site. Ironically, that facility was designed and built by the same package-dealer whose offer Tilling had declined at the outset. For Foster, however, the experience was not wasted, as ideas explored here would find vivid expression only a few years later at IBM Greenford and the Renault Distribution Centre.

David Jenkins

**Volkswagen advertising is unique in the history of automobile advertising, if not all advertising. Its tone, style, wit, irreverence have been imitated, mimicked, swiped, copied, misunderstood, and admired more than any campaign before or since … In the end, the manufacturing philosophy and the advertising philosophy became one and the same.** Bob Levenson, *Bill Bernbach's Book: A History of the Advertising That Changed the History of Advertising*, 1987

Far left: Bill Bernbach's 'Think small' campaign of 1962
Left: 'It's ugly, but it gets you there'; a special campaign to celebrate the moon landing of 1969.

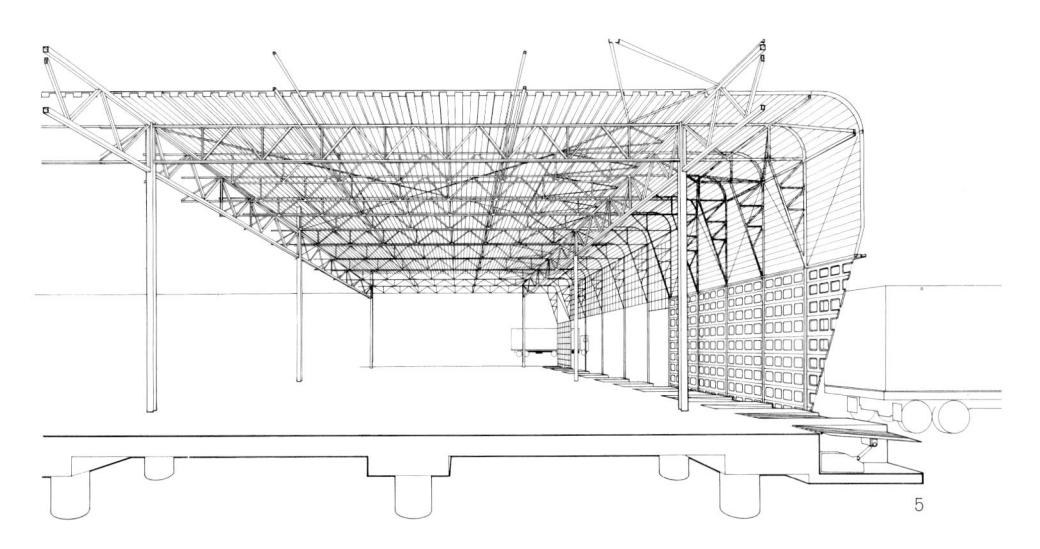

4. A Helmut Jacoby perspective of the VW-Audi project that succeeded the German Car Centre. Using only part of the Linford Wood site, the scheme was smaller but featured a warehouse with a 20-metre clear height.

5. The structural bay for the VW-Audi building was 17 metres square, which allowed the use of Warren trusses rather than the earlier space-frame. Profiled metal cladding wrapped over the building creating, on one side, a covered loading bay. To reduce its impact on the surrounding landscape, the building took advantage of a natural fall across the site and was dug in as much as possible. The project was still at an early design stage when cancelled.

# Meeting the Sainsburys
Norman Foster 1999

It was the morning of New Year's Day 1974 and I was standing in front of the door of number 5 Smith Square, for what I was told would be a brief meeting with Sir Robert Sainsbury about a possible museum project.

Before ringing the bell I remember feeling apprehensive, nervous. I was not to know the extent to which that meeting would influence both my future as an architect and my personal life. As it turned out the 'brief meeting' with Sir Robert carried on through lunch, when I was introduced to Lady Sainsbury, and continued until the end of the day.

Although it was more than twenty-five years ago I can remember it as if it were yesterday. I left with three lasting impressions. Firstly, their home which was surprisingly modest, intimate and discreet. Certainly the architecture was not spectacular, but every space was married with extraordinary works of art – paintings and sculptures. It was a combination of exquisite taste and restraint.

The second impression was the contrast between this very elegant couple and the radical nature of their works of art – especially when I heard how they had discovered them. For example there was a portrait of Lady Sainsbury by Francis Bacon hanging over the fireplace, which was very powerful – almost shocking. Bacon, Henry Moore and Giacometti were virtually unknown artists at the time the Sainsburys became their patrons.

Then there was Sir Robert's study, which had been beautifully designed by a young Dutch architect, Kho Lang Ie, who was to die tragically early. Here there were works by anonymous artists – tiny Eskimo carvings for example: objects, which at the time of their acquisition, were not even recognised as works of art in the traditional sense. I think Sir Robert playfully referred to them as his 'toys'.

The third impression was how those first conversations ranged so far and wide – I was getting early clues about their way of looking at things and I do not mean visually: it was as radical as those progressive artists they had encouraged. For me it was a mixture of independence, openness and conviction.

I was later to describe them both as the toughest clients that I had worked for – and I hasten to add that as an architect that was the highest compliment I could pay. Nothing came easily because everything was worked at hard. They made extraordinary efforts to research, to challenge and to support.

**Those first conversations ranged so far and wide – I was getting early clues about their way of looking at things and I do not mean visually: it was as radical as those progressive artists they had encouraged. For me it was a mixture of independence, openness and conviction.**

I say all this because frankly a building is only as good as the client, and the architecture of the Sainsbury Centre for Visual Arts is inseparable from the enlightenment and the driving force of the patrons behind it. It is not surprising then that the resulting building would challenge almost every preconception about what a museum should be.

For example, we selected a location which at that time was almost in the wilderness of the campus – away from the other arts buildings and next to the sciences – to encourage cross-fertilisation. And as a building it put all the varied functions and user groups – galleries and teaching spaces, students, academics and the public – together in a single space, under a single roof. It was a gallery without walls in the conventional sense.

**Sir Robert and Lady Sainsbury have had a long-standing relationship with the city of Norwich over the last 25 years. It is important that Norwich, as a regional centre for arts and culture and a city of European significance, recognises their outstanding personal contribution.** Councillor Barbara Simpson, Leader of Norwich City Council, speech on the occasion of the award of the Freedom of the City of Norwich to Sir Robert and Lady Sainsbury, 23 June 1999
Left: Sir Robert and Lady Sainsbury pictured with Norman Foster on the steps of Norwich City Hall, 23 June 1999. Sadly, Sir Robert Sainsbury died only ten months later, on 2 April 2000.

It was also an early example of a low-energy, 'green' architecture. These are fashionable buzz words today, but at the time the concept of 'sustainable buildings' was unheard of outside a fringe of society, which was mostly occupied by hippies and drop-outs.

I was recently in conversation with the critic Peter Buchanan who has identified a concept in our work, which he refers to as the 'urban room'. He explains this as a space that is egalitarian, accessible not just to the public but also to other specialist groups – 'urban' because it suggests a city microcosm with all the varied patterns of usage that concept implies. It is also about the relationship with nature – the movement of air, light and carefully considered views.

When Peter Buchanan made this observation I could see clearly that the Sainsbury Centre was not just our first public building but also the first of many 'urban rooms' that our studio has since created. But its influence on our work, and indirectly on the work of others, has also been far reaching in different ways.

For example, if you look up from inside the Sainsbury Centre you will see a structure that gently filters natural light. That is because all the pipes, ducts and machinery, which normally occupy the roof, have been discreetly located elsewhere, in the walls and below the floor.

**I was later to describe them as the toughest clients I had ever worked for – and I hasten to add that as an architect that was the highest compliment I could pay.**

This idea was further developed for Stansted Airport where we literally turned the traditional airport upside down. It has an undercroft, or basement, for all the machinery that drives the building, transparent walls to open up views; and a roof that lets in natural light. It is humanistic and ecological. Stansted has subsequently proved to be a model for a new generation of airport terminals worldwide, including our own Hong Kong Airport. In that sense, as well as in other ways, the Sainsbury Centre was a turning point.

Not too long after that first meeting at Smith Square there was an introductory design session with the Sainsburys and Kho Lang Ie. I knew his work and although we were almost contemporaries he was one of my design heroes. I took him to one side before the meeting and asked him how I should address Sir Robert and Lady Sainsbury. He laughed and said, 'but of course you must call them Bob and Lisa' – which I did there and then.

It was only afterwards that I realised how over-familiar that must have seemed, because Kho Lang Ie had built his relationship with them over many years. But I think they accepted my rashness with grace, because in all the ways that I hope mattered, it must have been obvious that I held them in the deepest respect. That respect has grown over time and the relationship has shifted from client to parental figures. And so this is a very privileged occasion on which to say 'thank you Bob and Lisa' and congratulations.

Concerned that display space at Smith Square was becoming increasingly congested – and eager that the wider public should be able to benefit from their collection – the Sainsburys began to consider alternative options. The collection was donated to the University of East Anglia in 1973.

1. Sir Robert and Lady Sainsbury photographed by Lord Snowdon in 1965 in the study of their house in Smith Square. Snowdon included Sir Robert Sainsbury in his survey of the London art world *Private View: The Lively World of British Art*.

2. The Sainsburys seated on a ledge in the stairwell in Smith Square. Jean Arp's *Dream Amphora* sits beside them, and two portraits of Lisa Sainsbury by Francis Bacon hang on the walls. (Photographs courtesy of Lord Snowdon.)

# Connections  Sainsbury Centre for Visual Arts

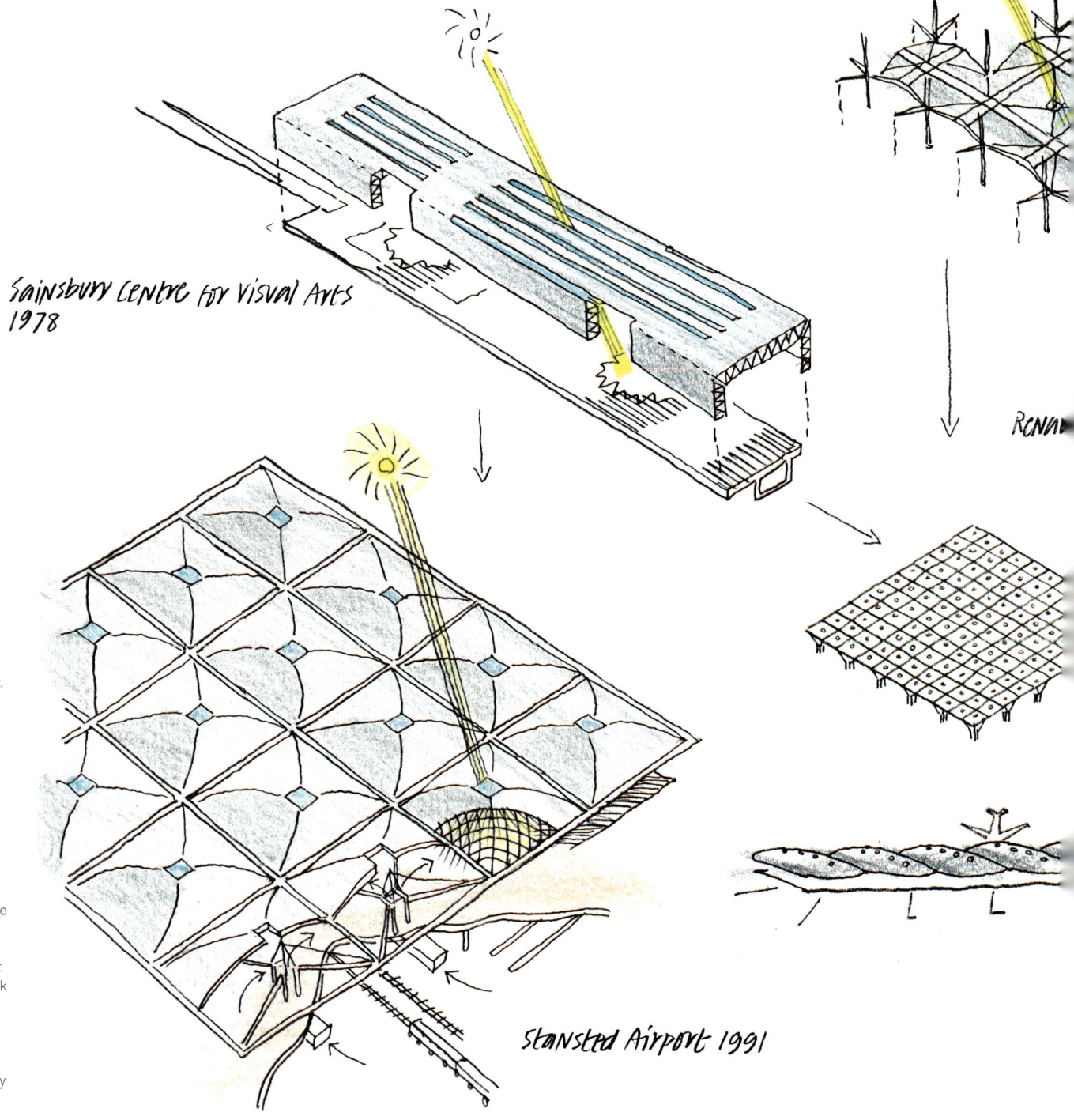

Sainsbury Centre for Visual Arts 1978

The Sainsbury Centre sought to combine flexible space with tuneable natural toplight and was the first of many roofs designed to capture and control sunlight. An integral part of the solar roof concept is a new way of looking at the building's services. By removing mechanical equipment and ductwork from the roof – and moving warmed or chilled air through the walls or floor – the roof can be concerned with light and lightness, becoming a point of reference changing by the hour and with the seasons. This strategy also brings savings in energy – sunlight is free! Stansted Airport took the solar concept further, placing all the mechanical equipment in a services undercroft. This strategy – since adopted as a model by airport designers worldwide – was re-explored in the design of Hong Kong International Airport.

Stansted Airport 1991

Typical pre-Stansted heavily serviced roof

Kawana House
Japan 1992

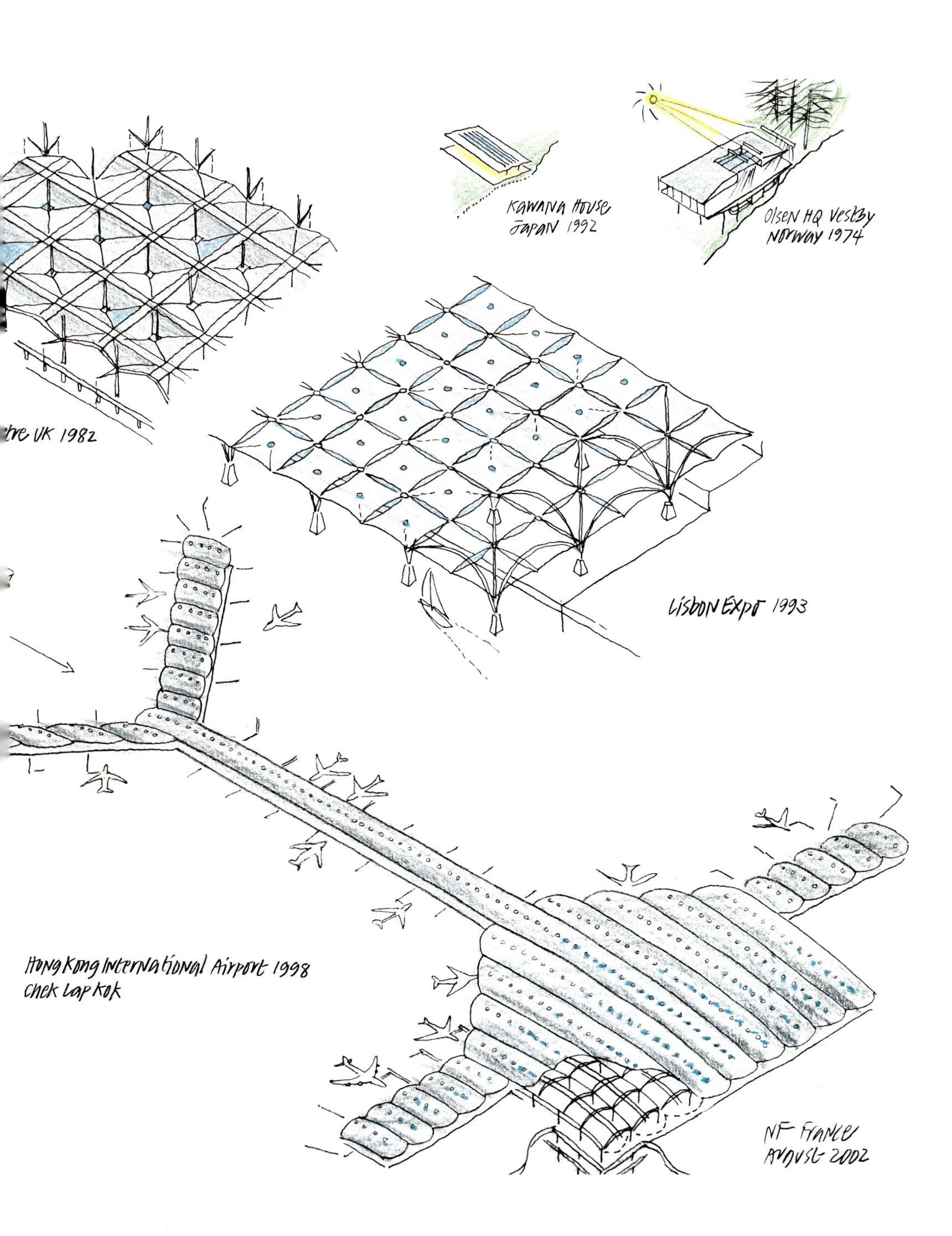

Olsen HQ Vestby
Norway 1974

...re UK 1982

Lisbon Expo 1993

Hong Kong International Airport 1998
Chek Lap Kok

NF France
August 2002

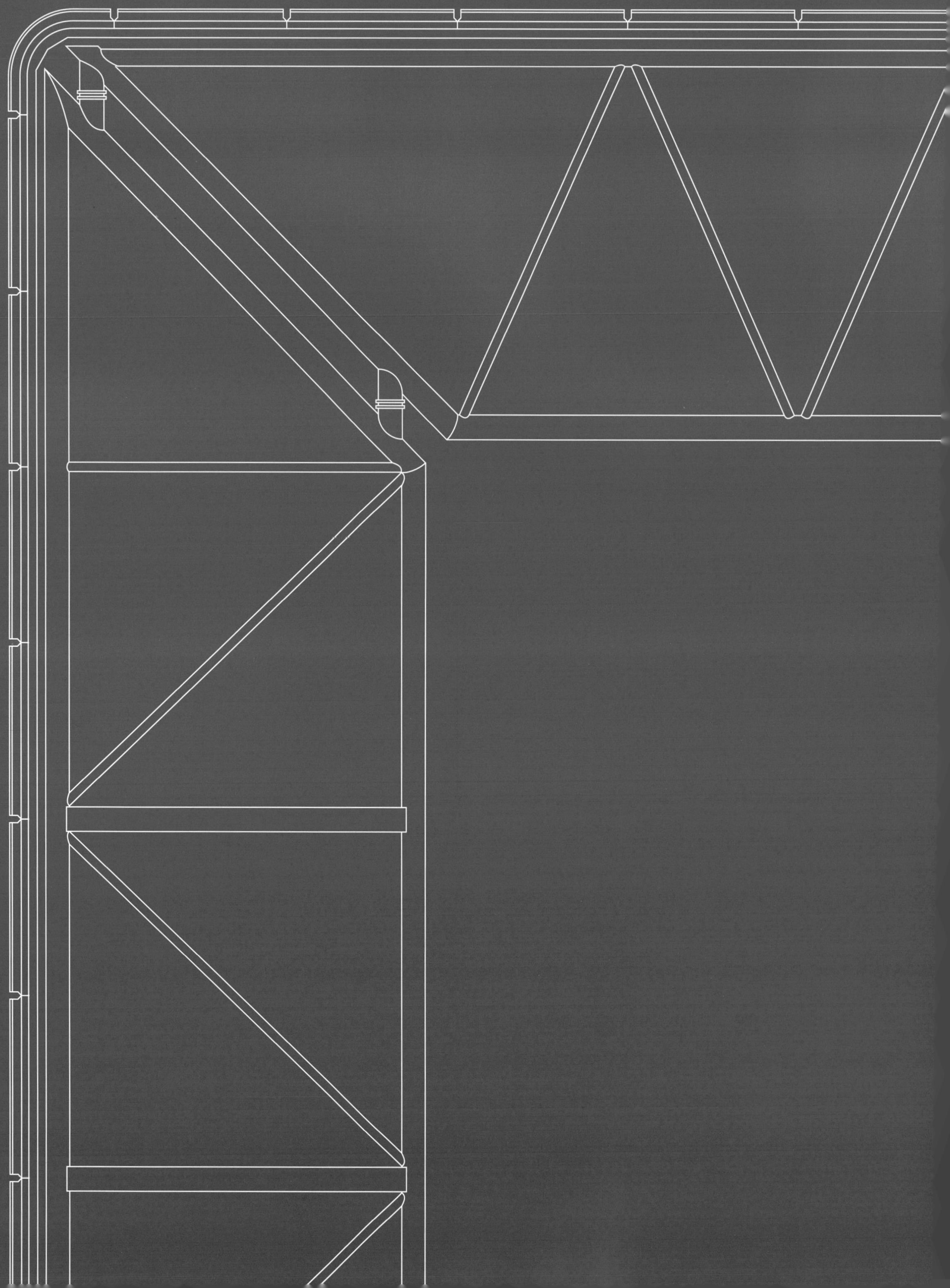

**Sainsbury Centre for Visual Arts**
Norwich, England 1974–1978

I have strong memories of my first meeting with the Sainsburys. Our initial conversations reflected their independence, openness and conviction. They were the toughest clients I have worked with – they made extraordinary efforts to research, to challenge and support. It is not so surprising then that the Sainsbury Centre challenges preconceptions about museums. All the varied functions and user groups – art galleries and teaching spaces, students, academics and the public – are integrated within a single unified space. It is a gallery without walls in the conventional sense. It is also an early example of low-energy design. All the heavy mechanical plant has been located discreetly in the walls and below the floor, leaving the roof structure free to filter natural light – an idea that was developed further for Stansted Airport, which literally turns the traditional terminal building upside down. In that sense, and in many other ways, the Sainsbury Centre was a turning point.

Norman Foster

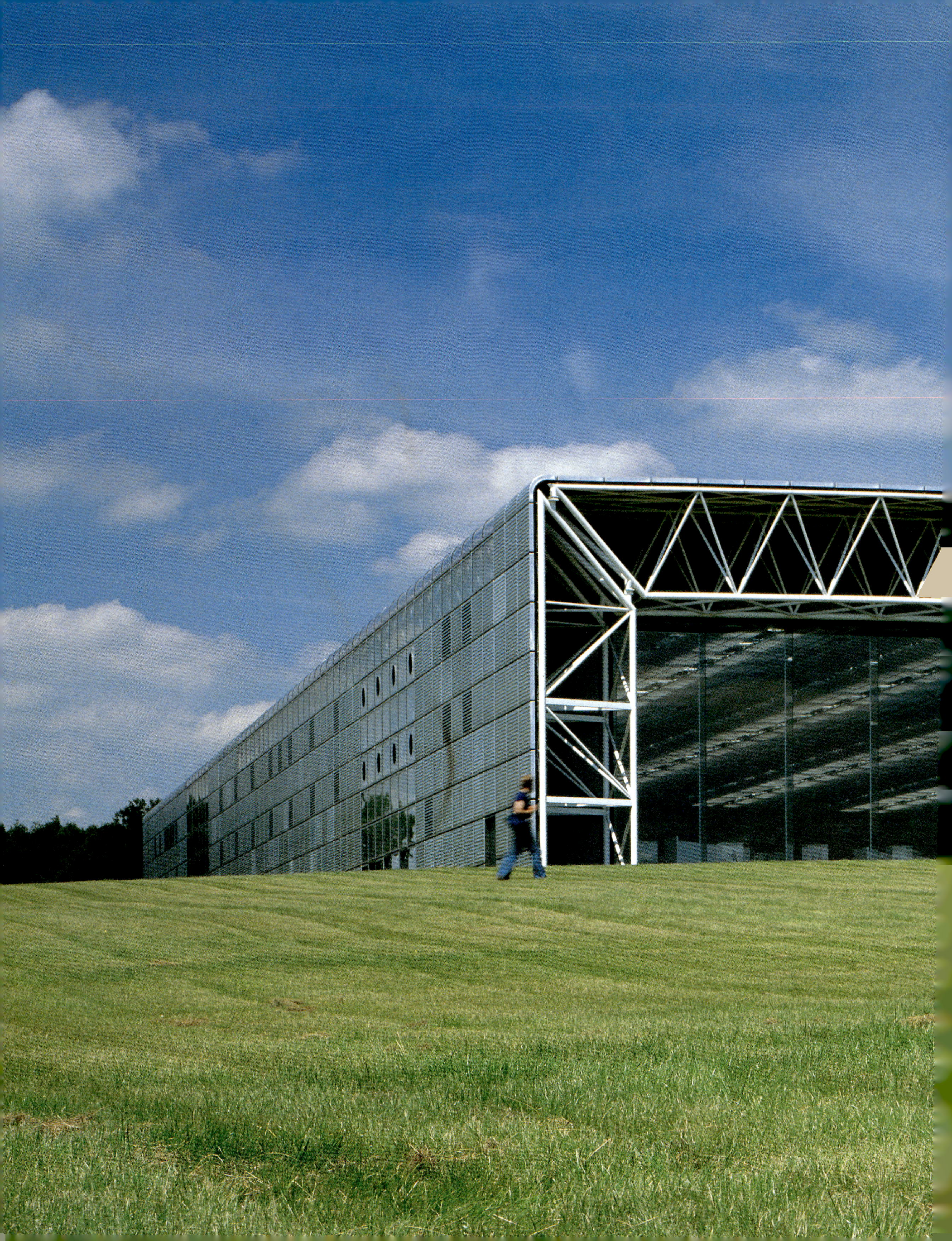

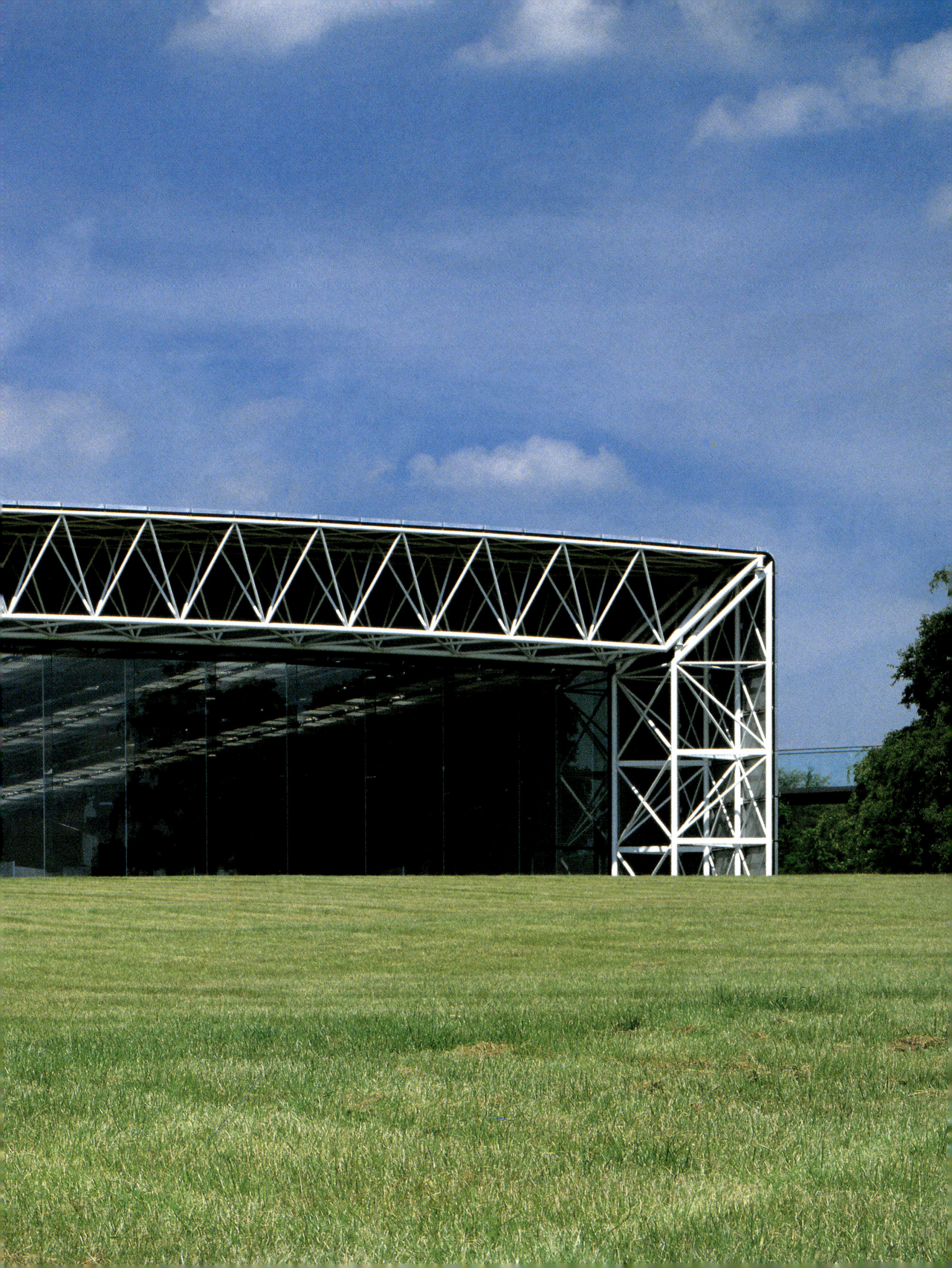

**There was a portrait of Lady Sainsbury by Francis Bacon hanging over the fireplace, which was very powerful – almost shocking. Bacon, Henry Moore and Giacometti were virtually unknown artists at the time that the Sainsburys became their patrons.** Norman Foster, speech on the occasion of the award of the Freedom of the City of Norwich to Sir Robert and Lady Sainsbury, 23 June 1999
Far left: Francis Bacon's *Portrait of R J Sainsbury*, 1955.
Left: Bacon's *Portrait of Lisa*, 1956.

The Sainsburys' remarkable collection ranges from modern European painting and sculpture to fine and applied arts from Africa, the Pacific, the Americas, Asia, Egypt, Medieval Europe and the ancient Mediterranean.

1. 'Fisherman's God' figure from the Cook Islands (late eighteenth or early nineteenth century). Acquired by the Sainsburys in 1949, this Polynesian sculpture is one of only seven of its type known to have survived.

2. Jacob Epstein's *Head of an Infant* (1904). In addition to being the earliest known sculpture by Epstein, this was the first sculptural work acquired by Sir Robert Sainsbury in 1931 or 1932.

Sir Robert and Lady Sainsbury's approach in collecting works of art has been characteristically straightforward: first and foremost any piece must make an emotional impact upon them. In a lecture at the Courtauld Institute Sir Robert once explained the process in this way: 'What I discovered, in my own way and in my own time, to be possibly the only valid art experience was my capacity to be tremendously stimulated by the particular plastic qualities of certain works of art, whilst being left completely cold by – although maybe greatly admiring – others which lacked that personal appeal.'

In the introduction to the first catalogue of the Sainsbury collection, published to coincide with the opening of the Sainsbury Centre for Visual Arts, Sir Robert explained this process further: 'I have never regarded myself as a collector in the most usually accepted sense of the word – that is to say, I have always refused to acquire something merely because it filled a gap or added to the representation of a particular art form. Rarity, as such, has had no attraction for me. If asked what I am looking for, I always say that I am not looking for anything. On the contrary, I have spent my life resisting temptation. For although denying that I am a collector, I have to admit that, first as a bachelor and then jointly with my wife, I have for over forty years been a passionate acquirer of works of art that have appealed to me, irrespective of period or style, subject only to the limitation of size – in relation to the space available – and naturally cash.'

These principles guided the Sainsburys through the acquisition of a major art collection, which at the time of the original donation, in 1973, comprised approximately five hundred pieces, a figure that has long since doubled. Though essentially varied and broad in scope, the collection may be clearly divided into two categories: late nineteenth and twentieth-century European art, including works by Alberto Giacometti, Henry Moore and Francis Bacon; and antique or ethnic sculptural objects.

A strongly anthropomorphic character, with an emphasis on heads and figurines, lends a balanced coherence to the collection, while his intuitive 'taste' identifies Sir Robert as a true collector in the sense once defined by Peggy Guggenheim as 'someone interested in art for his own self-ennoblement'.

Sir Robert Sainsbury had made it clear that he would like a permanent home for his collection and that it was to be considered a gift to the nation. Why then give it to a new university and house it in a Centre for Visual Arts rather than in a conventional museum or art gallery? Sir Robert answered that question thus: 'We want to give some men and women – and who better than undergraduates in a School of Fine Arts – the opportunity to look at works of art in the natural context of their work and daily lives, not just because they have been prompted to visit a museum or art gallery. To give them the opportunity, when young, of learning the pleasures of visual experience of looking at works of art from a sensual, not only an intellectual point of view: above all, of realising that certain artefacts are works of art as well as evidence of history. A new university clearly lends itself to our project in a way not possible at the older universities.'

The Sainsburys have acquired a significant body of work by the sculptor and artist John Davies, and their collection contains examples of virtually every aspect of his career.
Right: Davies' cryptic work *Bucket Man*, of 1974, is on permanent display in the main gallery space and exerts a particular fascination over visitors.
Far right: In 1973 John Davies completed the first of two portrait heads of Sir Robert Sainsbury, a work which is now on permanent display in the Sainsbury Centre.

The more significant unspoken message was that the Sainsburys' rationale was itself part of the gift, a rationale that could only be understood if the recipient could house the collection in a building that translated into spatial terms the cultural spirit of the donors.

Following an agreement in principle that the collection would indeed go to the University of East Anglia (UEA) initial discussions between the University and the Sainsburys centred upon the complex legal issues surrounding such a major gift. Meanwhile, the collection continued to be displayed exquisitely in the Sainsburys' house in Smith Square, London.

**I said that I was interested as a spectator in seeing works of art; I was not really interested in catalogues, though I enjoyed them in their own right. I was unhappy in a building that was monumental or pompous. I felt that the experience was all-important: the building should be a nice place to be in. It seemed that a certain common cause emerged as the discussion proceeded.**
Norman Foster

Under the terms of the gift, as well as donating the collection itself, the Sainsburys agreed to fund the construction of a building to house it. The University Grants Commission pledged to contribute to the cost in respect of the School of Fine Arts. Significantly, this arrangement assumed an overall budget rather than a building form.

When the time came to appoint an architect, Sir Robert Sainsbury visited a number of modern buildings and, like the decision-makers at IBM and Willis Faber & Dumas before him, went to see Foster's building for Fred Olsen at Millwall Dock. Both its fabric and its social ramifications impressed him greatly. Sir Robert and Lady Sainsbury invited Foster to Smith Square to discuss the project. Foster recalls: 'They asked me what I felt about galleries – it was a very personal exchange. I said that I was interested as a spectator in seeing works of art; I was not really interested in catalogues, though I enjoyed them in their own right. I was unhappy in a building that was monumental or pompous. I felt that the experience was all-important: the building should be a nice place to be in. It seemed that a certain common cause emerged as the discussion proceeded.'

3. Mexican jade mask in the Olmec style dating from the period 1200-400 BC. This piece was acquired by the Sainsburys in 1975, at roughly the same time as the brief for the Sainsbury Centre was being finalised.

4. Egyptian mummy portrait of a youth (c AD 100). This striking portrait image was formerly in the possession of the Pitt Rivers family and was purchased by the Sainsburys in 1966.

5. Mesoamerican terracotta effigy of a conch shell (AD 300-500). Ceramic effigies of this kind had a variety of ritual and practical uses in ancient Mesoamerica. This example was acquired by the Sainsburys in 1977.

**I recall moving through the Sainsburys' house for the first time: a Giacometti drawing and sculpture in the living room, a Henry Moore at the foot of the staircase, a Degas and several works by Francis Bacon at the head of the staircase; and in Sir Robert's study and the bedroom, African masks. This was a display that accepted a mixture of works of art in a very relaxed and curiously non-precious setting, despite the very evident importance and preciousness of the objects themselves.** Norman Foster, the Arthur Batchelor lecture at UEA, Norwich, 7 February 1978

**People have asked me 'Why a university?' 'Why a new university?' 'Why UEA?' … 'Why not a straightforward museum or art gallery?' It is because we wanted to give some men and women – and who better than undergraduates in a school of fine arts – the opportunity of looking at works of art in the natural context of their work and daily life … To give them the opportunity of learning the pleasures of looking at works of art from a sensual, not only an intellectual point of view … A new university clearly lends itself to our project in a way not possible at the older ones.** Sir Robert Sainsbury, *Architectural Design*, December 1978

The Sainsburys' collection on display at their London home in Smith Square. The comfortable integration of objects into this domestic space testifies to the deeply personal nature of the collection and the obvious pleasure that the Sainsburys derived from it.

1. A special cabinet designed by Kho Lang Ie for Sir Robert Sainsbury's study contained smaller pieces from the collection and was christened 'the toy department'.

2. Pablo Picasso's *Head of a Woman* (1926), a small pen and ink study painted on the back of an invitation card.

3. Francis Bacon's *Head of a Man* (1960), one of fifteen works by the artist acquired by the Sainsburys.

**I have never regarded myself as a collector in the most usually accepted sense of the word, although I have to admit that I have for over 40 years been a 'passionate acquirer' of works of art that have appealed to me, regardless of period or style.**
Sir Robert Sainsbury

**The Sainsburys had very strong ideas about the benefits that would follow from placing their collection with a university. In particular, they felt that there was not enough public exposure to works of art in the pure sense of an experience, and that, in an ideal world, more people ought to be exposed to works of art – not only people involved in the arts and humanities, but also scientists – the whole spectrum of study areas, if you like.** Norman Foster, the Arthur Batchelor lecture at UEA, Norwich, 7 February 1978

4. Henry Moore's sculpture *Mother and Child* (1932) at the foot of the staircase. Sir Robert Sainsbury bought this work from Moore's second exhibition at the Leicester Galleries in November 1933. He recalls being overwhelmed by the piece and only later worrying that he 'had bought a piece of sculpture that couldn't go inside the front door'.

5. Henry Moore's *Reclining Figure* (1930). Acquired in 1935, Sir Robert Sainsbury described this work as 'simply remarkable'.

6. Modigliani's *Head of a Woman* (1918-1919) acquired in 1935 (Moore's *Reclining Figure* is visible on the mantelpiece).

**I can still recall the study tour of galleries in Europe that Wendy and I undertook with the Sainsburys at the outset of the project. It was something of a research marathon. Only much later did I discover that each couple had, at the time, confided to their friends that they had difficulty in keeping up the pace set by the others!** Norman Foster, 'With Wendy', 1989

**We visited a number of museums. We wanted to get a feel for the way that they worked if you were visiting them to see works of art; or if you were guarding the works of art; or if you had the job of erecting the exhibitions.** Norman Foster, the Arthur Batchelor lecture at UEA, Norwich, 7 February 1978.
Left: Norman Foster's study tour photograph of Mies van der Rohe's New National Gallery in Berlin, with Lisa Sainsbury in the foreground.

1. Norman Foster has described the decision about where to site the Sainsbury Centre within the university campus as one of the most difficult aspects of the entire design process – there were all kinds of preconceptions from various quarters about where the best place for the building would be. As this sketch by Foster indicates, the site eventually chosen terminated the then major linear sequence of Denys Lasdun's UEA buildings, where it could enjoy views of the newly created lake, or 'broad'.

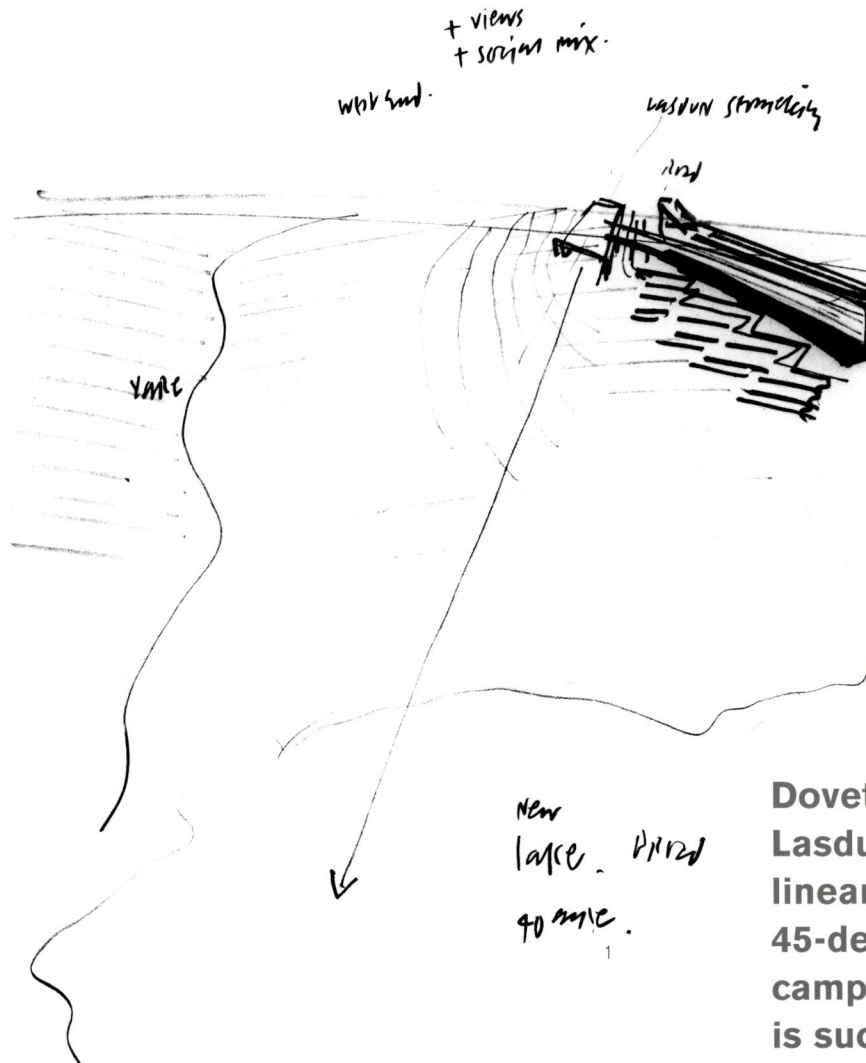

**Dovetailing with Denys Lasdun's masterplan, the linear plan follows the 45-degree geometry of the campus, but its orientation is such that views from inside frame the lake and woodland rather than the Lasdun buildings. Elevated on the brow of a hill, with a grassy meadow falling away towards the lake, the building's autonomous form is accentuated still further in the landscape.**
Graham Vickers

**Other galleries seemed dead when compared with the Louisiana Museum. It had a social ingredient, a focus. Everybody was there; everybody was enjoying it. It was a great fun place. The displays were also very exciting. They were not over-protected but were really respected. So somehow you had this feeling of vitality and exuberance but at the same time a kind of natural understanding and respect which didn't need iron bars between observer and works of art to preserve it.** Norman Foster, the Arthur Batchelor lecture at UEA, Norwich, February 1978
Left: Norman Foster's photograph of the Louisiana Museum of Modern Art in Denmark, taken during the study tour.

**At Aalborg ... on a late autumn afternoon, northern latitude and all, the quality of light was such that only afterwards did I realise that the building was windowless in the traditional sense of the word.** Norman Foster, *RIBA Journal*, July 1976
Left: Norman Foster's photograph of Alvar Aalto's ingeniously toplit Aalborg Museum.

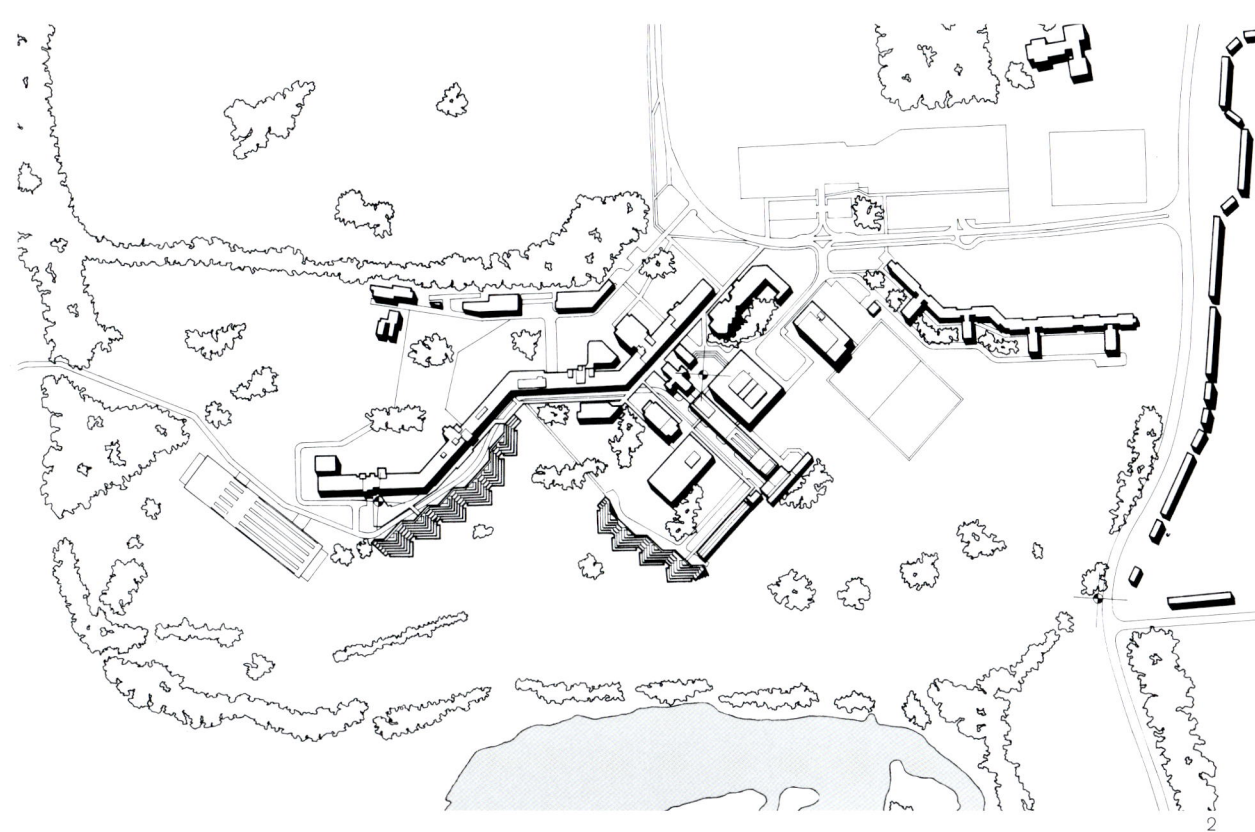

2, 3. The chosen location, away from the other arts buildings and next to the sciences, accorded with the Sainsburys' intention that the new building should contribute to the general life of the University; they did not want to encourage what Norman Foster characterises as an 'arts ghetto' on the campus – the university equivalent of a South Bank Centre. Pragmatically, a road link complete with services already existed on the site, in anticipation of future development. Working to a fixed budget, this had the added benefit of releasing the maximum funds for the building itself.

Sainsbury Centre for Visual Arts 379

**The Sainsbury Centre may evoke echoes from all over East Anglia, from temporary barns to old airship hangars, but it is crisply at variance with whatever traditions and visual habits have accumulated on the UEA campus.** Reyner Banham, *Foster Associates*, 1979

Left: The twin sheds at Cardington, constructed in 1931 to house the Shorts Brothers Engineering Company's airship-building programme. With an internal height of 157 feet and a length of 812 feet, each shed is tall enough to accommodate Nelson's Column and long enough to house an ocean liner.
Right: The airship Graf Zeppelin, photographed in 1928.

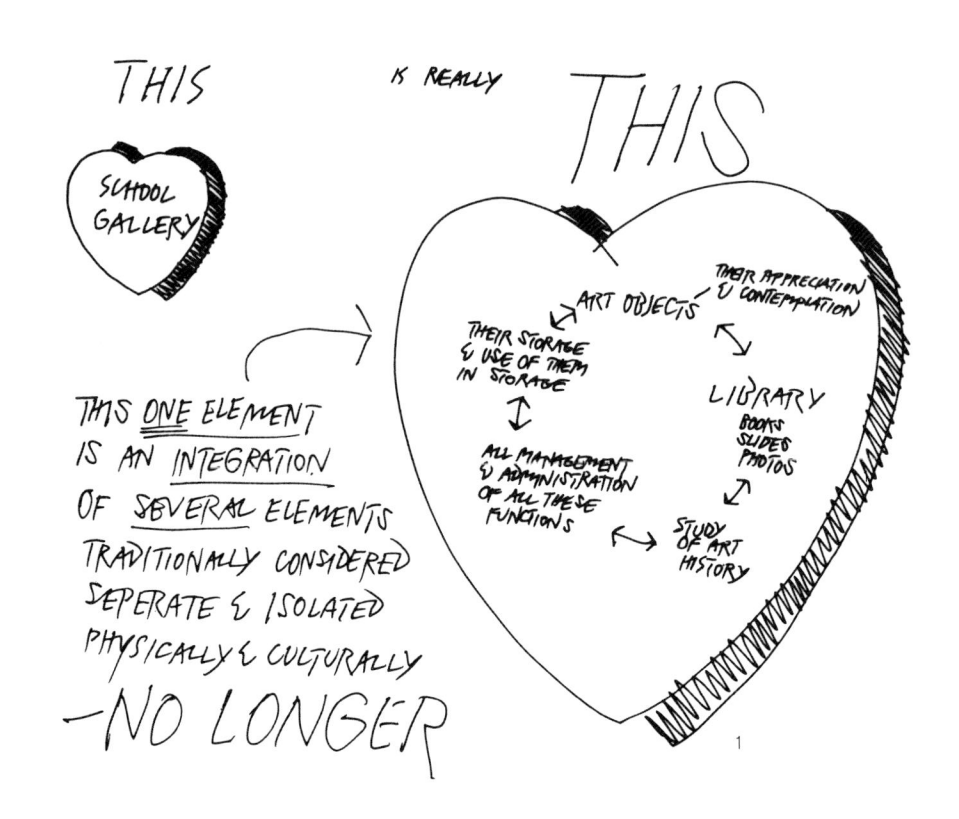

**Given the brief, you could have produced separate pavilions. Assuming a strong link between the collection, in terms of works of art, and a school teaching the history of art, you could fuse those two elements together; add to that a restaurant, a senior common room, and a special exhibition pavilion and you have a potential total of four buildings. On the other hand, you could make the leap and say that the linkage between all those elements was so strong that the case for making one building from them was overwhelming.**
Norman Foster

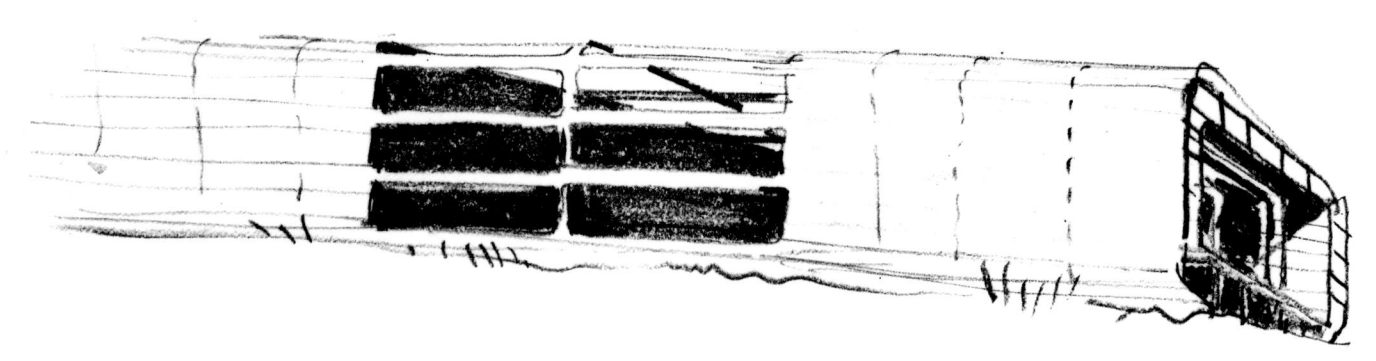

When Norman accepted the commission ... there was no written brief – in fact there never was one. Norman's task was to give substance to a somewhat ill-defined concept. We wanted him, in providing a home for our collection, to give members of the University and visitors the opportunity to look at works of art in the natural context of their daily work and life and, above all, to enjoy our collection as we have done. **Sensual enjoyment is no bar to the pursuit of knowledge or intellectual understanding. All this** called for a place in which people could relax, look at works of art in a leisurely manner if they so wished, work, read a novel or just dream away. Such a place would surely appeal equally to outside scholars and lay members of the public as to men and women in the University. That was Norman's brief ... and it was to be developed and elaborated in the course of many, many hours of discussion and travel during the planning stage.

Sir Robert Sainsbury, introducing Norman Foster as RIBA Royal Gold Medallist, London, 21 June 1983

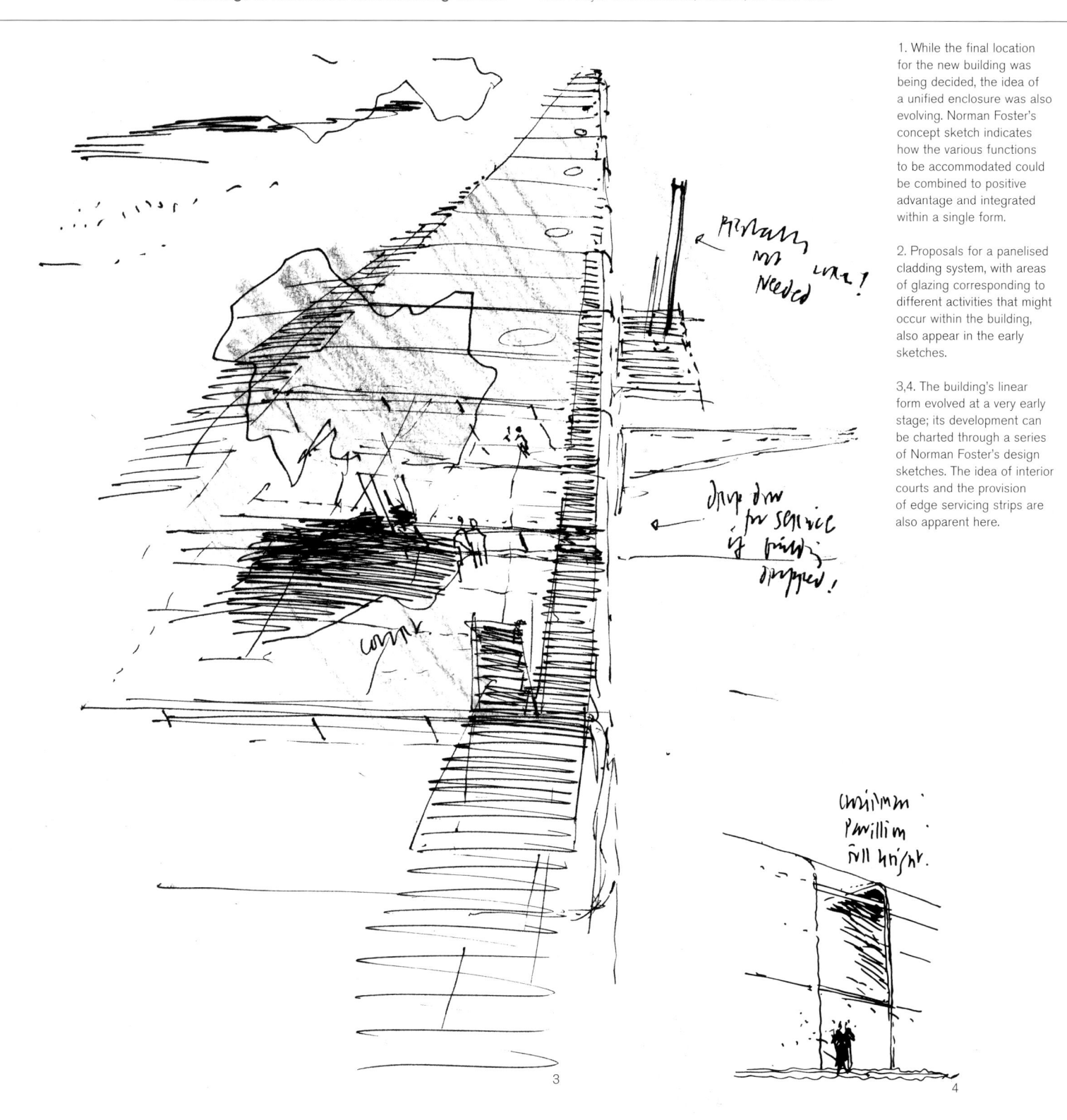

1. While the final location for the new building was being decided, the idea of a unified enclosure was also evolving. Norman Foster's concept sketch indicates how the various functions to be accommodated could be combined to positive advantage and integrated within a single form.

2. Proposals for a panelised cladding system, with areas of glazing corresponding to different activities that might occur within the building, also appear in the early sketches.

3,4. The building's linear form evolved at a very early stage; its development can be charted through a series of Norman Foster's design sketches. The idea of interior courts and the provision of edge servicing strips are also apparent here.

**Almost every gallery that we visited, whether it was in Berlin, Washington or Denmark, seemed to have a kind of regulation Calder. And so the Sainsbury Centre model sprouted its regulation Calder too. Although nobody had ever talked about having a Calder in the building we were obviously influenced by some of those early visits.**
Norman Foster, Arthur Batchelor lecture at UEA, Norwich, 7 February 1978
Left: A model of the early portal-frame structure proposal – complete with its 'regulation' Calder.

1. A portal-frame structure provided the clear span that Norman Foster had in mind for the building. The early drawings and models explored alternative engineering and cladding solutions to this basic form. In this model the cladding is placed within the portal frame; it allowed a smoother inner lining for the building's main spaces but the structure assumed an assertive nature and, being exposed, would have been more difficult to maintain.

2. External cladding was applied to a second model to allow a full comparison to be made.

Soon after that meeting a partnership was established between Foster and Kho Lang Ie, who had designed Sir Robert's study and its special display cases at Smith Square. The intention was that Kho Lang Ie would design the installation of the collection while Foster designed the building. Sadly this partnership was abruptly terminated when Kho Lang Ie tragically died while the project was still in its early stages. It was finally decided that Foster should continue alone with full responsibility.

The Sainsburys' sympathy of views with their architect is illustrated by their reluctance to impose a rigid brief. Rather, they preferred instead that the brief should develop out of a period of informed discussion. To facilitate this process, a series of visits to major European museums was undertaken by Sir Robert and Lady Sainsbury together with Norman and Wendy Foster.

Meanwhile, within the University campus, several potential sites were identified and studied. Regular meetings were established between Foster, the Sainsburys and representatives of the University headed by the vice-chancellor Frank Thistlethwaite, who was to be a powerful supporter of the project as it developed. As discussions proceeded the brief was expanded to embrace a number of related activities, including a senior common room, and a restaurant for both University and public use.

In view of the quite different nature of the separate functions to be accommodated, one might have assumed that several buildings would be required. Norman Foster, however, was always alert to the positive advantages of a single enclosure:

'Given the brief, you could have produced separate pavilions. Assuming a strong link between the collection, in terms of works of art, and a school teaching the history of art, you could fuse those two elements together; add to that a restaurant, a senior common room, and a special exhibition pavilion and you have a potential total of four buildings.

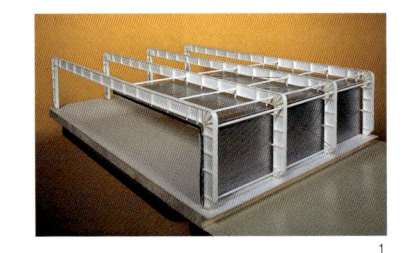

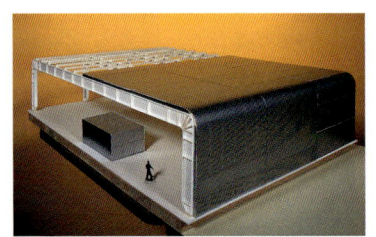

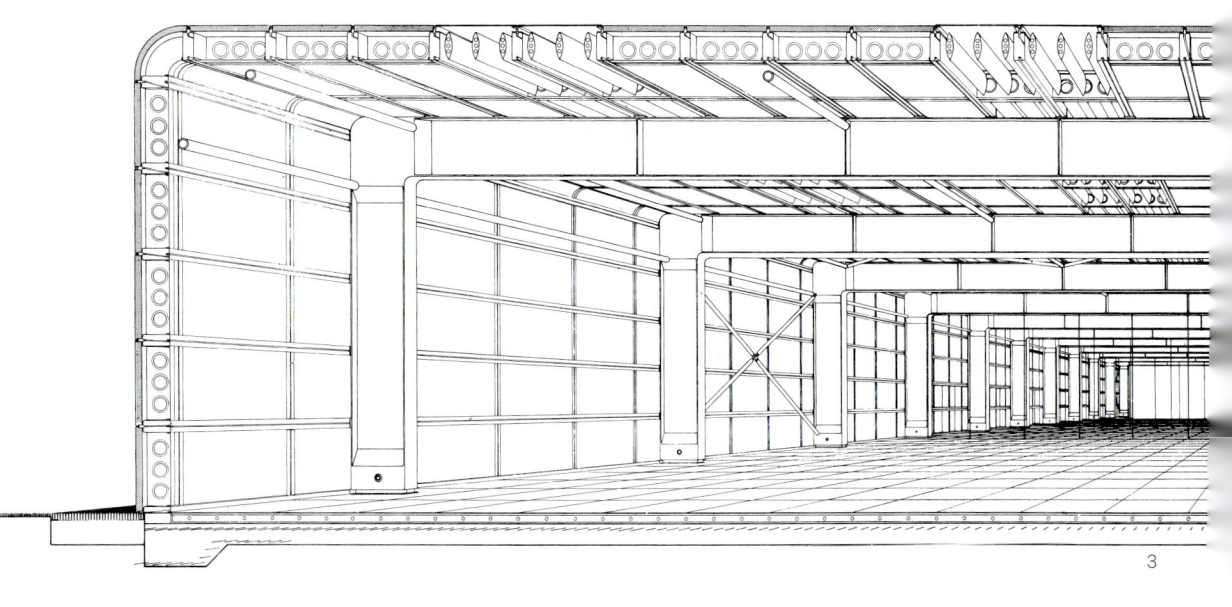

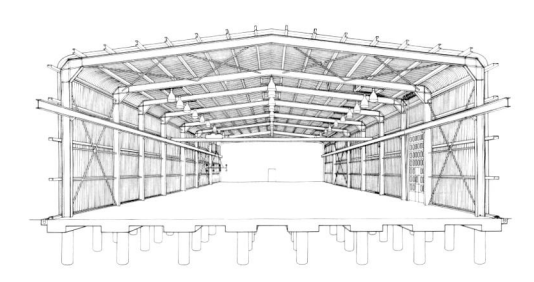

**Foster Associates' development of the modular pavilion from the industrial box is fascinating to behold ... After Reliance Controls there followed IBM Cosham, the Modern Art Glass warehouse and the Sapa aluminium extrusion plant – about as minimal and enigmatic a box as one could wish to see ... They are largely of academic interest as precursors to the Sainsbury Centre – the last word in sleek sheds and the end of the line for that particular built form.** Alastair Best, *The Architects' Journal*, 1 December 1982

Left: Initial proposals for the Sainsbury Centre's portal-frame structure clearly recalled the Modern Art Glass building of 1972-1973.

'On the other hand, you could make the leap and say that the linkage between those elements was so strong that the case for making one building out of them was overwhelming. If such a building could be a meeting place with the gallery providing a short-cut to the academic areas, then so much the better. Beyond these headlines the brief itself did not exist. The first design exercise was jointly to develop a schedule appropriate to such a project which, as far as we were aware, was without social precedent.'

The early visits to art galleries and museums had been undertaken to discover how various design solutions affected the task of the curator and the enjoyment of the visitor. The result was a list of positive responses, summarised by Norman Foster as follows: 'an awareness of the positive qualities of tuneable natural top lighting; the importance of flexibility for change and growth; the need for effective but not labour-intensive security; the value of usable storage space – most museums seemed to have as many works of art closeted away inaccessibly as on display; the need to service a gallery without disturbing either exhibits or users – changing and adjusting lamps and air filters for example; a desire to respect and integrate social elements; and a need to understand the furniture and installation of exhibits as integrated elements of the design.'

Added to this was the Sainsburys' strong distaste for the 'mausoleum' type of art gallery and the attendant approach to displaying works of art. Foster was strongly in agreement and, in a sense, the development of the brief had less to do with establishing a dialogue between patron and architect than with finding mechanisms that would serve their common goals. Situated a few miles to the west of Norwich, on a south-facing slope overlooking the River Yare, UEA was a new green-field university. The main campus was built by Denys Lasdun between 1964 and 1968. His distinctive plan utilised a 45-degree geometry that responded to the natural contours of the Yare Valley to form 'buildings conceived as architectural hills and valleys ... creating an architecture of urban landscape, rather than isolated campus buildings'. Established as part of the masterplan, the lake – or 'broad' – formed by damming the River Yare was, in fact, only created in 1975, just as the brief for the Sainsbury Centre was being finalised.

3. The initially favoured solution for the structure was a 300mm-deep steel portal frame. This frame supported a secondary system of pressed aluminium sections which in turn supported 75mm-thick insulated panels. Bolted together to form a matrix, the substructure incorporated lighting, acoustic panels and services.

4, 5. Structural engineer Anthony Hunt's exploratory drawings of the portal frame solution show a considered resolution of the foot and 'angle' details together with fixing points for the tubular steel connecting rods and cross-bracing elements.

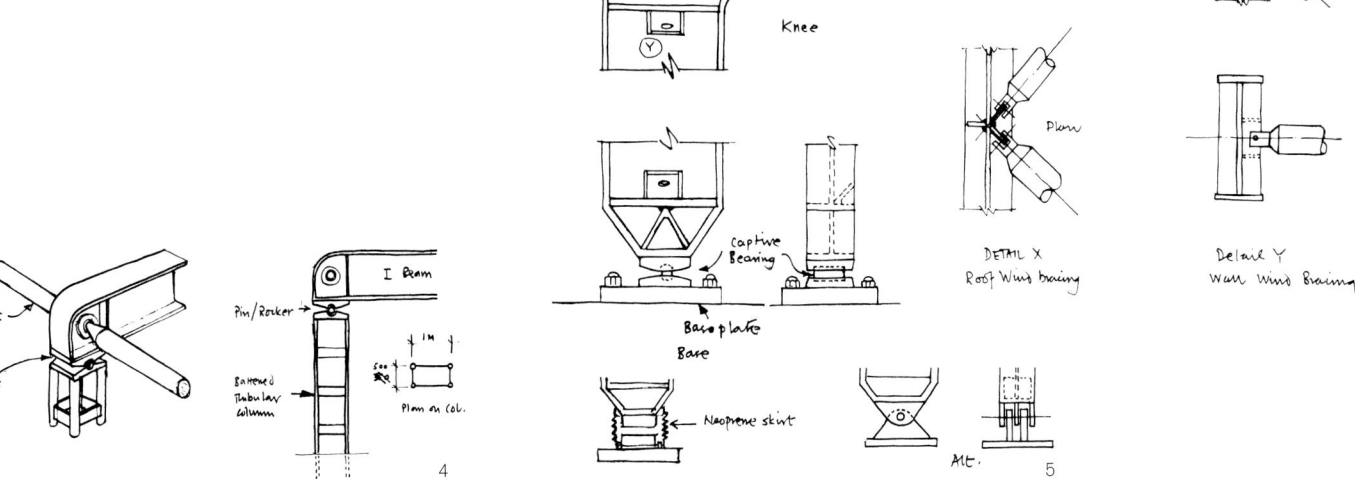

With about 3,000 square metres of floor space, fifteen lavatories, three kitchens and a capacity for up to 367 guests, this is surely a true building ... The surprisingly tiny but ruthlessly functional flight deck is a twinkling beauty and the layout is ergonomically efficient. At a more humdrum level the business-class toilets are admirably space efficient and are finely detailed pieces of industrial architecture. The galleys have a marvellous 'American diner' style – all stainless steel and black plastic ... There is a lot to learn from this building. In one sense you could say it is the ultimate technological building site. Norman Foster, *Building Sights*, 1995
Right: Norman Foster on the wing of a Boeing 747.

Right: The ergonomic efficiency of the Boeing 747 galley offered an example of how to configure the Sainsbury Centre's 'servant' spaces.
Far right: A photographic dark room and lavatories are housed within the building's 2.4-metre deep wall zone.

The process of resolving the subdivision of spaces, and the question of where to house the services installations within the building were to lead to the adoption of the 'double-skin' system, which is explained in Norman Foster's sketches.

1. Early design schemes grouped all activities on one level under a 'single-skin' roof. As a result the plan form was stretched, with many internal divisions and no clear relationship between major spaces.

2. Some of these difficulties were resolved by overlapping levels to create a semi-basement. The plan form was more compact, but the problem of relating major and minor spaces persisted.

3,4. The breakthrough came with the change from a single-skin roof to a double-layered wall and roof, with a 2.4-metre deep supporting structure, which could absorb the many small cellular spaces required. Mezzanines dramatically reduced the plan form. However, the location of all the storage and service areas at ground level remained a compromise, a problem that was resolved by the introduction of the basement spine.

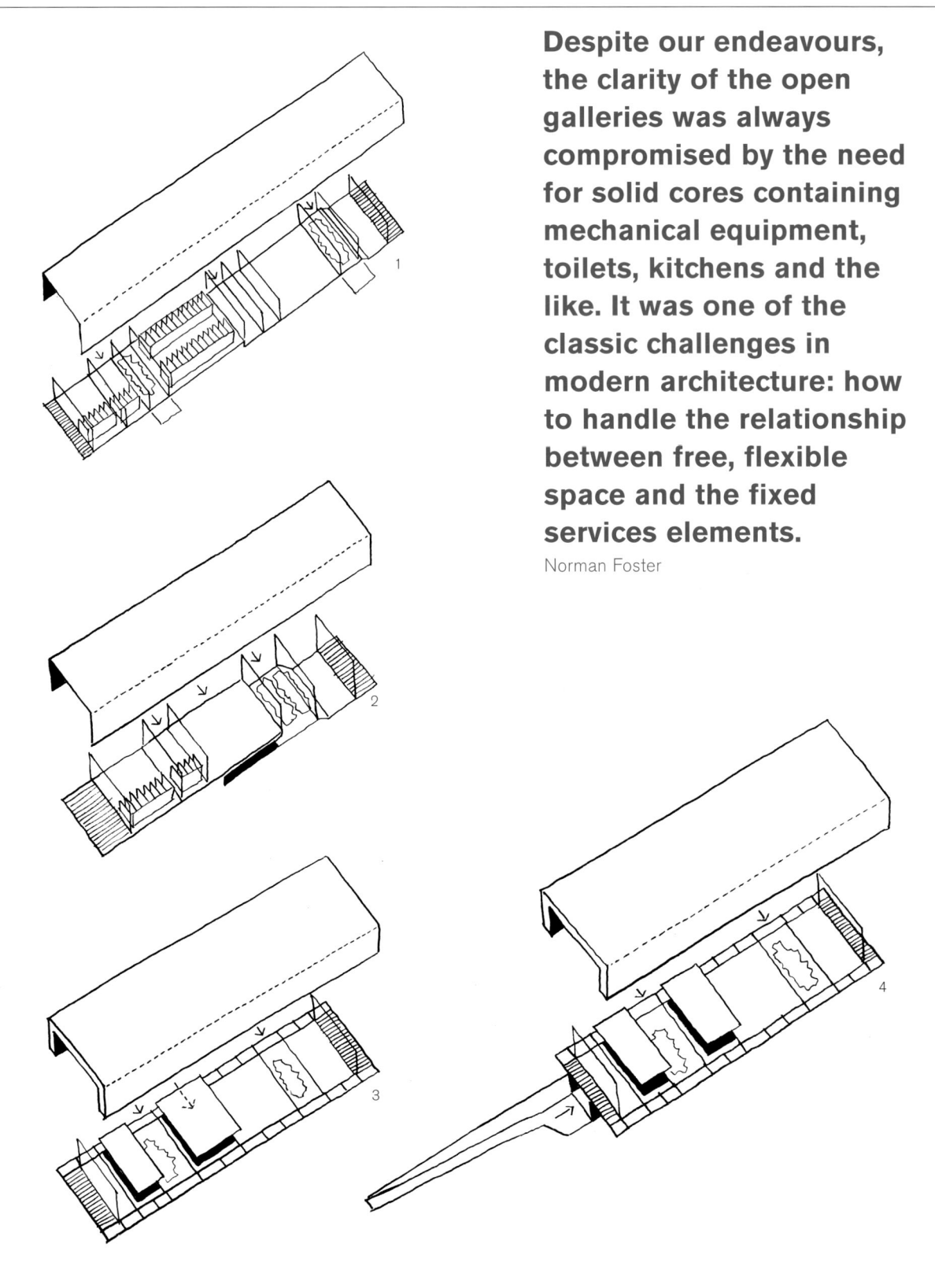

**Despite our endeavours, the clarity of the open galleries was always compromised by the need for solid cores containing mechanical equipment, toilets, kitchens and the like. It was one of the classic challenges in modern architecture: how to handle the relationship between free, flexible space and the fixed services elements.**

Norman Foster

**The considerable area and height requirements of the exhibition spaces dovetailed well with the absence of mechanical cooling, in that the warm air in summer would be able to rise, and thereby alleviate discomfort at floor level. Air conditioning, apart from being costly to install, is also costly to operate: two years after the opening of the building, financial cut-backs created a situation in which the University would have been forced to close the building if it had relied on a full air-conditioning system, because they could not have afforded to run it.** Loren Butt, lecture at the Construction Industry Conference, London 15 May 1980

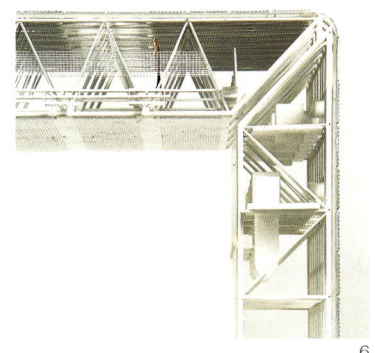

5, 6. Comparative models of the single and double-wall solutions were made at the same scale: the advantages of the deep-wall scheme are immediately apparent.

7. Norman Foster's sketch diagram of the final scheme shows how the various elements come together.

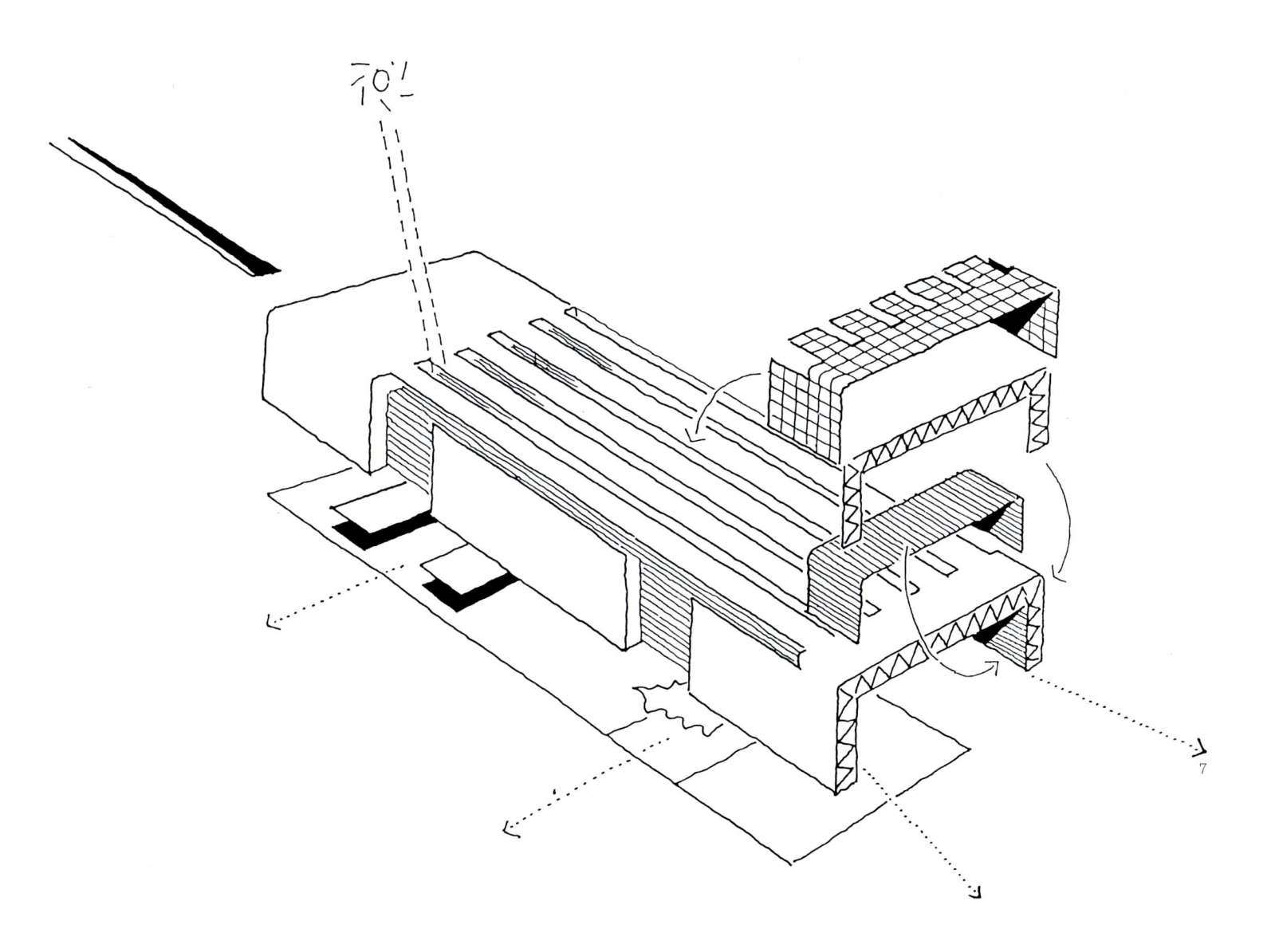

Sainsbury Centre for Visual Arts   385

**The conceptual key to the Sainsbury Centre is the membrane – a 2.4 metre 'extrusion' that forms the wall and the roof. It is constant and all-providing, [eliminating] the need for small rooms and special occurrences. It renders this building as the second generation of the 'well-serviced shed', where cubicles, capsules, things dangling down from the roof and crawling across the floor are apparently eliminated, or rather reduced to the status of apparatus within the membrane.**
Peter Cook, *The Architectural Review*, December 1978
Far left: The lower gangway of the airship Graf Zeppelin.
Left: The service catwalks installed at roof level of the Sainsbury Centre's truss provide yet another visual echo of the airship and its interior structure.

1. The 2.4 metre depth of the truss structure is used to conceal services and various back-up facilities in the wall zone and access to gallery lighting within the roof. These zones are broken into three main levels. General service rooms – including lavatories, small kitchens, storerooms and even a photographic dark room – are at the lowest level; immediately above is a zone for the transmission of pipes, ducts and wires along the entire length of the building. Mechanical, heating and ventilating plant, water services and electrical switchgear occupy the upper levels.

Seven locations were initially identified as possible settings for the new building. However, these were quickly reduced to four main strategies suitable for study. Norman Foster recalls:

'The original intention was that the building would go at the arts end of the campus, next to the Music Centre that Arup Associates had just completed. But we wanted to throw the whole thing wide open. We considered a 'gateway' site for the campus as a whole. We considered an almost subterranean building right in the middle. We looked at the arts corner and then at the site where the building finally settled. It was on a study trip, after we had visited Aalto's gallery at Aalborg, in Denmark, that we decided that the building should be where it ended up.

'Everybody liked the idea that it would be next to the science building and close to the student residences and that it would have an aspect onto the broad. There would be no need to spend a lot of money constructing new roads and services. The existing buildings indicated future growth along the line of the Yare Valley and, in anticipation of this, a network of roads, drainage, water, gas and so forth had already been provided.'

Concurrent with the choice of site, the concept of a single building was also being finalised. At this stage a detailed brief was still far from complete, but the main areas were clearly defined. They suggested a straightforward linear relationship, a theme introduced in Foster's earliest sketches. While dovetailing elegantly with Denys Lasdun's masterplan, the building's siting also encouraged a strong spirit of independence. The linear strip follows the 45-degree geometry of the main campus, but its orientation is such that views from inside frame the lake and woodland rather than the Lasdun buildings. Elevated on the brow of a hill with a grass meadow falling away towards the new lake, the building's autonomous form is accentuated further still.

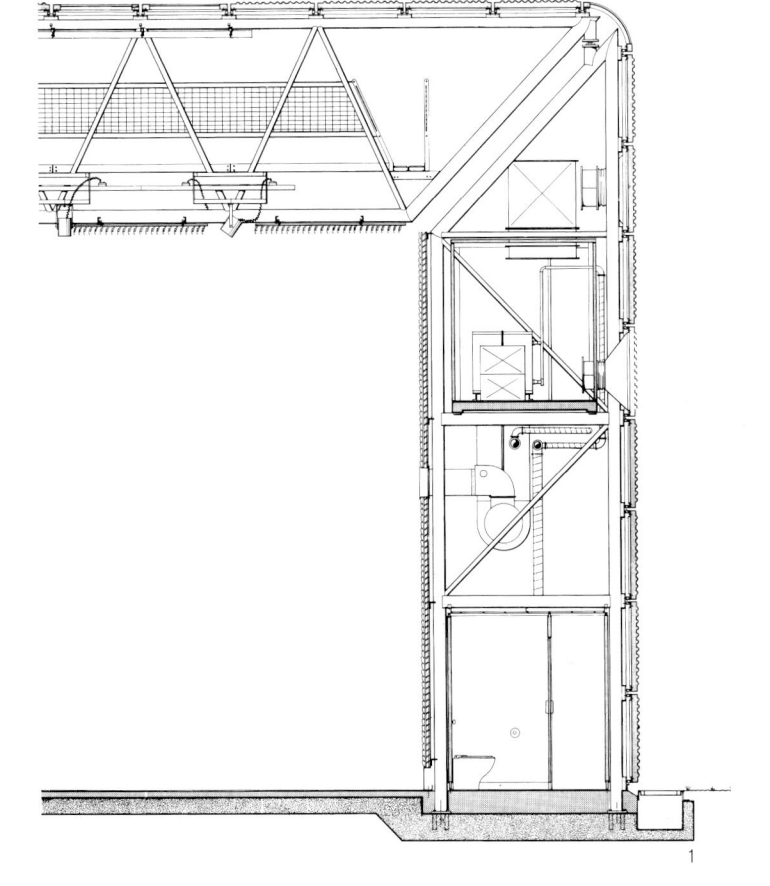

**Late in the day we seized upon an exciting new solution: by creating a double layer of wall and roof, the space between could absorb the secondary functions, leaving the primary spaces free and uncluttered. It was as if the original concept had suddenly flowered.**
Norman Foster

A grand entrance canopy, reminiscent both of an airplane hangar and of Le Corbusier's High Court at Chandigarh, transforms the trussed space into a gigantic portico, an expanded temple front. Amplification and simplicity, two rhetorical devices, are then combined with anamnesis (the recollection of things past) to produce a very dignified and haunting image, made more strange by the slick-tech aesthetic … Are we in a supermarket, an airplane hangar, a factory, a greenhouse, or an office building? Charles Jencks, *Current Architecture*, 1982

**Foster has decorated drawings of [his] buildings with helicopters or else his pure-white Caproni sailplane gliding overhead. These intrusions are significant. Most of Foster's best buildings are elegant machines, either complex in form (like the Renault Centre) or else simple, smooth skinned structures like a glider (Sainsbury Centre).**
Jonathan Glancey, *World Architecture*, April 1989
Left: Norman Foster's sketch of the Sainsbury Centre complete with Caproni sailplane.

2. At the building's open ends the all-glass walls are drawn back and the truss structure revealed at one of its most visually complex points: supplementary cross-bracing connects the two end trusses to provide stability to the entire structure.

3. The double-skin solution is explored in an early design sketch by Norman Foster; it anticipates an inner lining of louvres, and service plant is located within the space created. However, no clear structural form is yet suggested.

**The revelation that the Foster team, despite their reputation of coolness, is still attached to identifiable places and identifiable objects lies in the two 'window' conditions. The louvres are pared away, not just for the door, but right up the side of the building. As a result the ventilation apparatus becomes a sculptural object, framed against the sky, every bit as much as if it were a pediment, a carving, or some manipulation of the Classical repertoire that emphasises a particular patch of the facade. So the potential 'absoluteness' of this building is eschewed in favour of the old game of 'event'. And once again we have to be reminded iconographically of the joy of technology.**
Peter Cook, *The Architectural Review*, December 1978

**Look at Gresley's Pacific locomotives for the LNER, William Lyons' E-type Jaguar, and Mitchell's unparalleled Supermarine Spitfire. The sleek and the smooth, the thoroughbred, the well-mannered machine, mechanical successor to the racehorse. Now consider the Sainsbury Centre, probably Foster's best-known building. The form is sleek and smooth, the guts of the building, although beautifully detailed, largely hidden away from sight: note the complete resolution of the flowing surface, the sense of visual inclusion, of togetherness, propriety, good manners.**
Jonathan Glancey, *The Architectural Review*, July 1983

1. The double skin solution provided the key to the spatial success of the building. With servicing now achieved discretely from the wall and roof zones, the main area of the building achieves the single, clearly articulated volume aimed at in Norman Foster's first sketches.

Providing maximum flexibility within this overall form became a guiding principle. Added to that was the recognition that, in the lifetime of a building, certain items – the services and the cladding, for example – may be relatively 'short-life' items. Just as in an aircraft – to borrow one of Foster's favourite analogies – while the airframe may be designed to fly many thousands of hours, the engines and the avionics will be replaced or upgraded several times during its lifetime. The system of interchangeable cladding panels – glazed or solid on both roof and walls – reinforces this strategy. The building's elevations can be reconfigured at will, while within it various activities are able to develop, blend and change over time.

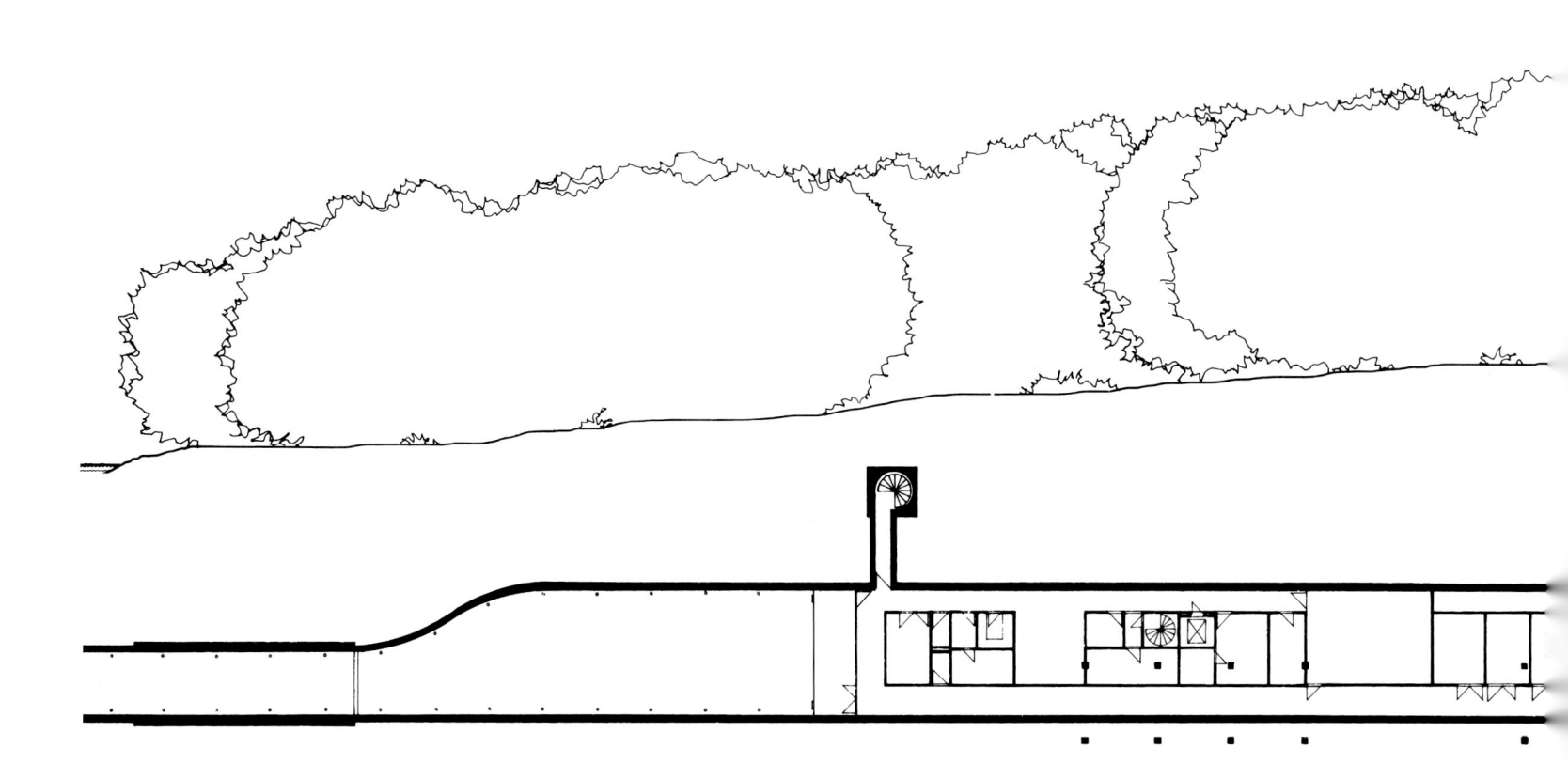

Far left: The 'sleek and smooth' Pacific locomotive designed by Sir Nigel Gresley (1876-1941), chief mechanical engineer of the London and North East Railway from 1923 to 1941. Gresley's many innovations included the design of the articulated carriage sets and the development of three-cylinder steam locomotives.
Left: The Supermarine Spitfire, designed by Reginald J Mitchell (1885-1937). This plane first saw service in the Battle of Britain, was still employed by the RAF as a front-line service aircraft well into the 1950s, and is, Norman Foster says, 'an absolute delight to fly'.

When discussing the planning of the building, Norman Foster draws on another machine-world analogy: 'Like a railway carriage, you can connect all the spaces internally, so that you can use the gallery as a short-cut to the school if you like. But you can also compartmentalise the spaces, just as you can close off the connections between one carriage and another. Each area is then private, secure and separate, because they may have different opening hours, or they may want to close one to do some kinds of work in private. You therefore have the option to open the thing up as a total entity, or close it off into a series of sealed areas.'

The eastern half of the building forms a public zone, comprising the main reception and cafeteria, a temporary exhibition area and the main gallery – or the 'living area', as it came to be known. It was planned that only a part of the collection would be displayed at any one time.

In order that the remainder would not be lost from view in storage, a study reserve area was integrated into the mezzanine adjacent to the main gallery from which it was separated by a glass wall. Here, in the days before the Crescent Wing provided greatly improved reserve facilities, students and staff enjoyed uninterrupted access, for study and research purposes, to those works not on public display.

While the gallery areas are public and highly permeable, accessed either at ground level or from a high-level walkway, the School of Fine Arts – located centrally in the plan – is protected by small 'buildings within buildings', which form two self-supporting mezzanine structures. These contain the variety of smaller, more private spaces required by the school. A temporary exhibition area and the senior common room make use of the open upper areas of the mezzanines, while a restaurant is placed next to the glazed wall at the western end of the building where diners can enjoy the afternoon sun and a view of the nearby woods.

2. Concealed beneath the main building, an extensive basement provides space for the necessary back-up facilities, which could not easily be housed in the principal areas above.

3. The basement runs the full length of the building to accommodate storage and workshop areas, together with smaller conservation laboratories and plant rooms. Main delivery access is by a ramp to an underground loading bay. Spiral stairs and lifts provide access to the gallery, school and mezzanine areas above, while two protected fire escapes lead to the outside, sheltered within the depth of the building's porticoes.

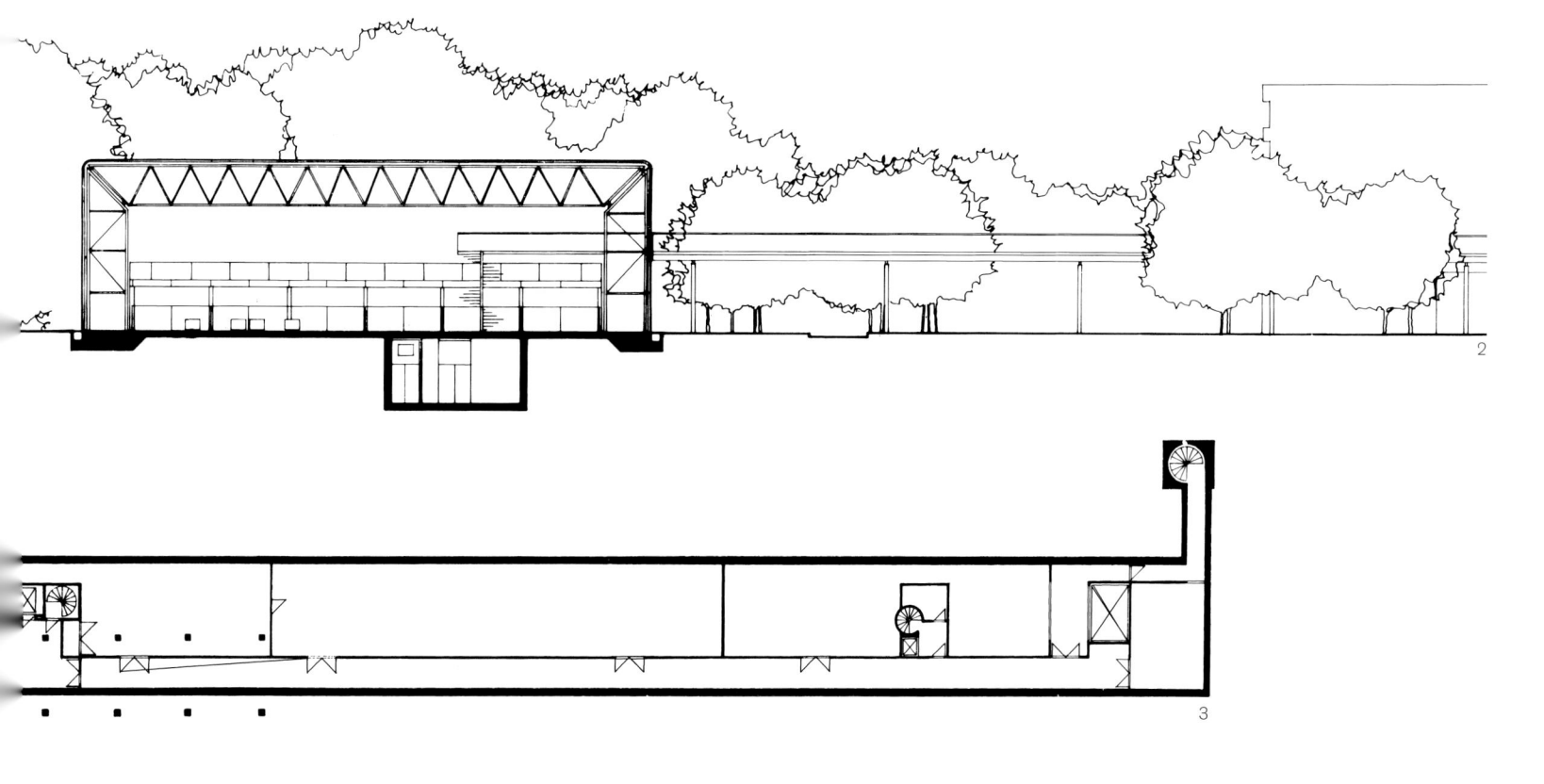

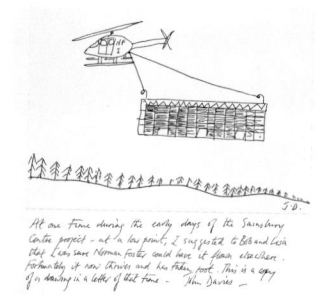

**At one stage during the early days of the Sainsbury Centre, at a low point, I suggested to Bob and Lisa that I was sure Norman Foster could have it flown elsewhere. Fortunately it now thrives and has taken root. this is a copy of a drawing in a letter of that time.** John Davies, annotation on a drawing presented as a card to Norman Foster on his sixtieth birthday by Sir Robert and Lady Sainsbury, 1 June 1995

**The interior of this vast shed stretches clear from one glass end wall to the other interrupted only by two low platforms. The plan would have any architecture school studio master hopping with agitation, so dramatic and apparently simplistic is it. Foster Associates have simply divided the floor into slices: no clever articulation of plan or ingenious circulation. The trouble, according to the administrators, is that it works extremely well.** Sutherland Lyall, *New Society*, 6 July 1978

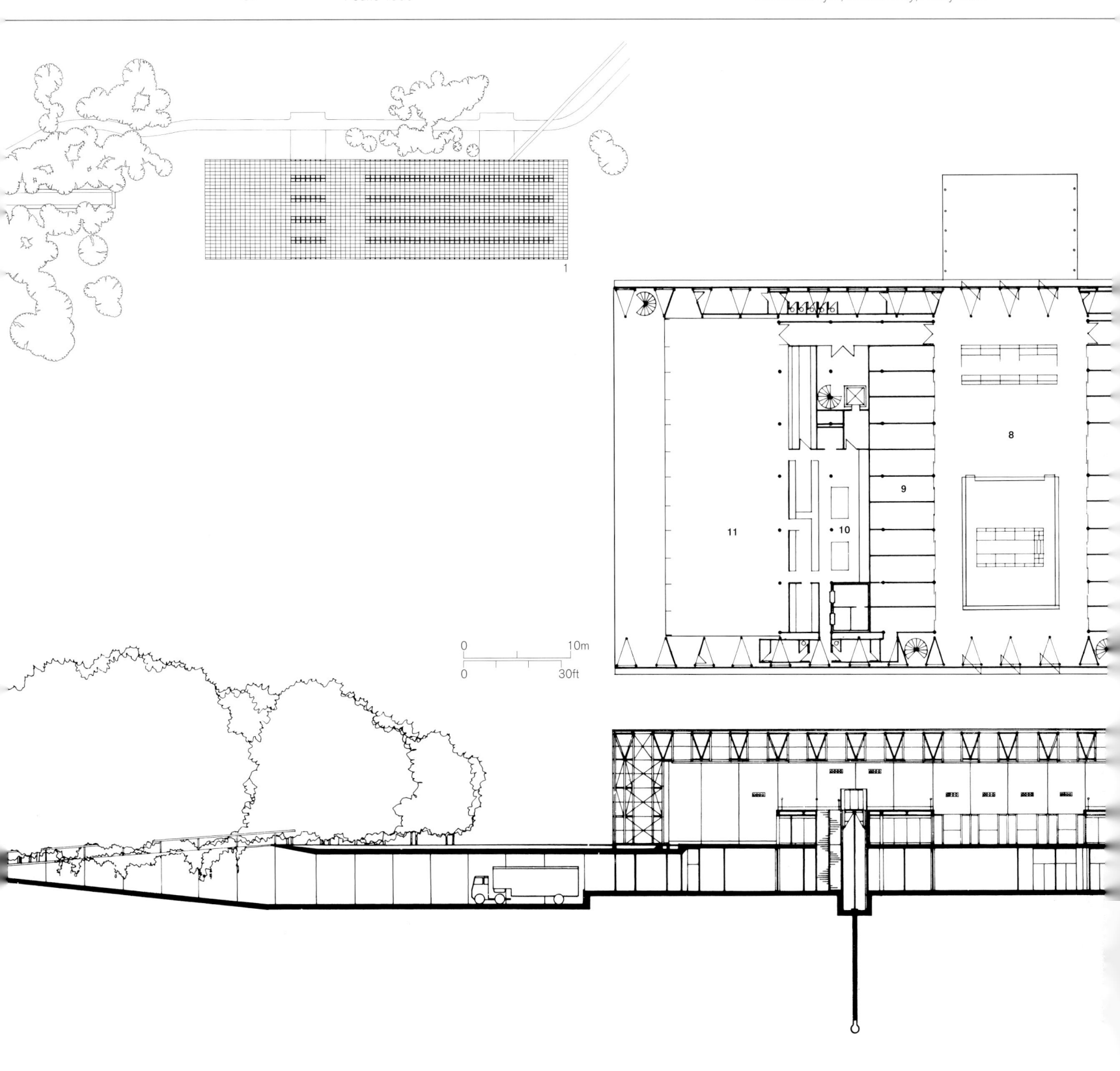

**In some respects the word 'gallery' could be a misnomer. There are in reality four main areas for display and related circulation. Arrival via the bridge and internal stair or through the front door is into an entrance conservatory, which combines the functions of reception, security, coffee bar and meeting place. To one side is an area for special exhibitions, to the other is the main 'living area'. This name was felt to express the spirit of the space with its easy seating and low tables for relaxed contemplation amid the collection, rather than the image of a traditionally formal gallery with its emphasis on art in isolation.** Norman Foster, *The Architectural Review*, December 1978

**The buildings that Foster enjoys most – Giuseppe Mengoni's Galleria in Milan, Decimus Burton's Palm House at Kew, the vehicular assembly building at Cape Canaveral … and the Bradbury Building in Los Angeles – are mostly from outside the narrow line of development of orthodox modernism. With their huge single-volume spaces they have clearly been an important influence on Foster. They were the products in the main of independent-minded inventors, people content to get things done and to leave the theorising to others.** Deyan Sudjic, *Norman Foster, Richard Rogers, James Stirling: New Directions In British Architecture*, 1986

Right: The Palm House, Kew Gardens, 1844-1848.

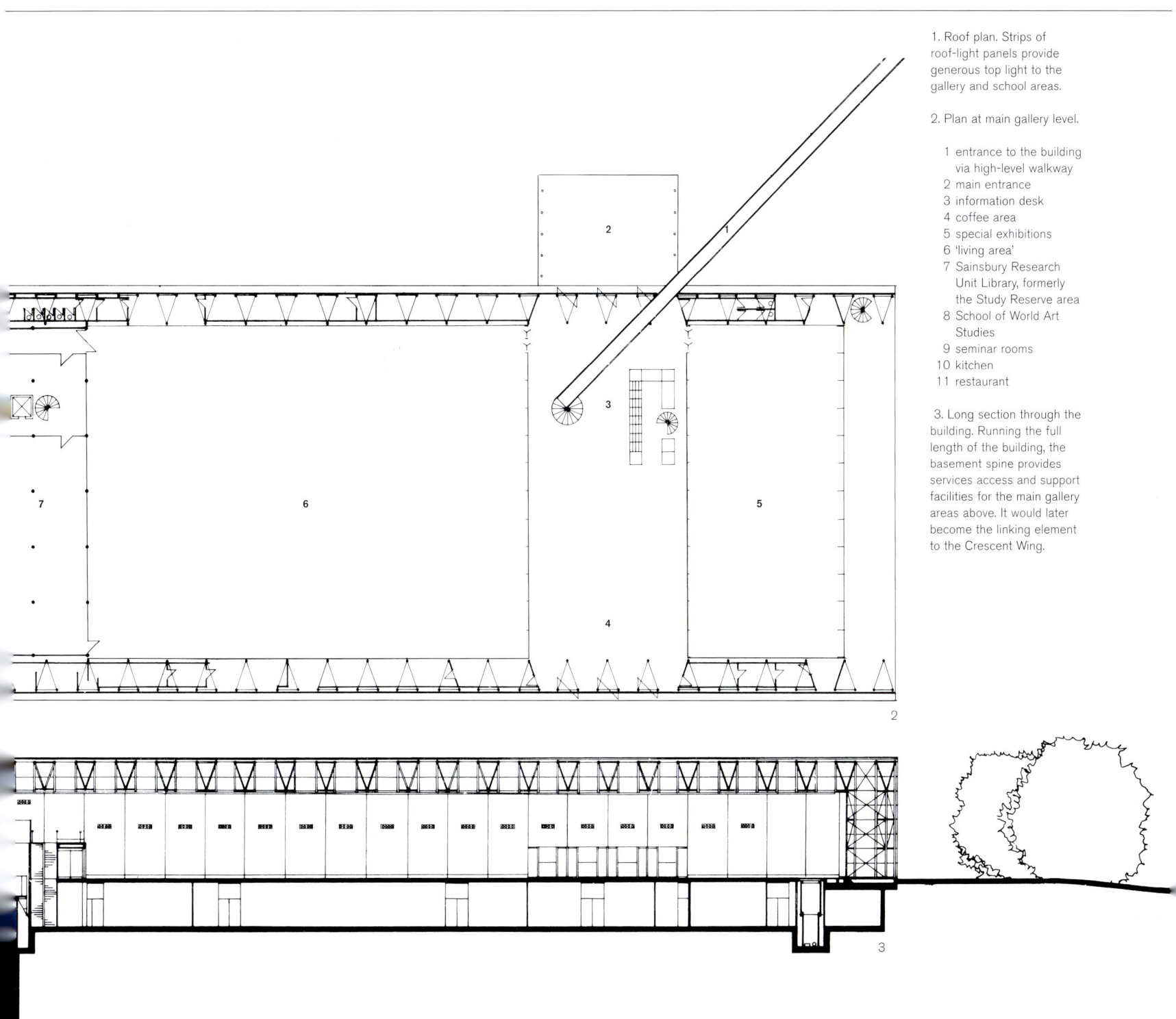

1. Roof plan. Strips of roof-light panels provide generous top light to the gallery and school areas.

2. Plan at main gallery level.

  1 entrance to the building via high-level walkway
  2 main entrance
  3 information desk
  4 coffee area
  5 special exhibitions
  6 'living area'
  7 Sainsbury Research Unit Library, formerly the Study Reserve area
  8 School of World Art Studies
  9 seminar rooms
10 kitchen
11 restaurant

3. Long section through the building. Running the full length of the building, the basement spine provides services access and support facilities for the main gallery areas above. It would later become the linking element to the Crescent Wing.

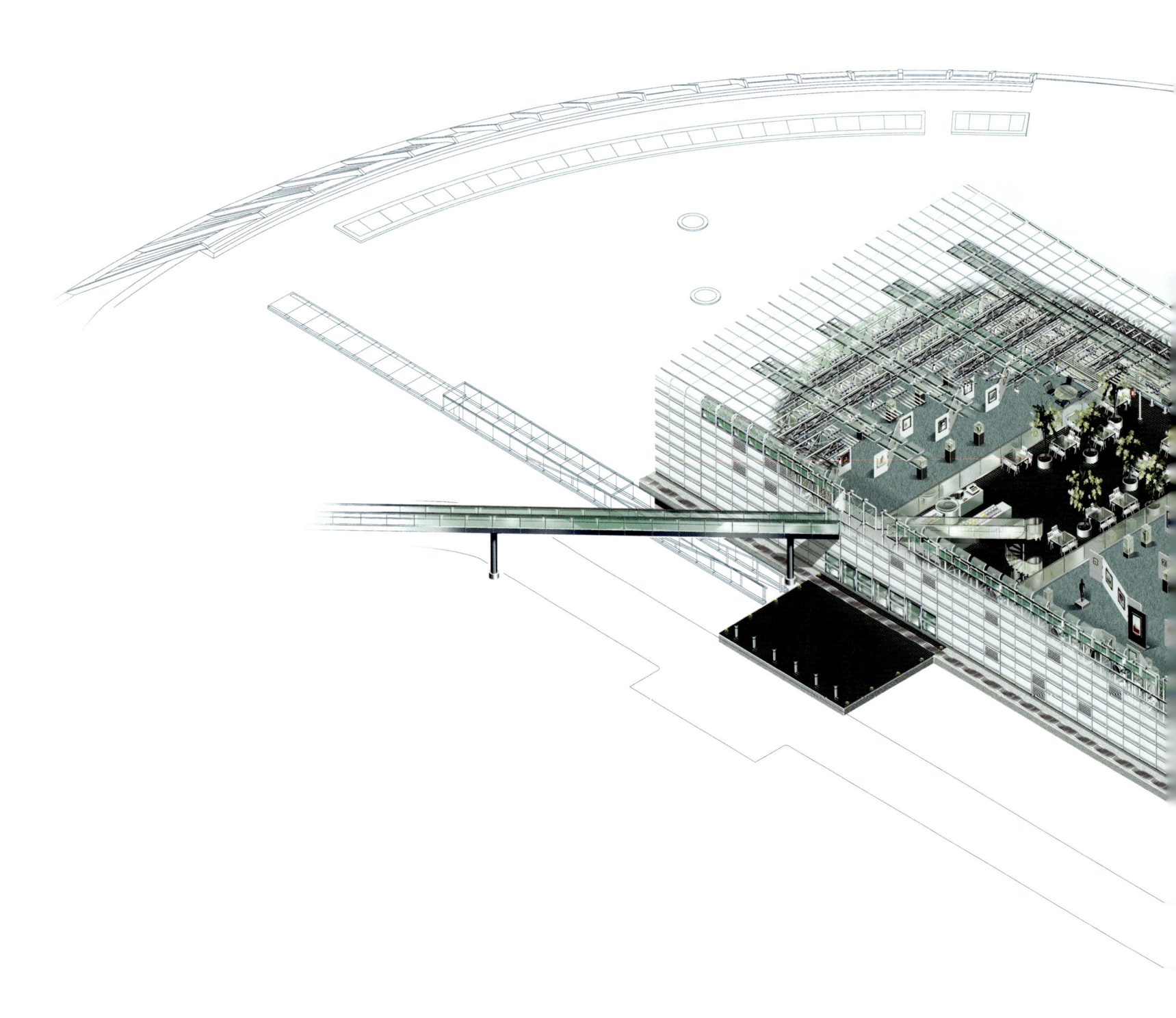

In this cutaway drawing the transparency between the public gallery areas and the various functions of the School of World Art Studies is revealed. The position of the Crescent Wing, which added enhanced facilities for the Study Reserve collection, together with conservation laboratories and conference facilities is shown in outline.

Sainsbury Centre for Visual Arts 393

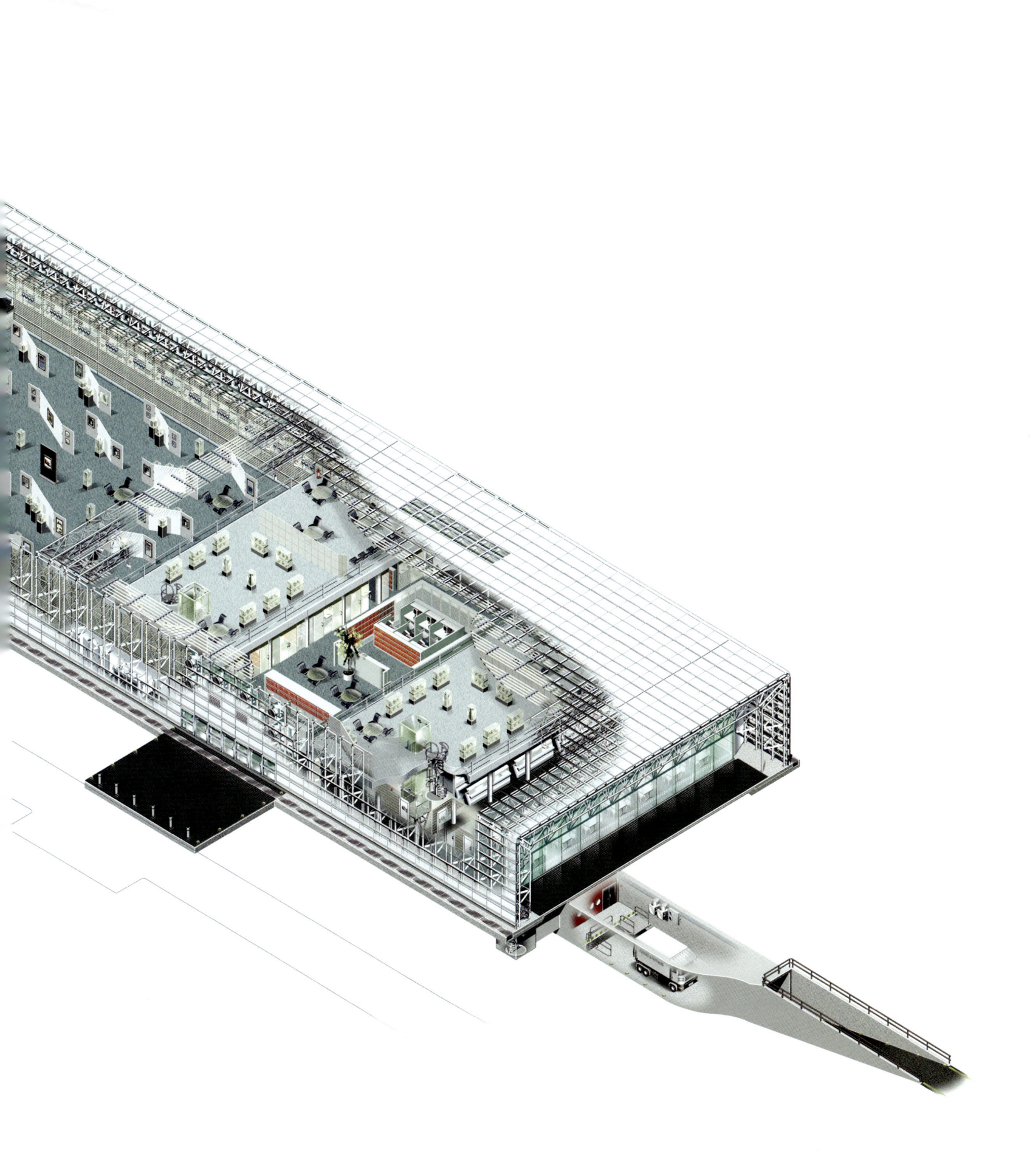

What is defined today as 'High-tech' in the field of construction is in reality a 'Zeppelin tech' transferred into our field. Light, often aluminium structures, modular construction ... prefabrication of elements and assembly, continuous and thin covering surfaces. Yet of course there is something more, and, for us architects, something unreachable in the structures of airships. Only the early avant-garde had imagined similar structures. Vittorio Gregotti, *Rassegna* 67, 1996
Left: The skeleton of the Graf Zeppelin in its assembly hangar at Friedrichshafen, Germany, in 1928.

The building is essentially a series of machine-made components and that relates to the realities of cost control, to the manner in which buildings are assembled, and the materials from which they are made. I am not saying that it's wrong to build from brickwork or anything like that – indeed the craftsmanship in the concrete basement areas is exceptional. But the main part of the building consists of machine-made, shop-assembled elements; and there's no short-cut here. If loving care is needed to put brick on brick, then to get a similar level of quality control using metal or glass components requires the same persistence from everybody involved. Norman Foster, Arthur Batchelor lecture at UEA, Norwich, 7 February 1978

1-10. The reinforced-concrete basement and ground slab were the only parts of the building requiring intensive site construction. The superstructure components were mostly prefabricated and brought to site for final assembly. The structural trusses and towers were fabricated at Tubeworkers' workshops in Warwickshire and were delivered complete with their final coat of paint. Only the roof trusses required on-site welding. Due to their size, they had to be transported to site in two sections. The welded connection was made with the truss raised into position and supported by a gantry at the mid-point.

We know before we've arrived that even if it looks like a shed [the Sainsbury Centre] is amazingly, intricately inventive; that wall or roof panels can be changed from door to solid to window and back in the blink of an eye; that vacuum-formed aluminium or mile-long neoprene strips are no mean feat; that, like all good Sainsburys, it is closed on Mondays ... But here, somehow, it's theatrically friendly; an intimate hugeness, spacious enough to take the different pursuits, but small; all at home within its shimmering louvred aluminium tent and black reflective gables. **I wonder what the Crystal Palace was like at night?** John McKean, *AD Profiles*, August 1978
Right: Workmen installing the glazing at Crystal Palace.

For Foster, Joseph Paxton's Crystal Palace was the greatest piece of architecture of the nineteenth century, and has still hardly been equalled. Yet Paxton ... was hardly considered an architect at all by his contemporaries. Of the twentieth-century pioneers, the names that Foster mentions as influences – Konrad Wachsmann, Charles Eames, Jean Prouvé, Buckminster Fuller – have also been on the edge of architecture, far away from the well-publicised debates about functionalism and modernism. From them, Foster has absorbed a passion for lightweight buildings, for flexibility and transparency. Deyan Sudjic, *Norman Foster, Richard Rogers, James Stirling: New Directions In British Architecture*, 1986

**The visual dimension of a structure is also its spiritual dimension: how it will look and how it will work become conceptually inseparable through the process of design.**
Norman Foster

Sainsbury Centre for Visual Arts 395

**Foster always thrives in these close-counting circumstances ... Recently he has had the temerity to answer Buckminster Fuller's non-rhetorical question, 'But what does your building weigh?' with a detailed breakdown of the Sainsbury Centre. It adds up to a remarkably modest total of 5,619 tonnes, or practically 70 cubic metres of building volume for every tonne of structural weight – a figure that grows more impressive when it is realised that around four fifths of that structural weight is the ground slab.** Reyner Banham, *Foster Associates*, 1979

Left: Buckminster Fuller and Norman Foster photographed during a visit to the Sainsbury Centre in 1978.

1. With the truss structure in place the process of installing the cladding could begin. The neoprene lattice, which forms a waterproof gasket for the cladding panels, is seen here draped over the roof of the building during construction. The lattice was delivered to site in manageable ladder-like sections, which were welded together to form the largest known continuous neoprene net in the world, weighing some 26 tonnes.

Beneath this main level, a basement spine runs the full length of the building. Underground loading docks, landscaped over, are connected by ramp to the University's main service road at the western end of the site. This basement provides a secure area for the unloading, preparation and storage of works of art for temporary exhibitions. It also contains workshops and technical support facilities for the other areas at ground level. Along its length there are staircases, lifts and – at the special exhibition end of the building – a hydraulic platform to connect the movement of people and exhibits between levels, including the two mezzanines.

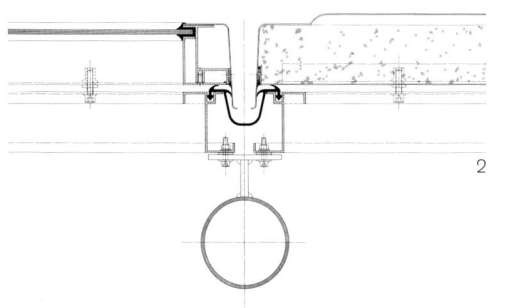

Structurally, welded tubular-steel trusses span a total of 35 metres to give a column-free enclosed space. The clear internal height of 7.5 metres was determined by a number of factors: a generous height was always envisaged to provide the correct sense of proportion to the building's large floor area; large works of art have to be accommodated; and a comfortable working height was required over the mezzanine areas.

The building's height is also a factor in its environmental control. The stack effect of air in an enclosure of such height means that warm air, collecting at the top, can be expelled or circulated by a simple fan system to maintain comfortable temperatures at ground level during the day; this means that air conditioning is not required. Excess heat is dissipated during the cooler nights, while the academic timetable ensures the building is at its least populated during the warmest months of the year. Significantly, this has been crucial to the building's low running costs – and its very survival as an institution. In the wake of the financial cut-backs of recent years, the University has calculated that it could not have afforded to run the building, had it been reliant on conventional heavily energy consuming air-conditioning systems.

The building as it stands seems so resolved, so absolutely 'right', that it is surprising to discover that several structural options were considered before the design team arrived at the solution one sees today. They initially looked at post and beam options before a portal frame emerged as an early favourite. This provided Foster with the clear span he was looking for, but as the design developed, the concept of providing a single open space for the main areas was constantly threatened with compromise by the complex demands of secondary service areas.

'Bucky asked us how much the building weighed. We didn't know but we worked it out and wrote to him; we learnt something from it as he predicted we would. The tiny basement, which is 8 per cent of the volume of the main space, weighs 80 per cent of the total, or about 4,000 tonnes. The main building itself, which weighs just over 1,000 tonnes, was built more quickly than the basement and its unit cost was about half that of the basement. It is miserable in the basement and very nice upstairs. I think Buckminster Fuller has a good point when he talks about the relationship between weight, energy and performance – to which I would also add 'joy'. Norman Foster, lecture at the Centre Pompidou, Paris, 26 February 1981

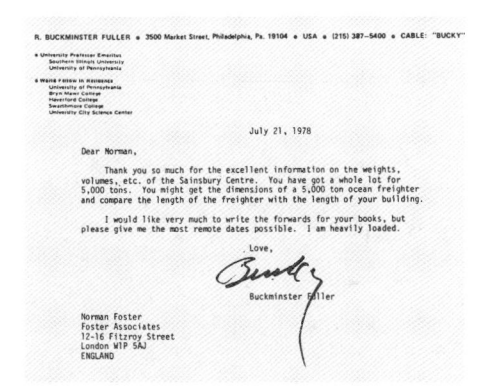

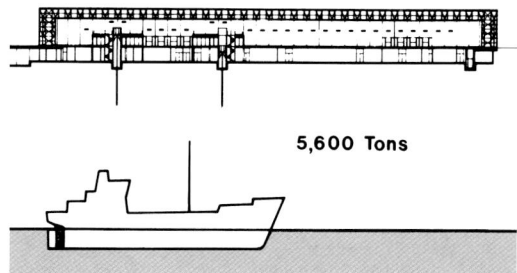

These demands were at first only partially met. The mezzanines, for example, solved such problems with regard to the school area. The upper parts of the truss structure could certainly contain the discreet distribution of services within their depth while, at ground level, that same depth could be used to contain some of the other smaller facilities common to all the main areas. There remained, however, a substantial amount of back-up facilities, which could not easily be accommodated within the main space.

As the structural form developed, other issues were also addressed. One area of particular interest was exactly how the system of interchangeable panels might be achieved. To ensure economical production, it was desirable to use the same panels for both roof and walls: with an appreciation of the benefits of top-lit gallery spaces, the ability to change from solid to glazed panels would be equally beneficial on both surfaces. Foster was also conscious that the building's extensive 'fifth elevation' would be overlooked by many of the existing campus buildings.

It was clear from the beginning that extensive mechanical and electrical services would have to be distributed through both walls and ceiling. The early panel proposals therefore adopted a composite arrangement, the panels combining with a supporting substructure to house basic ductwork, service runs and control systems. Models were made showing such a panelling system located both outside and, later, inside the portal frame. The external cladding solution clearly recalled Foster's earlier Modern Art Glass building, with the panels curving over from wall to roof, emphasising the continuous nature of the structure beneath. However, it is the second option, with the cladding inside the frame, which expresses the increasing reservations among the design team about the quality of space created by the portal frame solution and the ease of integrating the fixed services elements within it.

The planning requirements for both school and exhibition space specified a far more complex mix of spaces than had originally been assumed. Tackling the growing problems of how to subdivide the single-level space was resulting in deformations of the plan form. The numerous internal divisions were confusing any cogent relationship between major and minor spaces while, at a practical level, access for both goods and public was in danger of becoming poorly realised. One bid to resolve these difficulties resulted in the introduction of overlapping levels within the natural fall of the site to create a semi-basement. This generated a more compact plan, allowing secondary areas to be tucked away, but the difficulty of balancing major and minor spaces remained.

In the end it was the crucial decision, taken very late in the design process – or as Foster describes it, 'at five minutes to midnight' – to change to a double-skin system, which provided the key to the building's spatial success. It allowed service zones and other small facilities to be concealed within the thickness of the 'wall', so liberating the major space. Mezzanines provided the more private areas required by the school, offering concise groupings that clarified the overall plan-form. This left only certain storage and workshop areas to resolved. These were successfully accommodated with the introduction of the basement spine.

2. This section illustrates how the innovative neoprene gasket spans and seals the joint adjacent panels. The resulting gutter carries rainwater off the roof down to the drainage channels that run along the long sides of the building.

3. The original aluminium panels are fixed in place. This modular cladding system brought with it an added and unforeseen advantage: it allowed the contractor to fit temporary plywood sheeting to the frame, which formed a watertight enclosure, thus allowing the interior fit-out to proceed in parallel with the cladding operation.

Sainsbury Centre for Visual Arts 397

**The Airstream's polished aluminium exterior skin has the craftsmanly elegance of a Douglas aircraft; its miscellaneous doors and flaps and plug points and ventilators have that aptness and tidy detailing which is supposed to derive from unaffected engineering practice, but which actually requires enormous self-effacing sophistication on the part of the designer.**
Reyner Banham, *New Society*, 3 August 1978
Right: The Airstream caravan, designed by Wally Byam in the 1930s, and still in production sixty years later.
Far right: Norman Foster's sketch of the Airstream, just one of the influences which inspired and informed the Sainsbury Centre's original panel cladding system.

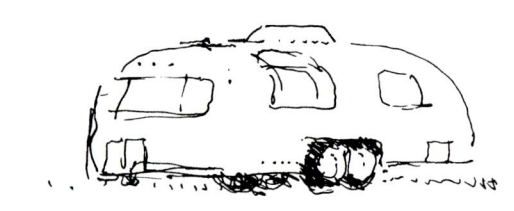

1-3. The original cladding consisted of 1.8 x 1.2 metre panels of insulated sandwich construction, with a moulded outer skin of highly reflective anodised aluminium. A core of 100mm Phenolux foam ensured a high insulation value. There are five types of panel: flat panels are available in glazed, solid or grilled forms, while special curved panels form the junction between wall and roof. All the flat panels are interchangeable and can be released by unfastening six bolts, which are easily accessible from inside the building. Any part of the roof or walls can be changed from solid to glass or vice versa as desired; the whole operation requires only two men and can be completed in as little as five minutes. Similarly, external entrances can be 'popped out' and moved to new locations as required.

The genesis of the double-skin solution can be clearly traced back to those early study models, which investigated the effects of a single layer of panels either inside or outside the portal frame. Each method had its good points, but Foster had realised that combining the two, and increasing the structural zone, would bring about major benefits. However, the portal structure restricted continuous access between the two skins and remained too shallow to conceal the many other small-scale facilities required. A Canadian triadetic system – a form of spaceframe – was briefly considered as an alternative, but rejected. A truss structure, on the other hand, with its open framework and greater depth, very neatly resolved both of those problems.

The truss structure is contained between an inner skin of perforated louvres and the outer system of interchangeable panels. In planning terms, one of the most positive effects of the truss solution was that it allowed service facilities – which by their nature are tolerant of a more fixed location – to be distributed evenly along each side of the building. In the wall zone at ground level, lobbies, lavatories, stores, small kitchen areas and a photographic studio are contained and concealed. For greater flexibility, these elements are housed in self-contained modules that can easily be dismantled and relocated if required.

The louvres that line the walls and ceiling are designed to function in harness with the interchangeable external panels and a companion system of artificial lighting. This solution, seemingly simple and elegant in its final form, was the outcome of an extensive period of study and research: conceptually, the inner skin had to fulfil many criteria, as Norman Foster describes:

'We wanted something that would line the inside of the building; something that would be neutralising; something that was not assertive if you were seeking the sympathetic display of a work of art; and something that was calm in terms of a background for study or relaxation. But at the same time we were looking for something that was semi-transparent; that was going to shield and be capable of adjusting – to respond, say, to the penetration of the sun; something that would work acoustically and would have a dampening effect; and something that could be easily removed.'

**The use of superplastic aluminium for the Sainsbury Centre's cladding panels was one of the first uses of the material in the construction industry ... The composite material can be stretch-formed into rigid shapes using low cost tools. The panels may look as though they were stamped out on expensive presses and mass-production lines in accordance with Modernist folklore (the raised surface of the original design is suggestive of the panels on the same Citroën vehicles that inspired Le Corbusier's naming of his 'Maison Citrohan' project) but they were not.** Chris Abel, 'From Hard to Soft Machines', 1989
Right: The Sainsbury Centre cladding panels.
Far right: The ribbed panelling of the Citroën 2CV.

Fixed louvres, concealing acoustic material, line the 'solid' wall areas, while a single layer of matching adjustable louvres continues across the glazed panel 'conservatory' areas and large end walls. Connected in motorised banks and linked to light sensors, the louvres adjust automatically to external light conditions. A similar arrangement lines the ceiling, while a supplementary layer of blinds is positioned beneath the roof-lights. This arrangement contributes significantly to the general feeling of airiness and space in the building. Aspects of the landscape are admitted or excluded as appropriate. Light is allowed in and is directed, augmented or occluded as circumstances dictate to allow an almost infinite degree of lighting control.

## While fixed panels had become an accepted part of construction techniques for walls, using the same system for roofing had never been attempted.

Mechanical and electrical services are located in the higher sections of the wall; again using localised plant spread evenly throughout the length of the building. Concealed behind the louvres lining the main space, the plant is accessible from within the truss zone so that routine maintenance can be carried out in complete isolation from any activities in the gallery or school areas. Similarly, when a more serious overhaul is necessary, external panels can be removed – just as you might lift the bonnet of a car – to allow direct access from the outside, again without affecting activities within the building.

At roof level, too, the possibility of concealed access within the depth of the truss offers enormous benefits, allowing one of the subtler lessons learned from the experiences of other museums to be put into practice. Catwalks within the 2.4-metre depth of each truss allow regular maintenance and fine tuning of both the artificial lighting and the adjustable louvres that automatically control the quality of daylight in the space. Perforated louvres, fixed in bands beneath the trusses, form a 'ceiling' to the main space, although ceiling is hardly an appropriate word in this instance. Here the vertical bands of louvres become translucent, celebrating the openness and lightness of the truss and allowing clear views up and through the length of the roof. The overall effect is one of remarkable finesse, the layers of white louvre, truss structure, catwalk grille and balustrade combining to create almost weightless architectural abstractions, constantly changing and suffused by daylight.

4. The glazed panels use the same moulded aluminium form as the solid panels around their edges, but this frame is attached to an aluminium subframe, which provides rigidity and also holds the glass. Special curved panels sweep up from the walls to form the roof. The curved panels could not be formed on a simple mould, so were constructed by cutting away the side flanges of a standard flat panel to which a new curved flange was attached and welded in place. The ribbed panels were affectionately inspired by the design of the Citroën van, but, in the case of the Sainsbury Centre, the ribbing served to disguise any imperfections in the panel surface rather than provide greater structural rigidity.

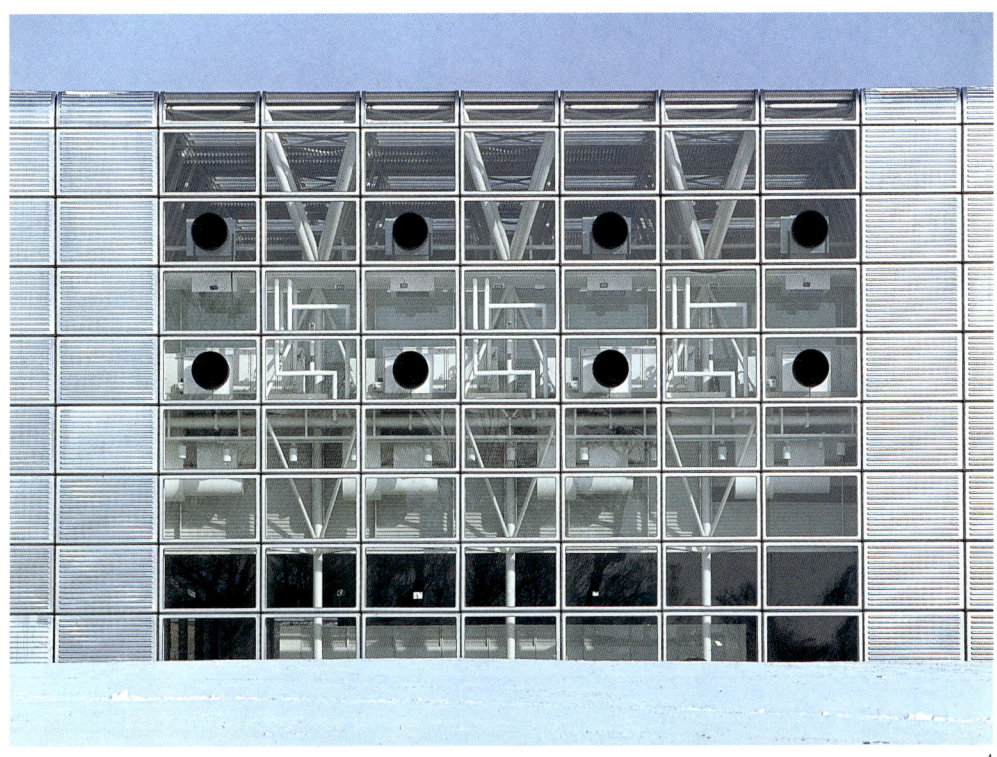

Sainsbury Centre for Visual Arts 399

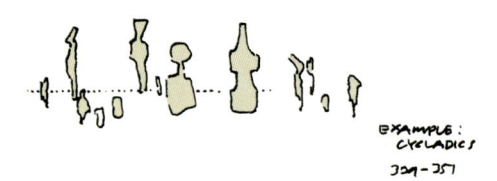

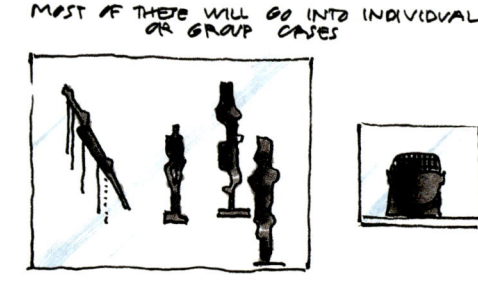

Above: Birkin Haward analysed the collection and techniques for its display in a sequence of freehand drawings. One of the main objectives in designing the display system was to preserve a 'living room' environment for the display of the collection, ensuring that the gallery area would, above all, be a 'nice place to be – quiet, easy to use, and informal'. The collection also demanded a display system that acknowledged its varied nature; some pieces were best seen in the round, other items were two-dimensional; some were very small, others quite large.

Structural engineer Anthony Hunt's elegant truss solution makes use of identical prismatic trusses with the same overall dimensions whether used vertically, for the supporting walls, or horizontally for the clear-span roof. As panel development had been proceeding in parallel with that of the structure, the late change to the truss solution meant that panel sizes were already clearly defined and the new structure could be tailored to match. The truss width was therefore set at 1.8 metres, matching the panels exactly. Working to a 300mm planning module, a dimension of 2.4 metres was determined to be the optimum depth, both providing structural stability and creating a suitably deep zone to house the various ancillary and service activities.

Although the structure is often described as 'folding over' the space, the trusses do not in fact form a continuous element. In order to make effective use of the potential space within the depth of the lattice trusses at ground level, it was necessary to omit the lowest diagonal elements, which means that the side trusses really act as vertical cantilevers.

The structure consequently adopts a 'post and beam' solution with the main roof truss connected to the lattice towers by only a pin joint on one side and a slip joint on the other. To allow for water run-off – and to counteract the illusion of sag perceived in perfectly horizontal spans – the main roof trusses are constructed with a slight entasis, arcing upwards by 150mm from their ends to their centre points.

The clear-span structure revealed hidden potential as construction progressed: the large space permitted protected assembly lines to be set up on site; and as Norman Foster recalls, the removable panel system also provided unexpected benefits:

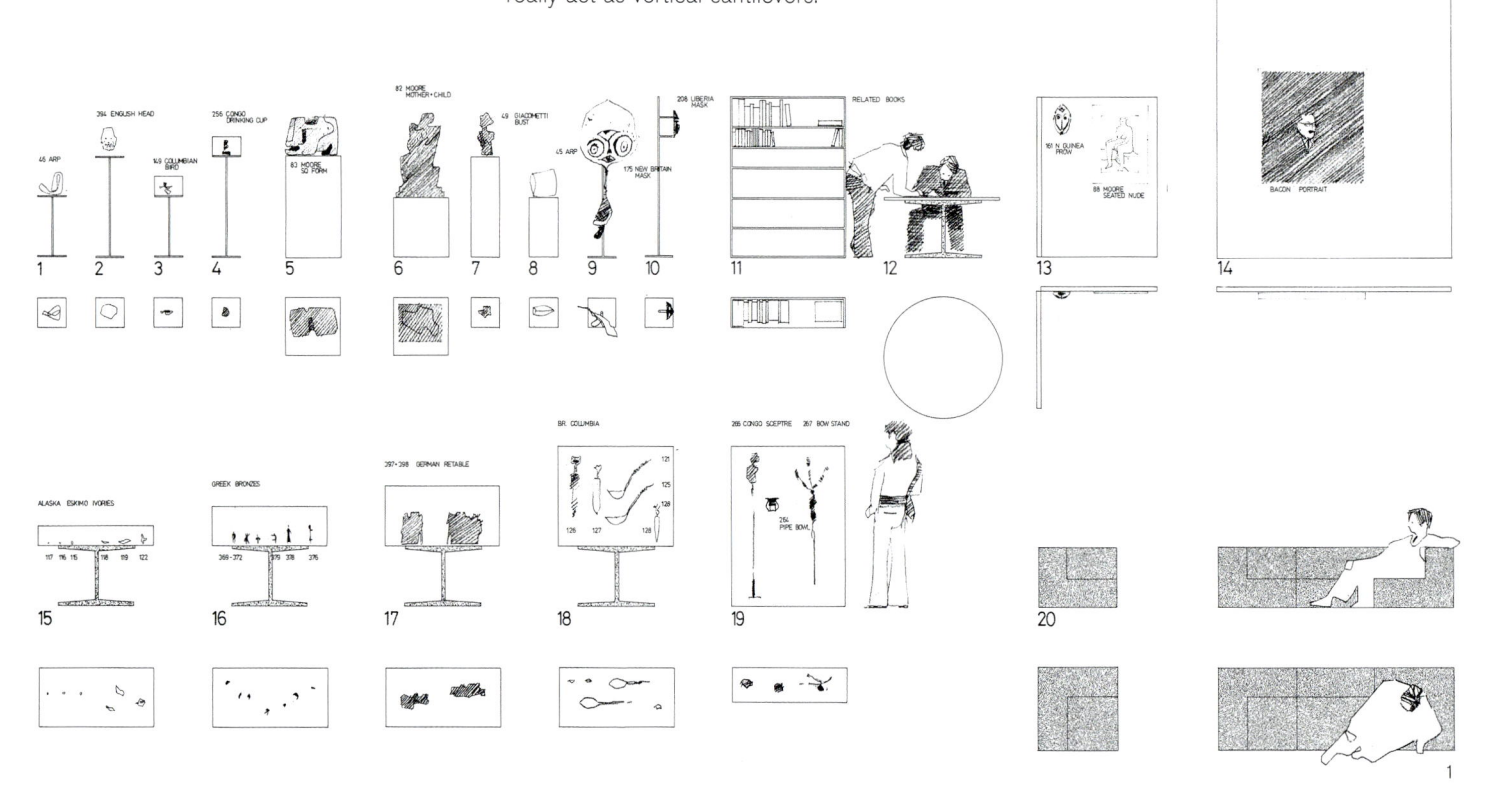

'The ability to bolt on a panel – any panel – enabled the contractor to take advantage of the system and just bolt on sheets of plywood. He wanted to get ahead of the game inside the building, but it had to be weathertight. He looked at the possibility and cost of waiting, and then he looked at the problem of draping polythene over the building on a large scale, but he finally came up with the idea that if he just cut sheets of plywood and bolted them into the system, it would result in a perfectly dry enclosure. This was certainly not something that we anticipated – and it produced some quite bizarre effects at the time.'

While fixed panels had become an accepted part of construction techniques for walls, using the same system for roofing had never been attempted. As discussions with the various manufacturers began, it became clear that many thought it was impossible. The design criteria were simple: panels should require the minimum of maintenance and be capable of being handled by one man. As a surface skin, steel was quickly discounted due to the regular maintenance that would be required to avoid corrosion. Similarly glass-fibre, with its poor surface durability, lack of proven performance and high fire risk, was also considered inappropriate. Anodised aluminium avoided these problems with the added benefit that, in its natural finish, it presented a highly solar reflective surface. Sandwich panels – in which thin skins of aluminium are bonded to a rigid foam core – were identified as the most promising solution.

A panel of 1800mm by 1200mm using a 100mm thick core of inert phenolic foam proved to be the optimum size. Structurally rigid but light enough to be carried by one man, it related well to available rolled-metal widths. Phenolic foam was specified as it combined excellent fire characteristics with an exceptional degree of insulation. Norman Foster describes it as, 'the kind of insulation you would normally associate with a cold store rather than anything to do with the building industry'.

While the panels themselves could be based on known technology, the way in which they might be brought together while providing a weatherproof seal was far more complicated. One early idea drew on the experience of Willis Faber & Dumas, proposing flat panels joined by a proprietary silicone sealant. A system was developed whereby panels would be factory-assembled on sub-frame modules 7.2 metres by 4.8 metres in size – a portal frame solution still being assumed at this point. Such a system, however, went against the concept of true flexibility as the panels would have to be cut free of the sealant and resealed each time they were moved.

1. An early proposal for the display system suggested a range of centrally supported stands. However, these were dropped in favour of plinths, which were able to offer greater stability and security.

2. The display system as finally designed comprises free-standing panels, hinged screens, display cases, stands and plinths. Together they comprise a kit of parts with its own simple rules. The display cases are based on plinths 600mm square, available in five different heights. Optically clear Perspex cases fix to the plinths, protecting the exhibits and allowing each to be individually climate controlled. The bases are made from mild steel with a stove-enamelled finish, into which a variety of floors – tailor-made for specific exhibits – can be installed. Labels applied by a silk-screening process are easily removed and replaced as necessary.

Left: Many models of the display system were built, leading to a series of full-scale mock-ups and prototype samples, prepared by different manufacturers as part of the tender process. (The final contract was awarded to a Swiss company.) Sir Robert and Lady Sainsbury were involved at every stage and are seen here with Norman Foster viewing the first prototype in the half-completed Sainsbury Centre.

Not long after arriving at the practice I was able to see Norman at work with Sir Robert and Lady Sainsbury on the new Sainsbury Centre, when they met to discuss carpets, display cabinets, turnstiles, and other interior details. I was really amazed at the sheer amount of effort required at that level to explore, convince people, and to develop a design. I also saw how very good Norman was at it. This early experience in the Foster studio left me with a conviction that has remained true over the years, which is that the design of interiors is by far the most difficult task in the entire building process. David Nelson, in conversation with Malcolm Quantrill, 1999

1. One of the objectives in designing the gallery areas was to encourage a rich, comfortable mix between people and art objects. Seating was an important ingredient in this regard, helping to create places simply to relax, read a book or quietly contemplate the works on display. Norman Foster's sketches explore different options for the display of two and three-dimensional works from the collection and the ways in which they might be viewed.

**Undoubtedly the building provides to a marked degree the sought-after environment. It equally satisfies the particular gallery needs of a somewhat eclectic collection containing a great deal of sculpture.** Sir Robert Sainsbury, introducing Norman Foster as RIBA Royal Gold Medallist, 21 June 1983
Right: Some examples of the 'eclectic' range of objects in the Sainsbury collection: a Mexican stone sculpture associated with the ballgame cult (AD 600-900), *Little Dancer aged 14* (1880-1881) by Edgar Degas, and a watercolour of a Deccani ruler, Sultan Jamshid Qutb Shah of Golconda (c. 1680).

2. Study models were used to explore various planning options for the gallery area. A balanced mix of relaxed seating areas and display cases was intended from the beginning.

3. Norman Foster's sketch shows how a system of self-supported screens can be used in the main space to create form and focus.

4, 5. As the fit-out of the gallery areas began, a detailed scale model was prepared as an aid to setting out the display system.

6. While display cases were standardised, each object in the collection required its own supporting armature to be specially made.

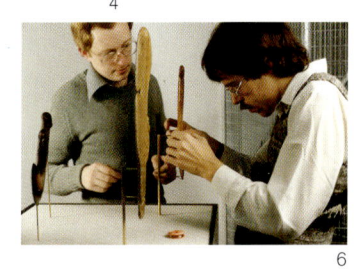

Sainsbury Centre for Visual Arts

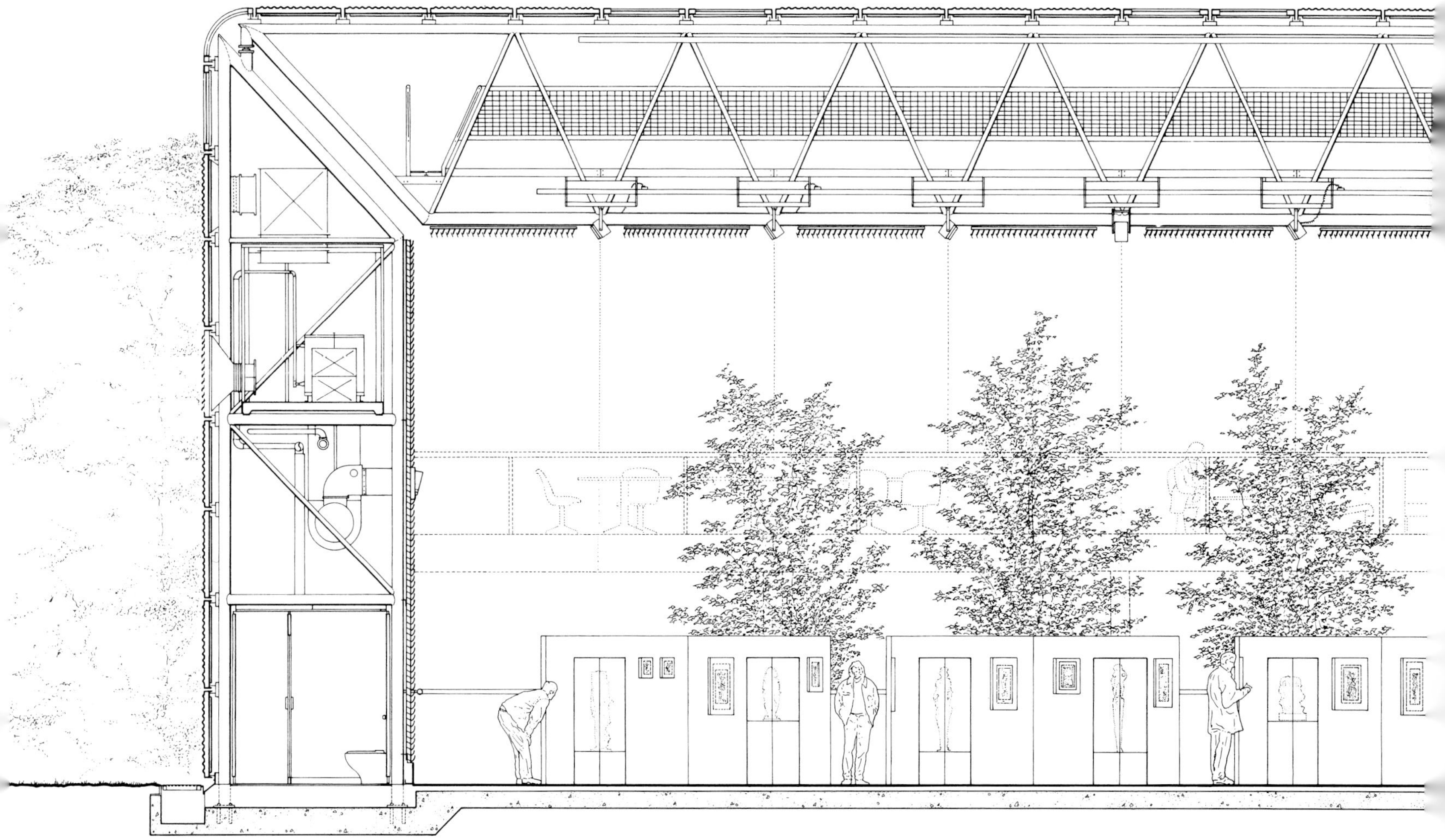

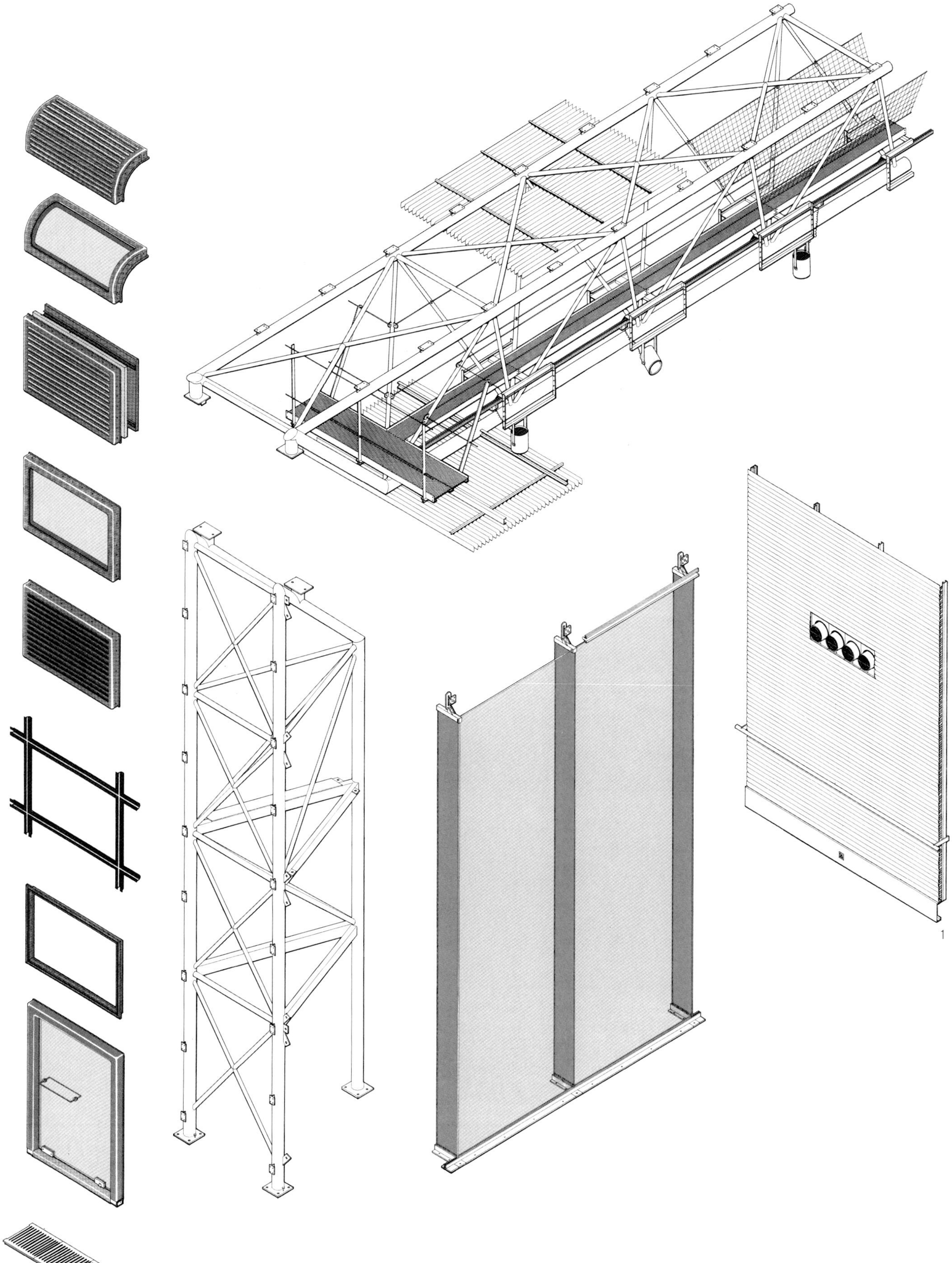

1

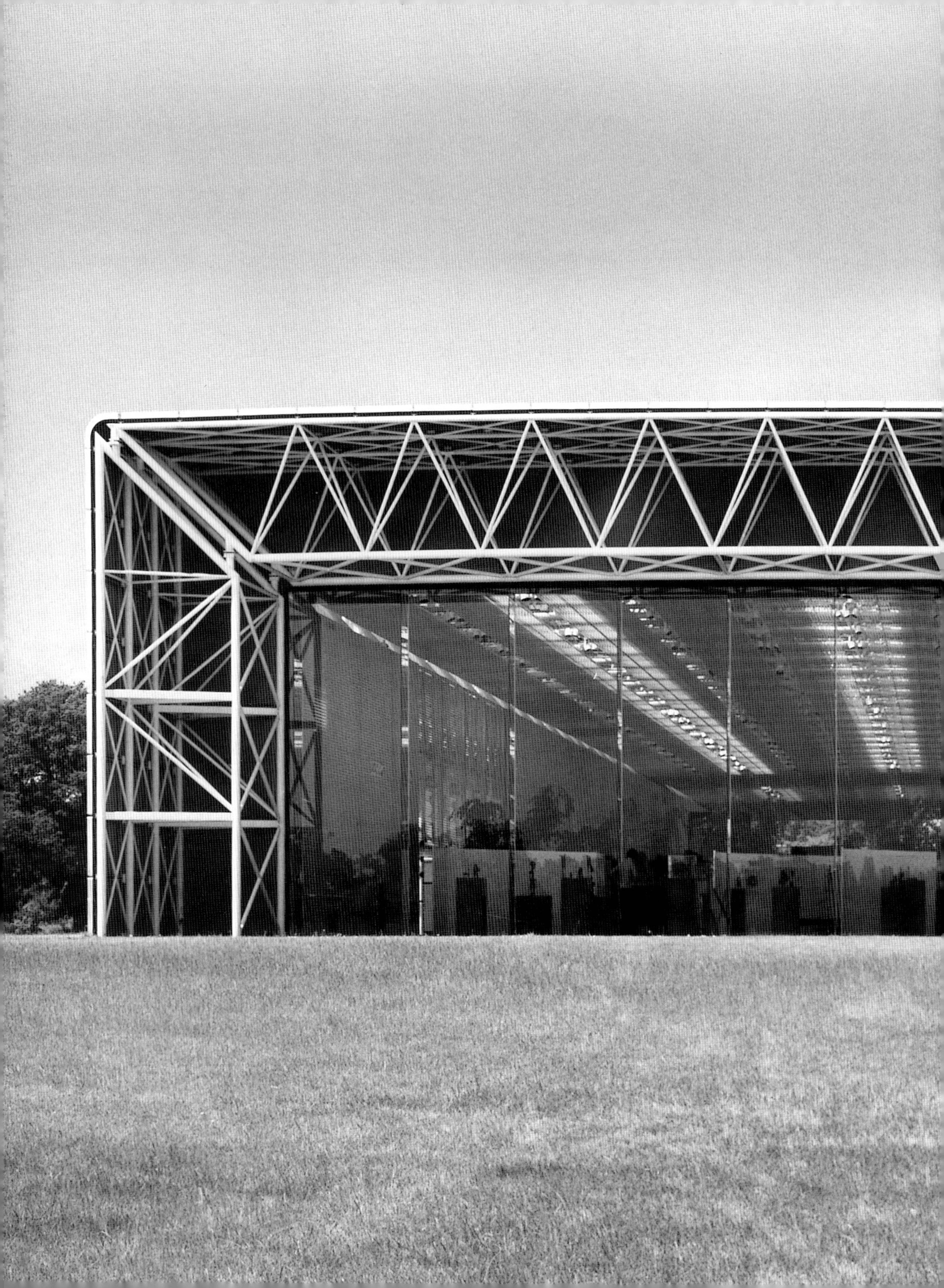

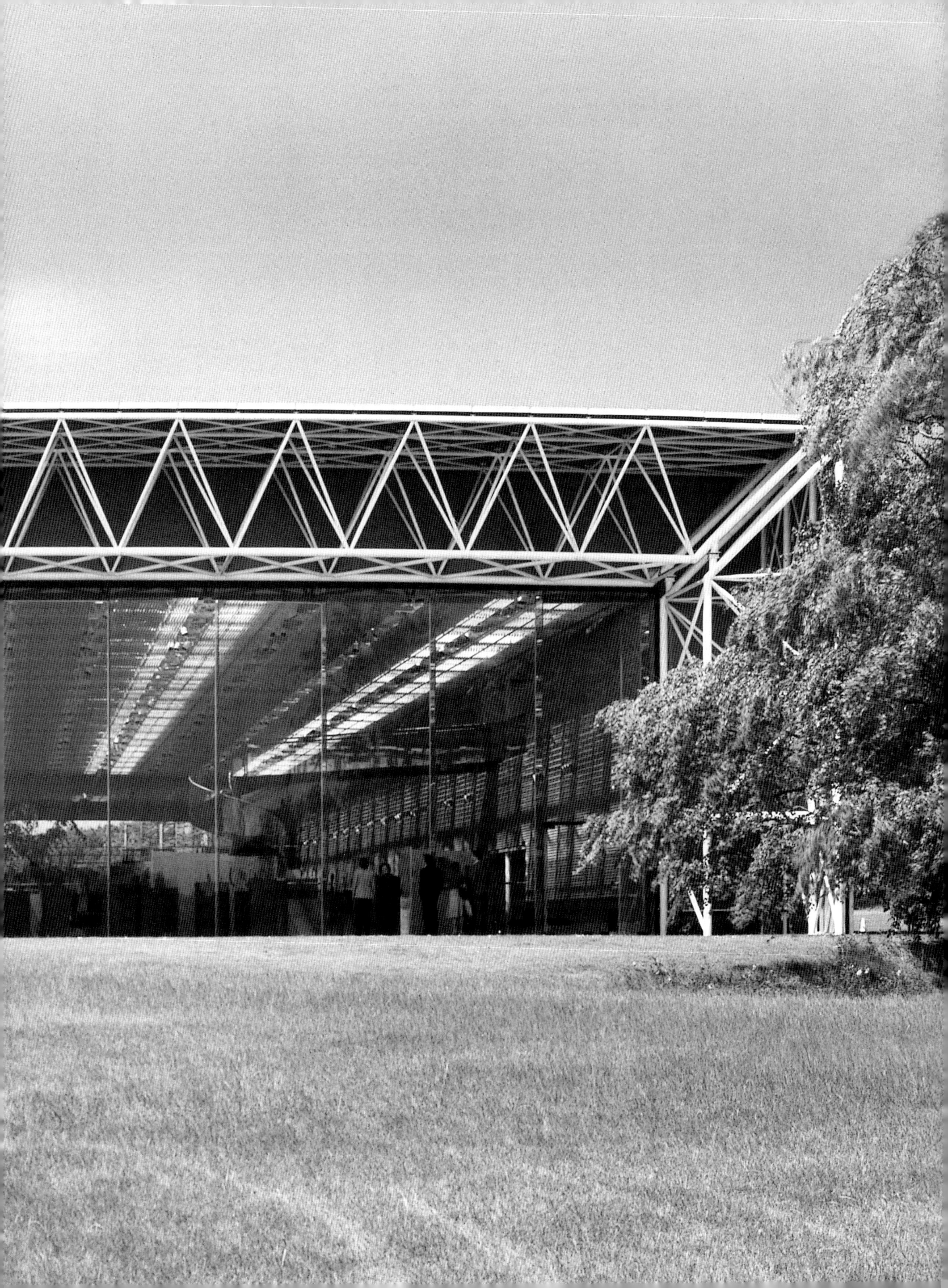

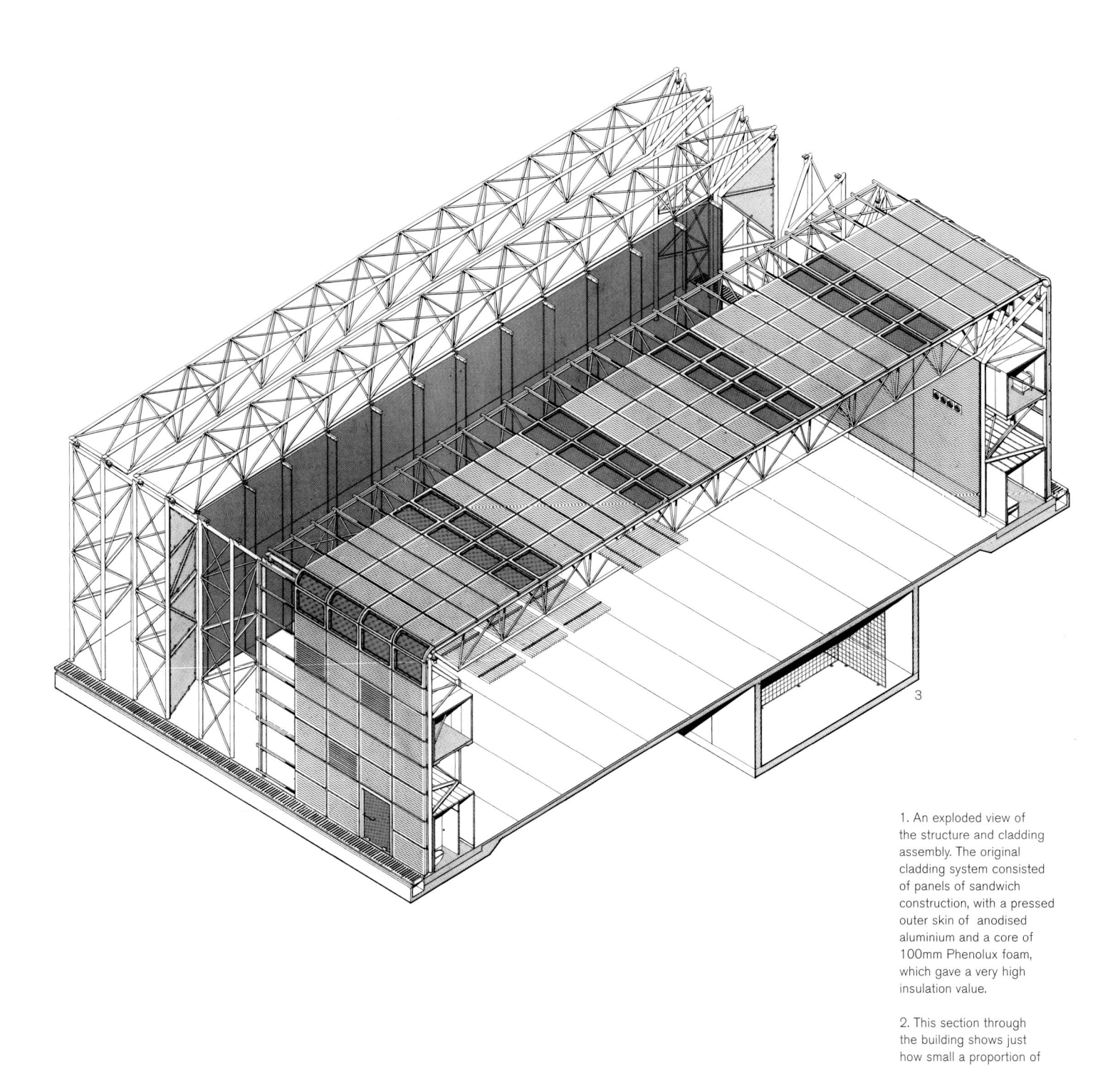

1. An exploded view of the structure and cladding assembly. The original cladding system consisted of panels of sandwich construction, with a pressed outer skin of anodised aluminium and a core of 100mm Phenolux foam, which gave a very high insulation value.

2. This section through the building shows just how small a proportion of its total volume is provided by the basement areas.

3. The main structure is a steel prismatic lattice framework with trusses of tubular steel, supported on triangular towers.

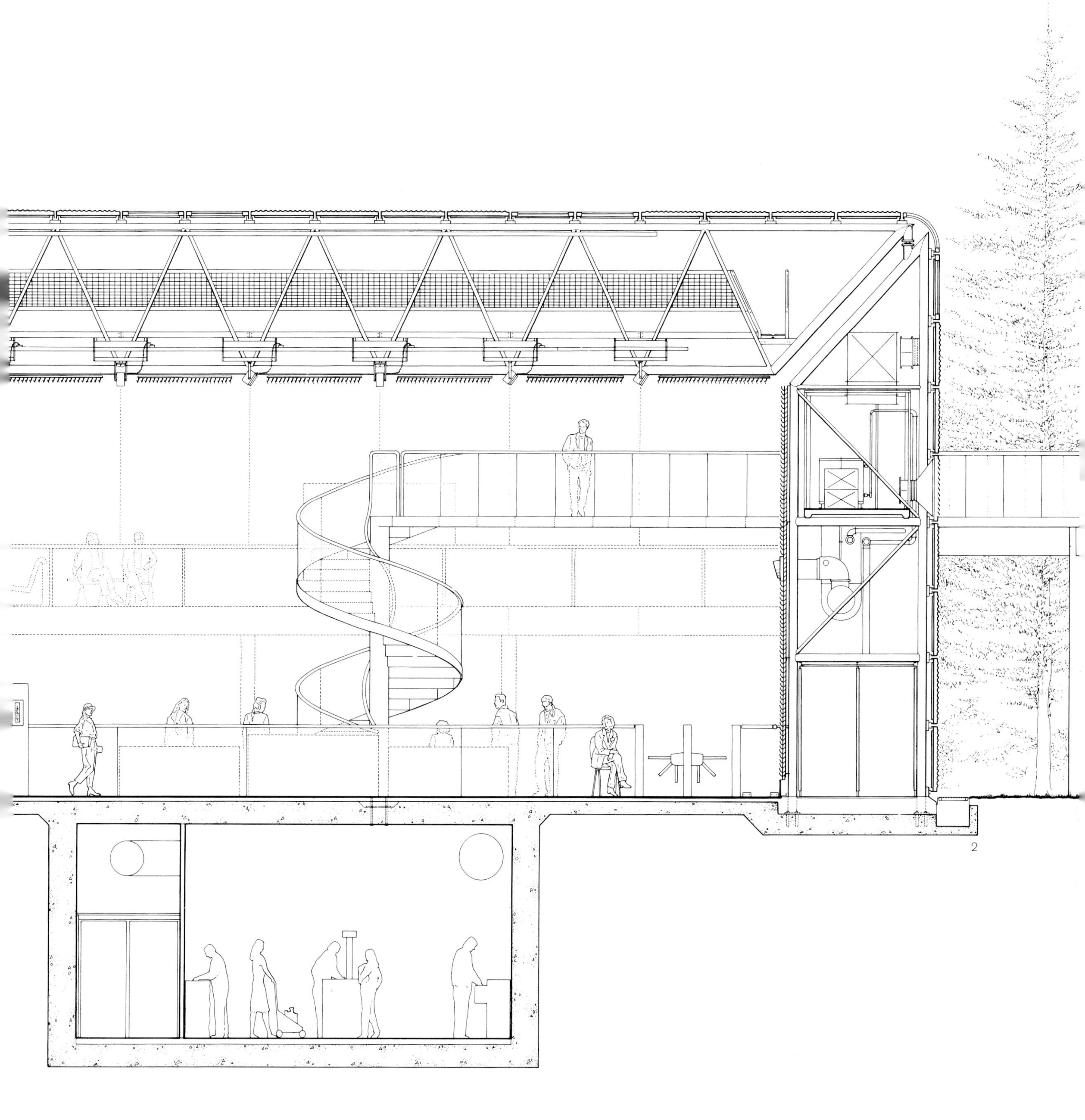

2

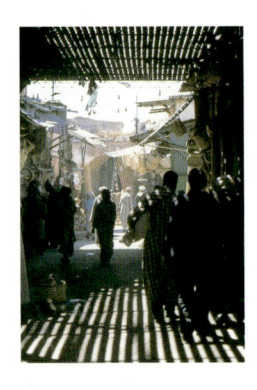

**I have a particular passion for natural light. I am interested in how it can be channelled and reflected – the way in which it is constantly changing and how this can inform and enhance the architectural experience. I am also fascinated by the manner in which a space can become a social focus – the drama of movement – the potential of a space to calm or stimulate, to recede or assert.** Norman Foster, *L'Architecture d'Aujourd'hui*, February 1986
Left: Norman Foster's photograph of the Kasbah in Morocco, a favourite reference image frequently used to illustrate the quality of light filtering into an interior.

Right, centre: The potential for introducing controlled daylight through the filter of the roof structure was further explored in the proposed scheme for the National Indoor Athletics Stadium at Frankfurt.
Far right: Stansted Airport pursues this idea together with another aspect of the Sainsbury Centre. Here all the major building services are accommodated in an undercroft which runs beneath concourse level so that the elegant umbrella roof is freed simply to admit light and keep out the rain.

1. The Sainsbury Centre is conceived as an infinitely 'tuneable' serviced container. Norman Foster's sketch encapsulates the concept of a clear, universal space that can be serviced with equal ease from all sides.

2. A view within the depth of the roof looking along the length of one of the main structural trusses. A catwalk provides access to lighting fixtures and the adjustable louvres, which control the amount of daylight entering through the roof-light panels.

3, 4. Artificial lighting is carefully coordinated with daylight admitted through the roof-lights. Ultra-violet light, the most damaging to art objects, is filtered out by means of specially tinted glazing. Spotlights are used to provide emphasis and create points of focus.

5. Seen from within the conservatory areas of the main reception and School of World Art Studies, the ventilation equipment mounted in the structural zone is silhouetted against the glazing panels, which are screened by a single layer of perforated louvres.

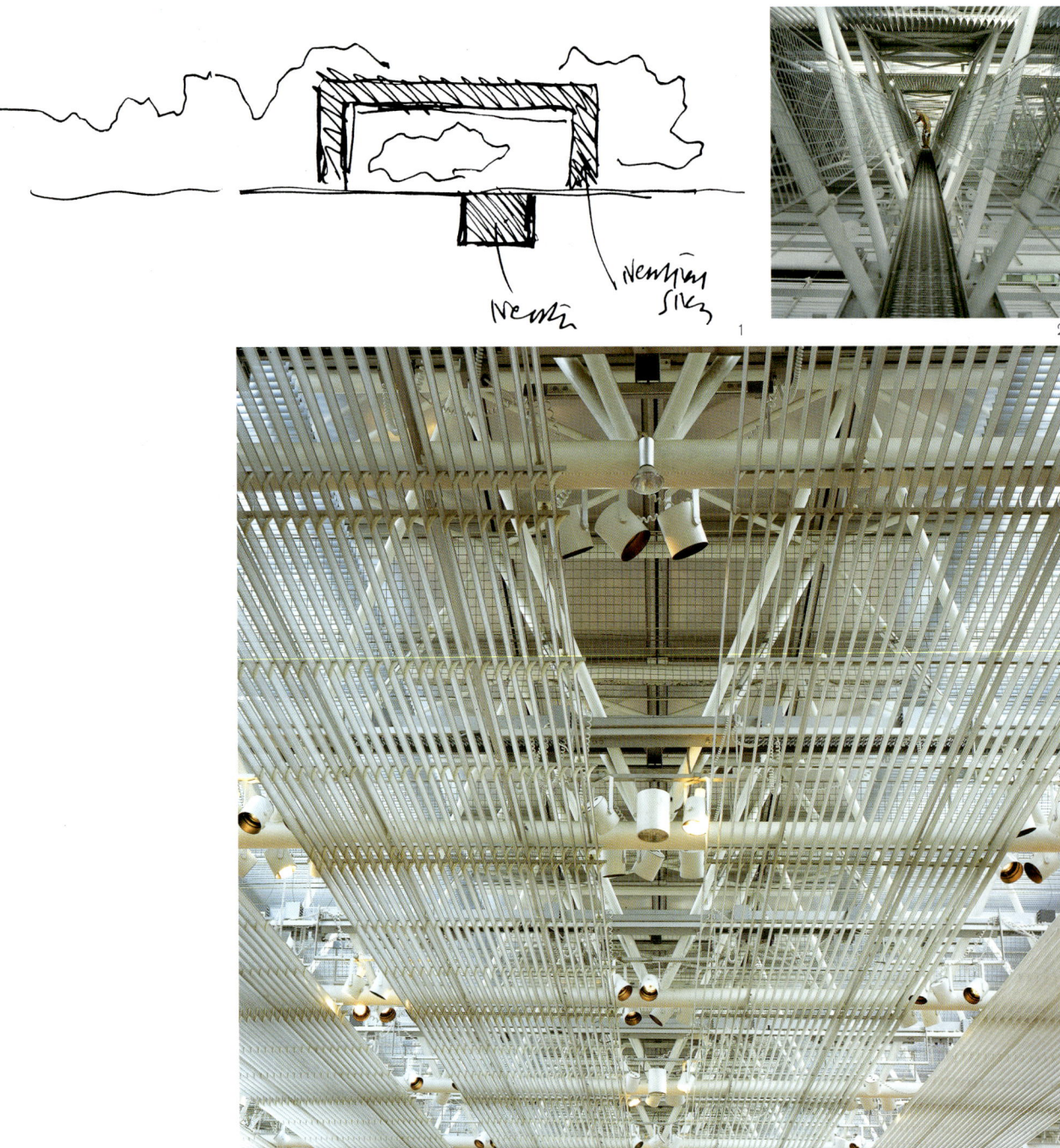

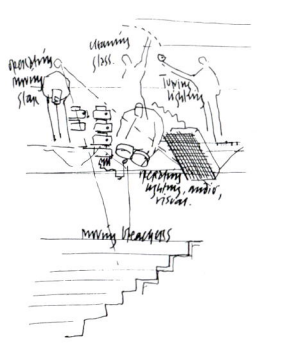

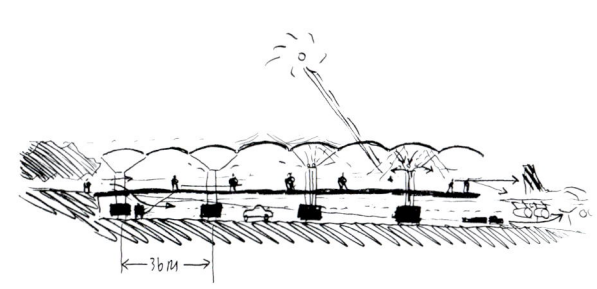

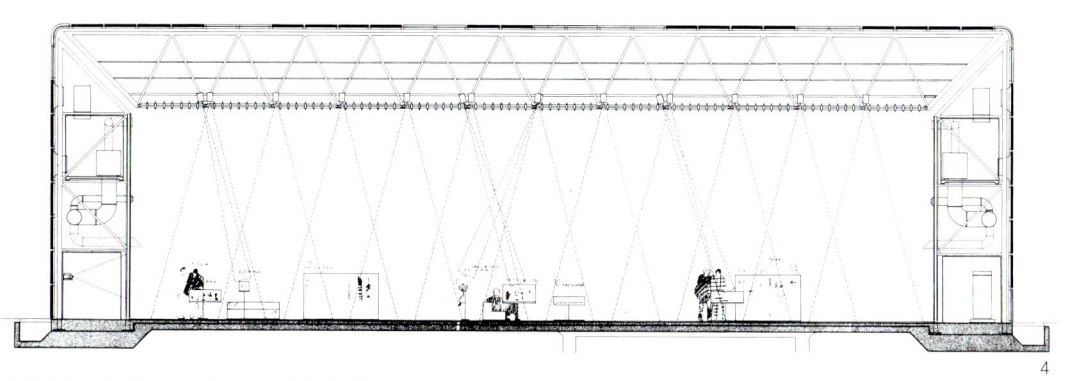

> The louvres become translucent, celebrating the openness and lightness of the trusses and allowing views up and through the length of the roof. The effect is one of remarkable finesse, the layers of louvre, truss structure, catwalk grille and balustrade combining to create weightless architectural abstractions, constantly changing and suffused by daylight.
>
> Graham Vickers

Sainsbury Centre for Visual Arts

The almost silent clatter of thousands of small plastic-coated parts every time a cloud goes by fascinates visitors to the new Sainsbury Centre ... This muted noise indicates that certain sections of the white louvres which line the whole of the interior, including the ceiling, of this vast hangar are adjusting themselves to changing light levels outside. Inside, apart from a flicker at the moment of adjustment, the light pours down deep and soft and even on the Sainsbury collection, assorted academics and students. Sutherland Lyall, *New Society*, 6 July 1978

Left: Ben Johnson's screenprint of the Sainsbury Centre captures the particular quality of light within the building.

Motorised louvres buzz overhead to set up optical as well as acoustic vibrations. A delicate, dappled, even light spills over the space, equating all parts. Wall, ceiling, and floor planes are equated by a similar silver finish, and so extreme isotropic space, the sign of equality and the sublime, is supported by isotropic surface, the sign of mass production. All activities are banished to the perimeter or dwarfed behind partitions as the universal space of Mies van der Rohe reigns triumphant over time, function and locale.
Charles Jencks, *Current Architecture*, 1982

There is an idea that small objects cannot be satisfactorily displayed in a tall building such as the Sainsbury Centre. I suggest that the height of a gallery is irrelevant ... provided that, as at UEA, the space is a comfortable one to be in and the objects can be displayed at the right height for the average adult. The same argument can be applied to paintings and drawings, all of which are displayed at UEA on screens related to the human scale. Sir Robert Sainsbury, introducing Norman Foster as RIBA Royal Gold Medallist, 21 June 1983
Left: Lady Sainsbury and Norman Foster in the Sainsbury Centre conservatory.
Right: Giacometti's *Standing Woman*, as first displayed in the Sainsburys' house in Smith Square, London.

**The louvres are controlled electronically but you can override them. You can adjust the lighting and preset it, so that when the sun comes out, motors whirr and the louvres open or close depending on the settings. You have a very positive control and, as far as we know, this hasn't been done before. The technology itself is simple; there are no computers or anything like that. It is fairly down to earth, but it is a sensitive machine.**
Norman Foster

1. The constantly changing play of light and shade across and through the louvred walls and soffit is one of the Sainsbury Centre's most distinctive characteristics. When used as a lining for the areas of solid wall, as in the gallery spaces, the louvres provide a calm, non-assertive background for intimately scaled works of art, such as Giacometti's *Standing Woman*, pictured here. Compare with the view of the same object above in a domestic setting.

2. When used to screen areas of open glazing, the louvres can be adjusted to control light levels or, as at the two ends of the building, retracted to allow views out. At the entrance points, as here in the 'conservatory' between the temporary exhibition space and the main 'living area' of the gallery, the louvres have been omitted altogether.

Right: In addition to the permanent display of the Sainsbury collection, the Centre is host to special exhibitions. These range from travelling exhibitions curated by national institutions to thematic exhibitions focusing on elements of the Sainsbury collection, which are curated in-house.

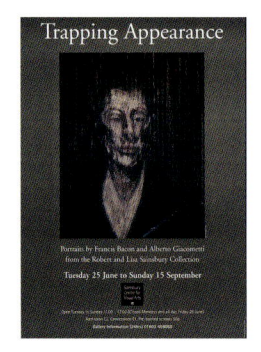

1. The gallery display system employs a combination of standardised screens and display cases which lend focus to individual objects whilst preserving the spirit of the Sainsburys' original domestic arrangement of the collection.

2. Screens take the form of hinged panels, which are easily moved by two people. Objects in cases can be placed in front of a panel, which then acts as a simple background. The smaller paintings and drawings can be hung on them, while large free-standing panels create points of emphasis in the space and support the larger paintings.

**The ceiling becomes Foster's *tour de force*. One's eye is constantly pulled up and out by its horizontal stretch of layered planes. The transparency and translucency created by the filigree of ceiling louvres, structure, ducts and catwalks, with strips of the glass and aluminium panels above, skilfully mesh to create a work of art.** Suzanne Stephens, *Progressive Architecture*, February 1979

**This building was a very considered attempt to design out mechanical refrigeration and therefore it is not air-conditioned in the traditional sense. There is no cooling as such, which seemed a sensible way to go. Aside from some of the more aesthetic desires, the Sainsburys and the University worked along the lines that here is an art collection, which has been built up over forty years; during that time, it has been in a country house or a town house in London, so why should it now have to go in a fridge?** Norman Foster, Arthur Batchelor lecture at UEA, Norwich, 7 February 1978

**It is not merely a reworking of the old Adolf Loos argument about creating a neutral white background for displaying objects, but a hint to the viewer that the big shed, providing it is heavily insulated, as here, and given the minimum of simple readily available environmental technology, does not have to go through the gymnastics of overly articulated and coloured peripheral equipment to make it work as a visual experience.** Sutherland Lyall, *New Society*, 6 July 1978

The Sainsbury Centre unites under one roof the contemplation of works of art in a gallery and the teaching of art history. It was interesting that the academics regarded it as absolutely outrageous that the two could come together and you would be able to teach in an informal manner in what was effectively a public gallery. Two years after the building was completed the Sainsburys suggested funding a lecture theatre in another part of the building and it met with howls of protest from those same academics who said that would be absolutely criminal because here we are in a building where it actually integrates works of art with the process of teaching ... Norman Foster, Aspen Design Conference, 16 June 1980

The studio often uses full-size mock-ups. They are a very useful working tool: a kind of staging post or stepping-stone between design drawings and small-scale models. This is a model of a teaching space in the Sainsbury Centre, which was used with visiting groups from the faculty: we were able to gauge their reactions and feed these back into the design process. Norman Foster, lecture at the Metropolitan Museum of Art, New York, 24 November 1982

1. The reception desk combines information and sales areas with the gallery's central environmental control panel. A spiral stair leads down to the staff facilities in the basement.

2. A high-level view, from the western end of the building, looking along the full length of the space over the two mezzanine floors. The senior common room and postgraduate desk area occupy the mezzanine in the foreground, overlooking the main study/library area of the School of World Art Studies beyond.

3, 4. Toughened glass enclosures to both lift-shaft and lift-cars minimise their visual impact in the main space, a quality further enhanced by setting the cars themselves on hydraulic rams so that all the drive machinery can be concealed at basement level. Norman Foster's sketch shows all-glass walls surrounding a minimal steel frame; a grilled ceiling in the lift-car provides maintenance access and supports the door-opening mechanism.

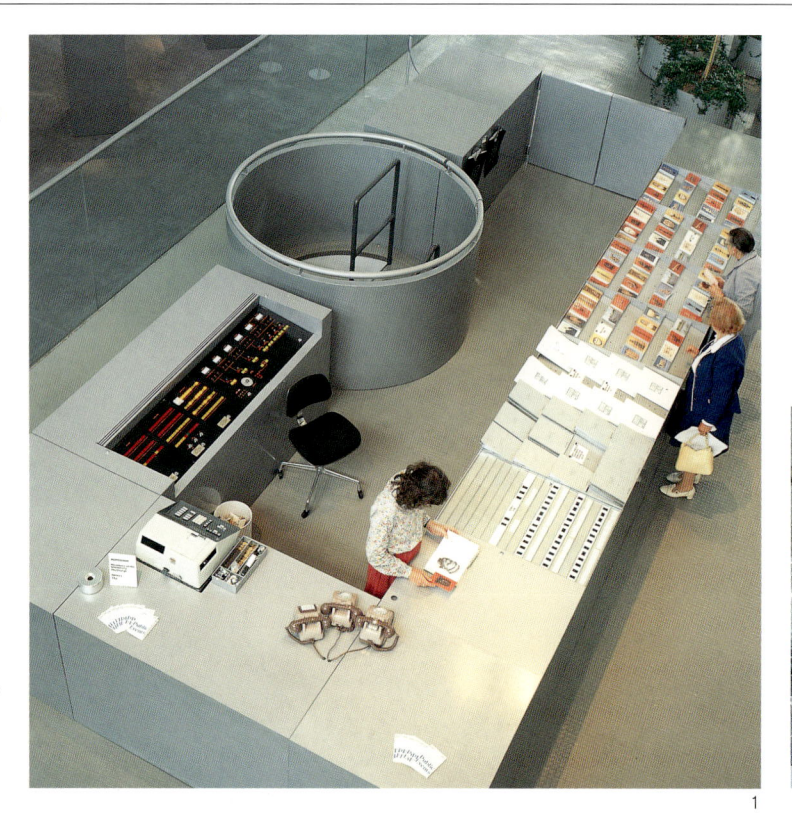

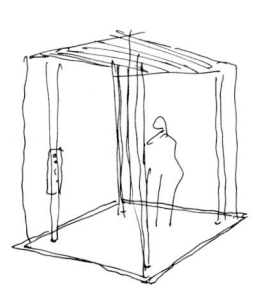

412  Norman Foster Works 1

There is an airy green haze reflected on the ceiling, its source hidden. The haze must surely be created by a strong light source beaming back from a highly pigmented carpet? But no, its source is that of the trees outside, framed and captured by the enormous open end of the box. And such is our elation, that the trees themselves can surely only be a superb, animated photomural. Peter Cook, *The Architectural Review*, December 1978

Even the staff, who were originally apprehensive about their exposed, strictly non-Oxbridge senior common room, now complain that it is too popular and are fending off an attempted take-over by students anxious to be able to share in the sensational high-level views down the hangar and out to the new lake in the landscape beyond. Sutherland Lyall, *New Society*, 6 July 1978

It is interesting to see the way that the building has evolved in terms of its use. It is used as a conference centre during summer, when the student accommodation becomes a hotel; it is used at the weekends for wedding receptions; it is used for dinners which combine occasionally with new shows – reflecting quite interesting, and unexpected, new patterns of use. Norman Foster, Aspen Design Conference, 16 June 1980

5. The Study Reserve area was originally housed in a secure area beneath the east mezzanine, visible from the main gallery through full-height glazing set into the sides of the mezzanine enclosure. Only about one third of the collection is on display at any one time, but regular changes ensure that the full collection is seen every two years, well within each student's normal time-span at the University. Following the construction of the Crescent Wing, this space is now occupied by the Sainsbury Research Unit Library.

6. The School of World Art Studies occupies the 'courtyard' between the two mezzanines.

7. Central to the School of World Art Studies is the extensive slide library. The cabinets were purpose designed and positioned to form a quiet enclosed area of study, which is further distinguished by being set 450mm lower than the surrounding floor.

8. The restaurant is located at the western end of the building where it enjoys expansive views through the glazed end wall to a stand of trees. Open to students and staff alike during the day it has also become a popular location for parties and private receptions in the evenings and at weekends.

Sainsbury Centre for Visual Arts 413

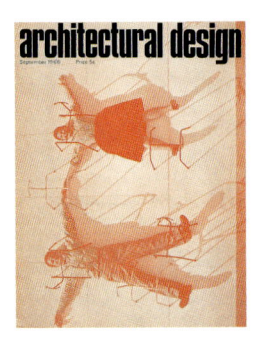

**The Eames's house in California of 1949 was ... assembled from standard parts and composed with a sensitive irregularity ... The 'shed' was subtly placed alongside a row of eucalyptus trees which filtered the light into an interior where judiciously selected objects were as much a part of the architecture as the building itself. The effect arose from the careful juxtaposition of 'ready-made' structural elements such as webbed trusses, from reflections and transparencies, and from an understatement which aspired towards ordinariness.** William J R Curtis, *Modern Architecture since 1900*, 1996

Far left and left: Charles and Ray Eames on the cover of *Architectural Design*, and at home.

1-6. 'Connections: The Work of Charles and Ray Eames' launched the programme of special exhibitions at the Sainsbury Centre. It opened in November 1978, a little over two months after the death of Charles Eames on 21 August 1978. Curated and designed by John and Marilyn Neuhart, it was divided into three categories: exhibitions, furniture and film and featured numerous examples of the Eames' pioneering work in these fields and the creative cross-fertilisation that existed between them.

**Foster is an architect of flexibility, and his instinct to design for the inevitability of change is rooted both in the unselfconscious factory sheds of England's Industrial Revolution and in the modest steel Case Study houses of Los Angeles by Pierre Koenig, Raphael Soriano, Craig Ellwood, and Charles and Ray Eames ... Instead of the Miesian temple, Foster adopted the Eamesian Tinkertoy model, which allowed a much looser, more spontaneous approach that also meant that plans could be easily changed.** Joseph Giovannini, *The Pritzker Architecture Prize, 1999: Norman Foster*, 2000

Right: The Eames' Case Study House #8 (1949) which Norman Foster first visited following his postgraduate studies at Yale University.

**The concept of connections is, according to Eames, intrinsic to design and architecture. It is also intrinsic to understanding the work of the Eames Office, but not to defining it ... Designers John and Marilyn Neuhart have resisted the curatorial urge to 'place' Eames and have tried to do something much more difficult ... to show how the work goes – which is to say how it goes together. It is, then, an attempt to exhibit process. The most important thing to say about connections is that they are made. The most important thing to show about connections is where and how they are made.** Ralph Caplan, *Making Connections: The Work of Charles and Ray Eames*, introduction to the exhibition catalogue, 1976

## The first special exhibition at the Sainsbury Centre focused on the work of Charles and Ray Eames – imagine having such a collection of remarkable objects at hand for use as a teaching resource.

Norman Foster

Right: In August 1978 *Architectural Design* magazine (then a bastion of Postmodernist thought) published a special issue on the newly completed Sainsbury Centre. It incorporated a critics' chorus of commentaries, which covered the spectrum from laudatory to censorious. As *AD* concluded: 'The excitement and contention that has been aroused by the Sainsbury Centre suggests that it is indeed a polemical work of architecture.'

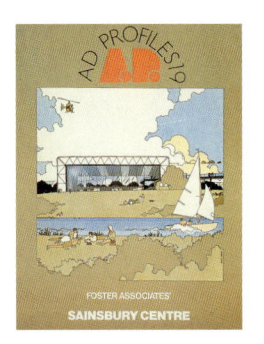

**The building ... should be understood for what it is – a fetishist expressionism. Like the sexual fetish of leather, this building celebrates the cladding of the object – the aluminium trappings, clips, straps and other paraphernalia ... The fascination with the six-bolted interchangeable aluminium, glass or louvred panel has kept Foster's team steadfastly (obediently?) at work – expressing and revelling in the cool feel and sight of the aluminiumed ass. Yet what a trivial and peripheral business is all that.** Doug Clelland, *AD Profiles 19*, August 1978

I think an 'industrial shed' or warehouse, however beautiful, is inappropriate to shelter artisanal art or cult objects, in the same way it is inappropriate to frame a classical landscape with an extruded aluminium profile ... Foster is forcing us to eat soup with a fork, and with a very well designed fork at that. Leon Krier, *AD Profiles 19*, August 1978

The criticisms of the Sainsbury Centre, and there have been some, often concern [its] metaphorical unsuitability. From the end elevation it looks like an 'aeroplane hangar' and even on the inside the grand space dwarfs the ... (relatively) minuscule works of art. Like the Centre Pompidou in Paris, a single, linear, spatial idea dominates all concerns. Charles Jencks, *AD Profiles 19*, August 1978

The year of the Sainsbury Centre was, as it happens, the first year I saw the Parthenon. Both experiences were exhilarating. Robert Maxwell, *AD Profiles 19*, August 1978

As night falls the Sainsbury Centre experiences a dramatic transformation.

1. The Sainsbury Centre at dusk, as seen from the far side of the 'broad', the lake created in the University parkland.

2,3. The vehicle delivery ramp emerges from the building's west end, but by using the natural contours of the land and the cover of trees for camouflage it remains invisible from the building itself. Concealed underground, the loading bays are provided with the best possible security.

**It is certainly true that Norman's building has aroused extraordinary passions among architects, writers and art historians. My personal prize goes to the description of the building as 'fetishist expressionism.'**
Sir Robert Sainsbury

Sainsbury Centre for Visual Arts 417

**There isn't anyone in America who could do something as good as the Sainsbury Centre. England has at once become the leader in the engineering and technology game.** Philip Johnson, lecture to the Architecture Club, New York, May 1979

**The Sainsbury Centre's design is shown to best effect in the rural setting rather than an urban one, for its sensitive siting means that the building opens out to views of the natural landscape. The building's scale, muteness and cool mien would deaden the urban context. In the pastoral milieu, this kind of form – minimal, lightweight, reflective and almost transparent from one end to another – intrudes only reticently on the landscape. Little more could be asked of it, except for it to be pushed to its logical conclusion and become virtually invisible.** Suzanne Stephens, *Progressive Architecture*, February 1979

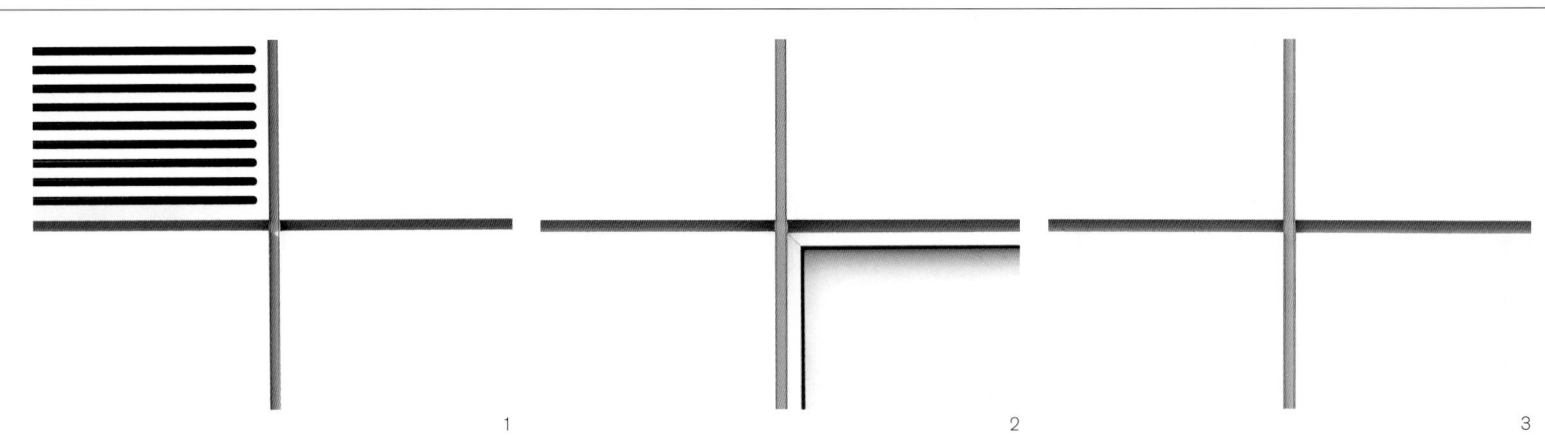

1-6. In 1988, following a detailed survey of the deterioration found in the cladding panels – caused by an unexpected chemical reaction between the supposedly inert phenolic foam insulation and the superplastic alloy of the outer skin – it was decided that the Sainsbury Centre's aluminium cladding would have to be replaced. The opportunity was taken to upgrade its technical specification. Advances in pressing technology meant that the new panels could be made completely flat. The new smooth white surface has lent a particularly sleek quality to the building.

Concern that the panels would be prone to site damage during construction had resulted in an approach to the glazing company, Modern Art Glass, who, apart from being an early Foster client, had been responsible for erecting the Willis Faber glazed wall. Modern Art Glass was itself involved in developing new systems and had recently entered into a consortium researching new glazing techniques based on aluminium frames and neoprene seals. Neoprene was by no means a new material – it had long been used to secure car windscreens, for example – but its application in a building context was usually restricted to small, simple elements.

Initial studies suggested individual neoprene seals for each panel clipping onto a gridded subframe of U-shaped aluminium channels. With these channels acting effectively as gutters however, there were insuperable problems of how acceptable tolerances between panel and main structure could be achieved while still maintaining a waterproof connection between the two. Overcoming this problem demanded that a single neoprene element be specially developed. It spans and seals two adjacent panels, which are supported by independent subframes. The neoprene itself forms the gutter – and being flexible can adjust the space between panels to take up any minor construction tolerances.

Joining individual neoprene lengths to create the four-way junction where panels meet was something that could be achieved in the factory. However, there remained the problem of how to achieve a continuous neoprene lattice to cover the entire structure. Fully vulcanised joins could, at that time, only be achieved with large factory presses, but transporting the completed lattice to site would have been impossible. A transportable vulcanising press was specially developed, which allowed manageable sections of lattice to be connected on site.

**Improved technology meant that the new panels could be completely flat. And so Foster opted to express the refit, giving the building a sleek new white livery that is more Boeing than Citroën.**

It is one of the ironies of the project that, while the complex neoprene gaskets have performed perfectly over the years, the apparently straightforward panels deteriorated prematurely, in circumstances that could not have been foreseen.

Architecture has always liked to eat itself as one style succeeds another. The re-facading of buildings down the centuries is sufficient proof of this: such as medieval timber-framed houses later clad in brick or stone, perhaps several times over. Unpeeling the layers became one of the most difficult challenges for building restorers in the 1990s. Re-facading continues today on a large scale … The re-cladding of the Sainsbury Centre, an exercise that passed virtually without comment, can be regarded as a discourse on the very nature of contemporary architecture and a prototype for the next generation of buildings – long predicted by techno-buffs – which will, we are assured, be capable of changing their appearance virtually at will as they respond to climate, light conditions and the needs of their users. Foster himself would probably prefer to see the exercise more pragmatically as little different from the lifetime maintenance schedules of aircraft, where the majority of components are replaced or upgraded by the end of the surprisingly long life of the average commercial flying machine. Hugh Pearman, *Contemporary World Architecture*, 1998

Right: The process of removing and replacing the original aluminium panels was greatly assisted by the ease and speed with which panels could be unbolted.

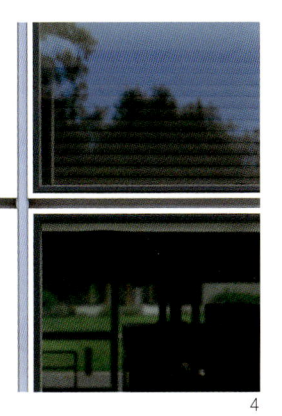

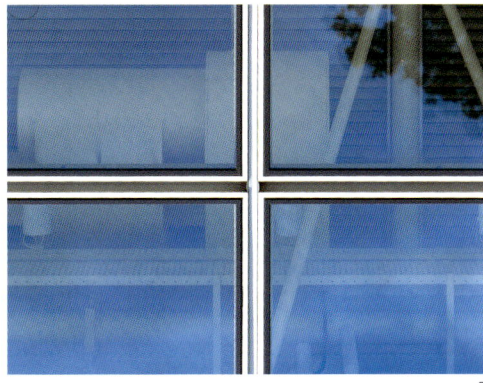

Tests carried out on isolated panels revealed an unexpected destructive chemical reaction taking place between the supposedly inert phenolic foam and the superplastic alloy of the outer shell. Following extensive research, which revealed the problem to be endemic, the decision was taken to replace all the panels.

Interestingly – perhaps presciently – the flexible nature of the cladding system ensured that the process of removing and replacing the panels was executed swiftly and easily. But rather than replacing 'to match existing' – a specification all too familiar in the building industry – Foster turned the aircraft analogy into reality, seizing the opportunity to improve the ultraviolet filtering of the glazed panels and to upgrade the specification and technical performance of the cladding overall.

The original silver panels had been ribbed to disguise imperfections in the smoothness of the finished surface caused by the limitations of the pressing process – creating, incidentally, an image that affectionately brought to mind the corrugated sides of Citroën vans. However, improved technology meant that the new panels could be completely flat. And so Foster opted to express this refit architecturally, giving the building a sleek new white livery that is more Boeing than Citroën. The new panels – constructed with a honeycomb aluminium core with rockwool insulation – have a smooth white PVF2 finish.

This process was funded by a grant from the Sainsbury family foundation and completed during the spring of 1988. The Sainsbury Centre reopened in June of that year with an exhibition of Chinese Bronzes. Meanwhile plans were already under way for the construction of a new extension, providing improved research and curatorial facilities, which would result in the creation of the Crescent Wing.

Perhaps as patron, of both the Sainsbury Centre and the Crescent Wing, the last word here belongs to Sir Robert Sainsbury. It is a mark of the close relationship that developed between the two men during the course of the project – one that continues to this day – that Sir Robert agreed to give the opening address on the occasion of Foster's investiture, in June 1983, with the RIBA's Royal Gold Medal. The following is an extract from Sir Robert's speech:

'Norman Foster has stated that the building attempts a sensitive but positive response to the collection. Undoubtedly the building provides to a marked degree the sought-after environment. It equally satisfies the particular needs of a somewhat eclectic collection containing a great deal of sculpture. I would add that as we find the building completely satisfying visually, we did not contradict the person who suggested that the building was the greatest work in our collection; although I wasn't wildly taken with a lady who looked around the Centre and said, "It's so beautiful – if only you didn't have these works of art in it".'

Graham Vickers, Ian Lambot

**A well-known architect recently asked me for the 'bucket' rating of the Centre. One bucket, two buckets, three buckets? I was pleased to be able to say that the Centre does not need buckets.**
Sir Robert Sainsbury, introducing Norman Foster as RIBA Royal Gold Medallist, 21 June 1983

**The glazed ends, with structure visible beyond the glass, embrace and frame a segment of the view, much as a Palladian portico would have done … It is a slightly disorienting compliment to the county that contains parks like Houghton and Holkham, and gave birth to Humphry Repton – disorienting because it seems so improbable in the context of this sleek and undeniably modern shed.**
Reyner Banham, *Foster Associates*, 1979

**This shimmering structure of superplastic aluminium whistles past the grim cement grey of the University buildings like the Paris to Marseilles Mistral Express, immaculate in its pure green landscape.** Stephen Gardiner, *The Listener*, 13 February 1983

**Set in parkland, the enigmatically anonymous shed sits as serene and uninvolved as Le Corbusier's ideal Villa Savoye, a white house in a green field.** Anthony Fawcett and Jane Withers, *The Face*, February 1983

# With Wendy
Norman Foster 1991

In 1963 I returned to England, after studying and working in the United States, to join Richard Rogers and two architect sisters, Georgie and Wendy Cheesman. We formed a practice based in Wendy's London flat, called Team 4 Architects, which lasted some four years before there was a parting of the ways. Almost from our first meeting Wendy and I had become inseparable, so there was a certain inevitability in our forming a new practice together: after much agonising we chose to call it Foster Associates. The name, with its overtones of a larger plurality, was a gesture of confidence in an uncertain future. Not only were there no associates, there were no commissions to build either.

The first Team 4 projects were mostly for friends and relations. It is only now, looking back, that one can marvel at the courage of those clients, as they subjected themselves to a level of social idealism that was matched only by our lack of real experience. Perhaps the most important asset for a designer, though, is the ability to recognise and accept the limits of personal knowledge, because this leads to the process of posing the right questions to the right people. In those early days this was a relatively slow and linear process, rooted in traditional trades and attitudes. However, the factory for Reliance Controls, which spanned the break up of Team 4 and the formation of Foster Associates, extended this challenge by introducing the commercial reality of time – in addition to financial and engineering constraints – as a fixed and limited resource. It set the stage for a way of working that has since become second nature.

Although all of Team 4's work received wide publicity and even national awards, we were still locked into a vicious circle: without the right kind of work to show, we lacked credibility; but how could we demonstrate credibility without first being given the opportunities? By the middle of 1968, after nearly a year occupied with small-scale conversion work and part-time teaching, Wendy and I – now with two very small sons – were talking about emigrating to a more receptive and open society. In the event, an established contact with the Fred Olsen company in London's Docklands came to the rescue. After long months of 'stop-go' – in competition not against other architects, but with contractors offering a package deal of 'design and build' – Fred Olsen decided to commission us to design his new buildings, a decision which became a major turning-point for us and was pivotal in establishing Foster Associates.

**The first Team 4 projects were mostly for friends and relations. It is only now, looking back, that one can marvel at the courage of those clients, as they subjected themselves to a level of social idealism that was matched only by our lack of real experience.**

The buildings that arose from this commission were born out of painstaking research into the operational processes of the company and the hardware of its ships, but they were also realised on extremely short timescales. The structures were later to be visited by clients such as Sir Robert and Lady Sainsbury, IBM and Willis Faber & Dumas. These visits were to prove instrumental in securing new opportunities for the future.

When the senior management of Willis Faber came to see the buildings, the outgoing chairman, Johnny Roscoe, was accompanied by Julian Faber, who was soon to take over from him. I introduced them to Mike Thompson, then the dock manager, who was later to become a director of the Olsen company. We sat down in the open office space, contemplating the activities around us, the paintings from Fred Olsen's personal collection that adorned the walls, and the ships beyond.

1

**Wendy rented an Edwardian two-roomed flat in Belsize Park. She slept and lived in one room and the other was our office. From the beginning we went from crisis to crisis. Within a few months, the only registered architect, Georgie had resigned … This left Norman, Wendy, Su and me with a letterhead that read 'Team 4 Architects'.**
Richard Rogers, 'Team 4', 1991
Left: Wendy Cheesman, Frank Peacock, Tony Hunt, Sally Appleby, Norman Foster, Richard Rogers, Su Rogers, and Maurice Phillips (left to right) photographed leaning out of the window of the flat at 16 Hampstead Hill Gardens that provided Team 4 with their studio.

**As Team 4 we were working out of Wendy's flat in Hampstead where the edges between our office life and domestic living were, to put it mildly, chaotically blurred!** Norman Foster, *Norman Foster: Sketches*, 1992

Johnny Roscoe, an outspoken individual, came quickly to the point: 'Well, is he any good?' he said, pointing at me. Mike Thompson squirmed with embarrassment and I got up to try to leave them to a private conversation. The chairman, persistent and visibly impatient, waved all this aside. Mike Thompson then entered into the spirit of the interrogation and conceded that, perhaps, I rated an 'A minus'. 'That's fine,' was the reply. 'Anything better and I wouldn't have believed it, anything less and it wouldn't be good enough.' Fred Olsen put it a different way – when quizzed about me he said simply: 'He asks the right questions.'

Trying to talk about those early days reminds me that some years ago, Wendy was supposed to have written an equivalent piece. I teased her then about what she might write. 'I'll say that you are a juggler,' she replied. 'You throw the balls higher than anybody else, and you let them fall lower before catching them.' That analogy is appropriate in trying to explain the component of time in the design process, and is perhaps best illustrated by another anecdote. It offers insights into the design process that are as fresh and relevant to us today as they were then.

It was the summer of 1975 and design work was progressing well on the Sainsbury Centre for Visual Arts, planned for the University of East Anglia. We proposed to integrate all the activities – public galleries for the collection donated by Sir Robert and Lady Sainsbury, as well as academic facilities – in one unifying enclosure. This had been greeted initially with some scepticism because it challenged the preconception of a group of separate buildings.

However, the principal parties to the venture had been united in this direction and there was a genuine excitement about the richer mix of cultures that would exist under the same roof. After many revisions as the project evolved, the design had finally settled down. The scheme had been approved by the client, the University and the planning authority, and everyone was relatively relaxed.

Behind the scenes, however, we as architects were struggling to resolve the detailed planning. Despite our best endeavours, the clarity of the open galleries was always compromised by the need for solid cores containing boilers, mechanical equipment, toilets and the like. In some ways it was one of the classic challenges in modern architecture: how to handle the relationship between free flexible space and the fixed elements such as toilets, kitchens and mechanical plant. Late in the day, however, we suddenly seized upon a new and exciting solution: by creating a double layer of wall and roof, the space in between could absorb the secondary functions, thereby leaving the primary spaces free and uncluttered. The double wall also had important environmental benefits, shielding the interior from solar gain and reducing the amount of energy required to service the spaces.

In our minds it was as if the original concept had suddenly flowered. It seemed like a new vision. In some ways the scheme responded to many of the directions that had surfaced at the regular design team meetings, but which we had so far failed to express in three dimensions. We rapidly explored the new idea through drawings and study models, which more than confirmed our expectations. To anybody who had felt the pulse of the project it was the culmination of all the work that had gone before.

1. The elegant simplicity and immaculate detailing of the Reliance Controls factory (1965-1966), Team 4's first project for a commercial client. Norman Foster recollects that the constraints imposed and discipline required by this project 'set the stage for a way of working which has since become second nature.'

2. The initial designs for the Fred Olsen Passenger Terminal. A cantilevered structure of tapered steel frames was to have been clad in horizontally profiled aluminium sheeting. The terminal was raised to provide a direct link to the passenger decks of docked ships and to allow work to continue unimpeded at quay level.

3. A view of the Olsen Amenity Centre, seen from the deck of an Olsen ship. This, the first of a string of projects Foster was to undertake for Fred Olsen, was pivotal in establishing the practice. Prior to this commission Norman and Wendy Foster were seriously contemplating leaving Britain to work in America.

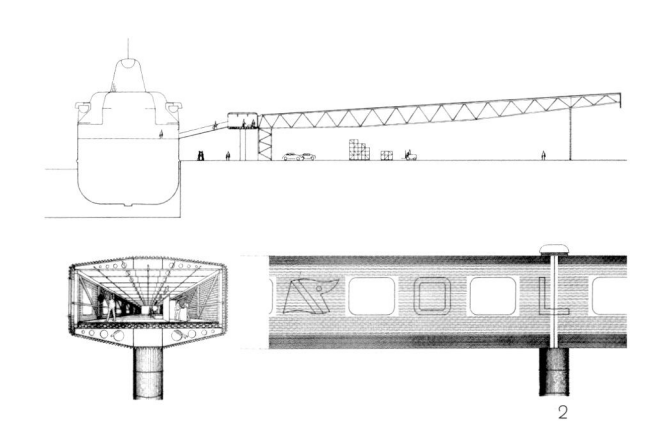

One of the engineers, while conceding that the new scheme was far better, suggested that it should be reserved for some future project. Wendy pointed out that such an opportunity might never occur – each scheme had to be the best thing we could achieve in the time, so 'let's do it now'. It pushed everyone to the brink but unlocked a creative energy that improved the design even further. Norman Foster, *Foster Associates*, 1991
Right: The advantages of the 'thick-skin' scheme, and its ability to accommodate the required services within the wall zone, are demonstrated in Norman Foster's sketch.

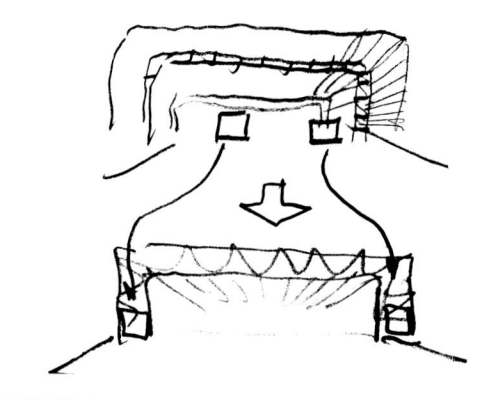

1. The eastern end of the Sainsbury Centre, its glass wall framed by the exposed 2.4-metre truss structure. The 'thick wall' scheme adopted at the eleventh hour was the key to the success of the building, freeing the interior space of fixed elements such as kitchens, mechanical plant and toilets.

At the next of our regular design team meetings with all the key individuals involved – architects, engineers and cost consultants – we unveiled the new proposals. As the full implications of the change became apparent, the mood of the meeting became very strained. The shift was so dramatic that it was apparent that it would entail a complete redesign of the structure and cladding. This was a dilemma. Everybody accepted that it was an infinitely better scheme. But dare we put the completion date at risk and threaten the goodwill and confidence of the client by proposing such far-reaching changes at such a late stage? Or should we forge ahead with the existing scheme, knowing that a significantly improved version existed, even if it was only in the mind and on scraps of paper and polystyrene?

**It was Wendy who polarised the discussion in her characteristically uncompromising manner: how could you possibly have your heart in a scheme that you knew was not the best one?**

To hold to the original date for starting on site would require a supreme effort by everyone. It would require the complete reworking of the many specialist drawings and schedules. Tony Hunt, a good friend and talented engineer whose firm has been responsible for the structures of many of our projects, shared everyone's sentiments. But he suggested that we should maintain our course, save these new directions for some future project, and complete the building to the original design.

It was Wendy who polarised the discussion in her characteristically uncompromising manner: how could you possibly have your heart in a scheme that you knew was not the best one? Furthermore, when it came to the next opportunity, we would all have moved on to newer ideas – each scheme had to be the best thing we could achieve at the time, so 'let's do it now'. By the time the meeting broke up, several hours later, Tony Hunt was already exploring the potential of a new prismatic structure and related panel geometry, which he had begun to sketch out; the services engineers were excited by the prospect of using the space within the structure; and the cost consultants could even see the scope for some savings in the equation.

Within a week of further intensive work, the clients had been persuaded of the new scheme's merits, the University had been consulted and a new application had been submitted for planning permission. All the original tender dates were held and the building works started on site on schedule. Looking back it was obviously the right course of action and no party to the project would ever disagree. In terms of the logistics of striving for the ultimate achievable quality within the fixes of time and cost, it was a supreme juggling act.

I tell the story for several reasons, which would be easy to take for granted, but which may not be so obvious to the reader. Firstly, it illustrates the importance of getting to the core of a situation. Wendy's pithy interventions always brought clarity to our thinking; sometimes only afterwards did this seem obvious and inevitable. But her role in the practice was much wider than her work on the projects. Reticently, behind the scenes, at so many important stages in the evolution of the practice, she was a strong and creative driving force, often sensing the need for change in the spaces we occupied and provoking appropriate actions – but always with kindness and a sense of humour that could verge on the mischievous. All of us took for granted her refusal to compromise on quality in everything the practice did: not just the architecture, but even down to the small things, such as the way a slice of bread might be served. Without Wendy, there would never have been a Foster Associates.

**Wendy challenged everything … She was determined to ensure that every avenue was explored to achieve the best possible solution. It was a remarkable experience to work with her, because of her extraordinary perception about design. She could always identify the heart of the matter with unerring acccuracy.** Spencer de Grey in conversation with Malcolm Quantrill, 1999

Secondly, the design evolution of our projects is rarely a simple linear route; the process is far more circuitous than might be imagined. Although our tools have become more sophisticated with the introduction of computer modelling, the evolution of a design is still as pragmatic as ever. The computer, like the pencil, is only as good as the person directing it. There is no doubt that the Sainsbury Centre, having undergone that final struggle, emerged as a visually simpler entity. But such simplicity can be deceptive, because the hidden circuitry behind those double walls proved to be far more responsive to the needs of the building and its users than the earlier versions of the design.

I still wonder at the contrast between the simplicity of the end product and the complexity of the explorations and debate that led up to it. The third point to be drawn is that the most important relationship behind any building is that between architect and client. When I went to see Sir Robert and Lady Sainsbury to explain our radical new ideas for the building, like the consultants, their first reaction was one of anxiety: 'Not again!' – how could we propose more changes just as everyone had grown accustomed to the scheme?

**No two projects are alike, and the same can be said for those people who commission them, whether they are individuals, corporate bodies or entrepreneurs. The most successful projects share that quality of enlightened concern called patronage.**

I urged them to consider the new scheme on its merits; after all, had they too not been responsible for changes during the evolution of the project? Had we not jointly agreed that we would strive to achieve the best possible building within the allotted time and cost? Twenty-four hours later we had a further meeting together and all the implications were set out in painstaking detail. The outcome was an even greater shared sense of purpose and enthusiasm for this new direction.

Over the years Sir Robert and Lady Sainsbury have become valued friends. But throughout our working relationship, their professionalism in the role of client remained undiminished. I can still recall the study tour of galleries in Europe and the United States that Wendy and I made with them at the outset of the project. It was something of a research marathon. Only much later did I discover that each couple had, at the time, confided to their friends that they had difficulty in keeping up the pace set by the others! That tour marked the start of a dialogue based on a common language of standards. No two projects are alike, and the same can be said for those people who commission them, whether they are individuals, corporate bodies or entrepreneurs. But the most successful projects share to some degree that quality of enlightened concern called patronage – and the Sainsburys were a role model.

2. Norman and Wendy Foster photographed in Foster Associates' Covent Garden studio, in Bedford Street, in the late 1960s.

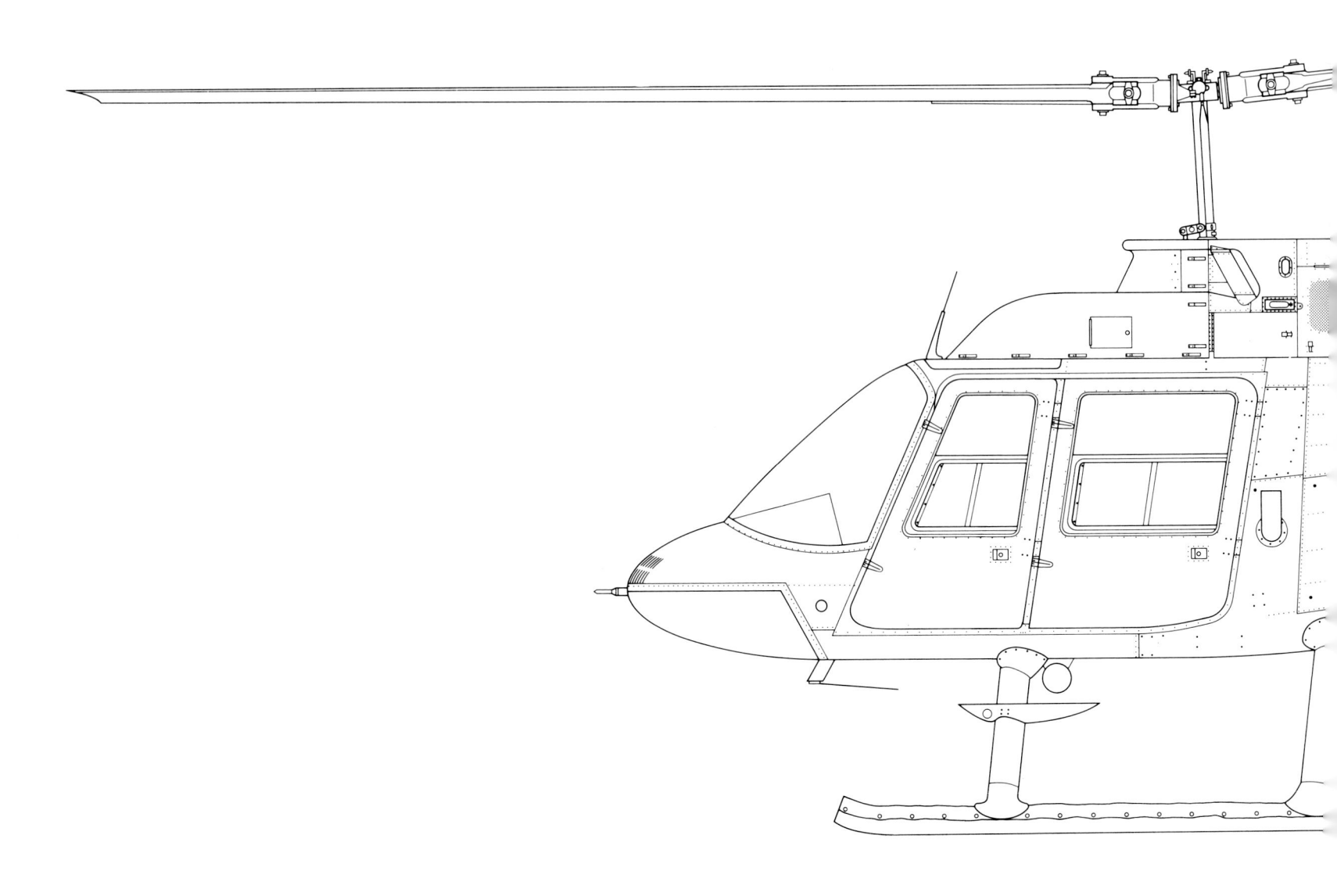

**The poetic ingredient of flight can lie close to the surface, even if it never emerges in conversation. In the same spirit, every decision in the design of a building is touched not only by reason but also by those intangible and poetic influences.**
Norman Foster

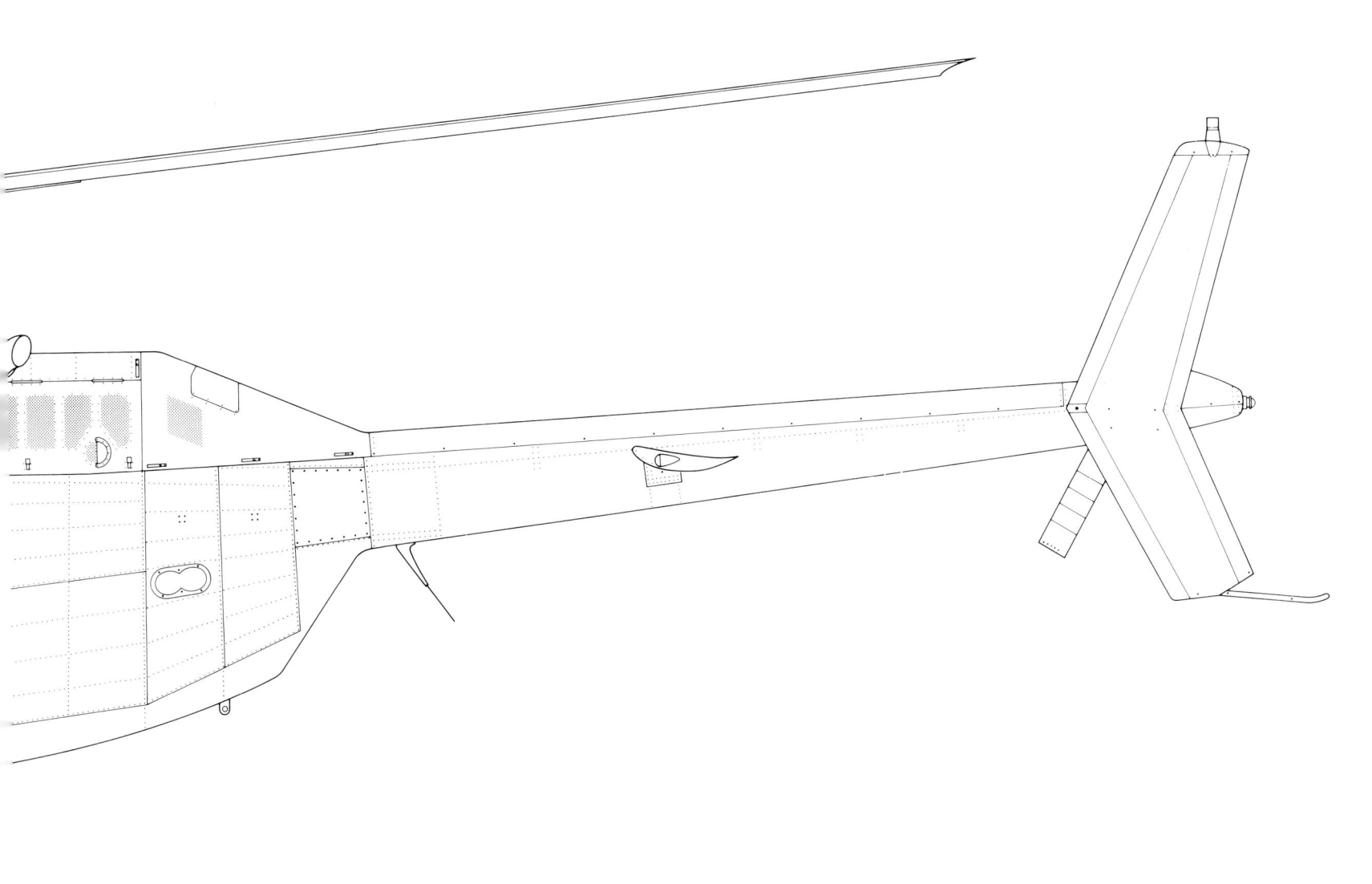

1-3. The Bell Jet Ranger helicopter is cited by Norman Foster as a model for true flexibility in design. It was first introduced in 1966, and although the technology of many of the individual parts, such as the engine and electronics, has changed quite dramatically, it has proved itself so responsive to the continuous process of change that it is still in production today. It has flown more hours and set more records than any other aircraft in the world.

With Wendy 427

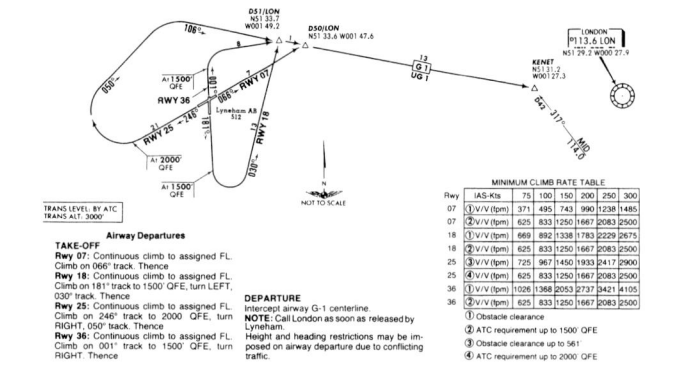

**The lessons from aviation for architecture are not confined to those buildings that host the aircraft and their users: they are operational, concerned with how people work together, as much as technological.** Norman Foster, 'Flight 347', 1989
Right: The graphic clarity of a flight plan.

Moving forward to the present, the teams now associated with the office, like those of the past, extend from a design-based core to embrace clients, users and a network of consultants and manufacturers. In the larger, more complex projects, which have evolved progressively from the earlier works, it is sometimes necessary to first design operational structures to bring the right people into the process at the right point in time; without a clear definition of needs, there is no basis on which to design. But often an honest 'don't know' is a far more precise acknowledgement of the reality of a situation than some spurious attempt to quantify an unknown future. Unlike the design of artefacts, buildings are conceived in the present for a volatile future but, culturally, they cannot be separated from the context of the past.

## Both flight and design involve unseen forces, obey certain rules, and for their realisation depend totally on communication.

Despite the differences between architecture and artefacts it can be helpful to draw comparisons to illustrate a point. Consider the helicopter for example. To fly a helicopter you have four controls. In front of the pilot is a stick called the cyclic; you push it forward to go forwards, back to go backwards, to the side to go sideways and so on. Next to the seat is a lever called the collective; you lift it up to ascend and push it down to descend. Depending on the movements of the helicopter it will require continuous adjustments of power, which in the most basic models is achieved by a twist-grip throttle on the end of the collective stick; you wind it up for more power and release it for less. All these control inputs act on the main rotor, which is overhead. Finally, the pilot's feet can move pedals connected to the tail rotor, which enables the helicopter to swivel on its own axis.

The helicopter, unlike a fixed wing aircraft, can describe almost any three-dimensional sequence of movement in space. To do so involves the movement of all the controls simultaneously; the adjustment of one input has consequences for all the others. You can pick apart the theory of this on paper or on a blackboard, but until the physical coordination of all these variables together, at the same time, becomes second nature, you simply cannot fly the machine. The relationship between the four controls is totally interactive.

To return to the design team and the issue of posing the right questions. If the development of a design is seen as a dynamic process in time, then all the variables – for example, massing, materials, inside, outside, structure, heating, lighting, cooling, cost, time – are, like the control inputs to that helicopter, entirely interactive. You cannot change one without affecting some or all of the others. To be able to pose the vital questions and assess the consequences requires a team of specialists who can come together and who are, each in their own way, able to share a vision.

The Sainsbury Centre story tells us something about the nature of communication and the way that individuals interact. It is the camaraderie and chemistry between members of the team that make such heroic efforts possible. I described a situation that was transparent in its openness; if the new idea had not been strong enough, it might well not have survived that cross-examination by the team. But when the idea took root, it was creatively expanded by everyone sparking off each other. The longer the participants are immersed in the design process, the easier it becomes for them to reshape the project at what might seem the eleventh hour. There is nothing capricious in this: it is merely optimising the shared knowledge of the team and using the resource of available time to its best advantage.

There is the potential for misunderstanding in all this. Such an approach is far removed from the grey world of design by committee. Although each individual may become committed to a common point of view, it is the personal chemistry and mutual respect within the team that enables anyone to challenge anything and everything in a forum that is open and volatile, but essentially sympathetic: nothing is too sacred. It is the opposite of much that has been academically taught.

**The way the practice works is that it really is a team of people – one team. It is not divided up into distinct groups. It has evolved as a team of like-minded people who continually search for excellence. There is a constant determination to ensure that we don't repeat experiences and produce the same scheme twice.** Ken Shuttleworth, in conversation with Malcolm Quantrill, 1999

**We all work here in London in a single studio so that communication is excellent throughout. This communication takes place both informally and formally. The chance discussion, the instant design comment or informal design review create a highly charged, creative atmosphere.** Spencer de Grey, in conversation with Malcolm Quantrill, 1999

Although strong leadership is important, the architect is not handing down from above, passing the parcel to the specialists who wait in line to be told what to do. Each individual has the potential for creative input. Paradoxically, the architect comes closer to the heart of the project because he is integrated into the 'how and why' of the making of the building. So the process extends out from the architect's studio, to the workplace where real people are making real things. And this must be right, because surely the essence of our culture is the making of things.

I told only part of the aviation story; flying is of course a much more complex interplay of all the senses. Aviation, like architecture, is also subject to legislation and prejudice. The flight can be tracked, via hidden lines of command, by controllers on the ground; they have the legal right of authority, although ultimate responsibility still rests with the pilot. When disasters occur, whether in airborne or ground-based structures, they provide a field-day for the media. The various parties are individually pilloried with scant regard for the totality of the system that caused the disaster, and of which they form an integral part. A flight, like a building, is only the visible tip of a vast iceberg of infrastructure.

When I fly an aircraft I can, in the same way that I analyse architecture, rationalise the event. Such factors as weight, load capacity, speed, range, fuel consumption and cruising altitude can be quantified into flight times and cost factors. I can even explain an aerobatic flight with blackboard theory. But striving to produce a graceful three-dimensional sequence of manoeuvres in space requires not only a grand decision but also continuous in-flight decisions to refine the performance. The poetic ingredient of flight can lie close to the surface, even if it never emerges in conversation. In the same spirit, every decision in the design of a building is touched not only by reason but also by those intangible and poetic influences. Although unspoken, and often taken for granted, it is this fusion which may explain my own passion for architecture. Like any love affair it is difficult to separate the heart from the mind.

Wendy's response at that design team meeting of 'let's do it now', with the emphasis on the now, also explains much about the nature of the practice then and today. I recall my spontaneous dash to the United States when British industry could not produce the goods to maintain the tight time schedule on the Olsen project. It never occurred to me to wait for time-consuming authorisations.

Taking the initiative to solve the problem rather than proffering apologies was very much in the spirit of 'doing it now'. That approach possibly explains the cross-section of the present office – with an average age of just 30, and commanding almost as many languages – as well as the early integration of other skills, especially model-making. It is also about the endless quest to improve a working lifestyle. I am reminded of a group who recently visited our studios, which overlook the Thames. 'Where do you work?' I was asked. I explained that I had the same space as anybody else at one of the long work-benches. 'But why don't you have your own office?' I was asked, almost in disbelief. I tried to explain that it was exactly what I did have, but I shared it with everyone else – I could never have had a space as grand as that just for myself. What I did not say was that the space was symbolic of the team. This has nothing to do with any theoretical attitude: it is simply a good place to be, to work alongside inspirational people. This grand dimension has taken many years to realise but, like all previous spaces that we have occupied, it was envisaged well ahead by Wendy when she identified the present site of Riverside. It is sad that she did not live to see it realised, but I am sure that she approves.

1. Norman Foster working on a design review in Foster and Partner's Riverside Three studio. Home to the practice since 1990, Riverside is a pioneering example of a building that combines living and working in one location. The Foster studio occupies the lower three levels of the eight-storey building, while apartments are located on the upper floors. The atmosphere in the daylit main studio is informal and energetic, with no division between design and production. The average age in the studio is 30 – and as many languages are spoken there. As Foster says, it is 'simply a good place to be, to work alongside inspirational people'.

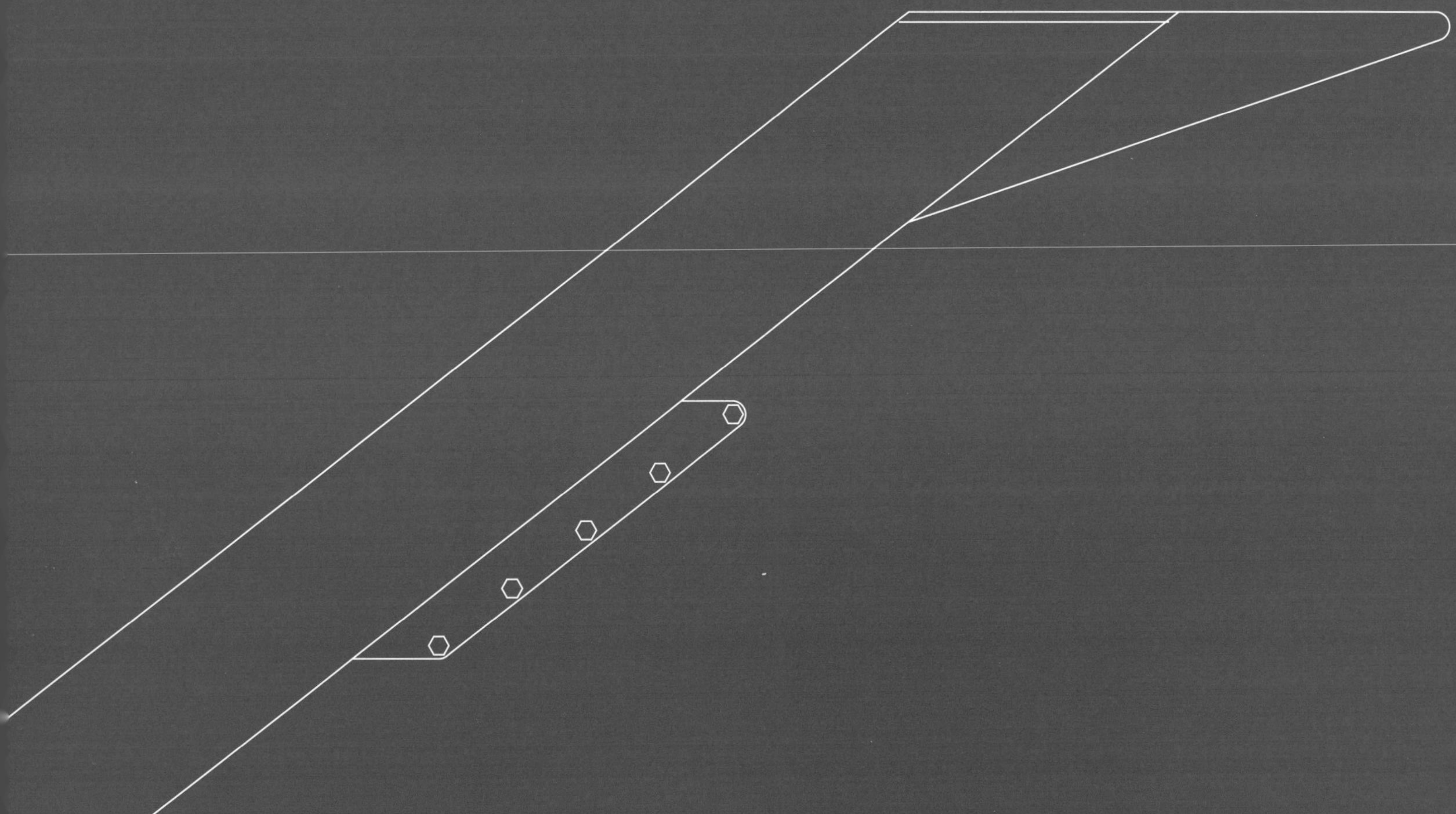

**The Crescent Wing**
Norwich, England 1986–1991

**Twelve years after we completed the Sainsbury Centre, a major new gift from Sir Robert and Lady Sainsbury gave us the opportunity to extend it. The brief included the reserve collection display – to be the best in the world – together with conservation facilities and a space for exhibitions and conferences, giving the Centre far greater flexibility. The obvious step was a linear extension. However, despite its open-ended nature the Sainsburys regarded the building as a finite object – 'perfect in itself' – and encouraged an approach that would preserve it intact. In the spirit of the 'cave' and the 'tent', the Centre is extended below ground. Roof-lights punctuating a level lawn, and a narrow ramp disappearing beneath the turf, provide clues; but only from the lake is the new wing's full extent apparent in a great sweep of glass. What is difficult to comprehend is that this extension is two-thirds the footprint of the original building!**
Norman Foster

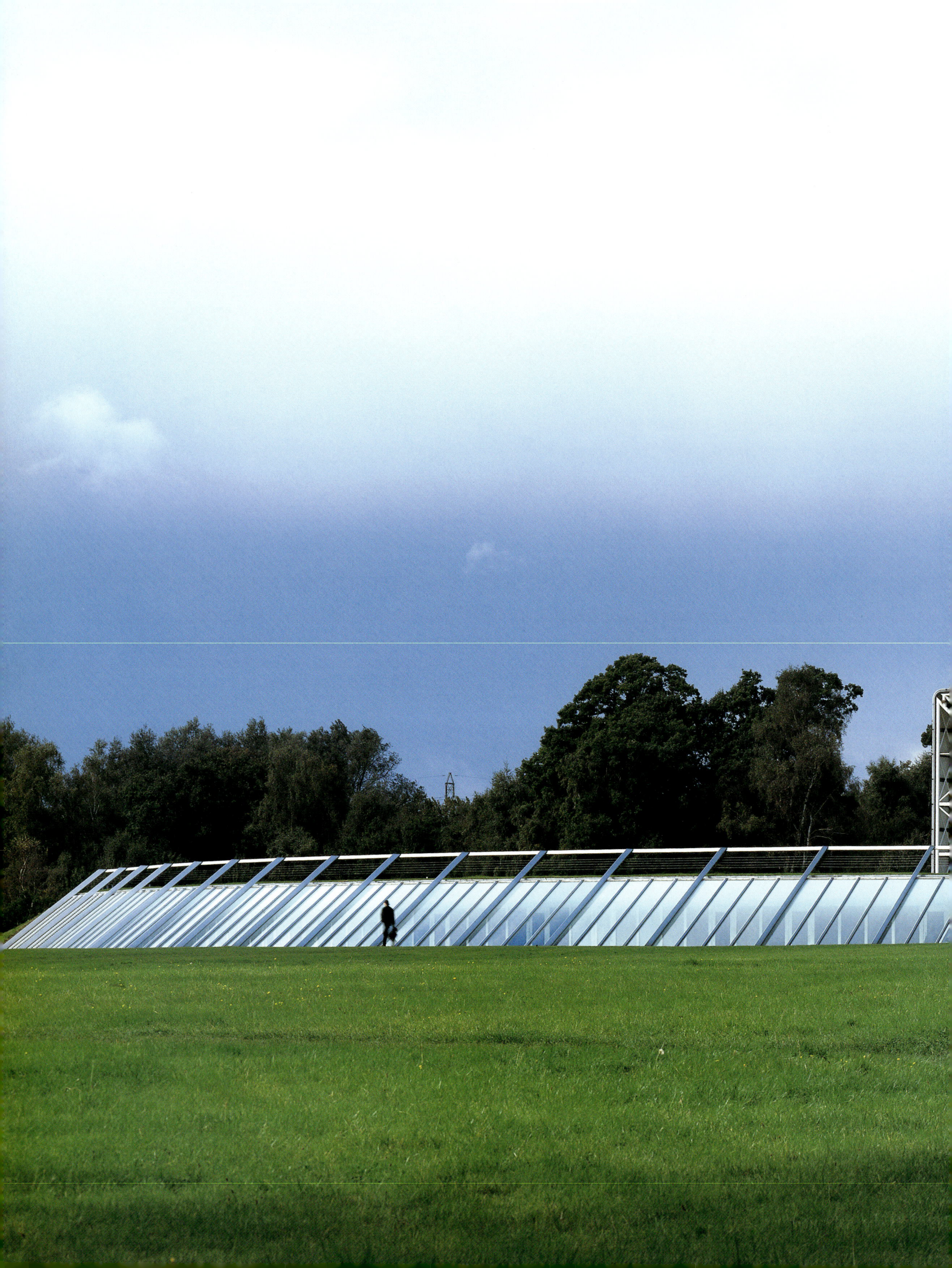

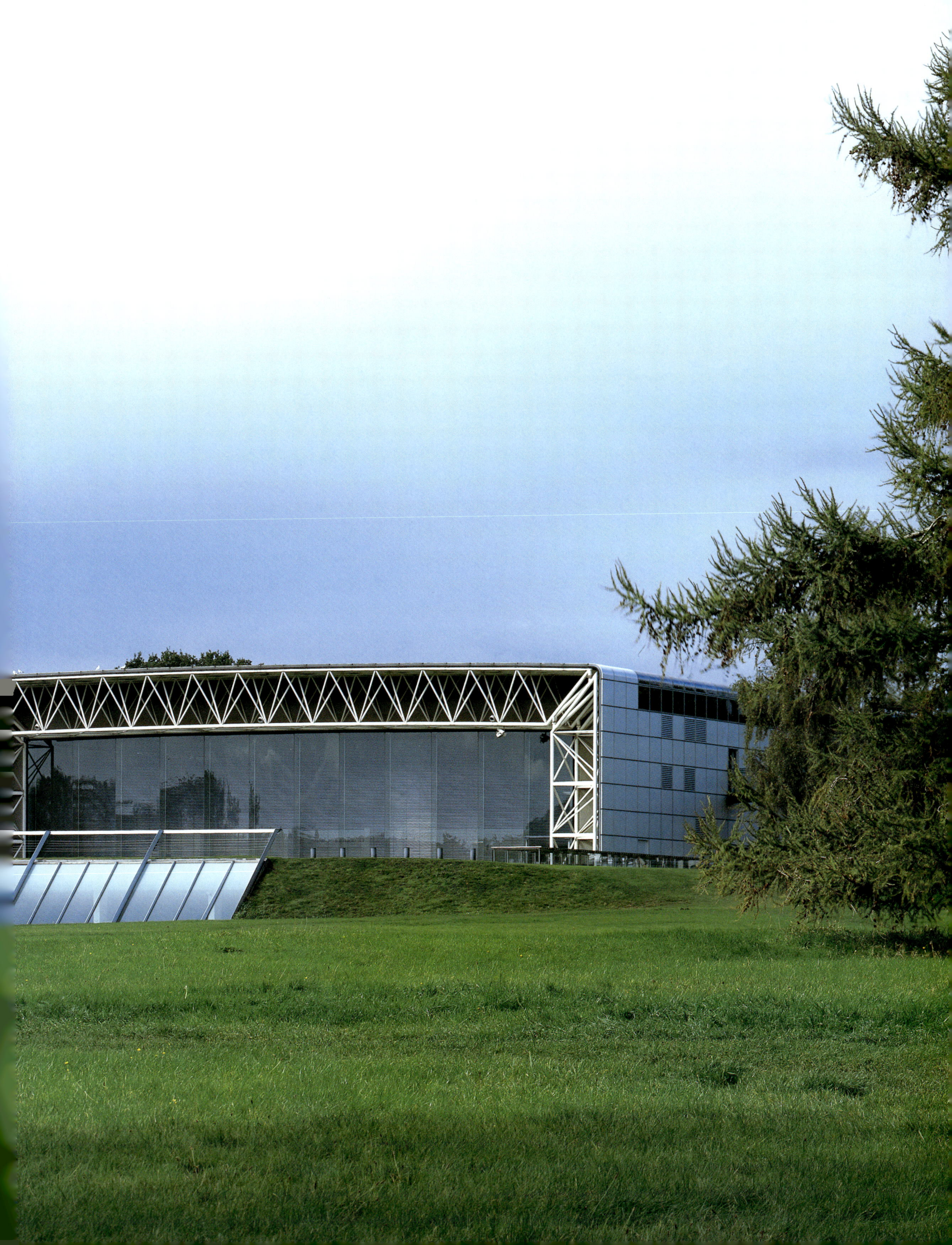

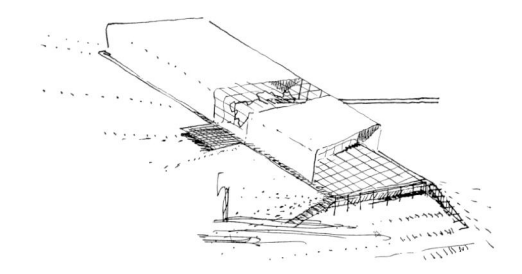

**It is interesting to see that the ideas behind the new wing were in circulation at the time of the first sketches for the original building.** Norman Foster, *Norman Foster: Sketches*, 1992
Left: One of Norman Foster's early design concept sketches for the Sainsbury Centre explores the potential for extending the undercroft at a later date.

It was no secret that Sir Robert and Lady Sainsbury considered the Sainsbury Centre building as one of the highlights of their collection, and they made it clear that they were reluctant to see it – or its relationship to the site – changed substantially.

1. In this sketch, Norman Foster investigated ways of expanding the original building. It soon became clear, however, that the brief made this approach inappropriate. The premise that the new accommodation provided by the Crescent Wing should be ancillary and subsidiary to the rest of the Sainsbury Centre became central to the continued development of the design.

The Sainsbury Centre for Visual Arts is one of Norman Foster's most completely satisfying achievements. Its impact is as immediate and, indeed, as sensational now as it was on the opening day in 1978. The serenity of the main gallery – or 'living area' – containing Sir Robert and Lady Sainsbury's extraordinary collection, remains total. The building itself, defined by the great extrusion that forms its walls and roof – conventional terms that hardly seem relevant – is utterly uncompromised by the smaller structures that sit beneath it.

The building is, however, underpinned – literally – by a domain that public and students never see. A narrow undercroft of storerooms, conservation laboratories and workshops runs the full length of the building, connected to the gallery level by lifts and inconspicuous spiral stairs, one of which emerges in the middle of the gallery's information and sales desk.

At the western end of the building, a ramp dives down below ground to provide vehicular access to a protected loading area. From the restaurant, looking westward through the glazed end wall, this great slit in the land is not seen but it is vital to the functioning of the centre.

The Crescent Wing, opened in 1991, can be seen in the context of the original Sainsbury Centre as a radical change in mood and direction. Yet the vital clues to its eventual form and character are clearly present in the 1970s building. In response to critics who suggest that the Crescent Wing is not the 'obvious' solution to the problem of extending a structure that had already attained near-canonic status, Norman Foster responds: 'We don't do the obvious – we are always open-minded, ready to discard our preconceptions'.

**The Sainsburys admired the study centre at the New York Metropolitan Museum of Art; the conviction grew that a similar facility should be created at the Sainsbury Centre. That this should be a quite distinct facility became the first element in the brief.**

Foster had always foreseen the possibility of an extension of the Sainsbury Centre to the east, taking advantage of the natural fall in the landscape towards the artificial lake – created as part of Denys Lasdun's UEA masterplan. When the idea of extending the building was first seriously discussed, however, in 1986, the scale of what was envisaged seemed to imply that the original building envelope would grow.

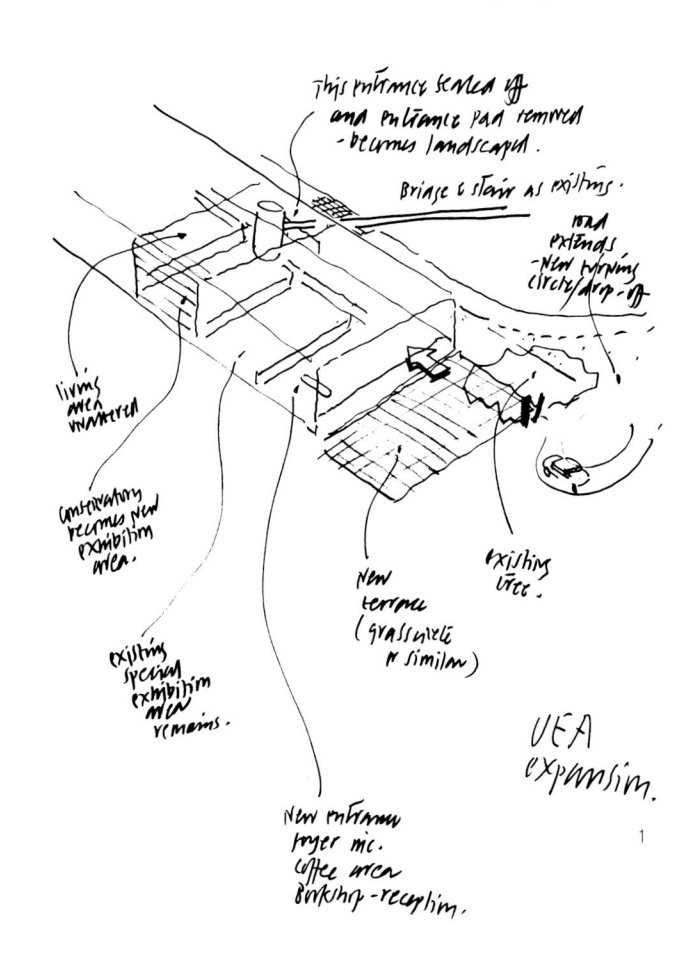

**The obvious answer [was] to extrude the construction for a few more bays, and hey presto, there's the extra space. However, in the Foster office a conception is never that simple. All the alternatives were considered. Linear growth was ruled out by the Sainsbury family, who saw the existing building as a complete entity, both a container for its art collection and its greatest prize. The family did not want it altered.**
David Jenkins, *The Architects' Journal*, 8 May 1991
Right: The definitive view from inside the Sainsbury Centre, looking out through the east portico over landscaped parkland towards the lake. The challenge in extending the building was to preserve this view intact.

Possible options for extending the shed, a natural enough solution, were sketched. 'If that approach had been right, we would have fought for it', Foster insists. But it soon became clear that there were sound reasons for adopting a very different approach, quite apart from the Sainsburys' great affection for the building as it stood – 'the greatest work in our collection' – and their reluctance to see it changed.

The brief for what became the Crescent Wing was well defined and quite distinct from that of the original building. Although the Sainsburys had donated a number of works of art to the Sainsbury Centre since its opening, there were no great pressures on the main gallery space. That said, there were very good arguments for rotating the items on display so as to avoid any impression of the Centre as a static entity.

However, there was a growing belief that it should also be possible for works in the Reserve Collection to be made available to a wider public, rather than just the small number of scholars that it was possible to cater for in the Centre's limited existing facilities. The Sainsburys had visited, and admired, the study centre at the Metropolitan Museum of Art, in New York, where pictures are kept secure but accessible in a system of sliding glass cases; the conviction grew that something similar should be available at the Sainsbury Centre. That this should be an attractive, but quite distinct, facility within the Centre became the first element in the brief.

The remaining elements fell quickly into place: the laboratories and workshops needed to be expanded and upgraded; office space was at a premium; and visiting exhibitions had increasingly come to play a central role in the Centre's activities, placing new environmental demands on its gallery spaces. None of these requirements could be very readily addressed merely by extending the existing building.

Implicit within the scheme that emerged was the realisation that the new space would be ancillary and subsidiary to the rest of the Centre. That being the case, one approach was to locate the new addition discretely in a nearby wood, thus responding to the Sainsburys' wish that the main building should remain uncompromised. An underground passage could link the two. However, in terms of security, convenience and economy that solution was quickly ruled out.

The way forward was to extend the existing basement level. The attractions of a basement level extension were manifold, not least in terms of economy. By taking advantage of the fall in the land towards the lake, the extension could be allowed to 'emerge' into daylight. In that way, both dark and daylit spaces could be provided and the new facilities would be only yards away from the main gallery.

2. Although the new building could not work completely independently of the Sainsbury Centre, it could work at one remove. Many options were explored, including building in the nearby woods, but the idea of an underground extension seemed to offer greater potential.

3. Placed at the eastern end of the Sainsbury Centre, where it was closest to the rest of the campus, the new extension was also able to take advantage of the fall in the land and emerge naturally into the daylight.

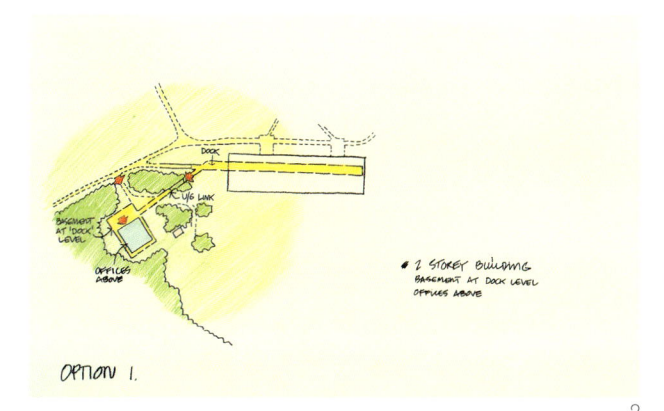

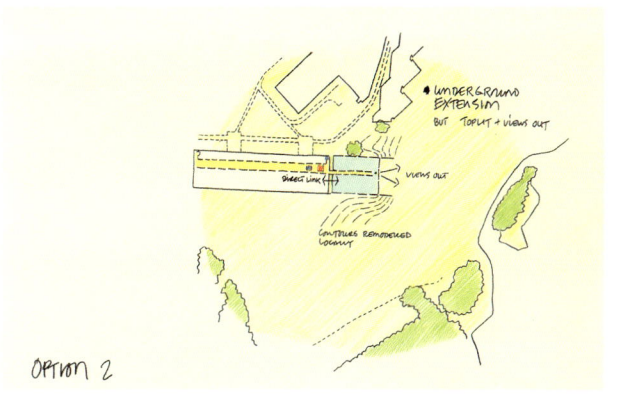

**The Sainsburys approached us with what seemed at first a very mundane assignment to discreetly site a storage shed to provide overspill space for the existing Sainsbury Centre on a nearby site. The beginnings of this project were quite humble, but the scale of the scheme changed as it evolved through discussion with the Sainsburys, the University, and the Keeper.** Norman Foster, *Norman Foster: Sketches*, 1992

Left: Sir Robert and Lady Sainsbury discuss the project with Norman Foster during a visit to the Foster studio.

Reconciling the needs of the brief with the natural slope of the land was the major challenge during the early stages of the design, and it was only resolved when the design team realised that the multi-purpose gallery would work equally well as a triangular space as one that was rectangular. The 'crescent' was born.

1. An extension of the undercroft had been considered during the design of the original building. Norman Foster's first sketches for the new Crescent Wing picked up where that long-forgotten proposal had left off.

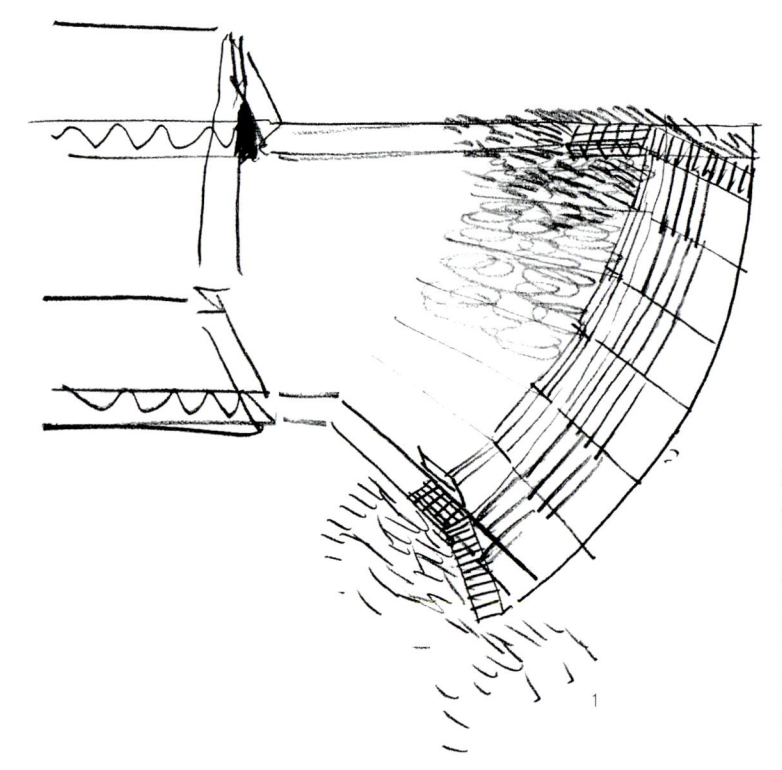

**In response to critics who suggest that the Crescent Wing is not the 'obvious' solution to the problem of extending a structure that had already attained near-canonic status, Norman Foster responds: 'We don't do the obvious – we are always open-minded, ready to discard our preconceptions'.**
Kenneth Powell

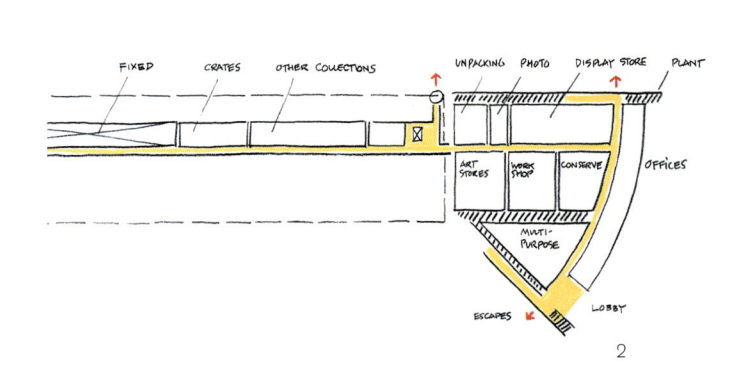

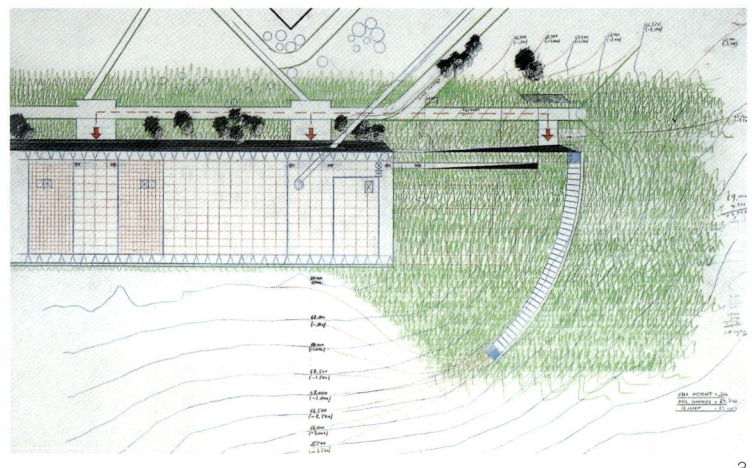

436  Norman Foster  Works 1

**The paradox of this extension lies precisely in that a building originally thought out for linear growth has achieved that idea of beauty which Alberti expressed as the impossibility of adding or removing a part without destroying the whole. Such impossibility has given rise to an intervention where the relationship between architecture and nature attains a spectacular balance.** Jorge Sainz, *A&V* 38, November-December 1992

With ecological issues increasingly to the fore, an earth roof also made sense, offering a high degree of natural insulation. Moreover, the grass could extend right up to the eastern elevation as it had always done, so that the view out would remain unchanged. The geometry of the extension, it was assumed, would reflect that of the original Centre: the new wing would terminate in a straight edge to the landscape. In July 1988, however, the brief was extended to include provision for a new lecture hall. In due course, this space was to be critical to the planning of the Crescent Wing.

As the concept design developed, the particular needs of the various spaces were more closely defined. Photographic darkrooms obviously needed to be capable of total black-out. Other spaces needed carefully controlled daylight, while in the offices good natural light was desirable. One drawback of following the existing building geometry was that the end elevation of the extension was relatively narrow, which limited the number of rooms that could benefit from daylight and views. Meanwhile the client was steadily adding to the office element of the brief, thereby increasing the demand for perimeter accommodation.

The revised brief suggested an extension of around 2,300 square metres, which implied a relatively deep building with limited exposure to natural light. In one of those adroit moves which underscores his claim to operate without preconceptions, Norman Foster thought again – and came up with the idea of the curve or the 'crescent', following the natural contours of the site. Foster describes this move as 'more radical than extending the original building: that was obvious. This was a response to real needs, not a mere gesture'.

It also offered a counterpoint to the shed – a 'cockpit', if you like, to the original 'hangar' – which echoed the little seaside Retreat Foster designed in his Team 4 days for the Brumwell family. In retrospect, the move away from a strictly rectilinear geometry seems forward-looking, a step towards a far more organic architecture and to themes that would become more apparent in the practice's architecture of the mid-1990s. Foster insists, however, that it was simply a response to a specific functional requirement, a 'natural' solution.

At a stroke, the central problem of how to incorporate an adequate area of daylit offices was solved: the offices were strung along the sweep of the crescent, looking out towards the park. Individually small in size, they could be all but square, with only a slight canting of walls to accommodate the curve.

The planning of the other spaces remained difficult, however. 'We struggled with the plan', admits Foster's partner Graham Phillips. It was illogical to have workshops and storerooms that were anything but rectangular. But the architects were coming up with some awkward spaces that seemed to bring into question the whole 'crescent' strategy. The lecture room, which was required to double-up as a gallery, became the pivot, on which the difficulties of the plan were resolved. By making the lecture room triangular, the design team was able to reconcile the two geometries – the rectangular, a continuation of the original building, and the curvilinear of the new extension.

2, 3. Once the idea of a triangular multi-purpose gallery cum lecture theatre had been accepted, the planning of the remaining internal spaces – and their relationship with the daylit offices that form the crescent – fell into place with relative ease. However, that is not to say that other options were not explored, including this early proposal that extended the undercroft of the original building right through the new wing.

4. Though it was useful in detailed planning terms, the presentation model proved less successful in conveying the spirit of the building in the landscape. However, this view of the model, internally lit, captures something of the drama of the building at night.

**Foster's design of this new wing marks a fresh episode in the singular relationship created by this architect … both rationally insular and sweetly participative.** Enrico Morteo, *Domus*, December 1992

**I recall a meeting with Norman and Wendy in 1987. At that time I was in charge of the Sainsbury Centre Crescent Wing, and this particular meeting was at the conceptual design stage … It was an incredibly productive meeting, with the result that the scheme took a great leap forward. I remember one observation in particular from that meeting: it was Wendy who said 'The speed of progress on a project is directly proportional to the frequency of design reviews.' At the time this didn't mean a great deal to me, but I've thought about it a lot since. Now I firmly believe that this observation really sums up how we work.** Graham Phillips, in conversation with Malcolm Quantrill, 1999

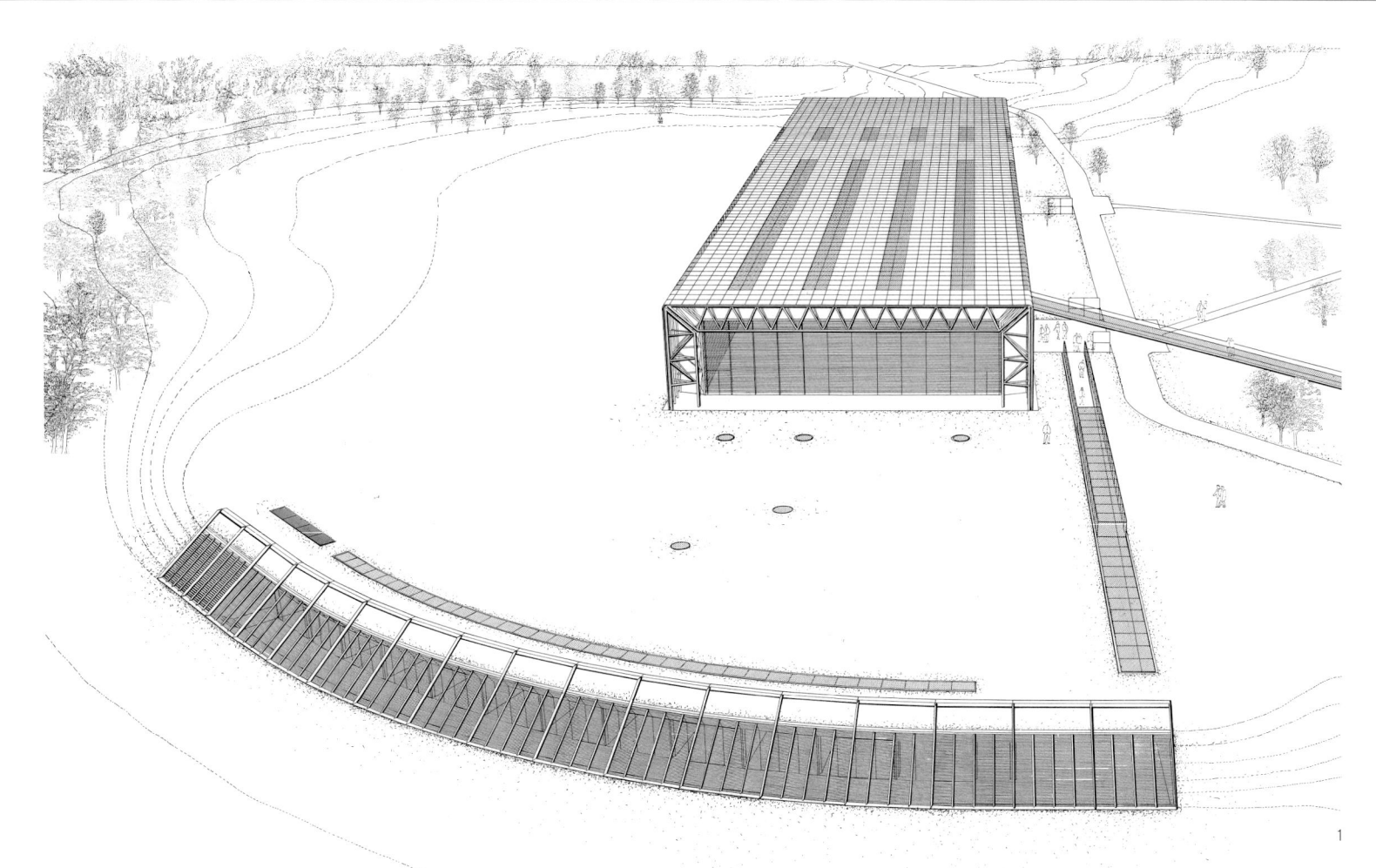

**The scale of the scheme changed as it evolved through discussion with the Sainsburys and the University. The new spaces are dramatic in their own right and complement the existing building – being ground hugging they make the original structure appear more tent-like.**

Norman Foster

**The quest for quality is very much an attitude of mind and the Sainsburys combine an unusual degree of deeply-held convictions with a refreshing open-mindedness ... The new Crescent Wing has sparked much of the same magic of working together which enthused the original development.**
Norman Foster, *Norman Foster: Sketches*, 1992
Right: The project team and Lady Sainsbury discuss the Crescent Wing's glazed wall during a design review.

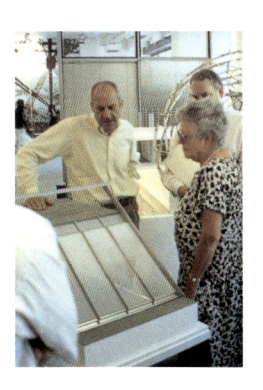

**It is in the spirit of the cave and the tent that the new Crescent Wing extension expands the original building almost invisibly into the landscape and enables through views to remain unchanged. What is difficult to comprehend is that this new extension is two-thirds the footprint of the original building!**
Norman Foster, *A&V* 38, November-December 1992

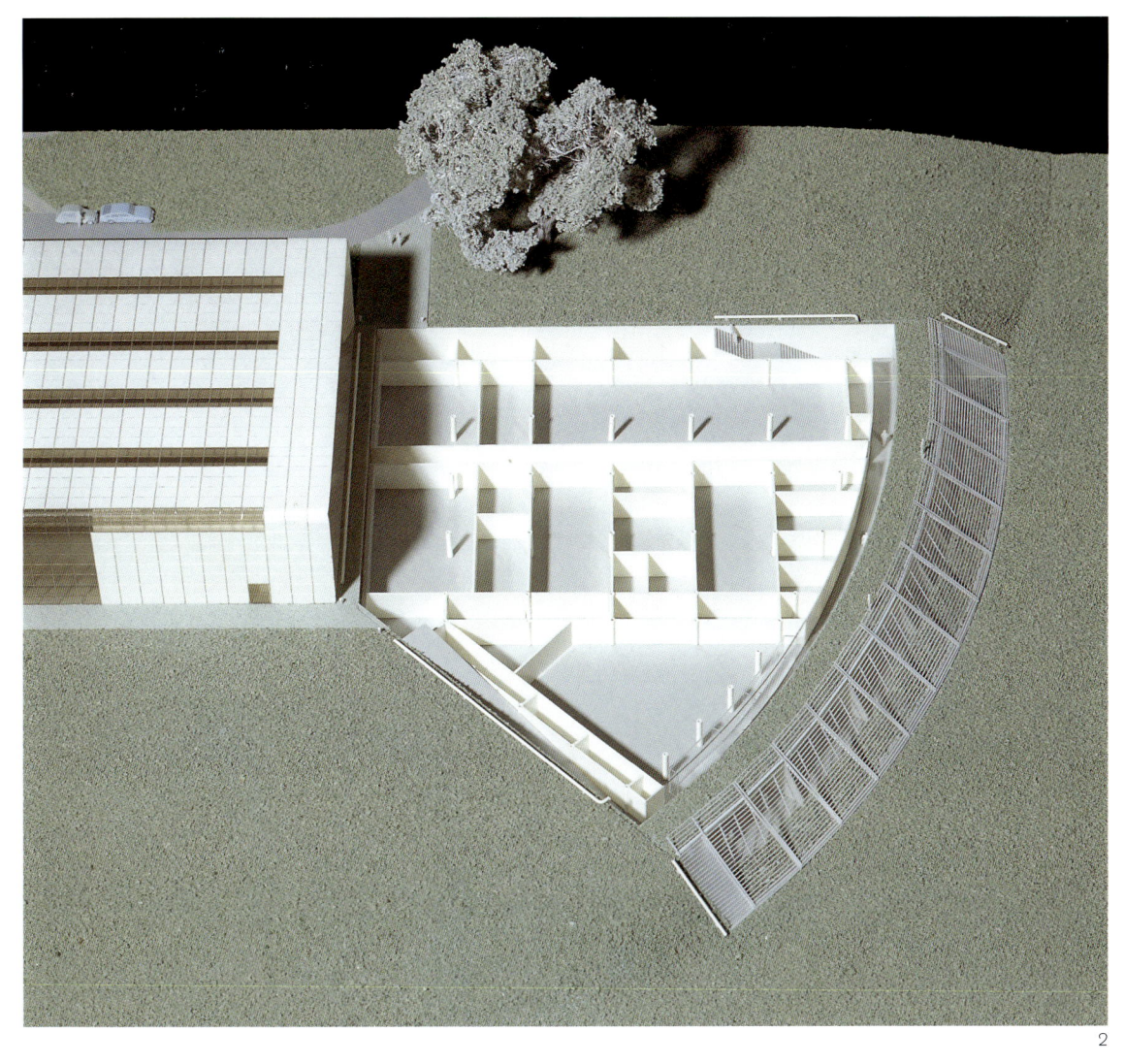

1. The Crescent Wing's curved glazed wall posed significant engineering and manufacturing challenges. The final radius and length of the glazing was calculated to match the contours of the site as closely as possible.

2, 3. The new wing is two-thirds the footprint of the original building. With so large an area, early plans assumed that two access ramps would be necessary for means of escape. But in the final design escape doors were incorporated in the glazing, allowing the second ramp to be omitted.

4, 5. A full-size mock-up of the escape door was constructed in the Great Portland Street studio to ensure that all the technical issues were resolved before construction began on site.

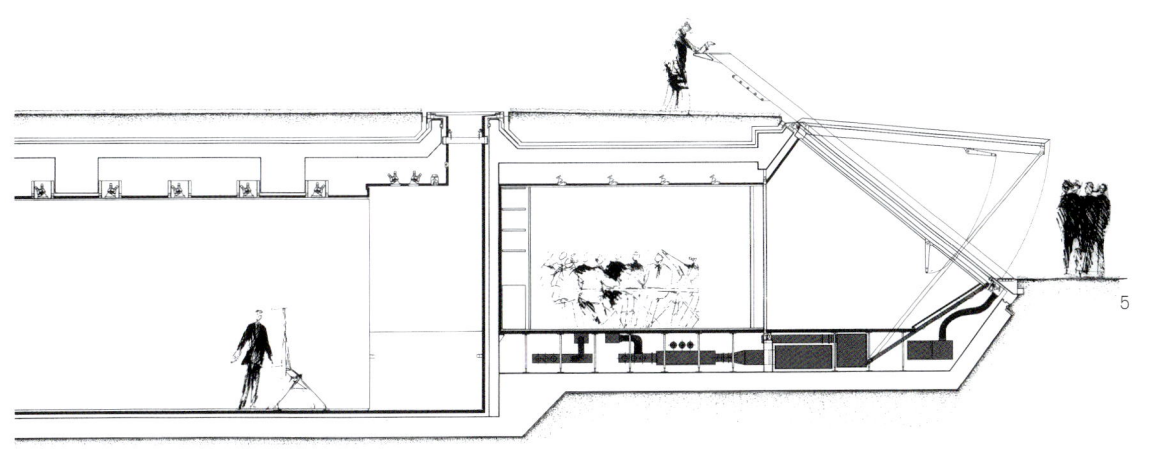

The Crescent Wing

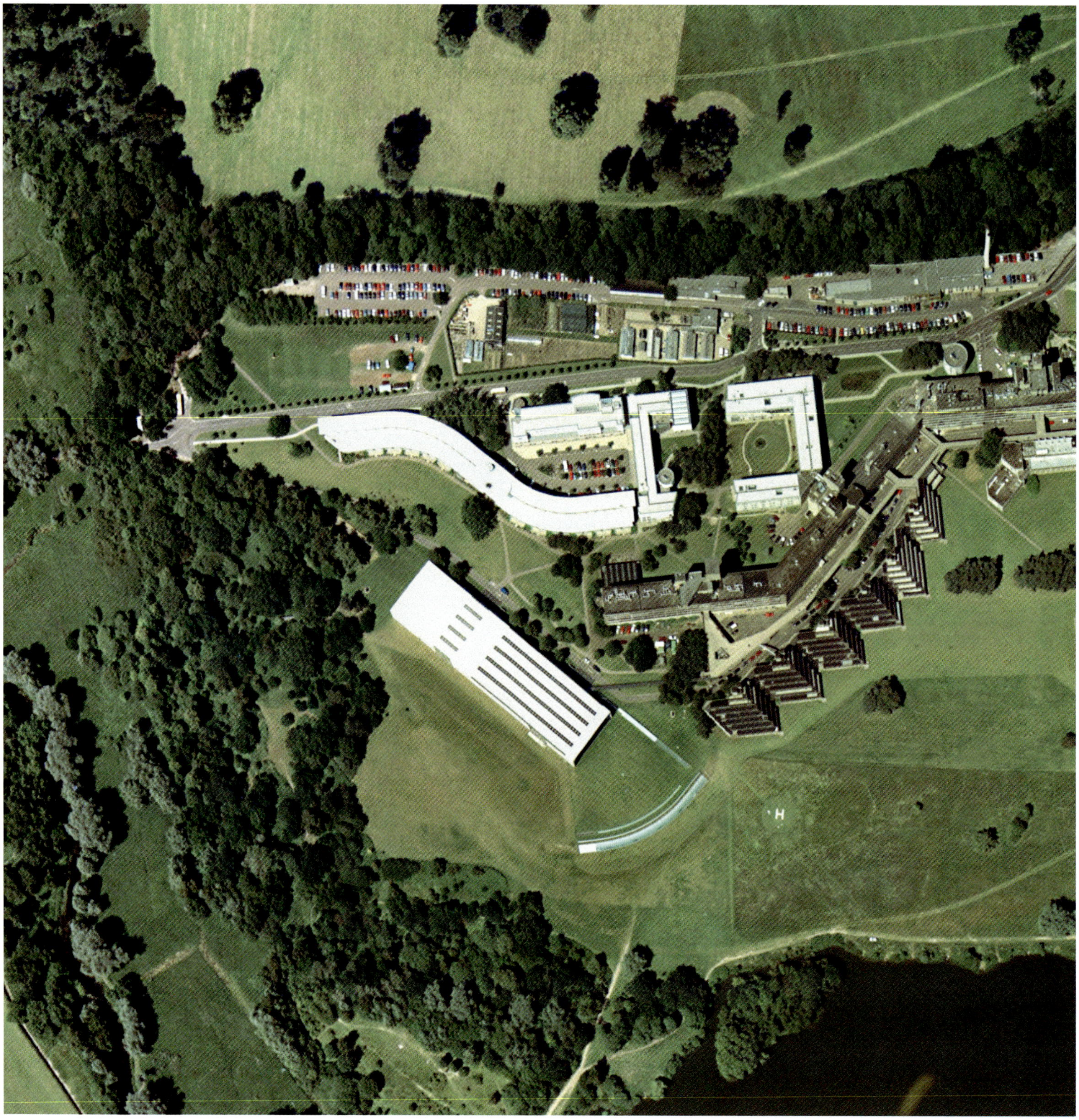

1

**Our work in the Sackler Galleries is clearly of its own time, using modern materials for modern ends. For me it demonstrates that contemporary interventions can enhance the old if they rely on sensitive juxtaposition rather than pastiche. In retrospect, the Royal Academy was almost a dress rehearsal for the Reichstag. It was also the first in a line of projects to pursue a clear philosophy about contemporary interventions in historical structures – establishing a meaningful relationship between old and new.** Norman Foster, *Rebuilding the Reichstag*, 2000
Left: The Sackler Galleries at the Royal Academy (1985-1991) designed at the same time as the Crescent Wing.
Right: The Reichstag (1992-1999).

In its final form, the plan combines an area of rectangular spaces connected by corridors – a projection of the footprint of the 1970s basement – counterpoised by the curve of the office wing. The space housing the reserve collection is curved to the east, where it abuts a ramp down to the lecture room. By setting the offices back from the external edge and providing access to them along a generous curved gallery on the perimeter, the need for an artificially lit internal corridor is removed, while the offices remain generously daylit.

## The Crescent Wing can be seen both to acknowledge the 'classic' status of its neighbour, and to reflect a developing attitude to context in Foster's work.

Since the Crescent Wing was conceived as ancillary to the original Sainsbury Centre, the need for a separate entrance might not seem obvious. However, the client insisted on separate access to the Crescent Wing, with the result that it offers a quite distinct experience from that of the main building. Architecturally, the decision allowed for a dramatic device: the long, glass-roofed ramp leading to a reception area which – far from being the dark underground space one might expect – opens dramatically onto a panorama of the lake beyond. From the reception area, the visitor can choose to go into the lecture room/gallery or the reserve collection.

The entrance foyer is equally the frontis to the Centre's administrative offices. The typical visitor is not normally given access to the office corridor and has to be content with a tantalising glimpse along its curving length. Though there was a case for making this a public space and, perhaps, relocating the Centre's public café there from its existing location a floor above, the determination to stress the ancillary nature of the new building remained firm. All the principal visitor facilities remain in the Sainsbury Centre proper. It is the administrative – and some academic – staff who benefit from the daylight and the views in this instance.

When the foyer is left behind and the visitor enters the enclosed world of the lecture room or reserve collection, the transition from 'above' to 'below' is total. This is as far as most people will go. Beyond is a secure zone of stores, workshops and laboratories, tailored to the specific needs of curators, conservators and technicians, and merging seamlessly with the 1970s undercroft. Yet there is nothing mean or second-rate about these spaces: indeed, they are generous in scale, well finished and well lit without being extravagant in detail or finish.

While the Sainsbury Centre is not air-conditioned, relying instead on natural ventilation, in the Crescent Wing extensive mechanical ventilation and cooling was always inevitable. Sophisticated extraction and filtration systems are required in the workshops and laboratories to cope with chemical fumes and dust, and to comply with health and safety regulations. However, because of the highly insulative nature of the building's turfed roof, the office spaces can be naturally ventilated, rather than air-conditioned, and they are each fitted with mechanically adjustable blinds to give individual occupants a degree of control over their environment.

1. An aerial view of the UEA campus, which shows the Sainsbury Centre and the Crescent Wing in context. Although designed on seemingly opposing principles, the two buildings have combined to create a composition that appears almost inevitable – a duality that Norman Foster has characterised as 'the cave and the tent'. It is also interesting to compare this view with that on page 379 and to see how Rick Mather's new University buildings make an inflection to the Sainsbury Centre of another kind by curving away respectfully.

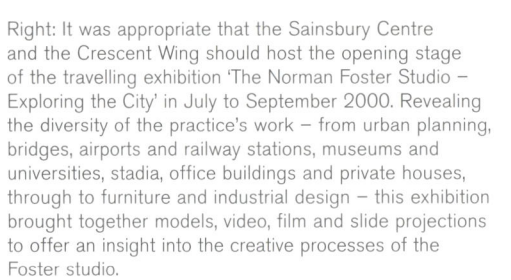

Right: It was appropriate that the Sainsbury Centre and the Crescent Wing should host the opening stage of the travelling exhibition 'The Norman Foster Studio – Exploring the City' in July to September 2000. Revealing the diversity of the practice's work – from urban planning, bridges, airports and railway stations, museums and universities, stadia, office buildings and private houses, through to furniture and industrial design – this exhibition brought together models, video, film and slide projections to offer an insight into the creative processes of the Foster studio.

The external face of the Crescent Wing is the curved, glazed wall looking out over the green parkland. Initially, this was designed to consist of vertical glass panels. The addition of a sloping bank of louvres was a device that not only helped to mould the elevation to the contours of the land, but was, in fact, also functionally necessary to act as a sun screen. By using fritted glass, a material pioneered by the practice to combat solar gain, Foster was subsequently able to dispense with the louvres and substitute inclined panes of glass – a far more elegant solution.

The engineering of this wall was far from straightforward, however. It was explored in drawings, models and finally in the form of a full-size mock-up. The double-glazed elevation also had to accommodate a fire escape door, but this has been successfully inserted in a way that does not disturb the serenity of the great sweep of glazing.

**In retrospect, the move away from a strictly rectilinear geometry seems forward-looking, a step towards a freer and more organic architecture and to themes that would become more apparent in the practice's architecture of the mid-1990s.**

Achieving a balance between natural and artificial lighting was a key element in the success of the final scheme. The flat, grass roof is pierced by five flush circular roof-lights, which bring daylight into internal workshop spaces. Daylight also floods into the depths of the building down the length of the long ramp. In contrast, the lecture room/gallery space is entirely artificially-lit. Indeed, it contains a highly sophisticated lighting system, which is adaptable to a wide variety of uses and occasions, thus providing a valuable learning resource for students of museum design.

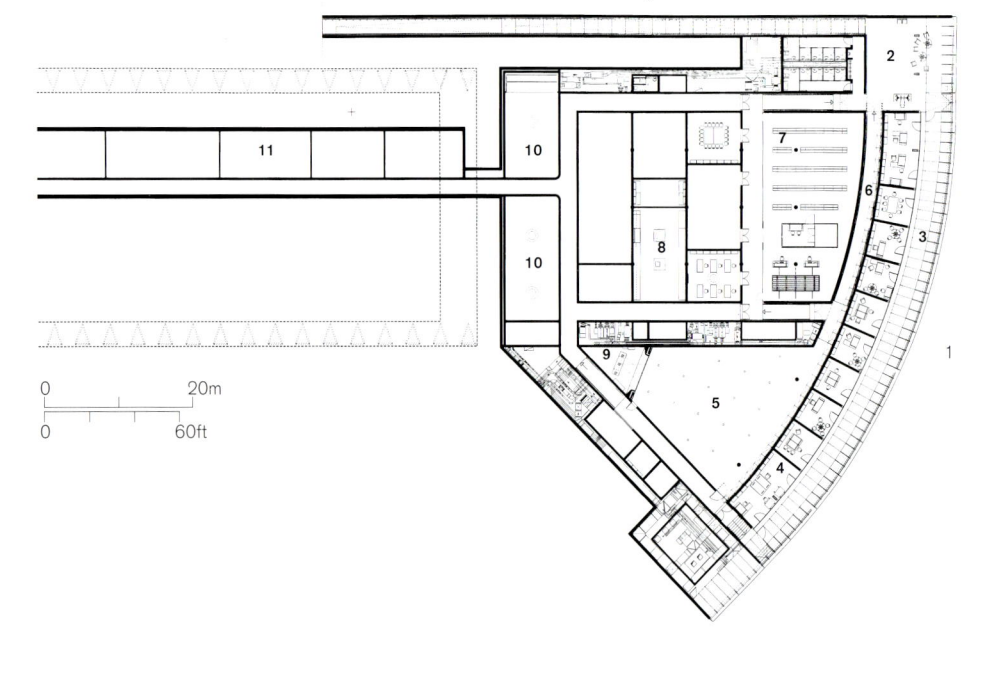

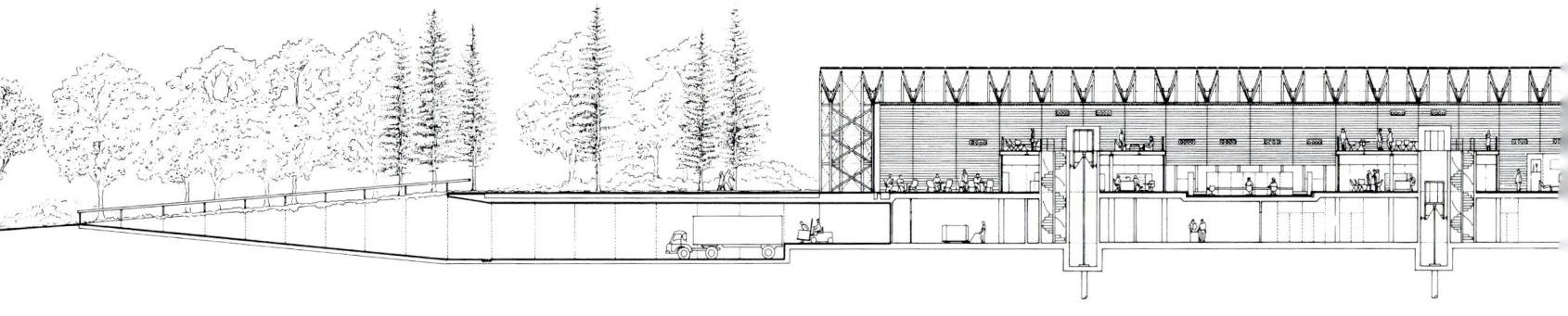

**The decisive shift in Norman Foster's work in the last decade has been a broadening of perspective. The studio has moved beyond a preoccupation with crafting the individual building and begun to operate at the scale of the city, as well as the spoon. In so doing it has of course drawn on concerns that were present in the practice's thinking even in the earliest days.** Deyan Sudjic, introduction to *On Foster … Foster On*, the book that accompanied the exhibition 'The Norman Foster Studio – Exploring the City' at the Sainsbury Centre, 2000

Lighting elsewhere ranges from recessed floor uplighters, on the entrance ramp, to low-voltage spots in the office corridor. Taking its cue from the Sainsbury Centre, all is carefully thought through to ensure the Crescent Wing makes highly effective but unshowy use of advanced building technology.

It would be easy to see the Crescent Wing as a symbol of changing attitudes to architecture in Britain between the 1970s and 1990s. By 1991, when the building was completed, Foster's Willis Faber building in Ipswich had been listed Grade I – ranking it alongside the likes of Ely Cathedral and Westminster Abbey. The merits of good contemporary architecture had begun to be perceived, and the value of modern 'classics' understood.

In assuming a character quite distinct from that of the Sainsbury Centre proper, the Crescent Wing can be seen to acknowledge the 'classic' status of its neighbour, and to reflect a developing attitude to historical context in Foster's work. This is manifested in projects such as the Sackler Galleries, inserted within the fabric of the Royal Academy, in London, and opened in the same year as the Crescent Wing, and more forcefully in the design of the rebuilt Reichstag, where new and old are elegantly juxtaposed. The fact that, in this case, the immediate context – more important than the landscape, or the much respected work of Lasdun – was an earlier building by Foster himself was immaterial, if a little ironic.

Foster's own description of the opposing relationship between the new and the old – the 'cave' and the 'tent' – is telling. The original Sainsbury Centre building is notable for its clarity, immediacy and single-mindedness. The overriding idea behind the building is expressed with a strength and conviction that overcomes the conflicting demands of a multiplicity of uses, subordinating all to a calm serenity.

The classical, even Platonic, qualities of the original building have been the subject of extended critical comment. It sits in the landscape with all the assurance of a Palladian country house. The Crescent Wing is, by comparison, reticent, subtle, complex, linked to its parent building yet with a life of its own.

From the south-east, the Sainsbury Centre now rises not from the grass, as it once did, but from a sweeping man-made ridge of glass, catching the sunlight by day and brilliantly lit after dark. Seen in this light, the Crescent Wing can be read not so much as the solid podium on which the Centre sits but as a narthex in the tradition of that which fronts the Romanesque cathedral at Durham. The visitor walking across the grass roof is unaware of the building below until he reaches the crest of the ridge and peers over the balustrade – a feature of aerodynamic elegance – onto the inclined planes of glass below.

Kenneth Powell

1. Invisible to the public, the Crescent Wing's stores and workshops serve as a continuation of the private world of the Sainsbury Centre's undercroft. The conservation laboratories form the core of the plan, around which are arrayed service areas, the reserve gallery and offices, and the multi-purpose gallery. Circulation is generous enough to ensure large works of art can be moved between the various areas with the maximum of ease.

   1 entrance ramp
   2 reception
   3 glazed corridor
   4 offices
   5 multi-purpose gallery
   6 internal corridor
   7 reserve gallery
   8 conservation laboratories
   9 projection room
   10 workshops
   11 original service area

2. This long section through the Sainsbury Centre and the Crescent Wing demonstrates how the extension forms a logical continuation of the undercroft level of the existing building.

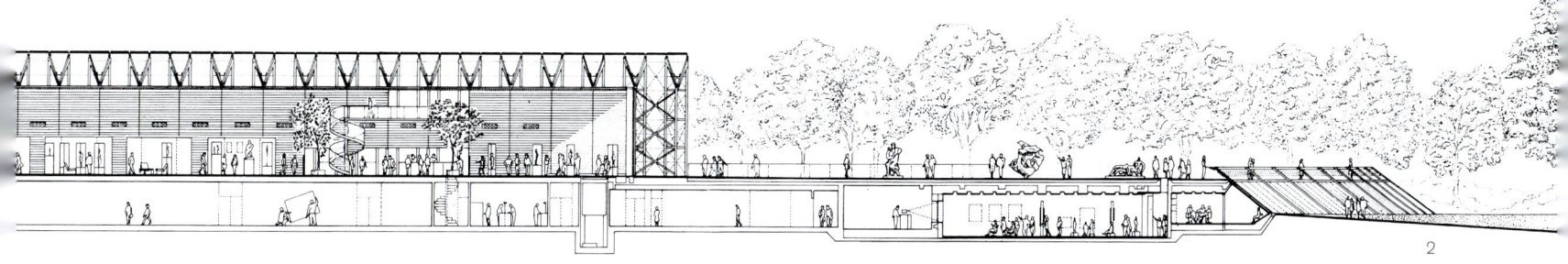

Right: The Reserve Collection Study Centre at the Metropolitan Museum of Art, in New York: a key reference point for Sir Robert and Lady Sainsbury in creating a brief for the Crescent Wing.

**Inside, the new wing is coldly impressive. The study collection is housed in jewel-like cases – beautifully made and lit. The conservation workshops, photographic studios and storage spaces are all so lavish and state-of-the-art as to make most museum curators salivate in envy.**
Alastair Best, *The Independent*, 8 May 1991

The Crescent Wing offers a generous and ingenious response to the prime requirement of the project brief – the expansion of the Sainsbury Centre's Reserve Collection study area, workshops and laboratories.

1, 3, 4. Items in the Reserve Collection are housed under the best environmental conditions in glass cases of various sizes, suitable for two and three-dimensional works, large and small. To maximise space, many of the cases were modified from the Bruynzeel storage system more usually used for books or files, allowing them to be stacked in groups and rolled out only when required. A specially-designed lighting system, in which the lamps are incorporated into easily demountable panels, has been installed throughout. The system offers a high degree of flexibility, and allows almost any lighting effect to be created.

2. New laboratories provide the Sainsbury Centre with state-of-the-art conservation facilities.

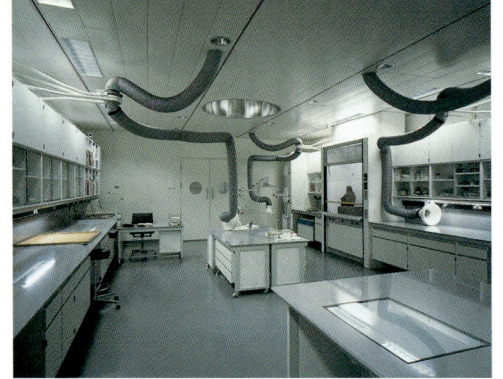

Close by is a spacious conservation room, quite unlike the cramped holes to which conservators are so often relegated, and a de-infestation room where exhibits can be deep frozen in order to rid them of their unwelcome visitors. Apart from all that, the study reserve is breathtaking. Glazed cabinets house the three-dimensional pieces, whilst rows of mechanically moveable frames, equalled only by the Metropolitan Museum in New York, house the larger two-dimensional work. Tony Warner, *Arts Review*, July 1991

The interior of the building, finished almost exclusively in non-reflective white, exudes an air of space-age hygiene. Low light levels, simple lines and hushed corridors prevail. Matthew Coomber, *Building*, 24 May 1991

Environmental controls are increasingly important in all buildings, not only art galleries. The new Crescent Wing is effectively an underground building, and for this reason it achieves a rate of heat loss only about one third of that of a conventional above-ground structure. Norman Foster, Tate Gallery lecture, London, 20 February 1991

Standing on this lawn, looking towards the lake, or from inside the original building, the new wing is virtually undetectable. Only the slender guardrail calls attention to its presence. However, from the lakeside the effect is dramatically reversed. The Sainsbury Centre now stands at the top of a shining cliff of glazing, which apparently lifts it above its drab neighbours. It seems that Foster's Parthenon has at last found its Acropolis. David Jenkins, *The Architects' Journal*, 8 May 1991

I have a concern to create spaces which work at different levels of experience – both functionally and aesthetically – spaces that might appeal to a wider range of our senses. I have a particular passion for natural light and how it can inform and enhance the architectural experience. Norman Foster, in conversation with Marc Emery, 1986

The only big gesture, ironically, is something the public will not see: the corridor that sweeps round in a curve beneath the glass windscreen. Tiger-striped with shadow, this is a marvellous piece of pure abstraction. Alastair Best, *The Independent*, 8 May 1991

1. Accentuating the streamlined form of the glass crescent, the protective handrail was formed by extending the mullions up to meet a generously wide ledge, perfect for leaning on and enjoying the view.

2. The 70-metre ramp linking the Sainsbury Centre to the new wing sinks gently into the landscape, protected only by a minimal glass enclosure. Underfloor heating ensures that it can never ice up in winter.

3. During the day the glazed corridor that provides access to the offices is an ethereal space dominated by its silent sweeping view over the Norfolk countryside.

**By exploiting the slope of the land away from the original building towards the lake it has been possible to gain an extraordinary lightness inside the building. The crescent of glass provides an uninterrupted view without itself constituting a visual obstruction, rather like the eighteenth-century device of the ha-ha wall.** Norman Foster, Tate Gallery lecture, London, 20 February 1991
Left: Sir Robert and Lady Sainsbury with Graham Phillips, project architect, on one of many site visits.

The Crescent Wing

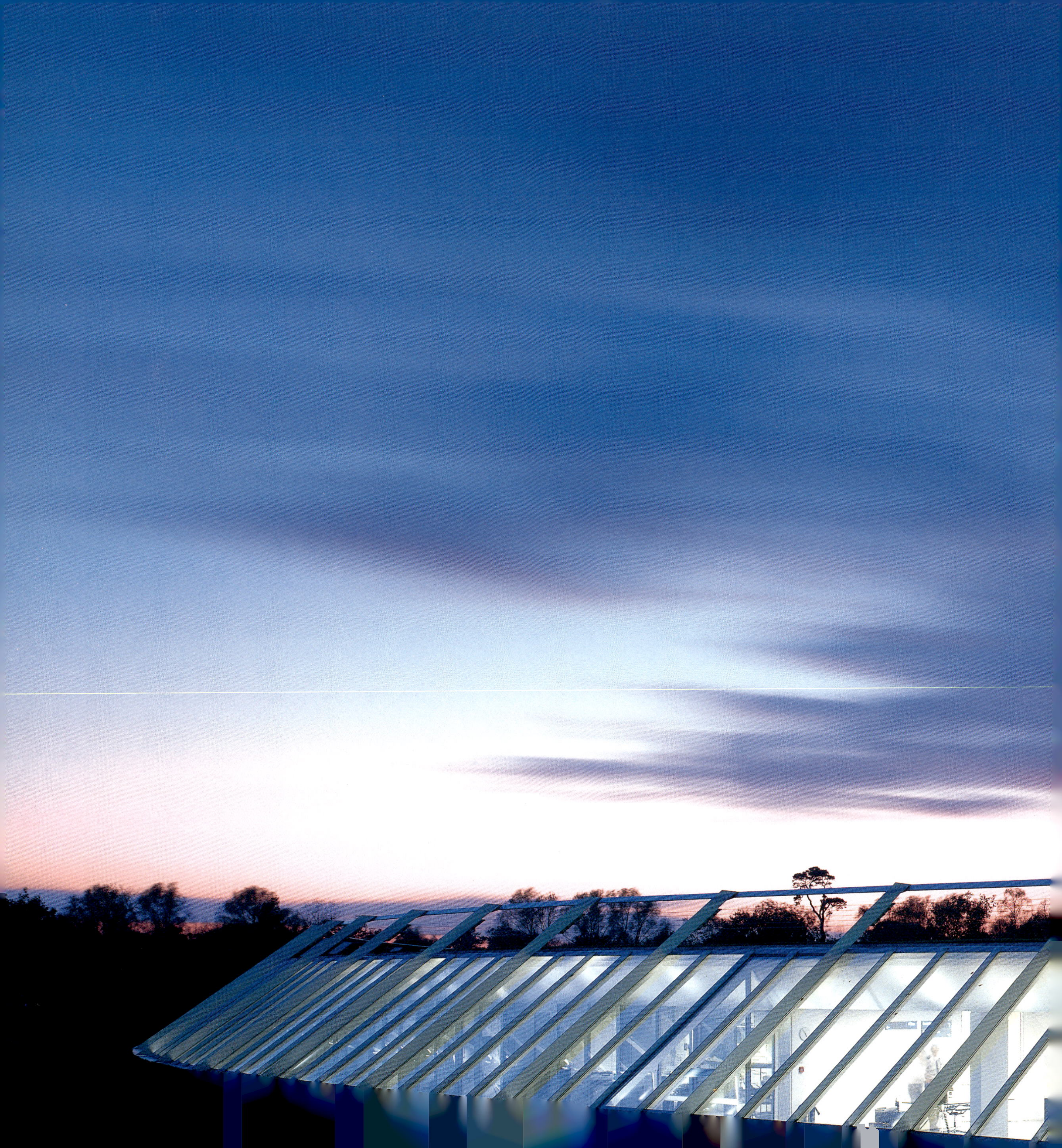

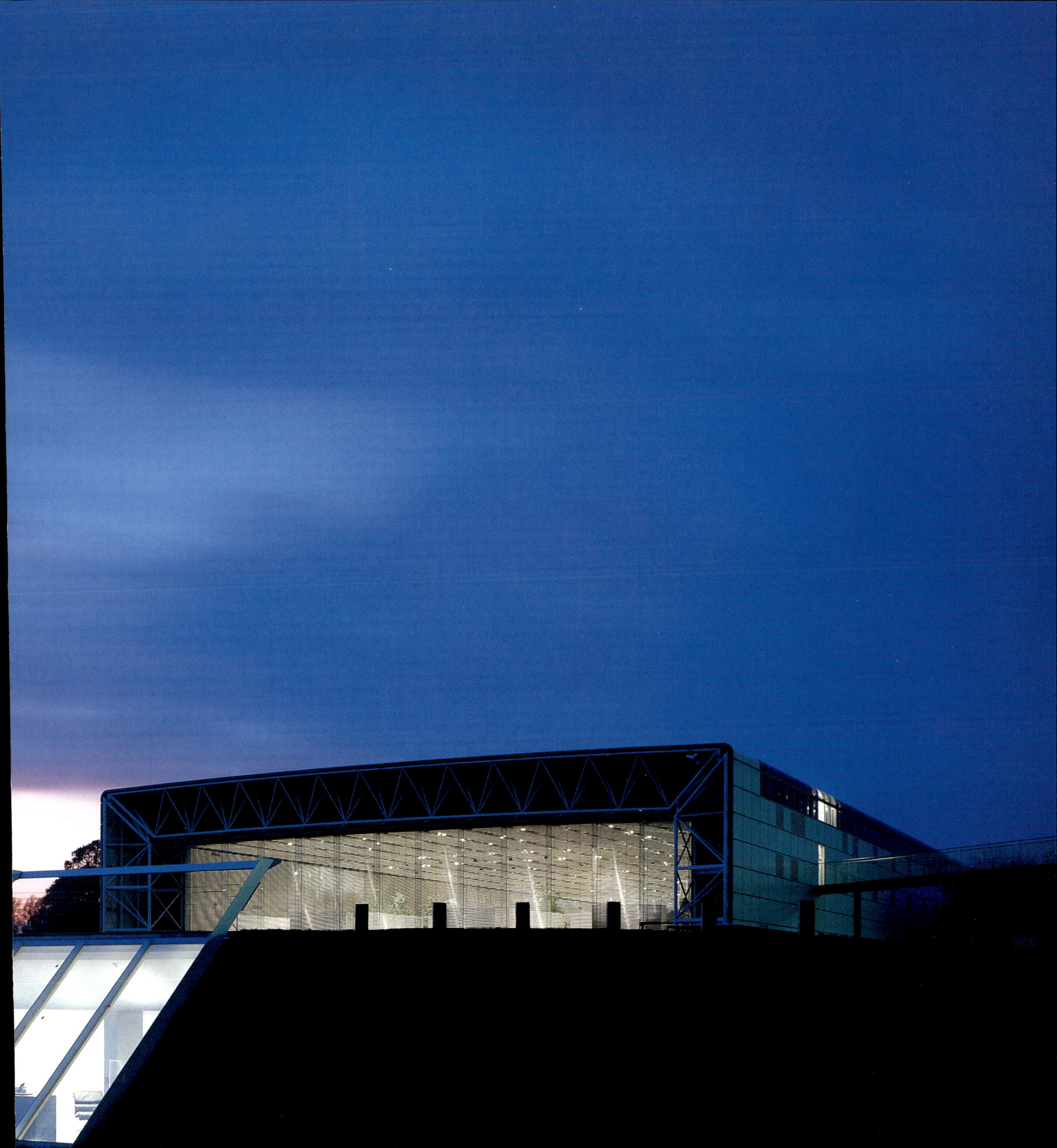

# Beyond the Yellow Bicycle
Reyner Banham 1985

It gives me, I think the right phrase is, peculiar pleasure, to be back in my home town and on this once sacred turf where I learned not the three 'Rs' but the three 'Ss'. One of those Ss was sledging. You can work out what the others were for yourselves. And it has also been of great interest to see how on this ancient turf this university has developed.

In the context of what had already been built here, the appearance of Norman Foster as the architect of the Sainsbury Centre was, I think, something of a surprise. Although given certain fancies and intellectual attitudes of what were once called the 'swinging sixties', the steady drift towards High-tech and high-finish as against the brut concrete, with which we began here, was only to be expected.

Nevertheless Foster was a strange choice in some ways because he is, or has been until the Hongkong Bank, among the least monumentally inclined of British architects. Or at least of that generation that tried to find an alternative to the precepts of an older Modernism by looking towards another kind of architecture, without following the Postmodernist retreat into the reassuring safety of historical revivalism, historical reminiscence, or quite frankly stylistic nostalgia. That is not an impossible route to go. The recent performances of James Stirling – particularly the Staatsgalerie in Stuttgart – show what a thoroughly modern architect can do with a body of historical knowledge, which he is prepared to apply in forms that quite clearly reveal their historicism, whatever else is going on.

But in some ways I think that the most interesting group – because they have operated largely against the fashionable tide – have been those so-called High-tech architects, Norman Foster and Richard Rogers, together with one or two slightly 'behind the scenes' people such as Cedric Price.

Somewhere in the middle of all this there stands a symbolic object, which suggested the title of this discourse. It is a yellow bicycle, leaning against the plate-glass window of the old Foster Associates office in Fitzroy Street. The yellow bicycle stands for many things in this set of references. It is a high performance device. It was not your ordinary old creaking Raleigh. It was a really flash, high-pressure, high-speed, pedal-back-up-to-Hampstead-in-two-minutes kind of bicycle. It was an elegant device in its own right, as all the better bicycles are. And its yellow colour was very much the flavour of the month. Or as someone said about the inhabitants of Foster's office in those days – 'all wearing the latest clothes and the moustache of the month'.

That point is worth emphasising. For Norman Foster, like Richard Rogers has been seen as a fashionable – one might say 'fashion-plate' – figure in some ways. But the seriousness, which one sometimes catches behind Foster's private utterances about architecture, has often been missed, especially by his critics. I think we might as well say right at the beginning, that 'yes, he has always been also a fashionable figure'. But the key word here is 'also'. To some extent I am going to use what you might call the decorative language, or the symbolic surface of his work, as a way of looking further into what seems to be going on.

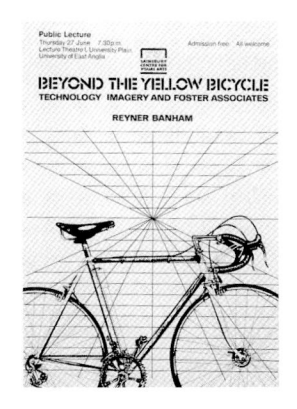

Left: The poster for Reyner Banham's lecture 'Beyond the Yellow Bicycle: Technology, Imagery and Foster Associates', delivered at the University of East Anglia on Thursday 27 June 1985. The bicycle in question is Norman Foster's own yellow racing model, which was habitually to be found outside the Fitzroy Street studio.

The visual character of the Sainsbury Centre, for example, is something that is thoroughly familiar to all Norfolk dumplings like myself. It is a large metal shed. The idea that this is somehow alien to the Norfolk scene, or not in the local vernacular is hogwash. It is one of the most thoroughly Norfolk buildings put up since Norwich Cathedral. It is the sort of metal shed that we — Western civilisation — covered the County in, particularly between 1939 and 1945. Stored therein were hay, B24s, poison gas and other engaging objects of that kind.

More than that it is also a mechanically serviced shed, as so many of our major agricultural monuments have been. It's a building that puts its remarkably sparse provision of machinery clearly on view. The London art critics mistook those devices hung over the entrance for air conditioners, whereas, of course, they are merely ventilators, for the building is not humidity controlled.

One could think through a number of very interesting points about the Sainsbury Centre. For instance, three quarters of its mass is below ground level. Although it is widely regarded as a super-High-tech, high-energy building, if you weigh it out, it is nothing of the sort. It is for the most part made of mineral materials extracted from the earth, bashed around a bit, mixed with water and poured back into the earth; it is a thoroughly traditional building for at least three quarters of its weight. Nevertheless what appears above ground makes certain challenges, offers certain promises: it is far from being an ordinary or old-fashioned kind of building.

Foster, in his lectures and literature, has always illustrated what for him have become symbolic or ritual objects. They are drawn not just from High-tech — I mean real tech-tech, not how architects believe high technology to be — but from an extraordinarily wide range. He will, for example, juxtapose a Vulcan bomber from the middle 1950s (an aircraft that could only do what it could do, by burning enormous quantities of fossil fuel) with a Caproni sailplane which does what it does without consuming any energy at all once it's up and flying. It flies almost on pure intellectual power. Seriously, it takes brains and sensibility, but not gasoline, to fly a glider.

I don't know which of these objects Norman actually admires the most. I think probably the glider. Of all the high performance objects that have passed through his hands, the glider more than anything else has satisfied his imagination, yet stretched it at the same time. Certainly it is the one about which he has raved loudest in my hearing. He did it leaning out of his Range Rover at the top of Tottenham Court Road. I was on my bicycle. It was an extremely dangerous location. And like the Ancient Mariner he held me there with glittering eye while he raved on about the Caproni while everything around us hooted and wailed and screamed. You know when you meet a real enthusiast.

**Norman Foster has been seen as a fashionable figure in some ways. But the seriousness behind Foster's private utterances about architecture, has often been missed by his critics. We might as well say right at the beginning, that 'yes, he has always been also a fashionable figure'. But the key word here is 'also'.**

But once you start looking at Foster's habitual mosaic of such images, there are some seemingly major visual contradictions. These two particular examples are objects of rather snug and tidy outlines. As indeed they must be because they pass through that elastic but pestiferous medium, the air. But you will also find things like this, which don't have to pass through the air, which are all legs and knobs and excrescences. They do not seem to satisfy the fairly obvious canon of elegance, which you can see is his inspiration in the airborne flying machine.

1. The Sainsbury Centre for Visual Arts (1974-1978). The building's relationship to its surroundings has led many commentators, including Banham, to describe it as shed-like, while its visual character invites comparisons with smooth-skinned aircraft and other such sleekly aerodynamic forms.

**The Caproni was the hottest two-seater sailplane at that particular time – it was unparalleled in terms of performance, but it was also a really beautiful object. Norman and I were lucky enough to be members of a consortium that jointly owned the only such sailplane in the country at the time and we put it to good use!** John Jeffries, in conversation with the editor, February 2002
Right: On 17 August 1975, flying their Caproni A-21S, Norman Foster and John Jeffries established the UK record for a 300km goal and return flight in a multi-seater sailplane.

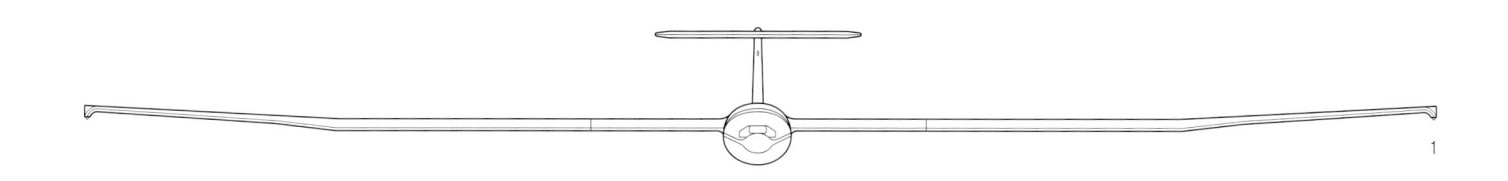

1-3. The Caproni Vizzola A-21S sailplane, whose superior aerodynamic characteristics and elegant profile have been a constant source of inspiration for Norman Foster. Caproni built its first glider in 1908 at its factory in Vizzola, in Italy, and manufactured the A-21S – designed in 1969 by Carlo Ferrarin and Livio Sonzio – between 1970 and 1982. This twin seater glider has a 20.38 metre wingspan and weighs approximately 450 kilograms. Its unique combination of a metal frame and fibreglass fuselage made for an extremely high-performance aircraft, capable of speeds of up to 65 miles per hour. It made its maiden flight on 23 November 1970, almost immediately establishing new world records for speed and distance. Approximately one hundred A-21Ss were built by Caproni and only one was imported to Britain in the late 1970s; Norman Foster owned a share in this glider. Although Caproni Vizzola ceased to operate in 1982 the A-21S is still produced by the German company Gomolzig.

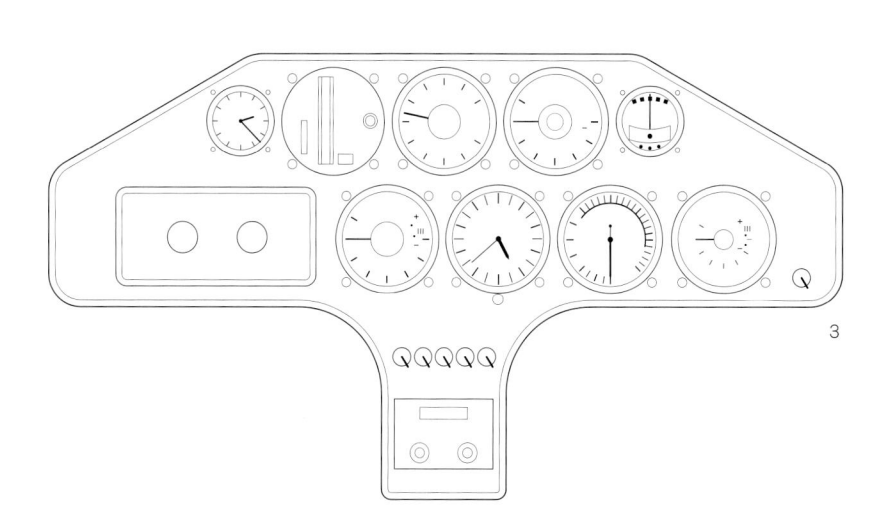

**If, at their peak, architecture and flight are about the spirit as well as physical practicalities, and the outcome of that fusion is a beautiful object, then there are links between architecture and aviation – even if one form is earthbound and the other traverses the earth.** Norman Foster, essay accompanying the First Day Cover of five Royal Mail postage stamps celebrating the 'Architecture of the Air', June 1997

Far left: The delta-winged Vulcan bomber of 1952.
Left: The Caproni sailplane which, as Reyner Banham speculates, Foster probably admires the most.

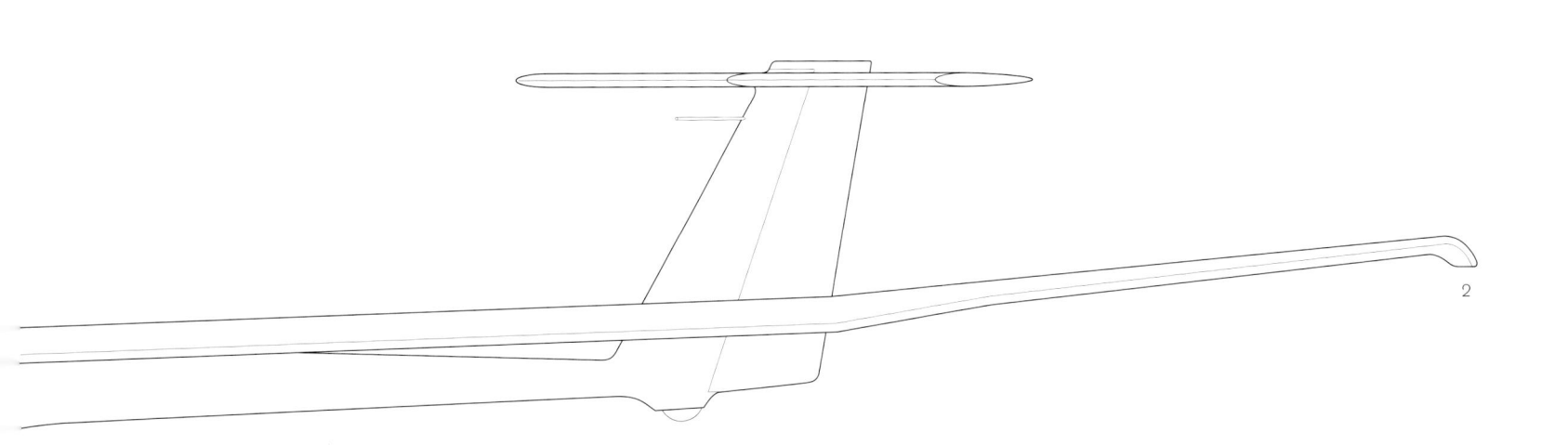

**Foster, in his lectures, has always illustrated what for him have become symbolic or ritual objects. He will, for example, juxtapose a Vulcan bomber with a Caproni sailplane which does what it does without consuming any energy at all once it's up and flying. It flies almost on pure intellectual power. Seriously, it takes brains and sensibility, but not gasoline, to fly a glider.**
Reyner Banham

Beyond the Yellow Bicycle 453

**Reyner Banham's background was as an engineer, and his training in the scholarship of art history at the Courtauld Institute represents two cultures that normally never come together ... but there is also another ingredient, which is special to Banham, and that is the entertainment value of his commentary, which always comes with some serious point just below the surface.** Norman Foster, introduction to the film 'Reyner Banham loves Los Angeles', shown on BBC 1 on 1 May 1988

These space vehicles seem almost to be the work of a different race of beings. Certainly they are the products of a different frame of mind. They do, however, have an elegance of their own. One, for example, is largely covered in gold leaf – a decorative effect more commonly associated with the Middle Ages or the Byzantine Empire. The American space operation decided to take that same material to the moon. How elegant can you get?

Whatever Foster derives from such sources of inspiration, it is not simply a language of forms to copy, or work over, or redo in the guise of architecture. Although that is, of course, a deeply ingrained twentieth-century tradition. Architects have long imitated the forms of advanced technology.

Foster, in contrast, starting from objects of this kind, appears to go off in a completely different direction. In fact, one supposes that these leggy bits and pieces are a side issue – objects of pure admiration – because his work, such as the Sainsbury Centre, most frequently takes the form of fairly snugly enclosed containers: if you must make formal comparisons in Foster's work, then it is more akin to a smooth-skinned aircraft than to NASA space vehicles.

One of the first sizeable products of Foster's practice was the Modern Art Glass warehouse, of 1972-1973. Like the Sainsbury Centre, of which it is the true ancestor, it is a very long metal shed. Its exterior cladding is corrugated metal. And in the middle of one side it has an extremely elegant door. I want to make only one point.

It is almost a standard, off-the-peg, as you find it, door. And somewhere lurking in the argument is the concept that out there, in real life land, beyond architecture, most of the things that you might need already exist. All you have to do is find them in the catalogue and go buy them.

It is something that Foster does not often do. But nevertheless it is a concept that has been effective in our times. I will come back to it later because it enables us to establish one position as a kind of polar opposite of the Foster approach.

But the door, as I say, is a standard off-the-peg affair. It is painted a standard industrial colour. And what makes the door elegant and decorative – the bright warning stripes across the bottom – are almost a standard set. Of course if they had been a standard set they would have been yellow and red. Not yellow and the base colour, the blue of the door. But all these are standard elements. They are things that exist outside the world of architecture and are simply and straightforwardly brought into that world. Simply and straightforwardly? Or is there some decorative intent in the way in which they have been worked upon?

It is interesting to compare this door with those of a standard factory unit building in Milton Keynes, for instance. What is the difference between the Foster and Milton Keynes examples? Well the real difference is that Foster thought of it first. And Milton Keynes is simply imitating. Furthermore, in Milton Keynes the whole thing quietly slides into a decorative symphony of muted colours. It is studiedly elegant but it is also derivative.

Now that we are in Milton Keynes another set of issues arises, chiefly concerning the so-called High-tech style and its history in our time. Milton Keynes, to me as an architectural historian, seems to be two things. It ought to be three things. That is to say, it is a question of whatever happened to that original permissive concept of its first planners, who saw Milton Keynes as, 'a modified Los Angeles system'? Hearing that celebrated phrase, practically every good grey town planner in England ran and hid. The idea that there should be anything orderly enough in Los Angeles as a system, and that it could be perceived and worse, modified, was anathema.

The first thing that Milton Keynes has become – and this is an English extension of an American catch-phrase in which Cambridge becomes Silicon Fen, Clydeside becomes Silicon Glen, and so on – is Silicon New Town. Secondly, it is also an extraordinary repository of the styles of the 1960s and 1970s. If you want to see what, on average, British architects think about the architecture of high technology, Milton Keynes is a great place to do it – that neat black glass box might look like a silicon chip plant, but you soon discover that it is in fact the town power station.

1

**The Digital Equipment Corporation designed in 1979 by M Arthur Gensler Associates ... is the ultimate black box; a rectangle of dark glass on a skinny plinth, standing in a mathematically precise plane of green lawn, interrupted only by the lower-case logo standing equally abstractly on its own plinth. And that's it ... a dark crystal on a green velvet mount.** Reyner Banham, *The Architectural Review*, May 1981

Left: Gensler Associates' Digital Equipment building, in Santa Clara, California, completed in 1979. As Banham observes, it is the direct descendant of Foster's pioneering 'black box' for IBM.

But it being, as it were, the most extreme form of the pure glass box – the pure black glass box – it makes an obvious connection to what you might almost call the 'International High-tech Style' as represented by the Digital Equipment Corporation, which actually is in Silicon Valley, in Santa Clara, California. The technology of the Digital building in fact is quite moderate. But it claims the anonymous elegance of the ultimate black box. After all it is not so long since 'black box' was probably the hottest topic in scientific thinking. Now of course it has been replaced by 'black hole'. It shows, I think, what has happened to Western attitudes in the science of the universe.

## IBM Cosham stands on almost nothing visible whatsoever. You just have a sheer glass wall.

The black box was something unknowable into which 'inputs' were put at one end and from which 'outputs' came at the other. You did not question what happened inside. The black hole alas, is something into which things are put, never to be seen again.

That anonymous black box is a simple building. It makes no great symbolic claims. Although over the door it says, 'through these portals pass only the finest computer engineers and programmers in the world.' With graphics like that you don't need to make architectural claims. It is one of the established images of high-technology architecture.

Question: Who thought of that? Answer: Foster Associates. Though the format here is rather different. Foster's building, the Advance Head Office building for IBM at Cosham, in Hampshire, completed in 1971 – eight years before Digital – is internally thoroughly conventional. The exterior, on the other hand, is an unbelievable performance. It is glass from top to bottom. There is almost no solid architecture visible. While Digital stands on a solid white brick plinth, IBM Cosham stands on almost nothing visible whatsoever. You just have a sheer glass wall. And most of what it does is reflect the surrounding landscape. It thus carries anonymity a stage further: when you look at it you see something else. It gives the building a very powerful image quality, of a very curiously negative or back to front kind, which Foster also exploited brilliantly in his Willis Faber & Dumas building in Ipswich, of 1970-1975.

What is offered here is the almost complete visual eclipse of the building. Foster is not alone in wishing to produce that kind of effect. High reflectivity is a fairly constant factor in high-technology architecture. For example, the WKBW Television in Buffalo, New York, completed in 1979 – the same year as Digital Industries – is entirely faced in satin finish stainless steel, which reflects spectacular sunsets across Lake Eerie. It is a photographer's joy. And it does seem to be saying something appropriate. That very high finish is still something that most people, particularly architects, feel appropriate to high technology.

1. Modern Art Glass (1972-1973), according to Banham the 'true ancestor' of the Sainsbury Centre. It is a steel portal-frame structure clad in profiled aluminium painted a distinctive blue. The double-height roller door is a proprietary component painted blue to match the cladding.

2. A presentation drawing of the glazed curtain wall at IBM Cosham (1970-1971) and its realisation in built form. The apparently insubstantial glass envelope is formed using aluminium box section glazing frames, with vertical mullions supporting 4 x 2 metre glass panels, tinted bronze. However no presentation drawing fully conveys the spectacular effect of the reflections produced by this glass skin.

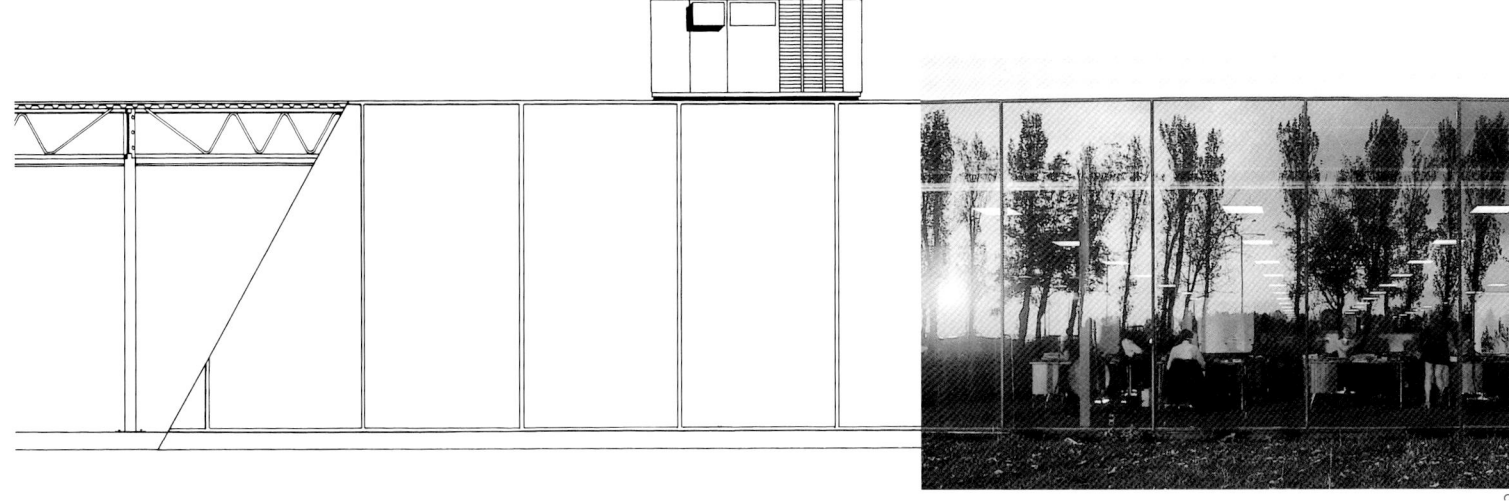

**The truest tradition of architecture is constructive, not decorative.** Reyner Banham, *New Society*, 28 July 1983

**The first High-tech buildings in Britain reflect mainly foreign influences. The seminal Reliance Controls factory of 1966, by Team 4, looks very Craig Ellwood, while Foster's subsequent projects again show clear inspiration from California, this time from the SCSD schools.** Peter Buchanan, *The Architectural Review*, July 1983

1. A photograph of Ezra Ehrenkrantz's iconic SCSD building was to be seen on the wall of Foster Associate's first studio in Bedford Street alongside images of the Foster's own buildings – evidence of its fundamental and lasting influence on the practice's design philosophy.

Those of us who have been engineers of course will know that engineers are not interested in finish, they are interested in its opposite which is tolerance. In other words engineers do not polish things for the sake of polishing them, they only polish them when they absolutely bloody have to. In fact engineers are chiefly concerned with seeing how bad a finish they can get away with and live to tell the tale. This is known in some quarters as the Australian aesthetic: 'She'll do'. As an aside here, there is a story that I think is worth telling occasionally. Norman Foster liked it very much when I told him, even though it goes against the grain of his kind of architecture.

During the Second World War the British Airforce decided that it could not make enough heavy machine guns to keep all those Spitfires and Hurricanes firing. They decided to use the American Browning 0.5 machine gun. They imported some to see what they were like, picked them up and they rattled. All loose bits inside. The Vickers people, who were going to manufacture them, were horrified. They said, 'We're going to make them into proper fine tolerances. Decent guns.' The Vickers version did not rattle. It also jammed solid after it had fired three rounds. Completely blocked up with black powder. The Americans knew, the Browning people knew, perfectly well what they were doing.

Generally speaking engineering is not interested in high finish. The appearance of high finish in engineering work has usually some very powerful economic or other cause, and not much to do with aesthetics. (But never quite, since all engineers think they have a good eye.) Take a straightforward engineering box, built to an engineering function, by those great American construction companies such as Butler. A standard Butler building is not made of particularly High-tech materials, although it is elegantly designed. It is an off-the-peg building of the utmost ordinariness. Nothing on the outside explains what it does at all. It just sits there buzzing quietly in the field. It doesn't even say Butler on it anywhere. It is one of the most anonymous structures there ever was. Put it in the right kind of landscape, however, and you suddenly begin to see what a good building it is.

But as I say, this attempt to deliver a completely neutral building is not such a brilliant ambition for an architect, unless he is in a situation where to be studiedly anonymous will in fact make oneself very visible. Anybody who is designing in those areas of human activity to which large tin sheds are native will, to some extent, have to pursue a rather interesting course, between being more anonymous than the competition or saying, 'to hell with it, let's do a shiny one, let's do a red one.' Or something like that.

The interesting thing is the way in which Foster has cut through this kind of thing. Take a look at the presentation drawings for IBM at Cosham. They could only be from the Foster office, they are so anonymous. The drawing shows sheets of glass. To the left it shows the internal structure, simple steel columns, simple steel zigzag trusses. On top, in red, is an air-conditioner pack.

That formula of columns, trusses and service packs is probably the most common in the whole world. Because outside peasant or tribal vernaculars it is how an ordinary American commercial building is made – quick, cheap and nasty – from exactly those elements. Now one sees what Foster has done. Taking those elements and turning them into something which is not cheap and nasty. You can see how he has transformed it. But the basic proposition is the same. It was the discovery out there in real life land – outside architecture – of how people were really building buildings in North America, which did as much as anything else to lay the foundations of what we nowadays regard as High-tech, architect-designed architecture.

> I think the SCSD system is very misunderstood because it is sadly associated with deep-plan schools. But the real liberation of the system was that it allowed you not to get hooked in any one particular corner; instead it has the capability of creating very very traditional plans as well as deep plans and courtyards. Norman Foster, 'Delight in Design' lecture, University of East Anglia, 27 November 1978

> With projects such as Willis Faber & Dumas and the Sainsbury Centre the concept of developing components was very much part of our thinking. This approach was influenced a lot by Norman and his education in the US. For example, projects like the California Schools by Ezra Ehrenkrantz were known to all of us. That ethos was very prevalent in the practice at the time. David Nelson, in conversation with Malcolm Quantrill, 1999

The translation from the ordinary and ugly to the elegant and sophisticated was made by one particular project – the School Construction System Development (SCSD) – designed by a team led by Ezra Ehrenkrantz, who had been here in England. It is interesting how the story loops back like that. Ehrenkrantz was in England in the middle and late 1950s, working with the Building Research Station down in Hertfordshire on things like the mathematics of interchangeable parts.

## Ehrenkrantz's SCSD system took the standard form of American supermarket construction and raised it to the level of extremely elegant architecture.

Ehrenkrantz's system took the standard form of American supermarket construction and raised it up to the level of extremely elegant architecture. His delicious little prototype is still there, standing in one corner of the Stanford campus, one of the great forgotten treasures of California. It became in 1964 the beau ideal of every young technology-minded architect on both sides of the Atlantic. Its influence on Foster and Rogers and others was absolutely enormous. It suddenly cleared up a whole lot of questions and above all it demonstrated a way of making sense of the rising tide of mechanical services, which was threatening to engulf architecture as we have known it. But as one of the design team said to me recently, 'Thank goodness we were in the corner of the campus, otherwise we would have had to do it Spanish colonial or possibly Lombardic.'

Ehrenkrantz contained most of the building's mechanical services in that deep overhanging roof slab – something that has been a mainstay of Foster thinking almost ever since. Foster's most elaborately worked out version of it can be seen in the Sainsbury Centre. All the gizmology is packed into about the depth of the trusses in the roof and walls. Tidied away. Made neat. Made anonymous.

Interestingly, the Rogers version of how to do this was almost literally to let it all hang out. If you compare Foster's approach with that of Piano and Rogers' Centre Pompidou in Paris, then the last thing that the Centre Pompidou wanted to do was to hide the gizmology. It is the architecture of that building. Sure there is a framework that holds things up – boring old horizontal floors for human beings to walk about on while looking at works of art. But to hell with it. Let all the gizmology – all the coloured ducts and things, all the people movers – drape down the outside.

But again its sources are American, although you will not find them in the history books. It only dawned on me fairly recently that the sources of the Pompidou aesthetic are to be found at Huntington Beach in California, in the power stations for Southern California Edison, designed by the Bechtel Corporation. They are great baroque exercises in piping and ducting. Now I can almost produce photographic evidence of at least three of the people (all members of the Chrysalis group in those days) who worked on Centre Pompidou with Richard Rogers standing looking at the Huntington Beach Power Station. Here is a complete vocabulary of forms for dealing with things like ducting and ventilating which have, as it were, the warrant of not being the product of architectural fantasy, but the result of strictly calculated, totally objective engineering thinking.

2. Ezra Ehrenkrantz's SCSD prototype on the campus of Stanford University (1964). The SCSD programme was to prove a key inspiration for Norman Foster, demonstrating that a standardised method of construction could be both supremely elegant and extremely cost effective.

**In contrast to Richard Rogers, whose work is an elaboration and a celebration of structure and connection, Foster's is about refinement, the omission of the inessential, smooth skins and sparing palettes.** Deyan Sudjic, 'Foster Mark Three', 1996

**Returning from America, some young English architects knew that they could and should make an architecture that was of the future – now ... Archigram emerged as the mouthpiece of this philosophy, Richard Rogers and Norman Foster emerged as its fashioners and engineers Peter Rice and Anthony Hunt emerged as its boffins. There was no need for a detached avant-garde: time for that could not be wasted if the future was really to happen – now.** Peter Cook, The Architectural Review, July 1983

1. The aerodynamic form of the Sainsbury Centre exemplifies a High-tech architecture that is both fully articulated and discreetly sophisticated. The building's truss structure is largely concealed beneath a sleek panel cladding system, but is revealed at either end of the building to frame full-height glazed walls.

These forms come from outside architecture. Somehow they have the authority that mere personal invention or fancy could not give them, which is perhaps why they are so admired by Foster. Now I've been an engineer and I know where this stuff is coming from. It is a path that I find it necessary to walk very warily indeed. But everybody from Le Corbusier and before has believed it. I wonder whether Corbusier ever met any engineers. Particularly as he describes them somewhere as, 'sane, virile, healthy'. He's got to be joking!

Engineers believe their eyes and their fantasies even in defiance of the facts. I remember when I worked for a Bristol airplane company. I was standing outside on the tarmac one day with my foreman, a chargehand who had been in the business for many years. We looked away to our left and there was the first Lockheed Constellation we had ever seen coming in slowly to land. The aircraft had a curious kind of droopy sausage shape. And he looked up at it and he said, 'Look at that bloody thing. That'll never bloody fly.' There it was 500 feet above ground having just flown the Atlantic. But I know exactly what he meant. It was an aesthetic offence to that man.

Engineers do have aesthetic sensibilities. They don't just admire sunsets and all the other anti-engineer jokes. But nevertheless people outside the art and mystery of engineering are inclined to endow their inventions, their forms, their usages with an aura of necessity and to admire them for it.

**In the Sainsbury Centre all the gizmology is packed into about the depth of the trusses in the roof and walls. Tidied away. Made neat. Made anonymous. Interestingly, the Rogers version of how to do this was almost literally to let it all hang out.**

Now this idea of objective engineering can be interpreted in another way. Since the beginning of the 1920s, there has been a suspicion in architecture that everything you need is already out there in the catalogue, if you know where to look. You don't have to keep designing things. All you have to do is design buildings.

I suppose the greatest exponent of this is Cedric Price. He plays this idea for, as it were, the folkloric virtues of ordinary objects, which have not been designed by people such as Michelangelo, nor by Norman Foster, or anybody you've ever heard of. Things like standard staircases, doors, windows and stuff like that, which anybody can go out and buy. His Interaction Centre is probably as High-tech a building as anything we've seen so far, with the possible exception of the power stations. It is put together out of perfectly ordinary stuff. And I think he would see that as its main virtue.

Nobody has wasted time designing things that don't need to be designed. The nut and bolt have already been invented and there is a huge amount of useful stuff out there. Already existing. Designed down to, or up to, economical standards, safety regulations and things like that. All you have to do is go out and buy it and bolt it together. Although you have to be some kind of genius to bolt it together in the way that Cedric Price does.

**Archigram were, simply, too avant-garde and at least a decade before their time. But their wilful and sometimes jokey 'impossibilities' have been crucial to two generations of real architectural adventurers.** Jay Merrick, *The Independent*, 14 February 2002

A driving force in the British architectural avant-garde of the 1960s, Archigram was founded by Peter Cook, Warren Chalk, Ron Herron, Dennis Crompton, Michael Webb and David Greene. The group expounded an experimental vision of High-tech architecture in a series of arresting pamphlets produced throughout the 1960s and early '70s which were heavily influenced by Pop Art and comic book imagery.
Right: Peter Cook's elevation of the 'Plug-in City', published in *Archigram*, 5 November 1964. This vast megastructure provided a framework into which standardised units for accommodation, transport, or services could be 'plugged', allowing the city to expand both upwards and outwards with infinite flexibility.

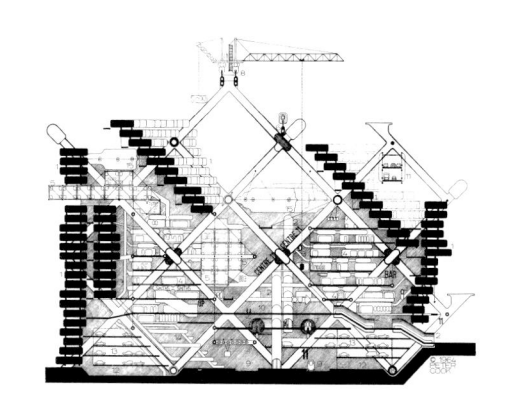

Many of these things happen in Foster's or Rogers' work, but in a sense the proposition is different. Not that they have required high style design. But they have required a kind of enlightened common sense in picking exactly the right things and bolting them together in exactly the right kind of way. Every now and again the aesthetic effect is surprisingly similar. There are vertical ducts. External staircases and things like that here. The one thing that is not ex-catalogue in most of these Cedric Price extravaganzas is the colours they are painted. Which brings us back to the question of that yellow bicycle.

There are certain colours that have quite clearly come to belong to the repertoire of High-tech and certain colours that have never made it. Blue, for example, is a dominant colour, which turns up persistently in both Foster's and Rogers' work. But certain primary reds and yellows come close behind. They very much belong. Are they necessary to this kind of off-the-peg technology? The answer is that they are not. Well possibly red lead underpaints although they're becoming unpopular for safety reasons nowadays. Red lead underpaint is almost the only colour of necessity in the whole of the repertoire. Everything else is a choice. Even a political choice. There is only one reason why the structural frame of Centre Pompidou is not bicycle yellow, which is that the President objected strongly on the grounds that he seemed to remember that had been the colour on which Gestapo posters had been printed during the Second World War in Paris. And that is why the structural frame is painted broken white. But it had been designed in bicycle yellow, as the original models show.

Bicycle yellow was one of the great colours of that particular period. But the interesting thing is that nearly the whole repertoire of colours is in fact traceable to one source. And one source only, I think. And that is the graphics of the Archigram Group. In Archigram's Plug-in City project, of 1963-1964, the whole basic High-tech colour range has already quite clearly appeared. The influence of Archigram on both Rogers and Foster is now generally admitted. You can see it in the Foster's Hammersmith project, for example. Parked on top of its towers are the permanently installed cranes, which would have serviced the building, exactly as they are in the Plug-In City.

But while we're down in yellow bicycle country, let's go back to the old Foster office in Fitzroy Street, with its conspicuously yellow and acid green interior. If you had looked through the window you would have seen a mysterious 'X' with a corrugated background – an image of the Reliance Controls building designed by Foster and Rogers while they were still together in Team 4. That diagonal bracer became almost a trademark. In his recent book on English architecture Sutherland Lyall pointed out that the Reliance Controls' diagonal bracer almost certainly comes from the house designed by Charles Eames for his own occupation at the end of the 1940s.

2. Piano and Roger's Pompidou Centre, Paris, of 1971-1977, is an exercise in overtly expressive structure, one in which the 'gizmology' of its servicing is literally allowed to hang out.

3. The 'baroque' piping and ducting of the Huntington Beach Power Station, built by the Bechtel Corporation in 1961, which, Banham suggests, inspired the Pompidou Centre.

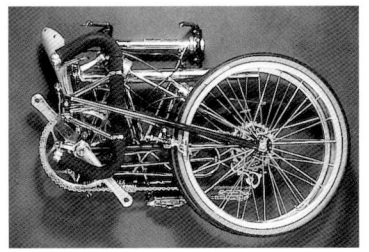

**This is a classic – a reinvention of the bicycle. It is light, separable, high performance – and it looks good.** Norman Foster, selecting a 'Product for the New Millennium', 1999

Left: The Moulton bicycle, designed by Alex Moulton and first launched in 1961, featured many design innovations: small wheels with high-pressure tyres; unisex, single-size frames with no top tubes, frame separability (with the ability to fold flat) and suspension front and rear. The Moulton bicycle was a reference point in the design of the Nomos table, not least because of the clear articulation of its various structural elements.

1. A view of the reception area of Foster Associates' Fitzroy Street studio, with a photograph of the iconic cross-bracing at Reliance Controls – a mysterious 'X' with a corrugated background. Other key reference images on display in the studio included the Eiffel Tower, the Apollo Lunar Lander, and Ezra Ehrenkrantz's SCSD prototype school.

Eames is a very significant figure here – another of the true American sources of the High-tech style. He has been dead barely seven years, but he is already a legend. He is probably the most brilliant and prolific designer that America has produced since Frank Lloyd Wright. His full impact cannot be assessed even yet, I think. The generation who came to first design maturity in the middle 1960s were nearly all fanatical admirers of Charles Eames. They saw and understood what it was that Eames had to offer: a freedom of form and experiment within the toughest technological disciplines. Eames' furniture answers all those principles of economy and so on. It does 'the most with the least', in Buckminster Fuller's phrase.

Within the tightest technical and economic disciplines Eames showed how much freedom for the designer there was. And that lesson has not been lost on the Foster office. You can see it in the marvellous bow-legged desk structures on which Foster displayed all the models in the Eames exhibition, which he designed. It is a piece of remarkable structural bravura, such as an engineer would not have done. (By the way, it also has diagonal cross-braces – that damned thing won't go away.) But I think it is justifiable.

It brings us back to one of the questions I raised at the very beginning. It is where Foster puts the other imagery to work. You will find these desks – used as drawing tables – in the present Foster studio in Great Portland Street, together with Eames chairs. There you will also find the corresponding image of the moonlander with its spread legs with the flat pads on the end. And it's all functionally justifiable, damn him! If it was just intellectual or aesthetic fancy you could say, 'Okay Norm, I take your point.'

But the thing is that the moonlander has legs with pads on because it has to be able to stand level wherever it lands. Remember the awful descriptions of the landing of the first lunar excursion module? There was a glitch in the computer and it came down in the wrong place. Instead of landing on flat dust it came down on a field of rocks. Nevertheless it came down on its spread legs and its pads and it stood secure. Now one thing an architect's drawing desk must do is stand secure. For one thing the architect will lean on it for much of his life and it would not be life enhancing if it kept falling on him. Furthermore his lines should not wobble.

**If you had looked through the window of the old Foster office in Fitzroy Street you would have seen a mysterious 'X' with a corrugated background – an image of the Reliance Controls building – that diagonal bracer became almost a trademark.**

But this device makes a big scene of standing secure. It takes you beyond mere necessity into the world of expressive necessity. You could design a lighter table. You could design a cheaper table. But you couldn't design a table that is quite so much fun. You could do a number of things but the result would not say in quite this way, 'Look at me I'm a High-tech drawing table. I'm the way of the future.' You have to admire it because you know it's also like that for perfectly good reasons.

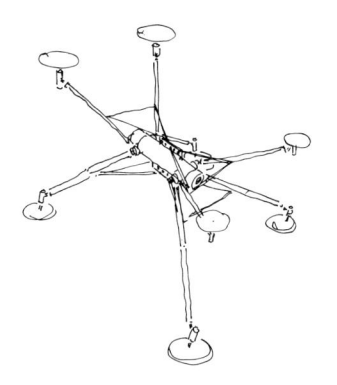

**Many critics and users have commented on the Nomos table's frame, suggesting references such as the lunar landing module. It is true that a large photograph of the craft adorned the walls of our studio at the time that the table was created, and it still remains a potent symbol.** Norman Foster, 'On Tables and Bicycles', 1999

Left: Norman Foster's sketch of the Nomos table's structural frame and spreading legs.
Right and far right: A detail of the Nomos table's foot compared with the Apollo Lunar Lander, of 1969. The legs of the Lunar Lander terminate in flat pads, which, like those of the Nomos table, ensure maximum stability regardless of the terrain on which it sits.

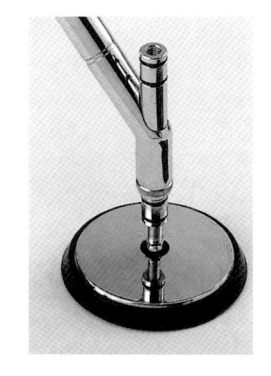

Now this business of moving from the functional to the expressively functional is, I think, taking very interesting forms in Foster's work at the moment. If I have appeared to suggest that he uses the smooth envelope for buildings and the leggy form for furniture that is perfectly true as far as we have gone. But if you look at the detailing of the Hongkong and Shanghai Bank (or Honkers and Shankers as the office calls it) you will see many of the same forms, including the weight-reducing holes pierced through the structural cantilevers.

So now Foster is beginning to make very large buildings out of what are almost furniture design components. I say 'almost' because quite clearly something more grandiose and more massive is going on. But certainly some of the work coming out of the office recently suggests the reclamation, as it were, of forms that come from the space vehicles via the furniture exercises. That kind of design thinking has recently produced the Renault Centre, for instance. Again you have the weight reducing holes and the tension members. (There must be some diagonal braces in there somewhere I think.) It is really a kind of superior circus tent system.

Organised in what must ultimately be a rectangular grid, it does not necessarily have to be tidy at the ends if the site does not require it. In what is seemingly a rigid geometrical system, it offers considerable opportunity to mess around at the ends as necessity requires. Each square unit is virtually self-contained, which means that you could omit units within the length or width of the building, at almost any point.

The emergence of these conspicuously lightweight structural elements – the spindly legs and the various diagonal members with their weight reduction holes – represents, I think, a major change in the way the Foster office has been working. And I am not quite sure where it may go – yet. I think we may have to wait until we can look at the Hongkong Bank in some detail. One of my concerns about the Hongkong Bank design visually, as a work of the art of architecture, irrespective of its functional or other aspects, is whether those skinny, lightweight details will sit happily with those enormously thick quadropods, which make the grand structure columns of the whole design.

## Foster is beginning to make very large buildings from what are almost furniture components. I say 'almost' because something far more grandiose and more massive is going on.

At Renault, however, there is no such contrast. Everything is fairly skinny, fairly light – or at any rate light looking – and bicycle yellow dominates the theme. The circus big-top aspect of the design is enhanced by the Renault cars on their flying trapeze, as well as the others cavorting on the ground. But there is no doubt that it is the apotheosis of bicycle yellow.

2, 3. A prototype folding Nomos table (1985-1987), complete with diagonal cross-braces. The Nomos concept originated in an adjustable table custom-designed for Foster Associates' Great Portland Street studio in 1981. Modified versions of this table were requested by the client for use in the Renault Centre, and in 1985 Italian furniture designer Tecno commissioned the practice to develop the design. Launched in 1987, the Nomos range has been in production ever since, with a new design, the Nomos 2000 Table, issued to mark the millennium.

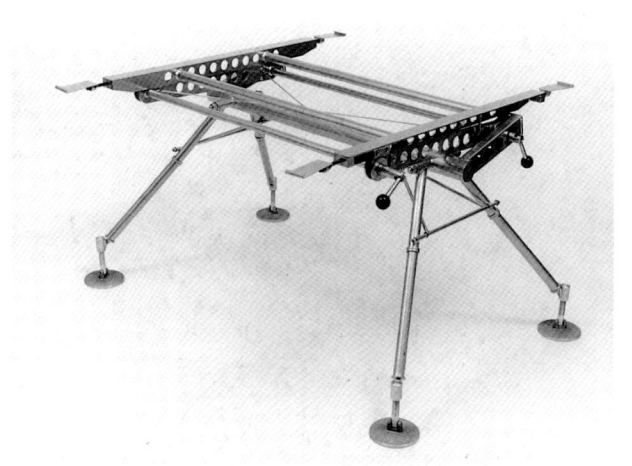

**People have come up with a range of theories regarding the colour of the Renault Centre in Swindon – is it a colour one enjoys because it is a friendly, cheerful colour, is it evocative of agricultural equipment, is it the house colour of Renault, or is it – if Peter Banham is here I know this embarrasses him – evocative of daffodils or buttercups?** Norman Foster, lecture at the Aspen Design Conference, 18 June 1986

**The sheer visual delight of the cladding details on the Bank ... is as much about aesthetics as water penetration and tolerances, but it is not about the architect as a remote aesthete removed from the production process.** Norman Foster, *L'Architecture d'Aujourd'hui*, February 1986
Left: Sunshade brackets on the curtain wall of the Hongkong Bank, with weight-reducing holes reminiscent both of Foster's earlier designs for furniture, and the structural members of the Renault Distribution Centre.

1. The bicycle-yellow exoskeleton of the Renault Centre (1982-1984), evokes, according to Banham, a 'superior circus tent system'. This building represented Norman Foster's most expressive structure to date and was interpreted by many critics as evidence of a significant change in direction.

Finally, to take us back to East Anglia, and the building which I think is to date the most satisfactory that the Foster office has done – the Willis Faber & Dumas building in Ipswich. It is I think an extraordinary brilliant performance. It may be more brilliant than they knew when they designed it. It does occasionally happen to architects that in Fuller's synergetic language, 'the whole turns out to be vastly more than the sum of the parts'. Not only vastly more, but rather different to the sum of the parts.

The building is a verbal description, the simplest possible verbal description. It is a glass walled office block – the very building type that the world has decided it can probably do without. But it does not look like any other glass walled office block known to me anywhere on the earth's crust. The reasons, I think, are concerned with its form, fairly obviously, with the way it's organised internally, with what it's roofed with and the visual benefits that come from acting on the phrase that Foster has used increasingly in recent years – 'appropriate technology'.

Now whatever is 'appropriate tech' for an office block for a reinsurance company? There is no helpful typological concept from the mighty past. Can anyone, for instance, think of a good Roman or Gothic block for a reinsurance company? It is a non-typology. The nearest you can get is 'office block', otherwise nothing is given. Given the form and the size of the site, it was perceived by Foster as an opportunity to create a building of modest height; and it is only a three-storey building. It is of course very much against the grain of conventional office block thinking, but nonetheless appropriate to this company. Instead of the lurking privacy of a bank of lifts, its escalators have turned internal circulation into a public spectacle.

The lift stack is not just destructive of community spirit, it breaks it down into a series of small conspiracies. The only person who knows anything about how the company runs is the man who services the lift when it goes wrong, because he hears the conversations on the other side of the door while he is trying to fix the machinery.

Here, however, all the late 1960s chat about community, togetherness and all that kind of thing, is delivered by a building with a very large open atrium (a thoroughly Roman concept of course) through which all the main vertical circulation ascends. Ultimately you are delivered to a rather attractive restaurant on the roof, which looks out upon a flat surface of, would you believe, grass.

That, I think, really upsets the kind of people who are upset by Foster's architecture. High-tech buildings do not have grass tops. The fact that the grass top was introduced into modern architecture by no less a person than Le Corbusier only makes the situation worse. Here is a building which on the outside is glass and therefore obviously energy wasteful, as every good architectural magazine editor knows. In fact, though, the performance of this building is energy moderate. And one of the reasons for that is that Foster cheated and put this damn turf roof on the thing. It is a brilliant insulator.

But where the building really jumps out of expectations and into the area I think of genius is not only does it have a 'traditional' grass roof – like Peer Gynt's house, or other well known peasant residences – but instead of defying medieval downtown Ipswich it slavishly follows the outlines of medieval downtown Ipswich. The plan is a funny fluid shape because it follows the given street pattern. What the result does to Ipswich, of course, is absolutely marvellous.

Just before Willis Faber was completed Theo Crosby had staged, in the Hayward Gallery in London, a well received exhibition called 'The Environment Game'. There was a long section, which explained that modern buildings were boring and injurious to your health because when you looked at them you didn't see any detailing. No Gothic pinnacles, no Baroque this that and the other, no Rococo curves, no Art Nouveau, no medallion brackets or anything like that.

The Maisons Jaoul's contrast with Le Corbusier's early works was dramatic, with their rough concrete frames, their curved Catalan vaults and their turfed roofs ... Peter Smithson, the English architect, characterised the combination of sophistication and primitivism nicely when he spoke of the Maisons Jaoul as being 'on the knife edge of peasantism'. William J R Curtis, *Modern Architecture since 1900*, 1996
Left: The turfed roofs at Maisons Jaoul, 1951-1954.

But here is a modern glass wall building. When you look at it you see nothing but detailing. But it's other people's detailing. The building is a great visual rip-off of boring old downtown Ipswich. But it raises it to the level of art by the process known as collage, in which pieces of Ipswich keep appearing in the wrong places. Because the plan is curved but the glass is flat, no two adjacent panels reflect parts of the same building. There are things, which appear in some reflections, which are not even in that part of Ipswich as far as I can work out. It is an extraordinary sort of surrealist decomposition and reconstruction of the Ipswich scene.

**High-tech buildings do not have grass tops. The fact that the grass roof was introduced into modern architecture by none other than Le Corbusier only makes the situation worse.**

Now to what extent this was clearly seen coming by the Foster office I think is still open to a degree of speculation and argument. But buildings must be judged for what they are rather than what they intend to be. And this one is easily the most original extraordinary and striking glass building in an urban setting seen anywhere in the world so far. It was arrived at by a process of overt rationalisations, shall we say, which are all about function and energy consumption. I don't think the words 'aesthetics', 'collage', or even 'surrounding scene', were mentioned anywhere in the architect's conversations or the brief.

Like all the architects who believe seriously in technology I think Foster proposed, quite seriously, quite honestly, to advance from a rational consideration of the client's needs and problems, to a rational solution to the good servicing of those needs and problems. But the man is an architect, not an engineer. The visuals will never go away. They are always in the head. They are always in the back of the eye.

Ask an architect a question and he will draw you a picture. Just watch. Any architectural conversation will destroy the average white tablecloth if there are no menus and things to write on. Ask an architect a question and if he can't actually find a piece of paper, even a pound note to draw on, then he is frustrated. He has no language with which he can speak. Architects are not great masters of prose style in most cases. They don't need to be. They have a marvellous means of expression of their own.

If Foster had simply been an engineer, if he had simply been a functionalist, goodness knows what he would have delivered. But being a man with an eye full of imagery, of which the yellow bicycle stands simply as one example, he could not in a sense help converting that rational, functional solution to the client's demands into a piece of sheer visual magic – which is the best kind of magic because you can see how the trick is done. Good architecture is transparent to the mind if not to the eye. Given the proposition on which Foster's architecture is based, this building – which is reflective to the eye and transparent to the mind – is about as good as you can get.

2. The grass roof of the Willis Faber & Dumas building (1971-1975). Unique in an office building at this time, the grass roof provided an additional amenity for users of the building, but also served as extremely effective thermal insulation.

3. The 'surrealist' collage of urban Ipswich reflected in Willis Faber's glass walls. The combination of distorted images of the past and partially perceived interiors, all overlaid by a grid of patch fittings, changes as constantly as the weather, revealing new compositions.

# Masterplan for St Helier Harbour
St Helier, Jersey 1976–1977

**The early studies revealed how little had been done to make the harbour an inviting place for visitors. The design team wanted to release the harbour's potential as a natural tourist amenity.**
Ian Lambot

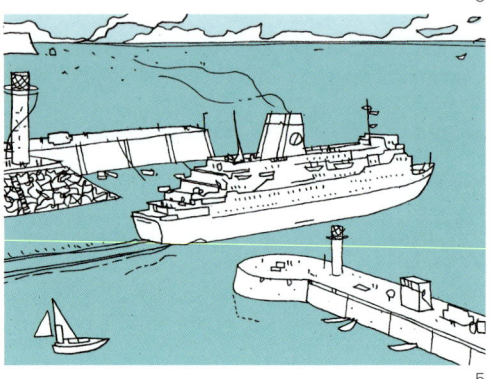

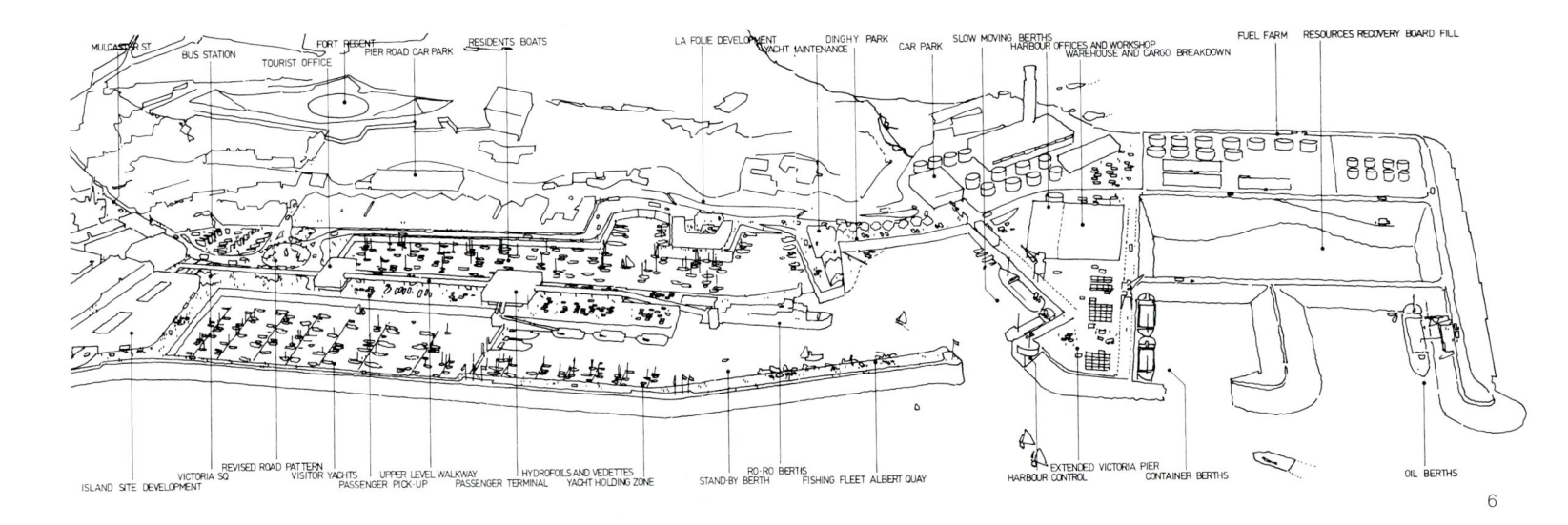

St Helier Harbour is located at the commercial centre of the town. It handles large numbers of tourists, many with their private cars, arriving by British Rail ferries and independent hydrofoil services. Most of the island's agricultural produce is shipped out by cargo vessels. All fuel supplies for the community are brought ashore in the harbour from bulk tankers. St Helier Harbour is used by the local fishing fleet and by local yachtsmen: there is also a rapidly growing demand for berthing facilities for visiting French and English yacht owners. Extract from Foster Associates' St Helier Harbour Masterplan report, 1976

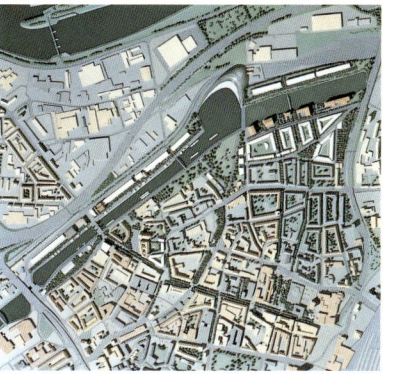

Our masterplan for the Duisburg Inner Harbour area has identified this quarter as having key regeneration potential. Older buildings which have run into disrepair are to be restored and upgraded, new buildings – including low-cost public housing – are being built, and the harbour itself will be cleaned and transformed into a new focus for the city. Norman Foster, lecture at the CABE conference, London, 6 February 2001
Left: A model of the 1991 masterplan for Duisburg Inner Harbour. Like the St Helier Masterplan, the scheme revitalises and brings new uses, including leisure facilities, to an area that had fallen into steep decline following the relocation of the harbour to alternative deep-water berths.

Spurred on by increasing concerns about the declining condition of the harbour and the immediate need to accommodate a new roll-on/roll-off ferry terminal, in March 1976, the Harbours & Airport Committee of the States of Jersey commissioned a masterplan for the development of the St Helier Harbour.

Research into the harbour's history and current working practices, combined with extensive consultation with harbour engineers, planners, and the port's main user groups, convinced the Foster team that a radical solution was required to see the harbour into the twenty-first century. Originally constructed to handle small cargo and passenger ships and a local fishing fleet, it was being rapidly outgrown as Jersey developed into a tourist destination. Old Victorian buildings continued in use despite extensive disrepair and dilapidation. Construction of a roll-on/roll-off ferry terminal on Albert Pier in the 1960s had done little to alleviate the situation. Some facilities were severely congested, while others were under-used; modern refreshment or lavatory facilities were lacking, while customs facilities and vehicle access were, at best, inadequate.

Keen to rationalise and expand existing facilities and release the harbour's potential as a natural tourist amenity, Foster proposed to locate a new terminal on New North Quay, while completely segregating pedestrian and vehicle traffic. Two pavilions raised above the quay housed waiting areas, baggage-handling facilities, a cafeteria and shops, booking and customs facilities, and tourist information services, leaving the quayside free for arriving, waiting and departing cars. Pedestrians made use of a high-level walkway which ran through the terminals, linking the ferry at one end with a new bus terminal at the other and offering generous views of the harbour and town beyond through a clear Perspex vault.

Freed of the existing terminal, Albert Pier – which enjoyed excellent views of the town and the harbour – could be given over to tourism. A new marina was to occupy the upper area of the main harbour, allowing yachts to berth within a few minutes' walk of the town centre. This strategy offered considerable commercial opportunities without placing further demands on the island's roads or fixed services. A wide variety of facilities and commercial units could be established on the pier, along with berths for the small local fishing fleet. To combat the upper area's tendency to dry out at low tide, dredging and waterproofing would be undertaken and a tidal gate installed across the harbour.

The repositioning of the terminal also facilitated a complete reorganisation of harbour use. Existing cargo ship moorings and warehouse facilities at the New North Quay were to be supplemented by development of expansion works already under way in the La Collette reclamation area to the south of the harbour. The old Victoria Pier was to be widened to accommodate new warehouses and deep-water berths. Only the Old Harbour would remain unchanged, providing permanent moorings for the island's residents.

Foster's scheme met the primary objectives in creating a harbour that provided the greatest benefits to the maximum number of users. The masterplan was completed in March 1977 and subsequently submitted to the Harbours and Airport Committee. Though the report was well received, its recommendations were not taken up – a familiar fate for many masterplan studies when there is a lack of political will.

Ian Lambot

1-5. As part of an interim report, Birkin Haward drew a series of sketches to illustrate proposals such as the harbour's potential for tourist development. A high-level walkway leading to the ferry incorporated a travelator for baggage and a clear vault to allow views across the town.

6. The final masterplan proposals were summarised in a single drawing. Founded largely on the reorganisation of existing facilities, only one new building was suggested – a ferry terminal relocated on New North Quay.

7. The Old Harbour provided a picturesque scene, but it would typically dry out to mud flats at low tide.

8. New North Quay had high-tide only moorings, which were unsuitable for modern container vessels, which required new, deep-water berths and improved quayside storage facilities.

# Hammersmith Centre
London, England 1977–1979

Take a site about the size of Trafalgar Square. Surround it by a large roundabout, slice it through on the diagonal with railway lines and make sure it lies on a high water table. While you're at it make it London's first major public transport interchange on the way in from Heathrow … These at least are the bare bones of the problem associated with the commission Foster Associates have just received from London Transport. *Building Design*, 3 February 1978

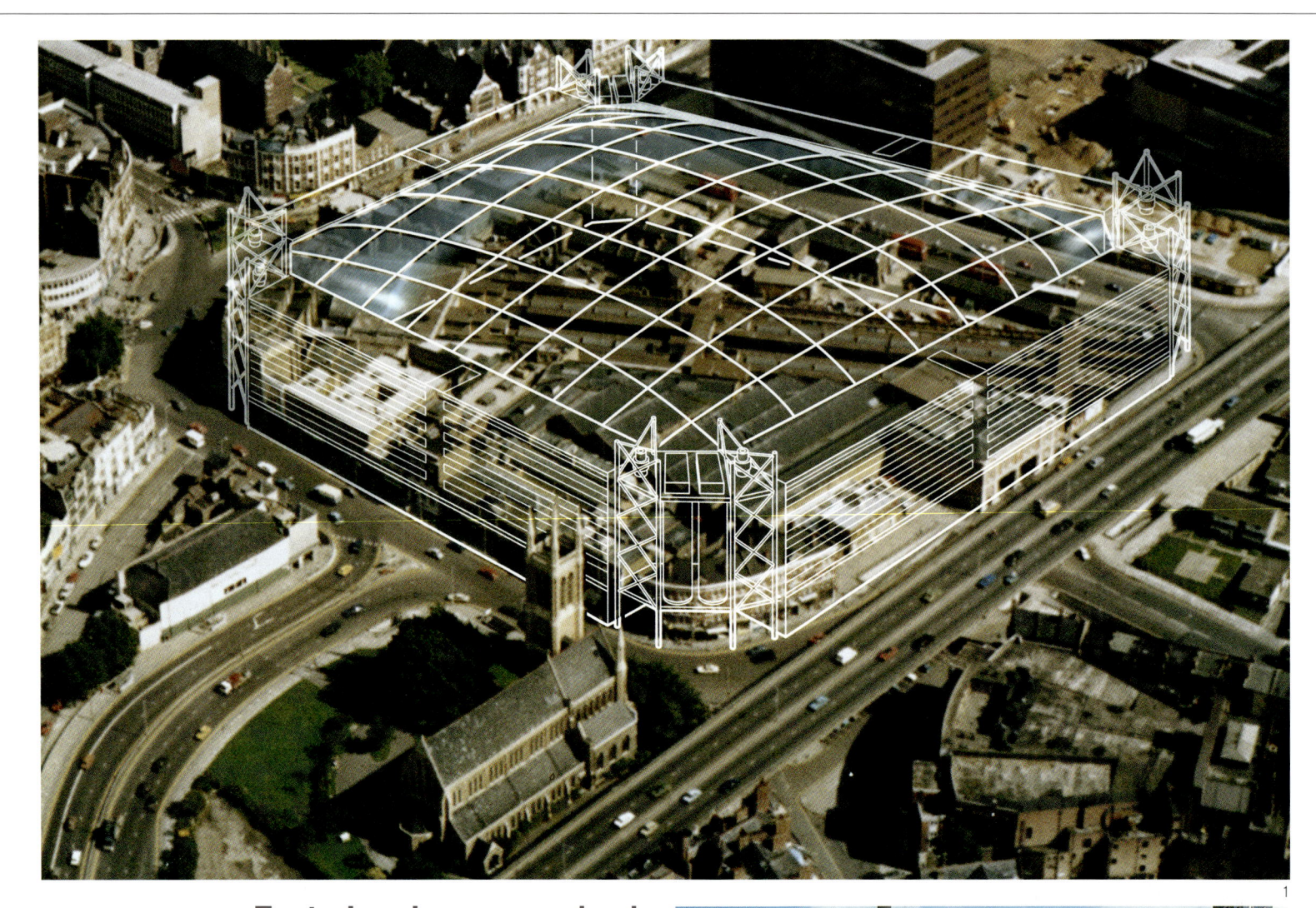

**Foster's scheme promised an elegant resolution to one of London's most complicated redevelopment problems; yet it was destined to become one of the great missed opportunities of post-war urban renewal.**
Tim Ostler

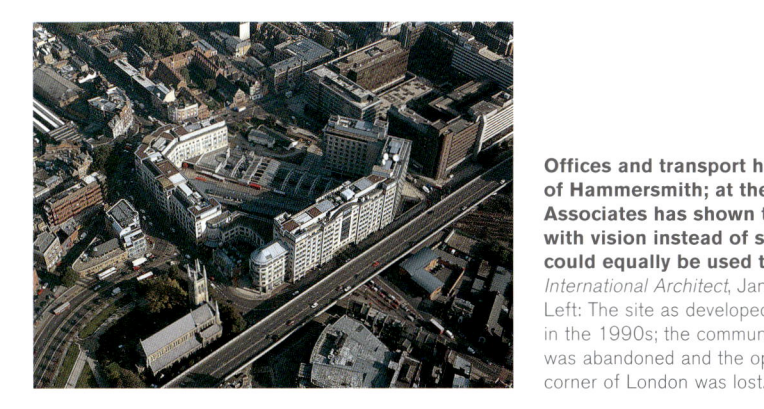

**Offices and transport have destroyed the heart of Hammersmith; at the eleventh hour Foster Associates has shown that, designed intelligently, with vision instead of short-sighted greed, they could equally be used to restore it.** Richard Padovan, *International Architect*, January 1979
Left: The site as developed commercially by Bredero in the 1990s; the community element of the scheme was abandoned and the opportunity to reclaim a forlorn corner of London was lost.

**The project had three main parameters: the commercial reality, the social acceptability in terms of producing a community benefit, and the complexities of the transportation network – often conflicting requirements by quite separate groups of people, all related to a situation of change around the road pattern.** Norman Foster, lecture at RIBA 'Frontiers of Design' conference, London, 28 September 1979

This ambitious London project for a transport interchange, office complex and enclosed public space – its sheer scale was not to be matched until the Hongkong Bank – was Norman Foster's first encounter with speculative commercial development. It was also the practice's first opportunity to design facilities for the public as a whole, rather than just for a client's employees. Ironically, it was the clash between these two interests that led to the project's demise. Foster's scheme promised an elegant resolution to one of London's most complicated redevelopment problems; yet it was destined to become one of the great missed opportunities of post-war urban renewal.

Hammersmith is not a pleasant place to spend an afternoon. Sandwiched between two major roads leading west out of London, the four-acre site housed a dilapidated bus garage and a motley collection of undistinguished turn-of-the-century structures. By 1977 it had become one of the busiest and most congested traffic intersections in Europe. Increasingly aggressive traffic had destroyed any lingering appeal the neighbourhood possessed, while a new shopping centre on nearby King Street had shifted Hammersmith's commercial centre of gravity westwards.

Foster's commission in February 1977 resulted from London Transport's desire to upgrade its existing facilities to create an integrated transport interchange, subsidised by a substantial office development. An admirably enlightened client, London Transport was firmly committed to finding a successful architectural solution. Its chairman, Kenneth Robinson, was particularly keen to ensure that any social benefits should not be superseded by the need to make the scheme pay for itself.

The brief was nonetheless demanding, and it was further complicated by several factors: two Underground railway lines bisected the site; London Transport wanted to maintain a working passenger interchange throughout the entire construction period; a newly devised traffic scheme proposed the relocation of the entire gyratory system one block to the east (which meant that Foster had to accommodate both existing and revised schemes); and finally, a high water table ran across the site, which meant that constructing deep basements could prove costly and extend the construction period considerably.

Foster's first response was to carry out a detailed study of the site and its surroundings. A review of the area's history revealed that successive developments had gradually encroached upon a large nineteenth-century garden at the centre of the site. Foster was determined that the reinstatement of this oasis-like space would be a major aim of the new development.

1. A view of London Transport's Hammersmith site with an outline of the final scheme superimposed.

2-5. The site contained a transport interchange between the Piccadilly and District Underground lines and a bus depot. Flanked by two major roads, it lay at the centre of one of Europe's busiest traffic roundabouts. Accessible only by pedestrian subways, much of the site had fallen into disuse. Any proposal had to respond to the social problems of the area as much as to the practical aspects of the brief.

# The story of the site seemed to be one of barriers – barriers generated by traffic.
Norman Foster

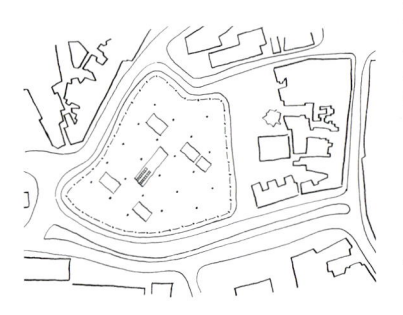

**At Willis Faber the whole structure is woven into the sinuous geometry of the medieval town; we allowed the street pattern to be the generator of the building's fluid form. Inside the building, you ascend through the office floors towards the light and the rooftop restaurant set on a big insulating quilt of grass – one of the reasons why the building is so energy efficient.** Norman Foster, lecture at Stuttgart University, 14 May 1997

Left: The economy with which the Willis Faber & Dumas building derived its plan form, by building up to the site boundaries, inspired a similar approach at Hammersmith. Right: The provision of a green space for occupants of the Willis Faber building was equally influential in the development of the Hammersmith scheme.

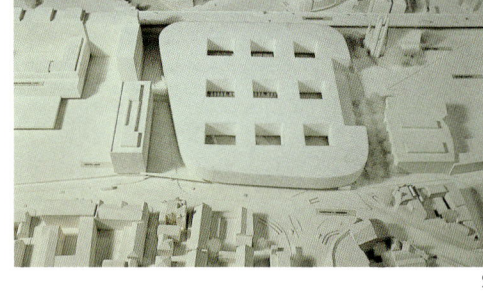

1, 2. Comparative models studied all the various options for the site including standard developer's blocks and a Willis Faber inspired deep plan.

3. A perimeter system around an open raised podium was the first option to be considered seriously, but even this went through many configurations.

4. Early proposals stepped in response to the surrounding streetscape.

5. A smooth form with fewer steps evolved, with openings in the podium to ventilate the bus depot below.

6. The first concrete proposal maintained a regular building height around the site, so as to achieve the full area of offices required.

The brief required a range of widely differing spaces, from small individual offices to a wide-span bus garage. The stacking of different span spaces in a multi-storey building would have necessitated a complicated and expensive structural solution, while the sheer quantity of office space required was hard to achieve without building to an excessive height or width.

**Foster had established both the strategy of tracing the street outline around an island site and using the roof level to provide a 'green oasis' with Willis Faber & Dumas. But Hammersmith's multi-functional brief presented a more complicated situation.**

The Foster team developed the scheme through a series of models that demonstrated the full range of approaches to the problem, from discrete blocks on a raft to total site coverage. Several of them were based on the 'perimeter theory' promulgated by Sir Leslie Martin and Lionel March's *Land Use and Built Form*, and it became clear that some variation of this solution would prove most effective.

In this instance, it would be achieved by locating the offices along the street frontage around the complete perimeter of the site. Other small-span zones could be grouped beneath the offices while long-span structures (the interchange and bus garage) could be enclosed within the 'wall' on a raft spanning the railway cutting at the centre of the site.

In addition to limiting problem areas where offices coincided on plan with the railway cutting, this scheme had a particular advantage: the central area above the large-span zone could be grassed over to create the sought-after public space.

Both the strategy of tracing the street outline around a fully-developed island site and the use of roof level to provide a 'green oasis' had been established with Willis Faber & Dumas. But Hammersmith's multi-functional brief, located within a dense pattern of circulation activity, presented a much more complicated situation; and its public dimension far exceeded the provision of leisure facilities for office staff at Ipswich. Perhaps the closest comparison is with New York's Rockefeller Plaza: an urban space funded by private sources, but colonised spontaneously by the wider public.

Foster was attempting to draw the idea of social responsibility into the commercial development mix. In architectural terms the most problematic result of 'working' the perimeter was its effect on the street frontage, where the edge of the central zone met the base of the office ring.

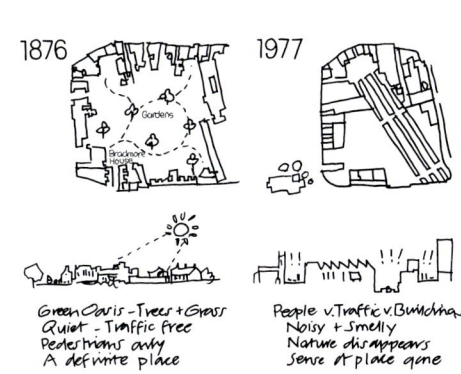

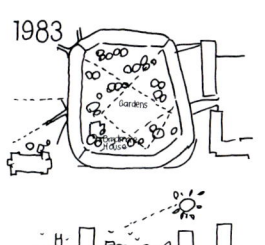

The challenge was to see how the ingredients could be transformed into providing a centre on a large site which had no public open space, and to see how the necessity of producing a developer's package could be realised without the attendant kind of developer's architecture horror-show which Hammersmith, and London Transport at that time, were very anxious to avoid.
Norman Foster, lecture at RIBA 'Frontiers of Design' conference, London, 28 September 1979
Left: A series of diagrams prepared for the Hammersmith project report illustrate how the scheme would remedy the impact of a century of ill-thought-out development.

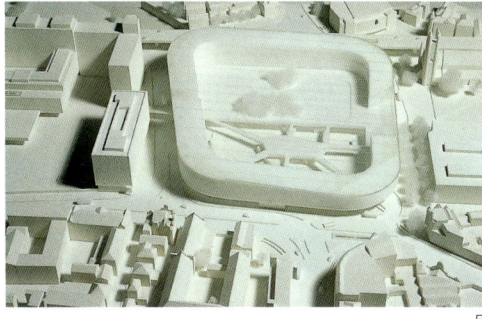

Foster's early sketches explored the architectural implications of combining the two distinct levels that emerged: a podium given over to interchange, garages and traffic; and above that, a ring of speculative offices giving on to the central space.

One option was to increase the span of the lower floors in the perimeter zone. Structural loads would be transferred above podium level to a larger-scale structure spanning the full width of the block between double-height pilotis, thereby ending the principle of stacking small spans one above the other. Nevertheless, dividing the elevation into two zones allowed the office ring above to remain smooth and impervious in contrast to the more animated treatment of the lower zone.

Although the elevations were never fully developed, sketches of this period suggest a cladding grid of bay-wide panels combining cladding and glazing – perhaps a development of the panels used at the Sainsbury Centre. Meanwhile, the divisions on the tall pilotis in the lower zone hint at a developing interest in the effect of cladding the primary structure itself, as witnessed at the Hongkong Bank.

As development proceeded the character of the office ring and the levels below diverged, with the offices forming a sheer wall at high level in contrast to the large-scale primary structure below. Concrete vehicular ramps and pedestrian decking were woven through the structure. In addition, another zone began to develop on the roof, creating a secondary leisure area directly related to the offices.

The large amount of office space required imposed considerable pressure to increase the number of floors and thus raise the height of the office ring. Foster's sectional sketches explored how the inner wall might be raked out over the open space thus increasing floor area in the upper storeys. Meanwhile, the podium structure had become completely detached from the surrounding ring of offices, forming a deck that covered the railway cutting. This, together with the optimum use of roof space, ensured that the absolute maximum of space on the site was brought into use. Meanwhile, office accommodation was organised in the most economical arrangement in order to liberate space on the 'ground' for public use.

Phasing construction was the next issue to be resolved. London Transport's proviso that perimeter offices should be placed on the market as soon as possible led to the adoption of a fast-track building programme using a uniform 'kit-of-parts' in fire-protected structural steel on an 8.1-metre square structural grid. Simple framing elements were supplemented by truss components for more difficult areas, such as bridging the railway cutting, or above the entrances to the bus station.

Although on the programme's critical path, the construction of the concrete raft over the railway cutting could not be significantly reduced, and it was decided to build this centre zone in in-situ reinforced concrete. This would also have the benefit of providing the requisite fire break between the garages and car parks of the podium and the open plaza above.

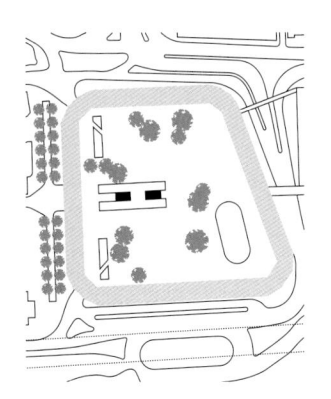

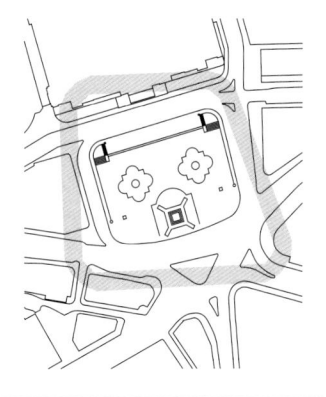

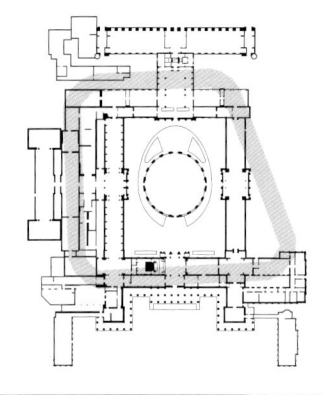

Left: The scale of the Hammersmith Centre project is demonstrated by these diagrams. The public space created would have been approximately equivalent to that of London's Trafalgar Square (centre). The practice was not to undertake a project on this scale in London until the Great Court at the British Museum (1994-2000).

1. The offices formed a continuous ring around the central area of the site, with rooftop areas landscaped for public use.

2. The scheme required the demolition of everything on the site – except the Underground railway lines. This was to be followed by the construction of a new transport interchange, bus depot and 55,750 square metres of offices, while, at all times, allowing free access and movement for cars, buses, trains and pedestrians across and around the site. First proposals placed the bus depot and interchange within a podium at ground level. Access roads, including ramps up to a first-storey car park, circulated in the zone beneath the offices.

Throughout these proposals, Foster considered it essential that the scale of the adjacent structures should be respected. A terraced roofline ensured that the building deferred to its more sensitive neighbours, yet rose to a peak opposite the flyover to form a protective barrier for the central space. At the same time it allowed more of the offices to make direct use of the roof zone. Gaps in the perimeter allowed invitational views from the surrounding streets into the central space and increased its accessibility.

The numerous perspective sketches gauging the effect of the project on its surroundings culminated in the first detailed model of the entire scheme. This showed a somewhat simplified, regularly stepped ring of offices, with its lowest point on the western side functioning to establish a clear link to a new park beside St Paul's Church and to connect the scheme through to King Street.

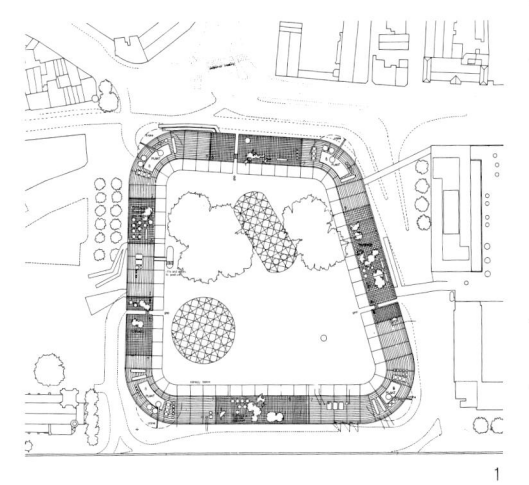

Although early proposals had placed no offices at the lowest point, in order to facilitate the visual link between the park and the central area, the sheer volume of offices required eventually forced the overall height of the offices upwards.

However, attempts to step the offices more frequently produced a somewhat amorphous effect, while the plan was neither particularly regular, nor quite random enough. The next major development decisively rejected such ambiguity, with more defined service cores moved to the 'corners' of the site. As before, the cores were not expressed externally – beyond plant rooms at roof level – but the offices between them were straightened out. At podium level, bridges and escalators linked the building with the surrounding streets.

With the realisation that the height of the offices would have to be maximised right around the site to maintain commercial viability, there was concern that the 'smooth' elevations would prove either monotonous or overbearing. The perspectives began to indicate a more articulated elevation, fully glazed but with columns standing free of the external wall.

Foster's sketches also began to explore how an increase in height might be balanced by clearly defined service towers breaking up the horizontal office elevations. With the roofline disciplined to a more constant height, the possibility of a fixed canopy – an option proposed in early sketches but disallowed by the adoption of the stepped roof profile – provided a radical change of direction.

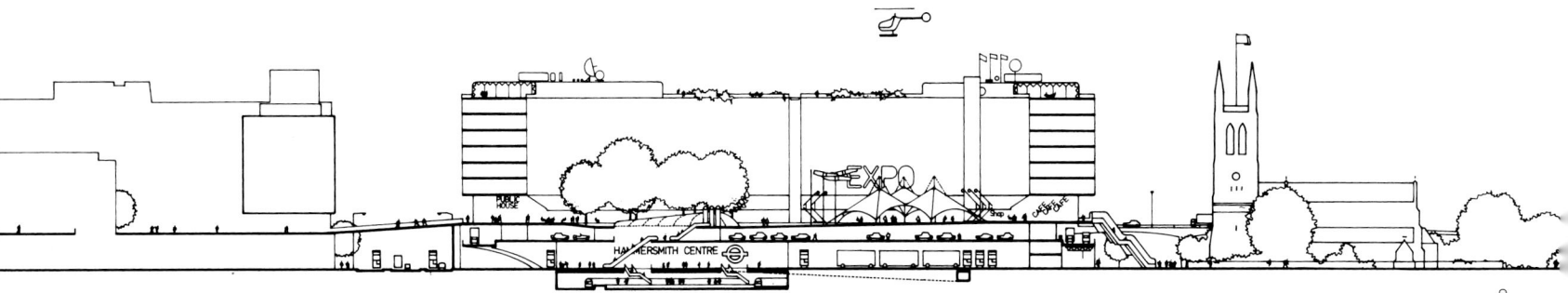

In its own way the Hammersmith scheme is as original an urban intervention as the Milan Galleria. It accepts not only elements of twentieth-century life that [traditionalists such as Leon] Krier are disgusted by – offices, motor cars, technology – but also a barbarously maimed site attractive to developers only by its very favourable position astride the main transport routes between Heathrow Airport and central London. But it transforms them into what could have been a highly civilised environment. Deyan Sudjic, *Norman Foster, Richard Rogers, James Stirling: New Directions In British Architecture*, 1986

Milan's Galleria Vittorio Emanuele II is a recurring reference, illustrating how a noble top-lit space has the potential to create enjoyable urban short-cuts with a richer mix of activities – in this instance the cafés and bookshops which line the route from the Piazza del Duomo to the Piazza della Scala.' Norman Foster, RIBA Royal Gold Medal address, London, 21 June 1983

Right: The Galleria Vittorio Emanuele in Milan (1865-1877) designed by Giuseppe Mengoni, which Foster cites as a reference point for the Hammersmith project.
Far right: The full potential of a light-flooded civic space would ultimately be realised by the practice in the Great Court at the British Museum (1994-2000).

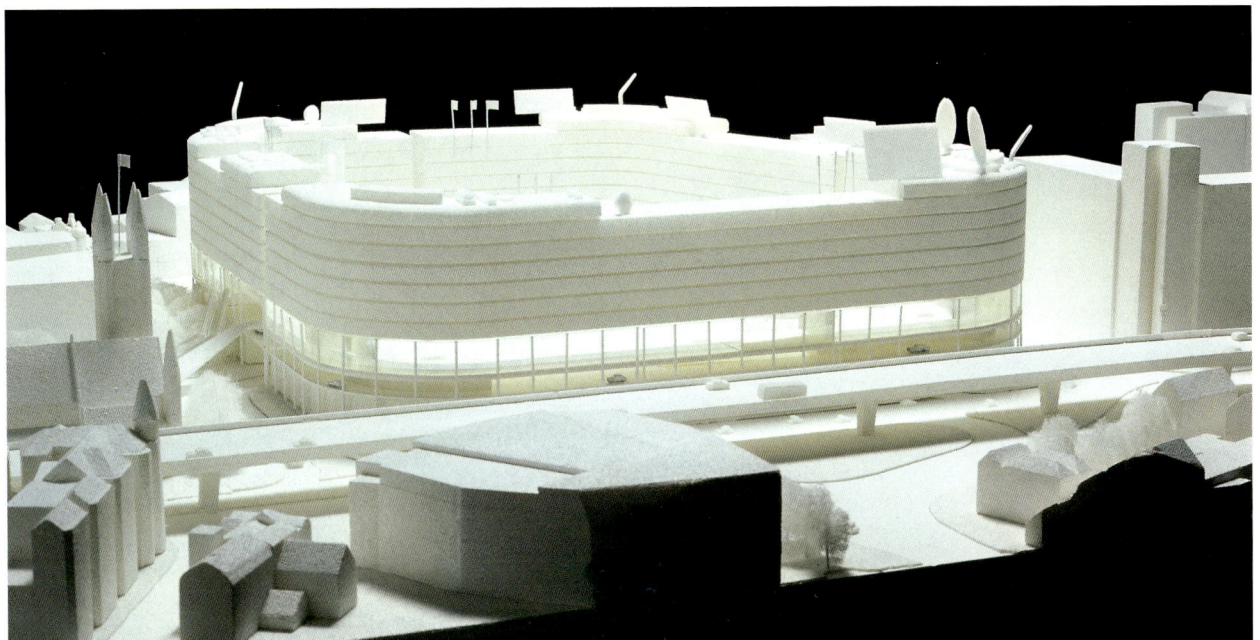

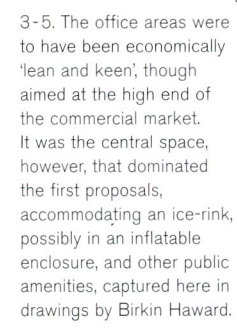

3-5. The office areas were to have been economically 'lean and keen', though aimed at the high end of the commercial market. It was the central space, however, that dominated the first proposals, accommodating an ice-rink, possibly in an inflatable enclosure, and other public amenities, captured here in drawings by Birkin Haward.

6. The model of the first proposal retained a stepped roof profile for the outer ring of offices.

7. Norman Foster's sketch explores the potential of the 'corners' of the site to be articulated as entry points to the public space within.

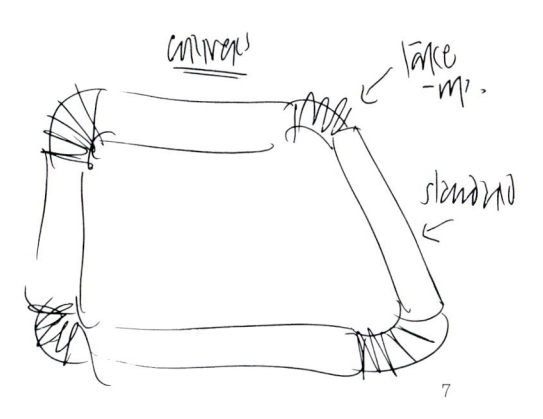

**Hammersmith had a public dimension that went far beyond the provision of leisure facilities for office workers. Here, Foster was attempting to draw the idea of social responsibility into the commercial development mix.**

Tim Ostler

In 1978 Foster Associates was invited to prepare proposals for a mixed-use development for the Whitney Museum of Art, in New York, to consist of a gallery expansion space – which would allow the Whitney to double its existing display area – and a residential tower intended to subsidise the project. As at Hammersmith, one of the challenges was to find an economical way of accommodating a variety of spatial conditions at different levels of the building.
Right: The diagonal struts of the Whitney proposal are clearly evoked in Foster's Hammersmith sketches (see below) which explore the possibility of using a splayed structure at the lower levels.

**In the Whitney Museum project … we were interested in revealing public glimpses into the galleries – the opposite of the closed form of the original Breuer building next door. This approach, with its emphasis on contrast, also respected the separate identity of the existing structure.**
Norman Foster, *Norman Foster: Sketches*, 1992

Norman Foster explored every aspect of the design through a series of sketches. For every sketch that considers the 'look' or the 'feel' of the design, another will explore the reality of how that might be achieved.

1, 2. The structural form of the Whitney redevelopment, which was being designed at the same time, is evoked in these sketches exploring the possibility of using a splayed structure at the lower levels of the building.

3. With the central podium area and main office entrances at a high level, ways of moving pedestrians above the surrounding traffic were investigated. In this sketch Foster explores the use of enclosed walkways ramping down to ground level and angled to coincide with existing pedestrian routes.

4. At two places in the ring of offices, a large-span element was required where it crossed the Underground railway lines beneath the site. This sketch proposes an elevated truss to support the offices, the structure for the traffic access routes being strong enough to be self-supporting.

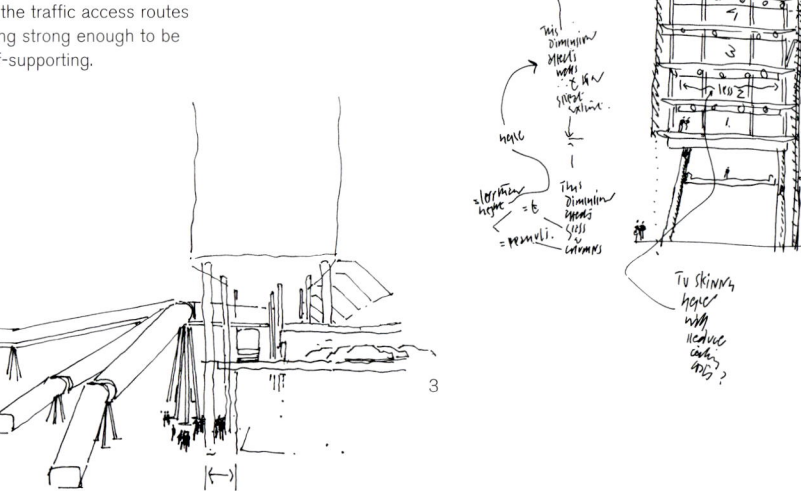

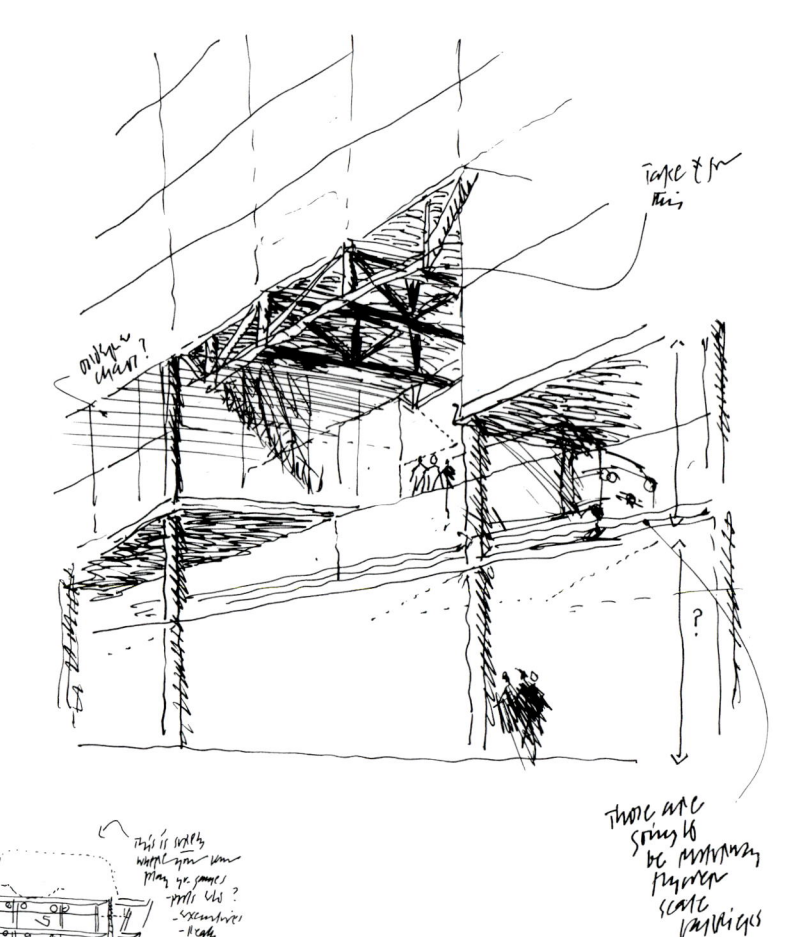

**The most problematic result of 'working' the perimeter was its effect on the street frontage where the edge of the central zone met the base of the office ring. Foster's early sketches explored the architectural implications.**
Tim Ostler

Part of our background research included a visit to the Omni Center, in Atlanta. Despite all the reasons why it should not work and why it should not attract people, it is immensely popular. I have never seen a development which so cuts through and across all social strata – where the fast-food outlet is cheek-by-jowl with a Gucci shop, and the most exclusive hotel in the city is surrounded by offices. Norman Foster, lecture at RIBA 'Frontiers of Design' conference, London, 28 September 1979
Left: The Omni Center, Atlanta, a monumental hotel, retail, office and entertainment complex designed by Thompson, Ventulett and Stainback and completed in 1976. Since acquired by Ted Turner, it has been renamed the CNN Center.

The abandoned Hammersmith project, although ostensibly concerned with the quality of urban life in a messy part of road-raped London, is essentially a glorious contemporary castle. It offers to protect those who use it cocooned inside a hermetic, if enjoyably hermetic, world. It makes few concessions, and perhaps it doesn't need to, to the surrounding urban chaos. Jonathan Glancey, *The Architectural Review*, July 1983

---

Here, at last, Foster had the opportunity to realise ideas originating in the Climatroffice project, developed with Buckminster Fuller seven years earlier, and apply them to a public space. The roof canopy represented a conceptual breakthrough that created a new set of architectural opportunities. It transformed the character of the internal space, bringing a Mediterranean flavour to the heart of an urban community.

Remarkably, it was calculated that the canopy would have paid for itself by obviating the need to weatherproof the internal office elevations. It also acted as a climatic buffer between one edge of the office floors and the outside atmosphere, thereby reducing mechanical plant requirements, and eliminated solar radiation from almost half the office elevations, while its low-insulation value dissipated heat by means of buoyancy stacking effects and night sky radiation. All of which meant that beneath the canopy the winter temperature would be suitable for activities such as ice-skating or exhibition viewing, with individual areas such as cafés boosted by radiant heaters if necessary.

The towers supporting the canopy's main structure served as symbolic gateways to the central public space, while their wall-climbing lifts and exposed service zones indicated a distinct shift towards greater expressiveness. The trend away from slick skins to a greater richness and variety was to be observed in several Foster projects at this time, which heralded the strongly articulated form of the Hongkong Bank.

By October 1979 the design had been approved by both London Transport and the local planning authority and was about to go to the Greater London Council for ratification. A series of public presentations had satisfied local residents' initial concerns and ensured broad popular support for the scheme. Yet in the same month Foster resigned the commission.

In retrospect it could be argued that the brief was excessively burdened by the need for the offices to subsidise both construction costs and those of the transport infrastructure. The departure of chairman Kenneth Robinson also deprived the scheme of an enlightened advocate within London Transport, a situation exacerbated by the appointment of the Dutch developer Bredero. Despite Foster's compelling demonstration that a shallower plan form would waste space and limit tenants' planning options Bredero refused to countenance the office plan because its 18-metre width departed from the then standard 12 metres. (The practice was to be vindicated by later developments: plan widths of 15-18 metres are now the norm.)

The proposals were thus paralysed by a set-piece battle between the notorious conservatism of the speculative office market and Foster's radical approach. Bredero was immovable and Foster was not prepared to dilute the design concept. Following Foster's departure, Bredero went on to develop the site with other architects and Hammersmith was condemned to join the unhappy family of prominent London sites that seem fated never to be satisfactorily resolved.

Tim Ostler

5. As the design developed, the structural hierarchy became clearly defined: a small-span office structure was raised up above podium level by means of a far heavier large-span system, with both of these quite separate from the podium structure they encircle. The floor profile clearly assumes a Willis Faber type solution with a suspended ceiling containing most services. As detail studies proceeded however, services were distributed beneath a raised floor, a system that was taken up two years later for the Hongkong Bank project.

6. The difference in elevational treatment between the office and podium levels is clearly demonstrated in Norman Foster's sketch. The nearby St Paul's Church was an important landmark and many of the early studies include it, both as a reference point and through a concern that it should not be overshadowed.

Right: Scale comparisons with comparable enclosed public spaces, past and present, researched during the design process. From left: the Hammersmith Centre; the USA pavilion for Expo 70, Osaka, Japan, 1970; the Uni-Dome, Iowa, USA, 1975; the Crystal Palace, England, 1851; the Norfolk Gardens Center, Virginia, USA, 1977; and Foster Associates' scheme for Expo 82, Knoxville, USA, 1978, designed with Buckminster Fuller. With a roof area of 15,200 square metres, the Hammersmith Centre was equal to the Uni-Dome and Expo pavilion. All, however, were dwarfed by the extraordinary Norfolk Gardens, with its roof covering 48,000 square metres.

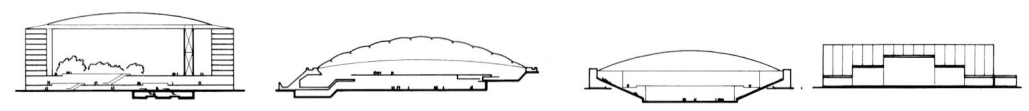

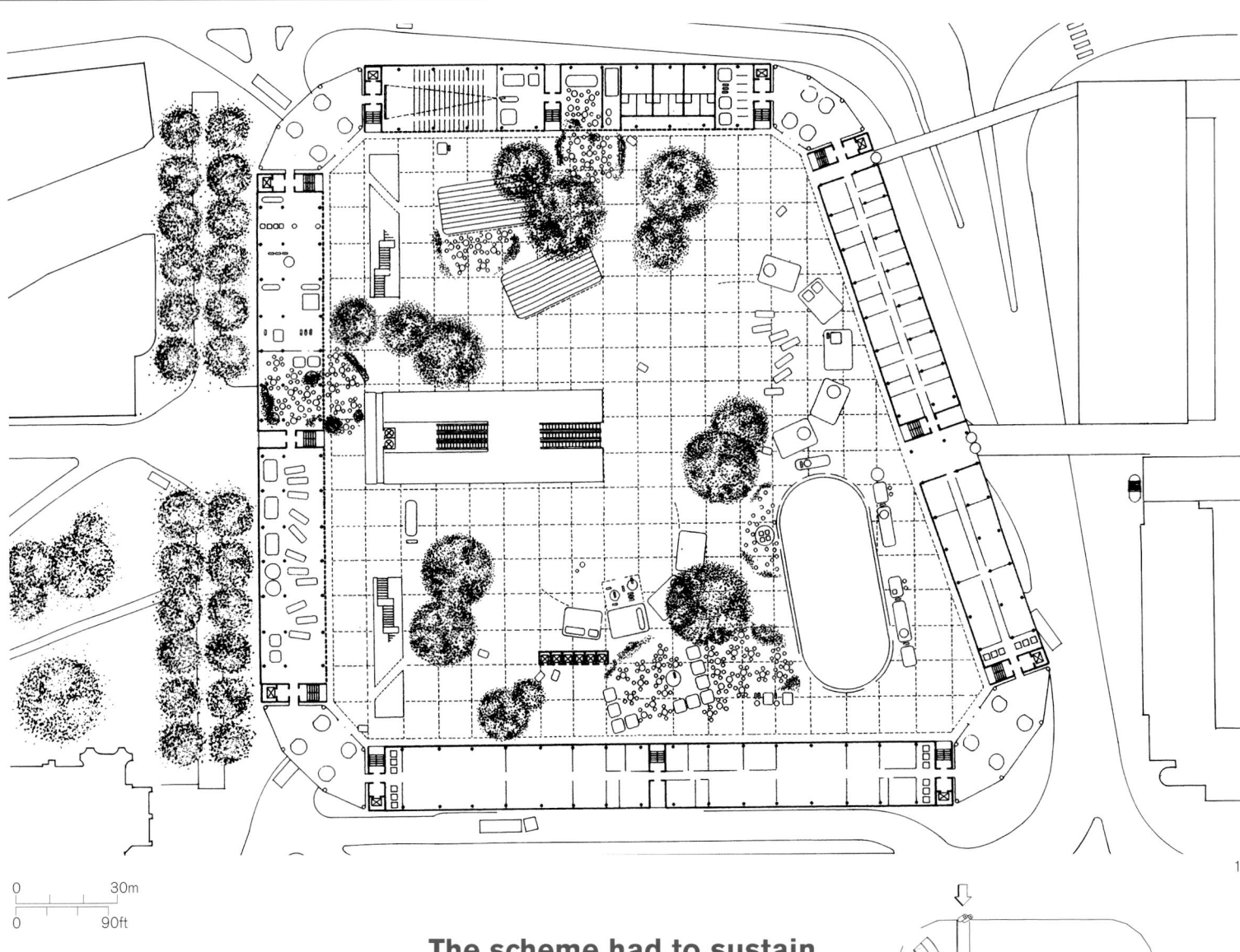

**The scheme had to sustain itself financially; it had to work as a transportation interchange for buses and tube trains; and it had to create something for the community – to work for people.**

Norman Foster

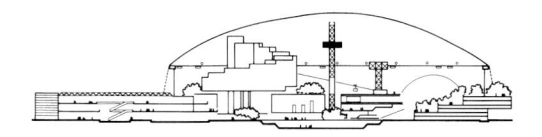

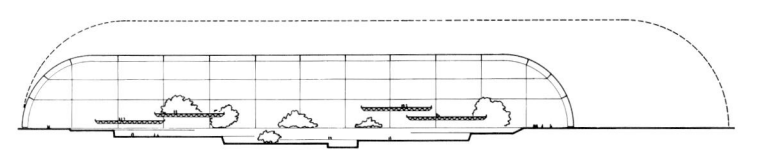

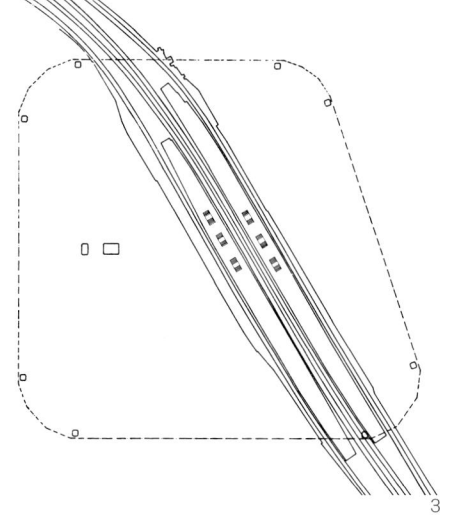

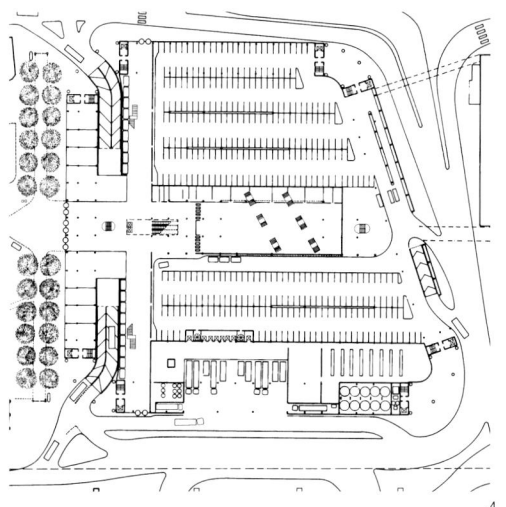

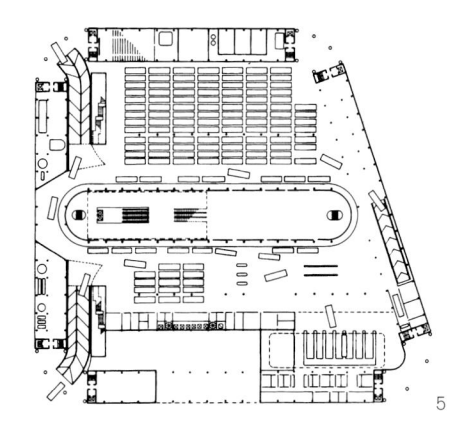

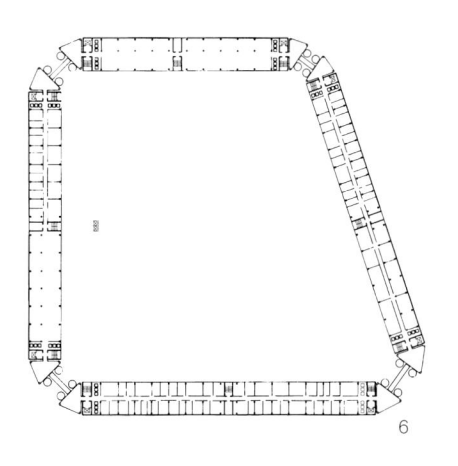

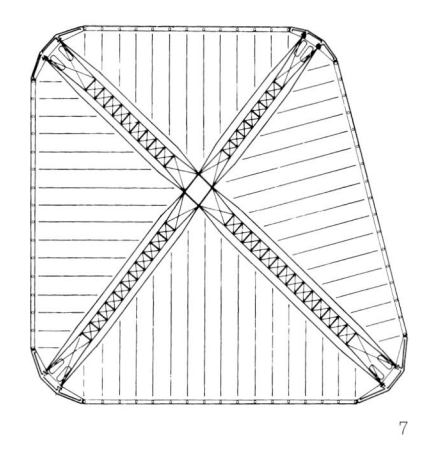

1, 2. The circulation 'spine', running east/west through the centre of the podium, doubled as the principal pedestrian access and the public interchange between the bus depot and the two Underground stations. This arrangement provided clear orientation for people using the development and created a transport interchange with direct connections between buses and trains.

3. Plan at Underground level.

4. The main, street-level entrance to the whole development was via wide, top-lit pedestrian malls lined with kiosks and shops coming from north and south, or directly from a new park adjacent to St Paul's Church to the west.

5. The bus concourse was elevated 3 metres above ground, with bus movements linked to the road system by vehicle ramps.

6. A typical office floor. Access to the offices was at podium level, with large reception areas at the corners of the central space. Vertical circulation to the different office levels was by 'wall-climber' lifts.

7. Roof plan. The lifts continued to roof level where there was the potential for restaurants and other public facilities beneath the shelter of the fabric canopy.

Hammersmith Centre 475

**The possible option of a lightweight roof over the plaza produced cost savings on other elements which balanced with the cost of the roof itself; it also offered the prospect of reduced cost-in-use through energy saving.** Norman Foster, letter to *The Architects' Journal*, 9 January 1980

Right: Comparative environmental studies illustrate how the enclosure would maintain an ambient temperature of 35 degrees Celsius during summer (right), and 15 degrees Celsius during the winter months (far right), ensuring the creation of an all-day, all-weather space, regardless of the season.

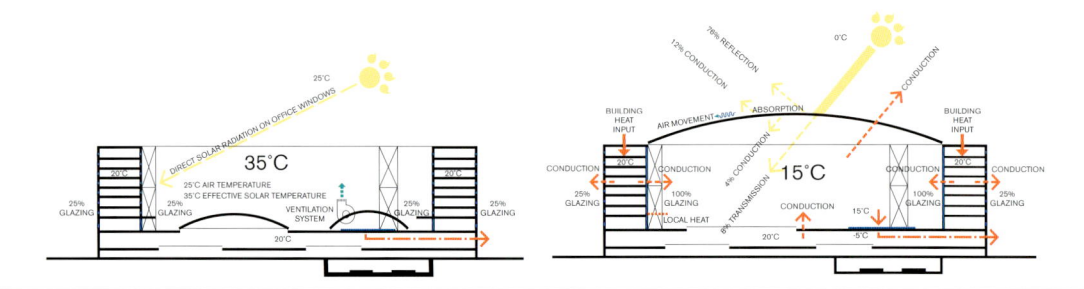

1. This model of the final scheme shows four service towers located at the 'corners' of the site, with offices between. The roof is modelled in clear plastic so that the interior can be seen; in reality, the fabric covering would have been opaque.

2, 3. Norman Foster's early sketches (2) explored the possibilities of a highly articulated facade. However, the final sketches (3) show a less assertive elevational treatment.

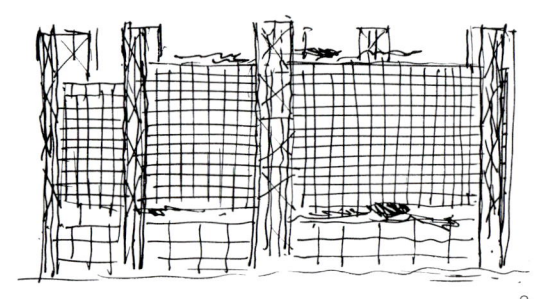

476 Norman Foster Works 1

A recurrent theme in Foster's oeuvre might be dubbed 'the urban room'. Typically this is a large, naturally lit space, an inward extension of the public realm into a corporate, cultural or institutional building ... It is an architectural type compensating for the loss of a conventional public realm and sometimes helping to regenerate this realm by forging vital new links within it.
Peter Buchanan, *On Foster ... Foster On*, 2000
Left: With its ethereal lightweight steel and glass roof enclosing a two-acre courtyard open to the public seven days a week, the Great Court exemplifies the concept of the 'urban room' and is the natural successor to the Hammersmith scheme.

[Foster] was left with one minor satisfaction: his Hammersmith Centre is one of the few modern buildings for which prominent local residents have held protest meetings not against but in favour. Felix Barker and Ralph Hyde, *London as it Might Have Been*, 1982

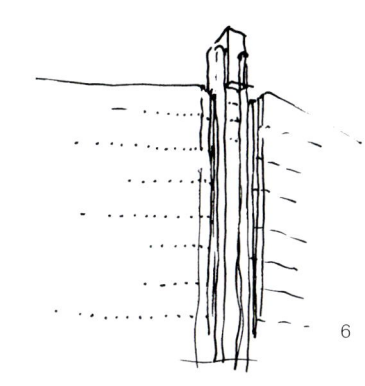

4. In the final scheme, the corner service zones are articulated into linked pairs of steel-lattice towers.

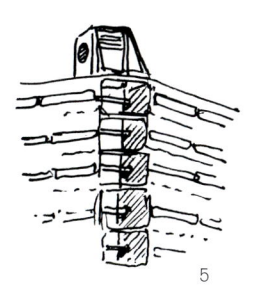

5-7. Earlier alternative options, explored here in Norman Foster's sketches, introduced a clear view through to the central space but repressed the service elements almost entirely.

Overleaf: Surrounded by eight storeys of offices and covering the equivalent of Trafalgar Square in area, the Hammersmith Centre's central space would have been one of the largest enclosed public volumes in Europe. This drawing by David Nelson, Ken Shuttleworth and David Morley, represents a synthesis of all the ideas inherent in the scheme. It was the first really big drawing that the practice had produced; in fact it was so large that it had to be taken off the usual Herman Miller desks in the Fitzroy Street studio and worked on in sections on flat work tables – heralds of the long benches in the present Riverside studio.

**The roof canopy was a conceptual breakthrough. At a stroke it resolved a series of problems and created a new set of architectural opportunities.**
Norman Foster

Hammersmith Centre 477

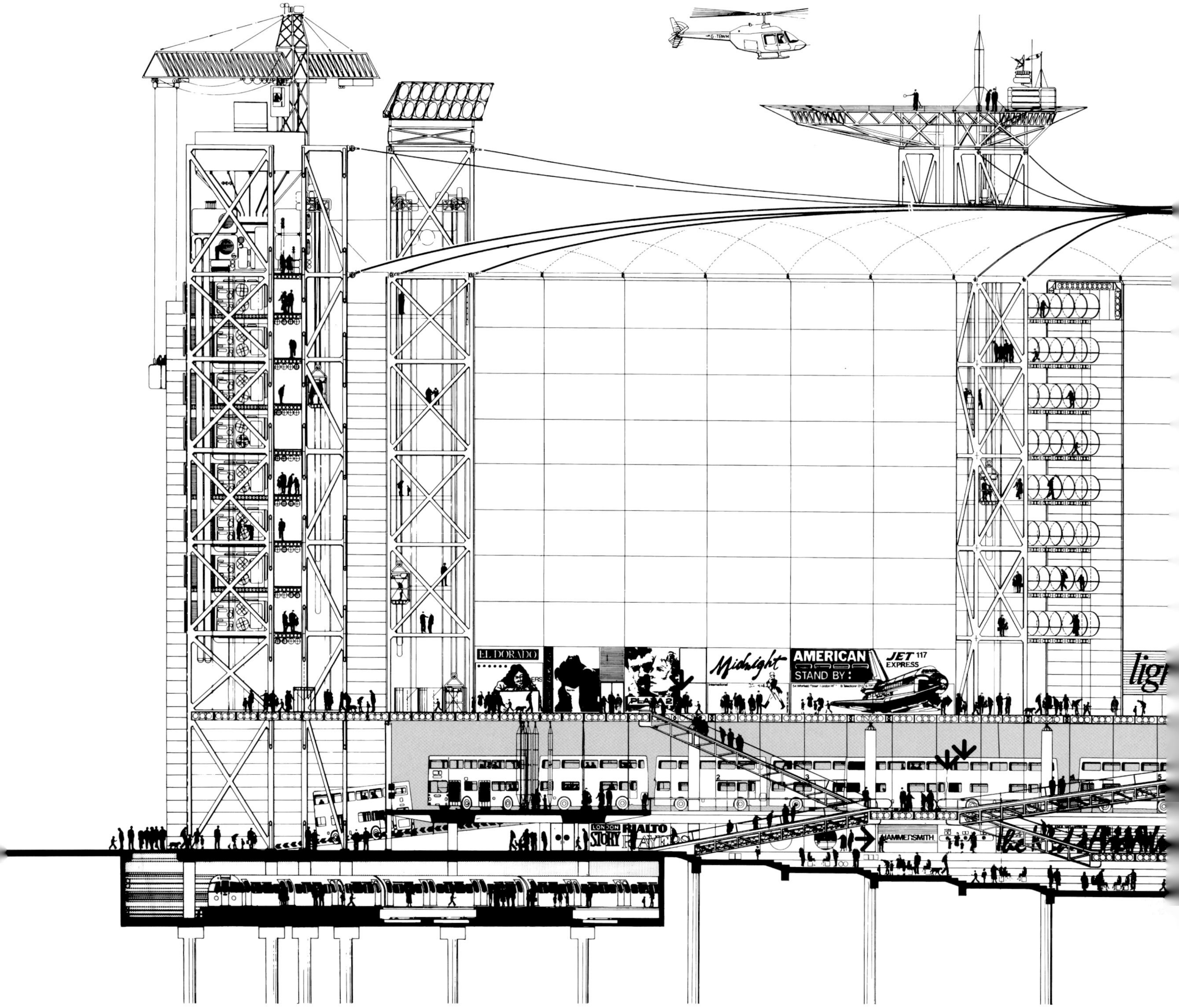
EL DORADO
Midnight
AMERICAN
STAND BY:
JET 117
EXPRESS
PLAZA 2
LONDON
STORY
RIALTO
HAMMERSMITH

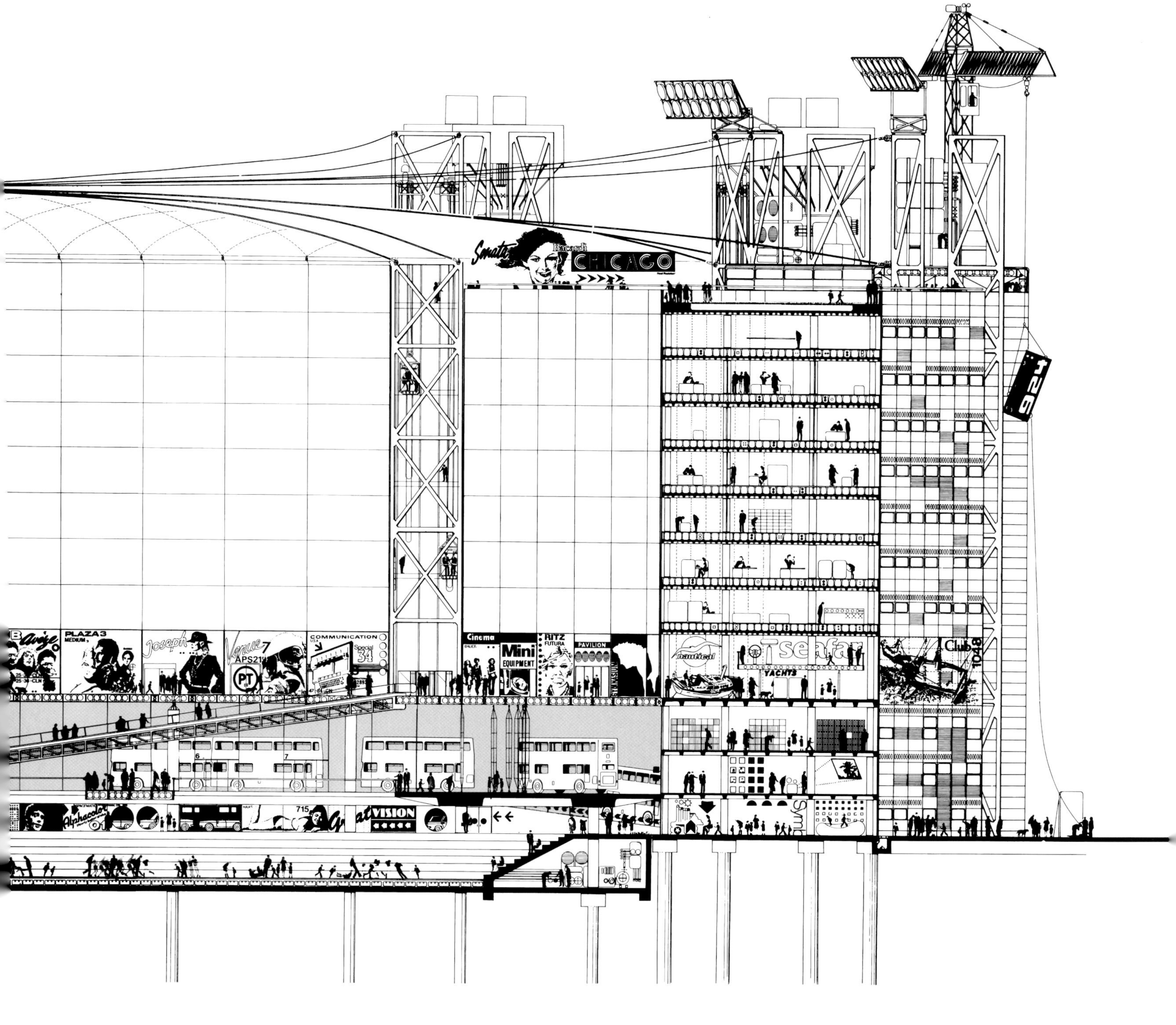
CHICAGO
PLAZA 3
MEDIUM
Joseph
APS21
PT
COMMUNICATION
Special
34
Cinema
Mini
EQUIPMENT
RITZ
FUTURA
PAVILION
nautical
seafar
YACHTS
Club
924
Alphacolor
715
VISION

# Joseph Shop
London, England 1978

The Joseph shop in Sloane Street was commissioned by the fashion retailer Joseph Ettedgui. Like Foster, he was an admirer of Pierre Chareau's Maison de Verre which, in its refined combination of steel, glass and studded rubber, was to prove a major influence on the design – the shop's hard 'industrial' framework offering a foil to the soft, colourful clothes.

The organising principle behind the project was a modest application of the 'perimeter theory'. A specially designed, double-height 'gantry' lining the perimeter utilised the full height of the space. In this way, it was possible to combine the maximum length of display and storage space with the creation of a large central area. Foster set out to reinterpret the way clothes might be displayed. Close attention was paid to every detail, including the size of members, so as to emphasise the lightness of the gallery structure. Painted dark grey, it created a subtle grid in which the clothes were given full expression.

Shops that seek to create an atmosphere appropriate to the goods they sell are by no means a new idea. The 1970s saw Biba introduce the idea into the fashion world, although Liberty had done much the same a century earlier. However, Joseph was one of the first shops to break certain conventions as to how 'designer' clothing should be displayed, and has since been much copied.

Tim Ostler

1. The premises had belonged to a well-known chain of shoe stores of the 'gilt chair and chandelier' variety. A false ceiling was stripped away and dummy columns removed to restore the Edwardian generosity of the original building, thereby creating a light and airy double-height space.

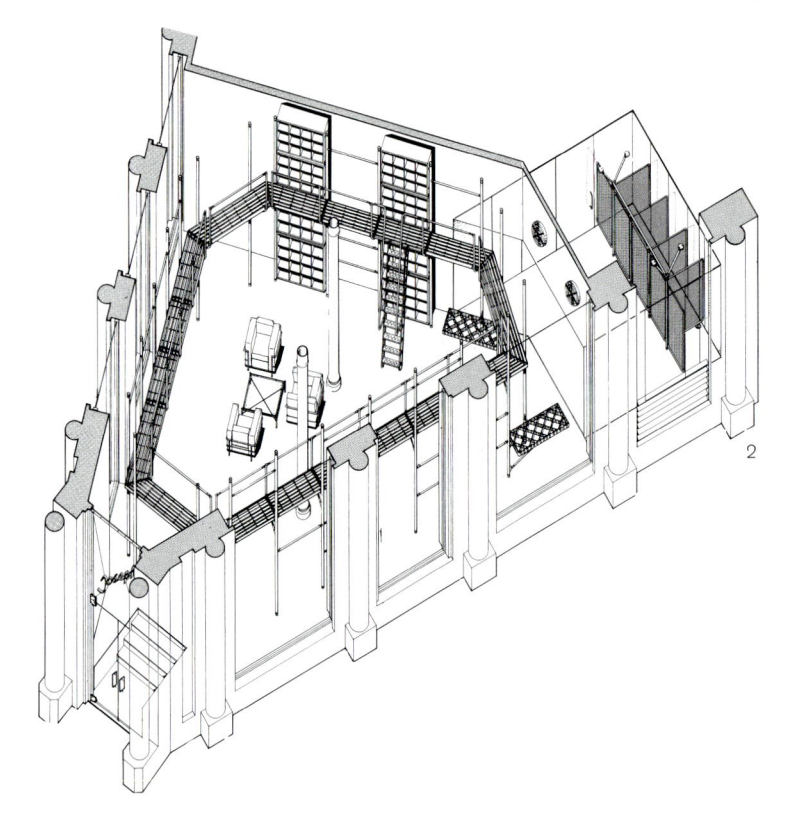

2. An axonometric drawing of the shop. By keeping the display to the edges of the plan a sense of spaciousness was created in what was, in reality, a very small floor area.

**This minimalist, functional environment reflected the understatement of Joseph's designs. At the time, this was considered a surprisingly 'masculine' setting for the display of women's clothing.**
Norman Foster

**Esprit's London agent was Joseph Ettedgui, so it was unsurprising when they proposed renovating the former Joseph shop on Sloane Street as their first shop in the capital. Where Joseph had used only the tall ground floor, however, Esprit preferred two floors of selling space, which meant descending into the previously unused basements.** Diana Periton, 'Esprit Shop', 1996

Far left, left: In 1987 Foster was commissioned to recast the Joseph shop as a new outlet for Esprit, the San Francisco-based clothing company. This involved piercing a circular aperture in the floor and unifying the two levels of retail space with a new glass staircase.

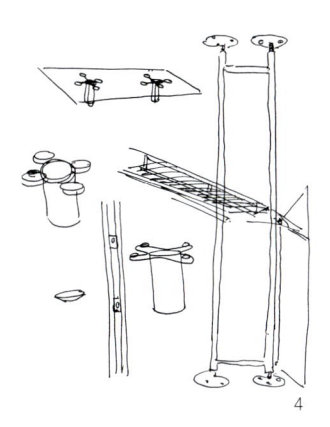

3-5. Norman Foster's own sketches illustrate the level of care and attention to detail in the development of the storage and display system. A 'kit-of-parts' approach and off-site prefabrication were essential if the very tight programme was to be achieved.

6. The elegant simplicity of the double-height display system, with its mezzanine walkway – consciously echoing Pierre Chareau's Maison de Verre – provided a discreet hanging frame on which the clothes were the focus of attention.

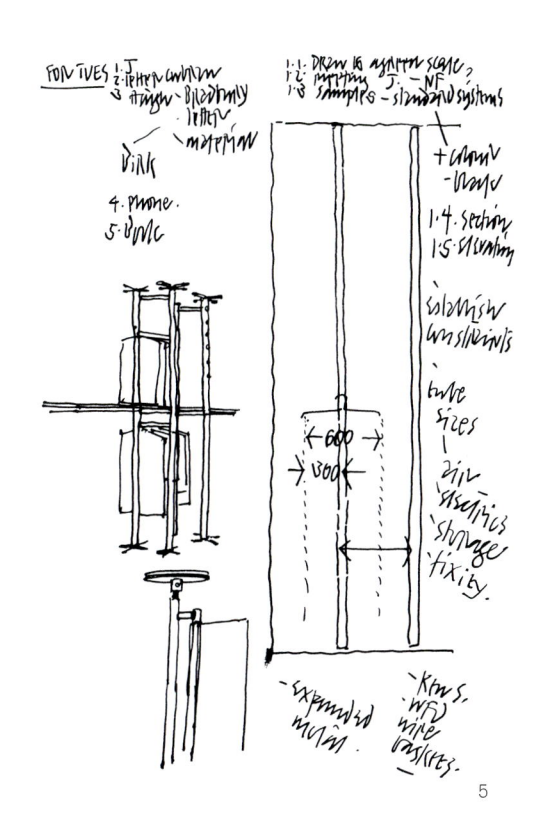

Joseph Shop   481

# Foster Residence

London, England 1978–1979

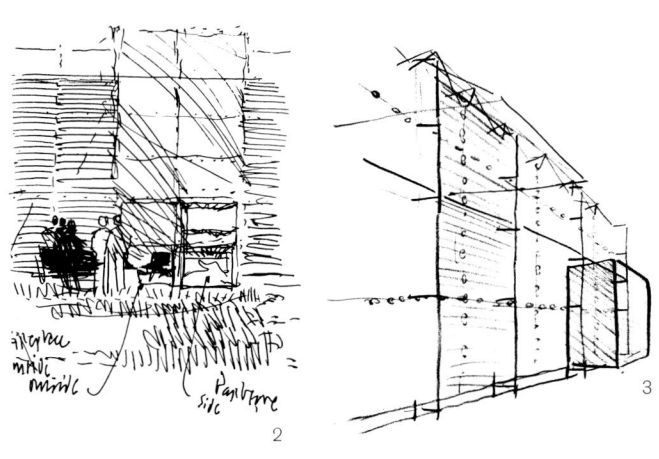

It would be more accurate to describe the studies on the house as an extension of Foster's already highly developed use of mock-ups, which nearly became a house, rather than a house design that was carried to mock-up stage.

Alastair Best

Charles and Ray Eames' seminal house of 1949 accommodated a variety of proprietary cladding elements in a lightweight steel frame to create informal spaces of great subtlety and character. Norman Foster first visited the house in the early 1960s, following his studies at Yale University, and it has proved a lasting influence. Left: Norman Foster's photograph of the Eames house.

**The plan can adjust to the circumstances in which we find ourselves as a family at this particular point in time, and can respond to patterns that we cannot possibly predict for the future: in terms of which of our children lives with us – which moves out, moves in or whatever; something that would enable us, if necessary, to create two buildings with a courtyard in between; something that would offer us that degree of flexibility.** Norman Foster, lecture at RIBA 'Frontiers of Design' conference, London, 28 September 1979

The Foster house was conceived during a relatively fallow period in the studio, coming as it did between the completion of the Sainsbury Centre and the start of the Hongkong Bank project. There was the time and space available to develop to a higher pitch some of the ideas embodied in the Sainsbury Centre, and the house was visualised as a series of private explorations that might have some application later on in public practice.

It was not necessarily Foster's intention to add to the existing canon of architects' pavilion houses. It would be more accurate to describe the studies on the house as an extension of his already highly developed use of mock-ups, which nearly became a house, rather than a house design that was carried to mock-up stage. In this, as in so many ways, Foster is much closer in his approach to Buckminster Fuller or Charles Eames than to other canonic house designers of the twentieth century.

The chosen site, a walled garden in Well Walk, Hampstead, shared an entrance with the adjoining house. The communal entrance was therefore treated in the form of a ha-ha, or sunken passage, and the site recreated as a descending series of platforms, with garaging embedded in the lowest level.

Foster has identified two chief shortcomings of the twentieth-century pavilion house. The first is the difficulty of relating it to its surrounding space and the second is the problem of relating subsidiary spaces to a central core.

The solution here was a clear-span box, made up of a primary skeleton of perforated aluminium plates braced by a secondary structure of aluminium tubes. On to this could be fastened an almost unlimited array of panels, pods and shells. As at the Sainsbury Centre, all the services elements were pushed to the periphery, partly in the interests of making a more expressive box, and partly to create a more luminous and open interior space, free from the spatial restrictions of a central core.

The Foster house carried the kit-of-parts idea to its logical extreme. It predates the Renault Centre at Swindon, but shares with it some of its functional expressionism. Before he abandoned the project under pressure of work on the Hongkong Bank, Foster had developed two mock-ups of the structural wall – one quite intricate, one less so. Later structural diagrams showed the design developing into something cooler and simpler.

Foster's studies for the house reveal a characteristic preoccupation with mock-ups and state of the art technology – the house would have incorporated packaged heat pumps and a raised computer-floor system – but they also reveal strong architectural preoccupations. The positioning of the pavilion on its terraced site, and the internal layering, are both influenced by his studies of Japanese houses and the struggle to achieve large, spatially fluid internal volumes – ideas that would continue to preoccupy him in the years ahead.

Alastair Best

1. The design studies carried out on the house emphasised its nature as a research project; indeed, the scheme was often referred to as a test rig. In this final model, the structural solution is clearly defined, supporting a grid of variable panels on its internal edge but with a secondary, external layer possible where required.

2. In Norman Foster's sketches of the cladding system the panels bear strong similarities to those used on the Sainsbury Centre, then recently completed.

3. Proposals for some form of external service 'pods' appear in Norman Foster's earliest sketches.

4. The long sloping garden site was to be terraced into a descending series of platforms, which would provide a sense of privacy for both the new house and the surrounding buildings. The services zone beneath the raised floor was sealed to provide a pressurised void for the distribution of warm or cool air.

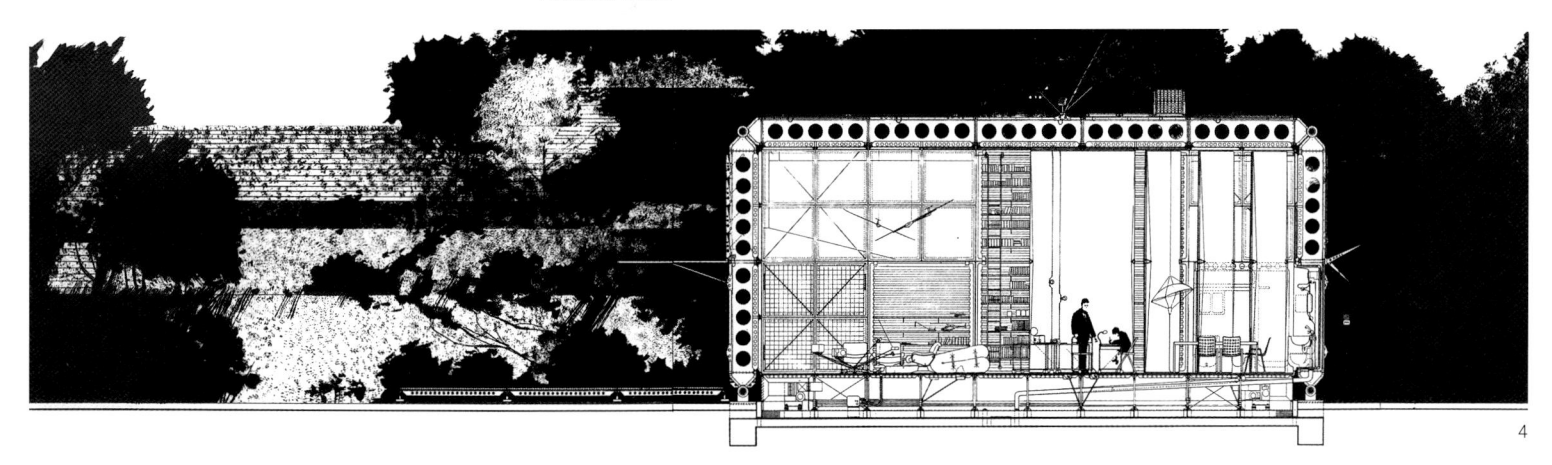

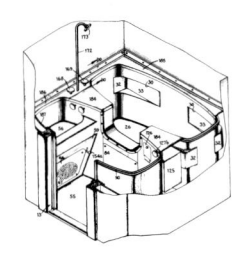

**In 1936, in the interests of exploring the development of prefabricated components for housing, Phelps-Dodge commissioned Fuller to design and assemble twelve prototype bathroom units based loosely on the assemblies he had proposed for the later versions of the Dymaxion House … pre-plumbed, pre-hand-welded copper sheet installations that could never have been economically produced, they attracted the hostile attention of organised labour when one or two were used in 'so-called Modernistic houses' as demonstration projects.** Martin Pawley, *Buckminster Fuller*, 1990
Left, right: Fuller's prototype bathroom module; Foster explored the use of similar modules in the house studies.

**The walls have interchangeable panels which can accommodate planting, or panels that can accommodate equipment. Within this concept you can then change that equipment; it may be bathrooms or heat pumps today, but we have no idea what it might be the day after.** Norman Foster, lecture at RIBA 'Frontiers of Design' conference, London, 28 September 1979

1. Working within the 1,200mm square panel coordinates, the lightweight structure provided a formal grid on to which an almost limitless range of cladding options could be clipped, zipped or bolted. Wall and roof modules embraced interchangeable solid, translucent or transparent panels – with an emphasis on high insulation values – through to wall elements, which provided packaged bathrooms, lavatories and storage. An edge zone provided the potential for a wide range of ancillary fittings including light diffusing louvres, blinds, moveable insulating quilts, solar panels, external lighting and planters.

2, 3. Full-size mock-ups of the house's main structural elements were produced and set up on an open site, where their relative scale and form could be properly appreciated.

4. Structural and cladding elements were to be the same whether used in the roof or the walls.

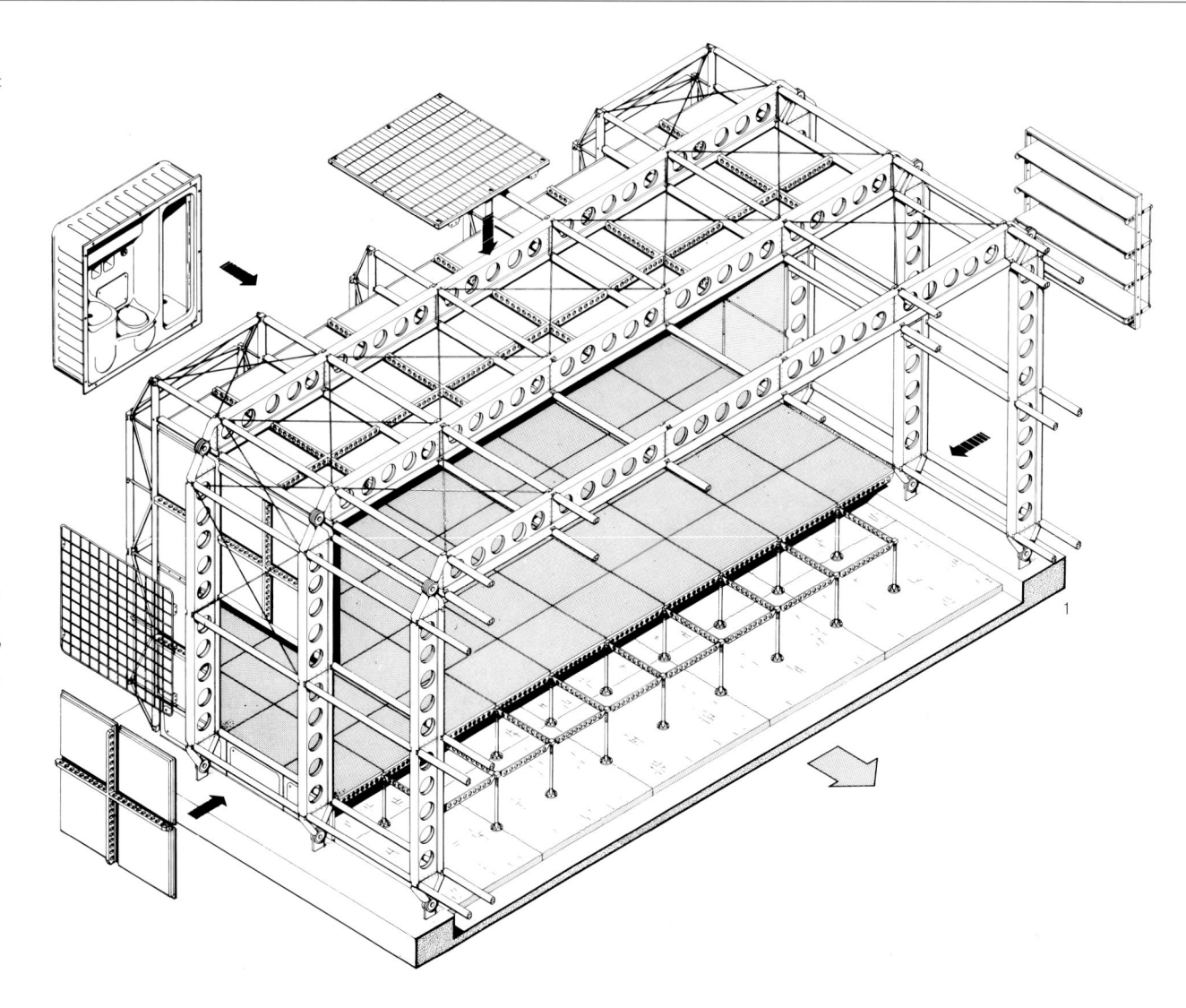

**As at the Sainsbury Centre, all the servicing has been pushed to the periphery to create a luminous and open interior, free from the spatial restrictions imposed by a central core.**
Alastair Best

**The manner in which the tatami mat and framed structure articulate interior spaces can be seen quite clearly in the Katsuro Imperial Villa ... There are many lessons to be learned about the possibilities of achieving a more subtle world in between the extremes of transparency and opacity – back to the exciting possibilities offered by the new generation of space-age materials and to the tradition of Pierre Chareau's classic Maison de Verre.** Norman Foster, RIBA Royal Gold Medal address, London, 21 June 1983
Left: The Katsuro Imperial Villa, in Kyoto – a powerful influence on the design of the Foster house.
Right: Pierre Chareau and Bernard Bijvoet's Maison de Verre (1928-1931).

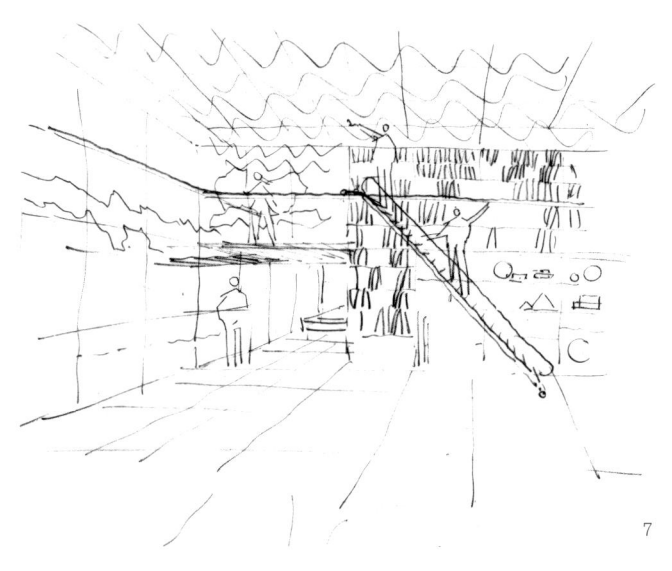

5. A model view of the main living space in the house.

6. The plan was organised on a basic 4.8-metre-square module, coordinated with the 1,200mm panel dimension. The fall across the site was exploited to create an undercroft at one side of the house for use as a covered parking area.

7. The influence on the house of Pierre Chareau's Maison de Verre is readily apparent in this sketch by Norman Foster; the mixture of double-height spaces and mezzanines and the detailing of the 'library' stair offer clear echoes.

Foster Residence

# London Gliding Club
Dunstable Downs, England 1978

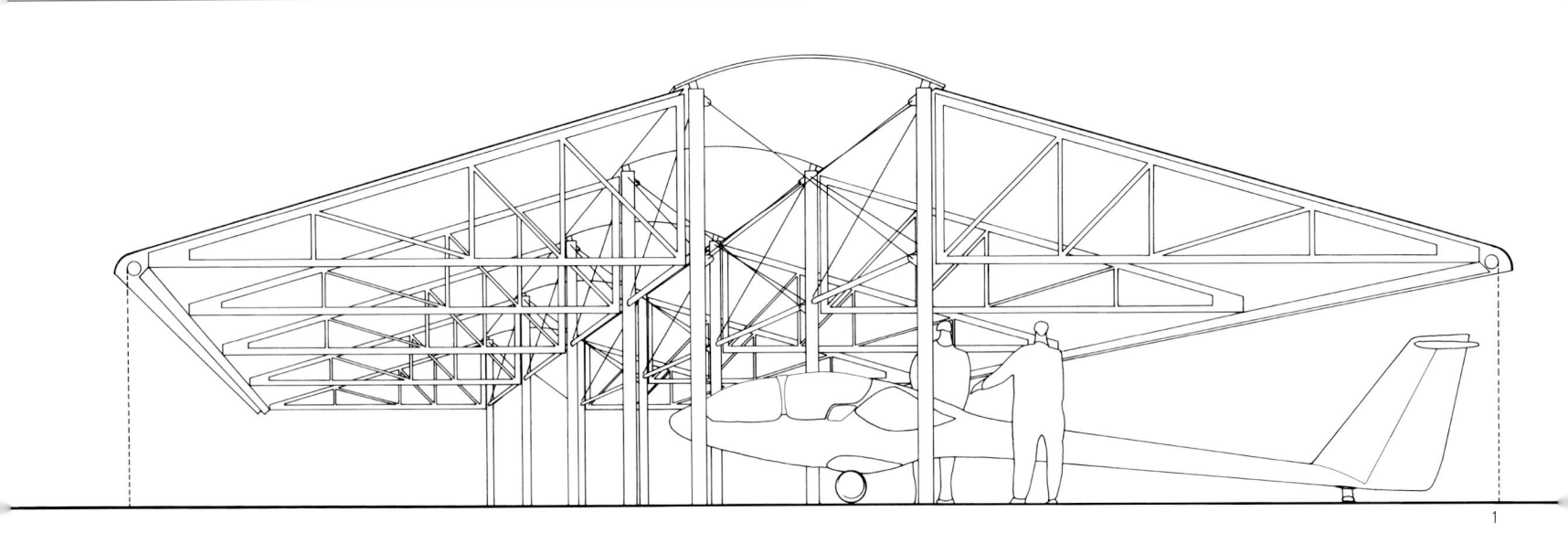

As a child I was obsessed with model aircraft and it can be no accident that the machines which give me most pleasure to fly are themselves like overgrown models.

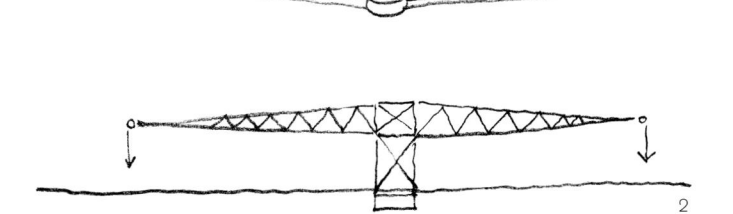

Norman Foster

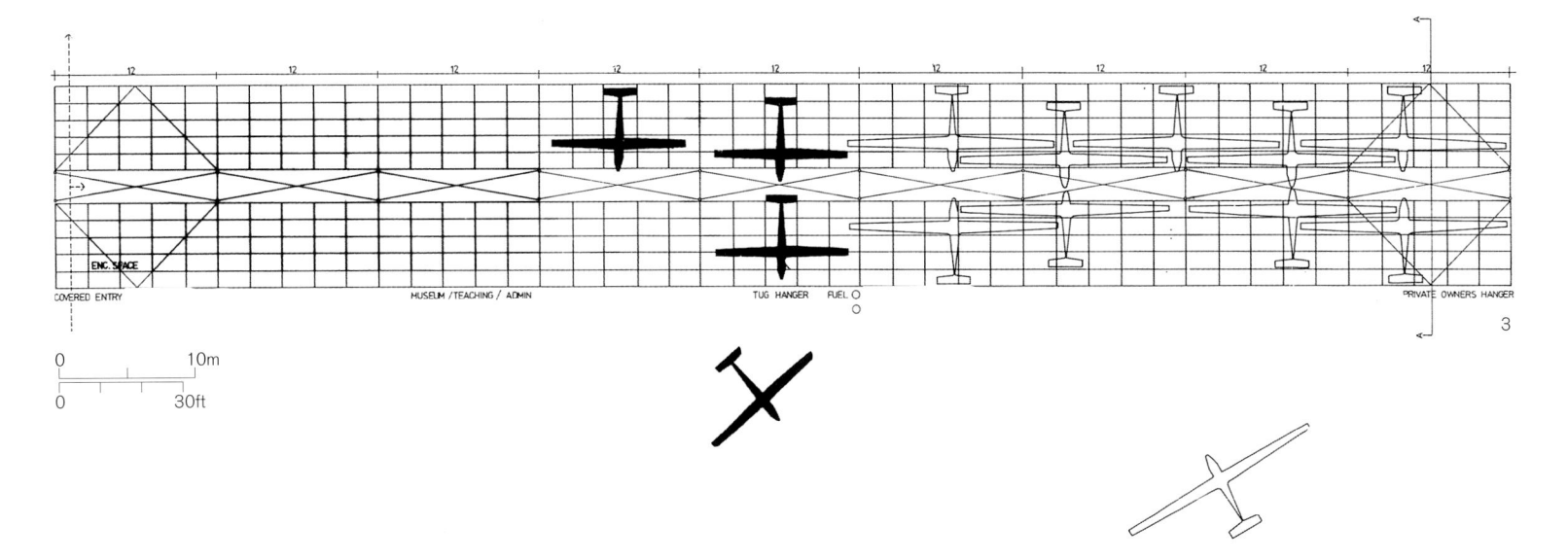

If you look at a racing sailplane in glass- or carbon-fibre, you'll see they are unbelievable. Beautiful. That's why I took to gliding in the first place; the actual tactile quality of the machine, even if it never flew, frozen in space.
Norman Foster, quoted in *The Architects' Journal*, 30 March 1983
Left: Norman Foster in his Libelle racing sailplane. Designed in 1964 by Wolfgang Hutter and Euggen Hanle, the Libelle was the first fibreglass sailplane. It revolutionised competitive soaring; in 1995 a fifteen year old Libelle sailplane set a world speed record of 126km per hour.
Right: One of Norman Foster's many sketches of a sailplane in flight.

Norman Foster's personal fascination with aircraft gives added relevance to the classic design analogy: just like a plane, when any designed product has finally integrated all the conflicting demands made upon it, it has to fly. Foster's informal response to a perceived need at the London Gliding Club at Dunstable Downs – where he used to fly his own glider – rather pleasingly brings together the concerns of aviation and architecture.

The somewhat restricted existing storage facilities for gliders at Dunstable were located beneath the clubhouse itself, a handsome 1930s building. Many of the surrounding auxiliary facilities had been acquired in a random fashion over the years, and there was a clear need for a fresh approach and a sympathetic new storage building. The need to accommodate gliders of differing wingspans militated against any sort of building supported by perimeter columns and Foster therefore proposed a cantilevered form, which would accept any number of stacking configurations.

Like the gliders it would store, the new enclosure was designed to be prefabricated and demountable, allowing the minimum on-site construction at an environmentally sensitive location. The steel frame was to be transported to site in simple, clearly articulated sections, designed to facilitate rapid assembly. The result not only offered an inexpensive and highly practical solution; it also provided a satisfying addition to the club by echoing the streamlined imagery of fuselage and wing.

Graham Vickers

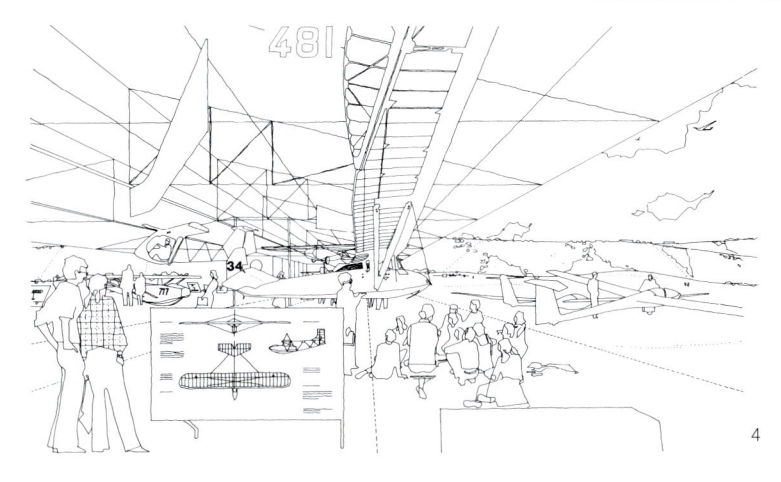

> **Like the gliders it would store, the new enclosure was designed to be demountable.**
> Graham Vickers

1. Gliders come in a variety of shapes and sizes. The new structure would have facilitated their storage in a number of configurations. Its width allowed aircraft to be 'overlapped' to maximise spatial efficiency, while the cantilevered form avoided the need for perimeter columns, which would have restricted access.

2. Norman Foster's sketch explores the analogy between the building's cantilevered roof form and the gliders it would house.

3. The linear plan form was both the most economic and the most flexible.

4. A perspective view, looking along the spine of the new hangar building.

5. Birkin Haward's drawing captures the spirit of the Dunstable Downs airfield.

London Gliding Club

# Open House
Cwmbran, South Wales 1978

Right: The Open House project, while founded on sound economic and practical considerations, was sadly not developed much beyond the conceptual stage. As such, it is Birkin Haward's series of sketches — produced to illustrate a fund-raising prospectus — that most memorably capture the spirit of the scheme.

**The final building also promised great efficiency in terms of environmental engineering. Recycled heat from the ice-rink would have satisfied most of the building's requirements for heating and hot water.**
Tim Ostler

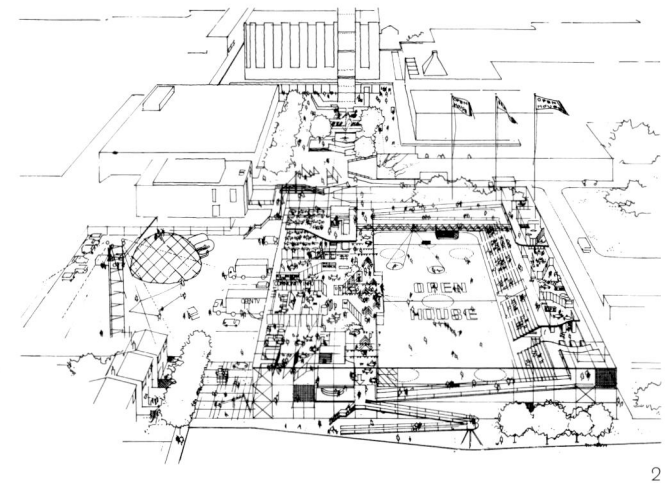

In 1978 Norman Foster was asked to design a combined community, arts and leisure centre for the new town of Cwmbran in South Wales. His client was Joe Miller, director of the Cwmbran Children's Trust and a former local community worker. In the words of Miller's initial fund-raising report, the aim of the project was, 'to generate and support community schemes throughout the region and to create new kinds of work, leisure and self-help'.

**With its multi-functional spaces and lack of social demarcation lines, the principles behind this project were quintessentially in tune with Foster's philosophy.**

At the time, unemployment in the region, and in the UK as a whole, was soaring and leisure was expected to occupy an increasingly dominant part of most people's lives. The Open House was a serious attempt to create the kind of social centre that this vision of the future implied. Included within it were facilities for community enterprises that would assist small businesses and unemployed school-leavers.

As a building it would be something quite new. The combination of activities it housed was intended to make the centre financially self-supporting. Perhaps the most novel feature in what was essentially to be a community centre was the inclusion of an ice-rink. As a 'non-elitist' facility, this was intended to draw in people who might then be persuaded to share in a range of other activities. The centre would also serve as a base for mobile community arts units, which would serve the surrounding area. With its multi-functional spaces and lack of social demarcation lines, the principles behind the project were quintessentially in tune with Foster's philosophy.

The site lay on an established route to the town centre from a nearby housing estate. Foster was keen to tap the flow of potential visitors on their way into town and draw them into the heart of the project. The plan form was therefore elaborated as a route, a configuration that recurs throughout Foster's work.

This linear path through the centre of the building was flanked, to the west, by shops, kiosks, markets, a coffee bar and a pub, while at the lower level, to the east, was the much larger space of the ice-rink. This arrangement offered many advantages: the smaller-scaled zone grouped together those areas that would be more intensively serviced; while, at a more practical level, the large-scale area could be used during construction as a covered builders' yard and storage area. Construction materials and techniques were selected to attract the maximum involvement of local firms and individuals. At the same time, however, the building – contained within a characteristic all-enveloping enclosure – also promised great efficiency in terms of environmental engineering. Calculations showed that heat extracted from the ice-rink, when recycled, would have satisfied most of the building's requirements for heating and hot water.

Sadly, sufficient funding for the project proved impossible to secure and work did not proceed beyond the initial development stage.

Tim Ostler

1. A model of the scheme prepared as part of the fund-raising process. The structural grid allowed the insertion of a choice of solid, glazed or louvred panels as appropriate.

2. The site lay on the route between Cwmbran town centre and a residential estate. It was proposed to bring this route through the centre of the new scheme, via a three-storey 'strip' of exhibition and information areas, cafeterias, local crafts shops, workshops and other small-scale community facilities. This route would have overlooked an ice-rink on one side and an open area on the other, which could be used for larger-scale outdoor activities and exhibitions.

3. A diagrammatic section shows high-level galleries extending right round the ice-rink enclosure.

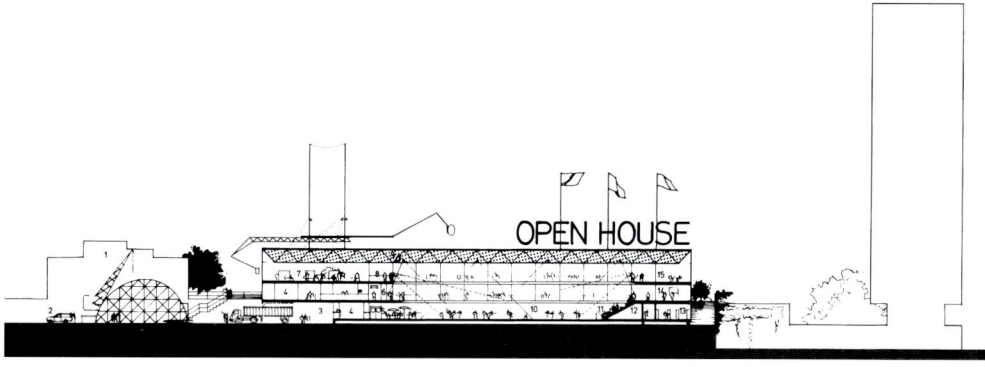

# Granada Entertainment Centre
Milton Keynes, England 1979

1. An early drawing of the Centre shows a far more elaborate tensile fabric enclosure than the simple 'squared' dome finally adopted. Self-supporting mezzanine structures within the enclosure could house almost any combination of leisure activities, while the suspended advertising wall that surrounds the enclosure – and hangs from the tension cables – is shown with a variety of display options including neon lighting systems and cantilevered signs.

2. On the final model the advertising wall provides the focus of attention. The vitality that could be created by such a system is becoming apparent.

3. Only the simplest of proposals for the internal arrangement were drawn. A swimming pool with wave machine and beach was proposed, but other areas were never fully resolved.

In 1979 Milton Keynes was emerging as one of Britain's most ambitious and populous New Towns. Granada, a firm specialising in leisure services, recognised the potential for an entertainment complex in the region and approached Foster Associates for ideas.

Norman Foster interpreted the brief on his own level. For him, as with a number of other architects who emerged in the 1960s, the idea of the 'fun palace' carried a powerful emotional charge. All of Foster's projects include, as an important part of their aims, the creation of an atmosphere of liberation and discovery among their users. In the case of the 'fun palace' this impulse occurs in its purest form, as the sole purpose of the building is to develop an atmosphere of spontaneity.

With the Granada Entertainment Centre Foster sought to create a completely free and open space for the building's various leisure activities. Following the Hammersmith project, there remained considerable enthusiasm in the office for the spatially liberating potential of a suspended roof and, in this respect, there are clear similarities between the two projects.

The building was broken down into two parts: a shelter for the various activities and, surrounding it, a vertical enclosure that gave it a public face. The shelter element was provided by a simple fabric 'bubble', hung from cables that were tensioned by diagonal props and secured in the ground outside the building's 'walls'. Hanging from the cables as they passed vertically into the ground were grids that supported panels for advertising. The physical aspect of the building, required to create a sense of identity and place, was thus reduced to the thinnest of structural supports and the ephemera of advertisers' signs.

The design was warmly received by Milton Keynes Development Corporation, but sadly Granada chose not to pursue the proposals. Although the idea of using advertising hoardings to generate a building form has not materialised elsewhere, it is interesting to note that, since this project, the idea of free-form lightweight structures enclosing and creating their own environment has been widely taken up as an appropriate form for leisure centres and swimming pools around the world.

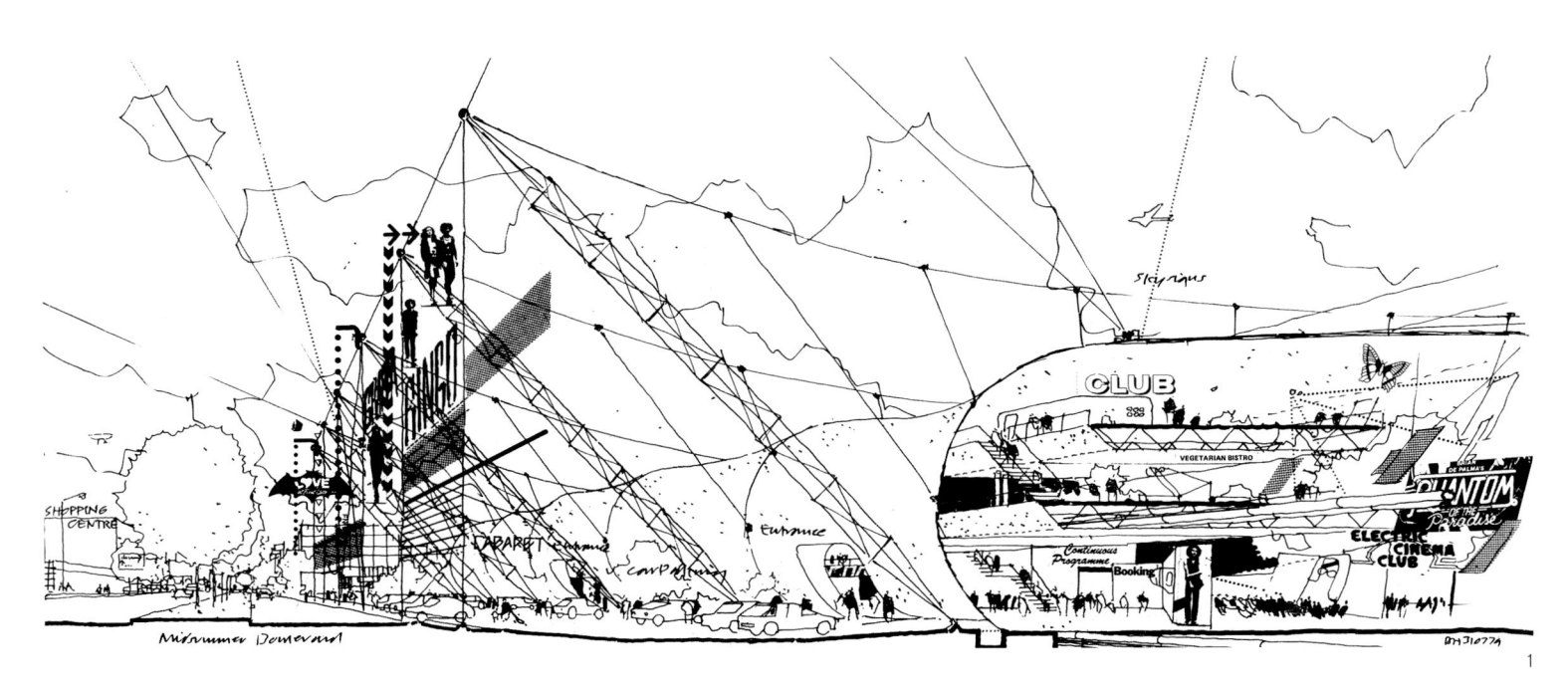

Tim Ostler

Left: A typical Los Angeles cluster of billboards, which are as much a part of the urban scene as the buildings behind them. Large-scale billboard structures such as these inspired the facade treatment of Foster's Granada Entertainment Centre; their changing content would have given the building an added dynamic dimension.

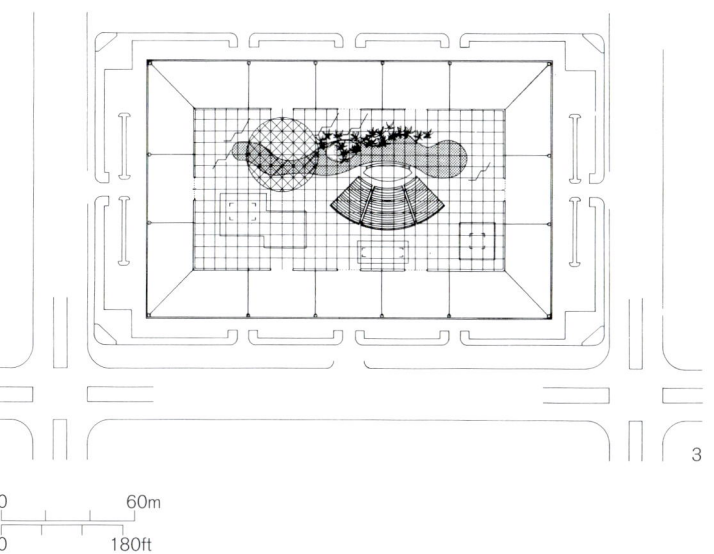

**All of Foster's projects include, as an important part of their aims, the creation of an atmosphere of liberation and discovery among the users.**
Tim Ostler

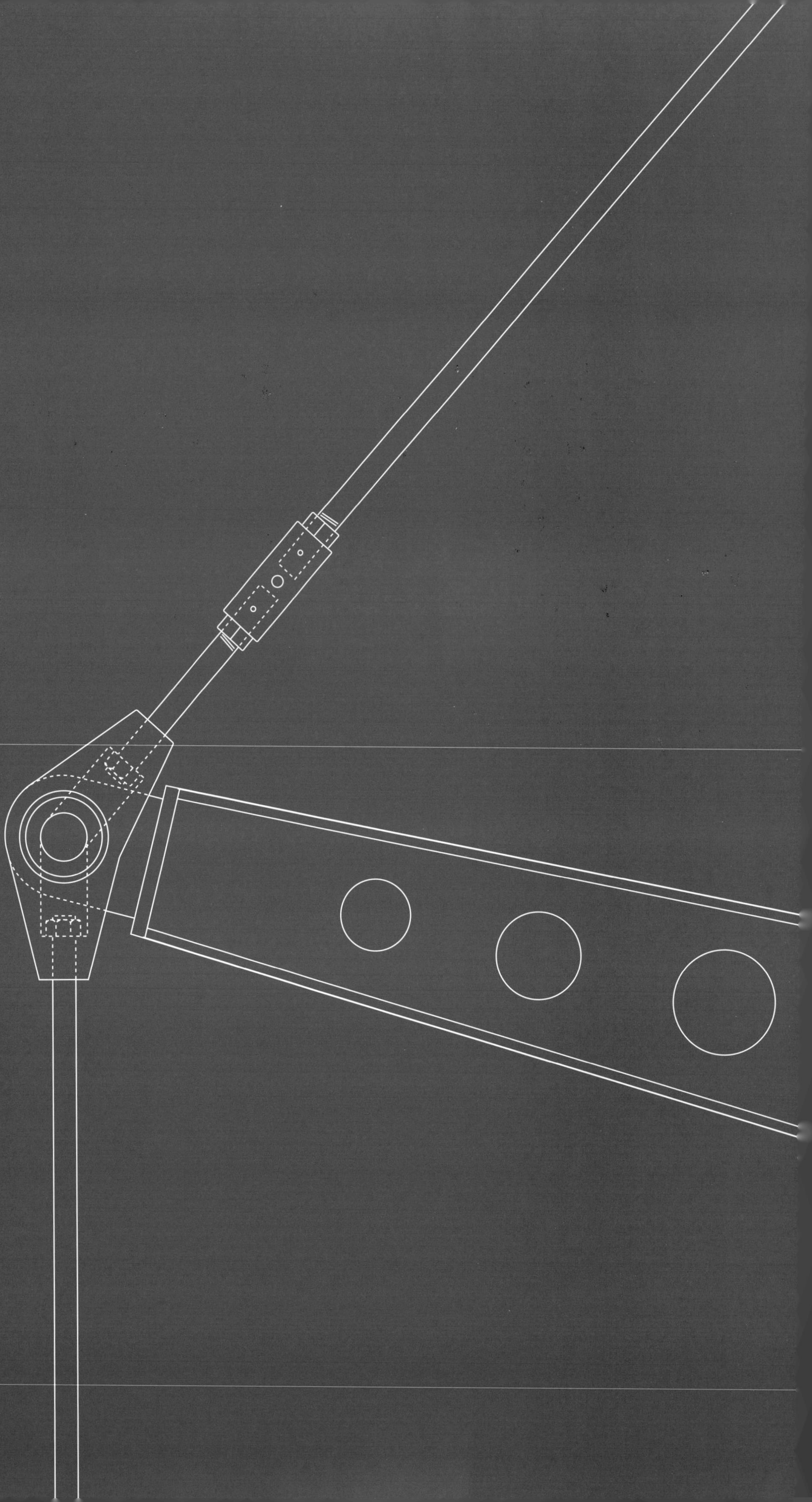

**Renault Distribution Centre**
Swindon, England 1980–1982

The Renault Centre has been described as the practice's most 'playful' structure, but its development owes much to earlier, perhaps more reticent schemes for clients such as Fred Olsen and Reliance Controls. The building forms a single enclosure, with a masted structure – painted 'Renault yellow'. Its generous internal clear height allows it to accommodate warehouse racking or be subdivided to contain two office floors. In plan the structural envelope steps back to a single, open bay which forms a *porte-cochère* alongside a double-height 'gallery'. Primarily a showroom, the gallery is also a focus for social events, encouraging wider community involvement in the life of the building. Significantly, the centre is alone among the company's buildings in not bearing its logo: it has become such a powerful icon that Renault even uses it in its corporate advertising.
Norman Foster

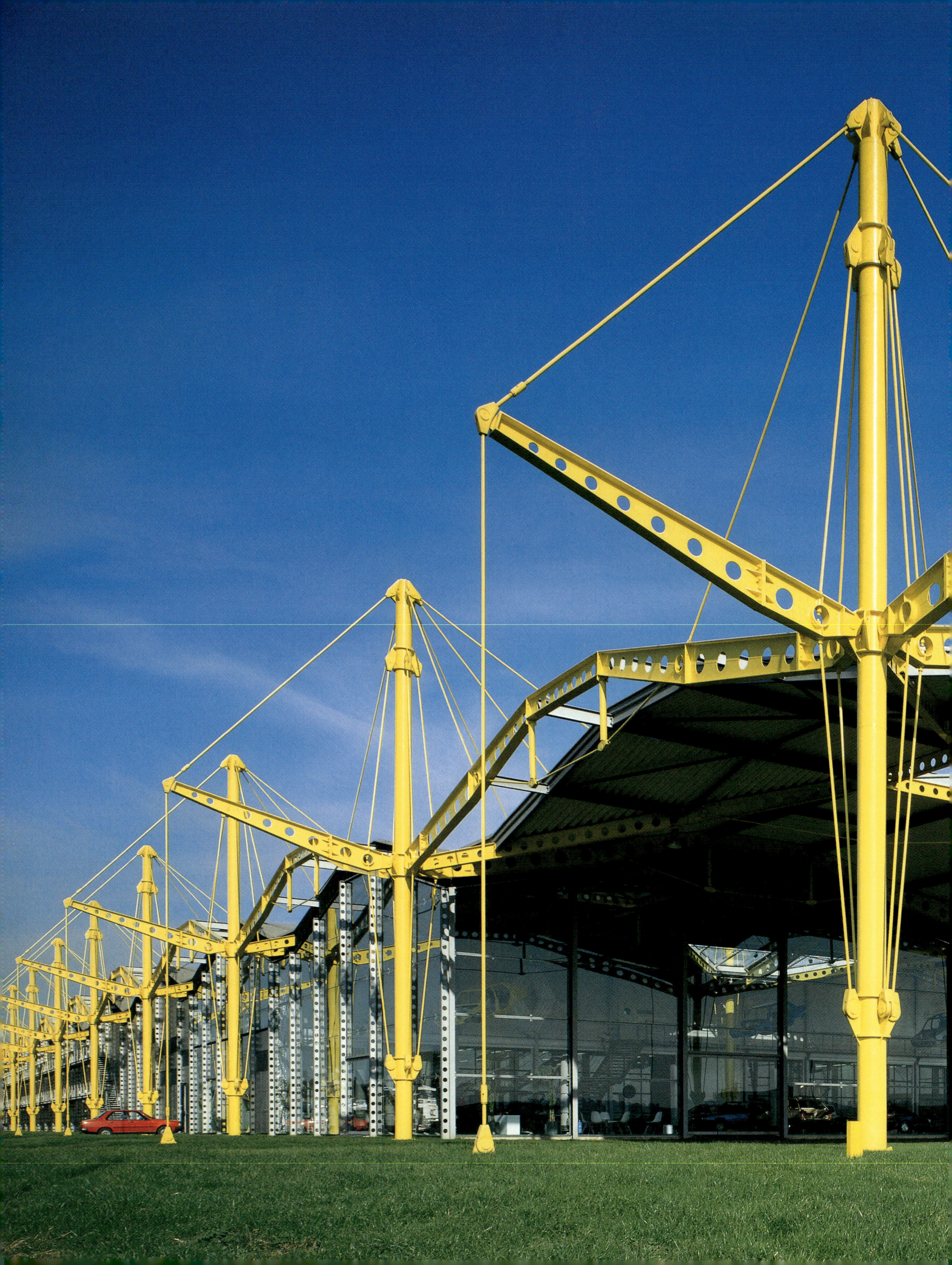

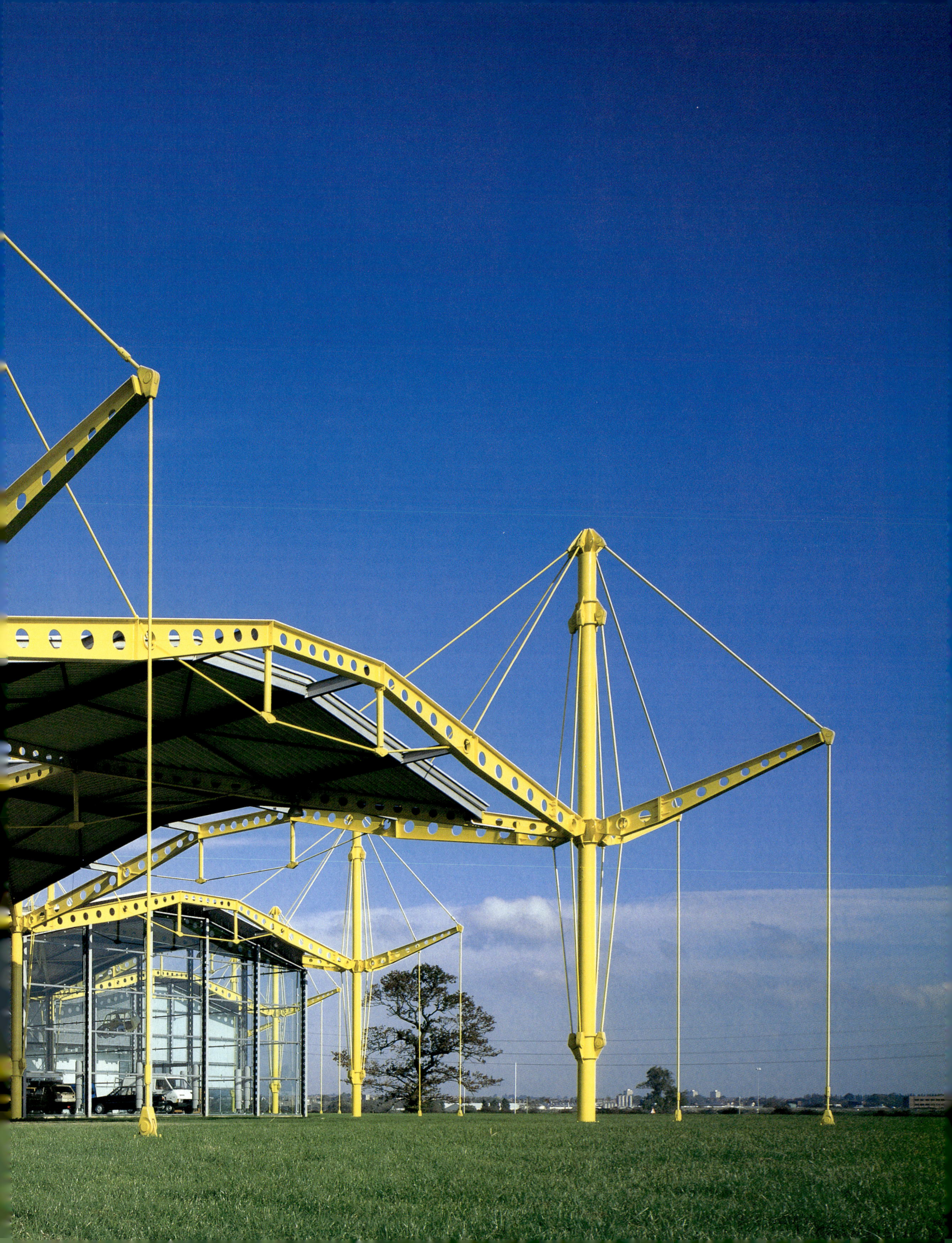

How Renault and Foster came together is something about which both parties prefer to remain coyly inscrutable. But there is really very little mystery about it. Foster is now the corporate architect 'de nos jours'. Any firm wishing to exhibit a keen design policy – which is precisely what Renault is attempting to do – will sooner or later be beating a path to his front door. Alastair Best, *The Architects' Journal*, 1 December 1982

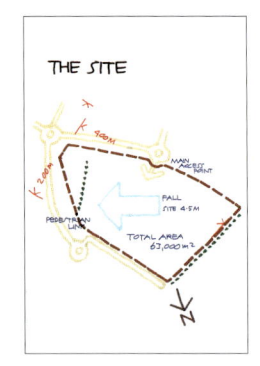

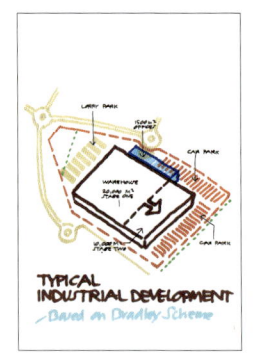

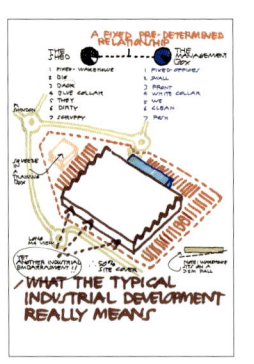

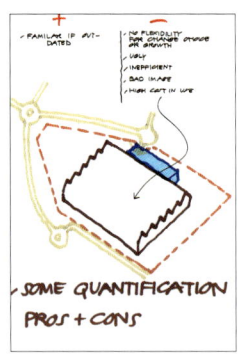

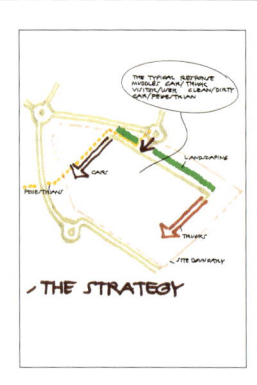

In 1979, Renault's share of the British car market was growing at such a rate that it looked unlikely that the company's national parts distribution centre in Reading would be able to meet future demand. Accordingly, surveyors were instructed to find a suitable location for a new centre. In October 1979, Renault UK purchased a 16-acre site in a new development area to the west of Swindon. The company was primarily interested in a replacement facility, which would be bigger but otherwise similar to its existing building.

Renault France, however, under its Coordinateur d'Expression Visuelle, Sébastien de la Selle, wanted to extend the company's reputation for design quality. Swindon's new Renault Centre presented him with the opportunity to do just that. It was clear that a conventional 'design and build' warehouse would not provide the required image. On the instructions of Renault France, therefore, Renault UK interviewed a number of leading architects. Foster Associates was one of the practices approached.

For Foster, the Renault commission offered the opportunity to continue the practice's exploration of factory systems begun in the early 1970s – with studies for unbuilt schemes such as the German Car Centre in Milton Keynes – and continued in the then newly completed Technical Park for IBM at Greenford.

For their part, the members of Renault's commissioning team visited Foster's buildings for Fred Olsen at Millwall Dock, Willis Faber & Dumas in Ipswich and IBM at Greenford, and came away highly enthusiastic. In Renault, Foster found a client body that was both positive and sympathetic.

## For Foster, the Renault project offered the opportunity to continue the practice's exploration of factory systems begun in the early 1970s.

Renault's requirements for the first phase of development were complex: a total of 20,000 square metres of warehouse space; a further 4,000 square metres of offices – housing the national after-sales service training school (relocated from London) and the south-west regional office (relocated from Reading) – together with a restaurant and a car showroom. However, the exact nature of each of these areas was not yet fully defined. It was therefore important to adopt a flexible planning strategy that would not impose too specific a mix of accommodation upon the building. Additionally, although Renault's sales were healthy in relation to the overall UK car-sales market, the market itself was depressed, which meant that the building budget was limited.

Left: Founded in Paris in 1899 by Louis Renault, inventor of the direct drive system, the Renault company rapidly expanded to become the largest manufacturing company in France and a major international contributor to automobile design and production. Early activities ranged from the production of vehicles as diverse as tanks and taxis, and the company has maintained this breadth of production.
Right: In addition to producing vehicles for the mass market Renault designs and constructs Formula 1 cars.

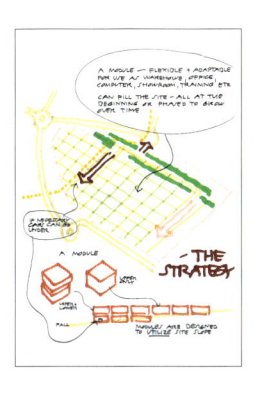

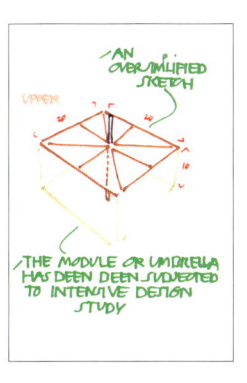

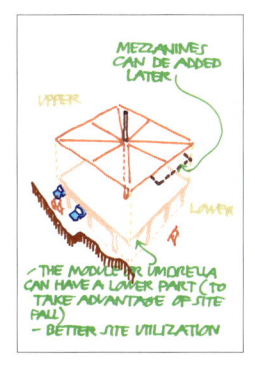

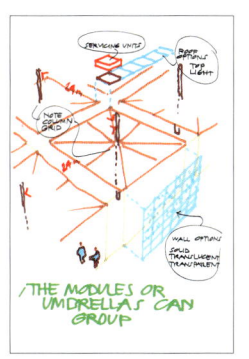

Foster's first presentation to Renault emphasised flexibility, speed of erection and low cost. A series of modular 'umbrella' structures was proposed, which would facilitate incremental growth in two directions, whilst allowing the overall shape of the building to respond to site boundaries. By implication it also recognised the requirement for future growth that the brief contained; but its square module contrasted with the linear plan of rectangular modules that had been adopted for similar projects in the past.

In Foster's eagerness to make maximum use of the site there was a hint of the strategy adopted at Willis Faber & Dumas, albeit with a far more articulated and expressive structure. Renault liked Foster's approach, but time was limited – Renault required a fully operational warehouse by the end of October 1982.

One early problem to resolve was the fact that the site had the capacity to accommodate about 40,000 square metres of floor area, yet the existing planning permission allowed Renault to develop only 30,000 square metres. However, Foster was optimistic that, if the scale and bulk of the building could be broken down, the planning authority might well be persuaded to increase this figure; that impression was confirmed during consultations with local planning officers. Like other towns in a time of growing unemployment, the local council was becoming increasingly proactive in marketing Swindon as a prime location for new industry. It was eager to raise the town's profile and to welcome Renault as a high-quality exemplar for future development.

Although it was in essence a 'green field', the site was bound by several physical constraints. Potentially all but one of the views was likely to be obstructed by future development, the one exception being the view to the south-east, which looked out across a neighbouring flood-plain. A site survey revealed a 5-metre fall along its length towards this plain. Furthermore, access was predetermined by the local authority in order to prevent traffic tailbacks on to the primary road system. Once on site, separate access was to be provided for goods and people – a requirement eventually satisfied by placing them at opposite ends of the building.

The mix of warehousing, administrative offices, training facilities, staff restaurant and car showroom specified in the brief implied 'blue-collar' and 'white-collar' accommodation. But Foster was determined to avoid such distinctions. Beginning with Reliance Controls, completed in 1967 (also in Swindon) Foster had pioneered the concept of democracy in the workplace in the UK, bringing assembly workers and administrative staff together in a single pavilion structure, with communal facilities specified to unprecedented standards. He speaks with conviction about 'reinventing the workplace'; and indeed, subsequent projects – such as those for Fred Olsen at Millwall Dock and for Computer Technology at Hemel Hempstead – are virtually built manifestos in this regard.

1. Buoyed by growing sales in the UK, Renault purchased a 16-acre site at Westlea Down – a development area to the west of Swindon – on which to construct a new national parts distribution centre.

2. This sequence of analytical sketches by Birkin Haward was presented at one of the first meetings with Renault. The sketches compare the problems generated by typical industrial developments – with their inefficient and fixed spaces – with a new approach, based on an 'umbrella' structure, that would embrace flexibility and growth over time.

**The local authority was really quite concerned about the possibility of a big box of a warehouse on the site. But the structural module concept broke down the scale of the building so effectively that they relaxed the planning regulations and raised the buildable area from 30,000 square metres to 40,000 square metres – which was an immediate bonus for Renault!**
Norman Foster, lecture at the Aspen Design Conference, 18 June 1986

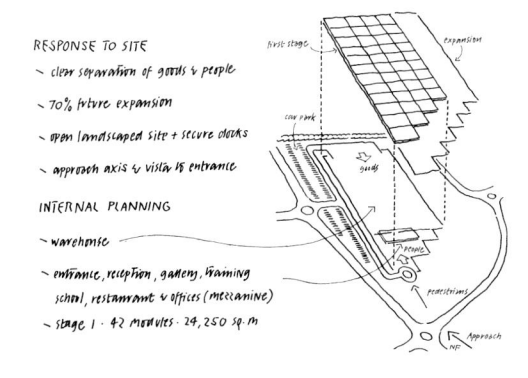

**Like most industrial sites, it isn't conveniently rectangular: the use of a square module is reminiscent in some ways of the Willis Faber building in its ability to respond to an amorphous site.** Norman Foster, lecture at the Aspen Design Conference, 18 June 1986
Left: Norman Foster's concept sketch shows how, if required, the Renault Centre's square planning module could be expanded carpet-like to cover the entire site.
Right: A series of early feasibility studies explored how the building might be extended in the future.

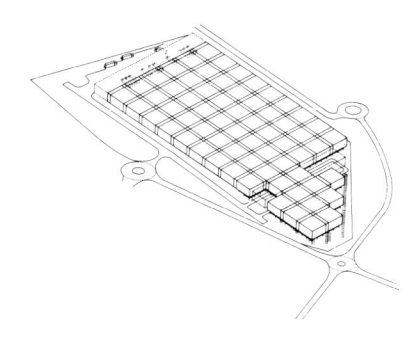

The fact that each specific area of the brief was not fully defined provided an added incentive for this flexible, democratic approach: a single envelope solution brought considerable practical advantages, allowing decisions such as how to subdivide the space to be left until relatively late in the programme. Once the envelope was decided, its interior could be 'tuned' to accommodate any variety of different requirements. This held true in both plan and section. A uniformly double-height space could be occupied by warehouse racking, or it could be divided to accommodate a mezzanine level in the office zone. It was determined that a structural bay of 24-metres square allowed the greatest degree of flexibility in laying out the various types of racking systems that Renault had specified.

**In Foster's eagerness to make maximum use of the site there was a hint of the strategy adopted at Willis Faber & Dumas, albeit with a more articulated and expressive structure.**

Although the idea of a modular 'umbrella' structure was considered from the outset, the decision to commit to this strategy did not come until fuller consideration had been given to all the options. These ranged from a conventional truss and rafters solution to grid-shells and suspension structures. These ideas are reflected in Norman Foster's sketches of the time, which also maintain a preference for some sort of suspended, centrally-supported umbrella. Although ground-based this might perhaps rise through a concrete floor sailing free of the fall in the site, providing protected access and parking areas.

Foster's choice of which option to pursue was made on quite consciously architectural grounds. (There are intimations, perhaps, of the mushroom columns at Frank Lloyd Wright's Johnson Wax building – an image that Foster discovered in the pages of Henry-Russell Hitchcock's *In the Nature of Materials* before he knew he would become an architect.) Ultimately, however, several factors flowed together to point in the direction of the tubular mast solution that Foster eventually adopted.

In retrospect, the first design presented to Renault can be seen to hint at the final scheme. The internal minimum height is set at 8 metres to accommodate the automatic material storage and retrieval systems specified by Renault. And although the structure is still clearly recognisable as a series of self-supporting umbrellas, elements such as the combined roof-light/smoke ventilators between the bays – which also light the interior – are in place.

Although it is masted, the overall effect of the final structure is more integrated, with each column braced against identical structures on all four sides. The masts are anchored at the ground with a pin-joint. The beams are connected to the masts by means of further pin-joints and are braced by two ties in each direction. The beams are angled upwards from the masts, partly because of drainage considerations, partly perhaps to suggest the 'umbrella' idea.

On plan, in this first scheme, the external envelope was to be located along the edges of the outermost structural bays. Consequently, the parapet is completely horizontal and the umbrella roof structures are largely hidden from view. Had it been pursued, the overall effect – with the intermittent full-height glazing and recessed entrance courtyard – might have been something akin to IBM Greenford; the major difference being that the cladding panels were to have been made from Kalwall – a translucent double-skin glass-fibre material – rather than the aluminium panels used at IBM. Outside the main envelope, loading bays were to be sheltered by a fabric canopy supported by umbrella structures identical to those within.

1. An aerial view of the completed Renault Centre demonstrates the extent to which its structural articulation invests a large slab of storage space with a rhythmic, tactile quality.

**If the Renault Centre is Foster's first unequivocal work of structural expressionism, it also marks a high point in the technological shift, begun at Willis Faber and continued at the Sainsbury Centre, from using ready-made to custom-made components from the factory. Almost all of the major component systems at Renault were designed and manufactured for the job in hand. Despite being custom-made, the use of a small variety of repetitive units and low-cost tools helped keep total building costs down to the same as those for a standard industrial 'shed'.** Chris Abel, 'From Hard to Soft Machines', 1989

**With the Renault building Foster seems to be attempting some kind of link with the structures of Victorian engineering: slightly ad hoc and overly chunky, because of the limitations of Victorian steel and iron specifications; overly elaborate around junctions – because they did not have welding. And slightly convoluted, partly because of the need to build in safety margins via redundant elements and partly because they had not yet developed the repertoire of economical or simple shapes which we now have.** Sutherland Lyall, *Building*, 10 June 1983

1-10. Conceptually, the Renault Centre's structure developed as a means of creating a system of self-sustaining modules, capable of grouping in any variety of configurations. The resulting umbrella would be able to respond to the demands of the site, or changing internal use, while allowing for future expansion. In collaboration with structural engineers Ove Arup & Partners, Norman Foster explored various structural options, which he elaborated in these early sketches. However, as the project developed the independent, centrally supported modules first proposed evolved into a more cohesive structure. But the original concept would go on to inform the design of the tree-like structural system that Foster would develop at Stansted Airport, a commission won shortly after the completion of the Renault scheme.

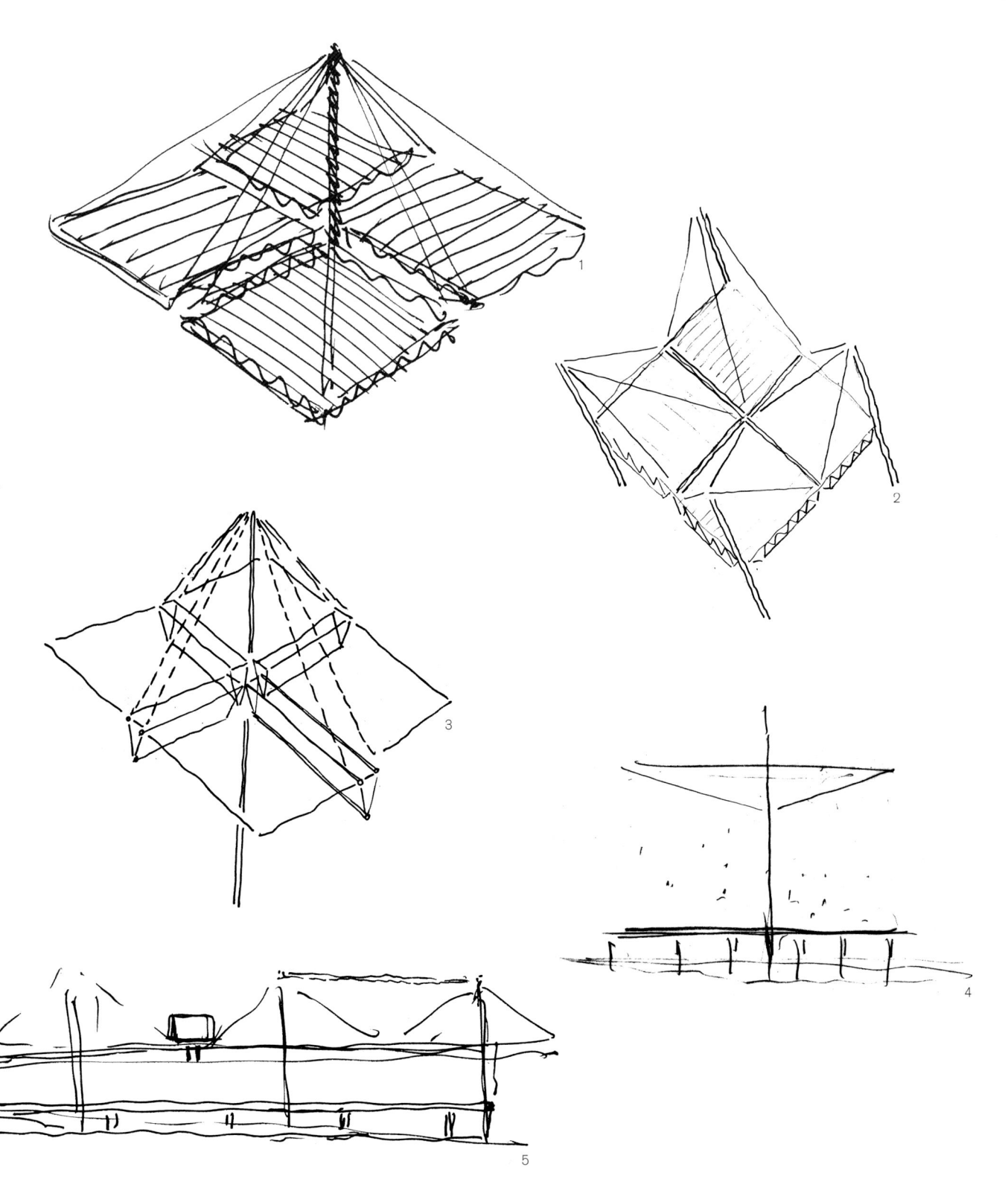

Foster's genius – the word is hardly too strong – is most apparent in his structural thought. He has often been called a High-tech architect, but actually, despite the complexity of some of his designs, the buildings don't brandish their technological language as gee-whiz metaphor; they use it as an essential tool of spatial effects and structural needs, always seeking the most elegant and succinct solution. Robert Hughes, *Time*, 19 April 1999

One of my passions is flying. In the years since the earliest prototypes were developed, there has been a refinement through streamlining, laminar flow, cantilevers and new materials such as glass-fibre. With each adaptation, horizontal speed increases and vertical speed decreases, and with each refinement the machines become more beautiful and the flying experience more amazing. I am continually seeking to apply my admiration of the technology of flight to designing buildings. Norman Foster, lecture at Stuttgart University, 14 May 1987
Left: Tensile structures have long been a source of reference for Norman Foster, whether hang-gliders, suspension bridges or modern agricultural machinery.

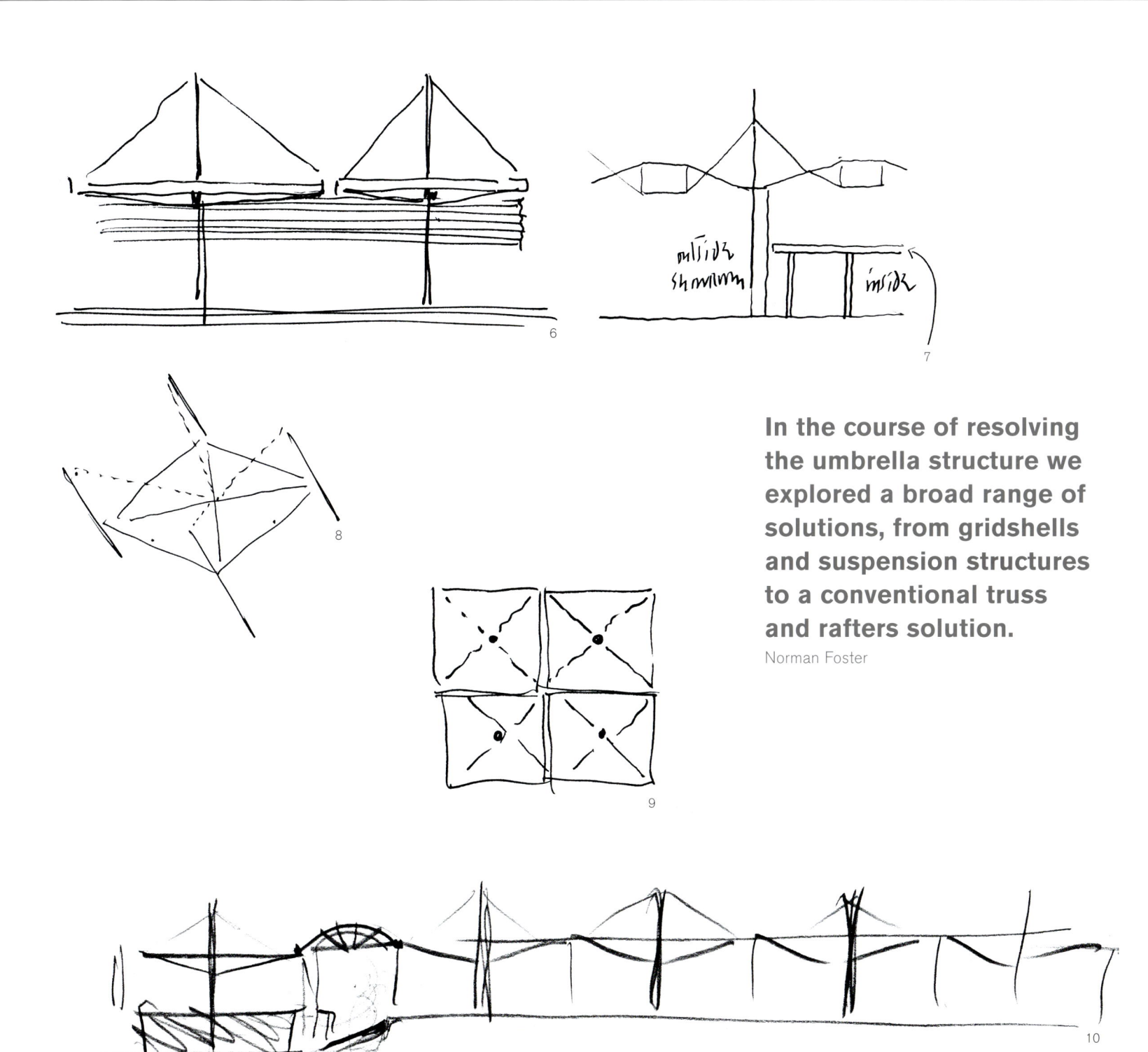

**In the course of resolving the umbrella structure we explored a broad range of solutions, from gridshells and suspension structures to a conventional truss and rafters solution.**
Norman Foster

Renault Distribution Centre 501

**All architects carry with them a mental store-house of their favourite architectural images, ready to dip into in times of need and, though his references are frequently unconventional, Norman Foster is no exception. The primary image the design team took with them to their first meetings with Ove Arup and Partners was that of Frank Lloyd Wright's graceful, free-standing concrete 'mushrooms' at the Johnson Wax administration building.** Chris Abel, *Architecture in Detail: Renault Centre*, 1991
Right: Frank Lloyd Wright's Johnson Wax Administration Centre, Racine, Wisconsin (1936-1939).

**As a schoolboy, my imagination was fired by the work of Frank Lloyd Wright as illustrated in the pages of Henry-Russell Hitchcock's *In the Nature of Materials* ... In particular, I remember being captivated by the science fiction images of the shimmering glass in the Johnson Wax building.** Norman Foster, RIBA Royal Gold Medal address, London, 21 June 1983

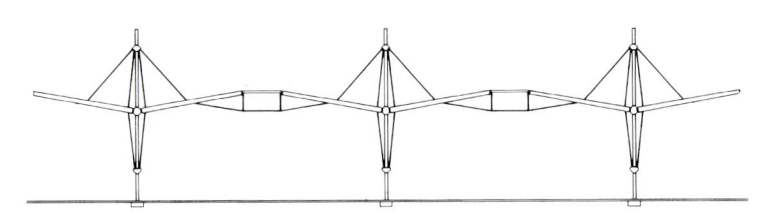

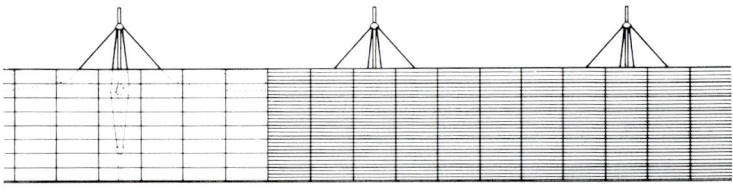

1. Initially, the structural system formed a series of self-supporting bays, with a central column. Each bay was independent from its neighbours, the zone of separation bridged by a roof-light. The undulating roofline was concealed behind a parapet.

2, 3. In the first scheme a 2-metre wide zone separated each bay. This zone was spanned by roof-lights, combined with louvres to provide ventilation.

One of the most distinctive features of this first scheme was the undercroft, which, it was proposed, could contain the after-sales service training school and car parking. Again, a parallel can be drawn with IBM Greenford and its bridge over the service road. There were other precedents also. Architecturally, the undercroft had the effect of detaching the building from the ground and thus accentuating the contrast between the green-field site and the pristine metal shed above. In this respect it refers to earlier Foster projects, such as the Country Office buildings for Fred Olsen at Vestby, in Norway, of 1973, in which Foster aimed to minimise the impact of the new buildings on their sensitive woodland setting by elevating them above the forest floor.

Foster was also conscious that the Renault building, located on the crest of a hill, would be visible from some distance. Cutting into the incline and raising the office/showroom end of the building would have allowed a more prominent approach, as well as better views out from the offices and restaurant. At the same time the loading bays would have been partially concealed by the rising ground.

Furthermore, the initial decision to raise the floor slab in this way was based on the assumption that pile foundations would be required, in which case it would have been necessary to span between pile caps in any event. It was only when a detailed survey of ground conditions indicated that elaborate foundations would not be required that the justification for the undercroft disappeared.

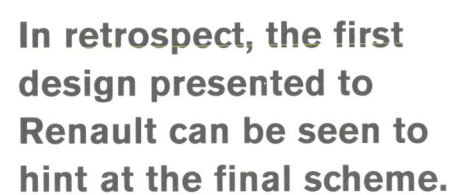

## In retrospect, the first design presented to Renault can be seen to hint at the final scheme.

The development of the structure was subject to similarly rigorous analysis. In order to provide the maximum flexibility, the original scheme had envisaged the structure as a series of independent modules. But it was clear that the sort of expansion Renault envisaged would be neither frequent nor informal. Providing for this extreme degree of flexibility has, in any case, usually been more of a rhetorical than a practical ideal: few buildings designed to be extended on a 'plug-in' basis have been added to in this way. It also implies a certain degree of structural redundancy: if it had been applied to the Renault Centre, each mast would have had to cantilever from the ground and would have been unable to enjoy the structural benefits that derive from linking elements together. In practical terms, there was nothing to be lost and much to be gained by making the modules act not individually, but together in the form of an integral 'table' structure.

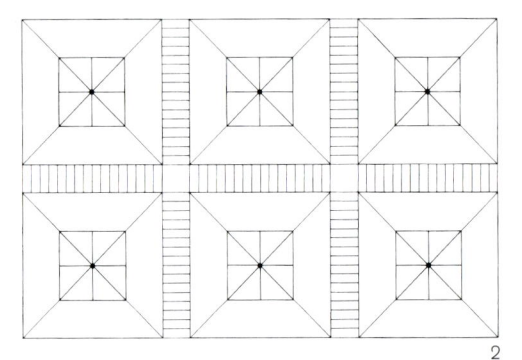

**Industry is notoriously subject to sudden expansion or contraction and industrial buildings must be able to cope with this. No industrial building can be too flexible. Even where the existing space is adequate, the building must be able to respond to changes in plant and production processes going on inside it. The nature of change is itself changing. The trend is now towards bigger spans, clearer floor space, improved insulation and, as a corollary, more artificial lighting. Clients themselves are becoming more specialised and more knowledgeable and need to be able to adjust their buildings to changing circumstances, tune them up in use.** *Industrial Buildings: A Client's Guide*, pamphlet produced by Foster Associates, 1977

**Our buildings have progressed from the self-contained pavilion towards a form which accommodates organic growth.** Norman Foster, *Building*, 22 October 1982

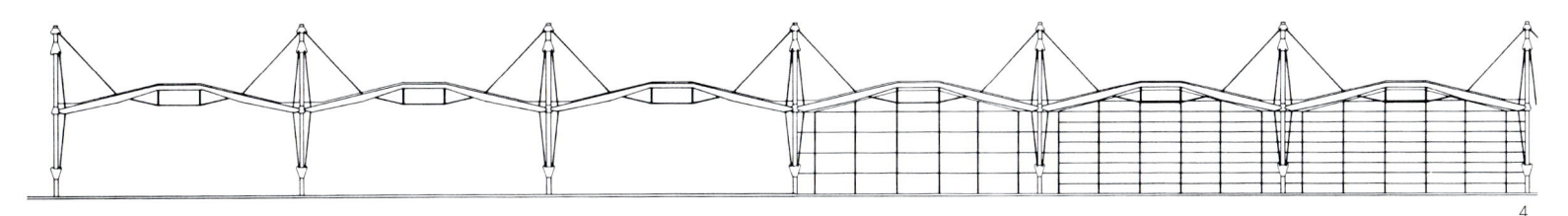

The adoption of a larger, table-like structure also implied a greater flexibility in positioning the cladding line on plan. Shifting the wall plane behind the column line allowed an elevational treatment that expresses the roof and structural profile. Gone is the austere horizontality of the first scheme, in which the cladding line followed the highest line of the structure. In its place is a more graceful undulation, which animates the eaves line and suggests comparison with the main facade of Foster's Palmerston Special School, completed in 1976.

The building is designed to be able to extend by up to six modules in width. With the wall line set in from the columns, such modular growth can occur with minimum disruption. New structural elements can be connected to the columns without disturbance to the existing envelope. It is simply a matter of unbolting the special side beams at their fixing plates, lengthening the upper ties with a turnbuckle, and bolting the new standard beams into place.

Rather than a linear arrangement between bays, as on the earlier scheme, natural light is introduced by means of glazed ventilators at the centre of each bay and wedge-shaped roof-lights just south of each mast. It is not only in terms of daylight and some measure of contact with the outside world that the benefits of this move are appreciated. In pursuit of Foster's goal of legibility, these roof-lights also reveal the essential elements of the structure to those working below.

This structure can be appreciated in its purest form in the building's *porte-cochère*; it is perhaps the Renault Centre's purest and most satisfying feature. But to describe it as an exercise in structural expressionism would be an overstatement. With the exception of the beams – which are an accurate reflection of their bending-moment forces – Renault's structure works rather differently from the way it looks. For instance, the struts facing out along the perimeter suggest that they are merely typical parts of the rest of the structure, and lead to an interpretation that the building comprises a series of semi-independent canopies, poised in formation like so many ballerinas. In fact, these struts are atypical, and the building's structure far more integrated than they imply. It is actually a set of portal frames, braced with pre-stressed ties. In other words, although the main beams are pin-jointed to the columns, the stressed ties above and below the joint form a fixed joint, the purpose of the pin being not to express movement but to facilitate quick assembly on site.

4. Eventually, the beams arching between columns became continuous rigid elements, the structure comprising a series of portal frames. By setting the cladding behind the columns the roof profile was revealed.

5. Roof-lights were placed at the centre of each bay.

6. The model of the first scheme omitted any linking structure between bays. Once compression beams and tension wires were inserted, however, it was a short step to the final 'portal frame' structure.

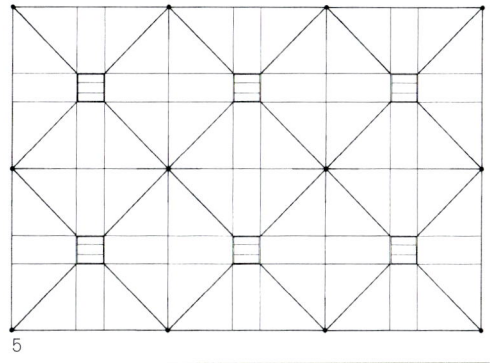

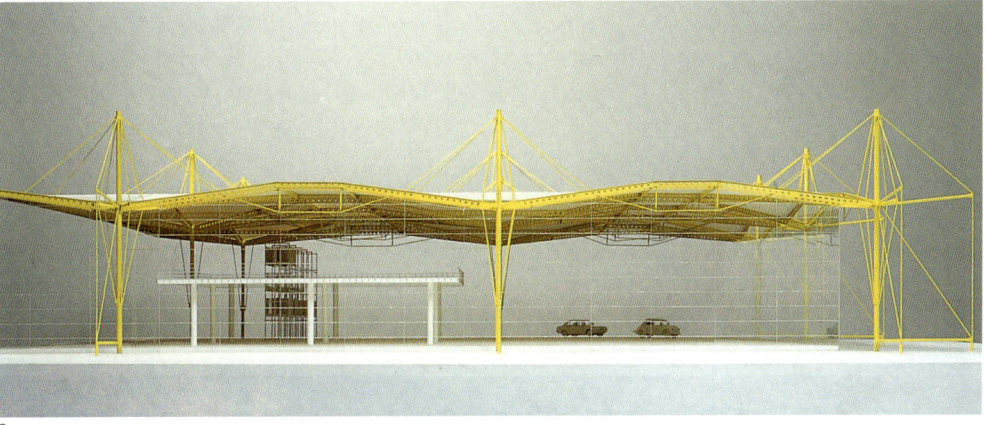

**During my time studying in America I was fascinated by lightweight agricultural structures, although they were not strictly architecture, or even designed. They had an extraordinary elegance and economy of means.** Norman Foster, lecture at Stuttgart University, 14 May 1987
Right: Norman Foster's photograph of agricultural silos, as discovered in the American Midwest.

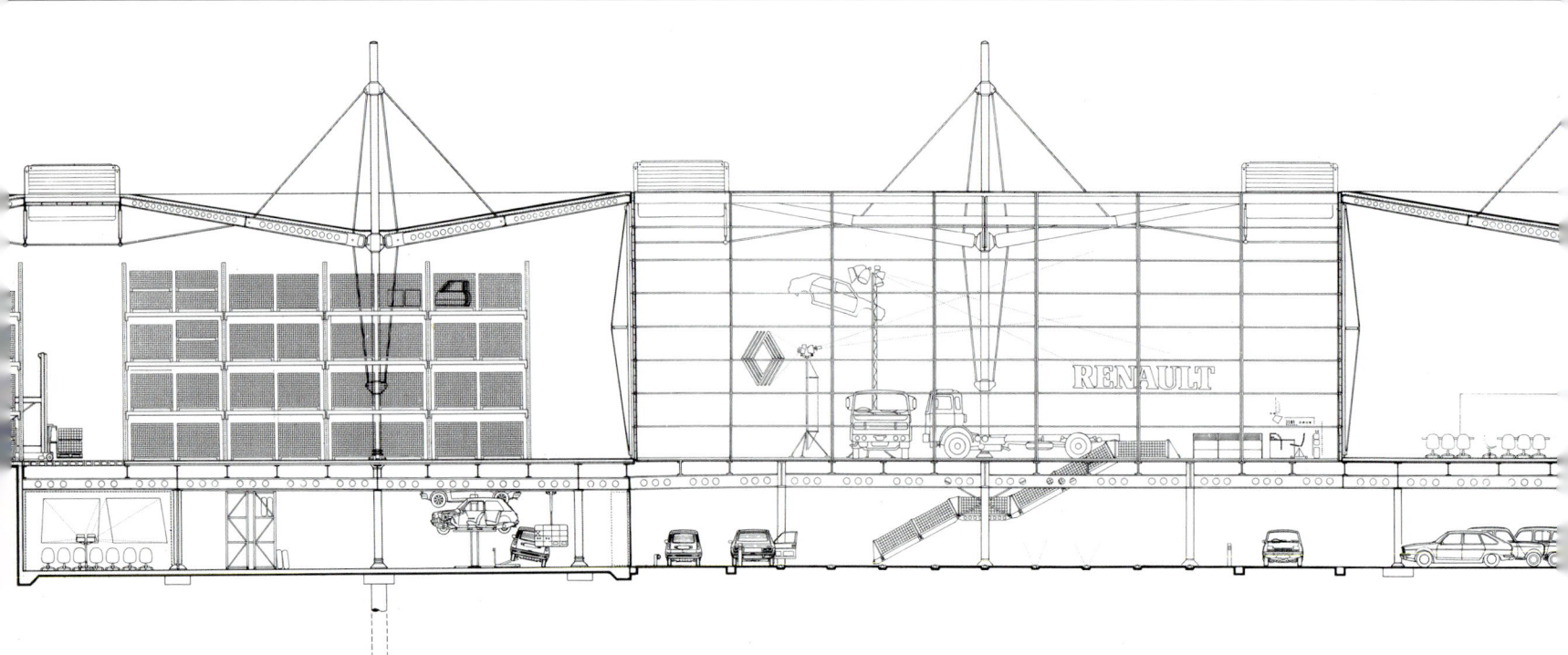

1. A part section through the developing scheme. Joint research with Renault yielded an optimum bay size of 24-metres square. Together with a minimum clear height of 7 metres – required by Renault's warehousing systems – this formed the basis for the first structural solution. The storage racks were based on Renault's own automated system. A cladding system of glazed, solid or translucent panels was initially proposed, suspended from the edge of the structural bay. This created a straight facade, which concealed much of the structure. A natural fall in the site was utilised to introduce an undercroft at one end of the building suitable for parking and, possibly, the after-sales service school.

Equally misleading is the fact that there is no differentiation between those ties that are pre-stressed and those that act exactly the way they seem to, that is, as cables in tension.

Another example that sheds light upon the difference between an architect's and an engineer's approach is the means of overcoming wind uplift on the roof. At Renault, this was found to be very nearly as great as the dead loads, and a pure engineering solution would have given equal emphasis to both. But an architectural solution implies a value judgement being made about which force should have priority of expression. The structural engineers, Ove Arup & Partners, suggested making the ties tubular so that they could take some compression. But Foster was anxious not to lose the quality of tautness in the ties, and instead asked Arup to engineer the beams to resist the uplift, even if this meant they had to be slightly larger. At the same time the roof's self-weight was increased, by specifying mineral wool, a relatively heavy roof insulation. In effect, gravity was considered more meaningful to the observer than the worst-case wind load, which might occur only once in fifty years.

If the elegance of the resulting structure suggests that Foster may have abdicated aesthetic decisions to his structural engineers, this would be mistaken. The Renault Centre is, above all, the product of a series of architectural, not merely structural, decisions.

Any impression to the contrary results from the fact that the architectural motifs deployed here also reinforce the structural symbolism. For example, the holes in the webs of the beams, a very important factor in achieving the building's remarkable 'lightness of touch', also have functional advantages. The tapered beams were constructed from parallel-flange beams cut at an angle along their length, reversed and welded back together again. The holes in the webs cut across this joint, thereby nearly halving the total length of weld required.

A key factor behind the building's rapid erection was the factory manufacture of components to fine tolerances. As a result, the manufacture of the steelwork could run concurrently with the foundations and slab site work. Site assembly of components was also accelerated, which brought corresponding savings in overall construction time.

**The anonymous industrial vernacular has long provided traditional source material for architects, for instance the pure white forms of grain elevators appeared in the earliest writings of Le Corbusier. More recent agricultural hardware shows a tensile use of materials to produce structures that are rigid, lightweight and easily transportable; virtues long advocated by Buckminster Fuller with his geodesic domes and tensegrity structures capable of encompassing total communities.** Norman Foster, *Creative Handbook Diary*, 1981

Left: A crop-spraying rig, photographed in the American Midwest by Norman Foster.

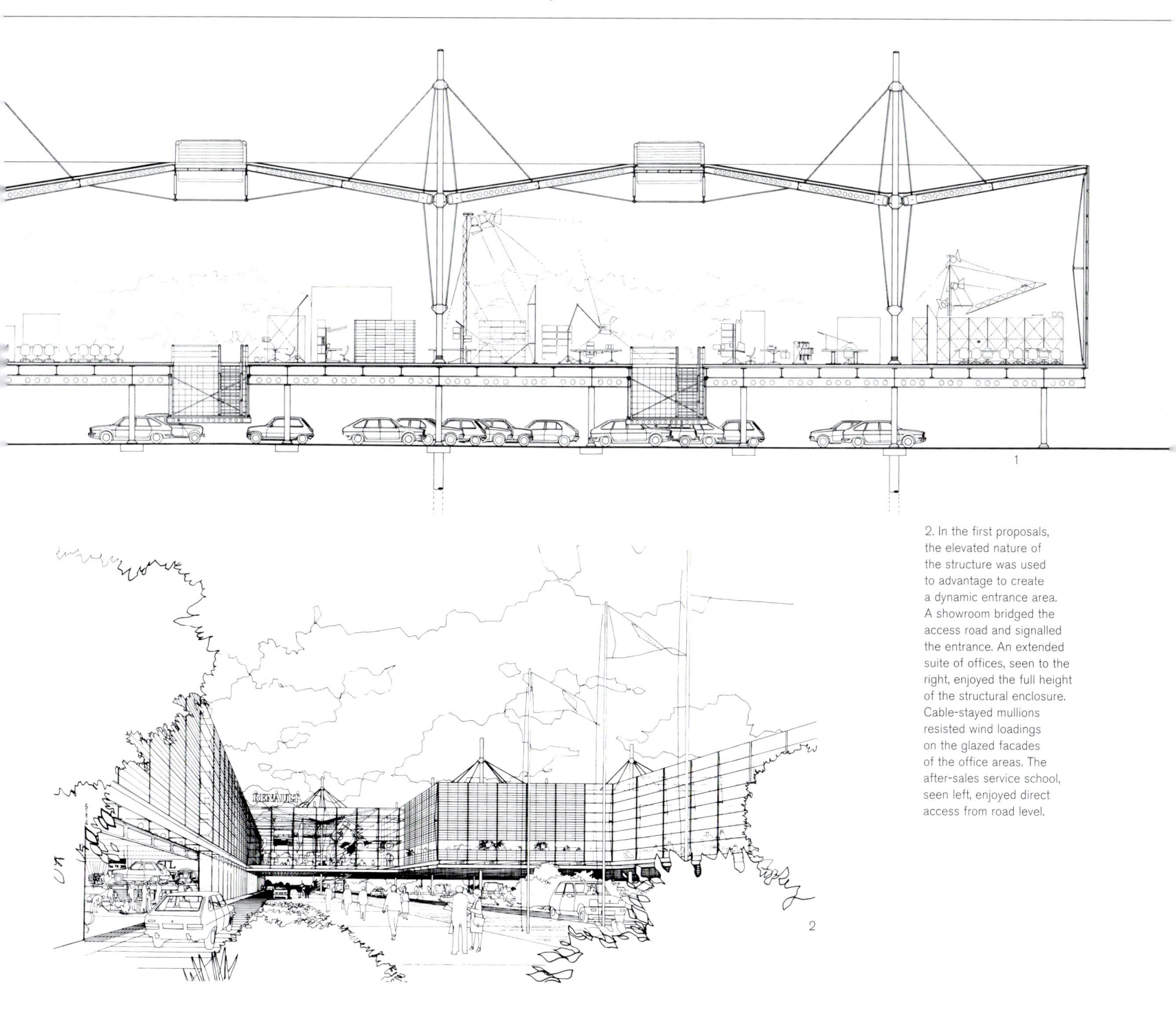

2. In the first proposals, the elevated nature of the structure was used to advantage to create a dynamic entrance area. A showroom bridged the access road and signalled the entrance. An extended suite of offices, seen to the right, enjoyed the full height of the structural enclosure. Cable-stayed mullions resisted wind loadings on the glazed facades of the office areas. The after-sales service school, seen left, enjoyed direct access from road level.

Renault Distribution Centre 505

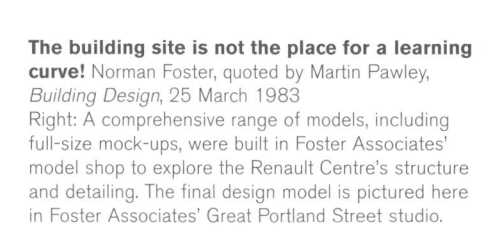

**The building site is not the place for a learning curve!** Norman Foster, quoted by Martin Pawley, *Building Design*, 25 March 1983
Right: A comprehensive range of models, including full-size mock-ups, were built in Foster Associates' model shop to explore the Renault Centre's structure and detailing. The final design model is pictured here in Foster Associates' Great Portland Street studio.

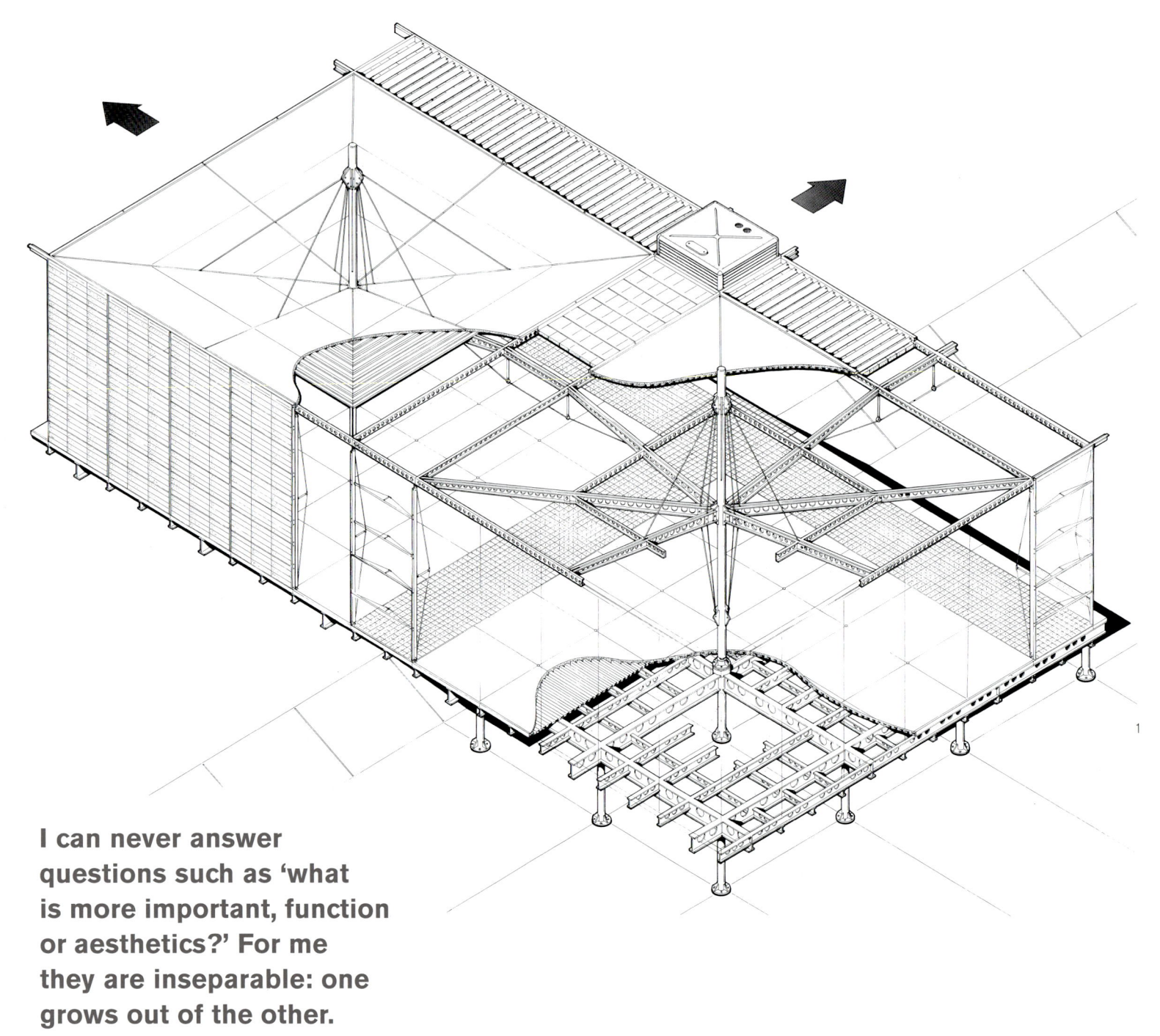

**I can never answer questions such as 'what is more important, function or aesthetics?' For me they are inseparable: one grows out of the other.**

Norman Foster

**It does not matter whether a building is about clear open space or whether it is divided up and cellular by nature – the structure will naturally impart its own order and make the building more legible and human in its scale.** Norman Foster, 'Architecture and Structure', written for the Architectural Association of Japan, November 1994

**The character and form of the steelwork were developed through an interactive process. The intention was to produce an essentially suspended lightweight roof with an undulating three-dimensional expression. Additionally, we wanted to connect the frame so that the advantages of continuity, so familiar to us in reinforced concrete and perhaps more difficult to achieve in structural steelwork, could be obtained. Having defined the location of the necessary structural elements in a qualitative way, the design was developed on the basis of refining the appearance and sizes of the members and their connections.** Martin Manning, project engineer for Ove Arup & Partners, *Building*, 22 October 1982

**I think that the whole Postmodern debate has raised some perfectly valid questions about certain aspects of architecture. I do not see this as being in any way irreconcilable with what we have been doing; but, on the contrary, it offers us greater possibilities for richness and diversity without stooping to pastiche. I like to think that our projects have become more balanced, although I am aware that as part of that balancing act some projects may overcompensate in one way or another. Renault is perhaps as 'expressive' as we are ever likely to go.** Norman Foster, Whitworth Exhibition catalogue, May 1984

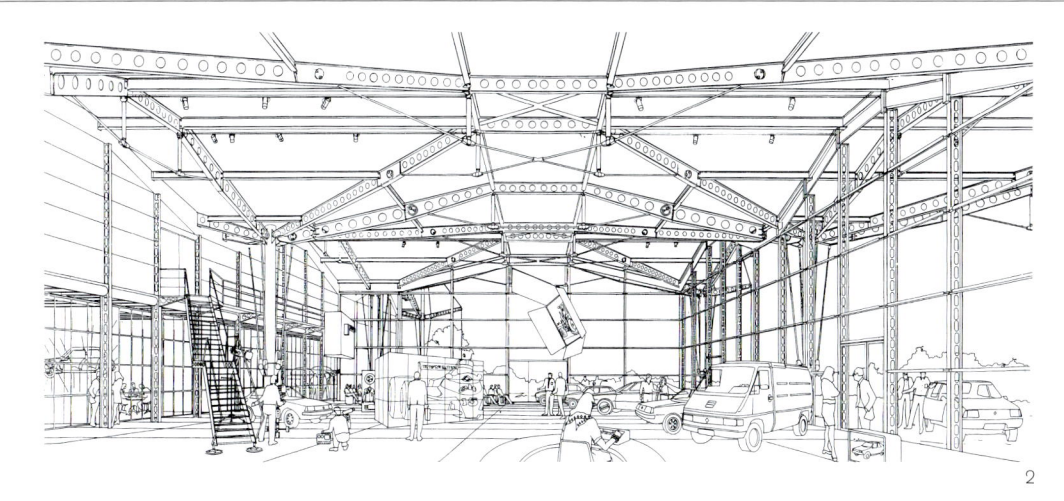

The fact that the steelwork subcontractor, Tubeworkers, had a background of working on Foster projects also helped. Past collaborations included the manufacture of the roof-top space-frame at Willis Faber, in 1974, and the main structures of both the Sainsbury Centre and IBM Greenford. Subsequently the firm was to be responsible for the primary structure at Stansted Airport.

As a relatively small team with a reputation for craftsmanship, Tubeworkers is exactly the kind of firm that Foster likes to work with. Interestingly, using craft-intensive production methods, the company was able to achieve the tight tolerances demanded far more cheaply than alternative approaches using more sophisticated levels of tooling. The Renault Centre was a particularly challenging job since it contained a number of details that, although visually the most elegant solution, in practice were far from easy to achieve. One such detail was the point at the tip of each mast where eight fins are connected. Here, each of the welds effectively concealed the next joint, making it difficult for the welders to see what they were doing. A simple jig solved the problem, holding each fin in the required position while it was welded in place.

The connector pieces that join each tie-rod to the mast were cast in spheroidal-graphite iron, a material which, although acting in a similar way to mild steel, is designed to be sand-cast, thus combining age-old casting techniques with newly-developed materials to achieve advanced technology design.

All the steelwork was fabricated and primed at Tubeworkers' workshops in Warwickshire and transported to site for final assembly. Bolted connections were used on site to avoid the use of site welding, and final painting was carried out after erection. By maximising the use of 'dry assembled' components in this way, the entire construction process was completed in just sixteen months.

1. In the initial scheme, a lightweight panel system was to be suspended from the edge of the roof structure by tubular mullions, cable-stayed to resist wind loads. Initial observations had indicated that the floor slab would need to span between pile foundations, in which case a raised floor would have been little different structurally to one at ground level. However, detailed studies revealed that a ground-supported slab was possible, thus removing the need for a complex floor structure and eliminating the possibility of an undercroft.

2. Ove Arup & Partners' computer provided three-dimensional views of the structure, which were animated to create a series of remarkably accurate perspectives.

3. A large-scale model was prepared to allow a more complete exploration of the various design options. An early version of the gallery showroom is shown here. The model was made before the detailed profile of the structural elements was resolved, but was accurate in most other respects.

It is sleek shed, slick-tech interior architecture of the kind which Foster does so immaculately. It is the result of loving care and attention to the fine detail of everything from the selection of the vast falls of perforated louvres and screen in the canteen to the design and shaping of the structural members and their connections. Sutherland Lyall, *Building*, 10 June 1983

Ad hoc Foster, Gothic Foster, playful, jolly Foster: these are not aspects of the architect we could have imagined before Renault. Peter Davey, *The Architectural Review*, July 1983

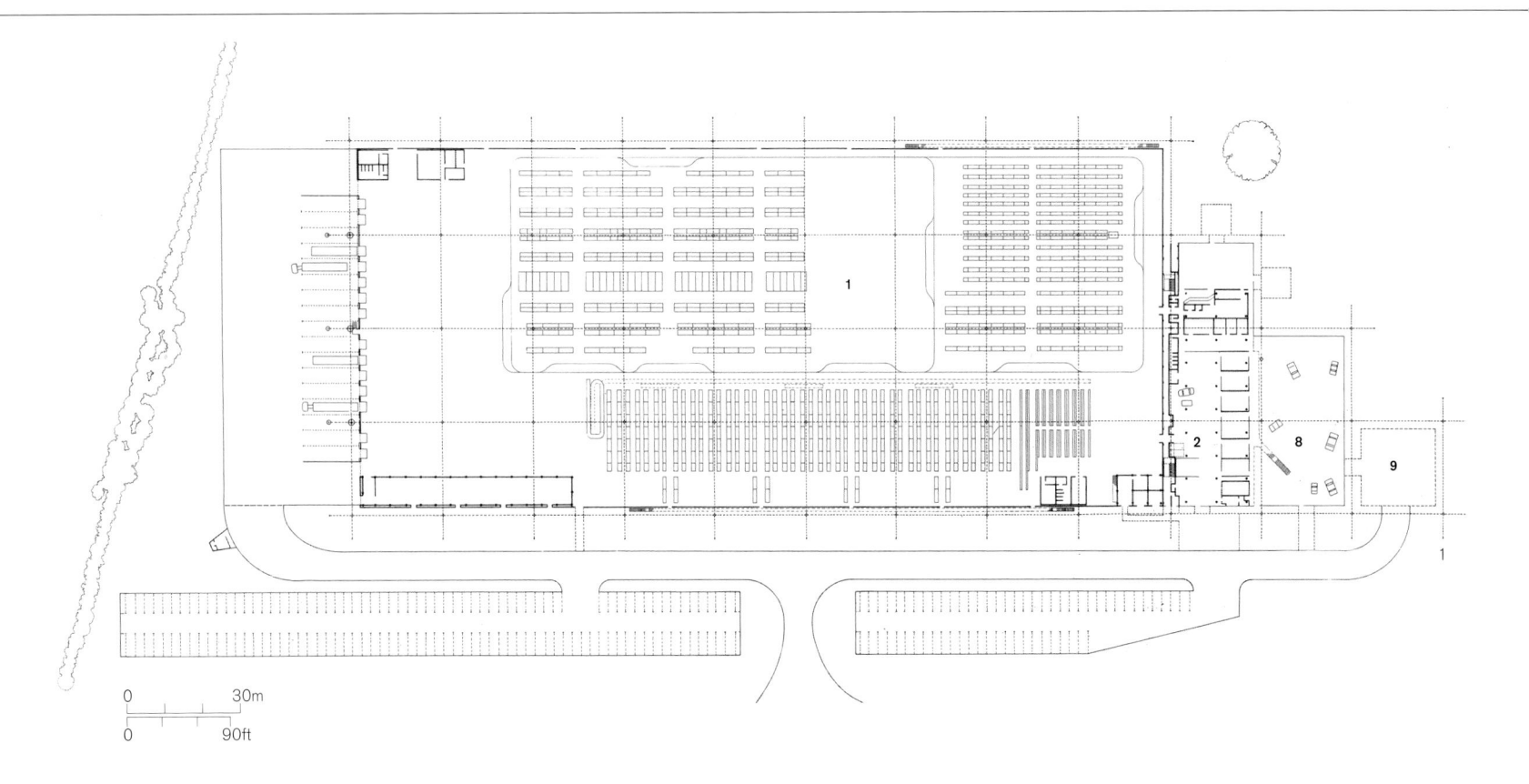

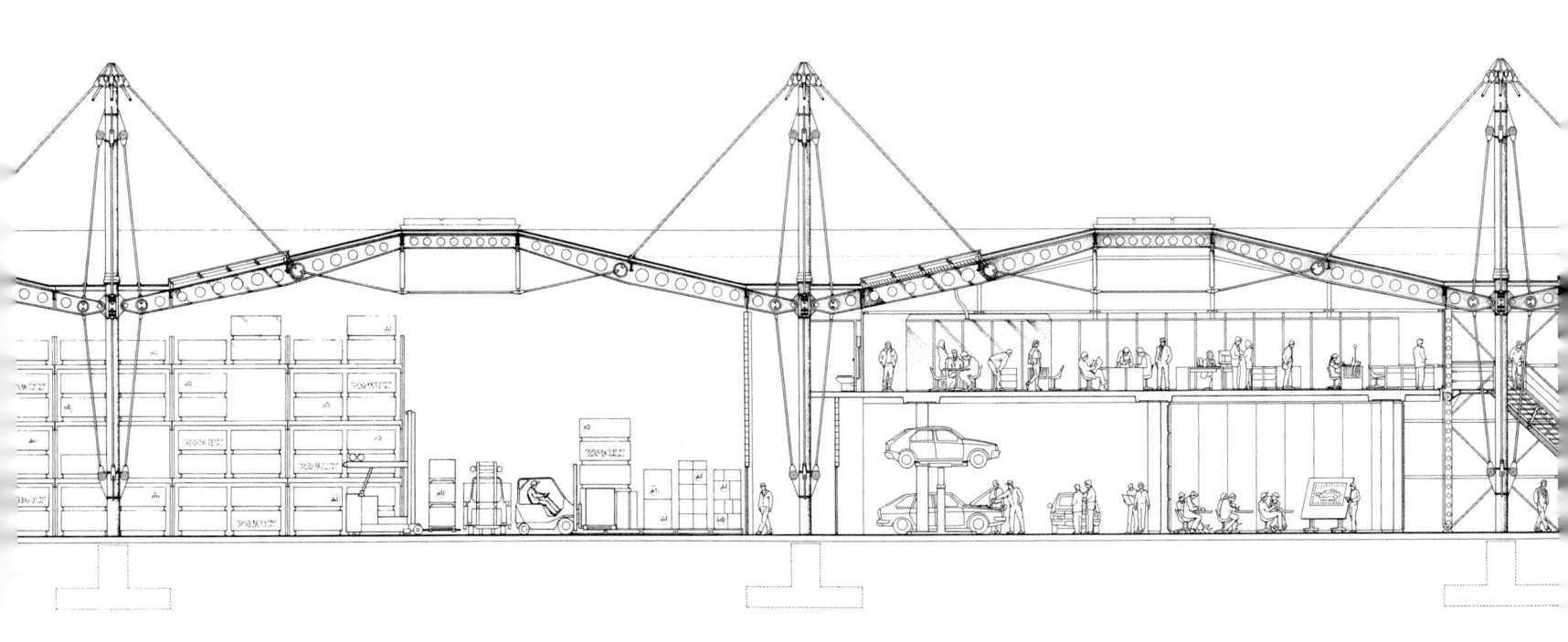

'Good design pays' is a cliché often used by architects when faced by tight-lipped clients wondering why on earth they should invest large sums in a building the like of which they have never seen before. The architect's unspoken prayer is that the client won't ask 'How?'. Not so Norman Foster, who is able to point out to the clients of his Renault Centre at Swindon that the planners have increased their permitted limit of site coverage from 50 to 67 per cent simply on the basis of the quality of his architecture. Faced by engulfment in a sea of lumpen banal industrial buildings (metal siding on top of a brick plinth with, perhaps, a bit of supergraphics smeared on) the planners of this rapidly expanding town in England's South-West saw a good thing and decided that they could do with more of it.'
Peter Davey, *The Architectural Review*, July 1983

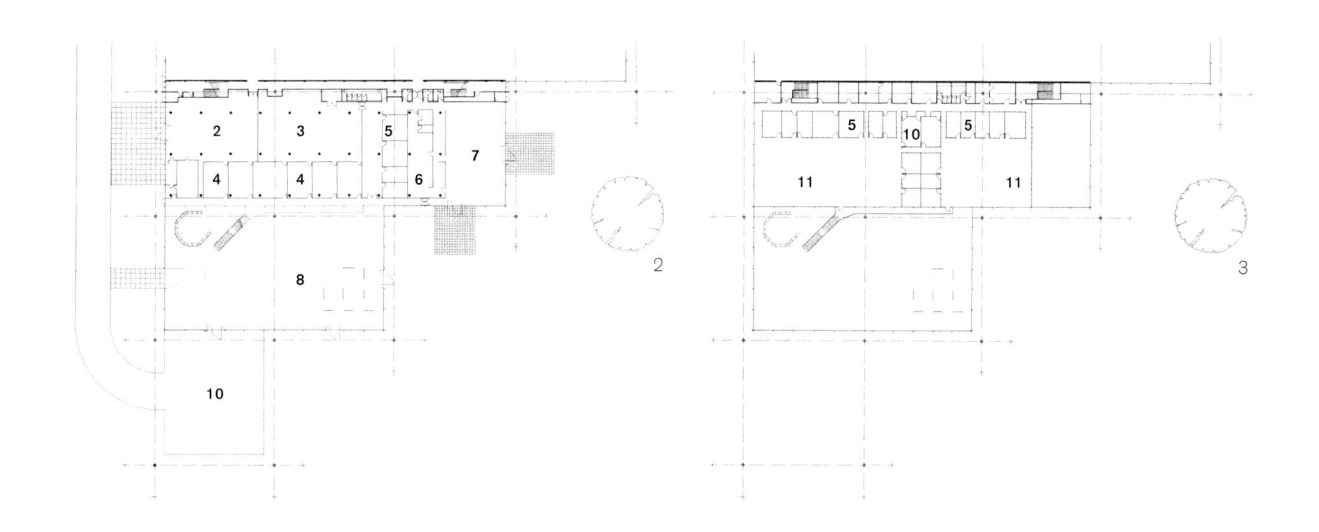

1. Ground floor plan.

2, 3. Detailed ground floor and mezzanine-level plans of the administrative areas.

1 warehouse
2 service bays
3 training school
4 lecture rooms
5 cellular offices
6 kitchen
7 restaurant
8 showroom/gallery
9 *porte-cochère*
10 conference room
11 open-plan offices

4. This section through the southern end of the building shows the final profile of the roof structure and the free-standing mezzanine which supports the office areas above the training school. The reinforced-concrete mezzanine structure was cast in-situ, that being the simplest way of providing the necessary fire separation.

**A flexible umbrella generated by the need for a warehouse also encompassed offices, training facilities, amenity areas and a showroom.**
Norman Foster

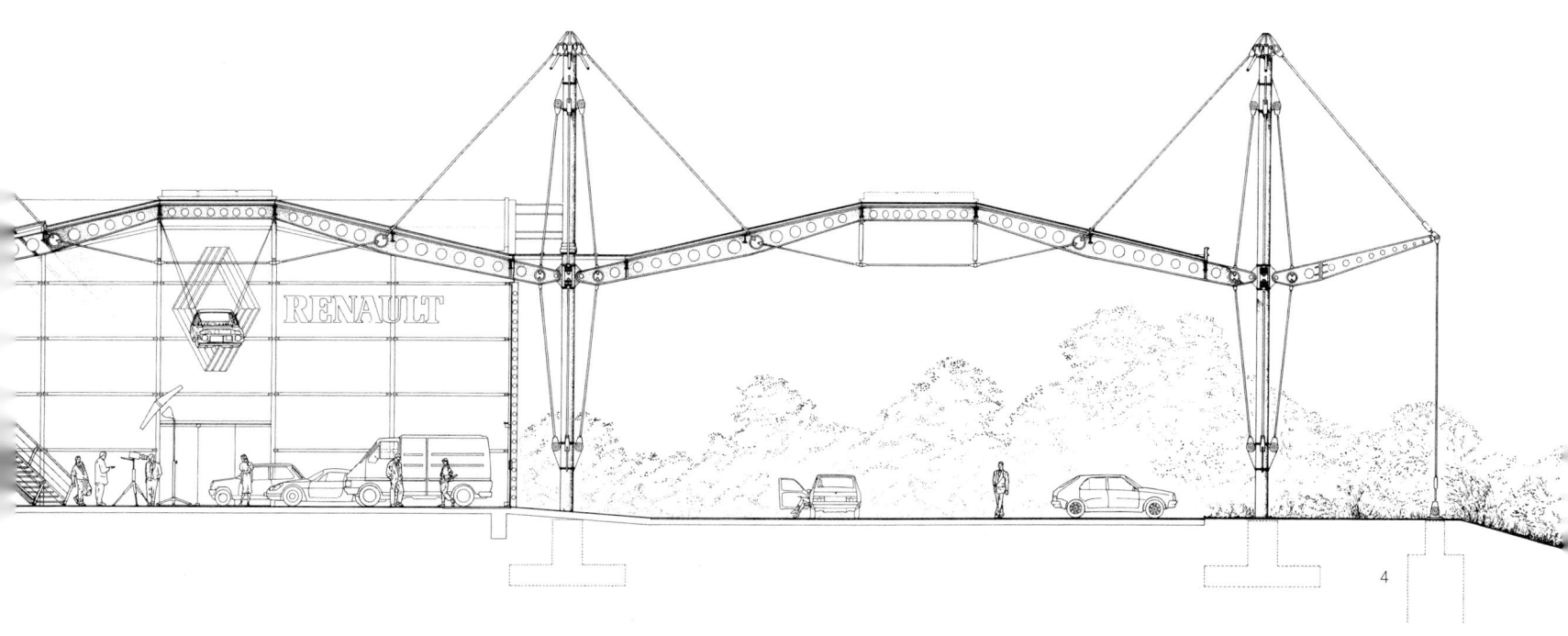

Renault Distribution Centre

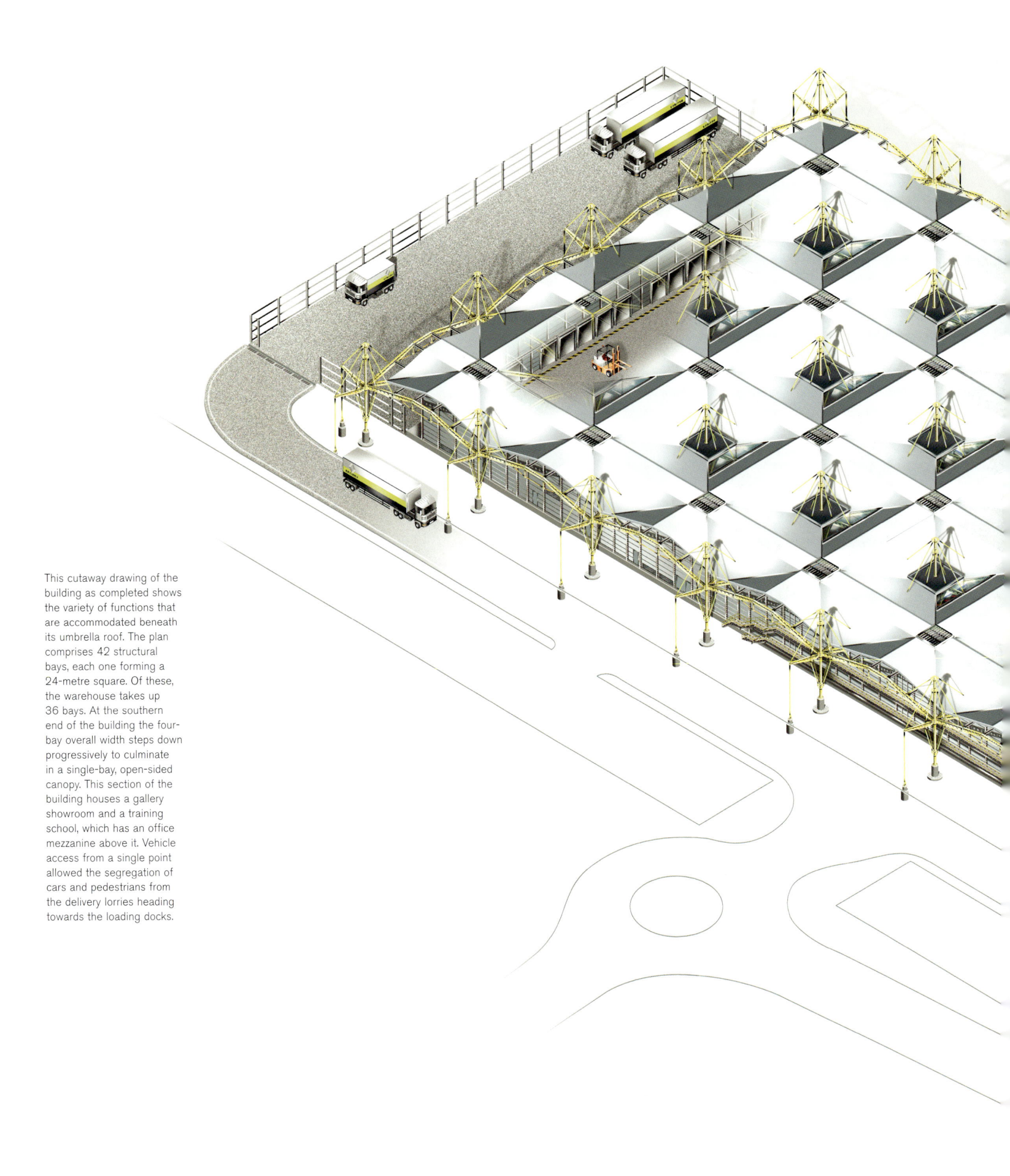

This cutaway drawing of the building as completed shows the variety of functions that are accommodated beneath its umbrella roof. The plan comprises 42 structural bays, each one forming a 24-metre square. Of these, the warehouse takes up 36 bays. At the southern end of the building the four-bay overall width steps down progressively to culminate in a single-bay, open-sided canopy. This section of the building houses a gallery showroom and a training school, which has an office mezzanine above it. Vehicle access from a single point allowed the segregation of cars and pedestrians from the delivery lorries heading towards the loading docks.

Renault Distribution Centre 511

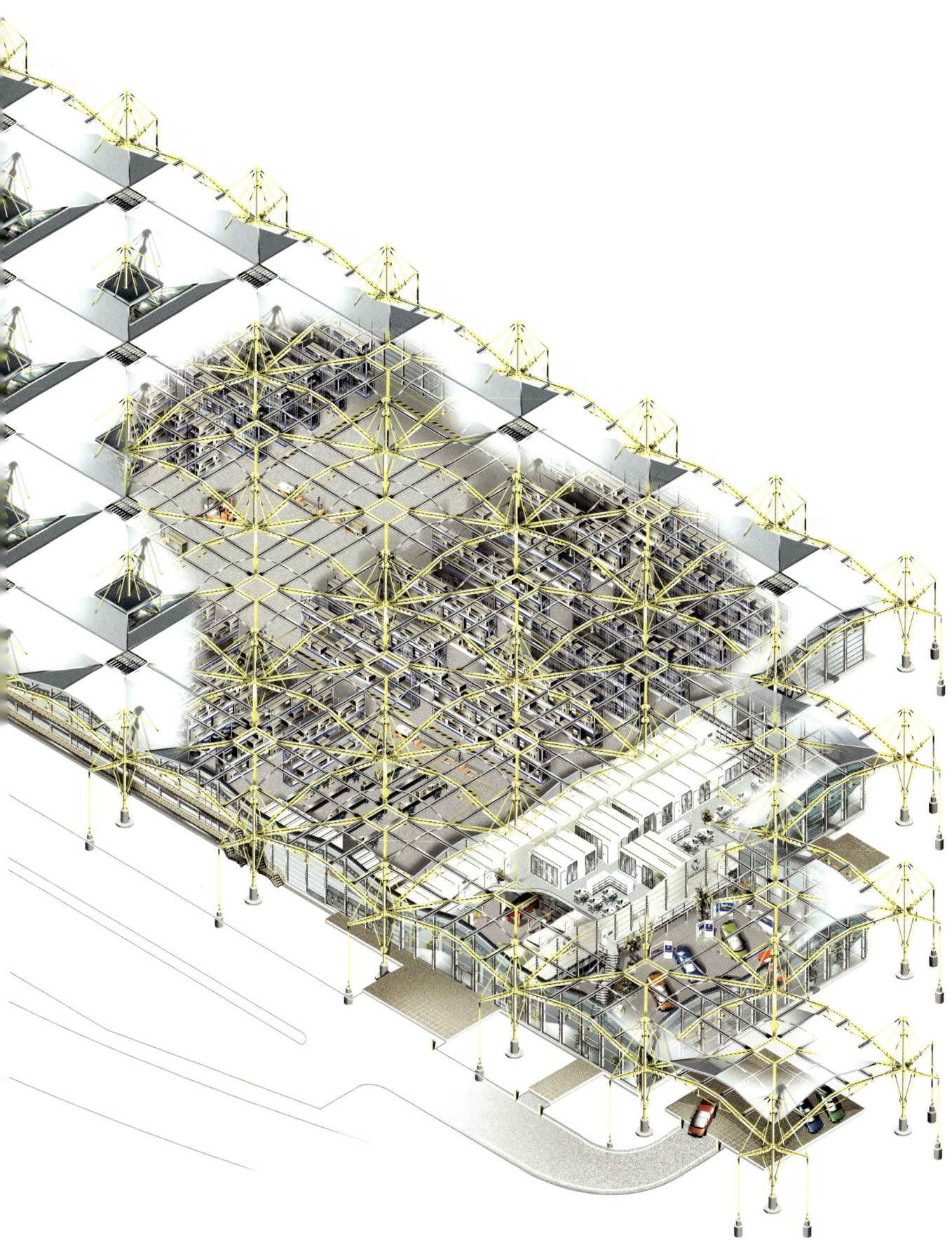

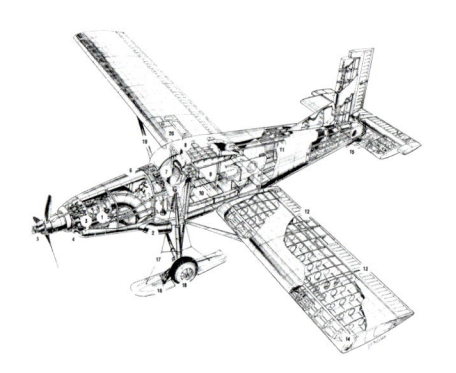

Norman Foster commissioned John Batchelor to draw the pull-out sheet in this issue of the *AR*. The name might not seem familiar in architectural circles, but a vast number of British architects born from the 1930s onwards will recognise his talent. Batchelor used to produce those superb cutaway drawings of rockets, ships, planes, cars, and trains for *Eagle*, probably the finest boy's comic ever published and an inspiration to a generation of architects and engineers.
Jonathan Glancey, *The Architectural Review*, July 1983
Left: John Batchelor's cutaway of the Swiss mountain rescue Porter aircraft, featured in *Eagle*, April 1963.
Right: Batchelor's drawing of the Renault Centre, and the cover of the magazine in which it was first published.

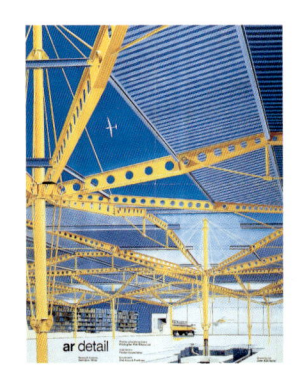

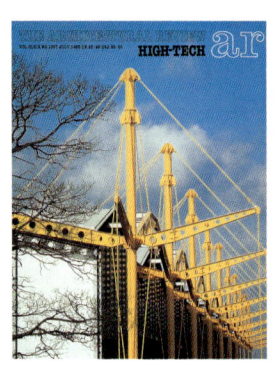

**Our tight construction schedule ruled out on-site welding and suggested a wholly prefabricated solution; the use of 'dry assembly' components ensured that the entire building was completed in sixteen months.**
Norman Foster

**Up here on the roof it's very other-worldly. I often come up here at the end of the day – it's the only place I can get some peace and quiet.** Renault Centre site agent, in conversation with Ben Johnson, 1982
Right: The Renault Centre roofscape at sunset.

**The roofscape evokes a range of images. Sand dunes deserted by the Bedouin who have left the frameworks of their tents dotted around a regular pattern of little oases. Or a seashore where a freak tide has suddenly uncovered the remnants of some mysterious Victorian structure poking out of a series of little rock pools. It is not a view that many people will get to see of the building during its life. It is a regret which Norman Foster himself shares and he talks about next time putting in observation bubbles.** Sutherland Lyall, *Building*, 10 June 1983

1, 2. Fabrication of the columns and beams in progress in the steelwork subcontractor's workshops.

3-5. The simplicity of the building's pin-jointed connections allowed on-site erection of the steelwork to be completed in six months.

6, 7. Steelwork was delivered to site with an undercoat only. The final coat of paint was applied on site, by hand, as soon after erection as practicable to provide the steelwork with the best possible protection.

8. Work progresses on installing the pvc roof membrane.

9. Only after each structural bay was complete could the final alignment of the columns and tensioning of the tie-rods take place.

Renault Distribution Centre  513

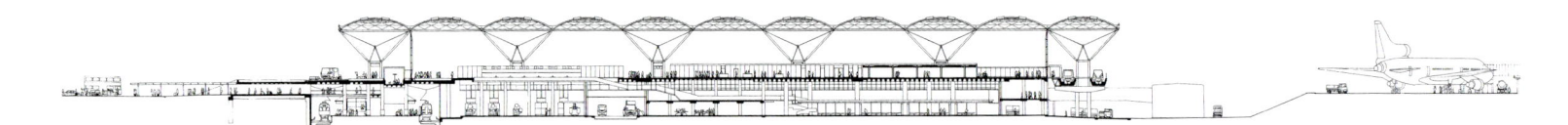

1-4. This sequence of aerial photographs shows the site over a thirteen-month period between December 1981 and January 1983, by which time the cladding and roof were completed and the warehouse was already in use. The design and construction programme ensured delivery to site of the first elements of the steelwork only twelve months after their formal commission in October 1980. The official opening took place in August 1983.

The early structure assumed that the cladding would be suspended from fixings at eaves level. However, as time went by, the difficulties this would have presented became clear. Wind uplift on the roof, in particular, would have caused major detailing problems as deflection under extreme conditions could amount to some 175mm. Additionally, all the weight of the cladding would have had to be taken through the roof structure and down the columns, resulting in thicker members in each instance. The choice would then have lain between over-designing all the structure in the building to conform with those elements on the perimeter, which took the load of the cladding, or treating the perimeter structure differently — a course that would have brought its own share of architectural problems.

In the meantime, on the grounds of cost and fire-resistance, the Kalwall cladding panels of the first scheme had been dropped in favour of steel sandwich panels. As this new system was developed, a 4-metre module was found to satisfy all the solid and glazed cladding conditions elegantly, both in terms of geometry and economy of materials.

There were three reasons for this. Firstly, the largest size in which it is normally possible to produce toughened glass is 4 x 2.1 metres: at Renault the sheets measure 3.9 x 1.86 metres, thereby minimising the need for joints and brackets. Secondly, the module could be spanned with steel sandwich cladding panels, connected without cladding rails by means of tongue and groove joints. Thirdly, it offered the optimum size for the vehicle loading bays.

As the glazing and cladding panels could not be suspended from the main roof structure, an alternative method had to be devised. Simplicity of detailing was deemed to be the most important criterion, on both aesthetic and cost grounds, and, indeed, the final system could not be more straightforward. Vertical I-beams, at 4-metre centres, cantilever up from a direct fixing to the edge of the concrete ground slab to form structural mullions which take all the gravity loadings of the cladding panels and the glazing.

The panels themselves and the horizontal glazing supports are fixed directly to these mullions which, as with the main structure, are drilled through the web with round holes. Lateral support in the wall plane is provided, in part, by the cladding panels, but this is supplemented by discreet cross-bracing at set points inside the building.

Left: A section through the passenger concourse of Stansted Airport terminal (1981-1991).
Right: Stansted's structural 'tree' system laid bare during the construction process. There is a strong family connection between the Stansted system and the independent, centrally-supported modules originally proposed for the Renault Centre.

**The Renault project gave Foster Associates the opportunity to further refine the performance and utility of its long-span steel-frame design by introducing mast-supported trusses to create even larger unobstructed floor spaces. The result is a building that consists largely of its own elaborate roofing system, which itself is an interesting precursor to the spectacular roof later designed for the passenger terminal at Stansted Airport … Like the Renault building, Stansted is a 'big shed'. But where Renault's PVC roof was penetrated by steel columns and tension rods, Stansted's 50,000 square metre PVC roof membrane is continuous.**
Martin Pawley, *Norman Foster; A Global Architecture*, 1999

The design team realised that if cladding rails could be eliminated (as Foster had done before at Reliance Controls) both economy and elegance would be improved considerably. For this to be achieved it was necessary to develop a sandwich panel that could span the full 4 metres between mullions. Normal calculations of structural strength for insulated panels are made on the basis of the metal profiles alone. However, tests carried out at Liverpool University on a variety of prototypes showed that such panels behave as composite structures, with the metal facing panels acting in conjunction with the foam between them. Some degree of profiling was needed to conceal inevitable variations and blemishes in panel finish, but deeper 'structural' corrugations in the panel were found to be unnecessary.

The profile eventually selected was one normally formed in aluminium to make caravan siding. The pressing tool was found not to be very robust, but after some difficulty the manufacturer managed to produce sufficient quantities in steel. The completed panels were screwed directly on to the mullions using self-drilling screws.

While the decision to place the cladding line just behind the columns simplified construction (if it had been positioned directly along the column line, providing a waterproof seal with the main structure would have been particularly difficult) sealing the eaves junction between the elevations and the undulating roof structure still posed an interesting problem. The solution was to develop a flexible neoprene gasket (inspired by the tie-down waterproof sheeting used on articulated trucks) which runs around the perimeter of the building.

The neoprene gasket sealing the gap between the mullion and the edge of each panel takes the form of a simple L-section, which is glued to the front corner of each edge of the panel and then curved round to press firmly against the mullion itself. For glazed areas, the gasket is only slightly different, the 'foot' of the 'L' being doubled to clip around the thickness of the glass.

Bright yellows, reds and blues are the colours of industrial machinery … Foster's umbrella columns for Renault refer, of course, to Renault yellow, but they are also uncontaminated by any reference to past architecture, to masonry columns … Each column has become a mast of joists and cables articulated, of all places, near the middle. The canary yellow further displaces the structure from tradition and, by extension, from the hidebound conventions of class and etiquette. This is an architecture of ships and holidays, of activity liberated from the weight of a past felt to be crushing. Charles Jencks, *The New Moderns*, 1990

The Renault Centre is the most romantic of Foster's buildings … At Swindon, the supports for the flexible wide-span portal roof structure project above the roof, masts and cables being freely displayed against the sky, creating a new sensation of suspended animation, unearthly quiet, frozen flight and supreme stability. François Chaslin, *Norman Foster*, 1986

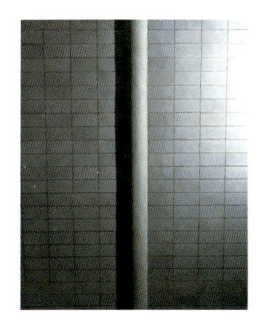

**For me, taking photographs is a form of meditation and concentration prior to painting. I use a plumb line and a spirit level so I can set the camera up to produce completely axial views, but the verticals are always vertical. I do this in order to orientate myself to the building so that I can respond to both formal and human space.**
Ben Johnson, 'Art and Architecture', 1991

Left: A blockwork wall had to be inserted between the warehouse and office/school areas to provide the necessary four-hour fire separation. Superbly detailed and built, the wall inspired Ben Johnson to take this photograph on one of his visits to the building when scouting for suitable subjects for paintings.
Right: Ben Johnson's screenprint *East Mast* of 1986.

The frameless glazing is a characteristically elegant instance of minimal detailing. Ten-metre high areas of flat bed armour-plated glass are suspended by means of countersunk bolts on cadmium-plated brackets, which were specially developed in collaboration with Pilkington, the glazing subcontractor. These brackets, in turn, are fixed to internal transoms, which span between the mullions. Each glass panel requires only two brackets to support the vertical loads: the rest take up lateral wind forces exclusively. As with the steel-faced cladding panels, joints between glass sheets are sealed with clear silicone.

## Simplicity of detailing was deemed the most important criterion for the glazing and cladding panels, on both aesthetic and economic grounds.

Within this elegant envelope, the space planning developed naturally as Renault's final requirements were established for each of the building's different zones. In its present form, the building is 42 bays long and mostly four bays wide. The warehouse occupies an area 36 x 4 bays. The remainder – three bays of offices, restaurant and training school, two bays occupied by a showroom and one by the *porte-cochère* – step down progressively from the four-bay width of the building at the south-east corner of the site. This corner offers the best views and, as the 'front' of the building, is the direction from which the main public image is determined.

Seated at the main entrance, the receptionist is able to receive visitors and at the same time supervise the space – which is, in effect, the ceremonial hub for the building. The overall impression is less a showroom or atrium and more a 'gallery'. This impression is reinforced by the installation of Renault car body shells, which are suspended from its undulating ceiling soffit, their colours chosen by the architects to counterpoint the yellow of the structure.

Unified within this space are a number of functions associated with the promotion of Renault's corporate image as a whole. This has broadened to encompass not only the reception of visitors, the display of cars and audio-visual sales presentations, but also activities such as exhibitions of school-children's paintings and other regular social and community events.

The community dimension was Foster's idea, and can be seen as part of the practice's constant commitment to the idea of providing social spaces and where possible using them to involve the users, their families and the wider community within the everyday life of the building. At Swindon, Renault responded enthusiastically, creating a new post of publicity officer specifically to administer these events.

The gallery is accessible to the workshop areas and training-school classrooms next door. Foster hoped that this would allow training staff to use the exhibitions and video display in the entrance space as teaching aids. Conversely, the sight of a national after-sales service training school in operation beyond the glass classroom walls is intended to promote Renault's reputation for quality of service amongst its visitors.

Having no need for direct access to the gallery, training school or warehouse, the administrative areas are located upstairs, where they are screened from workshop noise, and fire-separated by a structurally independent concrete mezzanine. The proportion of the plan devoted to cellular offices is larger in the finished building than in the original brief, but it provides a useful device for creating separate identities for the parts distribution centre and the regional sales office. Also, by giving the cellular spaces glass walls and 'lids', Foster was able to maintain the same quality of space and natural light inside them as in the main open-plan areas. Acting as a buffer between the offices and the warehouse is a 4-metre wide zone of service rooms such as lavatories, fire escapes and storage areas, with service runs accommodated above.

Opposite: A view towards the entrance *porte-cochère*, looking past the showroom and the flank wall of the warehouse. The steel superstructure sits on a concrete ground slab. Connections between columns and beams are pin-jointed, held rigid by tensioned stays so as to effect a portal-frame structure. From the beginning, the beams were shown tapered as a means of expressing the forces acting upon them. Early assumptions followed the simplest diagram, tapering evenly from the deepest point, where the beam is connected to the column. As design work progressed, however, this beam profile developed into a more accurate representation of the bending moment diagram, with the deepest section coinciding with the mid-point support cables, as seen here.

Left: A neoprene-coated nylon fabric normally used for hovercraft skirts was the only material that combined the flexibility and resilience required for the eaves detail. The poor thermal performance of the neoprene is offset by the higher than necessary U-values of the glazing or wall panel below.
Right: The tensioning detail at the eaves, which keeps the neoprene gasket taut, was inspired by the tie-down fixings on fabric-sided trucks.

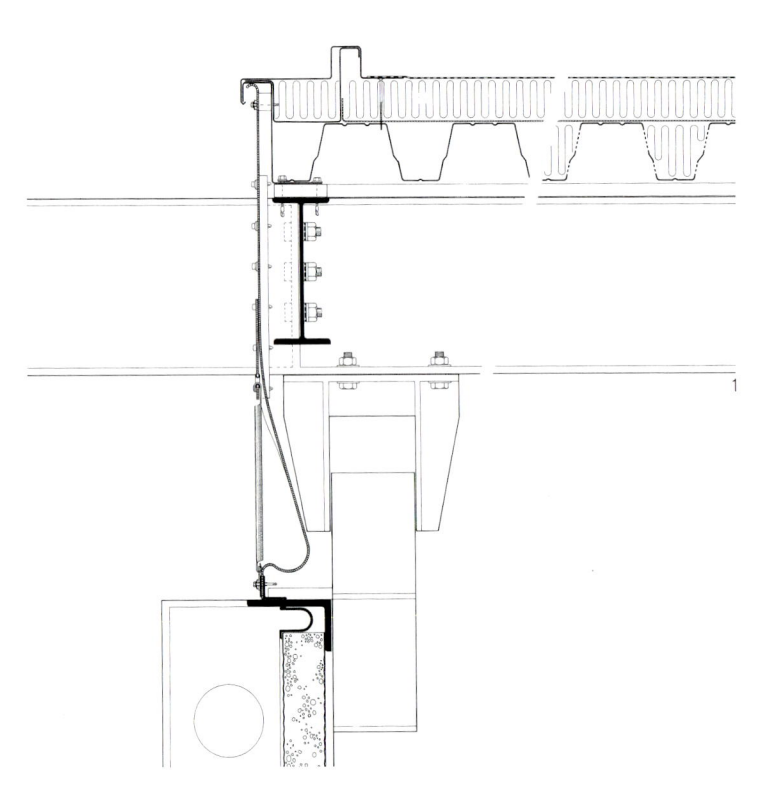

1. The 350mm-deep flexible neoprene gasket that seals the eaves is secured with stainless-steel coil springs to tension it against flapping – an idea inspired by the tie-down fixings on fabric-sided trucks.

2, 5. The external wall plane is recessed behind the line of the columns and the edge of the roof. These external elements cast crisp shadows upon the grey metal cladding panels.

3, 4. I-beam mullions, with holes drilled in their webs, support both the composite cladding panels and the clear glazing. The panels are fixed directly to the mullions, requiring no substructure. Intermediate transoms span behind the mullions to provide wind-loading support for the sheets of glass, which span 4 metres between mullions.

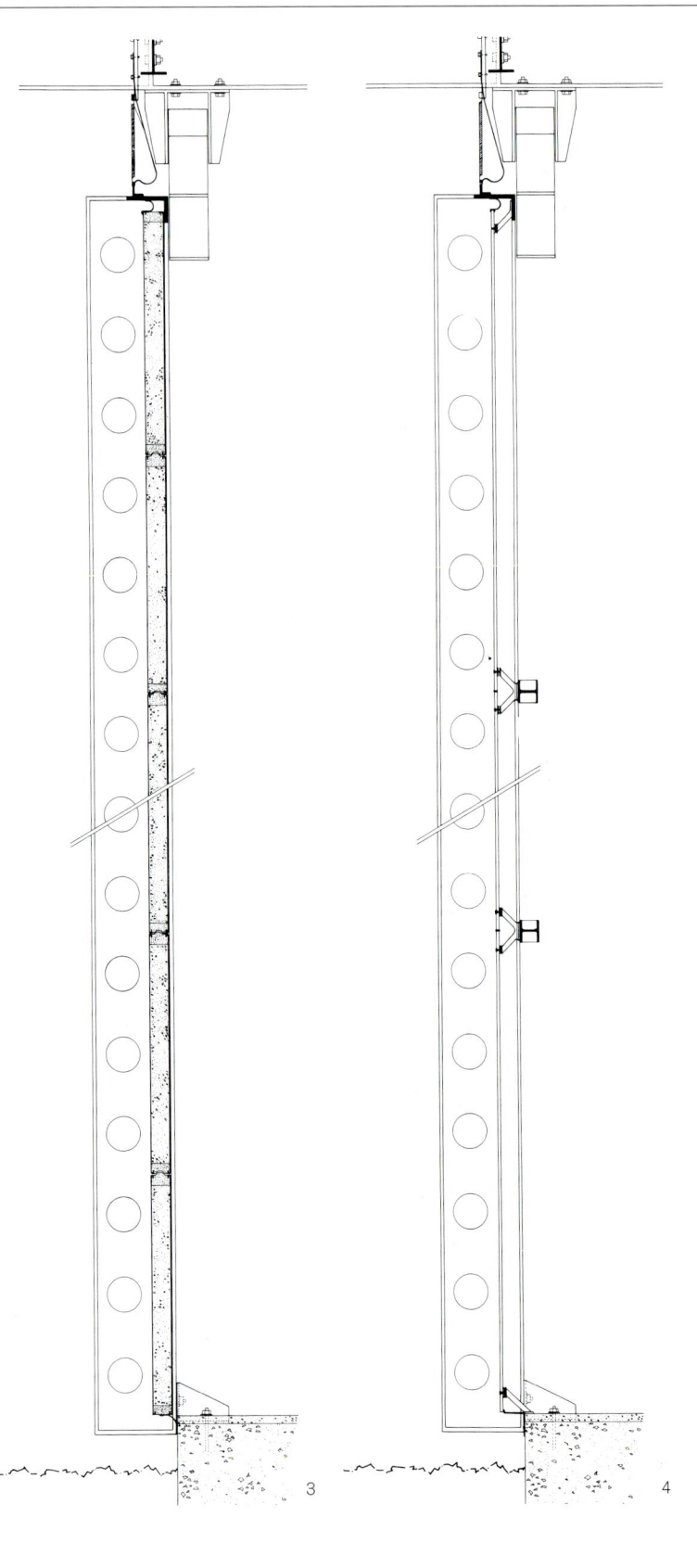

**The Renault Centre relies first and foremost on a yet more confident use of Foster's own brand of technology transfer whereby materials and methods are selected from the entire inventory of past and present techniques, not merely in construction or engineering but in such disparate fields as high-temperature steam technology, aerospace fire-proofing, heavy lorry-trailer side screen fixings and nineteenth-century cast-iron bridge building.** Martin Pawley, *The Architects' Journal*, 15 June 1983

**Renault's roofscape incorporates the metallic fabric more normally used to protect the airframe of a Harrier from the heat of its jet engine. To use it on a building to deliver a two-hour fire rating while also responding to movement tolerances involved special tests to prove the point; the test was, incidentally, stopped after two hours because it could apparently have performed almost ad infinitum!** Norman Foster, RIBA Royal Gold Medal address, London, 21 June 1983
Right: The Harrier jump jet, a single engine fighter bomber capable of vertical take-off, developed by Hawker Siddeley Aviation for use on aircraft carriers in 1966.

**Foster has allowed the skeleton to emerge from behind the flesh, the frame from behind the suppleness. At the Renault Centre, the exposed innards, the structural expression is reminiscent of the constructional forms – the *pattes de poulet* and the *pattes de cerf* metal joints – illustrated in Viollet-le-Duc's instruction manuals. It is a laying bare of the building's anatomy, a dissection of its structural properties, an architectonic stripping down of a kind completely unexpected from this supreme exponent of the smooth skin aesthetic.** François Chaslin, *Norman Foster*, 1986

Left, right: Illustrations from the *Dictionnaire raisonné de l'architecture française du XI$^e$ au XVI$^e$ siècle*, published by Viollet-le-Duc (1814-1879) in 1854-1868.

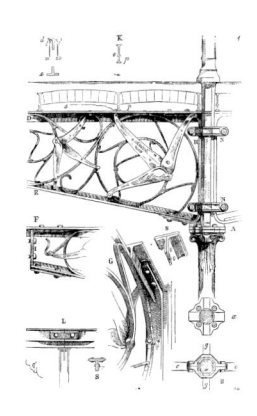

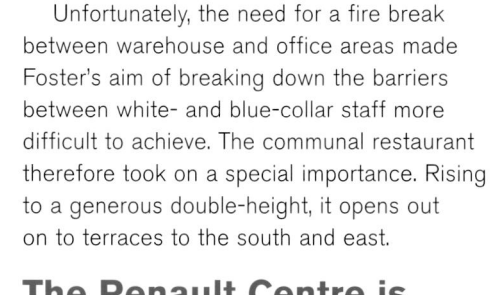

Unfortunately, the need for a fire break between warehouse and office areas made Foster's aim of breaking down the barriers between white- and blue-collar staff more difficult to achieve. The communal restaurant therefore took on a special importance. Rising to a generous double-height, it opens out on to terraces to the south and east.

**The Renault Centre is the product of a series of architectural, not merely structural, decisions. Any impression to the contrary results from the fact that the architectural motifs deployed also reinforce the structural symbolism.**

In August 1983, to mark the official opening of the centre, the French Secretary of State for Consumer Affairs, planted an oak tree. Also in attendance were the French Ambassador and Monsieur Bernard Hanon, president of the Renault Group. His comment, on first seeing the building was: 'It's a Cathedral!' Certainly it is magnificent. It is significant also that it is the only one of Renault's buildings that does not bear its logo. In fact, it is so closely bound up in the company's self-image, that Renault has used it in its product advertising.

For a cost no greater than a conventional design-and-build solution, Renault is the owner of a building whose beauty had the power to excite even those engaged in building it. The artist Ben Johnson, who has been inspired by many Foster projects, relates how, while he was up on the roof taking photographs, he met the site agent emerging from the twilight. 'It's very other-worldly', the agent said. 'I often come up here at the end of the day. It's the only place I can find peace and quiet.'

Tim Ostler

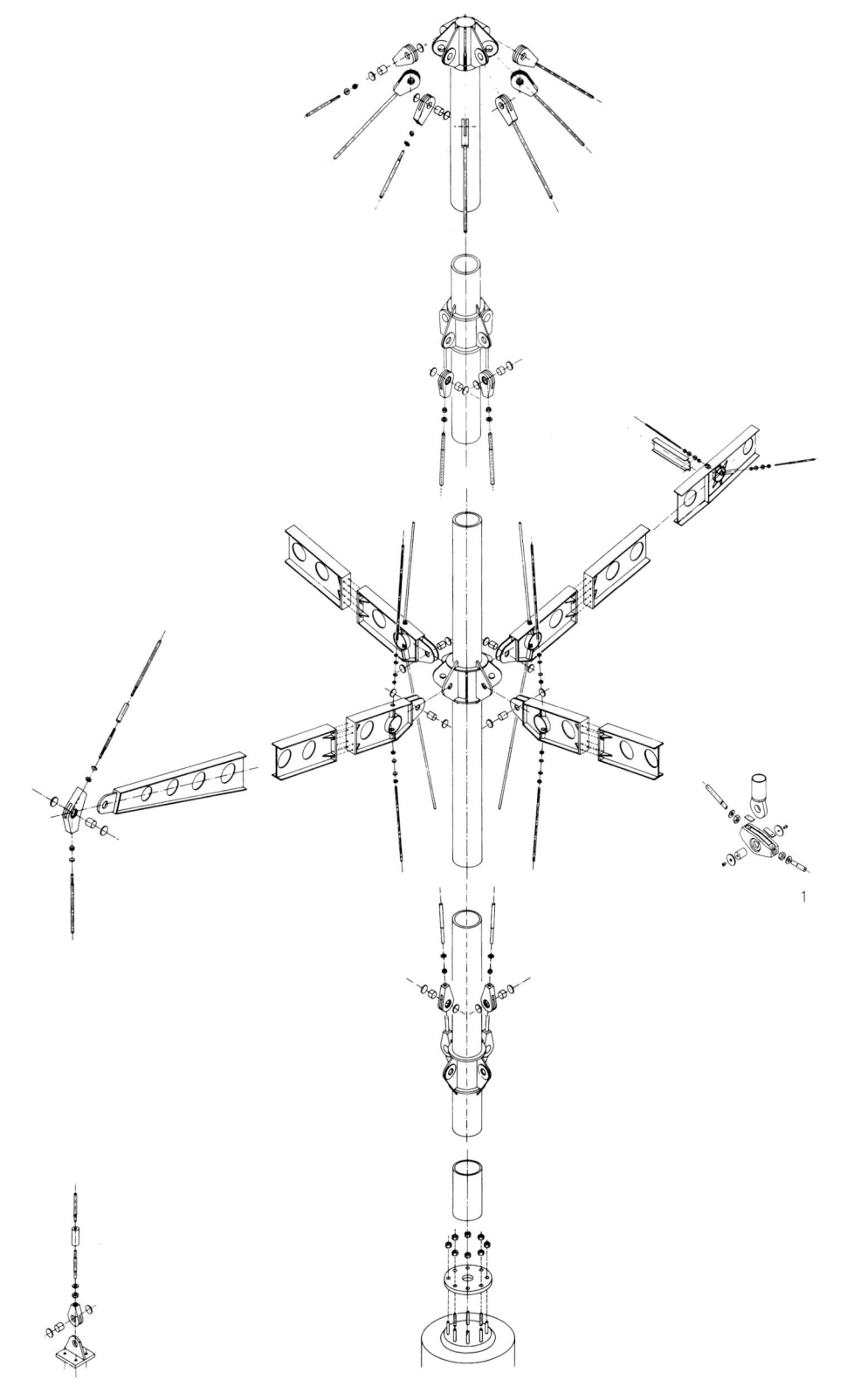

**I have strong recollections of many splendid buildings in Manchester ... In particular, I remember being excited by the tent-like tracery of the Barton and Lancaster Arcades, the latter sadly demolished in 1980.** Norman Foster, RIBA Royal Gold Medal address, London, 21 June 1983
Left: A detail of the Barton Arcade, the first glazed arcade to be built in Manchester, in 1871. The use of weight-reducing holes in its curved and tapering beams is reminiscent of the Renault Centre and demonstrates how this principle has been understood since the earliest days of iron and steel engineering.

**I see no conflict in embracing tradition and new technologies because for me they are both part of a single tradition. The most enduring structures, from any point in time, have always pushed the technology of the day to the limits whether they are man-made hills from pre-history, the Gothic stone cathedrals of Europe, the magnificent timber temples of Japan, the mosques of Islam, humble barns, or structures from ancient Rome.** Norman Foster, 'Architecture and Structure', article written for the Architectural Association of Japan, November 1994
Left: Another structural exemplar and inspiration is the Eiffel Tower, completed for the Paris 1889 Exhibition. A favourite image, an enlargement of this photograph hung in Foster Associates' Great Portland Street studio.

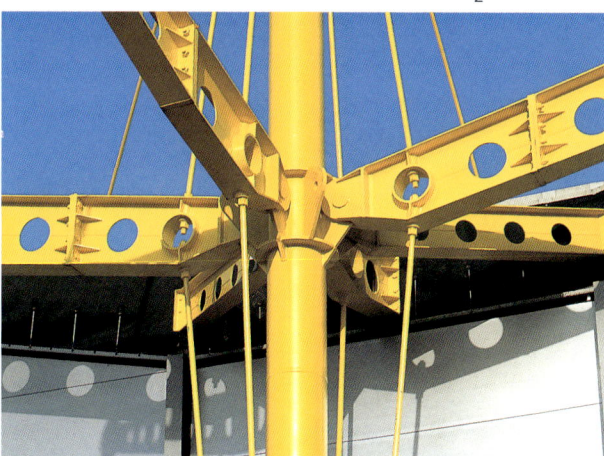

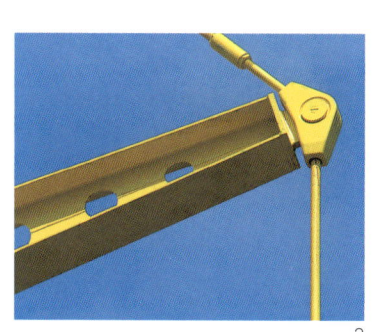

1. An exploded view of the structural assembly. Special elements, comprising eight radiating flanges welded to a central rod, cap the 457mm-diameter tubular steel columns. The tapered beams were made by cutting the web of a straight beam at an angle, reversing one section and re-welding the web. Holes into the beams help to reduce weight and the length of re-welding required. Annular flanges are welded into the holes in the beam webs at points where the ties are connected. These transfer the forces between the ties themselves and provide a solid bed against which the tensioning nuts can be tightened. A pre-drilled baseplate welded to the base of each column drops over a ring of high-tension bolts set into the foundation piles.

2-5. The use of pin-joints allowed the design of a very refined structure, capable of being erected quickly. Only three types of casting were required to cover all the different connection conditions. They are cast in spheroidal-graphitic iron, a material specially designed for sand-casting but with the performance characteristics of steel. To resist the uplift that can occur under severe wind conditions, tension rods at the edges of the building are attached to brackets set deep into bored foundations. Wind loads can impose far greater forces on the lower ties than those on top, so a special high-strength steel was specified accordingly.

Renault Distribution Centre 521

**Colour is regarded as something changing and evanescent which can be coaxed or teased out of (or into) a building, rather than as something that is 'applied'. Foster recounts flying an important visitor to see the Renault Centre at Swindon … As the helicopter landed outside the building they saw that the ground was densely covered with thousands of buttercups which visually echoed the yellow-painted steel structural supports of the Centre.** Paul Overy, *Norman Foster: Thirty Colours*, 1998

1. The steelwork reflects the company's house colour and is generally referred to as 'Renault yellow'. However, this photograph by Norman Foster suggests another, more poetic association.

2. In this sketch Norman Foster highlights the social potential of the showroom/gallery and the role that top-light plays in the building.

3. Exploded view of the roof and cladding assembly. The roof is covered with a welded pvc membrane with rainwater drainage taken in down-pipes within the hollow columns.

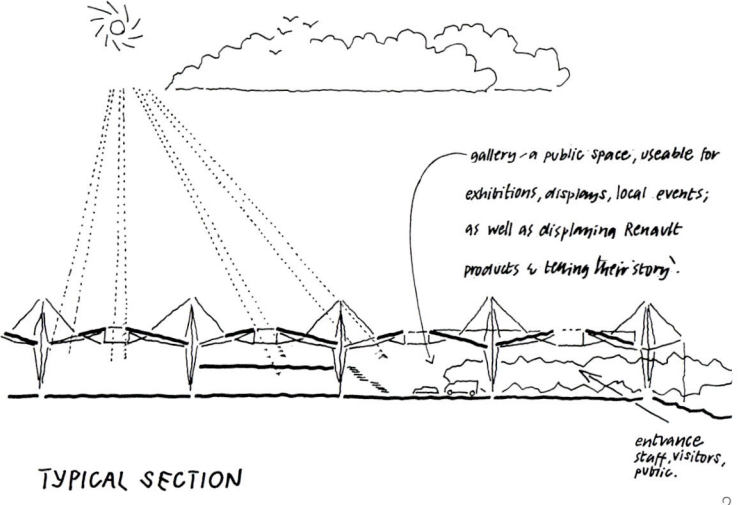

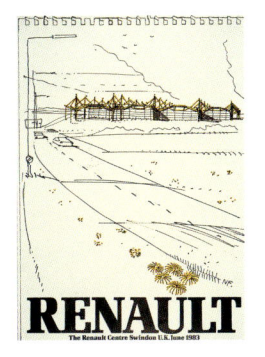

**It is the only building that Renault has which doesn't have the Renault sign on it; and it is the only building which Renault uses as part of its corporate advertising.** Norman Foster, lecture at the Aspen Design Conference, 18 June 1986
Left to far right: Examples from a range of promotional material produced by Renault featuring the building's distinctive yellow structure.

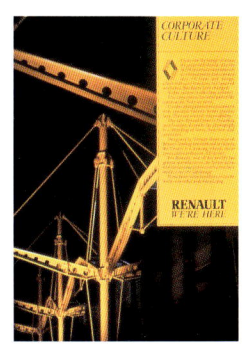

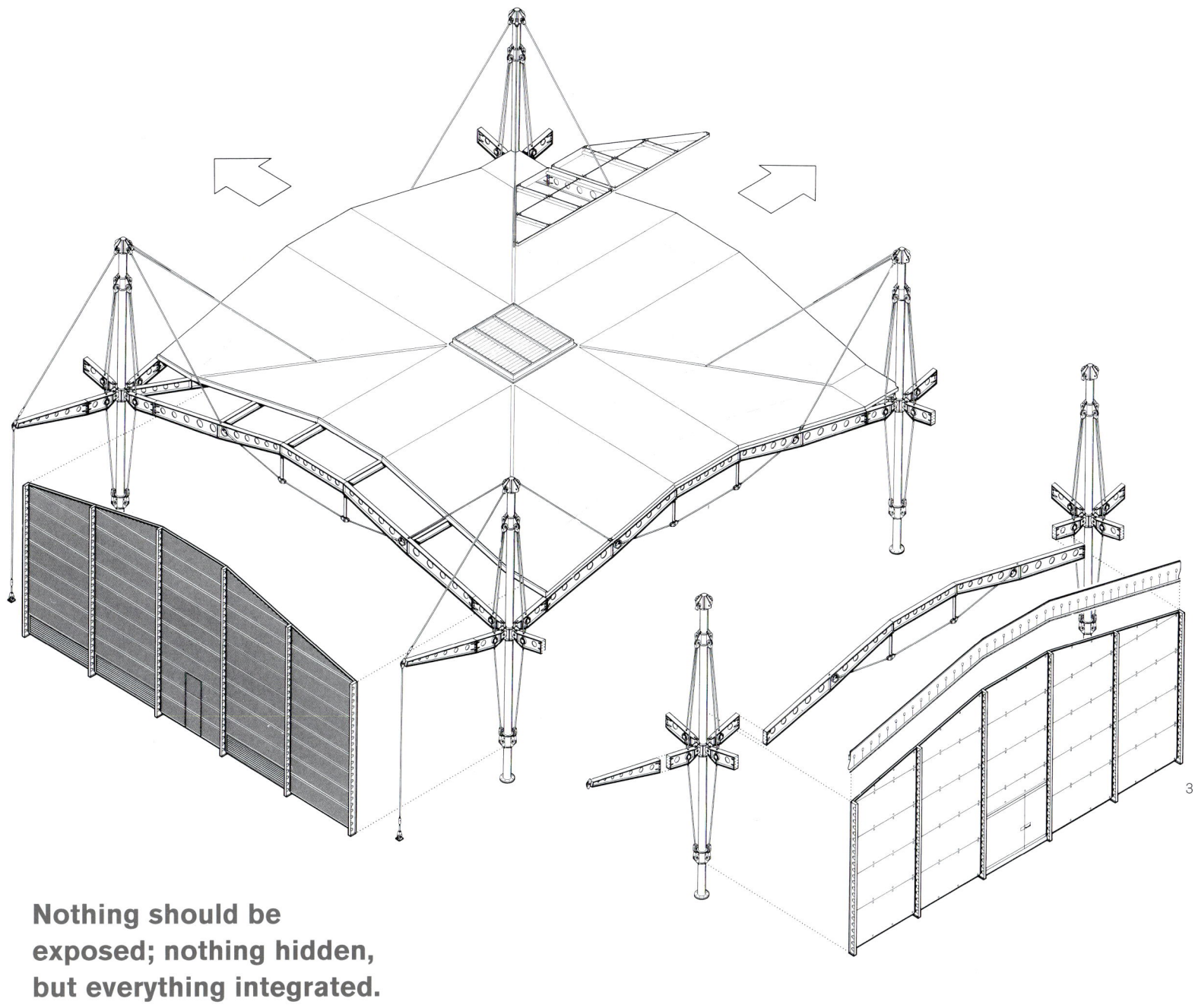

**Nothing should be exposed; nothing hidden, but everything integrated.**
Norman Foster

Renault Distribution Centre 523

**We meet again Mr Bond!**
Right: In addition to its regular appearances in company promotional material, the Renault Centre made its cinematic debut in 1985, when it was used as the location for 'Zorin Enterprises' computer chip factory in the James Bond film *A View to a Kill*.

1. A view of the newly completed warehouse space, shortly before the full-height racking was installed.

2, 3. The 19,500-square-metre parts warehouse encompasses a central services plant area, a fire-resistant enclosure for inflammable goods, a secure store for high-value goods, battery-changing facilities and lavatories. Two hundred people are employed within it, while truck deliveries average 45 a day. Materials handling is mainly by mobile mechanical equipment and manual order selection. Distribution within the warehouse is effected by means of robot trailer systems following tracks in the floor.

> **Renault's structure was designed as a means to an end: a way to span a given space and ensure flexibility of use of that space. And it was intended to achieve a sense of structural 'rightness'.**
> Norman Foster

**It's a cathedral!** Bernard Hanon, Président-Directeur Général, Régie Nationale des Usines Renault, on his first visit to the building, August 1983

**Inside the warehouse the undulating section of the roof structure, the tapering sections of the beams with their drilled webs, the reeded quality of the columns with their ties cannot but recall Gothic structure. The feeling of being inside some great church is enhanced by the racking which forces the perceived space up vertically into nave and multifarious aisles.** Peter Davey, *The Architectural Review*, July 1983

The Renault Centre fulfils Foster's intention of providing flexible, multi-use, well-lit space. It is as suitable for the storage of automobiles and their components as for the purposes of public reception, product display and the training of personnel. It not only serves its purposes adequately but also presents an effective technological image for an automobile company.
Kenneth Frampton, *On Foster … Foster On*, 2000

Ace joker Jeremy Beadle found hundreds of families fit for a game and a laugh at Swindon's Renault Centre open day on Saturday … the breezy TV personality played celebrity host to thousands of people joining in a promotion-packed fun day. Yellow Renault hats topped the heads of youngsters taking part in games and competitions with lots of give-away prizes … Centre manager Bob Gibbons said: 'It was super. We had a lot of fun and Jeremy Beadle was as mad as ever. A lot of people wanted to come and see what we do. We might hold another open day like this in the spring or the summer.' *Swindon Evening Advertiser*, 3 December 1984

**Foster hopes that the [gallery] space will be used by Swindoners to mount exhibitions of all kinds: concerts, sports events, film shows, and dances. In summer the events could spill out through the great glass doors into the space under the *porte-cochère*.** Peter Davey, *The Architectural Review*, July 1983

Right: The gallery/showroom at the Renault Centre with tables set out for a celebratory lunch on the occasion of the building's official opening in August 1983

**Renault presented the challenge of establishing a design quality that would extend from the product to embrace the working environment. That quest for excellence was pursued within demanding limits of time and cost, and also needed to accommodate the dynamic of change during the building's life.**
Norman Foster

1, 2. The gallery/showroom seen as it was completed. Body shells of some of Renault's then most recent models are suspended like acrobats from the ceiling, reinforcing the 'big-top' atmosphere of the space. The after-sales training school and service bays are visible through glazed screens, which line the internal wall of the space, their transparency aiming to demonstrate Renault's commitment to quality and service.

Renault Distribution Centre 527

**The expressionist bias evident in the Renault Centre exists in the furniture Foster has designed. The slender joints, splayed supports, clearly visible bolts, tie-rods and handles, resemblances to a water-boatman or a giant mosquito, give an almost parodic dimension ... Everywhere design sensuality pervades.** François Chaslin, *Norman Foster*, 1986

Left: The furniture systems designed for the Renault Centre were a development of those first used in the Foster studio in Great Portland Street.
Right: The Nomos system was developed in collaboration with the Italian company Tecno and entered production in 1987. Since then it has undergone a series of subtle modifications and refinements.

1-3. The restaurant is the social hub of the building. A double-height volume, with generous amounts of glazing, it is a light, airy space and enjoys the best views. Its internal wall is also glazed, the translucent panes concealing the kitchen and servery areas; the clear glass above allows views from the mezzanine offices at that level. Special tubular convector heaters, fixed to the inside edge of the wall mullions, heat the space efficiently. The glass-topped restaurant tables are a development of the furniture system first designed for the Foster Associates studio in Great Portland Street. The tables were later developed for commercial production as the Nomos system.

4, 5. The office areas house administrative and data-processing activities, as well as Renault's regional activities. The cellular offices and meeting rooms were installed as free-standing units with glazed 'ceilings' and side walls to maintain a sense of openness.

6. A range of office desks was also manufactured for Renault, together with a one-off reception desk in the showroom.

7. The service bays of the after-sales service school are located beneath the mezzanine-level offices. Supported on its own concrete columns, the mezzanine structure stands quite independently of the main steel-supported envelope. Extensive fire-protection equipment is installed at ceiling level.

**Living with the Nomos table has parallels with owning a bicycle – you discover the potential to modify the components. By varying the finishes it is possible to change the appearance, emphasising the frame or articulating the secondary structure for example.** Norman Foster, 'On Tables and Bicycles', essay written to celebrate the launch of the Millennium Edition of the Nomos table, December 1999

Right: The Nomos table is now available in a range of colours and finishes. To mark the millennium a new edition of the table was produced, far right, with the main frame picked out in a colour and the subsidiary elements articulated in chrome. As Norman Foster says, 'Without doubt this is the coolest!'

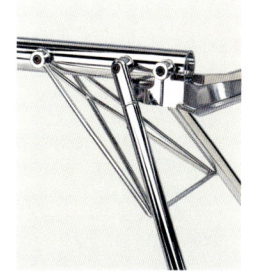

**Renault's director Pierre Jocou was so impressed by the furniture we had developed for Renault that he ordered a dining table from the range for his Detroit apartment.**

Norman Foster

Renault Distribution Centre   529

**Foster's structures are becoming more gutsy and expressive, even – unthinkable in early Foster – playful.** Alastair Best, *The Architects' Journal*, 1 December 1982

**For the first time, Foster's structure has come out. Instead of the smooth, non-committal, sheath that contained the works in his previous triumphs – Willis Faber & Dumas and Sainsbury Centre – at Swindon the jolly Renault-yellow structure dominates, suspending the roof and spilling over the side in a series of guy ropes. On its soon-to-be-green lawns, it is like nothing so much as a marquee, waiting for the festivities to take place.** Peter Davey, *The Architectural Review*, July 1983

**Sébastien de la Selle, 'Coordinateur d'Expression Visuelle' for Renault, contrasts the Renault Centre with what he says in French is called 'a shoebox in a beetroot field', waving his arm in the direction of the Anchor Butter warehouse a mile or so away.** Martin Pawley, *Building Design*, 25 March 1983

At Renault the protagonist is not the skin of mirror glass nor the classical proportions of the temple shed, but the structure of masts, perforated beams and multiple trusses painted in the bright yellow colour that is part of the French firm's corporate image … The image of this forest of wires in the middle of the green English countryside is of a visual poetry that is rare in industrial construction. Jorge Sainz, *A&V* 38, November-December 1992

The nautical joints between masts and guy rods, and the drilled-out webs of the mullions and main roof members which cast ever-changing patterns on the walls, all give the great shed human scale. Peter Davey, *The Architectural Review*, July 1983

# Richard Buckminster Fuller
Martin Pawley 1989

1. Richard Buckminster Fuller (1895-1983) photographed in 1967, in his study at the University of Southern Illinois, surrounded by models of geodesic dome structures.

It was fitting that Richard Buckminster Fuller, the great American engineer, poet, philosopher and polymath, who was himself the holder of the RIBA Royal Gold Medal for Architecture, should have given the oration on the occasion of Norman Foster's own Royal Gold Medal investiture in 1983. Fuller – known to generations of architecture students as 'Bucky' – sadly died in Los Angeles, at the age of 87, just ten days after the Gold Medal ceremony.

Though there was a difference of forty years in their ages, the two men had much in common and in the last twelve years of his life the great American sage was a friend and trusted advisor to the young English architect. They shared a mindset which Norman Foster describes as 'an impatience and an irritation with the ordinary way of doing things'. For both of them, this impatience was to lead to unique and unorthodox insights into environmental problems that have been expressed in remarkable achievements of anticipatory design.

Fuller understood the importance of what he called 'design science'. He saw that the needs of the world's burgeoning population could only be satisfied by the progressive ephemeralisation of goods and services so that higher standards of life support could be attained at a lower cost in terms of energy and resources; in other words: 'doing the most with the least'. It was an approach that Foster quickly identified with, for he could see history bearing it out.

Like Fuller, Foster believes that energy is the key to this issue. The energy question is ever present and sooner or later it is destined to reach another crisis that will make enormous demands on those few designers prepared to confront it. To this end Fuller strove, and Foster still strives, to remain open to influences and discoveries from widely different fields, suspicious that, in Fuller's words, specialisation is 'no more than a fancy form of slavery'.

**Fuller and Foster shared a mindset which Foster describes as 'an impatience and an irritation with the ordinary way of doing things'. For both of them, this impatience was to lead to unique and unorthodox insights into environmental problems, and remarkable achievements of anticipatory design.**

Born in 1895, the son of a wealthy Boston merchant, Fuller's aptitude for innovative design thinking grew out of his experience as an officer in the United States Navy during the First World War: 'Every ship designer knows what it means to shunt winds, tides, tension and compression to human advantage', he said years later. He spent much of the 1920s researching advanced methods of construction and for the rest of his life used his unusual skills, along with a whole range of unconventional architectural inspirations, to remain at the leading edge of design thinking for almost two-thirds of a century.

**Don't fight forces, use them.**
Richard Buckminster Fuller, *Shelter* 5, 1932

Sailor, machinist, comprehensive generalist, doer, new former, student of trends, technical editor, businessman, angel, quarterback, critic, poet, lecturer, experimental seminarist, random element, verb, comprehensive designer, inventor, engineer, architect, cartographer, philosopher, cosmogonist, choreographer, visionary, scientist, valuable unit, mathematician, air pilot, Navy lieutenant, affable genie, geometer, maverick thinker, gentle revolutionist, lovable genius, anti-academician, doctor of science, doctor of arts, doctor of design, doctor of humanities, amiable lunatic, prophet, custodian of a vital resource. A typically idiosyncratic curriculum vitae offered in Fuller's *An Autobiographical Monologue/Scenario*, 1980

Architecture is voodoo. The architects don't initiate anything; they just go to work when the client says so. They know how to draw, but they don't know how to design an airplane. They don't go to Douglas and say tell me what you've found out today about the tensile strength of the new steel or aluminium. They have approximately nothing to do with evolution. I think the younger architects may be changing. I think they **understand what I'm saying.** Richard Buckminster Fuller, *New York Times*, 23 April 1967

---

Today he is remembered as much for his prefabricated house design of 1927 and his revolutionary front-drive, rear-steering car of 1933 – both of which he called 'Dymaxion', a word coined from the combination of dynamic and maximum – as he is for the geodesic and tensegrity domes that were built in large numbers from the 1950s onwards. In 1935, the year of Norman Foster's birth, Fuller was already working on prototype production line service modules for dwellings. The battles he fought to try to establish such revolutionary solutions in the market place gave him a low opinion of the traditional construction industry. As he told his biographer Robert Marks: 'Craft building – in which each building is a pilot model for a design that never has a production run – is an art that belongs to the Middle Ages. All decisions in craft-built undertakings are based on methodological ignorance.'

While Foster's background was very different to Fuller's, he was drawn to similar – though less combative – conclusions. Born into a working-class family in the industrial city of Manchester he left school at sixteen and found a job as a clerical assistant in the City Treasurer's office before being called up for two years of military service in the Royal Air Force. It was not until he was in his twenties that he was admitted to Manchester University to study architecture, but his abilities were swiftly recognised. Upon graduation in the early 1960s he won a Henry Fellowship to Yale University. The experience of America influenced him deeply. When he returned to England he found that he had an energy and ambition he had not previously possessed.

'In England I was the odd one out – working-class background, early school leaver, a place in the university but no grant. I was an outsider', Foster told the audience at his American Institute of Architects Gold Medal investiture in Washington DC, in 1994. 'But when I came here I felt that I had come home. There was a pride in working and serving. I felt liberated. It is no exaggeration to say that I discovered myself through America.'

Fuller's lifetime experience and Foster's enthusiasm for American methods sparked off a fruitful synergy that bridged the age gap between them. Even before they met, in 1971, Foster had designed a perfect American steel box factory for an industrial estate in a provincial English town – the Reliance Controls building, in Swindon, completed in 1967 and since demolished. He had also begun to make a name for himself as an industrial architect, working with new, lightweight materials and novel techniques for the sunrise industries that were beginning to come to life all over England. In 1969 he wrote an article for BP's house magazine, *BP Shield*, that revealed the scale of his ambitions and the extent of his confidence in the potential of advanced technology architecture: 'Vast areas will soon be enclosed with lightweight space frame structures or inflatable plastic membranes', he predicted. 'Full climatic control is feasible; the polar regions can be tropicalised and desert areas cooled.'

## Fuller's experience and Foster's enthusiasm sparked off a fruitful synergy that bridged the age gap between them.

Vision of this calibre connected directly with Fuller's thinking, not least with the already famous image of a huge geodesic dome enclosing fifty blocks of Manhattan, and his realised design for the United States pavilion at the 1967 World Expo in Montreal. But inspiration and collaboration proved to be two different things. While the projects Fuller and Foster developed jointly during their collaboration exemplified the unorthodox thinking of which both men were capable, they did so with none of Fuller's gigantism.

2. Fuller's Dymaxion car, developed between 1933 and 1934, sought to give a fundamentally new architecture to the automobile. The car had three wheels – the single rear wheel did the steering, while power was provided through the the rigid front axle. The streamlined, aircraft-inspired body was developed in collaboration with the shipbuilder Sterling Burgess.

3. Fuller's Wichita House (1941-1946) was the culmination of his Dymaxion House concept, developed while Fuller was head engineer at the American Board of Economic Warfare. It aimed to provide a cost effective, easily constructed dwelling which could be deployed to meet housing needs during the Second World War. The aluminium-clad house consisted of industrial prefabricated units that could be assembled on site. Launched in 1945, 37,000 orders for the house were placed within six months of its unveiling.

**If industry would take it on, there are things we could do with geodesic domes that are spectacular. I haven't let much of it be visible, except that anyone looking at the geodesic dome in Montreal saw a very beautiful piece of mechanics. It did all kinds of things to your intuition … It would be perfectly possible to create a geodesic of very high frequency where each 'pore' could breathe air or let light in and the whole thing could articulate just as sensitively as a human being's skin. And I really think geodesic domes such as that will be developed.** Richard Buckminster Fuller, *Domebook*, 1971

**In architecture form is a noun; in industry form is a verb.** Richard Buckminster Fuller, *Nine Chains to the Moon*, 1938

**That we are endowed with such intuitive and intellectual capabilities as that of discovering genes and DNA … as well as nuclear energy and chemical structuring is part of the extraordinary design of Spaceship Earth, its equipment, passengers and internal support systems. It is therefore paradoxical but strategically inexplicable … that up to now we have been misusing, abusing, and polluting this extraordinary chemical energy-interchanging system for successfully regenerating all life aboard our planetary spaceship.** Richard Buckminster Fuller, *Operating Manual for Spaceship Earth*, 1969

1. Bucky's provocative question 'How much does your building weigh?' is authoritatively answered in this photograph of a geodesic dome structure being carried by helicopter. The broad potential of Fuller's immensely efficient structures was swiftly recognised by the US Marine Corps, amongst others, who worked with Fuller to develop new applications for these structures. A magnesium-framed geodesic dome developed to provide instant shelter in the field could be erected by untrained personnel in two hours, carried by ten men, and would withstand winds of up to 120 miles per hour.

The 1971 Samuel Beckett Theatre – the project that first brought Foster and Fuller together – was to have been a subterranean structure housing an auditorium, buried beneath the quadrangle of St Peter's College, Oxford, 'like a submerged nuclear submarine', as Foster put it. Unhappily the project failed to attract sufficient funding to proceed, although it aroused considerable professional interest and some of the preliminary design work on underground structures it involved was to feed into later projects.

This last characteristic was even more true of their second design collaboration in the same year. This was the 'Climatroffice', a much larger project based on a highly transparent tensegrity structured envelope enclosing landscaped office floors enjoying their own microclimate. The project, although it was essentially theoretical, not only inspired Foster's subsequent urban scheme for Hammersmith, but contributed to the next Fuller/Foster collaboration six years later, this time in the United States.

The project was to design a pavilion for the International Energy Expo to be held in Knoxville, Tennessee, in 1978. The solution here was another large tensegrity enclosure, this time a lozenge-shaped double-skin envelope designed to house the entire exhibition in a single controlled climate enclosure capable of serving the community as a public building once the exhibition was over.

Larger than Fuller's completed Expo '67 pavilion, the Knoxville project would have included within its double skin a wide range of solar heating, cooling and electricity generating devices so as to maintain optimum internal comfort conditions at all times. Unhappily this project failed to attract funding in time and was discontinued after preliminary design studies.

The final project jointly undertaken by Fuller and Foster cast the former in the role of client and the latter as architect. The project was for a residence – a working prototype – for Buckminster Fuller and his wife Anne in Los Angeles (Foster and his wife Wendy were to have an identical one in Wiltshire) that would have embodied Fuller's most advanced structural ideas. Like the Knoxville design it was to be double skinned but the two skins were to be independent. It was intended that the two concentric five-eighths spheres, the outer 15 metres in diameter, would be free to rotate in low-friction hydraulic races, so that little effort would be required to move them despite their considerable size.

Unlike Fuller's earlier geodesic domes this dome was structured using an interlocking series of identical frames following parallel segmental lines like the lines of latitude around the earth. Heating and cooling was to have been accommodated between the two skins and, since part of the aluminium skin of each part-sphere would have been opaque and part transparent, the house could have been darkened or lightened by means of its rotating action alone. In the same way, because the inner skin supported three intermediate floors, it would have been able to reorientate its accommodation to suit the position of the sun, direction of the wind or the occupants' preference.

A large-scale demountable model of this fascinating structure was made in the US and brought to London, where it was reassembled in Foster Associates' model shop, near the studio in Great Portland Street. After Fuller's death in the summer of 1983 work on the design ceased, but the model was exhibited in the Great Portland Street studio until the practice moved to Battersea in 1990, when it was again dismantled and placed in storage. It was reassembled again as the centrepiece of the Buckminster Fuller exhibition which travelled around the world during the course of 1999 and 2000, and later featured prominently in an exhibition of the work of the Foster studio at the British Museum in 2001.

**Bucky was a humanist and an optimist; he inspired a generation of people who were privileged to come into contact with him.** Norman Foster

**Bucky was fascinated by nature and plant structures. He would talk very eloquently of the way that trees were great hydraulic structures and would compare the elegance and beauty of a tree to the very crude adaptations of bits of stone and timber and brick.** Norman Foster, lecture at the Solar Energy Conference, Florence, 17 May 1993

**In 1970 we crossed a threshold where it could be demonstrated that if we took all the metals being put into armaments and put them into 'livingry', within ten years we could have all humanity living at a higher standard than anyone had ever known on a completely sustainable basis while phasing out all further use of fossil fuels and atomic energy. In 1970 it became evident in engineering that if we kept track of the whole thing on a planetary basis, for the first time in history it did not have to be you or me, it became adequate for both.** Richard Buckminster Fuller, closing address at Norman Foster's Royal Gold Medal investiture, London, 21 June 1983

2. Norman Foster photographed with a model of the Autonomous House designed in collaboration with Buckminster Fuller. Two such houses were planned: one was to be built in Los Angeles for Fuller and his wife Anne, and the other in Wiltshire for Norman and Wendy Foster. However, the project was discontinued following Bucky's death in 1983. Constructed by an American aircraft manufacturer, this model was returned to the Foster studio in 1983 and placed on display in the Great Portland Street studio.

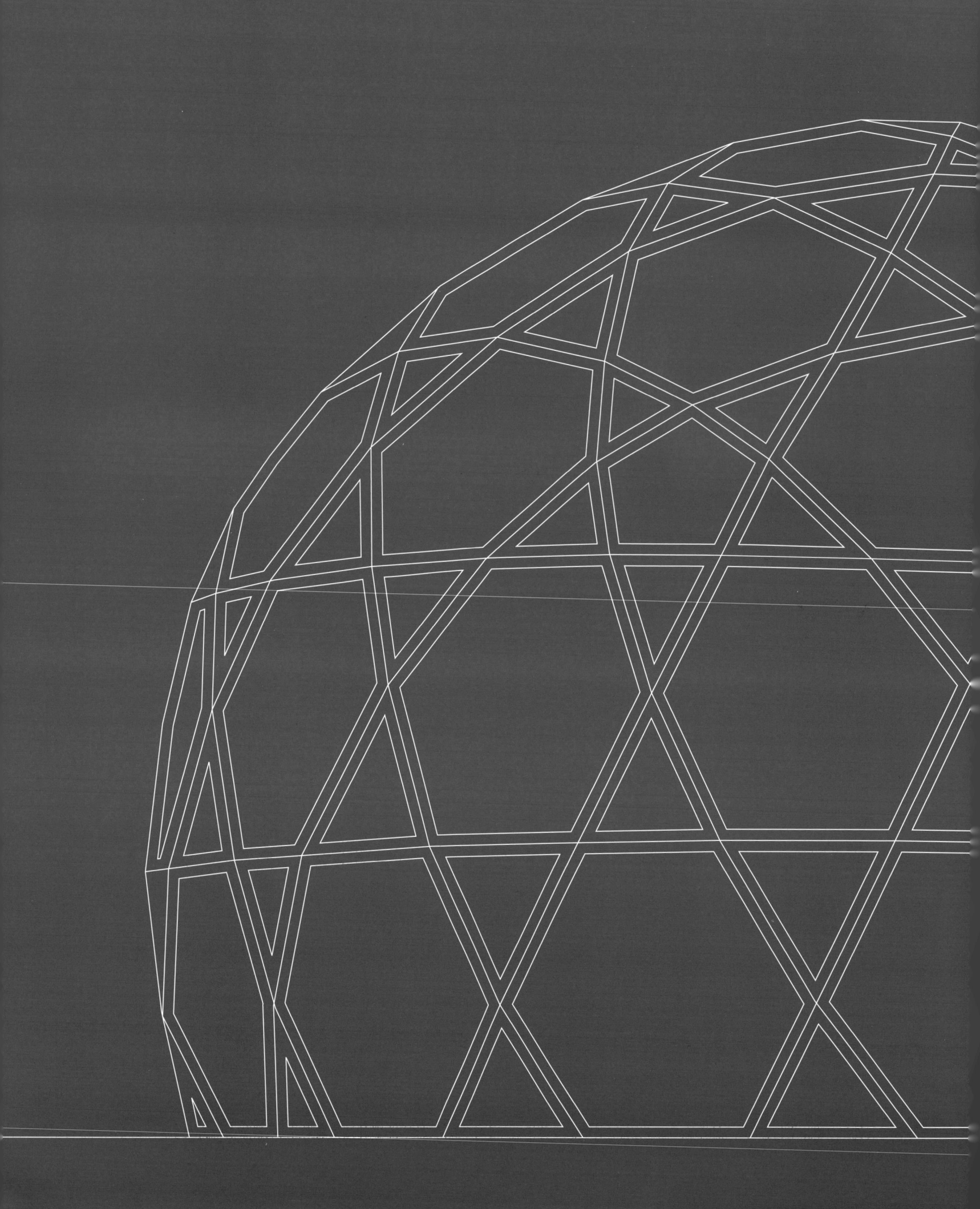

**Projects with Buckminster Fuller**
1971–1983

Our first project with Bucky was for an auditorium beneath the quadrangle of St Peter's College, Oxford. Although it did not proceed, it marked the beginning of a friendship and a shared approach to environmental issues, which is still very much alive today. The 'Climatroffice' – which sprang from design investigations for Willis Faber & Dumas – was a transparent tensegrity structure, with its own internal microclimate and landscaped office floors. These ideas were re-explored in a proposal for the Energy Expo in Knoxville. More recently they have influenced projects such as the Commerzbank and Swiss Re. Our last collaboration was for a prototype house. Formed from two concentric spheres – part opaque and part transparent – that rotated independently, it could be reoriented to suit the position of the sun. Work on the project ceased with Bucky's death, but the ideas it embodied would go on to inform the design of the Reichstag's new cupola, with its moveable sunshade.
Norman Foster

# Samuel Beckett Theatre
St Peter's College, Oxford, England 1971

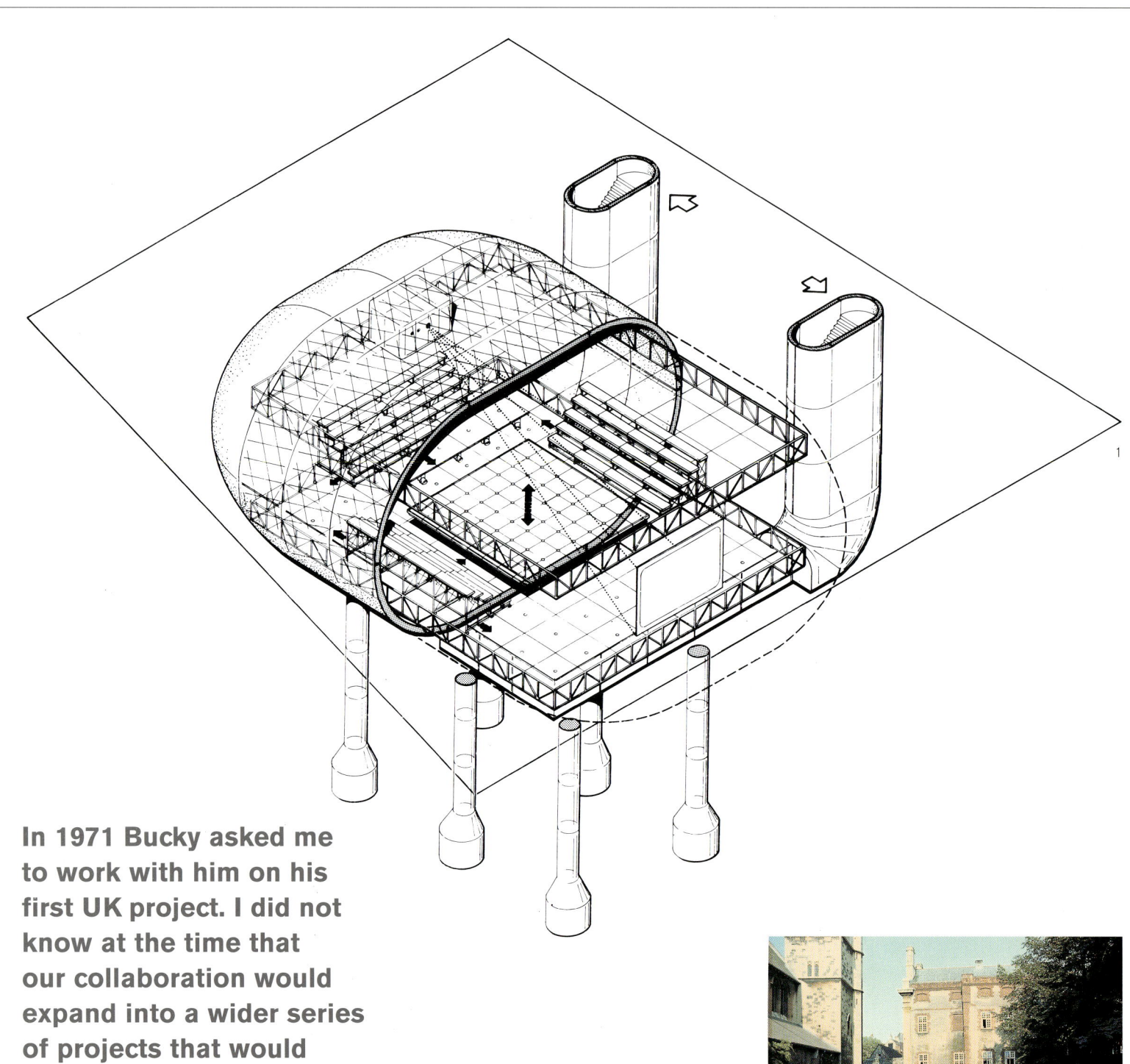

**In 1971 Bucky asked me to work with him on his first UK project. I did not know at the time that our collaboration would expand into a wider series of projects that would pose radical alternatives to conventional built forms.**
Norman Foster

**The theatre was really a complete break with the past in the context of Oxford. Instead of making a statement it hid itself discreetly below the lawn. Interestingly, one of the biggest questions, in terms of the structure, was how to resist flotation due to the high water table. I remember discussing this with Bucky and characterising the building as a 'nuclear submarine' – only the staircases, which broke the surface of the lawn like conning towers, would have revealed its presence in the quadrangle.** Norman Foster, in conversation with the editor, 2002
Left: The conning tower and hull of a nuclear-powered submarine break water.

**Bucky had a wonderfully evocative way of acting out how the forces of nature would work on his structures. On this occasion, suddenly – in the midst of trying to describe the form of the theatre – he ran into the bathroom and came back with a bar of soap, saying, 'This is what it would look like.' Inscribing the bar of soap 'Oxford Beckett Theatre', he signed it with a flourish.** Norman Foster, lecture at Stuttgart University, 14 May 1997
Right: The famous bar of soap bearing Bucky's signature. Duly photographed, the bar of soap went on to be used in several presentations to the college.

St Peter's College, Oxford, was the site of the first collaborative project between Norman Foster and Buckminster Fuller. Francis Warner, then a Fellow of St Peter's College and a long-time friend of Samuel Beckett, instigated the scheme in 1971 with the observation that the college, and Oxford, required a new, purpose-built experimental theatre which, he proposed, should be dedicated to the Nobel prize-winning dramatist. Richard Burton and Edward Heath, among others, were approached to head a fund-raising exercise and Buckminster Fuller was invited to prepare a series of outline proposals. Fuller invited Foster to collaborate with him on this, his first English project.

With his customary directness, Fuller proposed to build the theatre beneath the college quadrangle, suggesting, at the same time, that the scope of the scheme be expanded to maximise use of the new building by creating a multi-purpose space, adaptable for a wide range of theatre configurations but also capable of interpretation as a highly serviced teaching or exhibition space. The subterranean solution was a direct response to the lack of any suitable site at ground level; but it had the added benefit of placing the new space at the most central position possible within the college.

The scheme was destined to founder through lack of fund-raising support. Work continued, however, through to a prototype interior that proposed moveable, triangular blocks that could be rearranged to accommodate almost any configuration of seating layout and stage design.

Martin Pawley

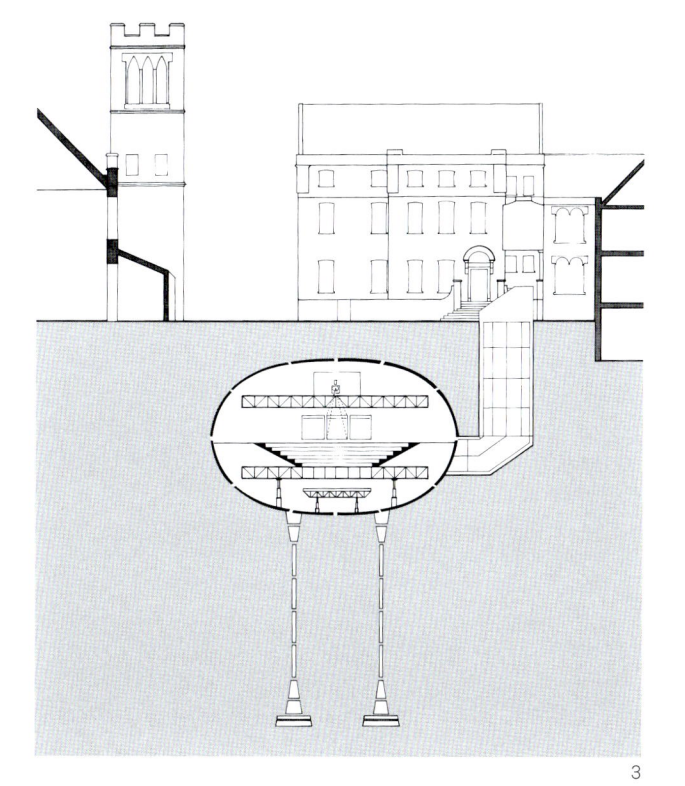

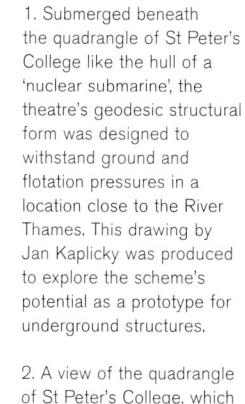

1. Submerged beneath the quadrangle of St Peter's College like the hull of a 'nuclear submarine', the theatre's geodesic structural form was designed to withstand ground and flotation pressures in a location close to the River Thames. This drawing by Jan Kaplicky was produced to explore the scheme's potential as a prototype for underground structures.

2. A view of the quadrangle of St Peter's College, which demonstrates the restricted nature of the site.

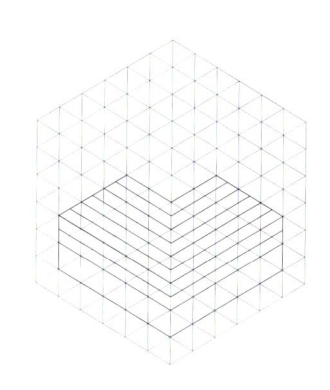

3. The theatre's only impact in its setting were the two entrance and ventilation turrets that broke through the surface of the lawn.

4. To facilitate flexibility in stage configuration a system of moveable plastic blocks was devised that could be deployed across the gamut of stage design – from Greek arena, through Elizabethan apron and Victorian proscenium arch, to theatre-in-the-round.

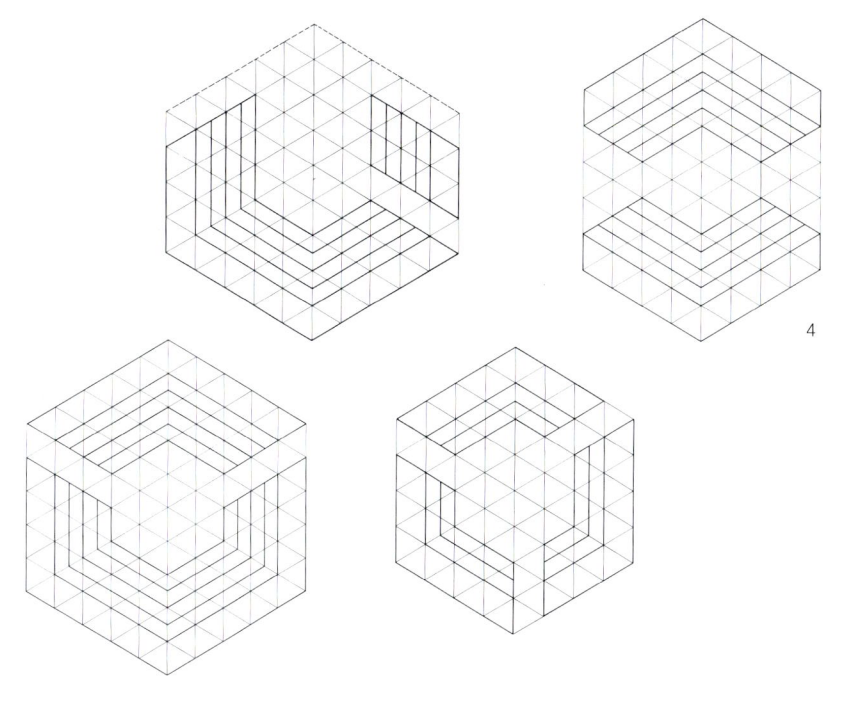

# Climatroffice
1971

> **Research is fundamental to the way we work; we frequently find that one building realises concepts previously explored only on the drawing board.**
> Norman Foster, in conversation with the editor, July 2001

> **Climatroffice points towards an architecture of 'interiorised' buildings, which live within an envelope so diaphanous that its presence is perceived as being closer to the sky or clouds than any conventional structure.**
> Norman Foster

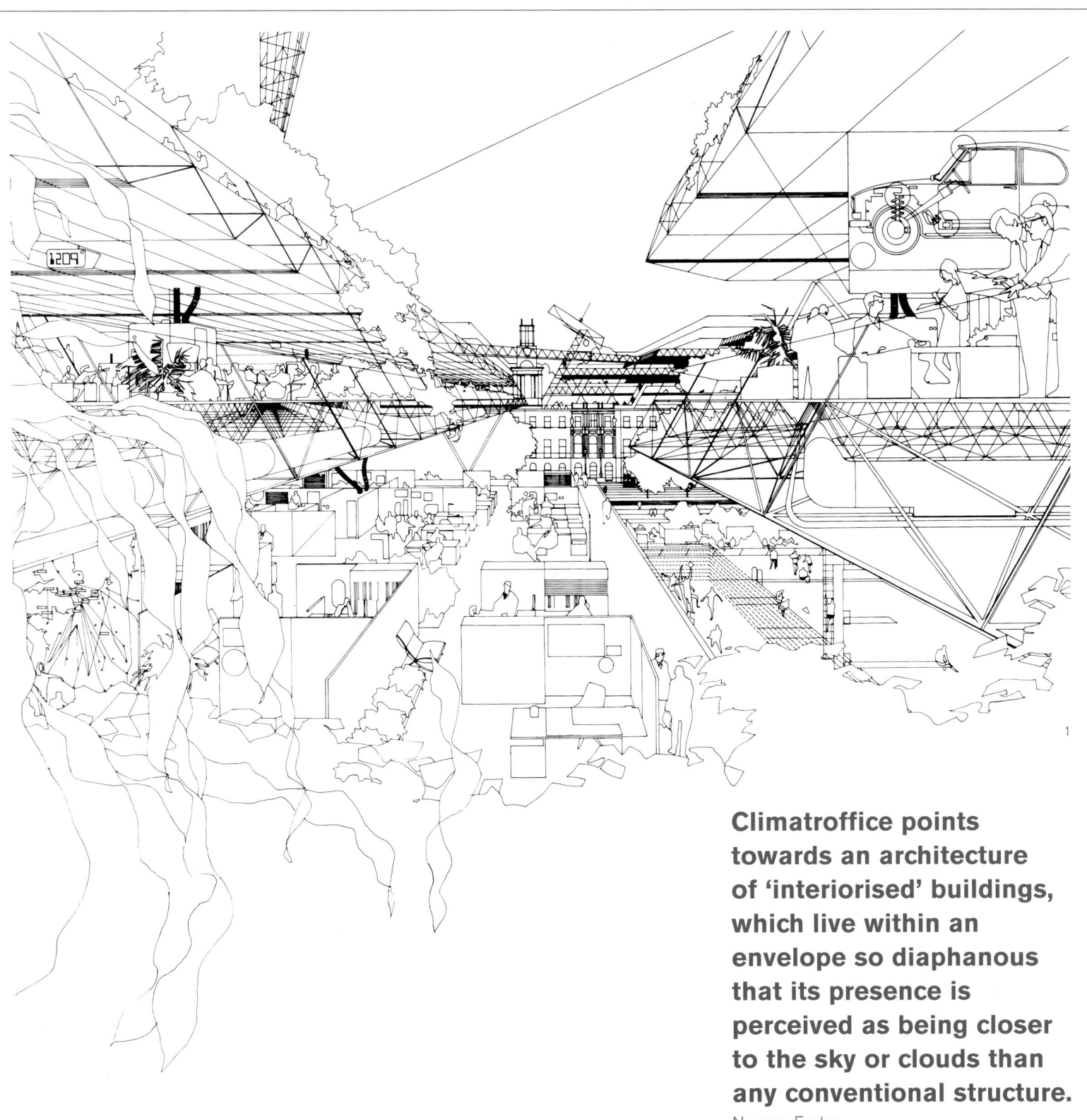

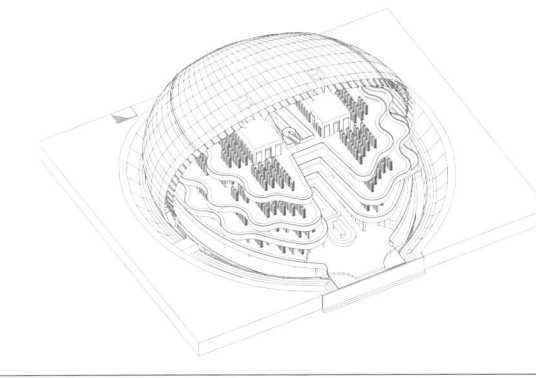

Left: The lessons of Climatroffice can be detected in the design of the library for the Faculty of Philology, at the Free University of Berlin (1997-2002). The five-storey building is enclosed within a free-form skin consisting of aluminium panels, ventilation elements and double-layered glass panels, supported on steel frames with radial geometry. The building's cranial form has earned it the affectionate nickname of 'the Berlin brain'.

**The Climatroffice looks at the scope for creating a rich mix of buildings, old and new, within a large-scale minimal enclosure; very much in the spirit of doing more with less. Such a form encloses the maximum volume with the minimum surface area, and creates a beneficial atmosphere within which change can take place gracefully and effortlessly outside of the elements.** Norman Foster, lecture at the RIBA Annual Conference, University of Hull, 14 July 1976

The Climatroffice concept arose during 1971 while Foster Associates was addressing both the St Peter's Theatre project, a collaborative effort with Buckminster Fuller, and the early stages of the Willis Faber & Dumas building. During a break in a working session on the theatre, the discussion turned to the difficulties involved in locating new buildings alongside existing ones – then the key challenge of the Ipswich-sited building for Willis Faber. Fuller suggested that one solution might be to build a large-scale enclosure which spanned and brought together all the buildings on the site, both new and old.

The appeal of such a solution – envisaged as a transparent, lightweight dome, containing its own planting ecology and microclimate – promoted the Climatroffice studies. These studies, very much in the spirit of Fuller's earlier work on the Montreal Expo Dome or the St Louis Climatron, were dedicated to the ideal of producing a 'living office' environment. 'It was an experiment,' notes Norman Foster, 'with the possibility of creating a microclimate within which there would be the option of flexibility. As far as possible, divisions between the inside and the outside worlds would be dissolved.'

Although it proved impractical to apply this thinking directly to the Willis Faber building, the Climatroffice project facilitated a clearer focus on issues close to Foster's own interests: flexibility of use, in the form of multi-function spaces; energy saving; the enclosure of the maximum space within the minimum external surface; lightweight envelopes; and an abundance of natural light and the enduring concept of the 'perfect space'. All these concerns were embodied in the Climatroffice project and all have continued to inform, and be reflected in, many of Foster's subsequent buildings, from unrealised projects such as the Hammersmith Centre, of the late 1970s, to schemes for Swiss Re and Berlin Free University completed in the early years of the new millennium.

Ian Lambot

1. The hard line drawings cannot do justice to what was always conceived as more of a theoretical exercise than a real building. It is Birkin Haward's almost abstract drawing that most memorably captures the spirit of the idea.

2. A modified oval plan form balanced the maximum volume enclosed by the minimum surface principle of the perfect sphere with the realistic creation of maximum usable floor area.

3. Within the indeterminate form of the enclosure, terraces of floors could be erected and changed at will. The central escalator atrium is an obvious reference to the Willis Faber project, which had prompted the Climatroffice studies.

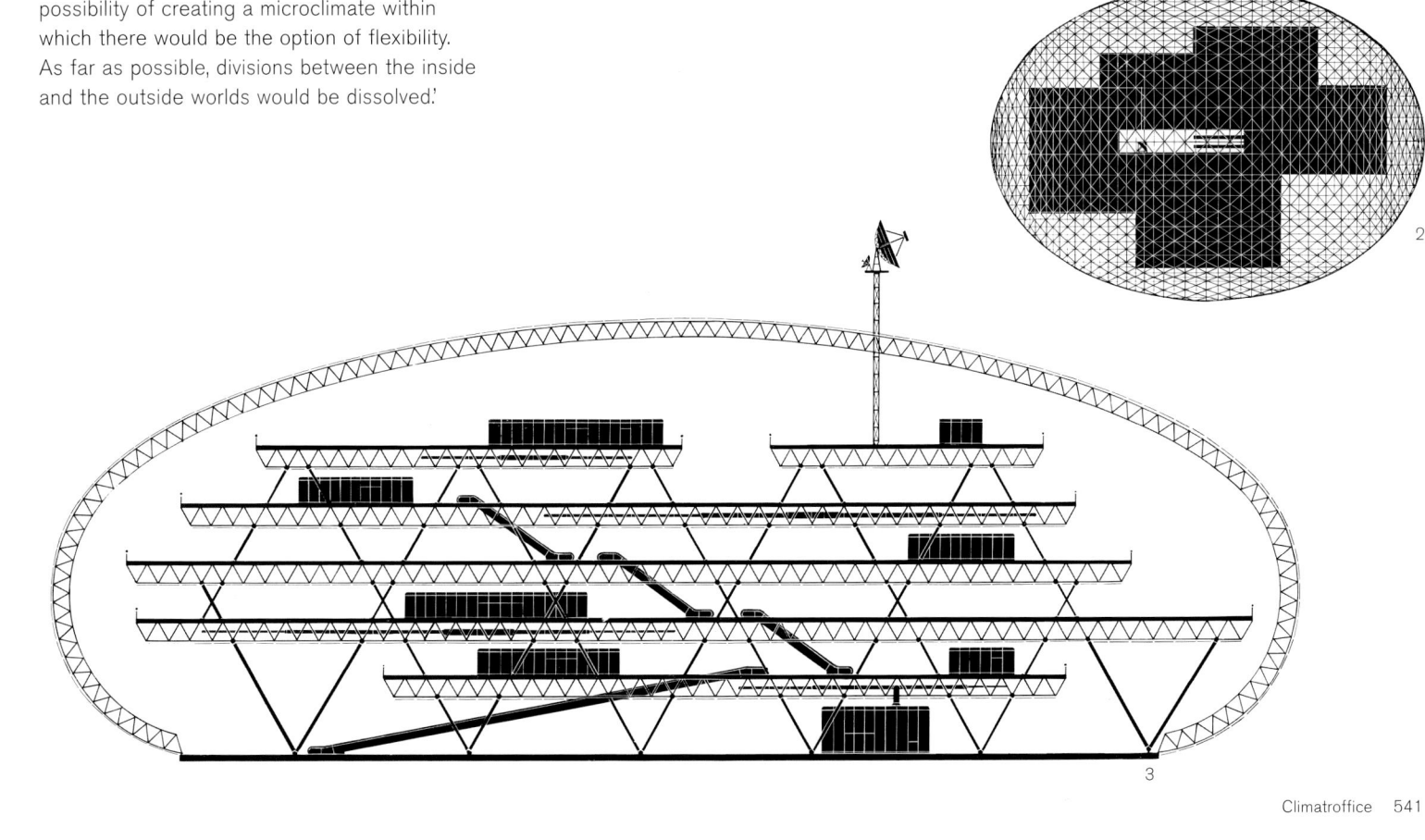

# International Energy Expo '82
Knoxville, USA 1978

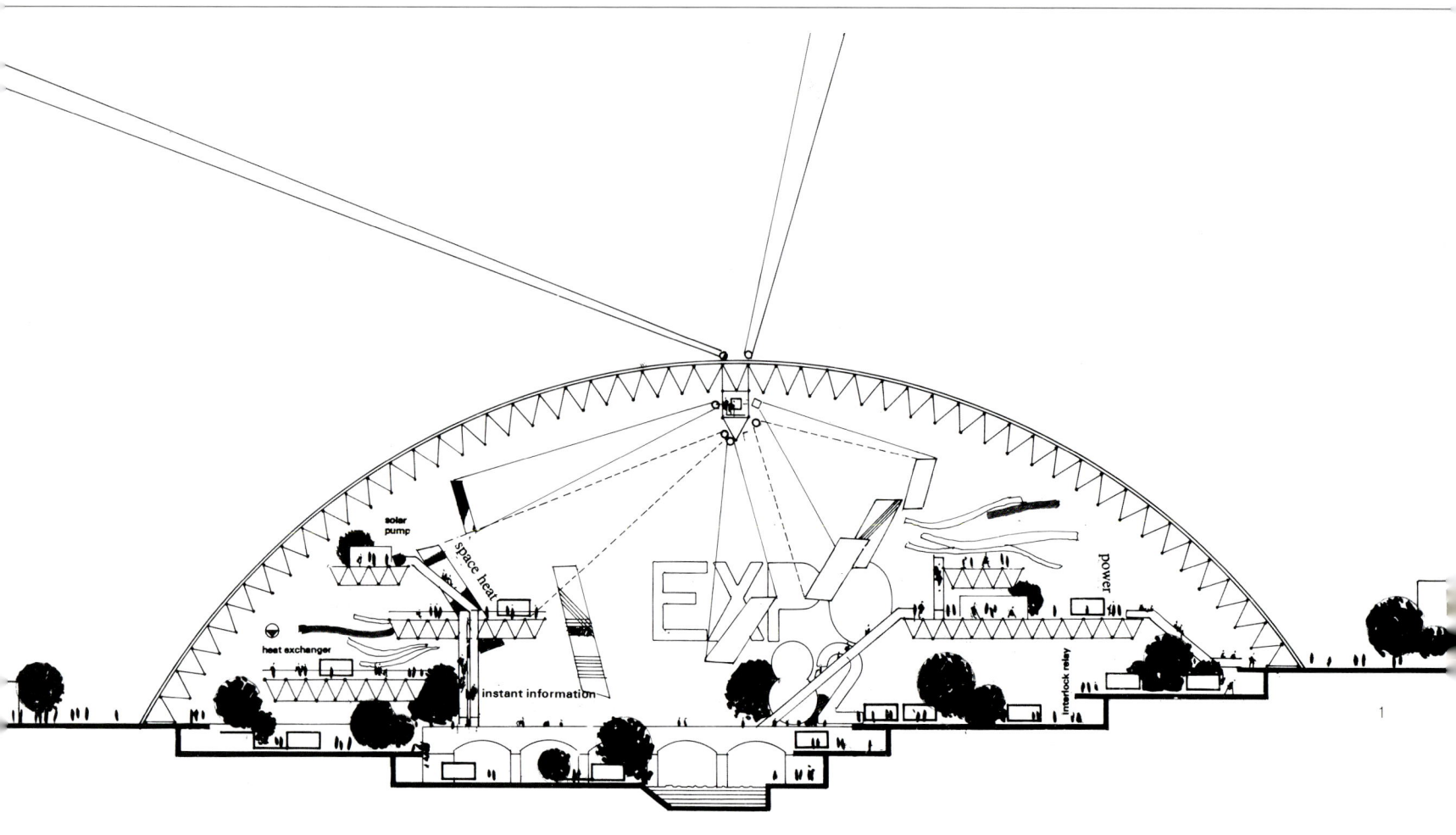

**The Knoxville project allowed us to explore further the Climatroffice concept of a large-span structure sheltering a range of structurally independent buildings.**
Norman Foster

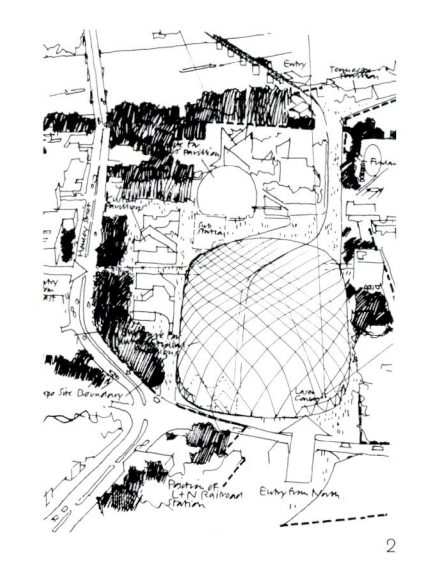

**Inside the dome the walls start going away from you; this has an extraordinary psychological effect of releasing you, for you realise that the walls are not really there ... I walked around and listened to what people had to say, and they seemed happy in this open but controlled environment. It was not done according to the aesthetics of architecture as it had been practised up to then; it was done simply in terms of doing the most with the least.** Robert Snyder, film maker, describing the experience of being inside Buckminster Fuller's United States pavilion at the 1967 Montreal Expo. Left: The Knoxville pavilion drew on Fuller's highly successful Montreal dome, which was retained as a popular landmark long after the exposition had closed.

Right: Possible future uses for the Knoxville building included a wide variety of public amenities, from winter garden or exhibition centre and museum, to convention centre and sports arena.

In 1978 the Knoxville Expo Committee invited proposals from Buckminster Fuller Associates, which brought together Buckminster Fuller himself from Philadelphia, Shoji Sadao from New York and Norman Foster from London. The team proposed a range of variations on large-scale, clear-span 'tensegrity' structures, within which exhibitors could lease ground, air or external roof space.

In exploiting current and new technologies in the construction and energy-conservation fields, the project was particularly appropriate to the theme of the exposition. The building was designed to provide passive energy savings through the shape and form of its double-skin enclosing structure and to accommodate solar-powered electricity generation and heat collection, which would be harnessed to provide space cooling in such a way that its internal environment would be wholly self-sustaining. In the spirit of the event, it was intended that the building itself would become the Expo's principal exhibit.

Unlike the more conventional arrangement of separate pavilions – which are usually demolished at the end of such events – it was hoped that such an energy-efficient enclosure would be of long-lasting benefit to the local community. Once the exposition had closed, the pavilion could easily be converted to suit a variety of alternative activities, from winter garden to sports arena.

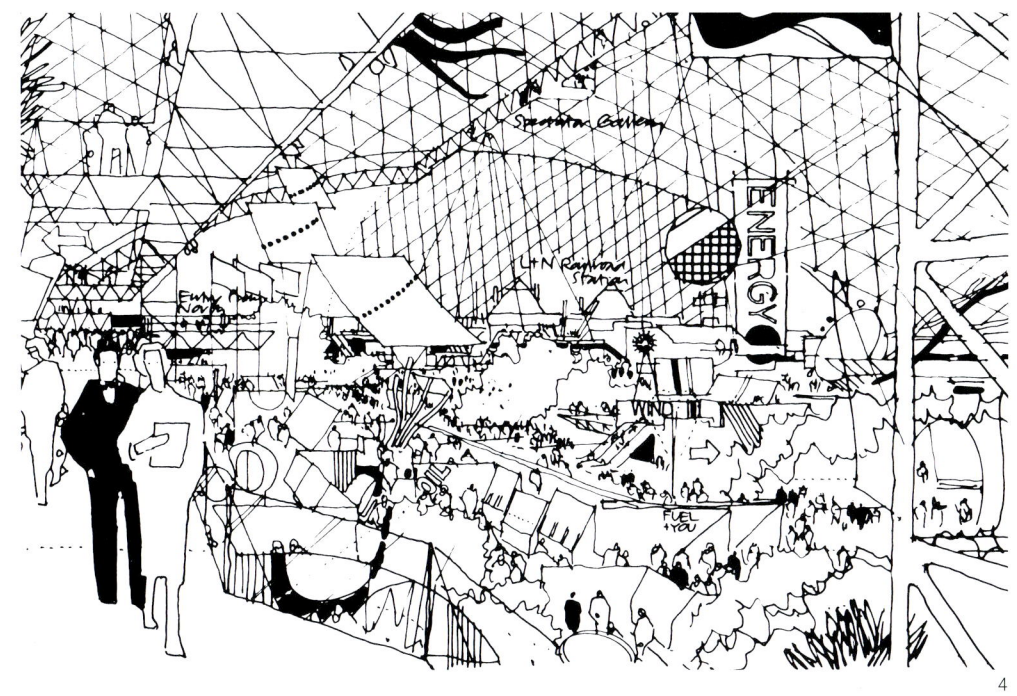

Martin Pawley

> **In the spirit of the event it was intended that the building itself would become the Expo's principal exhibit.**
> Martin Pawley

1. A single large tensegrity structure, spanning 130 metres, would have housed all the Expo's exhibits and been easily adaptable to a variety of alternative uses when the event ended.

2, 3. Aerial views of the dome and its Knoxville site.

4. Birkin Haward's sketch perspective captures the lightness of the interior and its diaphanous enclosure.

5. Included within the pavilion's double skin were a range of solar heating, cooling and generating devices, which would have allowed its comfortable internal environment to be wholly self-sustaining.

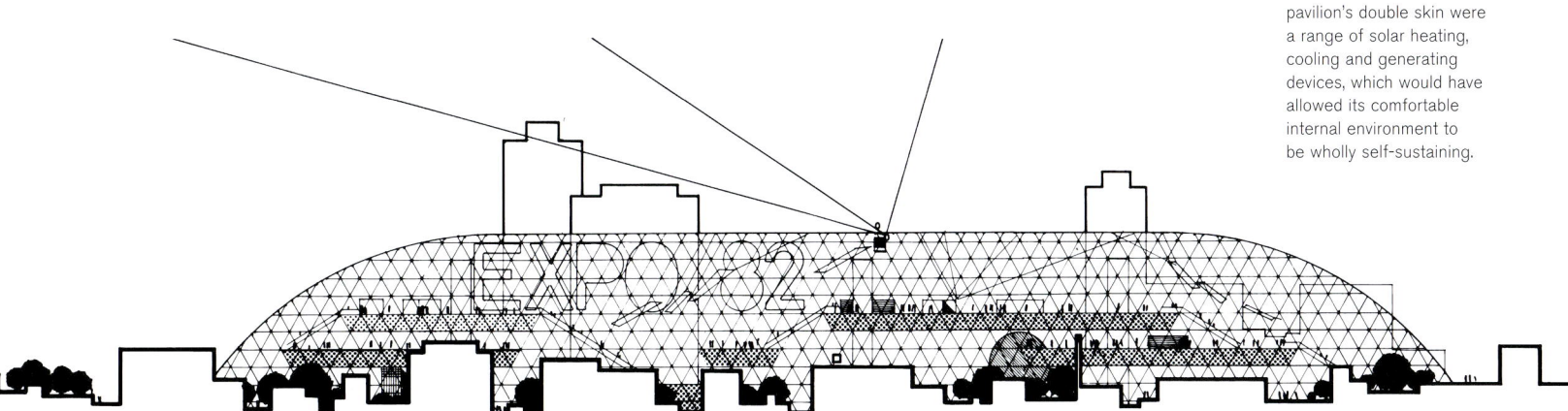

# Autonomous House

Los Angeles, USA 1982–1983

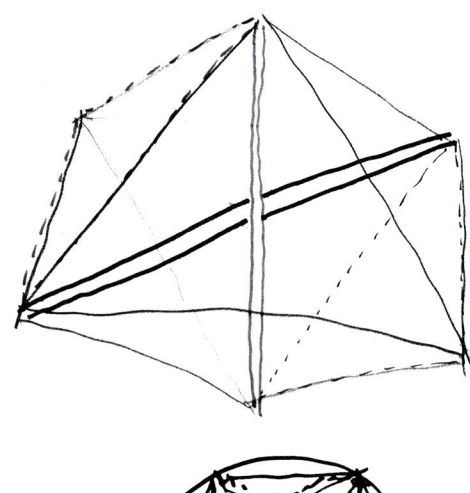

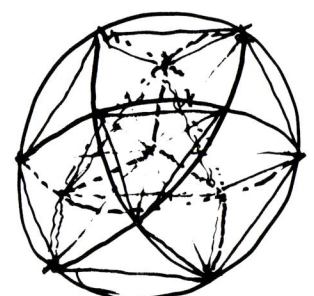

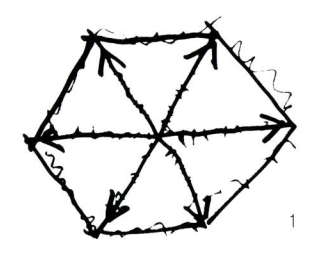

**Shortly before he died, in 1983, we were fortunate to work with Bucky on a design for an Autonomous House – a dome structure with its own microclimate.**
Norman Foster

**A home, like a person, must as completely as possible be independent and self-supporting, have its own character, dignity, beauty or harmony.** Richard Buckminster Fuller, 1928, quoted in *Buckminster Fuller*, Martin Pawley, 1990
Left: Fuller inspects a prototype dome produced in 1961 to provide emergency accommodation in the field for the Peace Corps. This was only one of numerous applications of Fuller's patented geodesic dome system to the field of mobile shelter and flexible, low-cost housing.

**Intuition of the resonances between natural and human structures is as old as the oldest surviving writings on architecture – even older if we take into account Aristotle's fascination with nature's 'constructivists', such as the cell-building bee and geometrically accomplished spider.** Martin Kemp, Professor of Art History, addressing the forum 'The Legacy of Buckminster Fuller in Science and Architecture', held at the Science Museum, London, 6 May 1998

Until Buckminster Fuller's death at the age of 87, just ten days after giving the oration at Norman Foster's RIBA Royal Gold Medal investiture in June 1983, the close friendship and working relationship between 'Bucky' and Foster had been extremely fruitful. Their last collaborative venture was an energy self-sufficient 'autonomous' dwelling based on a five-eighths sphere, double-skin dome generated by a new structural geometry that Bucky had recently developed. It was to have been developed as a house for Fuller and his wife Anne in Los Angeles; another was to have been built in Wiltshire, in England, for Norman Foster and his wife Wendy.

## The refinement of lightweight, high-performance structures had occupied Fuller throughout his career; with the design of the Autonomous House the concept reached its logical conclusion.

The external skin was to be a 15-metre diameter 'fly's eye' dome capable of rotating independently around a similar inner dome which would support the space-deck living floors. Each dome was to be half glazed and half solid – clad in polished aluminium panels – and capable of rotating with respect to the other, so that the house could be closed up at night, or track the sun during the day.

The continuous bottom tubes of the inner and outer domes 'floated' in a low-friction sealed hydraulic race which required very little fluid to support the structural load. It was a principle that Fuller had tested in the early 1970s with his 'rowing needles' – tubular hulled, catamaran scullers – which, as a keen oarsman, he had designed for his own use. In these, the water played the part of the hydraulic fluid. Using the same hydraulic principles for the house, it became possible to move the domes with very little effort, opening up a whole range of new possibilities.

It is an idea that can be traced back to Foster's rotating reflectors developed to trap the low Norwegian winter sun in the Vestby office project, in 1974 – a concept that would in turn inform the design of the 'sunscoop' in the Hongkong Bank and the louvred sunshade that revolves within the Reichstag's cupola. Between the two domes, the environment would be controllable, warm or cool air circulating between the two skins, depending on the outside air temperature. The interior was to be planted to create an internal microclimate.

1, 5. Extracts from Fuller's sketches of the house's geodesic geometry. It was configured as a double layered structure – a dome-within-a-dome – the interior rotating with respect to the exterior. The external surface was to be articulated as a series of flat polygonal panels with triangular infill.

2, 3. Fuller's last visit to London, in June 1983, was prompted by the address he was to give at Norman Foster's RIBA Royal Gold Medal investiture. The following day he spent time in Foster Associates' studio in Great Portland Street, discussing the details of the new house. He is seen here in the model shop.

4. Fuller and his American colleague John Warren, photographed in California with a model of the house's floor system.

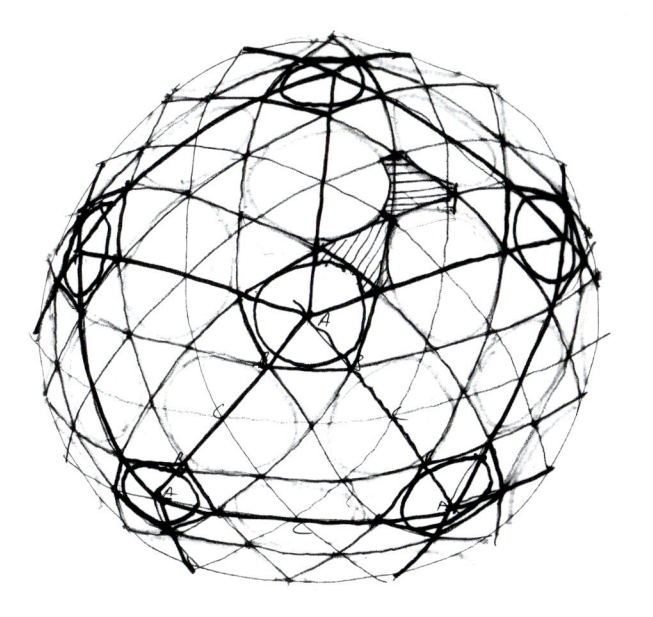

**When we developed the first geodesic dome, the two largest domes in the world were St Peter's in Rome and the Pantheon. St Peter's is around 30,000 tons – about the weight of the Queen Elizabeth 2. When I developed the first geodesic dome of 150 feet it came out at 30 tons – one thousandth of the weight of St Peter's. I have been trying very hard to get the world of architecture, the accrediting boards of the societies, to require that all drawings of any building made by any draughtsman or any architectural student always have the weights of the materials.** Richard Buckminster Fuller, closing address at Norman Foster's Royal Gold Medal investiture, London, 21 June 1983

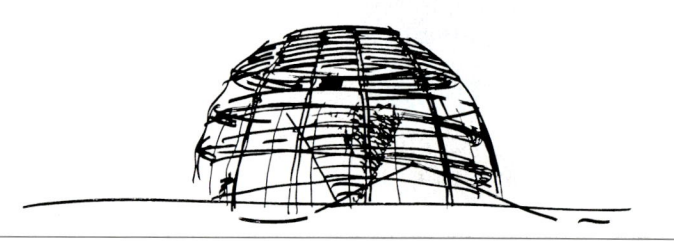

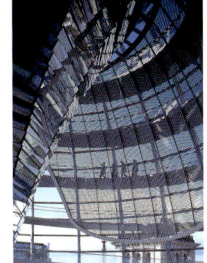

**The Autonomous House had its own microclimate and a double skin – the inner leaf of which moved in relation to the sun, providing shade in summer and drawing in light in winter. This idea has been developed further in the design of the Reichstag's new cupola; it houses a computer-controlled moveable sunshade that tracks the path of the sun to prevent glare and solar gain from penetrating the parliamentary chamber below.**
Norman Foster, lecture at Stuttgart University,
14 May 1997
Left: Norman Foster's sketch of the Reichstag's cupola and photographs of the completed structure illustrate the strong kinship between this remarkable form and the Autonomous House project.

The refinement of lightweight, high-performance structures had occupied Fuller throughout his career; with the design of the Autonomous House the concept reached its logical conclusion. Unlike Fuller's earlier geodesic domes, in which the surface is articulated as a structural pattern of triangulated polygons, here the two domes relied on a series of parallel, interlocking segmental lines to define the structure, an effect analogous to taking the equator and lines of latitude on the surface of the Earth, then tilting and repeating them at set intervals. These lines created a pattern of regular framed hexagons and triangles. Irregular pentagons were formed by the intersecting segments.

The design was advanced in a series of meetings with Fuller in London. A full set of design drawings was sent to Fuller's office in California, where the final complex three-dimensional geometry was calculated, and a large-scale model was made in the design studio of a US aircraft manufacturer. This was completely demountable into a kit, which Fuller brought with him to London.

Fuller was tremendously excited by the project and the success of his collaboration with the Foster team and felt that 'it was really going to happen'. But tragically he died while the project was still under development; it was inevitably shelved, although the model continued to hold pride of place in Foster's Great Portland Street studio until it was again dismantled when the practice moved to its new studio in Battersea in the summer of 1990.

Martin Pawley

1, 2. A large-scale model of the final version of the house was made in the workshops of a US aircraft manufacturer and brought to London in kit form. It was fitted with a selection of prototype cladding panels, both solid and transparent. Shortly after Fuller's death, the model was taken up to Dunstable Downs, in Wiltshire, and photographed against the evening sky, generating one of the most memorable images of Foster and Fuller's collaboration.

3. Studies for the internal arrangement of the house, from Norman Foster's sketchbooks, dated 20 September 1982. The space-deck floor structure allowed a variety of plan configurations.

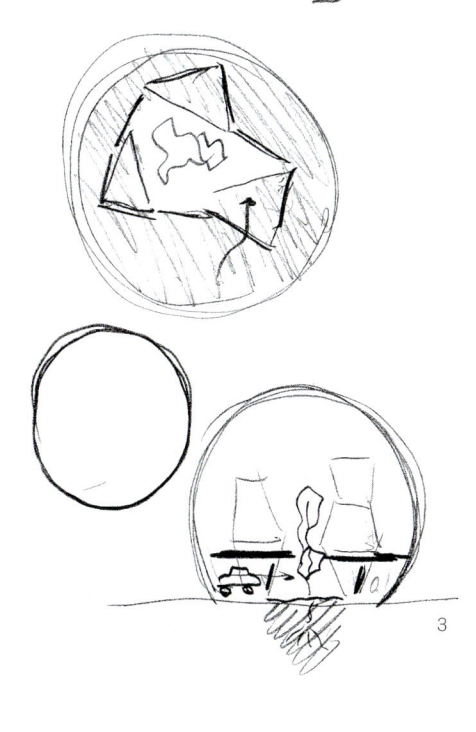

# Bucky and Beyond
Norman Foster 2000

I can remember vividly my first meeting with Bucky in 1971. He had been asked to design a theatre beneath the quadrangle of St Peter's College, Oxford and was looking for an architect to collaborate with him on the project. James Meller – a mutual friend – was helping by making some introductions. We met at the ICA, which at that time had a panelled dining room overlooking the Mall. In this elegant setting Bucky, James and myself talked through a long lunch. I had brought examples of our work to show him, and the studio was on stand-by in the hope that Bucky would visit us. In the event that was not necessary. Bucky decided on the spot that we should work together and then headed off to the next engagement on his ever-demanding schedule.

**Looking back over the twelve years of our collaboration and friendship, many papers could be written on the insights that Bucky was to offer. But perhaps the related themes of shelter, energy and the environment – which go to the heart of contemporary architecture – best reflect his inheritance.**

Only much later did I realise the extent to which Bucky was able to draw me out through that first conversation without my realising it. He got me to reveal attitudes to design, materials, research and other issues, which ranged far and wide. Looking back over the twelve years of our collaboration and friendship there are many papers that could be written on the insights that Bucky was to offer. But perhaps the related themes of shelter, energy and the environment – which go to the heart of contemporary architecture – best reflect his inheritance.

Bucky was a true master of technology, in the tradition of heroes such as Eiffel or Paxton. His many innovations – from the Dymaxion House to the geodesic dome – still surprise one with the audacity of their thinking. Yet, while his public image may have been one of the cool technocrat, nothing could have been further from the truth. What was never discussed was his deeply spiritual dimension. For me, Bucky was the very essence of a moral conscience, forever warning about the fragility of the planet and man's responsibility to protect it.

He was one of those rare individuals who fundamentally influence the way that you come to view the world. Bucky was the closing speaker on the occasion of my Royal Gold Medal investiture at the Royal Institute of British Architects, in June 1983. He used that occasion to address issues of survival: a message that today seems even more pertinent, as some of his most dire predictions are coming to life.

The world is changing rapidly around us but we are far from prepared for the consequences. The United Nations warned, in its report *Global Environment Outlook 2000*, of a series of looming environmental crises sparked by water shortages, global warming and pollution. It suggested that these trends can be reversed but only if the developed countries reduced their pattern of wasteful consumption of raw materials and energy by as much as 90 per cent.

An explosion in population growth is another crucial factor. Global population has doubled to six billion since 1960 and we are currently adding new humans to the planet at the rate of 78 million a year. That trend is expected to continue for at least the next decade.

Working sessions with Bucky and a mixed group of engineers and cost economists, more than twenty years ago, were remarkably similar to the meetings we have in the office today. The individuals may have changed, but the skills are the same, and there is still that appetite for cross-fertilisation, and an energy gained from shared values. Collaboration throughout the process, with the whole range of skills, is of the essence. Norman Foster, lecture at Stuttgart University, 14 May 1997
Right: Buckminster Fuller engaged in a design session for the Samuel Beckett Theatre in Foster Associates' Bedford Street studio, 1971.

Mexico City has a population of 22 million, 44 per cent of whom are living in slums. In a slum district like Chalco, where there are no pavings, no electricity, few sewers and no running water, clearly the motor car is an irrelevance. When we were in Mexico we had a discussion with the distinguished writer Octavio Paz about what should be done for the Chalcos of this world. His point was that everyone should do whatever is in their power to the best of their ability, and that includes architects. Norman Foster, lecture at Eindhoven University, 26 April 1996

By 2050 the UN predicts that the developed world will have 1.16 billion people, slightly fewer than today. But in the developing world in the same period, the population will have doubled from 4.52 billion in 1995 to 8.2 billion. As an illustration of what that means: the population of Africa in 1950 was half that of Europe; at the turn of the millennium it is equal; in fifty years time it is expected to be three times that of Europe. Alongside accelerating population growth is a shift towards living in cities. It is estimated that by 2030 two thirds of the world's population will be urban. We can already see the growth of a new generation of mega-cities of unprecedented size; and urban conurbations in excess of 25 million people are predicted in the next fifteen years. This trend introduces us to new dangers. In Latin America, where nearly 75 per cent of the population is urban, serious problems have already surfaced. Throughout the region, in cities such as Sao Paulo and Rio de Janeiro, air pollution causes an estimated 4,000 premature deaths a year. The reality behind these statistics, and the desperate state of our responses, was brought home to me when I was taken to see the Mexico City suburb of Chalco.

With a population of 1.5 million, Chalco is the size of many European cities. Yet there is a very significant difference. It is a place without transport infrastructure, sewage or drainage systems, mains water, gas or electricity. It has none of the basics that most of us take for granted. In one sense, however, the residents of Chalco are fortunate. Over one hundred million people around the world have no housing at all. This brings to life the estimate that, in the developing world, two billion people have no access to energy other than burning natural materials or animal waste. Add to that the fact that just 25 per cent of the world's population presently consumes 75 per cent of the energy and the future implications for energy and resources management are obvious.

In the developed world buildings consume half the energy we generate; the remainder is divided between transport and industry, with all the associated problems of pollution. So what will happen as the rest of the world catches up? We cannot afford to sit on our hands: we have a responsibility to act. Bucky was fond of quoting Theodore Larson: 'It is not to devise a better society so as to arrive at a finer architecture; it is to provide a better architecture in order to arrive at a more desirable society.'

> **Bucky was fond of quoting Theodore Larson: 'It is not to devise a better society so as to arrive at a finer architecture; it is to provide a better architecture in order to arrive at a more desirable society.'**

If those were not challenges enough to the design professions then surely it is a paradox that we have 'rapid responses' to war but no such responses to the social upheavals that follow. Certainly the needs of instant shelter for the victims of war, oppression or natural disaster should be high on our collective agenda. In 1999 the Kosovo conflict and devastating earthquakes in Turkey provided powerful demonstrations of the degree to which entire societies can be overwhelmed by sudden housing crises. But still we remain unprepared.

Architects, of course, are only part of the equation. But how do we break down the boundaries between the design professions, the politicians and industry; between conscience, provocation and action? As Bucky reminds us, in architecture 'form' is a noun; in industry 'form' is a verb. Architects and industrialists must be encouraged to work hand in hand, marrying innovation and production. But it is a partnership that has to be forged by political will.

1. Chalco, a sprawling suburb to the east of Mexico City, is occupied by people who cannot afford to live in the city itself. Its inhabitants live below the poverty line in an area lacking even the most basic infrastructure. Unsurprisingly, Chalco has the nation's highest child mortality rate. As Foster notes, residents of Chalco may indeed consider themselves 'fortunate'; over the last decade Mexico City has acquired another ad-hoc settlement named Carto Landia, or cardboard land, in which dwellings have been constructed from discarded cardboard boxes.

2. The Stenkovic Camp near Skopje, in Macedonia, which was administered by NATO and the UNHCR to provide temporary accommodation for up to 30,000 Kosovan Albanian refugees. This photograph was taken in April 1999 and the camp was disbanded later that year. In 1998 the world's population of refugees and internally displaced persons was estimated to stand at 30 million – an increase of more than 500,000 on the previous year.

**What is a house? ... The combined function of architect, industrialist and synchronising architect-engineer, since WHAT to do is known, is first to determine not causes but purposes, and then, acting within this knowledge, to evolve an adequate shelter design that will make possible the rational and spiritual self-realisation toward which man has ever so longingly striven.** Richard Buckminster Fuller, *Nine Chains to the Moon*, 1938

Left: In *Nine Chains to the Moon*, Fuller posited industrialised solutions to the housing question and outlined a technological strategy for maximising the social applications of energy resources.

However we might allocate the responsibilities, we must be able to do better than the tented cities which fill the pages of our newspapers, let alone the Chalcos of the future. Bucky himself said that, 'The proper goal of the architect-engineer is purposeful.' By that he meant forcing the pace, challenging accepted conventions or the intellectual status quo. Asia has shown us the 'can do' mentality in action. It presages a global shift that we will all soon face more out of necessity than by choice.

Hong Kong's International Airport at Chek Lap Kok is just one example. Rather than expand an overcrowded city airport you commit to building a new one. And when there is no remaining land on which to build it, you create its own island. And then, when the buildings are complete, you make the entire move from the old to the new overnight. The bravery of this thinking demonstrates the way forward; and if it can be applied to the epic scale of an airport, surely it can be focused on a solution to the problems of shelter that can arise at any time, almost anywhere in the world.

As early as 1939, in *Nine Chains to the Moon*, Bucky asked 'What is a house?' His response was an industrialised solution to housing provision. As ever, he backed words with deeds. He was a master of the art of 'technology transfer', harnessing new industries to produce pioneering solutions to old problems.

The Dymaxion Deployment Unit is just one example. Commissioned at the outbreak of war by the British War Relief Association, it anticipated the bombing of British cities and the urgent need for an emergency housing unit. Characteristically, Bucky looked outside the housing industry for manufacturing expertise and instead approached a company that specialised in making corrugated metal grain silos – the Butler Company of Kansas City – to build a prototype. He drew on the strengths of that industry but pushed it to achieve the sophistication and speed of manufacture he required. It is a lesson that we can still benefit from today.

**As Bucky reminds us, 'In architecture form is a noun; in industry form is a verb.' Architects and industrialists must be encouraged to work hand in hand, marrying innovation and production.**

Allied to his willingness to explore new techniques was a concern for economy of means. Bucky spoke frequently, for example, about the relationship between weight, energy and performance – of 'doing the most with the least' – and that has consistently been the story of technological progress, from the earliest cathedrals to the latest cellular phones.

I remember, in 1978, showing him our Sainsbury Centre for the Visual Arts and being startled when he asked: 'How much does your building weigh?' The question was far from rhetorical. He was challenging us to discover how efficient it was; to identify how much material enclosed what volume. We did not know the answer, but we worked it out and I wrote to him. We learned from the exercise as he predicted we would. The basement, which is only eight per cent of the volume of the main space, weighs 80 per cent of the total, or about 4,000 tonnes. The main building weighs just over 1,000 tonnes – less per cubic metre enclosed than a Boeing 747 – and was built far more quickly than the basement and for half the unit cost. There is also no comparison in terms of the quality of light and space.

1. Hong Kong's International Airport, at Chek Lap Kok (1992-1998), seen in the process of construction. In the absence of a suitable location in an overcrowded city, the airport was built on a reclaimed island site in one of the most ambitious construction projects of modern times. High-speed rail links ensure that the journey between city and airport can be completed in only twenty minutes.

**The Dymaxion House ... would be immediately available, erectable in a period measured by hours rather than by months. A house ... could be had for about $3000 and the application of the time-payment scheme would bring the house within the reach of practically all mankind.**
Buckminster Fuller, *Architecture*, June 1929
Far left: Model of Fuller's original pole-suspended single-unit Dymaxion House, developed in 1929.
Left: The Dymaxion Deployment Unit (DDU) commissioned from Fuller with the outbreak of the Second World War.
Right: Typical grain silos produced by the Butler Company, whose technical expertise with corrugated metal was harnessed by Fuller in the production of the DDU.

Back in the 1970s we made that calculation in simple volumetric terms. Today our understanding is far more sophisticated. We are familiar, for example, with concepts such as embodied energy and sustainability; and we know that some systems of construction are inherently more energy-efficient and environmentally responsible than others. Furthermore, there is a universal acceptance that the planet's natural resources are not only finite, but are dwindling. Bucky was one of the first people to advocate the recycling of source materials. He proposed that major manufactured items be rented from industry – cars for eight years, ships for twenty years and so on. In this way, he argued, the recycling process could be guaranteed. Only recently have major manufacturers taken steps in this direction – the automotive industry is a prime example – and begun to plan for recycling in a systematic way.

The pressure to 'do the most with the least', which has long been felt in the context of manufacturing industry, applies just as powerfully to energy production and consumption. Many years after Bucky first warned us, we have at last recognised that we must break the pattern of energy profligacy and pollution. We now acknowledge the fragility of the natural world and the destructive impact of our industrial installations. We know, for example, that power stations that burn fossil fuels to produce electricity are inherently wasteful and environmentally damaging. It is estimated that half the energy expended to generate electricity is lost in the form of waste heat that is dissipated into rivers and oceans, harming their natural ecology. These same power plants also deposit into the atmosphere huge amounts of carbon dioxide – a greenhouse gas – which has been a significant factor in global climate change.

The planet cannot naturally absorb the millions of tonnes of pollutants we currently tip into its oceans or pour into its atmosphere every year. As an illustration of the scale of the problem, it is calculated that one square kilometre of dense deciduous forest absorbs through photosynthesis approximately 570 tonnes of carbon dioxide per year. To throw this into sharper relief, you only have to take one of the coming mega-cities and consider its likely carbon dioxide emissions from burning fossil fuels alone. For a conurbation of 25 million people to be carbon dioxide neutral, that is to absorb all the carbon dioxide emissions from buildings, vehicles and industry at present levels, it would need to plant a forest with an area equivalent to fifteen times the entire metropolitan area of New York, or 114,000 times the area of Central Park. That is clearly impossible, so something fundamental must change.

Alternative energy sources have an important role to play. For example, if we were to produce all our energy by alternative means – by burning renewable fuels or by using wind and water turbines and solar panels – global carbon dioxide emissions could be reduced by approximately one third. This, allied with a proactive approach to energy conservation, begins to provide us with a solution.

**Bucky spoke frequently about the relationship between weight, energy and performance – of 'doing the most with the least' – that has consistently been the story of technological progress, from the earliest cathedrals to the latest cellular phones.**

I am reminded of Bucky's exhortation to 'Think global, act local'. Within my own practice, we have made significant steps in the direction of reduced energy dependency in the design of a new generation of ecologically sensitive projects. Among these is our proposal for the London headquarters of Swiss Re – one of the world's leading reinsurance companies – which will be the capital's first ecological high-rise building.

**One of the nice things about Bucky was his unquenchable optimism. He showed that technology's power to achieve more with less could create incredible leaps of performance so that, for example, a quarter-ton communications satellite could outperform by a long way 175,000 tons of copper cable laid on the ocean floor. In the very short time since Bucky died we are seeing satellites outperformed by another technological leap towards fibre optics.** Norman Foster, lecture at Eindhoven University, 26 April 1996

---

1, 2. The headquarters building for Swiss Re, in the City of London (1997-2004) realises principles first explored in the Climatroffice concept with Buckminster Fuller. The building suggests a new rapport between nature and the workplace. Each hub-shaped floor plate is rotated with respect to those above and below it, allowing the spaces between the radiating fingers of floors to combine to form 'gardens in the sky', which spiral up the height of the building. Socially, these spaces help to break down the scale of the structure. Environmentally, they act as the building's 'lungs', drawing in fresh air.

Swiss Re is rooted in the Bucky-inspired thinking that led to what I called the 'Climatroffice', designed in 1971. This concept suggested a new rapport between nature and workspace in which the garden setting helped to create an interior microclimate, which was sheltered by the most energy conscious enclosure. The ovoid forms employed were selected for their ability to enclose the maximum volume within the minimum surface skin – analogies might be drawn with the naturally efficient forms of birds' eggs – while conventional walls and roof were dissolved into a continuous skin of triangulated elements. Similarly, the Swiss Re building is derived from a circular plan which, over forty storeys, generates an elongated, beehive-like form that is fully glazed around a diagonally-braced structure.

Successive floors are rotated, allowing voids at the edge of each floor plate to combine in a series of spiralling atria or 'sky-gardens' which wind up around the perimeter of the building. These green spaces are the successors to the gardens we incorporated in the Commerzbank tower in Frankfurt. Socially they help to break down the internal scale of the building, while externally they add variety and life to its facades. They also represent a key component in regulating the building's internal climate.

The building's aerodynamic form generates large pressure differentials that greatly assist the natural flow of incoming and expelled air. Fresh air is drawn in at every floor via horizontal slots in the cladding and circulated through the gardens. This system is designed to be so effective that, weather conditions permitting, for the majority of the year, mechanical cooling and ventilating systems will not be required. As a result, energy consumption is reduced dramatically when compared with conventionally air-conditioned offices.

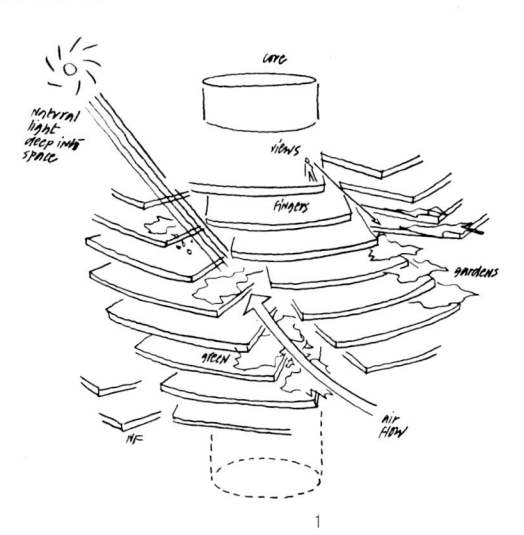

The rebuilt Reichstag in Berlin is equally progressive. It demonstrates the potential for a virtually non-polluting, wholly sustainable public building. It makes extensive use of natural light and ventilation, together with combined systems of cogeneration and heat recovery, and eschews fossil fuels in favour of renewable 'bio-diesel' – a refined vegetable oil derived from rape or sunflower seeds. The energy strategy for the building ensures that the minimum energy achieves the maximum effect at the lowest cost in use. In fact, because its own requirements are sufficiently modest, the Reichstag is able to perform as a local power station, supplying other buildings in the new parliamentary quarter.

Refined vegetable oil can be considered as a form of solar energy since the sun's energy is stored in the plants (the biomass). Furthermore, carbon dioxide emissions are considerably reduced in the long term as the growing plant absorbs almost as much carbon dioxide in its lifetime as is released during combustion.

Of all the honours heaped on Fuller in his later years, none was to equal the posthumous christening of a virtually indestructible carbon atom with his name. In 1985 Dr Harry Kroto, Dr Robert Curl, Dr Richard Smalley and their students at Rice University in Texas identified the smallest atoms of carbon in soot as consisting of … the pattern of hexagons and pentagons made familiar by the shape of the geodesic dome. Noting that this extremely strong arrangement … occurs even in the gas clouds between stars, the professors dubbed the atoms 'Buckminsterfullerenes'.
Martin Pawley, *Buckminster Fuller*, 1990

**Bucky was a person who inspired exploration, creative thought and innovation. But the fact that a newly identified molecular form should be named after him by a group of scientists is a testament to the incredible affection which he inspired in others, as well as his genuine insights into the world around us.** Norman Foster, speech at the Science Museum, London, 6 May 1998
Left: In May 1998, Norman Foster opened the exhibition 'Buckyballs and Beyond', which explored the scientific and practical applications of the spherical molecules affectionately named after Buckminster Fuller by Kroto and his colleagues.

Heating and cooling the Reichstag by burning bio-diesel produces an estimated 440 tonnes of carbon dioxide per annum as opposed to the 7,000 tonnes generated annually by its previous installations, installed in the 1960s – an astonishing 94 per cent reduction in emissions. As a further illustration, if the Reichstag were to burn natural gas instead of bio-diesel, its carbon dioxide emissions would be in the region of 1,450 tonnes per annum – more than three times the current amount.

**Bucky was a master of the art of 'technology transfer' – harnessing new industries to produce pioneering solutions to old problems. Allied to his willingness to explore new techniques was a concern for economy of means.**

As well as forming the public focus of the building, the Reichstag's cupola, or 'lantern', provides the key to our strategies for lighting and ventilating the assembly chamber. At its heart is a light-reflecting cone – a light 'sculptor' and a sculpture in its own right. The cone is covered with faceted mirrors that together form a giant Fresnel lens just as you might find in a searchlight or lighthouse. In fact the cone works as a lighthouse in reverse, reflecting daylight from a 360-degree horizon down into the chamber. An electronically controlled mobile sun-shade tracks the path of the sun to block solar gain and glare, but is designed to allow a little sunlight to dapple the floor of the chamber. In ventilation terms the cone and chamber together perform as a solar chimney, drawing air up naturally through the chamber and expelling it via the open top of the cupola.

In ecological terms, the Reichstag has shown how public buildings can challenge the status quo: big buildings do not have to be big consumers of energy or big polluters. And although it represents a minuscule first step in terms of the journey yet remaining, imagine the impact these strategies could have if they were applied more widely around the world. If every new building – public or private – were to follow this lead, the energy equation could be stood on its head. Rather than consuming energy, these buildings would be net providers; rather than emitting carbon dioxide, they would be broadly neutral. The savings in resources and running costs could be immense.

The cupola is the outward manifestation of these strategies, signalling a process of transformation. It represents the ultimate synthesis of old and new in the building and brings together all the elements that separately comprise our programme of renewal. Interestingly, it also carries more than a hint of the geodesic Autonomous House – an energy self-sufficient dwelling with a rotating, sun-screening inner skin – that we developed with Bucky shortly before his death. For me, with its environmental and democratic agenda, the cupola is certainly more closely related to Bucky's humanist vision of the future than it is to the symbolism of the past.

3. The new cupola of the rebuilt Reichstag (1992-1999) creates a civic space and a dramatic urban landmark but is also key to the building's environmental strategy. A mirrored 'light sculptor' reflects horizon light into the chamber below while a moveable sun-shield blocks solar gain and glare. A fan contained within the mirrored cone aids the extraction of stale air from the chamber below.

**To my beloved colleague and brilliant architect, the first printing of the most accurately detailed, non-visibly distorting map of the surface of planet Earth.** Buckminster Fuller's dedication to Norman Foster, inscribed on the Dymaxion Sky-Ocean World Map, 30 August 1980

Right: The Dymaxion Map represents the ultimate ephemeralisation of Fuller's ideas, casting the world itself in a new geometry. The Grip-Kitrick edition of the Fuller projection was published in 1980.

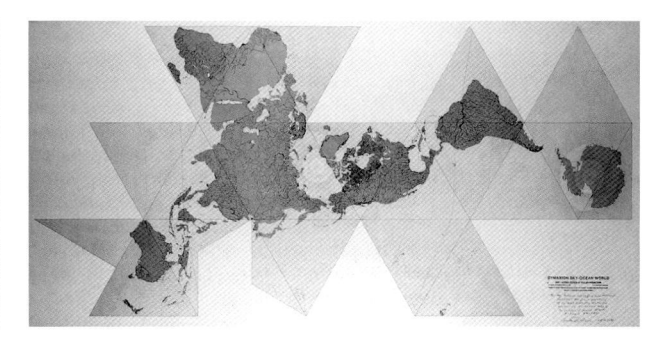

1. A view of the Business Promotion Centre, Duisburg (1990-1993). Located within the context of a newly created public park in a predominantly residential district of the city, the Centre forms part of a masterplan for a Microelectronic Park, which is designed to encourage the urban integration of the new technology companies that are gradually replacing the old heavy industries of the Ruhr heartland.

2, 3. An aerial study and exploded view of the library for the Faculty of Philology being created within the Free University of Berlin. The new building occupies a site created by uniting six of the University's courtyards and forms the centrepiece of a comprehensive programme of renewal within the campus.

As a practice we enjoy working in Germany, not least because of the enlightened attitudes that prevail there towards energy conservation and urban regeneration. By the early 1990s, when we entered the Reichstag competition, we had several German construction projects, including the Microelectronic Park in Duisburg – the first of our German projects to be realised – where we formulated a regenerative masterplan and designed a series of low-energy buildings. Of these, the Business Promotion Centre, which we completed in 1993, is the most radical. Its multi-layered outer skin is so thermally efficient that no heating is required, even in the coldest winter. And the building generates and harvests its own energy, burning natural gas to produce electricity by means of a cogenerator. The by-product of this process – heat that would normally be wasted – passes through an absorption cooling plant to produce chilled water. Instead of relying on conventional air conditioning, dramatic drops in temperature are achieved by distributing this cold water through miniaturised pipes embedded in the structure, in a system similar to the fins on a car radiator. This is not only an ecologically satisfying solution – of which Bucky would doubtless approve – but it makes economic sense too: in fact the developer makes a significant annual profit from energy management.

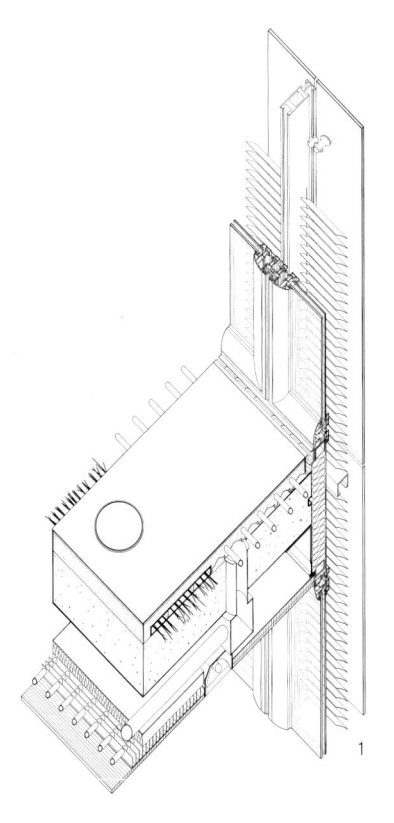

Those early projects in Germany seemed to encapsulate so many of the issues that were then coming to the fore in our work, not least the vital one of working with historical buildings and confronting the past, something that we did with the Reichstag and are doing again with the Free University, in Berlin. Since the end of the Second World War, the Free University has occupied a central role in the intellectual history of Berlin and it is one of its most symbolically important institutions – its foundation marking the rebirth of liberal education in the city. Today, with more than 60,000 students, it is the largest of Berlin's three universities. Our redevelopment of the campus includes the restoration of its Modernist buildings and the design of a new library for the Faculty of Philology.

The University's mat-like campus was designed in 1963 by the architects Candilis Josic Woods Schiedhelm. When the first buildings were completed in 1973 it was hailed as a milestone in modern university design. The facade was designed in collaboration with Jean Prouvé – another of my personal heroes. Its design followed Le Corbusier's Modulor proportional system and consisted of framed panels made in Cor-Ten steel, a material that, when used in the appropriate thickness, has self-protecting corrosive characteristics. The rusty appearance of these early buildings led to the affectionate nickname of '*die Rostlaube*' – the 'rust-bucket'.

However, in the elegant sections used by Prouvé the Cor-Ten steel was unfortunately prone to decay, which by the late 1990s had become extensive. As part of a comprehensive process of renovation we are replacing the corroded panels and framing with new elements made from patinated bronze. While the new cladding is faithful to Prouvé's original intentions, some details have been sensitively altered to meet contemporary technical requirements and energy-saving standards. The roof will be covered with vegetation – shades of Willis Faber – to improve insulation and microclimatic conditions.

Six of the University's courtyards have been united to form the site of a new library for the Faculty of Philology. The library building is perhaps the closest we have come to a direct realisation of the Climatroffice concept, which gave us a clearer focus on so many crucial issues: flexibility of use, in the form of multi-function spaces; energy saving; lightweight envelopes; and the use of natural light and ventilation. All of these concerns are encapsulated in the design of the library.

**Reshape the Environment; don't try to reshape Man.** Richard Buckminster Fuller, *New Forms vs Reforms*, 1963

[Bucky] liked to see himself as a hard-nosed engineer, who understood materials and tolerances, and an architect like Norman Foster … Instead he came to be seen as a guru, a visionary who saw the earth as a spaceship, someone who dreamed of things that never were and asked 'why not?' A polymath, like Coleridge, he was made Professor of Poetry at Harvard, his old university, in 1962. He could talk as fast, if not as eloquently as Coleridge. Even in his writings he never used a full stop where a semi-colon would do … Buckminster Fuller died last week, aged eighty-seven. The rest is silence. Obituary, *New Society*, 7 July 1983

The building's four levels are sheltered within a free-form skin consisting of aluminium panels, ventilation elements and double-layered glass panels, which are supported on steel frames with radial geometry. The cavity between the resulting double skin creates a 'solar motor', which assists a natural ventilation system to maximise energy efficiency. An inner membrane of translucent glass-fibre filters sunlight and creates an atmosphere of concentration, while scattered transparent openings allow momentary views of the sky and glimpses of sunlight. The bookstacks are arranged at the centre of each of the library's four floors, with reading desks arranged around the perimeter. The edges of the floors follow serpentine curves, which have the effect of lengthening the edge condition, and thus maximising the space available for private study. And because the profile of each floor swells or recedes with respect to the one directly above or below it, a continuous pattern of double-height volumes is established around the perimeter, creating generous, light-filled spaces in which to work.

Although it has not yet been built, it is amusing to note that the library's curving cranial form has already earned it an affectionate nickname of its own – 'the Berlin Brain'. Oh, and as Bucky would surely want to know, its lightweight structural envelope weighs just 640 tonnes.

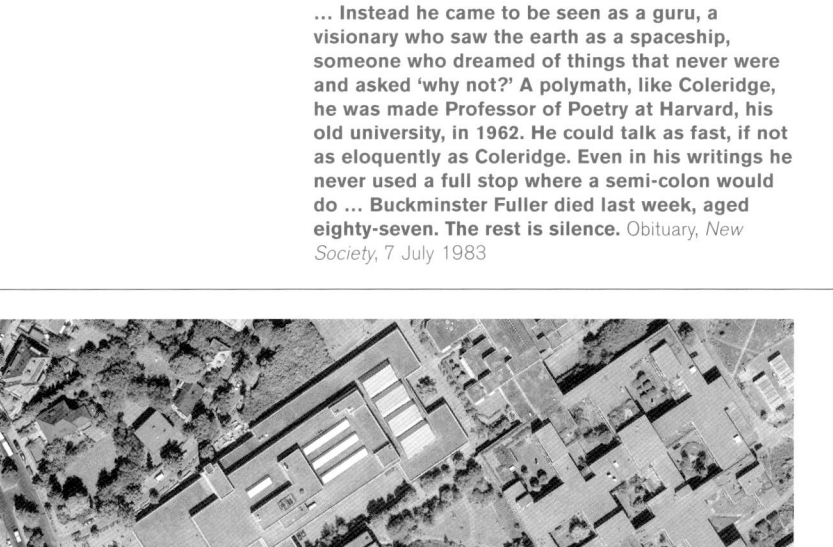

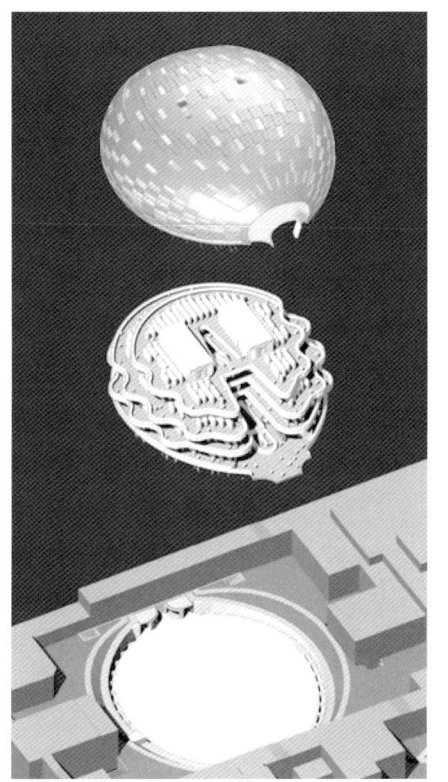

**The pressure to 'do the most with the least', which has long been felt in the context of manufacturing industry, applies just as powerfully to energy production and consumption. Many years after Bucky first warned us, we have at last recognised that we must break the pattern of energy profligacy and pollution.**

Norman Foster

Bucky and Beyond

**The Team**
1981

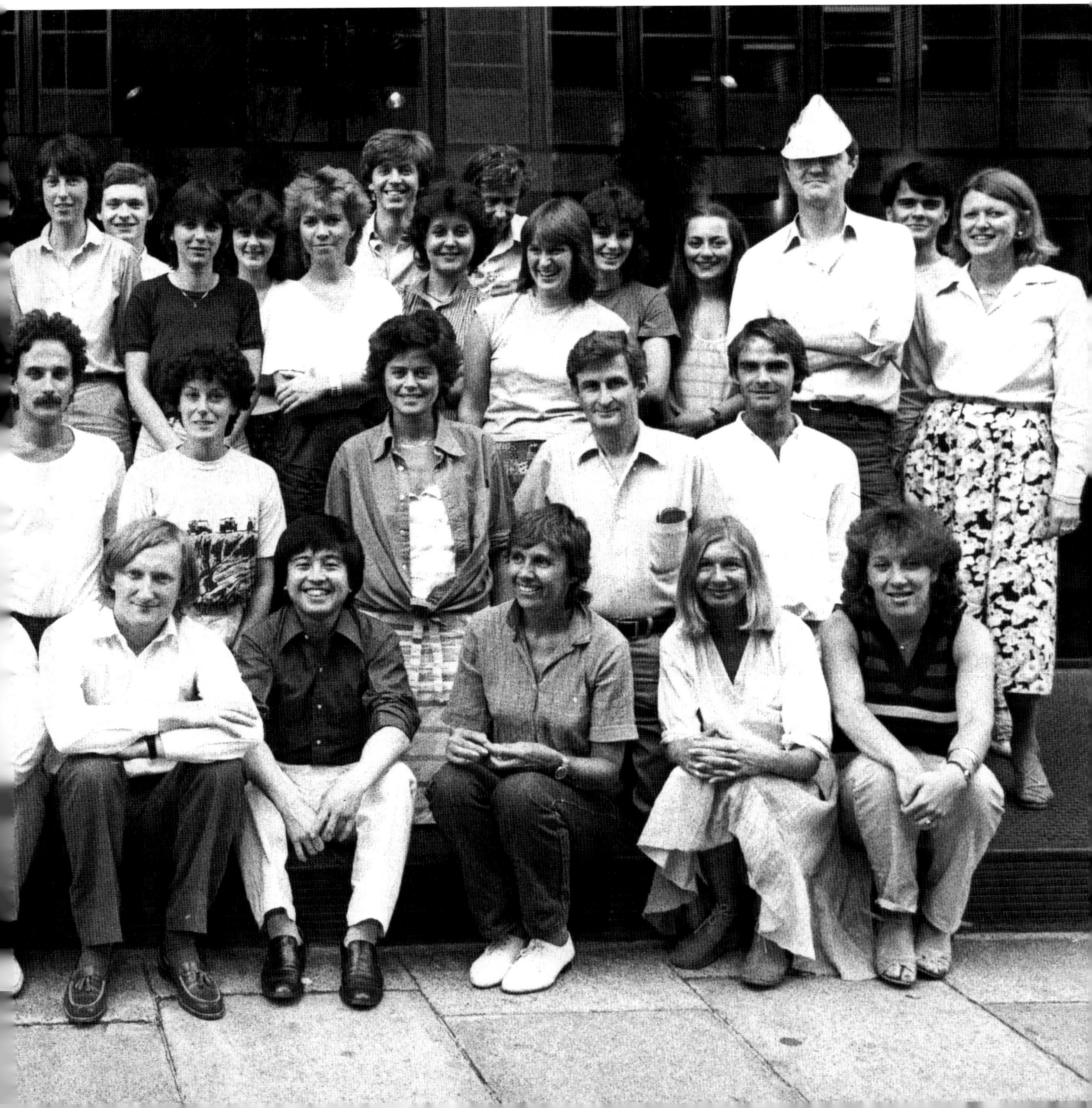

# Team 4

Previous pages: By 1981, after ten years in the Fitzroy Street Studio, larger premises had become essential and the move was made to Great Portland Street nearby. This team photograph was taken outside the Fitzroy Street offices shortly before they were vacated.

Editor's Note

Team 4 was founded in 1963 and dissolved in 1967, when Norman and Wendy Foster established Foster Associates.

The list of Foster Associates' staff given here includes all those employed in the London and Oslo offices during the period 1967-1983, which covers the projects detailed in this volume. The list does not include staff members who were based solely in the Hong Kong office, which was established during this time; details of Hong Kong staff are included in *Foster Works: Volume 2*.

For organisational reasons, this volume also includes the Sainsbury Centre Crescent Wing which falls outside the above timeframe. Team members for this project are included with the project credits on page 565.

**Partners**
Norman Foster
Wendy Foster
Richard Rogers
Georgie Wolton (1963-1964)


Laurie Abbott
Sally Appleby
Frank Peacock
Maurice Philips
Sophie Read
Su Rogers
Mark Sutcliffe
John Young

# Foster Associates

**Partners**
Norman Foster
Wendy Foster
Michael Hopkins (1970-1975)

**Associates**
Reg Bradley
Loren Butt
Chubby Chhabra
Spencer de Grey
Roy Fleetwood
Birkin Haward
Mickey Kuch
James Meller
Tomm Nyhuss
Norman Partridge
Frank Peacock
Graham Phillips
Mark Robertson
Mark Sutcliffe

Max Aiken
Sue Allen
Lucy Annan
Ken Armstrong
Reg Arney
Brian Atkinson
David Bailey
Nic Bailey
Ralph Ball
Julia Barfield
Prue Bell
Paul Berthon
Gill Bird
Peter Bradford
Arthur Branthwaite
Seanna Brennan
Tony Brohn
Peter Busby
John Calvert
Lorraine Caunter
David Chipperfield
Chris Clarke
Barry Copeland
Diane Copeland
Ray Crandon-Gill

Ian Davidson
Justin de Syllas
Giles Downes
Ian Dowsett
Tim Earnshaw
Nick Eldridge
Mike Elkan
Jim Elsdon
Anne Farrow
Georgina Fenton
Howard Filbey
Trish Flood
Robyn Foster
Vivian Fowler
Martin Francis
Muny Ganju
Paul Gibson
Mike Glass
Penny Glendinning
Diana Goddard
Barbara Goldstein
Mark Goldstein
Margot Griffin
Keith Griffiths
Pedro Guedes
Anthony Hackett
Vakis Hadji-Kyriakou
Di Haigh
Jane Hallam
Katy Harris
Dave Harriss
Jean Hawes
Paul Heritage
Eric Holt
Neil Holt
Richard Horden
Mavis Hudd
Peter Hufschmid
Jill Johncock
David Johns
Paul Jones
Jan Kaplicky
Cathy Kelly
Ben Kern
Lisette Khalastchi
Annette LeCuyer
John Leach

Alex Lifschutz
Ernst Lohzer
Robin Lorimer
Caroline Lwin
Paul Matthews
Tony Meadows
Clair Medhurst
Michael Millson
Orlando Modesti
Ian Montgomery
Nick Morgan
David Morley
David Nelson
David Nixon
Susan North
Gerry O'Conner
Jo Olsen
Jean Ovrum
Truls Ovrum
Robert Peebles
Archie Phillips
Graham Phillips
Louis Pilar
Tony Pritchard
Rosemary Ringrose
Ian Ritchie
Gayle Rose
Andy Scott
Carol Scott
Celia Scott
Mark Shapiro
Winston Shu
Ken Shuttleworth
Ian Simpson
Caroline Souroullas
Michael Stacey
Alan Stanton
Volker Stoecks
Christopher Taylor
Peter Terbüchte
Jill Townsend
Jamie Troughton
Jocelyne van der Bossche
Jo van Heyningen
Ron Walker
Judith Warren
Jenny Wharton

John Wharton
James White
Chris Wilkinson
Stuart Wilkinson
John Willcocks
Neil Winder
Chris Windsor
Arek Wozniak
John Yates
Paul Young
Bodo Zapp
Alison Zinzan

**Oslo Office**
John Calvert
Geoffrey Clark
Steiner Erikson
John Jones
Jørn Narud
Helger Saatvedt

# Project Credits

**Air-Supported Office**
Hemel Hempstead, England
1969-1970 (deflated 1971)
Client
  Computer Technology Ltd
Project Team
  Loren Butt
  Chubby Chhabra
  Norman Foster
  Wendy Foster
  Mickey Kuch
Consultants
  Structural Engineer:
  Anthony Hunt Associates
  Mechanical and Electrical
  Engineer: Foster Associates

**Autonomous House**
1982-1983
Client
  Richard Buckminster Fuller
Project Team
  Norman Foster
  Wendy Foster
  Richard Buckminster Fuller
  Paul Matthews
  James Meller
  John Warren
Consultants
  Structural Engineer:
  Fuller & Sadao Inc

**Bean Hill Housing**
Milton Keynes, England
1971-1973
Client
  Milton Keynes
  Development Corporation
Project Team
  Loren Butt
  Tim Earnshaw
  Roy Fleetwood
  Norman Foster
  Wendy Foster
  Birkin Haward
  Michael Hopkins
  Frank Peacock
  Jo van Heyningen
Consultants
  Structural Engineer:
  Anthony Hunt Associates
  Quantity Surveyor:
  Davis Belfield & Everest
  Landscaping: John Allen

**Climatroffice**
1971
Project Team
  Norman Foster
  Wendy Foster
  Richard Buckminster Fuller
  Birkin Haward

**The Cockpit**
Feock, England
1964
Client
  Mr & Mrs Marcus Brumwell
Project Team
  Norman Foster
  Wendy Foster
  Richard Rogers
  Su Rogers
Consultants
  Structural Engineer:
  Anthony Hunt Associates
  Principal Awards:
  1964 Architectural Design
  Project Award

**Creek Vean House**
Feock, England
1964-1966
Client
  Mr & Mrs Marcus Brumwell
Project Team
  Laurie Abbott
  Norman Foster
  Wendy Foster
  Frank Peacock
  Richard Rogers
  Su Rogers
Consultants
  Structural Engineer:
  Anthony Hunt Associates
  Quantity Surveyor:
  Hanscomb Partnership
  Principal Awards
  1969 RIBA Award

**Computer Technology**
Hemel Hempstead, England
1970-1971
Client
  Computer Technology Ltd
Project Team
  Loren Butt
  Lorraine Caunter
  Justin de Syllas
  Norman Foster
  Wendy Foster
  Martin Francis
  Dave Harriss
  Birkin Haward
  Mickey Kuch
Consultants
  Structural Engineer:
  Anthony Hunt Associates
  Mechanical and Electrical
  Engineer: G N Haden
  & Sons Ltd
  Quantity Surveyor:
  Hanscomb Partnership
  Drainage: G N Haden
  & Sons Ltd

**Factory Systems Studies**
Milton Keynes, England
1969-1972
Project Team
  Norman Foster

**Fitzroy Street Studio**
London, England
1971-1972
Client
  Foster Associates
Project Team
  Giles Downes
  Norman Foster
  Wendy Foster
  Birkin Haward
  Tomm Nyhuus
  Norman Partridge
  Archie Phillips
  Mark Shapiro
Consultants
  Mechanical and Electrical
  Engineer: Foster Associates
  Quantity Surveyor:
  Hanscomb Partnership
  Acoustics: Arthur Aldersley
  Williams
  Drainage: Adrian Wilder

**Fred Olsen Amenity Centre**
London, England
1969-1970 (demolished 1988)
Client
  Fred Olsen Ltd
Project Team
  Peter Bradford
  Barry Copeland
  Norman Foster
  Wendy Foster
  Tomm Nyhuus
  Norman Partridge

Consultants
  Structural Engineer:
  Anthony Hunt Associates
  Mechanical and Electrical
  Engineer: G N Haden
  & Sons Ltd
  Quantity Surveyor:
  Hanscomb Partnership
  Acoustics: Arthur Aldersley
  Williams/EDC
  Drainage: G N Haden
  & Sons Ltd
Principal Awards
  1969 Architectural Design
  Project Award
  1970 Financial Times
  Industrial Architecture
  Award Commendation

**Fred Olsen Country Offices**
  Vestby, Norway
  1973
Client
  Fred Olsen Group/Aker Gruppe
Project Team
  Loren Butt
  John Calvert
  Jim Elsdon
  Steiner Erikson
  Norman Foster
  Wendy Foster
  Birkin Haward
  John Jones
  Jørn Narud
  Tomm Nyhuus
  Helger Saatvedt
Consultants
  Structural Engineer:
  Multi-Consult A/S
  Mechanical and Electrical
  Engineer: Erichsen &
  Horgen/Foster Associates
  Quantity Surveyor:
  Hanscomb Partnership
  Drainage: Multi-Consult A/S

**Fred Olsen Passenger Terminal**
  London, England
  1969-1970 (demolished 1980)
Client
  Fred Olsen Ltd
Project Team
  Peter Bradford
  Barry Copeland
  Giles Downes
  Jim Elsdon
  Norman Foster
  Birkin Haward
  Tomm Nyhuus
  Norman Partridge
Consultants
  Structural Engineer:
  Anthony Hunt Associates
  Mechanical and Electrical
  Engineer: ZDB Engineering Ltd
  Quantity Surveyor:
  Hanscomb Partnership
  Acoustics: Arthur Aldersley
  Williams

**Fred Olsen Travel Agency**
  London, England
  1975
Client
  Fred Olsen Ltd
Project Team
  Anne Farrow
  Norman Foster
  Tomm Nyhuus
  Norman Partridge
Consultants
  Structural Engineer:
  Anthony Hunt Associates
  Mechanical and Electrical
  Engineer: Foster Associates
  Quantity Surveyor:
  Hanscomb Partnership

**Foster Residence**
  London, England
  1978-1979
Client
  Norman Foster
  Wendy Foster
Project Team
  Peter Busby
  Loren Butt
  Norman Foster
  Wendy Foster
  Richard Horden
  Tony Meadows
  Tony Pritchard
  Ken Shuttleworth
  Chris Windsor
Consultants
  Structural Engineer: Anthony
  Hunt Associates
  Mechanical and Electrical
  Engineer: Foster Associates
  Quantity Surveyor: Davis Belfield
  & Everest

**Forest Road Extension**
  East Horsley, England
  1966
Client
  Mrs R G L Cheesman
Project Team
  Norman Foster
  Wendy Foster

**German Car Centre**
  Milton Keynes, England
  1972-1974
Client
  Thomas Tilling & Co Ltd
Project Team
  Loren Butt
  Chubby Chhabra
  Norman Foster
  Wendy Foster
  John Wharton
Consultants
  Structural Engineer:
  Anthony Hunt Associates
  Mechanical and Electrical
  Engineer: Foster Associates
  Quantity Surveyor:
  Davis Belfield & Everest
  Materials Handling: Demag
  Systemtechnik AG/PE
  Consultancy Group

**Gomera Regional Planning Study**
  Gomera, Canary Islands
  1975
Client
  Fred Olsen
Project Team
  Norman Foster
  Wendy Foster
  Pedro Guedes
  Birkin Haward
  Neil Holt
  Pepe Martell
  Orlando Modesti
  Truls Ovrum
  Javier Ruiloba
  Fernando Saavedra
  Chris Windsor
Consultants
  Ecology: Kenneth Mellanby

**Granada Entertainment Centre**
　Milton Keynes, England
　1979
　Client
　　Granada Ltd
　Project Team
　　Roy Fleetwood
　　Norman Foster
　　Birkin Haward
　　Richard Horden
　　David Morley
　　David Nelson
　　Ken Shuttleworth
　Consultants
　　Acoustics: Tim Smith Acoustics

**Hackney Special Care Unit**
　London, England
　1970-1972
　Client
　　Spastics Society/Hackney
　　Borough Council/ILEA
　Project Team
　　Reg Bradley
　　Loren Butt
　　Justin de Syllas
　　Norman Foster
　　Wendy Foster
　　Birkin Haward
　　Frank Peacock
　　Jo van Heyningen
　Consultants
　　Structural Engineer:
　　Anthony Hunt Associates
　　Mechanical and Electrical
　　Engineer: Foster Associates
　　Quantity Surveyor:
　　Hanscomb Partnership
　　Drainage: Adrian Wilder

**Hammersmith Centre**
　London, England
　1977-1979
　Client
　　London Transport Executive
　Project Team
　　Arthur Branthwaite
　　Loren Butt
　　Spencer de Grey
　　Ian Dowsett
　　Roy Fleetwood
　　Norman Foster
　　Birkin Haward
　　Neil Holt
　　David Morley
　　David Nelson
　　Celia Scott
　　Ken Shuttleworth
　　Judith Warren
　　Chris Windsor
　Consultants
　　Structural Engineer:
　　Ove Arup & Partners
　　Mechanical and Electrical
　　Engineer: Foster Associates/
　　Brown Crozier & Wyatt
　　Civil Engineer:
　　Ove Arup & Partners
　　Quantity Surveyor: Davis
　　Belfield & Everest
　　Acoustics: Sound Research
　　Laboratories
　　Land Surveying: J A Storey
　　& Partners
　　Estates Surveying: Richard
　　Ellis/Jones Lang Wootton
　　Environmental Acoustics:
　　Shankland Cox Partnership
　　Financial Planning: Coopers
　　& Lybrand
　　Transport Planning:
　　Ove Arup & Partners

**High-Density Housing**
　Radlett, England
　1967
　Client
　　Anthony Jaffé
　Project Team
　　Norman Foster
　　Wendy Foster
　　Alan Stanton
　Consultants
　　Structural Engineer:
　　Anthony Hunt Associates
　　Quantity Surveyor:
　　Hanscomb Partnership

**IBM Pilot Head Office**
　Cosham, England
　1970-1971
　Client
　　IBM (UK) Ltd
　Project Team
　　Loren Butt
　　Chubby Chhabra
　　Barry Copeland
　　Norman Foster
　　Wendy Foster
　　Vivian Fowler
　　Dave Harriss
　　Michael Hopkins
　　Mickey Kuch
　　Tomm Nyhuus
　　Truls Ovrum
　　Norman Partridge
　　Frank Peacock
　　Andrew Scott
　　Mark Shapiro
　　Mark Sutcliffe
　　Judith Warren
　　Stuart Wilkinson
　　John Willcocks

Consultants
　Structural Engineer:
　Anthony Hunt Associates
　Mechanical and Electrical
　Engineer: R S Willcox
　Associates
　Quantity Surveyor:
　Hanscomb Partnership
　Lighting: Derek Phillips
　& Partners
　Acoustics: Arthur Aldersley
　Williams/Engineering Design
　Consultants Drainage:
　Adrian Wilder
Principal Awards
　1972 Structural Steel Award
　1972 RIBA Award

**IBM Technical Park**
　Greenford, England
　1975-1980
　Client
　　IBM (UK) Ltd
　Project Team
　　Loren Butt
　　Chubby Chhabra
　　Howard Filbey
　　Norman Foster
　　Wendy Foster
　　Michael Glass
　　Judith Hallam
　　Alex Lifschutz
　　Paul Mathews
　　David Nelson
　　Truls Ovrum
　　Frank Peacock
　　Graham Phillips
　　Michael Rayner
　　Ken Shuttleworth
　　Jamie Troughton

Consultants
  Structural Engineer:
  Anthony Hunt Associates
  Mechanical and Electrical
  Engineer: Foster Associates
  Quantity Surveyor: Northcroft
  Neighbour & Nicholson
  Acoustics: Sound Research
  Laboratories/Wolfson Unit,
  University of Southampton
  Landscaping: Michael Brown
  Partnership
  Transport Planning:
  Ove Arup & Partners/Freeman
  Fox & Partners
  Land Surveying: J A Storey
  & Partners
  Drainage: John Taylor & Sons
  Materials Handling: Modern
  Materials Management

**Joseph Shop**
  London, England
  1978
Client
  Lynx Mead Ltd
Project Team
  Georgina Fenton
  Norman Foster
  Wendy Foster
  Jan Kaplicky
  Frank Peacock
Consultants
  Structural Engineer: Anthony
  Hunt Associates
  Mechanical and Electrical
  Engineer: Foster Associates

**Knoxville Energy Expo**
  Knoxville, USA
  1978
Client
  International Energy
  Expo Committee
Project Team
  Norman Foster
  Richard Buckminster Fuller
  Michael Glass
  Birkin Haward
  James Meller
  Shoji Sadao
Consultants
  Structural Engineer:
  Fuller & Sadao Inc

**London Gliding Club**
  Dunstable Downs, England
  1978
Client
  London Gliding Club
Project Team
  Norman Foster
  Birkin Haward

**Modern Art Glass**
  Thamesmead, England
  1972-1973
Client
  Modern Art Glass Ltd
Project Team
  Loren Butt
  Lorraine Caunter
  Chubby Chhabra
  Norman Foster
  Wendy Foster
  Paul Gibson
  Mickey Kuch
  David Nixon
  Mark Sutcliffe
  John Wharton

Consultants
  Structural Engineer:
  Anthony Hunt Associates
  Mechanical and Electrical
  Engineer: Foster Associates
  Quantity Surveyor:
  Hanscomb Partnership
  Glazing Consultant:
  Martin Francis
  Drainage: Adrian Wilder
Principal Awards
  1974 Financial Times Industrial
  Architecture Award

**Murray Mews**
  London, England
  1965
Client
  Dr & Mrs Franklin
  Mr & Mrs Williams
  Mr D'Marco
Project Team
  Laurie Abbott
  Norman Foster
  Wendy Foster
  Frank Peacock
  Maurice Philips
  Richard Rogers
  Su Rogers
Consultants
  Structural Engineer:
  Anthony Hunt Associates
  Quantity Surveyor:
  Hanscomb Partnership

**Newport School Competition**
  Short-listed scheme
  Gwent, Wales
  1967
Project Team
  Norman Foster
  Wendy Foster
  Alan Stanton
  Mickey Kuch

Consultants
  Structural Engineer:
  Anthony Hunt Associates
  Mechanical and Electrical
  Engineers: Peter Jay and
  David Kut & Partners
  Quantity Surveyor:
  Hanscomb Partnership
  Acoustics: Arthur
  Aldersley Williams
  Component Consultant:
  Martin Francis

**Open House**
  Cwmbran, Wales
  1978
Client
  Cwmbran Children's Trust and
  Community Project Centre
Project Team
  Norman Foster
  Wendy Foster
  Birkin Haward
  Caroline Lwin
Consultants
  Mechanical and Electrical
  Engineer: Foster Associates
  Quantity Surveyor: Davis Belfield
  & Everest
  Acoustics: Sound Research
  Laboratories
  Management Consultants: LSD

**Orange Hand Shops**
England
1972-1975
Client
  The Burton Group
Project Team
  Loren Butt
  Chubby Chhabra
  Norman Foster
  Wendy Foster
  Dave Harriss
  Birkin Haward
  Mickey Kuch
  Jenny Wharton
  John Wharton
Consultants
  Structural Engineer: Anthony
  Hunt Associates
  Mechanical and Electrical
  Engineer: Foster Associates
  Quantity Surveyor: Davis Belfield
  & Everest

**P70 Unit**
Buckinghamshire
Client
  Milton Keynes
  Development Corporation
Architects
  MKDC Architects Department
Consultants
  Systems Analysis:
  Foster Associates
  Structural Engineer:
  Anthony Hunt Associates
  Mechanical and Electrical
  Engineer: Foster Associates
  Quantity Surveyor: Milton Keynes
  Development Corporation

**Palmerston Special School**
Liverpool, England
1973-1976 (demolished 1989)
Client
  City of Liverpool in association
  with the Spastics Society
Project Team
  Reg Bradley
  Loren Butt
  Chubby Chhabra
  Spencer de Grey
  Jim Elsdon
  Norman Foster
  Wendy Foster
  Birkin Haward
  Ron Walker
Consultants
  Structural Engineer:
  Anthony Hunt Associates
  Mechanical and Electrical
  Engineer: Foster Associates
  Quantity Surveyor:
  Flood & Wilson
  Acoustics: Sandy Brown
  Associates
  Drainage: Adrian Wilder
Principal Awards
  1976 International Prize
  for Architecture
  1977 RIBA Award
  Commendation

**Pavilion Leisure Centres**
Knowsley, England
Badhoevedorp, Holland
1972
Client
  MPC Associates Ltd
Project Team
  Loren Butt
  Chubby Chhabra
  Norman Foster
  Wendy Foster
  Ian Ritchie
  Jocelyne van den Bossche
Consultants
  Mechanical and Electrical
  Engineer: Foster Associates
  Quantity Surveyor:
  Hanscomb Partnership
  Transport Planning:
  Freeman Fox & Partners

**Reliance Controls**
Swindon, England
1965-1966
Client
  Reliance Controls Ltd
Project Team
  Norman Foster
  Wendy Foster
  Frank Peacock
  Richard Rogers
  Mark Sutcliffe
Consultants
  Structural Engineer:
  Anthony Hunt Associates
  Mechanical and Electrical
  Engineer: G N Haden
  & Sons Ltd
  Quantity Surveyor:
  Hanscomb Partnership
  Drainage: G N Haden
  & Sons Ltd
Principal Awards
  1966 Architectural Design
  Project Award
  1967 Financial Times Industrial
  Architecture Award

**Renault Distribution Centre**
Swindon, England
1979-1982
Client
  Renault UK Ltd
Project Team
  Sue Allen
  Nic Bailey
  Ralph Ball
  Julia Barfield
  Loren Butt
  Chubby Chhabra
  Ian Dowsett
  Nick Eldridge
  Roy Fleetwood
  Norman Foster
  Wendy Foster
  Paul Heritage
  Neil Holt
  Paul Jones
  Nick Morgan
  David Morley
  Ian Simpson
  Mike Stacey
  Chris Windsor
  Arek Wozniak
Consultants
  Structural Engineer:
  Ove Arup & Partners
  Mechanical and Electrical
  Engineer: Foster Associates
  Quantity Surveyor: Davis Belfield
  & Everest
  Acoustics: Tim Smith Acoustics
  Landscaping: Technical
  Landscapes Ltd
  Office Planning:
  Quickborner Team
Principal Awards
  1984 Structural Steel Award
  1984 Civic Trust Award
  1984 Financial Times
  'Architecture at Work' Award
  1986 Constructa Prize for
  Industrial Architecture in Europe

**Sainsbury Centre for Visual Arts**
  Norwich, England
  1974-1978
Client
  The University of East Anglia
Project Team
  Arthur Branthwaite
  Loren Butt
  John Calvert
  Chubby Chhabra
  Ian Dowsett
  Howard Filbey
  Roy Fleetwood
  Norman Foster
  Wendy Foster
  Birkin Haward
  Neil Holt
  Richard Horden
  Caroline Lwin
  David Nelson
  Tomm Nyhuus
  Ian Ritchie
  Judith Warren
  Chris Windsor
  John Yates
  Bodo Zapp
Consultants
  Structural Engineer:
  Anthony Hunt Associates
  Mechanical and Electrical
  Engineer: Foster Associates
  Quantity Surveyor:
  Hanscomb Partnership
  Lighting: Claude R Engle
  Acoustics: Sound Research
  Laboratories
  Landscaping: Lanning Roper
  Drainage: John Taylor & Sons
  Cladding: Tony Pritchard
  Display and Exhibition Lighting:
  George Sexton III
  Graphics: Minale Tattersfield
  Provinciali

Principal Awards
  1978 Structural Steel
  Finniston Award
  1978 RIBA Award
  1979 British Tourist
  Board Award
  1979 R S Reynolds
  Memorial Award
  1980 Museum of the
  Year Award
  1980 Ambrose Congreve Award
  1980 Sixth International
  Prize for Architecture
  (Brussels) Award

**Sainsbury Centre Crescent Wing**
  Norwich, England
  1986-1991
Client
  The University of East Anglia
Project Team
  Chubby Chhabra
  Chris Connell
  Norman Foster
  Carsten Grantz
  Richard Hawkins
  Heiko Lukas
  Graham Phillips
Consultants
  Structural Engineer:
  YRM Anthony Hunt Associates
  Electrical and Mechanical
  Engineers: J Roger Preston
  & Partners
  Quantity Surveyor: Henry Riley
  & Son
  Lighting: George Sexton
  Associates
  Acoustics: Acoustic Design

Principal Awards
  1992 Design Review Minerva
  Award – Commendation
  1992 RIBA Regional
  Architecture Award
  1992 Civic Trust Award
  1993 Citation Award from
  the International Association
  of Lighting Designers

**Samuel Beckett Theatre**
  Cambridge, England
  1971
Client
  St Peter's College, Oxford
Project Team
  Norman Foster
  Wendy Foster
  Richard Buckminster Fuller
  Michael Hopkins
  James Meller
  Tony Pritchard
Consultants
  Structural Engineer: Fuller
  & Sadao Inc/Anthony Hunt
  Associates
  Quantity Surveyor: Hanscomb
  Partnership

**Sapa Factory**
  Tibshelf, England
  1972-1973
Client
  Skandinaviska Aluminium
  Profiler AB
Project Team
Phase I:
  Max Aiken
  Loren Butt
  Chubby Chhabra
  Norman Foster
  Wendy Foster
  Diana Goddard
  Michael Hopkins
  Tony Meadows
  Tomm Nyhuus
  Norman Partridge
  John Yates

Phase II:
  Loren Butt
  Chubby Chhabra
  Mike Elkan
  Norman Foster
  Caroline Lwin
  Tomm Nyhuus
  John Yates
Consultants
  Structural Engineer:
  Anthony Hunt Associates
  Mechanical and Electrical
  Engineer: Foster Associates
  Quantity Surveyor:
  Hanscomb Partnership
  Drainage: Adrian Wilder

**Skybreak House**
  Radlett, England
  1965-1966
Client
  Mr & Mrs Anthony Jaffé
Project Team
  Norman Foster
  Wendy Foster
  Frank Peacock
  Maurice Phillips
  Richard Rogers
  Su Rogers
Consultants
  Structural Engineer:
  Anthony Hunt Associates
  Quantity Surveyor:
  Hanscomb Partnership

**Son Recreation Centre**
  Vestby, Norway
  1973
Client
  Fred Olsen Group
Project Team
  Loren Butt
  John Calvert
  Steiner Erikson
  Norman Foster
  Wendy Foster
  John Jones
  Jørn Narud
  Tomm Nyhuus
  Helger Saatvedt
Consultants
  Structural Engineer:
  Multi-Consult A/S
  Mechanical and Electrical
  Engineer:
  Erichsen & Horgen/Foster
  Associates
  Quantity Surveyor:
  Hanscomb Partnership
  Drainage: Multi-Consult A/S

**St Helier Harbour Masterplan**
  St Helier, Jersey
  1976-1977
Client
  Harbours and Airport Committee
  of the States of Jersey
Project Team
  Loren Butt
  Spencer de Grey
  Norman Foster
  Birkin Haward
  Jill Townsend
Consultants
  Mechanical and Electrical
  Engineer: Foster Associates
  Civil Engineer: Coode & Partners
  Quantity Surveyor:
  Davis Belfield & Everest
  Financial Planning:
  Coopers & Lybrand
  Transport Planning:
  Freeman, Fox & Associates

**Waterfront Housing**
  in association with Harry Gilbert
  Cornwall, England
  1965
Client
  Mr & Mrs Marcus Brumwell
Project Team
  Laurie Abbott
  Norman Foster
  Wendy Foster
  Richard Rogers
  Su Rogers
Consultants
  Structural Engineer:
  Anthony Hunt Associates
  Quantity Surveyor:
  Hanscomb Partnership
  Landscape: M. Branch
  Drainage: Tuke & Bell Ltd
  Principal Awards
  1964 Architectural Design
  Project Award

**Wates Housing**
  Coulsdon, England
  1965
Client
  Wates Built Homes Ltd
Project Team
  Norman Foster
  Wendy Foster
  Frank Peacock
  Richard Rogers
  Su Rogers
Consultants
  Structural Engineer:
  Anthony Hunt Associates
  Quantity Surveyor: Wates
  Ltd/Hanscomb Partnership
  Landscape: M Branch
  Drainage: Tuke & Bell Ltd
  Principal Awards
  1965 Architectural Design
  Project Award

**Willis Faber & Dumas**
  Ipswich, England
  1971-1975
Client
  Willis Faber & Dumas Ltd
Project Team
  David Bailey
  Reg Bradley
  Arthur Branthwaite
  Loren Butt
  Chubby Chhabra
  Ian Dowsett
  Roy Fleetwood
  Norman Foster
  Wendy Foster
  Birkin Haward
  Neil Holt
  Michael Hopkins
  David Johns
  Jan Kaplicky
  Rainer Koch
  Truls Ovrum
  Louis Pillar
  Tony Pritchard
  Ian Ritchie
  Ken Shuttleworth
  Mark Sutcliffe
  Judith Warren
  John Wharton
  John Yates
Consultants
  Structural Engineer:
  Anthony Hunt Associates
  Mechanical and Electrical
  Engineer: Foster Associates
  Civil Engineer: John Taylor
  & Sons
  Quantity Surveyor:
  David Belfield & Everest
  Acoustics: Sound Research
  Laboratories
  Glazing: Martin Francis
  Drainage: Adrian Wilder
Principal Awards
  1976 Business & Industry Award
  of the Royal Society of Arts
  1976 R S Reynolds
  Memorial Award
  1977 RIBA Award

# Project Bibliography

### Air-Supported Office
*Bauen und Wohnen*, No 1 1971, '730 m² Bürofläche in Acht Wochen Geplant und Gebaut'
*Business Management*, August 1970, 'White, Light and Airy'
*Design*, March 1970, 'Office Beneath the Skin' by Martin Pawley
*Queen*, April 1970, 'Liberty, Mobility, Modernity' by Janet Street-Porter

### Autonomous House
*Architecture and Urbanism*, Special Edition, 1986
*L'Architecture d'Aujourd'hui*, February 1986

### Bean Hill Housing
*Architects' Journal*, 9 May 1973, 'Bean Hill'
*Architectural Design*, November 1972, 'Housing at Bean Hill'
*Architecture and Urbanism*, July 1974, 'Bean Hill Housing'

### Climatroffice
*L'Architecture d'Aujourd'hui*, November 1973

### The Cockpit
*Daily Telegraph Magazine*, 28 March 1969, 'Putting the Family Out of the House' by Margaret Duckett

### Computer Technology
*Design*, October 1969, 'Computer Technology'
*Design*, October 1971, 'Conflict at Hemel Hempstead'
*Sunday Times*, 5 May 1968, 'Wall-to-Wall Carpet on the Factory Floor' by Nicholas Taylor

### Creek Vean House
*Architectural Review*, August 1968, 'Seaside House in Cornwall'
*Architecture and Urbanism*, October 1974, 'Brumwell House'
*Daily Telegraph Magazine*, 22 November 1968, 'Dream Houses Become Reality' by Margaret Duckett
*Die Kunst*, June 1979, 'Wohnhaus mit Dachgarten an der Küste von Cornwall'
*House and Garden*, March 1974, 'In Cornwall: Set Fair High Above Sea, River, Woods and Valley'

### Factory Systems
*Architectural Review*, November 1969, 'Manplan 3: Town Workshop', guest edited by Norman Foster

### Fitzroy Street Office
*Architectural Design*, November 1972, 'Fitzroy Street Project'
*Architectural Review*, September 1972, 'Project for Foster Associates'
*Créé*, September/October 1972, 'Aménagements Intérieurs'
*Domus*, October 1972, 'Architectural Office in London'

### Foster Residence
*Architects' Journal*, 31 October 1979, 'Foster at Home'
*Architectural Record*, mid-August 1979, 'Test-Rig House re-explores Panelization Energy Use'
*L'Architecture d'Aujourd'hui*, December 1980, 'Maison Test-Rig'
*Building Design*, 26 October 1979, 'A Cautious Practice' David Pearce and Norman Foster

### Fred Olsen Amenity Centre
*Architects' Journal*, 2 December 1970, Dock Buildings
*Architectural Design*, May 1970, Foster Associates' Recent Work
*Architectural Review*, October 1970, Operations-Amenity Centre for Fred Olsen
*Bauen und Wohnen*, January 1971, Verwaltungs und Freizeitgebäude Einer Schiffahrtsgesellschaft
*Créé*, November/December 1970, Amenity Centre
*Design*, May 1970, 'Just Arrived in Port: a New Deal for the Dockers' by Alastair Best
*Domus*, December 1970, Carico e Scarico Sul Tamigi

### Fred Olsen Passenger Terminal
*Architects' Journal*, 2 December 1970, 'Dock Buildings'
*Architectural Design*, February 1971, 'Fun, Cover and for Work'
*Design*, January 1971, 'Process Tube for Liner Passengers' by Jose Manser
*Guardian*, 26 October 1970, 'Berth Control' by Richard Carr
*Times*, 18 February 1970, 'The Olsen Line of Success' by Michael Bailey

### Hackney Special Care Unit
*Design*, July 1973, 'Lessons in Schooling the Handicapped' by Selwyn Goldsmith
*Domus*, October 1972, 'Da Londra: Due Progetti dei Foster Associates'
*The Observer Review*, 31 March 1974, 'Good Design, Happy Children' Stephen Gardiner

### Hammersmith Centre
*Architectural Record*, August 1979, 'A Four-Acre Fabric Roof Covers "Park" at Hammersmith'
*L'Architecture d'Aujourd'hui*, December 1980, 'Centre de Loisirs, Hammersmith'
*Building Design*, 3 February 1978, 'Powerhouse' by Stephanie Williams
*International Architect*, No 1 1979, 'Urban Context: Hammersmith Centre' by Richard Padovan

### High-Density Housing
*Architectural Review*, January 1968, 'The Warren, Radlett'

### IBM Pilot Head Office
*Archetype*, May 1974, 'Anti-Formalism in Contemporary British Architecture' by N. Ross Ramus
*Architectural Design*, August 1971, 'IBM Head Office' by Andrew Rabeneck
*Architectural Review*, January 1972, 'IBM Cosham' by Lance Wright
*Architecture Plus*, July 1973, 'Least is Most'
*Design*, October 1971, 'Two Problems Solved' by Alastair Best
*Deutsche Architektenblatt*, December 1980, 'In Deutschland Nicht Vorstellbar'
*Deutsche Bauzeitung*, June 1972, 'Büroumwelt'
*Domus*, January 1972, 'Scompare'
*Glass Age News*, 19 March 1973, 'Disappearing Buildings'
*Glasforum*, No 4, 1973, 'IBM-Versuchsbüro in Cosham'
*Techniques et Architecture*, September-October 1974, 'Siège IBM à Cosham'
*Werk*, June 1972, 'IBM-England in Cosham'

### IBM Technical Park
*Architectural Record*, August 1985, 'The Metal Skin Technology of Foster Associates'
*Architectural Review*, August 1980, 'IBM Greenford Green' by Christopher Woodward
*Baumeister*, April 1983, 'IBM Technical Park in Greenford'
*Building Design*, 3 February 1978, 'Stretching Glass'
*Decor and Contract Furnishing*, February 1979, 'Inscape' by Lesley Chisholm
*Design*, August 1980, 'Factories as Product Design: Architects Deliver the Goods' by Deyan Sudjic
*Designers' Journal*, May 1985, 'Noel Jordan: Company Man' by Peter Carolin
*Techniques et Architecture*, June 1982, 'Centre IBM à Greenford Green'

### Joseph Shop
*Building Design*, 11 May 1979, 'Foster's Shop Floor' by Maurice Cooper
*Progressive Architecture*, September 1980, 'High Fashion Tech' by Penny McGuire
*Viz*. No 4 1979
*Viz*. No 5 1979

### Modern Art Glass
*Architectural Review*, July 1974, 'Glass on the Marsh' by John Winter
*Bauen und Wohnen*, April 1975, 'Lagerbauten'
*Building*, 14 June 1974, 'Modern Art Glass Warehouse'
*Design*, August 1974, 'That Upstage Blue One' by Jose Manser
*Domus*, July 1974, 'Parc Urbano'
*Financial Times*, 4 March 1974, 'Modern Art's Glass House' by Jose Manser
*Guardian*, 5 March 1974, 'Blue Fit for the Planners' by Judy Hillman

### Newport School Competition
*Architectural Design*, May 1968, 'Learning' by Cedric Price
*Bauen und Wohnen*, No 2 1970, 'Optimale Flexibilität'
*Building*, 31 October 1969, 'School System–Sophisticated Package within DES Cost Limits'

### Open House
*Building Design*, 13 July 1979, 'Open House' by Deyan Sudjic

### Orange Hand Shops
*Baumeister*, August 1974, 'Orange Hand, London'
*Créé*, July/August 1973, 'A la Main Orange'
*Design*, May 1973, 'Shop Kit For a Roving Chain' by Ilse Gray
*Domus*, August 1974, 'Orange Land L'Immagine di un Negozio'

### Palmerston Special School
*Architectural Review*, November 1976, 'Low-Profile School' by Jane Hyde and Alastair Best
*L'Architecture d'Aujourd'hui*, November 1973, 'Ecole Spéciale de Palmerston'
*L'Architecture d'Aujourd'hui*, April 1981, 'Ecole pour Enfants Handicapés'
*Bauen und Wohnen*, May 1977, 'Schule für Behinderte Kinder'
*Design*, December 1976, 'Interiors'

### Reliance Controls
*Acier Stahl Steel*, December 1968, 'New Reliance Controls Factory at Swindon'
*Architects' Journal*, 19 July 1967, 'Factory'
*Bauen und Wohnen*, No 7 1968, 'Fabrik für Elektronische Geräte Reliance Controls Ltd'
*Baumeister*, No 3 1970, 'Tageslicht Gespart?'
*Bouwwereld*, May 1969, 'Gebouw Voor Wisselende Massafaricage'
*Daily Telegraph*, 30 December 1968, 'Anatomy of a Factory' by John Chisholm
*Design*, October 1969, 'Reliance Controls, Swindon'
*Domus*, February 1967, 'Electronic Factory for Reliance Controls in Swindon'
*Financial Times*, 30 November 1967, 'The Winning Design'
*Industrial Architecture*, February 1968, 'The 1967 Financial Times Award for Industrial Architecture'
*Observer*, 10 December 1967, 'Prize for Modesty' by Ian Nairn

### Renault Distribution Centre
*Architects' Journal*, 1 December 1982, 'Foster at Play' by Alastair Best
*Architects' Journal*, 15 June 1983, 'Renault Inspection' by Martin Pawley
*Architectural Design*, August 1982, 'British Architects'
*Architectural Review*, July 1983, 'Renault Centre' by Peter Davey
*L'Architecture d'Aujourd'hui*, September 1983, 'Centre Renault' by F Deslaugiers
*Architecture and Urbanism*, October 1983, 'Renault Centre' by Kenji Sugimura
*Baumeister*, No 1 1984, 'Ersatzteillager in Swindon'
*Building*, 22 October 1982, 'Framework for Renault' by Brian Waters
*Building Design*, 3 July 1981, 'The Umbrellas of Swindon' by Ted Stevens
*Building Design*, 3 September 1982, 'Renault's Umbrella over the Swindon Skyline'
*Building Design*, 26 November 1982, 'If You Ever Plan To Motor West' by Martin Pawley
*Detail*, July/August 1984
*Deutsche Bauzeitung*, No 10 1985, 'Good Design Pays'
*L'Industria della Costruzioni*, July/August 1984, 'Centro di Distribuzione Renault' by Aldo Benedetti
*Techniques et Architecture*, No 342, June 1982
*Techniques et Architecture*, No 350, November 1983

### Sainsbury Centre
*Architects' Journal*, 5 April 1978, 'Fostering the Arts'
*Architects' Journal*, 4 July 1984, 'Building revisits: Sainsbury Centre' by Martin Pawley
*Architectural Design*, August 1975, 'Sainsbury Centre' by Wendy Foster
*Architectural Design*, February 1979 'Architectural Design Profile 19: Sainsbury Centre' by Andrew Peckham and others
*Architectural Record*, mid-August 1979, 'Metal Shed with Savoir Faire encloses Arts Centre'
*Architectural Review*, December 1978, 'East Anglia Arts' by Peter Cook
*L'Architecture d'Aujourd'hui*, February 1981
*Architecture Intérieure/Créé*, December 1979, 'La Séduction du Vide'
*Der Architekt*, March 1979
*Bauen und Wohnen*, No 7/8 1979, 'Technologie und Architektur' by J. Joedicke
*Baumeister*, No 9 1979, 'Kunsthalle'
*Bolaffiarte*, No 81 1978, 'Hangar per l'Arte' by Lucio Cabutti
*Building*, 7 April 1978, 'Art-Shed' by Martin Spring

*Building Design*, 3 February 1978, 'Powerhouse' by Stephanie Williams
*Building Design*, 26 October 1979, 'A Cautious Practice' by David Pearce and Norman Foster
*Design*, July 1978, 'A Machine for Displaying Things In' by Alastair Best
*Domus*, March 1979, 'Per l'Arte All'Universita di East Anglia'
*L'Industria delle Costruzioni*, May 1980
*Modern Metals*, July 1979, 'Superplastic Aluminium goes Commercial in Prize-Winning Architecture' by James Bowe
*New Society*, July 1978, 'High/Low Technology' by Sutherland Lyall
*Progressive Architecture*, February 1979, 'Modernism Reconstituted'
*Space Design*, No. 8004
*Spectator*, 15 April 1978, 'Calm and Control' by Alastair Best
*Techniques et Architecture*, September 1979

## Sainsbury Centre Crescent Wing

*Architects' Journal*, 8 May 1991, 'Second Generation' by David Jenkins
*L'Architecture d'Aujourd'hui*, September 1991, 'New Crescent Wing'
*Architecture Interieure Créé*, August/September 1991, 'Extension du Centre Sainsbury'
*Artscribe*, September 1991, 'Madam, do you know how much your house weighs?' by Brian Hatton
*Arts Review*, 12 July 1991, 'Norman Foster' by Tony Warner
*Building*, 24 May 1991, 'Knight Light' by Matthew Comber
*Daily Telegraph*, 16 May 1991, 'Sir Norman Foster's Buried Treasure' by Kenneth Powell
*Deutsche Bauzeitung*, July 1991, 'Adel Verpflichtet' by Falk Jaeger
*Domus*, December 1992, 'The Crescent Wing' GA Document, No 31, November 1991
*Independent*, 8 May 1991, 'An Extension with More to it Than Meets the Eye', by Alastair Best
*Lichtbericht 39*, February 1992, 'Crescent Wing' by Monika Salzmann
*RIBA Journal*, July 1991, 'The Crescent Wing' by Richard Wilcock

## Samuel Beckett Theatre

*Daily Telegraph Magazine*, 10 July 1970

## SAPA Factory

*Architects' Journal*, 28 November 1973, 'Undecorated Shed'
*Architects' Journal*, 28 September 1977, 'Extrusion Plant's Expansion'
*Bauen und Wohnen*, May 1974, 'Fabrik als Container'
*Building Design*, 22 March 1974, 'Sophisticated Sheds'
*Domus*, July 1974, 'Per Lavorare: Structure-color'

## Skybreak House

*Architectural Review*, August 1968, 'Hertfordshire Suburban'
*Ville Giardini*, November 1973, 'Struttura a Gradoni'
*Werk*, January 1969, 'Haus in Radlett'

## Wates Housing

*Architectural Design*, April 1965, 'Housing at Coulsdon, Surrey'

## Waterfront Housing

*Sunday Times*, 14 April 1968, 'Planning on the Septic Tank Pattern' by Nicholas Taylor

## Willis Faber & Dumas

*AIA Journal*, April 1981, 'Evaluation: A building that succeeds in losing itself' by Annette LeCuyer
*Architects' Journal*, 4 June 1975, 'Foster in Ipswich' by Sutherland Lyall
*Architects' Journal*, 17 September 1980
*Architectural Design*, November 1972, 'Foster Associates: Recent Work'
Architectural Design, October 1977, 'The Design Philosophy of the WFD building' by Norman Foster
*Architectural Review*, January 1973
*Architectural Review*, September 1975, 'Ipswich Reflections' by Christopher Woodward
*L'Architecture d'Aujourd'hui*, December 1972/January 1973
*Architecture and Urbanism*, February 1974
*Der Architekt*, March 1979, 'Von der Technik zur Architektur' by Margrit Kennedy
*Bauen und Wohnen*, No 11 1973, 'Bürogebäude mit Freizeiteinrichtungen'
*Bauen und Wohnen*, No 2/3 1976 'Büro-und Verwaltungsgebäude'
*Baumeister*, No 10 1075, 'Versicherungsagentur in Ipswich'
*Building Design*, 3 February 1978, 'Thin-Skinned Conserver' by Stephanie Williams
*Building Design*, 26 October 1979, 'A Cautious Practice' by David Pearce and Norman Foster
*Design*, September 1975, 'Federated Skills'
*Domus*, November 1975, 'New England Uffici'
*Glass Age*, November 1975, 'Ipswich Spectacular'
*Harpers and Queen*, February 1976, 'Monday Morning Greens' by Tim Street-Porter
*Light and Lighting*, November/December 1975, 'Unique Lighting for a Unique Building'
*New Society*, 6 October 1977, 'Grass above, glass around' by Reyner Banham

# Contributors

**Chris Abel** is an architectural theorist, critic and educator, based in Sydney, Australia. He is the author of *Architecture and Identity: Responses to Cultural and Technological Change* and many other publications. He has taught in major universities in many different parts of the world and includes twentieth-century architecture in Asia Pacific and advanced production methods amongst his main interests.

**Peter Reyner Banham** (1922-1988) was a prolific journalist and critic whose writings on architecture and design appeared in journals from *New Society* to *The Architects' Journal*. He was Professor of Art History at the University of California, Santa Cruz, and, later, Sheldon H Solos Professor of the History of Architecture at the Institute of Fine Arts, New York University. His books include *Theory and Design in the First Machine Age* and *A Concrete Atlantis: US Industrial Building and Modern European Architecture*.

'LL/LF/LE v Foster' was first published in *New Society*, 9 November 1972.

'The Yellow Bicycle' lecture was given at the University of East Anglia on 27 June 1985. The transcript has been edited for inclusion in this volume with the kind permission of Mary Banham and the Banham Trustees.

**Alastair Best** is a writer, lecturer and broadcaster. He has edited *Design* and *Designers' Journal*, and written widely on architecture and design for *The Architectural Review*.

'In the Beginning' was first published as the introduction to *Norman Foster: Buildings and Projects*, Volume 1 (1991) and has been extensively revised for inclusion in this volume.

**Peter Buchanan** is a writer and critic who trained as an architect. He was deputy editor of *The Architectural Review* from 1983 to 1992 and is the author of *Renzo Piano Building Workshop*, Volumes 1 to 4.

**Francis Duffy** is an architect with a special interest in how organisations use space over time. In 1973 he founded DEGW with John Worthington and Luigi Giffone and now chairs the firm. He has edited *Facilities* magazine and is co-author of *Office Landscaping: Planning Office Space* and *The Changing City*.

'Systems Thinking' first appeared in *Norman Foster: Buildings and Projects*, Volume 1 (1991) and has been revised and updated for inclusion in this volume.

**Brian Hatton** is a journalist and lecturer. He is the London correspondent for *Lotus* magazine and has contributed to many journals on architecture and art. He teaches at the Architectural Association in London.

**Louis Hellman** trained as an architect before becoming a cartoonist. He has been the cartoonist for *The Architects' Journal* since 1967 and his work has also appeared in *Punch* and *Private Eye*. He has published several books, including *Archi-têtes*, and has written numerous articles for architectural magazines.

**David Jenkins** is an architect, editor and writer, now based in the Foster studio. He is a former buildings editor on *The Architects' Journal*, and was editorial director at Phaidon Press, responsible for architecture and design. His books include *Pierre Koenig*, co-written with James Steele, and *On Foster … Foster On*.

**Ian Lambot** originally trained and practised as an architect before turning to photography and the production of books. A resident of Hong Kong for fifteen years, he returned to Great Britain in 1995 and established his own publishing company.

**Tim Ostler** is a writer and critic. A regular contributor to *World Architecture*, his work has also appeared in *The Architects' Journal* and *Building Design*.

**Martin Pawley** is an architectural writer and critic. He was architectural correspondent of *The Guardian* and subsequently *The Observer*, and has edited the magazines *Building Design* and *World Architecture*. His books include *Theory and Design in the Second Machine Age* and *Norman Foster: A Global Architecture*.

'The Years of Innovation' first appeared in *Norman Foster: Buildings and Projects*, Volume 2 (1989).

**Kenneth Powell** is a contributor to many architectural journals and was formerly the architectural correspondent for *The Daily Telegraph*. He is consultant director of the Twentieth Century Society. His many books include *Stansted: Norman Foster and the Architecture of Flight*.

**Robert A M Stern** is an architect and writer. Founder of the firm Robert A M Stern in New York, he is also Dean of the Yale School of Architecture. His books include *New York 1900* and *Pride of Place*.

'The Impact of Yale' is adapted from a talk given at the seminar 'The Special Relationship: American and British Architecture since 1945', held at the Paul Mellon Centre for Studies in British Art, London, 29 October 1998.

**John Walker** is a quantity surveyor now based in Vancouver where he is senior principal of Hanscomb Canada.

'The Early Years' first appeared in *Norman Foster: Buildings and Projects*, Volume 1 (1991).

**Graham Vickers** is an author and journalist specialising in design and the built environment. He has contributed to publications such as *World Architecture* and *Management Today*, and was a contributing editor on *Creative Review*. His books include *Style in Product Design* and *Key Moments in Architecture: The Evolution of the City*.

**Norman Foster** was born in Manchester in 1935. After graduating from Manchester University School of Architecture and City Planning in 1961, he won a fellowship to Yale University, where he gained a Masters Degree in Architecture.

In 1963 he co-founded Team 4 and in 1967 he established Foster Assoicates, now known as Foster and Partners. The practice has its main studio in London, with project offices worldwide. Since its inception the practice has received more than 190 awards and citations for excellence and has won over fifty national and international competitions.

Norman Foster was awarded the Royal Gold Medal for Architecture in 1983, the Gold Medal for the French Academy of Architecture in 1991 and the American Institute of Architects Gold Medal in 1994. Also in 1994, he was appointed Officer of the Order of Arts and Letters by the Ministry of Culture in France. In 1999 he became the twenty-first Pritzker Architecture Prize Laureate; and in 2002 he was elected to the German Orden Pour le Mérite für Wissenschaften und Künste and awarded the Praemium Imperiale.

He was granted a Knighthood in the Queen's Birthday Honours List, 1990, and appointed by the Queen to the Order of Merit in 1997. In 1999 he was honoured with a life peerage in the Queen's Birthday Honours List, taking the title Lord Foster of Thames Bank.

'Design for Living' was first published in *BP Shield*, March 1969.

'Social Ends, Technical Means' was first published in *Architectural Design* 9-10, September-October 1977.

'Meeting the Sainsburys' is a transcript of a speech given at the presentation of the Freedom of the City of Norwich to Sir Robert and Lady Sainsbury, 23 June 1999.

'With Wendy' is a revised version of an essay first published in *Norman Foster: Buildings and Projects*, Volume 2 (1989).

'Bucky and Beyond' is a revised version of an essay first published in *Buckminster Fuller: Anthology for the New Millennium*, edited by Thomas Zung (2001).

# Index

Illustrations are indicated by italics except where they fall within a project sequence.

**A**+U
 IBM Pilot Head Office 231, 232
 IBM Technical Park 246, 258
 IBM Technical Park and SOM Chicago 256
 Modern Art Glass 352
 NF on Bean Hill 278
A&V 437, 439, 531
Aalborg Art Museum 121, 379, 386
Aalto, Alvar 22, 58, 72, 379, 386
 Aalborg Art Museum 121, 379, 386
 Muuratsalo Summer House 72
 Säynätsalo Town Hall 50, 58, 121
Abbott, Carl 19, 25, 26
Abel, Chris 140, 399, 500, 502
 on Reliance Controls 102-9
Adler, Alfred 283-5
agricultural structures 504, 505
Aicher, Otl 11
Aiken, Max 239, 240
air structures 125, 147, 205
Air-Supported Office, Hemel Hempstead 124, 200, 204-7
aircraft 426-9, 451-3, 458, 486-7, 501, 519
AIROH House 285
airships 380, 386, 394
 Cardington shed 380
 Zeppelin 380, 386, 394
Airstream caravan 171, 398
Aldersey-Williams, Hugh 106
Aldersley-Williams, Arthur G 164
Alexander, Christopher 30, 199
 see also Chermayeff, Serge
Alexandra Road housing, London 289
American Board of Economic Warfare 533
American Institute of Architects, Gold Medal 533
Anshen & Allen 30
Apollo Lunar Lander 460, 461
Appleby, Sally 35, 423
Appleyard, Bryan 58, 73, 87
Aram, Zeev 123
Archigram 103, 458, 459, 459
Architects' Co-Partnership 95
Architects' Journal 234-5, 351
 Bean Hill housing 278
 Crescent Wing 435, 446
 IBM Pilot Head Office 236
 NF on Hammersmith Centre 476
 NF on gliding 487
 NF 304
 Reliance Controls 114
 Renault Distribution Centre 496, 530
 Renault Distribution Centre and John Batchelor 512
 Reyner Banham on DC-3 170
 Sapa 347, 349
Architectural Association 119, 235, 236-7

Architectural Design (AD)
 Country Offices 173
 Charles and Ray Eames 414
 Foster Associates 237
 Modern Art Glass 201
 Newport School 133
 NF on Willis Faber & Dumas 298, 309, 315, 320, 330
 NF on Willis Faber & Dumas and Modern Art Glass 317
 Project Awards 78, 81, 164
 Robert Sainsbury on Sainsbury Centre 376
 Sainsbury Centre 395, 416, 417
 SCSD 197
 Waterfront Housing 78
Architectural Forum 21
Architectural Review 12, 15
 Archigram 458
 Reyner Banham on Volkswagen Beetle 291
 Computer Technology 209, 210
 Fitzroy Street Studio 239
 Hammersmith Centre 473
 IBM Pilot Head Office 221, 224
 IBM Pilot Head Office and IBM Technical Park 247
 IBM Technical Park 250, 252, 253, 259, 260, 263
 'Manplan 3' 138, 139, 141, 142, 143
 Modern Art Glass 199, 352
 Palmerston Special School 272, 273
 Reliance Controls 26, 456
 Renault Distribution Centre 287, 508, 509, 512, 525, 527, 530, 531
 Sainsbury Centre 386, 388, 391, 413
 Willis Faber & Dumas 304, 318, 322
Arnoldi, Per 11
Arup, Ove, Associates 228, 251, 386, 500, 502, 504, 507
ASPIRE Centre, Stanmore 269
'Astragal' (of Architects' Journal) 114, 235, 237, 278
Atelier 5 54, 68, 77, 119
Autonomous House, Los Angeles 534, 535, 544-5, 547, 553

**B**acon, Francis 366
 Head of a Man 376
 Portrait of Lisa 367, 374, 410
 Portrait of R J Sainsbury 374
Bailey, David 239
Banham, Peter Reyner 24, 235
 'Beyond the Yellow Bicycle' 450-63
 'LL/LF/LE v Foster' 234-7
 on air structures 125, 205
 on Air-Supported Office 207
 on Airstream Caravan 398
 on Digital Equipment Corporation building 455
 on Douglas DC-3 170
 on NF 146, 453
 NF on 235, 454, 462
 on Foster Associates 127, 171
 on Fitzroy Street studio 239-40

 on Huntington Beach Power Station 459
 on IBM Pilot Head Office 231, 290
 on Le Corbusier 91, 236, 458, 462
 on Minimalism 91
 on Reliance Controls and SDS 107
 on Renault Distribution Centre 461
 on Sainsbury Centre 380, 396, 420
 on Willis Faber & Dumas 313, 316, 318, 324, 328
Barker, Felix, and Hyde, Ralph 477
Barnett, Jonathan 19
barrage balloons 125
Barron, Iann 124, 209, 212
Batchelor, John 512
Bauen + Wohnen 328
Bauhaus, Dessau 253, 289
Bayes, Kenneth 271
BBC Radio Centre, London 116, 193, 282, 292
Bean Hill Housing, Milton Keynes 274-9
Beardshaw, John, & Partners 117
Beatles 119
Bechtel Corporation 457, 459
Beckett, Samuel 539
Bell Jet Ranger helicopter 427
Berco Corporation 284-5
Berlin
 Free University 541, 554, 555
 glass skyscraper project 313
 Philology Library 554-5
 New National Gallery 378
 Reichstag 10, 121, 175, 177, 194, 195, 441, 443, 537, 545, 546, 547, 552-3, 554
Bernbach, Bill 365
Best, Alastair
 'In the Beginning' 116-27
 on Bean Hill 286
 on Crescent Wing 444, 446
 on Fitzroy Street studio 240
 on Foster Residence 482-3
 on Olsen Amenity Centre 160, 164
 on Palmerston Special School 272, 273
 on Renault Distribution Centre 496, 530
 on influence of Paul Rudolph on NF 26
 on Sainsbury Centre 383
 on Willis Faber & Dumas 298
 on Willis Faber & Dumas and Daily Express Building 312
Bilbao Metro 38, 39
Bijvoet, Bernard see Chareau, Pierre
bio-diesel 552-3
Bland, Ken 77
Blue Cross-Blue Shield, Boston 26, 28
Boathouse project 96, 118
Boeing 747 384, 550
Bourn Mill, Cambridgeshire 16-17
BP Shield 104, 533
Bradbury Building, Los Angeles 307, 391
Bradley, Reg 240
Bredero 467, 473
Breuer, Marcel 19, 472
Bristol, Katherine G 288
'Bristow' cartoon strip 331, 333, 339-43

British Museum, London 195
 exhibition of work of Foster studio (2001) 534
 Great Court 10, 177, 470, 471, 477
Brumwell, Marcus and Rene 41, 45, 50, 50-6, 60, 67, 120, 437
Buchanan, Peter 367, 456, 477
 on Gomera Regional Planning Study 181-91
buckminsterfullerene 553
'Buckyballs and Beyond' (exhibition) 553
Building 445, 500, 503, 507, 508, 513
Building Bulletin 196
Building Design 188, 466, 506, 530
Building Research Station, Hertfordshire 196, 457
Building Sights 54, 384
Burgess, Anthony 87
Burgess, Sterling 533
Bürolandschaft 196, 200, 333
Burton, Decimus, Kew Palm House 391
Burton Group 361
Butler Company 550, 551
Butt, Loren 92, 93-4, 235, 237, 238, 239, 240
 on Computer Technology 211
 on energy conservation 237
 on IBM Pilot Head Office 221
 comparing IBM Pilot Head Office and Crystal Palace 225
 on IBM Technical Park 256
 on Sainsbury Centre 286, 385
 on Willis Faber & Dumas 321
Byam, Wally 398

**C**ambridge University, Faculty of Anthropology 18, 19
Camden Mews, London 35-7, 71, 74
Canary Islands 155, 180-91
Canary Wharf, London 156, 162
 Citibank 156, 195
 HSBC Headquarters 156
 Underground Station 39, 156, 157
Candilis Josic Woods Schiedhelm 554
Cape Canaveral 23, 30, 31
Caplan, Ralph 415
Caproni Vizzola sailplane 387, 451, 452-3
Camm, Sidney 42
Carrefour hypermarkets, France 357
Case Study houses, Los Angeles 30, 105, 111, 118, 196, 415
Casson, Sir Hugh 118
Chalco, Mexico City 548, 549, 550
Chalk, Warren 459
Chandigarh High Court Building 26, 387
Chareau, Pierre, and Bijvoet, Bernard 481, 485
Chaslin, François 304, 516, 520, 528
Cheesman, Georgie 10, 31, 422, 423
Chermayeff, Serge 11, 27, 29, 30, 35, 81, 89, 118
 Community and Privacy (with Christopher Alexander) 30, 79, 89
 House for Denis Cohen, London 30
Chesa Futura, St Moritz 174, 183
Chhabra, Chubby 240
Childs, David 19

Chisholm, John 24, *25*, 110
Chrysalis group 457
Cincinnati Milacron, Milton Keynes 140
Citibank, London *156*, 162, 195
Citroën 2CV *399*
City Academies *135*
Clapp, David *238*, 239
Clarke, Brian 335
Clelland, Doug 416
Climatroffice project 181, *290*, *301*, 305, 473, 534, 537, 540-1, 542, 552, 554
*A Clockwork Orange* 87
Cobb, Henry 19
Cochwillan barn, Llanllechid 13-14, *110*
Cockpit, Feock 10, *38*, 40-5, 50, *120*, 121, 176, 181
Cologne
    Glass Pavilion *313*
    Museum für Angewandte Kunst 43
    University of Applied Sciences 43
Combined Operations command centre *195*
Comet jet airliner 287
Commerzbank Headquarters, Frankfurt 10, 193, 292, *293*, 552
Computer Technology, Hemel Hempstead 95, 124-5, *125*, *128*, 147, 199, *200*, 201, 203-7, 209-13, 218, 246, 247, 281, 282, 355
'Connections: The Work of Charles and Ray Eames' (exhibition) *414*
Consortium of Local Authorities Special Programme (CLASP) 267
*Contemporary World Architecture* 419
Cook, Peter 386, 388, 458, 459
Coomber, Matthew 445
Copeland, Barry 155
Corten steel 554
Cordingley, Alan 23
Cordingly, Professor R A 118
Corsica House *38*, 59
Country Offices, Vestby, Norway 10, *85*, *120*, 121, 172-5, 176, 181, 183, 185, *369*, 502, 545
Cox, Anthony 95
Creek Vean House, Feock 35, *38*, 41, 46-65, *67*, 69, 71, 73, 83, 87, *120*, 120-1
Crescent Wing, Sainsbury Centre, Norwich *39*, 413, 419, 431-49, 558
Crompton, Dennis 459
Crosby, Theo 462
Cruickshank, Dan 332
Crystal Palace, London *193*, 222, *223*, 225, *395*, *474*
Curl, Dr Robert 553
Curtis, William J R 20, 24, 77, 200, *414*, 463
Cwmbran Children's Trust 489

**D**aily Express building, Manchester *312*
*The Daily Telegraph* 110
Davey, Peter 508, 509, 525, 527, 531
Davies, John 375, 390
de Grey, Spencer 11, 177, 271, 272, 359, 425, 429
de Maré, Eric 15
Deighton, Gerry 218
Demag 364
Derry & Toms, London 333, *334*
Design
    Air-Supported Office *124*
    Bedford Street studio 123
    Fred Olsen Amenity Centre 160, 164
    Fred Olsen Passenger Terminal 167, 171
    Fitzroy Street studio 240
    NF on Foster Associates 141
    IBM Technical Park 248, 256, 261
    Orange Hand shops 361
    Palmerston Special School 271
    Special Care Unit 268
Design Research Unit 50, 271
Dickens, Frank 331, 339
*Dictionnaire raisonné de l'architecture française du XIe au XVIe siècle* 520
Digital Equipment Corporation, California *455*
Dome over Manhattan project 290
*Domus* 111, *348*, 438
Donat, John 343
Douglas DC-3 aircraft *170*, *171*, 291
Downes, Giles *241*
Drexler, Arthur 322
Duffy, Francis
    'Systems Thinking Revisited' 192-201
Duisburg
    Business Promotion Centre *193*, 554
    Inner Harbour masterplan 465
    Microelectronic Centre *105*, 554
Dymaxion car *533*
Dymaxion Deployment Unit 550, *551*
Dymaxion House 55, 181, 484, *533*, 548, *551*
Dymaxion Sky-Ocean World Map 554

**E**agle comic 512
Eames, Charles and Ray 23, 30, 106, 121, 192, 395, *414*, 459, 460, 483
    Case Study houses 105, *111*, 118, *196*, *414*, *415*, 483
East Anglia, University of 375, 378, 383, 409, 423, *441*
    Arts Department 286, 389
    Music Centre 386
    School of World Art Studies 392, 406, 412, 413
    *see also* Sainsbury Centre for Visual Arts
Ede, Jim 55, 62
Education, Ministry of 196, 197
Education and Science, Department of 126, 131, 271, 272, 281
Ehrenkrantz, Ezra, School Construction Systems Development (SCSD) 30, 103, 121, 122, *132*, 135, 136, *140*, 196-7, 198, 271, 456-7, *457*, 460
Eiffel, Gustave 548
Eiffel Tower, Paris *521*
Einzig, Richard 83, *120*, *236*
Electronic Arts European Headquarters, Chertsey 292
Ellwood, Craig 19, 30, 121, 348, 415, 456
    Case Study houses 105
    Scientific Data Systems (SDS) *107*, *348*
Ely Cathedral, Norfolk *335*
Enercon wind turbine *16*, *17*
Engle, Claude *194*
'The Environment Game' (exhibition) 462
Esprit Shop, London *481*
Ettedgui, Joseph 280, 480-1
Evans, Eldred 19
*Evening Standard* 331

**F**aber, Julian 422
*The Face* 421
Factory Systems, Milton Keynes *129*, 138-43, *252*
Fallingwater, Pennsylvania 291
Farm Lane Estate, Fulham, London 89
Farnsworth House, Illinois 291
Fawcett, Anthony, and Withers, Jane 421
Ferrarin, Carlo 452
Financial Times Award for Industrial Architecture 113, 122, 211, 213, 354
Finsbury Health Centre, London 126
Fletcher, Banister, *A History of Architecture* 323
Fogg, Laurie *238*, 239
Forest Road Annexe, East Horsley 90-1
Forth Valley Community Care Village 269
Foster Associates 556-7
    Bedford Street studio *123*, 123-4, 196, *237*, 281, 425, *456*
    Fitzroy Street studio *234*, 234-7, 238-41, 281, 450, 459, *460*, 477, 558
    Great Portland Street studio *281*, 439, *460*, *506*, 521, 528, 534, 535, 545, 558
    RIBA Heinz Gallery exhibition 127
Foster (née Cheesman), Wendy 10, 31, *35*, 77, 86, 89, 93, 94, 95, 119, 122, *123*, 139, 151, 173, *237*, *239*, 275, 378, 382, 422-9, *423*, *425*, 438, 534, 558
Foster, Norman 8-9, *19*, *25*, 32-3, *35*, 92, *116*, *117*, *123*, *127*, *184*, *194*, *237*, *239*, *241*, *268*, *333*, *367*, *384*, *396*, *402*, *409*, *423*, *425*, *427*, *429*, *436*, 535, 553
    'Design for Living' 144-7
    'Bucky and Beyond' 548-55
    'Measured Drawings' 12
    residence 281, 482-5
    'Meeting the Sainsburys' 366-7
    'Preface' 10-11'
    'Social Ends, Technical Means' 338-43
    'With Wendy' 422-9
    on agricultural structures 504, 505
    on Alvar Aalto 58, 72, 121, 379
    on Air Supported Office 202, 204, 205, 207
    on Atelier 5 77
    on influence of America 19, 23, 31, 122, 204, 504
    on Autonomous House 544, 547
    on Reyner Banham 235, 454, 462
    on Bean Hill Housing 276, 278, 279
    on Boeing 747 384
    on Bourn Mill 16
    on Loren Butt 94
    on Bradbury Building 307
    on bicycles 460, 529
    on Cape Canaveral 23, 31
    on Serge Chermayeff 30
    on Climatroffice 301, 537, 540, 541
    on Cockpit 42, 43
    on Commerzbank 537
    on Computer Technology 202, 209, 210, 211, 212
    on Country Offices 172, 174, 175
    letter to Anthony Cox 95
    on Creek Vean 47, 50, 51, 55, 58, 59, 63
    on Crescent Wing 431, 434, 436, 439, 447
    on Crystal Palace 193
    on democracy in the workplace 102, 149, 158, 160, 161
    on Duisburg Inner Harbour Masterplan 465
    on Charles and Ray Eames 23, 415
    on Craig Ellwood 348
    on Ely Cathedral 335
    on Factory Systems 138, 142
    on flexibility 89, 141, 220, 228, 291, 332, 483, 484, 527
    on flying 426, 428, 453, 486, 487, 501
    on Wendy Foster 422-9
    on Foster Residence 483, 484
    on Buckminster Fuller 301, 397, 505, 534, 535, 537, 539, 548-55
    on German Car Centre 362, 364
    on glazing 314, 315
    on gliders 487
    on Gomera 149, 180, 182, 183, 188, 189, 190
    on Philip Johnson 27
    on Hackney Special Care Unit 268
    on Hammersmith Centre 467, 469, 473, 474, 476, 477
    on Hampstead Hill Gardens flat 93, 423
    on Harrier Jump Jet 519
    on High-Density Housing 88, 89
    on Hongkong and Shanghai Bank 28, 462
    on Tony Hunt 94
    on IBM Pilot Head Office 134, 137, 198, 215, 218, 220, 222, 228, 233
    on IBM Technical Park 137, 243, 248, 252, 257
    on Ipswich 298, 324
    on Charles Jencks 288
    on Joseph Shop 480
    on Louis Kahn 24
    on Katsuro Imperial Villa 485
    on Knoxville Energy Expo 537, 542
    on Le Corbusier 117
    on Leeds Corn Exchange 306
    on light 83, 85, 194, 306, 406, 446
    on Louisiana Museum 379
    on Lunar Lander 461
    on Maison de Verre 485
    on Manchester 117, 118, 119, 521
    on Manchester University 13, 117
    on Mexico City 549
    on Mies van der Rohe 23
    on Milan Galleria 471
    on mock-ups 309, 314, 412
    on Modern Art Glass 317, 352

Index 573

on Murray Mews 71, 75
on Newport School 122, 131, 132, 134, 135, 137, 222, 230
on Nomos table 461, 529
on office design 305
on Olsen Amenity Centre 122, 137, 149, 151, 154, 155, 158, 159, 160, 161, 162, 211, 493
on Olsen Passenger Terminal 149, 169
on Olsen Travel Agency 179
on Oslo offices 177
on Orange Hand shops 361
on Omni Centre 473
on Joseph Paxton 193
on prefabrication 276, 285
on Palmerston Special School 270
on Pruitt Igoe 288
on Regent Street Polytechnic 13
on Reichstag 194, 441, 537, 547
on Reliance Controls 94, 95, 99, 102, 107, 109, 110, 113, 115, 122, 493
on Renault Distribution Centre 462, 493, 498, 499, 501, 503, 506, 507, 509, 512, 519, 523, 524, 527, 529
on Paul Rudolph 20, 25, 27, 28, 29, 30
on Royal Academy Sackler Galleries 441
on Robert and Lisa Sainsbury 371, 374, 376-7, 378, 382, 431, 436, 439
on Sainsbury Centre 371, 377, 380, 384, 386, 391, 394, 395, 397, 409, 411, 412, 413, 415, 424, 431
on Samuel Beckett Theatre 537, 538, 539
on Sapa Factory 348
on Vincent Scully 21
on SCSD 230, 457
on shopping and leisure centres 357
on sketching 14
on Skybreak house 83, 86
on Stansted Airport 371
on James Stirling 22
on Swiss Re 537
on teamwork 126
on trucks 23
on vernacular architecture 521
on Waterfront Housing 66, 68, 69
on John Walker 94
on Willis Faber & Dumas 295, 298, 300, 301, 302, 306, 307, 314, 315, 317, 320, 323, 324, 328, 330, 332, 333, 334, 335, 338-43, 468, 537
on wind turbines 16
on windmills 16, 17
on Whitney Museum project 472
on working with engineers 94, 549
on Frank Lloyd Wright 23, 54, 117, 502
on Yale University 24, 25, 27, 28, 29, 30, 31, 54
Foster Residence, London 281, 482-5
Frampton, Kenneth 55, 526
Francis, Martin 122, 209, *314*, 355
Frankfurt am Main
  Commerzbank Headquarters 10, 193, 292, *293*, 552
  National Athletics Stadium *38, 41*, 281, *289, 406*

Franklin, Dr Owen 75
Franzen, Ulrich 19
Fred Olsen Amenity Centre, Millwall Dock, London 95, 122-3, 124, 131, 149-65, 167, 171, 172, 181, 198, 218, 221, 225, 260, 281, *283*, 299, 302, 335, 351, *354*, 375, 422, *423*, 429
Fred Olsen Passenger Terminal, Millwall Dock, London 166-71, 181, 190, 198, 282, *423*
Fred Olsen Travel Agency, London 178-9
Froebel, F W 267
Fuji Group pavilion, Osaka World's Fair 205
Fuller, Richard Buckminster 8-9, *396*, 532, 532-6, *545, 549*
  at Bedford Street studio *116*, 117
  Autonomous House 534, 535, 544-5, 547, 553
  bathroom module *484*
  Climatroffice project 181, *290, 301*, 305, 473, 534, 537, 540-1, *542*, 552, 554
  Dome over Manhattan project *290*
  Dymaxion car *533*
  Dymaxion Deployment Unit 550, *551*
  Dymaxion House 56, 181, 484, *533*, 548, *551*
  Dymaxion Sky-Ocean World Map *554*
  and Eames 460
  Expo 82, Knoxville, USA (with Foster Associates) *474*, 542-3, *543*
  geodesic domes 239, 505, *532*, 533, 534, 545, 546, 548
  influence on NF 11, 55, 183, 190, 192, 199, 395, 483, 532-4, 548-55
  and Law of Ephemeralisation 290
  NF on 126, 301, 397, 504, 535, 539, 548-55
  quoted 290, 533, 534, 535, 545, 546, 550, 551, 554, 555
  and RIBA Royal Gold Medal 532, 548
  Samuel Beckett Theatre 10, 93, 534, 538-9, 541, 548, 549
  and systems ideas 196
  tensegrity structures 505, 533, 534, 537, 543
  on NF at RIBA award ceremony 532, 545
  and weight of building 397, 534, 550, 555
  and *Whole Earth Catalogue* 183
  Wichita House 181, 183, *533*
  World Expo, Montreal (1967), US pavilion 533, 541, 543
  *Nine Chains to the Moon* 550
Futagawa, Yoshio 13, 54

**G***A Extra* 158, 162
Gabony, J H *161*
Galleria Vittorio Emanuele, Milan 391, *471*
Gardiner, Stephen 281, 324, 335, 421
Gensler, M Arthur, Associates 455
geodesic domes 239, *532*, 533, 534, *545*, 546
German Car Centre, Milton Keynes *128-9*, 140, 362-5, 496
Gibbons, Bob 526
Giovannini, Joseph 196, 415
Glancey, Jonathan 287, 307, 322, 387, 388, 473, 512

glass 232
  frameless glazing 517
  fritted 442
  steel mullion system 342, *354, 355*
  walls 123, 157, 161-2, 164, 167, *199*, 230, 307-8, 312-31, *327*, 335, 342, 351-5, *439*, 455, 463
glass skyscraper project 289, *313*
*Glasarchitektur* 313
gliders 451, *452-3*, 486-7
Gluck, Peter 19
Goddard, Diana *239*
Goldsmith, Selwyn 268
Gomera Regional Planning Study, Canary Islands 10, 126, 149, 175, 180-91, *280*, 281
Gowan, James 22, 23
Graf Zeppelin airship *380, 386, 394*
grain silos 550, *551*
Granada Entertainment Centre, Milton Keynes 490-1
Gray, Ilse 361
Great Court, British Museum, London 10, 177, *470, 471*, 477
Greater London Council 351, 473
Greene, David *459*
Gregotti, Vittorio 394
Gresley, Sir Nigel 388, *389*
Gropius, Walter 19, 23, 30, 89, 267
*The Guardian* 362
Guedes, Pedro 185, 187, 189
Gwathmey, Charles 19

**H**ACTL Superterminal, Hong Kong *292*
Ham Common Flats, Richmond 22, 23
Hammersmith Centre, London 10, 281, 286, 459, 466-79, 490, 534, 541
Hampstead Hill Gardens flat, London *93*, 94
Hanle, Euggen 487
Hanon, Bernard 520, 525
Hanscomb Partnership 93
Harbour Exchange development, London 162
Harrier jump jet *519*
Harris, John *127*
Harvard University 19, 30
Hatton, Brian
  on Camden Mews 35-7
  on Cockpit 41
  on Creek Vean House 50-5
  on Forest Road Annexe 90-1
  on Henrion studio 35
  on Murray Mews 71
  on Skybreak House 83-7
  on Waterfront Housing 67
Haward, Birkin 174, *175*, 176, 185, *186*, *187*, *188*, 198, 237, *241, 249, 267, 272*, 281, *314*, 400, *465, 471, 487, 488, 497, 541, 543*
Hawker Hurricane *42*
Hawker Siddeley Aviation 519
Hawkes, Dean 308
helicopters 426-7, *428*

Hellman, Louis 351
  cartoon 352, *353*
  on Palmerston Special School 271
  on Special Care Unit 267-8
Helmuth, Yamasaki & Leinweber 288
Henrion, F H K 35, *36*
Henrion Studio, London *34*, 35, *37*
Herron, Ron 459
Hertfordshire schools programme 197, 198
Hertzberger, Herman 200, *201*
  Centraal Beheer offices 200
High-Density Housing, Radlett 81, 88-9, 275
Hitchcock, Henry-Russell, *In the Nature of Materials* 116, *117*, 499, 502
Holborn Place, London *293*, 305
Hong Kong International Airport, Chek Lap Kok 10, *119*, 367, 368, *369*, 550
Hongkong and Shanghai Bank 200, *201*, 280, 283, *285*, 293, 450, *462*, 483
  articulation 473
  checklist for *284*
  cladding *462*, 469
  competition for 123, 287
  detailing 461
  and earlier projects 26, *28*, 281
  escalator atrium 263, *282*, 299, 307, 332
  and IBM 225
  prefabricated modules *201*, 277, 282, *285*
  raised floor 290
  and reinvention of tall building 124, 193
  sunscoop *121, 173*, 175, 545
  and Willis Faber & Dumas 299, 335
Hopkins, Michael 8-9, 10, 11, *116*, 117, *237, 241*, 251
Horden, Richard 286
Howe, George 19, 27
HSBC Headquarters, London *156*, 162
Hudson Institute 298, 338
Hughes, Robert 14, 222, 501
Hunstanton School, Norfolk *103*, 121
Hunt, Tony 8-9, 10, *35, 42, 92*, 92-4, 105, *116, 117, 141, 423*
  and Bean Hill Housing 276, 278
  on Bedford Street Studio 123
  on Creek Vean 51
  Peter Cook on 458
  and IBM Pilot Head Office 123, 222
  and Reliance Controls 103, 109, 111
  and Sainsbury Centre 383, 400, 424
  and Willis Faber & Dumas 319, 341
Huntington Beach Power Station, California 457, *459*
Hutter, Wolfgang 487
Huxtable, Ada Louise, *The Troubled State of Modern Architecture* 324

**I**BM
  Installation Support Centre (ISC) 247-51,
  262-3
  Pilot Head Office, Cosham 10, 95, 96, 97,
  105, 108, 123, 124, 125, 128, 131, 134, 140,
  157, 162, 172, 192, 195, 198, 198-9, 200, 209,
  211, 214-33, 235, 236, 246, 260, 280, 281,
  283, 290, 299, 302, 308, 335, 351, 354, 375,
  383, 422, 455
  Technical Park, Greenford 128, 129, 131,
  140, 200, 243-65, 363, 364, 496, 499, 507
  United Kingdom Distribution Centre
  (UKDC) 247-9, 252, 254-7, 259, 261, 262
Imperial War Museum, Duxford 38
Impington Village College 267
*The Independent* 444, 446, 459
*The Independent on Sunday* 120
*Industrial Buildings: A Client's Guide* 167,
222, 503
Industrial Construction Finance Corporation
(ICFC) 211
industrial estates 145
inflatable structures 124, 146, 147, 204-7, 247
Inner London Education Authority 268
*International Architect* 334, 467
International Energy Expo 82, Knoxville 475,
534, 537, 542-3
Ipswich
  Unitarian Meeting House 305, 307, 320,
  327, 340
  see also Willis Faber & Dumas

**J**acobsen, Arne 118
Jacoby, Helmut 274-5, 277, 354, 355, 365
Jaffé family 83, 87
Jeffries, John 452
Jencks, Charles
  on IBM Pilot Head Office  231, 232
  NF on 288
  on Olsen Amenity Centre 163
  and Pruitt Igoe 288
  on Reliance Controls 109
  on Renault Distribution Centre 516
  on Sainsbury Centre 387, 408, 417
Jenkins, David 4, 11
  on Bean Hill Housing 275-8
  on Country Offices 173-5
  on Crescent Wing 435, 446
  on Factory Systems 138-143
  on Fred Olsen Amenity Centre 150-62
  on Fred Olsen Passenger Terminal 166-71
  on German Car Centre 363-4
  on High-Density Housing 89
  on Modern Art Glass 351-5
  on Orange Hand Shops 361
  on Sapa 347
  on Shopping and Leisure Centres 356-8
  on Son Recreation Centre 176-7
  on Wates Housing 77-81
Jersey, Harbours & Airport Committee 465
Jewett Arts Centre, Massachusetts 19
Jocou, Pierre 529

Johnson, Ben 232, 288, 333, 513, 520
  *Cross-Bracing* 114
  *Dock Reflections* 163
  *East Mast* 517
  *Neoprene Gasket Supporting Curtain Wall
  Reflection* 232
  screenprint of Sainsbury Centre 408
  Willis Faber building, paintings of 330
Johnson, Philip 19, 22, 27, 29, 418
  Yale University, Kline Science Center 27
Johnson Wax building, Wisconsin 116, 117,
499, 502
Joseph Shop, London 280, 480-1
Judd, Donald 90, 91
  *Untitled* 91

**K**ahn, Herman 298, 338
Kahn, Louis 18-28, 29, 35, 78, 80, 201
  Richards Medical Research
  Laboratories 29
  Philadelphia Midtown Development 78, 80
  Yale University Art Gallery 20, 22, 24, 25
Kaplicky, Jan 539
Kasbah, Morocco 406
Katsuro Imperial Villa, Kyoto 485
Kawana House, Japan 368
Kemp, Martin 545
Kettle's Yard, Cambridge 55, 62
Kew Gardens, Surrey, Palm House 391
Kho Lang Ie 286, 366, 367, 376, 382
Kiln Farm, Milton Keynes 142, 143
Kingo Housing, Denmark 183
King's Cross masterplan, London 281, 286,
287, 288, 289
Kinross, Robin 36
Knight, Kenneth 299, 302, 308, 319, 335
Koenig, Pierre 111, 121, 415
  Case Study House #22 30, 111
Krier, Leon 417, 471
Kroto, Dr Harry 553
Kubrick, Stanley 87
Kuch, Mickey 122, 237

**L**a Selle, Sébastien de 287, 496, 530
La Tourette, Lyons 53
Lafayette Park, Detroit 81
Lambot, Ian 114, 185, 186
  on Climatroffice 541
  on Fred Olsen Travel Agency 179
  on Masterplan for St Helier Harbour 465
  on Sainsbury Centre for Visual Arts
  374-419
Larsen, Henning 19
Larson, Theodore 549
Las Vegas 103
Lasdun, Denys 251, 378, 443
  University of East Anglia 383, 386, 434
Le Corbusier (C E Jeanneret) 291
  in 1950s 234
  and Atelier 5 119
  Reyner Banham on 91, 236, 458, 462
  Chandigarh, High Court Building 26, 387
  and Louis Kahn 22

La Tourette 53
Maisons Jaoul 463
and NF at Yale 18, 27
NF on 505
quoted 55, 67
and Paul Rudolph 26
and Vincent Scully 20
and James Stirling 23
Villa Savoye 120, 291, 421
*Vers une architecture* 116, 117
Leeds Corn Exchange 306
Levenson, Bob 365
Libelle sailplane 487
*The Listener* 281, 324, 421
*Liverpool Echo* 273
Llewellyn, Walter 276
Lloyd, H M 161
Lockheed Constellation 458
London Bridge City offices 195
London Docklands Development Corporation
162, 165, 281
London Gliding Club, Dunstable Downs 486-7
London and North Eastern Railway (LNER)
388, 389
London Regeneration Consortium 287
London Transport 281, 467, 473
London Underground, Jubilee Line 157, 162
Long, M J 19, 22
Loos, Adolf 411
Lord's Hill Centre, Derby 356-9
Los Angeles 454, 491
  Bradbury Building 307, 391
  see also Case Study Houses
Louisiana Museum of Modern Art 379
Lowry, L S, *VE Day Celebrations* 118
Lubetkin, Berthold 126
Lyall, Sutherland 390
  Reyner Banham on 459
  comparing Eames house and Reliance
  Controls 106
  quoting Walter Gropius 89
  on prefabrication 276
  on Renault Distribution Centre 500,
  508, 513
  on Sainsbury Centre 408, 411
  *The State of British Architecture* 106
Lynton, Norbert 53
Lyons, William 388

**M**cCullough, David 21
McHarg, Ian, *Design with Nature* 183
McKean, John 304, 395
McKillop, Andrew 236
Mackintosh, Charles Rennie 53
Macmillan, Rt. Hon. Harold 329
*The Mail on Sunday* 331
Maison de Verre, Paris 481, 485
Maisons Jaoul, Paris 463
Malby, Clyde 239

Manchester 118
  Barton Arcade 117, 119, 521
  Daily Express building 117
  Lancaster Arcade 117, 119
  School of Art 117
  Town Hall 117, 119
Manchester University, School of Architecture
12, 13, 14, 18, 24, 110, 117-18, 533
Manning, Martin 507
*Manplan 3* 138, 139, 141, 142, 143
Manser, Jose 167
Manss, Thomas 11
Manufacture des Tabacs, Marseilles 168
Marks, Robert 533
Martell, Pepe 185
Martin, Sir Leslie and March, Lionel 468
Mason, Roy 24, 25
Masterplan for St Helier Harbour, Jersey 280,
464-5
Maxwell, Robert 258, 352, 417
May, Ernst 289
Mellanby, Professor Kenneth 185, 186-7
Meller, James 8-9, 10, 116, 117, 548
Melnikov, Konstantin 52
Mendelsohn, Erich 30
Mengoni, Giuseppe, Milan, Galleria Vittorio
Emanuele 391, 471
Merrick, Jay 459
Microelectronic Centre, Duisburg 105, 554
Mies van der Rohe, Ludwig 22, 26
  Farnsworth House 291
  glass skyscraper projects 289, 313
  Lafayette Park 81
  'less is more' 308
  New National Gallery 378
  and Fred Olsen projects 198
  and Reliance Controls 105
  and Sainsbury Centre 408
Millard House, California 54
Miller, Herman 234, 241, 477
Miller, Joe 489
Miller, John 54
Milton Keynes 141-2, 275, 454, 490-1
  Bean Hill Housing 274-9
  Factory Systems 138-43
  German Car Centre 140, 362-5, 496
  Kiln Farm 142, 143
  Olivetti headquarters 363, 364
  Unit P70 142
Ministry of Public Buildings and Works 125
Mitchell, Reginald J 388
Modern Art Glass, Thamesmead 161, 199, 273,
317, 324, 342, 350-5, 383, 397, 418, 454, 455
Modern Movement 102, 114, 124, 196, 234, 313
Modesti, Orlando 185
Modulor system 554
*Monografias de Architectura y Vivienda* 351
Moore, Charles 22
Moore, Henry 52, 366, 374, 376, 377
Morley, David 477
Morris, Henry 267
Morteo, Enrico 438
Moulton, Alex 460

Moulton bicycle 460
MPC & Associates 357, 358
Murata, Yakuta, Fuji Group pavilion, Osaka World's Fair 205
Murray Mews Houses, London 35, 37, 70-5, 121
MUST (Medical Unit, Self-contained Transportable) 146, *147*
Muuratsalo Summer House *72*

**N**airn, Ian 104
NASA 16
   space shuttle *287*
National Botanic Gardens of Wales, Great Glasshouse 10, 38, *39*, *120*, *176*, *177*, 181
Nelson, David 11, *194*, 402, 457, *477*
Neuhart, John and Marilyn *414*, 415
Neutra, Richard 30
*New Statesman* 24
*New Society*
   Air structures 125, 205
   Airstream caravan 398
   Sainsbury Centre 390, 408, 411, 413
   Willis Faber & Dumas 318, 324
New York
   Rockefeller Plaza 468
   Whitney Museum of Art *472*
   Metropolitan Museum of Art 434, *444*
Newby, Frank 125
Newport School competition 10, 96, *97*, 118, 122, *128*, 130-7, *139*, 140, *197*, 198, *200*, 221, *230*, 246, 263, 271, *281*
Nicholson, Ben 52, *53*, 62
   *Pill Creek by Moonlight* 52
Nîmes, Carré d'Art 195
Nomos table 460, *461*, *528*, *529*
'Norman Foster: architecture is about people' (exhibition) 43
'The Norman Foster Studio – Exploring the City' (exhibition) *442*, *443*
Norwich Cathedral 451

**O**bserver 212
Olivetti headquarters, Milton Keynes 363, *364*
Olsen, Fred 10, 11, 85, 95, 116, 120, 123, 126, 154-5, 157, *161*, 173, 177, 181, 185, 422, 423
Olsen, Fred, Ltd
   Amenity Centre, Millwall Dock 95, *122*, 122-3, 124, *128*, 131, 149-65, *167*, 171, 172, 181, *198*, 218, 221, 225, 260, *281*, *283*, 299, 302, 335, 351, 354, 375, 422, *423*, 429
   Fred Olsen Lines (travel agency) 178-9
   Offices, Oslo 176-7
   Passenger Terminal, Millwall Dock 166-71, 181, 190, 198, 282, *423*
   projects and masterplanning for 149, 198, 281
   and Renault Centre 496, 497
   Son Recreation Centre and Oslo offices 38, 176-7
   Vestby Country Offices 10, *85*, 120, 121, 172-5, 176, 181, 183, 185, 502, 545
Omni Center, Atlanta (later CNN Center) 473

Open House, Cwmbran 488-9
Orange Hand shops 360-1
Osaka World's Fair
   Fuji Group pavilion *205*
   USA pavilion *474*
Ostler, Tim
   on Granada Entertainment Centre 490-1
   on Hammersmith Centre 466-73
   on Open House 488-9
   on Renault Distribution Centre 496-520
Otto, Frei 19
Overy, Paul 522

**P**acific Locomotive *389*
Padovan, Richard 334, 467
Palmer House, Michigan 53
Palmerston Special School, Liverpool 126, 270-3, 503
Paragon Research and Development Centre, Woking 292
Paul-Huhne, Peter 197
Pavilion Shopping and Leisure Centres
   Badhoevedorp 128, *129*, 356-9
   Knowsley 356-9
Pawley, Martin
   'Richard Buckminster Fuller' 532-4
   'The Years of Innovation' 280-91
   on air structures 124
   on Autonomous House 545-7
   on 'big sheds' 351
   on Buckminster Fuller 484, 553
   comparing Creek Vean and Corsica House 59
   on IBM Technical Park 260
   on International Energy Expo 543
   quoting NF on Renault Distribution Centre 506
   on Fred Olsen 159
   on Reliance Controls 104
   on Renault Distribution Centre 515, 519, 530
   on Samuel Beckett Theatre 539
Paxton, Sir Joseph 193, 231, 395, 548
   Crystal Palace *193*, *223*, *395*
Paz, Octavio 549
Peacock, Frank 35, *237*, *241*, 423
Pearman, Hugh 419
Pennsylvania, University of 18, 21
   Richards Medical Research Laboratories 29
Periton, Diana 481
Perret, Auguste 55
*Perspecta* 22, 23
Petronas University, Malaysia 183
Phelps-Dodge 484
Philadelphia, Midtown Development 78, *80*
Phillips, Archie 240
Phillips, Graham 11, 239, 248, 251, 261, 437, 438, *447*
Phillips, Maurice 35, *423*
Piano, Renzo 457
Pilkington Glass *199*, 213, 239, 282, 317, 342, 355, 517
Piller, Louis 240

Pirsig, Robert M 145
Pitco T-wall system *259*, 351
Pittsburgh Plate Glass 161, *162*, 164
Planar system *354*
Plug-in City *459*
Pompidou Centre, Paris 286, 417, 457, *459*
Porsche, Ferdinand 283, 291
Porter aircraft *512*
Powell, Kenneth 50, 52, 63
   on Crescent Wing 434-43
prefabricated components 89, 276-7, 285, 289, *394*, 484, 500, 507, *512*, 533
Price, Cedric 131, 133, 192, 196, 450, 458, 459
Pritzker Prize 21
*Progressive Architecture* 411, 418
Prouvé, Jean 168, 171, 395, 554
   Manufacture des Tabacs *168*
Pruitt Igoe housing project, St Louis 288

**Q**uantrill, Malcolm 28, 35, 73, 93, 94, 177, 302, 332, 359, 402, 425, 429, 438, 457
Quick-Build system 276

**R**astorfer, Darl 258
Read, Sir Herbert 50, 119
Read, Sophie 119
Regent Street Polytechnic 119
Reichstag, Berlin 10, 121, 175, 177, *194*, 195, *441*, *443*, 537, 545, *546*, *547*, 552, *553*, 554
Reliance Controls Electronics Factory, Swindon 96, 73, *94*, 96-115, 121-2, 124, 151, *197*, *200*, 282, *422*, *423*
   and 1980s projects 200
   American influence on 118
   cladding *73*, 105, 515
   and Charles Eames 106
   and Financial Times Award 94, 122, 280
   Fuller's influence on 533
   as high-tech building 456, 459
   and IBM Cosham 221, *222*, 225
   and IBM Greenford 260, 263
   innovation in 119
   minimalism of 105
   and Newport School *136*
   and Olsen Amenity Centre 161, 165, 167, 170, 171
   and Renault Centre 493, 497
   and Paul Rudolph 26
   and Sapa Factory 347
   use of glass in 73
Renault, Louis 497
Renault Distribution Centre, Swindon *97*, 287, 288-90, *368-9*, 492-531
   Reyner Banham on 461
   as 'cathedral' 520, 525
   cladding 514
   colour 461, *462*, 516, 517, 522, 530-1
   functional expressionism 483, 500
   furniture systems 528-9
   and German Car Centre 363, *364*
   and Modern Art Glass 353
   NF on 221, 287
   official opening 527

   open day 526
   roofscape 513
   and Stansted Airport *192*, *193*, 281
   and umbrella structures 221, 281, 282, 499, 516
   warehouse 524, 525
Renault France 496, 497
   Renault logo 520, *523*
Repton, Humphry 420
Reynolds, R S, Memorial Award Citation 325
RIBA
   advice to Willis Faber 299
   awards 12, 16, 117, 120, 234, 280, 312, 419, 532, 545, 548
   Drawings Collection 127
   seminar on repair of post-war buildings 278
   Stockholm Conference 236
*RIBA Journal* 234-5
   NF on Air-Supported Office 207
   NF on Alvar Aalto 72, 121, 379
   NF on Computer Technology 211
   NF on Newport School 132
   NF on Sainsbury Centre 391
   Willis Faber & Dumas 308, 332
Rice, Peter 458
Richards, J M 12
   *The Functional Tradition* 15
Richardson, Henry Hobson 21
Ritchie, Ian *241*, 358
Riverside Three, London 10, *257*
Robinson, Kenneth 467, 473
Rock, Tim 139
Rockware Glass 246, 250
Roehampton Estate, London 119
Rogers, Richard 35, 121, 458
   Reyner Banham on 450, 457
   and break-up of Team 4 94, 280
   and Cockpit 41
   and Creek Vean 51, 52
   Ezra Ehrenkrantz and 457
   Lloyd's building 199
   Pompidou Centre 457, *459*
   quoted 51, 71, 423
   and Skybreak House 87
   and Team 4 31, *35*, 119, 422, *423*
   and Wates Housing 77
   at Yale with NF 10, *19*, 24, *25*, 27, 30, 118
   *see also* Team 4
Rogers, Su 24, 26, *35*, 54, 119, *423*
Ronan Point tower blocks, London *144*, 145
Roscoe, Johnny 302, 422-3
Royal Academy Sackler Galleries, London *177*, *441*, *443*
Royal Air Force 117
Royal Crescent, Bath *144*, 145
Rudofsky, Bernard, *Architecture without Architects* *172*, *173*, 183
Rudolph, Paul 11, 19-20, *20*, 23, 25-30, 35, 118
   Blue Cross-Blue Shield building 26, *28*
   Jewett Arts Centre 19
   Yale University Art and Architecture Building *20*, *26*, 30
Rufford Old Hall, Lancashire *12*, *13*

**S**aarinen, Eero 19, 21, 24, 107
Sackler Gallery, Museum of Israel, Jerusalem 39
Sadao, Shoji 543
Sainsbury Centre for Visual Arts, University of East Anglia, Norwich 96, 281, 282, *286*, 289, 291, 366-7, *368*, 370-421, 423-5, *450*, *458*
　akin to aircraft 387, 388, 394, 454
　cladding 388, 396-7, 469
　commissioned 123, 161, 375, 381
　and Computer Technology 213
　Crescent Wing *39*, 413, 419, 431-49, 558
　and double-skin system 397-9
　as 'integrated enclosure' 10, 119, 192, 221
　louvres 398-9, 406, 408-9
　and Modern Art Glass 352, 353
　patterns of use 413
　re-cladding 418-19
　and Renault Centre 287, 500
　Reserve Study Centre 413, 444
　and Sapa Factory 347
　services 399, 483
　sheath structure 530
　as shed structure 395, 417, 420, 421, 451
　weight of building 550
Sainsbury, Sir Robert, quoted 376, 381, 403, 409, 420
Sainsbury, Sir Robert, and Lady 11, 123, 286, *366*, 366-7, *367*, 374-7, 390, *402*, *409*, 411, 422, 423, 425, 434-6, *436*, *439*, 444, *447*
Saint, Andrew, *Towards a Social Architecture* 196, 197
St Helier Harbour, Jersey 280, 464-5
St Louis Climatron 541
Sainz, Jorge 437, 531
Samuel Beckett Theatre, St Peter's College, Oxford 10, 93, 534, 538-9, 541, 548, 549
Sapa Factory, Tibshelf *128*, 346-9, 383
Säynätsalo Town Hall 50, *58*, 121
Scheerbart, Paul 313
Schnelle brothers 196
School Construction Systems Development (SCSD) 30, 103, 121, 122, *128*, *132*, 135, 136, 140, 196-7, 271, 456-7, *457*, 460
Schweikher, Paul 19, 27
Scientific Data Systems (SDS) building, California *107*, *348*
Scottish Foundries 141
Scully, Vincent 19, 20-1, *21*, 23, 26, 118
　*American Architecture and Urbanism* 21
　*The Earth, the Temple and the Gods* 21
Sellers, David 19
services
　location 269, 384, 386, 397, 398-9, 457, 517
　replacing or upgrading 388
　roof-mounted 213, 224, 225, 226
shed structures 192, 199, 347, 395, 417, 420, 421, 451, 454, 515, 531
shopping and leisure centres *128*, *129*, 356-9
Shuttleworth, Ken 11, 263, 429, 477
Siedlung Halen, near Berne 54, 68, *77*, 119
Simpson, Barbara 367
Skybreak House, Radlett 35, *38*, 50, 71, 81, 82-7, 89

Smalley, Dr Richard 553
Smith, Peter 332
Smithson, Alison and Peter 23, 103, 121, 250, 463
Snowdon, Lord 367
Snyder, Robert 543
SOM Chicago 256
Son Recreation Centre *39*, 176, 181
Sonzio, Livio 452
Soriano, Raphael 30, 415
Southern California Edison 457
Spaeth, David 81
Spastics Society 126, 267, 268, 271, 272
Special Care Unit, London 126, 266-9, 271
Spence, Sir Basil 118
　Sussex, University of 119
Stanford University, California 196, 457
Stansted Airport, Essex 10, 124, 128, *129*, *192*, *193*, 200, 281, 358-9, *359*, 367, *368*, *406*, 500, 507, *514*, *515*
Stanton, Alan 122
Stenkovic Camp, Skopje *549*
Stephens, Suzanne 411, 418
Stern, Robert A M
　'The Impact of Yale' 18-31
Stirling, James 19, *22*, 22-3
　Ham Common Flats *22*, 23
　'The Functional Tradition and Expression' 23
　Olivetti Headquarters 363, 364
　Staatsgalerie, Stuttgart 450
Street-Porter, Tim 10, 116, 117, 123, 159, 238
'Structures Gonflables' exhibition, Paris 125
Sudjic, Deyan 54
　on NF and influences 391, 395
　on Foster and Partners 443, 458
　on Hammersmith Centre 471
　on IBM Technical Park 256, 261
　on industrial estates 248
　on Olsen Amenity Centre 164, 165
　on Reliance Controls 165
　on Richard Rogers and Norman Foster 458
Sullivan, Louis 21
*Sunday Telegraph* 16
*The Sunday Times* 67, 213
sunscoop 85, 173, 175, 545
Supermarine Spitfire 388, *389*
Sutcliffe, Mark 106, 107, 121, *237*, *238*, 239
Sutton, Trevor *237*
*Swindon Evening Advertiser* 526
Swiss Re building, London 194, *293*, 537, 541, 551-2, *552*
Systems Building for Industry 141-2

**T**aut, Bruno 313
　Glass Pavilion *313*
Tavistock Institute 196
Taylor, Nicholas 67
Team 4 31, 34-94, 103, 105, 108, 118, 122, 151, 197, 275, 280, 422, *423*, 558
Tecno 528
Tecton 126
tensegrity structures 505, 533, 534, 537, 543

Thistlethwaite, Frank 382
Thompson, Mike 151, 154, 155, 161, 422-3
Thompson, Ventulett and Stainback 473
Tilling, Thomas 362-5
*Time* magazine 14, 222, 501
Tinkertoy model 415
tower blocks 144-5
Tower Place, London *293*, *305*
trailer parks *146*
Trist, Eric 196
Troughton, Jamie *239*

**U**mbrella structures 221, 281, 357, 358, 359, 363, 497, 499, 500, 509, 510, 516
Uni-Dome, Iowa *474*
Unit P70, Milton Keynes 142
Unité d'Habitation, Marseilles 333
United Automobile, Detroit 141
United Nations, *Global Environment Outlook 2000* 548
University Grants Commission 375
urban room 367, 477
Utzon, Jørn 118, 183
　Kingo Housing 183

**V**an Heyningen, Joanna *239*
Varley, Eric 349
Venturi, Robert 22
　*Complexity and Contradiction in Architecture* 102, 103
Vickers, Graham 131, 256
　on Air-Supported Office 205-6
　on Computer Technology 209-13
　on IBM Pilot Head Office 218-28
　on IBM Technical Park 246-63
　on London Gliding Club 487
　on Newport School 130-7
　on Sainsbury Centre for Visual Arts 374-419
　on Willis Faber & Dumas 299-335
*A View to a Kill* 524
Villa Savoye, Poissy 120, 291, 421
Viollet-le-Duc, Eugène 520
Volkswagen Beetle *291*
Vulcan bomber 451, *453*

**W**achsmann, Konrad 358, 395
　*The Turning Point of Building* 358
Walker, Derek 142, 143, 275, 278, 363, 364
Walker, Hilary 93, 94
Walker, John 8-9, 10, *92*, 105, *116*, 117
　'The Early Years' 92-5
Wallace, John 155
Warnecke, John Carl 30
Warner, Francis 539
Warner, Tony 445
Warren, John 545
Waterfront Housing, Feock *38*, 66-9, 73, 77, 83, 183
Waterhouse, Alfred 119
　Manchester Town Hall 119
Wates Housing, Coulsdon 76-81, 89
Webb, Michael 459

Wellesley College, Jewett Arts Center 19
Wharton, Jenny *240*
Wharton, John *239*
Williams, Owen 117
　Daily Express building 117, 312
Williams, Stephanie 201
Willis Faber & Dumas, Ipswich 10, 105, 117, 123, 126, *137*, 157, 192, 193, 199, 200, 225, 231, 238, 239, 263, 281, 282, *283*, 285, 286-91, *291*, *292*, 294-337, 375, 401, 422, 455
　and Climatroffice project *290*, 541
　escalator atrium *282*, 306-7, 310, 328, 332, 335, 338, 339, 462, 541
　glass walls 313-31, 327, 335, *354*, *355*, 418, *463*
　and Hammersmith project *468*, *470*
　listed Grade I 443
　and Newport School *137*
　postage stamp featuring 325
　and Renault Centre 496, 497, 499, 500
　roof garden 333, 334, 335, 343, 462, *463*, 554
　swimming pool 298, 300, 305, 310, 320, 330, 331, 343
Wilson, Colin St. John 19, 23
wind turbines 16-17
Winter, John 199, 256, 352
WKBW Television, Buffalo, New York 455
Woods, Shadrach 19
Woodward, Christopher 247, 250, 253, 259, 260, 263, 304, 318
World Expo, Montreal (1967), US pavilion 533, 541
Wright, Frank Lloyd 18, 21, 23, 27, 53, 54, 55, 121, 291, 460
　Fallingwater 291
　Johnson Wax building 116, *117*, 499, *502*
　Millard House 54
　Palmer House 53
Wright, Lance 224
Wright, Terry 209

**Y**ale University 10, 11, *19*, 18-31, 35, 54, 79, 118, 131, 415, 533
　Art and Architecture Building *20*, 26
　Art Gallery 20, 22, *24*, 24, 25
　Gibbs Physics Laboratory 27
　Kline Science Center 27
　Pierson Sage Science Laboratories 27, 30

**Z**eppelin 380, 386, 394
zoning 271

# Credits

Photographs:
Aerofilms: 104(1), 156, 246(7), 250, 498
Arcaid/©Richard Bryant: 59 top (r), 64-65, 325(5), 387(2), 409(1), 410-411(2), 424(1), 477 top, 481 top (l,r), 524(2), 526-527(1), 529(4-6)
Arcaid/©Richard Einzig: 48-49, 50 top, 58(1-2), 59(3-5) top, 62(2), 63(4-6), 67 top, 82, 85(4-5), 86(1-3), 120(2), 134 top (r), 137 top (l), 152-153, 179(2), 223(4), 229 top (l,r), 230(2), 232-233, 234(1), 235(3), 283(4), 321(3), 455(2), 482(1), 485(5)
Architectural Association Photo Library/©Valerie Bennett: 235(2)
Architectural Association Photo Library/©M Handman: 119 top (r)
Architectural Design: 133 top (l,r), 237 top, 416 top
*Architects' Journal*: 236 top (l,r), 236(1-2)
*Architects' Journal*/PA Photos: 144(1)
*Architects' Journal*/de Burgh Galwey: 235 top
*Architects' Journal*/John R. Pantlin: 197 top
The Architectural Press, London: 15 top (l,r), 106 top (l,r)
*Architectural Review*: 138 top, 139 top (l,r), 142 top (l,r), 145(3), 239 top, 318 top, 512 top (m,r)
Arup: 512(1-2)
Courtesy of Atelier 5 (photo: Balthasar Burkhard): 77 top
Drawings and Archives, Avery Architectural and Fine Arts Library, Columbia University: 28 top (l)
©Hugh Ballantyne: 389 top (l)
©Evan Blandford/Studio St. Ives (photo: Tate Gallery Archive): 53 top (l)
*Bauen+Wohnen*: 328 top
Bauhaus Archiv, Berlin ©DACS 2002: 313 top (l)
BBC, photo: Chris Chapstick: 384 top (l)
Bechtel Corporation: 459(3)
©Bill Bernbach: 365 top (l,r)
Bildarchiv Foto Marburg: 313 top (r)
©2000 Boeing Management Company All Rights Reserved: 170 top
Clive Boursnell: 439(3)
*Building Bulletin*: 196 top (r)
The Burton Group: 361 top (r)
Geremy Butler: 127(2)
Butler Manufacturing Co: 551 top (r)
Camera Craft: 40(1)
Camera Press photograph by Snowdon: 366(1), 367(2)
©Gus Coral: 204(1)
Corbis/©John H Clark: 519 top
Corbis/©Howard Davies: 549(2)
Corbis/©George Hall: 538 top
Corbis/©Nic Wheeler: 473 top
Corbis/©Michael S Yamashita: 146(1), 335 top

©Richard Davies: 244-245, 249(3), 262(3), 263(5), 281 top, 287(2), 289(2), 385(5-6), 399 top (l), 407 top (l), 427(2), 437(4), 439(2), 446-447(3), 461(2-3), 462(1), 465 top, 471(6), 476(1), 477(4), 484(4), 491(2), 494-495, 503(6), 507(3), 518(2), 519(5), 521(2-5), 524(1), 528(1-2), 529(7), 530-531, 546-547(1), 547(2), 556-557
*Design*: 124 top
*Domus*: 348 top
©John Donat: 37 top (r), 41(3), 70, 73(3), 74(1-3), 75(4), 84 top, 142(1), 143 top, 143(2-3), 174(2), 175(6), 206 top (l-r), 207(1-3), 247(10-12), 270(1-2), 271(4-5), 272(2), 273 top (r), 273(4), 278 top, 279(1-3), 282(1), 286(1), 291(2), 308(1-3), 309 top, 309(5), 318(1), 324(1-2), 330, 332(1), 333(4), 334(2), 338(1), 340(1), 343(2), 344-345, 346, 348-349(2-6), 349 top (l,r), 376(1), 377(6), 382, 382(1-2), 409 top (r), 412 top, 435, 450(1), 463(2), 502(3), 525(3)
John Donat, ©Succession Picasso/DACS 2002: 376(2)
John Donat, ©Estate of Francis Bacon, All Rights Reserved, DACS 2002: 376(3)
John Donat, reproduced by permission of the Henry Moore Foundation: 377(4-5)
Doubleday, New York: 79 top (l,r), 172 top (l,r)
Duell, Sloan and Pearce, New York: 117 top (l)
©2000 Lucia Eames/ Eames Office (www.eamesoffice.com): 196 top (l), 414 top (l)
East Anglian Daily Times/Evening Star, Ipswich: 312(7), 313(10), 315 top
*Eastern Counties Newspaper*: 367 top
©Enercon: 17 top (l)
Esto/©Ezra Stoller, All Rights Reserved: 43(3-4), 44-45, 62(1,3), 120(1)
Esto/©Wayne Andrews, All Rights Reserved: 307 top
Mary Evans Picture Library: 193 top
Fondation le Corbusier ©FLC/ADAGP, Paris and DACS, London 2002: 117 top (r), 463 top
Norman Foster: 16 top (l), 23 top, 28(2), 29(5), 31 top (l,r), 62 top, 69(4), 73 top, 90(2-3), 91(4), 93 top, 94(1), 100-101, 109(3), 111 top (l), 112-113(1), 113(3), 115(1), 119 top (l,m), 121 top (l,m), 123 top, 180(1-2), 181 top, 181(3-5), 183 top, 184 top (r), 188 top, 190 top (l-r), 334 top, 357 top, 378 top, 379 top (l,r), 391 top, 406 top, 422(1), 444 top, 471 top, 483 top, 484(2-3), 485 top (l,r), 504 top, 505 top, 521 top (l,r), 522(1), 538(2), 539 top, 544(2), 545(3), 548(1), 554 top (l,r)

Foster and Partners: 25(2), 30 top, 32-33, 34(1), 35 top, 37 top (l), 51 top, 71 top, 77(1), 81 top, 86 top, 89 top, 102 top (l,r), 108(1), 113 top, 113(2), 115 top, 132, 135(5-7), 140 top (l,r), 165 top, 173(3), 182 top, 184 top (l), 198 top, 208, 209 top, 209(2), 223 top (l,r), 276 top, 279 top, 285 top (l), 287 top (l,r), 291 top, 298(1-2), 299 top (l,r), 307(5), 323 top, 351(2), 358(1), 363 top, 394-395(1, 3-7, 10), 396 top, 397 top (l), 397(3), 398 top (l), 402 top, 409 top (l), 423 top, 436 top, 439 top, 447 top (l,r), 452 top, 453 top (r), 456(1), 465(7-8), 466(2), 467 top, 467(3-5), 468-469(1-6), 487 top (l), 488(1), 501 top, 512(3-5), 513(6-9), 515 top, 518 top (l), 520 top (l,r), 542(3), 553 top
Foster Visualisation: 135 top, 174 top, 552(3)
The Flight Collection: 125 top, 384 top (r)
Courtesy the Estate of Buckminster Fuller, Sebastopol, CA: 484 top (r)
R. Buckminster Fuller Papers, M1090, Dept. of Special Collections, Stanford University Libraries, Stanford, California: 533(2-3), 534(1), 542 top, 545 top, 551 top (l,m)
©Geoffrey Gale: 162 top
Courtesy Galerie Patrick Seguin ©photo Marc Domage: 168 top
©Dennis Gilbert: 177 top, 193(2), 194(2), 359 top, 441 top (l,r), 444(2-3), 446(1-2), 448-449, 550(1)
Courtesy Arthur Gensler Associates (photo: Jeff Heller): 455 top
©Getmapping.com plc: 220, 304, 440
Getty Images – Stone: 518 top (r)
Handford Photography: 150, 151 top
Courtesy of Marion Henrion: 36 top (l)
Courtesy Architectuurstudio Herman Hertzberger, photo ©Willem Diepraam: 200 top
Hulton Archive: 395 top
Alan Howard: 314(2), 394-395(2,8-9), 396(1)
Pat Hunt: 210(1), 211(2)
©Alastair Hunter: 516, 527(2)
Imperial War Museum, London (A18473): 195 top
©Ben Johnson: 513 top, 517 top (l)
Jewish Museum, New York 'Primary Structures' April 27 – June 12 1966. Installation by Donald Judd, Untitled, 1966. Pasadena Art Museum, Pasadena California. Photo ©The Jewish Museum, New York. Art ©Donald Judd Foundation/VAGA, New York/DACS, London 2002: 91 top

©Ken Kirkwood: 108 top (r), 124(1), 216-217, 231(3), 256(1-2), 257 top (l), 257(6-8), 258(1,4), 259 top, 259(7), 260(1), 261(2-3), 264-265, 309(4), 322 top, 324(4), 329(3), 331(1), 332(2), 372-373, 379(3), 385 top (l), 386 top (r), 398(1-3), 399(4), 402(2), 403(4-6), 404-405, 406(2), 409(4), 410(1), 412(1-3,5), 413(6-8), 414(1-2), 415(3-6), 416(1), 417(2-3), 419 top, 427(4), 458(1), 480(1), 481(5), 506 top, 527 top, 528 top (l), 528(3)
©Balthazar Korab Ltd: 29 top, 502 top
©Ian Lambot: 28 top (r), 121 top (r), 173 top, 282(2), 285(2), 462 top
LAT Photographic: 399 top (r)
Jonathan Cape, London: 550 top
Heiko Lucas: 439(4)
Donald Luckenbill: 20(2)
Archive of the Luftschiffbau Zeppelin GmbH Friedrichshafen: 380 top (r), 386 top (l), 394 top
Simon Lyons Architects: 306 top
©Rudi Meisel: 194 top (l,r), 333(5), 429(1), 553(4)
MGM Clip and Still, A View to a Kill ©Danjaq, LLC and United Artists Corporation. All Rights Reserved: 524 top (r)
Alex Moulton Bicycles: 460 top (l,r)
Missouri Historical Society, St. Louis (Photo: Richard Moore): 288 top
Museum of Finnish Architecture/©G. Welin: 72 top
NASA: 182
NASA/Science Photo Library: 461 top (r)
National Archives and Records Administration (111-SC-640458&111-SC-640463): 147(2-3)
National Trust Photographic Library/©Matthew Antrobus: 13 top
John Nye: 201 top (r), 285 top (r),
Fred Olsen Ltd: 179 top
©Aidan O'Rourke: 312 top
©Mike Page: 333 top
©Eric Palmer: 333 top (l)
Frederick R Praeger, New York & Washington: 21 top (l)
Photo courtesy QinetiQ Ltd.: 380 top (l)
©Marvin Rand: 107 top
Reinhold: 358 top
Renault UK, Ltd: 497 top (l,r), 523 top (l-r)
RIBA Publications: 127 top
RIBA Library Photographs Collection: 30(1), 532(1)
©Simo Rista: 58 top
Su Rogers: 19(3)
The Royal Air Force Museum, Hendon: 389 (r), 453 top (l)
The Royal Mail: 325 top
Trustees of the Paul Rudolf Estate: 20 top, 20(1)

Sainsbury Centre for Visual Arts: 410 top (m,r), 442 top, 451 top
Sainsbury Centre for Visual Arts, ©Estate of Francis Bacon. All Rights Reserved, DACS 2002: 410 top (l)
Robert and Lisa Sainsbury Collection, University of East Anglia/James Austin: 374(1-2), 375 top (l-r), 375(3-4), 403 top (l-r)
Robert and Lisa Sainsbury Collection, University of East Anglia/James Austin, ©Estate of Francis Bacon 2002. All Rights Reserved, DACS: 374 top (l,r)
©Phil Sayer: 535(2)
©Sealand Aerial Photography: 144(2), 275 top, 514-515(1-4)
Courtesy of Jochen Seigemund, University of Applied Sciences, Cologne: 43 top
©Julius Shulman: 111 top (r), 414 top (r), 415 top
Simon Lyons Architects: 306 top
Courtesy of John Warren ©Jaime Snyder: 545(4)
Courtesy of Mary Stirling: 22(1)
Tim Street Porter: 8-9, 54 top, 87(4-5), 92(1), 116(1), 122(1), 123(2), 125(2), 126(1), 147 top, 158-159(1-8), 160 top, 160(3), 161 top, 161(4), 162(3), 163(4), 164-165, 166(1), 167 top, 168(1-2), 169(3,5-6), 170(1-2), 171(3-5), 178, 179(1), 199(3), 212 top, 212(1-2), 213(3), 228(1), 229(4-5), 230(1), 238(1), 239(2-6), 240 top, 240(1-6), 241(7-12), 266(1), 267(4-5), 268 top, 268(2), 269(3-5), 273 top (l), 283(3), 317 top (r), 329 top (l,r), 334(1,3), 335(4-6), 350, 352(1), 353(4), 354(1), 355 top (r), 355(3-4), 360(1), 361 top (l), 361(3,7), 423(3), 425(2), 454(1), 460(1), 468 top (r), 491 top, 549 top
©Peter Strobel: 461 top (m), 528 top (r), 529 top (l-r)
V&A Picture Library: 36 top (r)
Jocelyne van den Bossche: 324(3)
The Board of Trustees of the Victoria and Albert Museum ©Angela Verren-Taunt 2002 All Rights Reserved, DACS: 53 top (r)
©Angela Verren-Taunt 2002 All Rights Reserved, DACS: 52 top
VIEW/©Peter Cook: 445(4)
VIEW/©Grant Smith: 459(2)
©Morley von Sternberg: 269 top (l)
A Clockwork Orange ©1971 Warner Bros. Inc. and Polaris Productions, Inc. All Rights Reserved: 87 top (l,r)
©Jens Willebrand: 193(3)
Willis Faber/©W R Smith Ltd: 312-313(1-6), 312(8), 313(9,11)
Yale University/Michael Marsland: 19 top
Yale University Library, Manuscripts and Archives: 21(3-4), 24 top
Yale University Library, Manuscripts and Archives/©D A Lindley: 24(1)
Yale University Press, New Haven, CT: 21 top (r)

Nigel Young: 16 top (r), 17 top (m), 105 top, 120 top, 156 top (r), 157 top (r), 257 top (r), 269 top (r), 283(5), 296-297, 316(1), 317(2,5), 324-325, 331 top (l,r), 336-337, 341(2), 342(1), 355 top (l), 385 top (r), 406(3), 407(5), 408, 418-419(1-6), 420-421, 432-433, 443 top (l,r), 444(1), 463(3), 471 top (r), 547 top (l,r)

Drawings and Diagrams:
Kurt Ackermann/Stuttgart University: 520(1)
Arups: 507(2)
©John Batchelor: 512 top (l)
Reinfriede Bettrich: 426-427(1)
Birds Portchmouth Russum: 56-57, 60-61, 114-115(2), 157 top (l), 224-225(2), 326-327, 404-405 fold out, 442-443(2), 508-509(4)
Russell Clayton: 37(4), 73(4-5), 84(2), 88(1,3), 132-133(2-3), 133(1), 136(1), 137(2), 230 top
Walter Conquy: 328(2), 332(3), 339(2), 353(3)
Peter Cook, ©Archigram 1964: 459 top
Barry Copeland: 134(2), 151(1-3)
John Davies: 390 top
Spencer de Grey: 140(2)
Justin de Syllas: 170(6)
©Frank Dickens: 339 top (l-r), 340-341 top (l-r), 342-343 top (l-r)
Nick Eldridge: 504-505(1)
Norman Foster: 12-13(1-5), 14-15(1-3), 16(1), 17(2-5), 18(1-2), 26(1), 27(2), 28(1,3), 29(4), 31(2), 34(2), 35(3), 36(1-3), 37(5-6), 38-39, 40(2), 41 top, 42(1), 43(5), 50(1), 51(2-4), 52(1-2), 53(3-4), 59 top (l), 66(1-2), 67(3), 68-69 top (l-r), 68(1-3), 69(5), 71(1-2), 72(1-2), 74 top, 75 top, 78(1-2), 79(3-4), 80(1-2), 81(3-4), 83(1), 84(1), 85 top, 85(3), 88(2), 88-89(4), 90(1), 91(5), 96-97, 102(1-2), 103 top, 108 top (l), 109(2), 110 top, 111(3), 112 top, 118(1-2), 119(3), 128-129, 130(1-2), 131(3), 134(3-4), 138(2), 138-139(1), 141(5-6), 154(1-2), 155(4), 169 top (l,r), 173(2,4), 176 top, 176(2), 197(2), 204(2), 233 top (l), 246-247(1-5), 247 (8, 9), 248 top, 248(1-2), 252 top, 253 top, 258(2-3), 263(4), 266(2), 281(3), 282–283 top (l-r), 284 top, 290(1), 292–293, 300-301(1-16), 302(1), 303 (2-7), 306(2-3), 309(6-7), 315(5-6), 368-369, 378(1), 380(1-2), 381(3-4), 384(1-4), 385(7), 387 top, 387(3), 388(1), 397 top (r), 398 top (r), 402(1,3), 406(1), 407 top (m,r), 412(4), 423(2), 424 top, 434 top, 434(1), 436(1), 461 top (l), 468 top (l), 471(7), 472(1-5), 473(6), 476(2-3), 477(5-7), 481(3-4,6), 482(2-3), 485(7), 486(2), 487 top (r), 496-497(2), 499 top (l,r), 500-501(1-10), 522(2), 546 top, 547(3), 552(1-2)

Foster and Partners: 17 top (r), 42(2), 54(1), 55(2-3), 76, 77(2), 103(3), 110(1-2), 134 top (l), 134(1), 136 top (l), 137 top (r), 160(2), 161(5), 184(1), 192(1), 193(4), 194(1), 199 top, 200(1), 201 top (l), 201(2), 205(3), 206-207(4), 219 top, 222(1-2), 223(5), 224 top, 224(1), 225 top, 229(2), 241 top (l,r), 246(6), 249 top, 252-253(1-3), 258(5), 259(6,8), 262(1-2), 267(3), 273(3), 275(1), 277 top, 287(3), 299(3), 300 top, 302-303 top (l-r), 307(6), 314(1), 317 top (l), 317(3-4), 320(2), 322-323(1-6), 347(1), 349(8), 352(2), 357(5), 358(2), 363(4), 364(1-3), 379(3), 382(3), 386(1), 388-389(2-3), 390(1), 390-391(2-3), 396(2), 400(1), 401(2), 407(4), 436(5), 438(1), 439(5), 442(1), 466(1), 470(1), 474(2), 475(3-7), 480(2), 485(6), 491(3), 496(1), 502(1-2), 503(4-5), 508(1), 509(2-3), 514 top, 518(1,3-4), 523(3), 539(3-4), 541 top, 544(1), 545(5), 554(1), 555(2-3)
Martin Francis: 314(3), 315(4)
R Buckminster Fuller Papers, M1090, Dept. of Special Collections, Stanford University Libraries, Stanford, California: 290 top, 484 top (l)
Gregory Gibbon: 226-227, 254-255, 310-311, 392-393, 510-511
Pedro Guedes: 185 top, 189 top, 189(3-4), 190(2)
Birkin Haward: 140(1, 3-4), 151(4), 160(1), 162(1), 167 top (r), 171(7), 174(1, 3-4), 175 top (l-r), 175(5), 176(1), 183(1-2), 185(2-4), 186-187(2), 187 top (l-r), 188(1-2), 189(5-8), 190(1), 191(4-5), 198(1-2), 209(1), 210(1), 213(4), 219(4-5), 223(3), 229(4), 249(4), 267 top, 268(1), 270(3), 272-273(1), 272 top, 276(2), 280(1), 281(2), 301 top, 306(1), 307(4), 314 top, 365(5), 400-401 top (l-r), 455(2), 464(1-6), 469 top (l-r), 471(3-5), 486(1,3), 487(4-5), 488(2), 489 top (l-r), 489(3), 490(1), 505(1), 540(1), 542(1-2), 543 top, 543(4-5)
©Louis Hellman: 353 top (l-r)
John Hewitt: 6-7 fold out, 46, 98, 148, 155(3), 156 top (l), 179(3), 202, 210 top (l-r), 214, 218(1-3), 219(6), 242, 256(3-5), 294, 305 top (l-r), 354(2), 370, 430, 452-453(1-3), 470 top (l-r), 474-475 top (l-r), 476 top (l,r), 492, 536
Richard Horden: 470(2), 483(4)
Hetta Hunloke: 169(4), 474(1)
Anthony Hunt: 111(4-5), 319 top, 383(4-5)
Helmut Jacoby: 172(1), 177(3), 274, 288(1), 354 top, 356(1), 359(3,4), 362(1), 365(4), 472 top
Jeppesen & Co GmbH: 428 top
©Ben Johnson: 114 top, 163 top, 232 top, 330 top, 408 top, 517 top (r)
©1977 Louis I Kahn Collection, University of Pennsylvania and Pennsylvania Historical and Museum Commission: 80 top (l,r)
Jan Kaplicky: 318(2), 319(3), 328(1), 404 fold out, 405 fold out, 484(1), 506(1), 538(1), 541(2-3)
Orlando Modesti: 187(1), 191 top (l,r), 191(3)
David Morley: 478-479

David Nelson: 478-479
Norman Partridge: 348(7), 348-349(1), 383 top
Frank Peacock: 276(1), 277(3-4)
Graham Phillips: 435(2-3), 436(2)
Pittsburgh Plate Glass: 162(1)
Ian Ritchie: 356(2-4), 357(6-7)
Trustees of the Paul Rudolf Estate: 26 top
Ken Shuttleworth: 262 top (l,r), 478-479
Robin Spence: 320(1)
Mark Sutcliffe: 106-107, 108-109, 136 top (r)
Jo van Heyningen: 275(1)
John Wharton: 351(1), 360(2), 361(4-6), 362(2-3)

Every effort has been made to contact copyright holders. The publishers apologise for any omissions which they will be pleased to rectify at the earliest opportunity.

Editing: David Jenkins, Sophie Carter
Picture Research: Kate Stirling, Katy Harris, Sophie Hartley, Stephan Potchatek
Design: Thomas Manss & Company with Per Arnoldi; Thomas Manss, Lisa Sjukur
Research: Sophie Carter, Matthew Foreman
Proof-reading: Julia Dawson
Index: Christine Shuttleworth
Production Supervision: Martin Lee
Reproduction: Radstock Repro
Printed and bound in Germany